AUSTRALIAN

Fisheries Resources

AUSTRALIAN

Fisheries Resources

Patricia J. Kailola
Meryl J. Williams
Phillip C. Stewart
Russell E. Reichelt
Alex McNee
Christina Grieve

Bureau of Resource Sciences and the Fisheries Research and Development Corporation

ISBN 0 642 18876 9

Published by the Bureau of Resource Sciences, Department of Primary Industries and Energy, and the Fisheries Research and Development Corporation. Canberra, Australia.

Design
Julie Easton
Assistant design
Peter Moloney

Copy editing
Jean Norman

Production support
Kay Abel
Rob Brennan

The support provided by members of the Fisheries Resources Branch of the Bureau of Resource Sciences, Australian fisheries biologists and the Australian fishing industry is gratefully acknowledged.

Typesetting
Ruth Bosma,
The Typist, Canberra

Cartography
Graham Leahy,
Candata Pty Limited, Canberra

Cartographic reproduction
Tennyson Graphics, Melbourne

Film reproduction
H & H Colour Studios Pty Limited, Sydney

Printing
Inprint Limited, Brisbane

Title page photograph: Stuart Blight

This publication has been produced entirely in Australia.

Maps and graphics produced on Intergraph's Interactive Graphic Design Software (IGDS)
Desktop publishing on Ventura Publisher 3.0
Set in Garamond, text 10/12 pt medium and italic,
heading hierarchy from 12 pt to 20 pt bold and bold italic.
Captions set in Helvetica 9/10 pt.

Text printed on Media Satin 115 gsm

C o n t e n t s

F o r e w o r d

Australian Fisheries Resources is an outstanding publication written by Australian experts in fish biology and the fishing industry.

The Australian fisheries resources are small by world standards, but they provide an excellent array of fish, crustaceans and molluscs for both the world market and domestic consumption.

The development of the fishing industry and the growth in recreational fishing has been quite remarkable. It is an exciting industry which embraces technological advances in boats and gear which permit trawling for fish in depths down to 1500 metres as well as the use of delicate operations required to culture the world's finest South Sea pearls.

Much has been written about the fish and fisheries of Australia. This book draws together, into one very fine volume, our growing knowledge of the fish resources of the nation and their responses to exploitation.

Australian Fisheries Resources will be read widely by the Australian public. It contains up-to-date information on the distribution, life history, resource status and stock structure of more than 100 species of fish harvested in Australian waters. Facts about the fish species have been complemented with information on Australian fish habitats and fishing methods, fish quality, environmental issues affecting fisheries resources, and historical and current information on the Australian fishing industry and fisheries research.

The Bureau of Resource Sciences is to be congratulated on its initiative in preparing *Australian Fisheries Resources*. However, its task would have been impossible without the participation of a large group of experts from around Australia. Their collective commitment has been to ensure that the volume was of the highest quality in both text and illustrations.

I have a great deal of pleasure in commending *Australian Fisheries Resources* to all those interested in Australian fish and fisheries.

Bernard Bowen

Bernard Bowen AM FTS

Bernard Bowen is the former Chairman of the Fishing Industry Research and Development Council, recently replaced by the Fisheries Research and Development Corporation, that provided the majority of the financial support for *Australian Fisheries Resources*. He has extensive credentials in fisheries science and management, having been the Executive Director of the Western Australian Fisheries Department for many years, a Member of the Australian Marine Science and Technology Advisory Committee, and Member of the Advisory Committee on Marine Resources Research of the Food and Agriculture Organisation in Rome. Bernard Bowen is currently a Member of the Board of the Australian Fisheries Management Authority and Chairman of the CSIRO Division of Fisheries' Advisory Committee.

Source: SA Dept of Fisheries

The time is appropriate for a book such as *Australian Fisheries Resources*. The demand for an accessible and detailed description of Australia's major fisheries resources is greater than ever before and rising. There are major changes occurring in Australia and overseas in both fisheries and environmental science and management. An example of this is the increasing international interest in developing resource accounting systems, including systems for fisheries. In Australia there is a growing sense that all our resource-based industries should be managed according to the principles of ecologically sustainable development, which require an increased level of knowledge of the resources and their environment. The Bureau of Resource Sciences is in a unique position to produce this volume as its mission is to support the sustainable development of Australia's fishing, agricultural, mineral, petroleum and forestry industries by providing scientific and technical advice to government, industry and the community.

Recently there have been changes in Commonwealth fisheries management with the creation of the Australian Fisheries Management Authority and the Fisheries Research and Development Corporation. These two agencies are committed to the sustainable development of the Australian fishing industry, part of which includes the sound management of the fish stocks on which the industry is based. In addition, the 1992 Australian and New Zealand Fisheries and Aquaculture Council called for the Commonwealth and State fishery management agencies to undertake Fisheries Ecosystem Management assessments. These developments signal an increasing need to monitor and understand both our fisheries resources and the environment that sustains them.

Having said this, change is nothing new for Australian fisheries. Whaling and sealing, which dominated Australian fisheries of the 19th century, are no longer permitted. There have been huge fluctuations in the pearling industry in the past 100 years, and more recently there has been tremendous growth in fish trawling and lobster and prawn production. In the future, aquaculture production is likely to increase.

Source: Dave Evans

Other changes are difficult to predict but the present increasing emphasis on animal welfare is one area that may affect the fishing industry. This emerging issue should be seen as an opportunity rather than an obstacle to increased profits because in many agricultural industries this change has led to improved handling practices, better products and higher returns to the industry. The recent emphasis on the environment and ecologically sustainable development should similarly work in the industry's favour in the long term.

The future of Australian fisheries will depend, among other things, on improved management of resources. Many of the stocks that are presently overfished can be restored, and there is potential for increased profits in the industry through better handling and marketing of products. The benefit to fishery resource managers in using *Australian Fisheries Resources* as a reference tool is clear, however there should also be a number of benefits to the fishing industry. The information presented here will give fishers, managers and scientists a common language for debating resource issues and encourage future co-operation in research and data collection schemes.

As the title suggests, *Australian Fisheries Resources* focuses mainly on resources, but it also includes information on the Australian fishing industry, fishing gear and the environment.

The project has been ambitious from the outset, sometimes overwhelmingly so, when it was conceived by Meryl Williams. The project was financially supported by the Fishing Industry Research and Development Council and the then Bureau of Rural Resources. Early in the project the design was influenced by Professor Ed Miles of the University of Washington. At about the same time Patricia Kailola was recruited to co-ordinate the project that soon became widely known as the 'Atlas'. Patricia Kailola, as senior editor, was assisted by Phil Stewart, Alex McNee and Chris Grieve in compiling and analysing the scientific information for the book. Meryl Williams and Russell Reichelt contributed to the team through providing executive management and final scientific review. Members of the Fisheries Resources Branch have given their time and expertise generously to assist the 'Atlas team'. More than 350 contributors from all parts of Australia helped put the information together. During the final production stage the newly formed Bureau of Resource Sciences continued to support the 'Atlas' project.

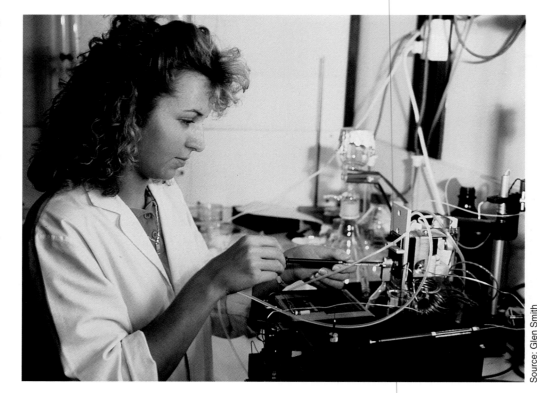

Source: Glen Smith

Source: Kevin McLoughlin

The book has been prepared entirely in digital form. The PostScript text and Intergraph maps, graphs and charts were merged digitally with the scanned photographs and line drawings to generate the colour-separated film of each 8 page spread ready for printing. Production of the book using this leading edge technology has already led to unforeseen benefits, eg a statistical bulletin resulted from the initial work of gathering fisheries production statistics. The distribution maps are already being transferred to a Geographic Information System from which they will be available for further analysis and improvement. It is possible that the next edition may appear as a CD-ROM. A digital 'Atlas' could include everything in this volume, but the information could be retrieved or updated more easily than through a printed product.

Much of the information presented in the book has been gathered from widely scattered sources that would otherwise be inaccessible to most people, including many scientists. In some cases the project has brought contributors together who were previously unaware of their colleagues' work. We view *Australian Fisheries Resources* as only the beginning in making fisheries resource information more readily available to all those who need it.

Meryl Williams
Russell Reichelt
Patricia Kailola

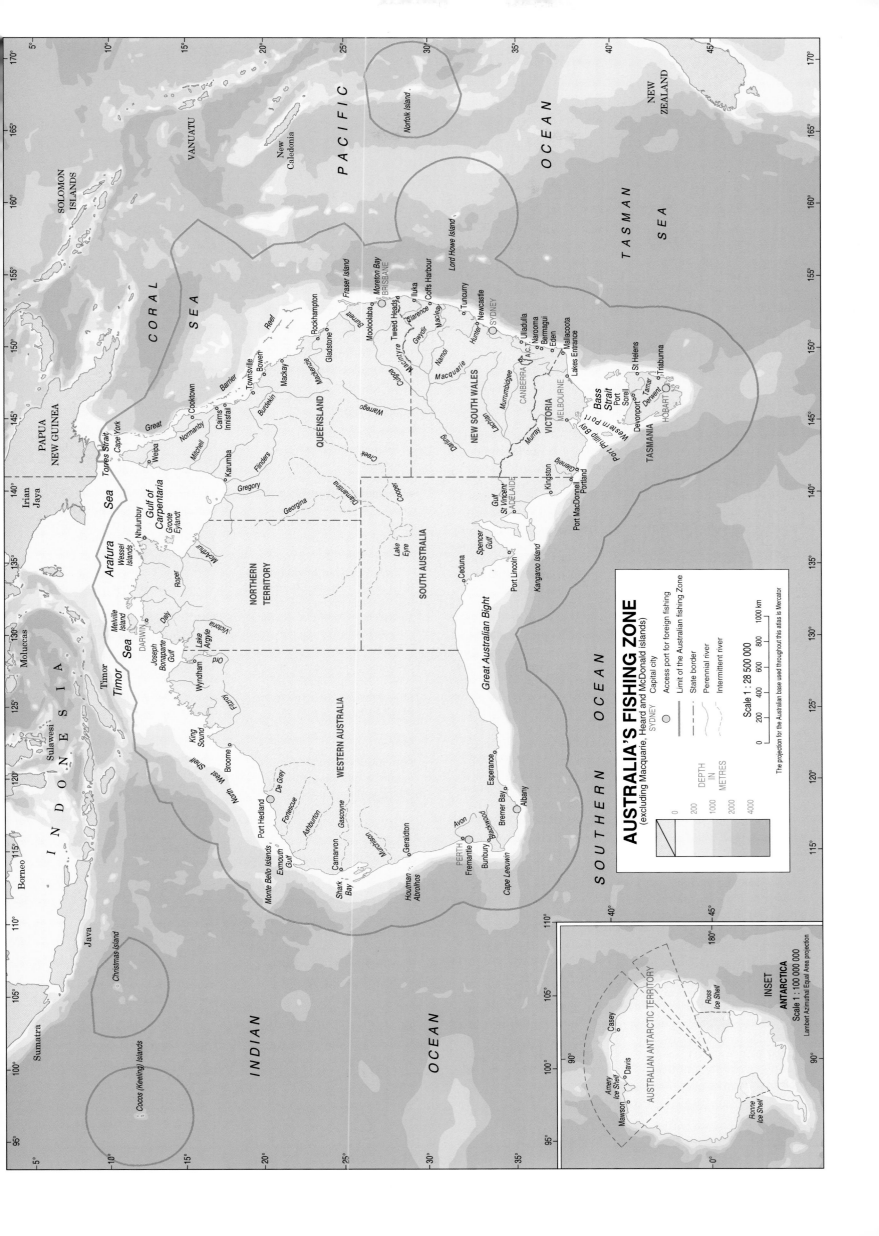

AUSTRALIA'S FISHING ZONE

(excluding Macquarie, Heard and McDonald islands)

SYDNEY ● Capital city

● Access port for foreign fishing

—— Limit of the Australian fishing Zone

—·—· State border

Perennial river

Intermittent river

Scale 1 : 28 500 000

0 200 400 600 800 1000 km

DEPTH IN METRES

0
200
1000
2000
4000

The projection for the Australian base used throughout this atlas is Mercator

INSET

ANTARCTICA

Scale 1 : 100 000 000

Lambert Azimuthal Equal Area projection

AUSTRALIAN ANTARCTIC TERRITORY

Ross Ice Shelf

Ronne Ice Shelf

Amery Ice Shelf

Casey

Davis

Mawson

Map labels

INDONESIA

Sumatra
Java
Borneo
Sulawesi
Moluccas
Irian Jaya

PAPUA NEW GUINEA

SOLOMON ISLANDS

VANUATU

New Caledonia

NEW ZEALAND

Christmas Island

Cocos (Keeling) Islands

Timor Sea
Timor
Arafura Sea
Arafura

Gulf of Carpentaria

Wessel Islands
Groote Eylandt

Torres Strait
Cape York

CORAL SEA

Great Barrier Reef

Norfolk Island

Lord Howe Island

PACIFIC OCEAN

TASMAN SEA

NORTHERN TERRITORY

QUEENSLAND

WESTERN AUSTRALIA

SOUTH AUSTRALIA

NEW SOUTH WALES

VICTORIA

TASMANIA

A.C.T.

CANBERRA

SYDNEY

MELBOURNE

ADELAIDE

PERTH

DARWIN

BRISBANE

HOBART

Great Australian Bight

INDIAN OCEAN

SOUTHERN OCEAN

Bass Strait

Place names and rivers

Nhulunbuy
Melville Island
DARWIN
Daly
Victoria
Lake Argyle
Ord
Joseph Bonaparte Gulf
Wyndham
Fitzroy
King Sound
Broome
North West Shelf
Monte Bello Islands
Port Hedland
De Grey
Fortescue
Ashburton
Exmouth Gulf
Gascoyne
Carnarvon
Shark Bay
Murchison
Houtman Abrolhos
Geraldton
Avon
Fremantle
PERTH
Bunbury
Blackwood
Bremer Bay
Esperance
Albany
Cape Leeuwin

Roper
McArthur

Weipa
Normanby
Mitchell
Karumba
Gregory
Flinders
Georgina
Diamantina
Cooper Creek
Lake Eyre

Cooktown
Cairns
Innisfail
Townsville
Bowen
Burdekin
Mackay
Mackenzie
Rockhampton
Gladstone
Burnett
Fraser Island
Moreton Bay
BRISBANE
Mooloolaba
Tweed Heads
Iluka
Clarence
Coffs Harbour
Gwydir
Macintyre
Condamine
Warrego
Darling
Namoi
Macquarie
Hunter
Newcastle
Tuncurry
Lachlan
Murrumbidgee
Murray
Uladulla
Narooma
Bermagui
Eden
Mallacoota
Lakes Entrance
Port Phillip Bay
Western Port
Glenelg
Kingston
Portland
Port MacDonnell
Spencer Gulf
Gulf St Vincent
Kangaroo Island
Port Lincoln
Ceduna

St Helens
Triabunna
Tamar
Port Sorell
Devonport
Derwent
HOBART

Ceduna

Sumatra

Australian Fisheries Resources has an emphasis on wild harvest fisheries but also presents information relevant to recreational fishing and aquaculture.

What's included

Species discussed in the book are only those naturally present in Australian waters or introduced species that are currently harvested.

As far as possible, species or species groups reviewed in detail are those for which the harvest is more than 100 t per annum or is valued at more than A$ 1 million per annum. The harvest need not be landed in Australia.

The book does not cover most of those species forming the pet fish trade.

To some extent, *Australian Fisheries Resources* picks up from the last overview of Australia's fisheries, which was a map and explanatory booklet published in 1965 by the then Department of National Development.

Decisions on the level of detail in the presentation for a species are based on the most accurate **fisheries statistics** available at the time the project was developing—1990. The editors ensured the completeness of these statistics where data were available. The time lag between planning and printing the book has been compensated for wherever possible by providing more recent catch figures and average fish prices in the text.

The information used in graphs indicating catch of a particular species are cited as 'Source: Fisheries Resources Atlas Statistical Database'. This database is described in detail in Stewart, P., Kailola, P. and Ramirez, C. (1991) *Twenty-five years of Australian fisheries statistics* (Bureau of

Rural Resources working paper WP/14/91). The data have been collected from a wide variety of sources and, unless indicated, the catch figures do not include landings by recreational fishers.

Text and figures

The term **'fish'** is sometimes used in its most general sense, ie it also includes invertebrates such as molluscs and crustaceans.

The species are arranged in the book in **phylogenetic order**, ie their evolutionary relationship based on recency of common descent. In tables, the fish are listed alphabetically.

The nominated **common name** of each species is almost always that accepted by the Australian commercial fishing industry through the Commonwealth's Recommended Marketing Names Committee's 1988 publication. We have not used the recommended name in the few cases where we have become aware that it is causing mis-identifications—for example, for blue eye and warehous.

The currently accepted **scientific name** identifies accurately each species or taxonomic group. Following normal scientific convention, genus names may be abbreviated to the first letter.

The **FAO name** for each species follows either: the FAO yearbook of fishery statistics, catches and landings 1988, volume 66 (*FAO Fisheries Series No. 34, FAO Statistics Series No. 92; 1990*); the FAO species catalogues, *FAO Fisheries Synopsis No. 125* series; or other FAO publications.

The **Australian species code** is a 6 digit identifier devised by the CSIRO Division of Fisheries and the Australian Museum, and widely used by Australian fisheries agencies for recording species catches.

Statements of fact are directly sourced to publications with **superscripts** indicating the references. Non-referenced information is the collective knowledge of the contributors and the compiler(s).

Weights in text and figures refer to live (that is, whole) weight, unless otherwise specified. Units are normally metric, and are abbreviated to the first letter, eg metres (m), tonnes (t).

We regard resource management as an integral part of a fishery. Statements on **management controls** are given in overview and are intended to show whether and how fisheries resources are being managed.

This overview should not be used as a formal statement of management arrangements. Such details should be obtained directly from relevant authorities.

Except where the editors have first hand expertise, we have avoided giving opinions or projections on likely future trends in a resource.

Maps

Distributions are plotted using information from verifiable fishing and museum records.

The **commercial fishing area** for each of the species shows the geographic distribution of fishing activity, and sometimes it may be the same as the species' geographic distribution. We considered an area as a true commercial fishing area for a species when the relevant species represents more than 10 percent of the catch from a fishing operation in that area.

The **Australian Fishing Zone** marks the limit of Australia's jurisdiction of fishing activity. Species distributions are marked only to the limit of the Zone—where applicable—and

these depictions are not meant to imply that the species inhabits waters only within the Zone.

Distributions are usually depicted only for the Australian mainland and Tasmania unless we know the species' distribution in other territorial waters. Distributional information in the Australian Fishing Zone for territories such as Lord Howe, Norfolk and Cocos islands is difficult to obtain so that often we do not know whether fish are present or absent in their waters.

Place names and positions were confirmed in the *Reader's Digest atlas of Australia* (first edition, 1977) and the *Australia 1:250,000 map series gazetteer* (Australian Government Publishing Service, 1975).

The **bathymetry** marked on the maps is at depths of 200, 1000, 2000 and 4000 m.

Various changes occurred while the book was being finalised in stages over 2 years. For example, some of the references that are cited as 'in press' have been published, and some organisations have changed names or been restructured. The Victorian Department of Conservation and Environment has become the Department of Conservation and Natural Resources. The South Australian Department of Fisheries split into the Fisheries Division, Department of Primary Industries, South Australia and the South Australian Research and Development Institute. The Western Australian Marine Research Laboratories have become the Bernard Bowen Fisheries Research Institute, Western Australian Marine Research Laboratories. We have cited the CSIRO Division of Fisheries in some places as 'CSIRO Marine Laboratories'.

by Meryl Williams
and Phillip Stewart

Introduction

ENCIRCLED by the Pacific, Indian and Southern oceans, Australia and its external Territories lie completely in the southern hemisphere. Thousands of different and fascinating types of organisms inhabit Australia's seas, rivers and lakes. Over 300 of these species are harvested by commercial, recreational and traditional fishers, and some are used for aquaculture. These harvestable living resources we call 'fisheries resources'.

Australian Fisheries Resources draws together our knowledge of these resources and their responses to harvesting. The volume concentrates on their uses over the past 3 decades.

In this introductory chapter, we present an overview of Australia's fisheries resources and describe the main groups of people using them, arrangements for their management, research on them and training in the fishing industry. Later chapters in the book describe the habitats occupied by the resources, the main fishing methods used, and the essentials of marketing them and preserving their quality as consumable products. The major part of this book describes the most abundant and valuable of Australia's commercial and recreational fisheries species, followed by a short chapter on the features of minor or presently underutilised fisheries resources. For each of the major species, this book provides a description of the species, its distribution and habitat, its life history, the fisheries which harvest it, the management controls applied, and its status as a resource.

Source: Glen Smith

Source: Glen Smith

Source: Ian Freeman

The resources

FISHING takes place throughout the large Australian Fishing Zone, a management zone of approximately 9 million square km that extends up to 200 nautical miles from the shore or coastal baselines and, in parts, adjoins the exclusive economic zones of Indonesia, Papua New Guinea, France (New Caledonia, and the Kerguelen Island adjacent to Heard and McDonald islands) and New Zealand. The Zone also encompasses waters around the Australian external territories of the Cocos, Christmas and Norfolk islands, and Macquarie, Heard and McDonald islands but not the Australian Antarctic Territory where only the activities of domestic vessels are controlled. It is the third largest fishing zone in the world after those of France and the United States of America. Correspondingly, the Australian coastline is one of the longest in the world at about 36 000 km. The waters fished comprise many different habitats, including inland rivers and farm dams, mangrove-lined creeks and estuaries, shallow coastal bays, coral reefs, the continental shelf and continental slope to over 1.5 km in depth.

Because of its long geographical isolation from other continents and its wide range of habitat types (refer Chapter 2), one of the most diverse marine faunas in the world has evolved in Australia's waters.[1,2] This fauna includes more than 3600 species of fish in 303 families and tens of thousands of species of aquatic molluscs.[1,2] The Decapoda, which is the most important crustacean Order for commercial fisheries, is represented by more than 2000 species in Australian waters. However, whereas Australian waters have representatives of most marine animal families, by world standards they have few freshwater animal species.

A wide selection of the Australian aquatic fauna is exploited for food, recreation and products such as pearl shell, fishing bait, pet food and stock feed. Commercial fish markets handle at least 200 commonly named species of fish.[3] In addition, the commercial and recreational catch includes more than 60 species of crustaceans, 30 species of molluscs and a few echinoderm species. The 101 species of fish, 26 species of crustaceans, 18 species of molluscs and 1 echinoderm species described in detail in this book (Chapter 5) together comprise 85 % of the total commercial catch by weight for 1990. A further 172 species are briefly described or noted.

Nearly half of the mollusc and crustacean species and about one third of the fish species discussed in this book are endemic to Australian waters. A further one third have a worldwide distribution. These include the large pelagic species such as tunas and marlins and the deepwater species such as orange roughy and oreos.

Although a majority of Australian species also inhabit the waters of other countries, only a few have populations that straddle the fishing zones of neighbouring countries. These shared taxa are chiefly the migratory tunas and billfishes, the ornate rock lobster in Torres Strait, and shark and other fishes inhabiting the waters between Indonesia, Australia and Papua New Guinea. The extent of intermingling between Australian and New Zealand populations of some pelagic species (eg school sharks) and deepwater fishes (eg orange roughy) has not been established.

In Australia, natural ('wild') fisheries resources have been supplemented since last century through the culturing of some species. Aquaculture production has increased markedly since the mid 1980s. Only 5 of 15 commercially cultured species described in this book are introduced (Pacific oyster, Atlantic salmon, rainbow trout, brown trout and goldfish). Aquaculture therefore contrasts with agriculture in this country in that almost all agricultural production is based on exotic species of plants and animals.

Australian waters also contain a wide diversity of aquatic plants, from the microscopic phytoplankton to flowering plants (the Angiospermae) such as seagrass and mangroves. These plants are not exploited to any great extent. Aquaculturalists grow algae as feed for early life stages of farmed species. Some macro-algae (eg kelp, *Durvillaea potatorum*) are harvested for food and food production in southern Australia. Early this century, there was an industry in South Australia making bags from the fibre in *Posidonia* species seagrass. Micro-algae (*Dunaliella salina*) are cultured in South Australia and Western Australia. Their natural pigment, beta carotene, is extracted for use as a colouring agent in various foodstuffs.

Fisheries production

Though they are diverse and occupy 1 of the largest fishing zones, Australia's fisheries resources are not as abundant or productive as those in many other parts of the world. This is thought to be because, on average, Australian waters are low in nutrients compared with waters in other world regions (refer Chapter 2). The generally low nutrient condition is due to a combination of factors including little run off from the dry Australian continent, a narrow continental shelf, the predominantly southwards (warm to cold) flow of the main Australian coastal currents and the lack of permanent upwellings. Off other continents, permanent upwellings are found where cold currents meeting warm water bring nutrients to the surface to form the basis of food webs supporting productive fisheries. Examples of these upwelling phenomena in the southern hemisphere are off the coast of Peru and off the west coast of South Africa. Fisheries resources supported by nutrient upwellings are usually dominated by fish of the Order Clupeiformes which includes sardines, herrings and anchovies. Australian seas contain few species and small populations of this fish group compared to those present in some other seas.

Despite Australia having the third largest fishing zone in the world, its 1988-89 commercial domestic catch of 201 709 t ranked only 55th in the world.[4] A further 19 500 t was taken from Australian waters by licensed foreign vessels, and an unknown quantity was caught by recreational fishers. Examples of catches by other nations were 10–12 million t by Japan, the Soviet Union (now the Commonwealth of Independent States, CIS) and China, and 2.7 and 0.5 million t by Indonesia and New Zealand, respectively, in 1989.

In the recent past, projections of Australia's fisheries potential were optimistic. In 1970, a Food and Agriculture Organisation (FAO) report[5] estimated that Australia's coastal and shelf waters could yield 2.3 million t annually. However the total Australian commercial catch has reached only about one tenth of this FAO prediction.

In total landed weight, Australia's fisheries catch is not expected to expand much beyond its present level. Few prospective areas of the Australian Fishing Zone are still to be explored although much still remains to be learned about the resources. For example, we are unable to determine the full effect of fishing on half of the species or groups described in this book. Only 9 of the species or groups are known to be under-exploited or capable of supporting higher catches without affecting their productive potential. A further 22 are considered heavily or fully exploited to the extent that higher average catches could start to affect the recruitment or stock replacement potential of their populations. Scientific assessments indicate that 9 species or groups

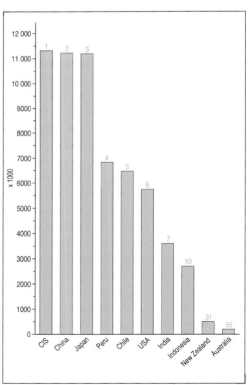

Total catch for selected fishing nations in 1989. The number above each bar indicates that country's rank in world production. (Source: Food and Agriculture Organisation of the United Nations[4])

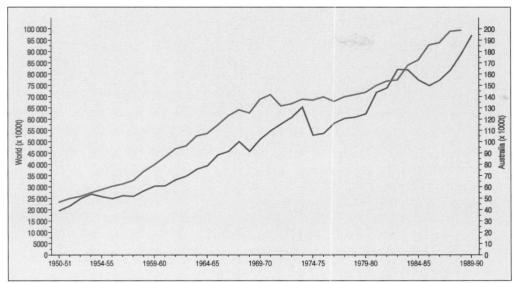

Australian fisheries production and world fisheries production for the period 1950–51 to 1989–90. (Source: Australian Bureau of Statistics, Australian Bureau of Agricultural and Resource Economics[20, 33] and Food and Agriculture Organisation of the United Nations[4])

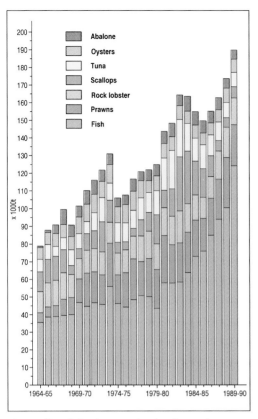

Australian fisheries production by main groups 1964–65 to 1989–90. (Source: Australian Bureau of Statistics and Australian Bureau of Agricultural and Resource Economics[20, 33])

are over-exploited. They could sustain greater catches if their populations were permitted to increase to more productive levels. None of Australia's commercial marine or freshwater species are so over-exploited that they are listed by the International Union for the Conservation of Nature as endangered animals. In 1985, however, 3 species of freshwater fish having commercial value were placed on an Australian list of threatened fish.[6]

For management purposes in Australia, fisheries resources are usually described and managed in units called a 'fishery'. A fishery is defined by a combination of the species caught (1 or several), the gear and/or fishing methods used, and the area of operation. About 70 fisheries were defined in Commonwealth and State government legislation in Australia in 1991, the majority of these on the basis of the species caught and the fishery area. Defined fisheries do not always cover the full extent of inter-breeding populations of each species and many single populations are managed as several different fisheries (eg the school shark and gummy shark fisheries in southern Australia are managed under the fisheries acts of the Commonwealth and 4 States).

Fisheries that are dominated by the catch of a single species are the exception rather than the rule in Australia. Some examples are western rock lobster, southern rock lobster, southern scallop, Sydney rock oyster, jack mackerel and southern bluefin tuna. Most species are caught and managed in association with several others, and often the lower value types are discarded on the fishing grounds — for example, in most demersal trawl fisheries. Most species may be taken by several types of fishing gear (refer Chapter 3). The interactions between species and gear in most Australian fisheries brings challenges in controlling incidental bycatches.

As fisheries have developed, particularly over the last 3 decades, Australian and foreign researchers and naturalists, and commercial and recreational fishers have discovered much about the species inhabiting Australian waters — their habits, distributions and sustainable production potential. Roughley[7,8] wrote some of the earliest detailed descriptions of Australia's fish and fisheries. A review by MacInnes[9] presented the state of knowledge just after World War II when the total commercial catch was 41 420 t. National fisheries resource maps produced in 1965 reflected the extent of fishing and research of the time and showed the limited development of northern fisheries. The growing body of knowledge on Australia's fisheries resources was documented also in *Australian Fisheries*,[10,11] by Pownall,[12] through the *Australian Journal of Marine and Freshwater Research*, and through scientific workshops such as those sponsored by the Australian Society for Fish Biology, the Bureau of Resource Sciences (formerly the Bureau of Rural Resources)[13,14,15,16,17,18] and the Fisheries Research and Development Corporation.

The increasing knowledge of fisheries resources has barely kept pace with the expansion of fishing. To assess the sustainable production from wild fisheries resources, biological information is needed on the abundance of populations and their productive capacity (growth, reproduction, recruitment and mortality) and information on the

Knowledge of Australia's fisheries resources

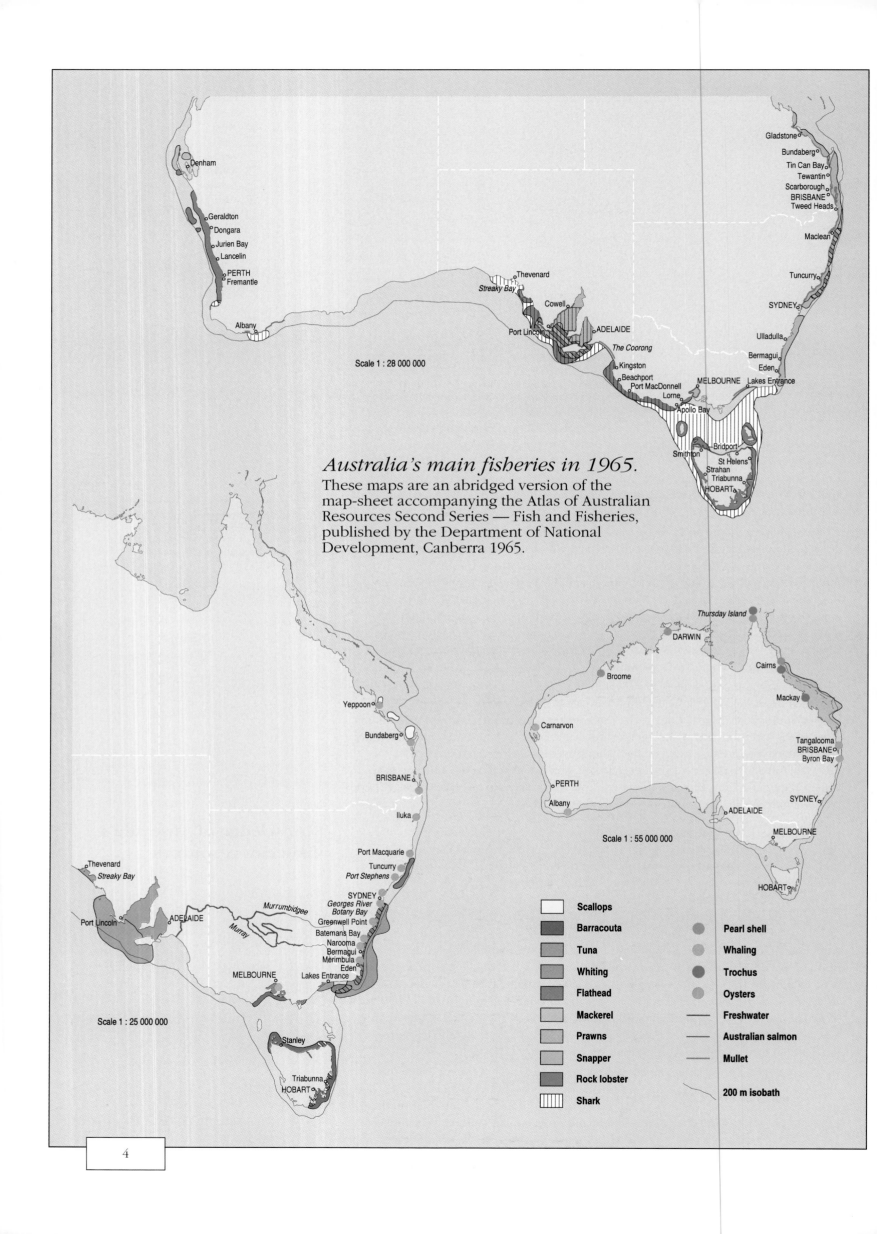

Australia's main fisheries in 1965.

These maps are an abridged version of the map-sheet accompanying the Atlas of Australian Resources Second Series — Fish and Fisheries, published by the Department of National Development, Canberra 1965.

Scale 1 : 28 000 000

Scale 1 : 55 000 000

Scale 1 : 25 000 000

Scallops	Pearl shell	
Barracouta	Whaling	
Tuna	Trochus	
Whiting	Oysters	
Flathead		
Mackerel	Freshwater	
Prawns	Australian salmon	
Snapper	Mullet	
Rock lobster		
Shark	200 m isobath	

response of the resource to fishing. Since the productive potential of a species may be affected by the variability of environmental factors and by interactions with other species, including predators, prey and parasites, some knowledge of these is also required. In Chapter 5, we show that the life history of each species is unique and that the biological characteristics of each species can vary considerably.

One example of species variation is longevity. On average, exploited fish species live longer than do molluscs and crustaceans. Over half of the fish (teleost) species described in this book live for more than 10 years but nearly all of the invertebrates live for less than 10 years. Some prawns are virtually 'annual crops'. In contrast, the longest lived fish species — orange roughy — grows slowly and appears to live for more than 100 years. The longevity of 22 of the 100 species or groups in this book is not yet estimated.

Growth is another example of species variation. The species featured in this book attain maximum sizes of from 150 g (prawns) to nearly 1 t (blue marlin). Age at maturity is as little as 5 months for grooved tiger prawns and as much as 30 years for orange roughy.

Ideally, fisheries resources would be best managed for economic and social gains if the levels of sustainable catch from each exploited resource could be predicted. However, it is difficult to achieve this ideal for most species because of the high level of knowledge required, variability in the distribution and abundance of each resource in space and time, and the complexity of interactions among living and non-living components of the aquatic environment.

Australia has a large number of fish resources but insufficient research resources to study them all. Allocation of research has been largely directed to the more valuable species, leaving many resources not well known. At present, there is sufficient knowledge to predict catches for western rock lobsters 4 years in advance and for some stocks of banana prawns in the Gulf of Carpentaria up to 2–3 months in advance of the season (refer Chapter 5). Knowledge of southern bluefin tuna, many penaeid prawn species and several fish species trawled in south-eastern Australia is improving to the stage where sustainable catch levels can be estimated.

To help predict the distribution and abundance of fisheries resources, an understanding is required of the spatial, seasonal and inter-annual relationships between species and their habitats — including factors such as water temperature, salinity and nutrients. In addition, knowledge of historical population levels is needed in order to understand the impact of past fishing on these populations. For many Australian species, these relationships are known broadly but not in sufficient detail to predict year to year variations. Thus, for example, a lower abundance of a population in a given area and year could be caused by the direct effect of oceanographic factors (eg higher than usual sea surface temperatures), smaller than usual recruitment of 1 or more year classes (eg caused by losses when ocean currents vary under El Niño conditions), fishing catches exceeding recruitment rates in previous years, the reduced carrying capacity of the habitat (eg by pollution or habitat degradation), or to a combination of the above factors.

The impact of global climate change on fisheries production in Australia cannot be fully predicted, even if forecasts of the direction and magnitude of climate change were possible. Nevertheless, a preliminary examination[19] of the likely impact of climate change on Australia's prawn, western rock lobster and south-eastern fisheries proposed that climate change was likely to affect prawn stocks through changes in critical coastal habitats; western rock lobster stocks through changes in oceanic circulation, particularly of the Leeuwin Current; and some of the south-eastern fisheries species through ocean temperature rises.

Using Australia's fisheries resources

AUSTRALIA'S fisheries resources are harvested by commercial, artisanal and recreational fishers (including game fishers and divers) and licensed foreign fishing fleets. Some sections of the resources are protected for conservation.

The different groups of fishers compete with each another for many resources but some resources are used by only 1 or 2 groups. For example, of the 100 species or

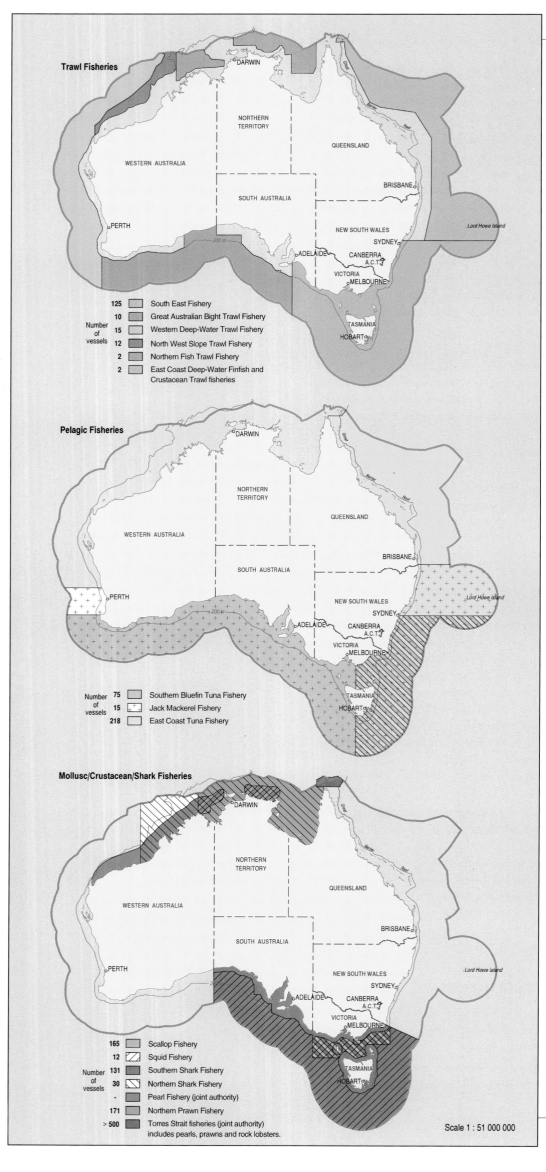

Trawl Fisheries

Number of vessels:
- 125 — South East Fishery
- 10 — Great Australian Bight Trawl Fishery
- 15 — Western Deep-Water Trawl Fishery
- 12 — North West Slope Trawl Fishery
- 2 — Northern Fish Trawl Fishery
- 2 — East Coast Deep-Water Finfish and Crustacean Trawl fisheries

Pelagic Fisheries

Number of vessels:
- 75 — Southern Bluefin Tuna Fishery
- 15 — Jack Mackerel Fishery
- 218 — East Coast Tuna Fishery

Mollusc/Crustacean/Shark Fisheries

Number of vessels:
- 165 — Scallop Fishery
- 12 — Squid Fishery
- 131 — Southern Shark Fishery
- 30 — Northern Shark Fishery
- - — Pearl Fishery (joint authority)
- 171 — Northern Prawn Fishery
- > 500 — Torres Strait fisheries (joint authority) includes pearls, prawns and rock lobsters.

Scale 1 : 51 000 000

species groups described in this book, 67 are taken both by recreational and commercial fishers and 27 are taken only or mainly by commercial fishers. The remainder are shared among commercial, recreational, aquacultural, indigenous and foreign users. None of the species described in this book is used solely by recreational fishers.

Control over access to and use of Australia's fisheries resources has been shared between the Commonwealth and State governments since Federation in 1901. The major commercial fisheries managed by the Commonwealth are the Northern Prawn Fishery, South East Fishery and Southern Bluefin Tuna and East Coast Tuna fisheries. The Southern Shark Fishery has both Commonwealth and State-managed components. The most valuable single fishery in Australia, the Western Rock Lobster Fishery, is managed by Western Australia. Other large fisheries managed by State governments are the Queensland East Coast Prawn, the Southern Rock Lobster, Abalone and all inshore net fisheries except for some trawl fisheries. Some fisheries are managed jointly by the Commonwealth and a State. Examples of joint management include the Torres Strait fisheries (Commonwealth and Queensland governments) and the Western Australian pearl fishery (Commonwealth and Western Australian governments).

Currently, the States manage wild fisheries worth about 58 % of the value of fisheries production in Australia. Aquaculture industries managed by States account for a further 18 % of fisheries production value.

Most recreational fishing is managed by the States where it takes place in inshore, estuarine and inland waters. However, game fishing for tunas, marlins and other pelagic fish species occurs well offshore and, with the exception of game fishing charter operations, is managed by the Commonwealth. The sheltered waters of the Great Barrier Reef also support important recreational fisheries and they are managed jointly by the Commonwealth through the Great Barrier Reef Marine Park Authority and the Queensland Government.

(left) Management areas for Commonwealth fisheries.

(opposite page) Major crustacean and mollusc fisheries managed by State fisheries authorities.

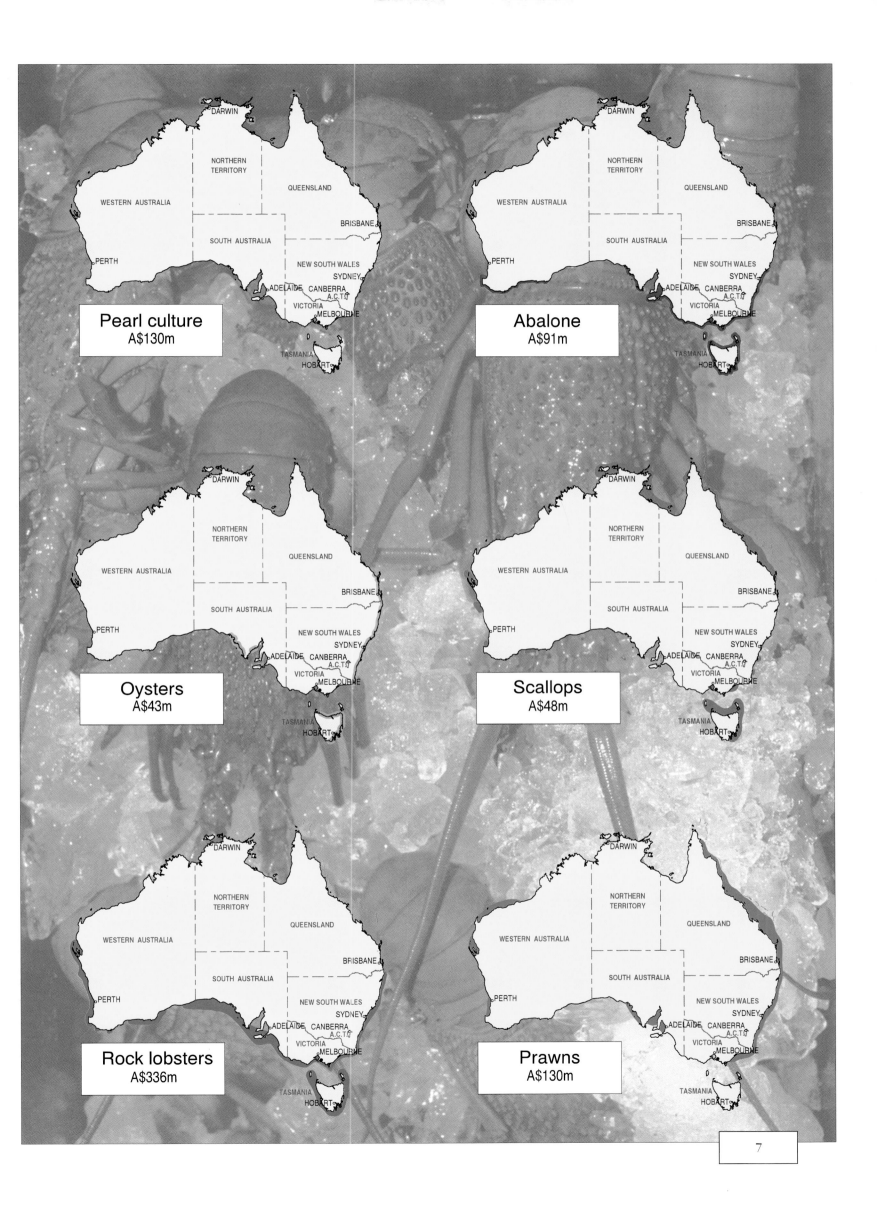

Pearl culture
A$130m

Abalone
A$91m

Oysters
A$43m

Scallops
A$48m

Rock lobsters
A$336m

Prawns
A$130m

Commercial fisheries

A brief history of commercial fisheries development

The commercial fishing industry ranks fifth in value amongst the rural industries in Australia after wool, beef, wheat and dairy (see figure, this page), although it provides only 4–5 % of the value of Australia's rural exports.[20] Fishing differs from most of the other rural industries because of its major reliance on wild stocks and the associated difficulties in their harvesting and management.

Despite having a small total production, Australia's fisheries are economically valuable. The total value of production from commercial wild fisheries and aquaculture has exceeded A$1 billion each year since 1988 and in 1991–92 was an estimated A$ 1289 million. This high value is generated because the commercial catch has a large component of highly priced shellfish species such as abalone, scallops, penaeid prawns and rock lobsters. In 1991–92 they provided 58 % of the total value of production.

Prior to British colonisation, indigenous Australians and lately visiting South-east Asians exploited the country's marine and freshwater resources for food and trade. Fish was a major dietary item in coastal Aboriginal and Torres Strait Islander communities. A wide range of fishing technologies including nets, hook and line, spears and fixed and moveable traps were used.[7] These historical fishing activities appear to have had little impact on fish populations and fish species' distributions.[2]

Commercial exploitation of fisheries resources expanded following British settlement in 1788. Whaling and sealing provided the first major industries and whale oil and whale bone, seal oil and seal skins were Australia's largest exports until overtaken by wool in 1834.[21] Exploitation of marine mammals (whales and seals), turtles, pearl oysters and inshore fisheries for oysters, prawns, crabs, rock lobsters and fish dominated fisheries until the 1920s. Now, marine mammals and turtles are protected from exploitation except by Aboriginal and Torres Strait Islander peoples.

The catching of additional species and the use of new fishing methods began in the early part of the 20th century. For example, barracouta was first exploited off the south-east coast in 1911. Steam trawlers owned by the New South Wales Government began operating in 1915. During the 1920s, the catching of school sharks with hooks began off southern Australia. Danish seiners were introduced in south-eastern fisheries in 1936 and the commercial exploitation of Australian salmon and southern bluefin tuna also commenced about this time. Whitebait (*Lovettia* species) was first exploited in Tasmania in 1941.

Until the end of World War II, sea mullet was the most common commercial fish and barracouta the second most common. Export of frozen rock lobster tails began in 1947 and the opportunities this presented led to expansions in the western rock lobster and southern rock lobster fisheries over the next few decades.

Larger scale commercial operations for fish, crustaceans and molluscs have developed in the last 40 years. Between 1951–52 and 1989–90, Australia's commercial catch increased by 470 %. Between 1964–65 and 1989–90 alone, the catch rose by 160 % compared with a total world increase of 80 % over the same period. In absolute tonnages, however, the Australian increase remains modest.

In the late 1950s prawn trawling began in New South Wales, southern Queensland and Shark Bay, Western Australia.

During the 1960s, Australian fishing activities diversified through developing new fisheries. Examples of these are the Gulf of Carpentaria banana prawn fishery in 1966, the Nickol Bay, Western Australia banana prawn fishery in 1967 and the Spencer Gulf king prawn fishery in South Australia in 1968, the saucer scallop fisheries in central Queensland and Western Australia and the Tasmanian and Victorian abalone fisheries in 1963. Gillnets were introduced into the Southern Shark Fishery in the late 1960s and, as a result, the catch of gummy shark began to increase. In the mid 1960s there was rapid development of the Port Phillip Bay scallop fishery in Victoria. The established fish, rock lobster and oyster fisheries also expanded. Most domestic fishing still occurred close to the coast. Although foreign fishing vessels and research ships from Japan, the Soviet Union, Taiwan and Korea had fished and explored offshore during the 1960s, little information about their activities was available.

Most fisheries development in the north of Australia did not commence until the mid 1960s. The only large scale fishery there was the pearl fishery.

In the 1970s, Australian abalone, scallop and fish catches all increased. Tiger prawn and endeavour prawn fisheries developed in the Gulf of Carpentaria and mixed prawn

Australian fisheries production compared to other rural industries for the year 1989–90. (Source: Australian Bureau of Agricultural and Resource Economics [20])

fisheries began in far north Queensland and off north-western Australia. Trawling for gemfish began in waters between 400 m and 600 m off the central New South Wales coast. Purse seining for southern bluefin tuna in the Great Australian Bight and off New South Wales was developed successfully in the mid 1970s.

Australia declared the 200 nautical mile Australian Fishing Zone in 1979. Under the principles embodied in the United Nations Convention on the Law of the Sea, Australia has made surplus resources within the Australian Fishing Zone available to a number of foreign fishing operations since then through fee fishing by foreign licensed vessels and Australian and foreign fleet joint ventures and feasibility fishing arrangements. Recent years have seen a marked decline in foreign fishing activity, however, as the Australian fishing industry has expanded its capacity to harvest the resources within the Zone.

Between 1980 and 1990, while the quantity of fish landed by Australian vessels trebled and rock lobster catches increased slightly, quantities in all other major fisheries categories declined. In the early to mid 1980s, deepwater fisheries for orange roughy, blue grenadier and oreos commenced off southern Australia, and for scampi and carid prawns off the North West Shelf.

By the early 1990s, most of Australia's inshore fisheries resources were fully developed. However, fisheries were developing in the more remote regions of the Australian Fishing Zone. Fishers were operating under developmental arrangements in the Western Deepwater Trawl, East Coast Deepwater Trawl, North West Slope Trawl, Northern Fish Trawl and Norfolk Island Deepwater fisheries. The most recent developmental phase of the trawl fishery in the Great Australian Bight ended in late 1992. However, investment in many of these developing fisheries is low and it remains to be seen whether discovery of productive grounds or declines in other fisheries will stimulate their more rapid growth.

Since 1965, trends in the overall composition of the commercial catch have masked events occurring in catches of individual species. Catches of some species remained stable – for example, for sea mullet and Spanish mackerel. Catches of other species fluctuated. Gemfish catches rose from small quantities in the early 1970s to peaks of 5000 t in the late 1970s and late 1980s and subsequently declined to below 1000 t. Barramundi catches rose from less than 200 t to over 1300 t and pilchard catches rose from less than 300 t to over 8000 t. Catches of Australian salmon fluctuated between 3000 t and 7000 t. Australian catches of southern bluefin tuna rose from 4770 t in 1965 to a peak of 20 330 t in 1983, and have since been reduced by quotas to about 5000 t. The deepest living commercial fish species in Australia, orange roughy, yielded 40 000 t in 1990 — only about 5 years after it began to be seriously exploited. This quantity was nearly one third of the total fish tonnage for Australia (under quota management, the orange roughy catch will be stepped down over the next 3 years).

The Australian commercial fleet operates a wide variety of fishing gear (refer Chapter 3). Due to the small size and diverse nature of most resources, many fishers use more than 1 type. For example, surveys in Queensland showed that nearly half of the licensed fishers employed 2 or more types of gear.[22]

Australia has about 10 000 commercial fishing vessels. Even though the number of vessels has changed little over the 25 years since 1965, there has been a significant increase in fishing power. For example, in 1990 Australian vessels longer than 15 m made up 14 % of the fleet, compared with only 4 % in 1964–65. Greater numbers of larger vessels represent a considerable increase in the fleet's fishing capacity, and reflects the expansion of fisheries into offshore areas where larger vessels are necessary. In recent times they have fished in waters down to 1500 m on the continental slope. The largest vessel in the Australian fleet is 85 m long.

The majority of fishing vessels however, are small and operated by 1 or 2 persons. Fishing boats less than 10 m long represented 65 % of the fleet in 1990, only 15 % fewer than the number in 1965–66. Small fishing vessels, such as otter trawlers, beam trawlers, gillnetters, trap and pot boats, are used in estuarine and inshore operations. New South Wales has the highest number of licensed fishing vessels but, on average, these are smaller in size than the vessels of other States.

Although some aspects of fishing methods, vessels and gear have not changed much since 1965, the Australian industry has embraced new technology rapidly in a number of ways. Vessel manufacture has advanced from producing mostly timber hulls to hulls of

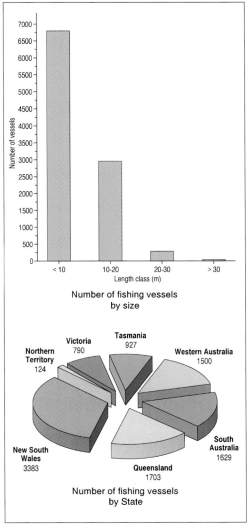

Numbers of Australian fishing vessels by size category and breakdown of Australian fishing vessels by State of registration. (Source: Fisheries Research and Development Corporation)

The fishing fleet and employment

Large otter trawlers such as these are typical of vessels now operating in Australia's prawn fisheries. (Source: Dave Evans, CSIRO Marine Laboratories, North Beach)

steel, aluminium or fibreglass. Australia leads the world in the design and construction of certain classes of fishing vessels such as prawn trawlers, and some otter trawlers are exported. The introduction of high powered diesel engines in the early 1970s saw the development of trawl vessels capable of fishing in deep waters offshore. Navigation, communications and fish location have been revolutionised by the advent of increasingly sophisticated electronic sonar and navigation systems (refer Chapter 3). Australia is also pioneering the use of satellite based transponders for fisheries surveillance. To best suit Australian fishing conditions and species, fishing gear such as trawl nets have been developed and refined by fishers and fishing companies, aided sometimes by a small amount of government-funded research.

A few fisheries such as the Northern Prawn Fishery and the North West Slope Trawl Fishery receive a significant investment from larger companies. However, most of the Australian fishing industry has a high percentage of private ownership and owner-operated vessels. Governments have not operated commercial vessels since before World War II when the New South Wales Government sold the steam trawlers it had operated in the South East Trawl Fishery.

Employment within the fishing industry has remained stable during the last 25 years. In 1964–65, approximately 13 000 people worked full-time in the catching sector. In 1990, 14 000 people fished full-time. In 1990, approximately 4000 people were involved in processing the Australian catch. Employment figures are not readily available for related industries such as vessel construction, maintenance services and fishing gear and electronic equipment suppliers.

Recreational fishing

Anglers at Fraser Island, southern Queensland. (Source: Ian Halliday, Fisheries Branch, Queensland Department of Primary Industries)

In addition to commercial fishers, anglers are the other main users of Australian fisheries resources. Recreational fishing is a very popular pastime in Australia and each year recreational fishers take a large but unquantified amount of fish, crustaceans and molluscs. The State and Commonwealth governments are developing a national recreational fishing policy which recognises the rights of access of recreational fishers to resources as well as the overall conservation and management needs of those resources.[23]

A 1984 survey[24] of participation in this sport revealed that nearly one third of Australians over 10 years of age go fishing each year. Recreational fishing is the third most popular outdoor activity in Australia after swimming and court sports (tennis, bowls, etc). Of all States, Queensland had the highest participation rate of all people fishing.[23] About 70 % of recreational fishers are male. A more recent study in Western Australia[25] confirmed the high rate of recreational fishing and estimated that between 80 000 and 100 000 jobs could be related to recreational fishing in Australia through tourism and small businesses in coastal towns.

The 1984 survey[24] estimated that about A$ 2000 million was spent in 1983–84 on fishing and related equipment, excluding accommodation costs.

The most popular fishing methods used in the recreational sector are fishing with bait (92 %), spinning with lures (26 %) and potting/ringing for crabs and prawns (18 %).[24] Most fishing is done in estuarine and marine waters and the most popular sites are from beaches and rocks (32 %), from boats in estuaries and bays (26 %) and from jetties and wharves (21 %).

Foreign fishing

Vessels from several nations fished within 200 miles of the Australian coast prior to the declaration of the Australian Fishing Zone. The most active were Japanese, Taiwanese and Indonesian.[26] Since 1979, Australia has had fee fishing arrangements with the governments of Japan (tuna longlining), Korea (squid jigging) and the Peoples' Republic of China (demersal trawling). Joint Australian and foreign venture agreements have operated with commercial operations from Taiwan (shark gillnetting, pair trawling, demersal longlining) and Thailand (demersal trawling).[27] In addition, there have been feasibility fishing ventures involving Korean, Norwegian, Russian and Polish trawlers, Japanese dropliners and purse seiners from the United States of America. In 1989–90 there were 290 foreign fishing vessels licensed to fish in the Australian Fishing Zone. Most of these were Japanese longline vessels.

In 1998–89 foreign licensed vessels from Japan, Korea, Taiwan, the People's Republic of China and Thailand fished in the Australian Fishing Zone. In the late 1970s, at the peak of foreign fishing activity in what are now Australian waters, Taiwanese pair trawlers caught an estimated 50 000 t of finfish.

In recent years, the fishing activities of foreign vessels have been reduced. Access to trawl grounds and to shark and Spanish mackerel resources through gillnetting in northern Australia has been curtailed and restrictions have been imposed on longline tuna fishing around Australia. Some Australian fishers are now operating in the waters of other countries and on the high seas. Prawn trawlers fish under agreements in several Middle Eastern and South-east Asian countries. Australian purse seiners have fished for skipjack tuna and yellowfin tuna in a number of central and western Pacific Ocean countries and on adjacent high seas.

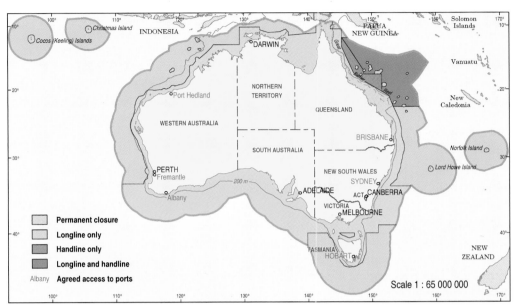

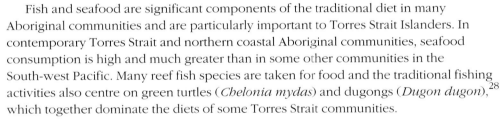

Management zones and port access for Japanese longline fishing vessels 1990–91. (Source: Australian Fisheries Management Authority)

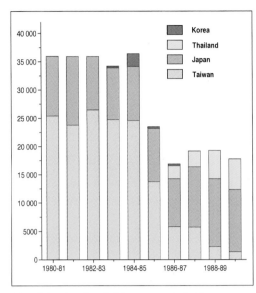

Catch by foreign fishing vessels in the Australian Fishing Zone by country for the period 1980–81 to 1989–90. (Source: Australian Fishing Zone Information System)

Fishing by Aborigines and Torres Strait Islanders

Fish and seafood are significant components of the traditional diet in many Aboriginal communities and are particularly important to Torres Strait Islanders. In contemporary Torres Strait and northern coastal Aboriginal communities, seafood consumption is high and much greater than in some other communities in the South-west Pacific. Many reef fish species are taken for food and the traditional fishing activities also centre on green turtles (*Chelonia mydas*) and dugongs (*Dugon dugon*),[28] which together dominate the diets of some Torres Strait communities.

Involvement of Islanders in commercial fishing activities is increasing although there is still potential for development of fisheries in Torres Strait. Islanders presently dispose of about half their catch of reef fish, trolled pelagic fish and tropical rock lobsters through commercial channels.[28]

Aquaculture and fishery enhancement

Aquaculture is a growing sector of the fishing industry. In 1989–90, aquaculture production represented A$ 190 million or 17 % of the total Australian fisheries production by value. This was a 31 % increase in real value since 1985.[29] Almost all of this was derived from 5 industries — trout, oysters, pearls, Australian salmon and ornamental fish — which, with the exception of Atlantic salmon, are all long established here. Brown trout were introduced to Australia in 1864 and Sydney rock oysters have been cultured since about 1870. Introduced between 1947 and 1952, Pacific oysters have gained acceptance lately as a viable species for culture in parts of eastern Australia.

Culturing of pearls in pearl oysters (*Pinctada* species) commenced in Australia in 1956 but cultured pearl production has become a major part of the Australian aquaculture industry only over the last 10 years. In 1989–90 cultured pearls accounted for almost half the value of aquaculture production. Cage culture of trout and Atlantic salmon in Tasmanian waters is another important sector of the industry.

The ornamental (pet) fish industry is based on small scale land-based operations. The value of production was estimated at A$ 0.9 million in 1990–91 with the majority of revenue obtained from exports. However, most of the ornamental fish sold in Australia are imported and there is scope for replacement of imports with Australian cultured fish, provided the costs of local production are competitive. Some fish (eg goldfish) are farmed increasingly in Australia. Research is being conducted into the efficient production of a range of tropical marine species.

Cage culture of southern bluefin tuna is being trialled in South Australia. (Source: Albert Caton, Bureau of Resource Sciences)

Aquaculture of prawns (mainly tiger prawns, *Penaeus monodon*) is developing in Australia but aquaculture production accounted for less than 5 % of the value of the total prawn harvest (wild plus cultured) in 1989–90.

With few exceptions (1 is Atlantic salmon) aquaculture production depends on the collection of juvenile stages or spawning stock from the wild. In the cases of pearl oysters and prawns, research is seeking techniques to complete the whole life cycle under hatchery conditions.

Stock enhancement programs for some wild fisheries resources are being developed in Australia. Several freshwater species (eg golden perch and Murray cod) are being re-seeded into natural waters from hatchery stock in New South Wales and Victoria. A program jointly run by the Tasmanian Government, Japan and Australian fishing interests is collecting scallop spat from the wild for rearing under field conditions. A similar program has been carried out for scallops at Jervis Bay in New South Wales. The tuna fishing industry, in conjunction with Japanese fishing interests and with Australian Government support, is developing methods for growing out juvenile southern bluefin tuna in inshore cages at Port Lincoln (South Australia) for the fresh 'sashimi' (raw fish) market.

Environmental issues and access to suitable sites are important to the growth of aquaculture in Australia. Much appropriate coastal land is now settled and production may be limited by the availability of low cost, unpolluted coastal sites. Aquaculture itself can be the cause of some local pollution problems.

Responsibility for management of the aquaculture industry rests with State or Territory fisheries authorities. With the participation of these authorities, the Commonwealth Government is co-ordinating a national aquaculture strategy to provide a framework for the orderly development of this industry.

Conservation and access to Australian fisheries resources

Commercial and recreational fishing are not the only uses of Australia's fisheries resources although they may be the only activities that directly 'harvest' them. Issues such as conservation are increasingly important in making decisions about access to some resources and habitats.

Whaling is the most prominent part of the Australian fishing industry to have disappeared over the last 25 years. It was reduced initially because of the declining global stocks of large whales. Whales were afforded complete protection in Australian waters in 1980 under the *Whale Protection Act* in response to community acceptance of the conservation value of whale species. Onshore whaling stations were present in Australia until the last station at Albany (Western Australia) closed in 1978 when policy changed from 'managed use' to 'protection'.

In the shark fishery in northern Australia, gillnetting by Taiwanese vessels was effectively eliminated in 1986 by gear restrictions aimed at reducing the bycatch of dolphins and other cetaceans. A more recent but related example of the impact of conservation values on fishing practices is the international moratorium on high seas large-scale driftnetting. Action against drifting gillnets was prompted by concerns over the incidental kill of whales, dolphins, turtles and seabirds, the poor quality of fish taken, and the excessive catching capacity of the gillnet fleets. Furthermore, tuna resources targeted by drifting gillnets can be harvested by more selective and less wasteful methods such as longlining and trolling.

Access to the aquatic environment may also be restricted through the setting aside of some areas as marine parks and reserves in which fishing is restricted. These reserves comprise less than 5 % of the area of the Australian Fishing Zone. Of the approximately 37.5 million ha of marine reserves in Australia, the largest marine park, the Great Barrier Reef Marine Park, accounts for 92 % of that area.[30] The Great Barrier Reef World Heritage Area stretches 2000 km along the Queensland east coast. It is the largest coral reef system in the world and is managed for sustainable multiple use, including commercial and recreational fishing, conservation and scientific values.

Coastal development, including recreational, tourism and urban, also restricts access to commercial and recreational fishing activities in some localities. The petroleum and mining industries may interact with the fishing industry when all 3 require access to the same marine areas. However, such interactions have so far had little impact on the use of Australian fisheries resources. Offshore petroleum and oil production occurs mainly in Bass Strait and on the North West Shelf. Similarly, shipping and communications can have priority over fishing activities in some areas.

Pollution affects both the quantity and quality of fisheries resources. Access to fisheries resources, including aquaculture, may be permanently or temporarily restricted by aquatic pollution including oil spills, sewage, other land outfalls and toxic algal blooms.

In the early days of European settlement in Australia, marine species introductions were due mainly to fouling organisms from ships' hulls. With the advent of modern shipping and the growth in Australia's bulk commodity exports, dumping of ballast water in Australia has introduced toxic dinoflagellates to harbours,[31] in turn leading to cases of paralytic shellfish poisoning and temporary closures of shellfish farms. There is growing concern over the introduction to Australian harbours of toxic dinoflagellates as well as exotic molluscs, crustaceans, echinoderms and fish and their associated pathogens and algae from the discharge of ships' ballast water and sediments. Voluntary Australian and international controls through the International Maritime Organisation of the United Nations have recently been implemented to encourage re-ballasting at sea (if feasible), regular cleaning of ballast tanks and de-ballasting outside of ports.

The distribution and abundance of fisheries resources may be changed by habitat changes due to natural and man-made effects (eg nutrient enrichment through organic discharges, construction of dams, marinas, canal estates and other forms of coastal development). The majority of Australia's human population lives on or near the coast and this places heavy demands on the coastal environment. Nutrient enrichment of coastal waters leading to enhanced aquatic plant growth is thought to have helped increase inshore populations of some herbivorous fish, such as luderick and yellow-eye mullet. Habitat disturbance by fishing activities (eg demersal trawling and scallop dredging) also have effects on the abundance of fisheries resources in addition to the direct impact of harvesting.[32] At the same time, nutrient enrichment is implicated in loss of seagrasses through increasing turbidity.

Inland waters are used in various ways, only 1 of which is fishing. Australia's fresh water areas are few owing to low rainfall and high rates of evaporation over most of the continent. Consequently freshwater fisheries resources are small. Management of river flow for irrigation, power generation, flood mitigation and human consumption all have effects on the commercial and recreational use of inland fisheries resources. The major environmental issues affecting inland water quality in Australia and hence resources, are eutrophication caused by excessive nutrient loads from urban sewage and agricultural run-off, salinisation and competition for alternative uses.

Fisheries products and markets

THE marketing of Australia's fish catch varies between fisheries and species. The Australian Quarantine and Inspection Service of the Commonwealth Government sets import and export product standards and regulations. The marketing and promotion of Australia's fisheries products for export and domestic markets (refer Chapter 4) is not co-ordinated nationally, as is the case for many other primary industries. Major wholesale markets exist in each capital city and are managed by either State government or commercial interests. Some 'generic' promotion of seafood is done through State fisheries authorities. For export markets, the larger catching and processing companies undertake their own market research and promotion, often using agents or brokers in the importing countries.

Fish export activities are carried out by private enterprise under prescribed conditions. Domestic handling and distribution of fisheries products is a matter for private enterprise, with State and Territory governments providing legislative framework for product standards and reporting.

Exports

The scale and nature of fisheries export products have changed considerably since 1964–65. In real terms the value of exports in 1989–90 was about 4 times that in 1964–65. The growth in export value occurred mainly in the period up until 1980 with only a marginal increase taking place between 1980 and 1990. In 1989–90 exports of edible fisheries products were valued at A$ 674 million and non-edible exports (chiefly pearls, earning A$ 101 million) were worth a further A$ 110 million.

There have also been changes in the proportions of exports by species. In 1964–65 rock lobsters dominated the export sector and accounted for approximately 80 % of the value. Prawns had become the most valuable export commodity by 1980 and were the main Australian fisheries exports up until the late 1980s. Abalone and fish, particularly orange roughy, have increased in importance as export products since 1985. The 2 most valuable fisheries (the Western Rock Lobster Fishery and the Northern Prawn Fishery) both rely on export markets to maximise their price.

The main destinations for Australia's fisheries exports are Japan, the United States of America, Taiwan and Hong Kong. Each country differs in its preference for species and product type. Japan is the major buyer of prawns, abalone and tuna, as well as of significant amounts of rock lobsters as whole product. The United States of America buys 90 % of the rock lobster tails exported by Australia and over 90 % of our fish fillets. Taiwan and Hong Kong are major buyers of Australian rock lobster and abalone.

Domestic markets

The domestic market is supplied mainly with fresh and frozen fish from the domestic catch. Most of the production from the South East Fishery, Southern Shark Fishery and numerous inshore fisheries is sold on these markets. However, significant imports of fisheries products are required to satisfy domestic consumption. In 1989–90 Australia imported A$ 422 million worth of edible fisheries products. In that year, Thailand, New

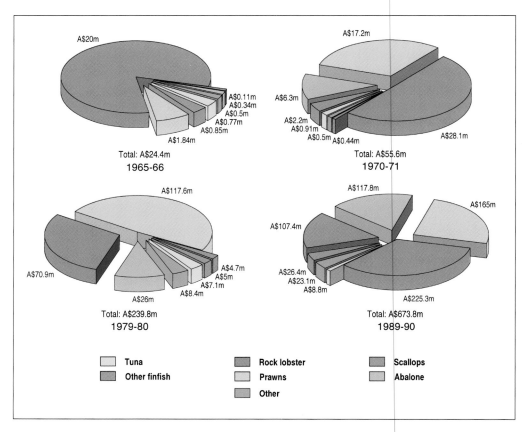

(right) Exports of edible fish products 1965–66, 1970–71, 1979–80, 1989–90.

(below) Proportion of total edible fish exports by country of destination 1989–90.

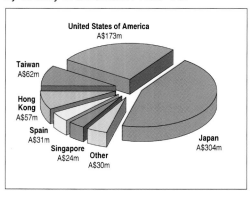

Zealand, Canada, Malaysia, the United States of America and Japan were the top 6 countries from which Australia imported fisheries products.[33]

Fish in the form of frozen fillets and canned fish accounted for the majority of fisheries imports. Fresh, chilled or frozen prawns were the other main fisheries imports. About 70 % of prawns consumed in Australia comprised imported, cheaper products.

Seafood is not a major source of protein in the diets of Australians, a trend which has been consistent over the last 25 years at least. Aboriginal and Torres Strait Islander peoples' seafood consumption is the exception in the national level (page 11). National surveys of seafood consumption were conducted in 1977[34] and 1991.[35] Results show that consumption of seafood by Australians at home increased only slightly between 1977 and 1991. The annual average consumption was 7 kg per person in 1977, rising to 7.5 kg in 1991. The consumption of fresh or frozen seafood increased within that figure but canned and smoked seafood declined. During the same period, consumption of poultry and pork increased significantly, an increase that could be attributed to their successful promotion. In Australia, seafood is infrequently promoted in the main food purchasing outlets such as supermarkets.[35]

There is little processing of most Australian fisheries products, including the most valuable. On the domestic market, fish are normally sold whole or in fillets because of market demands. Fisheries exports are usually frozen whole in bulk and processing occurs overseas (eg prawns, school whiting, eels). The highest prices are obtained for live rock lobsters, prawns, abalone and fish. For rock lobsters, whole cooked lobsters obtain the next highest export prices and frozen tails the least.

Depending upon the species, product value could be increased if there were more domestic processing of low value species, or if more live product of higher value species were offered for sale. There also appear to be opportunities in Australia for the processing of bycatch species from many fisheries as well as for the more productive use of waste from fish processing establishments.[36] Furthermore, little attention is being paid to using the by-products of targeted species; for example, the fins, skins and oil from many shark species. Some leather products are being made from fish skins.

Managing Australia's fisheries

CONCERNS over the exploitation levels of Australia's fisheries resources are not new. They arose in the late 1800s and early 1900s when Royal Commissions investigated the status of New South Wales and Tasmanian coastal fisheries[37] and northern pearl stocks.[38] The need to manage fisheries has accelerated in recent years as scientific evidence has shown increasing numbers of fisheries resources becoming fully exploited or over-exploited.

Like most countries today, Australia faces many challenges in managing its fisheries resources within sustainable limits while maintaining an economically efficient industry. The common property nature of the resources presents particular problems and governments are obliged to control access to the resources and their use on behalf of the community. Australia's fisheries resources appear to be particularly vulnerable to over-exploitation because, as revealed earlier, they are generally small and are harvested by a technically advanced, well developed industry and by many recreational fishers.

Fisheries are managed by a combination of methods designed to balance the exploitation levels to the productive capacities of the fisheries resources. Most Australian fisheries contain more catching capacity than is required to take the catch efficiently. For both commercial and recreational fisheries, the main management methods are by input controls (eg gear restrictions, limited entry licences, area closures and closed seasons), output controls (eg total allowable catches, transferable quotas, bag limits, legal minimum and maximum sizes[16]) and measures aimed at habitat and species protection (eg prohibitions on use of certain gear, on fishing in spawning areas, and on taking females of some species).

Legislation to manage fisheries was introduced in each Australian State and Territory from early this century including Commonwealth acts covering pearling and whaling activities. The first comprehensive Commonwealth fisheries act was passed only in 1952. The *Fisheries Act 1952* allowed the Commonwealth to regulate the activities of Australian fishing boats operating outside the 3 mile territorial sea while the States retained control over fishing in their territorial seas.

Responsibility for managing and exploiting Australia's fisheries resources has been shared between the Commonwealth and State governments since Federation in 1901. The States had the main responsibility until 1968, when 2 events significantly increased the responsibility of the Commonwealth in fisheries management. The first of these was a proclamation extending Australia's declared fishing zone to 12 nautical miles from the coast. This allowed the Commonwealth to regulate fishing by Australian and foreign boats within this zone. In the same year the *Continental Shelf (Living Natural Resources) Act* came into force. This Act extended Australia's jurisdiction to the edge of the continental shelf for sedentary marine species such as pearl oysters.

In 1979 Australia declared the Australian Fishing Zone. This move anticipated the 1982 United Nations Convention on the Law of the Sea provision that coastal States should have sovereign rights over living resources within a 200 nautical mile exclusive economic zone.

The situation of State management within the 3 mile territorial sea and Commonwealth management from 3 miles to 200 miles offshore caused fishers to hold multiple licences and complicated both fisheries management and enforcement in the Australian Fishing Zone. To overcome these problems and similar issues in other industries, the *Offshore Constitutional Settlement* was developed. This arrangement allowed for the exchange of powers between the Commonwealth and the States, and, following amendment of the *Fisheries Act 1952*, the fisheries component of this arrangement came into effect in 1983. It has not yet been fully implemented for all fisheries, with consultations to implement Offshore Constitutional Settlement agreements continuing in 1993.

Under the *Fisheries Act 1952* fishing licences permitted operations anywhere from 3 miles to 200 miles offshore. As fishing pressure increased it became necessary to limit entry to some fisheries. This was achieved by closing certain fisheries to all licence holders except those with specific endorsement. In 1985 the *Fisheries Act* was amended to allow implementation of fishery-specific management plans.

Following the 1989 release of a policy paper entitled 'New Directions for Commonwealth Fisheries Management in the 1990's', the *Fisheries Act 1952* was repealed and replaced with a new suite of fisheries legislation. The most important pieces of legislation were the *Fisheries Administration Act 1991* and the *Fisheries Management Act 1991*.[39] The main provisions of the *Fisheries Administration Act 1991* were to establish a statutory body, the Australian Fisheries Management Authority (commenced February 1992). This Authority is the body responsible for management of Commonwealth fisheries within the Australian Fishing Zone. Its responsibilities include licensing, policy development and surveillance. While it is an autonomous organisation with close links to the fishing industry, the Board of the Authority is responsible ultimately to the Minister for Primary Industries and Energy.

Commonwealth and State responsibilities

The *Fisheries Management Act 1991* is administered by the Australian Fisheries Management Authority and changes the emphasis in fisheries management from the fishing licence to development of specific management plans for each fishery. Management plans were in effect for some fisheries under the previous legislation, although the new Act requires plans to be drafted for all Commonwealth fisheries. Under the new legislation the fishing industry has greater involvement in management, primarily through representation on Management Advisory Committees.

Formal consultation between State ministers and the Federal Minister responsible for fisheries took place at meetings of the Australian Fisheries Council between 1967 and 1992. Prior to this, informal State-Commonwealth conferences were held from at least the 1940s but not annually. The Standing Committee on Fisheries was also created in 1967 and comprised the heads of each State and Commonwealth department overseeing fisheries administration. The Australian Fisheries Council and the Standing Committee Fisheries met annually and, despite changes in legislation, were the major forums for discussion of national fisheries policy. From 1993, the 2 bodies include the New Zealand Goverment as a full member and are called the Australian and New Zealand Fisheries and Aquaculture Council, and the Standing Committee on Fisheries and Aquaculture.

The *Offshore Constitutional Settlement* legislation has provided an additional formal means of negotiating co-operative fisheries management between States and the Commonwealth. *Offshore Constitutional Settlement* arrangements are now in place for most of Australia's important fisheries.

In addition to its responsibilities for domestic fisheries, the Commonwealth negotiates with foreign fishing nations for their access to the Australian Fishing Zone. The fishing capacity of the domestic fleets and the possible impacts of foreign fishing on local industries (including those other than the fishing industry) are considered before any foreign access agreements are approved. Foreign fishing vessels must comply with Australian licensing requirements, logbook and radio reporting and observer programs. These vessels are also charged management and access fees for the right to fish within the Australian Fishing Zone.[27]

Observers boarding a Chinese pair trawler.
(Source: Wade Whitelaw, CSIRO Marine Laboratories, Hobart)

Industry involvement

Close industry involvement is a key factor in Australian fisheries management. Fishing industry councils or organisations operate in each State and belong to a peak body, the National Fishing Industry Council. As well as these councils there are numerous industry organisations formed on a fishery basis — for example the South East Trawl Fishing Industry Association and the Australian Tuna Boat Owners' Association. In some States, industry bodies have direct involvement in fisheries management — such as the Commercial Fishing Advisory Council in New South Wales. Finally, for many fisheries there are well established management advisory committees which involve industry representatives, scientists and government managers.

International fisheries involvement

Australia is a member of several regional and global fisheries management and technical organisations. It is a member of the United Nations' Food and Agriculture Organisation (FAO) and of regional groupings under FAO including the Indo-Pacific Fisheries Commission and the Indo-Pacific Tuna Development and Management Programme. Australia is also a member of the Organisation for Economic Cooperation and Development, the Asia Pacific Economic Conference, the Pacific Economic Cooperation Conference, and the Convention for the Conservation of Antarctic Marine Living Resources. All of these bodies involve consideration of fisheries issues within their charter.

In the central and western Pacific Ocean region, Australia is a member of the Forum Fisheries Council under the South Pacific Bureau of Economic Cooperation. The Council operates the Forum Fisheries Agency in Honiara, Solomon Islands. Australia is also a member of the South Pacific Conference whose operations are executed by the South Pacific Commission in Noumea, New Caledonia. The South Pacific Commission conducts scientific and technical projects into tuna and billfish resources and their fisheries, and into inshore fisheries resources and their development.

Other regional fisheries management needs are handled through either bilateral arrangements with neighbouring countries (eg the Torres Strait Treaty with Papua New Guinea) or foreign fishing negotiations, or multi-laterally (eg the planned treaty on southern bluefin tuna with New Zealand and Japan).

Objectives of fisheries management

Australia has many examples of well managed fisheries and the economic gains through good management are illustrated in many of the species presentations in this book. In particular, the western rock lobster and most of Australia's penaeid prawn fisheries are internationally renowned for management which provides for biological sustainability and economic success. Current management policies have also been influenced by the failures of past attempts to regulate fisheries where non-intervention by management led to declines in stocks.

Fisheries management objectives are similar throughout Australia. For the Commonwealth, the fisheries management objectives stated in the *Fisheries Management Act 1991* are (paraphrased): exploitation of fisheries resources and related activities to be conducted in a manner consistent with the principles of ecologically sustainable development; efficient, cost effective fisheries management; maximisation of economic efficiency in the exploitation of fisheries resources; accountability to the fishing industry and the community in management of Commonwealth fisheries resources; and returns to the community through recovery of management costs according to Commonwealth targets.

Central to management objectives is compliance with the principles of ecologically sustainable development. The sustainable development concept broadens the conservation and utilisation aspects of fisheries objectives from that of single species and focused, single fishery management to include the effects of fishing on the environment at a national and global level. The concept also considers levels of natural capital, the stock of environmental assets such as clean water, maintenance of plant and animal species diversity, and acceptable stock levels of living and non-living natural resources. Reviews within State fisheries authorities have also expanded objectives of management plans to embrace ecologically sustainable development principles.

Fisheries research

FISHERIES research in Australia was funded at around A$ 49.9 million in 1988–89 and employed 729 people.[40] In 1992–93, an estimated A$ 48 million will be spent on fisheries research and development by Commonwealth and State research organisations and funding bodies. Research on Australian fisheries resources is carried out mainly in government research institutions and universities, although there is an increasing number of private consultancy firms involved in economic and market research.

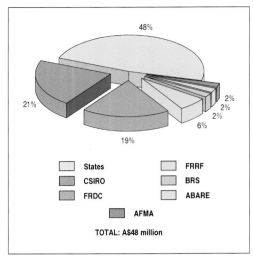

Estimated fisheries research funding by organisation for 1992–93. These figures exclude fisheries research directly funded by educational institutions. Code of abbreviations: CSIRO, Commonwealth Scientific and Industrial Research Organisation; FRDC, Fisheries Research and Development Corporation; FRRF, Fisheries Resources Research Fund; BRS, Bureau of Resource Sciences; ABARE, Australian Bureau of Agricultural and Resource Economics; AFMA, Australian Fisheries Management Authority (Source: Fisheries Research and Development Corporation)

The States and Territories provide around half of the total funding of research and about one third of these State funds derive from the fishing industry through access fees and other arrangements. Less than 5 % of costs is recovered from the industry for research on Commonwealth fisheries.

About 20 % of research funding is provided through the Fisheries Research and Development Corporation. The Corporation was established in mid 1991 under the *Primary Industries and Energy Research and Development Act 1989*. The function of the Fisheries Research and Development Corporation is to increase the economic and social benefits for the fishing industry and the people of Australia through planned investment in research and development in an ecologically sustainable development framework. In this context, the Corporation is a major priority setter for industry driven research. The Corporation obtains its funding — about 1 % of the gross value of production — from the Commonwealth Government and the fishing industry.

In 1989, 46 government and university centres carried out fisheries research, covering fish biology (25 centres), fisheries management and harvesting (23) and aquaculture (35). Some centres carried out research in all 3 disciplines.[41]

The largest fisheries research organisation in Australia is the Commonwealth Scientific and Industrial Research Organisation, which conducts major fisheries programs within its Division of Fisheries. Commonwealth fisheries research is also conducted by the Bureau of Resource Sciences and the Australian Bureau of Agricultural and Resource Economics (both within the Commonwealth Department of Primary Industries and Energy), the Australian Institute of Marine Science, the Commonwealth Scientific and Industrial Research Organisation's Division of Oceanography, and various State fisheries research institutions and universities on contract to the Commonwealth.

All State and Territory government fisheries organisations, except that of the Australian Capital Territory, have their own fisheries research agencies and most have a long history. Major expansions in research activities occurred throughout Australia in the late 1960s as fisheries exploitation increased, and most States now maintain more than 1 research station.

Fisheries research in Australia relies on national and international data gathering infrastructure including those providing taxonomic services (museums), tidal data (the Flinders Institute for Atmospheric and Marine Science), remote sensing information, navigation and fishing charts (the Hydrographic Service of the Royal Australian Navy and the offshore bathymetric map series of the Australian Geological Survey Organisation) and national geographic information centres (the National Resource Information Centre in the Bureau of Resource Sciences, and the Environmental Resources Information Network in the Department of the Environment, Sport and Territories).

Australia is among the top 10 countries in the world in output from its marine science research and development efforts, including fisheries research.[42] Fisheries researchers are represented in Australia by 2 professional bodies, the Australian Society for Fish Biology and the Australian Marine Sciences Association. The first of these is more concerned with fish and fisheries science; the second with a wider field of marine sciences, including botany, zoology, oceanography, chemistry and archaeology.

Location of fisheries research centres in Australia. (Source: Bureau of Rural Resources[41])

Fishing industry training

TRAINING and development for employment in the fishing industry have been conducted on a small scale and in a dispersed form, paralleling the nature of the Australian industry. For the majority of fishers, fishing skills are self-taught or learned 'on the job'. However, as fishing technologies have developed and the demands for greater efficiency of harvesting have increased, government and industry-supported training schemes have developed.

All States now have fishing industry training councils which are incorporated under a National Fishing Industry Training Council. All of the local fishing industry training councils are able to issue certificates for their training programs, which are conducted both 'on the job' and through formal training institutions. In addition, the National Fishing Industry Training Council was recently approved by the Commonwealth Government as a regular industry training agent and the councils are now *bona fide* providers with respect to the Training Guarantee Levy. The levy ensures that all employers spend at least 1.5 % of wages and salaries on training and development of staff.

Fishing industry training in Australia is carried out in colleges of Technical and Further Education and through the Australian Maritime College. The Australian Maritime College, established in 1980, is Australia's national maritime education centre and covers in-service, full-time education and training for the shipping, fishing and allied maritime industries. Situated in Launceston, Tasmania, it is the only Australian institution presently providing degree, diploma and masters' courses in fisheries. Australian secondary schools are also paying much greater attention to education in the marine sciences and industries, including fishing. In 1992 about 100 schools were conducting courses in maritime studies.

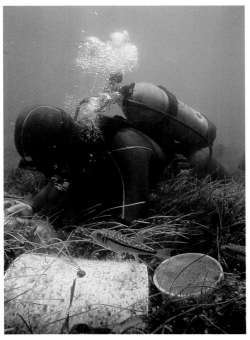

A researcher surveying seagrass beds off Seven Mile Beach, Western Australia. (Source: Dave Evans, CSIRO Marine Laboratories, North Beach)

The outlook

THE development and management of Australia's fisheries resources is entering a new stage of maturity.[43] We face the challenge of maintaining a productive and valuable resource base for all harvesters and users while taking account of changing community attitudes to the conservation values of aquatic species and ecosystems, as well as the welfare of harvested species. There is increasing emphasis on improving management of the total aquatic environment — including recognising that all users of the environment have a responsibility for its quality and maintenance. There is a move away from narrow and single species management of fisheries resources to management of all fish stocks, including those caught incidentally with the target species. Controlling the effects of pollution and environmental degradation is another essential to maintaining the quantity, quality and safety of Australia's fisheries resources.

Within this new framework, it is still essential to adequately control and manage the harvesting of exploited species. For many Australian fisheries, arrangements for managing the resources will need to change so that each population of a species is managed as a single unit and not as separate parts under various State and Commonwealth controls. In many cases, Commonwealth-State jurisdictional arrangements will have to be revised to satisfy this approach. Stronger controls on catch levels will be required also in some cases, thus raising the issues of who should have access to the resources, how this access should be shared and regulated and how incidental bycatch should be controlled. For example, competition between recreational and commercial fishers will probably become more common and recreational catches will need to be managed as a part of total fisheries resources management. Finally, foreign fishing in the Australian Fishing Zone is likely to decline even further with improvements in Australia's capacity to catch and use most species.

Australia is in a good position to manage its commercial fisheries even more strongly since most are closed to new entrants and are subject to catch and effort restrictions. Industry restructuring and further limits on catch and effort (where necessary after scientific, economic and social studies) should assist Australian fisheries managers to meet the challenge of achieving sustainability.

Within the restrictions on catch levels, however, there remains great potential to increase the value of fisheries by improving the handling and marketing of the catch

Source: Robert Lester

and by diversifying the range of products derived from the fisheries resources. Production too, can be increased as some depleted stocks recover under strong management regimes and as aquaculture production increases.

Above all, the wise use of fisheries resources will require access to the best available national and international information on the state of the resources, markets, research, management and training activities. This book is part of the effort to make information on Australian fisheries resources more accessible. It represents the first major attempt to draw together comprehensive information on the fisheries resources, to describe how the animals live in their aquatic environment and how they are used for economic, recreational, conservation and scientific purposes.

References

1. Paxton, J.E., Hoese, D.F., Allen, G.R. and Hanley, J.E. (1989) *Zoological catalogue of Australia. Volume 7, Pisces. Petromyzontidae to Carangidae.* Canberra: Australian Government Publishing Service. 664 pp.

2. Dyne, G.R. and Walton, D.W. (eds) (1987) *Fauna of Australia. Volume 1A. General articles.* Canberra: Australian Government Publishing Service. 339 pp.

3. Department of Primary Industries and Energy (1988) *Recommended marketing names for fish. A practical guide for fish marketing.* Canberra: Australian Government Publishing Service. 238 pp.

4. Food and Agriculture Organisation of the United Nations (1991) *FAO yearbook of fishery statistics — catches and landings, 1989.* Volume **68**. Rome. 516 pp.

5. Gulland, J.A. (ed) (1970) The fish resources of the oceans. *Food and Agriculture Organization of the United Nations, Fisheries Technical Paper* **97**. Rome. 425pp

6. Michaelis, F.B. (1985) Threatened fish. A report on the threatened fish of inland waters of Australia. *Australian National Parks and Wildlife Service Report* **3**. 45 pp.

7. Roughley, T.C. (1916) Fishes of Australia and their technology. *Technical Education Series* 21. Sydney: Government of New South Wales. 296 pp.

8. Roughley, T.C. (1966) *Fish and fisheries of Australia.* Sydney: Angus and Robertson. Revised edition. 328 pp.

9. MacInnes, I.G. (ed) (1950) *Australian fisheries: a handbook prepared for the second meeting of the Indo-Pacific Council, Sydney, April 1950.* Sydney: Halstead Press. 103 pp.

10. Pownall, P.C. (ed) (1968) *Australian Fisheries 1968.* Canberra: Department of Primary Industry. 73 pp.

11. Muir, T. (ed) (1973) *Australian Fisheries 1973.* Canberra: Department of Primary Industry. 40 pp.

12. Pownall, P.C. (1979) *Fisheries of Australia.* Farnham: Fishing News Books. 147 pp.

13. Williams, M. (ed) (1988) *Getting the message across.* Proceedings of the Australian Society for Fish Biology and the Bureau of Rural Resources workshop on scientific advice for fisheries management, Canberra, 10 July 1987. Canberra: Australian Government Publishing Service. 78 pp.

14. Hancock, D.A. (ed) (1988) *Tagging – solution or problem?* Australian Society for Fish Biology workshop, Sydney, 21–22 July 1988. *Bureau of Rural Resources Proceedings* **5.** 208 pp.

15. Pollard, D.A. (ed) (1989) *Introduced and translocated fishes and their ecological effects.* Australian Society for Fish Biology workshop, Magnetic Island, 24–25 August 1989. *Bureau of Rural Resources Proceedings* **8**. 181 pp.

16. Hancock, D.A. (ed) (1992) *The measurement of age and growth in fish and shellfish.* Australian Society for Fish Biology workshop, Lorne, Victoria, 22–23 August 1990. *Bureau of Rural Resources Proceedings* **12**. 310 pp.

17. Hancock, D.A. (1992) *Legal sizes and their use in fisheries management.* Australian Society for Fish Biology workshop, Lorne, Victoria, 24 August 1990. *Bureau of Rural Resources Proceedings* **13**. 135 pp.

18. Hancock, D.A. (ed) (1992) *Larval biology.* Australian Society for Fish Biology workshop, Hobart, 20 August 1991. *Bureau of Rural Resources Proceedings* **15**. 211 pp.

19. Parslow, J. and P. Jernakoff (eds) (1992) *Report of a workshop on managing Australia's fisheries under threat of climate change impacts, Hobart, 28–30 May 1991.* Canberra: Australian Government Publishing Service. 69 pp.

20. *Commodity statistical bulletin* (1991) Canberra: Australian Bureau of Agricultural and Resource Economics. 272 pp.

21. Ward, R.B. (1987) *Australia since the coming of man.* New York: St Martin's Press. 263 pp.

22. Williams, M.J. (1979) Survey shows prawn trawling is Queensland's most important fishery. *Australian Fisheries* **38**(8): 11–16.

23. National Recreational Fisheries Working Group (1992) *Recreational fishing in Australia. A draft national policy for public discussion.* Canberra: National Steering Committee on Recreational Fishing, Department of Primary Industries and Energy. 26 pp.

24. Australian Recreational Fishing Confederation (1984) *National survey of participation in recreational fishing, Report No. 1.* Melbourne: PA Management Consultants. 47 pp.

25. Lindner, R.K. and McLeod, P.B. (1991) The economic impact of recreational fishing in Western Australia. *Fisheries Department of Western Australia, Fisheries Management Paper* **38**. 44pp.

26. Foreign fishing vessel operations off Australia (1975) *Australian Fisheries* **34**(8): 8–25.

27. Cost recovery for managing fisheries (1992) *Industry Commission Report* **17**. 361 pp.

28. Johannes, R.E. and MacFarlane, J.W. (1991) *Traditional fishing in the Torres Strait Islands.* Hobart: CSIRO Division of Fisheries. 268 pp.

29. Treadwell, R., McKelvie, L. and Maguire, G.B. (1992) Potential for Australian aquaculture. *Australian Bureau of Agricultural and Resource Economics, Research Report* **92.2.** 81pp

30. Ecologically Sustainable Development Working Groups (1991) *Final report — fisheries.* Canberra: Australian Government Publishing Service. 202 pp.

31. Jones, M.M. (1991) Marine organisms transported in ballast water. A review of the Australian scientific position. *Bureau of Rural Resources Bulletin* **11**. 48 pp.

32. Craik, W., Glaister, J. and Poiner, I. (eds) (1990) The effects of fishing. Australia: CSIRO. 197 pp. Reprinted from *Australian Journal of Marine and Freshwater Research* **41**(1).

33. *Australian fisheries statistics* (1992) Canberra: Australian Bureau of Agricultural and Resource Economics. 36pp.

34. Department of Primary Industry (1978) *Fish and seafood consumption in Australia. A consumer survey 1976 – 77.* Canberra: Fisheries Division, Department of Primary Industry. 68 pp.

35. Peacock, G. (1992) *Key results from the national seafood consumption study and their implications for seafood marketing.* Paper presented at the *Fish marketing symposium, National Agricultural and Resources Outlook Conference, Canberra, 4–6 February 1992.* Canberra: Australian Bureau of Agricultural and Resource Economics.

36. Australian Science and Technology Council (1988) *Casting the net. Post-harvest technologies and opportunities in the fishing industry.* Canberra: Australian Government Publishing Service. 138 pp.

37. Harrison, A.J. (1991) The Commonwealth Goverment in the administration of Australian fisheries. *Royal Australian Institute of Public Administration, National Monograph* **6**. 96 pp.

38. Mckay, Captain J. (1908) *Report of the Royal Commission into the pearl-shell and beche-de-mer industries.* Brisbane.

39. Meany, F. (1992) AFMA brings changes. *Australian Fisheries* **51**(1): 6–13.

40. Department of Industry, Technology and Commerce (1992) *Australian science and innovation resources brief 1992. Measures of science and innovation 3.* Canberra: Australian Government Publishing Service. 72 pp.

41. Bureau of Rural Resources (1989) *Centres for rural research in Australia directory 1989.* Canberra: Australian Government Publishing Service.

42. Department of Industry, Technology and Commerce (1989) *Oceans of wealth? A report by the Review Committee on Marine Industries, Science and Technology.* Canberra: Australian Government Publishing Service. 188 pp.

43. Williams, M.J. and Reichelt, R.E. (1991) *Outlook for Australia's fisheries resources in 2001.* Paper presented at the 1991 national conference of the Environment Institute of Australia, *Towards environment 2001.* Canberra, 22–25 October 1991.

Contributors

Information and comments for this chapter were provided by (in alphabetical order) Bernard Bowen, Albert Caton, Mary Harwood, Burke Hill, Patricia Kailola, Bob Kearney, Rob Lewis, Frank Meany, Russell Reichelt and John Wallace.

compiled by Alex McNee

Introduction

AQUATIC environments in and around Australia provide a wide range of habitats for fish, depending on their requirements for food and shelter. Habitats used by fish can be broadly divided into the open ocean, reefs, estuarine and inshore areas, and freshwater.

The Australian Fishing Zone comprises an area 4 times the size of Australia's continental shelf, which is approximately 2 200 000 square km. It includes such a broad range of depths and latitudes that all major habitat types are represented.

The waters of the continental shelf support the majority of Australia's fisheries partly because of the amount of primary production in the zone of light penetration — the euphotic zone. The general productivity of any marine region is influenced by the area of shallow water around the continent along with the amount of nutrients supplied either by river run-off or upwelling from deeper waters. Furthermore, the transport of nutrients by ocean currents and tidal streams has a fundamental influence on the fisheries production of Australia.

This chapter describes the major characteristics of Australia's open ocean, coral reef, coastal and freshwater habitats. It concentrates on aspects which influence the distribution and abundance of fisheries resources and also addresses some key challenges in the conservation of fish habitats.

Oceans

AN area of ocean is characterised by 4 basic variables: **depth, currents, temperature** and **nutrients**. Of these only depth is constant. The other 3 depend on a variety of factors which are often themselves related to events that occurred a great distance away or a long time before the results are experienced in any particular location. There are many other variables involved in the ocean, but these 4 can give a good indication of what is happening.

The following sections summarise how the variables of depth, currents, temperature and nutrients are distributed in space and time. Taken individually, they provide a basic understanding of how and why fluctuations occur in the marine environment. When read together, they provide a good picture of the dynamic system that is the ocean around Australia, which affects and is extensively used by our mainly coastal dwelling population.

Source: Anne Coleman

Ocean depths and currents
by George Cresswell

(additional comments by Joe Doyle and Jason Middleton)

The continental shelf comprises a sloping sea floor and sub soil from the low water line to 200 m depth. Beyond the 200 m depth contour the continental slope falls away steeply to the deep ocean floor. The deepest part of the Australian Fishing Zone is north of Christmas Island, where it drops to approximately 6700 m. Off southern Australia, the deepest trawl fishery in the world harvests orange roughy to depths of about 1500 m.

The width of the continental shelf varies from less than 7 km wide (near North West Cape in Western Australia) to areas in the north of Australia where it extends beyond the boundary of the Australian Fishing Zone (200 nautical miles) and joins the continental shelf of Indonesia and Papua New Guinea.

Currents are primarily driven by winds acting over large areas of the ocean to pile water up in some areas and lower it in others. The consequent readjustment of sea level is also influenced by the earth's rotation and the coastal and sea floor topography. These factors cause currents to follow the paths that they do. In general, currents tend to follow the contours of the slowly changing sea surface levels — not the rapid changes caused by ocean waves and swells. Differences in sea surface elevation can be related to differences in water densities, where density depends on both temperature and salinity. Lower density waters stand 'taller' than those of higher density, and currents are strongest where the sea surface slope is steepest, ie where the density gradient is greatest. Tidal movements are driven by the influence of the sun and the moon. These

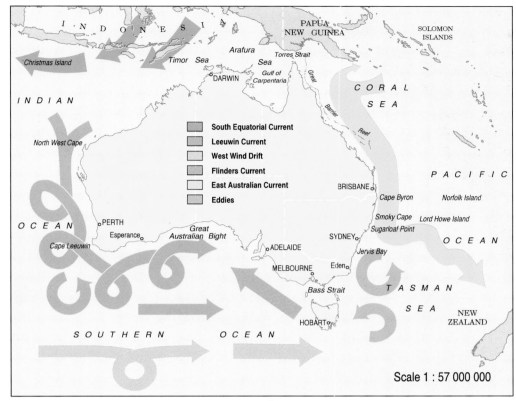

Schematic view of ocean currents around Australia. (Source: CSIRO Division of Oceanography)

are not important when considering the movement of water by currents, as their action is oscillatory and so there is no net movement of water over time.

The shape of the continental shelf affects current flow around the continent. Two examples are: 1) off the southern Queensland and New South Wales coasts where the shelf narrows to less than 10 km in places, the warm south-flowing East Australian Current moves close to the coast; 2) Bass Strait and the narrow continental shelf around Tasmania act as a barrier to the west-flowing circulation of the Antarctic Circumpolar Current in the Southern Ocean.

Australia's ocean surface waters have many sources. Two major currents that influence the waters off the coasts of Australia are the East Australian Current and the Leeuwin Current. There are also several minor currents such as the tropical Indian Ocean Current and the Pacific–Indian Ocean throughflow which filters water through the Indonesian Archipelago into the Timor Sea, the Flinders Current and the Antarctic Circumpolar Current (or West Wind Drift).

There are 2 deep currents that are also important. Ice melt and precipitation in the Southern Ocean create a descending cold, fresh plume of high density water that moves slowly down a density gradient northward and can be found off Australia at a depth of about 1000 m. Deeper still, at the sea floor, are cold salty waters that are produced near Antarctica during the winter freeze. This cold, high density brine spreads eventually into all the warm, high density waters of the world's oceans. This deep, cold water off the Australian continental shelf provides habitat for important commercial deep water fish species such as orange roughy.

The **East Australian Current** runs along Australia's east coast bringing water from the Coral Sea to the Tasman Sea off southern New South Wales. Because it forms on the western side of the Pacific Ocean, the East Australian Current is called a 'western boundary current'. It, and other western boundary currents such as the Gulf Stream in the north Atlantic Ocean and the Kuroshio ('black current') off Japan, receives an extra impetus from the earth's rotation. In the Coral Sea there is a westward flow towards Australia centred roughly at 18° S latitude. As it nears the Australian continent it splits, one branch flowing towards the Gulf of Papua and the other flowing southward to become the East Australian Current. By the time it enters the Tasman Sea the current is moving at speeds of up to 3 knots.

The Coral Sea waters are warmer and have a lower density than those of the Tasman Sea. This density difference makes the surface of the Coral Sea higher than that of the Tasman Sea. The boundary between the Coral and Tasman seas is not simply an

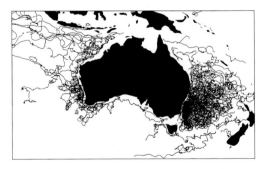

Spaghetti diagram — the paths followed by CSIRO satellite tracked drifters from 1975 to 1990. The eddies and meanders of the East Australian Current and the Leeuwin Current are clearly revealed by the drifters. Northwest of Australia there are a number of drifter tracks showing the South Equatorial Current flowing to the west and also, near Java, the South Java Current which flows eastward in summer and westward at other times. (Source: CSIRO Division of Oceanography)

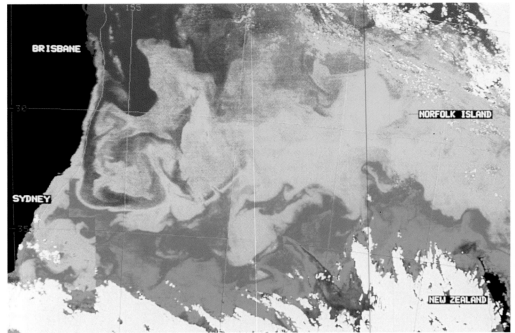

A satellite image showing the Coral and Tasman seas from Fraser Island to Eden and across to New Zealand. The East Australian Current can be seen in the top left as a warm (red) stream entering the Tasman Sea from the Coral Sea. It then loops and doubles back northwards before continuing to the south. Offshore from Sydney the current turns and flows to the east. Remnants of it continue along the Tasman Front (the boundary between green and yellow in the image), passing it to the south of Norfolk Island. South-east of Sydney is an eddy that is rotating anticlockwise. (Source: CSIRO Division of Oceanography)

east-west line. At its western end it reaches southward so that a ridge almost 1 m high and 200–300 km wide is formed in the sea surface. Furthermore, the ridge is not a static feature as it can extend southwards, sometimes as far as Bass Strait. Following a southward extension the ridge will retract northwards. The East Australian Current runs hundreds of km southward on the western side of this ridge to its southern-most extremity. The Current then veers anticlockwise, does a 'U'-turn and runs northwards on the eastern side of the ridge. Part of the Current rejoins the main current stream to flow down the New South Wales coast again, while the remainder flows eastward in the direction of New Zealand.

The East Australian Current includes a near-surface river of warm water up to 100 km wide and 100 m or more deep. The Current's surface speed can be greater than 4 knots, and at depths of hundreds of m the speed may have only decreased to half of this. As a further complexity, maximum current speeds may be encountered at about 50–100 m depth.

As it flows southward the East Australian Current frequently spreads across the continental shelf and moves close inshore, affecting the movement of bottom sediments. The edge of the Current leaves the coast and moves out to sea at Cape Byron, Smoky Cape, Sugarloaf Point and Jervis Bay. The rapid change in current speed across the 'front' that is formed between the clear, dark blue waters of the East Australian Current and the cooler, green local waters causes waves to steepen and

A vertical 'cut' out from Jervis Bay through the western side of an East Australian Current eddy showing the current speeds. The currents can be seen to peak at a speed of 3 knots in a band that is 15 km wide. Superimposed on the diagram are the temperature contours. These show warm water at the surface in the eddy and also cold water nearshore (less than 14˚C) that has either upwelled from a depth of more than 200 m or has been carried northward from Bass Strait. (Source: CSIRO Division of Oceanography)

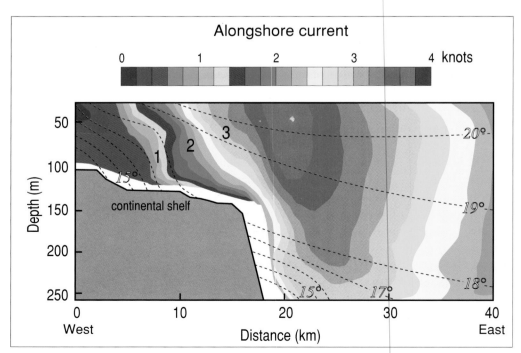

break. Upwelling of cold, nutrient-rich water can occur where the East Australian Current leaves the coast. This cold water can be entrained along the edge of the Current and carried tens of km out to sea.

There are times when the western edge of the ridge guiding the East Australian Current develops a series of 'waves' (as viewed from space) that cause small clockwise rotating eddies to form. These eddies can cause sections of the continental shelf to experience currents that flow northwards. To the south of Sydney there are 'warm core' eddies about 200 km in diameter. At the sea surface the eddies are 'hills' about 80 cm high and they are isolated from one another and from the East Australian Current stream. Retractions to the north following the occasional migrations of the ridge southward can cause the ridge to pinch off and produce 2 or 3 new or re-emerging eddies. These eddies rotate anticlockwise and have edge currents travelling at up to 4 knots. The effects of the eddy currents can reach the sea floor, even to 5000 m depth well offshore. Cooling at the surface of an anticlockwise eddy in winter can produce a deep lens-like layer of water extending to 400 m depth. This layer is isothermal (has the same temperature) and isohaline (has the same salinity).

While the eddies are usually isolated, there are times when they can be reconnected to the parent East Australian Current. This linking takes place when 'saddles' in the sea surface topography reach from the ridge to the eddy. The East Australian Current is then redirected to encircle the eddy. Another type of connection takes place when the southerly migration of the ridge causes 2 eddies to move close together, such that they eventually form a single larger eddy.

Eddies can last for more than a year and move along very complex paths. During its wanderings an eddy will occasionally collide with the continental shelf. The collision causes it to distort into an elliptical shape with strong currents along its western side. After it bounces away from the continental shelf edge the eddy eventually recovers its circular shape.

The East Australian Current has an important influence on the seasonal distribution of some fish species off eastern Australia, eg tunas and marlin.

The **Leeuwin Current** flows along the west coast, bringing water from north-western Australia to Cape Leeuwin. It then flows eastward around the southern coast to Esperance. From this point the coastline veers east-north-east while the Current continues in its easterly flow into the Great Australian Bight. The Leeuwin Current is called an 'eastern boundary' current because it flows along the eastern edge of the Indian Ocean.

The Leeuwin Current is considered unusual when compared to other eastern boundary currents because it flows the 'wrong way', ie southwards. Other eastern boundary currents in the southern hemisphere are the northward flowing, cold Benguela Current off south-west Africa and the Humboldt Current off the west of South

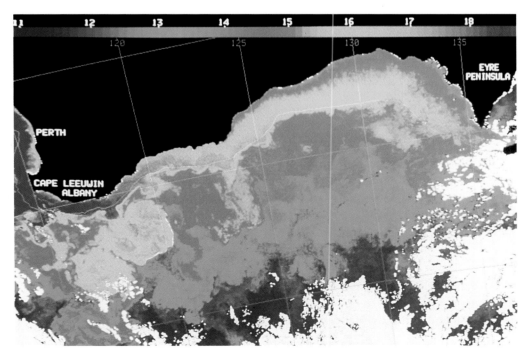

A satellite image showing the warm (red) waters of the Leeuwin Current flowing eastward 1800 km from Cape Leeuwin to the Eyre Peninsula. Note the offshoots where the flow becomes unstable and sections of the Leeuwin Current break out to sea. While the Leeuwin Current spreads shoreward across the continental shelf in the western half of this image, its speed is fastest just beyond the shelf edge where it can reach 3.5 knots. (Source: CSIRO, Division of Oceanography)

America. Both currents derive from the southerly winds that drive upwellings of nutrient-rich waters. The Leeuwin Current in contrast, flows *into* the southerly winds. Features that further distinguish the Leeuwin Current from other eastern boundary currents are the presence of a steep alongshore sea level gradient, and the strong transfer of heat from the ocean into the atmosphere rather than the reverse (which is the case for the other eastern boundary currents).

The Leeuwin Current is driven by a downward slope of the sea surface between north-western Australia and Cape Leeuwin. The high sea level off north-western Australia is caused by the flow of water from the Pacific Ocean to the Indian Ocean through the Indonesian Archipelago.

The Leeuwin Current's source is the warm, low salinity waters off north-western Western Australia. In this region it is broad and shallow (400 km wide by 50 m deep). As it flows southward to Cape Leeuwin, the Current tapers to less than 100 km wide and deepens to more than 100 m, while accelerating to 2 knots. The Current's speed increases as it flows eastward and speeds of up to 3.5 knots have been measured just beyond the edge of the continental shelf between Cape Leeuwin and Esperance. In this area the warm waters spread across the continental shelf and close to shore. Beyond Esperance the current speed drops considerably. Beneath the Leeuwin Current there is a reverse undercurrent, extending over a depth range of several hundred m, which moves at speeds of up to 0.5 knots.

The southward flow of the Current along the west coast is reflected in seasonal changes in sea levels. Sea level changes of up to 40 cm have been recorded, with maximum levels on the North West Shelf in March and in south-western Australia in May to June. The overall speed of the Current is relatively slow because of interactions with eddies and because of variations in flow rate. It is suggested that the fastest transit from North West Cape to Cape Leeuwin is about 2 months. It takes about another 3 months for the Current to cross the Great Australian Bight.

As it flows southward the Leeuwin Current both meanders and 'spins up' eddies. The Current provides the eddies with warm fresh waters, while taking cold salty waters from them. This mixing contributes to the cooling and increase in salinity in the Leeuwin Current as it flows. The eddies rotate both clockwise and anti-clockwise, are about 150 km in diameter, can last for up to 2 months and can have speeds of up to 2 knots.

After it 'turns the corner' and flows eastward the Leeuwin Current loses vast amounts of water into offshoots that can extend up to several hundred km southward. The offshoots are about 50 km wide and 150 m deep and are trough-shaped in cross section. On their western side the offshoots flow southward at up to 2 knots, while on their eastern side they flow northward at similar speeds.

The Leeuwin Current plays a significant role in the annual movement of several species of importance in Australian fisheries. It is thought to be a conduit, bringing juvenile southern bluefin tuna south from their spawning grounds in the triangle between north-western Australia and Indonesia. It also facilitates the eastward movement of juvenile Australian salmon and tommy ruff from spawning grounds off south-western Australia. The settlement of western rock lobster puerulus larvae on the near-shore reefs of Western Australia is higher in years when the Leeuwin Current is stronger.

Both the Leeuwin Current and the South Equatorial Current of the Indian Ocean appear to have their source in the triangle of the Indian Ocean formed by Indonesia and north-western Australia. This region receives the water that flows through the

Alongshore current

A vertical 'cut' southward from Albany through the Leeuwin Current showing the current speeds. The Current is flowing eastward and is very narrow, being only 10 km wide for speeds exceeding 1 knot. The maximum speed is over 3 knots. Superimposed on the diagram are the temperature contours. These show the warm water (more than 19°C) from the Leeuwin Current to spread in across the shelf and down to the shelf edge. Offshore there is a strong surface temperature front with a drop from 19°C to less than 16°C. (Source: CSIRO Division of Oceanography)

Indonesian Archipelago from the Pacific Ocean which is referred to as the **Pacific–Indian Ocean throughflow**.

The circulation of the upper water in the tropical Indian Ocean is very complex. This complexity is due to the monsoon cycle, the low latitude northern boundary of the Ocean, the many different water bodies formed through heating, rainfall and evaporation, and to the complex geography of the Indonesian Archipelago.

The cycling of the monsoons induces dramatic current reversals from the northern ocean boundary south to 10° S, as well as within the Indonesian Archipelago. In addition, there are upwellings and an alternating interchange of Indonesian waters and Pacific Ocean waters. Along the southern edge of the Archipelago the South Java Current reverses with the monsoons.

The **Flinders Current** flows north past western Tasmania, western Bass Strait and along the Victorian and South Australian coasts during the summer months. It may circle anticlockwise around a spiral current system (called a gyre) out to sea.

A summer upwelling occurs at the continental shelf near the South Australia–Victoria border. The upwelling has water temperatures as low as 12.5°C and it brings nutrient-rich waters to the surface from about 100 m depth. It is a major fishery area for rock lobsters, which may benefit directly from the rich waters. The upwelling results from the combined effects of the Earth's rotation and south-easterly winds that move surface waters offshore. The surface waters are replaced by deeper waters.

The last significant current affecting Australian seas is the eastward flowing **Antarctic Circumpolar Current**. It is driven by strong westerly wind in the Southern Ocean. This current has surface speeds of less than half a knot and the flow can break into eddies. It is a major component of global ocean circulation.

Sea surface temperatures
by Bob Edwards

There are 5 overlapping temperature zones recognised in the world's oceans: tropical, subtropical, temperate, subpolar and polar. The first 3 zones are represented around the shores of mainland Australia and a fourth, subpolar, is included by way of our external territories, Heard, MacDonald and Macquarie islands. The Australian Antarctic Territory lies in the polar zone. Some groups of fish are restricted to 1 zone, for example coral trout are found only in the tropical zone and blue eye are found only in the temperate zone. Other species, such as tuna, are more wide ranging and may be found in 3 zones. Sea surface temperatures therefore provide a strong indication by which the distribution of some fish species can be explained.

In shallow tropical waters during summer, sea surface temperatures reach about 32°C and south of Tasmania in late winter they drop to 9°C. If the waters around Australia's sub-Antarctic territories and the Australian Antarctic Territory are included, the minimum water temperature drops to 4°C and –1.5°C.

Seasonal differences in sea surface temperature vary markedly between tropical and temperate zones. In the Coral Sea the seasonal temperature difference is only 4°C, while south of Tasmania the difference can be over 9°C. This variation is related to the differences in the strength of solar heating in the 2 areas. In tropical areas, waters are warm and so temperature changes usually reflect changes in solar input. While solar heating is still important in temperate waters, large variations in temperature are caused by unusual inflows of water from warm tropical or cold sub-Antarctic sources.

The most apparent feature in sea surface temperature maps is a horizontal or zonal pattern that reflects the expected drop in temperature as distance from the equator

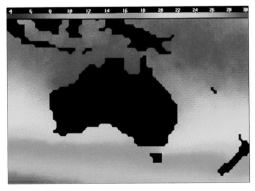 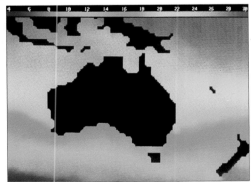

Long term averages of sea surface temperature for *summer* (left) and *winter* (right) for the Australian region. The data came from satellite images for February and August for the years 1984–1988. They can be thought of as climatic averages. (Source: CSIRO Division of Oceanography)

increases. The major departures from this pattern coincide with major current systems where the southward flow pulls warmer waters southward with it. Furthermore, the effect of currents varies depending on whether their flow patterns are permanent or seasonal.

The pattern of decreasing water temperature with increasing distance from the equator is a generalisation that fits well only for open oceans. Closer to shore these patterns can be disrupted by land effects and the effects of upwellings. In addition temperature conditions will vary in confined bodies of waters such as bays and gulfs due to reduced circulation, and in shallower waters, where heat is gained or lost more rapidly.

Land effects are most noticeable in summer months when the temperature of the land is well above that of the ocean. Waters near the shore are affected, especially those near river mouths and shallow bays. Ebb tide waters warmed by the land extend the thermal influence from 1 to tens of km offshore. This effect can be magnified in confined waterbodies where warm waters may be trapped. The reverse cooling effect occurs in winter months when near-shore waters tend to be cooler than those offshore, but the higher prevalence of winter storms means that the effect is not as noticeable as in summer.

In areas such as the Gulf of Carpentaria and Spencer Gulf and in confined water bodies such as Bass Strait and the Great Barrier Reef lagoon, water circulation is restricted. In summer the heat is trapped in the mixed layer of warm water that forms, and temperatures are higher than would be expected for the geographical location. When 'land effect' is added to this shallow waters such as those near Karumba in the Gulf of Carpentaria, the headwaters of the Spencer Gulf and the North West Shelf can have temperatures higher again. In winter, temperatures tend to be only slightly less than the geographic average for the reasons presented before.

Upwellings can occur in near-shore waters in summer months when there is a surface mixed layer of warm water overlying cooler water. Wind blowing across the water produces surface currents. If the wind moves the surface water away from the coast it is replaced by the cooler water underneath, ie water is lifted vertically to form an upwelling. This cool water, brought up from 30 or 40 m, is often richer in nutrients than the water it replaces. In other words such upwellings, if they are permanent occurrences, can be important to fisheries.

In Australia there are no permanent upwellings, although episodic ones occur near Laurieton and Evans Head on the central New South Wales coast, between Eden and

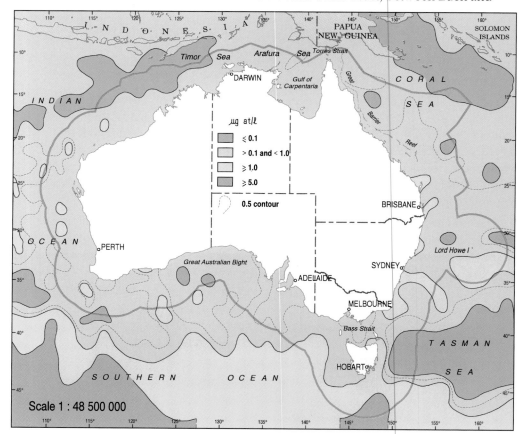

Concentrations of inorganic nitrogen in surface waters around Australia, measured in micromoles per l. (Source: Rochford, 1979)

Sale in south-eastern Australia and near Port MacDonnell in South Australia. Upwellings can result in drastic depressions in sea surface temperatures, often causing large thermal gradients over short distances.

Nutrients
by David Rochford

The productivity of ocean waters depends upon a continuous supply in the upper (50–100 m) water layer of nutrients such as nitrates, phosphates and to a lesser extent silicates and minor trace elements. To a large extent the potential productivity of ocean waters can be gauged from the amounts of these nutrients there.

Nitrates provide most of the basic nitrogen supply in the oceans for the production of organic matter. The productivity of Australian near-surface waters is constrained to low levels by the limited availability of essential nutrients. These nutrients are cycled within the sea. Because the cycling of nitrogen requires much more energy than that of phosphorous, nitrogen is often considered a limiting factor in primary production. Phytoplankton, the primary elements in marine food chains, utilise the available nutrients in near-surface waters. Their production is corrrelated with these nutrient levels, and their abundance affects the supply of nutrients throughout the chain. Ultimately it affects all species in the marine ecosystem. Nutrient availability must therefore be considered when managing any part (eg fishery resources) of the ecosystem. In the absence or near absence of nitrates, therefore, organic production in the ocean either ceases or is greatly retarded.

The general nutrient status of Australian waters is reflected by the distribution of nitrates. Long term average surface values of nitrates show that large areas of the oceans around Australia are virtual deserts (0.1 micromoles/l). South of 40° S (ie south of Tasmania) nitrates are more than 1 micromole/l but below 5 micromoles/l, a value not very rich when compared with nutrient levels in the world's highly productive waters (eg upwellings off the coast of south-west Africa where surface nitrates average 20–25

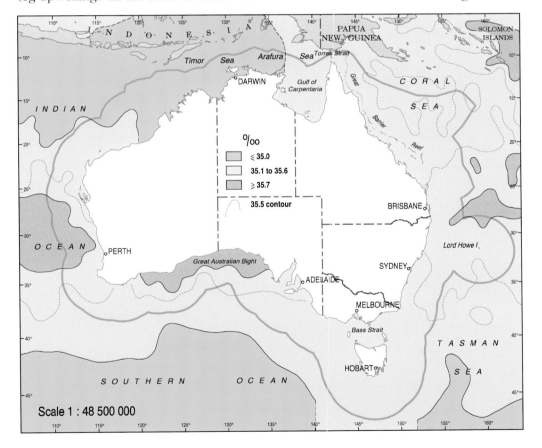

Major water masses at 100 m depth around Australia, as indicated by salinity concentrations measured in parts per thousand. (Source: Rochford, 1979)

micromoles/l). Everywhere else, except for isolated coastal regions of Tasmania and New South Wales and further offshore from Western Australia, nitrates are in the range 0.1–1.0 micromoles/l, a value typical of the low production sub-tropical belts of the world's oceans. In conjunction with the low nitrate levels, high salinity waters are present through the Coral and Tasman seas in the east, from the Great Australian Bight to about 40° S and from about 20° S to 40° S in the eastern Indian Ocean. These high salinity waters, which form a reservoir for the supply of surface nutrients, are themselves generally deficient in nutrients. The lack of nutrients in deep waters around Australia means that our near surface waters will always have low nutrient content.

Salinities at 100 m depth off north-western Australia to 20° S are typical of tropical, low salinity waters. Although much richer in nutrients than high salinity sub-tropical waters, these deeper waters are largely cut off from surface exchange by a very strong temperature gradient (thermocline).

Phosphates are associated with metabolic processes in living organisms. They are rarely a limiting factor on productivity because they are rapidly recycled in the upper layers of the ocean.

Despite the overall situation, there are processes that result in areas of nutrient-rich waters associated with some of Australia's coasts and continental shelf. These are: upwelling, coastal intrusions and North West Shelf enrichment.

Upwelling Within the outer margin of anticyclonic eddies in the western Tasman Sea and at the centre of cyclonic eddies off eastern Tasmania, deeper waters rise to the surface at various times of the year. Nutrient-rich waters that have been uplifted from depths of 200 m or more can often be found in the triangle formed between the coast and the East Australian Current. The surface temperature in these waters can be 5°C lower than those in the Current and can often be distinguished by a colour change from the deep blue of the nutrient-poor Current to the green of the phytoplankton rich upwelled waters. Another seasonal upwelling with unknown nutrient data occurs off south-eastern South Australia. Off Gippsland in Victoria, an intense coastal upwelling during autumn has limited nutrient enhancement. This is because the upwelled waters were originally nutrient-poor Bass Strait surface waters that sink during winter mixing. Satellite observations show other upwelling enrichment areas around Australia from surface temperature anomalies, but the nutrient value of these areas is unknown. Even so, the nutrient levels within Australian upwelled waters are less than 20 % of those in the world's richest upwelling systems.

Coastal intrusions Along the New South Wales coast south of Sydney incipient upwelling takes place when offshore nutrient-rich deeper waters are pushed into the near shore sea bed region by deviations in the shoreward meandering of the East Australian Current. For the most part, these nutrient-rich waters do not upwell to the surface and only contribute to surface nutrient enhancement when influenced by secondary processes such as wind mixing or internal wave disturbance. Similar coastal intrusions occur along the outer margin of the Great Barrier Reef. In this area however, fixed animal and plant communities (eg corals, algaes) quickly mop up the increased nutrients. They act as nutrient reservoirs in the periods between intrusions. The nutrients in these reservoirs are unavailable to higher life forms in the short term.

North West Shelf enrichment Productivity of North West Shelf waters is markedly seasonal. During summer and early autumn tropical waters rich in nutrients are carried southward into the offshore waters of this region. A variety of processes, including tidal currents and tidal mixing, combine to move pockets of these tropical waters into the coastal regions. Here the nutrients are quickly assimilated before the waters are dissipated by intense tidal mixing. During winter these North West Shelf waters are mainly sub-tropical in origin and poor in nutrients.

Further Reading

Cresswell, G.R. and Legeckis, R. (1986) Eddies off southeastern Australia. *Deep-Sea Research* **33**: 1527–1562.

Cresswell, G.R. (1991) The Leeuwin Current — observations and recent models. *Journal of the Royal Society of Western Australia* **74**: 1–14.

Edwards, R.J. (1979) Tasman and Coral Sea ten year mean temperature and salinity fields, 1967–76. *CSIRO Division of Fisheries and Oceanography Report* **88**. 40 pp.

Gibbs, C.F., Tomczak, M. Jr and Longmore, A.R. (1986) The nutrient regime of Bass Strait. *Australian Journal of Marine and Freshwater Research* **37**: 451–466.

Holloway, P.E., Humphries, S.E., Atkinson, M. and Imberger, J. (1985) Mechanisms for nitrogen supply to the Australian North West Shelf. *Australian Journal of Marine and Freshwater Research* **36**: 753–764.

Huyer, A., Smith, R.L., Stabeno, P.J., Church, J.A. and White, N.J. (1986) Currents off southeastern Australia: results from the Australian Coastal Experiment. *Australian Journal of Marine and Freshwater Research* **39**: 245–288.

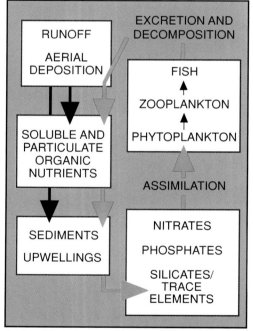

A simplified diagram showing cycling of inorganic nutrients in the sea, and the relationship of nutrients to the food chain.

Lewis, R.K. (1981) Season upwelling along the south-eastern coastline of South Australia. *Australian Journal of Marine and Freshwater Research* **32**: 843–854.

Pearce, A.F. (1991) Eastern boundary currents of the southern hemisphere. *Journal of the Royal Society of Western Australia* **74**: 35–45.

Rochford, D.J. (1979) Nutrient status of the oceans around Australia. *CSIRO Division of Fisheries and Oceanography Report* 1977–1979. Hobart. 20 pp.

Rochford, D.J. (1988) Seasonal influx of nitrates to the slope and shelf waters off north west Australia. *CSIRO Marine Laboratories Report* **191**. 23 pp.

Smith, R.L., Huyer, A., Godfrey, J.S. and Church, J.A. (1991) The Leeuwin Current off Western Australia, 1986–1987. *Journal of Physical Oceanography* **21**: 323–345.

Wolanski, E., Drew, E., Abel, K.M. and O'Brien, J. (1988) Tidal jets, nutrient upwelling and their influence on the productivity of Alga Halimeda in the Ribbon Reefs, Great Barrier Reef. *Estuarine, Coastal and Shelf Science* **26**: 169–201.

Coral reefs

by Peter Doherty

IN tropical Australia, the major hard substrate habitat for shallow water demersal fishes is provided by coral reefs. These environments are remarkable for their diversity of life forms (at least 1500 species of fish, 400 corals, 4000 other invertebrates) and their structural complexity.

Evolution has produced a variety of different forms of corals including branching forms, flat tabulate forms, flat encrusting forms, and rounded massive forms. The first 2 forms have the fastest linear growth rates and produce most of the 3-dimensional structure on the reef surface. They are therefore important in providing shelter for fishes. Ultimately, the massive forms contribute most of the durable reef framework, and the encrusting corals are more important in binding loose surface elements.

Unlike the rocky reefs of the temperate zone, coral reefs are dynamic structures, constantly growing and eroding. Growth is provided by the living corals, which are colonial animals related to sea anemones. Each coral colony consists of numerous polyps embedded in a calcareous honeycomb matrix. As these polyps multiply, they deposit a new skeleton and extend the size of the colony. After death, the skeleton is left behind. Much of the coral skeleton becomes incorporated into the framework of the

Reef growth and history

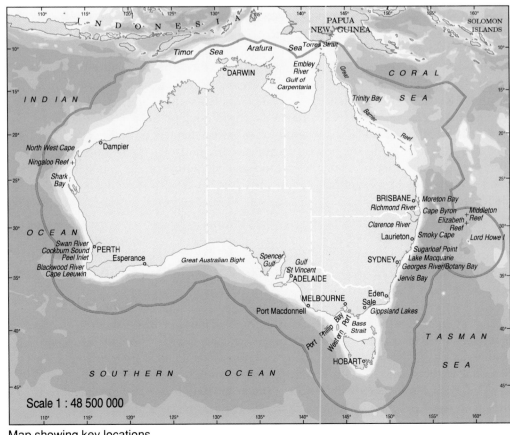

Map showing key locations.

Ribbon reefs in the Cairns section of the Great Barrier Reef Marine Park. (Source: Great Barrier Reef Marine Park Authority)

reef, where chemical processes eventually convert it to limestone. Some or all of it may also be reduced to rubble by wave action, assisted by a variety of living organisms such as sponges and worms that weaken the skeleton ('bioerosion').

The reef building activities of corals are made possible because of extra energy available to them from numerous tiny plant cells, called zooxanthellae, that are embedded in their tissues. Like all plants, zooxanthellae have the capacity through photosynthesis to make complex molecules from simple ones using the power of sunlight. Corals have evolved mechanisms for tapping some of this energy from the zooxanthellae, and without this association corals would not be able to deposit calcium carbonate fast enough to build reef structures. Reef building corals cannot flourish at depths where there is insufficient light to power the zooxanthellae's photosynthetic reactions. This 'critical' depth varies with turbidity (cloudiness) of the water, but in even the clearest water there is little reef growth below 100 m.

Temperature and changing sea level are other critical environmental controls that have been very important in the geological history of reefs in Australia. Reef building corals do not flourish in waters colder than 19°C, hence their association with the tropics. Until 75 million years ago, most of Australia was south of 40° S and the continent was surrounded by cold water. It was not until Australia separated from Antarctica and began drifting northwards into warmer waters that corals colonised this continent. While continental drift has determined *where* coral reefs could exist, fluctuating sea levels have determined *when* they could exist. During periods of low sea level, erosion from the land would have made the coastal seas turbid and unsuitable for most corals, although this erosion was building flat sedimentary plains around the continental margins. During subsequent periods of high sea level these plains were covered by water to form shallow continental shelves. In the warm northern waters, these shelves provided the ideal habitat for the formation of coral reefs.

As the Australian continent drifted further into the tropics, corals extended their range southward along the east and west coasts. For much of recent geological history, low sea levels have prevented extensive reef development; eg, reef growth has occupied only 180 000–360 000 of the last 1.8 million years, in 4000–14 000 year phases. Modern reef growth recommenced when sea levels began rising only 8000–9000 years ago. Sea level reached its present height around 6000 years ago, and corals would have reached the surface not long after. Thus, from a geological perspective, coral reefs are young and non-permanent habitats.

Distribution and geomorphology

Currently, coral reefs are well developed on both sides of Australia. The Great Barrier Reef off the east coast is the largest reef archipelago in the world. The Ningaloo Reef Tract off Western Australia is the largest fringing reef structure in Australia. Lord Howe Island is one of the southern-most fringing reefs in the world. Nearby, Elizabeth and Middleton reefs are the southern-most open ocean platform reefs in the world. On the North West Shelf there is evidence of buried barrier reefs suggesting that a structure like the Great Barrier Reef may have existed in the west during periods of lower sea level. Across the north of Australia, shallow turbid seas mean that reef growth is not as rich as might be expected. There are, however, extensive fringing reefs on the Coburg Peninsula. The other major reef type is the oceanic reef found off the continental shelf in deep water. The best examples of these are in the Coral Sea and off the North West Shelf.

The complexity of coral reef habitats is well illustrated by the vast Great Barrier Reef, which comprises almost 5000 reefs and shoals in an area of 230 000 square km. North of Cairns, the reefs have developed on a narrow continental shelf less than 50 km wide. In this region are linear ribbon reefs, some as long as 25 km, that line the edge of the continental shelf. Punctuated only by deep narrow passes with strong tidal flows, these reefs separate very deep water on the seaward side from a shallow coastal lagoon. Further north, the strong tidal currents of Torres Strait have resulted in complex deltaic reef structures with extensive reef flats covered with seagrasses. South of Cairns, the continental shelf is wider, reefs are more widely spaced and most are restricted to the outer half of the shelf so that the coastal lagoon becomes a prominent feature, critical to trawl fisheries. Further south, the shelf is more than 250 km wide and individual reefs are larger, some covering more than 100 km. These may be large and intersected by narrow, sheer sided channels with severe tidal currents; or be closely packed, with many reefs enclosing large central lagoons; or may be isolated with many examples of vegetated sand islands (cays). Despite the impression of vast tracts of coralline habitat, less than 10 % of the Great Barrier Reef area is covered by coral, the remainder being a mixture of sand and other substrate types.

Lord Howe Island and Elizabeth and Middleton reefs support a low diversity of corals, many at the southern-most limit of their distribution, but provide unique habitat for many fish species not found outside their area.

The 260 km long Ningaloo Reef Tract is not as extensive as those on the east coast. These reefs exist close to the mainland because the absence of large rivers in the area means there are no large sediment outflows to smother the coral.

Tropical reefs form many discrete habitats for demersal fishes, separated by large distances of deep water over which larval dispersal ensures the genetic unity of stocks of non-migratory fish.

Habitats

Despite the variety in the topography of coral reefs, the following habitats can be recognised:

windward reef slopes face the prevailing weather and are frequently dissected by buttress-like spurs and grooves. These are often steep walled, with rich coral and fish communities fed by the incoming water. Although the corals in this zone typically have the fastest growth rates, they also suffer the greatest damage from waves.

reef crests are shallow surf zones that often dry out at low tide. The harshness of the physical environment excludes most corals and this zone is typically dominated by a low pavement of algal-covered limestone. It is a zone of very high primary production and an important feeding ground during high tide for large schools of grazing fishes.

reef flats are broad areas of rubble and sand stretching downwind from the reef crest. These areas are constantly being extended by the coral debris being swept from and over the crest.

lagoons, when present, are 'sinks' for the finer sediments carried from the windward reef. They are constantly being infilled, but they provide many fish (schooling goatfishes [Mullidae], emperors, rays, etc) with a rich source of forage from organisms that live in the sediments. Most of the common nocturnal fishes (cardinalfishes [Apogonidae], squirrelfishes [Holocentridae]) also forage over the sand for plankton which rises into the water column at night. In addition, most lagoons contain large patch reefs that support a rich demersal fish fauna.

Hoskin Island and Reef, Great Barrier Reef Marine Park. (Source: Great Barrier Reef Marine Park Authority)

leeward reef slopes are expressed best on reefs that have a central lagoon, otherwise the backreef may be dominated by a sloping sand wedge. Generally these slopes are calmer environments. The coral communities on them show greater 3−dimensional structure, which offers more cover to fish. Although corals in this zone do not grow as quickly as those on windward slopes, their structure is more likely to remain in place after death. As a result, most coral reefs are actively growing downwind.

Productivity

With the exception of some coastal ecosystems, coral reefs are remarkable as systems of high productivity growing in clear, nutritionally poor waters. The keys to this production are constant entrapment of new energy by plankton-feeding animals from the water passing over reefs, and efficient recycling of nutrients within the ecosystem due to mechanisms like the coral−zooxanthellae symbiosis.

Estimates of productivity from reef systems often relate only to the area surveyed, because of the diverse nature of reef habitats and the range of depths. Collections have shown biomass of shallow water fishes of 93−239 t per square km on reefs of the central Great Barrier Reef. Generally, reefs seem able to sustain harvests of around 5 % of fish biomass, which suggests yields of 5–12 t per square km per year. Higher yields have been recorded from reefs in other parts of South-east Asia, but these figures are based on exploitation of all species and therefore are not directly comparable to the Australian situation where only the larger species are targeted.

The Great Barrier Reef supports the most productive reef fisheries in Australia. For example, 98 % of the total Australian commercial catch of coral trout is landed in Queensland.

Conservation and management

The effects of human actions are beginning to appear on some Australian reefs, but they are concentrated in coastal areas adjacent to centres of population. Of all the countries in the world bordering the tropics, northern Australia is unique in having relatively pristine coral reefs in proximity to areas of human activity.

The Great Barrier Reef Marine Park covers the area between 11° S and 24° S and is the largest multiple use marine park in the world. With dominion over more than 2500 separate reefs, the Great Barrier Reef Marine Park Authority has implemented an original scheme of zoning, generally of whole reefs, for compatible uses. Levels of reef protection in the Park vary from places where most extractive industries can be carried out to protected areas that are effectively closed to the public.

The only other coral reef area in Australian waters to receive similar treatment is the Ningaloo Reef Tract, managed by the Western Australian Department of Conservation and Land Management. Although the principles of multiple use management have been the same as in the Great Barrier Reef Marine Park, the Ningaloo Reef Tract provides a different set of problems as it lies for the most part within 2.5 km of the coast. This proximity to the coast means that Ningaloo Reef is much more accessible than parts of the Great Barrier Reef which gain some protection simply through remoteness, weather closures and sheer size.

Other smaller reef areas are also under legislative control. They include national nature reserves in the Coral Sea and Indian Ocean managed by the Australian National Parks and Wildlife Service. Such areas are difficult to manage actively because of their remoteness. However, they do not remain untouched. For example, Ashmore Reef, off the North West Shelf, is a traditional target of Indonesian fishers.

Further reading

Veron, J.E.N. (1986) *Corals of Australia and the Indo-Pacific.* North Ryde: Angus & Robertson Publishers. 644 pp.

The coastal environment

by Ron West

AUSTRALIA'S coastline traverses several climatic, geologic and oceanographic zones. This zonation produces a wide variety of habitats and environmental conditions, and a diverse and abundant marine flora and fauna.

The present coastline is thought to have formed about 6000 years ago, when sea level stabilised at its present height after a period of slow rises. Since that time there has been a gradual ageing of the coast. Local environmental conditions such as tides, rainfall and geology have played a major role in determining the type and variety of shorelines we see today.

In north-western Australia where the average temperature range is from 19°C to 33°C, monsoons drop an estimated 1250 mm of rain annually. There are large tidal ranges (3.7 to 11 m amplitude) with low wave energies. These remote shorelines are composed of rugged, deeply dissected sandstones, which form landlocked harbours, bounded by precipitous cliffs. Steep sided headlands alternate with mangrove-lined bays and intertidal mudflats. Large expanses of tidal flats are connected to the open sea by narrow straits which form spectacular tidal waterfalls that reverse in direction with the changing tides.

In contrast, the more populated south-eastern coastline has an average temperature range of 6°C to 26°C, an average rainfall of only 90 mm annually and follows no defined seasonal pattern. Tidal ranges are low (less than 2.5 m) but wave energy is high (storm

Deception Bay sunset. (Source: Glen Smith, Queensland Department of Primary Industries)

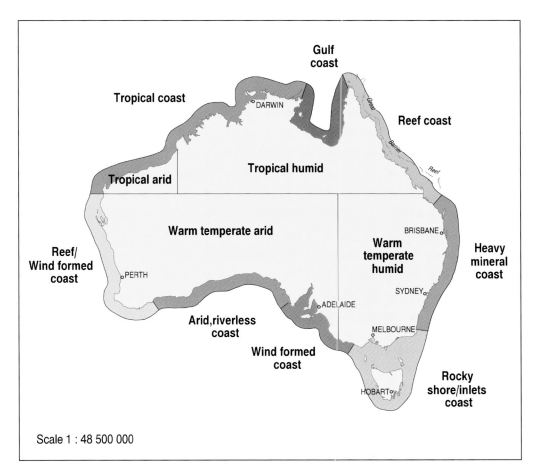

Coastal zones around Australia. (Source: Redrawn from Bunt, 1987)

Scale 1 : 48 500 000

generated wave heights of greater than 10 m have been recorded). Here the shoreline consists of long stretches of sandy beaches between rocky headlands, sometimes forming semi-enclosed embayments. These 'barrier' beaches and rocky headlands are interrupted only by the entrances to the more protected estuarine environments of the rivers, bays, and coastal lakes and lagoons.

The various coastal regions around Australia can be classified on the basis of their climate and geology. Even with this variability in environmental conditions, the basic building blocks of the coastline, sediment and rock, combine to form what could be termed the fundamental ecosystems of the shoreline: the beaches, the rocky foreshores and the estuaries.

Sedimentary shorelines in Australia are predominantly sandy beaches, although fine grain muds also form extensive tidal flats in northern Australia. About 70 % of Australia's coastline is beach and mudflat. Extensive barrier beaches extend along much of the eastern and western Australian coastlines.

Beaches

Beach sands are mixtures of materials that can include shell, coral debris and grains from various rock types. They vary in colour and grain size regionally due to local geology and climate, and also spatially along beaches as a result of sorting processes

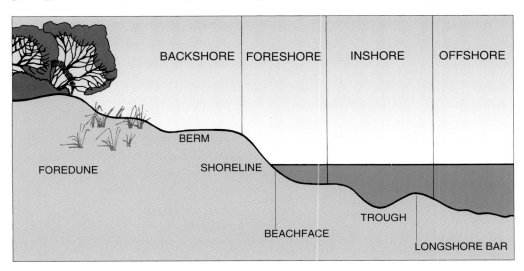

Cross section of a sandy shoreline.

caused by variations in wave energies. Much has been learnt concerning the dynamics and structure of beaches throughout Australia. However the fauna of beaches has not been extensively studied.

In eastern Australia, exposed barrier beaches form from marine-derived sands. Common benthic inhabitants are beach worms (Onuphidae), pipi (*Plebidonax* species) and a variety of small crustaceans called isopods and amphipods. There is virtually no scientific data concerning the ecology of fish in these habitats, and we presently rely on information from anglers and commercial fishers. Migrating schools of sea mullet, tailor, Australian salmon, and to a lesser extent yellowfin bream and sand whiting dominate both commercial and recreational catches from open beaches. Off southern beaches, anglers often catch mulloway. Rays and sharks are also common.

In Western Australia, the beach environment often is protected by offshore limestone reefs. This shallow, calm habitat gives rise to some of the world's most extensive and complex seagrass beds. The seagrass meadows off the Western Australian coastline occupy about 20 000 km and are made up of 25 different species. Extensive, though structurally less complex, seagrass beds occur in the sandy habitats within the South Australian gulfs. In Spencer Gulf, seagrass beds cover about 3700 square km. These seagrass beds support complex communities of fauna and flora, including many species important in recreational and commercial fishing. For example, in Shark Bay, Western Australia, 66 algal species and 40 animal species live on the seagrass leaves. Dugongs (*Dugong dugon*), turtles and crustaceans feed directly on the seagrass; however, the majority of the primary production from these seagrasses goes into a detrital food chain.

In north-western Australia, near Dampier, the inshore areas consist of 2 components: muddy mangrove-lined tidal flats and creeks, and igneous boulders interspersed with sandy beaches. The composition of the fish communities in these adjacent habitats is very different, probably the result of the differences in substrate (mud *versus* sand) and the presence of mangrove trees in 1 habitat and rocky reefs in the other. The inshore areas here are considered important nursery areas for adult fish inhabiting adjacent shallow (2–20 m) waters.

Another region where extensive muddy tidal flats are a prominent feature of the coastline is the Gulf of Carpentaria. Again, seagrasses are dominant communities, fringing the coastline for about 906 km. These habitats are considered to be critical in the life cycle of tiger prawns, endeavour prawns and ornate rock lobsters, which make up important commercial fisheries. Again in this region, seagrasses are also food for dugongs and green turtles (*Chelonia midas*).

Rocky foreshores

Extensive rocky foreshores exist in southern, western and eastern Australia, covering about 20 % of the coastline. They are composed of a variety of substrate types such as granite or sandstone. Very little information is available; however, rocky foreshores have been grouped into 4 major types:

- sandstones, shales and limestones, in the south-east of Australia;

- granitic and other igneous formations, along the Queensland coast;

- laterites, common in northern Australia; and

- Precambrian rocks, along the north-western coast.

Important factors determining the floral and faunal communities found on rocky foreshores are the degree of protection, tidal range, and local climate.

On many rocky shores there are discernible bands of invertebrate communities, such as barnacles, inhabiting intertidal zones. Large macro–algal beds

Cross section of a rocky shoreline.

LITTORAL   INTERTIDAL   SUBTIDAL

PERIWINKLES

LIMPETS

TUBE WORMS

ALGAL MAT

BARNACLES

SEA SQUIRTS

KELP

SEA URCHIN

HIGH TIDE

LOW TIDE

occur in southern and south-eastern Australia, containing genera such as *Cystophora, Phyllospora, Ecklonia, Sargassum* and *Durvillea*. Abalone, rock lobsters, sea urchins and turban snails (*Subninella* species) are commercially harvested from the waters around these rocky headlands. Recent quantitative and experimental work, particularly in south-eastern Australia, has shown that the patterns of vertical distribution of algae on rock platforms result primarily from the activities of grazing animals.

At many locations in southern Australia — for example along the coastlines of the eastern Great Australian Bight and western Victoria — the exposed cliffs drop directly to depths of 20–30 m. The water along these coastlines is extremely clean and, depending on substrate and degree of protection, algal and seagrass communities penetrate to depths of up to 70 m. Fish species such as tunas (Scombridae), Australian salmon and pilchards are seasonally abundant in these habitats.

Few reports of fish surveys in rocky reef areas exist for Australian waters, although over 100 fish species have been identified in rocky areas. Many of the permanent fish residents of rocky foreshores are herbivores or omnivores, and so also affect the distribution of the subtidal algal communities.

Rocky foreshores are popular with recreational anglers and divers. Commercial fish trapping may also occur there. Fish inhabiting these areas are generally from 2 groups: permanent residents, such as snapper, luderick, blue groupers (*Achoerodus gouldi*), wirrah (*Acanthistius* species), and rock cods; and migratory species such as tailor, Australian salmon and yellowtail kingfish. Many species of rays and sharks are common predators in these areas as well.

Estuaries and embayments

About 8 % of the Australian coastline consists of 'water', ie the entrances to estuaries and embayments. Australian estuaries have been classified into 3, based on climatic conditions. They are:

• estuaries dominated by discharges from summer rains and drought in winter (in northern Australia);

• estuaries which experience winter floods and summer drought and which are subject to micro-tidal conditions (in south-western Australia); and

• estuaries lacking a well-defined pattern of flooding (in south-eastern Australia).

Estuaries can also be classified in terms of their geomorphology into a number of different types: drowned river valleys, barrier estuaries and coastal lagoons. In many respects, semi-enclosed open embayments and inlets, such as Botany Bay, Moreton Bay, Shark Bay and Port Phillip Bay are best grouped with estuaries, as they contain many of the same types of ecological communities and experience similar management problems.

Estuaries and embayments are probably the best studied coastal areas in Australia, particularly in terms of their fish populations. Fish studies have been carried out at many estuarine sites throughout Australia, including:

• Trinity Bay, Moreton Bay and Embley River estuary in Queensland;

• Botany Bay, Lake Macquarie, Clarence and Richmond rivers in New South Wales;

• Western Port, Port Phillip Bay and Gippsland Lakes in Victoria; and

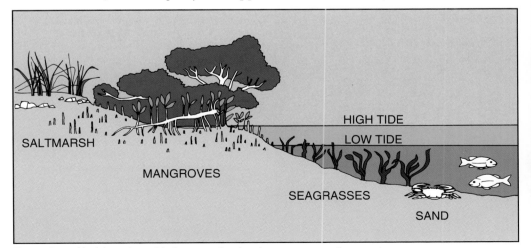

Examples of habitats found in bays and estuaries - cross section.

Kelp beds, South Australia.
(Source: South Australian Department of Fisheries)

- Blackwood and Swan rivers, Cockburn Sound, Peel–Harvey Estuary and Shark Bay in Western Australia.

Estuaries offer protected waters where intertidal and shallow-water plant communities, such as seagrasses, mangroves and saltmarshes, are found. Seagrasses include species such as common eelgrass (*Zostera capricornia*) and strapweed (*Posidonia australis*). These species form large beds in shallow estuaries, and, while considered a nuisance by many, are an important part of estuarine ecosystems. Seagrass beds contribute large amounts of organic material to estuarine food chains, provide food and shelter for many animals and act as buffers causing silt to settle from the water.

Mangroves line the shores of many estuaries, forming extensive forests in some areas. They contribute large amounts of organic material to estuarine food chains, and provide shelter and food for fish and crabs as well as for many species of birds and other animals. Mangroves also stabilise foreshore areas, acting as filters by trapping silt and sediments.

Saltmarshes are strips of land between tidal areas and dry land. They are dominated by plants such as salt wort (*Sarcocornia quinqueflora*), rushes (*Juncus* species) and sand couch (*Sporobolus virginicus*), which recover nutrients from upland runoff. These areas also act as buffers between estuarine areas and land developments.

Wetland communities are important providers of food and shelter to associated faunal communities. As shown by major reviews carried out on Australian seagrass and mangrove ecosystems, many fish species important to recreational and commercial fisheries use seagrass and mangrove habitats as settlement and nursery areas. For example, in eastern Australia juvenile yellowfin bream, snapper and luderick depend on seagrass beds for food and shelter. As adults, these species live predominantly in deeper water, such as around rocky reefs.

In some regions of Australia non-estuarine inshore areas also offer fish nursery habitats, eg protected inshore waters in some regions of south-western Australia.

Most permanent fish residents in estuaries tend to be small species which may serve as forage for transient populations of predominantly juvenile fish of larger species. Nevertheless, the importance of estuaries in contributing to total fish production must also be stressed. Commercial and recreational catches of many fish species and prawns are primarily taken in estuaries, including species such as sea mullet, bream, whiting and flathead.

Further Reading

Blaber, S.J.M, Young, J.W. and Dunning, M.C. (1985) Community structure and zoogeographic affinities of the coastal fishes of the Dampier region of north-western Australia. *Australian Journal of Marine and Freshwater Research* **36**: 247–266.

Bunt, J.S. (1987) The Australian marine environment. Pp 17–42, in *Fauna of Australia. Volume 1A, General articles*. Canberra: Australian Government Publishing Service.

Hutchings, P. and Sanger, P. (1987) *Ecology of mangroves*. St. Lucia: University of Queensland Press. 388 pp.

Larkum, A.W.D., McComb, A.J. and Shepherd, S.A. (eds) (1989) *Biology of Australian seagrasses*. Amsterdam: Elsevier. 841 pp.

Middleton, M. (1985) Estuaries — their ecological importance. *Department of Agriculture. New South Wales. Agfact* **F2.3.1.** 7 pp.

Pollard, D.A. (1981) Estuaries are valuable contributors to fisheries production. *Australian Fisheries* **40**: 7–9.

Underwood, A.J. (1981) Structure of a rocky intertidal community in New South Wales: patterns of vertical distribution and seasonal changes. *Journal of Experimental Marine Biology and Ecology* **51**: 57–85.

Mangroves at low tide. (Source: Fisheries Research Institute, NSW Fisheries)

Freshwater habitats

by John Koehn and Jenny Burchmore

AUSTRALIA is the driest continent after Antarctica, and with about 90 % of the rainfall lost through evaporation, fresh water becomes a limiting resource. The Murray and Darling rivers make up the largest river system and, with the larger tropical rivers in the north and rivers in Tasmania, accounts for about 80 % of the total annual runoff for Australia. The dry nature of the Australian continent has resulted in the evolution of a unique freshwater fish fauna, adapted to the temporary nature of the habitats that are Australian freshwater.

Rivers are continuous one way systems, with water flowing from source to mouth. Australian rivers can be divided into short, high gradient coastal streams (characteristic of those on the east coast) and the long, low gradient inland rivers. Runoff from inland rivers is low, relative to the size of the catchment, since flood waters have a long residence time as they spread out and cover large areas. The low and often unpredictable nature of flow in Australian rivers is one feature that distinguishes them from rivers elsewhere in the world.

With sparse water resources, the quality of water is a major concern. When water quality issues are considered, toxic pollutants and other highly visible and dramatic events are usually prominent. However, other less recognisable changes to water quality, such as water temperature, pH, dissolved oxygen concentrations, turbidity, suspended sediment levels, salinity and other chemicals may also affect fish populations.

Water temperature influences the physiology and behaviour of fish. Most fish species have optimal temperature ranges. Outside of this range they may suffer stress which reduces feeding or growth. Spawning in many species (eg Murray cod and golden perch) is related to rises in water temperature, or occurs between a narrow range of temperatures. Habitat modifications that alter thermal regimes (eg cold water outlets from storage) may reduce the ability of these species to spawn. Periods of low flow and reduced shading in the summer months can result in increases in water temperature above lethal levels for coldwater species.

Dissolved oxygen levels in the depths of dams and deep pools can often fall below levels needed for fish survival. Low level outlets on dams can result in the release of this deoxygenated water downstream. If stream flow is low, the opportunities for reoxygenation of water are few, and stagnant pools may persist in the river. High water temperatures and algal blooms will also reduce dissolved oxygen levels in the water.

Turbidity is an aspect of water quality that is often overlooked, although increases in water turbidity have been reported for most of our lowland waters. Increased turbidities are likely to affect growth rates of fish that rely on vision for feeding and increase their stress. Increased turbidity is generally a result of increased suspended sediment, which at high levels may be directly lethal to fish.

Salinity problems in farmland are only now receiving attention, particularly in the lower Murray–Darling Basin. Increased water salinities also may be affecting fish populations in the region, as each species has a particular salinity tolerance.

Freshwater habitats consist of more than just the water. Broad habitat zones can be identified throughout a length of stream, and microhabitats occur within the stream. Factors include diversity in channel shape and form, water velocity, water depth, substrate and objects providing cover (eg rocks, snags), aquatic vegetation and riparian vegetation. The stream channel provides the overall habitat perimeter and is the most stable component of the riverine habitats. Most freshwater fish species spend the greater part of their lives in rivers and streams.

Australia's freshwater fish biota has adapted to natural flow regimes dictated by seasonal rainfall and runoff. This century, many of these natural flow regimes have been altered by water storages and diversions. These often cause dramatic reductions in the amount of water available to flow downstream, and can result in the loss of large areas of habitat, especially the shallow riffle areas where invertebrate production is high.

The demand for irrigation water means that many rivers must accommodate constant high flows during summer, whereas their pre-impoundment summer flows were low.

Lake Coila, southern New South Wales.
(Source: John Matthews, Fisheries Research Institute, NSW Fisheries)

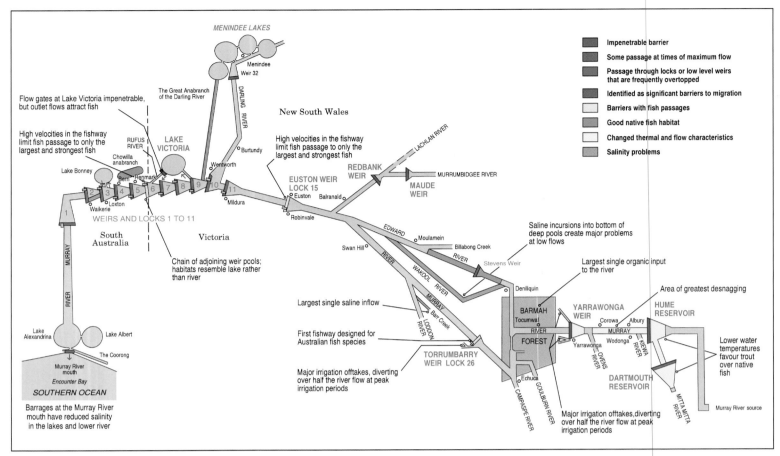

Schematic diagram of the Murray River system showing river regulation. (Source: Murray Darling Basin Commission)

Such reversals of the flow regime can affect various aspects of a fish's lifecycle, especially spawning and migration.

The stream substrate offers habitat such as pools, gutters and boulders. These provide spawning sites for many species, eg trout. In upland streams rocky substrates provide large areas for invertebrate production and the type of substrate and area of submerged stream bed will determine food production (ie the algae and invertebrates that occur).

The blanketing of the substrate by settled sediment is a major environmental problem. It fills pools and scour holes, decreases substrate variation and reduces useable habitat areas. Clogging of the substrate removes the spaces between particles, which are important as rearing and habitat areas for juvenile fish, small species and stream invertebrates. Eggs which are deposited in gravel substrate are liable to smothering by sediment and species such as Murray cod, which lay adhesive eggs, probably require clean sites for attachment.

There are 3 groups of aquatic plants which all provide important habitat for freshwater fish: submerged (eg ribbon weed, *Vallisneria* species); emergent (eg *Phragmites* species); and floating (eg *Azolla* species). These plants provide habitats with great structural complexity. Extensive plant areas may provide important migration corridors for some species (eg Australian bass, *Macquaria novemaculeata*). Aquatic plants are also sources of nutrients and oxygen, and act as physical filters and stabilise sediments.

Studies in other countries have shown that invertebrate and fish productivity is directly related to concentrations of aquatic plants. Shallow areas in dams and rivers are the areas where aquatic plants can grow.

Introduced species of aquatic plants such as *Salvinia* can cause problems. Their rapid growth and lack of natural predators can result in choking of waterways and eventually eutrophication. In many areas, herbicides are used to control outbreaks of 'weed' species. However, their uncontrolled use can affect fish populations.

'Riparian vegetation' is the vegetation that grows along the banks of rivers and creeks. The roots of trees bind and stabilise riverbanks, reducing erosion (and subsequent siltation) and stabilising channels. Vegetation can also act to filter out pollutants from the surrounding land. Overhanging trees provide, either directly or

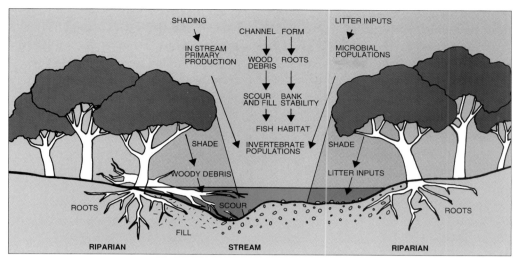

A diagrammatic representation of the influences of riparian vegetation on a stream. (Source: Adapted from Cummins, 1986)

indirectly, shelter, food and breeding sites for fish. Streams with well-developed riparian vegetation generally have a higher productivity than those lacking vegetation. Logs and debris that fall into streams provide fish with shelter, form a substrate for food and are also breeding sites for species such as Murray cod and river blackfish (*Gadopsis marmoratus*).

Native tree species provide the best riparian vegetation, rather than introduced species such as willows (*Salix* species), which tend to spread and choke waterways. Willows also form a dense canopy that prevents an understorey of shrubs, reeds and grasses from forming. Being deciduous, they also provide all their organic input to the water at once rather than spread throughout the year as most native species do.

The relationship between many fish species and their habitat is being increasingly well documented. The habitat requirements of each species are different and they may differ for each life stage. Species such as carp have very general habitat requirements and wide tolerance levels whereas other species have more specific needs. Murray cod, for example, use logs for spawning sites.

The removal of instream habitat by desnagging and stream clearing has been widespread in Victoria, and is particularly detrimental to species such as Murray cod. The forming of natural rivers into regular, smooth sided channels (channelisation) removes almost all instream habitat for fish, as does the drainage of wetlands. Such changes remove the diversity of habitat needed by different species.

Freshwater habitats are more than a river, its bed and banks. They also include temporary habitats such as floodplains and wetlands. Floodplains are important habitats for fish, at least for part of their lifecycles, and are associated with most rivers. They are of variable width, and on the vast plains of the Murray–Darling Basin they are extensive and can remain inundated for many weeks. When floodplains are inundated, nutrients are released and plankton develops. This plankton is an extremely important food source for fish, particularly as juveniles. Fish spawning and larval rearing success is increased after floodplain inundation. Some juvenile fish are thought to use floodplain habitats for many months. In addition, there is a recharge and flushing of wetland systems and increased movement of fish in and out of wetlands. Unrestricted access (eg without levees and floodbanks) to and from the floodplain enables fish to travel freely from the main channel.

Some species of fish such as silver perch (*Bidyanus bidyanus*), golden perch, bony bream, and spangled perch (*Leipotherapon unicolor*) can spawn on the floodplain. Their pelagic larvae develop rapidly. The dynamics of the plankton blooms are such that small zooplankton is available after the eggs hatch, with larger planktonic forms becoming available later in the flood peak when the fish have grown.

Wetlands are important ecosystems for fish, invertebrates, plants, birds and man. Wetlands are natural flood mitigation devices (ie they act as sponges); they absorb, recycle and release nutrients; they act as filters, improving water quality; and they increase the productivity of associated aquatic and terrestrial ecosystems. Freshwater wetlands provide feeding, spawning and nursery areas for many species of freshwater fish.

There are several types of freshwater wetlands in Australia, ranging from seasonal freshwater swamps to billabongs and shallow inland lakes. Freshwater wetlands can be characterised by trees (eg paperbarks, *Melaleuca* species), rushes and reeds, or floating and submergent aquatic plants. Most Australian wetlands are dry for some period and productivity falls if water levels are not allowed to fluctuate.

To be of use to fish, freshwater habitats must be available through unimpeded fish passage. Fish passage is necessary for spawning migrations, recolonisations, general movement and habitat selection.

Many of our native freshwater fish species have a migratory phase in their life cycle, particularly those in coastal rivers. Many of these migrate between coastal waters and fresh water for spawning (eg barramundi, freshwater eels), while others migrate wholly within fresh water (eg golden perch). In south-eastern Australia 70 % of the native fish species in coastal drainages have a migratory phase in their lifecycle. However, within this area about half the available aquatic habitat has been obstructed by barriers, excluding some species (eg Australian bass) from otherwise suitable habitat.

Further reading

Cadwallader, P.L. (1978) Some causes of the decline in range and abundance of native fish in the Murray–Darling River System. *Proceedings of the Royal Society of Victoria* **90**: 211–224.

Cummins, K.W. (1986) Riparian influences on stream ecosystems. Pp 45–55, in *Stream protection, the management of rivers for instream uses.* Ed by I.C. Campbell. East Caulfield: Water Studies Centre, Chisholm Institute of Technology.

Hall, D.N., Harrington, D.J. and Fairbrother, P.S. (1990) The commercial eel fishery in Victoria. *Victorian Department of Conservation, Forests and Lands. Arthur Rylah Institute for Environmental Research, Technical Report Series* **100**.41 pp.

Koehn, J.D. and O'Connor, W.G. (1990) *Biological information for management of native freshwater fish in Victoria.* Melbourne: Government Printer. 65 pp.

Koehn, J.D. and O'Connor, W.G. (1990) Threats to Victorian native freshwater fish. *Victorian Naturalist* **107**: 5–12.

Mackay, N. and Eastburn, D. (eds) (1990) *The Murray.* Canberra: Murray Darling Basin Commission. 363 pp.

McComb, A.J. and Lake, P.S. (1990) *Australian wetlands.* Sydney: Collins/Angus and Robertson. 258 pp.

Murray Darling Basin Commission (1988) *Proceedings of the workshop on native fish management.* Canberra. 174 pp.

Habitat changes

compiled by Alex McNee based on contributions by Jenny Burchmore, Peter Doherty, Ian Hamdorf and John Koehn.

THE close links between fish species and their habitat mean that any disturbance of the habitat can potentially change the distribution and abundance of fisheries resources. Changes to fish habitats can be classified into 2 groups: natural and human-induced.

Natural changes

Cyclones and typhoons are natural events which can damage or destroy fish habitats, particularly reef and inshore habitats. Large swells can cause considerable structural damage to reefs and shorelines. Storm tides can flood inshore areas, upsetting the balance in areas not accustomed to heavy wave action or high-salinity waters.

Thermal shocking is a natural event that can impact on fish communities. The effects of increased water temperatures during low flows in freshwater has been mentioned earlier. Large sudden influxes of cold water cause fish kills in reef habitats. Prolonged heating from abnormal current activities can cause deaths of corals, resulting in changes to the structure of reef habitats.

Changes in salinity can also cause stress problems. Large outflows of freshwater following heavy rains in coastal areas can result in loss of coral habitat. Conversely, storms or 'king' tides may push saline waters further into estuarine areas, resulting in high salinities in areas that may otherwise be fresh or brackish.

Disasters such as those above, while often resulting in fish kills or damage to habitat, are part of natural cycles, and environmental systems will recover from their impacts. It is when human actions add to the scale of such events that systems may be permanently damaged.

There are 2 main types of human-induced changes: ***pollutants*** and ***habitat modification.***

Pollutants can affect fisheries by direct changes to ecosystems. These then become unsuitable for fish by direct toxic effects or by the accumulation of contaminants in 'economic' species to sufficient levels to make them unsaleable. Issues related to pollution of the marine environment have caused concern among fisheries authorities, fishers and the public and these concerns are often highlighted in the media. Pollutants in fisheries may arise from the activities of humans (anthropogenic), or from the presence and accumulation of harmful levels of chemicals from natural background environmental sources, or from a combination of both these factors. Among the most notable sources are sewage effluent, plastics, oil spills and petrochemicals, tin-based antifoulants, heavy metals, persistent organochlorine compounds, ballast water and nutrient fluxes that lead to excessive plant growth (eutrophication).

Pollutants are classified as 'point' or 'diffuse' depending on the nature of their source and their distribution. Point sources are more easily controlled as they are usually effluent pipes or drains from urban or industrial sites. Diffuse sources are more difficult to control as they occur over wider areas and can have a large number of contributors. Examples are waste and rubbish tips, motor vehicle exhausts, and pesticide run-off from urban or agricultural areas.

Some pollutants cause concern among health authorities when they occur in human foodstuffs at concentrations above the current health guideline levels. This is particularly a problem as producers of fisheries products try to maintain a wholesome, clean food image. Where excess residues can be related to particular sources — more likely for point sources of anthropogenic pollution — fisheries may be closed. These closures negatively affect commercial ventures and recreational fishers. For some naturally occurring heavy metal pollutants which accumulate, other restrictions such as size/age limits can be applied to certain species or groups (eg sharks) in an attempt to keep the consumer product below legal food limits.

Persistent pollutants such as heavy metals and slowly degraded organic chemicals like polychlorinated biphenols (PCBs) may adversely affect aquatic organisms and ecosystems in general. These pollutants tend to move to 'environmental sinks' such as marine sediments, and aquatic organisms may be exposed to them even after their use ceases or is highly restricted. As well, aquatic organisms may often accumulate these pollutants to concentrations much higher than background levels. Commercially important marine species are likely to contain residues at concentrations above health guideline levels, or toxic ecosystem and foodchain effects may cause population decline from increased fish disease or mortality or decreased fecundity.

From time to time, problems may also arise due to pollution of the marine environment. Shellfish may build up toxic levels of heavy metals, pesticides and pathogenic viruses and bacteria. Some finfish may accumulate chemical pollutants, but the accumulation of human pathogens (ie disease organisms), even from contaminated water, is rare.

The effects of additional nutrients on an ecosystem are not always as noticeable as those of other pollutants. Increases in the naturally limited nutrients phosphorus and nitrogen can foster increased plant growth. This can lead to the clogging of channels or bays, or the overgrowth of reefs or rock habitats. An abundance of nutrients can often promote or contribute towards toxic algal 'blooms'. Excessive phosphorus loads create special problems in coral reefs because phosphorus interferes with the 'normal' calcification of corals: corals will preferentially accumulate phosphorus into their skeleton, resulting in a weaker matrix that is more susceptible to damage.

While most pollution problems are most visible in rivers or estuaries and inshore waters, pollution can also have major effects on the open ocean. Problems occur in the

Human-induced changes

Large blooms of toxic blue-green algae such as this are often the result of pollution of rivers with organic material such as sewage, fertilisers. (Source: Brian Lawrence, Murray Darling Basin Commission)

form of oil spills, contamination from sea dumping and discarded plastics and fishing gear.

Habitat modification The effects of habitat modification on fish population are often more easily seen in freshwater habitats. Construction of dams and weirs alters the natural flow patterns of rivers. These barriers reduce flooding, which is required by many species for spawning, and also act as physical barriers to those species that have a migratory phase in their lifecycle.

Over 80 % of Australians live along the coastal fringe. In many areas of Australia, this concentration of human population is affecting both fish populations and fish habitats. Changes to fish habitats include losses of seagrass beds in the river and bay, siltation of the river, addition of nutrients to the waters from sewage and other sources, dredging of large areas and reclaiming of intertidal foreshores. Dredging and reclamation works are major problems for coastal estuarine habitats such as coastal 'swamps' and mangroves, since they can cause the loss of important nursery areas for many fish species. In addition, remedial work to stabilise channels can alter the seasonal variation in water flow.

Land clearing and poor landuse practices in river catchments can affect fish habitats within the river, the estuary and offshore. Plumes of suspended sediment flowing down rivers can smother fringing reefs, and larger plumes may spread to offshore reefs.

Infestations of noxious plants or animals is another form of disturbance that can affect fish habitats. The effects of the introduced plant species *Salvinia* on river systems has been mentioned. Major population increases of the crown-of-thorns starfish (*Acanthaster planci*) have been recorded on the Great Barrier Reef over the past 20 years. Although these dramatic population increases may be a natural phenomenon as these starfish are highly fecund, it is possible that human action in altering the associated environments could be triggering these 'outbreaks' more frequently than in the past.

Ciguatera poisoning (an illness contracted by eating certain tropical fishes) may also be a natural phenomenon that is influenced by human activities. The fish become contaminated by toxins from particular dinoflagellates. These dinoflagellates are consumed by various herbivorous fishes and the toxins are concentrated in other fish that eat these herbivores. This concentration through the food chain has potentially disastrous effects for human consumers. Ciguatoxicity can be demonstrated in fish populations unaffected by human disturbance, and in this case it may arise from the effects of habitat destruction caused by cyclones. On the other hand, there is also evidence of chronic ciguatoxicity in fish from reefs that have been disturbed by human activities such as blasting reefs to create boat channels.

Fishing activities also impact on fish habitat. Commercial methods such as demersal trawling and dredging can modify the substrate, thereby reducing available habitat and often reducing water quality. The increasing popularity of recreational fishing modifies aquatic habitats. For example, anchor damage to reefs and sea beds, the impact of 4-wheel-drive vehicles on sand dunes and foreshores, the collection of bait in intertidal areas and lost fishing lines and lead sinkers are all seen as problems potentially damaging to fish habitats.

Modifications to habitats are sometimes beneficial to fish populations; for example, by establishing artificial reefs. Based on observations that communities of plants and animals will develop around wrecks, jetties, pylons and oil rig platforms over time, effort has recently been directed towards creating artificial reef habitats. Obsolete vessels, concrete pipes and specially designed structures, rubble, car tyres and car bodies have been placed on the sea floor in defined areas to artificially create these reef habitats. On monitored artificial reefs it has been observed that many species of fish are attracted, and many species of algae and plants established. These artificial structures need to be designed to withstand adverse weather and sea conditions.

At a global level, climate change is a potential threat to fish habitats in the future. Long term effects of climate change would include changes in sea level, water temperatures, tidal and current patterns, coastal erosion and storm patterns and effects of ozone depletion on oceanic food chains.

Further reading

Ecologically Sustainable Development Working Groups (1991) *Final report — fisheries.* Canberra: Australian Government Publishing Service. 202 pp.

Conclusion

AN overview of the different habitats available to fish and some of the problems confronting these habitats has been presented in this chapter. An understanding of the relationships between fisheries resources and their habitats is a sound background for any person trying to catch fish, especially when one's livelihood depends on it.

Commercial fishing today increasingly uses satellite imagery, sea surface temperature plots, and a host of onboard technology to increase the chances of catching fish. All of this equipment uses existing knowledge of the association between the resources and special features of their habitat to directly and indirectly locate fish. In addition, many of the observations made lead to new knowledge of how fishes use their aquatic habitats. Maintaining the quality of the habitat is 1 very important element in maintaining the abundance and distribution of our fisheries resources.

As Australia's major fisheries are located in coastal and continental shelf areas, loss of fish habitat through inappropriate use of the coastal zone could seriously affect these fisheries. However, the length of the Australian coastline and low population density along much of it has meant that problems have been concentrated near areas of intense settlement, leaving most coastal waters in a mostly undisturbed state.

The status of Australia's marine environment is presently being reviewed in a comprehensive State of the Marine Environment Report which will be released by the Commonwealth Government in 1993.

The Ecologically Sustainable Development Working Groups' report on fisheries stressed the importance of coastal zone management; and that all resource users and managers (land and water) should be involved in developing a framework for that management. The need for marine protected areas was also recognised in the report as important to maintain ecosystem diversity.

The report recognised the importance of at least 2 main areas to maintain ecosystem diversity:

Marine protected areas. The Great Barrier Reef Marine Park is a working example of a marine protected area. The park area is zoned for activities which cater for various user groups as well as conservation. Zones vary from areas of total environmental protection (limited access) to areas where extractive industries may operate.

Integrated catchment management in the conservation of freshwater environments. In summary, the effective management of land and water entails protection of habitat.

Conflict will always exist when there is competition for multiple use of a resource. Fisheries are no exception. Competition between commercial and recreational fishers for a common fish resource is the most common source of conflict. The variety of uses to which aquatic and marine habitats are put are another source of conflict.

Managing fish habitats must go hand-in-hand with managing fish populations. Sustainability in many fisheries may ultimately depend not on harvesting rates, closures and quotas, but on the success of fisheries managers in defending a more basic requirement — the key habitats of fish.

The isolation of much of the Australian continent has meant that any environmental problems that have occurred have been localised and are minor on a world scale. A wide diversity of aquatic habitats is represented here. Developments in ecosystem management and multiple use management need to be pursued to ensure the conservation of fish habitat and fisheries resources in our country.

3. Fishing gear

by Lindsay B. Chapman

Drawings by Henry Dekker

FISHING gear and methods are designed to take account of particular characteristics and behaviour of the species being sought. These include their feeding, spawning, shoaling and migratory behaviour, their ecology or relationship with their habitat, and their herding ability. In other words, the catchability of each species varies greatly depending upon the action of the gear. The composition of the catch from a particular fishing area therefore, may differ depending on the type of gear used.

There are many ways in which to classify fishing gear, and there is no Australian nor world standard. The terminology used in this chapter is based on that adopted by the Food and Agriculture Organisation of the United Nations Development Program's (FAO/UNDP) 1987 gear classification.[1]

The information is extracted from *Commercial fishing gear in Australia,*[2] and is not intended to be a comprehensive review of all fishing gear used in Australia. It does, however, cover the main fishing methods employed to catch those species of commercial importance that are included in this book. The chapter thus contains 5 sections: nets, hook and line, traps and enclosures, miscellaneous methods, and fishing vessel electronics.

Fishing craft designs are as many and varied as gear types. Many craft designs are categorised by the fishing gear used on them — for example, 'trawlers' and 'longliners'. On the other hand, many boats in Australian commerical fishing fleets are multi-purpose and can be rigged with different gear to operate in a number of fisheries.

The size of commercial fishing craft in Australia varies in length from 1.5 m to 85 m. The smaller craft such as punts, dinghies and 'runabouts' are primarily used in inshore waters by net, trap or handline fishers, and dories and skiffs are often employed in inshore or open water fisheries in conjunction with larger vessels — for example, in purse seine operations. The term 'fishing vessel' is usually applied to craft over 7 m long and which are moored on the water. Many of these vessels are designed to stay at sea for weeks at a time to maximise fishing effort. Such vessels are equipped with freezer or chiller space to store the catch.

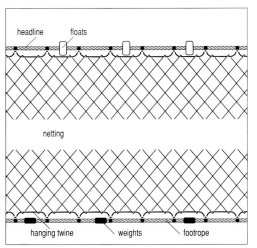

The main components of a common net.

Nets

NETS are responsible for the largest share of Australia's fish catches and are used in a wide variety of configurations and designs, depending on the species being targeted. The main components of a common net are described below.

The *netting* or *mesh* is the panel of net that fish will encounter and be retained in. In the past, natural fibres such as linen, sisal and hemp were used in the construction of netting material. Synthetic fibres such as monofilament nylon have now replaced natural fibres in net manufacture because of their greater strength and durability.

The top edge of the net is attached by *hanging twine* to a rope called the *headline* or *floatline* or *corkline*. Floats, usually made of cork, polystyrene or plastic, are attached to the headline to provide buoyancy.

The bottom edge of the net is attached by *hanging twine* to a rope called the *footrope* or *leadline*. Weights or *sinkers* made of lead or other materials attached to the footrope spread the net vertically in the water. The type and number of floats and weights used is chosen depending on whether the net is to be positively or negatively buoyant.

The 4 main types of fishing gear that use netting are gillnets and entanglement nets, surrounding nets, seine nets and trawl.

Gillnets and entanglement nets

These nets consist of a panel or panels of net held vertically in the water column, either in contact with the sea bed or suspended from the sea surface. The size of the mesh in the net determines the size range of the species caught, as smaller fish are able to swim through the meshes. The legal net length and the mesh size is set by individual State and

Federal fisheries authorities. Gillnets and entanglement nets are used in offshore and inshore waters, and in rivers and estuaries.

Fish are caught in gillnets or entanglement nets in 1 of 3 ways:

1) gilled, where the fish tries to swim through 1 or more mesh and if it cannot pass through it becomes caught behind its gill covers as it tries to back out of the net;

2) wedged, where the fish is tightly held in the net around the body by 1 or more meshes; or

3) tangled, where the fish is caught in the net by some part of its body, such as protruding fins or spines.

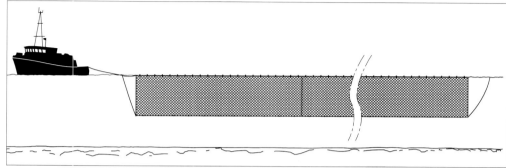

A surface set drifting gillnet.

Drifting gillnets are used in Queensland and the Northern Territory to target tropical sharks, although Spanish mackerel and threadfin salmon are also taken. Drifting gillnets are made up of individual net panels tied together, allowing for easy removal or replacement of damaged sections. They are set in open water and can be set with the headline on the sea surface (*positively buoyant*) or suspended below the surface from larger floats (*negatively buoyant*). A surface set drifting gillnet has very little weight on the footrope as it does not have to sink far or fast to straighten the net out. Sufficient flotation is required to support the weight of the net and the catch. Nets set below the surface require little or no flotation on the headline, and weight is used to sink the net to a pre-determined depth below larger surface set floats. This setting is used to reduce the chance of vessels running over the net and also to reduce the effects of wave action and surface turbulence on the net.

These nets are usually stored on *net reels* or *net drums* aboard fishing craft. The nets are set by putting 1 end through a *stern guide* and attaching a *dan buoy* (a buoy with a counter-weighted flag pole and flag) which is placed in the water as the vessel steams forward. The drag of the net in the water pulls the net freely off the net reel. If required, additional floats or weights can be clipped on as the net is set. The net is generally allowed to fish for 1–6 hours with 1 end of the net remaining attached to the vessel at all times. Hauling is the reverse of the setting process, with the net cleared of fish by hand as it is pulled over a *bow roller* and wound back onto the net reel.

Bottom set gillnets (also called shark nets, graball nets or mesh nets) are used in Victoria, South Australia, Tasmania and southern Western Australia to target school, gummy and whiskery sharks. They are also used to a lesser extent in the Northern Territory to target tropical sharks. Other species caught using this gear include morwong, warehous and tropical snapper.

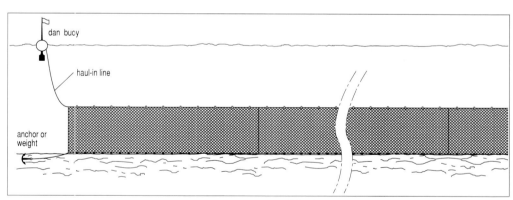

The basic design of a bottom set gillnet.

Bottom set gillnets are constructed and set in a similar manner to drifting gillnets. Unlike drifting gillnets, these nets are negatively buoyant and so they fish on the ocean floor. Each end of the net requires a dan buoy, an *anchor* or *weight* and a *haul-in line* of sufficient length to set the net on the sea floor. The boat does not remain attached to the gear, but usually remains in sight of it. The nets are set to fish for 1–6 hours, then the dan buoy and haul-in line are retrieved and the net is wound onto a net reel in a manner similar to that used for drifting gillnets.

Coastal, estuary and **river set gillnets** (also called swinger nets, mesh nets, running nets, offshore set gillnets) are set in estuaries and adjacent to the coast. They are used throughout Australia with the main target species being mullet, salmon, bream, trevallies and luderick. In Queensland, the Northern Territory and north-western Western Australia, barramundi and threadfin salmon are the target species. These types of gillnet are also used in the rivers and lakes of New South Wales and South Australia to target golden perch, bony bream, European carp and, to a lesser extent, Murray cod.

Estuary set gillnet used to catch barramundi in Queensland. One end of the headline is attached to the tree in the foreground.
(Source: Glen Smith, Southern Fisheries Centre, Queensland Department of Primary Industries)

When used in inland waters, the nets are often quite short because of the width of the rivers being worked.

Gillnets set adjacent to the coast on coastal mud flats are positively buoyant and are generally deeper than the water they fish in. This ensures that all fish moving in the area will encounter the net. These nets can be completely exposed at low tide. They start to fish as the tide rises and continue until the tide recedes.

Estuarine gillnets are set using small dinghies. The headline is tied to a tree or otherwise secured on the shore above the high water mark. The dinghy is used to set the net across the river at 90° to the shore line. A large float is attached to the other end of the headline, an anchor attached to the footrope, and both are released into the water. Several of these nets are set in an area and checked regularly by starting at 1 end of the net and pulling the dinghy along, taking out the caught fish as they are located. The nets are left in an area as long as there are reasonable quantities of fish being caught. When nets are to be moved, the float and anchor are retrieved and the net hand-hauled into the dinghy.

Offshore set gillnets are used in Queensland in the same fashion as coastal set gillnets, although regulations require that the shallow end of the net is set in a minimum of 2 m of water.

Running nets, used for prawns, are set in shallow water with a slight run-out current between the boat and a channel. The prawns are worked along the net to the boat anchored on the end of the net, where they are collected in *scoop nets*.

Swinger nets are used in South Australia to catch mulloway around river mouths. They are set from the shore. One end of the net is placed in the water and the tide, current and wind are allowed to pull the net out from the shore while the other end is held on the bank. The net swings around with the tide and is then hauled back onto the bank.

Ring nets (also called encircling gillnets, bull ringing, bunting nets, ring shots, power hauling, drain-off shots or round haul nets) are used in many parts of Australia to target species such as mullet, garfish, tommy ruff and whiting. They generally consist of a straight panel of netting (a *pocket* section may be incorporated) that is set around a school of fish sighted on the surface. When used in shallow water, they are deeper than the water so that the fish can only escape by either passing through the mesh, jumping over the net or swimming under the boat where there is no net. In deep water, the net is suspended from the surface and the success of the technique depends on the fishes' behavioural preference not to swim down and under the footrope of the net.

The ring net is set from a dinghy. A buoy attached to 1 end of the net is placed in the water. The dinghy then circles the school of fish, letting out the net and keeping far enough away so as not to scare the fish. An extra length of rope is attached to the headline in case the circle is larger than the length of net used. The first end of the net is picked up and the rope hauled in until both ends of the net are at the dinghy.

In shallow water the net ends are secured together and the dinghy moves inside the circle of netting. The fishers scare the fish into the net, then return to the ends of the net, attach 1 end to the dinghy's bow and haul the other over the stern. In deep water, the first end of the net set is secured to the bow of the dinghy while the other end of the net is slowly and quietly hauled in. Once the circle is reduced in size, hauling stops and the fish are scared into the net. Hauling then continues. If there is a large number of fish in the net, the headline and footrope are put together and the net hauled quickly to catch fish that are still swimming around inside the circle of netting.

The *round haul* or *bullring net* is a ring net with *purse rings* (a *purse line* runs through the rings) attached to the footrope along the first one quarter of the net. A school of fish is encircled and the net

The method of setting and hauling a round haul or bullring net.

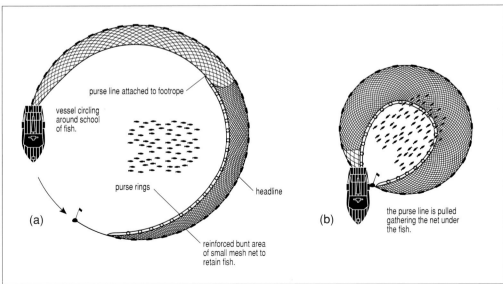

(a) purse line attached to footrope
vessel circling around school of fish.
purse rings
headline
reinforced bunt area of small mesh net to retain fish.

(b) the purse line is pulled gathering the net under the fish.

hauled to reduce the size of the circle until the purse line is reached. The purse line is then pulled, gathering the net under the encircled fish, thus trapping them. Hauling of the net continues until the fish are confined beside the vessel from where they are scooped onboard.

The **power hauling** method used in South Australia employs a long net with a pocket in 1 end. The pocket end is anchored and the net set in a straight line. Once set, the net is towed in a complete circle around the anchored end to sweep or herd the fish in that area. When the vessel is back to the starting point, the net is towed in a circle to collect the anchored end of the net. The net is then hauled, concentrating the fish into the pocket, which can be lifted onboard and emptied.

The **drain-off shot** method, also used in South Australia, involves 2 fishers using 2 nets set in a straight line parallel to the shore with 1 end of each net overlapping. The method targets fish moving offshore at day-break, on a falling tide. Each fisher tows the outside end of his net in a circle towards the centre. Once the 2 vessels are together they pull their nets as for a regular ring net.

Surrounding nets

These nets take advantage of the shoaling behaviour of pelagic fish. The nets work by enclosing schools of fish within walls of netting that prevent them from escaping both outwards and downwards.

Purse seine nets are used in the southern States of Australia to target high-volume fish species such as pilchards and jack mackerel. They are heavily constructed nets, with a smaller mesh size than the size of fish being targeted. They are positively buoyant, with sufficient flotation to support the expected catch. The end of the net that is set first (the *bunt*) is heavily reinforced, as this is where the fish will be concentrated when the net is hauled. The footrope of the net has purse rings attached at regular intervals by rope or chain. A purse line runs through the rings, which, when pulled, effectively closes the bottom of the net. Success of purse seining relies on surrounding the fish so that they cannot escape, whilst ensuring they do not become entangled or meshed in the netting.

Schools of fish are located by visual sighting, spotter aircraft or sonar. Once located the vessel circles the school, setting the net. The bunt end of the net is shot off the stern of the vessel by either attaching a large dan buoy or using a *skiff* (a small high powered vessel). An *overshoot line* is attached to the headline so that the start of the net can be retrieved. Once the first end of the net is retrieved, the overshoot line is winched in so that both ends of the net are beside the vessel. The purse line is then winched in from both ends, closing off the bottom of the net. The purse rings are detached in turn from the purse line as the net is hauled over a *power block* (a hydraulically powered block mounted on a boom over the back deck of the vessel) and stacked from the last end set until the catch is restricted in the bunt alongside the vessel.

Larger fish are lifted aboard in a large landing net arrangement (*brail*), while smaller fish are pumped aboard through a submersible pump. Once all the fish are removed from the net, the remainder of the net is hauled, stacked and the purse line passed through the purse rings and made ready for the next setting of the net.

Lampara nets (also called ocean garfish haul nets) are used in New South Wales, Victoria and Western Australia to catch pilchards and anchovy in inshore waters, and garfish offshore. They are a more specialised type of surrounding net with *wings* or long

Aspects of a purse seining operation: (below, left to right)
— the net is set around the school of fish;
— the fish are concentrated into the bunt of the net alongside the vessel;
— larger fish are brailed aboard. (Source: Mike Cappo, Australian Institute of Marine Science)

tapered panels of net added to each side of the bunt giving the net a characteristic scoop shape. Lampara nets are often used at night with lights or lamps.

The net is set around a school of fish as in purse seining. However, when both ends of the net have been retrieved the vessel tows the net forward. As the footrope is much shorter than the headline, it comes together first, effectively closing off the bottom of the net. The wings are then hauled, concentrating the fish into the bunt, from where the fish are lifted onboard.

Hauling a lampara net.

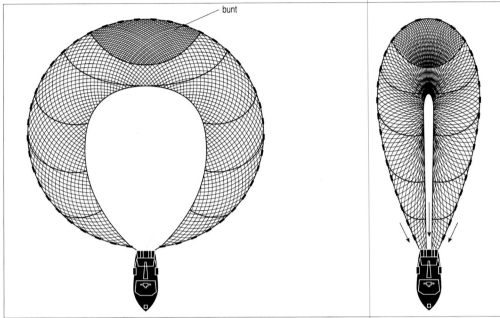

Seine nets

These nets usually have 2 long wings and a section in which to concentrate and retain the catch. Lengths of rope are added to the end of each of the wings. These ropes are negatively buoyant and extend the working area of the net while adding minimum drag to the hauling operation. The nets function on the principle that fish are reluctant to swim over a moving object in the water and instead try to swim in front of it. The fish are thus herded by the ropes and wing ends into the net. The wing ends of seine nets have a spreading device (*Dan leno*) between the headline and footrope to stop the net pulling together as it is hauled.

Beach seine nets (also called haul seines, pocket seines, baitfish seines, garfish seines, snapper seines, hauling seines, seines or estuary seines) are used Australia-wide to catch many species including mullet, whiting, Australian salmon, tailor and bream. The net may have a loose section of netting acting as the bunt area for retaining fish, or it may have a *bag* at 1 end of the net or in the centre. These nets often have a larger mesh size on the wing ends and a smaller mesh size around the bunt or bag area to reduce drag when the net is hauled. These nets are often used in shallow water and can be positively or negatively buoyant.

Beach seine nets can be set around a sighted school of fish, or set in an area where fish are known to congregate. The net is set from a dinghy with the first length of rope being set perpendicular to the shoreline, the net set parallel to the shore, and the second rope set back to the shore. The ropes are then hauled onto the beach evenly, herding the fish into the net. Hauling continues until the net and fish are dragged onto the shore, or the fish are concentrated in the bag. The bag is then lifted into the dinghy and emptied.

Boat seines (also called Australian Danish seine, haul nets or snigging seines). *Danish seining* is the main form of boat seine used in Australia. It is used in New South Wales, Victoria, Tasmania, South Australia and Western Australia to target a variety of species including morwong, flathead and redfish.

Danish seining gear is similar to a beach seine but is used on the continental shelf out to its edge (200 m) to fish along the sea floor. The nets are negatively buoyant and the lengths of rope used off each wing can be more than 40 times the length of the actual net. The principle of setting and hauling a Danish seine is also similar to that used for beach seining, only it is done from a boat rather than from the shore. The gear is set in a 'pear' shape with the net at the base of the 'pear' and the ropes making up the sides. Retrieval of the net uses a combination of the forward movement of the vessel to close the net and the hauling of the ropes using a powered winch. Hauling is slow initially to herd the fish, then speeds up to tire the fish and finally to concentrate them in the bag of the net.

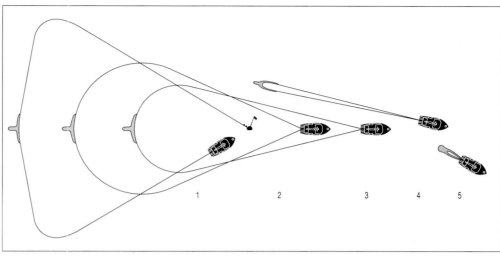

The hauling procedure for Australian Danish seining: **1.** the gear is set; **2.** towing commences; **3.** the gear begins to close up; **4.** the gear is closed; **5.** the net is hauled.

Haul nets are used in South Australia to catch snapper and garfish. They are similar to a Danish seine, with the net being positively or negatively buoyant depending on the target species. The gear is used from small vessels in shallow water (less than 5 m) and is set in the same manner as a Danish seine. The ropes are short and hand-hauled while the vessel is stationary.

Snigging seines are used in New South Wales bays and estuaries to catch bay prawns and school prawns. They are also similar to Danish seine; except that the net is negatively buoyant, has a smaller mesh and the ropes are quite short. They are set and hauled in the same manner as a Danish seine from small vessels.

Trawl

This is one of the most widely used commercial fishing methods in Australia. Trawling is performed in many ways, in depths of water ranging from just a few m to 1500 m. The design of trawl nets is more complex than the basic nets discussed earlier. Trawls are made up of components that perform specialised functions. The components of a fish trawl are described below.

1) *Warps* are wire ropes connecting the trawl boards to the vessel. They are stored on *winch drums* for ease of operation.

2) By acting as hydrodynamic kites, *trawl boards* (also called otterboards or trawl doors) keep the net open horizontally. They also provide weight required to keep the trawl at the desired depth of operation.

3) *Backstrops* are short lengths of wire or chain that connect the trawl boards to the sweeps.

4) *Sweeps* are used on demersal otter trawls to connect the backstrop to the bridle on each side of the net.

5) *Bridles* connect the sweep on each side of the net to the headline and footrope on the wing ends of the net.

6) *Ground gear* is a wire or chain which is attached to the footrope by short *chain droppers*. The ground gear has several rubber or steel *bobbins* and *spacers* threaded along its length. The object of the ground gear is to reduce damage from snagging by lifting the footrope and net clear of the sea bed.

7) *Body panels* are the panels of net that make up the body of the trawl, and comprise upper and lower sections.

8) The *codend* or bag is the last section of the net where fish are collected and held during trawling operations. This area has the smallest mesh size and it determines the

Two trawl configurations showing the main components.

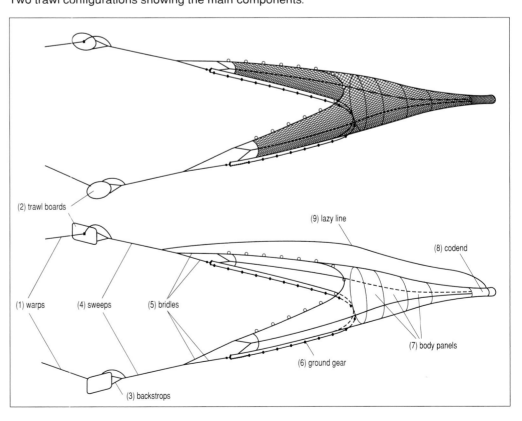

(2) trawl boards
(9) lazy line
(8) codend
(1) warps
(4) sweeps
(5) bridles
(7) body panels
(6) ground gear
(3) backstrops

Beam trawling in the Brisbane River (the solid headline of the net is visible). (Source: Glen Smith, Southern Fisheries Centre, Queensland Department of Primary Industries)

size of fish that the trawl will retain. The end of the codend is tied with a quick release knot so that the fish can be easily emptied from the net.

9) The *lazy line* is sometimes used to pull the codend onboard so that it can be emptied.

Beam trawls (also called dredge nets, beam tide nets or push nets) are used in Queensland, Victoria and New South Wales to catch school prawns and bay prawns. In north Queensland and the Northern Territory, a beam trawl is sometimes used to sample the catch in demersal otter trawl prawn fisheries, both before the larger demersal otter trawl gear is set and during the trawl itself to make sure the area being fished is still productive.

A beam trawl is simple in construction and can be used by small vessels, especially in restricted areas such as lakes and estuaries. It is constructed with 2 curved steel *end plates*; the height of the end plates determining the vertical opening of the net. A straight steel bar that connects the tops of the end plates acts as a solid 'headline' and also determines the horizontal net opening. The top of the netting is attached to the beam, while the footrope is attached to the back of the end plates.

A single beam trawl can be towed off the stern of a vessel, or *booms* can be used to allow 2 beam trawls to be towed. The warp is let out until the trawl is on the sea bed after which it is towed for from 10 minutes to several hours. When the trawl is retrieved only the codend is hauled onboard and emptied.

The beam trawl was once called a ***dredge net*** in Queensland where it was used to target saucer scallops and bay lobsters. These animals are now taken primarily by demersal otter trawls.

The ***beam tide net*** is used in Mandurah, Western Australia and is a variation of the beam trawl. Vessels anchor in shallow channels on a run out tide with the net set so that the headline is on the surface. When prawns are washed out of the rivers and rise off the bed of the shallow channels they get caught in the net that is suspended from the surface.

A variation on the beam trawl, a ***push net***, is used in Tasmania to catch garfish. Lights are placed on buoys or the shoreline at night to attract garfish. Once the garfish are aggregated around the light, a powered dinghy with a beam trawl net attached to the bow, pushes the net through the aggregated fish and traps them.

Demersal otter trawls for fish (also called stern trawling, bottom trawling, otter trawling or trawling) operate in south-eastern Australia, the south of Western Australia, the North West Shelf and some areas of the Northern Territory. Species taken in the southern fisheries include orange roughy, gemfish, blue grenadier and redfish. In northern Australia species taken include sea perch, emperors, rock cod and squid.

Demersal otter trawls work along the sea bed, in waters to a depth of 1500 m. The trawl boards, sweeps, lower bridle and ground gear are in contact with the sea bed. The net is held open horizontally by trawl boards being dragged along the sea bed spreading the sweeps, bridles and net wings. These in turn herd the fish towards the net. The fish then swim ahead of the net until they tire and fall back into the tapered bag where they are retained in the codend. The length of bridle and the buoyancy in plastic floats attached to the headline provide the net's vertical opening.

The net, ground gear, bridles and sweeps are stored on a net reel. During deployment, the net and trawl boards are 'shot away' from the vessel's stern as the boat steams forward on the fishing ground. Depending on the depth of water being worked, the length of warp let out is from 2 to 4 times the water depth. The gear can be towed for up to 6 hours before being hauled. Hauling is the reverse of the setting procedure. The codend is brought onboard either using the lazy line, or by winding the

A demersal trawl arrangement used for fish.

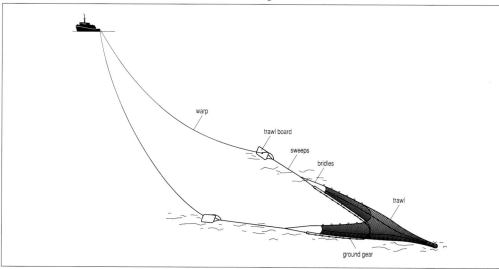

net onto the net reel, so that the catch can be emptied and sorted.

Demersal otter trawling for prawns (also called prawn trawl, trawling) takes place in all Australian States except Victoria and Tasmania. Tiger prawns, banana prawns, king prawns and endeavour prawns are the main species caught. Demersal otter trawls for prawns work along the sea bed. They resemble a fish trawl, except they do not employ long sweeps, backstrops or long wing ends. The gear used is generally smaller than that used for demersal fish trawling. The netting is a smaller mesh size, and the bridle is located in front of the trawl boards where it influences the horizontal rather than vertical opening of the net. The vertical net opening is created by the height of the trawl boards, and, except for banana prawn trawls, there are no headline floats used.

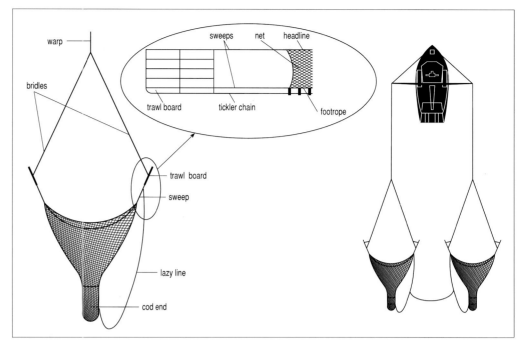

A double net arrangement used for demersal otter trawling for prawns.

Prawns burrow into or live on the ocean floor and do not 'herd' like fish, nor do they have the same escape capabilities. To compensate for this, a heavy chain (*tickler chain*) is used instead of the ground gear used on fish trawls. This chain hangs below the footrope to disturb the prawns, causing them to jump up into the path of the oncoming net.

Long booms extending out from each side of the boat allow *multiple* rigs to be used. These rigs can be in a double, triple or quad net arrangement. The gear and rig configuration used often depends on the fishers' preference and the regulations imposed in a particular fishing area. Shooting away and hauling the gear is similar to the method used in fish trawling. However, the trawl boards are winched to the outer ends of the booms when the nets are hauled. Only the codend is hauled aboard to empty the catch.

Two recent fisheries have been established using modified prawn trawl rigs. These are the saucer scallop fishery in southern Queensland and central Western Australia, and the scampi fishery off the North West Shelf. Both fisheries use a heavier tickler chain on a standard prawn trawl rig.

The **_semi-pelagic otter trawl_** (also called Julie Anne semi-pelagic trawl, semi-demersal trawl) has been adapted by the Northern Territory Department of Primary Industry and Fisheries as a more 'environmentally friendly' trawl for fish. The semi-pelagic otter trawl fishes close to the sea bed with only the trawl boards, *wing end weights* and chain droppers coming in contact with it. This trawl differs from conventional fish trawls in that there are no sweeps and the bridles are short. The lower bridle is connected directly to the backstrop on each trawl board, while the upper bridle is connected to the warp in front of the trawl board. The positioning of the upper bridle affects the net's orientation to the sea bed.

Mid-water trawling (also called pelagic trawling) has been trialled, mainly off eastern Australia, to target jack mackerel on the continental shelf and blue grenadier outside the continental shelf. Trawlers from Japan and the Commonwealth of Independent States of the former USSR use mid-water trawls in Australia's Antarctic Territory to catch krill and Antarctic fish. This method of trawling requires sophisticated electronic equipment, first to locate the fish, and then to position the gear at the desired depth to catch them.

Mid-water trawl nets resemble demersal trawl nets for fish except that they have a much larger mouth with short or no wings. The trawl boards are connected to the net via a long bridle and assist in giving the net its horizontal opening. Vertical opening of the net is achieved by flotation on the headline and weight on the footrope, as well as an additional weight on each lower bridle close to where it connects to the footrope. The position of the net in the water column is controlled by the length of the warp and by varying the speed of the vessel. The net is stored on a net reel and shot and hauled in the same fashion as a demersal fish trawl.

Demersal pair trawling was used in northern Australia by Taiwanese vessels to catch sea perch, tropical snappers, rock cod, emperors and squid. It requires 2 vessels to tow a single net. The vessels provide the horizontal opening of the net and replace the need for trawl boards. The net is the same as a demersal fish otter trawl, with long wings and a long bridle onto which the warp is attached. This method is no longer used in Australian waters.

The **dingo rig** was also a form of pair trawling used in Lake Wooloweyah and other sections of the Clarence River estuary to catch school prawns in the 1940s. Small powered vessels were used to tow a modified seine net with ropes, while hauling was done by hand.

Hook and line

FISH hooks, which come in an enormous range of types, are used to catch a variety of species and sizes of fish and are deployed by a wide range of configurations of fishing lines and rods. Fish hooks are known by their style and size.

Handlines, handreels and **powered reels** (also called set lines, rod-and-line or deepwater line fishing) are used commercially in all States. The main species targeted include coral trout and emperors in northern Australia and redfish, tailor, snapper and Westralian jewfish in southern Australia. Handlines are the simplest form of fishing, where 1 or more baited hooks are attached to a line. These may be used singly or several at a time. On a vessel, a 'V' shaped *jig stick* may be employed to set several lines at once. The jig stick can bend and will allow the line to slip through. Handreels are similar to handlines but can be mounted on the side of a vessel or attached to a rod. These reels are usually fitted with a *drag system* (a 'brake' system designed to create resistance in the reel as the fish takes out line). To reduce the time and effort involved in setting and hauling the line, electric or hydraulic motors are now fitted to some reels (*powered reels*).

Pole-and-line (also called pole-and-live bait) fishing mainly targets surface swimming tuna species in southern Australia, including southern bluefin tuna, skipjack tuna and yellowfin tuna. This technique involves attracting the surface schools of fish to the vessel, getting them into a feeding frenzy by throwing live or dead bait into the water and spraying water onto the sea surface to simulate the behaviour of small bait fish. Fishers stand at the side of the vessel or in a rack off the side or stern of the vessel. They use a fibreglass pole with a *trace* shorter than the pole, that terminates in a *barbless lure*. The lure is moved about on the water surface. When a fish strikes, the pole is raised, lifting the fish out of the water and 'poling' it onboard. Larger fish require 2 poles (2 people) attached to a single lure with the fish poled between the fishers. In some pole-and-line operations automatic poling machines are used.

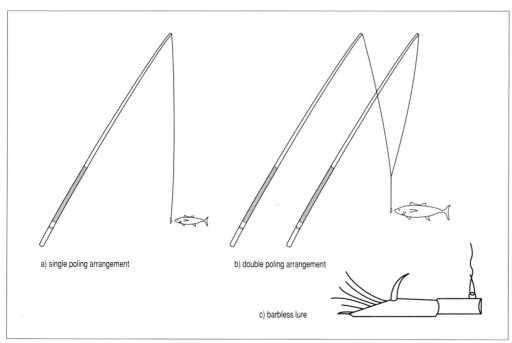

a) single poling arrangement

b) double poling arrangement

c) barbless lure

Equipment used in pole-and-line fishing operations.

Squid jigging is carried out in south-eastern Australia to catch arrow squid and occasionally calamary. Jigging is a night fishing method that exploits the squids' strong attraction to light. Powerful lights are positioned along the vessel to attract the squid. The squid congregate next to the vessel in the shadowed area created by the position and angle of the light, and dart into the lit area to feed.

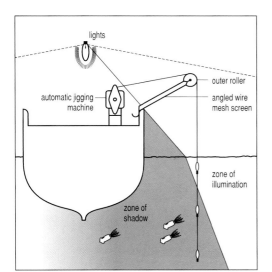

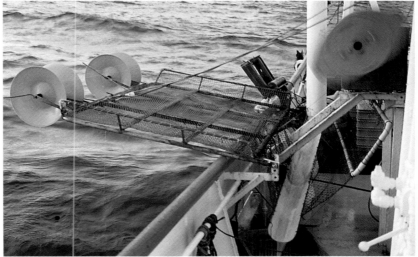

(left) Arrangement of equipment for squid jigging operations.
(right) Squid jigging machine in operation. (Source: Fisheries Research Institute, NSW Fisheries)

A line with several barbless lures is used off an elliptical spool. The rotation of the spool as the line is wound creates the jigging action. These spools are either automatic or hand operated. Squid caught on the lures are hauled over a roller, fall onto a wire mesh screen at the side of the vessel and slide onto the deck. Automatic machines continually wind up and down and need little attention.

Anchored longlines

Anchored longlines can be set vertically in the water column (droplines), horizontally along the sea bed (bottom set longline) or horizontally suspended off the sea bed (trotline).

Droplines are used mainly on the continental slope off south-eastern Australia to target blue eye and hapuku, although gemfish, school sharks, gummy sharks and pink ling are also taken. Off southern Western Australia, droplines are used on the continental shelf to target snapper and shark species. In the Northern Territory, tropical snappers and sea perch are targeted by droplining in waters over 80 m deep.

Droplines consist of a *mainline* of rope, wire or nylon anchored vertically in the water with a weight on the bottom and floats attached at the surface. Short lengths of twine, wire or nylon called *snoods* or *traces* have a clip attached to 1 end and a hook on the other. When being set for fishing, the desired number of pre-baited snoods (usually between 10 and 100) are clipped at regular intervals along the lower section of mainline as it is fed out. Alternatively, the snoods may be permanently attached to the mainline and are baited and lined up in order along individual '*shooting rails*' whilst the vessel is heading for the fishing grounds. When the weight is dropped overboard they are pulled off the rails in turn as the line is set.

In deeper water up to 10 lines may be set, usually before dawn, thus allowing the gear to fish through the fishes' dawn feeding time. Hauling commences 2–4 hours later. In shallower water, lines are set for only 10–20 minutes on fish schools located by an echo sounder. A *line-hauler* (powered winch) is used for hauling the gear, with the caught fish removed as the snoods come onboard.

Bottom set longlines (also called longlines or longlining) are used on the continental shelf and slope all around Australia to catch a variety of species including tropical sharks, school sharks, gummy sharks, sea perch and pink ling. This line differs from a dropline in that the mainline with the baited snoods attached is set along the sea bed. The gear is set from a moving vessel and a haul-in line is attached to each end of the mainline. One end of the haul-in line has a weight attached to anchor the end of the mainline, the other has a dan buoy and float. If the mainline is very long, extra haul-in lines, weights and buoys can be attached at about 1 km intervals. The line is left to fish for up to 6 hours. Setting of longlines can be mechanised, with the hooks passing through a tub of pre-cut bait pieces as the line feeds over the vessel's stern.

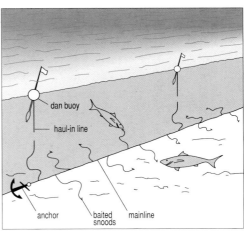

Arrangement of a bottom set longline.

Trotlines are used to target blue eye and hapuku on or beyond the continental shelf off south-eastern Australia. The gear is designed to fish over rough substrates. The mainline is set horizontally with small floats to suspend it off the sea bed so that it does not snag. At set intervals along the mainline's length, weighted short *droppers* or *trots* are attached, each containing up to 20 baited hooks. The droppers are set vertically in the water and act like a series of joined short droplines.

Drifting longlines

Drifting longlines are used off all States of Australia, except the Northern Territory, by both Japanese and Australian vessels. Species taken include tunas such as yellowfin, bigeye and southern bluefin, striped marlin and broadbill swordfish.

Drifting longlines have the mainline suspended horizontally in the water at a predetermined depth by *buoy lines* with floats spaced regularly every 200–400 m along its length. *Branch lines* 25–50 m long are attached at regular intervals along the mainline. Each branch line has a baited hook and fishes at a different depth depending on its position and the amount of slack in the mainline between floats.

Gear arrangement for a drifting longline.

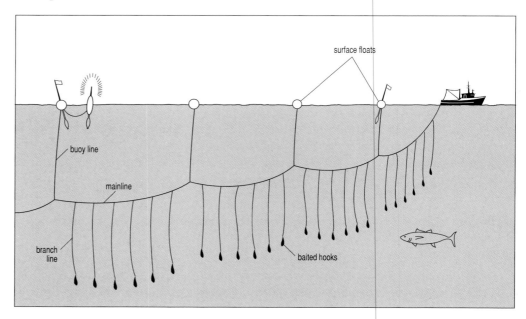

Drifting longlines are set while the vessel is moving ahead. The buoys and branch lines are attached as the mainline feeds out. The mainlines can range from 10 km to 80 km long, and can carry from 200 to 3000 hooks. The mainline takes 2–6 hours to set, whilst hauling may take 4–12 hours.

Trolling

Trolling is used Australia-wide to target species such as Spanish mackerel, coral trout, yellowtail kingfish and several tuna species. Trolling is a simple method of fishing in which lines with baits or lures are dragged behind a vessel as it moves along at a speed of 2–10 knots. Most commercial operations use lines rigidly mounted to the stern of the vessel or off *outriggers* or booms, and troll 3–18 lines at once. A variety of lines, rig designs and lures or baits are used for trolling. In New South Wales *leadlines* (lines with lead weights attached every 30 cm) are used to troll deeply for yellowtail kingfish. *Bowden cable* (galvanised cable of 1–1.5 mm diameter) is used to troll for Spanish mackerel in Queensland.

Traps and enclosures

TRAPS are devices which fish, crustaceans or molluscs enter voluntarily, but from which they are prevented in some way from escaping. Animals are enticed into a trap either by bait or because the trap appears to provide some form of refuge.

Most traps are set on the sea bed or river bed with a haul-in line, surface float and dan bouy to mark their position. They can have 1 or more entrances or openings on the top or sides, depending on the target species. A line hauler is used to pull traps for checking and re-baiting

Fish traps

Fish traps can be set in water from only a few m to hundreds of m deep. They are made in a variety of shapes and sizes depending on the target species. The shape of the trap and the number of entrances determines its orientation in the water during hauling. Before setting, suitable areas of either sea bed or fish schools are located with an echo sounder, and the speed and direction of the current are noted. Most baited traps are set on the sea bed, with at least 1 entrance facing down current. The traps are left to fish for from 20 minutes to 24 hours.

An **'O' trap** is used in Western Australia to target snapper, emperors, rock cod, sea perch and tropical snappers. The trap has a round steel frame covered with light wire mesh, and has 1 rounded entrance.

Modified **'O' traps** are used in parts of the Northern Territory and northern Western Australia to target tropical snappers and emperors. They are constructed in the shape of a 'D' of the same materials as the 'O' trap, with a rounded entrance on the flat side of the trap. Modified 'O' traps are most effective when set on schools of fish and left to fish up to 2 hours before hauling.

Arrow traps are also used in the Northern Territory. Their steel frame is in the shape of an arrow, and the tapered entrance is at the base of the arrow shape.

Rectangular traps with a wooden frame covered in light wire mesh are used in New South Wales to target snapper, bream, yellowtail kingfish and morwong. In South Australia, rectangular traps with a steel frame covered in wire mesh are used to target ocean jackets. Both trap designs may have 1 or more tapered oval entrances located on the trap's side towards the top. These traps are weighted so that they fish on the sea bed. In New South Wales, the same rectangular trap is suspended near the surface to target yellowtail kingfish. The top surface of these traps is covered with a material such as plywood to provide shading.

Other trap designs used in Australia are the **'Z' trap**, the **'S' trap**, the **beehive trap** and the **funnel trap** (used for cobbler in Western Australia).

Rock lobster and crayfish traps and pots

Lobster pots, Tasmania.(Source:Lindsay Chapman, Bureau of Resource Sciences)

Rock lobster pots are set in rocky or weedy areas for periods of from 6 hours to several days. The methods of rigging, setting and hauling are similar to those used for fish traps. Rock lobster pots are generally smaller than fish traps. Three main designs are used.

Batten pots are used mainly for western rock lobster. The pots are rectangular, with tapered sides and a single entrance at the top. They are constructed with a steel base with wooden slats or battens on the sides and top. The traps are baited, and undersized rock lobsters, which may enter the trap, can escape through the *escape gaps* near the base of the pot.

Beehive pots are used to target rock lobsters in southern Australia. They are dome-shaped, constructed of a wire frame over which tea tree sticks are woven. There is a single, cane lined entrance at the top, and 1–3 escape gaps for undersized rock lobsters near the pot's base.

Rectangular traps are primarily used in waters off New South Wales to target eastern rock lobsters. They are smaller than the rectangular fish traps, and have side entrances.

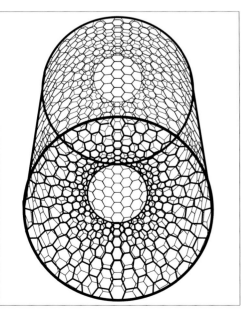

A yabby or crab trap.

Freshwater yabby or **crayfish traps** are smaller than rock lobster traps and come in a variety of shapes and sizes. They usually are made with a steel frame and wire mesh, and are often covered with hessian for darkness. The traps are baited and set in shallow water from the banks, and left to fish for several hours or longer.

Crab traps

There are many different shapes and sizes of crab traps, generally of a similar size to rock lobster pots. They are baited and left to fish for several hours to several days. Again, rigging, setting and hauling is similar to methods used with fish traps.

Mud crab trap designs come in 3 main styles — rectangular, cylindrical and half-moon. The traps are made of a steel frame covered with wire mesh. There is either 1 rectangular or cylindrical entrance on each end or a round, tapered entrance on top. Rectangular traps, which can be easily stacked, are the most commonly used.

Blue swimmer crab traps also vary in shape, and include the Japanese-style collapsible pot and the top entry pot. However, the most common trap design used is cylindrical. This trap has a steel frame over which wire mesh is stretched, and has 2 horizontal tapered entrances that are set opposite each other on the trap sides.

Dillies and snares

Dillies are used Australia-wide to catch crabs and yabbies. Snares are mainly used in Queensland and New South Wales to target spanner crabs and mud crabs. They may be set individually, or, for flat snares, in strings with 1 haul-in line connected to several snares. They are left to fish for several hours or overnight. Dillies and snares are set in a similar fashion to traps.

Dillies (also called hoop nets or crayfish rings in Tasmania) are generally round. They are set in coastal waters, bays or estuaries. They are also used in freshwater rivers, lakes, billabongs, irrigation canals, swamps, and farm dams when targeting yabbies. Dillies consist of a steel ring, up to 1 m in diameter, onto which some loose netting is attached to form a pocket or bag. When set, the netting lies flat on the substrate. The target species walks to the bait to feed and, when the dilly is hauled, becomes trapped in the loose netting that falls below the ring. A dilly is left set for 20 minutes to 2 hours before hauling.

A **drop net** is simply a dilly that has 2 rings and a collapsible side of netting. When set the 2 rings lie on the sea bed and the net works like a dilly.

A **witch's hat** (also called a cone snare) is an inverted dilly with a small float attached to the point of the netting holding it up off the bottom. When set, the ring rests on the sea bed and the netting forms a cone above it. Crabs are attracted to the bait, encounter the netting and get themselves tangled in it.

A **flat snare** (also called a tangle net) is used primarily to catch spanner crabs. The snares are constructed from a steel ring or a flat rectangular steel frame with netting loosely attached. They can be set in estuaries, bays and coastal waters to depths of 50 m. From 1 to 10 of these flat snares are attached at regular intervals to a single haul-in line. A weight is attached distal to the first and last flat snares to keep the snares set flat on the sea bed.

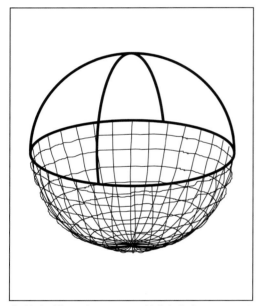 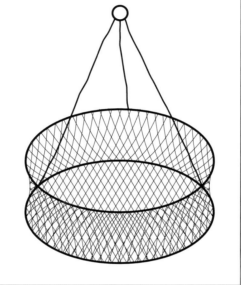

(left) A dilly or hoop net. (right) A drop net.

Octopus traps or pots

Octopus traps or pots are, or have been, used commercially in central and southern Western Australia, South Australia, Victoria and Tasmania. The trap or pot is a large-mouth pot made of plastic, pottery or polyvinyl chloride (PVC) tubing of around 100 mm diameter, cut into short lengths and weighted with a concrete plug in the middle. Octopus enter the traps or pots seeking safe refuges.

The pots are clipped along a common mainline at regular intervals, with up to 500 pots set on a single line. The mainline is weighted or anchored at both ends with a haul-in line and dan buoy attached to each weight or anchor. The pots are left to fish for up to 5 days, allowing the octopus to use them as a home.

Two styles of octopus trap used in Tasmania. (Source: Lindsay Chapman, Bureau of Resource Sciences)

Eel traps are used in the rivers of New South Wales, Victoria and Tasmania. There are 2 main styles of traps. The first is a rectangular shape similar in design to fish traps, except that the frame is covered by smaller mesh chicken wire and there are 1 or 2 entrances. After baiting it, the trap is left to fish for several days before checking. The second design is used in Tasmania to target migrating eels. The trap is set across a weir or creek and the eels are sieved from the water as it passes through the trap. The trap is open on the top and the catch is removed with a small scoop net.

Traps for eels
(also called weir traps)

Nets or netting material are used in many configurations to trap fish species.

Nets used as traps

Fyke nets are used in inland areas of New South Wales, Victoria, South Australia and Tasmania to target eels. Fyke nets are constructed from cane, aluminium or fibreglass hoops over which netting is secured. The outside hoop is generally a 'D' shape and the remainder are round. There are usually 2 or 3 internal funnels, each with an opening smaller than the one before. A wing of netting extends forward of the net opening. The eels encounter the wing and are directed towards the entrance of the net. Fyke nets are staked in position, usually in the afternoon or evening, and hauled the next morning.

Drum nets are used in inland fisheries to catch Murray cod, golden perch, European carp and bony bream. They are similar in construction to a fyke net, except that there is only 1 funnel leading to the codend and there are 2 wings. The net is usually checked several times a day by hauling the drum section of the trap and emptying the fish from the codend.

Glass eel nets are mainly used in Victoria to catch juvenile glass eels as they swim up the rivers. This trap is similar to a drum net, but has very small mesh netting. It is set and hauled in a similar fashion to the drum net.

Lift nets (also called hoop nets) are used in Victoria and southern Western Australia to target pilchards and tommy ruff. The net resembles a large dilly with a weight in the end, forming a long tapered bag. The net is set off wharfs or from small vessels, and can be used by night with a light or by day with berley to attract fish. The net is hauled vertically, trapping the aggregation of fish.

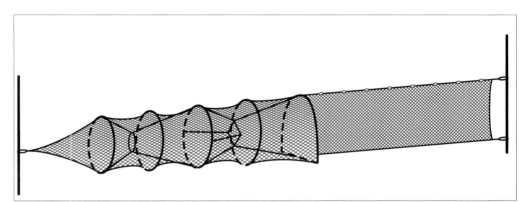

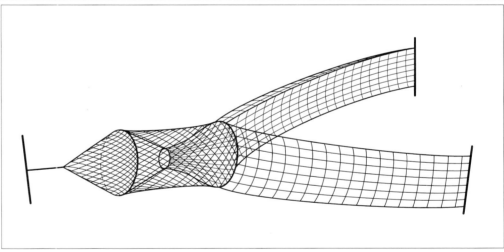

(top) A fyke net. (bottom) A drum net.

Tunnel nets are used along the coast or in estuaries in southern Queensland to target many species including mullet, tailor, flathead and luderick. The net is constructed of 2 long (up to 700 m) wings and a central pocket or 'tunnel'. An area in which fish concentrate, or a school of fish, is located at high tide and the net is staked in position to form a large arrow shape with the wing ends circling inwards to lead escaping fish back into the net. The net relies on fish encountering the net as they move with the receding tide. The fish become concentrated in the tunnel, which remains in the water at low tide. The tunnel section is finally lifted onboard a dinghy and emptied.

Arrow head traps are permanently set tunnel nets used in Queensland and Tasmania.

Stow nets (also called set pocket nets, pocket nets or stripe nets) are used in estuaries and rivers of southern Queensland and New South Wales to target school prawns and greasyback prawns. The gear resembles a small mesh prawn trawl and can be set in 2 ways. The first has the net staked by the wing ends across the current, using the current to open the net and wash the prawns into it. The second has the net set into

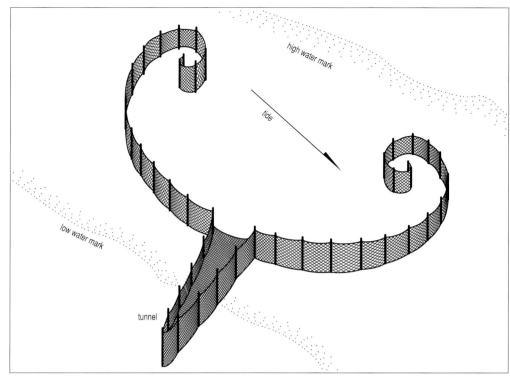

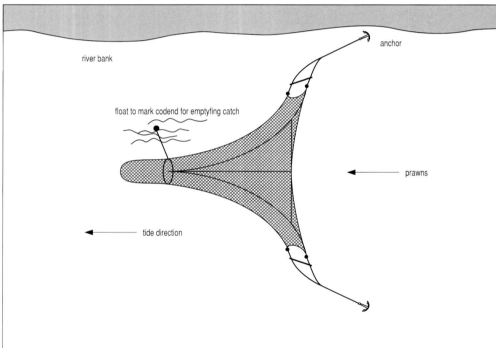

the current with stakes along the net to hold it open. The net is set close to the shore and catches the prawns as they move down the river into the incoming tide.

Trap nets are used in southern Western Australia to target tommy ruff and pilchards. The net may be a long straight panel or may include a pocket or bag at its inshore end. Trap nets are set in a configuration that resembles a '6' or 'G' and rely on the target species' natural circling behaviour to remain in the net. They are set during the migration period of the target species.

Trap nets are set in the afternoon and are left to fish all night, with hauling occurring after dawn. The seaward end of the net is brought ashore. If a straight net is used, it is hauled onto the beach like a beach seine. When the net has a pocket, only the seaward end of the net can be hauled to concentrate the fish in the pocket. The pocket is then either hauled ashore and emptied or lifted into a dinghy and emptied.

Pound nets are only used in certain locations in the Port Stephens area of New South Wales. They are mainly used to target bream and luderick. A pound net is a straight panel of net that is anchored in the shape of a rectangle or 'pound' off the shore and has 1 entrance. The entrance is on the shore side of the net and has a short *bank net* attached that runs in to the shore and guides the fish to the entrance. This gear concentrates small schools of the target species as they move along the shoreline over the course of a day. It is hauled and cleared every 24 hours.

(top left) A tunnel net showing the set in relation to tidal movements.
(bottom left) A stow net or set pocket net.

Miscellaneous

THIS section covers the use of gear such as dredges, diving, electricity and hand collection implements.

Dredges

Dredges (toothed mud dredges) have been used extensively in the waters off Victoria and Tasmania, including Bass Strait, to take southern scallop and blue mussels. Regulations have considerably reduced the use of dredges because of declining stocks and the suggested environmental damage the dredges cause.

The Australian-designed dredge consists of a heavy steel frame covered with steel mesh on all sides except the front, towed side. A *toothed bar* mounted across the lower front of the dredge helps to 'dig' the scallops out of the substrate. The weight of the dredge keeps it on the sea bed as it is towed. As the dredge is dragged across the sea bed the scallops or mussels in its path enter the dredge and are retained by the mesh. A drag can last for 10–60 minutes, after which the dredge is winched up to the back of the vessel. The dredge enters a *'tipper'* device on the back of the vessel and the contents are tipped onto a sorting table.

Diving

Diving as a method of fishing is carried out in all States of Australia. Species targeted include abalone, ornate rock lobsters, pearl oysters, sea urchins and occasionally southern scallops. The 3 styles of diving used in Australia are **snorkelling** (or free diving), **SCUBA** (Self Contained Underwater Breathing Apparatus) diving and **hookah** diving.

The 5 main gear components used in snorkelling or free diving are a *face mask*, *flippers* or *fins*, a *snorkel*, a *weight belt* and a *wet suit*. When free diving the diver's air supply is limited by lung capacity and so snorkelling is a shallow water activity. SCUBA divers carry *air tanks*, in addition to the basic snorkelling gear, which enable them to stay underwater longer and to work in deeper waters. Divers are still restricted by the amount of air that can be stored in the tank, so if long periods under the water are required hookah gear is used. Hookah divers are supplied with air via an *air line* from a *compressor* in a boat.

Divers in different fisheries also use several hand held implements to aid in collection. Abalone divers use a *chisel-like tool* to remove the abalone from the rocks and a *netting bag* to hold the abalone collected. Divers collecting blue mussels scrape them off pylons and rocks with a knife and place them in a bag. Divers collecting ornate rock lobsters use a short *hand spear* to spear the animal in the head (as only the tail is marketed). Divers collecting pearl oysters, sea urchins and southern scallops collect them by hand and place them in a bag similar to that used by abalone divers.

Electro-fishing

Electro-fishing techniques have been used commercially in the rivers and lakes of South Australia, New South Wales and Victoria to catch European carp, and, to a lesser extent, long-finned eels. There is little commercial electro-fishing carried out nowadays. However, scientists in most States use portable electro-fishing gear as a sampling tool for collecting fish in rivers and lakes.

Electro-fishing techniques use the natural conductivity of water. *Electrodes* connected to a *generator* or *battery pack* are put into the water and an electric current (direct current) is passed through the water, generating an electric field between the 2 electrodes. Fish caught within the field are attracted to the positive electrode (the *anode*), often attached to a scoop net. The strength of the electric field stuns the fish which can then be scooped into the boat.

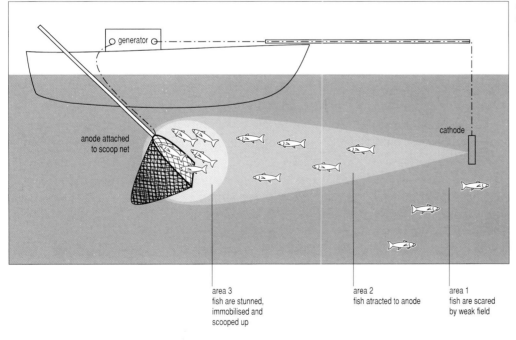

Gear arrangement for electro-fishing from a dinghy.

generator

anode attached to scoop net

cathode

area 3
fish are stunned, immobilised and scooped up

area 2
fish atracted to anode

area 1
fish are scared by weak field

Hand-held implements

Hand-held implements are used commercially to catch a few species of crustaceans and fish, although they are mainly used by recreational fishers.

Two types of **hooks** are used in north Queensland and the Northern Territory to catch mud crabs in mangrove areas. The hooks are made from a small diameter round steel bar with 1 end of the bar bent into a handle. The other end is bent into a right angle hook, which is hooked behind the crab to drag it out of its hole. Alternatively, the hook end of the bar is bent into a triangle and a piece of hessian is attached to it. The crab grasps the hessian and can be pulled out of its hole.

Rakes are used in South Australia to catch blue swimmer crabs. These rakes, which resemble garden rakes, are dragged across tidal sand flats, disturbing the crabs as they lie buried in the sand. When a crab moves the rake is used to hold it still until it is picked up.

Dab or scoop nets are used occasionally in South Australia to catch garfish. They consist of netting hung from a steel ring attached to a wooden handle. These nets are used at night, when the garfish are attracted to a light and scooped up into a boat. In South Australia, dab nets are used along with a rake to catch blue swimmer crabs.

Different designs of scoop or dab nets.

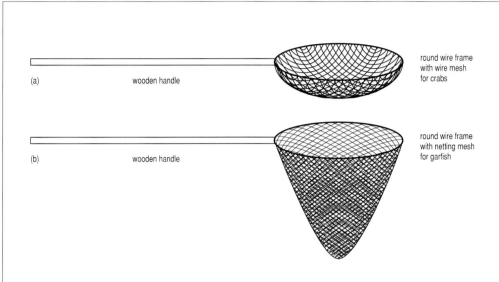

(a) wooden handle — round wire frame with wire mesh for crabs

(b) wooden handle — round wire frame with netting mesh for garfish

Fishing vessel electronics

THE use of fishing vessel electronics has advanced in Australia since the 1950s. Significant developments have been, and continue to be, made in the fields of navigation, communication and fish location. Many of these electronic devices can be interlinked or interfaced to enhance safety and fishing capabilities.

The introduction of ***radar*** revolutionised the shipping industry. The main advantage is that it allows vessels to navigate at night. Small electromagnetic pulses are transmitted through 360° radius from a *radar scanner unit* mounted on a high point of the vessel. The time taken for the echo of each pulse to return is measured. The different lengths of time translate as 'distance away'. Hence, a plan of the surrounding area can be plotted on a *display unit* mounted in the wheelhouse.

Radar, coupled with other innovations such as the ***gyro compass*** (a compass displaying 'true north' as opposed to 'magnetic north') and ***automatic pilots*** (a device that automatically steers the vessel on a pre-set course), allow fishing boats much greater flexibility of operation. ***Radar reflectors*** fitted to set fishing gear (eg longlines, traps) allow boats to locate the gear on returning to an area.

More recent developments in navigation stem from satellite technology. Making use of satellite signals, the ***Global Positioning System (GPS)*** can display a vessel's position (exact to 100 m), speed and heading. A plotter used with the Global Positioning System allows a fisher to plot a course on a monitor as well as view the course already followed.

Radio technology enables fishing vessels to communicate ship-to-ship, ship-to-shore and ship-to-air. This facility allows vessels to fish farther afield and to stay out longer, while maintaining regular radio contact with the shore or other vessels. Up to date aerial weather maps can be facsimiled to the vessel from coastal stations.

Sea surface temperature gauges let the fisher know the temperature of the water around the boat. This is useful when the water temperature preferences of the target species are known (eg for tunas). Satellite images showing sea surface temperatures can be used to locate likely fishable areas before setting out, and sea surface temperature gauges used to position the vessel when fishing.

Echo sounders are employed by fishing boats to determine water depth, bottom type (eg sandy, rocky), bottom gradient and the presence of fish. A pulse of sound is sent from a *transducer* attached to the bottom of the vessel. It travels through the water and, upon striking a medium of different density (eg air, rock, sand, fish), an echo pulse is reflected back to the transducer. The time taken for the signal to return is measured and a visual representation of this is displayed on a monitor in the wheelhouse. Stronger

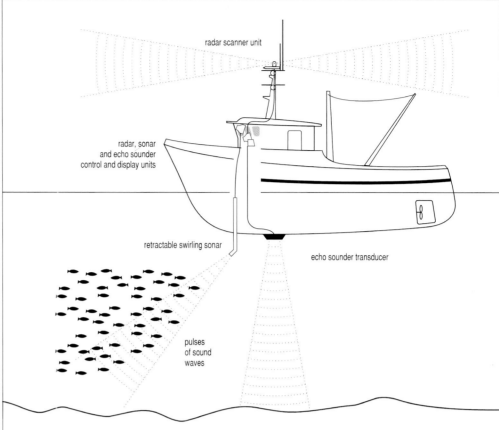

signals are received from fish with air-filled swim bladders than those with oil-filled swim bladders (eg orange roughy) or those without swim bladders (eg sharks).

Sonar works on the same principle as the echo sounder, except that the transducer is mounted on a retractable, movable arm and can scan through 360° around the vessel and 80° vertically. ***Net sounders*** have a transducer fitted to a trawl net and can determine net position in the water column, trawl opening/spread and the volume of fish entering the net. Soundings from transducers are displayed on a monitor via either a *cable* (cable system) or by a sound signal received by *hydrophones* towed by the boat (cable-less system).

(above left) Koden Radar Image.
(Source:Echo Radar Pty Ltd)
(above) Cut-away of a fishing vessel showing the location and use of radar, echo sounding and sonar equipment.

Conclusion

AUSTRALIAN commercial and recreational fishers use a very wide range of gears and technologies to capture fish. Many of the fishing systems used have been in existence for some time but most are in a constant state of modification to take advantage of new knowledge of fish behaviour and distribution, new materials and new technologies, especially in the field of marine electronics.

Increasingly complex changes in methodology and electronics are spreading through the Australian commercial fishing fleets. The sophistication of Australian vessels is rapidly approaching that of the Norwegian fleet, which is recognised internationally as perhaps the most progressive in its application of advanced methods and gear in its fishing operations.

References

1. Food and Agricultural Organisation (1987) *FAO catalogue of small-scale fishing gear.* Second edition. Surrey, England: Fishing News Books. 217 pp.

2. Chapman, L.B. (in preparation, 1993) *Commercial fishing gear in Australia.* Canberra: Bureau of Resource Sciences.

Compilers Alex McNee, Patricia Kailola and Mathew M. Maliel

4. Fish quality
and fish marketing

compiled by Patricia Kailola

Introduction

Global fish resources are limited, and there is increasing demand by human population for these resources. Within this sphere, Australia's diverse fish resources are vulnerable to over-exploitation, despite our small national population. Making good use of these resources is important, therefore, from both the aspects of domestic consumption and increased revenue through export.

Faced with stable or reduced quantities of fish in the commercial harvest, there is an imperative to maintain the quality of the harvested product. Many benefits accrue from careful handling of fish and fish products. They include higher monetary value, longevity of product, and — with controlled harvesting — sustainability of the resource for a longer period. The 'bottom line' is that with improved handling techniques and quality assurance, the benefit from Australia's limited fish resources can be maximised.

Fish are caught by a variety of means and the mode of fishing often influences the quality of the saleable item. Although many seafoods cannot yet be efficiently harvested by means other than those now in use, research into developing more 'environmentally friendly' capture techniques is increasing. Improvement in the quality of fish consumed may come from advances in *capture technology* (Chapter 3) but most importantly from *post-harvest technology*.

This chapter covers **post-harvest technology** (that is, what happens to the fish after it is caught), **domestic marketing of fish** (how the fish get from 'the boat' to retail outlets), **fish exports and imports**, **fish quality characteristics and handling** and **seafood in human nutrition**.

Fresh blue swimmer crabs, southern Queensland. (Source: Glen Smith, Queensland Department of Primary Industries)

Post-harvest technology

Information supplied by Felicia Kow

The large majority of fish sold on both domestic and export markets in Australia are offered frozen or chilled. They may be whole fish, gilled and gutted, in cutlet or fillet form. Crustaceans are offered fresh ('green') or cooked, either whole or as tails. Molluscs are offered fresh, chilled, or frozen. Less often, fish are marketed smoked, salted, boiled, pickled, raw ('sashimi', 'sushi') or as composite fish products ('surimi'). Some fish are sold canned. Fish may also be sold to the consumer alive and this practice is becoming popular in Australia. The different techniques used to 'process' fish for consumption in Australia are described below.

Handling High quality fish products can be achieved by careful, gentle handling and rapid chilling. These include: a) the rapid removal of live fish from the fishing gear; b) the fish not being thrown onto the deck or gaffed; c) large fish such as sharks and tunas being bled and spiked immediately ('ike-jime' is one very successful spiking technique) and immersed in ice slurry for rapid chilling; d) bled fish being gilled and gutted promptly, washed in clean sea water to remove excess blood and slime, and packed in fresh water ice. The optimum storage temperature of chilled fish is $-1°C$ to $4°C$; e) fish being packed with adequate protection to minimise temperature rise during transportation; and f) loading and unloading procedures being fast, efficient and hygienic.

Frozen and chilled product The distance offshore, duration of the fishing trip and the proximity of landing places for the vessel, influence the mode of freezing or chilling on board. Many products are marketed fresh chilled from nearby fishing areas. Ice made from fresh water is used on many vessels to produce fresh, chilled fish for the domestic market. Ice slurry is a fast way to chill fish and is used for high grade raw fish. The most widely used methods of chilling are a) melting ice, b) chilled sea water and c) refrigerated sea water. To obtain best results with *melting ice*, the iced product is layered with ice and placed in a cool room at a temperature no lower than –3°C. *Ice slurry* from chilled sea water (2 parts ice to 1 part sea water to 2 parts product) offers good contact between the chilling medium and the product and is a fast way to chill fish. Both chilled sea water and *refrigerated sea water* require agitation and circulation for maximum cooling efficiency. Rapid chilling also minimizes enzyme activity, which commences soon after or before death and starts the breakdown of body tissues.

On some vessels, frozen fish are stored in refrigerated holds. *Brine*, a mixture of water and salt, is another effective and popular method of freezing and keeping fish at sea for short periods.

Smoked fish Curing and smoking of fish is one of the oldest forms of food preservation. Smoked fish is treated with salt and then smoked with wood smoke. *Hot smoked fish*, whereby fish are generally cooked and smoked at temperatures of 80–90°C, destroys many bacteria and inactivates enzymes. These 'hard cured' products have a low moisture content and high salt levels. *Cold smoked fish* are lightly brined and smoked in temperatures less than 30°C. These low temperatures prevent the coagulation of protein, hence enhancing flavour (rather than preserving the flesh). Eel, trout and Atlantic salmon are often cold smoked.

Salted fish There are 3 basic ways to salt fish. In dry (or Kench) salting, dry salt is applied to fish in stacks. The salt penetrates the flesh while the extracted moisture drains away. After salting, the fish are washed in cold water and dried. Anchovies are often dry salted. In brine salting, the fish are soaked in a salt solution. Fish which are to be kept for long periods for use as bait (eg pilchards, mullet) are often brine salted. In pickling, dry salted fish become immersed in a pickle of extracted fluids. 'Gravlax' from Atlantic salmon is an example of pickled fish. Rollmops are made by salting and pickling fish in vinegar.

Canned fish Fish product is preserved through applying heat which both kills the vegetative cells and spores of bacteria and inactivates enzymes. The sealed container of food is heated for a period of time sufficient to kill micro-organisms in the food and the container. Australian salmon and tuna are often canned in Australia.

Live product Fish and crustaceans for the live market are kept in tanks of circulating sea water on vessels. Some groups of fish lend themselves to being marketed live, as they can stay alive for long periods of time out of water. Examples include crabs, mussels, oysters, octopus, carp and rock cod. Lowering the body temperature allows many animals to be transported in a minimum of, or sometimes no, water. This factor is very important when attempts are being made to minimise freight costs.

Fermented Sea urchin roe can be fermented. This process relies on a high salt concentration and the microbial population that develops to preserve the product.

Fishmeal Fishmeal can be produced from 'trash' fish (eg prawn bycatch), fish offal and fish wastes from processing operations, or fish caught solely for fishmeal production (eg jack mackerel, anchovies). The main steps undertaken in fishmeal production are: heating or cooking to coagulate protein and release water and oil; pressing to separate liquids from solids; drying; and grinding to produce a powdered or granular end product. The 2 main methods of processing are wet rendering or reduction (used primarily on fatty fish) and dry rendering (used on fish offal and low fat fish).

Sashimi, sushi 'Sashimi-quality' tuna and other seafood are eaten raw, either as *sashimi* (thinly sliced and served with soya sauce and Japanese horse radish, *wasabi*) or *sushi* (very thin slices served on balls of seasoned rice).

Surimi Fish with high gel-forming capacity, such as blue grenadier, are processed into *surimi* by mincing them and then subjecting the fish mince to several cycles of leaching with cold water. Cryoprotectants are then added to give the surimi resistance to freeze denaturation. Frozen surimi, after grinding with salt and other ingredients, can be steamed (*kamaboko*), fried (*tempura*) or broiled (*chikuwa*) and processed into surimi analogues such as imitation crabmeat and scallops.

Frozen tuna, Tsukiji Fish Market, Tokyo. (Source: Albert Caton, Bureau of Resource Sciences)

Jack mackerel are used almost exclusively for fishmeal production in Australia. (Source: Neil Klaer, Bureau of Resource Sciences)

Domestic marketing of fish

DOMESTIC markets accept all forms of fish products. The period of transition from water to retail outlet and the price of fish varies around Australia in response to the proximity of shore-based facilities and the distance between wholesale markets or buyers, but primarily with population size and distance.

Regulations on the marketing of fish in Australia are the responsibility of State governments. Most governments require fish for domestic consumption to be wholesaled at designated markets or sold to retailers and other end-users (eg restaurateurs) direct from the fisher for a fair price based on 'supply and demand' and the Consumer Price Index. Those fish destined for canning (eg some tunas, pilchards), fish meal and surimi products, and those from aquaculture production are usually sold direct to retailers or other end-users. Many commercial fishers belong to co-operatives which facilitate marketing and despatch of harvested fish. The mode of fish marketing for the Australian consumer varies from State to State.

New South Wales

(information supplied by Vince McDonnall and Terry Kennedy)

About 60 % of commercial fishers in New South Wales belong to 1 of the 22 co-operatives along the coast. Co-operative members in New South Wales cannot sell their catch direct from their vessels: they must market their catch through a co-operative or through the Sydney Fish Market. The only exemptions are for fishers in areas not serviced by co-operatives who are issued with Consents which allow them to sell to residents, restaurants, etcetera in the area where they live.

Auction floor, Sydney Fish Market. Dutch auction clock can be seen in right hand photo. (Source: Chris Nowak, Sydney)

Approximately 70 % of seafood caught in New South Wales is sold through the Sydney Fish Market. The remainder is sold either locally through the co-operatives' retail outlets, or to local wholesale customers, or exported (5 % of the New South Wales catch is exported). Fish are transported to market either under refrigeration in insulated trucks or landed directly in Sydney. High volume species (eg mullet, redfish, silver warehou) may bypass the auction system. They are sold direct to processors. Farmed fish and oysters are also exempt from the auction sales arrangements.

The Sydney Fish Market is administered by the New South Wales Fish Marketing Authority. It is the largest fish market in Australia with auctions held every weekday. The auctions run on a 'Dutch auction clock' system, where the price is set at a starting price and then reduced in cents until a buyer sitting at an electronic terminal is prepared to pay the price shown on the clock. The majority of buyers at the auctions are retailers or wholesalers. Most restaurateurs buy their seafood direct from these retailers and wholesalers.

The Sydney Fish Market also sources and sells fish from interstate and overseas, particularly fresh product from New Zealand.

Victoria

(information supplied by Fred Austin)

Victorian fishers have the option of selling their catch directly to restaurants, retail shops and processing plants or consigning their fish to the Melbourne Wholesale Fish Market. Fish and shellfish are boxed and iced and despatched from the port of landing to the Market from individual fishers, co-operatives and aquaculture operations. Products from interstate (mainly Tasmania and southern New South Wales) and overseas (primarily New Zealand) also feature in the Market.

The Melbourne Wholesale Fish Market is owned and managed by the Melbourne City Council and operates at 3 levels: agents, provedores and processors. The *agents* auction fish on a commission basis for fishers and co-operatives. The commission charged varies depending on the fish species, the volume of fish being auctioned and the supplier. Many of the fish are sold prior to auction to fill specific orders. *Provedores* are processors and/or wholesale merchants who work from the fish market and sell seafood and other goods to retailers, fishmongers and restaurateurs. They buy fish from the auctions and fillet them for sale to retailers/restaurateurs who require small quantities of seafood. The *processors* are small scale fish processors who work within the market complex. They buy fish from the auctions and process them immediately on the auction floor.

Tasmania
(information supplied by Des Wolfe)

There is 1 fishermen's co-operative in Tasmania, at Stanley. In the absence of a wholesale fish market, most scalefish fishers market their own catch to individual buyers or to 1 of the registered processing plants. Many Tasmanian fishers consign fish to agents in the Melbourne Wholesale Fish Market, or to Victorian processors and wholesalers.

There are several destinations and processes for the marketing of Tasmania's main fish harvest. Abalone are bought from individual fishers by a wide range of private, licensed factories who in turn sell them on the international market. Some abalone divers also have an export licence. Most live or chilled product, such as southern rock lobsters and Atlantic salmon, are transferred to the mainland to link with international flights. Many of the deep water trawl species taken off Tasmania are landed in Victorian ports although some of the catch of gemfish, blue grenadier and orange roughy is processed into fillets or portions for export at large Tasmanian factories (eg at Stanley, Bridport and Hobart). Farmed oysters and blue mussels are sent from the farms to the mainland live in bags or frozen on the half shell.

South Australia
(information supplied by Tom Angelakis and Keith Jones)

Most of the catch landed in South Australia is of inshore fish. The catch is boxed and iced and sent on refrigerator trucks to Adelaide by the individual fishers, usually on a daily basis. There are no fishermen's co-operatives in South Australia.

At a wholesale market operated by SAFCOL, fish are auctioned on a commission basis for individual fishers. However, most of the catch is sold direct to wholesale buyers for onsale to retail outlets. 'Supply and demand' regulates prices.

The products of some fisheries (eg southern rock lobsters) are bought directly at the point of landing. They are processed in local plants prior to export.

Western Australia
(information supplied by Marshall Thomson, Theo Kailis and Malcolm Anderson)

Successful marketing in Western Australia has to take account of big distances — eg transporting fish from Broome and Esperance, up to 2500 km away from Perth. Fish are put into large bins, iced and sent by refrigerated road transport to major regional centres such as Bunbury, Geraldton and Perth. About 70–80 % of the State's total finfish catch is destined for a major wholesale centre in Perth (A.J. Langford's Pty Ltd) where it is auctioned on behalf of fishers on a commission basis. This market is a private operation with no direct government involvement. Fish that go through the market are sold to wholesalers and retailers. The remainder is consigned by the fisher direct to wholesalers, restaurants and processors. Some of these fish are trucked directly interstate as fresh chilled product.

Shellfish such as prawns, rock lobsters, abalone and scallops are sold direct to either licensed processors, individual retailers or licensed retailers who export most of them to Japan, Taiwan and the United States of America. The Western Australian 'wet fish' (finfish) fishery is worth about A$ 25 million annually while the crustacean and mollusc fisheries (including pearls) are worth about A$ 375 million.

Northern Territory
(information supplied by Christine Julius, Alf Mikolajczyk and Rex Pyne)

In the Northern Territory there are no intermediate marketing structures such as auction floors or co-operatives between fishers and the wholesalers and retailers. There is currently 1 fish processing plant in the Territory, although limited processing is also undertaken by local retailers and wholesalers. Fishers in the Territory may sell their product to any buyers. On the other hand, Northern Territory processors, wholesalers and retailers need a licence to buy fish from Northern Territory fishers. Restaurateurs also require a retail licence which is issued free of charge.

Approximately 65 % of seafood product landed in the Northern Territory is frozen. Because of the small local market, most of the frozen and nearly all the fresh seafood is sold interstate. Chilled fish is available in small quantities at local markets.

The difficulties of distance are reflected in the marketing of fish in the Territory. Chilled, fresh product not sold locally is airfreighted to southern markets — mainly Sydney and Brisbane — by individual fishers who negotiate costs with the airlines.

Frozen seafood for interstate markets is road freighted. All the frozen prawns for overseas markets are trucked directly interstate for export. Fresh fish and mud crabs are air-freighted regularly to Brisbane and, more recently, Sydney markets.

Queensland

(information supplied by Mark Lees and Pat Appleton)

Up until 1982 the majority of wet fish was traded through a statutory organisation known as the Queensland Fish Board. Separate fishermen's co-operatives operated independently of the Board in various Queensland ports but, with the exception of at least 3 fishermen's co-operatives still operating, have generally not been strongly supported by fishers. Since 1982 until the present, individual fishers may either sell directly to retailers if they hold the appropriate licences or to privately owned processing and wholesale operations that function under guidelines set down by the Queensland Fish Management Authority. There are a number of marketing operations (ie processors or wholesalers) in most of the provincial centres along the Queensland coast as well as in Brisbane. These operations tend to be small scale. Prices for wet fish are based largely on 'supply and demand'.

Fish exports and imports

ALL Australian processing operations wishing to *export* fish and fishery products (including freezer vessels which process catch onboard for direct export) need to be registered with the Australian Quarantine and Inspection Service, a group of the Department of Primary Industries and Energy. Fishery products intended for export are subject to the requirements of the Commonwealth's Export Control Act of 1982 and its associated legislation which is administered by the Australian Quarantine and Inspection Service. This legislation requires and the Service ensures (by various inspection methods) that products are fit for human consumption, meet the requirements of the destination countries, and are accurately described. Western Australia is the only State that applies licences to exporters. This regulation is primarily to control foreign entry into the western rock lobster fishery. The Commonwealth Government does not have a marketing strategy for fish exports but does encourage it.

Foreign vessels fishing in Australian waters have to comply with Australian export requirements only if their catch is landed in Australia prior to export.

The major fisheries products exported by Australia are rock lobsters, prawns, abalone, pearls and finfish. The majority of Australian landings of the first 3 groups are exported: for example, 95 % of the western rock lobster catch. High value live and chilled products — such as live rock lobsters and eels and fresh chilled sashimi grade tuna, snapper and farmed Atlantic salmon — are exported by air freight from international airports in capital cities. Frozen products are loaded into refrigerated containers at registered processing establishments and shipped to the nearest port for overseas shipment by sea cargo. Examples include orange roughy fillets, whole school whiting, prawns and abalone. Canned and preserved products are similarly shipped but in unrefrigerated containers.

Many fishing vessels in the rock lobster and prawn fisheries are registered as approved export processing establishments. Their catch is processed on board and frozen into bulk packs which may be either landed then transported to the nearest port for shipping, or repacked onshore by another approved processor.

Australia has strict quarantine regulations on *imported* fish and fish products, largely designed to protect our environment and fish from the introduction of disease organisms not present in Australia. By virtue of its global position and palaeohistory, Australia is naturally free from many diseases found in fish populations and present in the waters of other countries, especially north America, Europe and Asia. Permission to import fish and fish products is granted by the Commonwealth Government based on recommendations from the Advisory Committee on Live Fishes, a committee within the Government's Standing Committee on Fisheries and Aquaculture. Regulations are enforced by the Australian Customs Service and the Australian Quarantine and Inspection Service. *Live fish* imports (mainly for the pet fish trade) are restricted to certain species, the consignments are quarantined before becoming accessible to local buyers and the transporting water is chemically treated. *Frozen and fresh fish* may be imported only from 'disease free' waters and imported *fish products* must have been

Rock lobsters being loaded for trans-shipment prior to export. (Source: Paul Browne, Australian Quarantine and Inspection Service)

prepared by approved methods, and through registered fish processors. For example, cold smoked salmon from north America may not be imported. It has been shown that the smoking method used does not kill all potentially harmful pathogens which may affect Australia's trout and salmon populations.

Fish quality characteristics and handling

COMMERCIAL fish and shellfish can be grouped generally by flesh quality, texture, body shape and flavour. Information on these and other characteristics of fish can be extremely useful to the exporter, vendor (eg wholesaler) and purchaser (eg consumer, restaurateur, dietician). It enables alternative seafoods to be selected and guides the nutritionist, even though objective information on, for example, flavour and fat content of foods is not easy to gather as so much of it depends on individual taste preferences and cooking methods.

Consequently, comments on flesh colour, texture, moisture and fat content, flavour and presentation for all of the major finfish resources included in this book (except for bony bream and Antarctic fish) are presented in tabular form below. Similar information on Australia's main shellfish (molluscs and crustaceans) resources precedes the table. The information was gathered from a variety of sources, including published material and comments by individual fishing industry experts, particularly **Nick V. Ruello**, **Peter Doyle** and **Felicia Kow**. No doubt some of the information presented here would be disputed depending on individual tastes.

Squid, calamari, cuttlefish and octopus have a delicate and mild to sweet flavour. They have a low oil content, yet there is large individual variation in their flesh texture. These animals have an ink sac and their flesh can be tough, requiring tenderising by either marinating or tumbling, and by not overcooking.

Shellfish

Scallops, oysters and mussels have a high mineral content (especially of iron and zinc) and a very low fat content. Their flesh is moist, very versatile, and the flavour varies from 'fishy' to mild and delicate.

Prawns are highly nutritious and have a rich, often sweet taste, due mainly to glutamic acid in their body protein. They are low in saturated fat, high in protein and also have a high level of cholesterol of the type that is not implicated in heart disease. Variations in flavour and texture are shown in royal red prawns, which have a very soft flesh and texture, peel very easily, and have an iodoform flavour when boiled; and in greasyback prawns and endeavour prawns which have a firm shell, while the large roe in females gives them a distinctive taste.

Crabs and freshwater crayfish have white flesh of mild to sweet flavour. The flesh texture varies from fine (eg crabs) to medium (lobsters). Lobster flesh is moist and rich in flavour.

(left) Unloading frozen tuna, Eden. (Source: Bureau of Resource Sciences)

(centre top) Unloading fish at Bicheno, north-eastern Tasmania. (Source: Lindsay Chapman, Bureau of Resource Sciences)

(centre) Weighing and packing western rock lobsters. (Source: Paul Browne, Australian Quarantine and Inspection Service)

(below) Southern scallops being moved into a factory for processing. (Source: Paul Browne, Australian Quarantine and Inspection Service)

Name	Colour of raw fillet	Texture/ firmness	Fat content	Flavour	Comments on retail presentation, preparation and eating quality
albacore	pinkish — paler than other tunas	medium firm; softer than other large tunas	medium to high	mild and delicate; 'meaty' if overcooked	sold as fillets or steaks; excellent as steaks if not overcooked; 'chicken of the sea' if cooked very rare
anchovy	dark	medium texture; very soft — firmed by salting	oily (medium fat)	distinct, strong fishy flavour	sold whole; usually salt cured; can be eaten whole, as fillets or garnish
Atlantic salmon	pale to dark pink; reddish pink	medium-sized flakes; soft	high	mild, distinct flavour	sold whole, or as cutlets or fillets; best as cutlets; excellent smoked, as 'gravlax' or as sashimi, also pâté; few bones; has a good shelf life; good eating, yet dry if overcooked
Australian salmon	dark	coarse to medium texture; firm	low to medium	strong fishy taste; distinct flavour	sold whole; can be eaten whole, or as cutlets or fillets, more commonly canned; best newly caught, having been bled soon after capture; has a short shelf life; cook rare with dark meat removed; good in fish cakes
barracouta	dark	medium texture	low to medium	mild yet distinct flavour	usually slices are taken from fillets; often canned; is very suitable for smoking and fish cakes; was a popular 'fish-and-chips' species; has long, large bones; flesh can be 'milky'
barramundi	white	large, firm flakes; tender	low to high — varies with season	distinct, mild flavour	sold whole or as fillets, eaten as cutlets or fillets; best skinned; has few or large bones; excellent eating yet may have an 'earthy' taste in some areas or under certain conditions
blue eye	pale pink	large flakes; firm to medium	medium to high	mild, pleasant flavour; tasty	sold as fillets or cutlets; usually sold skin-on but best skinned; has few bones; presents well; versatile; care needed not to overcook
blue grenadier	off white	delicate, soft texture; tends to flake easily into medium flakes	low to medium	delicate to mild fishy flavour	sold as fillets or cutlets, skin-on or skinned; need deep skinning to remove fat layer just under the skin; has few bones; good for surimi and 'fish finger' manufacture
bream	white	fine texture; soft to firm	medium to high	mild or bland; sweet, delicate	sold whole or as fillets; often have hard white fat layer along the belly wall; has short shelf life as not gutted; has fine bones; fish from estuaries have a coarser flavour
broadbill swordfish	creamy white	firm	medium to high	delicate to mild	sold as fillets or steaks; must be skinned; high quality table fish and good for barbecue; care needed not to overcook
carp	white to dark pink	firm	high	bland to mild; distinct fishy flavour	sold whole or as fillets; bony; often prepared as minced product; poor table fish; can have an 'earthy' taste; flavour can be improved ('cleaned') by feeding with pollard in a bath for several days
cobbler	off white	very fine flakes; very soft texture	low	pleasant, mild	sold head-off; must be skinned; best eaten fresh
coral trout	very white	fine flakes; firm to medium	low to medium	delicate, mild sea flavour, distinct	sold as fillets or whole; best when skinned; fine eating, especially when very fresh; a top table fish
dories	white	fine texture; firm to tender	low to medium	delicate; mild to sweet	sold whole or as fillets, skin on or off; no or few bones in fillets; easily boned; John Dory especially good eating; supreme table fish
freshwater eels	white to pink	firm to medium	variable; can be very oily	delicate, fishy flavour	sold whole when fresh but usually smoked and sold as cutlets; small eels skinned and grilled are a luxury item in Japan
emperors	white	fine and firm	medium	varies from sweet to mild to strong	sold whole or as fillets; long shelf life; good eating
flathead	white	flakes easily; soft, tender (tiger flathead) to firm (dusky flathead)	low	distinct, mild flavour	sold whole or as skin-on fillets, with or without 'wings'; best when boned; short shelf life
garfish	translucent with silver stripe; off white	fine to medium texture; soft	low to medium	sweet to mild; good flavour	sold whole or as 'butterfly' fillets; best as fillets, skin-on; when sold whole gut must be removed promptly to avoid staining by seagrass; has very fine bones that usually can be chewed up

Name	Colour of raw fillet	Texture/ firmness	Fat content	Flavour	Comments on retail presentation, preparation and eating quality
gemfish	white to pink	delicate to medium texture; flakes easily into firm and chunky flakes	medium	distinct mild fishy flavour	usually sold as fillets or cutlets, skin-on; has few, large bones; excellent smoked; a versatile fish
golden perch	white	firm	medium to high –– varies with season	mild, distinct flavour	usually sold whole; can have fat layer in body cavity
jack mackerel	dark	medium texture; soft	medium to high –– varies with season	'meaty' flavour	good smoked; should be bled promptly for best quality
kingfish	variable: white to pink or reddish; dark	firm texture, coarse in larger fish	low to high	mild to distinct, strong flavour	usually sold as fillets or cutlets; when whole, can be stuffed and baked; also sold as sashimi; a versatile fish; dry if overcooked; better from colder waters and when smaller
luderick	off white; pale grey or dark	firm to soft texture	medium to high	distinct or strong fishy flavour	sold whole or as fillets; best to remove rib bones; should be bled and skinned immediately; tasty fish if prepared correctly
black marlin & blue marlin	pale pink	firm	medium to high	mild; blue marlin may have an iodine taste; 'meaty' if overcooked	sold as fillets or steaks; good as sashimi; domestic sales are banned in some States
striped marlin	reddish pink	firm texture; medium	high	mild;'meaty' if overcooked	sold as fillets or steaks; not sold for domestic market in NSW and WA; esteemed by Japanese as sashimi (receives a higher price than do blue or black marlins)
morwong	white to pale pink; creamy pink	medium to firm texture	low to medium	mild, distinct fishy flavour	sold whole or as fillets; best to remove rib bones; good table fish—versatile; often sold as 'sea bream' or 'sea perch'
sea mullet	pinkish grey, darker after spawning period	flakes easily; medium firm, always tender	seasonally high fat content	rich, distinct taste; strong fishy flavour	usually sold whole, sometimes as fillets; roe is delicious; rib bones must be removed; deep skinning removes the dark, fatty tissue under the skin; sea run fish are fine eating but often have short shelf life; fish from estuaries have a 'muddy' flavour; excellent barbecued or smoked; flesh rich in omega-3 fatty acids, low in cholesterol
yellow-eye mullet	grey to dark pink	flakes easily; delicate and soft	medium to high	strong, fishy flavour	sold as fillets or whole; excellent barbecued
mulloway	white to pale pink	large flakes; soft to medium	low	mild to very distinct flavour	sold as cutlets or whole; excellent table fish
Murray cod	white	firm	medium to high –– varies with season	distinct, delicate flavour	sold whole or as cutlets or fillets; small fish always sold whole; large fish very fatty
ocean jacket	white to cream	firm and dense texture, chunky	low	mild to sweet	sold skinned, headed and gutted; must be skinned; few bones, so easy eating
ocean perch	white to pale pink	soft to firm texture	low to medium	pleasant, mild flavour	sold whole or as fillets; fillets de-boned; attractive fish, especially with skin on; beware sharp spines
orange roughy	pearly white	coarse flakes; medium to firm	medium to high (oil content high)	delicate to mild or bland	sold as boned fillets; needs deep skinning to remove fat layer under the skin; attractive and versatile fish for a range of cooking styles; often sold as 'sea perch'
oreos	white	doesn't flake easily; dense, firm	medium	delicate, good	sold as boneless fillets; must be skinned; holds together well with cooking
pilchard	dark; reddish	medium to firm texture; soft	oily (medium fat)	distinct or strong fishy flavour	sold whole; bony; best grilled, or floured and fried crisp; highly versatile
pink ling	white	dense, large flakes; medium firm	low to medium	mild to bland; tasty	sold whole or as fillets; best skinned as skin is thick and slimy; has few bones; excellent smoked
redfish	white to pale pink	fine, large flakes; tender to firm	medium to high	delicate to mild to slightly sweet	sold whole, as cutlets or fillets; best skinned; slightly bony; bones fine
rock cod	white	large, soft to firm flakes	low	sweet to mild, fishy flavour	sold as fillets or cutlets, smaller fish sold whole; best when skinned; has good shelf life

Name	Colour of raw fillet	Texture/ firmness	Fat content	Flavour	Comments on retail presentation, preparation and eating quality
sea perch (*Lutjanus* species)	white	fine and firm	low to medium	varies from sweet to mild to strong	usually sold as cutlets or fillets, smaller ones sold whole; red skin attractive; has long shelf life
shark ('flake')	white to translucent pink	fine and firm texture, tends to be flaky	low	mild to moderate fishy flavour	sold as slices from fillets; boneless; must be skinned; can have an ammonia 'off' flavour if not handled correctly; short shelf life
silver trevally	pinkish with dark lines; reddish	medium texture; medium to firm	medium to high	mild or subtle fishy flavour	sold whole, sometimes as fillets or steaks; best when skinned; has few bones; needs to be bled immediately for peak quality; can be a fine sashimi fish; inclined to be dry when cooked
snapper	white to pinkish	medium flakes (coarse in large fish); soft	low to medium	delicate, sweet to mild; distinct fishy flavour	sold whole or as cutlets or fillets; best in fillets without rib bones; excellent smoked and becoming popular for sashimi; longer shelf life if chilled immediately; usually served whole in restaurants; high quality snapper are excellent eating
Spanish mackerel	pearly pink to white	medium to large flakes; smooth and firm	medium to high	good rich fishy 'sea' flavour	sold as cutlets or fillets; care needed when handling chilled mackerel that the flesh doesn't soften; inclined to be dry if overcooked
tailor	pink to dark grey	soft to medium texture	medium and slightly oily	distinct or strong 'fishy' flavour	sold whole or as fillets; should be bled on capture to prevent flesh softening; best as fillets and when eaten very fresh; excellent smoked
threadfin salmon	white	very large flakes; firm	medium	sweet; very fine flavour	sold as fillets; best skinned; bones in fillets; good shelf life if processed immediately
tommy ruff	pinkish	firm	medium	sweet and delicate when fresh; strong, fishy flavour if frozen	sold whole or as fillets; best eaten very fresh; excellent split and smoked
tropical snapper	white to pale pink	firm	medium	delicate to mild	sold whole or as fillets; pink skin attractive; has long shelf life
trout	white to pink	soft and delicate	high	mild — the pinker the better	sold whole, occasionally as fillets; have fine bones; farmed trout generally have a good shelf life; needs salt in cooking; good smoked; a top table fish; 'ocean trout' are particularly good eating
bigeye tuna	pink to red	firm or soft	low to high	rich; mild and 'meaty' when cooked	high quality sashimi fish; rarely eaten cooked; good as steaks
skipjack tuna	dark red	medium	low to high	mild and 'meaty' when cooked	sold mostly canned but sold fresh either whole or as steaks; major item in Japan prepared as smoked/dried 'katsuobushi' as base for soups and stocks; liver oil is rich in Vitamin D
southern bluefin tuna	pink to red	medium to firm with attractive coarse grain	low to high	rich; mild and 'meaty' when cooked	top grade sashimi fish
yellowfin tuna	pink to red	soft to firm	low to high	rich; mild and 'meaty' when cooked	best as sashimi; sometimes sold as steaks
warehou	white to off white	medium to large flakes; firm	medium to high	distinct fishy flavour	usually sold as fillets; best skinned
Westralian jewfish	white	tender, soft and fine	low to medium	delicate, sweet to mild	sold whole or as cutlets
whiting	white	fine texture; tender to firm	low to medium	delicate, slighly sweet (and 'peppery' in King George whiting)	sold whole or as fillets; good shelf life; versatile fish; King George whiting particularly good eating

Seafood in human nutrition

Information supplied by Stephen Thrower

SEAFOOD — that is, all edible products from marine and fresh waters — has been a major source of human food for thousands of years. Seafood in general is highly nutritious and beneficial to human health. In recent years it has been suggested that 2 components of oils found in seafood ('marine oils'), eicosapentaenoic acid (EPA) and docosahexaenoic acid (DHA) — sometimes referred to as the Omega 3 fatty acids — can help reduce the incidence of atherosclerosis, or fatty hardening of the arteries. In addition, work has been done to show that fish oils are beneficial for inflammatory and immunological diseases (eg rheumatoid arthritis and asthma), multiple sclerosis and cancer. Furthermore, different parts of fish contain different nutrients. These fall into 2 broad categories:

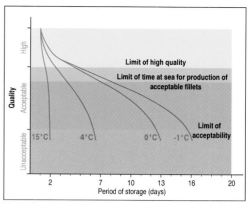

Hypothetical figure for changes in quality of undamaged orange roughy. (Source: Thrower and Bremner, 1987)

- **Macronutrients** Fish is generally a good source of quality *protein*. The muscles of fish and shellfish typically contain 15–20 % protein, which is usually readily digestible, and is rich in essential amino acids (lysine, methionine and cysteine).

The level of *lipids*, usually referred to as 'oils', in fish muscle can vary considerably. The flesh of lean or 'white' fish such as shark, which store their oils in their viscera, is low in lipids. The level is typically 1 % or 2 %. Fatty fish such as mackerel or mullet, which store oil in their flesh, may contain much higher levels but the levels vary with size of the fish, season and the fish's condition. The level of oil in jack mackerel for example, varies from 2 % to 17 % over a year. Furthermore, dark muscle tissue usually contains more fat than light tissue. Whilst some marine oils are readily digested and absorbed by humans, lipids stored as 'wax esters' in some deepsea fish such as orange roughy are not absorbed.

Health conscious consumers seeking to increase their intake of EPA and DHA need to consider the level of lipid in the fish, the level of EPA and DHA in that lipid, how these vary with fish size and season, and whether they are in a form that can be absorbed.

The levels of *carbohydrate* in fish are fairly low, but those in shellfish, which tend to store energy as the complex carbohydrate glycogen rather than as lipid, can be quite high. Like the level of lipid in fish, the level of glycogen in shellfish can vary greatly with size of the animal, condition and season. For example, the glycogen level in abalone meat varies from 0.2 % to 7.5 % over a year.

- **Micronutrients** Seafood is also a good source of vitamins and minerals. The level of oil in the flesh determines the level of the *fat soluble vitamins A and D* and the *antioxidant vitamin E*, sometimes referred to as tocopherol. Fatty fish are one of the best sources of these vitamins. Fish is also a good source of *water soluble vitamins* such as the *B-complex vitamins* and, in some species, *riboflavin* and *niacin*.

Iodine is present in all seafood. Other minerals at high levels include *phosphorus*, *potassium* and *calcium*. Certain shellfish are good sources of *iron*, *copper* and *zinc*.

Proximate composition of fish The 'proximate' composition of the edible portion of fish is based on the relative proportion of moisture, protein, lipid and ash in the tissue. Dieticians, nutritionists, and animal feed processors all require knowledge on the proximate composition of fish. Unfortunately, there is little of this information for Australian fish.

Variations in the proximate composition of fish are mainly due to variations in fat content. Fish generally fall into 2 categories: fatty or oily (composed of 5 % or more fat) and lean (less that 5 % fat). Fatty or oily fish include pilchards, jack mackerel, tailor, and tuna. Lean fish include flathead, bream, snapper, dories, blue grenadier and pink ling.

Quality deterioration The time needed for transportation and handling means that *very* fresh fish often do not reach the consumer. Some deterioration takes place despite care. The processes of deterioration may be biochemical or microbiological in nature.

- **Biochemical deterioration** Harvested fish are considerably stressed physiologically during their capture and subsequent death, and these phenomena use large amounts of energy. This energy is supplied by the breakdown of energy-rich compounds called *nucleotides* (eg adenosine triphosphate, ATP) in the muscle.

Depending on the rate and extent of this breakdown, the fish's flavour deteriorates to some degree.

In addition to nucleotide breakdown, other *enzymic processes* may occur. Enzymes may be released within the muscle cells and break down the proteins, and digestive enzymes in the gut may begin to attack the gut wall, eventually leaking out and attacking the flesh.

• **Microbiological deterioration** In the later stages of spoilage, fish are subject to bacterial attack. The bacteria on living fish are confined to the skin, gills and gut, and are held in check by the fish's immune system. After the fish dies the bacteria begin to multiply, producing compounds which have unpleasant flavours and odours. These compounds and eventually the bacteria themselves, invade the fish flesh, making it unfit for consumption.

Poor handling and storage Product deterioration will be exacerbated by poor handling and poor hygiene on vessels and in processing plants. Spoilage can best be reduced by reducing the temperature. Chilling fish can greatly increase their 'shelf life', for example 1 day's storage at 10°C is equivalent to 4 days on ice at 0°C. Much longer shelf life can be achieved by frozen storage; for example at –18°C fatty fish can be kept 2-3 months and white (lean) fish can be kept 3–5 months with little deterioration in quality.

Some quality deterioration does take place during freezing, frozen storage and thawing, eg dehydration and oxidation leading to 'freezer burn' and rancidity. Enzymic reactions also continue in the cold store — even at –30°C (albeit at a slow rate). Deterioration can be reduced by fast freezing and thawing, good moisture-tight packaging and glazing, and maintenance of constant, low temperatures in the cold store.

Preparation for consumption The nutritional status of seafood can be affected by the way it is prepared. Protein may be lost by excessive fluid losses during freezing and cooking. The highly unsaturated marine oils in fish may be lost by heating processes such as frying and canning, and replaced by oils of much lower nutritional value from the cooking fat or oil used to fill the can. Vitamins may also be lost with oil and water. In addition, some vitamins such as riboflavin and niacin are destroyed by heat, while thiamine can be destroyed by processing and tocopherol is lost as fats oxidise.

Assessing seafood quality Considerable variation in quality can be expected in seafoods, and buyers need to be able to form judgements of the raw material on offer. Buyers assess seafood quality by smell, sight, touch and, sometimes, taste. For example,

• **in whole fish**, the gills should be a bright red colour, the skin should be bright, firm and shiny with some iridescence, and the eyes should be convex and clear;

• **in a fish fillet**, the flesh should be firm and elastic and appear translucent;

• **freshly cooked prawns (crustaceans)**, should have bright colours, a clear carapace and black, smooth eyes. Their flesh should be firm and elastic, the head firmly attached to the body and they should have no or very little smell. Melanosis or 'black spot', which can occur in prawns and lobster, does not affect eating quality, but can indicate temperature abuse. (Melanosis can be prevented by dipping in properly measured levels of antioxidants such as sodium metabisulphite, or controlled by storing the prawns under cold water to minimise their exposure to the oxygen in the air);

• **in molluscs**, the shells should be shut and fairly full of pale, creamy meat and the mantle should be bright and moist. The quality of live molluscs such as scallops and abalone can be judged by how quickly they contract their muscular foot to avoid an intruding knife. The relative firmness and elasticity of the muscular foot also can indicate the animal's freshness. Bright, iridescent colours indicate that intact squid and octopus are in good condition. Fresh cleaned and skinned squid 'tubes' are usually white.

Contaminants In general, seafoods are amongst the safest of foods, as most marine pathogens are not toxic to humans. There are 2 main types of contaminants that may accumulate in fish products: biotoxins and chemicals. *Biotoxins*, such as ciguatera and paralytic shellfish poisons, usually occur when oceanographic conditions favour the growth of 'blooms' of marine algae, which may produce these toxins. The algae are eaten by filter feeding shellfish which in turn can accumulate the toxins to levels causing poisoning in consumers. *Chemicals* may be accumulated by seafood organisms, often through biomagnification along the food chain. Of public concern are organic pollutants such as polychlorinated biphenyls, and trace metals such as cadmium and mercury. Food standards set the maximum limits for these substances in seafood and their occurrence is monitored by State and federal programs to assure consumer confidence.

Further reading

Australian Science and Technology Council (1988) *Casting the net. Post-harvest technologies and opportunities in the fishing industry. A report to the Prime Minister.* Canberra: Australian Government Publishing Service. 138 pp.

Bremner, H.A. (1985) A convenient easy to use system for estimating the quality of chilled seafoods. *DSIR Fish Processing Bulletin* **7**: 59.

Brown, A.J., Roberts, D.C.K. and Truswell, A.S. (1989) Fatty acid composition of Australian marine fin fish: a review. *Food Australia* **41**: 655.

Fisheries Research and Development Corporation (1992) *National seafood consumption study: summary report.* West Perth: PA Consulting Group. 83 pp.

Huss, H.H. (1991) Public health aspects of seafood consumption. Special report. *Infofish International* **3**: 27–32.

Mikolajczyk, A. (1991) Recommended handling methods for fresh tropical reef fish. *Northern Territory Department of Primary Industry and Fisheries.* 16 pp.

Miezitis, O. and Wright, A.D. (1979) Variations in the chemical composition of jack mackerel (*Trachurus declivis* (Jenyns)) from commercial fishing for FPC production 1973–1974. *Tasmanian Fisheries Research* **22**: 30.

New South Wales Fishing Industry Training Council Ltd (1989) *Onboard handling of sashimi quality fish for export.* Sydney. 16 pp.

Palmas Seafood Distributors Pty Ltd (1992) *Seafood handbook. A comprehensive buying guide for the food service industry.* Victoria. 80 pp.

Poole, S. Williams, D. and Knight, C. (1990) The iced storage lives of selected commercial inshore and offshore reef fish from Northern Territory waters. *Northern Territory Department of Primary Industry and Fisheries, Fisheries Report* **23**. 47 pp.

International Atomic Energy Agency (1989) Radiation preservation of fish and fishery products. Final results of a co-ordinated research programme of the joint FAO/IAEA Division of Nuclear Techniques in Food and Agriculture. *Technical Reports Series* **303**. Vienna. 139 pp.

Seafood catering manual (in press, 1993) Brisbane: Queensland Department of Primary Industries.

Smith, P. and Read, C. (1993) Efficiency of Australian seafood marketing. *Australian Bureau of Agricultural Research and Economics, Research Report* **93.1**. 134 pp.

Stansby, M.E. (ed) (1990) *Fish oils in nutrition.* New York: AVI, Van Nostrand Reinhold. 313 pp.

The 1990 Australian market basket survey (1991) Canberra: National Health and Medical Research Council and the National Food Authority. 109 pp.

Thrower, S J. (1984) *Recommended code of practice for the hygienic handling, stowage and transport of fresh fish.* Tasmanian Fisheries Development Authority.

Thrower, S.J. and Bremner H.A. (1987) Orange roughy — a guide to handling, chilling and processing. *Australian Fisheries* **46**(11): 22–28.

Vleig, P. (1984) Proximate analysis of 10 New Zealand fish species. *New Zealand Journal of Science* **27**: 99.

Williams, S.C. (1988) Marketing chilled fish in Japan. *Queensland Department of Primary Industries Information Series* **Q187022**. 66 pp.

Contributors

In addition to the contributors named above, the following people provided information on various aspects of fish quality and handling: Paul Browne, Albert Caton and Ian Hamdorf.

Source: Stephen Thrower

MOLLUSCS *are a group of mainly aquatic invertebrates with a soft, unsegmented body and often a shell. Most have a radula (a rasping ribbon of teeth on the 'tongue'), a large muscular foot—modified to 'arms' in squid, octopus and their relatives—and a fleshy mantle covering the internal organs which, in some forms, secretes a thin shell. Most forms possess 1 or 2 gills. Examples are oysters, scallops, abalone, periwinkles, limpets, cuttlefish, squid and octopus.*

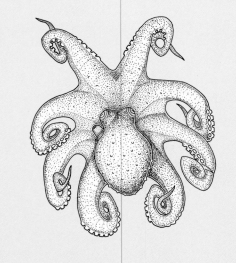

CRUSTACEANS *are a group of mainly aquatic invertebrates with a hard exoskeleton, 2 pairs of antennae and jointed, double-branched limbs. Crustaceans grow by moulting (or shedding) their hard exoskeleton and forming a new one. Most crustaceans have gills, although smaller forms breathe directly through their exoskeleton. Examples are crabs, lobsters, prawns, sea lice and barnacles.*

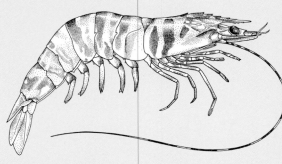

ECHINODERMS *are exclusively marine invertebrates with an internal skeleton of calcareous plates that often bear spines. Echinoderms have a unique hydraulic water vascular system which operates tube feet used for feeding and locomotion. Their bodies are generally radially symmetrical with the body divided into 5 parts around a central axis. Echinoderms are nearly all bottom-dwelling. Examples are star fish, feather stars, brittle stars, sea urchins and sea cucumbers.*

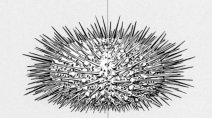

ELASMOBRANCHS *are fishes whose internal skeleton is mainly cartilaginous, sometimes calcified but never ossified. Their skull is without sutures. Elasmobranchs have placoid scales and their upper jaw is not fused to the cranium. They have numerous teeth that are not usually fused to the jaws and are replaced serially. Elasmobranchs have a spiracle (respiratory pore) and 5–7 separate gill openings on each side, no swim bladder and males bear claspers for internal fertilisation. This group includes sharks, skates and rays.*

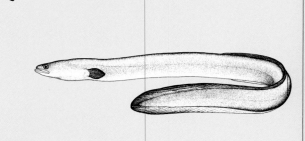

TELEOSTS *are fishes whose internal skeleton is constructed mainly of true bone. Their skull is sutured and the teeth are usually fused to the jaw bones. The posterior tip of their vertebral column turns upwards and terminates in a bony plate. Their scales are usually thin and bony. Teleosts have external nostrils, a single gill opening on each side, and usually have a swim bladder or lung. Examples include sardines, eels, bream and tunas.*

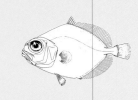

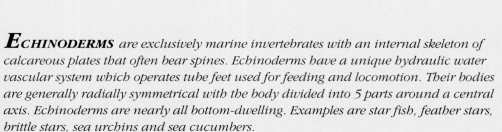

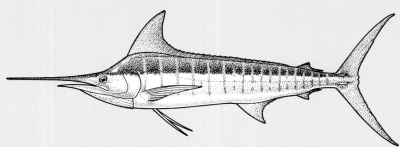

5. Fisheries resources

Greenlip abalone

Haliotis laevigata

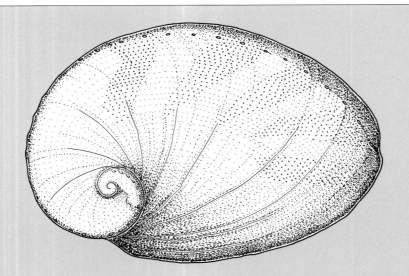

Haliotis laevigata Donovan

Greenlip abalone

There are no other common names.
FAO: no known name
Australian species code: 662002

Family HALIOTIDAE

Diagnostic features Greenlip abalone have a large shell which is broad and 'ear' shaped. The outside of the shell surface is smooth. The shell's spire is moderately elevated, and there is a series of small holes along the left side of the shell following the course of the spire. The inside of the shell is silvery and rather smooth.[1] The foot has a distinct green lip that gives this species its name.

Distribution

Greenlip abalone are endemic to Australian waters, distributed from Corner Inlet in Victoria across the southern coast of the mainland to Cape Naturaliste in Western Australia. They also inhabit waters off the coast of Tasmania including the islands in Bass Strait.[2]

Greenlip abalone live in waters from 10 m to 30 m, occasionally to 40 m, deep. They inhabit inshore rocky reefs, often in the lee of headlands or islands, or in gutters and clefts in rough waters at the base of cliffs. In more sheltered sites they may live in shallower water on rocks near sand. Greenlip abalone are often found in or near seagrass beds.[2] Their distribution is not continuous, but rather they occur in clusters on favourable habitat, separated by areas of unsuitable habitat.[2] Whereas blacklip abalone (*Haliotis rubra*) have a nearly continuous distribution along rocky coastlines of southern Australia, greenlip abalone tend to be more patchy. Distance between populations can be as much as tens of km.[3]

Life history

Abalone are normally solitary but aggregate during the spawning season.[4]

Greenlip abalone spawn from October to March or April.[5] They are termed 'broadcast spawners', as their eggs and sperm are released and fertilised in open water. They produce large numbers of eggs, with fecundity (egg number) increasing in larger abalone.

The fertilised eggs are not buoyant but can be moved around by water currents. The abalone grow quickly through 3 mobile larval phases[6] before settling after 2–6 days, depending on the water temperature. Greenlip abalone larvae are often found on various coralline algae species including *Sporolithon* species, *Lithothamnion* species and *Mesophyllum* species.[7] The larvae remain on the algae until they are about 5 mm long when they move to adjacent rock habitats.[7] Larval dispersal in greenlip abalone is in the order of hundreds of m and adult migration is in the order of tens to hundreds of m.[3]

Abalone are not permanently attached to substrates. Juvenile greenlip abalone hide under rocks and crevices, moving into more open environments as they grow. Growth is estimated at 1.5–2 mm a month for the first 5 years[8] and is usually greatest in the spring and summer months. Growth rates vary with location; for example, in areas with significant water movement abalone grow more quickly than in still water. Females grow faster than males. After 1 year, greenlip abalone average 2–5 cm in length.[9] They grow to 15–22 cm in length, with both males and females maturing after 3 years. As many as 70 % of young greenlip abalone die in their first year of life.[10]

The diet of adult greenlip abalone is dominated by drift algae. The abalone feed by adopting a posture with the front of their shell slightly raised. As a piece of weed drifts by, the front part of the 'foot' extends to grasp it. The abalone feed

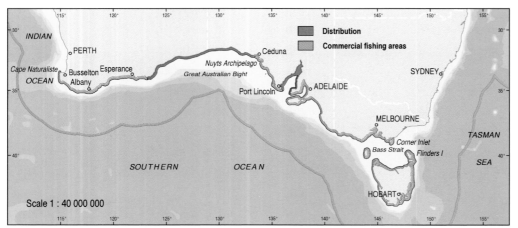

Geographic distribution and commercial fishing areas for greenlip abalone.

selectively, taking only red algae (*Asparagosis armata*) and seagrass leaves (including *Hetrozostera tasmanica, Posidonia sinuosa* and *Amphibolis antarctica*).[11] Their main predators are stingrays (Myliobatoidei).

Stock structure

Abalone populations show an increase in genetic variation with increasing geographic distance between them ('isolation by distance'). Gene flow between populations is largely dependent on dispersal of larvae which in turn is dependent on ocean currents and coastal topography. Aggregations of greenlip abalone have been found to be genetically discrete.[3]

Commercial fishery

Greenlip abalone are taken by commercial abalone divers working off many localities along the coasts of Tasmania, Victoria and South Australia and off Esperance in Western Australia. In southern Western Australia and western South Australia, greenlip abalone, blacklip abalone and Roe's abalone (*Haliotis roei*) are all taken in the abalone fishery. Greenlip abalone is the dominant species in the catch from these coasts. Both greenlip abalone and blacklip abalone are fished in Victoria and Tasmania, but in those States the catches are dominated by blacklip abalone.

Abalone are collected by divers operating from boats and primarily using hookah gear, but also some SCUBA gear. The abalone are prised from the rocks using an 'abalone iron' or screw driver.[12]

Abalone diver at the surface with the catch. (Source: Department of Foreign Affairs and Trade)

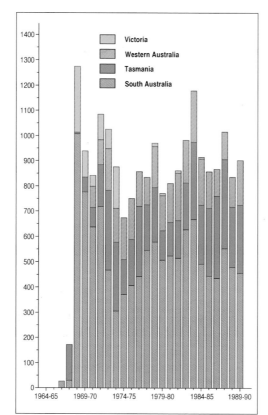

Total annual catch in t of greenlip abalone for the period 1964–65 to 1989–90 in Australia. Figures are unavailable for Victoria from 1974–75 to 1977–78 and 1985–86 to 1989–90. (Source: Fisheries Resources Atlas Statistical Database)

The boats used are often small and launched from trailers, allowing divers access to remote stretches of coastline.

All abalone are landed whole and then shucked (de-shelled), cleaned and processed. The meat is graded and then either bulk frozen, cooked in brine and canned,[12] or parboiled and then frozen.[6] A small amount is frozen whole on the shell. The meat yield is 30–40 % by weight after shucking and cleaning.[12]

The entire greenlip abalone catch is exported. Frozen abalone is exported to Japan and Hong Kong, with canned abalone sold in Japan, Hong Kong, Singapore and the United States of America. There is also a small market for live abalone in Japan and an erratic market for the shell in Asia.[3] Fishers in Tasmania received up to A$ 32.00 kg for greenlip abalone in 1992–93, and in South Australia the early 1993 average wholesale price per kg (for meat only) was A$ 95.00.

Management controls In all States there is limited entry to the abalone fishery and transferable licences and individual transferable quotas apply. All States have minimum size limits on greenlip abalone. Divers in South

Australia and Tasmania are required to undergo yearly medical examinations.

Because of the patchy distribution of greenlip abalone populations and their genetic structure, aggregations or local populations need to be managed as individual stocks so that local genetic diversity is maintained.

Aquaculture

Exploratory work on the culture of greenlip abalone and blacklip abalone has been carried out in Tasmania, South Australia and Victoria. Several methods have been tried, including 1 common method that is land-based, using a pond or raceway system. The juvenile abalone are either grown out in tanks onshore or re-seeded onto the sea bed.[13]

Recreational fishery

Abalone are harvested by recreational divers throughout their natural range. Greatest effort is centred on inshore coastal waters around rocks and headlands, especially near towns. The abalone are collected using snorkelling or SCUBA diving gear. The larger, more visible adults are the major targets. The amount of greenlip abalone taken by recreational divers is probably substantial.

Management controls The number and the minimum size of abalone that can be taken recreationally is regulated by each State. In Western Australia abalone may only be taken by divers using snorkelling gear.

Resource status

Greenlip abalone stocks are fully exploited and will not sustain an increase in fishing effort. However, increases in

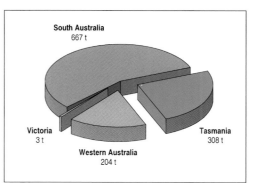

Proportion of the catch of greenlip abalone in each Australian State for the year 1983–84. (Source: Fisheries Resources Atlas Statistical Database)

recreational catches and an undetermined amount of poaching activity are potential extra drains on abalone stocks.[6]

References

1. Macpherson, J.H. and Gabriel, C.J. (1962) *Marine molluscs of Victoria.* Victoria: Melbourne University Press. 475 pp.

2. Shepherd, S.A. (1973) Studies on southern Australian abalone (genus *Haliotis*). I. Ecology of five sympatric species. *Australian Journal of Marine and Freshwater Research* **24**: 217–257.

3. Shepherd, S.A. and Brown, L.D. (in press, 1992) What is an abalone stock?: implications for the role of refugia in conservation. *Canadian Journal of Fisheries and Aquatic Sciences.*

4. Shepherd, S.A. (1986) Studies on southern Australian abalone (genus *Haliotis*). VII. Aggregative behaviour of *H. laevigata* in relation to spawning. *Marine Biology* **90**: 231–236.

5. Shepherd, S.A. and Laws, H.M. (1974) Studies on southern Australian abalone (genus *Haliotis*). II. Reproduction of five species. *Australian Journal of Marine and Freshwater Research* **25**: 49–62.

6. Ward, T.J. (1986) Abalone biology and fisheries in Australia: a review of research. *Australian Fisheries Service, Department of Primary Industries and Energy, Fisheries Paper* **86-12**. 33 pp.

7. Shepherd, S.A. and Turner, J.A. (1985) Studies on southern Australian abalone (genus *Haliotis*). VI. Habitat preference, abundance and predators of juveniles. *Journal of Experimental Marine Biology and Ecology* **93**: 285–298.

8. Shepherd, S.A. (1988) Studies on southern Australian abalone (genus *Haliotis*). VIII. Growth of juvenile *H. laevigata. Australian Journal of Marine and Freshwater Research* **39**: 177–183.

9. Shepherd, S.A. and Hearn, W.S. (1983) Studies on southern Australian abalone (genus *Haliotis*). IV. Growth of *H. laevigata* and *H. ruber. Australian Journal of Marine and Freshwater Research* **34**: 461–475.

10. Shepherd, S.A. and Godoy, C. (1989) Studies on southern Australian abalone (genus *Haliotis*). XI. Movement and natural mortality of juveniles. *Journal of the Malacological Society of Australia* **10**: 87–95.

11. Shepherd, S.A. and Cannon, J. (1988) Studies on southern Australian abalone (genus *Haliotis*). X. Food and feeding of juveniles. *Journal of the Malacological Society of Australia* **9**: 21–26.

12. Abalone (1982) *Demersal Mollusc Research Group, South Eastern Fisheries Committee, Fishery situation report* **10**. 22 pp.

13. Cropp, R.A. (1989) Abalone culture in Tasmania. *Division of Sea Fisheries, Tasmania, Technical Report* **37**. 26 pp.

Close-up of greenlip abalone. (Source: Warwick Nash, Division of Sea Fisheries, Tasmanian Department of Primary Industry and Fisheries)

Contributors

The information on this species was originally provided by Scoresby Shepherd and supplemented by (in alphabetical order) Ian Knuckey and Warwick Nash. Drawing by Leslie Newman. (*Details of contributors and their organisations are given in the Acknowledgements section at the back of this book.*)

Compilers Alex McNee and Christina Grieve (maps)

Blacklip abalone

Haliotis rubra

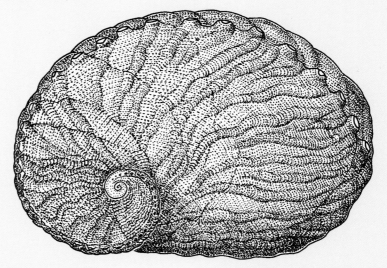

Haliotis rubra Leach

Blacklip abalone

Another common name is **brownlip abalone**.
FAO: **blacklip abalone**
Australian species code: 662001

Family HALIOTIDAE

Diagnostic features Blacklip abalone have a large shell which is obliquely wrinkled and spirally ridged, with some ridges larger than others. The ridges are crossed by feeble growth lines. Their shell is slightly angular at the row of holes near its margin and below this it is markedly excavated. The inside of the shell is corrugated and silvery in colour.[1] The foot of the abalone has a distinct black lip that gives this species its name.

Distribution

Blacklip abalone are endemic to Australian waters and are found from Coffs Harbour in New South Wales, around the south of the continent to Rottnest Island (off Perth) in Western Australia. The coastal waters of Tasmania and the Bass Strait islands are included in this area.[2]

In the warmer part of their range blacklip abalone live in crevices and caves on reefs in up to 10 m of water, although they are most common in less than 5 m of water.[3] Around Tasmania they occupy water to 40 m depth. Throughout their range, blacklip abalone inhabit crevices and horizontal and vertical rock faces. They can live in both rough and sheltered waters if the habitat is suitable, and unlike greenlip abalone (*Haliotis laevigata*), their distribution is more or less continuous along rocky coastlines.[2]

Life history

Blacklip abalone have an extended spawning period from October to March.[4] The exact time of spawning varies between localities and the environmental cues that trigger it are unknown. In Tasmania, blacklip abalone are in peak reproductive condition in March, although ripe animals may be found throughout the year. Abalone are termed 'broadcast spawners', as their eggs and sperm are released and fertilised in open water. A 6-year-old female can produce more than 1 million eggs.[5]

The larval stage of blacklip abalone is short. It lasts from 4 to 10 days, depending on water temperature. Larvae are free swimming, although the dispersal during this phase is limited.[6] What induces larval settlement is unknown.

After settlement the juveniles shelter in rock crevices, moving out at night to feed. Abalone can move around, ie they are not permanently attached to substrates.

Growth rates vary seasonally and with location. Blacklip abalone grow to at least 21 cm in length. Maturity is related to age, not size.[7] Blacklip abalone in South Australia have been estimated to mature at from 3 to 4 years when 7.5–12 cm long.[4] Tasmanian populations mature at from 6 to 10 years of age[7] when 9–11 cm long.[8] Whether this reflects a true difference in age at maturity or differences in ageing techniques is unknown.

As abalone mature they emerge from cryptic habitats into the open where they are more available for capture. Mortality is as high as 90 % in the first year but declines with age.[9]

In areas where drift algae collect and are abundant, they are consumed by blacklip abalone, which catch and feed on them in a similar manner to greenlip abalone. Their diet is dominated by red algae *(Asparagosis armata)*.[2] In areas where drift algae are scarce, however, blacklip abalone graze on seagrass leaves and algae growing on rocks.[3]

Blacklip abalone are preyed upon by crabs (Portunidae), starfish (Asteroidea),

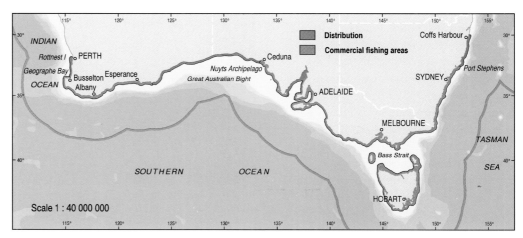

Geographic distribution and commercial fishing areas for blacklip abalone.

stingrays (Myliobatoidei), wobbegong sharks (Orectolobidae) and possibly rock lobsters (*Jasus* species).

Stock structure

Blacklip abalone populations show an increase in genetic difference with increasing geographic distance between them, ie 'isolation by distance'. These differences are insufficient for identification of distinct stocks.[10] Gene flow between populations is largely dependent on larval dispersal, which in turn is dependent on ocean currents.[6,11] In the high energy waters generally inhabited by abalone, larval dispersal is mostly limited to the spawning locality. In less turbulent waters, however, it is possible for larvae to be transported well away from the spawning site.

Breeding populations of blacklip abalone appear to be large, with nearly continuous distributions. Locally distinct populations are known to occur however, separated by as little as 1.5 km of unsuitable, uninhabited territory.[10]

Commercial fishery

Blacklip abalone are taken by commercial divers in the coastal waters from Port Stephens in New South Wales southwards around the east, south and west coasts of Tasmania to the Nuyts Archipelago off Ceduna. Small amounts are also taken in the south-west of Western Australia. In Victoria they are fished from inshore reefs along the coastline as well as from reefs inside Port Phillip Bay. The divers use hookah gear, based on small trailer-launched boats that allow access to remote areas of the coastline. Some divers also use SCUBA gear or snorkels.

In New South Wales the fishery is for blacklip abalone only. In Victoria, Tasmania and South Australia, greenlip abalone are also taken. Catch in Victoria and Tasmania is dominated by blacklip abalone. However, in South Australia blacklip abalone is the dominant species taken in the east of the State, while greenlip abalone dominate in the west.[12] Divers target mature adults generally greater than 13 cm long. The abalone are landed live and processed onshore, except in South Australia where they are shucked (meat is removed from the shell) at sea. They are shucked, cleaned and either sorted and frozen, or cooked in

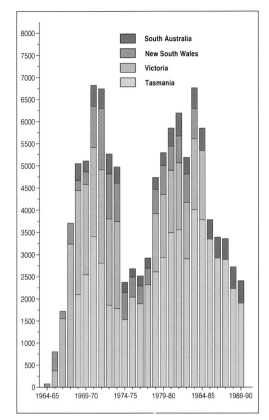

Total annual catch in t of blacklip abalone for the period 1964–65 to 1989–90. Figures are unavailable for: New South Wales from 1984–85 to 1989–90; Victoria for 1964–65, 1974–75 to 1977–78 and 1985–86 to 1989–90; and Tasmania for 1964–65 to 1967–68. Catches for States that average less than 5 % of the total for all States are not shown. (Source: Fisheries Resources Atlas Statistical Database)

Abalone diver helping to haul a blacklip abalone catch on board. (Source: Warwick Nash, Division of Sea Fisheries, Tasmanian Department of Primary Industry and Fisheries)

brine and canned. Frozen and canned abalone is exported to Japan, Hong Kong and Singapore. Some of the abalone is frozen whole in the shell, or cooked and frozen. There is a small live export trade with Japan, and an erratic market for the shell in Asia, where it is used as a substitute for mother-of-pearl (*Pinctada* species). Greenlip abalone command a higher price than blacklip abalone on Japanese markets. On average, Tasmanian and South Australian fishers were receiving A\$ 16.00 to A\$ 18.00 per kg for abalone in 1990, but this return has doubled in recent years. The average price for abalone at the Sydney Fish Market in 1992 was A\$ 16.00 per kg.

Management controls The Victorian and South Australian fisheries are divided into zones, with divers licensed to work in only 1 zone. There is limited entry to abalone fisheries in all States[10] and the minimum sizes for abalone are set out in State regulations. Different minimum size limits are set for different areas within Tasmanian and Victorian waters in recognition of the abalone's different growth rates.[5,7] Individual transferable quotas are applied to divers in all States.[12]

Aquaculture

Experimental culture of both blacklip abalone and greenlip abalone is being tested in Tasmania, South Australia and Victoria. Spat, the newly settled juvenile abalone, are reared in hatcheries or collected from the wild.[13] There are 2 hatcheries operating in Tasmania. One is growing blacklip abalone in tanks to a commercial size of 10–11 cm for sale in Japan. The other hatchery is raising and selling juveniles, 1–2 mm long.

Recreational fishery

Blacklip abalone are taken throughout their range by sport divers using both snorkelling and SCUBA diving gear. Fishing effort is greatest in the areas around coastal towns during the summer months. Effort is concentrated on rock shelves and outcrops or reefs in inshore waters. Divers target large adult abalone. Amateur catch is considerable: in New South Wales it is estimated to be equivalent to 6 % of the commercial catch.[14]

Management controls State regulations set bag limits and minimum size limits for abalone caught by recreational fishers. In

Western Australia abalone may only be taken by divers using snorkelling gear.

Resource status

The abalone resource cannot support heavier fishing pressure and measures are in place in most States to protect stocks. Abalone poaching by 'shamateurs' (unlicensed fishers selling their catch) is significant. For example, it has been estimated that the illegal catch of abalone in New South Wales is as much as twice the commercial catch.[14]

Recognising the existence of locally distinct populations of blacklip abalone and the desire to conserve regional gene pools, management of the resource is applied by zoning. Some of the management zones extend for several hundred km of coastline.[11]

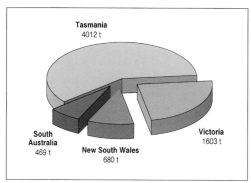

Proportion of the catch of blacklip abalone in each Australian State for the year 1983-84. (Source: Fisheries Resources Atlas Statistical Database)

References

1. Macpherson, J.H. and Gabriel, C.J. (1962) *Marine molluscs of Victoria.* Melbourne: Melbourne University Press. 475 pp.

2. Shepherd, S.A. (1973) Studies on southern Australian abalone (genus *Haliotis*). I. Ecology of five sympatric species. *Australian Journal of Marine and Freshwater Research* **24**: 217–257.

3. Shepherd, S.A. (1975) Distribution, habitat and feeding habits of abalone. *Australian Fisheries* **34**(1): 12–15.

4. Shepherd, S.A. and Laws, H.M. (1974) Studies on southern Australian abalone (genus *Haliotis*). II. Reproduction of five species. *Australian Journal of Marine and Freshwater Research* **25**: 49–62.

5. McShane, P.E. (1989) Stock assessment of blacklip abalone (*Haliotis rubra*) in Victoria. *Victorian Department of Conservation, Forests and Lands, Fisheries Division, Internal Report* **176**. 15 pp.

6. Prince, J.D., Sellers, T.L., Ford, W.B. and Talbot, S.R. (1987) Experimental evidence for limited dispersal of haliotid larvae (genus *Haliotis*; Mollusca: Gastropoda). *Journal of Experimental Marine Biology and Ecology* **106**: 243–263.

7. Nash, W. (1990) Abalone mature with age, not size. *Fishing Today* **3**(2): 38–39.

8. Prince, J.D., Sellers, T.L., Ford, W.B. and Talbot, S.R. (1988) Recruitment, growth, mortality and population structure in a southern Australian population of *Haliotis rubra* (Mollusca: Gastropoda). *Marine Biology* **100**: 75–82.

9. Shepherd, S.A. and Godoy, C. (1989) Studies on southern Australian abalone (genus *Haliotis*). XI. Movement and natural mortality of juveniles. *Journal of the Malacological Society of Australia* **10**: 87–95.

10. Brown, L.D. (1991) Genetic variation and population structure in the blacklip abalone, *Haliotis rubra. Australian Journal of Marine and Freshwater Research* **42**: 77–90.

11. McShane, P.E. (1992) Early life history of abalone: a review. Pp 120-138, in *Abalone of the world: biology, fisheries and culture. Proceedings of the 1st international symposium on abalone.* Ed by S.A. Shepherd, M.J. Tegner and S.A. Guzmán del Próo. Oxford: Fishing News Books.

12. Prince, J.D. and Shepherd, S.A. (1992) Australian abalone fisheries and their management. Pp 407-426, in *Abalone of the world: biology, fisheries and culture. Proceedings of the 1st international symposium on abalone.* Ed by S.A. Shepherd, M.J. Tegner and S.A. Guzmán del Próo. Oxford: Fishing News Books.

13. Cropp, R.A. (1989) Abalone culture in Tasmania. *Division of Sea Fisheries, Tasmania, Technical Report* **37**. 26 pp.

14. Madden, T. (1990) Spotlight on the abalone black market. *Professional Fisherman* **12**(4): 9–10.

Contributors

The information on this species was supplemented by comments from (in alphabetical order) Ian Knuckey, Warwick Nash and Scoresby Shepherd. Drawing by Leslie Newman. (*Details of contributors and their organisations are given in the Acknowledgements section at the back of this book.*)

Compilers Alex McNee and Christina Grieve (maps)

Blue mussel

Mytilus edulis planulatus

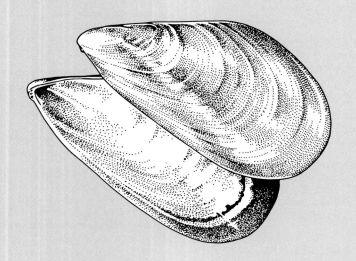

Mytilus edulis planulatus
(Lamarck)

Blue mussel

There are no other common names.
FAO: **Australian mussel**
Australian species code: 652001

Family MYTILIDAE

Diagnostic features Blue mussels are approximately wedge shaped and are broad and rounded at the posterior end. Their valves (shells) are of equal size. The exterior of the shell is purplish black (brown in juveniles) and the interior is bluish white.[1]

Distribution

Blue mussels live on the southern coast of Australia, from Cape Hawke on the east coast to Fremantle on the west coast, including the waters around Tasmania. They also inhabit New Zealand waters. The parent species to blue mussels, *Mytilus edulis*, has a circumpolar distribution in temperate and sub-polar waters of the northern and southern hemispheres.[2]

Blue mussels inhabit a wide range of estuarine and marine environments. They are sessile and attach to rocks, jetties and piers, or sometimes form dense beds on sandy flat substrates. Blue mussels can be found from the low tide level to a depth of 10 m.[3] Their distribution is limited by high water temperatures and low salinities (lower limit 15 parts per thousand).[4] They prefer sites with significant water movement.[5]

Life history

Blue mussels have a minor spawning period in June followed by a second, extended spawning period[6] from August to January. Spawning occurs at water temperatures of 14°C. It peaks in spring in

the northern and western populations[3] and in summer in Tasmanian populations. Blue mussels are 'broadcast spawners', releasing eggs and sperm simultaneously into the water with fertilisation taking place in open water. The sexes are separate although hermaphrodites occur occasionally. The fertilised eggs are planktonic, averaging 0.07 mm in diameter, and develop into unshelled larvae within a day.

Larvae are free swimming and the planktonic stage can last from 2 weeks to several months, although most larvae settle 3–4 weeks after spawning.[7] Before settlement the larva is called a 'pediveliger'. The pediveliger periodically settles to the bottom to test for suitable substrate. If none is found, the pediveliger re-enters the plankton.[8] The larvae are approximately 0.2 mm long on settlement, when they attach themselves to filamentous substrates (algae) by the 'byssus', a thread-like structure. The settled larvae are called 'spat'. Throughout life the blue mussels can move by releasing from the substrate and re-attaching to a new site by secreting new byssus threads.

Growth rates of blue mussels vary but can be rapid. Blue mussels can reach 32–92 mm in length after 12 months and 53–110 mm after 18 months. Blue mussels have been known to live for 25 years, although commercial harvest usually occurs after 1–2 years. As in scallops, the meat condition changes seasonally during the growing period.[2] Male and female blue mussels mature within 2 years of age, at 4.5–5.0 cm in length. Mortality is highest during the free-floating larval stage of the life cycle.

Blue mussels are filter feeders, straining plankton from the water. They are preyed on by crabs (Portunidae), starfish (Asteroidea), leatherjackets (Monacanthidae), pufferfish (Tetraodontidae) and flat worms (Turbellaria).

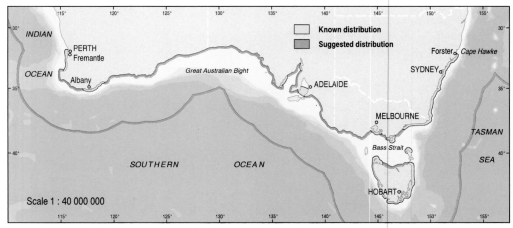

Geographic distribution for blue mussels in Australian waters.

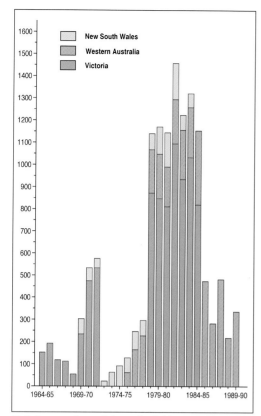

Total annual catch in t of wild harvest blue mussels for the period 1964–65 to 1989–90. Figures are unavailable for: New South Wales from 1964–65 to 1968–69 and 1984–85 to 1989–90; and Victoria from 1972–73 to 1977–78 and 1985–86 to 1989–90. Catches for States that average less than 5 % of the total for all States are not shown. (Source: Fisheries Resources Atlas Statistical Database)

Stock structure

As the blue mussel's larval phase is free swimming, its distribution is dependent on tide and current. Individual beds are not separate stocks. There has been no research undertaken to determine whether populations in Western Australia are different from those in eastern States.

Commercial fishery

Until 1986 the major blue mussel fishery in Victoria was the dredge fishery in Port Phillip Bay. This has since closed, and blue mussel culture areas have been established in the Bay. The only commercial operations still harvesting wild stocks of blue mussels are small dive fisheries at Jervis Bay in New South Wales, Lakes Entrance in Victoria and Cockburn Sound in Western Australia. These operations involve divers using SCUBA or hookah equipment to collect mussels from the sea floor.

Management controls Divers in all States must hold commercial fishing licences. In addition, the Western

Australian fishery is limited entry, with a limit of 1 diver per boat.

Aquaculture

Blue mussels are cultured in Jervis Bay in New South Wales; in 3 areas of Port Phillip Bay and Western Port in Victoria; in Oyster Bay and the D'Entrecasteaux Channel in Tasmania and in Cockburn Sound, Warnbro Sound and Geographe Bay in Western Australia. All farmed blue mussels are grown using long line techniques, with spat collected via natural settlement. 'Collector' ropes are hung in the water from August to September. The young blue mussels are stripped from the ropes in January and February and then attached to new ropes in 'socks' at a density of approximately 250 per m. These socks are hung back in the water and the blue mussels continue growing

Mussel farming: mussels naturally settle on weighted lines hung vertically in the water column. (Source: John Tompkin, Marine Science Laboratories, Victorian Department of Conservation and Environment)

for a further 7–10 months. Harvesting occurs between July and February. Production is seasonal, with wild harvest mussels providing supplies during the winter months.

In Tasmania farmed blue mussels have been produced since 1977. Production is low, rising from 1–2 % of the total wild catch in early years to 12 % of the total wild catch in 1990. By comparison, farmed blue mussel production in Victoria for 1990 was nearly double the total wild catch. It has remained static at about 600 t over 1990–92.

In Western Australia all blue mussel spat is collected in Cockburn Sound. Growth is greatest in this area, so settlement lines are left in the water for as long as possible. The lines are then stripped and the blue mussels transported to the other growing areas where they are re-attached to lines which are hung back

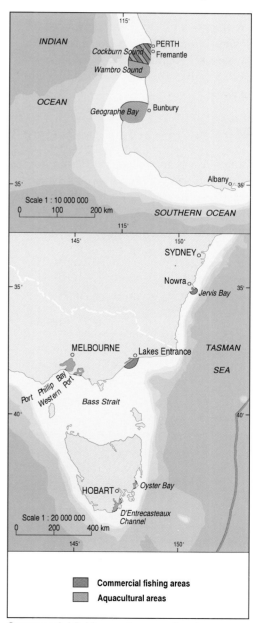

Commercial fishing and aquacultural areas for blue mussels in Australian waters.

in the water where the mussels continue to grow. The first year of production for Western Australian was 1990, when 35 t of blue mussel was harvested. The industry in the State has grown considerably since then, with 266 t harvested in 1991–92.

Blue mussels are harvested when around 5 cm in length. All farmed production is sold live and whole in the shell. Small blue mussels are either re-attached to ropes for continued growing or sold for bait. In 1992 Victorian blue mussel farmers received A$ 2.50 per kg at market. Eighty percent of the Victorian blue mussels are sold to a single Sydney wholesaler, with the remainder sold through the Melbourne markets. All Australian farmed blue mussels are sold domestically.

Management controls There are 20 entitlements for blue mussel farming within Port Phillip Bay and farm numbers are frozen at this level pending a future review of operations. Western Australian farmers are required to meet specified performance criteria in developing culture facilities.

Recreational fishery

Blue mussels are collected by hand from rocks and jetties within their natural

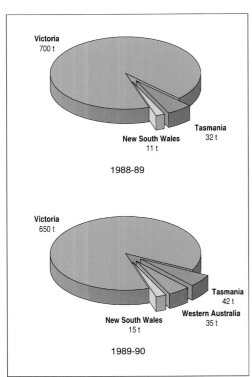

Production of farmed blue mussels in New South Wales, Victoria, Tasmania and Western Australia in 1988–89 and 1989–90 as a proportion of total Australian farm production. (Source: O'Sullivan[9] and O'Sullivan[10])

Harvesting farmed mussels: removing the mussels from growing lines on shore. (Source: John Tompkin, Marine Science Laboratories, Victorian Department of Conservation and Environment)

range. The majority is collected during the summer months by anglers for use as bait. There is no information on the number of blue mussels harvested by recreational fishers but it is not considered to be large.

Management controls The collecting of mussels in parts of Port Phillip Bay is prohibited. There are no regulations on blue mussel gathering in other areas.

Resource status

Past dredging activity has removed or altered available mussel habitats within Port Phillip Bay. Natural spatfall still occurs however, and there are large annual variations in mortality. As blue mussel farming involves settlement on artificial habitats the resource can be considered stable. Commercial divers are still harvesting beds at Lakes Entrance but the extent of the stock there and elsewhere is unknown. Existing Western Australian stocks appear to be fully exploited.

References

1. Macpherson, J.H. and Gabriel, C.J. (1962) *Marine molluscs of Victoria.*Victoria: Melbourne University Press. 475 pp.

2. Dix, T.G. (1980) Biology of mussels. Pp 11–21, in *Tasmanian mussel industry seminar. Report of proceedings.* Hobart: Tasmanian Fisheries Development Authority.

3. Wilson, B.R. and Hodgkin, E.P. (1967) A comparative account of the reproductive cycles of five species of marine mussels (Bivalvia: Mytilidae) in the vicinity of Fremantle, Western Australia. *Australian Journal of Marine and Freshwater Research* **18**: 175–203.

4. Nell, J.A. and Gibbs, P.J. (1986) Salinity tolerance and absorption of 1-Methionine by some Australian bivalve molluscs. *Australian Journal of Marine and Freshwater Research* **37**: 721–727.

5. MacIntyre, R.J. (1980) The Australian mussel industry — its development. Pp 6–10, in *Tasmanian mussel industry seminar. Report of proceedings.* Hobart: Tasmanian Fisheries Development Authority.

6. Sause, B.L. and Hickman, N.J. (1983) Culture of blue mussel *Mytilus edulis planulatus* in Port Phillip Bay, Victoria, Australia. II. The reproductive cycle. *Victorian Ministry for Conservation, Fisheries and Wildlife Division, Internal Report* **59**. 20 pp.

7. Hickman, N.J. and Sause, B.L. (1984) Culture of blue mussel *Mytilus edulis planulatus* in Port Phillip Bay, Victoria, Australia. III. Larval settlement. *Victorian Ministry for Conservation, Fisheries and Wildlife Division, Internal Report* **75**. 25 pp.

8. Bayne, B.L. (1965) Growth and delay of metamorphosis of the larvae of *Mytilus edulis* (L). *Ophelia* **2**: 1–47.

9. O'Sullivan, D. (1990) *Aquaculture downunder. Status & prospects for Australian aquaculture (1989–90).* Tasmania: Dosaqua. 66 pp.

10. O'Sullivan, D. (1991) Status of Australian aquaculture in 1989/90. *Austasia Aquaculture* **1991** (June): 2–13.

Contributors

The information on this species was originally provided by Rob Cordover and supplemented by (in alphabetical order) Ray Clarke, Rick Fallu, Neil Hickman and Simon Stanley. Drawing by Rhyllis Plant. (*Details of contributors and their organisations are given in the Acknowledgements section at the back of this book.*)
Compilers Alex McNee, Phillip Stewart (statistics) and Christina Grieve (maps)

Distribution

Pearl oysters are distributed across northern Australia, from Carnarvon in Western Australia to south of Cairns in Queensland.[1] They are also widely spread across the central Indo-Pacific region from India to New Guinea and the Philippines.[2,3]

Pearl oysters live on the sea bed from the low water mark[2] to a depth of 85 m on the continental shelf,[3] preferring areas with fast flowing currents. They inhabit a variety of substrates, from mud, sand and gravel to deepwater reefs, beside sponges, soft corals and whip corals (a 'garden bottom'). The loose substrates contain fragments of shell and coral to which pearl oysters and other organisms attach themselves.[4] They have also been found in seagrass beds.[5]

Life history

Pearl oysters spawn at water temperatures around 29˚C,[2,6] and fertilisation occurs externally in open water. Populations of pearl oysters in Western Australia spawn from September to April,[7] with peaks from late October to December and from February to March.[8] Torres Strait populations commence spawning slightly later, in October.[6] Their first spawning peak is from November to December and the second is from January to March.[6,9] Spawning periods of Northern Territory and east Queensland pearl oyster populations are unknown.

Larvae develop within 8 hours of fertilisation.[9] They are free floating and are distributed on tidal currents.[4] The larvae settle as 'spat' after approximately 21 days, at which stage they have developed 2 thin shells.[4] The spat are capable of short movements, and on settling they attach themselves by byssus

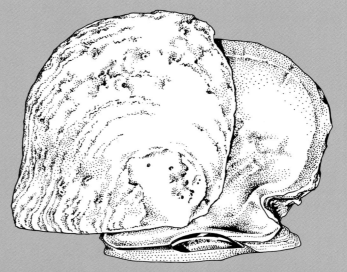

Pearl oyster

Pinctada maxima

Pinctada maxima (Jameson)

Pearl oyster

Other common names include **gold lipped pearl oyster** and **silver lipped pearl oyster**.
FAO: no known name
Australian species code: 658001

Family PINCTADA

Diagnostic features Pearl oysters have a convex left valve (shell) and a flat or slightly convex right valve. Growths resembling overlapping scales form radial markings across the shell in younger oysters. These growths may be worn away in older oysters. The outside of the shell is usually pale fawn although it may vary through dark green, dark brown or purple. The inside of the shell has a rich, clear lustre and may have a distinct gold or silver band of varying widths along its margin.[1]

threads to fragments of stone or coral[4] or even to the shells of adult pearl oysters.

Pinctada maxima is the largest of the Australian species of pearl oyster. Pearl oyster growth is highly variable and dependent on environmental factors.[2] As a rule high water temperature will promote faster growth. At about 3 years of age pearl oysters are 170–200 mm long,[2] and at this size they release their hold on the substrate and lie free on the bottom.

A substantial proportion of pearl oysters are protandrous hermaphrodites, ie they change from being functional males to functional females as they age.[4] A survey in Torres Strait showed that after the second year most of the young oysters surveyed had developed as males. In subsequent years the population shifted back towards a 50–50 male–female split.[4,6] Similarly in Western Australian populations, 30–40 % of the population that survive to larger sizes change sex from male to female.[10] Both males and female pearl oysters mature in their first year. In Western Australian populations males were found to be mature at approximately 110 mm in length and females at approximately 135 mm.[10]

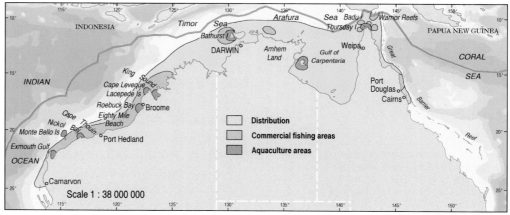

Geographic distribution, commercial fishing areas and aquaculture areas for pearl oysters in Australian waters.

Pearl oysters are filter feeders, with both adults and juveniles feeding on organic detritus. Juveniles are preyed upon by marine snails, starfish (Asteroidea), octopus (*Octopus* species), crabs (Portunidae), and rays (Batoidea). Adults are vulnerable to stingrays (Myliobatididae), octopus, and a range of internal parasites, boring worms and sponges.[2]

Stock structure

No studies have been conducted on the stock structure of pearl oysters in Australian waters.

Commercial fishery

For more than 100 years pearl oysters have been fished from the north-west coast of Western Australia, and early this century Broome was a major world pearling centre.

Pearl oysters were harvested for mother-of-pearl, with any natural pearls found being considered a bonus. As a result, pearl oysters are often referred to as 'shell'. In the late 1950s the first cultured pearls produced in Australia were harvested from a farm lease north of Broome.[10] This event marked a shift in the Australian pearl industry from the wild harvest of pearl oysters for shell towards the production of cultured pearls. Pearling activity in Australia now centres on Broome, and on Darwin in the

Packing harvested pearl shell into mesh panels. (Source: Ian Knuckey, Fisheries Division, Northern Territory Department of Primary Industry and Fisheries)

Northern Territory and Thursday Island in Torres Strait.

Western Australia records the largest harvest of shell in Australia. The Western Australian fishery extends from the Lacepede Islands in the north to Exmouth Gulf in the south. Most fishing effort is centred off Eighty Mile Beach in waters from 10 m to 37 m deep.[11]

Northern Territory pearl grounds are divided into eastern and western fishing grounds. The eastern grounds stretch from Goulburn Island to the Crocodile Islands along the Arnhem Land coast. They were historically important but have not produced many pearl oysters in recent years.[11] The western grounds, west of Bathurst Island, are the main source of pearl oysters in the Northern Territory.

In Torres Strait the main fishing ground lies to the west of Badu Island. Small quantities have also been taken from the Warrior Reefs. Some pearl oysters have been taken in Torres Strait since the 1970s, much of it as a bycatch of the rock lobster (*Panulirus* species) fishery. There is also a small pearl oyster fishery in north-east Queensland around the Cooktown area.

Pearl oysters are collected by hand by divers free diving or using hookah diving equipment. The divers drift behind a vessel moving at about 1 knot.[5] Divers usually work at neap tides when visibility is best. In Western Australia pearl oysters are collected between March and November.[10] In the Northern Territory

they are collected between September and December and in Torres Strait, between October and March.

The pearl culture industry prefers pearl oysters between 120 and 160 mm shell height. These sizes therefore dominate commercial catches. Divers are usually paid by the shell. In 1988 this ranged from A\$ 3.00 to A\$ 4.00 per shell.[12]

Management controls Pearl beds in Western Australia, the Northern Territory and Torres Strait are jointly managed by State and Commonwealth governments. Pearl farms are the responsibility of the States.

There is a minimum size for pearl oysters harvested and there are quotas on the numbers of pearl oysters that may be collected. The Northern Territory fishery also is limited entry and separate licences are required for both the collection and the culture of pearl oysters. There are also limits on the number of pearl oysters that may be introduced into the culture operations from the wild each year. In the Torres Strait fishery entry criteria also apply.

Aquaculture

There are pearl farms in Western Australia, the Northern Territory and Queensland, although most Australian cultured pearls come from Western Australia.

Pearl oyster aquaculture is presently based on collecting pearl oysters from the wild during the fishing season and then transporting them to farms for use in the

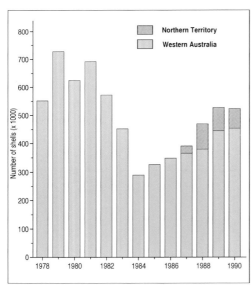
Wild harvest in numbers of pearl oysters for the period 1978 to 1990. Western Australian figures are only for the area between Cape Touin and Cape Leveque. Figures are unavailable for the Torres Strait fishery. (Source: Fisheries Division, Northern Territory Department of Primary Industry and Fisheries; and Fisheries Department of Western Australia)

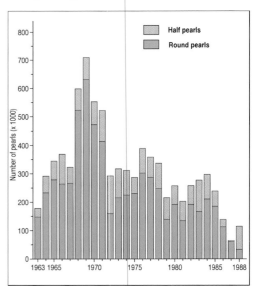
Production of round pearls and half pearls from Australian pearl culture operations for the period 1963 to 1988. (Source: Australian Bureau of Statistics and Department of Primary Industries and Energy)

production of cultured pearls. Round pearls are produced by inserting a pearl nucleus into the body of the oyster. Half pearls are produced by attaching appropriately shaped nuclei to the inner side of the pearl oyster's shell. Oysters producing round pearls are left in the water for 2 years. Half pearl growth takes less time, these oysters being harvested 8 to 12 months after seeding. Some pearl oysters used for round pearl production can be reused, but pearl oysters used in the production of half pearls are killed.[13]

Harvested pearl oysters are stored in steel framed, mesh-covered 'panels' which are placed on the sea bed near the fishing grounds, clipped to weighted lines. After 2–4 months the panels are retrieved and the operation to insert nuclei into the pearl oysters is carried out ('seeding'). The pearl oysters are put back into the panels after seeding and returned to the sea bed. After a period of 1–2 months they are again collected and transported to farms in coastal embayments 80 km to 320 km from the fishing grounds.

The main holding method used in Australian pearl culture is a floating 'longline' technique. Here, net panels containing pearl oysters are suspended vertically in the water from a horizontal longline. This technique is used in Western Australia, the Northern Territory and areas in Torres Strait. Some farmers in Torres Strait are using a raft culture technique. In it, the pearl oysters are placed in wire baskets which are hung below a floating raft.

The pearl industry is Australia's most valuable aquaculture industry, estimated to be worth A$ 96.5 million in 1989–90. Most of the revenue comes from pearl production, with 1991 prices for round pearls being A$ 40.00 to A$ 45.00 per g. Half pearls were worth A$ 5.00 to A$ 50.00 a piece depending on size and quality. In 1992, pearl prices were reduced significantly by economic conditions in Japan and competition from Asian producers. Mother-of-pearl not used in the production of half pearls are sold mostly on Asian and European markets. Its export value in 1992 was A$ 10 000 per t. There is also a small market for adductor muscle meat, which is considered a delicacy in parts of Asia. In 1988 this was worth up to A$ 80.00 per kg.[12]

Recreational fishery

There is no recreational fishery for pearl oysters.

Resource status

The present pearl oyster fishery is generally fully exploited. Australian pearl fisheries yielded much larger, but unsustainable, catches up until the 1960s. Prior to World War II, Australian production of shell averaged more than 2000 t per year. The chances of finding new grounds are remote and the resource is now being fished at increasing depths. The Western Australian stocks appear to be stable, but the fishery in Torres Strait appears to be in decline.

Pearl oyster stocks are subject to natural variation and there are records of pearl beds being wiped out by cyclones.

Notes

Hatcheries are currently being established in Australia to produce pearl oyster spat. The spat will be used on certain strictly managed pearl farms, primarily to produce round pearls.

Recent surveys[5,11] identified 7 species of pearl oyster in Torres Strait including *Pinctada maxima* and *P. margaritifera*. This second species is cultured successfully in the South Pacific to produce black pearls, but is not cultured commercially in Australia.[5]

Pearl oysters wedged open prior to seeding with pearl nuclei. (Source: Ian Knuckey, Fisheries Division, Northern Territory Department of Primary Industry and Fisheries)

References

1. Hynd, J.S. (1955) A revision of the Australian pearl shell genus *Pinctada* (Lamellibranchia). *Australian Journal of Marine and Freshwater Research* **6**: 98–137.

2. Wada, S. (1953) *Biology and fisheries of the silver lip pearl oyster*. NSW: Division of Fisheries and Oceanography, Harold Thompson Library, CSIRO. 86 pp.

3. George, D. (1978) *The pearl. A report to the government of Papua New Guinea, the FAO and the Asian Development Bank*. Papua New Guinea: Mr D. George.

4. Hynd, J.S. (1957) *Biology and economics of* Pinctada maxima, *the golden or silver lip pearl oyster*. Unpublished CSIRO report. Australia: CSIRO Division of Fisheries. 7 pp.

5. Colgan, K. and Reichelt, R. (1991) Torres Strait pearl bed survey 1989. *Report to the Torres Strait Fishing Industry and Islanders Consultatative Committee and Torres Strait Fisheries Management Committee, May 1991, Cairns*. Canberra: Bureau of Rural Resources. 61 pp.

6. Tranter, D.J. (1958) *Reproduction in Australian pearl oysters*. Unpublished MSc thesis, University of Queensland. 143 pp.

7. Rose, R.A., Dybdahl, R.E. and Harders, S. (1990) Reproductive cycle of the Western Australian silverlip pearl oyster, *Pinctada maxima* (Jameson) (Mollusca: Pteriidae). *Journal of Shellfish Research* **9**(2): 261–272.

8. Rose, R.A. and Baker, S.B. (1989) Research and development of hatchery and nursery culture for the Pearl oyster, *Pinctada maxima*. *Western Australian Marine Research Laboratories. FIRTA Project 87/82, Final Report*. 26 pp.

9. Minaur, J. (1969) Experiments on the artificial rearing of the larvae of *Pinctada maxima* (Jameson) (Lamellibranchia). *Australian Journal of Marine and Freshwater Research* **20**: 175–187.

10. Dybdahl, R. and Rose, R.A. (1986) The pearl oyster fishery in Western Australia. Pp 122–132, in *Torres Strait seminar, Port Moresby, 11–14 February 1985*. Ed by A.K. Haines, G.C. Williams and D. Coates. Canberra: Australian Government Publishing Service.

11. Colgan, K. and Reichelt, R. (1991) Northern Territory pearl bed survey 1989. *Report to the Northern Territory Government/Pearling Industry Meeting, June 1991, Darwin*. Canberra: Bureau of Rural Resources. 36 pp.

12. Scoones, R. J. S. (1988) An overview of pearl oyster culture in Western Australia. Pp 266–282, in *Proceedings of the first Australian shellfish aquaculture conference, Perth, 1988*. Ed by L.H. Evans and D. O'Sullivan. WA: Curtin University of Technology.

13. Cultured pearl techniques (1991) *Austasia Aquaculture* **4**(6): 13.

Contributors

The information in this presentation was provided originally by Kathy Colgan and Russell Reichelt and supplemented by (in alphabetical order) Lindsay Joll, Ian Knuckey and Rosemary Lea. Drawing by Rhyllis Plant. (*Details of contributors and their organisations are given in the Acknowledgements section at the back of this book.*)

Compilers Alex McNee and Christina Grieve (maps)

Pacific oyster

Crassostrea gigas

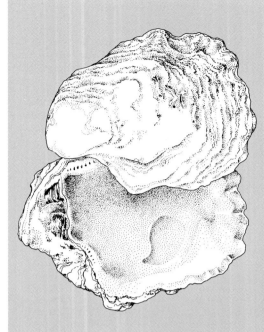

Crassostrea gigas (Thunberg)

Pacific oyster

Another common name is
Japanese oyster.
FAO: **Pacific cupped oyster**
Australian species code: 653002

Family OSTREIDAE

Diagnostic features Pacific oysters have a thin shell. Their exterior surfaces are rough, with spiky lobes and long protusions. There are no hinge teeth on the oyster's inner, upper shell. The mantle edges are black and the adductor muscle scar is purple or brown.[1]

These oysters are cultured intertidally and subtidally (deep water culture).

Life history

Pacific oysters spawn in water temperatures over 18°C. At Port Stephens in New South Wales spawning occurs from October to May. Pacific oysters are broadcast spawners, ie their male and female gametes are released into the water, where fertilisation occurs. The fertilised eggs sink and the free-swimming larvae hatch after 6 hours. The larvae settle after about 2 weeks, and assume the appearance of adult oysters. The settled larvae are known as 'spat', and Pacific oysters are characterised by large spat falls.

Growth in Pacific oysters is more rapid than in the native Sydney rock oysters (*Saccostrea commercialis*). They reach the marketable size of 50 g in 10 months to 2 years, in contrast to the 2 to 3 years required for Sydney rock oysters. Pacific oysters are hermaphrodites that mature at 1 year of age. There is no information on the maximum age of animals in Australian waters, but they are known to reach 30 cm in length (an exceptional animal).

Pacific oysters are plankton feeders, straining planktonic algae and other flora

Distribution

Pacific oysters are native to Japan, but have been introduced elsewhere in the world for culture. They are cultivated in the west coast of Canada, United States of America, South America, United Kingdom, France, China, Korea and throughout the South Pacific and Indian oceans.[1] Pacific oysters were first introduced to Western Australia and Tasmania between 1947 and 1952. The Western Australian population did not survive but oysters from southern Tasmania did and were transplanted to Port Sorell. These oysters colonised the Tamar River estuary and now form the basis of the Tasmanian commercial fishery. They were also introduced to

Mallacoota Inlet in Victoria and Coffin Bay in South Australia.[1]

In New South Wales Pacific oysters were first recorded in the Pambula River in 1967. By the mid 1970s they had been found as far north as Moreton Bay in southern Queensland,[1] although the present limit of breeding populations is Wallis Lake on the New South Wales central coast.

Pacific oysters will settle on any hard substrate in the intertidal zone. Adult oysters are sessile. They prefer brackish waters in sheltered estuaries, yet will tolerate moderately turbid waters and a wide range of environmental conditions. Settlement from the wild occurs in the mid to low parts of the intertidal region.

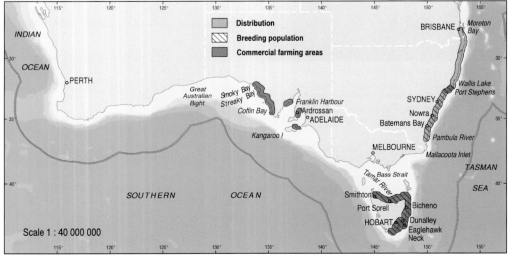

Geographic distribution and commercial farming areas of Pacific oysters in Australia.

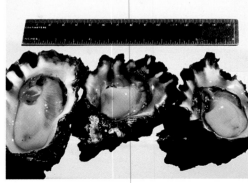

Open Pacific oysters. (Source: Peter Wolfe, Sydney, New South Wales)

from the water. Adult oysters are preyed upon by bream (*Acanthopagrus* species), toadfish (Tetraodontidae), octopus (*Octopus* species), stingrays (Myliobatoidei), crabs (Portunidae) and starfish (Asteroidea).

Stock structure

Three strains of Pacific oyster, the Miyagi, Hiroshima and Kumamoto, were introduced to Australia prior to 1970. The Miyagi strain is now being farmed in Tasmania, South Australia and Victoria. Pacific oysters in New South Wales are thought to be also of the Miyagi strain.[2]

Commercial fishery

There is no commercial harvesting of wild Pacific oysters.

Aquaculture

Tasmania and South Australia are outside the natural range of Sydney rock oysters and so Pacific oysters were introduced as an ideal culture species in these areas. Pacific oysters are farmed commercially in estuaries along the north and east coasts of Tasmania, and in several areas in South Australia. They have also begun to penetrate New South Wales oyster growing estuaries, particularly Port Stephens. Here they have become well established, replacing native Sydney rock oysters in many areas. Port Stephens is the only region in New South Wales where farmers are permitted to grow

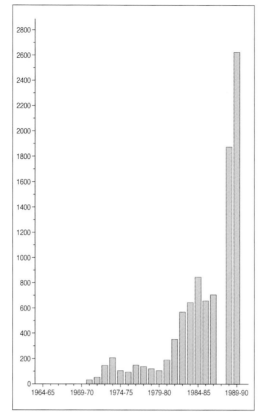

Total annual harvest in t of Pacific oysters for the period 1964–65 to 1989–90. Figures are unavailable for Tasmania for 1987–88. South Australian harvest averages less than 5 % of the total Australian harvest and is not shown. (Source: Fisheries Resource Atlas Statistical Database)

Pacific oysters commercially. In Victoria the only culture of Pacific oysters is land-based, using pond culture techniques.

In Port Stephens, Pacific oysters are grown on intertidal trays. In Tasmania most Pacific oysters are grown in plastic baskets set out on intertidal racks,

Using a boom spray to clean up oyster trays before harvest. (Source: Ian Smith, Brackish Water Fish Culture Research Station, NSW Fisheries)

although a few farmers are using deep water raft culture. In raft culture, young oysters are set out on racks or trays hung on long, vertical lines below a floating raft.[3] Farmers in South Australia also use a form of 'longline' culture, where the oysters are grown in wire mesh bags clipped to horizontal steel wires. The height of the bags in the water can be adjusted to maintain the oysters in the correct depth of water.[4]

The Tamar River estuary in Tasmania is the main source of natural spat for farming of Pacific oysters. Irregular spat falls led to the establishment of a commercial hatchery there in 1979 to ensure continuity of supply. There are now 2 hatcheries operating in Tasmania at Bicheno and Dunalley, and they produced about 150 million seed oysters in 1990 to supply farmers in Tasmania and South Australia. The industry has developed using intensive culture systems and hatchery reared stock, with less reliance on wild stocks. Pacific oyster culture in South Australia is based entirely on hatchery reared stocks.

Oysters are grown all year. Pacific oysters for the food market are harvested at 60–100 g weight, usually when 1–2 years of age. Most Tasmanian production is sold domestically, with 77 % of market sized oysters going to Victoria. All South Australian production is sold locally. The United States of America also accounts for a small export market taking 5–6 % of production. Initially restricted to exporting frozen oysters, farmers have recently received approval to export live and chilled Pacific oysters.[5] There is also considerable trade in small oysters sold to other farmers for further growth. Market sized Pacific oysters were wholesaling for about A$ 3.40 per dozen in 1992, in New South Wales. Sale of hatchery seed is a major part of the industry, seed oysters selling for A$ 12.00 to A$ 18.00 per thousand.

Tray culture of Pacific oysters in South Australia. (Source: Peter Wolfe, Sydney, New South Wales)

Management controls Pacific oysters have been declared noxious in New South Wales. Farmers are required to remove them from their leases — except those in Port Stephens. It is illegal to grow Pacific oysters in Victorian waters. All Victorian culture is carried out in land-based pond operations.

Recreational fishery

There is no recreational fishery for Pacific oysters in Australia.

Resource status

As an introduced species, all Pacific oyster spat for culture is provided from Tasmanian hatcheries.

Notes

Because of their large spat falls and rapid growth, Pacific oysters can potentially replace the endemic Sydney rock oysters — particularly in New South Wales waters. In many New South Wales estuaries where settlement of Pacific oysters has occurred, they are considered pests and removed. In Port Stephens, Pacific oyster spat settles in areas used for ongrowing Sydney rock oysters and problems of 'overspatting' occur. The Pacific oysters' rapid growth also causes crowding on sticks. Total removal of the oysters is difficult, so commercial culture is permitted, rather than closing the whole fishery.

References

1. Holliday, J.E. and Nell, J.A. (1987) The Pacific oyster in New South Wales. *Department of Agriculture, New South Wales. Agfact* **F2.1.3.** 4 pp.

2. Holliday, J.E. and Nell, J.A. (1985) Concern over Pacific oysters in Port Stephens. *Australian Fisheries* **44**(11): 29–31.

3. Witney, E., Beumer, J. and Smith, G. (1988) Oyster culture in Queensland. *Queensland Department of Primary Industries, Fisheries Management Branch, Information Series* **QI88017**. 27 pp.

4. SA farmers pioneer open water oyster techniques (1991) *Austasia Aquaculture* **5**(7): 3–4.

5. Oysters set for US tables (1989) *Fishing Today* **2**(5): 6.

Contributors

Most of the information on this species was originally provided by John Nell, and supplemented by (in alphabetical order) Patrick Hone, Ian Smith and John Wilson. Drawing by Rhyllis Plant. (*Details of contributors and their organisations are given in the Acknowledgements section at the back of this book.*)
Compilers Alex McNee and Christina Grieve (maps)

Sydney rock oyster

Saccostrea commercialis

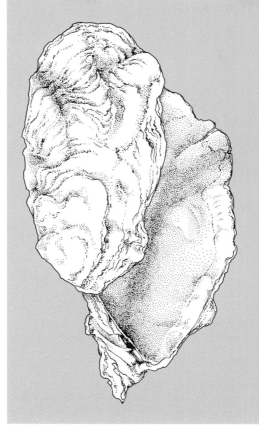

Saccostrea commercialis
(Iredale and Roughley)

Sydney rock oyster

There are no other common names.
FAO: no known name
Australian species code: 653001

Family OSTREIDAE

Diagnostic features Sydney rock oysters have a thick shell with a smooth exterior surface. There are hinge teeth on the inner margin of their upper shell. The mantle edges and adductor muscle scar are pale-coloured.

Distribution

Sydney rock oysters are endemic to Australia and are found in bays, inlets and sheltered estuaries from Hervey Bay in Queensland to Wingan Inlet in eastern Victoria.[1]

Sydney rock oysters are capable of tolerating a wide range of salinities. The oysters occupy the intertidal zone to 3 m below the low water mark. Within this range they are common on hard rocky substrates, but can survive and grow on soft substrates.[2]

Life history

Sydney rock oysters generally spawn in summer.[2] Peak spawning occurs at water temperatures of 21–23°C, and time of spawning varies between localities. The main spawning season at Port Stephens in New South Wales is from October to April. Oysters are termed 'broadcast spawners', as their male and female gametes are released into open water, where fertilisation occurs.[2] Within hours of fertilisation the eggs develop into free swimming planktonic larvae. The larvae swim in estuarine and coastal waters for

up to 3 weeks during which they develop transparent shells and a retractable foot. The larvae then settle on a clean substrate, using the foot to find a suitable site. The foot is resorbed once the larva is attached, the shell darkens and the small animal takes on the appearance of an adult oyster.[3] Settled, footless oyster larvae are known as 'spat'. Adult oysters are sessile, ie they are fixed to the substrate.

Growth rates vary with local conditions. Sydney rock oysters generally reach 40–60 g in 2 or 3 years. They have been recorded to live for up to 10 years.[3] Spawning first occurs at 1 year of age. Sydney rock oysters change sex during life. They first function as males but later change to females. A later sex reversal is possible but generally 75 % of prime eating oysters are female.[2]

Sydney rock oysters are filter feeders, straining planktonic algae from the water. Mortality is highest in the free living and early settlement phases.[3] At this stage oysters are prey to a variety of fish. Once the shell has hardened they are less vulnerable to fish predation but stingrays (Myliobatoidei), mud crabs (*Scylla serrata*), whelks (Neogastropoda) and starfish (Asteroidea) all feed on adult oysters.[2]

Stock structure

There have been no studies on the stock structure of wild populations of oysters from individual estuaries.

Sydney rock oysters with their upper shell removed. (Source: Fisheries Research Institute, NSW Fisheries)

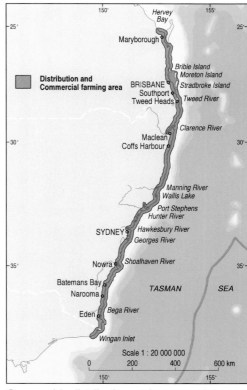

Geographic distribution and commercial farming area for Sydney rock oysters.

Commercial fishery

There is no commercial harvesting of wild Sydney rock oysters.

Aquaculture

Aborigines were the first to harvest Sydney rock oysters from intertidal areas. Oysters later proved popular as a food source amongst the early European colonists, who also burnt the shells to provide lime for building mortar. In 1868, legislation was introduced to prohibit the burning of live oysters to protect rapidly depleting stocks. Soon after, the first attempts at oyster culture in Australia began.

Sydney rock oysters are now cultured in estuarine areas and rivers of Queensland and New South Wales. In Queensland there are 134 commercial banks,[4] with concentrations at Hervey Bay, Bribie Island, Moreton Island, Canaipa and Myora on Stradbroke Island and Southport.[1] In New South Wales commercial leases exist in most river estuaries or tidal lakes along the coast. Most Sydney rock oyster production is from leases at Wallis Lake, Port Stephens,

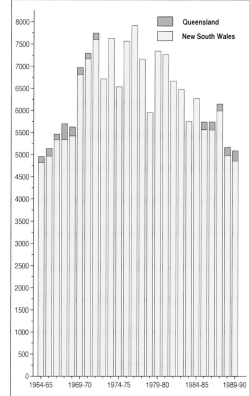

Total annual harvest in t of Sydney rock oyster for the period 1964–65 to 1989–90. Figures are unavailable for Queensland from 1972–73 to 1984–85. (Source: Fisheries Resources Atlas Statistical Database)

Hawkesbury River and Georges River.[2] Most spat are collected in the areas where commercial growing operations take place; however some oyster growers may purchase spat from other areas. There is no commercial hatchery production of spat.

The most popular method of growing Sydney rock oysters is the 'stick and tray' culture. Hardwood sticks 1.8 m in length are coated in tar and made into frames with sticks 10 cm apart and 5 or 6 layers deep. The frames are set out on intertidal racks in spat-catching areas from January to May to collect the fresh spatfall. The spat attach themselves to the sticks. When the spat are firmly attached the frames are moved to racks further up the estuary where they are left until the spat are 25–30 mm long. The frames are then broken up and the sticks spread out in a single layer on racks. The oysters remain on the sticks until they grow to marketable size.[2]

At harvest time, the oysters are removed from the sticks and sorted according to size.[1] Plate grade[1] oysters are between 40 and 60 g whole weight. Those between 30 and 40 g whole weight are opened and used in the bottled oyster trade. Smaller oysters are laid out on trays and returned to the water to continue growing.[2]

In Queensland loose oysters are laid out on 'ground' banks (ie firm intertidal surfaces) for ongrowing to marketable size.[3] Experimental work has also been carried out with 2 other methods — mesh cylinders that are suspended in the water,[3] and raft culture where trays of oysters are suspended below floating rafts in deep water.

Plate grade oysters are sold to the restaurant trade on either the full or half shell. Oysters on the half shell are sold in boxes of 10 dozen.[3] In 1992 average prices (Sydney) were A$ 3.20 per dozen wholesale and A$ 9.00 to A$ 10.00 per dozen retail. All Queensland production is sold within the State, while oysters produced in New South Wales are sold on both local and interstate markets.

Management controls In Queensland farmers are issued licences under the *Fisheries Act* that entitle them to occupy an oyster bank and conduct oystering operations.[3] In New South Wales oyster leases are issued under the *Fisheries and Oyster Farms Act*. As all production is cultured, no closures apply to the fishery.

Harvesting Sydney rock oysters at Moreton Island in Queensland. (Source: Glen Smith, Southern Fisheries Centre, Queensland Department of Primary Industries)

Recreational fishery

Sydney rock oysters are gathered by recreational fishers from intertidal areas throughout their natural range. Most harvesting is carried out near population centres, particularly around popular holiday centres.

Management controls Public harvesting of Sydney rock oysters is permitted on shorelines that are not leases or private land, but they may not be removed from the area and must be consumed where they are gathered. There are no minimum size limits set for this species.

Resource status

Potential production in the oyster industry is limited by lease space and efficiency. There is little space available for new leases in New South Wales. Current development is directed towards finding more efficient ways of using lease space, for example through deep water culture techniques. In Queensland there has been no increase in the area available for lease space, and lease holders are encouraged to find more efficient ways of using the existing space.

The Sydney rock oyster industry in New South Wales has been threatened by the introduction of the Pacific oyster (*Crassostrea gigas*) into the area, as that species often settles on the newly settled Sydney rock oysters, often dislodging them.

The resource status of wild Sydney rock oyster stocks is unknown and no data are available concerning the impact of recreational harvesting on these stocks.

Notes

Sydney rock oyster growers in southern Queensland and northern New South Wales have had major stock losses as a result of 'QX' disease, caused by the microscopic parasite *Marteilia sydneyi*. This disease may cause the oysters to starve but is not harmful to humans. It is possible to reduce the risk of 'QX' disease by keeping the oysters out of the water for a period of time, particularly in the months from December to March. Unfortunately, this step reduces the oysters' growth and increases heat stress and so is not a commercial option.[3] In southern New South Wales Sydney rock oysters are affected by 'winter mortality', caused by the parasite *Mikrocytos roughleyi*. Low temperatures and high salinities are also thought to contribute to increased oyster mortality.[5]

The spread of Pacific oysters is a major problem for New South Wales oyster farmers. The Pacific oysters' proliferation in Port Stephens, a major source of Sydney rock oyster spat for growers in New South Wales and Queensland, has led to their introduction to many estuaries via transfers of stock. Many growers are now looking to other areas as sources of stock.

Western rock oysters, *Saccostrea* species, are morphologically very similar to Sydney rock oysters. They are found from southern Western Australia to Darwin and possibly further east.

References

1. Moxon, A.J. (1986) Economic survey of the oyster industry in southern Queensland. *Queensland Department of Primary Industries, Fisheries Management Branch, Report* **FMB-010**. 19 pp.

2. Malcolm, W.B. (1987) The Sydney rock oyster. *Department of Agriculture, New South Wales. Agfact* **F3.1.1**. 12 pp.

3. Witney, E., Beumer, J. and Smith, G. (1988) Oyster culture in Queensland. *Queensland Department of Primary Industries, Fisheries Management Branch, Information Series* **QI88017**. 27 pp.

4. Quinn, R., Barlow, C. and Witney, E. (1991) Aquaculture in Queensland continues to grow. *Austasia aquaculture* **5**(7): 9–12.

5. Nell, J.A. and Smith, I.R. (1988) Management, production and disease interaction in oyster culture. Pp 127–133, in *Fish diseases. Refresher course for veterinarians. Proceedings* **106**. University of Sydney: Post Graduate Committee in Veterinary Science.

Contributors

The information on this species was originally provided by John Nell and supplemented by (in alphabetical order) Ian Smith and Eve Witney. Drawing by Rhyllis Plant. (*Details of contributors and their organisations are given in the Acknowledgements section at the back of this book.*)
Compilers Alex McNee, Phillip Stewart (statistics) and Christina Grieve (maps)

Stick culture of Sydney rock oysters in a New South Wales estuary. (Source: Fisheries Research Institute, NSW Fisheries)

Southern scallop

Pecten fumatus

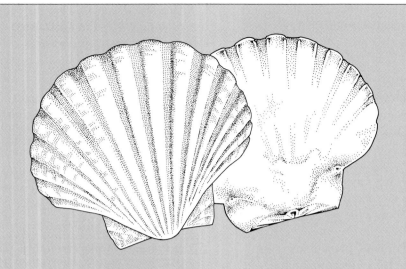

Pecten fumatus Reeve

Southern scallop

Other common names include
Tasmanian scallop and **commercial
scallop.**
FAO: no known name
Australian species code: 651001

Family PECTINIDAE

Diagnostic features Southern
scallops have a thin shell, nearly circular
in outline, and strengthened by about 15
radiating ribs. In life the scallops rest on
their paler, more convex lower valve
which slightly overlaps the darker, flat or
slightly concave upper valve. The fine
sculpturing and the brownish colour
pattern of the shells are variable
features within this species.[1]

Distribution

Southern scallops inhabit Australia's
southern waters. They occur from
Tuncurry on the New South Wales coast,
south through Bass Strait, along the east
and north coasts of Tasmania to South
Australia, across the south coast and
along the west coast of Western Australia
as far north as Shark Bay.[2]

As with the other species of scallops,
southern scallops live in discrete beds and
are found to depths of at least 120 m, over
bare, soft sand or mud.

Life history

Spawning of southern scallops is thought
to be initiated by a sudden rise in water
temperature. Spawning occurs over an
extended period during winter and
spring, with peaks in activity varying
between locations. In Jervis Bay in New
South Wales spawning activity peaks
between December and April,[3] in Bass
Strait spawning peaks in early spring[4] and
in Port Phillip Bay spawning peaks in late
spring.[5] Southern scallops are
hermaphrodites and 'broadcast spawners',
with male and female gametes released
into the water. Fertilisation occurs in open
water and to avoid self fertilisation there
is a delay between the release of eggs and
sperm.[3] Spawning is prolific with up to 1
million eggs produced by an individual.
The orange coloured eggs are planktonic.[6]

Larval scallops (spat) drift as plankton
for up to 6 weeks before first settling, and
by moving in the water column they
influence where they settle. At first
settlement they attach themselves to
seaweed or mussel or oyster shells, and
remain attached until about 6 mm long.
The small scallops then detach and settle
into the sediment, burying themselves so
that only the top shell is visible.[3]

Growth in southern scallops is slower
than in saucer scallops, *Amusium* species.
Populations in New South Wales have
been recorded to reach 40 mm height in 1
year, 70 mm after 2 years and 77 mm and
80 mm after 3 and 4 years respectively.[3]
Growth rates in populations in different
parts of Tasmania are highly variable and
range widely around the figures reported
above. On average, Tasmanian scallops
are about 50 mm in height after 1 year.
Southern scallops can live for more than
10 years, reaching a height of 145 mm.[7]
Southern scallops mature after 1 year but
do not spawn until the second year.[8] Each
year, 20 % to 50 % of southern scallops
die naturally. Juvenile scallops are
susceptible to low salinities, temperature
extremes, deoxygenation and siltation.[3]

Scallops feed by filtering plankton and
detritus from the water. They are preyed
upon by starfish (eg *Cascinasterias
calamaria*) and octopus (*Octopus*
species).

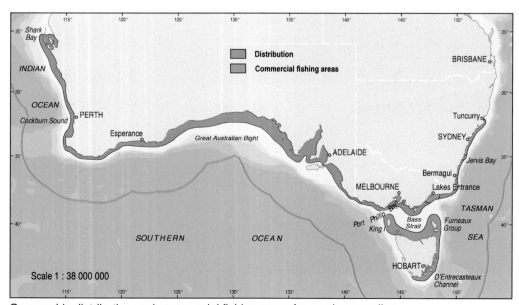

Geographic distribution and commercial fishing areas for southern scallop.

Stock structure

Southern scallops were once considered to belong to 4 species — *Pecten fumatus* from New South Wales, *P. albus* from Victoria and South Australia, *P. meridionalis* from Tasmania and *P. preissiana* (sometimes called *P. modestus*) from Western Australia. However, recent genetic analysis[9] has determined that the New South Wales, Victorian, Tasmanian and South Australian populations are all included in the species *P. fumatus*. The west coast populations have a greater degree of genetic distinction than that found between other populations however, and this warrants investigation.

Commercial fishery

Southern scallops are taken commercially in New South Wales, Victoria and Tasmania. In Victoria the main areas fished are Port Phillip Bay and off Lakes Entrance. In Tasmania fishers work inshore along the north and east coasts around the Furneaux Island group. The waters around King Island and western Bass Strait are managed by the Commonwealth of Australia and are fished by boats from Victoria and Tasmania. Catch from the Commonwealth managed zone was about 5 t in 1990[10] and so is minor compared with catch from other areas. Victorian boats operate year round, while the Tasmanian fishery is seasonal, with most fishing carried out during the winter months. There are also small dive fisheries at Jervis Bay and Bermagui in New South Wales.[8] Southern scallops are occasionally taken in Western Australia as a bycatch in the saucer scallop fisheries. There was a limited dredge fishery in Cockburn Sound in 1971 but it closed quickly.

Southern scallops are caught using box-shaped mud dredges, 2 m to 3.5 m wide. 'Keta-ami' dredges are also used in Tasmania. The dredges may be fitted with teeth. As the dredge is dragged along the bottom, the teeth dig into the mud, lifting the scallops so that they are caught in the dredge basket. Each dredge run lasts up to 15 minutes, after which it is lifted and emptied. The boat then reverses direction and fishes back the other way.[11] The catch efficiency of the toothed mud dredge has been estimated at between 1 % and 28 %, depending on the size of

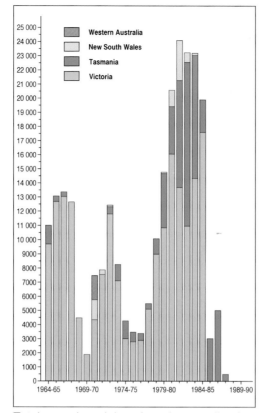

Total annual catch in t of southern scallop for the period 1964–65 to 1989–90. Figures are unavailable for: New South Wales from 1964–65 to 1969–70, 1974–75 to 1978–79 and 1984–85 to 1986–87; Victoria from 1985–86 to 1989–90; and Tasmania for 1967–68 and 1970–71. (Source: Fisheries Resources Atlas Statistical Database)

scallop, density of the beds, sea bed type and vegetation, and the duration of each dredge pass.[12] Recently, researchers have been looking at dredge types used elsewhere in the world to see if any are more efficient and less damaging than those being used in Australia.[11]

The scallops are stored whole in bags before being processed onshore where the meat and gonads are removed from the shell. Most processors look for a meat count of around 100 pieces per kg. For the export markets 90 pieces per kg is preferred. The meat is cleaned, washed and weighed and either packed fresh, individually or bulk frozen, or canned. The scallops are sold locally (fresh or frozen), or exported (frozen). The major export destinations are France, the United States of America, Hong Kong and New Zealand.[8] Southern scallops were selling for A$ 12.00 to A$ 13.00 per kg (wholesale) in mid 1992.

Management controls The fisheries in Victoria and Tasmania are limited entry fisheries. Tasmania has a volumetric unit quota that sets allowable catch for each fisher based on the length of the vessel (up to a maximum quota). In addition, boats wishing to fish in the central zone of Bass Strait require a Commonwealth

Scallop fishing boat with its catch on deck at Lakes Entrance, Victoria. (Source: Australian Department of Foreign Affairs and Trade)

A full scallop dredge on the back of a vessel, Jervis Bay, New South Wales. (Source: John Matthews, Fisheries Research Institute, NSW Fisheries)

licence with a Bass Strait scallop endorsement. There are seasonal closures in both Victoria and Tasmania. Victoria also has restrictions on the number of fishing days per week. In Port Phillip Bay dredging is banned in shallow water. The Tasmanian region of Bass Strait has been closed to commercial scallop fishing since 1987.[13] Dredging is banned in Western Australia.

Aquaculture

Following research prompted by the decline in wild stocks in the mid 1980s, a commercial aquaculture operation based on southern scallops was set up on the east coast of Tasmania. Scallop spat is obtained from the wild using spat collectors, or from stock reared in hatcheries. The spat are grown through the 'attached' phase until they are about 10 mm long. They are then harvested and transferred to midwater cages for an intermediate culture phase before being re-seeded onto the sea floor — either over natural beds that have been depleted or in new areas considered suitable for scallop growth. There have also been attempts to raise scallops to commercial

size in deep water cages, but as yet there has been no commercial production.

Recreational fishery

In Victoria southern scallop are collected by recreational divers using SCUBA equipment. The recreational scallop dive fishery in the D'Entrecasteaux Channel in Tasmania is for the doughboy scallop, *Chlamys (Mimachlamys) asperrimus* and the queen scallop, *Chlamys bifrons*.

Management controls There is a bag limit on the number of scallops that may be collected in Port Phillip Bay, but not for other Victorian waters. Southern scallop are protected in Tasmania as part of management aimed at encouraging the recovery of commercial stocks, and cannot be taken.

Resource status

The southern scallop fishery is characterised by highly variable catches and, overall, it is over exploited. Heavy fishing pressure and poor recruitment have seen some areas in Tasmanian and Victorian waters closed to fishing to allow stocks to recover.[7] Less destructive fishing methods may assist this fishery.

Notes

There is a dive fishery for the queen scallop in South Australia. Divers work in 5 zones: Coffin Bay, western and eastern Spencer Gulf, Kangaroo Island, and western Gulf St Vincent, usually only working to water depths of about 20 m. The dive fishery was opened in 1985, and catches have increased to the current level of around 120 t.

References

1. Macpherson, J.H. and Gabriel, C.J. (1962) *Marine molluscs of Victoria*. Victoria: Melbourne University Press. 475 pp.

2. Joll, L.M. (1989) History, biology and management of Western Australian stocks of the saucer scallop *Amusium balloti*. Pp 30-41, in *Proceedings of the Australasian scallop workshop*. Ed by M.L.C. Dredge, W.F. Zacharin and L.M. Joll. Hobart, Tasmania.

3. Hamer, G. (1987) Scallop biology and management. *Department of Agriculture, New South Wales*. Agfact **F1.0.2**. 8 pp.

4. Young, P.C., Martin, R.B., McLoughlin, R.J. and West, G. (1989) Variability in spatfall and recruitment of commercial scallops (*Pecten fumatus*) in Bass Strait. Pp 80–91, in *Proceedings of the Australasian scallop workshop*. Ed by M.L.C. Dredge, W.F. Zacharin and L.M. Joll. Hobart, Tasmania.

5. Coleman, N. (1989) Spat catches as an indication of recruitment to scallop populations in Victorian waters. Pp 51–60, in *Proceedings of the Australasian scallop workshop*. Ed by M.L.C. Dredge, W.F. Zacharin and L.M. Joll. Hobart, Tasmania.

6. Dix, T.G. and Sjardin, M.J. (1975) Larvae of the commercial scallop *Pecten meridionalis* from Tasmania, Australia. *Australian Journal of Marine and Freshwater Research* **26**: 109–112.

7. Zacharin, W.F. (1988) Scallops. *Fisheries Division research reviews*. Unpublished report.

8. Dix, T.G. (1982) Scallops. *CSIRO Marine Laboratories, Cronulla, Fishery Situation Report* **8**. 11 pp.

9. Woodburn, L. (1990) Genetic variation in southern Australian *Pecten*. Pp 226–240, in *Proceedings of the Australasian scallop workshop*. Ed by M.L.C. Dredge, W.F. Zacharin and L.M. Joll. Hobart, Tasmania.

10. Australian Fisheries Service (1991) *Department of Primary Industries and Energy, Fisheries Paper* **91/6**. 42 pp.

11. Zacharin, W. (1989) Alternative dredge designs and their efficiency. Pp 92–102, in *Proceedings of the Australasian scallop workshop*. Ed by M.L.C. Dredge, W.F. Zacharin and L.M. Joll. Hobart, Tasmania.

12. McLoughlin, R.J., Young, P.C., Martin, R.B. and Parslow, J. (1991). The Australian scallop dredge: estimates of catching efficiency and associated indirect fishing mortality. *Fisheries Research* **11**: 1–24.

13. Zacharin, W.F. (1991) Slow recovery for Bass Strait scallops. *Australian Fisheries* **50(1)**: 28–30.

Contributors

Most of the information on this species was originally provided by Will Zacharin and supplemented by (in alphabetical order) Noel Coleman, John Johnson and Lindsay Joll. Drawing by Rhyllis Plant. (*Details of contributors and their organisations are given in the Acknowledgements section at the back of this book.*)

Compilers Alex McNee and Christina Grieve (maps)

Saucer scallops

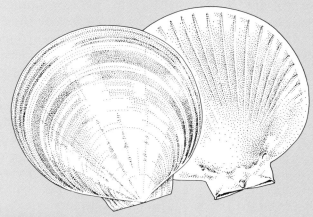

Distribution

Ballot's saucer scallops are present off the Queensland and New South Wales coasts from Innisfail to Jervis Bay. They also inhabit New Caledonian waters. Western saucer scallops are distributed along the Western Australian coast from Esperance to Broome.[1] The warming effect of the Leeuwin Current is thought to be responsible for the species' greater southern range extension in Western Australia compared with saucer scallops on the east coast. Delicate saucer scallops inhabit inshore northern waters from Montague Sound in the Bonaparte Archipelago in Western Australia through the Gulf of Carpentaria to Yeppoon in central Queensland. Their distribution also includes the Indo-Pacific region.[2]

Saucer scallops in Australia live on bare sand, rubble or soft sediment surfaces. They inhabit waters from 10 m to 75 m deep,[2] with the smaller delicate saucer scallops mostly in waters shallower than 20 m.[2] Within their broad geographic distribution, saucer scallops occur in discrete 'beds', up to 15 km in length, at densities of up to 1 per m^2. Beds are separated by areas in which no or few saucer scallops live.

Life history

Spawning in Australian species of saucer scallops coincides with changes in water temperature in the range 18° to 23°C.[3] Spawning times vary and spawning can take place more than once each season. The western saucer scallop population in Shark Bay, Western Australia, spawns between April and December, whilst the Houtman Abrolhos population spawns between August and March.[1] In Queensland, Ballot's saucer scallops spawn between May and September[3] with peaks in June and August. Saucer

Saucer scallops

This presentation is on 2 species and one of these has 2 subspecies. They are **Ballot's saucer scallop, western saucer scallop** and **delicate saucer scallop**.

Ballot's saucer scallop,
Amusium balloti balloti
   (Bernardi)

Other common names include **northern scallop** and **tropical scallop**.
FAO: no known name
Australian species code: 651002

Western saucer scallop,
Amusium balloti
   (new subspecies)

Other common names include **northern scallop** and **tropical scallop**.
FAO: no known name
Australian species code: 651004

Delicate saucer scallop,
Amusium pleuronectes
   (Linnaeus)

Other common names include **Asian moon scallop, sun scallop** and **mud scallop**.
FAO: no known name
Australian species code: 651003

Family PECTINIDAE

Diagnostic features The shells (valves) of saucer scallops are medium to large, thin, rather flat and circular and have a number of radiating ribs inside. There are small 'ears' on the anterior and posterior margins at the ends of the hinge, and both shells gape slightly at the anterior and posterior borders. The outer shell surfaces are smooth and polished. Ballot's saucer scallop and western saucer scallop look almost identical, having straight-edged ears and about 50 internal ribs. The delicate saucer scallop however (pictured), has ears with more rounded edges and only about 30 internal ribs. In Ballot's saucer scallop and western saucer scallop, the right valve is pale and generally plain white on its outer surface, while the left valve is striped and banded in shades of brown and/or red (darker in western saucer scallop). In the delicate saucer scallop, the right valve is generally white, while the left valve has a complicated colour pattern of dark-edged spotted rays on a dull pink background.

scallops are termed 'broadcast spawners' as they release their eggs and sperm into the water where fertilisation occurs. Delicate saucer scallops are functional hermaphrodites. Sexes are separate in western saucer scallops and Ballot's saucer scallops,[4] although hermaphrodites do occur.

Saucer scallop eggs are positively buoyant. Eggs of western saucer scallops are significantly bigger than those of Ballot's saucer scallops. The short larval phase lasts from 12 to 18 days and, under laboratory conditions, larval settlement occurs after 22 days.[5] There is no information on the larval phase of delicate saucer scallops.

Saucer scallops are active swimmers[6] and random dispersal movements have been recorded in Australian species,[7] but there is no evidence of regular migrations.

Growth rates in Australian adult saucer scallops vary, due to seasonal changes in their condition associated with reproductive development and as a function of location. In Queensland, Ballot's saucer scallops which occur in deeper water with swift tidal flow grow more slowly than do those in shallow water with less tide.[7] Early growth is rapid.[7] Young Ballot's saucer scallops and western saucer scallops average 8.5 cm long after 28–35 weeks and 9 cm long after 33–42 weeks.[1,4,7] Ballot's saucer scallops and western saucer scallops live for a maximum of 3–4 years[2,8] and can reach 14 cm in length. There is no information on growth rates in delicate saucer scallops, although they are smaller animals, growing to about 8 cm in length.[9] Saucer scallops become sexually mature in their first year, with most mature animals having a shell height greater than 9 cm.[3]

Saucer scallops feed by filtering microscopic particles from the water. Known predators of saucer scallops are, on the west coast, snapper (*Pagrus auratus*) and possibly octopus (*Octopus* species); in the north, threadfin salmon (Polynemidae); and in the east, bay lobsters (*Thenus* species) and starfish (Asteroidea).

Stock structure

Saucer scallops of Australia consist of 2 species, *Amusium balloti* and the smaller *A. pleuronectes*. However, recent research in Queensland has shown that there are differences in the genetic make-up of the eastern and western populations of *Amusium balloti*. The degree of difference indicates that there is probably no interbreeding between the 2 and, since they are separated in their distribution across northern Australian waters, they are regarded as separate sub-species while work on their taxonomic status continues.

Commercial fishery

The first commercial fishing for Australian saucer scallops, using dredge nets, began off Hervey Bay in Queensland in the 1950s. In the mid 1960s, saucer scallops were taken in the prawn (Penaeidae) catches in Shark Bay in Western Australia, but it was not until 1969–70 that vessels in that area began targeting saucer scallops.

In Queensland waters, Ballot's saucer scallops are fished between Townsville and southern Hervey Bay[10] at depths of

25 to 55 m.[2] They are also taken off Tin Can Bay.[10] All prawn trawlers in the State may fish for saucer scallops, but only about 200 of the approximately 1000 otter trawlers participate in the fishery.[2] Few rely on them for a primary source of income. Delicate saucer scallops are taken in coastal waters of the Northern Territory, from around Melville Island to west of Karumba and an area around Weipa, as bycatch of the Northern Prawn Fishery. Approximately 40 % of northern prawn trawlers retain their catch of saucer scallops for sale.[11] The species is also taken in prawn catches from Princess Charlotte Bay to Bowen in Queensland but they are processed intermittently. Western saucer scallops are fished mainly in Shark Bay and the Houtman Abrolhos, with small target fisheries in Geographe Bay and off Esperance. They are also taken in the Nickol Bay prawn fishery.[1]

In Australia saucer scallops are caught by demersal otter trawling. Most boats in the east coast fishery are designed for multispecies trawling, targeting either prawns or saucer scallops, depending on the season. Bay lobsters comprise a bycatch in some areas. Dredges used to catch other species of scallop cannot catch saucer scallops: these scallops are capable of swimming out of the path of

dredges. Saucer scallops can be trawled 24 hours a day. The fisheries target resting (post-spawning) or pre-spawning adults because at this time, meat yield and scallop condition are at their best.[1] Incidental commercial catches from saucer scallop fishing include large crabs,[4] squid and cuttlefish (*Sepia* species).

Saucer scallops are sold whole or shucked (shell removed). All the Northern Territory catch and up to 20 % of the Queensland and Western Australian catches are sold through local markets or shipped to markets in southern States. Most of the Queensland and Western Australian catch is exported, sold as 'roe off' meat, mainly in South-east Asia but also in the United States of America.[2] In 1992, Queensland fishers received from A$ 12.00 to A$ 15.00 per kg of meat, depending on the number of pieces per kg. Prices are higher for larger scallops. In Western Australia fishers were paid between A$ 10.00 and A$ 14.00 per kg in 1992. All prices are for saucer scallops landed in the shell.

Management controls In the Northern Territory there are no regulations specific to delicate saucer scallops, with fishing controlled under the Northern Prawn

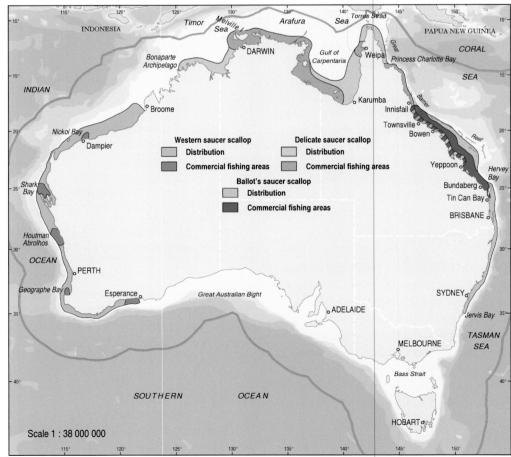

Geographic distribution and commercial fishing areas for saucer scallops in Australian waters

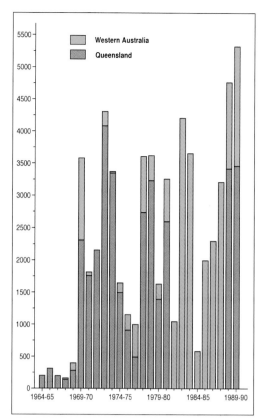

Total annual catch in t of saucer scallops for the period 1964–65 to 1989–90 in Australia. Figures are unavailable for Queensland from 1981–82 to 1987–88. Catches for States that average less than 5 % of the total for all States are not shown. (Source: Fisheries Resources Atlas Statistical Database)

Fishery regulations. State regulations apply in Western Australia and Queensland where daylight bans on trawling have been introduced. In Western Australia, both the Shark Bay and Houtman Abrolhos fisheries are limited entry fisheries,[10] and open only for limited seasons. The Shark Bay fishery coincides with the prawn fishery in that area and the Houtman Abrolhos fishery is timed to coincide with the western rock lobster (*Panulirus cygnus*) fishery.[1] There are no minimum shell size limits. Net mesh size is specified in Western Australian regulations[1] and season opening times are deliberately set to capture scallops of appropriate sizes. Seasonal minimum size limits are used to protect breeding stocks in Queensland.

Recreational fishery

There is no recreational fishery for saucer scallops.

Resource status

Saucer scallop densities in many Queensland beds have been reduced[2] from about 1 animal per m[2] to 1 per

150 m[2]. This reduction has probably been caused by intense fishing, which also removes large numbers of young, pre-spawning scallops from the population. The open habitats occupied by the scallops and their occurrence in discrete beds also make stocks vulnerable to depletion under heavy fishing pressure. Measures such as a daytime ban on trawling and variable size limits have been introduced to protect stocks.

Annual saucer scallop catches in Western Australia and Queensland vary according to the success of the previous year's recruitment (ie survival of larvae).[12] This appears to be determined by environmental factors in Western Australia, but is not understood in Queensland waters. The resource is believed to be secure. Timing of harvesting seasons in the Houtman Abrolhos fishery ensures that only post-spawning individuals (older than 1 year) are targeted. However the Shark Bay fishery targets pre-spawning (less than 1-year-old) saucer scallops as well.

References

1. Joll, L.M. (1989) History, biology, and management of Western Australian stocks of the saucer scallop *Amusium balloti*. Pp 30–41, in *Proceedings of the Australasian scallop workshop*. Ed by M.L.C. Dredge, W.F. Zacharin and L.M. Joll. Hobart, Tasmania.

2. Dredge, M.C.L. (1988) Recruitment overfishing in a tropical scallop fishery? *Journal of Shellfish Research* **7**(2): 233–239.

3. Dredge, M.C.L. (1981) Reproductive biology of the saucer scallop *Amusium japonicum balloti* (Bernardi) in central Queensland waters. *Australian Journal of Marine and Freshwater Research* **32**: 775–787.

4. Joll, L.M. (1987) The Shark Bay scallop fishery. *Fisheries Department of Western Australia, Fisheries Management Paper* **11**. 123 pp.

5. Rose, R.A., Campbell, G.B. and Sanders, S.G. (1988) Larval development of the saucer scallop *Amusium balloti*, Bernardi (Mollusca:Pectinidae). *Australian Journal of Marine and Freshwater Research* **39**: 133–160.

6. Joll, L.M. (1989) Swimming behaviour of the saucer scallop *Amusium balloti* (Mollusca: Pectinidae). *Marine Biology* **102**: 299–305.

7. Williams, M.J. and Dredge, M.C.L. (1981) Growth of the saucer scallop, *Amusium japonicum balloti* Habe in central eastern Queensland. *Australian Journal of Marine and Freshwater Research* **32**: 657–666.

8. Heald, D. (1978) A successful marking method for the saucer scallop *Amusium balloti* (Bernardi). *Australian Journal of Marine and Freshwater Research* **29**: 845–851.

9. Habe, T. (1964) Notes on species of the genus *Amusium* (Mollusca). *Bulletin of the Natural Science Museum of Tokyo* **7**: 1–5.

10. Dredge, M. (1989) How far can a scallop population be pushed? Pp 68–79, in *Proceedings of the Australasian scallop workshop*. Ed by M.L.C. Dredge, W.F. Zacharin and L.M. Joll. Hobart, Tasmania.

11. Pender, P.J. and Willing, R.S. (1990) Northern prawn fishery bycatch with market potential. *Northern Territory Department of Primary Industry and Fisheries, Fishery Report* **20**. 52 pp.

12. Lenanton, R.C., Joll, L., Penn, J. and Jones, K. (1991) The influence of the Leeuwin Current on coastal fisheries of Western Australia. *Journal of the Royal Society of Western Australia* **74**: 101–114.

Contributors

Information on this species was originally provided by Mike Dredge with additional comments by (in alphabetical order) Lindsay Joll, Clive Keenan, Rosemary Lea and Shirley Slack-Smith. Drawing by Rhyllis Plant. (*Details of contributors and their organisations are given in the Acknowledgements section at the back of this book.*)

Compilers Alex McNee, Patricia Kailola and Christina Grieve (maps)

Sorting a catch of saucer scallops on board a trawler, Queensland. (Source: Mike Dredge, Southern Fisheries Centre, Queensland Department of Primary Industries)

Inshore squid and calamary

Loligo and *Sepioteuthis* species

Inshore squid and calamary

This presentation is on 4 species, **mitre squid**, **north-west pink squid**, **southern calamary** and **northern calamary**.

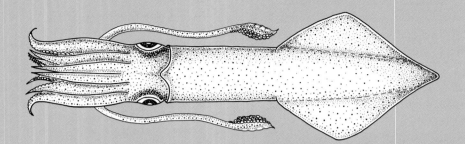

Mitre squid, *Loligo chinensis* Gray

Other common names include **Asian squid, pencil squid** and **calamary**.
FAO: **mitre squid**
Australian species code: 600004

North-west pink squid, *Loligo edulis* Hoyle

There are no other common names.
FAO: **swordtip squid**
Australian species code: 620002

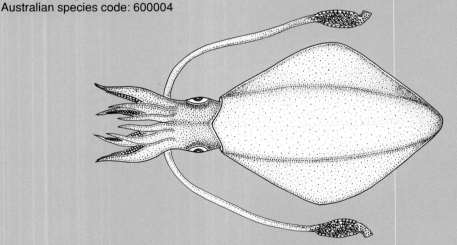

Southern calamary, *Sepioteuthis australis* Quoy and Gaimard

There are no other common names.
FAO: **southern reef squid**
Australian species code: 600003

Family LOLIGINIDAE

Diagnostic features Squid of the family Loliginidae are cephalopods with eyes covered by a transparent corneal membrane. Their funnel is connected with the mantle by a pair of simple, straight locking apparatus — grooves on the funnel and ridges on the mantle. They have 8 arms and 2 tentacles around the mouth. Each arm has 2 rows of suckers,

Northern calamary, *Sepioteuthis lessoniana* Lesson

There are no other common names.
FAO: **bigfin reef squid**
Australian species code: 620011

while there are 4 rows on each of the tentacular clubs. There are no hooks on any of the suckers. *Loligo* species have an elongate mantle with rhombic terminal fins. Calamary have a more robust mantle with a rounded posterior end and long, rounded fins extending nearly the whole length of the mantle.[1] Illustrated species are mitre squid (top) and southern calamary (bottom).

Distribution

Mitre squid, north-west pink squid and northern calamary inhabit northern Australian waters. Mitre squid are distributed from Shark Bay to Botany Bay, while north-west pink squid are distributed from Shark Bay to Townsville. Northern calamary inhabit waters from Geraldton to Moreton Bay. Southern calamary are distributed around southern Australia, including the waters around Tasmania, from Brisbane on the east coast to north of Dampier on the west coast.

Mitre squid inhabit shallow water on the continental shelf as well as coastal bays and inlets, but they have been caught in waters as deep as 300 m.[2] North-west pink squid inhabit continental shelf waters to a depth of 170 m.[3] Both northern and southern calamary are inshore species that inhabit coastal waters and bays and inlets, usually in less than 100 m of water.[2,4]

All 4 species occur elsewhere in the Indo-Pacific region. Mitre squid live throughout the western Pacific to Japan, including the south and east China Seas. North-west pink squid range from the western Pacific Ocean through the Philippine Islands to southern Japan.[1] Southern calamary has the most restricted distribution, inhabiting only Australian and northern New Zealand waters. Northern calamary, the most wide ranging species, are distributed throughout the Indo-Pacific region from the Red Sea and eastern Africa to Japan and the Hawaiian Islands.

Life history

Little is known of the life history of mitre squid and north-west pink squid in Australian waters. In the western Pacific Ocean mitre squid spawn throughout the year, although activity peaks in February to May and August to November.[1] North-west pink squid from the same area over-winter in deep waters and migrate inshore in spring and summer. They aggregate, prior to spawning, over sandy substrates in 30–40 m of water.

Southern calamary spawn throughout the year, although spawning activity peaks in summer and winter in South

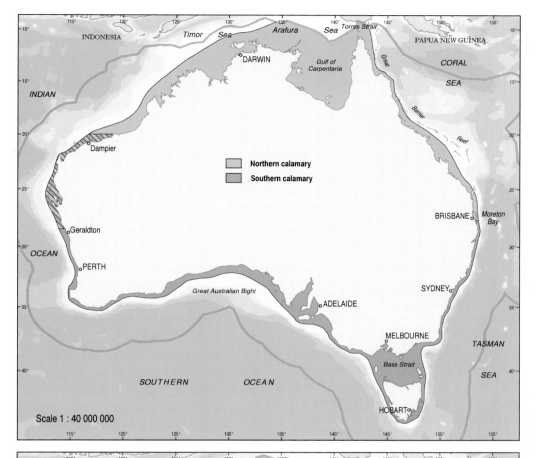

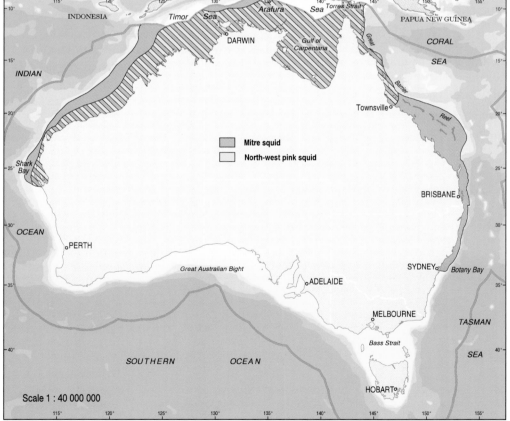

(top) Geographic distribution of northern and southern calamary in Australian waters.
(bottom) Geographic distribution of mitre squid and north-west pink squid in Australian waters.

Southern calamary eggs are laid in groups of 4–5 in finger-like capsules. The capsules are attached to rocky substrates, algae or seagrasses, often in masses of 50 to several hundred capsules.[5,7] On hatching, the larval calamary swim to the surface and remain among the plankton. The juvenile calamary remain in these hatching areas until they reach a mantle length of about 7 cm.[5] It is known that northern calamary eggs hatch after 35 days at temperatures of 20°C to 24°C.[2]

Southern calamary are short lived and quick growing and live for about 18 months.[8] They mature at 12 months of age,[9] at a mantle length of about 16 cm. They can reach a mantle length of 38 cm[1] and weigh up to 2.1 kg.[6] There is no information on the growth of mitre squid, north-west pink squid and northern calamary.

Southern calamary feed on prawns and fish. They feed voraciously when aggregating, often eating small calamary.[5] Nothing is known about the diet of mitre squid, north-west pink squid and northern calamary.

Stock structure

There is no information on the stock structure of mitre squid, north-west pink squid or northern calamary. There has been no detailed assessment of stock structure of southern calamary, although distinct summer and winter breeding groups are recognised in South Australian waters.[5] Limited tagging studies there have indicated no significant movement of southern calamary.

Commercial fishery

There are no target fisheries for mitre squid and north-west pink squid. They are taken incidentally in demersal otter trawl catches in northern Australia. During the 1970s and 1980s most of the cephalopod catch in northern Australia was taken in the Arafura Sea and Gulf of Carpentaria by Taiwanese (and some Thai) pair trawlers and stern trawlers.[10]

Jigging is the only fishing method that specifically targets calamary and squid. In fisheries using other methods calamary are taken as part of a mixed species catch, although they may be targeted at certain times of the year (eg when spawning aggregations occur).

Australia,[5] and between August and January off Victoria. Spawning is known to occur in summer off Tasmania.[6] It takes place in shallow waters, usually less than 15 m deep. In South Australia, summer spawning predominates in areas of shallow water immediately adjacent to deep water, while in large areas of shallow water, such as seagrass (eg *Zostera* species) meadows, winter spawning will dominate.[5] Less is known about northern calamary, but eggs have been collected in September in southern Queensland.[2]

Squid egg mass. (Source: South Australian Department of Fisheries)

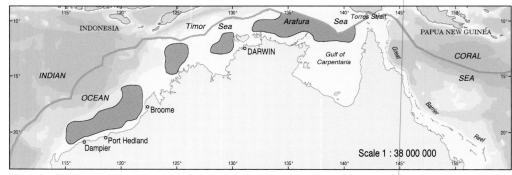

Historical demersal trawl fishery for *Loligo* species in northern Australian waters.

Although primarily a bycatch of Queensland prawn fisheries, mitre squid are occasionally targeted by prawn trawlers in Moreton Bay. Prawn fishers will target squid when prawn catches are low, although squid catch rates are limited by the ability of the local market to absorb the catch. Best catches are achieved by bottom trawling during daylight hours when squid species aggregate near the sea bed.[2] The Moreton Bay fishery catches squid of 7 cm to 18 cm mantle length,[2] and these are sold either as seafood or as bait.

Northern calamary represent a minor bycatch of prawn trawling in Queensland.[2] 'Squid' (probably a mixture of mitre squid, north-west pink squid and northern calamary) are reported as bycatch in the Northern Prawn Fishery and Western Australian prawn fisheries.

In southern Queensland, southern calamary are caught incidentally by fishers using tunnel nets in the intertidal zones of Moreton Bay and Great Sandy Strait. Most of this catch is taken between April and October, and incidental catch from prawn trawling is also highest at this time.[2]

In New South Wales, southern calamary are taken as a bycatch of demersal trawling for fish and prawns.

In Victoria the largest catches of southern calamary are taken in Port Phillip Bay, mostly by beach seining[6] and hand jigging.[11] Beach seining is carried out throughout the year, but southern calamary catches are greatest in winter months when targeting shifts from other species. Jigging effort is concentrated from October to December when the calamary aggregate to spawn.[11] Southern calamary are also caught by beach seining from Western Port, Corner Inlet and off the southern coast, and as incidental catch of Danish seiners and trawlers off the south east coast.[6]

In Tasmania large schools of southern calamary are occasionally targeted by hand jigging, while incidental catches are taken in haul seine nets off the south and east coasts.[6]

Southern calamary are taken from Spencer and St Vincent gulfs and sheltered bays along the south-east and west coasts of South Australia.[5] It appears that the largest catches in the north of the gulfs are taken in autumn and winter, while in the south of the gulfs they occur in spring and summer.[12] Most southern calamary are caught in hauling nets or by hand jigging. Spawning aggregations are targeted, although small quantities are taken as incidental catch throughout the year.[5,8] Hand jigging is the dominant method for summer catches in South Australia, while most autumn–winter catches are taken in hauling nets.[12]

Southern calamary of 7–16 cm mantle length are taken as bycatch in the prawn fisheries.

Calamary are sold on domestic markets for human consumption or bait. In 1991-92 the average price for calamary at the Sydney Fish Market was A$ 5.48 per kg.

Management controls Mitre squid, north-west pink squid, northern calamary and southern calamary are primarily taken as bycatch or incidental catch of other fisheries (eg the Northern Prawn Fishery, the East Coast Trawl Fishery, South East Fishery) and as such are regulated by the controls imposed on the parent fishery. In South Australia the application of a total allowable catch for calamary, as part of the catch in the Marine Scale Fishery, is under consideration.[8]

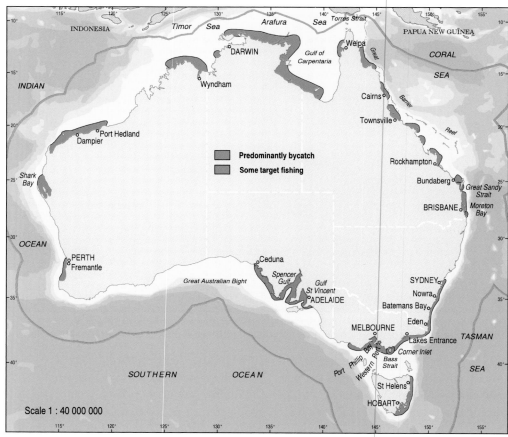

Commercial fishing areas for inshore squid and calamary in Australian waters.

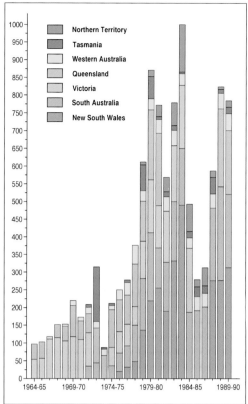

Total annual catch in t of all squid species (including arrow squid, *Nototodarus gouldi*) for the period 1964–65 to 1989–90 in Australia. Figures are unavailable for: New South Wales from 1964–65 to 1974–75 and 1984–85 to 1986–87; Victoria for 1972–73, 1973–74 and 1985–86 to 1989–90; Queensland for 1966–67 and 1981–82 to 1987–88; and South Australia from 1964–65 to 1970–71 and for 1973–74. (Source: Fisheries Resources Atlas Statistical Database)

Recreational fishery

Mitre squid, northern calamary and southern calamary are often caught by recreational fishers from coastal waters within their respective ranges. They are primarily caught on baited jigs or lures used from boats or from jetties. Fishing effort is greatest around population centres such as Moreton Bay, Port Phillip Bay and Spencer and St Vincent gulfs. There is no recreational fishery for north-west pink squid.

Management controls Regulations on recreational squid fishing exist in Victoria and South Australia only. A daily bag limit on recreational squid catch applies in Victoria, while in South Australia consideration is being given to the introduction of bag limits for recreational squid fishing.[8]

Resource status

Catches of squid and calamary do not meet domestic demand. In 1989–90 Australia imported 4300 t cephalopods,

consisting mainly of cleaned squid 'tubes'. In most areas in their Australian distribution, the resources are considered under-exploited. In South Australia, where there is substantial commercial and recreational calamary fishing effort, commercial catches have stabilised. This may indicate that the stock is nearly fully exploited.[8]

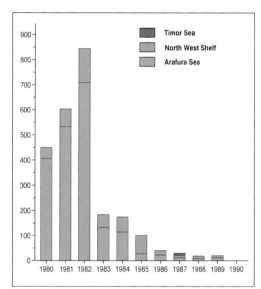

Squid (*Loligo* species) catch in t from the northern sector of the Australian Fishing Zone for the period 1980 to 1990. (Source: Ramm, Lloyd and Coleman[10])

References

1. Roper, C.F.E., Sweeney, M.J. and Nauen, C.E. (1984) FAO species catalogue. Vol. 3. Cephalopods of the world. An annotated and illustrated catalogue of species of interest to fisheries. *FAO Fisheries Synopsis No. 125*, **3**. 277 pp.

2. Winstanley, R.H., Potter, M.A. and Caton, A.E. (1983) Australian cephalopod resources. *Memoirs of the National Museum of Victoria* **44**: 243–253.

3. Wadley, V. and Swainston, R. (1990) *Squid from the west and north west slope deepwater trawl fisheries.* Marmion: CSIRO Division of Fisheries. 30 pp.

4. Lu, C.C. and Tait, R.W. (1983) Taxonomic studies on *Sepioteuthis* Blainville (Cephalopoda: Loliginidae) from the Australian region. *Proceedings of the Royal Society of Victoria* **95**(4): 181–204.

5. Jones, G.K., Hall, D.A., Hill, K.L. and Staniford, A.J. (1990) *The South Australian marine scale fishery. Stock assessment, economics, management.* South Australian Department of Fisheries, Green paper. 186 pp.

6. Winstanley, R.H. (1979) *Squid.* Demersal and Pelagic Fish Research Group, South Eastern Fisheries Committee, Fishery Situation Report. 12 pp.

7. Parry, G.D., Campbell, S.J. and Hobday, D.K. (1990) Marine resources off east Gippsland, southeastern Australia. *Victorian Department of Conservation and*

Environment, Fisheries Division, Technical Report **72**. 166 pp.

8. Rohan, G., Jones, K. and McGlennon, D. (1991) *The South Australian marine scale fishery.* South Australian Department of Fisheries, Supplementary green paper. 170 pp.

9. Smith, H.K. (1983) The development potential of the southern calamary (*Sepioteuthis australis*) fishery. South Australian Department of Fisheries, unpublished. Cited in Hall, D.N. and MacDonald, C.M. (1986) Commercial fishery situation report: net and line fisheries of Port Phillip Bay, Victoria, 1914–1984. *Victorian Department of Conservation, Forests and Lands, Fisheries Division, Marine Fisheries Report* **10**. 121 pp.

10. Ramm, D.C., Lloyd, J.A. and Coleman, A.P.M. (1991) *Demersal trawling in the northern sector of the Australian Fishing Zone: catch and effort 1980–1990.* Northern Territory Department of Primary Industry and Fisheries, unpublished draft fisheries report.

11. Hall, D.N. and MacDonald, C.M. (1986) Commercial fishery situation report: net and line fisheries of Port Phillip Bay Victoria, 1914–1984. *Victorian Department of Conservation, Forests and Lands, Fisheries Division, Marine Fisheries Report* **10**. 121 pp.

12. Smith, H. (1980) *The development potential of the southern calamary squid* (Sepioteuthis australis) *fishery.* Progress Report, South Australian Department of Fisheries, unpublished. 14 pp.

Contributors

The information on this species was supplemented by Malcolm Dunning and C.C. Lu. Drawings by Leslie Newman. (*Details of contributors and their organisations are given in the Acknowledgments section at the back of this book.*)

Compiler Alex McNee

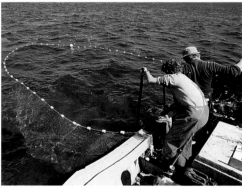

Net fishing for southern calamary in South Australia. (Source: South Australian Department of Fisheries)

Arrow squid

Nototodarus gouldi

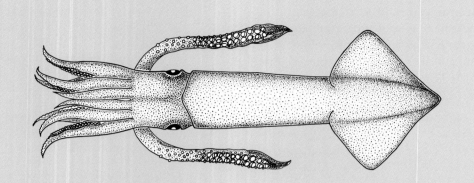

Nototodarus gouldi (McCoy)

Arrow squid

Other common names include
**Gould's squid, aeroplane squid,
aero squid, seine boat squid** and
torpedo squid.
FAO: **Gould's flying squid**
Australian species code: 636006

Family OMMASTREPHIDAE

Diagnostic features Arrow squid have
a heavily muscled mantle which tapers
gradually to the fins, then sharply to the
tail. The mantle skin is smooth and light
brown to brick red with a bluish purple
dorsal stripe. The eyes do not have a
covering membrane. The cartilage that
locks the mantle to the funnel is in the
shape of an inverted 'T'. The largest
suckers on the 2 tentacles have 12–15
sharp teeth of about equal size. The 8 arms
also have large suckers with 10–14
triangular teeth grading to a single large
tooth in the area furthest from the mouth.[1,2]

Distribution

Arrow squid are distributed through
southern Australian waters from latitude
27° S in southern Queensland to
Geraldton in Western Australia, including
Bass Strait and Tasmania. They also
inhabit northern waters of New Zealand.

Arrow squid inhabit waters from
estuaries to ocean depths of about 500 m[3,4]
for most of their distribution, although they
have been caught in depths as great as 825
m in the Great Australian Bight.[4] They are
most abundant over the continental shelf
from 50 m to 200 m.[4] In Australia, arrow
squid inhabit waters with sea surface
temperatures from 11°C to over 25°C.[5]

Arrow squid are schooling animals
that tend to aggregate near the sea bed
during the day and disperse throughout
the water column at night. Following
concentrations of prey species, they will
often aggregate near the thermocline at
night or migrate to the surface to feed.
Catch rates usually decrease at the surface
during the full moon period.[4]

Life history

Arrow squid spawn throughout their
Australian distribution.[5,6] In south-eastern
Australia, spawning occurs in all months,
although 2 or 3 peaks in spawning activity
are indicated by length-frequency studies.
Male arrow squid transfer bundles of
sperm called spermatophores to the
female's buccal membrane during mating,
but it is not known how long the
spermatophores are retained before
fertilisation occurs.[4] The eggs are released
in a jelly-like egg mass, although it has
not been confirmed whether the egg mass
is attached to the sea bed or released into
the water. Hatching occurs between 1 and
2 months after fertilisation depending on
the sea temperature, and the larvae are
most abundant in continental shelf waters
of 50–200 m depth.[5] Little else is known
of early life history for arrow squid or
other squids from the same family in
Australia.

Arrow squid are relatively short-lived,
probably reaching a maximum age of only
12 months.[4,7] Growth rates have been
estimated by length-frequency analysis at
up to 4 cm per month in south-eastern
Australia.[5] Male arrow squid mature at a
smaller size than do females but size at
maturity seems to vary with region. Most
males of 22 cm mantle length and most
females of 30 cm mantle length are
reported to be mature in south-eastern
Australia.[4] Females grow more quickly
than males and reach a maximum size of
40 cm mantle length and a weight of
1.6 kg, compared with 35 cm mantle
length and 1.2 kg for males.[6,7,8]

Limited tagging studies of arrow squid
in Bass Strait showed that their movement
may be quite significant, up to 60 nautical
miles in 3 days, but the results did not
indicate any significant migratory
pattern.[4,6]

Arrow squid feed mainly at night.
They eat pelagic crustaceans, fish and

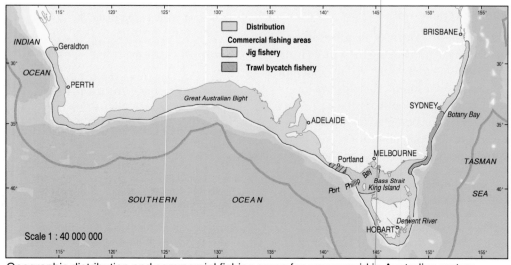

Geographic distribution and commercial fishing areas for arrow squid in Australian waters.

squid.[4,9] Cannibalism is common in larger arrow squid but the prey is normally less than half the size of the predator.[9] In Bass Strait the most important fish species in the diet are pilchards (*Sardinops neopilchardus*) and barracouta (*Thyrsites atun*).[9]

In south-eastern Australian waters arrow squid are eaten by a number of fish species including school shark (*Galeorhinus galeus*), gummy shark (*Mustelus antarcticus*), whiskery shark (*Furgaleus macki*) and John dory (*Zeus faber*).[10]

Stock structure

There are at least 3 broods each year in the Bass Strait arrow squid population.[11] Limited studies of arrow squid in Bass Strait showed no genetic difference between spring and summer broods, but these results were inconclusive in determining stock structure.[12]

Commercial fishery

The first significant catches of arrow squid in Australia were taken in the Derwent estuary in December 1972 and January 1973. About 30 Tasmanian vessels with improvised gear caught 154 t during the 2 months.[13] The existence of a significant arrow squid resource in south-eastern Australian waters was known prior to the 1970s but this species was mainly taken as bycatch of demersal otter trawling, Danish seining and trolling.

Between 1977 and 1988 resource surveys and feasibility fishing by jigging vessels from Japan, Korea and Taiwan confirmed the extent of arrow squid resources off Victoria, Tasmania and South Australia.[4,7] The highest catch rates were obtained in western Bass Strait and off northern Tasmania.[4] Feasibility fishing off Western Australia in the summer of 1979–80 produced much lower catch rates than those recorded in south-eastern waters.[4]

Arrow squid are caught in a seasonal jigging fishery off western Victoria and in western Bass Strait,[7] and as a bycatch in the South East Fishery. The jig fishing season lasts from October to April in western Bass Strait, with the best catches being taken late in the season. Most of the jigging vessels are converted scallop or shark boats. The jig fishery commenced in

1986–87 with a single vessel and by 1990 included 14 vessels.

The annual catch from the jig fishery is between 200 t and 300 t. Jigging for arrow squid is carried out at night over the continental shelf in depths between 50 m and 150 m.[14] Most of the squid catch is made with automatic jig machines but a small proportion is taken by hand-jigging. Some fishers target arrow squid only during the months when southern scallop (*Pecten fumatus*) or shark catches are lowest. There is a small (less than 1 %) bycatch of red ocean squid (*Ommastrephes bartrami*) and Southern Ocean arrow squid (*Todarodes filippovae*) taken by squid jigging in Bass Strait.

Within the South East Fishery arrow squid are caught as a bycatch by demersal otter trawling and Danish seining for fish in depths between 50 m and 300 m. Most of the catch is taken between Botany Bay and western Bass Strait and from grounds off western Victoria. The arrow squid catch from the South East Fishery

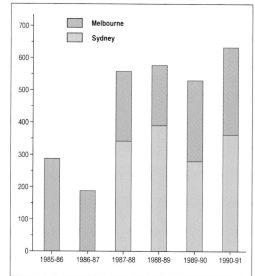

Total annual sales in t of arrow squid at the Sydney Fish Market and the Melbourne Wholesale Fish Market for the period 1985–86 to 1990–91. The 1985–86 and 1986–87 totals for Sydney are not presented due to variation in the accounting period. (Source: NSW Fish Marketing Authority and Melbourne City Council.)

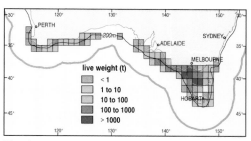

Total arrow squid catch in t by 1-degree block for the period 1979–80 to 1986–87. The indicated catch is the total taken by all foreign fishing vessels. (Source: Australian Fishing Zone Information System)

An automatic squid jigging machine retrieving a catch of arrow squid. (Source: Ken Graham, Fisheries Research Institute, NSW Fisheries)

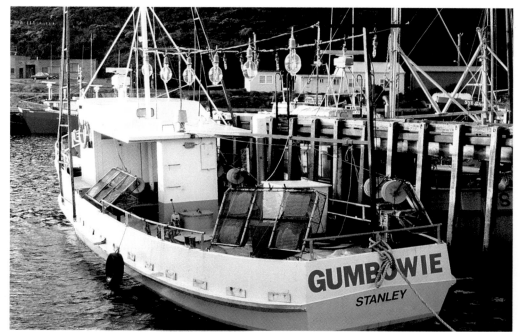

An Australian fishing vessel rigged for squid jigging. (Source: Lindsay Chapman, Bureau of Resource Sciences)

probably ranges between 300 t and 500 t in most years.

Small quantities of arrow squid are caught as a bycatch of hand-jigging for southern calamary (*Sepioteuthis australis*) in Port Phillip Bay.[15,16] They may also be taken as bycatch of beach seine and trolling fisheries in Victoria, Tasmania and South Australia.[15]

Most of the Australian catch of arrow squid is sold on the domestic market, through the Sydney Fish Market, the Melbourne Wholesale Fish Market or directly to processors. The catch by jig vessels is normally frozen on board, while the trawl catch is chilled. Arrow squid caught by the jigging method is generally of higher quality than trawl-caught product and attracts higher prices. Despite the destination of locally harvested product, most of the squid consumed in Australia is imported. In 1989–90, imports of cephalopods (mainly squid) amounted to 4300 t. In 1991–92, arrow squid wholesale prices ranged from A$ 1.30 to A$ 1.70 per kg on the Melbourne Wholesale Fish Market. The average wholesale price for arrow squid at the Sydney Fish Market was A$ 1.83 in 1991–92.

Squid jigging machines on the upper deck of a Japanese vessel. (Source: Gabrielle Nowara, Western Australian Marine Research Laboratories, Fisheries Department of Western Australia)

Management controls Fishers targeting arrow squid by jigging within 3 nautical miles of the coast are subject to management regulations of the appropriate State Government. In waters outside 3 miles, fishers are required to hold a Commonwealth Fishing Boat Licence. The South East Fishery is managed by the Commonwealth of Australia through a management plan including limited entry licensing and individual transferable quotas for the main target species.

Recreational fishery

Arrow squid are not normally a target species of recreational fishers, although they may be caught as a bycatch of some fishing methods. Anglers hand-jigging for southern calamary in Victorian bays catch some arrow squid but normally discard the catch in preference for the calamary. Arrow squid may also be taken by fishers trolling for fish species such as barracouta and Australian salmon (*Arripis* species).

Management controls A daily bag limit of 10 individuals of any squid species (including calamary and cuttlefish, *Sepia* species) applies in Victoria.[17] There are no regulations specific to arrow squid in other States.

Resource status

There is insufficient biological information for estimation of biomass or sustainable yield for arrow squid in Australian waters. Stock assessments for arrow squid are also difficult because of the animal's short life span, and variability in population levels within and between years. Information from foreign fishing ventures indicates that the resource in Bass Strait is considerably under-exploited at current catch levels.

Notes

A jig fishery for arrow squid and another species, *Nototodarus sloanii*, has existed in New Zealand waters since 1972.[18] The fishery was developed by Japanese, Taiwanese and Korean jig vessels under licence agreements and joint venture arrangements. The total jig catch has varied between 10 000 t and 70 000 t since 1980. Between 30 000 t and 40 000 t of arrow squid are also caught by demersal otter trawlers in New Zealand each year.

There is considerable scope for harvesting of other ommastrephid squid species within the Australian Fishing Zone. The Hawaiian arrow squid (*Nototodarus hawaiiensis*) is a bycatch of demersal otter trawling for scampi (*Metanephrops* species) and deepwater prawns in the North West Slope Deepwater Trawl Fishery. Hawaiian arrow squid inhabit northern Australian waters in depths of 100–710 m[1] and are also reported from Hawaii, the Midway Islands and the South China Sea.[5]

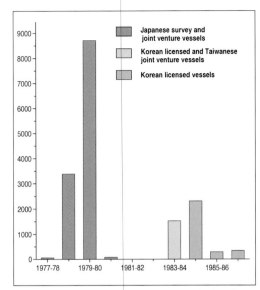

Total annual catch in t of arrow squid for the period 1977–78 to 1986–87 taken by foreign fishing vessels in the Australian Fishing Zone. (Source: Australian Fishing Zone Information System)

Landings of this species from the North West Slope reached 34 t in 1986–87. Hawaiian arrow squid are usually discarded in favour of the high value scampi and prawns but are retained when catches of those crustaceans are low. The squid are frozen whole in blocks on board and processed onshore for the domestic market.

Red ocean squid is another ommastrephid squid which has commercial potential. This species grows to a larger size than does the arrow squid and inhabits surface waters of the continental slope off southern Australia.

Squid jigging machines in operation on a Japanese vessel. (Source: Gabrielle Nowara, Western Australian Marine Research Laboratories, Fisheries Department of Western Australia)

Mesh netting trials in Bass Strait in 1981 showed that red ocean squid could be successfully targeted with this method.[19] Exploratory fishing by a Japanese research vessel during the same year showed that jigging methods could also be used to catch this species in deep water.[20] Red ocean squid is the main commercial species in the North Pacific, where the Japanese catch was 188 000 t in 1980.

References

1. Wadley V. and Swainston, R. (1990) *Squid from the west and north west slope deepwater trawl fisheries.* Marmion: CSIRO Division of Fisheries. 30 pp.

2. Lu, C.C. and Dunning, M. (1982) Identification guide to Australian arrow squid (Family Ommastrephidae). *Victorian Institute of Marine Sciences Technical Report* **2**. 29 pp.

3. Roper, C.F.E., Sweeney, M.J. and Nauen, C.E. (1984) FAO species catalogue. Vol. 3. Cephalopods of the world. An annotated and illustrated catalogue of species of interest to fisheries. *FAO Fisheries Synopsis No. 125*, **3**. 277 pp.

4. Winstanley R.H., Potter, M.A., and Caton A.E. (1983) Australian cephalopod resources. Pp 243–253, in *Proceedings of the workshop on the biology and resource potential of cephalopods, Melbourne, Australia, 9–13 March 1981. Memoirs of the National Museum of Victoria* **44**.

5. Dunning, M.C. (1988) *Distribution and comparative life history studies of deepwater squid of the family Ommastrephidae in Australasian waters.* Unpublished PhD thesis, University of Queensland. 288 pp.

6. Machida, S. (1983) A brief review of the squid survey by *Hoyo Maru No. 67* in southeast Australian waters in 1979/80. Pp 291–295, in *Proceedings of the workshop on the biology and resource potential of cephalopods, Melbourne, Australia, 9–13 March 1981. Memoirs of the National Museum of Victoria* **44**.

7. Molloy D.(1988).The squid resources of Bass Strait. Pp 57–65, in *Proceedings of the squid seminar, Melbourne, Victoria, April 11, 1988.* Victorian Department of Industry, Technology and Resources, Victorian Department of Agriculture and Rural Affairs, Victorian Fishing Industry Council.

8. Ichikawa, W. (1980) Report of feasibility study 1978 on squid jigging fisheries in the southwestern Pacific Ocean. *Japan Marine Fishery Resource Research Center Report* **19**. 178 pp.

9. O'Sullivan, D. and Cullen, J.M. (1983) Food of the squid *Nototodarus gouldi* in Bass Strait. *Australian Journal of Marine and Freshwater Research* **34**: 261–285.

10. Coleman, N. and Mobley, M. (1984) Diets of commercially exploited fish from Bass Strait and adjacent Victorian waters, south-eastern Australia. *Australian Journal of Marine and Freshwater Research* **35**: 549-560.

11. Harrison, A.J. (1979) Preliminary assessment of a squid fishery off Tasmania. In *Squid Outlook Tasmania 1979/80.* Ed by H.E. Rogers. Tasmanian Fisheries Development Authority. 60 pp.

12. Richardson, B.J. (1983) Protein variation in *Nototodarus gouldi* from southeastern Australia. Pp 199–200, in *Proceedings of the workshop on the biology and resource potential of cephalopods, Melbourne, Australia, 9–13 March 1981. Memoirs of the National Museum of Victoria* **44**.

13. Wolfe, D.C. (1973) Tasmanian surveys put to good use. *Australian Fisheries* **32**(3): 6-9.

14. Smith, H.K. (1983) Fishery and biology of *Nototodarus gouldi* (McCoy, 1888) in western Bass Strait. Pp 285–290, in *Proceedings of the workshop on the biology and resource potential of cephalopods, Melbourne, Australia, 9–13 March 1981. Memoirs of the National Museum of Victoria* **44**.

15. Winstanley, R.H. (1979) *Squid.* Demersal and Pelagic Fish Research Group, South Eastern Fisheries Committee, Fishery Situation Report. 12 pp.

16. Hall, D.N. and MacDonald, C.M. (1986) Commercial fishery situation report: net and line fisheries of Port Phillip Bay, Victoria, 1914–1984. *Victorian Department of Conservation, Forests and Lands, Fisheries Division, Marine Fisheries Report* **10**. 121 pp.

17. MacDonald, C.M. and Hall, D.N. (1987). A survey of recreational fishing in Port Phillip Bay. *Victorian Department of Conservation, Forests and Lands, Fisheries Division, Marine Fisheries Report* **11**. 40 pp.

18. Paul, L. (1986) *New Zealand fishes. An identification guide.* Auckland: Reed Methuen. 184 pp.

19. Jameson, J. (1981) Bass Strait trials show mesh-netting for red ocean squid has potential. *Australian Fisheries* **40**(12): 20–29.

20. Dunning, M., Potter, M. and Machida, S. (1981) *Hoyo Maru* survey shows oceanic squid could have potential. *Australian Fisheries* **40**(12): 26–29.

Contributors

Most of the information on this species was provided by (in alphabetical order) Malcolm Dunning, C.C. Lu, David Molloy and Vicki Wadley. Drawing by Leslie Newman. (*Details of contributors and their organisations are given in the Acknowledgements section at the back of this book.*)

Compiler Phillip Stewart

Octopus

Octopus species

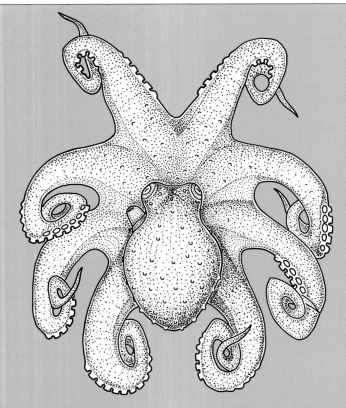

Octopus

This presentation is on 4 species, **southern octopus**, **Maori octopus**, **pale octopus**, and **gloomy octopus**.

Southern octopus, *Octopus australis* Hoyle

There are no other common names.
FAO: no known name
Australian species code: 645001

Maori octopus, *Octopus maorum* Hutton

There are no other common names.
FAO: no known name
Australian species code: 645002

Pale octopus, *Octopus pallidus* Hoyle

There are no other common names.
FAO: no known name
Australian species code: 645003

Gloomy octopus, *Octopus tetricus* Gould

There are no other common names.
FAO: **Gloomy octopus**
Australian species code: 645004

Family OCTOPODIDAE

Diagnostic features Octopus are cephalopods with 8 arms. They lack fins on the mantle. Those in the family Octopodidae can be distinguished from other octopus by having a firm body, no cirri on the arms and the web normal, reduced or absent. Southern octopus have long, approximately equal arms with slender tips. Maori octopus have long arms with slender tips but of unequal lengths. Pale octopus are chunky in appearance, with stout arms sub-equal in length.[1] Gloomy octopus have long arms unequal in length, with slender tips.[2]

Distribution

Three of these octopus — southern octopus, Maori octopus and pale octopus — are distributed in temperate waters around south-eastern Australia. Southern octopus and pale octopus have a similar distribution around the mainland from Sydney to west of Ceduna in South Australia. These 2 species are also present off the north and east coasts of Tasmania.

The distribution of the Maori octopus is similar, but it extends as far north as Tuncurry in New South Wales and around Tasmania. Gloomy octopus are common along the eastern and western coasts of the continent from Brisbane to Eden on the east coast, and from Albany to Exmouth Gulf on the west coast.[2] All 4 species are endemic to Australian waters.

Southern octopus inhabit seagrass beds in bays and coastal waters.[3]

Similarly, gloomy octopus inhabit seagrass beds as well as coastal reefs.[4] Pale octopus are primarily an inshore species where they live on sandy substrates, but they have been recorded in a depth of 275 m.[5] Maori octopus live both inshore on coastal reefs and as far as off the continental shelf, and the species has been recorded from a depth of 549 m.

Life history

All octopus have a short life cycle in which each female produces 1 egg mass and dies soon after the eggs have hatched. Gloomy octopus females store the spermatozoa for 2–16 weeks following copulation.[6] A 2.1 kg female will produce up to 150 000 eggs,[6] which average 2.4 mm long and are usually laid in darkness over a period of several days. The eggs are attached to the substrate in strings[7] or 'festoons'; the planktonic larvae hatch 4 to 9 weeks later.[6] The female octopus dies 5–20 days after all the eggs have hatched.[6]

Female Maori octopus produce large numbers of small ovoid eggs (a brood of 7000, 4–6 mm long eggs has been reported).[8] The eggs are attached to the substrate in clusters of 3–10 eggs and hatching occurs 11 weeks after laying. The larvae are approximately 7 mm long when they hatch and they swim towards light. The larvae swim actively near the surface in the days following hatching. In common with many other octopus species, Maori octopus females exhibit strong care of the egg brood, and eat little during this period.

Southern octopus and pale octopus produce considerably larger eggs, at 9 mm to 14 mm[9] (southern octopus) and 11 to 13 mm[5] (pale octopus) in length. In each species, the eggs are attached singly to the substrate.[5,9] A female southern octopus produces only 1 brood of 50 to

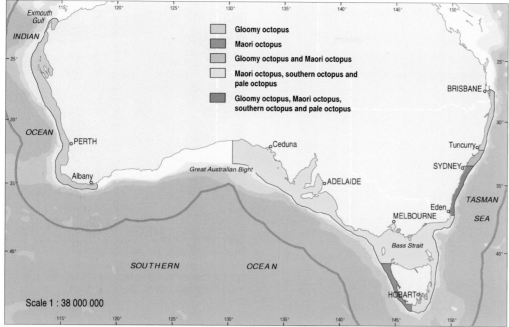

Geographic distribution for southern octopus, Maori octopus, pale octopus and gloomy octopus.

Gloomy octopus
Maori octopus
Gloomy octopus and Maori octopus
Maori octopus, southern octopus and pale octopus
Gloomy octopus, Maori octopus, southern octopus and pale octopus

130 eggs in summer. The eggs are attached to old oyster (*Saccostrea* species) shells or similar substrates and hatch after about 14 weeks. The larvae weigh less than 0.1 g and are thought to be benthic dwellers.[9]

Maori octopus are the largest of the 4 species, growing to 120 cm in total length and weighing up to 9 kg.[1] Gloomy octopus grow to 80 cm in total length (mantle length 16 cm) and weigh up to 3 kg.[2] Males mature at 100–150 g weight with females being larger at maturity. Southern octopus reach 35 cm in total length and 300 g in weight.[1] Males grow considerably larger than females yet mature earlier, at 10–13 g (females weigh 40–60 g at maturity).[3] Pale octopus grow to 35 cm total length (mantle length 15 cm) and a weight of 800 g. Males of this species mature when 5 cm in mantle length, while females mature at 6 cm mantle length.[5]

Southern octopus are solitary animals, and are often very active during daylight. They live for 18 to 20 months.[3] Similar information on the life span of the other species is lacking.

Maori octopus and gloomy octopus are major predators of rock lobsters (Palinuridae). The smaller southern octopus feed mainly on isopod crustaceans, although the diet includes other crustaceans, gastropod and bivalve molluscs, polychaete worms and other octopus.[9] There is no information on the diet of pale octopus. In turn, whiskery shark (*Furgaleus macki*) is a major predator of octopus.[10]

Stock structure

There is no information on the stock structure of these octopus species. The taxonomic status of Australian octopus species is unclear.

Commercial fishery

Generally, interest in commercial harvesting of octopus in Australia is based on reducing predation within the valuable rock lobster fisheries. In New South Wales, octopus are a significant bycatch in trawl fisheries, especially for prawns.

In Victoria, pale octopus are taken as an incidental catch by inshore demersal otter trawlers and Danish seiners. Danish seiners also take small quantities of other octopus species. Small quantities of southern octopus have also been taken in scallop dredges and beach seining operations in Port Phillip Bay. This species is of little commercial value due to its small size and it is usually sold as bait.[3]

There is also a small-scale fishery for pale octopus in Tasmania. Long lines are set with plastic pots along the north and east coasts and they take most of the commercial catch. Small amounts are landed as incidental catch from southern rock lobster (*Jasus edwardsii*) pots. There is also a seasonal catch in the south-east of Tasmania where inshore aggregations of octopus are targeted.

Large quantities of octopus, mainly Maori octopus, are caught in South Australia where they form a major bycatch of the rock lobster fishery.[11] A similar situation exists in the Western Australian western rock lobster (*Panulirus cygnus*) fishery.[12]

In Western Australia there is a small developmental fishery targeting octopus between Augusta and Shark Bay. It takes mostly gloomy octopus. The octopus traps are set on long lines and cleared once or twice a week.[13] Traditional earthenware pots have been replaced by traps made from PVC pipe as they are more robust and easier to handle. The pipes have multiple openings that increase catch rates and efficiency.[14] Catches are best between January and June.[11,12] The octopus are either landed

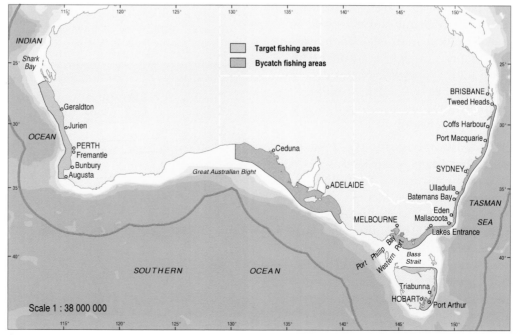

Target fishing areas
Bycatch fishing areas

Commercial fishery areas for southern octopus, Maori octopus, pale octopus and gloomy octopus.

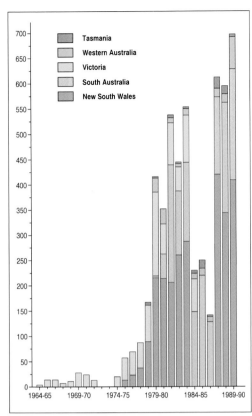

Total annual catch in t of octopus for the period 1964–65 to 1989–90 in Australia. Figures are unavailable for: New South Wales from 1984–85 to 1986–87; and Victoria from 1972–73 to 1973–74 and 1985–86 to 1989–90. Catches for States that average less than 5 % of the total for all States are not shown. (Source: Fisheries Resources Atlas Statistical Database)

live or processed at sea and frozen on landing. The total octopus catch from Western Australia in 1991–92 was 93 t. Most of the catch is exported to Japan.

Experimental commercial trapping of octopus has also been carried out in Tasmania and Victoria.[3,15]

Apart from the Western Australian catch, most octopus caught are sold on the domestic market, either for human consumption or for bait. The mid 1992 price at the Sydney Fish Market averaged A$ 2.90 per kg (whole). In Western Australia, 1992 prices averaged A$ 3.00–4.50 per kg.

Management controls The Western Australian fishery is managed as a developmental fishery. The fishery has limited entry with restrictions on the number of pots that can be set. The fishery is opened for a restricted season to coincide with the opening of the western rock lobster fishery. As the catches in other States are bycatch and incidental, the restrictions that apply to the parent fishery (eg the southern rock lobster fishery) apply also to the octopus harvest. There are no controls specific to octopus.

Recreational fishery

There is no recreational fishery for octopus, although they may be taken occasionally for use as bait.

Resource status

No studies have been conducted on the size of the octopus resource in Australia.

References

1. Stranks, T. (1986) Study of the octopuses of south-eastern Australia. *SAFISH* **10**(3): 9.

2. Roper, C.F.E., Sweeney, M.J., and Nauen, C.E. (1984) FAO species catalogue. Vol. 3. Cephalopods of the world. An annotated and illustrated catalogue of species of interest to fisheries. *FAO Fisheries Synopsis 125*, **3**. 277 pp.

3. Winstanley, R.H., Potter, M.A. and Caton, A.E. (1983) Australian cephalopod resources. Pp 243–253, in *Proceedings of the workshop on the biology and resource potential of cephalopods, Melbourne, Australia, 9–13 March 1981. Memoirs of the National Museum of Victoria* **44**.

4. Joll, L.M. (1977) Growth and food intake of *Octopus tetricus* (Mollusca: Cephalopoda) in aquaria. *Australian Journal of Marine and Freshwater Research* **28**: 45–56.

5. Stranks, T.N. (1988) Redescription of *Octopus pallidus* (Cephalopoda: Octopodidae) from south-eastern Australia. *Malacologia* **29**(1): 275–287.

6. Joll, L.M. (1976) Mating, egg laying and hatching of *Octopus tetricus* (Mollusca: Cephalopoda) in the laboratory. *Marine Biology* **36**: 327–333.

7. Joll, L.M. (1983) *Octopus tetricus*. Pp 325–334, in *Cephalopod life cycles. Vol. 1. Species accounts*. Ed by P.R. Boyle. London: Academic Press.

8. Batham, E.J. (1957) Care of eggs of *Octopus maorum. Transactions of the Royal Society of New Zealand* **84**(3): 629–638.

Commercial octopus catch; a traditional clay pot trap can be seen on the deck. (Source: Australian Fisheries Management Authority)

Tasmanian fishers use these cast plastic octopus pots which are more durable than traditional clay pots. (Source: Lindsay Chapman, Bureau of Resource Sciences)

9. Tait, R.W. (1982) A taxonomic revision of *Octopus australis* Hoyle, 1885 (Octopodidae: Cephalopoda), with a redescription of the species. *Memoirs of the National Museum of Victoria* **43**(1): 15–23.

10. Stevens, J.D. (1991) Preliminary study of Western Australian commercial sharks. *CSIRO Division of Fisheries, Marine Laboratories, Internal Report.* 16 pp, 12 figs.

11. Jones, G.K., Hall, D.A., Hill, K.L. and Staniford, A.J. (1990). *The South Australian marine scale fishery: stock assessment, economics, management*. South Australian Department of Fisheries, Green paper. 186 pp.

12. Joll, L.M. (1977) The predation of pot-caught western rock lobster (*Panulirus longipes cygnus*) by octopus. *Western Australian Fisheries and Wildlife Report* **29**. 58 pp.

13. Kimura, Y. (1980) *Report on the second-phase survey for commercial harvesting of octopuses in Western Australian waters*. National Federation of Fisheries Cooperative Associations of Japan. 47 pp.

14. Kimura, Y. and Isomae, H. (1981) *Report on the third-phase survey for commercial harvesting of octopuses in Western Australian waters*. National Federation of Fisheries Cooperative Associations of Japan. 77 pp.

15. Winstanley, R.H. and Kearney, J. (1982) Experimental and exploratory octopus trapping in Port Phillip Bay, December 1980–April 1981. *Victorian Fisheries and Wildlife Division, Commercial Fisheries Report* **7**. 13 pp.

Contributors

The information on this species was originally provided by Tim Stranks. General drawing by Leslie Newman. (*Details of contributors and their organisations are given in the Acknowledgements section at the back of this book.*)

Compilers Alex McNee and Patricia Kailola

Antarctic krill

Euphausia superba

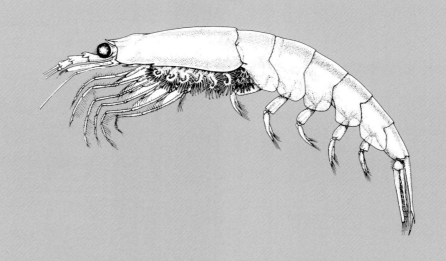

Euphausia superba Dana

Antarctic krill

Another common name is **krill**.
FAO: **Antarctic krill**
Australian species code: 905301

Family EUPHAUSIIDAE

Diagnostic features Antarctic krill are large euphausiid shrimps, similar in appearance to other decapod shrimps. However, they have luminous organs at the base of each pair of swimming legs and feathery gills exposed at the base of the carapace. Krill vary in colour from transparent or white to red[1] or green (after feeding).

Distribution

Antarctic krill are distributed in the waters of the Antarctic continental shelf and as far north as the Antarctic Convergence (the oceanic front caused by the sharp change in water temperature when cold Antarctic waters meet warmer northern waters). Antarctic krill are most abundant south of latitude 60° S.[2] They usually live in the top 40 m of the water column, although there are anecdotal accounts of their presence in the hyperbenthic layer

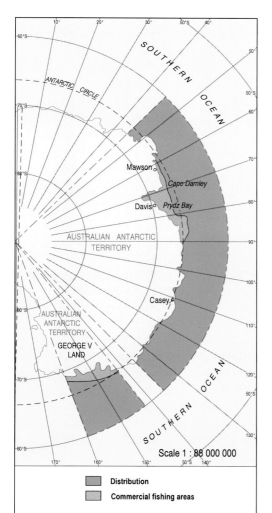

Geographic distribution and commercial fishing areas for krill in Australian Antarctic Territory waters.

(ie just above the sea floor) at depths greater than 500 m. They are often associated with the edge of the continental shelf, island groups and oceanic frontal features. Adults have been found associated with the underside of ice in winter, spring and early summer.

Krill often live in vast swarms which can be tens of km long and have a biomass of thousands of t.

Life history

Spawning takes place from November to March each year in surface waters over the continental shelf. Up to 10 000 eggs can be shed into the water column by a single spawning female. Females are capable of producing over 20 000 eggs during the spawning period, and spawning may take place several times in this period.

The 0.8 mm diameter eggs may sink to depths greater than 3000 m. On hatching the developing larvae swim towards the surface layer of the water[2] where they complete their larval and juvenile development. The larval krill grow through several stages in the first year and schooling begins in the later larval stages. The pelagic juvenile krill inhabit waters both on and beyond the continental shelf.

Antarctic krill are one of the larger euphausiid shrimps and have been recorded up to 6 cm in length and 1 g in weight. Male and female krill mature at 2 years of age when they are 3 cm long and weigh 0.4 g and 0.5 g respectively. The maximum recorded age of Antarctic krill from laboratory studies is 11 years.

Antarctic krill are strong vertical migrators. They can be found from depths of 10 m to 40 m (occasionally as deep as 150 m) during the day, moving to within 10 m of the surface at night. Being near the surface enables them to feed on the abundant phytoplankton, and at the same time reduces the risk of predation. This surface aggregation also allows swarms of Antarctic krill to intermix for mating.[2] Antarctic krill may also form daytime surface aggregations for reasons which are unknown. Swarms may be predominantly adults, juveniles, a single sex,[2] or a mixture of these. They can be quite concentrated, at densities of up to 20 kg of krill in 1 cubic m of water.[3] Horizontal migrations by krill of hundreds of km have also been observed, but these may be caused by water movements rather than by active swimming.

Both juvenile and adult Antarctic krill feed on phytoplankton and ice algae. Antarctic krill are an important food item in Antarctic food chains, forming a large part of the diet of baleen whales (Mysticeti), crabeater seals (*Lobodon carcinophagus*), penguins (Spheniscidae) and other seabirds, fish and squid.[2]

Stock structure

Despite the occurrence of population concentrations in several well separated areas, no significant genetic difference between these populations has been demonstrated. Analysis of the mitochondrial DNA of krill is currently being used to determine stock structure. At present it appears unlikely that there are separate stocks.[4]

Commercial fishery

The Antarctic krill fishery began in the early 1970s and peaked in the early 1980s. Most of the commercial Antarctic krill catches are made by vessels from Japan or the Commonwealth of Independent States (CIS) of the former USSR. Within the Australian Antarctic Territory catches of Antarctic krill have been taken by pelagic trawling in the Prydz Bay region and off George V Land, with most fishing effort concentrated on the shelf break. Historically, most of the commercial catch has come from the Atlantic sector of the Southern Ocean, but the Indian Ocean sector, which encompasses the Australian Antarctic Territory, has also yielded high tonnages in some years. Almost any region of the Southern Ocean can yield commercial quantities of Antarctic krill.

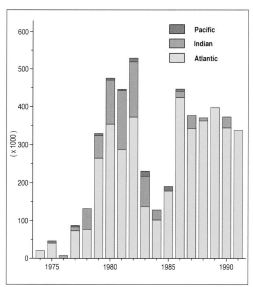

Total annual catch in t of Antarctic krill for the period 1974 to 1991 by sectors of the Southern Ocean. (Source: Steve Nicol, Australian Antarctic Division)

Lowering an experimental midwater krill trawl for sea trials. (Source: Steve Nicol, Australian Antarctic Division)

Antarctic krill decompose rapidly when out of the water and need to be processed or frozen within 3 hours of capture for human consumption or within 10 hours for animal feed products. Therefore, Antarctic krill fishing vessels are large (70 to 100 m) freezer-trawlers, equipped for onboard processing.[3] Mid-water trawling using a conventional stern trawler rig towing a fine mesh net with a large mouth area (400–500 m^2) has been found to be the most efficient method of catching Antarctic krill.[5] Swarms of Antarctic krill are located using echo sounders. The trawl nets are set on these targets, towing at speeds of less than 3 knots. The Japanese vessels aim to take 7 t to 10 t per haul, while vessels from the CIS take 3 t to 8 t. Vessels limit the duration of trawls to avoid catching more Antarctic krill than they can process. New fishing grounds are sought when catches fall below 50 t per day.[3]

Antarctic krill are fished in the Indian Ocean in the summer and autumn months and off South Georgia in the Southern Atlantic Ocean in winter and spring. Swarms of non-feeding adults are targeted for capture. Fishers avoid areas where Antarctic krill are feeding as the catch will be tinted green and have a 'grassy' taste.[3] Japanese fishers may target egg bearing females as they are considered to be a prime product with the richest flavour.

The main problem with using Antarctic krill for food is that there are extremely high levels of fluoride in the shell, so the animals must be peeled

before they can be processed into a food product. Many Antarctic krill products have been tried, including protein pastes and minced krill. The most valuable products are based on the whole animal.[3] There are established markets in Japan and the CIS for Antarctic krill, mainly as peeled tails, frozen and tinned, and also boiled or frozen whole. Antarctic krill are also processed to produce meal for domestic animals and for aquaculture. Using current technology in onboard peeling, Japanese fishers achieve yields of 10 to 25 % tail meat. The meat is light pink in colour, has a shellfish aroma, a springy texture and a sweet shellfish taste.[6] The Antarctic krill catch from all sectors of the Southern Ocean was estimated to be worth A\$ 300.00 per t in 1990.

Several by-products of the Antarctic krill fishery, although not currently used, may in the future prove to be worth more than the meat product. Antarctic krill contain several protein-destroying enzymes which could be used in the treatment of wounds and ulcers. Chitin in the shells can be altered to form 'chitosan' which has the ability to coagulate protein and bond with heavy metals, giving it possible uses in the treatment of waste water. When used in human wound dressings, chitosan has also been found to accelerate healing.[5]

Management controls All resources in Antarctic waters are under the control of the international Convention for the Conservation of Antarctic Marine Living Resources (CCAMLR), as well as under national governments to the extent of their jurisdiction. At present, there are no catch restrictions in force in Australian Antarctic Territory waters, but vessels wishing to fish in these waters require permits, as resources are protected under the Commonwealth Antarctic Marine Resources Act. CCAMLR is currently debating catch limitations on the krill fishery. Any limits on total allowable catch are likely to be considerably above the current catch levels.

Recreational fishery

There is no recreational fishery for Antarctic krill.

Resource status

The current catch of Antarctic krill from all sectors of the Southern Ocean is nearly 400 000 t per year.[2] Catch levels have fluctuated, even while processing technology has been developed for Antarctic krill. The size of the Antarctic krill stock is uncertain, but estimates have put it as high as 7000 million t. It is estimated that late last century whales consumed around 190 million t of Antarctic krill a year. Intensive whaling activity and the consequent decline in

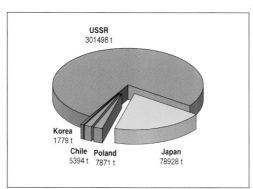

Proportions of Antarctic krill catch taken by each fishing nation in 1988–89. (Source: Steve Nicol, Australian Antarctic Division)

whale numbers may have resulted in a huge surplus of Antarctic krill (millions of t) that can be harvested by man. Much of this resource, however, is being consumed by other Antarctic animals whose numbers have increased.

There is a large potential fishery for Antarctic krill in the Southern Ocean, provided that the harvesting and processing operations are economic.[3] Catches have remained stable for the last 4 years and are likely to remain at this level for a few more years as the market becomes accustomed to Antarctic krill. There is, however, serious concern over the effects of the fishery on the other animals of the Antarctic ecosystem — most of which depend on krill, directly or indirectly, for food.

References

1. Nicol, S. (1991) Krill fishing in Antarctica, is it a no-frill affair? *Australian Fisheries* **50**(9): 30–31.

2. Kirkwood, J.M. (1982) A guide to the Euphausidae of the Southern Ocean. *ANARE Research Notes* **1**. 45 pp.

3. Nicol, S. (1990) Antarctic marine living resources. *Maritime Studies* **53**: 1–10.

4. Miller, D.G.M. and Hampton, I. (1989) Biology and ecology of the Antarctic krill, *Euphausia superba* (Dana): a review. *BIOMASS Scientific Series* **9**. 166 pp.

5. O'Sullivan, D. (1983) Fisheries of the Southern Ocean. *Australian Fisheries* **42**(7): 4–11.

6. Nicol, S. (1989) Who's counting on krill? *New Scientist* **1690**: 38–41.

Contributors

Most of the information on this species was originally provided by Steve Nicol. Drawing courtesy of FAO, Rome. (*Details of contributors and their organisations are given in the Acknowledgements section at the back of this book.*)
Compilers Alex McNee and Christina Grieve

Royal red prawn

Haliporoides sibogae

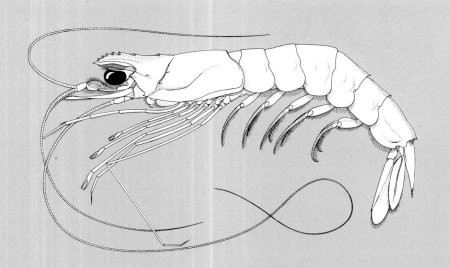

Haliporoides sibogae (de Man)

Royal red prawn

Other common names include **pink prawn, royal red** and **jack-knife prawn**.
FAO: **jack-knife shrimp**
Australian species code: 701004

Family SOLENOCERIDAE

Diagnostic features Royal red prawns are uniformly pale pink. Their antennae are equal in length and cylindrical in cross-section. The rostrum extends forward past the eye and there is 1 small tooth below the rostrum tip. There are 3 small spines on the side of the carapace.

Life history

Two spawning periods have been identified for royal red prawns off New South Wales: February to April and July to August. Little is known of spawning behaviour or larval development and individuals smaller than 20 mm carapace length are not usually found in trawl catches.[7] Preliminary results from biological sampling of prawns in New South Wales waters indicate the presence of a spawning ground north of latitude 33° S. Royal red prawns tend to produce fewer eggs than do other prawn (Penaeidae) species but their eggs are larger.

Distribution

Royal red prawns live in the Indian and western Pacific oceans in the waters of New Zealand, Madagascar, Japan and Australia.[1] The species has been recorded from the eastern and western waters of the Australian Fishing Zone. In the east, royal red prawns have been caught on the Queensland Plateau, east of Cairns[2] and from the Saumarez Plateau off Rockhampton[3] to the east of Lakes Entrance in Victoria, with some unconfirmed reports of catches further south off the Tasmanian coast. In western waters the distribution extends from the northern limit of the continental slope south to Fremantle.[4]

Royal red prawns are reported to inhabit depths from 100 m to 1500 m[1] although they have only been caught in waters of 230 m to 825 m in the Australian Fishing Zone.[5] Abundance is normally greatest between 365 m and 550 m with some evidence of a movement to the shallower depths during winter.[6] The prawns are found on mud substrates close to the sea bed with no evidence of migration through the water column.

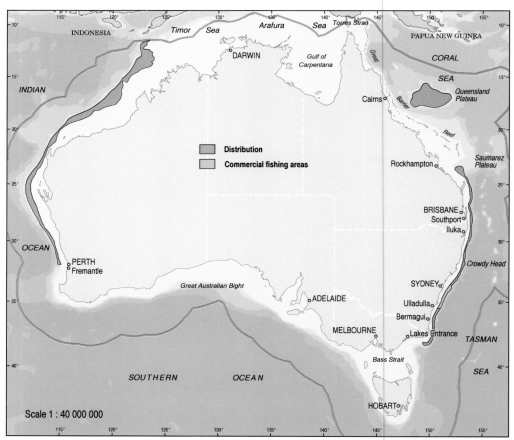

Geographic distribution and commercial fishing area for royal red prawns in Australian waters.

Royal red prawns appear to be long-lived in comparison with penaeid prawn species and at least 3 size classes can be distinguished in catches. However, it is unclear whether these size classes represent the annual recruitment into the fishery.[7] Different growth patterns are evident for each sex, with females reaching a maximum size of 200 mm total length (49 mm carapace length) and males 165 mm (33 mm carapace length).[1,5] Royal red prawns are sexually mature at about 25 mm carapace length (females) and 21 mm carapace length (males). Male prawns appear to spawn only once but females may spawn on a few occasions during their lifetime. The ratio of males to females is approximately 1:1 in depths where abundance is highest but varies with size of the prawns and depth of capture. Furthermore, there is some evidence that sex reversal occurs in royal red prawns.

Royal red prawns have a diet similar to other prawns, feeding on small molluscs, crustaceans and polychaete worms. They are preyed upon by demersal fish species such as blue grenadier (*Macruronus novaezelandiae*), pink ling (*Genypterus blacodes*), gemfish (*Rexea solandri*), ocean perch (*Helicolenus* species) and blue eye (*Hyperoglyphe antarctica*).

Stock structure

Taxonomic studies of royal red prawns from eastern Australia have confirmed that they represent a distinct subspecies from the royal red prawns from the Indian Ocean, and they have been named *Haliporoides sibogae australiensis*.[8] The taxonomic status of royal red prawns from Western Australian waters is presently unclear.

Commercial fishery

A survey of deepwater trawl grounds off New South Wales carried out by the NSW Fisheries research vessel *Kapala* in 1971 confirmed the presence of commercial quantities of royal red prawns.

Exploitation of the grounds began in 1975 with only a few trawlers, but since 1980 more fishing effort has been devoted to target fishing for the prawns. The main fishing ground for royal red prawns lies off the central New South Wales coast between latitudes 34° S and 35° S in depths of 400 m to 500 m. This limited

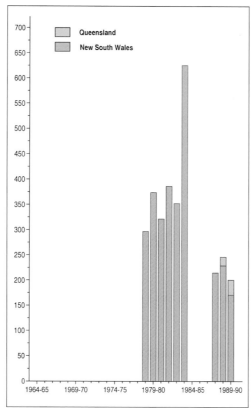

Total annual catch in t of royal red prawns for the period 1964–65 to 1989–90. Figures are unavailable for: New South Wales from 1964–65 to 1977–78 and 1984–85 to 1986–87; Queensland from 1964–65 to 1986–87; and Western Australia for 1964–65 to 1989–90. (Source: Fisheries Resources Atlas Statistical Database)

area is subject to target fishing by trawlers using single demersal otter trawl nets. The vessels used are primarily fish trawlers that target the prawns during summer.[6]

Royal red prawns are also present on grounds from Crowdy Head to Sydney but they are not usually targeted because of the presence of significant inshore resources of penaeid prawns. Prawns are also caught by prawn trawl vessels operating off Iluka on the north coast of New South Wales. The north coast vessels use triple-rigged demersal otter trawls and target the royal red prawns when catches of school prawns (*Metapenaeus macleayi*) and eastern king prawns (*Penaeus plebejus*) on inshore grounds are low. Some commercial catches have been taken by trawlers working off Southport in southern Queensland.

Off north-western Australia, royal red prawns are also caught by trawl vessels in continental slope waters. The fishery has developed only since early 1985 and was originally for scampi (*Metanephrops* species). Now it is a fishery based on scampi and deepwater prawns. The main prawn species in this North West Slope Trawl Fishery is the red prawn (*Aristaeomorpha foliacea*). The royal red prawn catch has ranged between 20 t and 50 t since 1985–86, representing between 5 % and 10 % of total catches for the fishery.[9,10] Some catches of royal red prawns have been taken in the Western Deep-Water Trawl Fishery further south to as far as Fremantle,[4] but development of this fishery has been slower than the North West Slope Trawl Fishery.

Large catch of royal red prawns taken by FRV *Kapala*. (Source: Ken Graham, Fisheries Research Institute, NSW Fisheries)

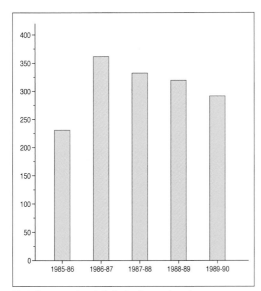

Total annual catch in t of royal red prawns from the South East Fishery for the period 1985–86 to 1989–90. Catch records for 1985–86 are incomplete. (Source: Australian Fishing Zone Information System)

A number of other prawn species are taken in association with royal red prawns, mainly the red prawn, scarlet prawn (*Plesiopenaeus edwardsianus*) and a smaller related species (*Haliporoides cristatus*) in eastern waters.[6] Dogfishes (Squalidae) and ocean perch are the main fish bycatch in New South Wales.[6] In Western Australian waters royal red prawns are taken with red prawn, scarlet prawn, scampi, pink-striped prawn (*Aristeus virilis*) and 2 species of carid prawn, *Heterocarpus sibogae* and *H. woodmasoni*.[9] Squid comprise the bulk of the non-crustacean catch in western waters. Small numbers of royal red prawns are also caught as bycatch in demersal fish trawls.

Annual catches of royal red prawns from New South Wales waters are currently in the range of 300 t to 350 t. Some is being exported to Japan. Royal red prawns are sold as uncooked whole prawns or in packs of frozen meat. They require more care in handling than do other prawn species due to their fragile shell.[11] However, prompt sorting and refrigeration of the prawns will yield a quality product with excellent flavour. The average price to fishers for frozen royal red prawns in mid 1992 was A\$ 3.07 per kg.

Management controls Management of the royal red prawn stocks is a responsibility of the Commonwealth of Australia as part of the South East Fishery in New South Wales waters south of latitude 33°25' S. Fishers trawling for royal red prawns in northern New South Wales are regulated by the State Government. The North West Slope Trawl Fishery and the Western Deep-Water Trawl Fishery are administered by the Commonwealth of Australia.

Recreational fishery

Royal red prawns are not caught by recreational fishers.

Resource status

Catch rates for royal red prawns in New South Wales have been consistent since the start of the fishery, indicating that the exploited stock has not been significantly affected by earlier levels of fishing.[7,12] However, more information about royal red prawn behaviour and patterns of abundance is required. The status of the resource off Western Australia is unknown.

References

1. Holthuis, L.B. (1980) FAO species catalogue. Vol. 1. Shrimps and prawns of the world. An annotated catalogue of species of interest to fisheries. *FAO Fisheries Synopsis No. 125*, **1**. 261 pp.

2. Williams, G. (1990) Exploratory fishing on Queensland Plateau. *Australian Fisheries* **49**(1): 30–31.

3. Dredge, M. and Gardiner, P. (1984) Survey discovers new central Qld prawning grounds. *Australian Fisheries* **43**(1): 16–19.

4. Jernakoff, P. (1988) The western and north west shelf deep-water trawl fisheries: research priorities. *Bureau of Rural Resources Bulletin* **1**. 33 pp.

5. Gorman, T.B. and Graham, K.J. (1975) Deep water prawn survey off New South Wales. Pp 207–212, in *First Australian national prawn seminar*. Ed by P.C. Young. Canberra: Australian Government Publishing Service.

6. Graham, K.J. and Gorman, T.B. (1985) New South Wales deepwater prawn fishery research and development. Pp 231–243, in *Second Australian national prawn seminar*. Ed by P.C. Rothlisberg, B.J. Hill and D.J. Staples. Cleveland, Australia.

7. Baelde, P. (in press, 1992) Royal red prawn. In *The South East Trawl Fishery: a scientific review with particular reference to quota management*. Ed by R.D.J. Tilzey. *Bureau of Resource Sciences Bulletin*.

8. Kensley, B., Tranter, H.A. and Griffin, D.J.G. (1987) Deepwater decapod crustacea from eastern Australia (Penaeidea and Caridea). *Records of the Australian Museum* **39**: 263–331.

9. Wallner, B. and Phillips, B. (1988) From scampi to deepwater prawns: developments in the North West Shelf deepwater trawl fishery. *Australian Fisheries* **47**(9): 34–38.

10. Phillips, B. and Jernakoff, P. (1991) The north west slope trawl fishery. What future does it have? *Australian Fisheries* **50**(7): 18–20.

11. Freeman, D.J., Gorman, T., Whitfield, F.B. and Graham, K. (1981) Royal red prawns reward careful handling. *Australian Fisheries* **40**(10): 47–49.

12. Baelde, P. (1991) Assessment of the Australian deep-water royal red prawn stock using commercial catch and effort data. *Fisheries Research* **12**: 243–258.

Contributors

Most of the information on this species was provided by Pascale Baelde and supplemented by (in alphabetical order) Ken Graham, Kevin Rowling, Richard Tilzey and Geoff Williams. Drawing by W. Richard Webber. (*Details of contributors and their organisations are given in the Acknowledgements section at the back of this book.*)

Compiler Phillip Stewart

Royal red prawn. (Source: David Evans, CSIRO Marine Laboratories, North Beach)

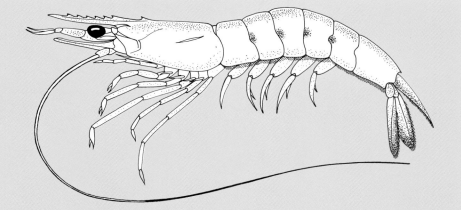

Greasyback prawn

Metapenaeus bennettae

Metapenaeus bennettae
Racek and Dall

Greasyback prawn

Other common names include
greentail prawn, bay prawn and
greasy.
FAO: **greentail shrimp**
Australian species code: 701323

Family PENAEIDAE

Diagnostic features Greasyback prawns
are small, inshore prawns distinguished
from other species of *Metapenaeus* by the
absence of obvious spines on the telson.
They have an ischial spine (as a small,
blunt angle) on the inside edge of the first
legs. The sides of the abdomen have
well-defined areas of fine hair. The body is
semi-transparent and speckled with dark
brown, the antennae are red to brown and
there are green tips on the uropods and
pleopods on the underside of the abdomen.[1]

Distribution

Greasyback prawns are endemic to
eastern Australian shallow coastal waters
from Rockhampton in Queensland to
eastern Victoria.[1] The greatest abundance
of greasybacks is between latitudes 32°S
and 37°S, and they generally live over
soft, muddy bottoms rich in organic
detritus. Greasyback prawns are found
predominantly in embayments in
estuaries and coastal lakes, and to sea in
depths to 22 m, as well as in coastal rivers.

Greasyback prawns live in different
habitats depending on their life cycle
stage. Postlarvae inhabit calm upstream
waters, mangrove canals or intertidal
seagrass areas, preferring a warm,
sheltered locality with abundant algal
cover and salinity below 20 parts per
thousand.[2] They have been found as far
as 35 km upstream in the Noosa River.[3]
Subadults inhabit shallow mangrove
creeks. Adult habitat extends from rivers
out to sea. Prawns caught in coastal
waters are generally larger than those
caught in rivers. Juvenile male greasyback
prawns tend to leave rivers during
periods of heavy rainfall, forming
concentrations outside river mouths.[2]
Mature female greasyback prawns inhabit
coastal embayments, bays or exposed
waters.[2,4]

Life history

There has not been a detailed study of the
reproduction of this species. Mating
probably occurs in or around river
mouths and shallow coastal waters, and
eggs may be spawned in comparatively
shallow water, possibly around the full
moon.[5] Spawning in the Moreton Bay
region appears to be either extended or to
occur throughout the year, as juvenile
greasyback prawns are present in nursery
grounds almost all year.

The eggs sink to the bottom and after
12–24 hours hatch into a non-feeding

nauplius larval stage. After 2 more larval
stages lasting up to 2 weeks, the
postlarval stage is reached. Postlarvae
enter shallow nursery grounds about 3 or
4 weeks after hatching.

The age at sexual maturity for
greasyback prawns is estimated as 12–15
months, at 16 mm carapace length (or
about 4 g weight) for males and 20 mm
carapace length (about 6 g) for females.[2]
Females attain 110 mm total length and
males reach 80 mm.[6] Studies of these
prawns in rivers[2,3,4] revealed difficulties
in measuring their growth. Because there
is a significant relationship between
greasyback prawn size and distance
upstream from a river mouth,[4] it is
deduced that those greasyback prawns
that enter rivers grow as they move
downstream. This species does not
perform a large-scale migration.

The diet of greasyback prawns has not
been analysed, but they are probably
opportunistic omnivores (ie they feed on
the variety of mainly detrital organic
matter as it becomes available).
Greasyback prawns are probably eaten
by many inshore finfish, including skates
and rays (Batoidea).

Stock structure

Because of the lack of tagging and other
migratory studies on greasyback prawns,

it is not possible to comment on specific
stock differentiation. A study[1] on the
genetic structure of greasybacks from 6
locations from Rockhampton to Lake
Macquarie indicated that stocks differ
over large distances. Therefore, there is
probably only very limited migration and
'mixing' of gene pools.

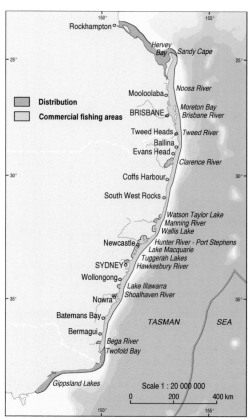

Geographic distribution and commercial
fishing areas for greasyback prawns.

Commercial fishery

In Moreton Bay, greasyback prawns have been of major commercial importance since 1949. They are the most abundant prawn species trawled from the rivers in south-eastern Queensland, including Moreton Bay. For example, about 100 t were taken from the Brisbane River alone in 1983.[4] To the present day, greasyback prawns have contributed significantly to the trawled prawn landings in Moreton Bay: estimated to range from 38 % to 56 % of landings.[7] Because fishers do not sort or record their prawn catches on a taxonomic basis, there is uncertainty of the actual (or species specific) landings of this and other prawn species for Queensland.

Greasyback prawns are trawled mainly at night. The species is exploited principally by beam trawl in rivers and by demersal otter trawl in Moreton Bay. Prawns caught by beam trawling are small and usually supply the bait market. Otter trawl vessels are up to 14 m in length and capture prawns of a larger size and in greater depths within Moreton Bay. Greasyback prawns caught by otter trawl are marketed for local consumption as fresh 'bay prawns'. Smaller prawns are known locally as 'bays' while larger prawns are classed as 'bay kings'.

In New South Wales, greasyback prawns are the fourth most important species taken in the State's prawn fishery,[8] although they comprised only 2 % by weight and value of the State prawn catch between 1983–84 and 1986–87. They are taken by several methods including set pocket netting, haul seining and snigging from boats 4–14 m long.[9]

Management controls In Moreton Bay, there are limitations on the number and size of trawl nets per vessel, mesh size and boat length. A limited number of licences is issued for the Queensland east coast, and there are area, seasonal and weekend closures within Moreton Bay. The number of river beam trawlers is limited and net size and mesh limitations apply. Similar limits on vessel numbers and areas are in effect in New South Wales. The prawn fishery in Queensland is closed to further entry.

Recreational fishery

There is no significant recreational fishery for greasyback prawns in Queensland, although small catches may be taken by cast nets off jetties or from small boats in very shallow water. There is no information on the species composition of prawn catches by recreational fishers in New South Wales.

Management controls There are no restrictions.

Resource status

The status of greasyback prawns is unknown. In Queensland, there appear to be several times more greasybacks taken by otter trawl in Moreton Bay than by beam trawl in adjacent rivers. However, an accurate assessment of landings is not available because fishers sort their catches by size rather than by species.

Beam trawler, Brisbane River. (Source: Glen Smith, Southern Fisheries Centre, Queensland Department of Primary Industries)

2. Dall, W. (1958) Observations on the biology of the greentail prawn *Metapenaeus mastersii* (Haswell) (Crustacea: Decapoda: Penaeidae). *Australian Journal of Marine and Freshwater Research* **9**: 111–134.

3. Coles, R.G. and Greenwood, J.G. (1983) Seasonal movement and size distribution of three commercially important Australian prawn species (Crustacea: Penaeidae) within an estuarine system. *Australian Journal of Marine and Freshwater Research* **34**: 727–743.

4. Hyland, S.J. (1987) *An investigation of the nektobenthic organisms in the Logan River and Moreton Bay, Queensland with an emphasis on penaeid prawns.* Unpublished MSc thesis, University of Queensland.

5. Morris, M.C. and Bennett, I. (1952) The life history of a penaeid prawn (*Metapenaeus*) breeding in a coastal lake (Tuggerah, New South Wales). *Proceedings of the Linnean Society of New South Wales* **76**: 164–182.

6. Grey, D.L., Dall, W. and Baker, A. (1983) *A guide to the Australian penaeid prawns.* Darwin: Department of Primary Production of the Northern Territory. 140 pp.

7. Haysom, N.M. (1975) The Moreton Bay permit system. An exercise in licence limitation. Pp 240–245, in *First Australian national prawn seminar.* Ed by P.C. Young. Canberra: Australian Government Publishing Service.

8. Montgomery, S. (1988) Trends in New South Wales prawn catch. *Australian Fisheries* **47**(8): 24–30.

9. Montgomery, S. and Winstanley, R.H. (1982) Prawns (east of Cape Otway). *CSIRO Marine Laboratories, Fishery Situation Report* **6**. 15 pp.

10. Dall, W. (1957) A revision of the Australian species of Penaeinae (Crustacea: Decapoda: Penaeidae). *Australian Journal of Marine and Freshwater Research* **8**:136–231.

Contributors

Information on this species was originally provided by Tony Courtney and supplemented by Steven Montgomery and Derek Staples. Figure redrawn by Peter Moloney after Dall.[10] (*Details of contributors and their organisations are given in the Acknowledgements section at the back of this book.*)

Compilers Patricia Kailola and Christina Grieve (maps)

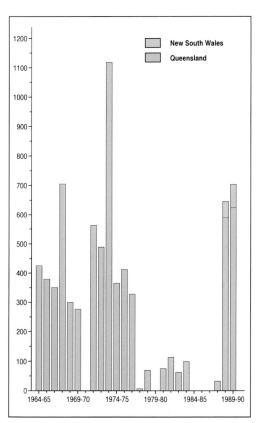

Total annual catch in t of greasyback prawns for the period 1964-65 to 1989-90. Figures are unavailable for: New South Wales from 1964–65 to 1977–78, 1979–80, 1984–85 to 1986–87; and Queensland for 1970–71 and from 1978–79 to 1987–88. Queensland figures to 1977–78 are based on a mixture of species, mostly *Metapenaeus bennettae*. The 1988–89 and 1989–90 Queensland figures are solely *M. bennettae*. (Source: Fisheries Resources Atlas Statistical Database)

References

1. Salini, J. (1987) Genetic variation and population subdivision in the greentail prawn *Metapenaeus bennettae* (Racek and Dall) [sic]. *Australian Journal of Marine and Freshwater Research* **38**: 339–349.

Endeavour prawns

This presentation is on 2 species, **blue endeavour prawns** and **red endeavour prawns**.

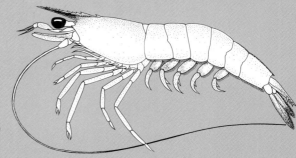

Blue endeavour prawns,
Metapenaeus endeavouri
(Schmitt)

Another common name is **blue tail endeavour prawn**.
FAO: **endeavour shrimp**
Australian species code: 701320

Red endeavour prawn,
Metapenaeus ensis
(de Haan)

Another common name is **offshore greasyback prawn**.
FAO: **greasyback shrimp**
Australian species code: 701322

Family PENAEIDAE

Diagnostic features Blue endeavour prawns can be distinguished from other *Metapenaeus* prawns by having 3 pairs of conspicuous movable spines on the telson (the sharp, triangular spike at the end of the abdomen) and by body colouration. They are generally pale brown or yellow to pink and the antennae, rostrum and abdominal ridges are red. The uropods (tail fan) are light brown to yellow-green and brilliant blue at the extremities. There are irregular patches of short hairs on their body that make it feel greasy to touch. Red endeavour prawns lack movable spines on the telson. Their body is pale brown to bright pink. Their antennae are bright red, the legs pink to red (sometimes striped) and the uropods are red.[1]

Distribution

Both species of endeavour prawns are distributed from Shark Bay in Western Australia, across northern Australia to New South Wales. Blue endeavour prawns range only as far south as Ballina in northern New South Wales, while red endeavour prawns are found in waters south to Nowra. Outside Australian waters, blue endeavour prawns inhabit only the Gulf of Papua, while red endeavour prawns are distributed throughout the Indo-West Pacific region, from Sri Lanka through Indonesian and New Guinea waters to southern China and Japan.[1]

Juvenile blue endeavour prawns are most commonly associated with seagrass beds in shallow estuaries,[2] although they occasionally are found in other areas. Juvenile red endeavour prawns occupy a wide range of habitats including seagrass beds, mangrove banks, mud flats and open channels.[2] Adult blue endeavour prawns can be found from inshore waters to depths of 50–60 m, while red endeavour prawns have been found as deep as 95 m in Joseph Bonaparte Gulf in the Northern Territory. Larger blue endeavour prawns live over sandy or sand-mud substrates. Red endeavour prawns prefer muddy substrates.[3]

Life history

Endeavour prawns spawn year round. In central Queensland, spawning peaks in March and September for blue endeavour prawns and from September to December for red endeavour prawns.[4] Blue endeavour prawns in the eastern Gulf of Carpentaria are thought to spawn offshore between September and December,[5] appearing not to undertake a shoreward migration to spawn.[6] Immature endeavour prawns in central

Queensland waters have been found in deeper water than mature prawns, but they may be moving inshore to mature and spawn.[4]

There is little information on larval development in blue endeavour prawns.[7] There are more juveniles (less than 5 mm carapace length) in inshore nursery grounds in the Gulf of Carpentaria and north Queensland between October and November than at other times of the year.[5] Small blue endeavour prawns (less than 20 mm carapace length) appear in commercial catches in the Gulf of Carpentaria between October and June. This suggests that juveniles spend only a short time in nursery areas and that migration to adult habitats occurs at a small size.[3,6] The main movement of red endeavour prawns out of nursery areas occurs between January and June.[8]

Female blue endeavour prawns are reported to grow to 47 mm carapace length,[4] while males are smaller, growing to 37 mm carapace length. Growth rates in blue endeavour prawns (at half their maximum size) from the western Gulf of Carpentaria have been estimated at 0.52 mm and 0.71 mm carapace length per week for females and males respectively.[6] Female red endeavour prawns reach 41 mm carapace length[4] and males may achieve 33 mm carapace length.

Size at maturity varies between areas. In the Gulf of Carpentaria, female blue endeavour prawns mature when quite small, at 18 mm carapace length, while female red endeavour prawns mature at 22 mm carapace length.[8] By comparison, female blue and red endeavour prawns from Queensland mature at 26 mm and

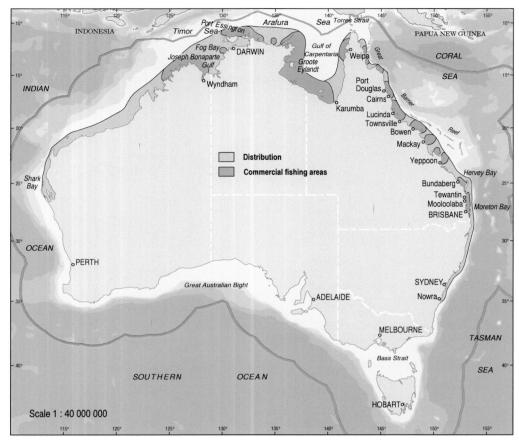

Geographic distribution and commercial fishing areas for red endeavour prawns in Australian waters.

24 mm carapace length respectively.[4] Male blue endeavour prawns in the Gulf of Carpentaria are between 19 mm and 26 mm carapace length at maturity.[8]

Endeavour prawns are benthic feeders. They are primarily carnivorous, their diet including small crustaceans, molluscs, polychaete worms and Foraminifera.[9] Endeavour prawns are eaten by squid (Loliginidae), cuttlefish (*Sepia* species) and a variety of demersal fish species.[10]

Stock structure

Studies on populations of blue endeavour prawns from Exmouth Gulf and the Gulf of Carpentaria indicate a high degree of genetic isolation between them.[11] There is only one stock in Torres Strait. There is no information on the status of endeavour prawn populations from other areas.

Commercial fishery

Blue and red endeavour prawns are taken commercially in Western Australia, the Northern Territory and Queensland (including Torres Strait). Commercial catch records do not separate the 2 species, and the proportion of each species in the catch varies between localities.

The largest catches of endeavour prawns are taken in the Gulf of Carpentaria in the Northern Prawn Fishery. In Torres Strait, blue endeavour prawns are the second most important commercial species, constituting 40 % to 50 % of the catch. The combined value of the endeavour prawn catch from the Northern Prawn and Torres Strait fisheries was A$ 8 million in 1991. By comparison, in the Queensland east coast otter trawl fishery the combined endeavour prawn catch was 21 % of the total prawn catches in 1989.[12] In Western Australia endeavour prawns are a small proportion of the mixed species catch in Shark Bay, Exmouth Gulf and the Kimberley coast areas.

Endeavour prawns are taken mostly at night by demersal otter trawling.[7] Beam trawlers are also used in rivers and specified inshore areas in the east coast otter trawl fishery.[13]

Endeavour prawns are normally taken in multi-species fisheries in which tiger prawns (*Penaeus esculentus, P. semisulcatus*) are the main target species. In Western Australian fisheries, western king prawns (*Penaeus latisulcatus*) are a major part of the catch. Saucer scallops (*Amusium* species) are also taken in conjunction with prawns in the east coast otter trawl fishery. Moreton Bay bugs (*Thenus* species), blue swimmer crabs (*Portunus pelagicus*), calamary (*Sepioteuthis* species) and whiting (*Sillago* species) are important bycatch species caught in these fisheries.[13]

Most of the catch from the Northern Prawn Fishery is exported to Japan. Catch from the east coast otter trawl fishery is exported (to Japan and Spain) or sold through domestic markets. Export prawns are usually frozen and packed in bulk. Prawns for the domestic market are cooked and stored in brine or on ice. Beam trawlers in the east coast otter trawl fishery provide cooked prawns for domestic markets, with smaller prawns being sold for bait. The average wholesale price for endeavour prawns from the Northern Prawn Fishery in 1991–92 was A$ 6.00 per kg.

Management controls The Western Australian, Northern Prawn, Torres Strait and Queensland fisheries are all limited entry. Permanent, seasonal and area closures and gear restrictions also apply. There are 2 seasonal closures (summer and winter) in the Northern Prawn Fishery.

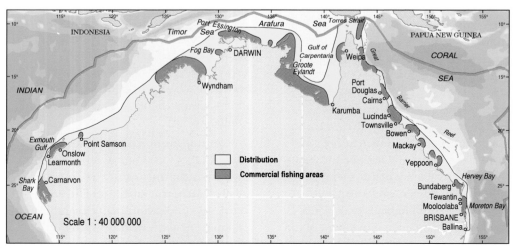

Geographic distribution and commercial fishing areas for blue endeavour prawns in Australian waters.

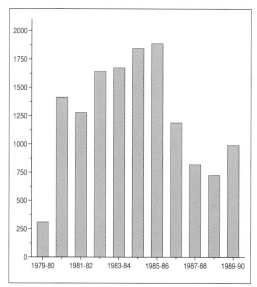

Total annual catch in t of endeavour prawns (*Metapenaeus endeavouri* and *M. ensis*) for the period 1979–80 to 1989–90 from the Northern Prawn Fishery. (Source: Australian Fishing Zone Information System)

Recreational fishery

There are no recreational fisheries for endeavour prawns in Australia.

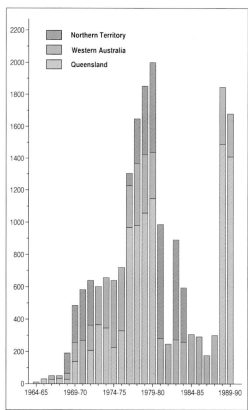

Total annual catch in t of endeavour prawns (*Metapenaeus endeavouri* and *M. ensis*) for the period 1964–65 to 1989–90. Figures are unavailable for: Queensland for 1970–71 and 1980–81 to 1987–88; Western Australia for 1964–65 to 1965–66; and the Northern Territory for 1964–65 to 1966–67, 1972–73 to 1975–76, 1981–82 and 1984–85 to 1989–90. Catches for States that average less than 5 % of the total for all States are not shown. (Source: Fisheries Resources Atlas Statistical Database)

Resource status

Endeavour prawn stocks in Western Australia are considered fully exploited and stable. Catches of endeavour prawns in the Northern Prawn Fishery have declined in recent years, although there are no assessments to suggest whether this is a reflection of changes in stock levels or management practices. An estimated sustainable yield for the Torres Strait stock is 685 t.[14] Catches of blue endeavour prawns in Torres Strait have increased since the mid 1980s, possibly reflecting their increasing export value.

References

1. Grey, D.L., Dall, W. and Baker, A. (1983) *A guide to the Australian penaeid prawns.* Darwin: Department of Primary Production of the Northern Territory. 140 pp.

2. Staples, D.J., Vance, D.J. and Heales, D.S. (1985) Habitat requirements of juvenile penaeid prawns and their relationship to offshore fisheries. Pp 47–54, in *Second Australian national prawn seminar.* Ed by P.C. Rothlisberg, B.J. Hill and D.J. Staples. Cleveland, Australia.

3. Somers, I.F. (1987) Sediment type as a factor in the distribution of the commercial prawn species of the western Gulf of Carpentaria, Australia. *Australian Journal of Marine and Freshwater Research* **38**: 133–149.

4. Courtney, A.J., Dredge, M.C.L. and Masel, J.M. (1989) Reproductive biology and spawning periodicity of endeavour shrimps *Metapenaeus endeavouri* (Schmitt, 1926) and *Metapenaeus ensis* (de Haan, 1850) from a central Queensland (Australia) fishery. *Asian Fisheries Science* **3**: 133–147.

5. Coles, R.G. and Lee Long, W.J. (1985) Juvenile prawn biology and the distribution of sea grass prawn nursery grounds in the south-eastern Gulf of Carpentaria. Pp 55–60, in *Second Australian national prawn seminar.* Ed P.C. Rothlisberg, B.J. Hill and D.J. Staples. Cleveland, Australia.

6. Buckworth, R.C. (in press, 1992) Movement and growth of tagged blue endeavour prawns, *Metapenaeus endeavouri* (Schmitt 1926), in the western Gulf of Carpentaria, Australia. *Australian Journal of Marine and Freshwater Research* **42**.

7. Somers, I.F., Poiner, I.R. and Harris, A.N. (1987) A study of the species composition and distribution of commercial penaeid prawns of Torres Strait. *Australian Journal of Marine and Freshwater Research* **38**: 47–61.

8. Buckworth, R.C. (1988) *Biological summary, prawn fishery monitoring, western Gulf of Carpentaria. Attachment 1. Western Gulf of Carpentaria, prawn fishery monitoring study.* Fisheries Division, Northern Territory Department of Primary Industry and Fisheries. 27 pp.

9. Moriarty, D.J.W. and Barclay, M.C. (1981) Carbon and nitrogen content of food and the assimilation efficiencies of penaeid prawns in the Gulf of Carpentaria. *Australian Journal of Marine and Freshwater Research* **32**: 245–251.

10. Salini, J.P., Blaber, S.J.M. and Brewer, D.T. (1990) Diets of piscivorous fishes in a tropical estuary, with special reference to predation on penaeid prawns. *Marine Biology* **105**: 363–374.

11. Mulley, J.C. and Latter, B.D.H. (1981) Geographic differentiation of tropical Australian penaeid prawn populations. *Australian Journal of Marine and Freshwater Research* **32**: 897–906.

12. Trainor, N. (1990) Review of the east coast otter trawl fishery. *The Queensland Fisherman.* **8**(9): 25–32.

13. Queensland Fish Management Authority (1990) *A review of the East Coast Trawl Fishery and proposed management arrangements.* A discussion paper. 16 pp.

14. Bureau of Rural Resources (1992) *Torres Strait prawns.* Fishery Status Report, February 1992. 4 pp.

15. Dall, W. (1957) A revision of the Australian species of Penaeinae (Crustacea: Decapoda: Penaeidae). *Australian Journal of Marine and Freshwater Research* **8**: 136–231.

Contributors

Information on this species was provided by (in alphabetical order) Rik Buckworth, Kurt Derbyshire and Clive Turnbull. Drawing of red endeavour prawn courtesy of FAO, Rome; and figure of blue endeavour prawn redrawn by Peter Moloney after Dall.[15] (*Details of contributors and their organisations are given in the Acknowledgements section at the back of this book.*)
Compilers Alex McNee and Christina Grieve (maps)

Prawn trawler cleaning its nets between trawls, Fog Bay, Northern Territory. (Source: Neville Gill, Fisheries Division, Northern Territory Department of Primary Industry and Fisheries)

School prawn

Metapenaeus macleayi

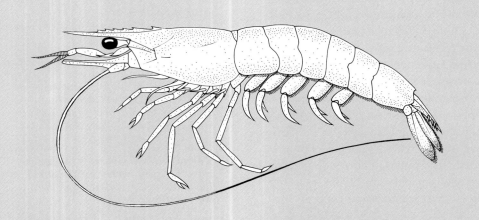

Metapenaeus macleayi
(Haswell)

School prawn

Other common names include **New South Wales school prawn** and **eastern school prawn**.
FAO: **eastern school shrimp**
Australian species code: 701321

Family PENAEIDAE

Diagnostic features School prawns have very few or no hairy patches on their body and the telson has 4 pairs of conspicuous mobile spines. Males bear a notch near the tip of the fifth walking leg. Their colour is translucent with irregular brown or green spots (especially in those individuals living in estuaries) and the antennae are brown.[1]

Distribution

School prawns are endemic to waters off the east coast of Australia and have been recorded from Tin Can Bay in Queensland to Corner Inlet in Victoria in depths from 1 m to 55 m.[2]

Postlarval to adolescent school prawns inhabit estuaries[3] and can be found in waters with salinities as low as 1 part per thousand.[4] Adult school prawns may also occur in estuaries, but are found predominantly in oceanic waters.[3]

Juvenile school prawns prefer to live in seagrass areas within estuaries although they are also present on bare substrates[4] of fine to moderately coarse sand.[5] Adult school prawns are most abundant in turbid marine waters arising from estuarine discharge after heavy rainfall or river floods.[2]

Life history

Between February and May, school prawns spawn in the sea off New South Wales in waters of about 40–55 m depth.[3,6]

The larval stage of the school prawn life cycle is about 2–3 weeks. As with other prawns (Penaeidae),[7] the planktonic nauplius larvae hatch from eggs and develop through a series of moults into postlarvae, the transitional phase before the benthic living juvenile stage. The postlarvae enter rivers during summer and early autumn and the juveniles move upstream.[2] The juveniles

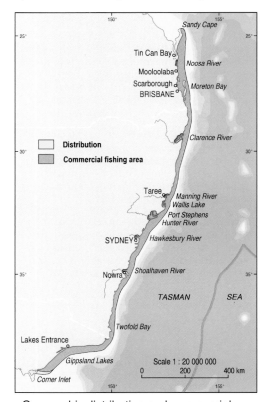

Geographic distribution and commercial fishing areas for school prawns.

remain in the estuaries and rivers through the autumn and winter, buried in the bottom sediment.

By about October, adolescent and maturing prawns begin moving downstream, and between November and April each year they move out to oceanic waters to breed. Data from tagging studies[8] suggest that the school prawns move along the coast in a northerly direction. The longest recorded migration by these prawns is 120 km.[8] However, most individuals stay within approximately 70 km of the estuary from which they migrated.

School prawns live for 12–18 months. Almost no growth takes place during the colder months of the year, but rapid growth begins when the waters warm in spring (September).[2] Females are usually larger than males,[2] growing to 160 mm total length, whilst males grow to 130 mm total length. Sizes at maturity may vary along the coast of New South Wales. For example, sexual maturity is first evident in Clarence River school prawns at 18–30 mm carapace length (mean 22.5 mm),[9] and school prawns in the Hunter River are mature at 25 mm carapace length for males and 23 mm carapace length for females.[6]

Rainfall is thought to be an important environmental cue in the life cycle of school prawns. For example, researchers have noted the following occurrences after rain: enhanced seaward movement of school prawns in response to the disturbance of bottom sediments by increased river flow; increased quantities of nutrients being transported into estuaries and adjacent coastal areas via freshwater runoff; a strong freshwater inflow to the estuaries which stimulates the school prawns' ovaries to mature; increased density of prawns at sea after good rainfall which improves the prawns'

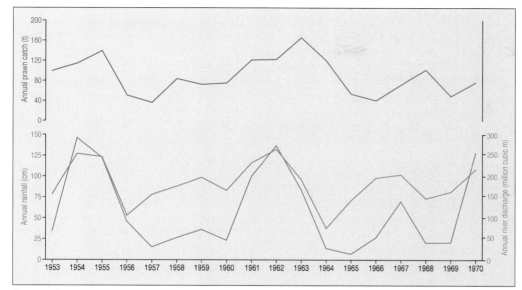

Comparison of the catch of school prawns with fluctuations in the rainfall and river discharge in the Hunter River region between 1953 and 1971. (Source: redrawn from Ruello.[2])

chances of mating and spawning; and changes in salinity in coastal waters produced by freshwater discharge which facilitates the movement of larvae and postlarval school prawns from the sea to the estuaries.[2,10]

School prawns are bottom-feeding, opportunistic omnivores; in other words they eat a variety of food as it becomes available. Food items include small crustaceans, polychaete worms, bivalve molluscs and detritus.[5] They are preyed on by a variety of finfish.

Stock structure

Of the estimated 60 estuarine populations of school prawns in eastern Australia there are 6 major populations, centred around the Noosa River in Queensland and the Clarence, Manning, Hunter, Hawkesbury and Shoalhaven rivers in New South Wales.[8] Electrophoretic[11] and tagging studies[8] show that the school prawns in each of these and nearby rivers constitute individual sub-stocks although they appear to be genetically similar.

Commercial fishery

School prawns are harvested on grounds in offshore waters by demersal otter trawling, carried out predominantly during the day. The boats are from local ports. The size of the landed catch of school prawns from offshore waters is correlated with the river discharge of the previous year.[2,10] Catches are highest from November to May,[2,8] and juveniles comprise much of the catch for the first few months. In the estuaries, there is also a higher catch rate of juvenile prawns several days after a full moon.[10] In most estuaries where they occur, school prawns are harvested by various methods: demersal otter trawling, beam trawling, set pocket netting, hauling and seining, or with running nets or dingo rigs.

Fish, octopus, bay lobster (Scyllaridae) and crabs (Portunidae) are caught as bycatch of the school prawn fishery.

School prawns are marketed locally and in the Sydney and Brisbane markets. They are sold uncooked (green) or cooked. The average 1991–92 price per kg at the Sydney Fish Market was A$ 5.22 (green) and A$ 5.98 (cooked).

Management controls There are limits on the numbers of vessels licensed to fish for prawns off New South Wales and Queensland. There are also vessel size, gear, area and seasonal constraints. In Victoria also, inshore vessels need an endorsement to fish for prawns. Estuarine and offshore prawn fisheries are managed under different arrangements in all States.

Aquaculture

The possibility of farming school prawns has been investigated[12] and school prawns have been cultured in northern New South Wales for a number of years. However, a recent trend has favoured the culture of tiger prawns (*Penaeus monodon, P. esculentus*) rather than school prawns.

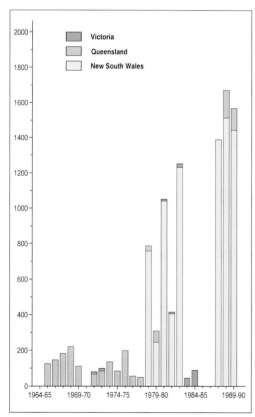

Total annual catch in t of school prawns for the period 1964–65 to 1989–90. Figures are unavailable for: New South Wales from 1964–65 to 1977–78 and 1983–84 to 1986–87; Victoria from 1964–65 to 1965–66, 1974–75 to 1977–78 and 1985–86 to 1989–90; and Queensland for 1970–71 and from 1980–81 to 1987–88. Catches for States that average less than 5% of the total for all States are not shown. (Source: Fisheries Resources Atlas Statistical Database)

Catch of school prawns on a trawlers sorting tray, northern New South Wales. (Source: John Matthews, Fisheries Research Institute, NSW Fisheries)

Recreational fishery

School prawns are taken recreationally from most east coast estuaries within their distribution. Methods of harvesting include scoop nets, scissor nets, cast nets or 6 m drag nets.

Management controls There are restrictions in both New South Wales and Queensland on the size of net mesh and gear used.

Resource status

School prawn populations are exploited heavily and there are concerns that they are being overfished. Reduced freshwater flow into estuaries because of weir or dam construction and divergence of river water also probably decreases the size of the resource.

References

1. Grey, D.L., Dall, W. and Baker, A. (1983) *A guide to the Australian penaeid prawns.* Darwin: Department of Primary Production of the Northern Territory. 140 pp.

2. Ruello, N.V. (1973) The influence of rainfall on the distribution and abundance of the school prawn *Metapenaeus macleayi* in the Hunter River region (Australia). *Marine Biology* **23**: 221–228.

3. Racek, A.A. (1959) Prawn investigations in eastern Australia. *State Fisheries Research Bulletin* **6**: 1–57.

4. Young, P.C. (1978) Moreton Bay, Queensland: A nursery area for juvenile penaeid prawns. *Australian Journal of Marine and Freshwater Research* **29**: 55–75.

5. Ruello, N.V. (1973) Burrowing, feeding, and spatial distribution of the school prawn *Metapenaeus macleayi* (Haswell) in the Hunter River region, Australia. *Journal of Experimental Marine Biology and Ecology* **13**: 189–206.

6. Ruello, N.V. (1971) *Some aspects of the ecology of the school prawn* Metapenaeus macleayi *in the Hunter River region of New South Wales.* Unpublished MSc thesis, University of Sydney. 145 pp.

7. Garcia, S. and Le Reste, L. (1981) Life cycles, dynamics, exploitation and management of coastal penaeid shrimp stocks. *FAO Fisheries Technical Paper* **203**. 215 pp.

8. Ruello, N.V. (1977) Migration and stock studies on the Australian school prawn *Metapenaeus macleayi. Marine Biology* **41**: 185–190.

9. Glaister, J.P. (1978) Movement and growth of tagged school prawns *Metapenaeus macleayi* (Haswell) (Crustacea: Penaeidae), in the Clarence River region of northern New South Wales. *Australian Journal of Marine and Freshwater Research* **29**: 645–657.

10. Glaister, J.P. (1978) The impact of river discharge on distribution and production of the school prawn *Metapenaeus macleayi* (Haswell) (Crustacea: Penaeidae) in the Clarence River region, northern New South Wales. *Australian Journal of Marine and Freshwater Research* **29**: 311–323.

11. Mulley, J.C. and Latter, B.D.H. (1981) Geographic differentiation of eastern Australian penaeid prawn populations. *Australian Journal of Marine and Freshwater Research* **32**: 889–895.

12. Maguire, G.B. (1980) *A review of the farming and biology of penaeid prawns with emphasis on juvenile school prawns.* New South Wales State Fisheries. 80 pp.

13. Dall, W. (1957) A revision of the Australian species of Penaeinae (Crustacea: Decapoda: Penaeidae). *Australian Journal of Marine and Freshwater Research* **8**: 136–231.

Contributors

Information on this species was originally provided by Steven Montgomery and supplemented by (in alphabetical order) John Glaister and Derek Staples. Figure redrawn by Peter Moloney after Dall.[13] (*Details of contributors and their organisations are given in the Acknowledgements section at the back of this book.*)

Compilers Patricia Kailola and Christina Grieve (maps)

The life cycle of a penaeid prawn. (Source: Redrawn by Peter Moloney from original by Rik Buckworth)

Prawn trawlers, Sydney Harbour estuary.(Source: Gary Henry, Environment Protection Authority, NSW)

126

Tiger prawns

This presentation is on 2 species, **brown tiger prawns** and **grooved tiger prawns**.

Brown tiger prawn,
Penaeus esculentus
Haswell

Another common name is
tiger prawn.
FAO: **brown tiger prawn**
Australian species code: 701308

Grooved tiger prawn,
Penaeus semisulcatus de
Haan

Other common names include
green tiger prawn and **northern
tiger prawn**.
FAO: **green tiger prawn**
Australian species code: 701307

Family PENAEIDAE

Diagnostic features Brown tiger prawns are generally brown with dark banding. Their rostrum and antennae are also banded. Grooved tiger prawns are dark green to dark brown, with darker banding on the abdomen, legs, antennae and rostrum. Brown tiger prawns lack a distinct groove in their postrostral ridge, and their adrostral ridge (alongside the postrostral ridges) only extends to the level of their first rostral tooth. By comparison, the postrostral ridge of grooved tiger prawns has a small groove and the adrostral ridge extends behind the first rostral tooth.[1]

Distribution

Brown tiger prawns are endemic to Australian waters,[1] while grooved tiger prawns are found in the Indo-West Pacific region from southern Africa to Japan. Populations have also established in the eastern Mediterranean following migrations through the Suez Canal.[1] Both species of tiger prawns are present around the west, north and east coasts of Australia. Brown tiger prawns have the greatest range, distributed from Shark Bay in Western Australia to Wallis Lake in New South Wales. Grooved tiger prawns are restricted to more northerly waters, from Collier Bay in northern Western Australia to Yeppoon in Queensland.

Adult brown tiger prawns are found to depths of 200 m, but are mostly trawled in 10–20 m of water,[1] over coarse sediments.[2] Grooved tiger prawns have been trawled from depths to 130 m.[1] They are found in fine mud sediments in the Gulf of Carpentaria.[2] Within the Gulf of Carpentaria, larval brown tiger prawns are distributed along the coast, while larval grooved tiger prawns are distributed both along the coast and offshore. Juveniles of both species are found in shallow waters associated with seagrass beds,[3] sometimes on top of coral reef platforms.[4]

Life history

Brown tiger prawns spawn in the Gulf of Carpentaria throughout the year with a peak between July and October, in both inshore and offshore areas.[5] In Western Australia spawning takes place from July–August through to March, with peak activity in October. Most spawning females are found in 13–20 m of water.[6] Grooved tiger prawns in the Gulf of Carpentaria exhibit a major peak in spawning in August–September and a

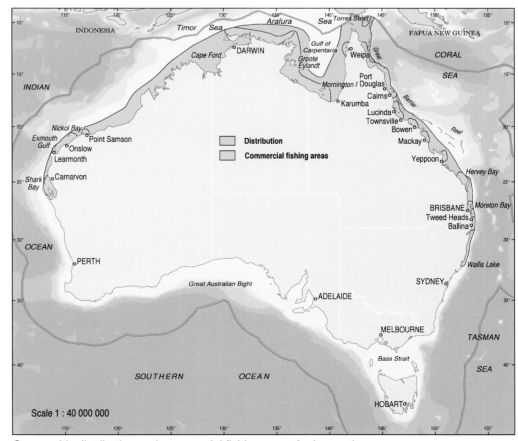

Geographic distribution and commercial fishing areas for brown tiger prawns.

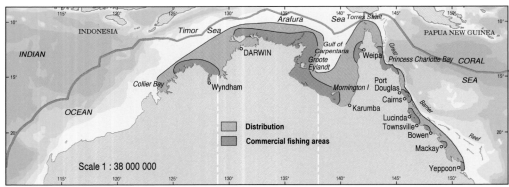

Geographic distribution and commercial fishing areas for grooved tiger prawns in Australian waters.

minor peak in February.[5] Grooved tiger prawns spawn only in offshore areas.[5] Fecundity of both species is high, with a female brown tiger prawn of 32 mm carapace length producing about 186 000 eggs, while a female grooved tiger prawn of 39 mm carapace length produces about 364 000 eggs.[5]

In the Gulf of Carpentaria the life cycle of both species of tiger prawns is similar. Larval phases (nauplius, zoea and mysis) are found in less than 50 m of water. The larvae remain in the plankton for about 3 weeks, before settling on inshore nursery grounds.[7]

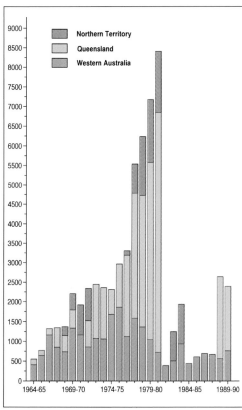

Total annual catch in t of tiger prawns (*Penaeus esculentus* and *P. semisulcatus*) for the period 1964–65 to 1989–90. Figures are unavailable for Queensland for 1970–71 and 1981–82 to 1987–88; and the Northern Territory for 1964–65 to 1966–67, 1972–73 to 1975–76, 1981–82 and 1984–85 to 1989–90. Catches for States that average less than 5 % of the total for all States are not shown. (Source: Fisheries Resources Atlas Statistical Database)

Developing juveniles of both species remain in nursery areas for several months, where they grow to about 20 mm carapace length before migrating offshore.[7] In the Gulf of Carpentaria brown tiger prawns migrate offshore between November and February while grooved tiger prawns migrate between January and April.[8] In Torres Strait migration from the nursery areas takes place between January and June.[9]

The minimum size at first maturity for female brown tiger prawns from the Gulf of Carpentaria is 26 mm carapace length. Female brown tiger prawns grow to 55 mm carapace length while males grow to 40 mm carapace length.[7] Female grooved tiger prawns from the same area are slightly larger, at 30 mm carapace length, at first maturity.[8] Grooved tiger prawns first spawn when 5–7 months old.[5] Female grooved tiger prawns grow to 50 mm carapace length while males grow to 39 mm carapace length.[10] Grooved tiger prawns in the northern Gulf of Carpentaria live for 18 to 24 months.[10]

Both brown and grooved tiger prawns feed primarily at night.[11] Their similar diets are dominated by molluscs, crustaceans and polychaete worms. There are changes in the importance of dietary items in tiger prawns from different areas and there are changes in diet as they grow. Juveniles of both species have a similar diet to adults, although gastropod molluscs dominate in the diet of juvenile brown tiger prawns, while bivalve molluscs and crustaceans dominate in the diet of juvenile grooved tiger prawns.[11]

Tiger prawns are prey to squid (*Loligo* species), cuttlefish (*Sepia* species) and a variety of demersal fish species. Estuarine fish such as barramundi (*Lates calcarifer*), king threadfin (*Polydactylus sheridani*) and catfish (Ariidae) are major predators of juvenile grooved tiger prawns.[12]

Stock structure

Genetic studies[13] have shown no evidence of different stocks of either species in Australian waters.

Commercial fishery

Brown and grooved tiger prawns are taken commercially in Western Australia, the Northern Territory and Queensland, with the largest catches being made in the Northern Prawn Fishery. In areas where both species are taken, the catch is recorded as 'tiger prawns' with no separation of species.

In Western Australia brown tiger prawns are caught in Shark Bay, Exmouth Gulf and Nickol Bay as part of multi-species prawn fisheries that also take western king prawns (*Penaeus latisulcatus*). Brown tiger prawns are also caught in a local fishery in waters west of Cape Ford. Brown tiger prawns dominate catches in the south-eastern Gulf of Carpentaria and the Torres Strait fishery.[14] Grooved tiger prawns dominate catches around Groote Eylandt and Weipa, Gulf of Carpentaria. In the Queensland multi-species east coast otter trawl fishery, tiger prawns comprise about 30 % of the catch.[15] The catch from waters north of Yeppoon is a mixture of brown and grooved tiger prawns while only brown tiger prawns are taken from southern Queensland waters.

Tiger prawns are caught at night[6] using demersal otter trawls. Beam trawls are used in some areas of the east coast

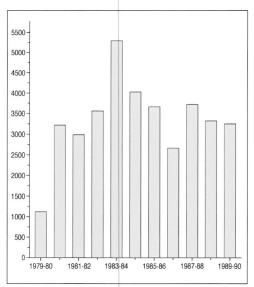

Total annual catch in t of tiger prawns (*Penaeus esculentus* and *P. semisulcatus*) for the period 1979–80 to 1989–90 from the Northern Prawn Fishery. (Source: Australian Fishing Zone Information System)

fishery. Endeavour prawns (*Metapenaeus endeavouri, M. ensis*) are taken with tiger prawns in many fisheries, and banana prawns (*Penaeus merguiensis, P. indicus*) may be an alternative target species for some vessels in the northern fisheries. Saucer scallops (*Amusium* species), bay lobsters (*Thenus* species), blue swimmer crabs (*Portunus pelagicus*), and calamary (*Sepioteuthis* species) are all valuable bycatch.

Most of the tiger prawn catch is exported,[7] with Japan the major destination.[14] The prawns are packed as frozen whole, 'green' (uncooked) prawns which have been either boxed and frozen on board, or chilled in brine on board and processed onshore. Smaller prawns may be cooked on board. Prawns are graded by size. On-board boxing results in 'bulk' 10-12 kg packs, which, depending on market demand, may be processed and broken down into smaller lots. Wholesale prices for tiger prawns in 1991–92 varied from A$ 8.00–18.00 per kg. Tiger prawns caught in the Northern Prawn Fishery were worth an estimated A$ 54 million in 1991–92.

Management controls All prawn fisheries managed by the States and the Commonwealth of Australia are limited entry, with permanent seasonal and area closures and gear restrictions. There are 2 seasonal closures (summer and winter) in the Northern Prawn Fishery.

Recreational fishery

There is no recreational fishery for tiger prawns in Australia.

Resource status

Tiger prawn resources in all States are considered fully utilised. In the Exmouth Gulf fishery in Western Australia and the Northern Prawn Fishery stocks were considered overexploited in the 1980s. Stocks are recovering however, after the imposition of severe management restrictions in 1983–84 in Exmouth Gulf and 1987 in the Northern Prawn Fishery.

References

1. Grey, D.L., Dall, W. and Baker, A. (1983) *A guide to the Australian penaeid prawns.* Darwin: Department of Primary Production of the Northern Territory. 140 pp.

2. Somers, I.F. (1987) Sediment type as a factor in the distribution of commercial prawn species in the Western Gulf of Carpentaria,

(top) Aquarium photograph of brown tiger prawns. (Source: Glen Smith, Southern Fisheries Centre, Queensland Department of Primary Industries)

(bottom) A prawn trawler at anchor in Joseph Bonaparte Gulf. (Source: Rik Buckworth, Fisheries Division, Northern Territory Department of Primary Industry and Fisheries)

Australia. *Australian Journal of Marine and Freshwater Research* **38**: 133–149.

3. Staples, D.J., Vance, D.J., and Heales, D.S. (1985) Habitat requirements of juvenile penaeid prawns and their relationship to offshore fisheries. Pp 47–54, in *Second Australian national prawn seminar.* Ed by P.C. Rothlisberg, B.J. Hill and D.J. Staples. Cleveland, Australia.

4. Turnbull, C.T. and Mellors, J.E. (1990) Settlement of juvenile *Penaeus esculentus* (Haswell, 1879) on nursery grounds in Torres Strait. Pp 29–37, in *Torres Strait prawn project: a review of research 1985–1987.* Ed by J.E. Mellors. *Queensland Department of Primary Industries, Information Series* **QI90018**.

5. Crocos, P.J. (1987) Reproductive dynamics of the tiger prawn *Penaeus esculentus*, and a comparison with *P. semisulcatus*, in the north-western Gulf of Carpentaria. *Australian Journal of Marine and Freshwater Research* **38**: 91–102.

6. Penn, J.W. and Caputi, N. (1985) Stock recruitment relationships for the tiger prawn, *Penaeus esculentus*, fishery in Exmouth Gulf and their implications for management. Pp 165–173, in *Second Australian national prawn seminar.* Ed by P.C. Rothlisberg, B.J. Hill and D.J. Staples. Cleveland, Australia.

7. Kirkwood, G.P. and Somers, I.F. (1984) Growth of two species of tiger prawn, *Penaeus esculentus* and *P. semisulcatus*, in the western Gulf of Carpentaria. *Australian*

Journal of Marine and Freshwater Research **35**: 703–712.

8. Buckworth, R.C. (1985) Preliminary results of a study of commercial catches, spawning and recruitment of *Penaeus esculentus* and *P. semisulcatus* in the western Gulf of Carpentaria. Pp 213–220, in *Second Australian national prawn seminar.* Ed by P.C. Rothlisberg, B.J. Hill and D.J. Staples. Cleveland, Australia.

9. Blyth, P.J., Watson, R.A., and Sterling, D.J. (1990) Spawning, recruitment and life history studies of *Penaeus esculentus* (Haswell, 1879) in Torres Strait. Pp 38–50, in *Torres Strait prawn project: a review of research 1985–1987.* Ed by J.E. Mellors. *Queensland Department of Primary Industries, Information Series* **QI90018**.

10. Somers, I.F. and Kirkwood, G.P. (1991) Population ecology of the grooved tiger prawn, *Penaeus semisulcatus*, in the north-western Gulf of Carpentaria, Australia: Growth, movement, age structure and infestation by the bopyrid parasite *Epipenaeon ingens. Australian Journal of Marine and Freshwater Research* **42**: 349–367.

11. Wassenberg, T.J. and Hill, B.J. (1987) Natural diet of the tiger prawns, *Penaeus esculentus* and *P. semisulcatus. Australian Journal of Marine and Freshwater Research* **38**: 169–182.

12. Salini, J.P., Blaber, S.J.M. and Brewer, D.T. (1990) Diets of piscivorous fishes in a tropical estuary, with special reference to predation on penaeid prawns. *Marine Biology* **105**: 363–374.

13. Mulley, J.C. and Latter, B.D.H. (1981) Geographic differentiation of tropical Australian penaeid prawn populations. *Australian Journal of Marine and Freshwater Research* **32**: 897–906.

14. Watson, R.A., Channells, P. and Blyth, P.J. (1990) Commercial prawn catches in Torres Strait. Pp 13–19, in *Torres Strait prawn project: a review of research 1985–1987.* Ed by J.E. Mellors. *Queensland Department of Primary Industries, Information Series* **QI90018**.

15. Trainor, N. (1990) Review of the east coast otter trawl fishery. *The Queensland Fisherman* **8**(9): 25–32.

16. Dall, W. (1957) A revision of the Australian species of Penaeinae (Crustacea: Decapoda: Penaeidae). *Australian Journal of Marine and Freshwater Research* **8**: 136–231.

Contributors

Information on this species was supplemented by (in alphabetical order) Mike Dredge, Ian Somers and Clive Turnbull. Figure of brown tiger prawn redrawn by Peter Moloney after Dall;[16] drawing of grooved tiger prawn courtesy of FAO, Rome. (*Details of contributors and their organisations are given in the Acknowledgements section at the back of this book.*)

Compilers Alex McNee and Christina Grieve (maps)

Banana prawns

Penaeus species

Banana prawns

This presentation is on 2 species, **white banana prawns** and **red-legged banana prawns**.

White banana prawn,
Penaeus merguiensis
de Man

Other common names include **banana prawn** and **white prawn**.
FAO name: **banana prawn**
Australian species code: 701901

Red-legged banana prawn,
Penaeus indicus
H. Milne Edwards

Another common name is **Indian banana prawn**.
FAO name: **Indian white prawn**
Australian species code: 701306

Family PENAEIDAE

Diagnostic features These are large, white prawns with characteristics in common with other species of the genus *Penaeus*. White banana prawns have a poorly defined gastro-orbital ridge and high, toothed rostral crest. Their body is pale yellow or translucent, and speckled with reddish brown dots. Red-legged banana prawns have a well-defined gastro-orbital ridge and low, toothed rostral crest. Their body is yellow or translucent with dark ridges and their legs are often reddish pink.[1]

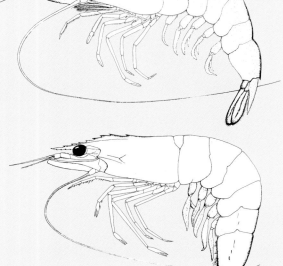

Distribution

Banana prawns inhabit tropical and subtropical waters. Both species are distributed through the Indo-West Pacific region and South China Sea to northern Australia. White banana prawns extend westwards as far as the Middle East, and red-legged banana prawns extend as far as south-east Africa.[1] In Australia, white banana prawns are present from Shark Bay in the west to the Tweed River in northern New South Wales,[1] and red-legged banana prawns are present from south of Broome in northern Western Australia as far east as the north-western margin of the Gulf of Carpentaria.

The preferred habitat of white banana prawns is coastal waters from shallow estuaries and intertidal areas to a maximum depth of 45 m. They live in turbid waters for most of their lives, over muddy substrates in estuaries and muddy sands offshore. Juveniles inhabit small creeks and rivers in a sheltered mangrove environment in waters ranging from almost fresh to highly saline (more than 70 parts per thousand).[2] Adult white banana prawns inhabit medium and low energy coastlines, although they can withstand high energy cyclonic events. In northern Australia, schools of adults frequently occur in depths between 16 m and 25 m.[1] They also form aggregations which in some areas become extremely dense and are known as 'boils'.

In Australia, red-legged banana prawns inhabit deeper water than white banana prawns, from about 35 m to a maximum of 90 m. There is no information on juvenile habitat in Australian waters, although in Africa, India and Bangladesh juveniles live in shallow lagoons. Schools of adults in north-western Australia are located in deep water over muddy or sandy substrates. By day or night these prawns form aggregations which appear to contain a range of size classes.

Life history

White banana prawns can become sexually mature at about 6 months of age (26–34 mm carapace length for females). Sex ratios are overall 1:1, although local deviations from this figure can occur in certain seasons and localities. Spawning occurs throughout all of the shallow coastal zone inhabited by adults, and older adults may migrate shorewards at the time of spawning. Mating occurs during moulting. Eggs are shed into the

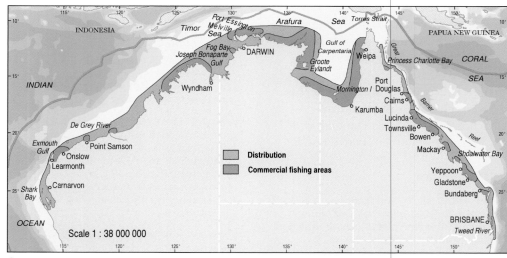

Geographic distribution and commercial fishing areas for white banana prawns in Australian waters.

water prior to the moult and are fertilised externally by sperm from the spermatheca implanted by the male. Individual prawns are partial spawners and each female can lay several batches of eggs each year. Fecundity ranges from 100 000 to 400 000 eggs.[3] Although spawning occurs throughout much of the year there are 2 main periods based on the monsoon: the late dry season (September–November) and late wet season (March–May). In the Gulf of Carpentaria, it is mainly the prawns from the September–November spawning which survive through to adulthood and contribute to the commercial fishery.[4]

White banana prawn eggs are demersal and hatch into the first of 3 larval stages, the nauplius, in approximately 15 hours. The nauplius, zoea and mysis larval stages are pelagic and are able to move towards the coast by undertaking daily vertical migrations. This process takes 2–3 weeks. There is no information on the larval and juvenile stages of Australian populations of red-legged banana prawns.

Postlarval white banana prawns settle in the creeks of mangrove swamps and over a few weeks develop into juvenile prawns. Two or 3 months later, mainly during the wet season in northern Australia, the juveniles migrate offshore into deeper water. There is a direct relationship between the amount of rainfall and the number of juvenile prawns moving out of the estuaries.[5]

The juvenile growth rate is rapid in white banana prawns, with increases of approximately 1.2 mm carapace length per week.[6] In Gulf of Carpentaria waters, the maximum carapace length is achieved at about 12 months of age.[7] Moulting is continuous throughout the life of these prawns and is tied to temperature fluctuations.

The maximum life span for white banana prawns is 12–18 months. The maximum recorded total length is 240 mm (approximately 60 mm carapace length) for females and 200 mm total length (approximately 50 mm carapace length) for males. Female banana prawns can weigh up to 69 g, males up to 59 g.

There is no recent information on the life span, fecundity, maximum size and growth rates in Australian populations of red-legged banana prawns, although they follow a similar life cycle pattern to white banana prawns. Females are reported to

Tipping the codend, Gulf of Carpentaria banana prawn fishery. (Source: Mike Dredge, Southern Fisheries Centre, Queensland Department of Primary Industries)

attain 230 mm total length and males to reach 190 mm.[1]

Juvenile white banana prawns are mainly opportunistic feeders, food items consisting of benthic organisms such as small bivalve molluscs, crustaceans, polychaete worms and Foraminifera.[8] Adult prawns, also benthic feeders, tend to be more carnivorous, eating greater amounts of polychaetes and bivalves. There is no information on the diet of Australian populations of red-legged banana prawns.

The main predators of adult banana prawns in the Gulf of Carpentaria include blue-spot trevally (*Caranx bucculentus*) and 4 species of sharks and rays (elasmobranchs).[9] Juvenile banana prawns in the estuaries are eaten mainly by queenfish, (*Scomberoides* species), catfish (*Arius proximus*), barramundi (*Lates calcarifer*) and king threadfin (*Polydactylus sheridani*).[10] Predation rates appear to be very high and account for a large part of the high natural mortality of the species.

Stock structure

Because the white banana prawn is an annual species which recruits seasonally (mainly during the wet season), the adult population is largely composed of prawns of similar age: 6–12 months old. Within this group, there are often several cohorts representing waves of recruits from the nursery areas. This stock structure is probably also true of red-legged banana prawns.

Commercial fishery

White banana prawns are fished commercially across most of the species' range. Its fishery in Australia is one of the country's most lucrative single species trawl fisheries. The main fishery for white banana prawns is centred on the Gulf of Carpentaria and operates from about April through May. Several smaller fisheries operate in Queensland estuaries. In some areas, such as Joseph Bonaparte Gulf and around Melville Island,

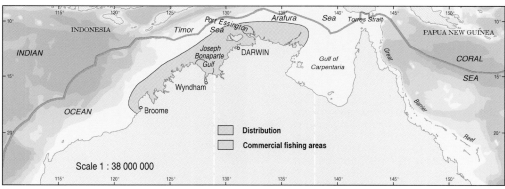

Geographic distribution and commercial fishing areas for red-legged banana prawns in Australian waters.

red-legged banana prawns are fished with white banana prawns and recorded in catch statistics as 'banana prawns'.

The main capture method is by demersal otter trawling. The vessels are twin-rigged, and use 2 high-flying modified Yankee Doodle nets. Other fishing methods include beam trawling, pocket netting and beach seining in Northern Territory and Queensland waters. Aggregations of white banana prawns are often detected by echo sounders and spotter aircraft have been used to locate 'boils'. Most fishing is carried out by day. The size of vessels engaged in the fishery varies, larger ones (up to 21 m) working the more remote Northern Prawn Fishery.

Like white banana prawns, red-legged banana prawns are fished only by demersal otter trawling and an echo sounder is used to detect the schools of prawns. They can be fished day and night, although the catches are generally higher during daylight hours. The Joseph Bonaparte Gulf fishery operates from April to May. Fishing is conducted when currents are less (on neap tides), as the

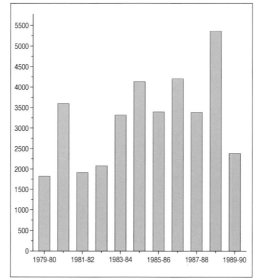

Total annual catch in t of banana prawns (*Penaeus merguiensis* and *P. indicus*) from the Northern Prawn Fishery for the period 1979–80 to 1989–90. (Source: Australian Fishing Zone Information System)

large tidal movement in that region makes fishing very difficult. The remoteness of the region, distance of the fishery from the coast, exposure to weather, large tides and depth of fishing dictate that only the largest boats in the Northern Prawn Fishery fleet engage in fishing for red-legged banana prawns.

Endeavour prawns (mainly *Metapenaeus endeavouri*) and tiger prawns (mainly *Penaeus esculentus*) are incidental and alternative target species for white banana prawns. The main bycatch of finfish is generally non-commercial, although bay lobsters (*Thenus* species) and some saucer scallops (*Amusium* species) are kept for sale. As well as these species, squid

(Loliginidae) form a useful bycatch of trawling for red-legged banana prawns.

Most of the banana prawn catch from northern Australia is exported to Japan. The remainder of the northern catch and some Queensland banana prawns are sold on local and interstate markets. The main product consists of frozen, 12–15 kg packs of head-on green prawns, although there is a trend to smaller consumer packs for both the domestic and export markets. Wholesale prices per kg for Northern Prawn Fishery banana prawns in 1992 ranged from A\$ 6.50 to A\$ 8.00. On the east Queensland coast, the wholesale price in 1991–92 was about A\$ 8.00 per kg.

Currently, white banana prawns and red-legged banana prawns tend to be packaged separately. Red-legged banana prawns receive a better price than white banana prawns because of their colour, slightly better flesh yield, their more regular supply, and their landings being offered in a narrower size range which includes larger prawns.

Management controls The Northern Prawn Fishery is Commonwealth-managed. A limited licence scheme has been operating in it since 1978, and a similar scheme operates along the Queensland coast. The main trawl fisheries are also regulated by strict seasonal closures as recommended by the Northern Prawn Fishery Management Advisory Committee and, in Queensland, by the Department of Primary Industries and the Great Barrier Reef Marine Park Authority. The opening date for the first period of the Northern Prawn Fishery was

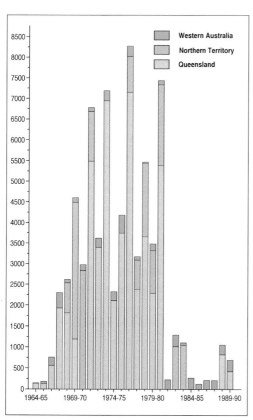

Total annual catch in t of banana prawns (*Penaeus merguiensis* and *P. indicus*) for the period 1964–65 to 1989–90. Figures are unavailable for: Queensland for 1970–71 and from 1981–82 to 1987–88; and Northern Territory from 1964–65 to 1966–67, 1972–73 to 1975–76, 1980–81, and from 1984–85 to 1989–90. (Source: Fisheries Resources Atlas Statistical Database)

Sorting the banana prawn catch from trash fish, Gulf of Carpentaria. (Source: Northern Territory Department of Primary Industry and Fisheries)

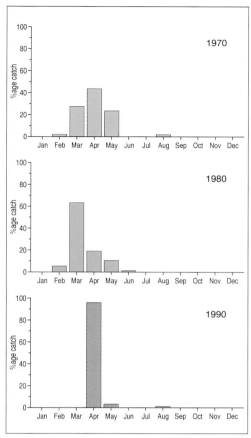

Monthly distribution of catch over the whole Gulf of Carpentaria at 10-yearly intervals from 1970 to 1990. Catch is expressed as percentage of total catch in each year. Closed seasons have applied since 1970–71 and they are varied slightly each year. (Source: Australian Fishing Zone Information System and Ian Somers, CSIRO Marine Laboratories, Cleveland)

set at 1 April from 1992. Closures in the associated tiger prawn fishery also impose on the banana prawn fishery.

Recreational fishery

A popular recreational fishery for white banana prawns occurs each year in the Darwin area and also along most of the Queensland coast. It is extremely seasonal, with peak catches occurring from February to March, which is at the end of the wet season. Recreational fishers use beach seines and cast nets to target subadult prawns during their migration from juvenile nursery areas to the adult offshore habitat.

There is no recreational fishery for red-legged banana prawns.

Management controls Both the Northern Territory and Queensland restrict the types of net used to beach seines and cast nets. Length, drop and mesh size restrictions apply for beach seines. In the Northern Territory, nets must not be anchored, staked or otherwise fixed and may not be used in rivers.

Resource status

The white banana prawn resource is fully utilised over all of its range. Catches show extreme year-to-year variation that can be linked to rainfall,[10] with good catches occurring in years of high rainfall. The resource status of red-legged banana prawns is uncertain and studies are continuing.

Notes

Attempts to culture white banana prawns in Australia have so far been exploratory, although they are cultured in some other countries — such as China.

References

1. Grey, D.L., Dall, W. and Baker, A. (1983) *A guide to the Australian penaeid prawns.* Darwin: Department of Primary Production of the Northern Territory. 140 pp.

2. Staples, D.J. and Vance, D.J. (1978) Comparative recruitment of the banana prawn, *Penaeus merguiensis,* in five estuaries of the south-eastern Gulf of Carpentaria. *Australian Journal of Marine and Freshwater Research* **38**: 29–45.

3. Rothlisberg, P.C., Staples, D.J. and Crocos, P.J. (1985) A review of the life history of the banana prawn, *Penaeus merguiensis* in the Gulf of Carpentaria. Pp 125–136, in *Second Australian national prawn seminar.* Ed by P.C. Rothlisberg, B.J. Hill and D.J. Staples. Cleveland, Australia.

4. Robertson, A.I. (1988) Abundance, diet and predators of juvenile banana prawns, *Penaeus merguiensis,* in a tropical mangrove estuary. *Australian Journal of Marine and Freshwater Research* **39**: 467–478.

5. Staples, D.J. and Vance, D.J. (1986) Emigration of juvenile banana prawns, *Penaeus merguiensis,* from a mangrove estuary and recruitment to offshore areas in the wet-dry tropics of the Gulf of Carpentaria, Australia. *Marine Ecology in Progress Series* **23**: 15–29.

6. Staples, D.J. (1980) Ecology of juvenile and adolescent banana prawns, *Penaeus merguiensis,* in a mangrove estuary and adjacent offshore area of the Gulf of Carpentaria. II. Emigration, population structure and growth of juveniles. *Australian Journal of Marine and Freshwater Research* **31**: 653–665.

7. Crocos, P.J. and Kerr, J.D. (1983) Maturation and spawning of the banana prawn *Penaeus merguiensis* de Man (Crustacea:Penaeidae) in the Gulf of Carpentaria, Australia. *Journal of Experimental Marine Biology and Ecology* **69**: 37–59.

8. Brewer, D.T., Blaber, S.J.M. and Salini, J.P. (1991) Predation on penaeid prawns by fishes in Albatross Bay, Gulf of Carpentaria. *Marine Biology* **106**: 231–240.

9. Salini, J.P., Blaber, S.J.M. and Brewer, D.T. (1990) Diets of piscivorous fishes in a tropical Australian estuary, with special reference to predation on penaeid prawns. *Marine Biology* **105**: 363–374.

10. Vance, D.J., Staples, D.J. and Kerr, J. (1985) Factors affecting year-to-year variation in the catch of banana prawns (*Penaeus merguiensis*) in the Gulf of Carpentaria. *Journal du Conseil international pour l'Exploration de la Mer* **42**: 83–97.

Contributors

The information on white banana prawns was originally provided by Derek Staples, and that on red-legged banana prawns by Rik Buckworth. Additional contributions were provided by (in alphabetical order) Mike Dredge, Ian Somers and Russell Willing. Drawings courtesy FAO, Rome. (*Details of contributors and their organisations are given in the Acknowledgements section at the back of this book.*)

Compilers Patricia Kailola, Christina Grieve (maps) and Phillip Stewart (statistics)

A 'boil' of white banana prawns (appearing as an area of murky water) in the Gulf of Carpentaria. (Source: Derek Staples, Bureau of Resource Sciences)

Western king prawn

Penaeus latisulcatus

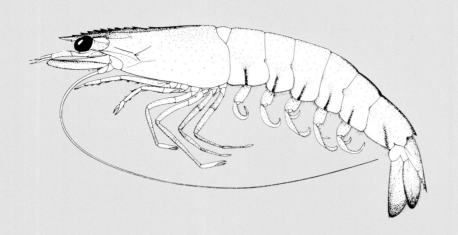

Penaeus latisulcatus Kishinouye

Western king prawn

Another common name is
blue-legged king prawn.
FAO: **western king prawn**
Australian species code: 701904

Family PENAEIDAE

Diagnostic features Western king prawns are grooved prawns, ie they have a pair of parallel grooves running the length of the upper surface of the carapace. The gastrofrontal groove is divided into 3 posteriorly, and the postrostral groove is long. There is an accessory pair of ridges on the blade of the rostrum. Their body is generally light yellow to brown and dark brown along the ridges and rostrum. Their legs and tail tips are blue. They can be distinguished from eastern king prawns by having no cross bands on the body.[1]

Distribution

Western king prawns are widely distributed throughout the Indo-Pacific region, from Madagascar to Japan and Australia.[1]

In Australia, western king prawns are present along the west, north and east coasts of Australia, from Cape Leeuwin in Western Australia to Ballina in northern New South Wales. They also inhabit the gulfs and associated waters in South Australia west to Ceduna. There has been no sampling to determine if the distribution is continuous across the Great Australian Bight. Populations of western king prawns tend to occur in concentrated pockets which are often associated with hypersaline waters of marine embayments such as Shark Bay, Exmouth Gulf, the Gulf of Carpentaria, Gulf St Vincent and Spencer Gulf.[2]

Western king prawns show a preference for sandy substrates,[3] yet are also found over mud, gravel or hard substrates.[1] Adult prawns inhabit deeper open waters of depths to 90 m,[1] while juveniles can be found in shallow coastal areas frequently characterised by extensive sandflats.[4]

Life history

Studies[4,5] have shown some relationship between the commencement of spawning and water temperature. There is most likely a threshold temperature below which spawning will not occur, and a sequence of cues such as temperature and day length stimulates the onset of spawning. For populations in Western Australia, spawning coincides with a rise in water temperature above 17°C.[5] Off the west coast of South Australia, where water temperatures near the sea bed do not exceed 17°C, day length may also influence spawning.[4] As with other *Penaeus* species spawning takes place in offshore waters.

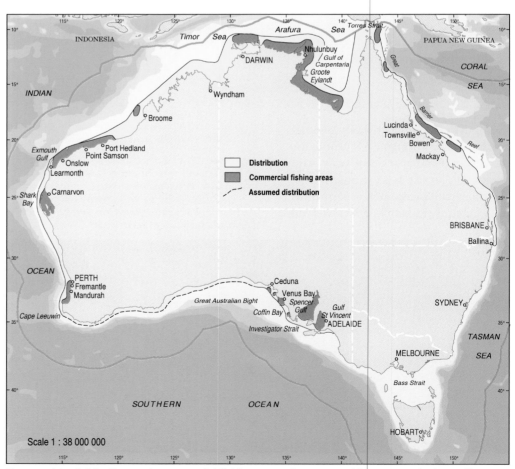

Geographic distribution and commercial fishing areas for western king prawns in Australian waters.

Timing of spawning varies around the country. In Western Australian temperate waters, south to 36° S, western king prawns spawn between October and March.[5] In warmer northern waters, between 22° S and 26° S, spawning occurs throughout the year.[5] Western king prawn populations in the Gulf of Carpentaria have 2 spawning peaks: in September and between January and March.[6] On the east coast, spawning takes place between April and August.[7] In South Australia the spawning period extends from October to March with an apparent peak in the State's west coast waters in November–December[4] and 2 peaks for Spencer Gulf populations in December and January–February.

Western king prawns are capable of multiple spawning, both within a season and in successive seasons.[5] They are able to produce large numbers of eggs: from an average of 237 000 eggs at 40 mm carapace length to 1 540 000 eggs at 71 mm carapace length.[8] The larvae hatch and remain in offshore waters for about 2 weeks before moving into high-salinity, sheltered, inshore and estuarine waters on incoming tides.[9] Juvenile development takes place in these nursery areas.

Juvenile western king prawns remain in shallow nursery areas[10] for 3 months to 1 year. Juveniles spawned in early spring will move out of the nursery habitats in late autumn, while those spawned later may remain until the following spring.[4] In southern Western Australia, movement of western king prawns out of nursery areas may be intensified by the flushing action of winter rains. Juveniles are thought to move offshore under the influence of ebb tides.[9]

Western king prawns can live for up to 4 years. In Western Australia males grow to a maximum size of 51 mm carapace length and females grow to 76 mm carapace length. In South Australia maximum reported sizes are 55 mm carapace length for males and 72 mm carapace length for females. In tropical areas, western king prawns mature within their first year. However, in temperate waters (such as in South Australia) maturity is reached in their second year. Mature males measure up to 23 mm carapace length.[5] Mature females range from 25 mm carapace length in Western Australia[5] and South Australia to 26–27 mm carapace length in Queensland.[6]

Western king prawns feed on detritus, ie decayed organic matter. They are prey to numerous juvenile and adult fishes including tailor (*Pomatomus saltatrix*), cobbler (*Cnidoglanis macrocephalus*), mulloway (*Argyrosomus hololepidotus*) black bream (*Acanthopagrus butcheri*) and snapper (*Pagrus auratus*).

Stock structure

Populations of western king prawns sampled from the Gulf of Carpentaria differ genetically from populations sampled in Western Australia and South Australia.[2] However, there are no significant differences between sampled populations from South Australia and Western Australia.[2] Studies on South Australian stocks[11] from Gulf St Vincent and the Investigator Strait detected no evidence of geographic isolation between them, but it is possible that sub-populations, separated by different spawning periods, may exist.[11]

Commercial fishery

The main commercial fisheries for western king prawns are in South Australia and Western Australia.

In South Australia the main fisheries are in Spencer Gulf, Gulf St Vincent[4] and bays along the west coast. Fishing usually takes place in November and December and from March to June, during the dark moon phase, as catch rates decline during the full moon phase. Although western king prawns are the only prawn species in the South Australian prawn fisheries, a

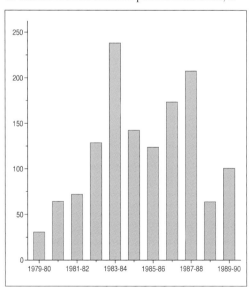

Total annual catch in t of king prawns (*Penaeus latisulcatus* and *P. longistylus*) for the period 1979–80 to 1989–90 from the Northern Prawn Fishery. (Source: Australian Fishing Zone Information System)

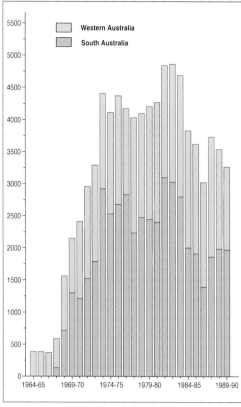

Total annual catch in t of western king prawns for the period 1964–65 to 1989–90. Figures are unavailable for South Australia from 1964–65 to 1966–67. Catches for States that average less than 5 % of the total for all States are not shown. (Source: Fisheries Resources Atlas Statistical Database)

bycatch of other commercially important species is taken. Bycatch species include leatherjackets (Monacanthidae), western school whiting (*Sillago bassensis*), pilchards (*Sardinops neopilchardus*), barracouta (*Thyrsites atun*), flounders (Bothidae), blue swimmer crabs (*Portunus pelagicus*)[12] and southern calamary (*Sepioteuthis australis*).

In Western Australia the principal fisheries are in Shark Bay and Exmouth Gulf, with smaller fisheries off Broome, at Nickol Bay and in the Onslow area. These are generally multi-species fisheries with tiger prawns (*Penaeus esculentus*) and banana prawns (*P. merguiensis*).

In northern Australia western king prawns form a minor part of the catch in the banana prawn fishery and the tiger prawn (*P. esculentus, P. semisulcatus*) and endeavour prawn (*Metapenaeus endeavouri, M. ensis*) fishery.[13] They are also a minor component of the catch in the multi-species Torres Strait and Queensland east coast prawn fisheries. In the Queensland fishery, although king prawns form a major part of the catch (30 % in 1989),[14] 3 species are involved: western king prawns, red spot king prawns (*P. longistylus*) and eastern king prawns (*P. plebejus*).[14] This prawn fishery is offshore, near reef habitat in 40 m to 60 m of water. Fishing is carried out between May and October. Endeavour prawns are also harvested and scallops (*Amusium balloti balloti*) and Moreton Bay bugs (*Thenus orientalis*) form a valuable bycatch that may occasionally be targeted.

Western king prawns are harvested usually at night, by demersal otter trawls in deeper waters in all States, and by beam trawling in Queensland inshore waters. In Spencer Gulf and along the west coast of South Australia fishers use double rigged otter trawl gear and in Gulf St Vincent they use triple rigged gear.

Western king prawn catches are recorded as 'king prawns' as fishers do not distinguish them from red spot king prawns and eastern king prawns when processing the catch. Most of the western king prawn catch is exported, primarily to Japan. However, some of the catch is sold through domestic and local markets. In 1991–92 fishers received an average price of A$ 9.04 per kg for prawns from Spencer Gulf and A$ 11.17 per kg for prawns from the west of South Australia. The wholesale price paid in Western Australia in 1992 varied from A$ 8.50 to A$ 10.50 per kg depending on the size of the prawns.

Management controls The South Australian and Western Australian prawn fisheries are limited entry fisheries with restrictions applying on vessels and gear. Seasonal, monthly and area closures also apply in both States.[15,16] In the Northern Prawn Fishery and the Queensland east coast prawn fishery, limited licence schemes operate. The main prawn trawl fisheries are also regulated by strict seasonal closures recommended by the Northern Prawn Fishery Management Committee and, in Queensland, by the Department of Primary Industries and the Great Barrier Reef Marine Park Authority. There are 2 seasonal closures (summer

Tray of processed western king prawns, South Australia. (Source: Mervi Kangas, South Australian Department of Fisheries)

and winter) in the Northern Prawn Fishery.

Recreational fishery

Western king prawns are taken by recreational fishers in Western Australia from estuaries and inshore waters. Fishing takes place at night, with fishers using scoop nets or small hand trawl nets to collect prawns. Western king prawns caught by recreational fishers are generally smaller than those caught commercially as recreational fishing activity is restricted to within or near the nursery areas. There is no recreational fishery for western king prawns in South Australia.

Management controls In Western Australia, only hand-held scoop nets or hand-held trawl nets may be used for recreational prawning. A daily bag limit applies and there are closed seasons in some estuaries.

Resource status

The South Australian west coast and Spencer Gulf prawn fisheries are considered fully exploited at current levels of fishing effort.[3] The Gulf St Vincent prawn fishery has been overfished and is closed until November 1993. Western king prawn resources in other States are considered fully exploited.

References

1. Grey, D.L., Dall, W. and Baker, A. (1983) *A guide to the Australian penaeid prawns.* Darwin: Department of Primary Production of the Northern Territory. 140 pp.

2. Mulley, J.C. and Latter, B.D.H. (1981) Geographic differentiation of tropical penaeid prawn populations. *Australian Journal of Marine and Freshwater Research* **32**: 897–906.

3. Somers, I.F. (1987) Sediment type as a factor in the distribution of the commercial prawn species of the western Gulf of Carpentaria, Australia. *Australian Journal of Marine and Freshwater Research.* **38**: 133–151.

4. Wallner, B. (1985) *An assessment of the South Australian west coast western king prawn* (Penaeus latisulcatus) *fishery.* South Australian Department of Fisheries. 82 pp.

5. Penn, J.W. (1980) Spawning and fecundity of the western king prawn, *Penaeus latisulcatus* Kishinouye, in Western Australian waters. *Australian Journal of Marine and Freshwater Research* **31**: 21–35.

6. Rothlisberg, P.C., Jackson, C.J. and Pendrey, R.C. (1987) Larval ecology of penaeids of the Gulf of Carpentaria, Australia. I. Assessing the reproductive activity of five

species of *Penaeus* from the distribution and abundance of the zoeal stages. *Australian Journal of Marine and Freshwater Research* **38**: 1–17.

7. Courtney, A.J. and Dredge, M.C.L. (1988) Female reproductive biology and spawning periodicity of two species of king prawns, *Penaeus longistylus* Kubo and *Penaeus latisulcatus* Kishinouye, from Queensland's east coast fishery. *Australian Journal of Marine and Freshwater Research* **39**: 729–741.

8. Dall, W., Hill, B.J., Rothlisberg, P.C. and Staples, D.J. (1990) The biology of the Penaeidae. *Advances in Marine Biology* **27**. 489 pp. Ed by J.H.S. Blaxter and A.J. Southward. London: Academic Press.

9. Penn, J.W. (1975) The influence of tidal cycles on the distributional pathway of *Penaeus latisulcatus* Kishinouye in Shark Bay, Western Australia. *Australian Journal of Marine and Freshwater Research* **26**: 93–102.

10. Carrick, N. (1982) Spencer Gulf prawn fishery — surveys increase our knowledge. *SAFIC* **6**: 1–33.

11. Richardson, B.J. (1982) Geographical distribution of electrophoretically detected protein variation in Australian commercial fishes. III. Western king prawn, *Penaeus latisulcatus* Kishinouye. *Australian Journal of Marine and Freshwater Research* **33**: 933–937.

12. Rohan, G., Jones, K. and McGlennon, D. (1991) *The South Australian marine scale fishery.* South Australian Department of Fisheries, Supplementary green paper. 170 pp.

13. Haysom, N.M. (1985) Review of the penaeid prawn fisheries of Australia. Pp 195–203, in *Second Australian national prawn seminar.* Ed by P.C. Rothlisberg, B.J. Hill and D.J. Staples. Cleveland, Australia.

14. Trainor, N. (1990) Review of the east coast otter trawl fishery. *The Queensland Fisherman* **8**(9): 25–32.

15. Carrick, N. (1988) The role of industry and fleet manipulation studies in the Spencer Gulf prawn fishery. *SAFISH* **12**(4): 4–9.

16. Penn, J.W. and Caputi, N. (1985) Stock recruitment relationships for the tiger prawn, *Penaeus esculentus*, fishery in Exmouth Gulf, Western Australia, and their implications for management. Pp 165–173, in *Second Australian national prawn seminar.* Ed by P.C. Rothlisberg, B.J. Hill and D.J. Staples. Cleveland, Australia.

Contributors

The information on this species was originally provided by James Andrews and Mervi Kangas. Additional comments were made by (in alphabetical order) Neil Carrick, Neil Gribble and Jim Penn. Drawing courtesy of FAO, Rome. (*Details of contributors and their organisations are given in the Acknowledgements section at the back of this book.*)

Compilers Alex McNee and Christina Grieve (maps)

Red spot king prawn

Penaeus longistylus

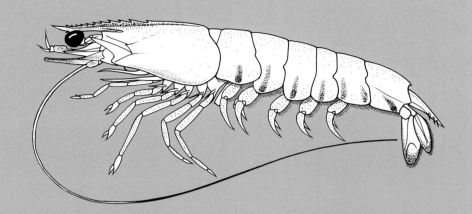

Distribution

In Australian waters, red spot king prawns are common from Shark Bay in Western Australia along northern Australia to near Yeppoon, Queensland. They are also recorded from Lord Howe Island.[2] A single specimen recorded from Cockburn Sound in Western Australia (32°11' S) probably represented larvae brought south of the species' normal distribution by tropical water.[3] On the east coast, isolated individuals have been recorded as far south as Moreton Bay(27°25' S). Red spot king prawns are rare in the Gulf of Carpentaria, especially along the eastern part of the Gulf. The species' distribution includes South-east Asia from the South China Sea to Malaysia and Indonesia.[1]

In Western Australia, red spot king prawns are associated with sponges, soft corals (eg large gorgonians), coarse sand or shell grit substrates, coral reefs and coral rubble.[3] On the Queensland east coast, they are rarely found more than 30 km from coral reef systems.[4] Through much of Queensland, red spot king prawn juveniles inhabit coral reef lagoons in depths of 1–3 m,[4] yet in north-eastern Queensland the juveniles live in estuaries and on reef tops.[4] Adults inhabit inter-reef channels and adjacent waters in depths from about 18 m to 60 m, often on sand-mud substrates.[5]

Life history

Red spot king prawns have an extended spawning period between May and October.[6] Sexual maturity increases steadily from about April to a peak in July–August when a maximum ovary weight is attained. There are also increases in ovary weight in January and November–December.[6] The main peak in population fecundity correlates with low

Penaeus longistylus Kubo

Red spot king prawn

Another common name is **red spotted prawn**.
FAO: **redspot king prawn**
Australian species code: 701303

Family PENAEIDAE

Diagnostic features Red spot king prawns are grooved prawns, ie they have a pair of parallel grooves running the length of the upper surface of the carapace. The gastrofrontal groove is divided into 3 posteriorly, and the postrostral groove is long. There is an accessory pair of ridges on the blade of the rostrum. Red spot king prawns can be distinguished from western king prawns by having a red abdominal spot and blue-red over cream body markings (blue over cream in western king prawns).[1,2] The presence of an extended spine on the first walking leg is a useful feature for identifying juveniles.

sea bed water temperature (to 23.6°C) from June to September.[6] Spawning in the Gulf of Carpentaria takes place during June to September,[7] and in Torres Strait, quarterly samples showed high proportions of sexually mature female red spot king prawns present in March, June and September,[8] and a low proportion in December.

There is no information on the prawn's larval form and maximum age. However, red spot king prawns appear to be unusual in that, unlike some other prawns, they do not require estuarine or coastal environments for the successful completion of their life cycle.[4] Red spot king prawn larvae are transported to reef tops and settle as postlarvae on shallow sandy areas. Settlement takes place between September and May.[5] Juvenile red spot king prawns emigrate from reef tops into deeper water[9] when they are 15–20 mm in carapace length. Movement is generally local, with apparently random longer movements.[3,9] Adult red spot king prawns are sedentary, which makes them unique among prawns.

These prawns grow more slowly than do eastern king prawns, *Penaeus plebejus*.[9] Growth rates in red spot king

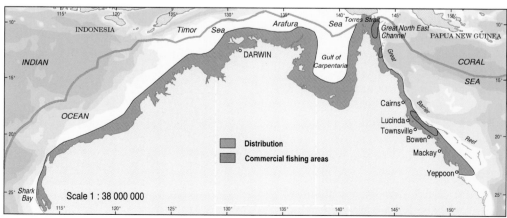

Geographic distribution and commercial fishing areas for red spot king prawns in Australian waters.

prawns vary year by year and females grow more quickly than males.[9] At 1 year of age, females weigh about 40 g and have a carapace length around 44 mm. Females attain a larger size than males; they have been recorded at up to 180 mm total length. Males are reported to reach 150 mm total length.[1]

Red spot king prawns are sexually mature by 33 mm carapace length in central Queensland waters,[6] although in Torres Strait sexually mature red spot king prawns as small as 24 mm carapace length have been recorded.[8] Ripe females grow to 54.5 mm in length.[6] Mating by red spot king prawns can take place when the prawns are as small as 26 mm carapace length. Generally, a high proportion (more than 80 %) of females in the population carry sperm packets at any one time of the year.[6] The proportion of early mature and ripe females in the Queensland central east coast population never exceeds 10 % in any month.[6]

The red spot king prawn diet conforms to the general penaeid pattern, and includes active selection and opportunistic feeding.[4] They consume detritus, molluscs, crustaceans, polychaete worms, brittle stars and basket stars (Ophiuroidea). These prawns are predatory, and will chase smaller crustaceans and polychaetes. They also scavenge.[4]

Stock structure

No studies on the stock structure of red spot king prawns have been conducted.

Commercial fishery

The commercial fishery for this species is primarily in the eastern Queensland part of its range. The main fishing area is between about Lucinda and Bowen (18°–21° S) on the central coast, over a 20–30 km wide strip to the west of the Great Barrier Reef.[4] Commercial catches were first taken in this area in the late 1970s. Although annual catches of king prawns fluctuate in this area, the fishery has developed rapidly. In 1983, 300 vessels took 650 t[10] of red spot king prawns. Between 1984 and 1990, annual landings have varied between about 600 t and 1800 t.

Red spot king prawns are caught by demersal otter trawlers operating at night. The main fishing effort is expended in

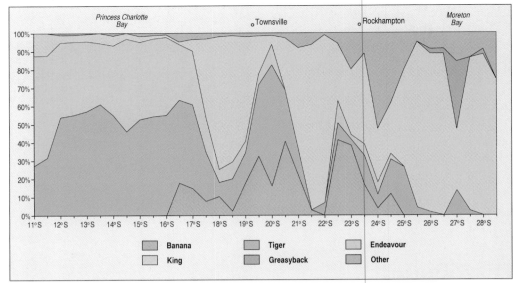

Percentage catch composition of prawn groups in the Queensland east coast fishery from 11°00' S to the New South Wales border for the period 1988–1989. (Figure adapted from Trainor.[15])

open water in depths of 40–60 m, in the vicinity of coral reefs.[10,11] Red spot king prawns are the major components of the 'king prawn' fishery on the central Queensland coast, with western king prawns (*Penaeus latisulcatus*) making up the remaining 20–30 %.[4,10] More than 70 % of the catch in this fishery is taken between May and September.[4] In 1985–86, red spot king prawns and western king prawns comprised 36 % by weight of the catch from the central prawn trawl fishery,[11] which includes the coastal fisheries for tiger prawns (*P. esculentus, P. semisulcatus*) and endeavour prawns (*Metapenaeus endeavouri, M. ensis*). The 'tiger prawn' fishery does not overlap with the 'king

prawn' fishery in the same area, as it is centred on inshore waters 10–30 m deep and takes place from March to June[11] (or even August). Also, there is no interaction between the fisheries for red spot king prawns and eastern king prawns in Queensland waters. In the fishery for red spot king prawns about 22–23° S (eg, off North West Island, 23°18' S) at 40–60 m, eastern king prawns only occur in depths of more than 150 m.

The total east coast king prawn (red spot and western) catch was 2257 t in 1988, 2272 t in 1989 and 2357t in 1990.

Other fisheries for red spot king prawns take place off far north-east Queensland and in the Great North East Channel area of Torres Strait. In Torres

Prawn trawlers in the early morning, south-eastern Queensland. (Source: Glen Smith, Southern Fisheries Centre, Queensland Department of Primary Industries)

Strait, red spot king prawns are an incidental catch of the brown tiger and endeavour prawn fishery: logbook data indicates that king prawns form only 1–10 % of the total prawn catch.[12] The catches of king prawns in Torres Strait are almost exclusively red spot king prawns — between 96–98 % of the king prawn catch.[8] In the south-eastern Gulf of Carpentaria, red spot king prawns form only a small component (less than 1 %) of the Northern Prawn Fishery.[13]

Bycatch in the king prawn fishery includes species such as blue endeavour prawns (*M. endeavouri*), sand bugs (*Thenus* species), saucer scallops (*Amusium balloti balloti*) and coral prawns (*Metapenaeopsis* species, *Trachypenaeus* species).[10]

Red spot king prawns and western king prawns are not differentiated in catches and are marketed together. Prices for these 2 species are generally close to, but slightly less than, those for eastern king prawns — averaging A$ 10.00–13.00 per kg wholesale in 1992. The market for these prawns does not form a niche of its own. Red spot king prawns are sold both on domestic and overseas markets.

Management controls There are no specific controls for red spot king prawns. They are managed as part of the Queensland multi-species trawl fishery to which restrictions on gear size, vessel size and boat numbers apply.

Recreational fishery

There is no recreational fishery for red spot king prawns.

Resource status

Stable catch rate data indicate that recruitment is reasonably steady under increasing fishing pressure.[4] However, annual landings between 1983 and 1990 have varied by a factor of 3.

References

1. Grey, D.L., Dall, W. and Baker, A. (1983) *A guide to the Australian penaeid prawns*. Darwin: Department of Primary Production of the Northern Territory. 140 pp.

2. Holthuis, L.B. (1980) FAO species catalogue. Vol. 1. Shrimps and prawns of the world. An annotated catalogue of species of interest to fisheries. *FAO Fisheries Synopsis No. 125*, **1**. 261 pp.

3. Penn, J.W. (1980) Observations on length-weight relationships and distribution of the red spot king prawn, *Penaeus longistylus* Kubo, in Western Australian waters. *Australian Journal of Marine and Freshwater Research* **31**: 547–552.

4. Dredge, M.C.L. (1988) Queensland's near reef trawl fisheries. 15 pp, in *Workshop on Pacific inshore fishery resources, 15–25 March 1988, Noumea, New Caledonia*. Noumea: South Pacific Commission.

5. Robertson, J. (1990) *Habitat selection, distributional overlap and coexistence of two king prawn species*, Penaeus longistylus *Kubo and* Penaeus latisulcatus *Kishinouye, off the central Queensland Coast*. Unpublished PhD thesis, University of Queensland. 123 pp.

6. Courtney, A.J. and Dredge, M.C.L. (1988) Female reproductive biology and spawning periodicity of two species of king prawns, *Penaeus longistylus* Kubo and *Penaeus latisulcatus* Kishinouye from Queensland's east coast fishery. *Australian Journal of Marine and Freshwater Research* **39**: 729–743.

7. Rothlisberg, P.C., Jackson, C.J. and Pendrey, R.C. (1987) Larval ecology of penaeids of the Gulf of Carpentaria, Australia. I. Assessing the reproductive activity of five species of *Penaeus* from the distribution and abundance of the zoeal stages. *Australian Journal of Marine and Freshwater Research* **38**: 1–17.

8. Somers, I.F., Poiner, I.R. and Harris, A.N. (1987) A study of the species composition and distribution of commercial penaeid prawns of Torres Strait. *Australian Journal of Marine and Freshwater Research* **38**: 47–63.

9. Dredge, M.C.L. (1990) Movement, growth and natural mortality rate of the red spot king prawn, *Penaeus longistylus* Kubo, from the Great Barrier Reef lagoon. *Australian Journal of Marine and Freshwater Research* **41**: 399–410.

10. Robertson, J. and Dredge, M. (1986) Redspot king prawn research off central Queensland. *Australian Fisheries* **45**(6): 18–20.

11. Jones, C.M. and Derbyshire, K. (1988) Sampling the demersal fauna from a commercial penaeid fishery off the central Queensland coast. *Memoirs of the Queensland Museum* **25**(2): 403–415.

12. Watson, R.A., Channells, P. and Blyth, P.J. (1990). Commercial prawn catches in Torres Strait. Pp 13–19, in *Torres Strait prawn project: a review of research 1985–1987*. Ed by J.E. Mellors. *Queensland Department of Primary Industries, Information Series* **QI 90018**.

13. Robertson, J.W.A., Coles, R.G. and Goeden, G.B. (1985). Distribution patterns of commercial prawns and reproduction of *Penaeus esculentus* around the Wellesley Islands in the southeastern Gulf of Carpentaria. Pp 71–75, in *Second Australian national prawn seminar*. Ed by P.C. Rothlisberg, B.J. Hill and D.J. Staples. Cleveland, Australia.

14. Dall, W. (1957) A revision of the Australian species of Penaeinae (Crustacea: Decapoda: Penaeidae). *Australian Journal of Marine and Freshwater Research* **8**: 136–231.

15. Trainor, N. (1990) Review of the east coast otter trawl fishery. *The Queensland Fisherman* **8**(9): 25–32.

Contributors

Information on this species was originally provided by (in alphabetical order) Tony Courtney, Mike Dredge, John Robertson, Neil Trainor, Clive Turnbull and Reg Watson. James Andrews provided comment. Figure redrawn by Peter Moloney after Dall.[15] *(Details of contributors and their organisations are given in the Acknowledgements section at the back of this book.)* **Compilers** Patricia Kailola and Christina Grieve (maps)

Prawn net repairs, Queensland. (Source: Glen Smith, Southern Fisheries Centre, Queensland Department of Primary Industries)

Eastern king prawn

Penaeus plebejus

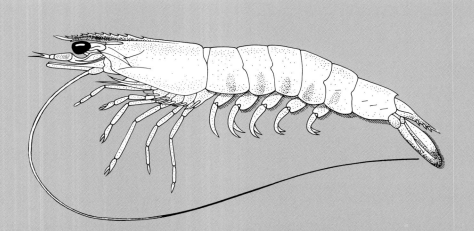

Penaeus plebejus Hess

Eastern king prawn

Another common name is **king prawn**.
FAO: **eastern king prawn**
Australian species code: 701304

Family PENAEIDAE

Diagnostic features Eastern king prawns are grooved prawns, ie they have a pair of parallel grooves running the length of the upper surface of the carapace. The gastrofrontal groove is divided into 3 posteriorly, and the postrostral groove is long. There is an accessory pair of ridges on the blade of the rostrum. Their body is cream to yellow and the ridges are dark brown. There are short brown stripes on the sides of the tail segments. The tips of the antennal scales and uropods (tail fan) are blue with red fringes.[1]

Distribution

Eastern king prawns are endemic to Australia. They inhabit the east coast between Mackay in Queensland and north-eastern Tasmania in water depths ranging from 1 m to 220 m, and they are also present around Lord Howe Island.[2]

Postlarval to adolescent eastern king prawns inhabit areas of higher salinity within estuaries and possibly oceanic waters than do juveniles of many other prawn species.[3] Eastern king prawns have been found on both bare and vegetated substrates, but where both substrate types occur in the one area, prawn abundance is greatest on vegetated areas.[4,5]

Life history

Eastern king prawns spawn at sea,[2,3] and the northern, warmer waters of the prawns' range between northern New South Wales and Swain Reefs in Queensland appear to be the most important spawning areas.[6] Eastern king prawns spawn over most of the year, but mainly between January and August,[3,7] in depths greater than 90 m.

The larval phase of the eastern king prawn life cycle lasts about 3 weeks.[8] The larvae are found near the edge of the continental shelf, mostly near the sea floor by day and higher in the water

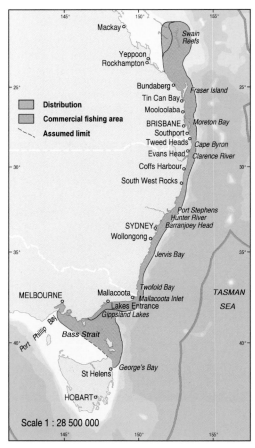

Geographic distribution and commercial fishing area for eastern king prawns.

column at night.[9] The planktonic nauplius larvae hatch from the eggs[8] and develop through a series of moults into postlarvae. They settle in coastal lakes and estuaries along the entire coast to the south of the main spawning area, from about Tin Can Bay to Lakes Entrance, and they are in greatest abundance between February and October.[4,5] The postlarvae are carried across estuary and river bars by tidal currents in the first few hours of flood tide.[5] The area ultimately inhabited by the benthic juveniles probably varies according to the spawning location and winds and currents, such as the East Australian Current.[2,10] For example, females spawning close to the shore (within 10 km) in water shallower than about 50 m contribute the majority of recruited postlarvae to the local population.[10]

After about 12 months,[3] older juvenile eastern king prawns in New South Wales move out of coastal lakes and estuaries to offshore, deeper waters. Prawns in more northerly areas such as Moreton Bay are probably younger when they emigrate. The offshore migration takes place in summer, the prawns moving out in the surface waters of the night ebb tide, during the darker half of the lunar cycle.[2] The size of the emigrating prawns varies considerably with season and from one region to another.[2,7] The differences probably reflect variations in local temperature, salinity and food abundance, or a combination of these factors.[2] The prawns reach sexual maturity within several months of leaving the estuaries, at between 12 and 18 months of age.[2,3]

The movement pattern of eastern king prawns out of estuaries into deeper marine waters and northwards along the coast has been documented by tagging studies.[2,7] It is possible that this is a spawning migration,[2] although prawns

Measuring eastern king prawns. (Source: John Matthews, Fisheries Research Institute, NSW Fisheries)

may spawn as far south as Jervis Bay.[7] Prawns from some regions move offshore to water deeper than about 70 m before migrating north (eg from the Hunter River), whereas prawns from other regions stay close to the coast (eg Clarence River), at least during the early part of the migration.[2] The schools of migrating prawns travel rapidly[2] and generally at a uniform rate.[7] It is likely that they move in shallower water south of Cape Byron and in deeper water north of Cape Byron.[7] The Fraser Island–Mooloolaba area is the endpoint in the migration of most eastern king prawns from Moreton Bay and estuaries as far south as Sydney.[2,11] Migration distances recorded from recaptured tagged eastern king prawns are the longest reported for any prawn species.[7] For example, the longest recorded migration is 1193 km in 407 days from a release site in the Gippsland Lakes.[7]

As with other penaeid prawn species, the growth rate of eastern king prawns is generally high, and females have a higher growth rate than males.[2] The life span for eastern king prawns is 1–2 years or perhaps even 3.[2,11] A growth model for this species predicts that female prawns grow to a mean maximum length of 59.5 mm carapace length and male prawns to 45.5 mm. The longest prawn measured during research studies has been 71 mm carapace length. The longest recorded total lengths are 300 mm for females and 190 mm for males.[1] Although the length by which 50 % of female

eastern king prawns are mature varies along the New South Wales coast, the average is 40 mm carapace length.[12]

Eastern king prawns are opportunistic omnivores. Food items include small crustaceans, polychaete worms, bivalve molluscs and Protozoa. They are eaten by most carnivorous marine species, including rays (Batoidea), flathead (Platycephalidae), cobbler (*Cnidoglanis macrocephalus*), dolphins (Cetacea) and seals (Pinnipedia).[3]

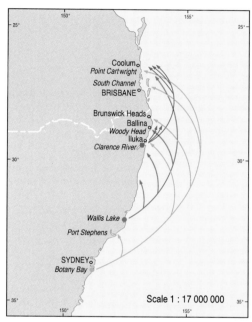

Eastern king prawn migration pathways inferred from studies by Ruello[2] and Montgomery[8] (redrawn). The point of release is indicated by a circle. Each arrow represents at least 1 prawn.

Stock structure

Electrophoretic[13] and tagging[2,7] studies indicate that the eastern king prawn population is a unit stock. It comprises a single adult population supported by prawns from many estuaries along the east coast.

Commercial fishery

The eastern king prawn is the prawn species of most economic importance in eastern Australia, and has been exploited for more than 50 years.[14] There are fishing grounds in offshore waters and in some estuaries from east of Swain Reefs in Queensland to the Gippsland Lakes in Victoria. Approximately 60 % of the average total catch comes from Queensland waters and 93 % is taken north of the Clarence River.[11] Small catches are taken from areas such as Twofold Bay and Lakes Entrance.[2]

In Queensland, most of the catch comes from southern areas. The prawn fleet is separated into 2 components — an inshore, shallow water fleet which fishes sub-adult prawns, and an offshore fleet which fishes mainly adult prawns. The inshore catch of eastern king prawns is very seasonal, whilst the offshore boats fish king prawns year round. The large fishery in southern Queensland is supported by a substantial contribution of migrating eastern king prawns from New South Wales.[2]

In New South Wales, the prawns are caught as juveniles in estuaries during spring and summer, and as sub-adults and adults on the continental shelf from 60 m depth and deeper. The adults are fished in waters shallower than 100 m south of Cape Byron, and deeper than 182 m north of Cape Byron.[7] They are targeted from midsummer through winter in southern waters but a year-round fishery exists north of Coffs Harbour.[7,14] Because of their northerly migration, eastern king prawns are targeted sequentially by local fleets as the prawns move along the coast, and fishing fleets follow the prawns into deeper water as the season progresses.[11]

Eastern king prawns are harvested by numerous methods within estuaries (demersal otter trawling, set pocket and running netting, hauling, seining and hand netting) whilst offshore they are harvested exclusively by demersal otter trawling. Species of finfish, octopus, squid (Loliginidae), bay lobsters (Scyllaridae) and crabs (Portunidae) are caught as bycatch.

In Queensland, prawns from the inshore fishery are sold either fresh or frozen to local markets. Larger prawns from the offshore fishery are exported green, frozen and headed, mainly to Spain and Japan. Prices per kg to fishers range from A$ 3.00 for small eastern kings sold as part of a mixed catch of so-called 'bay prawns', to A$ 15.00 for large, frozen eastern kings. The Sydney Fish Market price per kg for eastern king prawns during 1991–92 averaged A$ 12.18 (green) and A$ 13.27 (cooked).

Management controls There is a limit on the number of vessels licensed to fish for prawns off New South Wales and Queensland. Restrictions are also placed on the number of vessels, engine horsepower, vessel length and the total headline length of net towed. The prawn fishery in Queensland is closed to further

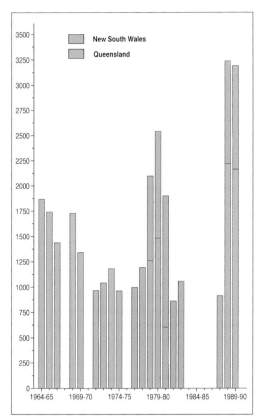

Total annual catch in t of eastern king prawns for the period 1964–65 to 1989–90. Figures are unavailable for: New South Wales from 1964–65 to 1977–78 and 1983–84 to 1986–87; and Queensland for 1967–68, 1970–71, 1975–76 and 1981–82 to 1987–88. Catches for States that average less than 5 % of the total for all States are not shown. For most years, the Queensland catch figures include an unknown amount of red spot king prawns (*Penaeus longistylus*). (Source: Fisheries Resources Atlas Statistical Database)

limits on gear, vessel size and vessel replacement. Area and seasonal closures are also a significant component of management in both States.

Recreational fishery

Eastern king prawns are exploited within estuaries from Noosa Heads in Queensland to north-eastern Tasmania.

Methods of harvesting include fishing with scoop nets, scissor nets or 6 m drag nets.

Management controls There are restrictions in New South Wales on the size of mesh and gear used.

Resource status

The eastern king prawn population is heavily exploited. There are concerns that both biological and economic overfishing is occurring. A recent study[14] suggested that further increases in fishing effort would only cause lower catch rates.

References

1. Grey, D.L., Dall, W. and Baker, A. (1983) *A guide to the Australian penaeid prawns.* Darwin: Department of Primary Production of the Northern Territory. 140 pp.

2. Ruello, N.V. (1975) Geographical distribution, growth and breeding migration of the eastern Australian king prawn *Penaeus plebejus* Hess. *Australian Journal of Marine and Freshwater Research* **26**: 343–354.

3. Racek, A.A. (1959) Prawn investigations in eastern Australia. *State Fisheries Research Bulletin* **6**: 1–57.

4. Coles, R.G. and Greenwood, J.G. (1983) Seasonal movement and size distribution of three commercially important Australian prawns species (Crustacea: Penaeidae) within an estuarine system. *Australian Journal of Marine and Freshwater Research* **34**: 727–743.

5. Young, P.C. and Carpenter, S.M. (1977) Recruitment of postlarval prawns to nursery areas in Moreton Bay, Queensland. *Australian Journal of Marine and Freshwater Research* **28**: 745–773.

6. Potter, M.A. and Dredge, M.C.L. (1985) Deepwater prawn resources off southern and central Queensland. Pp 221–229, in *Second Australian national prawn seminar.* Ed by P.C. Rothlisberg, B.J. Hill and D.J. Staples. Cleveland, Australia.

7. Montgomery, S.S. (1990) Movements of eastern king prawns, *Penaeus plebejus*, and identification of stock along the east coast of Australia. *Fisheries Research* **9**: 189–208.

8. Preston, N. (1985) The effects of temperature and salinity on survival and growth of larval *Penaeus plebejus*, *Metapenaeus macleayi* and *M. bennettae*. Pp 31–40, in *Second Australian national prawn seminar.* Ed by P.C. Rothlisberg, B.J. Hill and D.J. Staples. Cleveland, Australia.

9. Rothlisberg, P.C. (1982) Vertical migration and its effect on dispersal of penaeid shrimp larvae in the Gulf of Carpentaria, Australia. *Fishery Bulletin (U.S.)* **80**: 541–554.

10. Rothlisberg, P.C., Church, J.A. and Fandrey, C.B. (submitted, 1992) A mechanism for nearshore concentration and estuarine recruitment of postlarval *Penaeus plebejus* (Decapoda, Penaeidae). *Estuarine, Coastal and Shelf Science.*

11. Glaister, J.P., Lau, T. and McDonall, V.C. (1987) Growth and migration of tagged eastern king prawns *Penaeus plebejus* Hess. *Australian Journal of Marine and Freshwater Research* **38**: 225–241.

12. Glaister, J.P. (1983) *Dynamics of the eastern Australian king prawn population.* Unpublished PhD thesis, University of New South Wales. 208 pp.

13. Mulley, J.C. and Latter, B.D.H. (1981) Geographic differentiation of eastern Australian penaeid prawn populations. *Australian Journal of Marine and Freshwater Research* **32**: 889–895.

14. Glaister, J.P., Montgomery, S.S. and McDonall, V.C. (1990) Yield-per-recruit analysis of eastern king prawns *Penaeus plebejus* Hess, in eastern Australia. *Australian Journal of Marine and Freshwater Research* **41**: 175–197.

15. Dall, W. (1957) A revision of the Australian species of Penaeinae (Crustacea: Decapoda: Penaeidae). *Australian Journal of Marine and Freshwater Research* **8**: 136–231.

Contributors

Information on this species was originally provided by Steven Montgomery. It has been supplemented with comments from (in alphabetical order) David Die, John Glaister, Peter Rothlisberg and Derek Staples. Figure redrawn by Peter Moloney after Dall.[15] (*Details of contributors and their organisations are given in the Acknowledgements section at the back of this book.*)
Compilers Patricia Kailola and Christina Grieve (maps)

Prawn trawlers at Brunswick Heads, northern New South Wales. (Source: John Glaister, Fisheries Branch, Queensland Department of Primary Industries)

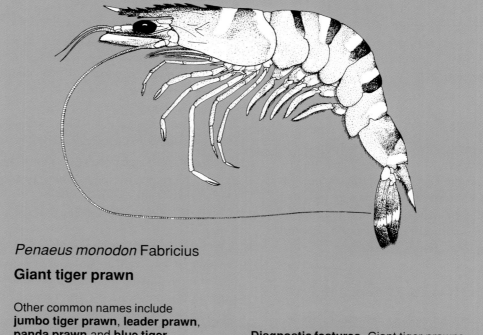

Giant tiger prawn

Penaeus monodon

Penaeus monodon Fabricius

Giant tiger prawn

Other common names include **jumbo tiger prawn**, **leader prawn**, **panda prawn** and **blue tiger prawn**.
FAO: **giant tiger prawn**
Australian species code: 701908

Family PENAEIDAE

Diagnostic features Giant tiger prawns can be distinguished by their large size and distinctive black and white stripes across their abdomen. Adults are coloured light brown to red and juveniles are dark grey to bluish.[1]

Distribution

Giant tiger prawns are distributed from Shark Bay in Western Australia through Northern Territory and Queensland waters to the Hawkesbury River in New South Wales. Sometimes, individuals have been found near Perth in Western Australia but these prawns are thought to have been transported there in ships' ballast water. Giant tiger prawns are also distributed throughout the western Pacific and Indian oceans.

Larval giant tiger prawns live in estuarine waters, in seagrass beds and mangrove areas. From these nursery areas, the juveniles migrate to deeper coastal waters. Giant tiger prawns have been caught in waters as deep as 110 m but they usually live in less than 30 m of water. They inhabit mud, silt and sand substrates.

Life history

Little is known of the life history of giant tiger prawns in the wild in Australia. Most of the information on life history is based on research into commercial farming of the species. However, it is known that in the wild, spawning is initiated by rising water temperatures. In warmer tropical waters there is an extended spawning period with peaks between August and November and March and April. Spawning occurs in deeper coastal waters.

Under hatchery conditions females spawn at night. Optimum water temperatures for spawning are between 28°C and 30°C. The eggs hatch after 10 to 14 hours. The larvae grow through several developmental stages in the next 10 days. The eggs, larval and postlarval prawns are planktonic for the first 2 weeks of life. In the wild, the larvae move on coastal currents to nursery areas in shallow embayments and mangrove fringed estuaries where they settle onto

the substrate. They remain in this habitat until about 80 mm long.

The older juvenile giant tiger prawns migrate out of the nursery habitat to

deeper waters where they continue to grow. This migration can be extensive: giant tiger prawns have been taken in trawls up to 72 km from shore. Females

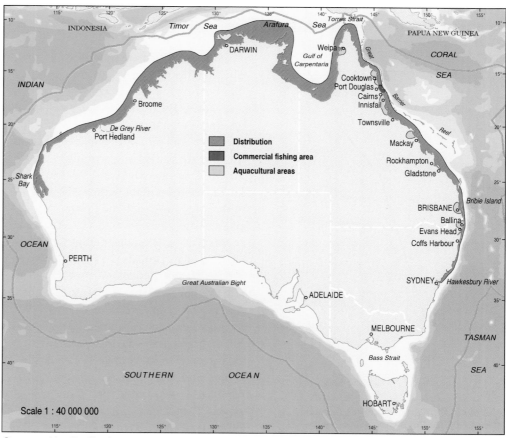

Geographic distribution, commercial fishing area and aquacultural areas for giant tiger prawns in Australia.

are reported to grow to 336 mm total length, and males are generally smaller. Giant tiger prawns have also been recorded up to 150 g in weight, but in farming operations they are generally harvested at between 100 mm and 130 mm total length, weighing between 20 g and 30 g.

Stock structure

Recent genetic examinations have found that populations of giant tiger prawns from the De Grey River in the north-west of Western Australia are significantly different from those present throughout the Northern Territory, north Queensland, and New South Wales.[2,3]

Commercial fishery

Giant tiger prawns are uncommon in Australian waters[1] and generally are caught only as bycatch of other prawn fisheries — particularly the banana prawn fisheries — in Queensland, the Northern Territory and Western Australia. Giant tiger prawns are combined with other tiger prawns in catches, so there are no separate catch figures recorded for them.

A commercial operator working out of Cairns is landing live giant tiger prawns for sale to hatcheries as broodstock. The operator uses a small otter trawl to catch the prawns, which are immediately transferred to shore and air-freighted to

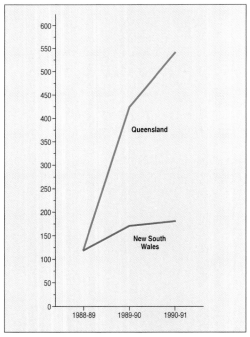

Australian farm production of penaeid prawns in t for the period 1988–89 to 1990–91. Figures for 1990–91 are estimates. (Source: Gillespie[8] and O'Sullivan[9,5])

the buyers. The fishery is intermittent, depending on demand and availability, and provides 90 % of wild-caught spawning females sold to farmers. In 1990, 2000 animals were sent to hatcheries. The best monetary return is for females in spawning condition, which were worth A$ 50.00 to A$ 80.00 each in 1990. For the same year non-spawning females (called 'blanks') were worth A$ 20.00 to A$ 40.00 each while males were worth A$ 10.00 to A$ 15.00 each.

Management controls Fishers catching giant tiger prawns in the Northern Prawn Fishery are regulated by the Commonwealth of Australia, and those operating in the Western Australian and Queensland prawn fisheries are regulated by their State Governments. The prawn fisheries are 'limited entry' licence issue and regulations apply for gear types, boat length, closed seasons and areas.

Aquaculture

The giant tiger prawn is the species used in 95 % of the commercial prawn farming ventures in Australia. These are mainly in Queensland and northern New South Wales. The largest concentration of farms is on the north Queensland coast between Cooktown and Townsville.[4] There are 30 farms, 23 in Queensland and 7 in New South Wales. There is also an experimental farm in the Northern Territory.[5]

At present all spawning stock is obtained from the wild either as egg-bearing females or 'blank' females and males. The 'blank' females and males are kept in maturation tanks at the hatchery until required, while egg-bearing females are placed in spawning tanks on arrival. Once spawned and hatched, the larval prawns remain in the spawning tanks until they reach the first larval phase, when they are transferred to larval rearing tanks. The nursery tanks are stocked at 15 animals per l and the larvae are fed algae (*Chaetoceros gracilis*), brine shrimp (*Artemia* species) and, in many operations, commercial microencap-sulated diets. The postlarval juveniles are either stocked directly into ponds at densities of 15–20 animals per square m or transferred to intensive nursery ponds for 2 to 3 weeks before being stocked into ponds. Ponds are prepared to ensure phytoplankton blooms prior to and during stocking. Farmers also feed

Breeding tanks at a prawn aquaculture research facility. (Source: Stewart Frusher, Division of Sea Fisheries, Tasmanian Department of Primary Industry and Fisheries)

prawns with commercial food pellets during the pond grow-out stage.

Ponds can either be selectively harvested by netting or trapping, or completely harvested by draining. Growth rates in aquaculture operations are dependent on water temperatures. The time to grow from spawning to harvestable size varies from 6–7 months in Queensland to 7–10 months in New South Wales. However, by stocking with postlarval juvenile prawns, farmers are able to grow the prawns to commercial size in 6–9 months, depending on water temperatures. Farmers in north Queensland are capable of growing 2 crops of prawns a year from these stockings, whereas those further south will get only 1 crop per year.[4] Yields for 1988–89 were low on average, at 1.7 t per ha per year. However, some farmers recorded yields over 6 t per ha per year, indicating that it is possible to increase yields without developing additional ponds.[6]

The prawns are harvested, sorted into size categories, packed into crushed ice and sent to local markets within 24 to 48 hours. Some farms have the ability to cook prawns before packaging, depending on market requirements, but about 50 % are packaged uncooked. Most of the production is sold through fish markets in the major capital cities in the eastern States. Small amounts are sold to local restaurants or as farm gate sales for local consumption. Trial consignments of live prawns from Queensland to restaurants in southern States have met with limited success. In 1992 farmers were receiving A$ 10.00 to A$ 12.00 per kg for giant tiger prawns.

As well as farms concentrating on grow-out of commercial size prawns there are specialised hatcheries in southern and central Queensland producing postlarval juveniles for sale to farmers for ongrowing. Several farms in Queensland and New South Wales also operate hatcheries as well as grow-out ponds. In 1989–90 an estimated 110 million postlarval juveniles were produced and sold for between A$ 17.00 to A$ 20.00 per thousand.[7] Postlarval prawns from hatcheries were sold to farmers in Queensland, New South Wales and overseas.[6]

Management controls People wishing to run aquaculture operations require permission from relevant State or local government authorities. They also require licences to access, pump and discharge water and wastes. An aquaculture permit is required to produce and sell prawns to wholesalers. Potential aquaculturists in New South Wales also require a fish farming permit that covers the rearing and sale of cultured animals. There are also regulations covering the interstate transfer of breeding and grow-out stock.

Recreational fishery

There is no target recreational fishery for giant tiger prawns. Their low abundance in Australian waters means that they would occur rarely in mixed prawn catches, but occasional juveniles may be taken.

Resource status

Aquaculture production of giant tiger prawns is a developing industry in Australia currently valued at about A$ 6 million. Production is still low and costs are high relative to other countries that are farming prawns. However, costs are falling as experience and technology improve, and if farmers can increase production and maintain quality there is a demand for this product in the domestic market.[8]

References

1. Grey, D.L., Dall, W. and Baker, A. (1983) *A guide to the Australian penaeid prawns.* Darwin: Department of Primary Production of the Northern Territory. 140 pp.

2. Benzie, J.H., Frusher, S.D. and Ballment, E. (in press, 1992) Geographic variation in allozyme frequencies of *P. monodon* (Crustacea:Decapoda) populations in Australia. *Australian Journal of Marine and Freshwater Research.*

3. Benzie, J.H., Ballment, E. and Frusher, S.D. (in press, 1992) Genetic structure of *P. monodon* populations in Australia. *Aquaculture.*

4. Robertson, C.H. (1988) Prawn farming in Queensland — problems and progress so far. Pp 17–27, in *Proceedings of the first shellfish aquaculture conference, 1988.* Ed by L.H. Evans and D. O'Sullivan. Western Australia: Curtin University of Technology.

5. O'Sullivan, D. (1991) Status of Australian aquaculture in 1989/90. *Austasia Aquaculture.* 1991 (June): 2–13.

6. Quinn, R., Barlow, C. and Witney, E. (1991) Aquaculture in Queensland continues to grow. *Austasia Aquaculture* **5**(7): 9–12.

7. Kenway, M. (1991) The quality and production of post larval prawns in Australia. *Proceedings of the third intensive tropical animal production seminar, Townsville, August 1991.* Queensland Department of Primary Industries.

8. Gillespie, N. (1991) Domestic market to soak up prawn farm harvest. *Austasia Aquaculture* **5**(7): 5–7.

9. O'Sullivan, D. (1990) *Aquaculture downunder. Status & prospects for Australian aquaculture (1989–90).* Tasmania: Dosaqua. 67 pp.

Contributors

The information on this species was originally provided by Stewart Frusher and supplemented by (in alphabetical order) Geoff Allan, Chris Barlow, Noel Gillespie, Matt Kenway, Derek Staples and Lindsay Trott. Drawing courtesy of FAO, Rome. (*Details of contributors and their organisations are given in the Acknowledgements section at the back of this book.*)

Compiler Alex McNee

Larval rearing tanks at a prawn aquaculture research facility. (Source: Stewart Frusher, Division of Sea Fisheries, Tasmanian Department of Primary Industry and Fisheries)

Y a b b y

Cherax destructor

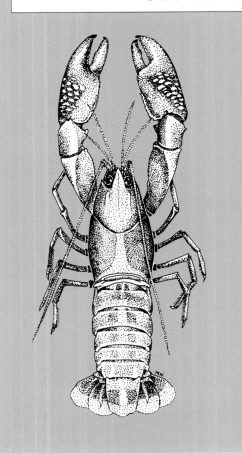

Cherax destructor (Clark)

Yabby

There are no other common names.
FAO: no known name
Australian species code: 704002

Family PARASTACIDAE

Diagnostic features Yabbies are freshwater crayfish which are distinguished from others by having 4 low ridges along the head and a short, smooth rostrum. Their claws are broad and spade-like, with serrations along their inner edge. The claws are sometimes covered with a matt of fine hairs. Body colour ranges from pale to dark brown and there is a distinctive mottled pattern on the outer edge of the claws.

(fecundity) increases with the size of the female parent and it is not uncommon to find 1000 eggs on a large female. Repetitive spawning is common and females can produce 2 or 3 broods a year.[1]

Following spawning, the female carries the eggs under her tail, where they incubate for 3 weeks at water temperatures of 23–24°C, longer at lower temperatures.[1] Larval development occurs within the egg and juveniles emerge as miniature adults. They remain attached to the female for a further 2 or 3 weeks before becoming independent.[1] At this stage they are 3–4 mm total length.[2]

Like all crustaceans, yabbies have to moult as they grow, the frequency decreasing as they grow older.[1] Newly hatched juveniles moult frequently.

Distribution

Yabbies are widely distributed throughout central and southern inland Australia. There is also a translocated population in the south-west of Western Australia.

Yabbies live in both temporary and permanent habitats including rivers, creeks, billabongs, lakes, irrigation canals, farm dams, swamps and bore drains.[1] Generally they inhabit turbid, slow flowing or still, shallow water but they can be found in waters up to 5 m deep,[2] depending on the levels of dissolved oxygen. Juveniles are often found associated with macrophytes — ie large emergent aquatic plants — in the shallower parts of waterbodies.[2,3] In the Murray River basin yabbies occupy offstream floodplain habitats.[2] Temperature limits for yabbies are between 0°C and 36°C.[3] Yabbies can survive periods of drought by burrowing in damp soil and they remain in their burrows until the next rains.[1]

Life history

Yabbies spawn from October to March, with a peak in activity between December and February.[3] Spawning is induced by

an increase in day length and water temperature — to above 15°C.[1] Yabbies spawn in the afternoon into early evening. The number of eggs produced

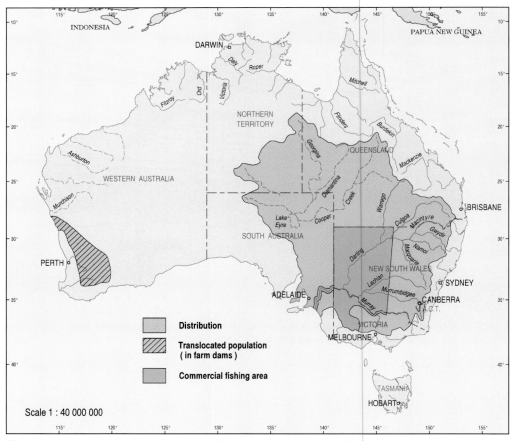

Geographic distribution and commercial fishing area for yabbies in Australian inland waters, including translocated populations.

Weight can increase by up to 50 % with each moult. Growth in yabbies is highly variable and is related to water temperature and food availability. Under ideal conditions maximum growth occurs at water temperatures around 28°C.[3] Yabbies can grow to 60 g in their first 6 months after hatching. Growth is stunted in crowded conditions and ceases below 10°C. Yabbies grow best in semi-permanent water bodies that expand during flooding. Both male and female yabbies mature when 2–3 months old, with the females slightly bigger (40–50 mm carapace length) than males (30 mm carapace length).[1]

Feeding activity peaks at dusk and dawn. As juveniles, yabbies filter food from the water. As adults, their diet is dominated by detritus, plant material and small invertebrates.[3] Yabbies are cannibalistic and smaller animals often fall prey to larger animals, particularly when moulting. Yabbies are also preyed on by fish, water rats (*Hydromys* species), fresh water tortoises (Chelidae), and water birds. Water birds, particularly cormorants (*Phalacrocorax* species), can be a major pest in commercial pond operations.

Stock structure

While yabbies are distributed throughout a wide area, they are not highly mobile and many isolated populations exist. Many of these populations were originally described as different species but recent work suggests that many may just be local variations of the one species.[4]

Commercial fishery

Yabbies are commercially fished in New South Wales, Victoria and South Australia. In New South Wales the fishery is centred on the western rivers and lakes, particularly those associated with the Darling River. In South Australia most of the catch is taken in the Murray River, with a small amount taken in Lake Alexandrina. In Victoria the western lakes Albacutya, Hindmarsh and Walla Walla are the only waters open to commercial yabby fishing.

The fishery is seasonal, operating from November to May in western Victoria. Catches are highly variable.[3] Baited pots are set at dusk and left out over night. Drop nets may also be used. Fishing effort

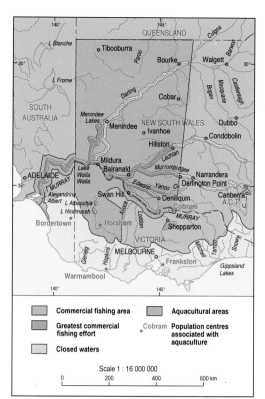

Commercial fishing area and aquacultural areas for yabbies in inland waters.

intensifies following flooding, as in dry years many lakes cease to exist. Fishers in New South Wales supply only local markets such as restaurants, and restrict

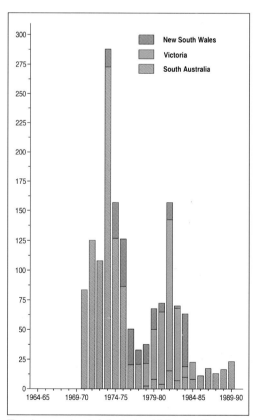

Total annual catch in t of yabbies for the period 1964–65 to 1989–90. Figures are unavailable for: New South Wales from 1964–65 to 1972–73 and 1984–85 to 1989–90; Victoria from 1964–65 to 1977–78 and 1985–86 to 1989–90; and South Australia from 1864–65 to 1969–70. (Source: Fisheries Resources Atlas Statistical Database)

their fishing effort to supply those markets.

Most yabbies are sold whole and cooked, and the size at which they are marketed varies. For the Australian market, 60 mm carapace length is preferred (weight between 30–45 g). Local prices vary. In 1992, yabbies sold in New South Wales for the restaurant trade returned A$ 6.00–8.00 per kg. Preferred size for overseas markets varies from the German preference for larger animals over 80 g to the French preference for smaller animals around 30–40 g. Animals for the export market averaged A$ 10.00 per kg (wholesale) in 1992.

Management controls State regulations control the numbers of traps or pots used by commercial fishers. There is no restriction on the number of animals that can be taken and no size limits. In Victoria only 3 lakes are open to commercial fishing and all rivers are closed. In New South Wales the main channel of the Darling River is closed to commercial fishing, as are the Lachlan River upstream from Hillston and the Murrumbidgee River upstream from Darlington Point and reaches of the Murray and Murrumbidgee rivers around major towns.[5]

Aquaculture

One method of yabby farming uses shallow (less than 1 m deep) ponds with an average area of 0.25 ha. A plant crop, usually clover, is grown when the ponds are empty. This crop provides food for the yabbies as the ponds are flooded. Supplementary foods may also be used. The yabbies are initially stocked at a density of 3 per m[2] in early or mid-spring (August–October). The water level in the ponds is gradually increased, flooding the vegetation. Most Victorian operations use wild-caught broodstock in their breeding ponds. From them, juveniles are harvested and transferred to 'grow-out' ponds. Animals in grow-out ponds are harvested at 1 year of age, weighing about 50–80 g.[6]

The distribution of yabby farms in 1991 was as follows: New South Wales — 38; Victoria — 100, but only 24 producing;[7] South Australia — 112; Western Australia — 57. The location of farming areas is generally controlled by access to wild-caught broodstock and distance to market.

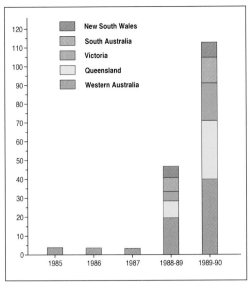

Total cultured production in t of all freshwater crayfish for calendar years 1985 to 1987 and financial years 1988–89 to 1989–90. Figures are unavailable for Queensland, Victoria, South Australia and New South Wales from 1985 to 1987. (Source: Martin Smallridge, University of Adelaide; Rick Fallu, Victorian Department of Conservation and Environment; Fisheries Department of Western Australia; O'Sullivan;[7] Quinn et al;[8] O'Sullivan[6])

In Victoria there are hatcheries at Cobram and Frankston, and several farmers maintain ponds specifically for the production of juveniles. Extensive culture farms are located in the Wimmera area (around Horsham), while intensive culture is centred in the Goulburn valley area (near Shepparton). In South Australia most farming is centred around Bordertown in the south-east.

A Western Australian company operates by periodically harvesting yabby

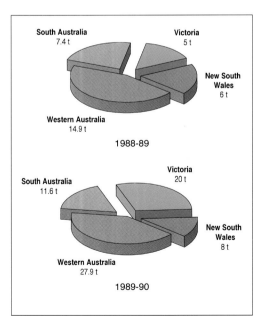

Proportion of cultured yabby production by State for the years 1988–89 and 1989–90. Western Australian figures include production of koonacs. (Source: Martin Smallridge, University of Adelaide; Rick Fallu, Victorian Department of Conservation and Environment; Fisheries Department of Western Australia; O'Sullivan;[6] Quinn et al;[8] O'Sullivan[7])

populations in farm dams. Farmers receive a set amount per kg for the harvest. This arrangement started as a wild stock fishery, but now the operator supplies farmers with additional management information designed to improve yields. The other species of freshwater crayfish farmed in Western Australia are marron (*Cherax tenuimanus*) and koonacs (*Cherax plebejus, Cherax glaber*).

The major problems encountered by yabby farmers are oxygen depletion and bird predation. Oxygen depletion occurs when overfeeding leads to excessive algal growth, and can be avoided by proper management and pond design. Bird predation is reduced by constant vigilance at the ponds or by having bird netting over the ponds.

Yabbies are marketed both locally and overseas. The best local prices are obtained through direct sales to restaurants. Prices for farmed yabbies in 1992 averaged between A$ 10.00 and A$ 20.00 per kg, highest prices being received in South Australia and Western Australia. The major export destinations are Hong Kong and Singapore.

Recreational fishery

Recreational fishing for yabbies occurs throughout their natural range. Yabby pots and hoop nets are the main gear used. The fishery is seasonal and highly opportunistic with greatest activity at periods of highest numbers, ie following flooding when population numbers increase rapidly. Large adults are targeted.

Harvesting yabbies from a drained pond, South Australia. (Source: Martin Smallridge, University of Adelaide)

Management controls No size or bag limits apply. Gear restrictions and closed waters are set out in State regulations. In Victoria pots are banned in inland waters except in those lakes open to commercial fishing. In all States females carrying eggs must be returned to the water.

Resource status

The level of exploitation of this species is difficult to determine due to its seasonal availability and the opportunistic way in which it is fished.

References

1. Johnson, H.T. (1988) Crayfish farming. Pp 2–9, in *Crayfish farming*. Ed by G. Ryder. Sydney: NSW Department of Agriculture and Fisheries.

2. Lake, P.S. and Sokal, A. (1986) Ecology of the yabby, *Cherax destructor. Australian Water Resources Council, Technical Paper No.* **87.** 186 pp.

3. Mitchell, B.D. and Collins, R. (1989) *Development of field-scale intensive culture techniques for the commercial production of the yabby* (Cherax destructor/albidus). Centre for Aquatic Science, Warrnambool Institute of Advanced Education, unpublished report. 253 pp.

4. Morrissy, N.M., Evans, L.E. and Huner, J.V. (1990) Australian freshwater crayfish: aquaculture species. *World Aquaculture* **21**(2): 113–122.

5. O'Connor, P.F. (1989) Fisheries management in inland New South Wales. Pp 19–23, in *Proceedings of the workshop on native fish management.* Ed by B. Lawrence. Canberra: Murray–Darling Basin Commission.

6. O'Sullivan, D. (1990) *Aquaculture downunder. Status & prospects for Australian aquaculture (1989–90).* Tasmania: Dosaqua. 67 pp.

7. O'Sullivan, D. (1991) Status of Australian aquaculture in 1989/90. *Austasia Aquaculture* 1991 (June): 2–13.

8. Quinn, R., Barlow, C. and Witney, E. (1990) Aquaculture in Queensland continues to grow. *Austasia Aquaculture* **5**(7): 9–12.

Contributors

The information on this species was provided originally by Martin Smallridge, and supplemented by (in alphabetical order) Ray Clark, Rick Fallu and John Timmons. Drawing courtesy of the Murray–Darling Basin Commission. (*Details of contributors and their organisations are given in the Acknowledgements section at the back of this book.*)
Compiler Alex McNee

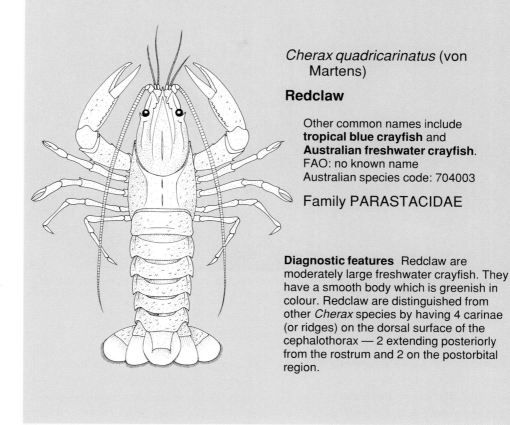

Redclaw

Cherax quadricarinatus

Cherax quadricarinatus (von Martens)

Redclaw

Other common names include **tropical blue crayfish** and **Australian freshwater crayfish**.
FAO: no known name
Australian species code: 704003

Family PARASTACIDAE

Diagnostic features Redclaw are moderately large freshwater crayfish. They have a smooth body which is greenish in colour. Redclaw are distinguished from other *Cherax* species by having 4 carinae (or ridges) on the dorsal surface of the cephalothorax — 2 extending posteriorly from the rostrum and 2 on the postorbital region.

Distribution

Redclaw live in rivers of northern Australia, from the Daly River in the Northern Territory eastwards to the Normanby River on the eastern side of Cape York Peninsula. They have also been found in rivers in south-eastern New Guinea.[1]

Redclaw inhabit permanent fresh water to a depth of 5 m and are abundant in the headwaters sections of rivers. They can live in a variety of habitats, from shallow, clear, fast flowing creeks to the deep, still and often turbid waters of billabongs.[2] Redclaw prefer sites with abundant aquatic vegetation that provides cover. They leave the water regularly and can exist in stagnant or poor quality waters.

Life history

Redclaw spawn throughout the year, although there is less spawning activity in May and June. In southern Queensland, where redclaw are aquacultured, farmers have reported a shorter spawning season of about 6 months. Spawning is stimulated by water temperature rising above 20°C, and is possibly also influenced by an increase in day length. Females are capable of producing up to 3 broods in a spawning season. Fecundity varies with the size of the female parent and they produce from 300 to 1000 eggs per brood.[1]

During mating the male deposits a sperm mass on the female's shell between her walking legs. The female curls her tail to form a temporary brood chamber, into which she releases the eggs 12 to 24 hours later. The sperm mass is broken and fertilisation occurs, with the eggs becoming attached beneath the female's tail. The 2 mm long oval eggs are carried beneath the female's tail for 6 to 10 weeks. The larval redclaw develop within the eggs before emerging as miniature adults.[1]

At hatching, larval redclaw are 9.5 mm long on average. They remain attached to the female for 1–2 weeks, making independent feeding forays of increasing duration until they become totally independent about 3 weeks after

Natural distribution of redclaw in Australian inland waters and centres of aquaculture production in Queensland.

Distribution
Aquacultural areas
• Cairns Population centres associated with aquaculture

Scale 1 : 40 000 000

Catch of commercial sized redclaw from the research ponds at the Northern Fisheries Centre at Walkamin near Cairns. (Source: Clive Jones, Fisheries Branch, Queensland Department of Primary Industries)

hatching.[1] In optimum conditions the larvae weigh 0.5–1 g after 50–60 days. Redclaw live for 4 to 5 years, reaching 90 mm carapace length and usually weighing around 300 g, although they have been recorded up to 600 g.[1] Both males and females mature after the first year.

Larval redclaw have a diet that includes zooplankton and detritus and the adult diet is dominated by detritus.[1] Cormorants (*Phalacrocorax* species), herons (Ardeidae), eels (*Anguilla* species) and water rats (*Hydromys* species) are major predators on pond stock.

Stock structure

Redclaw populations are dispersed throughout their natural range. This dispersal pattern suggests use of a preferred habitat rather than any genetic differences between redclaw populations. Populations exhibiting morphological and colour differences have been identified from rivers in Queensland and the Northern Territory but their genetic and specific status is unknown.

Commercial fishery

There is no commercial fishery for redclaw, primarily due to their remote distribution. However, there is limited collection from wild stocks to provide broodstock and juveniles for aquaculture operations.

Aquaculture

The commercial aquaculture of redclaw only commenced in 1985.[3] By 1990, there were 80 licensed farmers in Queensland with 140 ha of pond area.[4] Of these only 20 were 'serious' redclaw farmers and only 3 had produced significant yields. Until 1990 most farming activity centred on southern Queensland but recently larger farms have been established in far northern Queensland. There are also trial farms in northern New South Wales and the Northern Territory.

Commercial aquaculture of redclaw uses earthen 'grow-out' ponds, each 500 m to 1 ha in area and 1–2 m deep. The ponds are stocked with juveniles that are taken from the wild or are hatchery-reared. Some operations maintain broodstock ponds that contain naturally reproducing populations. Juveniles are harvested from these ponds and stocked into grow-out ponds. They are stocked at a size of 0.1–2 g at densities of 2–10 per m². Temperatures of 23–30°C and dissolved oxygen concentrations greater than 5 parts per million are ideal for redclaw growth. Under these conditions they will reach 50–100 g after 1 year.[1] It takes between 1 and 3 years for a stock to reach commercial size. The redclaw are harvested from the ponds by either trapping them or draining the ponds.[1]

Redclaw are harvested when they reach 50–100 g or 100–150 g in size, depending on the market.[5] The main market is for whole live animals which

are sold to restaurants. Some redclaw are also sold frozen, either whole or split. Market prices for redclaw ranged from A$ 10.00 to A$ 20.00 in 1992. Currently 80 % of production is sold locally with the remaining 20 % exported, mainly to Hong Kong, Singapore, Europe and the United States of America.

With commercial operations only recently established, production is still quite low. Seven t of redclaw were produced in 1988.[6] This rose to 31 t by 1989–90[6] and approximately 50 t in 1990–91. Estimates for 1991–92 are up to 150 t with more ponds in large scale operations in northern Queensland becoming productive.

Management controls All aquaculture operations must be licensed. The requirements vary between States but usually cover aspects of water quality, as well as permits to produce and sell redclaw. It is illegal to fish commercially for redclaw in Queensland natural waters but permits are issued to collect a limited number of animals as breeding stocks for aquaculture operations. All animals sold have to be certified to show that they are farm produced and not taken from the wild. At present there is no minimum legal saleable size.

Recreational fishery

Recreational fishing for redclaw is limited to the areas near population centres

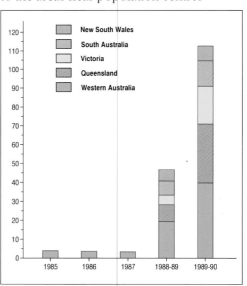

Total cultured production in t all of freshwater crayfish for calendar years 1985 to 1987 and financial years 1988–89 to 1989–90. Figures are unavailable for Queensland, Victoria, South Australia and New South Wales from 1985 to 1987. (Source: Martin Smallridge, University of Adelaide; Rick Fallu, Victorian Department of Conservation and Environment; Fisheries Department of Western Australia; Quinn et al;[6] O'Sullivan;[8] O'Sullivan[7])

within their natural range. Fishing is carried out throughout the year and larger adults are targeted. Fishing effort is low, primarily due to the isolation of natural populations of redclaw. However, it may increase as the market for cultured redclaw develops.

Management controls There are no bag limits or minimum sizes set for this species in Queensland or the Northern Territory. In Queensland redclaw may only be taken by recreational fishers using baited lines and must be eaten at the site of capture.

(below) Drained redclaw pond in south-eastern Queensland. Car tyres are used to provide a sheltered habitat. (Source: Clive Jones, Fisheries Branch, Queensland Department of Primary Industries)

Resource status

Wild redclaw populations have not been reduced significantly. If markets for farm produced stock are expanded, potential for illegal exploitation of wild stocks would exist, either by commercial or recreational fishers.

Notes

The high densities of animals required for commercial aquaculture operations can increase the risk of disease outbreaks. Export potential of Australian freshwater crayfish depends on the absence of crayfish plague, *Aphanomyces astaci.* Keeping Australian farms free of this

disease will ensure that the demand for Australian crayfish species overseas is maintained.

References

1. Jones, C.M. (1990) *The biology and aquaculture potential of the tropical freshwater crayfish*, Cherax quadricarinatus. Brisbane: Queensland Department of Primary Industries. 130 pp.

2. Horwitz, P. (1990) The conservation status of Australian freshwater crustacea. *Australian National Parks and Wildlife Service, Report Series* **14**. 121 pp.

3. Jones, C.M. (1990) Commercial production of redclaw. *Australian Fisheries* **49**(11): 18–21.

4. Gillespie, J. (1990) Redclaw, a hot new prospect. *Australian Fisheries* **49**(11): 2–3.

5. Jurgensen, T. (1990) Marketing challenges need to be faced. *Australian Fisheries* **49**(11): 40–41.

6. Quinn, R., Barlow, C. and Witney, E. (1990) Aquaculture in Queensland continues to grow. *Austasia Aquaculture* **5**(7): 9–12.

7. O'Sullivan, D. (1991) Status of Australian aquaculture in 1989/90. *Austasia Aquaculture* 1991 (June): 2–13.

8. O'Sullivan, D. (1990) *Aquaculture downunder. Status & prospects for Australian aquaculture (1989–90).* Tasmania: Dosaqua. 67 pp.

Contributors

The information on this species was originally provided by Clive Jones. Drawing by Charles Hausman. (*Details of contributors and their organisations are given in the Acknowledgements section at the back of this book.*)
Compiler Alex McNee

Marron

Cherax tenuimanus

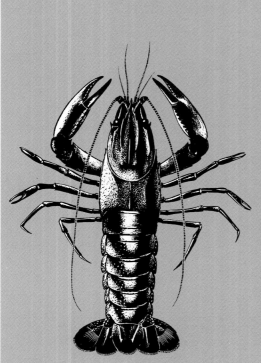

Cherax tenuimanus (Smith)

Marron

There is no other common name.
FAO: no known name
Australian species code: 704004

Family PARASTACIDAE

Diagnostic features Marron are distinguished from other freshwater crayfish by having 5 ridges on the head and 3 pairs of spines on the rostrum. Their claws are narrow and pincer-like. There are 2 small spines on the central segment of the tail fan. Large marron are usually jet black. Juveniles are brown but may be variegated.

Distribution

Marron inhabit the river systems of south-western Western Australia, from Esperance in the east to the Hutt River north of Geraldton. Prior to European settlement marron were probably restricted to the larger permanent rivers of the south-west, from the Kent River westward to the Harvey River north of Bunbury. Their range was subsequently extended by the deliberate seeding of rivers and stocking of large irrigation and farm dams with juvenile and adult marron. Clearing, habitat modification, and poor agricultural practices since then have caused the range of marron to contract towards the coast.[1]

Marron live in fresh to brackish water (salinity less than 6–8 parts per thousand), including deep pools in rivers and some natural and artificial lakes and farm dams. They favour areas with a sandy bottom, with logs and debris for cover.[1]

Marron have been translocated to southern Queensland, northern New South Wales and South Australia for farming purposes. They have also been introduced to the United States of America, the Caribbean, Zimbabwe, South Africa, New Zealand, China and Japan where experimental culture is being assessed.[2]

Life history

Marron usually first spawn at 2 years of age or older, although 1-year-old

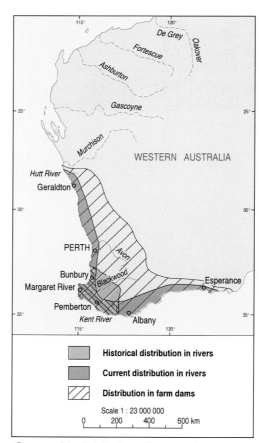

Geographic distribution of marron in Australian inland waters, including extensions to the range through translocation to rivers and farm dams.

▨	**Historical distribution in rivers**
▨	**Current distribution in rivers**
▨	**Distribution in farm dams**

Scale 1 : 23 000 000
0   200   400   600 km

egg-bearing females have been recorded. Mating is stimulated by rising water temperature and starts any time after mid-July when the water temperature reaches 12°C.[3] Spawning normally occurs from September to October. Fertilisation is external and the female carries the fertilised eggs, which measure 2.5 mm or larger in diameter,[4] in a mass attached to the swimmerets beneath her tail. The eggs hatch in October and November but the larvae remain attached, hanging head down beneath the female's tail for a further 3–5 weeks. They are released from the female when they reach about 10 mm in length.[1]

Growth in marron is related to competition for space and food.[5] This is shown by the difference in recorded growth rates between populations in rivers, dams and research cultivation ponds. Growth is faster in dams, marron growing to approximately 76 mm carapace length in 2 years. However, juvenile survival is greater in river populations. Growth is maximised at a water temperature of 24°C. Young marron moult every 10 days, the interval between moults increasing to 2 months as the marron grow.[1] Marron can live for over 10 years, growing to 38 cm in total length (17 cm carapace length), and a weight of 2.2 kg.[1]

Male marron mature between 1–2 years of age at about 30 mm carapace length. Females are smaller (25 mm carapace length) at maturity, some maturing at 1–2 years of age but most at 2–3 years. Females produce 50–750 eggs per brood, with larger animals producing more eggs. Egg development is slow and females will produce only 1 brood a year.[2]

Juvenile marron move to deeper water in their first year of life, but there are no regular migrations upstream or downstream. In clear water marron feed at night, with most activity in the hours following dusk. Marron are opportunistic scavengers and will feed on detritus, plant and animal material and aquatic invertebrates. They have been known to leave the water and feed along the banks.[1]

Protective cover is very important to juveniles as mortality from both predators and cannibalism is quite high. Predators include water rats (*Hydromys* species), cormorants (*Phalacrocorax* species), kookaburras (*Dacelo* species) and several larger species of freshwater fish.[1]

Stock structure

Marron are non-migratory, and separate stocks can be identified in individual pools along the length of a river. Over time, there is limited movement by marron both upstream and downstream from these pools, and this allows for some intermixing of stocks.[3]

Commercial fishery

The commercial fishery on wild marron stocks was closed in the 1950s and has not been reopened.

Aquaculture

The development of an inland aquaculture industry for freshwater crayfish began in the late 1960s with experiments on the culture of marron and yabby, *Cherax destructor*.[2] Marron culture has been carried out in Western Australia for 20 years. Recently farms have been established in Queensland, New South Wales and South Australia. Most Queensland farmers have switched to production of redclaw (*Cherax quadricarinatus*) however, a tropical freshwater crayfish that is more suited to warmer climates.

Marron are cultured both extensively and semi-intensively in Western Australia. Extensive culture is private culture in existing farm dams and natural water bodies. Stock may be added initially if natural populations do not exist. The dams are harvested periodically, mostly for personal use. Supplementary feeding, stock and water quality management and predator control may be used to increase yields.[6]

Semi-intensive culture employs purpose-built ponds and is the method preferred for commercial production. A farm usually has several small, shallow

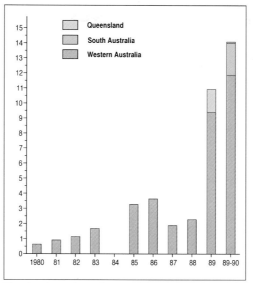

Total cultured production in t of marron for calendar years 1980 to 1989 and financial year 1989–90. Figures are unavailable for Western Australia for 1984. (Source: Fisheries Department of Western Australia; O'Sullivan;[7] O'Sullivan[9])

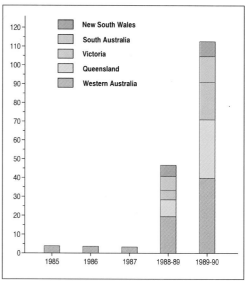

Total cultured production in t of all freshwater crayfish for calendar years 1985 to 1987 and financial years 1988–89 to 1989–90. Figures are unavailable for Queensland, Victoria, South Australia and New South Wales from 1985 to 1987. (Source: Martin Smallridge, University of Adelaide; Rick Fallu, Victorian Department of Conservation and Environment; Fisheries Department of Western Australia; O'Sullivan;[7] O'Sullivan;[9] Quinn et al[10])

ponds, which are easy to manage and harvest. The farmer requires a reliable supply of clean, well-aerated water, and sufficient cover to reduce predation. Removable artificial habitats are useful, particularly in juvenile rearing operations, as they ease the harvesting of smaller animals. Larger scale operations have small broodstock ponds for the production of juveniles and several 'grow-out' ponds with animals at various stages of growth. This capacity ensures a constant supply to markets.[6] Ponds are stocked with juveniles at up to 10 per m^2 with most stocked at 5 per m^2.

The only other farming method for marron currently being investigated is intensive battery culture. This involves the rearing of juvenile marron in individual compartments housed within a larger tank.

The marron farming industry supplies 2 main markets. The first is for direct human consumption through retailers and restaurants within Australia and to export markets. About 23 % of marron production is exported mainly to South-east Asia and Europe. The second market is for juvenile marron which are stocked for commercial or private culture.[7] In 1992 the average price received by marron growers was about A$ 27.00 per kg.

Sorting a marron catch. (Source: Dos O'Sullivan, Dosaqua)

Management controls In 1975 amendments to the Western Australian *Fisheries Act* provided for the licensing and control of commercial fish farming activities within the State. The legislation included regulations controlling the commercial sale, farming and processing of marron. A legal minimum size was also applied to marron sold for human consumption. In 1986, following a review of licensing governing freshwater aquaculture in Western Australia, several changes were implemented. The changes allowed the sale of undersized marron to the food market and the harvesting of broodstock from private impounded waters. These measures have facilitated further development of the commercial aquaculture industry as indicated by increased production in recent years.

The commercial harvest of broodstock from the wild is not permitted.

Recreational fishing

Marroning is an important recreational activity in the rivers and lakes of south-western Western Australia, with approximately 25 000 licences issued in 1990. Catches declined from an estimated 150 t in the 1970s to an estimated 53 t in

Harvesting marron from a drained pond at Margaret River Marron Farm, Western Australia. (Source: Dos O'Sullivan, Dosaqua)

1986–87. Declining catches combined with a period of low water levels, saw the fishery closed in 1987 to allow stocks to recover.[3] It was reopened in 1989–90 for a very restricted season. The dates for the opening of the season are now set each year and publicised prior to the opening.

The best time to catch marron is in the hours following sunset. Chicken feed pellets and meat are popular baits. In shallow waters along dam shores, scoop nets are the most common fishing methods. In deeper waters drop nets are used. These are more effective in deep river pools and can be used later into the night when the marron are more active. Sections of the Warren and Shannon rivers near Pemberton are open only to fishing with pole snares,[8] a popular method for catching larger marron that forage during daylight.[3]

Management controls Licences are required for marroning, and a legal minimum size applies. State regulations set out bag limits and allowable gear. Undersized animals and females carrying eggs must be returned to the water. The use of boats or diving gear is illegal.[8]

Resource status

Marron culture in Western Australia is still a small industry. The ban on harvest of wild stocks to provide brood stock has meant that the industry is self-supporting. Barring any major disease outbreaks or other problems, the future of the industry resource should be good.

Wild stocks are subject to fishing pressure from recreational fishers, fluctuations in water supply (both natural and induced by humans) and deteriorating water quality through changes in catchment use. These factors have had adverse effects on the abundance and range of marron.

References

1. Marron (1989) *Fisheries Department of Western Australia, Fishing WA* **8**. 4 pp.

2. Morrissy, N.M., Evans, L.E. and Huner, J.V. (1990) Australian freshwater crayfish: aquaculture species. *World Aquaculture* **21**(2): 113–122.

3. Morrissy, N.M. and Fellows, C.J. (1990) The recreational marron fishery in Western Australia, summarised research statistics, 1971–1987. *Fisheries Department of Western Australia, Fisheries Research Report* **87**. 27 pp.

4. Morrissy, N.M. (1970) Spawning of marron, *Cherax tenuimanus* Smith (Decapoda: Parastacidae) in Western Australia. *Fisheries Department of Western Australia, Fisheries Bulletin* **10**. 23 pp.

5. Morrissy, N.M. (in press, 1992) Density-dependent pond growout of year class cohorts of a freshwater crayfish, *Cherax tenuimanus* (Smith) to two years of age. *Journal of World Aquaculture Society*.

6. Morrissy, N.M. (1985) Marron and marron farming. *Fisheries Department of Western Australia, Fisheries Information Publication* **4**. 31 pp.

7. O'Sullivan, D. (1990) *Aquaculture downunder. Status & prospects for Australian aquaculture (1989–90)*. Tasmania: Dosaqua. 66 pp.

8. *Marron fishing in Western Australia* (1989) Fisheries Department of Western Australia. 2 pp.

9. O'Sullivan, D. (1991) Status of Australian aquaculture in 1989/90. *Austasia Aquaculture* 1991 (June): 2–13.

10. Quinn, R., Barlow, C. and Witney E. (1990) Aquaculture in Queensland continues to grow. *Austasia Aquaculture* **5**(7): 9–12.

Contributors

Most of the information on this species was provided originally by Noel Morrissy, and supplemented by (in alphabetical order) Heather Brayford and Ray Clarke. Drawing by Roger Swainston. (*Details of contributors and their organisations are given in the Acknowledgements section at the back of this book.*)

Compiler Alex McNee

Southern rock lobster

Jasus edwardsii

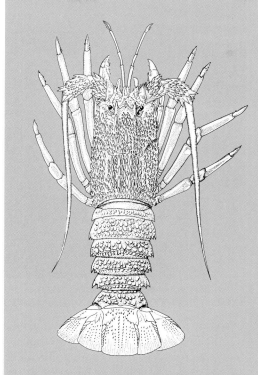

***Jasus edwardsii* (Hutton)**

Southern rock lobster

Other common names include **rock lobster**, **red rock lobster** and **crayfish**.
FAO name: no known name
Australian species code: 703014

Family PALINURIDAE

Diagnostic features Southern rock lobsters have 2 distinct, long supraorbital spines on the upper anterior part of the carapace, and their other carapace spines are narrow and raised. The medial antennules have short flagella. The abdominal segments are sculptured into scale-like shapes before each transverse groove. Southern rock lobsters vary in colour from usually reddish-purple and orange in shallow water to purple and creamy yellow in deeper water, and often there are pale bands on the antennal flagella.

Distribution

Southern rock lobsters are distributed from Coffs Harbour in northern New South Wales, around Tasmania, across southern Australia, to Dongara in Western Australia. They are also present throughout New Zealand waters.[1] These rock lobsters live in a variety of reef habitats on the continental shelf, in water from 1 m to approximately 200 m deep.

Life history

Southern rock lobsters mate primarily between April and July. Fertilisation is external, the male depositing a spermatophore under the female's body.[2] Very shortly after, the eggs are extruded and the female carries the fertilised eggs under the abdomen (ie is 'in berry') for 4 to 6 months. The number of eggs carried varies with the female's size. A female lobster with a carapace length of 74 mm can carry 69 000 eggs and a female with a carapace length of 124 mm can carry 400 000 eggs.[3] Most eggs hatch between September and November. Mating and egg hatching tend to occur earlier in southern waters of the species' distribution.

Southern rock lobsters have several recognised life stages. The eggs hatch into naupliosome larvae which quickly moult into the phyllosoma larval stage. The thin, leaf-like phyllosoma larvae are planktonic and become widely dispersed during a lengthy oceanic phase, estimated to last up to 23 months.[1] During this period they can be carried by ocean currents at least 1100 km from land.[1] The phyllosoma larvae change into transparent puerulus larvae, which resemble miniature adult lobsters in shape. The pueruli swim onto the continental shelf where they settle in coastal waters. The highest settlement rates in South Australia occur during July

and August,[4] 8 or 9 months after hatching. Soon after settlement, the pueruli moult into bottom-living juvenile lobsters.

Growth rates of southern rock lobsters differ greatly between locations and also between mature males and females. There is a general trend for the growth rate and resulting size of rock lobsters to decrease from northern Tasmanian to southern Tasmanian waters, and from the south-east of South Australia towards western South Australia. For example, in Tasmanian studies between 1987 and 1990, the carapace lengths of the largest rock lobsters caught in pots were 208 mm (male) and 197 mm (female) at King Island in the north, and 144 mm (male) and 114 mm (female) on the south coast.

Southern rock lobsters are known to live for at least 20 years and grow to at least 230 mm carapace length.

The size at which females reach sexual maturity varies and is approximately 112–114 mm carapace length in western South Australia[5] and 75–80 mm in south-eastern South Australia.[5] About half the females are mature at 115 mm carapace length at King Island, northern Tasmania, and at about 65 mm in southern Tasmania. Females appear to reach sexual maturity at between 3.5 and 4.5 years of age. The age or size at maturity of males is unknown.

There is currently no evidence for mass migrations by southern rock lobsters in Australian waters. However,

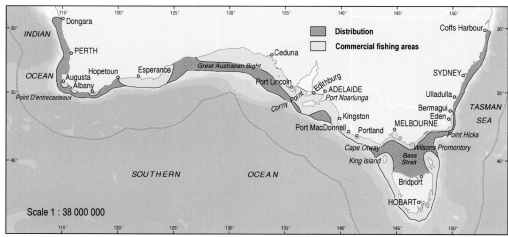

Geographic distribution and commercial fishing areas for southern rock lobsters in Australian waters.

movements of up to 89 km have been reported,[6,7] as well as shorter distances from inshore to deeper offshore waters. In many locations, rock lobsters show little recorded movement.[6]

Southern rock lobsters are carnivorous and eat molluscs, small crustaceans, echinoderms and other benthic invertebrates.[3]

Major predators of both adult and juvenile southern rock lobsters are octopus (*Octopus* species) and gummy sharks (*Mustelus antarcticus*).[8] Other predators are fish such as southern rock cod (*Physiculus* species), flathead (Platycephalidae), wrasse (Labridae), morwong (Cheilodactylidae), conger eels (*Conger* species) and rock ling (*Genypterus* species).[8]

Stock structure

Recent studies[1] have shown no genetic or morphological evidence for discrete stocks of southern rock lobsters in Australian and New Zealand waters. The Australian form was previously known as *Jasus novaehollandiae*.

Commercial fishery

The southern rock lobster commercial fishery is based primarily off South Australia, Tasmania and Victoria. Small catches are also taken around Esperance in Western Australia and in southern New South Wales. In Tasmania, the fishery takes place along the entire coast and Bass Strait islands, except for the central north coast. In Victoria, 80 % of the catch is taken west of Cape Otway, where the grounds extend up to 42 km offshore. Between Cape Otway and Wilsons Promontory the fishery is confined to a narrow strip of inshore reef up to 7 km offshore; and further eastwards there are only sparse patches of reef offshore including a very narrow coastal reef east of Point Hicks. In South Australia, commercial fishers operate in all continental shelf waters except the 2 gulfs and near estuaries.

Fishing for southern rock lobsters is permitted all year in New South Wales but in other States harvesting is from early October to the end of April or from mid-November to the end of August. The rock lobsters are caught in wood, cane or steel pots baited with whole fish or fish heads. The pot shapes vary from beehive

A southern rock lobster and a beehive pot, the most common type of pot used in the Tasmanian fishery. (Source: Australian Department of Foreign Affairs and Trade)

to square to rectangular. The entrance is usually on the upper surface of the pot, but some fishers use pots with a side neck and these increase the incidental catch of finfish. In most States, gaps are fitted in the pots so that undersized rock lobsters can escape. Individual pots are set in water up to 200 m deep on suitable sea beds, located with the aid of an

echo-sounder or sonar or global positioning system (GPS) (satellite) navigation equipment. Because rock lobsters are most active at night, pots are usually set late in the afternoon and hauled in early the next day. However, during periods of high catch rates in Tasmania, pots are also set and hauled during the day. Boats often stay out for 10–14 days at a time, and the live catch is stored in their wells or tanks. Crayfish ring nets are also used to catch southern rock lobsters in shallower waters around Tasmania.

Small numbers of giant crabs (*Pseudocarcinus gigas*), finfish and octopus comprise the incidental catch.

Approximately half of the southern rock lobster catch is exported, mainly to Japan, Taiwan and the United States of America. The remainder is sold on interstate and local markets. The rock lobsters are marketed cooked, live or frozen, and as tails or whole. The beach price for southern rock lobsters tends to rise during the fishing season. In Tasmania during the first half of 1992 the beach price averaged A$ 18.84 per kg. It rose by up to A$ 10 per kg later in the season.

Management controls In New South Wales, any of the state-licensed fishing vessels may take southern rock lobsters. In other States, entry to the southern rock lobster fishery involves the purchase of an existing entitlement. In most States, there are restrictions on the number of pots which may be used per boat, on the size and design of pots and the type of escape

Total annual catch in t of southern rock lobsters for the period 1964–65 to 1989–90. Figures are unavailable for Victoria for 1986–87, 1988–89 and 1989–90. Catches for States that average less than 5% of the total for all States are not shown. (Source: Fisheries Resources Atlas Statistical Database)

gaps. Furthermore, there are legal minimum size restrictions which are set at or above the size at first maturity. The fishing season is strictly controlled in the southern States.

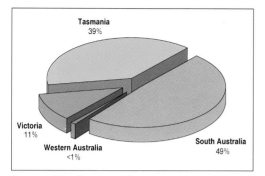

Comparison between the mean annual State catches of southern rock lobsters from 1980-81 to 1984-85 expressed as a percentage of the total catch. (Source: Fisheries Resources Atlas Statistical Database)

Recreational fishery

Southern rock lobsters are taken by recreational fishers throughout their range, although usually from relatively shallow and sheltered waters. The rock lobsters are caught by hand (when diving), baited pots and ring or hoop nets. In Tasmania, the recreational catch is estimated to be approximately 13 % of the commercial catch.

Management controls The States have different restrictions on gear type, daily catch and possession limits, licensing, and the amount of gear per vessel or gear in use simultaneously.

Resource status

The southern rock lobster fishery is believed to be fully exploited, as catches remain relatively stable while effective fishing effort continues to increase. Management is centred around the need to reduce and stabilise fishing effort and protect breeding stock.

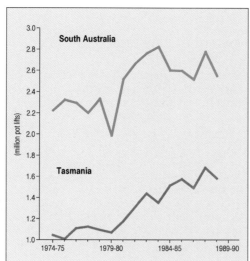

Comparison of fishing effort in the southern rock lobster fishery in South Australia and Tasmania as measured in millions of pot lifts, for the period 1974–75 to 1988–89. (Source: Tasmanian Department of Primary Industry and Fisheries and South Australian Department of Fisheries)

References

1. Booth, J.D., Street, R.J. and Smith, P.J. (1990) Systematic status of the rock lobsters *Jasus edwardsii* from New Zealand and *Jasus novaehollandiae* from Australia. *New Zealand Journal of Marine and Freshwater Research* **24**: 239–249.

2. MacDiarmid, A.B. (1988) Experimental confirmation of external fertilisation in the southern temperate rock lobster *Jasus edwardsii* (Hutton) (Decapoda: Palinuridae). *Journal of Experimental Marine Biology and Ecology* **120**: 277–285.

3. Hickman, V.V. (1946) Notes on the Tasmanian marine crayfish, *Jasus lalandii* (Milne-Edwards). *Papers and Proceedings of the Royal Society of Tasmania*, 1945: 27–38.

4. Lewis, R.K. (1977) Rock lobster puerulus settlement in the south-east. *SAFIC* No. 13: 9–11.

5. Lewis, R.K. (1981) Southern rock lobster (*Jasus novaehollandiae*) — a review of the Zone S fishery. *SAFIC* **5**(5): 31–43.

6. Winstanley, R.H. (1977) Results of recent research on southern rock lobster in south east Australia. *Victorian southern rock lobster fishery seminar papers, Portland Arts Centre, 9–10 June 1977*, Paper 3. Victorian Ministry for Conservation, Fisheries and Wildlife Division. 9 pp.

7. Lewis, R.K. (1975) Report on studies of the western population of the southern rock lobster. *SAFIC* No. 4: 9–14.

8. Winstanley, R.H. (1977) Biology of the southern rock lobster. *Victorian southern rock lobster fishery seminar papers, Portland Arts Centre, 9–10 June 1977*, Paper 1. Victorian Ministry for Conservation, Fisheries and Wildlife Division. 9 pp.

Contributors

Most of the information on this species was originally provided by Robert Kennedy and supplemented by (in alphabetical order) Rhys Brown, Rob Lewis, Dave Molloy, Steve Montgomery, Jenny Ovenden, Alex Schaap, Bruce Wallner and Ross Winstanley. Drawing by Rosalind Poole. (*Details of contributors and their organisations are given in the Acknowledgements section at the back of this book.*)
Compilers Patricia Kailola, Christina Grieve (maps) and Phillip Stewart (statistics)

Southern rock lobster vessels, Bridport, north-eastern Tasmania. (Source: Bureau of Resource Sciences)

Eastern rock lobster

Jasus verreauxi

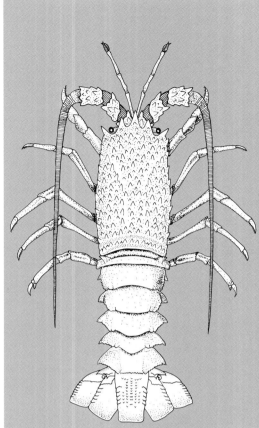

Jasus verreauxi
(H. Milne-Edwards)

Eastern rock lobster

Other common names include **eastern crayfish, green lobster, marine crayfish** and **packhorse rock lobster**.
FAO: **green rock lobster**
Australian species code: 703013

Family PALINURIDAE

Diagnostic features On the upper anterior part of the carapace, eastern rock lobsters have a moderately large rostrum and 2 equally large supraorbital spines, 1 on each side of the rostrum. There are short flagella on the medial antennules. Their abdominal segments are smooth and unsculptured on their dorsal surface. Eastern rock lobsters have a green body and brownish legs.[1]

Distribution

Eastern rock lobsters inhabit the continental shelf along the east coast of Australia from Tweed Heads in New South Wales, through Bass Strait, around Tasmania and as far west as Port MacDonnell in South Australia. Eastern rock lobsters are also present in New Zealand waters, mainly around the North Island.

Eastern rock lobsters live in rocky areas and reefs, commonly with vegetative cover, and they hide in holes and crevices. Juvenile eastern rock lobsters inhabit shallow waters along the shoreline.[2] Although there is no information on the large-scale movement of this species in waters off New South Wales, they move long distances in waters off New Zealand.[3] Eastern rock lobsters move into deeper water during early winter, and return to shorelines in late August.[2]

Life history

Breeding takes place during the colder months.[2] In waters north of Port Stephens on the central New South Wales coast, most spawning takes place between

September and January each year[4,5] and it is thought that all spawning occurs in water shallower than 50 m. It is known that female lobsters in New Zealand breed once each year,[6] but no information is available for Australian populations. A female eastern rock lobster may carry up to 2 million eggs[7] under her abdomen, and the larger the female the more eggs she can carry.

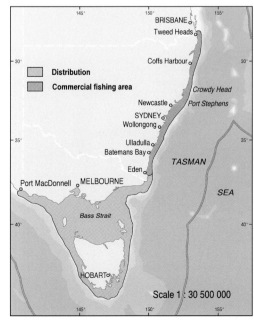

Geographic distribution and commercial fishing areas for eastern rock lobsters in Australian waters.

Females are in berry (ie carry eggs) for 3 months. Larvae hatch between September and February.

There are several planktonic larval stages of the eastern rock lobster's life cycle and the whole planktonic phase is thought to last for 8–12 months.[8] The puerulus, the stage after the larva, settles to become the bottom-living juvenile.

Eastern rock lobsters live for over 10 years, attain a maximum length (ie whole body with antennae) of 1 m and a weight in excess of 8 kg. The maximum recorded length of the eastern rock lobster in Australian waters is 262 mm carapace length. This species is the largest spiny lobster known;[9] it matures at a larger size and carries more eggs than does any other species of spiny lobster.

In New South Wales, eastern rock lobsters attain a carapace length of 104 mm after 3–4 years. The lobsters grow by a series of moults, ie they shed their shell. Studies under laboratory conditions have shown that individuals of 100–110 mm carapace length grow about 12 mm a year, although the growth rate slows in larger individuals.[6] The size at which lobsters reach sexual maturity varies along the New South Wales coast. The length at which 50 % of females carry eggs is 167 mm carapace length.

Eastern rock lobsters are omnivorous. They eat benthic (ie bottom living) organisms such as molluscs and crustaceans on rocks and among seagrass, and scavenge dead organic matter.[2] Octopus (*Octopus* species) and gummy sharks (*Mustelus antarcticus*) are their major predators, but small juveniles are sometimes eaten by fish.

Stock structure

There is no information on the stock structure of eastern rock lobsters. It is possible that larvae from Australia contribute to the New Zealand stock.[8]

Commercial fishery

Rock lobsters have been exploited in New South Wales waters since 1873.[5] Four species are caught, of which the eastern rock lobster comprises in excess of 97 % of the annual landings.[5] The other species are southern rock lobster (*Jasus edwardsii*), painted rock lobster (*Panulirus longipes*) and ornate rock lobster (*P. ornatus*).[5]

Eastern rock lobsters are targeted between Tweed Heads and Eden in New South Wales. Fishing grounds in depths up to 50 m are exploited seasonally or year-round, and comprise the inshore fishery. This fishery operates between September and January off Crowdy Head, between June and April off Sydney, and year-round off Batemans Bay.[5] Fishing grounds in deeper waters, approximately 51–220 m, comprise the offshore fishery. These deeper grounds also are exploited seasonally or year-round — between March and July off Crowdy Head and between December and February off Sydney and Batemans Bay.[5] The fishing season for eastern rock lobsters begins earlier in northern New South Wales waters. Catch rates are highest from March to September in northern ports and from October to February in southern ports.[5] A recent study[5] has shown that the legal minimum length, 104 mm carapace length, is shorter than the size at which female eastern rock lobsters first breed.

Fishing is carried out almost exclusively with baited traps, and the trap design varies from the traditional style with an entrance in the top used in the inshore fishery, to larger, rectangular traps with entrances in the side. The traps are set for 1–2 days in the inshore fishery and up to 2 weeks in the offshore fishery. A negligible bycatch, mostly of leatherjackets (Monacanthidae) and morwong (Cheilodactylidae), is made with these traps. A small proportion of the commercial catch is taken by divers from waters less than 10 m deep.[5]

Eastern rock lobsters comprise a very incidental catch in the southern rock lobster fishery off Tasmania, Victoria and South Australia. They are sold as part of the southern rock lobster catch. Eastern rock lobsters are also an incidental catch of demersal otter trawlers and Danish

Fishers operating off central New South Wales in the inshore fishery for eastern rock lobsters. (Source: Steven Montgomery, Fisheries Research Institute, NSW Fisheries)

seiners operating in deeper New South Wales waters.

Most eastern rock lobsters are sold whole on local fresh seafood markets, either fresh chilled or cooked. The average price in the Sydney Fish Market in 1991–92 was A$ 27.28 per kg for green (fresh) lobsters and A$ 26.04 per kg for cooked lobsters. Reported landings of the 4 lobster species caught off New

South Wales are worth A$ 3 million a year.[5]

Management controls The number of vessels licensed to fish in any fishery in State waters off New South Wales is restricted and lobsters may be targeted only with traps or by hand. Berried lobsters may not be retained and there is a legal minimum carapace length for retained lobsters.

Recreational fishery

Eastern rock lobsters are exploited by recreational fishers to a depth of approximately 30 m by diving and trapping. The traps are similar in design to commercial traps.

Management controls Bag and gear limits are imposed. For example, SCUBA or hookah gear cannot be used to collect lobsters and each fisher is permitted to use only one trap.

Resource status

Eastern rock lobsters are heavily exploited. Unreported landings are estimated to be approximately 70 % of the catch in the fishery.[5] The annual catch per unit effort for New South Wales declined over the 19-year period to 1987–88, and individuals harvested in the inshore fishery are shorter than those from the offshore fishery. Approximately 64 % of the average total landings of rock lobsters in New South Wales come from areas where all eastern rock lobsters sampled in

Total annual catch in t of eastern rock lobsters for the period 1964–65 to 1989–90. Figures are unavailable for 1984–85 to 1986–87. (Source: Fisheries Resources Atlas Statistical Database)

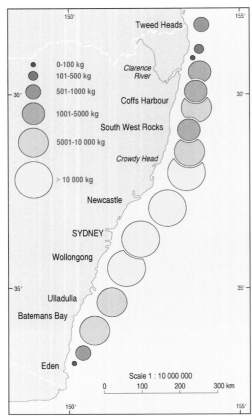

The average annual landings of rock lobsters for the period 1979–80 to 1983–84. The circles represent different categories of landings by weight. Major ports of landings of rock lobster are shown. (Source: Montgomery[5])

a recent study were immature.[5] There is no information from which to determine optimum levels of yield and fishing effort.

References

1. George, R.W. and Kensler, C.B. (1970) Recognition of marine spiny lobsters of the *Jasus lalandii* group (Crustacea: Decapoda: Palinuridae). *New Zealand Journal of Marine and Freshwater Research* **4**: 292–311.

2. *Commercial fisheries of New South Wales* (1982) NSW State Fisheries. 60 pp.

3. Booth, J.D. (1984) Movements of packhorse (*Jasus verreauxi*) tagged along the eastern coast of the North Island, New Zealand. *New Zealand Journal of Marine and Freshwater Research* **18**: 275–281.

4. Lee, C. (1969) *Preliminary study on the fishery and biology of* Jasus verreauxi *(H. Milne Edwards) (Crustacea: Decapoda: Palinuridae)*. MSc qualifying thesis, University of New South Wales. 30 pp.

5. Montgomery, S.S. (1990) Preliminary study of the fishery for rock lobsters off the coast of New South Wales. *Fisheries Research Institute, Department of Agriculture, New South Wales. FIRDC Project 86/64, Final Report*. 22 pp.

6. Booth, J.D. (1984) Size at onset of breeding in female *Jasus verreauxi* (Decapoda: Palinuridae) in New Zealand. *New Zealand Journal of Marine and Freshwater Research* **18**: 159–169.

Catch of eastern rock lobsters, southern New South Wales. (Source: Steven Montgomery, Fisheries Research Institute, NSW Fisheries)

7. Kensler, C.B. (1967) Fecundity in the marine spiny lobster *Jasus verreauxi* (H. Milne Edwards) (Crustacea: Decapoda: Palinuridae). *New Zealand Journal of Marine and Freshwater Research* **2**: 143–155.

8. Booth, J.D. (1986) Recruitment of packhorse rock lobster *Jasus verreauxi* in New Zealand. *Canadian Journal of Fisheries and Aquatic Sciences* **43**: 2212–2220.

9. Phillips, B.F., Cobb, J.S. and George, R.W. (1980) General biology. Pp 2–82, in *The biology and management of lobsters. Volume 1. Physiology and behaviour*. Ed by J.S. Cobb and B.F. Phillips. New York: Academic Press.

Contributors

The information on this species was originally provided by Steven Montgomery and supplemented by (in alphabetical order) Robert Kennedy and Dave Molloy. Figure redrawn by Peter Moloney after *Commercial fisheries of New South Wales*.[2] (*Details of contributors and their organisations are given in the Acknowledgements section at the back of this book.*)
Compiler Patricia Kailola

Western rock lobster

Panulirus cygnus

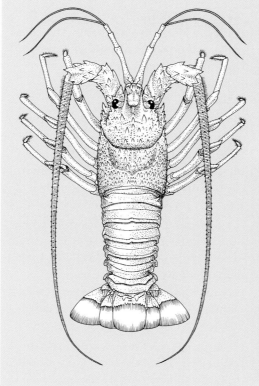

Panulirus cygnus George

Western rock lobster

Another common name is **Western Australian crayfish**.
FAO: **western rock lobster**
Australian species code: 703999

Family PALINURIDAE

Diagnostic features Western rock lobsters are spiny lobsters with long antennular flagella. The anterodorsal aspect of the carapace bears 2 distinct, smooth supraorbital spines and behind them are 2 rows of 4–8 smaller spines. Each abdominal segment has a transverse groove. The older juveniles and adult lobsters (except 'whites') assume a reddish-purple colour with each moult. The carapace is uniformly coloured without obvious spots and markings, although the abdomen is spotted dorsally and laterally. Each walking leg has a broad, pale longitudinal stripe on its dorsal surface. The 'white' phase lobsters (see text) are light coloured.[1]

Distribution

Western rock lobsters live only in Western Australia, from Albany to North West Cape. They are also present in the Houtman Abrolhos, about 80 km off Geraldton.

From post-larval stage to adult, western rock lobsters inhabit the continental shelf in water from 1 m to approximately 200 m deep, although most live in waters shallower than 60 m. Juveniles live in caves and under ledges of limestone patch reefs surrounded by seagrass beds (eg *Halophila* species, *Amphibolis* species)[2] in water generally 10–30 m deep. Adults can be found in similar habitats in deeper water. At the Houtman Abrolhos, lobsters shelter in holes and under clumps of coral.

Life history

Mating takes place between July and December, and the female carries the black 'tar-spot' of spermatophores on her abdomen until the eggs are spawned. This occurs between August–September and January. Many individuals spawn twice in a season. Depending upon the female's size,[3] 100 000 to 1 million eggs are produced.[4] These eggs are carried on the underside of the female's abdomen until hatched, which may take up to 10 weeks depending on the water temperature.[4] Egg-bearing females are said to be 'berried'.

Western rock lobsters have several different life stages: an egg, a phyllosoma larva, a puerulus postlarva, a juvenile and an adult rock lobster.

The larvae are planktonic and are carried into the Indian Ocean, up to 1500 km from the Western Australian coast. The larvae moult into the puerulus stage after 9–11 months. The return of the pueruli to the continental shelf depends on shifts in ocean currents. The number

of pueruli settling (which also indicates the recruitment level to the fishery about 4 years later) is correlated with annual fluctuations in the sea level. These fluctuations are associated with the strength of the Leeuwin Current.[5] Between September and January, the pueruli settle in inshore coastal waters

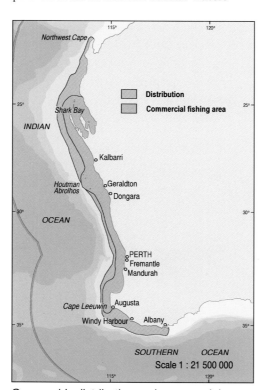

Geographic distribution and commercial fishing area for western rock lobsters.

where they moult within 2 weeks into juvenile rock lobsters. When they are between 4 and 6 years old, the juveniles move out of the shallow coastal nursery areas to deeper adult habitats.[6,7] This movement commences in late November each year and continues into January.[6] The greatest recorded migration is approximately 170 nautical miles. These newly moulted migrating lobsters are called 'whites' because their shell is lightly coloured.

The size at which western rock lobsters reach sexual maturity has been assessed only for females and varies with location of subpopulations and growth rate. Along the coast, 50 % of females are sexually mature at approximately 5–6 years of age, at a carapace length of 90–95 mm. In the Houtman Abrolhos, females mature at a smaller size, around 65 mm carapace length.

The maximum recorded length and weight of western rock lobsters are 200 mm (carapace length) and at least 4.5 kg. The maximum age — based on an arbitrary 'birthday' of 1 January[6] — is in excess of 20 years.

Growth rates vary considerably along the coast and between the coast and the Houtman Abrolhos. In general, pueruli

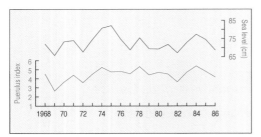

Annual mean data for the Fremantle sea level and index of puerulus settlement at Seven-Mile Beach, Dongara from 1968 to 1986. (Adapted from Pearce and Phillips[5])

settle at approximately 8 mm carapace length. One year after settlement, juveniles are about 25 mm in carapace length.[8] A study in 1981 at Seven Mile Beach (Dongara)[9] recorded 3-year-old juvenile lobsters of 39–55 mm carapace length, 4-year-olds between 56–68 mm carapace length, and 5-year-old and older animals with a carapace length greater than 69 mm.

Western rock lobsters are omnivorous and feed at night, locating their food by tactile response and chemoreception.[1,10] Their diet changes according to moult stage, season and habitat. Postmoult rock lobsters prefer epiphytic coralline algae (eg *Corallina* species, *Metagonolithon* species)[2] and intermoult forms prefer molluscs.[9] Adults eat food similar to but larger than that of juveniles — epiphytic coralline algae, molluscs (such as the trochid *Cantharidus lepidus*[2,11]), small crustaceans, polychaete worms and peanut worms (Sipunculida).[2]

Finfish, sharks and octopus (*Octopus* species) prey on juvenile and adult western rock lobsters.[12]

Stock structure

There is only 1 stock of western rock lobsters. The variability in ocean currents ensures mixing of the larvae prior to settlement.

Commercial fishery

Western rock lobsters were first fished commercially in the late 1800s. They now make up one of the major rock lobster fisheries in the world and the most valuable single-species fishery in Australia.[13]

The commercial fishery for western rock lobsters extends from Augusta near Cape Leeuwin to Shark Bay. The bulk of the catch is harvested along the Western Australian coast between Mandurah and Kalbarri and at the Houtman Abrolhos.

Regulations specify the periods when rock lobsters may be fished. Fishers target 'white', migrating lobsters from November to mid-January, and switch to 'red', non-migrating lobsters at the beginning of February. The average catch over the past 20 seasons has been about 10 000 t.

Western rock lobsters are caught in baited pots. The most commonly used pot designs and materials are batten pots (usually made of wood with steel bottoms) and beehive pots (usually made of tea-tree and cane). The pots have only one entrance and, by regulation, must have at least 3 escape gaps in designated positions on the pot. Baited pots are usually set on 1 day, pulled the next and reset, weather permitting. When deeper water is being fished, pots may be left for up to 5 days before being lifted.[13] Pots are baited with fish and other organic matter such as cattle hocks and hide.

A variety of fishes, wobbegong shark (*Orectolobus* species) and octopus comprise the small bycatch.

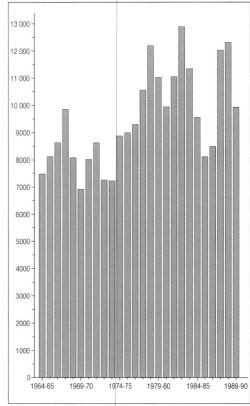

Total annual catch in t of western rock lobsters for the period 1964–65 to 1989–90. (Source: Fisheries Resources Atlas Statistical Database)

Almost all of the western rock lobster catch is exported. Forty per cent is sent as frozen, raw tails to the United States of America and 60 % is exported to Japan and Taiwan as live or whole, cooked or raw (frozen) product. Only a very small quantity of whole cooked animals is kept for the domestic (Australian) market.

The tail yield per rock lobster is approximately 40 % of the live weight. Prices vary between seasons, the average price to fishers in the 1991–92 season being about A$ 20.00 per kg.

Management controls Regulations proclaiming limited entry to the fishery were introduced in 1963. At that time, there were 835 boats and 76 632 pots in the fishery. As a result of a pot reduction scheme, the number of vessels and pots in the commercial fishery was reduced to 700 boats and 70 608 pots by 1990.[13]

Western rock lobsters may not be fished between 1 July and 14 November along the coast and between 1 July and 14 March at the Houtman Abrolhos. The fishery is limited by licence (total number of boats), with restrictions on the taking of berried females, a legal minimum size, the number of pots, pot size and pot construction.[13]

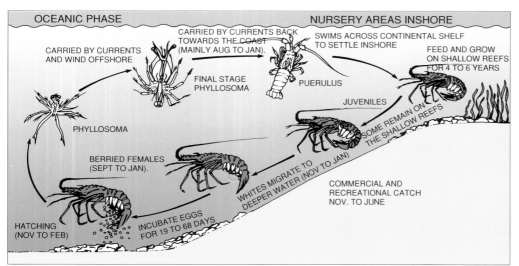

Life cycle of the western rock lobster. (Redrawn by Peter Moloney from original by B.F. Phillips)

Juvenile western rock lobster on a seagrass bed. (Source: Dave Evans, CSIRO Marine Laboratories, North Beach)

Management is centred on reducing or stabilising levels of fishing effort to protect the breeding stock.

Recreational fishery

The recreational fishery for western rock lobsters, although confined to shallow waters along the coast, covers the same period and area as the commercial fishery. The rock lobsters are caught by pot or by hand (when diving or walking on reefs).

An extensive survey of recreational lobster fishers conducted since 1986–87 estimated that the recreational catch is between 2 % and 5 % of the commercial catch. The number of recreational licences issued in 1989–90 was 23 374.[13]

Nearshore habitat for western rock lobsters. Aerial view of Seven-Mile Beach, Dongara — compiled. (Source: Dave Evans, CSIRO Marine Laboratories, North Beach)

Management controls Controls are the same as those applied to the commercial fishery, but with added restrictions on pot numbers, bag limits, boat limits and selling.

Resource status

The western rock lobster fishery has been extensively researched and is closely monitored. It is considered to be fully exploited. Although catches remain relatively stable, effective fishing effort continues to increase. Further increases in exploitation rate may lead to reduced catch rates.

Notes

Puerulus, juvenile and adult western rock lobsters can be kept under laboratory conditions. There is interest in raising larvae in these conditions with a view to aquaculture.

References

1. Phillips, B.F., Morgan, G.R. and Austin, C.M. (1980) Synopsis of biological data on the western rock lobster *Panulirus cygnus* George, 1962. *FAO Fisheries Synopsis* **128**. 64 pp.

2. Edgar, G.J. (1990) Predator–prey interactions in seagrass beds. I. The influence of macrofaunal abundance and size-structure on the diet and growth of the western rock lobster *Panulirus cygnus* George. *Journal of Experimental Biology and Ecology* **139**: 1–22.

3. Morgan, G.R. (1972) Fecundity in the western rock lobster *Panulirus longipes cygnus* (George) (Crustacea: Decapoda: Palinuridae). *Australian Journal of Marine and Freshwater Research* **23**: 133–141.

4. Chubb, C.F. (in press, 1992) Measurement of spawning stock levels for the western rock lobster, *Panulirus cygnus*. *International workshop on lobster ecology and fisheries, Cuba, 1990. Revista de Investigaciones Marinas* **12** (1–3).

5. Pearce, A.F. and Phillips, B.F. (1988) ENSO events, the Leeuwin Current, and larval recruitment of the western rock lobster. *Journal du Conseil international pour l'Exploration de la Mer* **45**: 13–21.

6. Morgan, G.R., Phillips, B.F. and Joll, L.M. (1982) Stock and recruitment relationships in *Panulirus cygnus*, the commercial rock (spiny) lobster of Western Australia. *Fishery Bulletin (U.S.)* **80**: 475–486.

7. Ford, R., Phillips, B.F. and Joll, L.M. (1988) Experimental manipulation of population density and its effects on growth and mortality of juvenile rock lobsters, *Panulirus cygnus* George. *Fishery Bulletin (U.S.)* **86**: 773–787.

8. Phillips, B.F., Campbell, N.A. and Rea, W.A. (1977) Laboratory growth of early juveniles of western rock lobster *Panulirus longipes cygnus. Marine Biology* **39**: 31–39.

9. Fitzpatrick, J.F., Jernakoff, P. and Phillips, B.F. (1989) An investigation of the habitat requirements of the post puerulus stocks of the western rock lobster. *CSIRO Marine Laboratories. FIRTA Project 86/83, Final Report.* 80 pp.

10. Jernakoff, P. (1987) Foraging patterns of juvenile rock lobsters *Panulirus cygnus* George. *Journal of Experimental Marine Biology and Ecology* **113**: 125–144.

11. Edgar, G.J. (1990) Predator–prey interactions in seagrass beds. III. Impacts of the western rock lobster *Panulirus cygnus* George on epifaunal gastropod populations. *Journal of Experimental Marine Biology and Ecology* **139**: 33–42.

12. Howard, R.K. (1988) Fish predators of western rock lobster (*Panulirus cygnus* George) in a nearshore nursery habitat. *Australian Journal of Marine and Freshwater Research* **39**: 307–316.

13. Brown, R.S. (in press, 1992) A decade (1980–1989) of research and management for the western rock lobster (*Panulirus cygnus*) fishery of Western Australia. *International workshop on lobster ecology and fisheries, Cuba, 1990. Revista de Investigaciones Marinas* **12** (1–3).

Contributors

Most of the information on this species was originally provided by (in alphabetical order) Rhys Brown, Chris Chubb, Peter Jernakoff and Bruce Phillips. Drawing courtesy of FAO, Rome. (*Details of contributors and their organisations are given in the Acknowledgements section at the back of this book.*)
Compiler Patricia Kailola

Ornate rock lobster

Panulirus ornatus

Panulirus ornatus (Fabricius)

Ornate rock lobster

Other common names include
**ornate spiny lobster, tropical
rock lobster** and **crayfish**.
FAO: **ornate spiny lobster**
Australian species code: 703034

Family PALINURIDAE

Diagnostic features Ornate rock
lobsters are spiny lobsters with long
antennular flagellae. The bases of
the antennae are separated by a
broad plate bearing 2 pairs of
spines. The abdominal segments
are smooth. The body colour varies
between greenish blue and reddish
brown and the front of the carapace
has orange spines and is marked
with narrow pale and dark
undulating lines. The eyes are
ringed with blues and pinks. Each
abdominal segment has a large
pale spot on each side, the 2nd to
4th segments bearing an additional
pair of elongate pale spots. There is
no transverse white band along the
posterior margin of each abdominal
segment, although each bears a
dark band across its middle. The
legs have regular bands of distinct
pale and dark rings and blotches.[1]

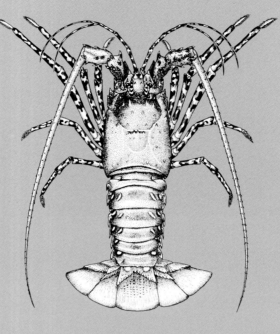

Distribution

Ornate rock lobsters are widely
distributed throughout the Indian and
western Pacific oceans: from the Red Sea
and southern Africa to Kiribati and Samoa
in the Pacific.[2] In Australia they are
normally found from the North West Cape
– Ningaloo Reef region, through northern
Australia to Sydney. Individuals have
occasionally been collected south of
North West Cape, even as far south as
Albany.[3]

Ornate rock lobsters inhabit a range of
turbid, rocky areas on the continental
shelf — from those exposed to oceanic
waters, sheltered waters of lagoons and
backreefs among luxuriant coral growth,
to silted rubble areas near river mouths
and mangroves.[4] Ornate rock lobsters are
found in water depths ranging from about
1 m on reef tops, over reef slopes and off
the continental shelf to 200 m.[4] Juveniles
live on rocky sea beds which may support
coverings of seagrass, algae and sponges.
In Torres Strait, ornate rock lobsters live
in holes and crevices in rocky
weed-covered inter-reef areas, on reef
tops, or under rocks and coral bomboras.[5]

Life history

The breeding season of ornate rock
lobsters at Yule Island in Papua New
Guinea extends from November to
April.[2,5] On the east Queensland coast,
berried (ie egg- bearing) females are
sometimes found between December and
April.[5]

Ornate rock lobsters do not breed on
the reefs of central and northern Torres
Strait.[6] They and north-east Queensland
lobsters undertake an annual breeding
emigration; and tagging studies[5] have
shown that the Torres Strait animals move
great distances, up to 511 km.[2,5] They
begin to move off the reefs in the Strait
during August and the emigration appears
to take place in waves about 2 weeks
apart, up until October–November.

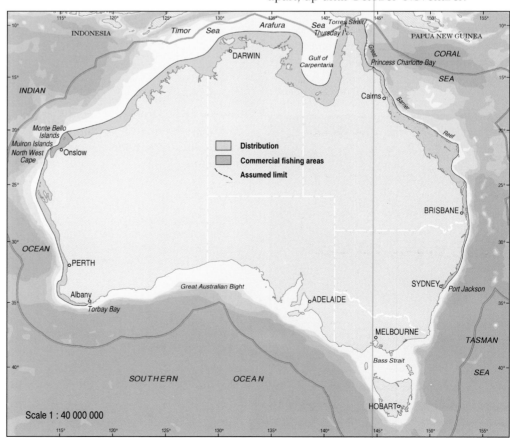

Geographic distribution and commercial fishing areas for ornate rock lobsters in Australian
waters.

164

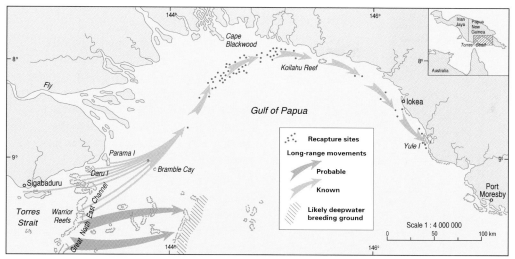

Representation of the annual breeding emigration of ornate rock lobsters. (Source: adapted from Moore and MacFarlane[2])

Some of the migrating rock lobsters move north-eastward across the Gulf of Papua to breeding grounds near Yule Island. A large number of mature animals from Torres Strait however, may move to deep (40–120 m) water reefs on the edge of the continental shelf outside the far northern Great Barrier Reef.[7,8]

The emigrating breeding rock lobsters are mostly 2.5–3 years of age and 80–130 mm carapace length.[2,5] There are approximately twice as many females as males in the groups of emigrants.[2] Large lobsters (often males) and first year class juveniles do not emigrate.

Rock lobsters emigrating across the Gulf of Papua form compact aggregations and rarely interrupt their walk.[5] They have been trawled at particular depth lines from 14 m to at least 80 m.[2] Trawlers used to target these aggregations, and would catch from hundreds to 60 000 individuals[2] before the aggregations were depleted or dispersed. There is no return migration to Torres Strait from Yule Island after breeding.[2,6] Rock lobsters arriving on eastern Gulf of Papua reefs are in very poor condition[7] and suffer catastrophic mortality after breeding.[7,9] It is not known whether the rock lobsters on the northern Great Barrier Reef grounds also die after breeding.

Ornate rock lobsters on the north-east Queensland coast move mostly in a southerly or south-easterly direction from about March to mid-May.[5] Journeys are shorter (average 70 km[5]) than those undertaken by the Torres Strait animals and demersal otter trawlers report catching ornate rock lobsters migrating in small groups in March–April. The lobsters also may move into deep water[7] near the outer Great Barrier Reef,[5] where breeding probably takes place.[7] The animals range in size from 75 to 95 mm carapace length.

General movements into deeper water associated with breeding probably occur throughout the animal's range in Australia.

Ovary development, copulation and egg deposition take place during the emigration. During copulation the male rock lobster places a sperm packet, or 'tar-spot' on the female's body between the last 2 pairs of legs. When the eggs exit the female's body, they are fertilized as they pass the then ruptured tar-spot. The eggs attach to the female's pleopods ('swimmerettes') where they remain until hatching about 1 month later. As many as 3 broods[6] may be carried and reared by a female ornate rock lobster during 1 spawning season, new eggs being deposited sometimes within a few days of earlier eggs hatching. The average

Tagging and measuring ornate rock lobsters, Torres Strait. (Source: Geoff Williams, Bureau of Resource Sciences)

fecundity ranges from 225 000 eggs for females of 70–80 mm carapace length to 840 000 for females of 130–140 mm carapace length,[6] and it declines with subsequent broods through the season.[4,6]

Ornate rock lobster larvae are released at the end of the adult emigration in the Gulf of Papua.[2] Information from other breeding areas is lacking. Ornate rock lobster larvae are pelagic and undergo about a dozen leaf-shaped phyllosoma stages. The dispersal of the phyllosoma larvae onto the continental shelf is probably assisted by a combination of prevailing wind and ocean currents.[5] After the pelagic phase, which lasts 4–10 months,[4] the puerulus postlarvae settle to a benthic existence at 6–8 mm carapace length.[10] Studies in Cairns Harbour showed that the settlement of rock lobsters is seasonal, with newly settled animals first appearing in April–May, being most abundant from June to August, and continuing to settle as late as October.[10] This settlement pattern probably occurs in Torres Strait also. Ornate rock lobsters remain in the rocky, inter-reef habitat until adulthood. Resident Torres Strait rock lobsters are nomadic, continually moving within a reef complex.[2]

Ornate rock lobsters are fast growing, attaining 40–60 mm in carapace length in the first year after settlement, and adding 25–35 mm in the second year. There are no reliable maximum size estimates for ornate rock lobsters in Australian waters. A few individuals of 130–140 mm carapace length are found in Torres Strait and are estimated to be 5 years old.[10]

Female ornate rock lobsters on the Queensland east coast are sexually mature from about 2.5–3 years of age (85–95 mm carapace length), most mature females being 110–120 mm carapace length[5,6] or greater. In the Gulf of Papua, the smallest female recorded with developed ovaries was 67 mm carapace length.[6]

Ornate rock lobsters are carnivorous, feeding mostly on molluscs but also crustaceans and echinoderms.[11] The rock lobsters feed at night, often in deeper water but also on shallow reef tops or between reefs. They return to shelter during the day. Rock lobsters also forage on seagrass beds and sand flats,[2] and eat carrion. Octopus (Octopus species), some sharks and large rock cods (Serranidae) are known to prey on ornate rock lobsters.

Stock structure

Genetic studies have shown that the Torres Strait and east Queensland populations of ornate rock lobsters are part of the same stock.[5,7] Ocean currents can disperse larvae to both areas — at least from 10°24' S to 25°58' S.[6] There is no information on the population structure of ornate rock lobsters in other areas of the species' Australian distribution.

Commercial fishery

Ornate rock lobster are fished commercially on the north-east Queensland coast and in Torres Strait. In Torres Strait, the commercial fishery for ornate rock lobster is shared by Papua New Guinea and Australia. The breeding population of ornate rock lobsters also supports a small, artisanal fishery near Yule Island for 2–4 months each year.

The ornate rock lobster fishery in Torres Strait began in the late 1960s and is mostly worked by Torres Strait Islanders. The fishery is based on Thursday Island and the main fishing grounds are around Thursday Island, Orman Reef (09°54' S, 142°17' E) and the Warrior Reefs. This species does not enter pots or traps. They are caught with short hand spears in water depths to 15 m. Divers work singly or in pairs from outboard- powered dinghies. The fishers either free dive or use breathing equipment: SCUBA or hookah gear (which allows access to deeper water on the reef edges). Most fishing takes place during neap tide when currents are slower and the water is clearer. The average daily catch for 1 dinghy is about 16 kg of tails (equivalent to about 40 lobsters).[4]

Freezer boats with attendant vessels fish the reefs of Torres Strait and north-east Queensland, as far south as Princess Charlotte Bay.[12] This fishing system began in the early 1980s, and by 1986 freezer boats were processing about 66 % of all diver landings.[12] Freezer barges anchored near islands on the major fishing grounds receive catch from freezer boats and dinghies and are regularly serviced by mother ships from Thursday Island and mainland ports.[12]

Ornate rock lobsters were also targeted by demersal otter trawlers in the Gulf of Papua between September and December each year and in eastern

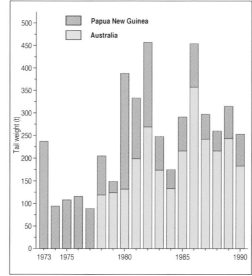

Total annual catch in t tail weight of ornate rock lobsters for the period 1973–90. Figures are unavailable for Australia from 1973 to 1977. Partial and total trawling bans applied in Papua New Guinea in 1977, 1979 and 1985–90. (Source: Channells, Phillips and Bell;[12] Rob Coles, Australian Fisheries Management Authority; Andy Richards, Forum Fisheries Agency)

Torres Strait (eg the Great North East Channel) from September to October.[13] In August 1984 however, a total ban on trawling was brought in to protect the spawning migration.[13] Until recently, incidental catches have been made by demersal otter trawlers fishing for prawns (Penaeidae) off north-east Queensland.[12]

The fishery operates all year in Torres Strait and far north-east Queensland, with best catches between March and August.[12] At least 15 % of the annual Australian diver catch of ornate rock lobsters is taken from east coast reefs.[13]

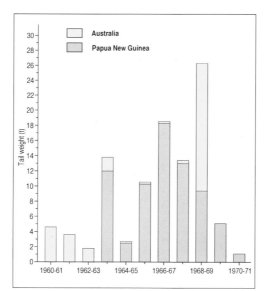

Total annual catch in t tail weight of ornate rock lobsters from the diver fisheries for the period 1960–61 to 1970–71. Figures are unavailable for Papua New Guinea from 1960–61 to 1962–63; and Australia from 1969–70 to 1970–71. (Source: Channells, Phillips and Bell[12])

The tail weight of rock lobsters taken in the dive fishery ranges from about 250 g to 450 g. The animals enter the commercial dive fishery 1.5–2 years after hatching, when they have grown to the legal minimum size of 100 mm tail length (ie at approximately 75 mm carapace length). Rock lobsters recruit to the fishery in Torres Strait from November to February.

Less than 1 % of the catch in the rock lobster dive fishery is formed by other species (mainly painted spiny lobster, *Panulirus versicolor*). All rock lobsters are marketed together as 'tropical rock lobster'. Pearl oysters (*Pinctada* species) are also taken incidentally by rock lobster divers.

There are incidental dive fisheries for ornate rock lobsters in the Northern Territory and much of Western Australia. There is a small, localised dive fishery for rock lobsters around the islands and reef chains from approximately the Muiron to the Monte Bello islands. This fishery focuses on the most common species, the painted spiny lobster. Generally, divers use hookah gear and a hand-held hook. The product is landed at Onslow. For the 5 years from January 1986 this fishery yielded 7.2 t whole weight of rock lobsters.

All rock lobster tails from the Torres Strait and north-east Queensland fisheries are snap frozen. Most are exported to Japan and the United States of America, and although the domestic market is small, its value is significant. Tails from the Western Australian and Northern Territory fisheries and a few from Queensland are sold on the domestic markets. The mid-1992 wholesale price per kg in Brisbane averaged about A$ 32.00 for tails.

Management controls Management of the Torres Strait rock lobster fishery is the responsibility of the Australian and Papua New Guinea governments through the Torres Strait Treaty. Non-Torres Strait Islanders are discouraged from participating in the fishery. Management arrangements for the Australian area include limiting freezer vessel numbers and a total ban on taking rock lobsters by any method other than diving using hand-held spears (this includes incidental catch from trawlers). A minimum legal size, bag limits and sometimes a boat licence apply to traditional fishers. Limited access to the fishery in the

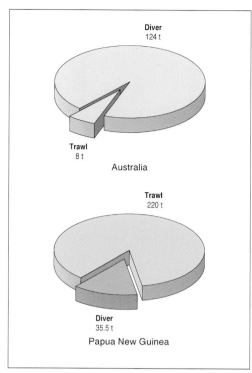

Comparison of the 1980 catch in t tail weight by method between Papua New Guinea and Australian ornate rock lobster fisheries. (Source: Channells, Phillips and Bell;[12] Andy Richards, Forum Fisheries Agency)

Australian area by Papua New Guinean fishers is controlled by both governments according to negotiated catch sharing arrangements.

In Western Australia the number of tropical rock lobster licences issued is fixed, and a minimum size limit applies.

Recreational fishery

Throughout the species' range in Australia, tourists and local residents collect ornate rock lobsters by free diving, using SCUBA and 'reef walking' at night.

Management controls In Western Australia licence restrictions and bag limits apply. Berried females may not be kept. There are no bag limits for the Torres Strait Protected Zone. Queensland fishers may take rock lobsters only by hand or hand-held spears and no bag limits apply. The entire tropical rock lobster fishery south of 13° S is managed by the Queensland Fish Management Authority as a recreational fishery.

Resource status

Total effort in the ornate rock lobster fishery in Torres Strait has increased since 1974,[12] and the catch rate per hour has decreased to about one third of the level realised in the early 1970s.

A 1989 study showed that the ornate rock lobster population in Torres Strait and adjacent areas numbered about 14 million animals, of which 7–9 million were of legal size — ie a potential yield of 2200–3350 t of tails. The total catch in that year was only 240 t — approximately 10 % of the possible yield. Analyses show that a 4-fold increase in catch could yield a long-term average of 800 t, still leaving about 74 % of the population to emigrate and breed. This estimate is conservative. Surveys in 1990 and 1991 showed that the actual yield would vary from year to year because of recruitment fluctuations.[7,14] Predictions could be made for each following year however, based on the numbers of juveniles recruiting.

An important observation is that the Torres Strait fishery removes individuals that are sub-adult and have not spawned.

Trawl catch of ornate rock lobsters from Torres Straight. The commercial trawl fishery for ornate rock lobsters ceased in the mid-1980s. (Source: Geoff Williams, Bureau of Resource Sciences)

References

1. Holthuis, L.B. (1984). Lobsters, in *FAO species identification sheets for fishery purposes. Western Indian Ocean (Fishing Area 51)*. Prepared and printed with the support of the Danish International Development Agency. Rome, FAO, vol. 5, pag. var.

2. Moore, R. and MacFarlane, J.W. (1984) Migration of the ornate rock lobster, *Panulirus ornatus* (Fabricius), in Papua New Guinea. *Australian Journal of Marine and Freshwater Research* **35**: 197–212.

3. Western Fisheries (1990) *Breaking all records, the continuing saga of the ornate lobster*. May/June edition: 24–25.

4. Pitcher, C.R. (in press, 1992) Biology, ecology and fisheries for spiny lobster in the south-western Pacific. In *Inshore marine resources of the South Pacific: information for development and management*. Ed by L. Hill and A. Wright. Forum Fisheries Agency. Fiji: University of the South Pacific.

5. Bell, R.S., Channells, P.W., MacFarlane, J.W., Moore, R. and Phillips, B.F. (1987) Movements and breeding of the ornate rock lobser, *Panulirus ornatus*, in Torres Strait and on the north-east coast of Queensland. *Australian Journal of Marine and Freshwater Research* **38**: 197–210.

6. MacFarlane, J.W. and Moore, R. (1986). Reproduction of the ornate rock lobster *Panulirus ornatus* (Fabricius) in Papua New Guinea. *Australian Journal of Marine and Freshwater Research* **37**: 55–65.

7. Pitcher, C.R., Skewes, T.D. and Dennis, D.M. (1991) Research for management of the ornate tropical rock lobster, *Panulirus ornatus*, fishery in Torres Strait: summary report on CSIRO research, 1987–1990. *CSIRO Marine Laboratories Report*. 9 pp.

8. Prescott, J. and Pitcher, R. (1991) Deep water survey for *Panulirus ornatus* in Papua New Guinea and Australia. *The Lobster Newsletter* **3**(2): 8–9.

9. Dennis, D.M., Pitcher, C.R., Prescott, J.H. and Skewes, T.D. (in press, 1992) Severe mortality in a breeding ornate rock lobster, *Panulirus ornatus*, population at Yule Island, Papua New Guinea. *Journal of Experimental Marine Biology and Ecology*.

10. Trendall, J.T., Bell, R.S. and Phillips, B.F. (1988) Growth of the spiny lobster *Panulirus ornatus*, in the Torres Strait. *South Pacific Commission workshop on Pacific inshore fishery resources, Noumea, 14–25 March 1988. Working Paper* **BP 90**.

11. Joll, L.M. and Phillips, B.F. (1986) Foregut contents of the ornate rock lobster *Panulirus ornatus*. Pp 212–217, in *Torres Strait fisheries seminar, Port Moresby, 11–14 February 1985*. Ed by A.K. Haines, G.C. Williams and D. Coates. Canberra: Australian Government Publishing Service.

12. Channells, P.W., Phillips, B.F. and Bell, R.S. (1987) The rock lobster fisheries for the ornate rock lobster, *Panulirus ornatus* in Torres Strait and on the north-east coast of Queensland, Australia. *Australian Fisheries Service, Department of Primary Industry and Energy, Fisheries Paper* **87/8**. 34 pp.

13. Prescott, J.H., Phillips, B.F. and Bell, R.S. (1986) Rock lobster research in Torres Strait. *Australian Fisheries* **45**(1): 2–4.

14. Pitcher, R., Skewes, T. and Dennis, D. (1991) *Progress report to the Torres Strait Fisheries Scientific Advisory Committee meeting, April 1991*. Cleveland: CSIRO Division of Fisheries. 6 pp.

Contributors

The information in this presentation was originally provided by Roland Pitcher. Additional comments were made by (in alphabetical order) Peter Channells, Chris Chubb, Bruce Phillips, Jim Prescott, Andy Richards, Tim Skewes, Derek Staples and Geoff Williams. Drawing courtesy FAO, Rome; redrawn by Karina Hansen. (*Details of contributors and their organisations are given in the Acknowledgements section at the back of this book.*)
Compiler Patricia Kailola

Bay lobsters

Thenus species

Bay lobsters

This presentation is on 2 species, **mud bugs** and **sand bugs**.

Mud bug, *Thenus orientalis* (Lund)

Other general common names include **bug, slipper lobster** and **squat lobster**, and a specific common name is **Moreton Bay bug**.
FAO: **flathead locust lobster**
Australian species code: 700002

Sand bug, *Thenus* species

Other general common names include **bug, slipper lobster** and **squat lobster**, and a specific common name is **reef bug**.
FAO: no known name
Australian species code: 700004

Family SCYLLARIDAE

Diagnostic features Bay lobsters have a flattened body top to bottom with a rough carapace and their antennae are short, broad and platelike.[1] Their eyes are sunken into the front margin of the carapace, and are widely spaced at the front corners. The 2 *Thenus* species can be distinguished as follows: mud bugs (pictured) are brown overall and a bit 'furry', their legs are vertically striped and their tail swimmerettes are yellow; sand bugs

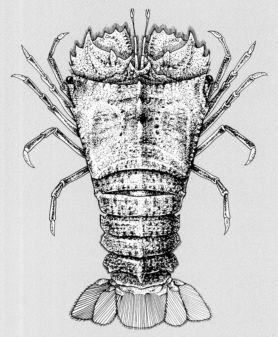

are speckled overall, including their legs and their tail swimmerettes are brown.[2] Shovel–nosed lobsters (*Ibacus* species) are also members of the Scyllaridae but differ from bay lobsters mainly in having eyes that are close together and located near their body midline.[1]

August–September to January–February. A peak in spawning activity occurs in spring,[3] and there is a minimum of 3 months between spawnings. The male deposits a spermatophore under the female's abdomen and fertilisation occurs as the eggs emerge. Separate mating and sperm deposit precedes each spawning. The eggs attach to the female's pleopods and are incubated within a brood chamber formed by the flexed tail fan and the abdominal sections. Approximately 10 weeks after emerging, planktonic phyllosoma larvae are hatched. Mud bugs produce 4000–25 000 (average 12 500) eggs per brood and sand bugs produce 16 000–60 000 (average 32 000) eggs per brood. Up to a carapace length of 65 mm, mud bugs produce a relatively higher number of eggs than do sand bugs of similar sizes.[3]

Distribution

Bay lobsters are found along the entire northern coast of Australia from Shark Bay in Western Australia to Coffs Harbour in northern New South Wales. They are distributed generally throughout the tropical Indo-West Pacific Ocean approximately between latitudes 20°N and 30°S, and longitudes 40°E and 155°E.

Bay lobsters live on the sea bed, that is, they are benthic. Mud bugs live in turbid inshore coastal waters from 10 m to 30 m depth in eastern Queensland[3] and to 60 m depth in northern Australia[4] over soft, unconsolidated muds and fine sand and silt particles. Sand bugs, however, prefer the clear, 30–60 m deep waters of the coastal shelf and offshore areas, over hard, medium–coarse sand between reefs.[3]

Life history

Two spawnings per female bay lobster are common, and possibly more take place throughout the summer period from

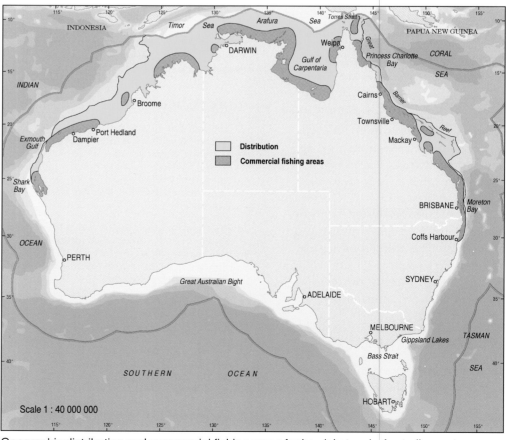

Geographic distribution and commercial fishing areas for bay lobsters in Australian waters.

Some phyllosoma larvae have been collected near the edge of the continental shelf, possibly carried there by ocean currents. They may also attach to small medusae (jellyfish – Coelenterata). Ocean currents probably carry the phyllosoma larvae and the medusae inshore. The planktonic phase lasts for about 3 months before the larvae settle to the sea floor.

Growth is initially rapid, but it slows down in larger animals. Both species attain a size of 45–50 mm carapace length at 9–12 months.[3] The maximum recorded carapace length is 90 mm (average 42 mm) for mud bugs and 100 mm (average 60 mm) for sand bugs.[3] The maximum recorded weight for mud bugs is 420 g but the average size is about 80 g in catches. For sand bugs the maximum recorded weight is 560 g with most harvested bugs averaging 120 g. Both mud bugs and sand bugs can reach an age in excess of 7 years. Bay lobsters attain sexual maturity at 1–2 years of age, from a size of about 52 mm carapace length for female mud bugs and from about 58 mm carapace length for female sand bugs.[3]

Bay lobsters are active at night, remaining buried in bottom sediment with only their eyes and antennules, or 'feelers', exposed during the day.[3] They are highly mobile, and can move great distances (up to 50 nautical miles).[3] Bay lobster density varies between areas, and between species.[3] For example, mud bugs are less abundant in Queensland waters than are sand bugs. Bay lobsters are capable of continuous swimming and

complex manoeuvres, and generate lift when moving through the water by a series of short 'hops'.[5] No other group of lobsters swims like this.

Juvenile bay lobsters feed on small benthic animals. The adults are selective foragers and will capture live prey including fish, crustaceans and molluscs. Both juvenile and adult bay lobsters exhibit a preference for bivalve molluscs in their diets. Predators of bay lobsters are bottom-dwelling fish and shovel-nose rays (*Rhina* species) and stingrays (*Dasyatis* and *Himantura* species).

Stock structure

Discrete groups of bay lobsters are defined by their preferred habitat association with species of prawn (Penaeidae), or prawn and saucer scallop (*Amusium*) species. Mixing of the larvae from these discrete groups during the planktonic phyllosoma phase probably sustains a single Australia-wide stock.

Commercial fishery

Although bay lobsters have been harvested in Moreton Bay in association with prawn trawling since the late 1800s,[6] they were not marketed until the mid-1930s.

Bay lobsters are not targeted by fishers even though they are available all year round. They are a bycatch of prawn or prawn and saucer scallop fisheries — although in Northern Territory waters at

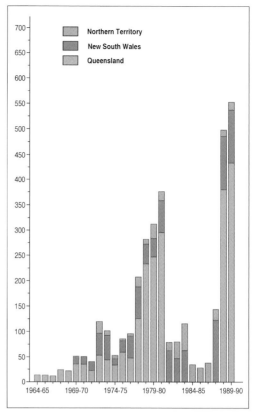

Total annual catch in t of bay lobsters (*Thenus* species) and shovel-nosed lobsters (*Ibacus* species) for the period 1964–65 to 1989–90. Figures are unavailable for: New South Wales from 1964–65 to 1968–69, 1984–85 to 1986–87; Queensland for 1981–82 to 1987–88; and the Northern Territory from 1964–65 to 1967–68 and 1969–70 to 1971–72. Catches for States that average less than 5 % of the total for all States are not shown. (Source: Fisheries Resources Atlas Statistical Database)

least, they are the most sought after of all bycatch products.[7] Interest in targeting bay lobsters in previously untrawlable areas is increasing, some fishers using traps or old otter trawl gear for this purpose.

Bay lobsters are caught by demersal otter trawls and with dredge nets. Mud bugs are caught in localised prawn fisheries targeting tiger prawns (*Penaeus esculentus, P. semisulcatus*), endeavour prawns (*Metapenaeus endeavouri, M. ensis*) and school prawns (*Metapenaeus macleayi*) in Moreton Bay. Sand bugs are caught in prawn fisheries targeting red spot king prawns (*Penaeus longistylus*) and western king prawns (*Penaeus latisulcatus*) and saucer scallops.

Mud bugs comprise most of the bay lobster catch in the tiger prawn and endeavour prawn fishing grounds along the Northern Territory coastline, in the western and eastern Gulf of Carpentaria and Torres Strait, Princess Charlotte Bay, central Queensland and southern Queensland. Sand bugs comprise less than 5 % of the catch from these fishing

Trawl gear coming aboard, Northern Prawn Fishery area. (Source: Anne Coleman, Fisheries Division, Northern Territory Department of Primary Industry and Fisheries)

grounds. However, where king prawns and saucer scallops are targeted in central and southern Queensland, sand bugs comprise up to 80 % of the catch.[3] In 1980–81 surveys,[4] catch rates off northern Australia were highest in depths between 11 m and 60 m, reaching 217 bugs per half hour trawl; and in a 1988 survey[7] highest catch rates were obtained in the western Gulf of Carpentaria. Overall, the estimated proportions by weight of the annual commercial catch in the central Queensland prawn trawl fishery are 10 % for sand bugs and 4 % for mud bugs.[8] Small individuals are discarded from catches.

Bay lobsters are sent to wholesalers usually frozen, whole and green (uncooked). Sand bugs fetch higher prices than do mud bugs.[3] Bay lobsters retail as green whole, cooked whole, green tail and uncooked meat. In 1992, wholesale prices in Queensland averaged A$ 11.00 per kg for whole cooked bugs, A$ 16.50 per kg for green tails and A$ 26.00 per kg for meat only. At the Sydney Fish Market, the average 1991–92 price for whole green bugs (*Ibacus* and *Thenus* species) was A$ 7.78 per kg. Approximately 5 % of the catch is exported to the United States of America; and of the Queensland catch, 70 % goes to Sydney and Melbourne markets and 25 % is sold in local restaurants.

Management controls There are no specific State controls except that in Queensland, the keeping of berried females is prohibited. Otherwise, the restrictions in the associated State and Commonwealth-managed prawn fisheries control the bay lobster fishery. Juveniles and berried females are voluntarily returned to sea by many trawler operators.[7]

Recreational fishery

There is no recreational fishery for bay lobsters.

Resource status

Bay lobsters are heavily exploited where prawns are targeted and evidence of overfishing comes from reduced catch rates and average size of caught individuals. For example, average bay lobster size and catch per unit effort were significantly less in 1983 than they were 20 years earlier, probably because more are retained for sale than in early years. However, there are extensive areas that are not suitable for prawn fishing (due to rough ground and/or low prawn densities) which do support bay lobster stocks. In such areas, bay lobsters could be targeted using alternative catching methods such as traps. The full potential of the bay lobster resource may not yet have been realised.[6]

References

1. Holthuis, L.B. (1985) A revision of the family Scyllaridae (Crustacea: Decapoda: Macrura). I. Subfamily Ibacinae. *Zoologische Verhandelingen* **218**. 130 pp.

2. Jones, C.M. (1990) Morphological characteristics of bay lobsters *Thenus* Leach species (Decapoda: Scyllaridae) from north-eastern Australia. *Crustaceana* **59**(3): 265–275.

3. Jones, C.M. (1988) *The biology and behaviour of bay lobsters*, Thenus *spp. (Decapoda: Scyllaridae), in northern Queensland, Australia*. Unpublished PhD thesis, University of Queensland.

4. Okera, W. and Gunn, J.S. (1986) Exploratory trawl surveys by FRV *Soela* in the Australian fishing zone sector of the Timor–Arafura Seas and in the Gulf of Carpentaria, 1980–81. *CSIRO Marine Laboratories Report* **150**. 104 pp.

5. Ritz, D.A. and Jacklyn, P.M. (1985) Believe it or not — bugs fly through the water. *Australian Fisheries* **44**(6): 35–37.

6. Jones, C.M. (1984) Development of the bay lobster fishery in Queensland. *Australian Fisheries* **43**(9): 19–21.

7. Pender, P.J. and Willing, R.S. (1990) Northern prawn fishery bycatch with market potential. *Northern Territory Department of Primary Industry and Fisheries, Fishery Report* **20**. 52 pp.

8. Jones, C.M. and Derbyshire, K. (1988) Sampling the demersal fauna from a commercial penaeid prawn fishery off the central Queensland coast. *Memoirs of the Queensland Museum* **25**(2): 403–415.

Contributors

Information on mud bugs and sand bugs was originally provided by Clive Jones and some additional comments were made by Russell Willing. Figure redrawn by Peter Moloney and Julie Easton from an illustration supplied by Clive Jones. (*Details of contributors and their organisations are given in the Acknowledgements section at the back of this book.*)
Compiler Patricia Kailola

Lateral view of a bay lobster in an aquarium. (Source: Clive Jones, Fisheries Branch, Queensland Department of Primary Industries)

Spanner crab

Ranina ranina

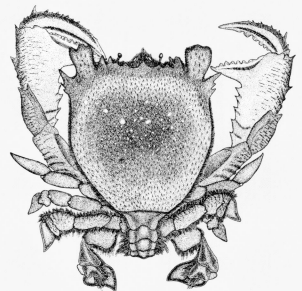

Ranina ranina (Linnaeus)

Spanner crab

Other common names include **frog crab** and **red frog crab**.
FAO: no known name
Australian species code: 702002

Family RANINIDAE

Diagnostic features Spanner crabs have an elongate carapace (shell) with convex sides. The carapace is very broad at the front where there is a series of prominent triangular teeth. The crabs' abdomen can be seen from above. The first legs are 'spanner'-shaped and the remaining legs are flattened with numerous short bristles. The body colour varies from orange to red. Movement is forwards-backwards (unlike other crabs).

Distribution

Spanner crabs inhabit coastal waters of several countries in the Indian and Pacific oceans, from the east coasts of southern Africa to Hawaii. In Australia they live along the east and west coasts: from Yeppoon in Queensland to Nowra in New South Wales and from Quinns Rocks north of Perth to the Houtman Abrolhos and Geraldton in Western Australia. There have also been unconfirmed reports of spanner crabs on the northern reefs of the Great Barrier Reef. In Australia, distribution is patchy.

These crabs prefer bare sandy areas.[1] They inhabit intertidal waters to depths of more than 100 m, from sheltered bays to surf areas.

Life history

Spanner crabs aggregate to spawn during the warmer months of the year, from October to February. They may mate at any stage in their moult cycle[2] and females store sperm until the eggs are extruded. At spawning, females often bury themselves to incubate and protect the egg sponges. Large female spanner crabs produce at least 2 batches of eggs each season with an average number of 120 000 per batch, and the eggs remain attached to the female for 4–5 weeks before hatching.[2]

Spanner crabs pass through 8 larval stages during the following 5 to 8 (longer in higher latitudes) weeks of their life, then settle during 1 further stage before metamorphosis to the recognisable spanner crab form.[3]

Newly settled crabs grow rapidly, attaining 30 mm carapace length within 3 or 4 weeks.[3] Studies of growth rates of crabs in the New South Wales commercial fishery show males increasing in carapace length by 12–16 mm per moult and females increasing by 5–9 mm per moult, and there is an average of 1 moult per year. Spanner crabs may live for 7 to 9 years, with males reaching a size of 150 mm carapace length and 900 g, while females are smaller, reaching a maximum size of 120 mm carapace length and 400 g.[3]

Female crabs are mature at approximately 2 years of age or 70–75 mm carapace length and approximately 100 g, although they may be as small as 64 mm carapace length when mature.[3] Ovarian development is more rapid in warmer, northerly waters.[3]

Spanner crabs remain completely buried in the sand for most of each day.

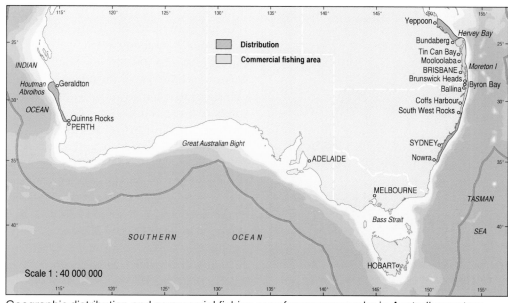

Geographic distribution and commercial fishing area for spanner crabs in Australian waters.

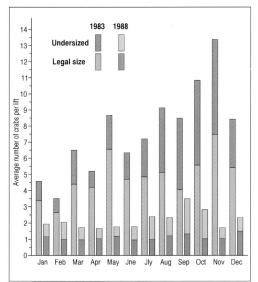

Estimate of monthly abundance of spanner crabs in Moreton Bay for 1983 and 1988, measured as numbers of crabs per pot-lift. (Source: Fisheries Branch, Queensland Department of Primary Industries)

They emerge rapidly when food appears.[1] Spanner crabs are opportunistic feeders, ie they eat whatever is available. Adults eat heart urchins (Echinoidea) and a variety of small bivalve molluscs, crustaceans, polychaete worms and fish.[2,3] Spanner crabs are often found in areas where there is an intensive night time prawn trawl fishery, suggesting that discards from the trawl catch may form a significant part of their diet.[3]

There is evidence that sharks and turtles (Chelonidae) feed on spanner crabs and turtles take advantage of crabs being caught in nets.

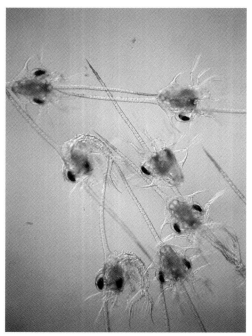

Planktonic spanner crab larvae (zoeae) just after hatching. (Source: Glen Smith, Southern Fisheries Centre, Queensland Department of Primary Industries)

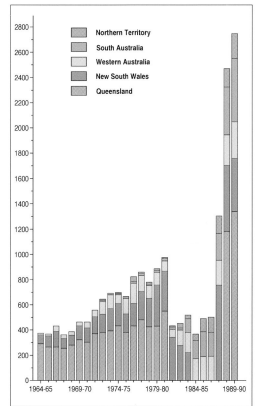

Total annual catch in t of all crabs for the period 1964–65 to 1989–90. Figures are unavailable for: New South Wales from 1984–85 to 1986–87; Queensland from 1981–82 to 1987–88; and South Australia for 1964–65, 1965–66 and 1971–72. Catches for States that average less than 5 % of the total for all States are not shown. (Source: Fisheries Resources Atlas Statistical Database)

Stock structure

The stock structure of Australian spanner crabs is unknown, although genetic studies are being undertaken. New South Wales populations exhibit variability in both location and depth.[4]

Commercial fishery

The spanner crab fishery has developed only recently — since 1980 in Queensland and 1982 in New South Wales. It is now one of the largest spanner crab fisheries in the world. New South Wales landings were 445 t in 1987–88, 219 t in 1988–89 and 192 t in 1989–90; and Queensland landings were 374 t in 1988–89 and 505 t in 1989–90. Fishing effort was initially concentrated near Moreton Island in southern Queensland and later spread northwards along the coast to Hervey Bay and southwards to New South Wales areas including Brunswick Heads, Byron Bay, Ballina and Coffs Harbour.[4] Most of the New South Wales catch is landed at Ballina.

Spanner crabs are caught throughout the year using baited tangle nets, set during daylight hours. Usually several nets are deployed on a trotline from small speedboats and fish for 30–60 minutes at a time. Crabs of legal size — 3 years old and older[3] — are available throughout the year. Catches are higher around new moon, and the total catch is higher from July to October due to the recruitment of smaller crabs to the fishery.[2] Spawning and feeding aggregations are targeted,[2,5] and fishers generally target male crabs as females are often less than the legal minimum size restriction. Because of concern about high mortality in discarded, undersized crabs damaged in the process of removal from tangle nets,[5] other methods of fishing are being investigated.

Demersal otter trawlers fishing for prawns occasionally catch large numbers of spanner crabs from a moving aggregation during the spawning period but rarely catch buried crabs.

Most of the spanner crab catch is sold as whole crabs on the domestic market. Some is sent interstate and exported overseas to Hawaii and South-east Asia. Wholesale prices in Queensland in 1992 averaged about A$ 4.00 per kg for cooked crabs. The average wholesale price paid at the Sydney Fish Market in 1991–92 was A$ 3.20 per kg.

Management controls Females bearing eggs may not be taken. Both Queensland and New South Wales impose a minimum legal carapace length, gear restrictions and a short closed season.

Recreational fishery

There is a small recreational fishery in Queensland and New South Wales parallelling the commercial fishery, although it is closer to coastal towns and more common in the summertime. Gear similar to commercial gear is used.

Management controls There are bag limits and a restriction on the number of tangle nets used.

Resource status

A large proportion of the spanner crab population is exploited[4] in southern Queensland and northern New South Wales, where it is heavily fished. The northward move by the fishery in

Queensland in recent years is due to declining catch rates in the original fishery in the more southern areas. The status of the resource is uncertain.

References

1. Skinner, D.G. and Hill, B.J. (1986) Catch rate and emergence of male and female spanner crabs (*Ranina ranina*) in Australia. *Marine Biology* **91**: 461–465.

2. Brown, I.W. (1986) South Queensland's spanner crabs — a growing fishery. *Australian Fisheries* **45**(10): 3–7.

3. Brown, I.W. (1986) Population biology of the spanner crab in south-east Queensland. *Southern Fisheries Centre, Queensland Department of Primary Industries. FIRTA Project 81/71, Final Report.* 106 pp.

4. Kennelly, S.J. (1989) Effects of soak-time and spatial heterogeneity on sampling populations of spanner crabs *Ranina ranina. Marine Ecology in Progress Series* **55**: 141–147.

5. Kennelly, S.J., Watkins, D. and Craig, J.R. (1990) Mortality of discarded spanner crabs *Ranina ranina* (Linnaeus) in a tangle-net fishery — laboratory and field experiments. *Journal of Experimental Marine Biology and Ecology* **140**: 39–48.

Contributors

Most of the information on this species was originally provided by Ian Brown and Steve Kennelly and supplemented by (in alphabetical order) Peter Davies and Roger Springthorpe. Drawing by Jack Hannan, courtesy Fisheries Research Institute, NSW Fisheries. (*Details of contributors and their organisations are given in the Acknowledgements section at the back of this book.*)
Compilers Kay Abel, Patricia Kailola and Christina Grieve (maps)

Meshed spanner crabs, Moreton Bay. (Source: Glen Smith, Southern Fisheries Centre, Queensland Department of Primary Industries)

Blue swimmer crab

Portunus pelagicus

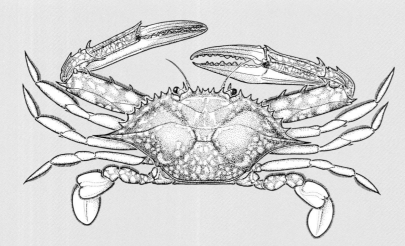

Portunus pelagicus (Linnaeus)

Blue swimmer crab

Other common names include **sand crab**, **blue manna crab**, **blue crab** and **sandy**.
FAO name: **sand crab**
Australian species code: 702003

Family PORTUNIDAE

Diagnostic features Sand crabs are swimming crabs and, like mud crabs (*Scylla serrata*), they have their last pair of legs modified as swimming paddles. Their carapace (shell) is rough in texture. It is very broad and has a prominent projection on each side. The crabs' claws are long and slender. Sand crabs vary in colour from brown through blue to purple with pale mottling.

Distribution

Blue swimmer crabs are very widely distributed throughout the Indo-West Pacific region from east Africa to Japan, Tahiti and northern New Zealand. They are also present in the Mediterranean Sea.

In Australia, blue swimmer crabs inhabit coastal waters from Cape Naturaliste in Western Australia around the north of Australia to the south coast of New South Wales. They are also present around Lord Howe Island and in the warmer waters of the South Australian gulfs, as far south as Barker Inlet in Gulf St Vincent.[1]

Blue swimmer crabs live in a wide range of inshore and continental shelf areas, including sandy, muddy or algal and seagrass habitats, from the intertidal zone to at least 50 m depth.[2,3] Blue swimmer crabs move to deeper water as they age[4] and in response to changes in water temperature and inshore salinity. Only juveniles live in intertidal habitats. Adults are generally found in salinities between 30 and 40 parts per thousand, though in upper Spencer Gulf (South Australia) both juveniles and adults are present in summer salinities of more that 45 parts per thousand. Female, egg-bearing blue swimmer crabs in

Moreton Bay migrate to deeper, oceanic waters in the Bay.[5] Blue swimmer crabs are active swimmers, but when inactive, they usually bury in the bottom sediment, leaving only their eyes, antennae and gill chamber opening exposed.

Life history

Blue swimmer crabs form breeding pairs[6] and mating takes place during the late summer (January to March) moult of the females.[4,6] Mature males moult some weeks before the maturing females, and each carries a female clasped beneath him for 4–10 days before she moults. Mating occurs immediately after the female has moulted and when her shell is still soft.[6] Males can mate with a number of females during the season.[7]

Female crabs spawn up to 2 million eggs per batch, larger crabs producing more eggs than smaller crabs. Spawning takes place all year in tropical and subtropical waters[5,8] although spawning females are more prevalent in the dry season (July to October) in the tropics (eg Gulf of Carpentaria) and in spring

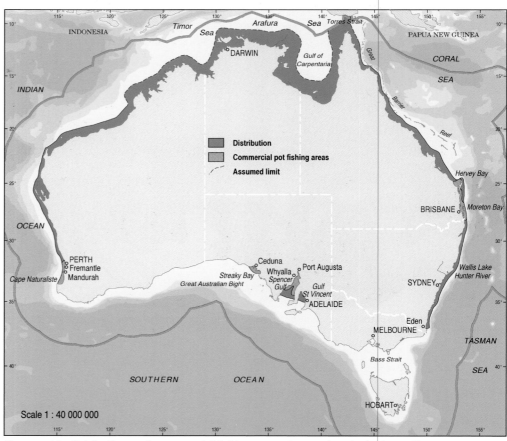

Geographic distribution and commercial fishing areas for sand crabs in Australian waters.

(August to October) in subtropical latitudes (eg Moreton Bay). In temperate waters, females store sperm until spawning takes place in spring or summer (November to January) when there is a spawning peak.[6] Female crabs may spawn several times a season using sperm from 1 mating,[7] even as frequently as 2 or 3 times over a few months.[9]

Blue swimmer crab eggs and larvae are planktonic. The eggs hatch after about 15 days at 24°C water temperature. The blue swimmer crab larval phase consists of 5 stages. During the larval phase, the crabs may drift as far as 80 km out to sea before returning to settle in shallow, inshore waters.[2] Newly settled blue swimmer crabs are about 15 mm in carapace width.[6] One-year-old juveniles move out of estuaries in winter in the Peel–Harvey Inlet near Mandurah, Western Australia[4] and to deeper water in summer in southern Queensland.[5]

Blue swimmer crabs usually moult 1 or more times within each of their several distinct life stages. Male and females grow at similar rates and reach similar maximum ages and sizes for given locations. The maximum recorded age for blue swimmer crabs is 3 years.[9] The maximum size recorded in Australian waters is 218 mm carapace width.[7] However, these crabs rarely reach 200 mm and in the Gulf of Carpentaria and South Australia[6] they seldom reach 150 mm carapace width. Adult blue swimmer crabs usually weigh about 500 g but have been recorded up to 1 kg.

Blue swimmer crabs mature at about 1 year of age.[6,7] The size at which maturity occurs varies with latitude[8] and within individuals at any location. The range of sizes at maturity for female crabs is illustrated below. Males mature at

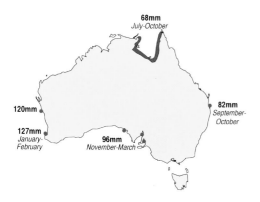

Geographic variation around Australia of blue swimmer crab size at first sexual maturity and the period of peak spawning activity. (Source: Potter et al;[4] Potter et al;[5] Smith[6])

68mm
July-October

82mm
September-October

120mm

127mm
January-February

96mm
November-March

85–157 mm carapace width in the Peel–Harvey Inlet;[4] 80 mm and larger in the Gulf of Carpentaria; 95–150 mm in Moreton Bay;[8] and 105–140 mm in South Australia.[6,10]

Blue swimmer crabs are bottom-feeding carnivores and scavengers and they are most active in foraging and feeding at sunset.[9,11] Their diet chiefly consists of a variety of sessile and slow moving invertebrates, including bivalve molluscs, crustaceans, polychaete worms and brittle stars (Ophiuroidea).[2,3] Seagrass (eg *Zostera* species) and algae may be eaten occasionally. In some localities, fish and squid (Loliginidae) discarded from prawn trawlers may be important sources of food.[11]

Little is known of predation on blue swimmer crabs but turtles (Chelonidae), sharks, rays (Batoidea) and large fish are probably the most common natural predators. Crabs are most vulnerable to predation immediately after moulting.

Stock structure

The stock structure of blue swimmer crab populations in Australia has not been investigated although it has been observed that blue swimmer crabs from different parts of the species' range vary considerably in appearance. The planktonic egg and larval stages probably enable population mixing and dispersion. In South Australia, separate stocks of blue swimmer crabs have been identified in Streaky Bay, Spencer Gulf and Gulf St Vincent. The stocks appear to be isolated by cooler waters to the south.[10]

Commercial fishery

Moreton Bay, Hervey Bay and other inshore areas of southern Queensland account for approximately half of the commercial catch of blue swimmer crabs in Australia. Other important commercial grounds are along the New South Wales coast and include Wallis Lake and the lower Hunter River. Spencer Gulf and Gulf St Vincent in South Australia, and the Peel–Harvey Inlet and Cockburn Sound near Fremantle and the Swan–Avon River near Perth in Western Australia are all important commercial grounds. Streaky Bay in South Australia periodically supports a small fishery.

Fishing takes place on offshore sand banks, channels and deeper water up to

Sand crabs trawled in Moreton Bay being tagged for study of growth and migration. (Source: Glen Smith, Southern Fisheries Centre, Queensland Department of Primary Industries)

25 m deep. Catches are highest from about January to March.[4] Blue swimmer crabs are caught in cylindrical wire traps or pots and folding traps, preferably baited with mullet (Mugilidae).[9] Hoop nets, drop nets and sunken crab gillnets are also used. Rakes and dab nets are employed in very shallow water.

Blue swimmer crabs form a significant part of the bycatch of many prawn trawlers and in Queensland it has been estimated that between one third and one half as many crabs are caught in prawn trawls as are caught in the target pot fishery.[9] Blue swimmer crabs are caught incidentally with rock lobsters and in finfish fisheries. Due to the seasonal nature of the fishery, blue swimmer crab fishers usually engage in other fishing activities as well, such as catching spanner crabs (*Ranina ranina*).

Most of the catch is marketed within Australia as whole, cooked crab or crab meat. There is a small export market for blue swimmer crabs. The average 1991–92 price per kg for blue swimmer crabs at the Sydney Fish Market was A$ 4.86 (green) and A$ 5.54 (cooked).

Management controls In most States, regulations limit the types and quantity of fishing gear which may be used and the size and/or sex of crabs which may be taken. In Queensland, for example, no females and only males over 150 mm carapace width may legally be taken. The

Commercial sandcrabber, Moreton Bay.
(Source: Glen Smith, Southern Fisheries Centre,
Queensland Department of Primary Industries)

number of licences is limited in many
areas and seasonal closures are common.
The minimum legal size varies from State
to State, as does the method of
measurement. Females in berry are
protected in all States.

Aquaculture

There have been successful attempts at
culturing blue swimmer crabs in Australia.
The species is cultured in Japan and other
Asian countries.

Recreational fishery

There is a substantial recreational fishery
in the same areas as the commercial
fishery, but concentrated in the more
accessible inshore areas. Recreational
fishers use cylindrical pots and tangle nets
('dillies') as well as rakes, dab nets, baited
hoop nets and drop nets. Blue swimmer
crabs are often caught by fishers targeting
prawns.

Management controls The recreational
fishery is managed by restrictions on the
number of pots or nets as well as bag
limits on the number of crabs. Berried
females may not be kept.

Resource status

The long-established blue swimmer crab
fisheries in Queensland, New South

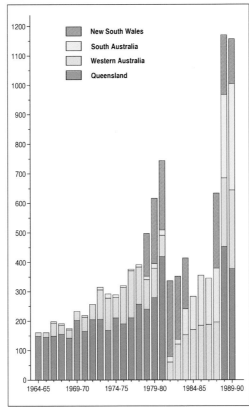

Total annual catch in t of blue swimmer
crabs for the period 1964–65 to 1989–90.
Figures are unavailable for: New South
Wales from 1964–65 to 1977–78 and
1984–85 to 1986–87; Queensland for
1981–82 to 1987–88; and South Australia for
1964–65, 1965–66 and 1971–72. Catches
for States that average less than 5 % of the
total for all States are not shown. (Source:
Fisheries Resources Atlas Statistical Database)

Wales and Western Australia show no
evidence of overfishing with relatively
stable catches in recent years. Since 1982,
the blue swimmer crab fishery in South
Australia has increased in importance.

Notes

A rhizocephalan parasite, *Sacculina
granifera*, infects up to 11 % of crabs in
Moreton Bay and the Gulf of Carpentaria,
rendering them unmarketable.[12]

The 'sand crab' in South Australia and
Victoria is a different species, *Ovalipes
australiensis*.

References

1. Stephenson, W. and Campbell, B. (1959)
The Australian portunids (Crustacea:
Portunidae). III. The genus *Portunus*.
*Australian Journal of Marine and
Freshwater Research* **10**: 84–124.

2. Williams, M.J. (1982) Natural food and
feeding in the commercial sand crab
Portunus pelagicus Linnaeus, 1766
(Crustacea: Decapoda: Portunidae) in
Moreton Bay, Queensland. *Journal of
Experimental Marine Biology and Ecology*
59: 165–176.

3. Edgar, G.J. (1990) Predator–prey
interactions in seagrass beds. II.
Distribution and diet of the blue manna
crab *Portunus pelagicus* Linnaeus at Cliff
head, Western Australia. *Journal of
Experimental Marine Biology and Ecology*
139: 23–32.

4. Potter, I.C., Chrystal, P.J. and Loneragan,
N.R. (1983) The biology of the blue manna
crab *Portunus pelagicus* in an Australian
estuary. *Marine Biology* **78**: 75–85.

5. Potter, M., Sumpton, W. and Smith, G.
(1987) Qld sand crab study highlights a
need for changes in management.
Australian Fisheries **46**(6): 22–26.

6. Smith, H. (1982) Blue crabs in South
Australia — their status, potential and
biology. *SAFIC* **6**(5): 6–9.

7. The blue manna crab (1990) *Fisheries
Department of Western Australia,
Fishing WA* **7**. 4pp.

8. Campbell, G.R. and Fielder, D.R. (1986) Size
at sexual maturity and occurrence of
ovigerous females in three species of
commercially exploited portunid crabs in
S.E. Queensland. *Proceedings of the Royal
Society of Queensland* **97**: 79–87.

9. Smith, G.S. and Sumpton, W.D. (1987) Sand
crabs a valuable fishery in south east
Queensland. *The Professional Fisherman*
5 (1): 13–15.

10. Grove-Jones, R. (1987) Catch and effort in
the South Australian blue crab (*Portunus
pelagicus*) fishery. *South Australian
Department of Fisheries. A discussion
paper.* 47 pp.

11. Wassenberg, T.J. and Hill, B.J. (1987)
Feeding by the sand crab *Portunus
pelagicus* on material discarded from prawn
trawlers in Moreton Bay, Australia. *Marine
Biology* **95**: 387–393.

12. Sumpton, W.D., Potter, M.A. and Smith,
G.S. (1989) The commercial pot and trawl
fisheries of sand crabs (*Portunus pelagicus*
L.) in Moreton Bay, Queensland.
*Proceedings of the Royal Society of
Queensland* **100**: 89–100.

Contributors

The information on this species was originally
provided by Wayne Sumpton and
supplemented by (in alphabetical order) Rod
Grove-Jones, Steve Kennelly and John Short.
Drawing by Clare Bremner. (*Details of
contributors and their organisations are given
in the Acknowledgements section at the back
of this book.*)

Compilers Kay Abel, Meryl Williams, Patricia
Kailola and Christina Grieve (maps)

Distribution

Mud crabs are widely distributed throughout the Indo-West Pacific region from the east coast of Africa to northern Australia, and across the western Pacific to Tahiti. They were introduced to Hawaii more than 55 years ago.

In Australia, mud crabs inhabit tropical to warm temperate waters from Exmouth Gulf in Western Australia to the Bega River in New South Wales. They are present only in isolated populations south of Broome in Western Australia and Sydney in New South Wales, associated with pockets of mangrove (eg *Avicennia marina*, *Aegiceras* species, *Rhizophora stylosa*) habitat.

Mud crabs commonly inhabit sheltered estuaries, the tidal reaches of some rivers, mud flats and mangrove forests, although females in berry (ie carrying eggs) are present in deeper waters up to 50 km offshore. These crabs favour a soft muddy bottom, often below low tide level.

Life history

Mating occurs when the female mud crab is in the soft-bodied condition following moulting. Sperm is stored until eggs are ready to be fertilised. Female mud crabs in Australian populations migrate offshore to spawn and are rarely seen.[1] Multiple spawnings in the 1 season may follow a single mating, and 2–8 million eggs are shed in each spawning . The abdominal flap is folded outwards to accommodate the large egg mass which is incubated for 2–4 weeks before the eggs hatch, depending on temperature.[2]

Over the 12–15 days after hatching, the crabs pass through 4 planktonic larval stages requiring salinity above 30 parts per thousand and water temperatures of 26°C–30°C.[3] At the next developmental stage, the mud crabs are 3 mm long and

Scylla serrata (Forsskål)

Mud crab

Other common names include **mangrove crab, muddy** and **black crab**.
FAO: **mud crab**
Australian species code: 702001

Family PORTUNIDAE

Diagnostic features Mud crabs are large crabs with a smooth, broad carapace. They have 9 even-sized teeth on each side of their eyes. Their 2 hind legs are flattened for swimming. In the most common form, the colour varies from very dark brown to mottled green. The other, generally smaller, form has a deeper body and is reddish brown.

move inshore to settle. Mud crabs assume the adult form within 4 weeks of hatching. Juveniles 20–80 mm carapace width typically shelter under stones in the upper intertidal areas,[2] and are found in the shelter of seagrass beds and around

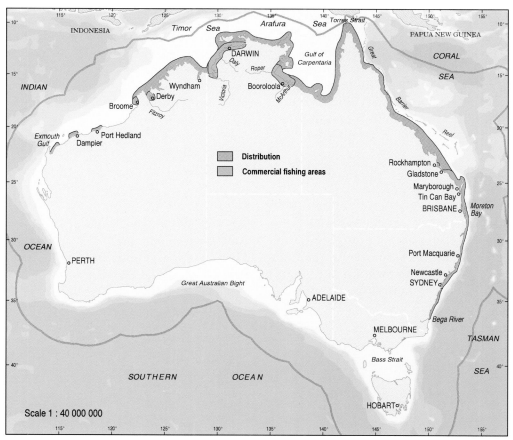

Geographic distribution and commercial fishing areas for mud crabs in Australian waters.

mangrove roots.[4] Large numbers of these small mud crabs have sometimes been seen on sandbars at the wide mouths of tropical rivers.

During moulting or mating periods mud crabs spend most of the day in mud burrows they have excavated below the low tide mark. These burrows may be up to 2 m long.[1] Growth rates and maturity vary with temperature. There is little or no growth in winter (May to August) and more rapid growth in spring (September to November). Mud crabs in the tropics mature at about 18 months of age whilst those in warm temperate areas mature at about 2 years. Mud crabs live for up to 3 years, reaching a maximum size of 24 cm carapace width (the largest crab of the red-brown variety recorded was only 14 cm[5]). At the Queensland markets, mud crabs are usually between 0.7 and 1.25 kg weight, although crabs of up to 3.25 kg have been noted.

Juvenile mud crabs eat planktonic animals, benthic molluscs and crustaceans of various types. Adults feed at night on a variety of bivalve and gastropod molluscs including mussels (*Mytilus* species) and pipis (*Plebidonax* species), small crabs (eg marine crabs, Grapsidae, and hermit crabs, Paguridae), and polychaete worms.[1,4,7] Mud crabs are also attracted to dead fish and meat in traps. The mud crab's large claws are used for crushing and cutting their prey. If lost, these claws may grow again in successive moult cycles.

Natural predators of mud crabs include sharks, crocodiles (*Crocodylus* species), turtles (Chelonidae), rays (Batoidea), large fish such as rock cods (Serranidae) and barramundi (*Lates calcarifer*);[6] also herons (Ardeidae).[8]

Stock structure

Since there is little movement between adjacent inshore habitats, each mud crab population appears to be discrete. However, the stocks may show a high degree of genetic mixing as a consequence of their offshore spawning and having planktonic larvae.[9]

Two distinct forms of mud crab are present in Australia. Their specific identity has not been fully investigated.

Commercial fishery

The commercial fishery is in the estuaries and lower reaches of rivers. The Western

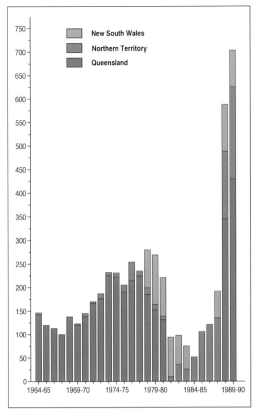

Total annual catch in t of mud crabs for the period 1964–65 to 1989–90. Figures are unavailable for: New South Wales from 1964–65 to 1977–78; and Queensland from 1981–82 to 1987–88. Catches for States that average less than 5 % of the total for all States are not shown. (Source: Fisheries Resources Atlas Statistical Database)

Australian mud crab fishery is largely limited to a small area in the north of the State, centred on Broome and Derby. The Northern Territory fishery has expanded from the area near Darwin in recent years and fishing is now concentrated in the south-west Gulf of Carpentaria in the region around and between the Roper and McArthur rivers. The major mud crab fishery in Queensland is south of Rockhampton, particularly between Maryborough and Gladstone. The fishery in New South Wales is principally between Newcastle and Port Macquarie although mud crabs are fished from the Queensland border to Sydney.

Mud crabs are caught in wire mesh pots baited with meat or fish. Pots are usually set from small runabouts. Drop nets are also used in Western Australia. Other methods used in the fishery are dillies and witches' hats, and hooking in burrows with a piece of wire, sometimes mounted on a pole. Occasionally blue swimmer crabs (*Portunus pelagicus*) and bottom dwelling fish such as flathead (*Platycephalus* species), bream (Sparidae), rock cod, pike eels (*Muraenesox* species), catfish (Ariidae) and sharks are caught in the traps. Mud

Setting traps for crabs, Northern Territory estuary. (Source: Fisheries Division, Northern Territory Department of Primary Industry and Fisheries)

crabs also form a bycatch of the coastal set gillnet fishery for barramundi and threadfin salmon (Polynemidae).

In Queensland the mud crab catch is higher in summer (December to May). However, the wet season from December to March makes many areas inaccessible in the Northern Territory so the peak mud crab season there is from May to November.

Live, adult mud crabs are sold on local markets and exported interstate to the major population centres.[6] Some of the catch is frozen and sold whole or as crab meat. A small quantity is exported to Japan.[6] In 1992, wholesale prices for mud crabs in Queensland averaged about A\$ 9.00 per kg.

Management controls The fishery is managed by the States and the Northern Territory. Mud crab burrows are protected in Queensland and there are restrictions on the number of licences available and the number of pots fishers may use. Minimum sizes apply in all States. The smaller red-brown form is prevalent in sufficient numbers in some parts of Western Australia to warrant a separate, lower minimum size limit there. Different regulations apply to the taking of female mud crabs in different States (no restrictions in the Northern Territory). Females in berry are protected in New South Wales and all females are protected in Queensland and Western Australia.

Aquaculture

Investigations directed at establishing mud crab aquaculture in Australia have been undertaken, and so far crabs have been reared to the juvenile stage.[10] However, costs of fishing natural populations of mud crabs are low in Australia compared with the development and production costs of mud crab farming.

Recreational fishery

There is an extensive recreational mud crab fishery in the same locations used by commercial fishers. In some areas, such as Moreton Bay in southern Queensland, the recreational mud crab fishery is larger than the commercial fishery. Recreational fishers use similar methods to the commercial fishers.

Management controls Bag limits and limits on the number of pots (or nets, in Western Australia) per person or per boat are imposed.

Resource status

The stocks are heavily exploited by both commercial and recreational fishers. Though an overall assessment of the resource status is difficult, it is believed that some areas such as Moreton Bay and Maryborough–Tin Can Bay in southern Queensland, and some areas near Darwin, have been overexploited at times.[6,11]

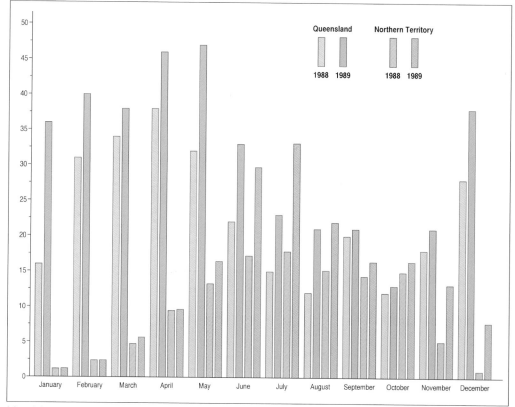

Monthly commercial catch in t of mud crabs for 1988 and 1989 in Queensland and the Northern Territory showing variation in catching effort due to inaccessibility to regions because of rains. (Source: Northern Territory Department of Primary Industry and Fisheries and Queensland Department of Primary Industries)

References

1. Fielder, D.F. and Heasman, M.P. (1978) The mud crab. *Queensland Museum Booklet* **11.** 15 pp.

2. Heasman, M.P. (1980) *Aspects of the general biology and fishery of the mud crab* Scylla serrata *(Forskål) in Moreton Bay, Qld.* Unpublished PhD thesis, University of Queensland.

3. Hill, B.J. (1974) Salinity and temperature tolerance of zoeae of the portunid crab *Scylla serrata. Marine Biology* **25**: 21–24.

4. Hill, B.J. (1979) Aspects of the feeding strategy of the predatory crab *Scylla serrata. Marine Biology* **55**: 209–214.

5. Taylor, M.L. (1984) New species of mud crab found in Western Australia. *FINS* **17**(2): 15–18.

6. Mounsey, R. (1989) Northern Territory mud crab fishery investigation. *Northern Territory Department of Primary Industry and Fisheries, Fishery Report* **19**. 73 pp.

7. Hill, B.J. (1976) Natural food, foregut clearance-rate and activity of the crab *Scylla serrata. Marine Biology* **34**: 109–116.

8. Mukherjee, A.K. (1971) Food habits of water birds of the Sundarban, West Bengal. II Herons and bitterns. *Journal of the Natural History Society, Bombay* **68**: 37–64.

9. Hyland, S.J., Hill, B.J. and Lee, C.P. (1984) Movement within and between different habitats by the portunid crab *Scylla serrata. Marine Biology* **80**: 57–61.

10. Cowan, L. (1984) Crab-farming in Australia — there's potential, but some way off. *Australian Fisheries* **42**(2): 47–50.

11. Heasman, M.P. and Fielder, D.R. (1977) The management and exploitation of the Queensland mud crab fishery. *Australian Fisheries* **36**(8): 4–8.

Contributors

Most of the information on this species was originally provided by Stuart Hyland. Other contributions were provided by (in alphabetical order) Jim Craig, Steve Kennelly and Ian Knuckey. Drawing by Clare Bremner. (*Details of contributors and their organisations are given in the Acknowledgements section at the back of this book.*)

Compilers Kay Abel, Patricia Kailola, Christina Grieve (maps) and Phillip Stewart (statistics)

Mud crabs being boxed for sale, Northern Territory. (Source: Fisheries Division, Northern Territory Department of Primary Industry and Fisheries)

Purple sea urchin

Heliocidaris erythrogramma

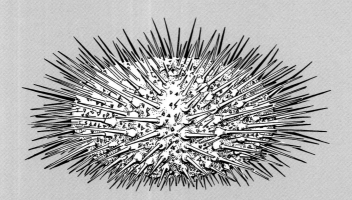

Heliocidaris erythrogramma
(Valenciennes)

Purple sea urchin

Other common names include **white urchin** and **red sea urchin**.
FAO: no known name
Australian species code: 711002

Family ECHINOMETRIDAE

Diagnostic features Sea urchins are in the same group of animals as starfish, brittle stars and sea cucumbers. Members of this group have tube feet, a water vascular system and a body comprising 5 symmetrical segments. The sea urchin has a hard external skeleton (or test) surrounding the body organs, and the mouth is located on the underside. Purple sea urchins have numerous striated primary and secondary spines. The primary spines are 10–25 mm long and taper to a point. The secondary spines have blunt or slightly widened tips. The urchins vary in colour from white to shades of green, purple and black, and 2 colour forms are often seen. The spines are often differently coloured from the test.

Distribution

Purple sea urchins are endemic to Australian waters. They are distributed from Caloundra in southern Queensland to Shark Bay in Western Australia, including all of Tasmania. These sea urchins inhabit coastal waters from the shoreline to approximately 35 m deep and are generally abundant in south-eastern Australia.

Sea urchins are benthic animals, ie they live on the sea floor. They are generally confined to depths of less than 15 m and are most common in water shallower than 10 m.[1,2] Purple sea urchins usually inhabit areas that are not fully exposed to wave action, where they can be found on top of or under rocks and stones in reef areas and sandy mud, or in seagrass beds (eg *Posidonia* species). In moderately exposed areas they tend to inhabit crevices or burrows.[2,3] Purple sea urchin densities are often higher in areas where abalone (*Haliotis* species)[3] and southern rock lobsters (*Jasus edwardsii*) are absent or low in numbers.[4]

Life history

Sea urchins have separate sexes. Sperm and eggs are shed into the water during spawning. Spawning by purple sea urchins takes place over an extended period, from summer (December) to early autumn (March) in Port Phillip Bay[5] and

Tasmania.[6] It seems to be triggered by the presence of warmer water (17°C or warmer). Spawning is asynchronous, ie it does not take place at the same time by all individuals.[5,6,7] It is not known whether individuals spawn once or repeatedly over a single season.[6,7]

The eggs are buoyant.[7] The larvae remain in the plankton for 3–5 days[7] and they are likely to settle relatively close to the parent reef.

Purple sea urchins can grow up to 14 cm in test diameter but commonly range in size from 5 cm to 9 cm when they are probably between 4 and 8 years old.[1] The size attained depends on food supply and exposure to wave action.[5] Purple sea urchins probably start spawning when 4–5 cm in diameter[6] which, for Port Phillip Bay animals, would be at about 3 years of age.[5]

Some data have been obtained on recruitment of purple sea urchins in Port Phillip Bay and, as with other sea urchins,[8] recruitment seems to be highly variable from year to year.[5]

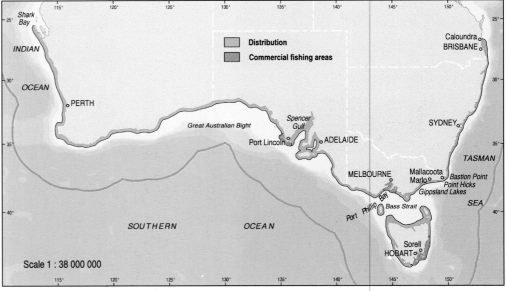

Geographic distribution and commercial fishing areas for purple sea urchins.

Purple sea urchin adults either actively graze rock surfaces or trap drift seagrasses and algae.[9] The juvenile diet has not been recorded. Sea urchin predators include octopus (*Octopus* species), southern rock lobsters, Port Jackson sharks (*Heterodontus* species), leatherjackets (Monacanthidae), snapper (*Pagrus auratus*) and Pacific gulls (*Larus pacificus*).[9]

Stock structure

There is no information on purple sea urchin stock structure.

Commercial fishery

Sea urchins are harvested for their gonads or roe, which is found as 5 skeins adhering to the inside test wall of both male and female urchins. In various parts of the world, sea urchin roe is considered a delicacy and returns very high prices.[10] It is eaten as a side dish mainly in Japan, Korea and other Asian countries, after being prepared in various ways[11] including chilled when fresh, salted, cooked and fermented.

In Victoria, the sea urchin fishery has been operating for more than 10 years[12] as an adjunct to the abalone industry. It is centred between Marlo and Mallacoota in the east of the State. Reefs east of Point

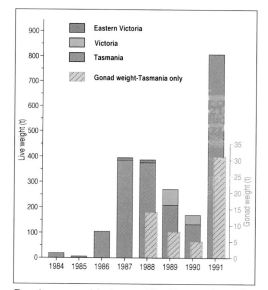

Purple sea urchin harvest for Tasmania and Victoria in t live weight for the period 1984 to 1991. The total Victorian harvest is unavailable for 1984 to 1988 and 1991, and the Tasmanian figures for 1991 are incomplete. The Tasmanian harvest is also presented as gonad weight in t for the period 1988 to 1991. (Source: Division of Sea Fisheries, Tasmanian Department of Primary Industry and Fisheries and Marine Science Laboratories, Victorian Department of Conservation and Environment)

Steps in the processing of purple sea urchins for export to Japan:
(top) unloading sea urchins at the factory;
(middle) opening the sea urchins and scooping out the roe;
(bottom) salt water washed sea urchin roe ready for grading and packing. (Source: Ken Yasuda, Oceania Trading Pty Ltd, Sorell, Tasmania)

Hicks,[12] such as Bastion Point, yield 98 % of the State's catch. Sea urchins are also collected from Port Phillip Bay.[12] In Tasmania, purple sea urchins have been harvested since about 1985.[4] In 1988, 356 t of purple sea urchins, yielding almost 13.8 t of roe, were harvested in Tasmania. Small but increasing catches of purple sea urchins have also been taken in South Australia — from 905 kg in 1986–87 to 3562 kg in 1990–91. Most of the catch is taken in a small area to the west of Spencer Gulf, mainly as a bycatch of Queen scallops (*Chlamys* species).

The fishery for purple sea urchins is seasonal, being based on the reproductive period of the sea urchins. They are harvested just before they spawn, when roe yields are greatest. Gonads have a low marketability during the spawning period when they absorb water, and after spawning when they are small and flaccid.[10] At harvest, purple sea urchins are between about 6 and 12 cm in

diameter.[2] However, gonad weight is not related to the size of the sea urchin.[2]

Sea urchins are collected by hand by divers using SCUBA and hookah breathing equipment, usually working from boats. Many divers work part-time. Sea urchins also comprise an incidental catch, primarily for divers targeting abalone and scallops (*Pecten* species, *Chlamys* species). After collection, the sea urchins are transported live to land-based processing plants. Here the test is split and opened using a knife or hammer, the gonads are carefully scooped out, rinsed in salt water, cleaned and sorted and the roe is packed. For the Japanese market, fresh roe is packed onto wooden trays in a traditional layout, each tray containing roe which are uniform in size and colour. Highly priced fermented roe, prepared to make 3 different products, is also air-freighted to Japan.[10]

In Victoria, harvesting of purple sea urchins takes place between June and January. The season is generally longer in Tasmania where the peak harvesting period is September–December.[2] In a Tasmanian study,[2] harvest rates varied between northern and eastern coasts, with a mean rate of 40–50 kg whole weight per diver per hour at sites not previously harvested.

Product quality (and resultant high prices) of the sea urchin roe depend on rapid post-harvest processing and transport. Quality is measured by gonad taste, size, colour and texture.[1] The preferred colour is bright or pale orange-yellow. Best quality roe is also firm and smooth, whole and has a preferred skein length of less than 5 cm.[10] Darker or brown gonads receive a low price or are discarded.[11] Factors known to affect gonad quality, in addition to reproductive state, are harvest location and the urchin's nutritional status.[10] The recovery rate of roe from purple sea urchins varies from 3–10 % of the whole animal's weight.[2,4] In Port Phillip Bay, about 80 purple sea urchins are needed to yield 1 kg of roe. The average whole weight of a purple sea urchin is 208 g.[2]

Prices paid depend on quality, texture and season. The price paid to divers in Tasmania averaged A$ 15.00 per kg in 1988, and the average price paid for processed roe was A$ 75.00 per kg. The value of the purple sea urchin fishery in Tasmania rose in 1988 to an estimated A$ 1.25–1.5 million (for processors) and

A\$ 296 000 (for divers).[4] In 1992, the price paid for processed roe ranged from A\$ 80.00 to A\$ 120.00 per kg. Whole sea urchins sold on Melbourne markets for domestic consumption were worth about A\$ 2.50 per kg in 1992.

Japan is a major importer of sea urchin roe and, in 1988, roe sold in Japan for up to A\$ 160.00 per kg. Premium quality roe can sell for as much as A\$ 400.00 per kg in Japan.[10] Most urchin roe produced in Australia is sold in Japan and other Asian countries such as Korea and Taiwan, with only a small proportion being sold for domestic consumption. Fresh roe is air-freighted chilled to Japan and marketed within 48 to 60 hours of harvesting.

Management controls A logbook system for divers has been introduced in Tasmania. Divers', fishers' and fishing boat licence fees are required in Victoria and Tasmania. The South Australian fishers hold a scallop licence.

Recreational fishery

This fishery is small. People gather purple sea urchins and black sea urchins (*Centrostephanus rodgersii*) in New South Wales, Victoria and Tasmania. These harvesting activities tend to be concentrated on reef areas near cities.

Management controls There are no management controls.

Resource status

The size of the resource in south-eastern Australia is unknown.

There has been an increase in demand for purple sea urchins by processors in Tasmania over recent years, and much more coastline is being accessed.[4] Although the fishery in Australia is largely unexploited, the need for skilled labour and associated high costs, and the variability in quality and yield of roe,[3,4] constrain the industry's development.

Notes

Black sea urchins, *Centrostephanus tenuispinis* and *Heliocidaris tuberculata*, are also harvested commercially in Australia. They are caught as a bycatch of the abalone and inshore prawn fisheries. In Victoria, harvesting of black sea urchins takes place between February and July, mainly around the Gippsland Lakes. Large black urchins are very abundant in New South Wales and eastern Victoria, and give a greater roe yield than do purple sea urchins. For example, 20–24 urchins yield 1 kg of roe at Mallacoota. However, the colour, texture and taste of the roe is generally unacceptable to the Asian market.

C. rodgersii and *H. tuberculata* are eastern species, while *C. tenuispinis* is distributed from Spencer Gulf in South Australia to Shark Bay in Western Australia.

Black sea urchins are known to create 'urchin barrens', ie areas devoid of kelp and other larger brown seaweeds or macro-algae (mainly Laminariales) and containing only encrusting coralline algae (Corallinaceae).[9,12] This phenomenon has also been observed with purple sea urchins in Spencer Gulf, South Australia.[9]

References

1. Dix, T. (1977) Survey of Tasmanian sea urchin resources. *Tasmanian Department of Agriculture, Sea Fisheries Division, Tasmanian Fisheries Research* **21**: 1–14.

2. Dix, T. (1977) Prospects for sea urchin fishery in Tasmania. *Australian Fisheries* **36**(7): 18–22.

3. Shepherd, S.A. (1973) Competition between sea urchins and abalone. *Australian Fisheries* **32**(6): 4–7.

4. Furlani, D. and Gibson, J. (1988) *Sea urchins. FIRDTA proposal.* Tasmanian Department of Sea Fisheries, Fisheries Division research reviews, 1988. Pp 24–34.

5. Constable, A.J. (1989) Resource allocation in the sea urchin, *Heliocidaris erythrogramma.* Unpublished PhD thesis, University of Melbourne. 147 pp.

6. Dix, T. (1977) Reproduction in Tasmanian populations of *H. erythrogramma* (Echinodermata: Echinometridae). *Australian Journal of Marine and Freshwater Research* **28**: 509–520.

7. Williams, D.H.C. and Anderson, D.T. (1975) The reproductive system, embryonic development, larval development and metamorphosis of sea urchin *Heliocidaris erythrogramma* (Val.) (Echinoidea: Echinometridae). *Australian Journal of Zoology* **23**: 371–403.

8. Ebert, T.A. (1983) Recruitment in echinoderms. *Echinoderm Studies* **1**: 169–203.

9. Connolly, R. (1986) *Behaviour and ecology of the sea urchin* Heliocidaris erythrogramma *(Valenciennes).* Unpublished Honours thesis, University of Adelaide. 73 pp.

10. Mahoney, D. (1991) *The seafood manual. A study guide for students undertaking training in the Seafood Technology Section.* Ed by F. Kow. 3rd edition. Launceston: School of Fisheries, Australian Maritime College. 219 pp.

11. Ward, J. (1975) Sea urchins — a new Victorian industry? *Australian Fisheries* **34**(1): 16.

12. Parry, G.D., Campbell, S.J. and Hobday, D.K. (1990) Marine resources off east Gippsland, southeastern Australia. *Victorian Department of Conservation and Environment, Fisheries Division, Technical Report* **72**. 166 pp.

Contributors

This presentation was assisted by information provided by (in alphabetical order) Neil Andrew, Rod Connolly, Andrew Constable, Dianne Furlani, Fred Glasbrenner, Les Gray, Dorothy Huber, Loisette Marsh, Peter Millington, Scoresby Shepherd, Angelo Tsolos, Geoff Williams, Ken Yasuda and Alex Ziolkowski. Drawing by Rhyllis Plant. (*Details of contributors and their organisations are given in the Acknowledgements section at the back of this book.*)
Compiler Patricia Kailola

Sea urchin roe being graded and priced at the Tsukiji Fish Market in Tokyo, Japan. (Source: Nick V. Ruello, Ruello & Associates, Sydney)

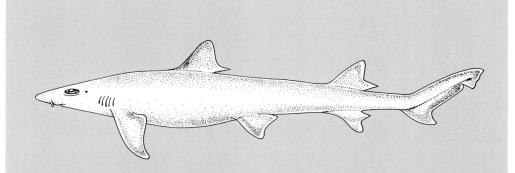

Furgaleus macki (Whitley)

Whiskery shark

Other common names include **sundowner** and **reef shark**.
FAO: whiskery shark
Australian species code: 017003

Family TRIAKIDAE

Diagnostic features Whiskery sharks are stocky, moderately deep-bodied hound sharks. They have a prominent, slender barbel on each nostril and the teeth in the upper jaw are triangular and sharp. The dorsal fins are approximately the same size and they are larger than the anal fin. Whiskery sharks are grey or bronze with darker blotches on the upper half of the body.

Distribution

Whiskery sharks are endemic to Australia. They inhabit continental shelf waters from eastern Victoria and Tasmania to Shark Bay in Western Australia, possibly as far as Exmouth Gulf. These sharks live on or near the sea bed in rocky, rough 'coral', seaweed and kelp areas, and are more common in deeper continental shelf waters to about 220 m.[1]

Life history

Whiskery sharks are ovoviviparous — ie they hatch from eggs which mature internally and are born live. Ovulation and early pregnancy in the Western Australian population takes place between January and March[1] and gestation probably lasts for 9–12 months. Females give birth to 4–24 young[1] which are 20–25 cm long at birth.[2,3] Individual females probably do not breed every year.

The maximum recorded size of whiskery sharks is 160 cm total length. There are no reasonably accurate growth and ageing assessments for the species. Both males and females are sexually mature at about 120 cm total length.[1]

Whiskery sharks feed mostly on octopus (*Octopus* species), although squid, fish, rock lobsters (Palinuridae), peanut worms (Sipunculida) and seagrass are also consumed.[1,2,3]

Stock structure

No studies have been undertaken. The nominal species *Furgaleus ventralis* (Whitley) is a junior synonym (ie it is the same species).[3]

Commercial fishery

Commercial exploitation of sharks in Western Australia commenced in 1941[2,4] and by 1949 the catch was beginning to be significant. Fishing activities expanded considerably between 1950 and the early 1970s. Concern about mercury levels in sharks caused a drop in fishing effort and catch between 1972 and 1976. Shark fishing resumed its expansion from then into the early 1980s.[4]

Most shark fishing activities extend from about Eucla on the Western Australian border, west and north to Geraldton.[5] About 25 species of shark are consistently caught in the Southwest Shark Fishery and the 3 most important of these are whiskery sharks, dusky whalers (*Carcharhinus obscurus*) and gummy sharks (*Mustelus antarcticus*). Whiskery sharks and dusky whalers are more abundant in west coast catches and gummy sharks are more important in catches on the south coast.[4] About half of the total Western Australian catch comes from the Busselton region.

In Western Australia, whiskery sharks are exploited over their entire range, and mainly adults are targeted.

Bottom set longlines were the main gear used to catch sharks in Western Australia until the early 1960s, when

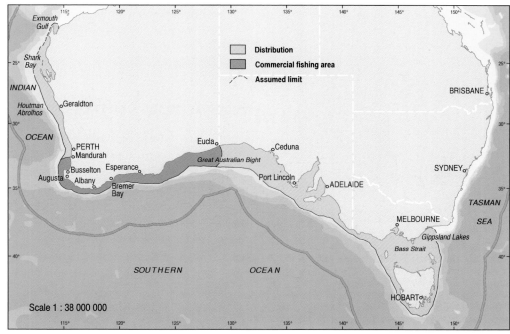

Geographic distribution and commercial fishing area for whiskery shark.

elasmobranchs

monofilament gillnets were introduced. Bottom set gillnets, longlines, handlines and droplines are the main methods used in the Fishery today. Gillnets take most of the catch and individual gillnets can vary in length from about 100 m to nearly 3 km,[4] depending on the region. Gillnet sets vary from 1 to 24 hours in duration, with an average of nearly 10 hours per day. Long sets are usually made overnight.

Longline sets may be up to 12.8 km long, although the average is 6.8 km with about 970 hooks.[4] Oily fish, such as mullet (Mugilidae), pilchards (*Sardinops neopilchardus*), Perth herring (*Nematalosa vlaminghi*), or squid or octopus are used for bait. The average depth fished is 24 m.[4] Handlines fish at about 50 m, usually near rocks or over broken substrate.[4]

Whiskery sharks are an incidental catch of demersal otter trawlers on the continental shelf off South Australia where they are caught in waters deeper than 100 m. Fishers targeting other shark such as dusky whalers and gummy sharks with longlines and large mesh gillnets also catch small quantities of whiskery sharks in the South Australian gulfs.

Fishing harbour, Albany, Western Australia.
(Source: Kevin McLoughlin, Bureau of Resource Sciences)

Whiskery sharks are sold at local and Perth markets, and much of the catch from the Esperance region is sold interstate.[4] Fillets are sold in fish shops and restaurants under a variety of names. The 1992 wholesale price per kg of whiskery shark at the Perth metropolitan markets averaged A$ 4.50. Gummy shark carcasses are sometimes sold with those of whiskery shark.

Management controls The west coast south of 33° S to the 200-mile Australian Fishing Zone is managed as a limited entry fishery. Management steps introduced by the Western Australian Government in the Southwest Shark Fishery include restricted access, gear limitations, transfer of licences and introduction of a system of time-gear access units which controls the number of nets and time they may be used over a year.

Recreational fishery

There is little recreational fishing activity for whiskery sharks. The largest whiskery shark caught by a recreational angler was 12.9 kg from near Perth (Australian Anglers Association record).

Management controls There are none.

Resource status

In the 1960s, whiskery sharks were estimated to comprise up to 40 % of the shark catch in metropolitan fish markets in Western Australia. However, from the early 1980s the catch per unit effort of whiskery shark and their average individual length and weight have fallen[2,4] and a recent estimate[6] puts the stock at about 18 % of virgin (ie unfished) biomass.

Whiskery shark stocks are very heavily fished and are over-exploited in Western Australia.[7] The relative scarcity of

knowledge on whiskery shark life history provides no guarantee for the future of the fishery.[5]

References

1. Stevens, J.D. (1991) Preliminary study of Western Australian commercial sharks. *CSIRO Division of Fisheries, Marine Laboratories, Internal Report.* 16 pp.

2. Heald, D.I. (1982) The WA shark fishery. *Fishing Industry News Service [FINS]* **15**(3): 16–21.

3. Compagno, L.J.V. (1986) FAO species catalogue. Vol. 4. Sharks of the world. An annotated and illustrated catalogue of shark species known to date. Part 2 — Carcharhiniformes. *FAO Fisheries Synopsis No. 125*, **4**(2): 251–655.

4. Heald, D.I. (1987) The commercial shark fishery in temperate waters of Western Australia. *Fisheries Department of Western Australia Report* **75**. 71 pp.

5. Lenanton, R., Millington, P. and Smyth, C. (1989) Shark and chips. Research and management into southern WA's edible shark fishery. *Western Fisheries* **May/June**: 17–23.

6. Fisheries Department of Western Australia (1990) *Southern demersal gillnet and demersal longline fishery management advisory committee. Chairman's report, November 1990.* 6 pp.

7. Fisheries Department of Western Australia (1991) *Southern demersal gillnet and demersal longline fishery management advisory committee. Chairman's report, May 1991.* 3 pp.

8. Whitley, G.P. (1944) New sharks and fishes from Western Australia. *Australian Zoologist* **10**(3): 252–273.

Contributors

Most of the information on this species was originally provided by John Stevens and supplemented by (in alphabetical order) Rod Lenanton, Peter Millington, Kevin McLoughlin and Gina Newton. Figure redrawn by Peter Moloney from Compagno[3] and Whitley.[8] (*Details of contributors and their organisations are given in the Acknowledgements section at the back of this book.*)
Compiler Patricia Kailola

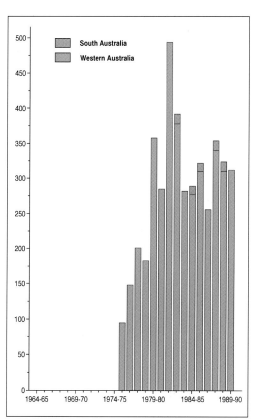

Total annual catch in t of whiskery shark for the period 1964–65 to 1989–90. Figures are unavailable for: Western Australia from 1964–65 to 1974–75; and South Australia from 1964–65 to 1975–76. Catches for States that average less than 5 % of the total for all States are not shown. (Source: Fisheries Resources Atlas Statistical Database)

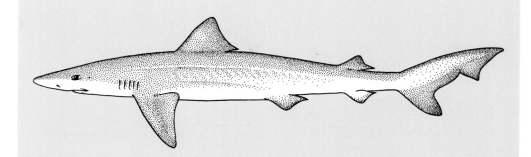

School shark

Galeorhinus galeus

Galeorhinus galeus (Linnaeus)

School shark

Other common names include **snapper shark, eastern school shark** and **tope**.
FAO: **tope shark**
Australian species code: 017008

Family TRIAKIDAE

Diagnostic features School sharks are slender and long-nosed. The second dorsal fin is smaller than the first and is about as large as the anal fin; and the ventral caudal fin lobe is very long. The mouth is broadly arched and there are several rows of similar teeth in both jaws.[1] Their teeth are blade-like, strongly notched and coarsely serrated on the outer side. School sharks are grey or brown on the back and upper sides, and white below.

Distribution

School sharks are distributed on the continental shelf and slope around southern Australia, from Moreton Bay in Queensland to the Houtman Abrolhos in Western Australia, including Bass Strait and Tasmania.[1] Nearly all of the commercial catch is taken from waters off Victoria, Tasmania and South Australia. Other populations of school sharks are present around Lord Howe Island and New Zealand, and off Europe and the west coasts of South America, North America and Africa.[1]

School sharks have been captured at depths to 550 m but most live at depths of less than 200 m.[2] Catch data for 1975 indicate that 3 % of the weight of school sharks captured are from the 0–24 m depth-range, 11 % from 25–49 m, 54 % from 50–74 m and 32 % from more than 75 m. They are active, strong-swimming sharks, often found well offshore as well as at the surfline.[1]

Life history

School sharks are ovoviviparous — ie, they are born live from eggs that develop and hatch internally. Ovulation occurs in early summer and parturition is complete by January of the following year. These events indicate that gestation is seasonal and lasts for about 12 months.[3] Pregnant sharks larger than 140 cm length carry 15–43 young (average 30), and the litter size increases with the size of the mother.

Records of the occurrence of school sharks bearing early and mid-term embryos suggest that pregnant sharks from south-eastern Australia move to waters off South Australia,[3] particularly the Great Australian Bight, and remain there for the period of gestation. They return eastwards to give birth, moving

into the shallow bays and estuaries of eastern Bass Strait, eastern Victoria, and eastern and southern Tasmania.[4] There are relatively few young sharks in waters off South Australia compared with Bass Strait and eastern Tasmania.[4,5] After pupping, the females move away from the coast into deeper water.

Shallow water 'nursery areas' have been identified where large aggregations of newborn and older juvenile sharks, 30–70 cm long, are present. These are Port Sorell, the Pitt Water Estuary, Frederick Henry Bay and Georges Bay in Tasmania, and areas near Portarlington, Port Phillip Bay in Victoria.[6] The young school sharks remain in these nursery areas until the late summer months, when they gradually move to deeper coastal waters to over-winter. In the following spring, most return to their former nursery

areas. Juveniles aged 2 years and older do not return to nursery areas but move instead to eastern Bass Strait where the bulk of the immature stock is centred.

School sharks move over a wide area of the continental shelf and form schools of predominantly 1 sex and 1 size. Although many remain in the deeper waters of Bass Strait and at the edge of the continental shelf around Tasmania, much of the population migrates to the warmer waters of South Australia and New South Wales in the late summer and winter months. The return movement commences during October or November.[4]

The average length of full-term school shark embryos is 32 cm.[3,4] The maximum recorded total length of school sharks in Australian waters is 171 cm for males and 175 cm for females,[7] and the maximum

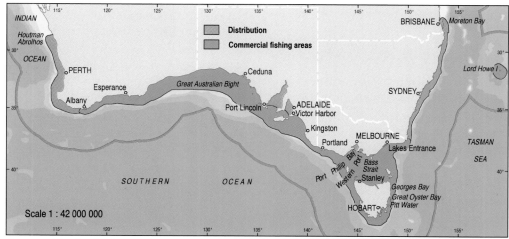

Geographic distribution and commercial fishing areas for school shark in Australian waters.

recorded weight is 32.7 kg.[2] School sharks are thought to have a life span of more than 50 years.[8] A male school shark tagged in Victorian waters was recaptured almost 42 years later, only 194 km away off north-west Tasmania.[8] Tagging and ageing studies indicate that male and female sharks have similar growth patterns. School sharks grow rapidly during the first 10 years of life. After about 15 years, the growth rate is negligible.[9] At maturity, female school sharks are about 140 cm long (and about 12 years of age) and males are marginally smaller.

School sharks feed on fish at any level in the water column, but the wide range of benthic organisms found in school shark stomach contents shows that they also feed on the sea bed. In south-eastern Australia, at least 64 species of fish and invertebrates have been recorded from school shark stomachs.[10] Of these, bony fish (teleosts) contribute 47 % by weight to the diet, followed by squid and octopus (Cephalopoda) which make up 37 %. The 4 most important species of prey items are barracouta (*Thyrsites atun*), Gould's arrow squid (*Nototodarus gouldi*), octopus (*Octopus* species) and southern calamary (*Sepioteuthis australis*), all of which are fished commercially. The diet of juvenile school sharks includes worms (Annelida), molluscs and crustaceans.[4]

Stock structure

Evidence of rapid and large movements of tagged school sharks across southern Australia suggests the presence of a single stock.[4] Recent population studies have assumed a unit stock but the possibility of local depletion in parts of the Southern Shark Fishery has also been considered. Five New Zealand tagged school sharks recaptured in Australian waters in 1991[8] provide evidence of Tasman crossings.

Commercial fishery

The Southern Shark Fishery is based on school sharks, gummy sharks (*Mustelus antarcticus*) and several other less abundant temperate-water species of shark. This Fishery currently produces over 3000 t (carcass weight) of sharks annually, valued at up to A$ 15 million to fishers in Victoria, Tasmania and South Australia. Most of the catch is marketed in Victoria. School sharks comprise only a

very small amount of the shark fishery in Western Australia.

School sharks have been caught and marketed in Victoria since the State's bays-and-inlets fishery began, immediately after European settlement. In

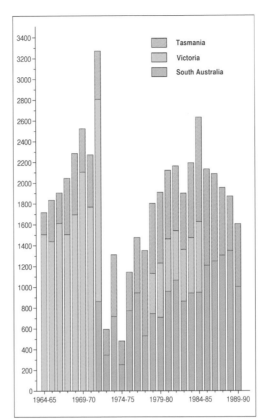

(above) Total annual catch in t of school shark for the period 1964–65 to 1989–90. Figures are unavailable for: Victoria from 1972–73 to 1977–78 and 1985–86 to 1989–90; and South Australia from 1964–65 to 1970–71. (Source: Fisheries Resources Atlas Statistical Database)

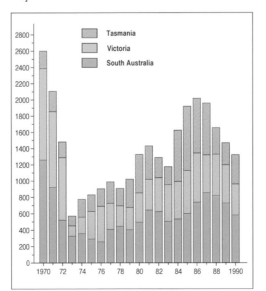

(below) Production in t measured in carcass weight of school shark from the Southern Shark Fishery by State of landing, for the period 1970 to 1990. (Source: Southern Shark Monitoring Fishery Database, 16 May 1991). The large fall in catch in the early 1970s followed the mercury levels regulations.[12,13] [conversion factor of carcass to live weight applied in the Fishery is 1.5]

the mid 1920s, Victorian fishers began operating in offshore waters in response to an increasing demand for fresh shark fillets, particularly by Melbourne consumers. During the Second World War, when Australia became dependent on shark for the supply of liver oils of high vitamin A content, fishers based in Tasmania and South Australia entered the school shark fishery.[11]

Until the 1960s, shark fishers used longlines up to 10 km long and took mainly school sharks. In 1964 gillnets were introduced in the fishery and by the early 1970s, most of the catch was taken by this method. This step, coupled with the 1972 banning of the sale of large school sharks in Victoria because of their mercury content,[12,13] led to gummy shark replacing school shark as the dominant species in the Southern Shark Fishery catch.

School shark catches peaked in 1969 and were still high at the end of the 1980s, but by then the fishing effort required to take this catch was 3 times that in the late 1960s. Today, gummy sharks and school sharks are of equal importance in the catch, most of which is taken by specialist shark fishers. Small quantities of these sharks are taken by fishers for rock lobsters (*Jasus* species), scallops (*Pecten fumatus*) and inshore finfish. These fishers target sharks when their main fishery is affected by seasonal closures or poor catch rates.

Shark fishers in Bass Strait mainly employ gillnets of 6-inch mesh, but most off South Australia use 7-inch mesh gillnets as the sharks in those waters are generally larger. Gillnets are more selective of fish size than hook fishing. Most Tasmanian shark fishers still take school sharks by longline. Small quantities of school sharks are taken in southern Australia as a bycatch of fish trawling. For example, in 1989–90, 10 t were recorded as landed catch from the South East Fishery.

Significant bycatches in the Southern Shark Fishery are 2 species of saw sharks (*Pristiophorus cirratus* and *P. nudipinnis*) and elephant fish (*Callorhynchus milii*). Over the last 20 years the annual catch of saw sharks has fluctuated between 44 t and 325 t, and that of elephant fish between 4 t and 119 t.

School sharks are marketed fresh, chilled, headed and gutted. The carcasses are skinned and filleted, and the flesh sold mostly under the name of 'flake'. This product is very popular in the 'fish-and-chips' trade, particularly with consumers in Victoria and Tasmania. The average carcass price per kg at the Melbourne Wholesale Fish Market in June 1991–92 ranged from A$ 4.70 to A$ 7.00.

Management controls Management of the Southern Shark Fishery is shared by both the Commonwealth and the governments of Victoria, Tasmania and South Australia. It is directed towards the total shark stock and no distinction is made between species.

Management controls have been based on several strategies: a closed fishing season during October or November, the months prior to sharks giving birth; legal maximum and minimum lengths of marketed shark (the former to reduce the average mercury concentration in the catch[13] and the latter to protect young sharks[6]); a legal minimum gillnet mesh size; reductions in the amount of gillnet used; and the closure to fishing of inshore areas around Tasmania (to protect new-born and young sharks).

In the mid-1980s the Southern Shark Fishery was assessed as overfished and there was scientific advice that fishing effort should be reduced. In September 1984 the first step was taken towards licence limitation. A management plan adopted in April 1989 brought a reduction in the number of gillnets set and carried, and the number of vessels operating in the Fishery. Subsequent controls have limited the shark catch by longlining and

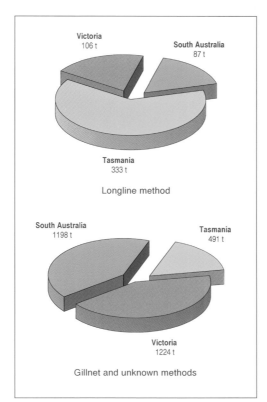

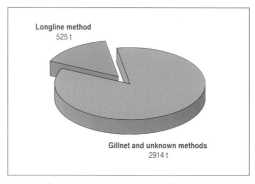

(above) Average annual production in t carcass weight of gummy and school shark combined from the Southern Shark Fishery, for the period 1986 to 1990 by fishing method. (Source: Southern Shark Monitoring Fishery Database, 16 May 1991) [conversion factor of carcass to live weight applied in the Fishery is 1.5]

(left, top and bottom) Average annual production in t carcass weight of gummy shark and school shark combined from the Southern Shark Fishery, for the period 1986 to 1990 by State and fishing method. (Source: Southern Shark Monitoring Fishery Database, 16 May 1991) [conversion factor of carcass to live weight applied in the Fishery is 1.5]

trawling, and have further reduced gillnet effort.

After a stock assessment review in 1992, further controls are seen to be necessary and a new management plan is being developed.

Recreational fishery

A small number of school sharks are taken along ocean beaches by recreational fishers using handlines, rod-and-line and gillnets (only in Tasmania), and in coastal bays. The largest school shark taken by a

recreational angler was 33.5 kg, caught in South Australia (Australian Anglers Association record).

Management controls Many of the sheltered bays and estuaries around Tasmania have been designated shark nursery areas, where the taking of either school sharks or gummy sharks has been prohibited. Additionally, controls on the use of gillnets have been introduced in these areas to reduce incidental mortality of sharks caused by recreational gillnet fishing and poaching.[6] Legal minimum lengths of retained shark apply in some States.

Resource status

Natural mortality of school sharks has been estimated at 10 % per annum from tagging experiments.[9]

Trends in catch per unit of effort and fishery simulation models indicate that overfishing has occurred in the Southern Shark Fishery. In 1991 and 1992 assessments of the Fishery concluded that both school and gummy sharks were overexploited. Evidence suggests that school sharks are more severely overfished than gummy sharks and that school sharks in Bass Strait have been particularly reduced in abundance. Sustainable yield at present stock sizes was estimated to be about 1200 t per annum (carcass weight; school and gummy shark combined). This is less than half the present catch of both species.

Hauling a shark gillnet, eastern Tasmania. (Source: Lindsay Chapman, Bureau of Resource Sciences)

However, this figure carries a high degree of uncertainty as the assessments are complicated by the changing spatial pattern of the Fishery over many years, the difference in biology of school and gummy sharks and the inadequate data for the 50 years prior to the 1970s.

Sharks generally live a long time, grow slowly and produce only a few offspring. Therefore, the stocks are characterised by a close relationship between parent stock and recruitment, and by a low capacity to recover from overfishing. Furthermore, sharks which bear their young live have a long gestation period and recruitment to the Fishery takes even longer. Hence, several years elapse before the effects of reduced parent stock are reflected in recruitment. School and gummy shark stocks are also affected by other fisheries such as trawling, offshore longlining, the bay-and-inlet fisheries in Victoria, Danish seining and the recreational fishery in Tasmania where specialised gillnets are used.

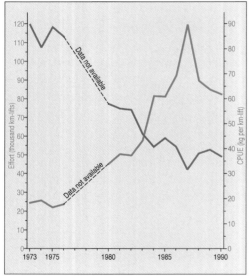

Estimates of total fishing effort and catch per unit effort (CPUE) for combined gummy shark and school shark in the Southern Shark Fishery for the period 1973 to 1990. Effort is expressed as equivalent gillnet effort. Data is not available from 1977 to 1979. (Source: Southern Shark Monitoring Fishery Database, 16 May 1991)

References

1. Compagno, L.J.V. (1984). FAO species catalogue. Vol. 4. Sharks of the world. An annotated and illustrated catalogue of the shark species known to date. Part 2 — Carcharhiniformes. *FAO Fisheries Synopsis No. 125*, **4**(2): 251–655.

2. Scott, T.D., Glover, C.J.M. and Southcott, R.V. (1974). *The marine and freshwater fishes of South Australia. Handbook of the flora and fauna of South Australia.* 2nd edition. Adelaide: South Australian Government. 392 pp.

3. Walker, T.I., Moulton, P.L. and Saddlier, S.R. (1989) Reproduction studies of four species of shark and one species of elephant fish commercially fished in southern Australian waters. 88 pp, in *Southern shark assessment project, Final FIRTA Report, Part B. Department of Conservation, Forests and Lands, Fisheries Division, Internal Report* **175b**.

4. Olsen, A.M. (1954) The biology, migration and growth rate of the school shark, *Galeorhinus australis* (Macleay) (Carcharhinidae) in south-eastern Australian waters. *Australian Journal of Marine and Freshwater Research* **5**: 353–410.

5. Moulton, P.M., Walker, T.I. and Saddlier, S.R. (in press, 1992) Age and growth studies of gummy shark, *Mustelus antarcticus* Günther, and school shark, *Galeorhinus galeus* (Linnaeus) from southern Australian waters. *Australian Journal of Marine and Freshwater Research* **43**.

6. Williams, H. and Schaap, A.H. (1992) Preliminary results of a study into the incidental mortality of sharks in gillnets in two Tasmanian shark nursery areas. *Australian Journal of Marine and Freshwater Research* **43**: 237–250.

7. Walker, T.I. (1989) Fishery situation report — southern shark. 34 pp, in *Southern shark assessment project, Final FIRTA Report, Part B. Department of Conservation, Forests and Lands, Fisheries Division, Internal Report* **175b**.

8. Coutin, P. (1992) Sharks ... and more sharks. *Australian Fisheries* **51**(6): 41–42.

9. Grant, C.J., Sandland, R.L. and Olsen, A.M. (1979) Estimation of growth, mortality and yield per recruit of the Australian school shark, *Galeorhinus australis* (Macleay), from tag recoveries. *Australian Journal of Marine and Freshwater Research* **30**: 625–637.

10. Walker, T.I. (1989) Stomach contents of gummy shark, *Mustelus antarcticus* Guenther, and school shark, *Galeorhinus galeus* (Linnaeus), from south-eastern Australian waters. 24 pp, in *Southern shark assessment project, Final FIRTA Report, Part B. Department of Conservation, Forests and Lands, Fisheries Division, Internal Report* **175b**.

11. Olsen, A.M. (1959) The status of the school shark fishery in south-eastern Australian waters. *Australian Journal of Marine and Freshwater Research* **10**: 353–410.

12. Victoria bans taking and sale of shark (1972). *Australian Fisheries* **31**(9): 14.

13. Walker, T.I. (1976) Effects of species, sex, length and locality on the mercury content of school shark *Galeorhinus australis* (Macleay) and gummy shark *Mustelus antarcticus* Guenther from south-eastern Australian waters. *Australian Journal of Marine and Freshwater Research* **27**: 603–616.

Contributors

Information on this species was originally provided by Terry Walker. Additional comments were provided by (in alphabetical order) the Southern Shark Assessment Group, John Stevens, Richard Tilzey and Howel Williams. Drawing courtesy of FAO, Rome; redrawn by Karina Hansen. (*Details of contributors and their organisations are given in the Acknowledgements section at the back of this book.*)

Compilers Kevin McLoughlin, Russell Reichelt, Patricia Kailola, Christina Grieve (maps) and Phillip Stewart (statistics)

Male school shark caught in Tasmanian waters. (Source: John Stevens, CSIRO Marine Laboratories, Hobart)

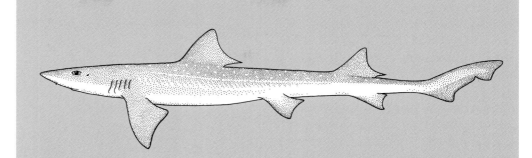

Gummy shark

Mustelus antarcticus

Mustelus antarcticus Günther

Gummy shark

Other common names include
Australian smooth hound and **sweet
William**.
FAO: **gummy shark**
Australian species code: 017001

Family TRIAKIDAE

Diagnostic features Gummy sharks
have a slender body and short head.
Their second dorsal fin is nearly as large
as the first and the ventral caudal fin
lobe is short. Their mouth is short and
angular with numerous rows of blunt,
flattened teeth arranged like pavement
stones. Gummy sharks are grey or
grey-brown above and white below, with
white spots on the back and upper
sides. On some individuals a few small
black spots are interspersed among the
white spots. An undescribed species of
Mustelus from northern Australia is
almost identical in colour and
morphology to gummy sharks.[1]

Distribution

Gummy sharks are endemic to the temperate waters of the continental shelf and slope off southern Australia, from approximately 28° S in northern New South Wales, around Tasmania and through Bass Strait, to approximately 30° S in Western Australia. Their distribution possibly extends northwards to southern Queensland and Shark Bay in Western Australia. The limit of the northern distribution is confused because of the species' similarity to an undescribed species whose southern distribution extends to Dampier (20°40' S) (possibly Shark Bay) in the west and Bowen (20° S) (possibly Coffs Harbour) in the east. This *Mustelus* species inhabits the outer continental shelf and upper slope at depths of 120–400 m.

Gummy sharks are demersal (ie remain on or near the sea bed) and are found from intertidal waters to about 80 m, although they have been recorded as deep as 350 m. Catch data provided by Victorian-based commercial fishers in 1975 indicate that 12 % of the weight of gummy sharks captured were from a depth-range of 0–24 m, 42 % from 25–49 m, 42 % from 50–74 m, and 4 % from more than 75 m.

Life history

Gummy sharks are ovoviviparous — ie they develop from eggs which mature internally, and are born live. Ovulation occurs between October and December or between November and early February in Western Australia. Parturition is complete by December of the following year, indicating that gestation is seasonal and lasts 11–12 months. Pregnant sharks carry between 1 and 38 young (average 14) and older mothers carry more embryos than younger mothers.

Newborn and juvenile gummy sharks aggregate in many areas across southern Australia but there is presently no knowledge of well defined shallow-water nursery areas. Young and adult gummy sharks are distributed widely.[2]

Female gummy sharks achieve a larger total length (175 cm) than males (145 cm),[3] and maximum recorded weight is 24.8 kg. Tagging and ageing studies indicate that gummy sharks can live as long as 16 years. The growth of male sharks is negligible after 10 years of age, whereas female sharks continue to

grow until the end of their lives.[4] The smallest female shark recorded as mature was 84.5 cm long, but the length at which 50 % of female sharks mature is 120–130 cm. Male sharks are considerably shorter than female sharks when they become mature.[5,6] The length at first maturity and the proportion of pregnant female sharks longer than this length increases from east to west, such that in waters west of longitude 132° E most female gummy sharks are pregnant.

Gummy sharks do not exhibit well-defined migration patterns but a number

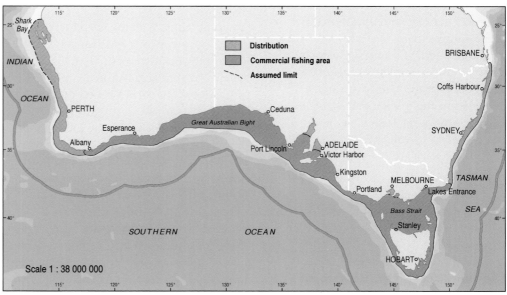

Geographic distribution and commercial fishing areas for gummy shark.

of large female gummy sharks leave Bass Strait and move to waters off South Australia and perhaps Western Australia. Whether any return is not known. Possible emigration from Bass Strait to waters off South Australia is supported by evidence that gummy sharks inhabiting waters off South Australia are generally larger than those inhabiting Bass Strait;[5] and by records of 7 tagged female gummy sharks moving from Bass Strait to waters off South Australia,[3] and 1 tagged female shark moving from Bass Strait to waters off Western Australia. Juvenile male and female gummy sharks have similar rates of movement, but as the sharks grow larger, the females travel longer distances than the males.[3]

Gummy sharks have blunt, flattened teeth suitable for crushing prey. Gummy sharks are non-selective feeders on demersal species from areas of sandy and, to a lesser extent, rocky substrate. Larger gummy sharks may also feed in the water column.

Studies of stomach contents show that gummy sharks in Bass Strait feed on at least 95 species and that squid and octopus (Cephalopoda) contribute most weight (36 %) to their diet. Crustaceans contribute 25 % by weight, bony fish 11 %. The remaining 28 % consists of 12 other classes of organism and unidentifiable material.[7] Gummy shark prey items that are also commercial fish species include octopus, southern rock lobsters (*Jasus edwardsii*), southern calamary (*Sepioteuthis australis*), arrow squid (*Nototodarus gouldi*) and barracouta (*Thyrsites atun*).

Stock structure

Tagging,[3] genetic[8] and morphometric[9] studies suggest that there is a single stock of gummy shark in southern Australia. However, the possibility of regional stock differences has not been discounted.[8,10,11] The relationship of the other *Mustelus* species in Western Australia to gummy shark is being investigated.

Commercial fishery

Gummy sharks, along with school sharks (*Galeorhinus galeus*) and several other less abundant temperate-water shark species, provide the resource for the Southern Shark Fishery. This Fishery currently produces approximately 3000 t

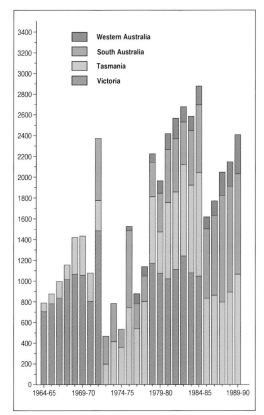

Total annual catch in t of gummy shark for the period 1964–65 to 1989–90. Figures are unavailable for: Victoria from 1972–73 to 1977–78 and 1985–86 to 1989–90; South Australia from 1964–65 to 1970–71; and Western Australia for 1964–65 to 1966–67 and 1968–69 to 1974–75. Catches for States that average less than 5 % of the total for all States are not shown. (Source: Fisheries Resources Atlas Statistical Database.)

(carcass weight) of shark annually, valued at up to A$ 15 million to fishers in Victoria, Tasmania and South Australia. Most of the catch is marketed in Victoria.

Gummy sharks have been caught and marketed in Victoria since the State's bays and inlets began to be fished, immediately after European settlement. Early in the Southern Shark Fishery, fishers targeted school sharks with bottom set longlines, a method not selective for gummy sharks. With the introduction of gillnets to the Fishery in 1964, the catch of gummy sharks increased. After 1972, when a ban was placed on the sale of large school sharks in Victoria because of their mercury content, gummy shark replaced school shark as the predominant species in the shark catch. Today, gummy sharks and school sharks are of equal importance in the catch, which is taken both by specialist shark fishers and by other fishers. These other fishers are primarily engaged in fisheries such as those for southern rock lobsters, scallops (*Pecten fumatus*) and inshore finfish, and target shark when their main fishery is affected by closed seasons or poor catch

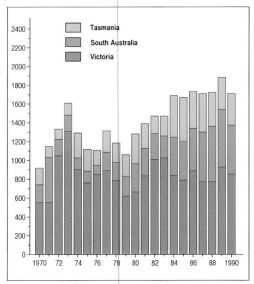

Production in t measured in carcass weight of gummy shark from the Southern Shark Fishery by State of landing, for the period 1970 to 1990. (Source: Southern Shark Monitoring Fishery Database, 16 May 1991). [conversion factor of carcass to live weight applied in the Fishery is 1.5]

rates. A small amount of gummy shark is taken as bycatch by demersal otter trawlers in the South East Fishery.

In New South Wales, some gummy sharks are caught by longline vessels although most are taken as a bycatch of demersal otter trawl and inshore finfish fisheries.

About 10 % of the total Australian catch of gummy shark comes from waters off Western Australia.[6] Gummy shark is one of the dominant species in the Esperance and Albany regions of the Western Australian Southwest Shark Fishery[11,12] and in 1983–84, it comprised approximately 11 % of the shark catch from that area.[11] The sharks are mainly caught with monofilament gillnets hundreds of m long, and a small proportion are caught on longlines of several hundred hooks. Handlines and droplines are also used. Gummy sharks averaging 60–68 cm total length and 4–6 kg are targeted.[11] Fishing effort on gummy sharks in Western Australia has been increasing since 1976–77, and the Fishery has developed rapidly over the last 5 years.

With the introduction of bottom set gillnets to the Southern Shark Fishery, other shark species became more abundant in the catch. Among these, saw sharks (2 species, *Pristiophorus cirratus* and *P. nudipinnis*) and elephant fish (*Callorhynchus milii*) comprise a significant bycatch. The saw shark catch in the Southern Shark Fishery rose from

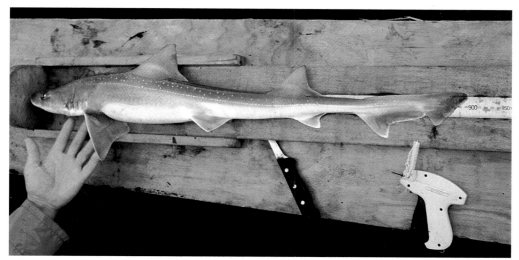
A live gummy shark being measured and tagged before release. (Source: Grant Pullen, Division of Sea Fisheries, Tasmanian Department of Primary Industry and Fisheries)

52 t in 1970 to a peak of 325 t in 1987 and stood at 183 t in 1990. The elephant fish catch is smaller, ranging from 4 t to 119 t over the same period (58 t in 1990). Small quantities of saw sharks are also part of the bycatch of the gummy shark fishery in Western Australia.

By the early 1970s most of the catch in the Southern Shark Fishery was taken by gillnets, which tend to take sharks of a particular size range and are relatively more selective than hook fishing.[13] Fishers in Bass Strait operate mainly 6-inch mesh gillnets to target sharks, and fishers in South Australia use mainly 7-inch mesh gillnets to target larger sharks. Most Tasmanian fishers take sharks (mostly school sharks) by longline.

Sharks are marketed as fresh, chilled carcasses (headed and gutted). These are filleted and the meat is sold mostly under the name of 'flake'. It is very popular with consumers in Victoria and Tasmania, especially in the 'fish-and-chip' trade. The average price per kg at the Melbourne Wholesale Fish Market in 1991–92 ranged from A$ 4.70 to A$ 7.00.

Management controls Management of the Southern Shark Fishery is shared by the Commonwealth and the southern States. It is directed towards the total stock of shark and no distinction is made between species.

Management controls have been based on several strategies: closed fishing seasons during October or November, the months before sharks give birth; legal maximum length of marketed shark; a legal minimum gillnet mesh size; and inshore areas (around Tasmania) closed to fishing to protect new-born and young sharks.

In the mid-1980s the Fishery was assessed as overfished and the scientific advice was that fishing effort should be reduced. In September 1984 the first step was taken towards licence limitation. A management plan adopted in April 1989 has brought a reduction in the total number of nets set and carried, and the number of vessels operating in the Fishery. More controls introduced since then have further reduced gillnet effort and placed limits on the catch by longline and trawlers.

After a stock assessment review in 1992, further controls were seen to be necessary and a new management plan is being developed.

Management steps introduced by the Western Australian Government on the Southwest Shark Fishery include restricted access, gear limitations, transfer of licences and introduction of a system of time-gear access units which controls the number of nets and time they may be used over a year.

Recreational fishery

Small numbers of gummy sharks are taken by recreational fishers from bays, inlets and ocean beaches. They are caught with handlines and gillnets (only in Tasmania). The record size of a gummy shark taken by a recreational angler is 23.9 kg from Western Australia (Australian Anglers Association records).

Management controls The same legal minimum lengths imposed for the commercial fishery apply to recreational fishing.

Since the early 1960s, many sheltered bays and estuaries around Tasmania have

been designated shark nursery areas, where the taking of either gummy sharks or school sharks has been prohibited. Recently, the level of commercial and recreational gillnetting within shark nursery areas has been curtailed because of concern at the level of incidental mortality of sharks caused by recreational gillnet fishing and poaching.[14]

Resource status

Natural mortality and catchability have been estimated by cohort analysis, tagging studies and fishery simulation models. Estimates range for natural mortality from 11% to 18% per annum.[2]

Trends in catch per unit of effort and fishery simulation models indicate that overfishing has occurred in the Southern Shark Fishery. In 1991 and 1992 assessments of the Fishery concluded that both school and gummy shark were overexploited. Sustainable yield at present stock sizes was estimated to be about 1200 t per annum (carcass weight; school and gummy shark combined). This is less than half the present catch of both species. However, this figure carries a high degree of uncertainty as the assessments are complicated by the changing spatial pattern of the Fishery over many years, the difference in biology of school and gummy shark and the inadequate data for the 50 years prior to the 1970s. The downward trend in gummy shark catch per unit effort in the Southwest Shark Fishery in Western Australia suggests that the resource is fully exploited in that part of its range.[11,12]

Sharks are generally long-lived and slow-growing and produce only a few offspring. Therefore, stocks are characterised by a close relationship between parent stock and recruitment, and by a low capacity to recover from overfishing. Recruitment is also slow because sharks bear their young live and have a long gestation period, so that several years elapse before the effects of reduced parent stock can be seen. The bycatch of shark taken by trawlers, the Danish seine fishery, offshore longlining, bay and inlet fisheries (in Victoria), and recreational fishing also affect gummy and school shark stocks.

References

1. Stevens, J.D. and McLoughlin, K.J. (1991) Distribution, size and sex composition, reproductive biology and diet of sharks

Gummy sharks being trimmed, Melbourne Wholesale Fish Market. (Source: Ignatius Duivenvoorden, Victorian Department of Conservation and Environment)

from northern Australia. *Australian Journal of Marine and Freshwater Research* **42**: 151–199.

2. Walker, T.I. (1989) Fishery situation report — southern shark. 34 pp, in *Southern shark assessment project, Final FIRTA Report, Part B. Department of Conservation, Forests and Lands, Fisheries Division, Internal Report* **175b**.

3. Walker, T.I. (1984) Investigations of the gummy shark, *Mustelus antarcticus* Günther, from south-eastern Australian waters. *Report to FIRC, June 1983*. 94 pp, in *Proceedings of the shark assessment workshop, South East Fisheries Committee Shark Research Group, Melbourne, 7–10 March 1983*. Canberra: Department of Primary Industry.

4. Moulton, P.M., Walker, T.I. and Saddlier, S.R. (in press,1992) Age and growth studies of gummy shark, *Mustelus antarcticus* Guenther, and school shark, *Galeorhinus galeus* (Linnaeus) from southern Australian waters. *Australian Journal of Marine and Freshwater Research* **43**.

5. Walker, T.I., Moulton, P.L. and Saddlier, S.R. (1989) Reproduction studies of four species of shark and one species of elephant fish commercially fished in southern Australian waters. 88 pp, in *Southern shark assessment project, Final FIRTA Report, Part B. Department of Conservation, Forests and Lands, Fisheries Division, Internal Report* **175b**.

6. Lenanton, R.C.J., Heald, D.I., Platell, M., Cliff, M. and Shaw, J. (1989) Aspects of the reproductive biology of the gummy shark, *Mustelus antarcticus* Günther, from waters off the south coast of Western Australia. *Australian Journal of Marine and Freshwater Research* **41**: 807–822.

7. Walker, T.I. (1989) Stomach contents of gummy shark, *Mustelus antarcticus* Günther, and school shark, *Galeorhinus galeus* (Linnaeus), from south-eastern Australian waters. 24 pp, in *Southern shark assessment project, Final FIRTA Report, Part B. Department of Conservation, Forests and Lands, Fisheries Division, Internal Report* **175b**.

8. MacDonald, C.M. (1988) Genetic variation, breeding structure and taxonomic status of the gummy shark *Mustelus antarcticus* in Australian waters *Australian Journal of Marine and Freshwater Research* **39**: 641–648.

9. Heemstra, P.C. (1973) A revision of the shark genus *Mustelus* (Squaliformes: Carcharhinidae). Unpublished PhD thesis, University of Miami, Florida.

10. Walker, T.I. (1976) Effects of species, sex, length and locality on the mercury content of school shark *Galeorhinus australis* (Macleay) and gummy shark *Mustelus antarcticus* Guenther from south-eastern Australian waters. *Australian Journal of Marine and Freshwater Research* **27**: 603–616.

11. Heald, D.I. (1987) The commercial shark fishery in temperate waters of Western Australia. *Fisheries Department of Western Australia Report* **75**. 71 pp.

12. Lenanton, R., Millington, P. and Smyth, C. (1989) Shark and chips. Research and management into southern WA's edible shark fishery. *Western Fisheries* **May/June**: 17–23.

13. Kirkwood, G.P. and Walker, T.I. (1986) Gill net mesh selectivities for gummy shark, *Mustelus antarcticus* Günther, taken in south-eastern Australian waters. *Australian Journal of Marine and Freshwater Research* **37**: 689–697.

14. Williams, H. and Schaap, A.H. (1992) Preliminary results of a study into the incidental mortality of sharks in gill-nets in two Tasmanian Shark Nursery Areas. *Australian Journal of Marine and Freshwater Research* **43**: 237–250.

Contributors

Information on this species was originally provided by Terry Walker. Additional comments were made by (in alphabetical order) Mick Bishop, Rod Lenanton, the Southern Shark Assessment Group, John Stevens, Richard Tilzey and Howel Williams. Drawing courtesy of FAO, Rome; redrawn by Karina Hansen. (*Details of contributors and their organisations are given in the Acknowledgements section at the back of this book.*)
Compilers Kevin McLoughlin, Russell Reichelt, Patricia Kailola, Christina Grieve (maps) and Phillip Stewart (statistics)

Dusky and bronze whalers

Carcharhinus species

Dusky and bronze whalers

This presentation is on 2 species, **dusky whalers** and **bronze whalers**.

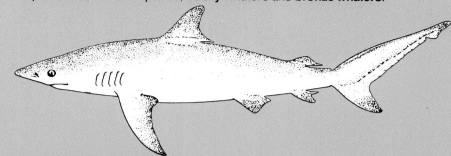

Dusky whaler, *Carcharhinus obscurus* (LeSueur)

Other common names include **dusky shark, common whaler** and **black whaler**.
FAO: **dusky shark**
Australian species code: 018003

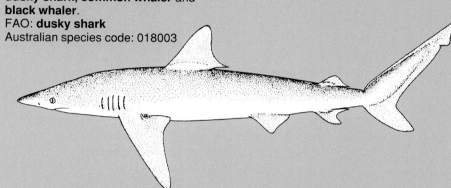

Bronze whaler, *Carcharhinus brachyurus* (Günther)

Other common names include **bronze whaler shark, cocktail shark, copper shark, bronzie** and **cocktail whaler**.
FAO: **copper shark**
Australian species code: 018001

Family CARCHARHINIDAE

Diagnostic features Dusky whalers are often confused with bronze whalers. Dusky whalers have 13–14 broad teeth on each side of their upper jaw. The snout is broadly rounded, and there is usually a low ridge running along the back between the 2 dorsal fins. Bronze whalers have 15–16 narrow teeth on each side of their upper jaw. The snout is slightly pointed or angular, and there is usually no ridge between the 2 dorsal fins. Body colour for both species varies from dark grey to bronze over the back and upper sides.[1,2]

Distribution

Dusky whalers inhabit all Australian continental shelf waters as far south as Hobart.[2] Elsewhere, dusky whalers are present in the eastern Pacific Ocean, the Atlantic Ocean, western Indian Ocean and some regions of the western Pacific.[1] Bronze whalers inhabit warm-temperate[1] coastal waters in Australia, from Coffs Harbour in New South Wales, along southern Australia to Jurien Bay in Western Australia.[2] Reports of the species off eastern Tasmania are unconfirmed. They have a similar global distribution to dusky whalers, except that they are also present in New Zealand.

Dusky whalers and bronze whalers are generally common in offshore waters of the continental shelf. Both species occasionally enter large coastal bays and inshore areas, as far inshore as the surf line. Dusky whalers inhabit waters from the surface to a depth of 400 m,[1] and bronze whalers range from the surface to a depth of at least 100 m.[2] Bronze whalers sometimes enter estuaries, but dusky whalers tend to avoid estuaries and areas of reduced salinities.[1]

Life history

These sharks are viviparous, — ie they produce live young and have well-developed placenta. A dusky whaler litter contains 3–14 pups,[2] possibly more, born at about 70–100 cm total length. The number of pups in a bronze whaler litter varies from 7 to 20,[2] and they are born when 59–70 cm long.[1] In both species, birth may occur at any time of year, but there is a peak in births in summer. Gravid females of both species move inshore to drop their young.[1] A known pupping site for bronze whalers is just north of Adelaide in Gulf St Vincent.

Dusky whalers reach a maximum size of about 370 cm total length. The largest recorded in Australia weighed 323.5 kg and measured 345 cm.[2] Adult dusky whalers mature between 14 and 18 years[3] when about 280 cm total length[1,2] and live at least 35 years.[3] Bronze whalers reach a maximum size of about 295 cm total length[2] and a maximum age of 30 years (males) and 25 years (females).[4] The largest recorded individual caught in Australia weighed almost 227 kg and measured 295 cm.[5] Preliminary calculations of bronze whalers' ages at first sexual maturity are 13 years (males) and 19 years (females).[4]

Dusky whalers and probably also bronze whalers migrate, following the warmer water southwards in the spring and summer and northwards in the autumn and winter. There are records of dusky whalers migrating long distances in Western Australia: from the region between Augusta and Shark Bay, individuals have migrated to as far away as Rowley Shoals off the north-west coast and Esperance on the south-east coast.[6] Dusky whalers may also migrate in groups of the same sex and age class.[1] In Western Australia and South Australia both species are common inshore only during summer and autumn. Seasonal, inshore–offshore movements also occur — especially by pregnant females moving from outer continental shelf regions onto the inner shelf to pup, and returning.

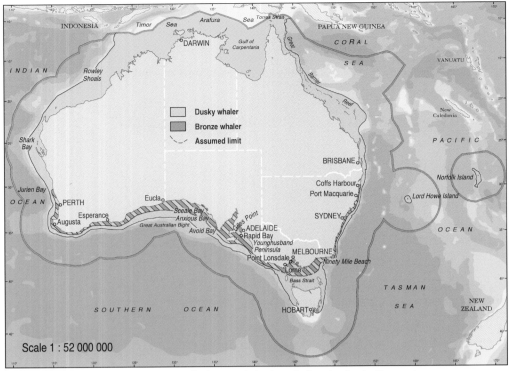

Geographic distribution of bronze whalers and dusky whalers in Australian waters.

Immature sharks, usually less than 150 cm total length, may remain resident in nursery areas, independent of season.[1]

Dusky whalers eat a variety of bony fishes from reefs, the sea floor and pelagic zones. Bronze whalers feed on a variety of bony fishes, including pilchards (*Sardinops neopilchardus*), trevallies (Carangidae) and mullet (Mugilidae); also spiny dogfish (*Squalus* species), squid and cuttlefish (*Sepia* species).[1] Young dusky whalers form large feeding aggregations. Both species commonly eat eagle rays (*Myliobatis australis*) in southern Australian waters, and 'packs' of 20–30 large individuals about 2 m long, have been observed preying heavily on schools of pilchards and Australian salmon (*Arripis truttaceus*) off South Australian beaches in summer (eg Sceale Bay, Anxious Bay, Avoid Bay),[7] and schools of tailor (*Pomatomus saltatrix*) off New South Wales beaches. Young

dusky whalers are preyed upon by other large sharks such as white pointers (*Carcharodon carcharias*) and tiger sharks (*Galeocerdo cuvier*).

Stock structure

There is no information on stock structure of either species in Australian waters, although their migratory behaviour suggests they each comprise a single stock.

Commercial fishery

The major commercial fishery for dusky and bronze whalers is in Western

Australia. A smaller fishery exists in South Australia.

The Western Australian Southwest Shark Fishery extends from the Western Australian–South Australian border to south of Shark Bay (about 27° S). Most fishing is carried out off the south and south-west coasts to depths of about 80–100 m.[6,8] The Fishery consistently catches about 25 species of shark,[6] of which the most important are dusky whalers, gummy sharks (*Mustelus antarcticus*), whiskery sharks (*Furgaleus macki*), sandbar sharks (*Carcharhinus plumbeus*) and wobbegong sharks (Orectolobidae). Bronze whalers are confused with dusky whalers in catch records but comprise only about 5 % of the 'dusky whaler' catch, which makes up about 29 % of the entire shark catch in south-western Western Australia.[2,8] Dusky whalers are caught mainly between the Albany and Busselton regions of the Southwest Shark Fishery.

Whaler sharks are caught mainly with bottom set gillnets several km long, and a small proportion are caught on bottom set longlines of several hundred hooks. They are also caught on droplines and handlines. Fishing effort in the Southwest Shark Fishery in Western Australia has been increasing since about 1976–80. It increased by 274 % from 1980–81 to 1987–88.[6] Catch rates stabilised in 1987–88, and remain stable. The Fishery has developed rapidly over the last 5 years.

Dusky and bronze whalers are primarily exploited as newly born and small juveniles of around 100 cm total length, in what are probably their nursery areas.[2,6] Hence, annual catch variations

Individual upper jaw teeth. Left: 210 cm dusky whaler, front view. Right: 265 cm bronze whaler, reverse view. [Lengths are total length.] (Source: Mike Cappo, Australian Institute of Marine Science)

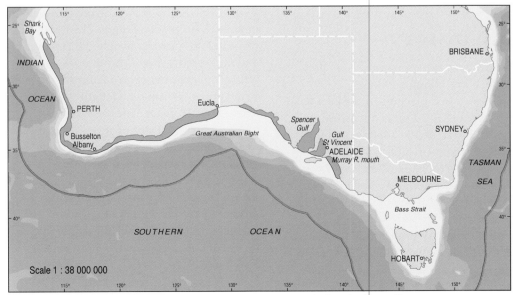

Commercial fishing areas for bronze whalers and dusky whalers in Australian waters.

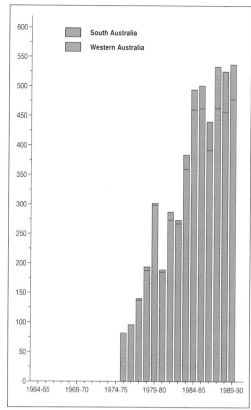

Total annual catch in t of dusky and bronze whalers (combined) for the period 1964–65 to 1989–90. Figures are unavailable for: South Australia from 1964–65 to 1975–76 and Western Australia from 1964–65 to 1974–75. Catches for States that average less than 5 % of the total for all States are not shown. (Source: Fisheries Resources Atlas Statistical Database)

are likely to be related to the number of new recruits available to the fisheries in any one year.[6,8]

Dusky and bronze whalers comprise an incidental catch of demersal otter trawling off southern Australia.

Bycatches of the dusky and bronze whaler fishery other than sharks include large quantities of finfish, such as queen snapper (*Nemadactylus valenciennesi*), snapper (*Pagrus auratus*) and silver trevally (*Pseudocaranx dentex*).[6]

In the South Australian inshore fishery, both species are targeted in west coast bays, Spencer Gulf and Gulf St Vincent, off the Murray River mouth and the south-east coast. The catch mainly comprises juveniles of less than 150 cm total length. The whalers are caught with large mesh bottom set gillnets and bottom set longlines.

Dusky whalers and bronze whalers are sold on domestic markets for their flesh in the 'fish-and-chip' trade. In 1991–92 in Perth markets, fishers received A$ 4.00–5.00 per kg for whalers.

Management controls Management steps introduced by the Western

Australian Government on the Southwest Shark Fishery include restricted access, gear limitations, transfer of licences and introduction of a system of time-gear access units which controls the number of nets and the period of time they may be used over a year. In South Australia there are limits on the number of hooks on longlines and on entry to the inshore fishery.

Recreational fishery

Whaler sharks are frequently targeted by gamefishers. They use moderately heavy lines with wire or light chain traces, and gamefishing tackle, often fishing from jetties (such as at Giles Point and Rapid Bay in South Australia, and Lorne and Point Lonsdale in Victoria). Often the sharks are first attracted by berley. Much 'blind' (untargeted) fishing takes place with surf fishing tackle on long beaches such as Ninety Mile Beach in Victoria and Younghusband Peninsula in South Australia, where mulloway (*Argyrosomus hololepidotus*) and Australian salmon are the principal target species. Dusky whalers comprise about 5 % of all sharks caught by New South Wales gamefishing clubs between Port Macquarie and Sydney, and sharks in this group (Carcharhinidae) comprise only 24 % of all sharks caught.[9]

Management controls There are no controls on recreational fishing.

Resource status

The fisheries are based on juveniles, probably in nursery areas. The extent of these areas is not known and little is known of the level of exploitation of adults. It is known that the relative abundance of juveniles is about 25 % of the unfished population in Western Australia.[10] If the sharks' migratory behaviour means that stocks are not being fished over the extent of their Australian distribution, then current levels of fishing may be sustainable.[6] Whalers, in common with other shark species, have low fecundity, a late age of sexual maturity, slow growth rates and a long gestation period.

References

1. Compagno, L.J.V. (1984). FAO species catalogue. Vol. 4. Sharks of the world. An annotated and illustrated catalogue of the shark species known to date. Part 2 — Carcharhiniformes. *FAO Fisheries Synopsis No. 125*, **4**(2): 251–655.

2. Last, P.L. and Stevens, J.D. (in press, 1992) *Sharks and rays of Australia*. Melbourne: CSIRO.

3. Natanson, L.J. (1990) Relationship of vertebral band deposition to age and growth in the dusky shark, *Carcharhinus obscurus*, and the little skate, *Raja erinacea*. Unpublished PhD thesis, University of Rhode Island.

4. Walter, J.P. and Ebert, D.A. (1991) Preliminary estimates of age of the bronze whaler *Carcharhinus brachyurus* (Chondrichthyes: Carcharhinidae) from southern Africa, with a review of some life history parameters. *South African Journal of Marine Science* **10**: 37–44.

5. Hutchins, B. and Swainston, R. (1986) *Sea fishes of southern Australia. Complete field guide for anglers and divers*. Perth: Swainston Publishing. 180 pp.

6. Lenanton, R., Millington, P. and Smyth, C. (1989) Shark and chips. Research and management into southern WA's edible shark fishery. *Western Fisheries* **May/June**: 17–23.

7. Cappo, M. (1992) Bronze whaler sharks in South Australia — how many species? *SAFISH* **17**(1): 10–13.

8. Heald, D.I. (1987) The commercial shark fishery in temperate waters of Western Australia. *Fisheries Department of Western Australia Report* **75**. 71 pp.

9. Pepperell, J.G. (in press, 1992) Trends in the distribution, species composition and size of sharks caught by gamefish anglers off south-eastern Australia, 1961–90. *Australian Journal of Marine and Freshwater Research* **43**.

10. Hall, D.A. (1991) A discussion of options for effort reduction. Report, Southern Demersal Gillnet and Demersal Longline Fishery Management Advisory Committee. *Fisheries Department of Western Australia, Fisheries Management Paper* **43**. 6 pp.

Contributors

Most of the information on this species was originally provided by (in alphabetical order) Mike Cappo, Rod Lenanton, Kevin McLoughlin, Julian Pepperell and John Stevens. Additional comments were made by Barry Bruce, Kerrie Deguara, Dave Hall, Keith Jones and Trevor Rule. Drawings courtesy of FAO, Rome. (*Details of contributors and their organisations are given in the Acknowledgements section at the back of this book.*)
Compiler Patricia Kailola and Christina Grieve (maps)

Tropical sharks

Carcharhinus species

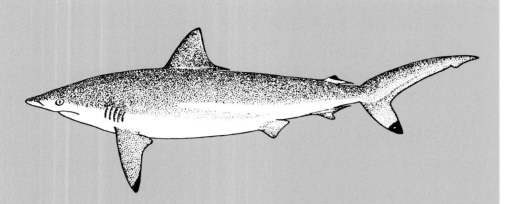

Tropical whaler sharks

This presentation is on 2 species, **blacktip shark** and **spot-tail shark**.

Blacktip shark,
Carcharhinus tilstoni
(Whitley)

Other common names include
**Australian blacktip shark,
Whitley's blacktip shark** and
blacktip whaler.
FAO: no known name
Australian species code: 018014

Spot-tail shark,
Carcharhinus sorrah
(Valenciennes)

Other common names include
sorrah shark, spot-tail whaler and
school shark.
FAO: **spot-tail shark**
Australian species code: 018013

Family CARCHARHINIDAE

Diagnostic features Blacktip sharks are bronzy-grey on the back and most fins have black tips. They are long-snouted sharks with slender, erect, serrated upper teeth, the first dorsal fin origin about over the pectoral fin insertions, and no interdorsal ridge. Spot-tail sharks (pictured) are bronze to greyish brown on the back and have conspicuous black tips to the pectoral, second dorsal and lower caudal fins. Their teeth are oblique, triangular and serrated, the first dorsal fin origin is about over the rear free tip of the pectoral fin, and they have an interdorsal ridge.[1]

produced in January after a 10-month gestation period. The average litter size is 3 pups, the range for blacktip sharks being 1–6, and for spot-tail sharks being 1–8. Average total lengths at birth are 60 cm for blacktip sharks and 50 cm for spot-tail sharks.[3]

In comparison with many other shark species, young blacktip and spot-tail sharks grow rapidly, increasing in length by about 20 cm (blacktip) and 25 cm (spot-tail) in the first year. Sexual maturity in blacktip sharks is attained at 3–4 years of age at 110–115 cm length and 8–10 kg. In spot-tail sharks, sexual maturity is achieved at 2–3 years of age at 90–95 cm length and 4–5 kg. Blacktip sharks reach a maximum size of 200 cm total length and 52 kg, and live to 12 years. Spot-tail sharks reach 160 cm total length, 28 kg and live for at least 8 years.[3,4]

Tagging studies showed that most movements of blacktip sharks and spot-tail sharks were within 50 km of the tagging site, although some sharks travelled as far as 1100 km in less than 1 month at large.[5] Immature blacktip sharks travel greater distances than do mature sharks. Blacktip sharks also appear to aggregate, the groups tending to be dominated by one sex or size class.

Distribution

Both species are present throughout northern Australian waters from about Shark Bay in Western Australia (spot-tail sharks) or Exmouth Gulf (blacktip sharks) to Gladstone in southern Queensland.[1] Blacktip sharks are endemic to Australia, but spot-tail sharks have a wide Indo-West Pacific distribution from Africa and the Red Sea to the Solomon Islands.[2]

These whaler sharks inhabit continental shelf waters, to about 80 m (spot-tail sharks) and 150 m (blacktip sharks). Spot-tail and blacktip sharks occur throughout the water column but are more common near the sea bed during the day and near the surface at night.

Life history

Both species are viviparous, — ie they produce live offspring and have well-developed yolk sac placenta. They breed once each year, the pups being

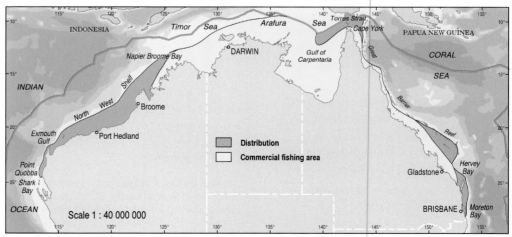

Geographical distribution and commercial fishing areas for blacktip sharks and spot-tail sharks in Australian waters.

Tagging whaler sharks aboard F.V. *Rachel*, northern pelagic shark survey program. (Source: Stephanie Davenport, CSIRO Marine Laboratories, Hobart)

Sharks are both predators and scavengers. Blacktip sharks feed mostly on finfish and to a lesser extent on cephalopods such as squid, octopus and cuttlefish (*Sepia* species). Spot-tail sharks eat finfish, some cephalopods and crustaceans.[4]

Stock structure

Tagging and electrophoretic studies have indicated that there is only 1 stock of blacktip sharks and spot-tail sharks in Australian waters.[6]

Commercial fishery

Whaler sharks have been fished off northern Australia from the early 1970s. Between 1975 and 1977, more than 7500 t were taken annually by Taiwanese gillnetters. This drifting gillnet fishery operated until mid-1986, targeting principally shark, longtail tuna (*Thunnus tonggol*) and Spanish mackerel (*Scomberomorus* species).[7,8] Initially, 8 km long nets were used but by 1986 the nets were 20 km or more long and 15 m deep. Sharks comprised 65–76 % of the total catch, and of them, blacktip sharks and spot-tail sharks comprised 90 % of the catch. More than 20 species made up the remaining shark catch, including several species of whaler sharks (eg *C. macloti, C. amboinensis*), milk sharks (eg *Rhizoprionodon acutus*) and hammerhead sharks (*Sphyrna* species). Similar species proportions make up the

current shark fishery. Most shark caught in the Taiwanese fishery were retained except for very large sharks (fins were kept) and very small ones.

Because of concerns over decreasing shark catch rates and high incidental catches of dolphins (Delphinidae), limitations on gillnet length were introduced in 1986. This step effectively made the Taiwanese operation uneconomic and despite some attempts to switch to longlining as an alternative, fishing by the Taiwanese drifting gillnet fleets had ceased within the Australian Fishing Zone by mid-1986.

An Australian gillnet and a drifting longline fishery has operated between about Napier Broome Bay and eastern Gulf of Carpentaria in inshore waters off northern Australia from the late 1970s. Catches of predominantly small sharks are harvested and the current catch is about 500 t. Catch rates for sharks are higher (by about 2.3 times) at night than during the day.[8] Sharks are also taken in small numbers as a bycatch of dropline fishing in this area. Sharks caught by Australian gillnetters are generally sold on domestic retail markets only for their meat. They are processed on board and either frozen, chilled, or put in brine, and landed as trunks or fillets. The shark is sold as 'flake' in fillet form. In Darwin, nearly all shark is marketed as 'blacktip shark'. The Queensland, wholesale price for shark in 1992 averaged A$ 2.00–3.00 per kg. Fins are retained predominately from hammerhead sharks. Dried or frozen, they are either exported (mainly to Chinese markets) or sold locally. In 1990,

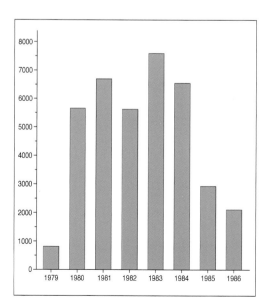

Annual catch data from the Taiwanese gillnet fishery in Australian waters, from 1979 to 1986. (Source: Taiwanese Annual Reports, in Stevens and Davenport[7])

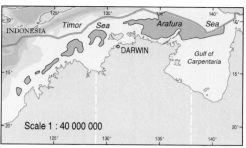

Area of the historical Taiwanese gillnet fishery for shark in northern Australian waters, 1979–86. (Source: Australian Fishing Zone Information System logbooks)

shark fin sold in Australia fetched A$ 12.00–65.00 per kg when dried (Darwin wholesale prices). During 1992, the overseas price for dried, top quality shark fin exceeded A$ 100.00 per kg.

Sharks and rays comprise about 10 % by weight of the bycatch from the Northern Prawn Fishery but very little is retained.[9] Sharks also form a bycatch of barramundi (*Lates calcarifer*) and threadfin salmon (Polynemidae) fisheries. A small fishery targeting large sharks operates off northern Western Australia as far south as Broome.

The developing Queensland East Coast Shark Fishery mostly takes small whaler sharks less than 1 m total length. Sharks are caught with coastal and offshore set gillnets and drifting gillnets up to 1200 m long all along the coast but are targeted north of Hervey Bay. Nets are set at dawn and dusk. Handlines are also used to catch shark from trawlers at night. Sharks are either sold wholesale as trunks for A$ 1.50–3.00 per kg or processed on board and sold direct to restaurants and retail outlets for A$ 4.50–6.00 per kg. In some areas, fins, jaws and skins are also marketed.

Management controls At present no foreign fishing fleets are allowed into the shark fisheries. A development plan is in place to encourage Australian participation in the Northern Shark Fishery which is managed by the Commonwealth of Australia. The plan initially ran from mid-January 1992 to mid-January 1993. Fishing endorsements are required in the 3 defined zones of the Northern Shark Fishery which extends from 120° E to the eastern Gulf of Carpentaria.

Inshore shark fishers in Queensland and the Northern Territory require endorsements for different shark fishing methods. Restrictions on net length, mesh size and areas also apply. There are no

Repairing a gillnet on board a Taiwanese gillnetter, northern Australia. (Source: John Stevens, CSIRO Marine Laboratories, Hobart)

Drying shark fins hanging in the rigging of a Taiwanese pair trawler, North West Shelf. (Source: Glen Smith, Southern Fisheries Centre, Queensland Department of Primary Industries)

limits on tropical shark fishing in other Western Australian waters.

Recreational fishery

Whaler sharks are caught by game fishers, mostly off Queensland. These are usually small individuals up to 2 m and about 60 kg weight. Fishers targeting larger whaler sharks make use of a berley trail and fish with heavy handlines with wire trace, or rod-and-reel. Whalers are also taken by trolling using lures and fish baits. The largest whaler shark (Carcharhinidae) caught by a recreational fisher in Australia was from New South Wales, and weighed 378 kg (Game Fishing Association of Australia records).

Management controls No restrictions apply in any State.

Resource status

Assessments of historical Taiwanese catch and effort data in 1986 showed that the stocks were being overexploited,[7] and indicated[5] that the sustainable catch for the offshore waters of the fishery would have been about 2400 t live weight over 1980–84. Since 1986 (with the exception of Taiwanese longlining in 1989), fishing effort has declined and sustainable catch in these waters may be somewhat higher than the 1980–84 estimate. The inshore northern region is probably only lightly exploited and tagging studies suggest that the maximum sustainable catch for both species combined in these waters is about 1500 t live weight.[5] Considerable quantities of whaler sharks are caught as bycatch of demersal otter trawl fisheries,[9] and the impact of these catches on the resource is unknown. Furthermore, Taiwanese and Indonesian gillnetting vessels continue to fish for sharks outside the Australian Fishing Zone to the north.

The status of whaler shark populations off the east coast of Queensland is unknown.

Notes

The other shark species caught in northern Australia belong to the families Triakidae, Hemigaleidae, Sphyrnidae and Carcharhinidae. A study[10] of 17 of these species indicates that for the majority, reproduction is distinctly seasonal. Individual females give birth each summer after a gestation period of 9–12 months. The average length at birth varies from 27–75 cm and the average litter size varies from 2 to 34 pups. Diet ranges from omnivorous to highly selective.

Blacktip sharks are very similar to common blacktip sharks, *C. limbatus*, which are widespread in tropical waters of the Indo-Pacific and Atlantic oceans. The 2 species can currently only be distinguished on enzyme systems and vertebral counts.[1,4] Common blacktip sharks are very rare in Australian waters.

References

1. Last, P.L. and Stevens, J.D. (in press, 1992) *Sharks and rays of Australia*. Melbourne: CSIRO.

2. Compagno, L.J.V. (1984) FAO species catalogue, vol. 4. Sharks of the world. An annotated and illustrated catalogue of the shark species known to date. Part 2 — Carcharhiniformes. *FAO Fisheries Synopsis No. 125*, **4**(2): 251–655.

3. Davenport, S. and Stevens, J.D. (1988) Age and growth of two commercially important sharks (*Carcharhinus tilstoni* and *C. sorrah*) from northern Australia. *Australian Journal of Marine and Freshwater Research* **39**: 417–433.

4. Stevens, J.D. and Wiley, P.D. (1986) Biology of two commercially important carcharhinid sharks from northern Australia. *Australian Journal of Marine and Freshwater Research* **37**: 671–688.

5. Northern pelagic fish stock research (1990) *CSIRO Division of Fisheries FIRDC Projects 83/49 and 86/87, Final Report*. 325 pp.

6. Lavery, S. and Shaklee, J.B. (1989) Population genetics of two tropical sharks, *Carcharhinus tilstoni* and *C. sorrah*, in northern Australia. *Australian Journal of Marine and Freshwater Research* **40**: 541–557.

7. Stevens J.D. and Davenport, S. (1991) Analysis of catch data from the Taiwanese gill-net fishery off northern Australia, 1979 to 1986. *CSIRO Marine Laboratories Report* **213**. 51 pp.

8. Lyle, J.M. and Timms, G.J. (1984) Northern Australia's multi-species shark fishery. Exploratory fishing survey of shark and other pelagic fish resources found in Northern Territory inshore waters. *Northern Territory Department of Primary Production, Fishery Report* **12**(4). 75 pp.

9. Pender, P.J., Willing, R.S. and Ramm, D.C. (1992) Northern Prawn Fishery bycatch study: distribution, abundance, size and use of bycatch from the mixed species fishery. *Department of Primary Industry and Fisheries, Fishery Report* **26**. 70 pp.

10. Stevens, J.D. and McLoughlin, K.J. (1991) Distribution, size and sex composition, reproductive biology and diet of sharks from northern Australia. *Australian Journal of Marine and Freshwater Research* **42**: 151–199.

Contributors

This presentation was originally prepared by Stephanie Davenport. Additional information was provided by (in alphabetical order) Jeff Blaney, Rusty Branford, Jeremy Lyle, Colin Olson, Colin Simpfendorfer, Dick Slack-Smith and John Stevens. Drawing courtesy of FAO, Rome. (*Details of contributors and their organisations are given in the Acknowledgements section at the back of this book.*)

Compilers Patricia Kailola and Kevin McLoughlin

Bony bream

Nematalosa erebi

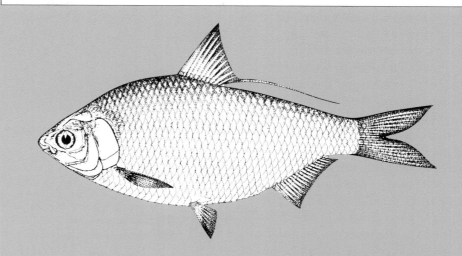

Distribution

Endemic to Australia, bony bream are present and widespread in all mainland warm water catchments.[1] Within this broad geographic range distribution may be patchy, with fish locally abundant. The Murray River below Yarrawonga Weir is the species' southern limit. Bony bream do not occur in rivers that drain east of the Great Dividing Range, nor in Tasmania or the south-west of Western Australia.

Bony bream live in a variety of habitats including shallow backwaters and artesian bores, over mud, clay or sand. In northern Australia they inhabit floodplain lagoons as well as main river channels and sandy lowland creeks.[2] Adults live in water depths from 10 cm to

Nematalosa erebi (Günther)

Bony bream

Other common names include **hairback herring**, **pyberry**, **melon fish** and **tukari**.
FAO: **Australian river gizzard shad**
Australian species code: 085019

Family CLUPEIDAE

Diagnostic features Bony bream have a deep, compressed body. Their head is scaleless with a blunt snout, a small toothless mouth and large eyes. Body scales are generally smooth but there are sharp serrated ridges along the fish's back and belly profiles. The last dorsal ray is elongated. Individuals vary in colour, the back from greenish to grey, the sides lighter and the belly silvery to white.

at least 3 m, although juveniles are more commonly found near the surface. Bony bream are not found in the cool, fast flowing, high altitude reaches of rivers.

They live in still or slow flowing stretches of water, and can tolerate water clarity that varies from clear to extremely turbid. Adult fish prefer open water, whilst juveniles may be found near macrophytes (large aquatic plants) and submerged terrestrial vegetation. Juveniles will often congregate by day in shallow backwaters or bays, a habit resulting in downstream colonisation during flooding.[3]

Life history

Bony bream in the lower Murray River spawn from spring to early summer when water temperature rises above 21°C. Spawning in Lake Alexandrina occurs off sandy shores.[4] In northern Australia, bony bream spawn in muddy, lowland lagoons.[2] In the northern and arid zone populations, spawning is intensified by flooding: it may occur in spring, summer or autumn and take place up to 3 times per season per individual. Although the fish aggregate to spawn, there is no evidence of spawning migration. Fecundity in bony bream is high: a 90 g female can produce 33 000 eggs, and a 595 g female can produce 880 000 eggs.[4] Bony bream eggs are small (average 0.83 mm diameter) and initially are demersal and adhesive. They may later

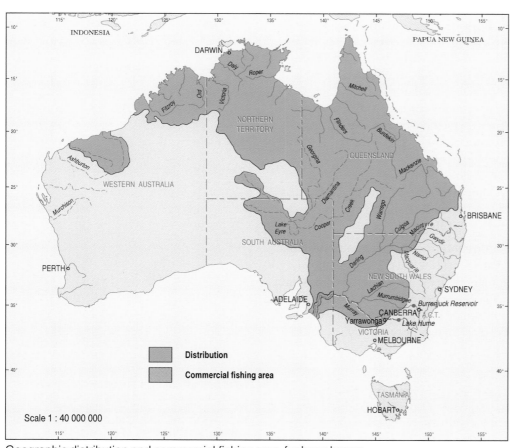

Geographic distribution and commercial fishing area for bony bream.

Distribution
Commercial fishing area

Scale 1 : 40 000 000

become semi-buoyant.[4] Both larval and juvenile bony bream are pelagic.[1]

Bony bream are thought to live for more than 10 years[5] but to date, age classes have not been validated beyond 3 years. Growth rates and spawning activity vary between northern and southern populations because of different environmental conditions. In northern populations most growth takes place during the wet season.[2] Growth rates also differ slightly between males and females. In the lower Murray River the average total length at 1 year is 8 cm, at 2 years it is 15 cm, and at 3 years it is 24 cm for males and 25 cm for females.[4] The largest recorded fish, taken in the lower Murray River, was 48 cm long.[5]

In the lower Murray River the earliest recorded sexual maturity for bony bream is at 13 cm length for males and 15 cm length for females. The median lengths at maturity are 16 cm (males) and 20 cm (females).[4] Fish from northern populations are about the same length at first maturity.[2]

Juvenile bony bream initially feed mostly on zooplankton. They switch to a diet of detritus and algae when they reach 5–6 cm length.[6] Adult fish are primarily herbivorous, feeding on algae and aquatic plants, although occasionally they eat insects and small crustaceans.

Bony bream are one of Australia's most important freshwater forage species. Both juvenile and adult fish form a major part of the diet of birds such as pelicans (*Pelecanus conspicillatus*), cormorants (*Phalacrocorax* species), fork-tailed (black) kites (*Milvus migrans*), whistling kites (*Haliastur sphenurus*); and fish such as golden perch (*Macquaria ambigua*), redfin (*Perca fluviatilis*), Murray cod (*Maccullochella peelii*), mulloway (*Argyrosomus hololepidotus*), barramundi (*Lates calcarifer*) and fork-tailed catfish (Ariidae).

Stock structure

Bony bream from different areas were originally described as separate species.[7,8] No studies on stock structure have been conducted.

Commercial fishery

Bony bream are taken commercially only in South Australia. There have been intermittent reports of catches of up to 2 t

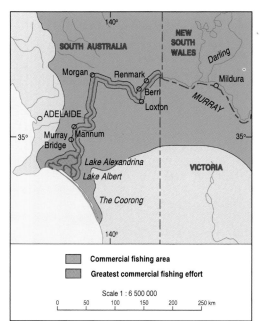

Inland waters commercially fished for bony bream, showing areas of greatest fishing effort.

from Victoria, but these are probably only as bycatch from European carp (*Cyprinus carpio*) fisheries. In recent years most of the catches have come from lakes Albert and Alexandrina and the Coorong, with a small amount taken by fishers working the lower reaches of the Murray River. The lake fishers take most of their catch in gillnets whereas the catch in the river fishery is taken mainly in drum nets.[9] Gillnets are set in still water and left overnight, while drum nets are set in flowing water during the day.

Bony bream make up about 47 % of the total inland fish catch for South Australia.[10] The fishery for bony bream targets only adult, non-spawning fish. The fish are used as bait for the southern rock lobster (*Jasus edwardsii*) fishery.[4] There is potential for the use of bony bream as a forage species in aquaculture operations. High value future products may include using bony bream fillets for pickling or 'rollmops'. In 1992, returns to fishers for whole bony bream averaged about A$ 0.30 per kg.

Management controls South Australian fishers must hold a licence, and the number of these issued each year is being held constant or reduced. Commercial fishers may only take fish from area(s) listed on their licences, using specified gear.[9]

Recreational fishery

Bony bream are rarely taken by anglers. According to the Australian Anglers Association records, the largest bony

bream taken by angling weighed 1.86 kg and was caught in the Murray River in South Australia.

Resource status

There are no concerns about the current viability of the bony bream stock in the Murray River, as they appear to be thriving under modified river conditions.[9] It is unlikely that the increase in their abundance is related to the decline in numbers of Murray cod, a major predator.[4] Bony bream densities in the lower Cooper Creek (where there is a variety of natural predators) far exceed those in the lower Murray River. They die in large numbers following rapid drops in water temperature.[11] Accordingly, it has been suggested that the release of cold water from Burrinjuck and Hume reservoirs is responsible for the disappearance of bony bream from sections of the river downstream from these structures.[11]

Bony bream densities have so far remained high in spite of heavy fishing pressure. However, as there are no monitoring or research programs on this species, reliable conclusions on their status cannot be made.

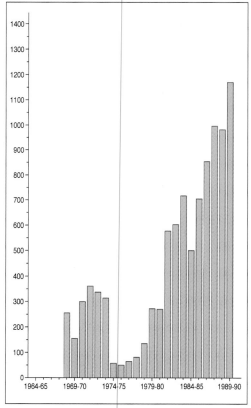

Total annual catch in t of bony bream in South Australia for the period 1964–65 to 1989–90. Figures are unavailable for 1964–65 to 1967–68. Catches for States that average less than 5% of the total for all States are not shown. (Source: Fisheries Resources Atlas Statistical Database)

Using a fine mesh seine net to trap small fish in the backwaters of Cooper Creek, South Australia. (Source: Jim Puckridge, University of Adelaide)

Notes

In bony bream populations in the lower Murray River the condition of juvenile fish deteriorates markedly over winter while that of adults does not.[5] These populations also suffer from regular early spring epidemics of the water fungus, *Saprolegnia parasitica*. This infection affects only adults and involves 10–64 % of that population.[12]

References

1. Puckridge, J. (1986) *The reproductive biology of bony bream in the lower Murray.* Abstract, Australian Society for Fish Biology Conference, 13–18 August 1986, Darwin.

2. Bishop, K.A., Allen, S.A., Pollard, D.A. and Cook, M.G. (in press, 1992) Pp 107–117, in *Ecological studies on the freshwater fishes of the Alligator Rivers Region, Northern Territory. Research report 4,* **3**: *Autecology.* Canberra: Office of the Supervising Scientist for the Alligator Rivers Region.

3. Puckridge, J.T. and Drewien, M. (1988) The aquatic fauna of the north-west branch of Cooper Creek. Pp 69–108, in *The Coongie Lakes study.* Ed by J. Reid and J. Gillen. Adelaide: South Australian Department of Environment and Planning.

4. Puckridge, J.T. and Walker, K.F. (1990) Reproductive biology and larval development of a gizzard shad, *Nematalosa erebi* (Günther) (Dorosomatinae:Teleostei) in the River Murray, South Australia. *Australian Journal of Marine and Freshwater Research* **41**: 695–712.

5. Puckridge, J.T. (1988) *The life history of a gizzard shad, the bony bream* Nematalosa erebi *(Günther) (Dorosomatinae, Teleostei) in the lower River Murray, South Australia.* Unpublished MSc thesis, University of Adelaide.

6. Atkins, B.A. (1984) *Feeding ecology of* Nematalosa erebi *in the lower River Murray.* Unpublished Honours thesis, University of Adelaide.

7. Munro, I.S.R. (1956) Handbook of Australian fishes, number 6. Pp 25–28. *Fisheries Newsletter, Sydney* **15**(12): 15–18.

8. Nelson, G.J. and Rothman, M.N. (1973) The species of gizzard shads (Dorosomatinae) with particular reference to the Indo-Pacific region. *Bulletin of the American Museum of Natural History* **37**: 653–756.

9. Rohan, G. (1989) River fishery (South Australia) — review of management arrangements. Pp 37–54, in *Proceedings of the workshop on native fish management, Canberra 16–17 June, 1988.* Ed by B. Lawrence. Canberra: Murray–Darling Basin Commission.

10. Catch, effort and value of production of South Australian fisheries (1990) *SAFISH* **15** (2): 16–26.

11. Lake, J.S. (1971) *Freshwater fishes and rivers of Australia.* Sydney: Thomas Nelson (Australia) Limited. 61 pp.

12. Puckridge, J.T., Walker, K.F., Langdon, J.S., Daley, C. and Beakes, G.W. (1989) Mycotic dermatitis in a freshwater gizzard shad, the bony bream, *Nematalosa erebi* (Günther), in the River Murray, South Australia. *Journal of Fish Diseases* **12**: 205–221.

Contributors

The information on this species was originally provided by Jim Puckridge. Drawing courtesy of FAO, Rome. (*Details of contributors and their organisations are given in the Acknowledgements section at the back of this book.*)

Compiler Alex McNee

Pilchard

Sardinops neopilchardus

Sardinops neopilchardus (Steindachner)

Pilchard

Other common names include **blue pilchard, sardine, bluebait** or **mulies** (if used as bait)
FAO: **Australian pilchard**
Australian species code: 085002

Family CLUPEIDAE

Diagnostic features Pilchards are moderately elongate and slender and they have a serrated belly profile. Their head length is greater than their body depth. The body scales are very deciduous. The ventral fin begins opposite the middle of the single dorsal fin, which consists entirely of soft rays. Pilchards are steely blue above and silvery yellow below and they have a row of dark spots along the upper sides of their body.[1,2]

Distribution

Pilchards are schooling fish which inhabit the temperate waters of most continents. In Australia the pilchard group is represented by *Sardinops neopilchardus*, which is distributed from Hervey Bay in southern Queensland, around southern Australia to Red Bluff in Western Australia.[1,2] Pilchards are also found in Bass Strait, across the north coast of Tasmania and along the east coast to Hobart. This species also inhabits waters around the North and South islands of New Zealand.

Pilchards are usually found in bays, inlets, and waters from inshore to the edge of the continental shelf.[2,3,4] They are distributed from the surface to depths of up to 200 m.[2] Pilchards prefer clear marine waters, with salinities of 34–37 parts per thousand and mean annual temperatures between 9° and 21°C.[5]

Life history

Many aspects of pilchard life history vary with locality. In Victorian waters, pilchards shoal and spawn at the surface during spring and summer,[2,3] while in South Australia[4] and southern New South Wales[6] spawning occurs later, during summer and autumn. Spawning takes

place from autumn to early spring in the northern parts of the species' range in New South Wales, as well as along the south coast of Western Australia.[2,3,6] It is not known whether pilchards undertake extensive spawning migrations, yet there is evidence of surface schooling at this time. It was believed that individual Australian pilchards only spawn once or twice in a season,[5,7] but research on related species suggests that they may spawn a number of times.[8] Spawning has been recorded only when surface temperatures are between 14° and 21°C.[1,5]

Pilchard eggs have been found from just offshore, in bays and estuary mouths, out to the edge of the continental shelf and even slightly beyond.[5] The eggs are planktonic and hatch 45–58 hours after fertilisation at water temperatures of 18–20°C.[9] Batch fecundities range from about 10 000 eggs in 13 cm long females to about 45 000 eggs in females of about 18 cm.[2]

At hatching, larvae are 2–3 mm long. Larvae have been recorded from the edge of the continental shelf and from depths to 100 m but are generally most abundant within 10 km of the coastline.[2] The postlarvae are presumed to move inshore to bays, inlets and estuaries after about 5 months.[6] Juveniles remain in this region for between 8 and 12 months and then move out to join adult schools[4] with the onset of sexual maturity.[2]

Pilchards from New South Wales waters grow rapidly, reaching a total length of 14–15 cm in 3 years. By comparison, fish in Victorian populations grow more slowly, reaching a length of 12 cm in 3 years.[2,7] Pilchards from Australian waters have been recorded to reach

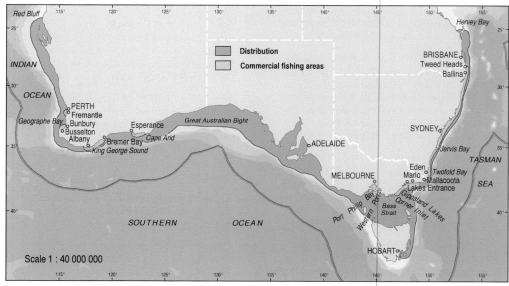

Geographic distribution and commercial fishing areas for pilchards in Australian waters.

21 cm standard length[1] and they can live up to 6 years. The size and age at maturity also vary with locality, generally occurring between 7 and 13 cm total length and an age of 1–3 years.[2,4] In New South Wales waters, males are smaller than females at maturity. At Lakes Entrance and Port Phillip Bay, females mature at 8 cm and 10 cm total length respectively.[3]

Pilchards mainly feed on a variety of planktonic crustaceans, but also take molluscan larvae, gastropod molluscs, polychaete worms and phytoplankton (diatoms).[1,2,4] Both juvenile and adult pilchards are prey to many species of fish such as tunas (Scombridae), flathead (Platycephalidae), tailor (*Pomatomus saltatrix*), barracouta (*Thyrsites atun*), Australian salmon (*Arripis* species) and tommy ruff (*Arripis georgianus*). Birds (eg gulls (Laridae), mutton birds (Procellariidae) and little penguins (*Eudyptula minor*)) and dolphins (Delphinidae) also feed on pilchards.[2,3]

Stock structure

Genetic studies on pilchards are being conducted at the University of New South Wales. Early work[10] proposed the existence of at least 3 separate breeding populations of pilchards in Australian waters. These population units were based on differences in spawning periods, vertebral counts and growth rates. The populations included an eastern unit, distributed along the New South Wales and Queensland coasts; a south-eastern unit, found along the Victorian and probably the Tasmanian coastlines; and a south-western unit along the south coast of Western Australia. There was insufficient evidence to categorise those populations of South Australia or the west coast of Western Australia.

Commercial fishery

In Australia, exploitation of pilchards began in the 1800s, although the development of a fishery was hampered by the lack of a substantial or consistent market. Since the 1970s, fishing for pilchards has intensified.[2]

The largest pilchard fisheries are located in Western Australia with major fisheries in the coastal regions off Fremantle, in King George Sound and the surrounding Albany region and Bremer

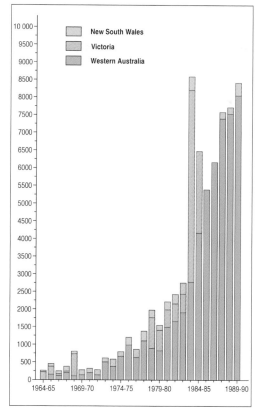

Total annual catch in t of pilchards for the period 1964–65 to 1989–90. Figures are unavailable for: New South Wales from 1984–85 to 1986–87; and Victoria from 1969–70 to 1977–78 and 1985–86 to 1989–90. Catches for States that average less than 5 % of the total for all States are not shown. (Source: Fisheries Resources Atlas Statistical Database)

Bay. Smaller pilchard fisheries are located in Geographe Bay and Esperance areas in the south-west,[11] and in other States. In Queensland, pilchards are taken occasionally as part of a mixed catch in beach seine fisheries.[12] Pilchards are also harvested along the length of the New South Wales coast, although most of the catch is taken from waters between Ballina and Tweed Heads, Jervis Bay and south of Eden. In Victoria, pilchards are fished in waters within 1 km of shore east of Lakes Entrance, in eastern Bass Strait and in Port Phillip Bay. Small catches are also taken from Western Port and waters outside Port Phillip Bay.[3,11] The only fishery for pilchards in South Australia is bait fishing by tuna pole-and-line fishers.[11]

In Western Australia the biggest catches of pilchards are made in winter.[11] Most fishing is done in the early morning or late afternoon using echo sounders and sonar to locate schools, and pollard ('wheat germ' or chicken feed) to attract the fish. In Victoria, pilchards are fished all year with the largest catches being made during late summer, autumn and early winter.[3,13] Commercial purse seiners fishing for pilchards there and in New South Wales work mainly at dusk or after dark using lights to attract the fish.[11]

Purse seine nets are the main gear used in pilchard target fisheries.[11,13] In Western Australia, a small quantity of pilchards is caught for bait by part time fishers and rock lobster and tuna fishers.[11] They use lampara nets, hand hauled purse nets and beach seine nets.[11] The average size of pilchards caught varies among locations but, in general, fish are between 14 cm and 16 cm long and 2–5 years old.

Pilchards have a high oil content which increases with the size of the fish.[3] The condition and fatness of fish are important for canning or oil production. Pilchards are used either for bait for anglers, rock lobster pots and fish traps, pet food, or canned as 'sardines' for human consumption.[11,12] There is also a small but increasing market for fresh pilchards in capital city fish markets.[12] Most of the New South Wales catch is sold

Pilchard fishing in Western Australia: hauling a purse seine net. (Source: Rick Fletcher, Western Australian Marine Research Laboratories, Fisheries Department of Western Australia)

through the Sydney Fish Market or processed into pet food.[11] Substantial quantities of pilchards were canned for human consumption or processed as fish meal in Victoria during the 1960s, 1970s and early 1980s. They are now used mainly as pet food with small quantities sold as recreational fishing bait or as fresh fish for human consumption. Pilchards from Western Australia are sold primarily for pet food or bait.[11] The average price for pilchards at the Sydney Fish Market in 1991–92 was A$ 1.54 per kg.

Management controls In New South Wales and Victoria, pilchard catches are part of multi-species, multi-method limited entry commercial fisheries. In Western Australia, there are specific management and development plans for all regions where pilchard fisheries are located.[11] For example, the fishery is managed by a limited entry scheme with additional controls on boat and net sizes in Fremantle, and in the Albany region (including King George Sound) there is a limited number of licences with a total allowable catch broken up on an individually transferable quota basis. The Augusta, Esperance and Geographe Bay regions are presently managed as developing fisheries but only a limited number of development licences has been issued and total allowable catches have been imposed.

Recreational fishery

There is no recreational fishery for pilchards in any Australian State, although small quantities are occasionally gathered for bait.

Resource status

There is inadequate knowledge of the pilchard stock size (or biomass) in most fishing areas. However, it is likely that most Australian stocks (at least until recently) are under-exploited. The exception to this is along the south-west coast of Western Australia, where pilchards are heavily exploited.

References

1. Whitehead, P.J.P. (1985) FAO species catalogue. Vol. 7. Clupeoid fishes of the world (Suborder Clupeoidei). An annotated and illustrated catalogue of the herrings, sardines, sprats, shads, anchovies and

Brailing a catch of pilchards onboard in Western Australia. (Source: Rick Fletcher, Western Australian Marine Research Laboratories, Fisheries Department of Western Australia)

   wolf-herrings. Part 1 — Chirocentridae, Clupeidae and Pristigasteridae. *FAO Fisheries Synopsis No. 125*, **7**(1): 1–303.

2. Fletcher, W.J. (1990) A synopsis of the biology and exploitation of the Australasian pilchard, *Sardinops neopilchardus* (Steindachner). Part I: Biology. *Fisheries Department of Western Australia, Fisheries Research Report* **88**. 45 pp.

3. Blackburn, M. (1950) Studies on the age, growth and life history of the pilchard, *Sardinops neopilchardus* (Steindachner), in southern and western Australia. *Australian Journal of Marine and Freshwater Research* **1**: 221–258.

4. Dredge, M.C.L. (1969) *Aspects of the biology of the Australian pilchard*, Sardinops neopilchardus *(Steindachner) relating to commercial exploitation of stocks in South Australia*. Unpublished Honours thesis, University of Adelaide. 34 pp.

5. Blackburn, M. (1960) Synopsis on the biology of the Australian and New Zealand sardine, *Sardinops neopilchardus* (Steindachner). Pp 245–264, in *Proceedings of the world scientific meeting on the biology of sardines and related species. Vol 2. Species synopses*. Ed by H. Rosa and G. Murphy. Rome: FAO.

6. Blackburn, M. (1949) The age, rate of growth and general life history of the Australian pilchard (*Sardinops neopilchardus*) in New South Wales. *Bulletin of the Science and Industry Research Organisation* **242**: 1–86.

7. Joseph, B.D.L. (1981) *Pilchard fishery at Jervis Bay — biology, fishery and population dynamics*. Unpublished MSc thesis, University of New South Wales. 135 pp.

8. Hunter, J.R. and Goldberg, S.R. (1980) Spawning incidence and batch fecundity in northern anchovy, *Engraulis mordax*. *Fishery Bulletin (U.S.)* **77**: 641–652.

9. Baker, A.N. (1972) Reproduction, early life history, and age-growth relationships of the New Zealand pilchard, *Sardinops neopilchardus* (Steindachner). *Fisheries Research Division of New Zealand, Fisheries Research Bulletin* **5**: 1–64.

10. Blackburn, M. (1951) Races and populations of the Australian pilchard, *Sardinops neopilchardus* (Steindachner) in southern and western Australia. *Australian Journal of Marine and Freshwater Research* **2**: 179–192.

11. Fletcher, W.J. (1991) A synopsis of the biology and the exploitation of the Australasian pilchard, *Sardinops neopilchardus* (Steindachner). Part II: History of stock assessment and exploitation. *Fisheries Department of Western Australia, Fisheries Research Report* **91**. 55 pp.

12. SCP Fisheries Consultants (1988) Economics and marketing of Western Australian pilchards. *Fisheries Department of Western Australia, Fisheries Management Paper* **22**. 26 pp.

13. Hall, D.N. and MacDonald, C.M. (1986) Commercial fishery situation report: net and line fisheries of Port Phillip Bay Victoria, 1914–1984. *Victorian Department of Conservation, Forests and Lands, Fisheries Division, Marine Fisheries Report* **10**. 121 pp.

Contributors

The information on this species was originally provided by Murray MacDonald and supplemented by (in alphabetical order) Rick Fletcher, Augy Syahailatua and John Virgona. Drawing courtesy of FAO, Rome. (*Details of contributors and their organisations are given in the Acknowledgements section at the back of this book.*)
Compilers Ebenezer Adjei, Alex McNee and Christina Grieve (maps)

Anchovy

Engraulis australis

Engraulis australis (White)

Anchovy

Other common names include
southern anchovy, **whitebait**
and **smig**.
FAO: **Australian anchovy**
Australian species code: 086001

Family ENGRAULIDIDAE

Diagnostic features Anchovy have a
rounded, moderately elongate body
lacking keeled scutes along the belly
profile. They have a pointed, fleshy
snout, and an inferior mouth which
extends well back behind the eye.
The dorsal and anal fins are short-based
and the caudal fin is forked. Anchovy
are purplish-green on the back and
upper sides and silvery white below.
They have a broad silver band along
their sides. [1,2,3]

Distribution

Anchovy are distributed from Cape
Capricorn in Queensland[3] around
southern Australia, including Tasmanian
coastal waters,[3] to Shark Bay in Western
Australia.[2] It is not known whether
distribution is continuous in the Great
Australian Bight.[3] Anchovy probably also
inhabit the waters around Lord Howe and
Norfolk islands, and those around most of
New Zealand.[3]

Anchovy are caught from shallow
inshore waters to depths of 20 m but their
maximum depth limit is unknown. They
are pelagic, schooling fish, preferring low
to moderate energy habitats such as
sheltered bays and inshore and open
coastal waters.

Life history

In southern Australia (Victoria and
Tasmania) adult anchovy appear to
migrate from coastal waters into bays and
inlets during spring prior to their summer
spawning.[4] Spawning occurs there when
salinities exceed 15 parts per thousand.[5]
The main spawning period in southern
Australia is from October to April with
peak activity in January.[4,6,7] Spawning
occurs earlier in northern populations.[4]

Anchovy eggs are ellipsoid[3] and
buoyant. Eggs and larvae are abundant in
the summer plankton layer in the
Gippsland Lakes[6] and Port Phillip Bay.[7]
Larval and juvenile anchovy inhabit bays,
inlets and brackish estuaries.[3,4] Mature,
older fish (2 years old or more) move into
open coastal waters in winter and back
inshore in spring, although some adults
remain in bays and inlets during winter.[3,4]

Both male and female anchovy mature
when 1-year-old at a total length of
6–7 cm.[4] In southern Australian waters,
anchovy exhibit a seasonal growth
pattern with faster growth in spring and
summer. They reach an average total
length of 6–7 cm at 1 year, 7.5–8 cm at 2
years and 8.5–9 cm after 3 years.[4]
Anchovy probably live for at least 6
years,[8] growing to a maximum length of
15.7 cm.[4]

Anchovy feed on zooplankton,
particularly copepods.[3] They are preyed
upon by large fish, dolphins
(Delphinidae) and many birds. Anchovy
also form an important component of the
diet of little penguins (*Eudyptula minor*)
in Victorian waters.

Stock structure

Early studies[4] using verterbral counts
suggested the existence of at least 3
different breeding populations of
anchovy in Australia. The distribution of
the 3 subspecies is: Queensland and New
South Wales north of Twofold Bay;
southern New South Wales, Victoria,
Tasmania and South Australia; and
Western Australia. No subsequent studies
have been performed.

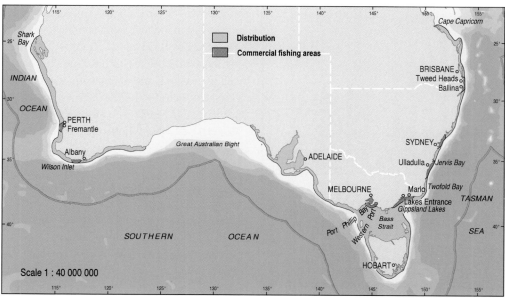

Geographic distribution and commercial fishing areas for anchovy in Australian waters.

Commercial fishery

Since about 1910 anchovy have been caught for bait in Port Phillip Bay,[4] mainly using hoop nets.[3] Catches increased in the 1950s with the popularity of haul seine and purse seine nets and the establishment of fish paste processing plants nearby. Purse seine catches of anchovy in Bass Strait waters grew substantially in the late 1960s following the establishment of a processing plant at Lakes Entrance, but declined in the late 1970s and early 1980s and ceased following the closure of the plant in 1985.

Anchovy are now caught commercially in New South Wales, Victoria and Western Australia. In New South Wales they are fished from Tweed Heads to Ballina, Sydney Harbour and Jervis Bay. In Victoria they are taken from bays, inlets and coastal waters between Lakes Entrance and Marlo,[5] in the Gippsland Lakes, Port Phillip Bay and Bass Strait. Most fishing effort centres on Port Phillip Bay.[8] In Western Australia there are small fisheries at Wilson Inlet and Fremantle. Anchovy are also harvested occasionally in inshore Tasmanian waters by tuna and rock lobster fishers for use as live bait.

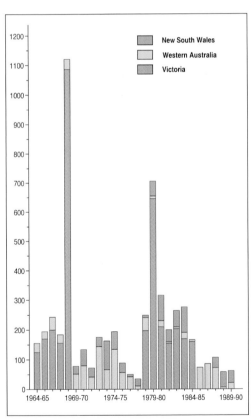

Total annual catch in t of anchovy for the period 1964–65 to 1989–90. Figures are unavailable for: New South Wales from 1964–65 to 1968–69 and 1984–85 to 1986–87; and Victoria from 1969–70 to 1977–78 and 1985–86 to 1989–90. Catches for States that average less than 5% of the total for all States are not shown. (Source: Fisheries Resources Atlas Statistical Database)

Hauling a purse seine net at night. (Source: Rick Fletcher, Western Australian Marine Research Laboratories, Fisheries Department of Western Australia)

Anchovy are caught primarily by purse seining in Port Phillip Bay, Bass Strait and off Fremantle. Haul seines are used in the Gippsland Lakes and at Wilson Inlet. Haul seines and hoop nets are also used in Port Phillip Bay. Anchovy can be fished all year with catches fluctuating depending on the availability of fish, market conditions and the attractiveness of other types of fishing. Most catches are made from March to September.[6] Adult fish are targeted and catches sometimes contain small fish such as sprats (eg *Spratelloides robustus*) and pilchards (*Sardinops neopilchardus*).

Most anchovy are sold either locally or interstate as bait fish although there is a small market for human consumption. Anchovy caught in Victoria are mostly sold whole and salted. Anchovy flesh is soft and oily and salting helps make it firmer. In 1992 Victorian wholesale prices for anchovy ranged from A$ 1.00 to A$ 1.60 per kg. In Western Australia most anchovy are now processed (canned and fish paste) for human consumption.

Management controls In New South Wales, regulations cover the size and type of haul nets and purse seine nets that may be used. In Victoria, anchovy are managed as part of the limited entry, multi-species fishery in bays and inlets. There are also restrictions on the use of haul seine nets as well as seasonal and area closures in these areas. No Victorian regulations are specific to anchovy. A similar situation exists in Western Australia, where anchovy are taken in a limited entry, multi-species fishery.

Recreational fishery

There is no recreational fishery for anchovy in Australia, but recreational fishers purchase large amounts of commercially caught anchovy for bait, and some may catch small quantities of fresh anchovy for the same purpose.

Resource status

The status of the eastern Australian anchovy resource is unknown, although the Victorian resource is thought to be underutilised in coastal waters. Western Australian stocks do not appear to be as large as those in Victoria.

References

1. Last, P.R., Scott, E.O.G. and Talbot, F.H. (1983) *Fishes of Tasmania*. Hobart: Tasmanian Fisheries Development Authority. 563 pp.

2. Hutchins, B. and Swainston R. (1986) *Sea fishes of southern Australia. Complete field guide for anglers and divers*. Perth: Swainston Publishing. 180 pp.

3. Whitehead, P.J.P., Nelson, G.J., and Wongratana, T. (1988) FAO species catalogue. Vol 7. Clupeoid fishes of the world (Suborder Clupeoidei). An annotated and illustrated catalogue of the herrings, sardines, pilchards, sprats, shads, anchovies and wolf herrings. Part 2 — Engraulididae. *FAO Fisheries Synopsis No. 125*, **7** (2): 305–509.

4. Blackburn, M. (1950) A biological study of the anchovy, *Engraulis australis* (White) in Australian waters. *Australian Journal of Marine and Freshwater Research* **1**: 3–84.

5. Parry, G.D., Campbell, S.J. and Hobday, D.K. (1990) Marine resources off east Gippsland, southeastern Australia. *Victorian Department of Conservation and Environment, Fisheries Division, Technical Report* **72**. 166 pp.

6. Arnott, G.H. and McKinnon, A.D. (1985) Distribution and abundance of eggs of the anchovy *Engraulis australis antipodum* Günther, in relation to temperature and salinity in the Gippsland Lakes. *Australian Journal of Marine and Freshwater Research* **36**: 433–439.

7. Jenkins, G.P. (1986) Composition, seasonality and distribution of ichthyoplankton in Port Phillip Bay, Victoria. *Australian Journal of Marine and Freshwater Research* **37**: 507–520.

8. Hall, D.N. and MacDonald, C.M. (1986) Commercial fishery situation report: net and line fisheries of Port Phillip Bay, Victoria, 1914–1984. *Victorian Department of Conservation, Forests and Lands, Fisheries Division, Marine Fisheries Report* **10**. 120 pp.

Contributors

Information on this species was originally provided by Murray MacDonald and supplemented by Rick Fletcher. Drawing courtesy of FAO, Rome; redrawn by Julie Easton. (*Details of contributors and their organisations are given in the Acknowledgements section at the back of this book.*)
Compilers Alex McNee and Christina Grieve (maps)

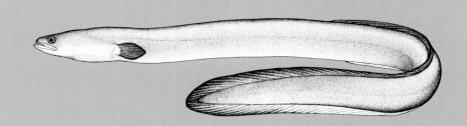

Distribution

Shortfin eels are present in coastal streams and tributaries from Pine River in south-eastern Queensland to the Murray River in South Australia, including Flinders Island in Bass Strait and all of Tasmania except for the central western plateau.[1] They also occur around Norfolk Island and New Zealand and may inhabit streams of Fiji and Tahiti. Longfin eels inhabit coastal streams and tributaries from the Jardine River, Cape York, to Wilsons Promontory in Victoria[2] as well

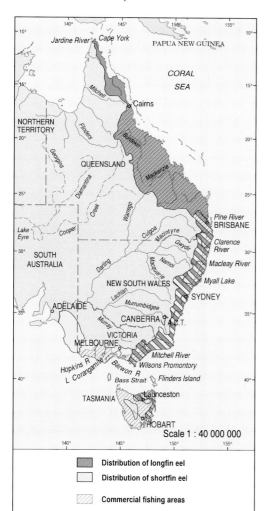

Geographic distribution and commercial fishing areas for longfin eel and shortfin eel in Australian waters.

Freshwater eels

This presentation is on 2 species, **shortfin eels** and **longfin eels**.

Shortfin eel, *Anguilla australis* Richardson

Other common names include **short-finned eel** and **silver eel**.
FAO: **short finned eel**
Australian species code: 056001

Longfin eel, *Anguilla reinhardtii* Steindachner

Other common names include **long-finned eel**, **spotted eel** and **conger eel**.
FAO: no known name
Australian species code: 056002

Family ANGUILLIDAE

Diagnostic features Shortfin eels (pictured) are a uniform golden-olive to olive-green on the back and sides with a greyish to silvery-white belly, with fins similar in colour to the back. Longfin eels are olive-green to brown and paler on the belly, with darker blotches or mottling on the upper body. Their pectoral fins are yellowish and other fins are dark brown. Shortfin eels have a dorsal fin which originates only slightly forward of the anal fin while in longfin eels the dorsal fin commences well forward of the anal fin.

as northern and eastern Tasmania. They also live in New Caledonian waters. The abundance of longfin eels is greatest in Queensland and New South Wales while shortfin eels are most common in Victoria and Tasmania.[3] Both species are present on Lord Howe Island.

Freshwater eels are diadromous, ie they move from marine to fresh waters as juveniles and return to the sea as adults. These eels live in a variety of freshwater and estuarine environments including coastal lagoons, rivers, creeks, swamps, lakes and farm dams.[2] Longfin eels prefer riverine habitats while shortfin eels are more likely to inhabit slow flowing streams or still waters.[4]

Life history

Freshwater eels probably spawn in Coral Sea waters deeper than 300 m, although the exact location of spawning grounds remains unknown. Estimates of age for freshwater eel larvae indicate that the 2 species spawn at different times.[3] Females of both species produce between 5 and 10 million pelagic eggs. Within 2–10 days the eggs hatch into pelagic larvae called 'leptocephali'.[5] The leptocephali are carried by ocean currents to the continental shelf where they develop into 'glass eels' — toothless, unpigmented forms which move into estuaries with the assistance of currents and tides. Glass eels of shortfin eels move into estuaries between late autumn and spring, and glass eels of longfin eels enter estuaries mainly in summer and autumn. The difference in migration period seems to reflect differing peaks in rainfall and river flow within each species' distribution.[3]

The larval period probably lasts from 12 to 18 months after which glass eels develop pigmentation and functional teeth and are called 'elvers'.[2] A second migration is evident when glass eels and elvers move from the estuaries into lakes, swamps and the freshwater reaches of rivers and creeks. This migration takes place during spring and summer, and movement occurs mainly at night. A

A catch of freshwater eels in a fyke net. (Source: Des Harrington, Fisheries Division, Victorian Department of Conservation and Environment)

Transferring undersized eels to an impoundment for extensive culture. (Source: Des Harrington, Fisheries Division, Victorian Department of Conservation and Environment)

number of age classes may be involved in this mass migration, with the age of elvers increasing with distance from the sea.[6] Some elvers remain in estuaries and the lower reaches of rivers and tend to develop into males, while most eels inhabiting fresh water mature as females.[2] Following the second migration freshwater eels enter a sedentary feeding stage when they are known as 'brown eels' or 'yellow eels'.[5]

As freshwater eels reach maturity they move downstream to the entrances of rivers and creeks prior to commencing their spawning migration. A number of changes occur in the eels as they mature. The dorsal surface becomes grey-green and the belly silvery-white, the pectoral fins and eyes enlarge, the lateral line becomes prominent and the skin thickens. Internally, the gonads enlarge, the stomach degenerates and the anus constricts to reduce water loss. Mature eels are referred to as 'silver eels' and do not feed.[5] The age at which eels mature may vary considerably and estimates of ages for migrating silver eels are from 8 to 12 years for males and from 10 to 30 years for females.[5,7] Silver eels leave the estuaries from late summer to autumn. Some eels swim distances greater than 3000 km before reaching the Coral Sea spawning grounds. The mature eels probably all die following spawning.[5]

Growth rates of freshwater eels vary depending on habitat, population density and food availability.[5] Eels from still waters display more rapid growth than do those from running waters. Females of both species grow faster than males. The oldest estimated age is 32 years for a shortfin eel and 41 years for a longfin eel.[8] Male shortfin eels have been recorded up to 54 cm total length and females to 106.5 cm. Female longfin eels reach 158 cm.[2] There are no records of maximum size in male longfin eels.

Freshwater eels are mainly nocturnal feeders and they have a well developed sense of smell for locating prey. The diets of shortfin eels and longfin eels are very similar and include crustaceans, molluscs and aquatic and terrestrial insects.[9] Large eels of both species also prey upon fish such as native trout (*Galaxias* species) and commonly feed upon shortfin or longfin elvers.[8,9]

Stock structure

Both species of freshwater eels in Australian waters probably consist of single stocks.

Commercial fishery

The main Australian freshwater eel fishery is located in Victoria where eels have been caught commercially since 1914.[2] The annual Victorian catch has averaged 225 t since 1976 with shortfin eels comprising 95 % of the total. Most of the catch is taken during spring and early summer from waters west of Melbourne, particularly in the Hopkins River, Barwon River and Lake Corangamite basins.[2] Smaller catches are taken from central and eastern Victoria. Eels in Victoria are caught almost exclusively using fyke nets. Aluminium dinghies with outboard motors are used to set up to 50 nets per licensed holder.[2]

The Tasmanian eel fishery has operated since 1965–66 with catches in most years ranging between 20 t and 40 t. Shortfin eels account for 97 % of the Tasmanian catch, caught between October and March.[10] The catch is taken mainly from coastal lagoons and farm dams with fyke nets. Fyke nets are prohibited from most streams and lakes because they take a high bycatch of trout (Salmonidae). Traps are used in some

rivers, including weir-type traps to harvest migrating silver eels.

Longfin eels are the main species caught in the New South Wales and Queensland eel fisheries. The New South Wales annual catch has averaged just over 100 t during the 3 years up to June 1990, with 60 % of the eels being caught from the Clarence River, Macleay River and the Myall Lakes. Traps, including weir-type traps, are used to catch eels in tributaries, flood drains and swamps but are excluded from main river courses in New South Wales.

In Queensland the recorded annual catch is approximately 35 t. Fishing is restricted to impoundments, located between Cairns and the New South Wales border. Only 1 operator is allowed to fish each impoundment using traps baited with mullet (Mugilidae) or other oily fish. The traps consist of trawl mesh hung over a frame forming a single funnel leading to a bag. Fyke nets are prohibited in Queensland due to their bycatch of recreational species.

Most of the Australian eel catch is destined for export markets, with 290 t exported in 1988–89. The shortfin eel

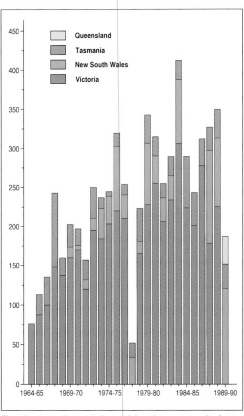

Total annual catch in t of freshwater eels for the period 1964–65 to 1989–90. Figures are unavailable for: New South Wales from 1984–85 to 1986–87; Victoria for 1977–78 and 1989–90; and Queensland from 1964–65 to 1988–89. The Victorian catch figures include aquacultured product. (Source: Fisheries Resources Atlas Statistical Database)

catch is purged in fresh water, eviscerated and snap frozen for export, mainly to Germany.[2] Longfin eels are exported live or chilled to Hong Kong and Taiwan, or frozen for the French market. 'Free on board' export prices for shortfin eels in 1991–92 varied between A$ 3.00 and A$ 10.00 per kg; and live longfin eels obtained up to A$ 18.00 per kg on the Asian markets. In 1991–92, exported product was valued at approximately A$ 2 million free on board. A small proportion of both species is smoked and sold on the domestic market.

Management controls Regulations implemented by each State fisheries body limit the number of licences or permits issued, number of traps or nets used and the manner of their use. There are also restrictions on the bycatch species which may be retained in each State. Minimum legal sizes apply in Queensland, Victoria and Tasmania.

Aquaculture

Shortfin eels are farmed using 'extensive' culture techniques in Victoria and Tasmania.[11] In Victoria, Japanese glass eel nets are used to capture shortfin elvers which are then transferred to natural closed water bodies such as freshwater lakes and swamps.[2] Some undersized brown eels are also released into these water bodies. The eels are harvested using fyke nets when they reach a marketable size. Eight lakes, with an area of 5500 ha, are used for extensive culture of eels in Victoria. They are all located west of Melbourne and produce about 25 % of the catch in that State.[2]

Extensive culture of shortfin eels is also conducted in northern Tasmania. About 30 t were produced by culture there during 1988–89.[11] Some Tasmanian fishers are licensed to trap elvers for stocking of Tasmanian and Victorian lakes.

Cultured shortfin eels are handled and marketed by the same methods as in the commercial fishery.

Longfin eels are not cultured on a commercial basis at present, but a number of pilot projects are under way.

Management controls Permits are required in Victoria and Tasmania for culture of freshwater eels in public and private waters. Licences or permits are

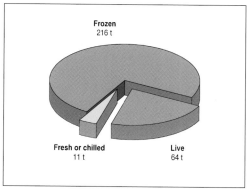

Breakdown of freshwater eel exports for 1988–89 by product type. Values are in t product weight. (Source: Australian Bureau of Statistics; Australian Bureau of Agricultural and Resource Economics)

also required by fishers who retain undersized eels for stocking in approved water bodies.

Recreational fishery

Freshwater eels are commonly caught by anglers when line fishing for other species in estuaries or freshwaters.[4] They can be targeted by using introduced garden snails (Helicidae) as bait.[5] The Australian Anglers Association record for freshwater eel is a longfin eel of 8.9 kg caught in northern New South Wales.

Management controls Minimum legal sizes apply in Queensland, Victoria and Tasmania.

Resource status

The shortfin eel resource in Tasmania and Victoria will not support heavier fishing pressure and any increase in production is likely to come from expansion of culture operations.[2] The longfin eel catch in Queensland is probably below sustainable levels but the expansion of that fishery is dependent on regulations aimed at protecting other valuable commercial and recreational fish species. There is no information on the status of New South Wales eel resources.

References

1. Sloane, R.D. (1984) Distribution and abundance of freshwater eels (*Anguilla* spp.) in Tasmania. *Australian Journal of Marine and Freshwater Research* **35**: 463–470.

2. Hall, D.N., Harrington, D.J. and Fairbrother, P.S. (1990) The commercial eel fishery in Victoria. *Victorian Department of Conservation and Environment, Arthur Rylah Institute for Environmental Research, Technical Report* **100**. 41 pp.

3. Beumer, J. and Sloane, R. (1990) Distribution and abundance of glass-eels *Anguilla* spp. in east Australian waters. *International Revue der Gesamten Hydrobiologie* **75**: 721–736

4. McDowall, R.M. and Beumer, J.P. (1980) Family Anguillidae: freshwater eels. Pp 44–47, in *Freshwater fishes of south-eastern Australia*. Ed by R.M. McDowall. Sydney: A.H. & A.W. Reed Pty Ltd.

5. Beumer, J. (1987) Eels: biology and control. *Queensland Department of Primary Industries, Leaflet Series* **QL87018**. 4 pp.

6. Sloane, R.D. (1984) Upstream migration by young pigmented eels (*Anguilla australis australis* Richardson) in Tasmania. *Australian Journal of Marine and Freshwater Research* **35**: 61–73.

7. Sloane, R.D. (1984) Preliminary observations of migrating adult freshwater eels (*Anguilla australis australis* Richardson) in Tasmania. *Australian Journal of Marine and Freshwater Research* **35**: 471–476.

8. Sloane, R.D. (1984) Distribution, abundance, growth and food of freshwater eels (*Anguilla* spp.) in the Douglas River, Tasmania. *Australian Journal of Marine and Freshwater Research* **35**: 325–339.

9. Beumer, J.P. (1979) Feeding and movement of *Anguilla australis* and *A. reinhardtii* in Macleods Morass, Victoria, Australia. *Journal of Fish Biology* **14**: 573–592

10. Sloane, R.D. (1982) The Tasmanian eel fishery — some facts and figures. *Australian Fisheries* **41**(12): 14–17.

11. O'Sullivan, D. (1990) *Aquaculture downunder. Status & prospects for Australian aquaculture (1989–90)*. Tasmania: Dosaqua. 66 pp.

Contributors

Information on this species was originally provided by (in alphabetical order) John Beumer, Doug Hall, Des Harrington, Allan Kaufmann, Viv Spencer and John Virgona. Drawing by Jeffrey Davies. (*Details of contributors and their organisations are given in the Acknowledgements section at the back of this book.*)

Compiler Phillip Stewart

Trout and salmon

Salmo species and *Oncorhynchus mykiss*

Trout and salmon

This presentation is on 3 species, **brown trout**, **rainbow trout**, and **Atlantic salmon**.

Brown trout, *Salmo trutta* Linnaeus

Other common names include **trout** and **sea trout**.
FAO: **sea trout**
Australian species code: 094004

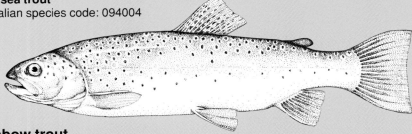

Rainbow trout, *Oncorhynchus mykiss* (Walbaum)

Another common name is **steelhead**.
FAO: **rainbow trout**
Australian species code: 094003

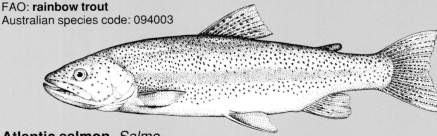

Atlantic salmon, *Salmo salar* Linnaeus

There are no other common names.
FAO: **Atlantic salmon**
Australian species codes: 094001

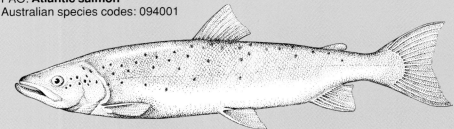

Family SALMONIDAE

Diagnostic features Brown trout are thick bodied, with a large head and mouth. Their eyes are moderate to large. Their dorsal fin has 12–14 rays and the caudal fin is almost truncate. Body colour is variable: sea run fish are generally silvery and have a darker olive back, with indistinct dark spots; and freshwater fish are silvery but darker, their back is dark brown to olive, and the spots are distinct, well-separated and darker brown. They have a plain caudal fin. Rainbow trout have a more compressed body than brown trout, with a moderate size head and eyes. Their dorsal fin has 10–12 rays, and the tail is slightly forked.

Body colour is variable, being predominantly silvery with a darker, greenish olive or steel blue back. They have many small, dark, round spots on the back and upper sides, and also on the caudal fin. They often have a pink stripe along the sides on their gill covers. Atlantic salmon very closely resemble brown trout, and the 2 are often difficult to tell apart. Atlantic salmon have a forked tail, a small mouth not extending past the eyes, and their body scales are small. Their back is blue to silvery blue, to brownish olive. Their sides are silvery, their belly silvery white[1] and they have small dark spots on the back and sides.[2]

Distribution

Brown trout are native to waters in Europe, Iceland and Western Asia. Rainbow trout are naturally distributed in the Pacific coastal drainages of North America from Alaska to Mexico.[3] The first successful introduction of trout into Australia occurred in 1864 when brown trout ova (eggs) were brought to Tasmania from England. A breeding program commenced and by 1872 eggs and fry raised in Tasmania were being sent to New South Wales, Victoria and New Zealand.[4]

Trout were introduced to Australian inland waters, primarily for their sporting value. They are cool water (4–19°C) species, restricted mainly to alpine and sub-alpine waters. Self maintaining populations of brown and rainbow trout occur in the higher altitude waters of New South Wales, Victoria and Tasmania. Populations are maintained by stocking in warmer rivers and reservoirs throughout New South Wales and Victoria. Cooler waters in Tasmania mean that trout are common down to sea level.[1] Trout populations are also present in rivers and reservoirs around Adelaide in South Australia and in the south-west of Western Australia. Populations in Western Australia are largely maintained by continued stocking as there is an absence of suitable natural spawning sites. There are also isolated populations of sea run trout in Tasmanian and Victorian streams.

Atlantic salmon are native to cool to cold waters flowing into the North Atlantic Ocean.[1] Atlantic salmon eggs were included with the trout eggs in the 1864 shipment but their introduction into Victoria, Tasmania and New South Wales was not successful as the fry liberated into rivers migrated to the sea and as adults failed to return to the rivers. Atlantic salmon were again imported to New

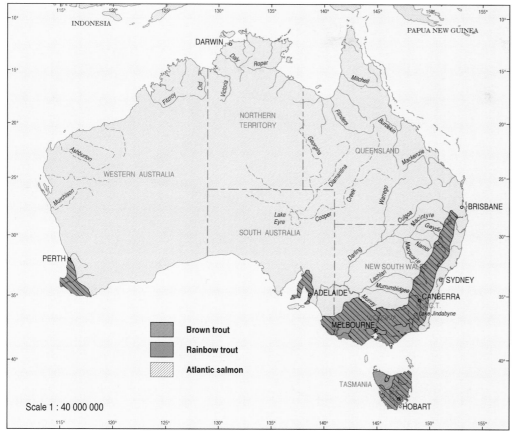

Geographic distribution of brown trout, rainbow trout and Atlantic salmon in Australian waters.

South Wales in 1963, and they have been reintroduced recently to Tasmania as part of commercial aquaculture operations. Currently there are populations in Tasmania and Lake Jindabyne in New South Wales.

All 3 species require moderate to fast flowing, well oxygenated waters for breeding, but they also live in cold lakes. Rainbow trout survive better in lakes than in streams,[1] while brown trout are hardier, and usually predominate in streams.[5]

Life history

The general life history characteristics are similar for all 3 species. Trout and salmon are characterised by their annual spawning runs. In Europe and North America salmon spend most of their lives at sea, but migrate back to freshwater to spawn. Brown trout and rainbow trout also have sea dwelling populations known as 'sea trout' and 'steelhead', respectively. Sea trout occur in Tasmania. Land-locked populations of trout in Australia still undergo spawning migrations. Lake populations migrate into feeder streams, while riverine populations often move upstream to shallow waters to spawn. There is little evidence of natural spawning by land-locked populations of

Atlantic salmon in Australia, and populations are maintained by stocking.[1]

Brown trout spawn from early April to July,[6,7] whereas rainbow trout spawn from August to October or early November.[5,6] Brown trout migrate at water temperatures from 6° to 10°C generally under all flow conditions, while rainbow trout migrate at water temperatures of 5° to 11°C, generally under high flow conditions.[6] Homing behaviour has been recorded in spawning brown trout.[7] There is no information on spawning in the wild for Atlantic salmon in Australian waters.

Spawning occurs in clear, flowing waters, usually less than 30 cm deep, over clean gravel. Fertilised eggs are deposited in a depression in the gravel made by the female.[7] Brown trout have large, orange eggs, 4–5 mm in diameter. Hatching of the eggs is temperature dependent, varying from 21 weeks at 2°C to 4 weeks at 12°C.[8] Rainbow trout eggs are smaller, 3–5 mm in diameter. Development is more rapid in rainbow trout, the eggs hatching within 4–7 weeks.[8]

Larval brown trout are 12 mm long at hatching.[9] They remain in the gravel for 2–3 weeks until they are about 25 mm long, when they emerge to begin feeding in the water column.[8] Larval rainbow trout become free swimming fry after 3–7

days.[5] Initially they remain near the bottom, rising into the water column to feed. Brown trout are territorial and begin establishing territories as juveniles.[8] Juvenile trout from lake populations move from their natal inlets to lakes during the first 2 years of life.

Brown trout can live for up to 12 years,[5] growing to a fork length of 140 cm and a weight more than 20 kg. Fish from Australian populations tend to be smaller, growing to about 90 cm fork length and 14 kg.[1] Rainbow trout live for about 8 years,[5] growing to 110 cm in length and 18 kg. Again fish from Australian populations are smaller, growing to 90 cm and 8 kg.[1] In Australia, it is rare for brown trout to survive beyond 9 years, and rainbow trout beyond 5 years. Atlantic salmon grow to 150 cm fork length, weighing up to 38 kg. Fish from Australian populations are much smaller, rarely over 2 to 3 kg in weight.[1] Growth rates of trout and salmon vary with environmental conditions. Growth is optimal at water temperatures between 7° and 17°C, and Australian populations of trout and salmon may grow more rapidly than those in the northern hemisphere due to a longer growing season here.[10]

The average age at maturity for male brown and rainbow trout is 2 to 3 years old. Female brown and rainbow trout usually mature at 3 years of age.[5]

Young brown trout feed on a variety of small invertebrates, such as insects, molluscs and crustaceans, while young rainbow trout feed predominantly on zooplankton.[5] Adults of both species usually consume similar food, which includes both aquatic and terrestrial insects, molluscs, crustaceans and small fish.[5]

Stock structure

Because of their history of introduction into Australia, rainbow trout and Atlantic salmon can genetically be considered as single stocks. However, more than one variety of brown trout has been introduced, and their genetic status is unclear.

Commercial fishery

There is no commercial fishery for wild stocks of trout or Atlantic salmon in Australian waters.

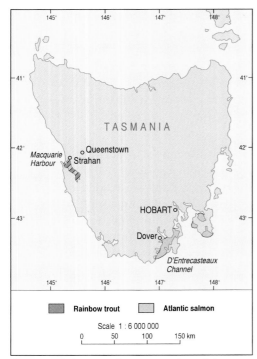

Commercial aquaculture areas for rainbow trout and Atlantic salmon in Australian waters.

Traps for collecting trout fry. (Source: Australian Fisheries Management Authority)

Aquaculture

Only rainbow trout and Atlantic salmon are cultured commercially in Australia, although brown trout fry and fingerlings are produced by hatcheries for stocking. There are trout farms in New South Wales, Victoria, Tasmania, South Australia and Western Australia, most producing 'pan' sized (250 g to 300 g) fish in freshwater.[11] Many farms and some State governments operate hatcheries.[1]

Some trout farms also operate 'fish-out' ponds as well as producing pan sized fish for sale to restaurants and markets. These ponds are stocked with fish 200–250 g in size, and then opened to the public. Fishing tackle is provided and anglers are guaranteed a catch that is sold to them at a set price per kg.[12]

The 2 most common designs of systems for cultured production of trout in freshwater are raceways and circular ponds. Circular ponds create more uniform flow and water quality conditions than do raceways, causing the fish to be distributed more evenly within each pond.[13] Trout in freshwater systems grow to marketable size in 10–18 months after stocking into grow-out ponds.[14]

Commercial culture of Atlantic salmon is carried out only in Tasmania, where sea cage farming of Atlantic salmon and rainbow trout has become a major part of the aquaculture industry. In 1991–92 over 3400 t were produced, valued at over A$ 40 million. Young rainbow trout and Atlantic salmon are reared in freshwater hatcheries until they weigh between 70 and 100 g. They are gradually acclimatised to salt water over a period of 5 to 7 days, before being transferred to floating, net sea cages in coastal bays for continued growing.[11] In Tasmania, Atlantic salmon and rainbow trout are raised in bays along the south and east coasts and at Macquarie Harbour on the west coast.

For sea cage culture stocking rates vary according to fish size.[15] Artificial feeds containing up to 50 % fish meal are used in all trout and salmon farming. Major problems can occur with sea cage culture if there is inadequate water movement or overstocking. Build-ups of accumulated waste (both animal and unused food) under cages can increase the risk of disease outbreak.

The value of trout and salmon products varies widely. Atlantic salmon is the highest value product, in 1992 selling for A$ 11.00 to A$ 16.00 per kg of whole fish. At the same time ocean trout were worth around A$ 10.00 per kg, while freshwater trout were sold for A$ 5.00 per kg.[11] Trout and Atlantic salmon are sold as whole fish, chilled and gutted, or in a variety of processed forms including whole smoked, cutlets, fillets and pâté. Approximately 60 % of the Atlantic salmon produced in Tasmania is exported to South-east Asia, principally Japan. The Australian industry has the advantage of being able to supply fresh fish outside of the northern hemisphere growing season. Furthermore, there is an increasing demand for trout eggs from Australian hatcheries due to the high quality, disease free nature of these stocks.[12]

Management controls All fish farms are licensed under relevant State legislation that controls farm operations even including water supply and discharge. To maintain the disease free status of Australian trout and salmon products, there is a total ban on imports of trout and salmon products, other than those canned

Harvesting Atlantic salmon from sea cages in Tasmania. (Source: Australian Department of Foreign Affairs and Trade)

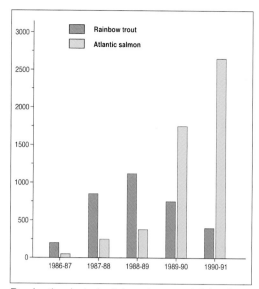

Production in t of rainbow trout and Atlantic salmon in Tasmania for the period 1986–87 to 1990–91. (Source: Tasmanian Salmonid Growers Association)

or hot smoked. However, this ban is constantly being challenged by foreign exporters.

Recreational fishery

Trout were introduced to Australia for their sporting qualities. They have been released into rivers, lakes and impoundments throughout southern Australia. Many populations are self reproducing but others are maintained in marginal waters by continued stocking (eg many Western Australian rivers). The rivers and lakes of alpine and sub-alpine areas of New South Wales, Victoria and Tasmania are the major centres for recreational trout fishing.

Recreational fisher with a 7 kg brown trout, Tasmania. (Source: Bureau of Resource Sciences)

Trout are taken primarily on rod-and-line using bait, lures or flies. The method used varies, depending on the angler and the waters. Both trout species are considered excellent angling fish, with larger adults being targeted. The Australian Anglers Association records are an 8 kg rainbow trout and a 12.7 kg brown trout, both from Tasmania; but larger fish have been unofficially recorded.

Management controls All States where trout occur impose minimum legal sizes on fish caught by anglers, and bag limits apply except in Victoria. There are closed seasons to protect breeding fish in New South Wales, Tasmania, and Western Australia. Amateur licences are required by anglers in Tasmania and Victoria.

Resource status

Both brown trout and rainbow trout have established breeding populations in many rivers, lakes and impoundments in Australia. Stocking of waterways is still carried out by many State fisheries agencies. Freshwater angling is a major recreational industry, and trout are the species most sought after. The major threats to trout fisheries come from habitat loss and degradation through pollution, siltation, and water extraction.

Notes

The success of trout in Australian waters is largely attributable to the similarity of Australian and ancestral habitats, and the absence of large, coldwater predatory native fish.[10] However, trout are thought to have displaced native trout (*Galaxias* species) from many waters.[16]

Two other species, brook trout (*Salvelinus fontinalis*) and chinook salmon (*Oncorhynchus tshawytscha*), have also been introduced to Australia but neither has established populations as successfully as have brown trout and rainbow trout. A wild population of brook trout is established in a lake in Western Tasmania.[2] Releases of these 2 species are regularly made in that State, New South Wales and South Australia.

References

1. McDowall, R.M., and Tilzey, R.D.J. (1980) Family Salmonidae, salmons, trouts and chars. Pp 72–78, in *Freshwater fishes of south-eastern Australia.* Ed by R.M. McDowall. Sydney: A.H. & A.W. Reed Pty Ltd.

2. Fulton, W. (1990) *Tasmanian freshwater fishes.* Tasmania: Fauna of Tasmania Committee. 80 pp.

3. French, G. (1987) *Trout fishing in Tasmania.* Tasmania: Mercury Walsh. 242 pp.

4. Walker, J. (1988) *Origins of the Tasmanian trout.* Tasmania: Inland Fisheries Commission. 48 pp.

5. Cadwallader, P.L. and Backhouse, G.N. (1983) *A guide to the freshwater fish of Victoria.* Melbourne: Government Printers. 249 pp.

6. Davies, P.E. and Sloane, R.D. (1987) Characteristics of the spawning migrations of brown trout, *Salmo trutta* L., and rainbow trout, *S. gairdneri* Richardson, in Great Lake, Tasmania. *Journal of Fish Biology* **31**: 353–373.

7. Tilzey, R.D.J. (1977) Repeat homing of brown trout (*Salmo trutta*) in Lake Eucumbene, New South Wales, Australia. *Journal of Fisheries Research Bulletin Canada* **34**(8): 1085–1094.

8. Frost, W.E. and Brown, M.E. (1967) *The trout.* London: Collins. 286 pp.

9. Farragher, R.A. (1986) Trout in New South Wales. *Department of Agriculture,* New South Wales, *Agfact* **F3.2.1.**: 8 pp.

10. Tilzey, R.D.J. (1977) Key factors in the establishment and success of trout in Australia. Pp 97–105, in *Exotic species in Australia — their establishment and success.* Ed by D. Anderson. *Proceedings of the Ecological Society of Australia* **10**.

11. O'Sullivan, D. (1991) Status of Australian aquaculture in 1989/90. *Austasia Aquaculture, 1991 (June)*: 2–13.

12. McGlennon, D. (1988) Trout farming in South Australia. *SAFISH* **13**(12): 13–15.

13. Morrissy, N.M. and Cassells, G. (1985) A guide for trout farming in Western Australia. *Western Australian Fisheries Information Publication* **5**. 21 pp.

14. O'Sullivan, D. (1991) Year-round production key to trout farm's success. *Austasia Aquaculture* **5**(10): 3–6.

15. Hortle, M. (1981) *Sea water culture of rainbow trout.* Tasmania: Tasmanian Fisheries Development Authority. 47 pp.

16. Fletcher, A.R. (1986) Effects of introduced fish in Australia. Pp 231–238, in *Limnology in Australia.* Ed by P. De Dekker and W.D. Williams. Melbourne: CSIRO Australia.

Contributors

The information on this species was originally provided by (in alphabetical order) Peter Davies, Simon Stanley and Richard Tilzey. Drawings courtesy of Wayne Fulton. (*Details of contributors and their organisations are given in the Acknowledgements section at the back of this book.*)
Compiler Alex McNee

Carp and goldfish

Cyprinus carpio and *Carassius auratus*

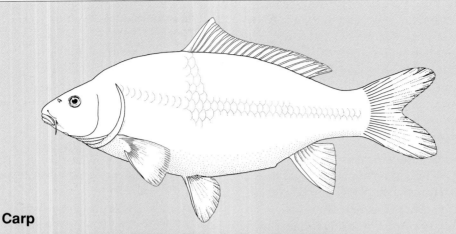

Carp

This presentation is on 2 species, **European carp** and **goldfish**.

European carp, *Cyprinus carpio* Linnaeus

Other common names include **carp**, **common carp**, **German carp** and **Asian carp**.
FAO: **common carp**
Australian species code: 165003

Goldfish, *Carassius auratus* (Linnaeus)

Other common names include **golden carp** or **native carp**.
FAO: **goldfish**
Australian species code: 165001

Family CYPRINIDAE

Diagnostic features European carp (pictured) have a small mouth with no teeth and 1 pair of barbels at each corner of the mouth. The body scales are large and there are 33–40 lateral line scales. The dorsal fin is long with 3 or 4 spines and 15 to 24 rays. There is a serrated spine on the anal fin. Usually carp are olive green to golden along the back with paler sides and a brassy or silvery yellow belly.[1,2] Colour variations are quite common in wild populations. Goldfish are a smaller, similar looking fish distinguished by an absence of barbels at the corners of the mouth.[1]

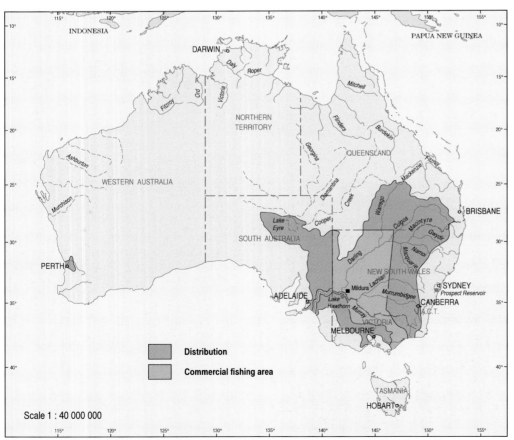

Distribution
Commercial fishing area

Scale 1 : 40 000 000

Geographic distribution and commercial fishing area for European carp in Australian waters.

Distribution

Both European carp and goldfish are introduced species and are now distributed throughout southern Australia. European carp are present from the Warrego River in Queensland south to the Murray River mouth including most rivers in the Murray–Darling basin. They are also found in several Victorian and South Australian coastal streams[3] and from Lake Frome in the arid region of South Australia. European carp were introduced into Tasmania in 1960 or 1961,[3] but have since been eradicated there. Goldfish inhabit rivers from as far north as the Fitzroy River in central Queensland,[4] throughout South Australia to the south-west of Western Australia.[1]

Both species are native to Asia. European carp are thought to have originated in central Asia, and goldfish originated in China and Japan. Both species have since been introduced throughout the world.

European carp and goldfish prefer warm waters in lakes and slow flowing rivers.[4] They usually live over soft, muddy river beds, in areas with soft submerged vegetation.[4] European carp are tolerant of a variety of environmental conditions including high salinities and low oxygen concentrations. They have been observed to gulp air at the surface of oxygen-depleted waters.[2]

Life history

European carp spawn from spring to late summer at water temperatures between 17° and 25°C, with a breeding group consisting of 1 female and 2–3 males. Large females may spawn more than once in a season. Spawning occurs in shallow water, less than 2 m deep, at the edges of lakes and rivers. A 0.9 kg female can produce 100 000 eggs while a 4–5 kg female can produce 1 million eggs. The eggs are demersal, up to 2 mm in diameter, and adhere to rocks, logs and aquatic plants.[1] Little is known of the biology of goldfish in the wild but spawning is thought to occur in spring and summer at water temperatures of about 15°C. Eggs are smaller than those of European carp and adhere to submerged aquatic plants.[5]

European carp hatch within 2–6 days at water temperatures of 18–30°C. The larvae sink to the bottom where they attach themselves to plants.[1] In a further 2–6 days they become free swimming and start feeding on zooplankton.

Growth rates in European carp vary with temperature and availability of food. Maximum growth rates recorded from Victorian waters are 1.5 mm per day.[6] In Australia, European carp are thought to live for 20 years, grow to 85 cm total length and weigh more than 15 kg. Males mature at 2–4 years of age when about 20 cm long. Females mature between 3 and 5 years of age at about 25 cm length. Goldfish reach a maximum size of about 20 cm length.[5] They are mature at 1 year of age.

European carp are active swimmers that can leap obstacles up to 1 m high and negotiate torrential flows.[1]

European carp feed on benthic invertebrates, insects and aquatic plants. They feed by 'roiling', ie straining material from the mud. They will also take aquatic plants and insects from the surface.[1] Goldfish feed on aquatic plants, detritus and aquatic insects.[6] Golden perch (*Macquaria ambigua*), Murray cod (*Maccullochella peelii*) and redfin (*Perca fluviatilis*) feed on small European carp, as do water rats (*Hydromys* species) and some water birds.

Stock structure

There are 3 distinct stocks (or strains) of European carp in Australia. They are thought to represent 3 separate introductions rather than derivatives of a single introduction.[7] The 'Prospect group' is confined to Prospect Reservoir near Sydney. The 'Yanco' (or 'Singapore') stock is confined to the waters of the Murrumbidgee Irrigation Area. The 'Boolarra' stock is distributed throughout the Murray–Darling drainage basin,[7] and dominates catches. There is no

information on the genetic status of wild goldfish in Australia.

Commercial fishery

European carp first appeared in commercial catches in inland fisheries in the early 1970s (catch records for carp before this date are thought to consist of a mixture of goldfish and European carp). In Victoria in 1971 special licences were issued to fishers for European carp in rivers normally closed to fishing. These fishers used electro-fishing gear, and were based at Echuca and Koondrook. They worked the rivers in the Murray River valley.[8] Low catches have seen electro-fishing activities cease there in recent years.[6] In the Gippsland Lakes, European carp are taken using electro-fishing gear, beach seines and gillnets. Catches for the State fluctuated widely between 1964–65 and 1983–84, peaking at 487 t in 1975–76 and 464 t in 1979–80. For the same period, 66 % of the European carp catch came from the Gippsland Lakes.

In the rivers of New South Wales and the Murray River in South Australia European carp and goldfish are taken in

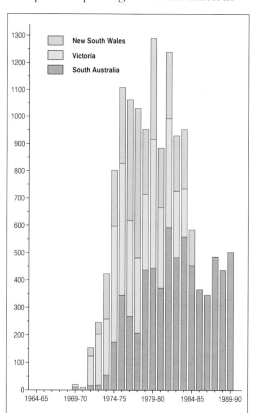

Total annual catch in t of European carp for the period 1964–65 to 1989–90. Figures are unavailable for: New South Wales from 1984–85 to 1989–90 and Victoria from 1985–86 to 1989–90. Catches for States that average less than 5 % of the total for all States are not shown. (Source: Fisheries Resources Atlas Statistical Database)

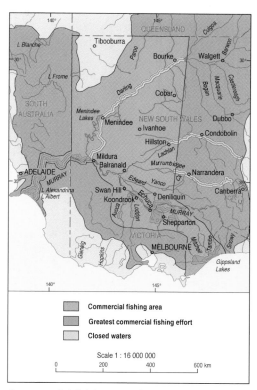

Commercial fishing area for European carp showing locations of greatest fishing effort and waters closed to commercial fishing.

drum nets. In Lake Albert and Lake Alexandrina in South Australia fishers use gillnets and electro-fishing gear.

Best quality fish larger than 1.5 kg are sold through the fresh fish markets of Melbourne, Sydney and Adelaide, with a small amount sold locally. The remainder are sold for use as bait in the rock lobster (*Jasus* species) fisheries in south-eastern Australia. Some used to be sold to pet food processors in Victoria. The average value to fishers of European carp sold in South Australia (for bait and human consumption) in 1991–92 was A$ 0.34 per kg, yet the average price at the Sydney markets in 1991–92 was A$ 1.10 per kg. Goldfish are not useful as a food and are of little commercial value.[1] They are taken as a bycatch of the European carp catch, and probably sold for rock lobster bait.

Management controls Individual State regulations set out the types and amount of gear that may be used. While there are no closures specific to European carp, in Victoria nets can only be used in those waters open to net fishing. Similarly there are no catch or size limits for European carp.

European carp have been declared noxious fish in most Australian States. Management is therefore directed towards eradication and restricting the spread of populations. Total eradication is impossible, but in an attempt to reduce

Biologists using hand held electro-fishing gear in a shallow river backwater, south-eastern Australia. (Source: Australian Fisheries Management Authority)

the species' spread there are prohibitions on its use as live bait, its return to the water and its transfer between States.

Recreational fishery

Traditionally not a popular angling species, European carp are now being targeted by an increasing number of anglers. They are said to provide good sport when hooked and due to their prolific spread they are often more available than more 'desirable' species. They are taken on rod-and-line and handlines from rivers and lakes throughout their range. The largest European carp recorded by the Australian Anglers Association is a 10.2 kg fish taken in New South Wales in 1988. Goldfish are of no sporting value.

Management controls It is illegal to return European carp to the water, so all catch must be retained. There are no bag or size limits or water closures specific to European carp in any State.

Resource status

European carp have been introduced to Australia several times in the last 150 years. The 'Prospect group' were introduced in the late 1850s.[6] It is only since the most recent introduction in 1959–60 that European carp have become widespread, establishing populations in

many areas within the Murray–Darling River system. Experience in the United States of America suggests that European carp will eventually find their way into all waters in which they are able to survive.[3]

European carp population numbers have declined since the peak levels in 1974–76, but the range of the species continues to expand. Large local concentrations still exist and there is a possibility that with several 'good' years population numbers could increase again.[9]

It is illegal to breed European carp for sale in Victoria[6] and South Australia. Because goldfish are important in the aquarium trade there are no restrictions on their importation (except into Tasmania) and breeding. It is unfortunate

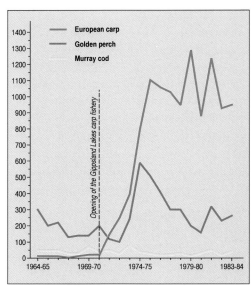

Comparison of the total Australian catch in t of European carp, golden perch and Murray cod for the period 1964–65 to 1983–84. (Source: Fisheries Resources Atlas Statistical Database)

that much of the spread of goldfish in Australia is a result of accidental liberations of pet fish from aquariums.

Notes

There is little evidence of either positive or negative interactions between European carp and native species. For example, it has been suggested that European carp increase water turbidity through feeding and mating activities and as a result make habitat less suitable for native species. However, many Australian streams are naturally turbid. European carp are preyed upon by golden perch and Murray cod and may well have a positive effect by providing food for these species.

Goldfish ulcer virus (*Aeromonas salmonica*) has been found in wild

goldfish populations. While this disease does not affect native fish species, it does affect trout (Salmonidae) populations which form an important recreational fishery. The importation of goldfish into Tasmania is prohibited to prevent the spread of the disease to both wild and farmed trout and salmon populations.

References

1. Merrick, J.R. and Schmida, G.E. (1984) *Australian freshwater fishes. Biology and management.* Adelaide: Griffin Press. 409 pp.

2. de Moore, I.J. and Bruton, M.N. (1988) Atlas of alien and translocated indigenous aquatic animals in southern Africa. *South African National Scientific Programmes Report* **144**. 310 pp.

3. Fisheries and Wildlife Division, Victorian Ministry for Conservation (1976). *Common (European) carp*, Cyprinus carpio, *Linnaeus, in Australia*. A joint situation report to the Australian Government Standing Committee on Fisheries. 32 pp.

4. Pollard, D.A., Llewellyn, L.C. and Tilzey, R.D.J. (1980) Management of freshwater fish and fisheries. Pp 227–270, in *An ecological basis for water resource management*. Ed by W.D.Williams. Canberra: ANU Press.

5. McDowall, R.M. and Shearer, K. (1980) Family Cyprinidae. Pp 84–85, in *Freshwater fishes of south-eastern Australia*. Ed by R.M. McDowall. Sydney: AH & AW Reed Pty Ltd.

6. Hume, D.J., Fletcher, A.R. and Morison, A.K. (1983) *Final report, carp program.* Arthur Rylah Institute for Environmental Research, Fisheries and Wildlife Division, Victorian Ministry for Conservation. 213 pp.

7. Shearer, K.D. and Mulley, J.C. (1978) The introduction and distribution of the carp, *Cyprinus carpio* Linnaeus, in Australia. *Australian Journal of Marine and Freshwater Research* **29**: 551–563.

8. Fisheries and Wildlife Division, Ministry for Conservation (1976) *The European carp fishery in Victoria*. Pp 17–20, in *Fisheries management in Victoria*.

9. Morison, A.K. and Hume, D.J. (1990) *Cyprinus carpio* in Australia. Pp 110–113, in *Introduced and translocated fishes and their ecological effects*. Ed by D.A. Pollard. *Bureau of Rural Resources Proceedings* **8**.

Contributors

Most of the information on this species was originally provided by Sandy Morison and supplemented by Les Gray. Drawing by Rosalind Poole. (*Details of contributors and their organisations are given in the Acknowledgements section at the back of this book.*)

Compiler Alex McNee

Cobbler

Cnidoglanis macrocephalus

Cnidoglanis macrocephalus
(Valenciennes)

Cobbler

Another common name is **estuary catfish**.
FAO: no known name
Australian species code: 192001

Family PLOTOSIDAE

Diagnostic features Cobbler have scaleless bodies. They have 4 pairs of barbels around the mouth and the front nostril in the border of the upper lip points downwards. The eye is small. They have 1 anterior dorsal fin and a continuous fin made up of the second dorsal fin, caudal and anal fins. There is a branching, fleshy 'dendritic organ' behind the anus. The body is blackish grey or mottled with pale and dark patches.

Distribution

Cobbler are endemic in Australian waters. They are present along both eastern and western Australian coasts, from Kirra in southern Queensland to Jervis Bay in New South Wales, and from Kingston in South Australia to the Houtman Abrolhos in Western Australia.

Cobbler inhabit estuaries, sheltered inshore waters[1] up to 30 m deep, bays and surf beaches. Favoured habitats have clear to turbid water and substrates of sand, rocks and weeds. By day, cobbler are most often found in holes and on ledges in banks.

Life history

Cobbler begin to mature in August and spawning takes place over a protracted period between spring and early summer, from about October to December.[2] They spawn in burrows, in inshore waters and estuaries,[2] the female laying between 500 and 3500[2] eggs in a nest constructed by the male. The eggs are large, 4.0–9.5 mm in diameter, and the male guards them for an unknown period. There is only 1 spawning each season.

There is no information on the larval stage. The drift weeds found in inshore marine waters, protected inshore marine environments and estuaries act as nursery areas for cobbler. Cobbler enter these areas during their first year of life[3] and often remain there for long periods.[1,3]

Growth is rapid in summer and autumn, and slower in winter and early spring.[2] One-year-old fish have a total length range of 18–28 cm, 2-year-olds of 29–35 cm and 3-year-olds of 30–42 cm.[2,4] Although the growth rate varies from year to year, regional growth differences are more significant. For example, cobbler generally grow faster in the northern part of their range than in the south, and

cobbler inhabiting inshore, marine areas grow more slowly on average than do cobbler living in estuaries. The maximum recorded total length for cobbler is 76 cm. The maximum age estimated from otolith readings is 13 years and the maximum weight is 2.5 kg.

Cobbler reach maturity at about 38.5 cm total length for males and 40.5 cm for females.[2] Most fish are mature at 3 years of age, but some individuals may reach maturity at 2 years.

Cobbler are opportunistic,[5] mainly carnivorous[1,2] feeders, feeding primarily at night. They eat bivalve and univalve molluscs, crustaceans (small prawns and amphipods), polychaete worms, algae and organic debris.[5] Juveniles eat more crustacea — often from among drifting macrophytic algae[1] — and adults eat more molluscs and polychaetes. Cobbler

predators include birds such as cormorants (*Phalacrocorax* species) and pelicans (*Pelecanus conspicillatus*).[1]

Stock structure

Although it has been suggested that marine and estuarine populations of cobbler form independent populations, this has not been substantiated. The nature of the stock structure is unknown.

Commercial fishery

Cobbler have been exploited since the inception of the inshore, estuarine fishery in Western Australia, but targeted only in the last 20 years.

The commercial cobbler fishery is concentrated in southern waters between Perth and Albany. The Swan–Avon and

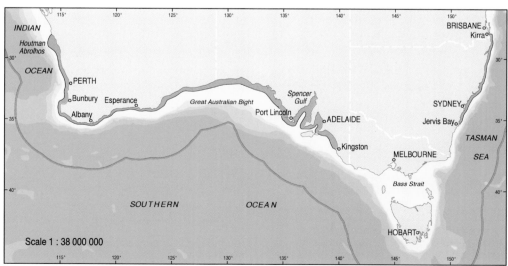

Geographic distribution of cobbler.

Peel–Harvey estuaries are the traditional centres of the fishery. However, over recent years Wilson Inlet has become the major contributor to the overall catch.

The fishery is mainly located in the lower and middle sections of estuaries,[6] with a few fish caught in marine embayments around Albany. The youngest fish taken in the fishery are between 2 and 3 years of age. Fishing goes on all year, although the catch per unit effort varies markedly with the season. The annual catch and catch per unit effort also fluctuate widely between years.[2,4,6] Generally, cobbler together with sea mullet (*Mugil cephalus*) and yellow-eye mullet (*Aldrichetta forsteri*) comprise between 70 % and 90 % of the annual commercial catch from the south-west estuaries.

Cobbler are caught at night, with bottom set gillnets and haul nets, bunting and funnel traps. The bycatch often comprises flathead (Platycephalidae) and mullet (Mugilidae).

The catch is consumed locally, mostly in Perth. Cobbler are marketed headed, gutted and on ice, and reach the market within 3 days of capture. In 1992 the average wholesale price for whole or gutted cobbler varied between A$ 5.00 to A$ 7.00 per kg.

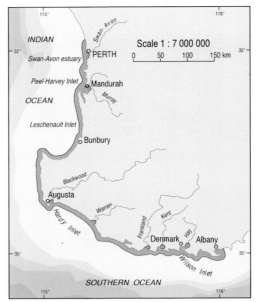
Commercial fishing area for cobbler.

In South Australian waters, small numbers of cobbler are taken as a bycatch of the haul net fishery, mainly in southern Spencer Gulf. The recorded annual catch ranged from 6 to 72 kg over the last 9 years. Cobbler is infrequently sold on local fresh fish markets in South Australia.

Management controls There is restricted entry into the estuarine fishery. In Western Australia, regulations also control the minimum legal mesh size of nets and the minimum legal fish length.

Recreational fishery

In Western Australia, cobbler are popular with recreational fishers. Along the south coast, most cobbler are caught with gillnets. On the west coast handlining is becoming increasingly popular, especially in the Swan–Avon and Peel–Harvey estuaries and from the ocean around Hillary's Beach (Perth). Cobbler are also caught with hand spears at night.

In southern Spencer Gulf (South Australia), cobbler are taken occasionally by recreational fishers. They are generally considered a nuisance, as they are difficult to remove from nets.

Management controls The mesh size regulations and minimum legal fish size that apply to commercial fishing also apply to recreational fishers.

Resource status

The resource status is largely unknown. Cobbler catches from the south-western estuaries have declined in recent years, and recreational fishing pressure is increasing in inshore coastal waters.

References

1. Lenanton, R.C.J. and Caputi, N. (1989) The roles of food supply and shelter in the relationship between fishes, in particular *Cnidoglanis macrocephalus* (Valenciennes), and detached macrophytes in the surf zone of sandy beaches. *Journal of Experimental and Marine Biology and Ecology* **128**: 165–176.

2. Nel, S.A., Potter, I.C. and Loneragan, N.R. (1985) The biology of the catfish *Cnidoglanis macrocephalus* (Plotosidae) in an Australian estuary. *Estuarine and Coastal Shelf Science* **21**: 895–909.

3. Lenanton, R.C.J. and Potter, I.C. (1987) Contribution of estuaries to commercial fisheries in temperate Western Australia and the concept of estuarine dependence. *Estuaries* **10**(1): 28–35.

4. Lenanton, R.C.J., Potter, I.C., Loneragan, N.R. and Chrystal, P.J. (1984) Age structure and changes in abundance of three important species of teleost in a eutrophic estuary (Pisces:Teleostei). *Journal of Zoology, London* **203**: 311–327.

5. Thomson, J.M. (1957) The food of Western Australian estuarine fish. *Western Australian Department of Fisheries, Fisheries Bulletin* **7**. 13 pp.

6. Loneragan, N.R., Potter, I.C. and Lenanton, R.C.J. (1989) Influence of site, season and year on contributions made by marine, estuarine, diadromous and freshwater species to the fish fauna of a temperate Australian estuary. *Marine Biology* **103**: 461–479.

Contributors

The information in this presentation was originally provided by Laurie Laurenson and Rod Lenanton and supplemented by (in alphabetical order) Keith Jones and Ian Potter. Drawing by Roger Swainston. *(Details of contributors and their organisations are given in the Acknowledgements section at the back of this book.)*
Compilers Patricia Kailola and Christina Grieve (maps)

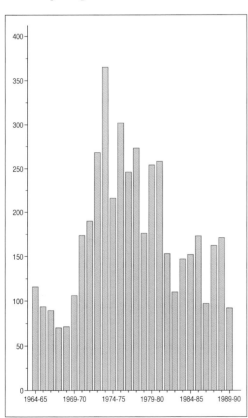
Total annual catch in t of cobbler for the period 1964–65 to 1989–90. Catches for States that average less than 5 % of the total for all States are not shown. (Source: Fisheries Resources Atlas Statistical Database)

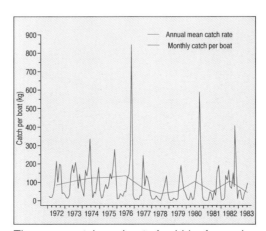
The mean catch per boat of cobbler for each month between January 1972 and July 1983, and annual means of monthly catch rates, in the Swan–Avon estuary. (Source: Nel et al[2])

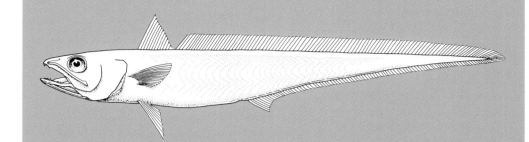

Blue grenadier

Macruronus novaezelandiae

Distribution

Blue grenadier are distributed through southern Australian waters from Broken Bay, New South Wales[1] to the western region of the Great Australian Bight.[2] This species is also distributed over the continental slope off New Zealand.[3]

In Australian waters adult blue grenadier normally inhabit continental slope waters between 200 and 700 m[4] although they have been recorded at a depth of 1000 m.[5] Blue grenadier form dense schools near the sea bed during the day and disperse into the water column at dusk, ascending to within 50 m of the surface.[6] Juveniles are common in estuaries and bays of southern Tasmania.[7]

Life history

The main spawning ground for blue grenadier is centred off Cape Sorell on the west coast of Tasmania. The presence of larvae off north-eastern Tasmania in some years suggests that a second ground may be used by a small proportion of the stock.[8] Adult blue grenadier are thought to migrate to the main spawning ground from all regions of the species' Australian distribution. Spawning occurs in winter and early spring, and there is evidence that the onset of spawning varies according to differences in water temperature between years. Female blue grenadier produce about 1 million eggs on average, which are all released at once. The eggs are pelagic, spherical, and about 1 mm in diameter.[9] Fertilised eggs hatch within 55 to 60 hours, releasing pelagic larvae.[9] The duration of the pelagic phase is not known. Some of the larvae are carried southwards by offshore currents and may be carried around the southern tip of Tasmania to eventually settle in estuaries and bays on the east

Macruronus novaezelandiae (Hector)

Blue grenadier

Other common names include **blue hake**, **whiptail**, **New Zealand whiptail** and **hoki**.
FAO: **blue grenadier**
Australian species code: 227001

Family MERLUCCIIDAE

Diagnostic features Blue grenadier have bodies which are blue-green or purple above and silvery below. Their fins are dark blue. The first dorsal fin has a short base and the elongated second dorsal and anal fins are joined to the tail. Tiny scales cover the smooth skin, and they are easily dislodged.

coast.[10] However, it is likely that most larvae settle offshore from the Tasmanian west coast.[5,10]

Blue grenadier reach a total length of approximately 40 cm during their second year. Females become mature at a total length of 73 cm, which corresponds to a range of ages between 4 and 7 years.[11] The maximum age reached by blue grenadier in Australian waters has been estimated from otolith readings at 25 years, although ageing was only validated for juvenile fish. Females grow more slowly than males but reach a greater maximum size. Ageing studies and estimates of mortality rates indicate that female blue genadier also live longer than males.[5] Blue grenadier are reported to reach a maximum size of about 110 cm standard length.[3,7]

Blue grenadier feed mainly at night. The main prey items are fish (particularly the lanternfish *Lampanyctodes hectoris*), prawns including royal red prawns (*Haliporoides sibogae*), krill (*Euphausia* species) and squid.[6] Adults will prey on juvenile blue grenadier during periods of high juvenile abundance.[6] Pink ling (*Genypterus blacodes*) are also predators of juvenile blue grenadier.

Stock structure

Electrophoretic studies of Australian blue grenadier indicate a single Australian stock.[12] However, comparison between Australian and New Zealand samples of blue grenadier (for example, on growth patterns[5]) showed significant differences, probably due to genetic isolation of the 2 groups.[12]

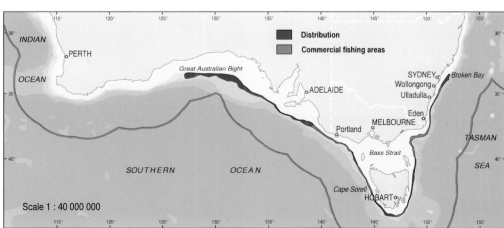

Geographic distribution and commercial fishing areas for blue grenadier in Australian waters.

Commercial fishery

The Australian blue grenadier fishery has operated since the late 1970s when the first large catches were taken in Tasmanian waters. The fishery has since become an important component of the South East Fishery with catches ranging between 1500 and 2800 t liveweight. A small amount (up to 50 t per year) of blue grenadier is caught by trawlers in the Great Australian Bight Trawl Fishery.

Blue grenadier are caught throughout the South East Fishery by vessels using demersal otter trawl gear in depths of 300 to 600 m[13] but the main fishing ground is located near the spawning area off western Tasmania.[5] Fishers also catch significant quantities throughout the year in southern and south-eastern Tasmanian waters and off Portland on the Victorian coast.[13] Mid-water trawling for blue grenadier has also been tried. Off western Tasmania, most of the blue grenadier

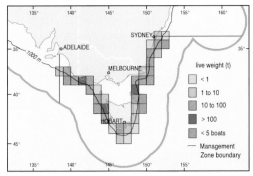

Total blue grenadier catch in t by 1-degree block from the South East Fishery for 1989–90. The catch for blocks fished by fewer than 5 boats is not shown. (Source: Australian Fishing Zone Information System)

Wholesale Fish Market. The fish are mainly processed as fillets or cutlets; however there is potential for development of markets for manufactured fish products ('surimi') which utilise blue grenadier. Some of the blue grenadier catch is also exported as frozen fillets to the United States of America. In 1991–92, wholesale prices for

blue grenadier on the Melbourne market normally ranged between A$ 2.00 and A$ 2.50 per kg.

Management controls The fishery for blue grenadier is managed by the Commonwealth of Australia through the South East Fishery Management Plan with associated limited entry provisions, boat replacement policy and gear restrictions. A total allowable catch limit and an individual transferable quota system have applied to blue grenadier catches in the South East Fishery since January 1992. Vessels operating west of the South East Fishery boundary are managed under the Great Australian Bight Trawl Fishery Management Plan.

Recreational fishery

Blue grenadier are infrequently caught by anglers.

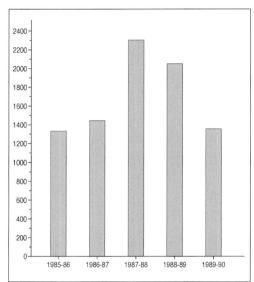

Total annual catch in t of blue grenadier from the South East Fishery for the period 1985–86 to 1989–90. The catch records for 1985–86 are incomplete and most of the recorded catch is in headed-and-gutted form. (Source: Australian Fishing Zone Information System)

catch is taken during winter when spawning fish are most abundant. Catches taken from the spawning ground also tend to have a higher percentage of large female fish compared to catches for other areas of the Fishery. Most of the blue grenadier catch results from targeted fishing. The main bycatch species are pink ling (*Genypterus blacodes*), mirror dory (*Zenopsis nebulosus*) and blue eye (*Hyperoglyphe antarctica*).[5]

Blue grenadier are usually sold on the domestic fresh fish market, with most product marketed through the Melbourne

A catch of blue grenadier taken off the west coast of Tasmania. (Source: Jeremy Lyle, Division of Sea Fisheries, Tasmanian Department of Primary Industry and Fisheries)

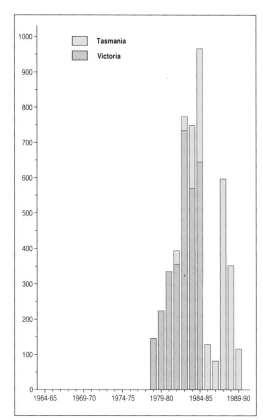

Total annual catch in t of blue grenadier for the period 1964–65 to 1989–90. Figures are unavailable for Victoria from 1970–71 to 1977–78 and 1985–86 to 1989–90. Catches for States that average less than 5 % of the total for all States are not shown. (Source: Fisheries Resources Atlas Statistical Database)

Resource status

There are no reliable estimates of stock size for this species. However, current estimates of sustainable yields for blue grenadier suggest that the Australian fishery may be able to sustain catches higher than historic catch levels.[5]

Notes

The size of the New Zealand blue grenadier resource greatly exceeds the known stock in Australian waters. For example, the 1989–90 catch from the New Zealand fishing zone was approximately 210 000 t. It was taken mainly by large factory trawlers which processed the catch onboard into surimi or headed-and-gutted product.

References

1. Paxton, J.E., Hoese, D.F., Allen, G.R. and Hanley, J.E. (1989) *Zoological catalogue of Australia. Volume 7, Pisces. Petromyzontidae to Carangidae.* Canberra: Australian Government Publishing Service. 664 pp.

2. Newton, G. and Klaer, N. (1991) Deep-sea demersal fisheries resources of the Great Australian Bight: a multivessel survey. *Bureau of Rural Resources Bulletin* **10**. 71 pp.

3. Paul, L. (1986) *New Zealand fishes. An identification guide.* Auckland: Reed Methuen. 184 pp.

4. May, J.L. and Maxwell, J.G.H. (1986) *A field guide to trawl fish from temperate waters of Australia.* Hobart: CSIRO Division of Fisheries Research. 492 pp.

5. Smith, A.D.M. (in press, 1992) Blue grenadier. In *The South East Fishery: a scientific review with particular reference to quota management.* Ed by R.D.J. Tilzey. *Bureau of Resource Sciences Bulletin.*

6. Bulman, C.M. and Blaber, S.J.M. (1986) Feeding ecology of *Macruronus novaezelandiae* (Hector) (Teleostei: Merlucciidae) in south-eastern Australia. *Australian Journal of Marine and Freshwater Research* **37**: 621–639.

7. Last, P.R., Scott, E.O.G. and Talbot, F.H. (1983) *Fishes of Tasmania.* Hobart: Tasmanian Fisheries Development Authority. 563 pp.

8. Gunn, J.S., Bruce, B.D., Furlani, D.M., Thresher, R.E. and Blaber, S.J.M. (1989) Timing and location of spawning of blue grenadier, *Macruronus novaezelandiae* (Teleostei: Merlucciidae), in Australian coastal waters. *Australian Journal of Marine and Freshwater Research* **40**: 97–112.

9. Bruce, B.D. (1987). Larval development of blue grenadier, *Macruronus novaezelandiae* (Hector), in Tasmanian waters. *Fishery Bulletin (U.S.)* **86**: 119–128.

10. Thresher, R.E., Bruce, B.D., Furlani, D.M. and Gunn, J.S. (1988) Distribution, advection, and growth of larvae of the southern temperate gadoid, *Macruronus novaezelandiae* (Teleostei: Merlucciidae), in Australian coastal waters. *Fishery Bulletin (U.S.)* **87**: 29–48.

11. Kenchington, T.J. and Augustine, O. (1987) Age and growth of blue grenadier, *Macruronus novaezelandiae* (Hector), in south-eastern Australian waters. *Australian Journal of Marine and Freshwater Research* **38**: 625–646.

12. Milton, D.A. and Shaklee, J.B. (1987) Biochemical genetics and population structure of blue grenadier, *Macruronus novaezelandiae* (Hector) (Pisces: Merlucciidae), from Australian waters. *Australian Journal of Marine and Freshwater Research* **38**: 727–742.

13. Tilzey, R.D.J., Zann-Schuster, M., Klaer, N.L. and Williams, M.J. (1990) The South East Trawl Fishery: biological synopses and catch distributions for seven major commercial fish species. *Bureau of Rural Resources Bulletin* **6**. 80 pp.

Contributors

Most of the information on this species was provided by Tony Smith and supplemented by Jeremy Lyle and Richard Tilzey. Drawing by Rosalind Poole. (*Details of contributors and their organisations are given in the Acknowledgements section at the back of this book.*)
Compilers Phillip Stewart and Christina Grieve (maps)

Pink ling

Genypterus blacodes

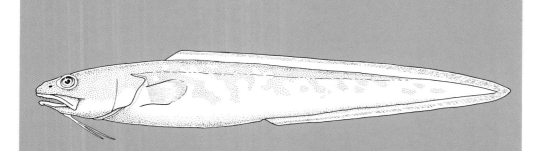

Genypterus blacodes (Forster)

Pink ling

Another common name is **ling**.
FAO: **pink cusk-eel**
Australian species code: 228002

Family OPHIDIIDAE

Diagnostic features Ling have long and tapered (or eel-like) bodies with very small scales. Their bodies are covered with thick mucus. Their upper jaw extends only a short distance beyond the eye and the gill openings are 'normal', on each side of the body behind the head. The 2-rayed ventral fins are positioned on the chin and the dorsal, caudal and anal fins form a continuous fin. The overall body colour is pinkish to orange, with irregular brown bands on its upper two-thirds.[1]

Distribution

Pink ling inhabit the south-west Pacific waters of New Zealand and temperate Australia, and are also recorded from South America.[2] In Australia they are present in continental shelf and slope waters from Crowdy Head in New South Wales to Albany in Western Australia.[3]

Pink ling are demersal and inhabit a depth range of 20 to 800 m, being most abundant between 300 m and 550 m. Juveniles (fish less than 40 cm total length) are present in shallower shelf waters. Pink ling occur over a variety of substrates, from rocky ground to soft sand and mud[4] in which they burrow.

There are no records of regular migrations by pink ling. Changes in pink ling catch rates indicate a shift into deeper water in winter and spring.[5] However, larger catches of pink ling in deeper water largely reflect the associated targeting for other fish such as gemfish (*Rexea solandri*) and blue grenadier (*Macruronus novaezelandiae*).[6] Twice as many female as male pink ling are present in commercial catches to the east of Bass Strait except in February, when there are slightly more males than females.[7] This ratio could suggest that spawning-related migrations may take place.

Life history

There is little information on the spawning of pink ling. To the west of Bass Strait spawning probably takes place in late winter–early spring. Based on seasonal catch by depth data, pink ling may move into deeper waters to spawn.[5] Pink ling in New Zealand waters spawn between August and October.[2] The fecundity (number of eggs produced) of pink ling appears to be moderately low.

Ocean currents may carry the larvae into shallow shelf waters and inshore. A study in Tasmanian waters found that ling larvae decreased in abundance with an increase in depth, and there were no ling larvae caught in offshore sampling locations. Larvae have been collected from all areas of coastal Tasmania, and in all months except June. The largest catches of larvae were made from the northern west coast and mid east coast during September–October, with a secondary peak in abundance in January–February. Although the specific identity of very small *Genypterus* larvae has not yet been determined, it appears that more than 1 species contributes to these peaks of larval abundance. It is not known if each peak represents a single species.

The maximum reported total length for pink ling is 1.6 m, and maximum weight is 20 kg.[1] A recent unvalidated calculation of growth rate, based on counting of otolith rings, showed that pink ling grow to 135.5 cm by 21 years of age.[7] This slow-growing species[7] apparently exhibits no significant difference in growth rate between sexes.

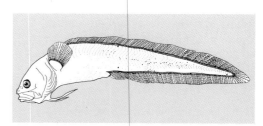

Line drawing of 24.6 mm pink ling larva.
(Source: Dianne Furlani, CSIRO Marine Laboratories, Hobart)

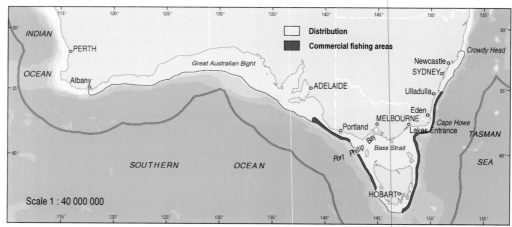

Geographic distribution and commercial fishing areas for pink ling in Australian waters.

Pink ling are active predators, feeding on crustaceans such as royal red prawns (*Haliporoides sibogae*) and a variety of fish including gemfish and blue grenadier.

Stock structure

Biomass estimates of pink ling in Bass Strait suggest a uniform distribution of individuals on the continental shelf break and along the slope.[4,6] It is assumed that pink ling in south-eastern Australia comprise one stock. However, difference in catchability around southern Tasmania suggests discrete stocks.[8] Presence of the morphologically similar rock ling (*Genypterus tigerinus*) in catches and larval samples has confused analysis and identification of stocks.

There is evidence, from the distribution of larvae and different depth preferences of adults, that pink ling consists of 2 'forms', 1 on the shelf (ie to less than 200 m) and 1 in deeper slope waters. The identity of the deeper form — which constitutes virtually all of the South East Fishery catch — is yet to be determined.

Commercial fishery

Pink ling are taken year-round by demersal otter trawlers on the continental slope. It has become an important component of the South East Fishery since the Fishery expanded onto continental slope waters. Nevertheless, only 35 % of the South East Fishery catch of pink ling is targeted. Most is taken as bycatch in the Fishery, mainly by fishers targeting gemfish and blue grenadier.[5] South East Fishery catches of pink ling come mainly from waters off New South Wales, off Victoria from Lakes Entrance to Cape Howe and the west of the State, and off north-western Tasmania.[5,8] In this Fishery, pink ling are caught in depths from approximately 100 m to 650 m, mostly between 350 m and 550 m. Around Tasmania catches for pink ling are highest in the 550–600 m depth range.[5] Catch rates by demersal trawl are generally low, averaging less than about 50 kg per hour. Catch rates are highest to the west and south-east of Tasmania during spring and summer,[8] rising to over 150 kg per hour.

Pink ling catches are a small component of trawl landings from the Great Australian Bight Trawl Fishery, with

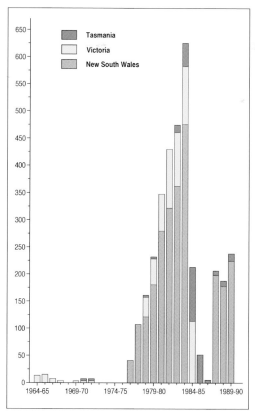

Total annual catch in t of pink ling for the period 1964–65 to 1989–90. Figures are unavailable for: New South Wales from 1964–65 to 1975–76 and 1984–85 to 1986–87; Victoria from 1972–73 to 1977–78 and 1985–86 to 1989–90; and Tasmania for 1964–65, 1965–66 and 1967–68. Catches for States that average less than 5 % of the total for all States are not shown. (Source: Fisheries Resources Atlas Statistical Database)

only 8 t taken in 1989–90. In a survey of the Great Australian Bight demersal fish resources[3] the average catch rate for pink ling was highest at 400 m, where it was 11 kg per hour. A maximum rate of 120 kg per hour was achieved in the eastern Bight.[3]

Droplining and bottom set longlining methods are also employed to catch pink ling on the continental shelf and upper continental slope. Most of the dropline catch of pink ling is a bycatch of the blue eye (*Hyperoglyphe antarctica*) fishery. Pink ling are also an incidental catch of the Southern Shark Fishery using bottom set longlines and gillnets off Victoria.[5]

Pink ling is caught by all methods off New South Wales southwards from Ulladulla.

Pink ling are probably at least 3 years old before they are caught in the trawl fishery.[7] Average biomass of pink ling throughout the year at depths of 300 to 800 m has been estimated at 600 kg per square km in eastern Bass Strait.[4]

Compared with many other fishes harvested in the South East Fishery, pink ling have a high market value. They are

Catch of pink ling in the hold of a trawler, Portland, Victoria. (Source: Australian Fisheries Management Authority)

marketed locally as fresh and chilled whole fish, and they are also smoked. The average annual value for pink ling over 4 recent years from the Fishery was approximately A$ 2 million. In 1991–92 the average wholesale price for pink ling at the Sydney Fish Market was A$ 3.49 per kg. Prices at the Melbourne Wholesale Fish Market normally ranged between A$ 3.00 and A$ 4.00 per kg in 1991–92. In New Zealand, pink ling skins are occasionally tanned for leather.[2]

Management controls Capture of pink ling is controlled under limited entry

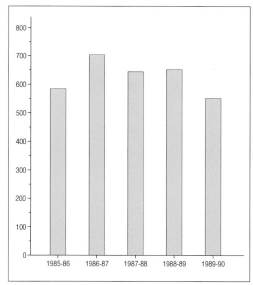

Total annual catch in t of pink ling for the period 1985–86 to 1989–90 from the South East Fishery and Great Australian Bight Trawl Fishery. South East Fishery catch records for 1985–86 are incomplete. (Source: Australian Fishing Zone Information System)

regulations in the Commonwealth-managed Great Australian Bight Trawl Fishery. A catch quota is now operating in the South East Fishery, which is also managed by the Commonwealth.

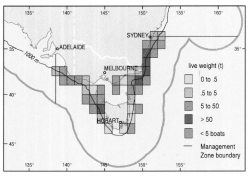

Total pink ling catch in t by 1-degree block from the South East Fishery for 1989. Catch for blocks fished by fewer than 5 boats is not stated. (Source: Australian Fishing Zone Information System)

Rows of snoods arranged along the shooting rails of the automatic bottom set longline system being trialed in Tasmania for pink ling. (Source: Lindsay Chapman, Bureau of Resource Sciences)

Recreational fishery

Pink ling are rarely caught by recreational fishers because these fish inhabit deep water.

Management controls There are no management controls.

Resource status

The current status of the resource is unclear. Indirect evidence from the commercial fishery suggests that only one-third of the pink ling catch comes from targeted fishing. Pooled length frequencies of pink ling caught by research trawls off southern New South Wales from 1975–77 to 1979–81 suggest a decrease in size (and presumably age).[5] However, length frequencies from the Sydney Fish Market from 1986 to 1991 showed no decline.

Notes

Rock ling are often confused with pink ling. They can be distinguished by their variable, mottled body colour, usually with a darker mottled pattern, and an upper jaw extending well past the eye. Rock ling are an endemic, reasonably common species in southern coastal waters from Newcastle (New South Wales) to Garden Island near Perth, Western Australia. They occupy waters shallower than 60 m, rocky reef areas and seagrass beds in estuaries, and can grow to 1.2 m and 9 kg.[1]

Rock ling are caught by Danish seines, bottom set gillnets, bottom set longlines and cray pots (shallow water). Between 0.1 and 22 t of rock ling were taken commercially in Port Phillip Bay, Victoria, between 1914 and 1984.[9] Rock ling comprise only a very small proportion of the recorded 'pink ling' catch from the South East Fishery.

Rock ling are especially important on the Melbourne Wholesale Fish Market. They are popular with recreational anglers, and have been completely removed from some popular fishing areas in Tasmania.[10]

References

1. Last, P.R., Scott, E.O.G. and Talbot, F.H. (1983) *Fishes of Tasmania*. Hobart: Tasmanian Fisheries Development Authority. 563 pp.

2. Paul, L.J. (1986). *New Zealand fishes. An identification guide.* Auckland: Reed Methuen. 184 pp.

3. Newton, G.N. and Klaer, N. (1991). Deep-sea demersal fisheries resources of the Great Australian Bight: a multivessel trawl survey. *Bureau of Rural Resources Bulletin* **10**. 71 pp.

4. Wankowski, W.J. and Moulton, P.L. (1986) Distribution, abundance and biomass estimates of commercially important demersal fish species in eastern Bass Strait, Australia. *Victorian Department of Conservation, Forests and Lands, Fisheries and Wildlife Service, Technical Report* **62**. 57 pp.

5. Tilzey, R.D.J. (in press, 1992) Pink ling *Genypterus blacodes*. In *The South East Fishery: a scientific review with particular reference to quota management.* Ed by R.D.J. Tilzey. *Bureau of Resource Sciences Bulletin.*

6. Tilzey, R.D.J., Zann-Schuster, M., Klaer, N.L. and Williams, M.J. (1990) The South East Trawl Fishery: biological synopses and catch distributions for seven major commercial fish species. *Bureau of Rural Resources Research Bulletin* **6**. 80 pp.

7. Withell, A.F. and Wankowski, J.W.J. (1989) Age and growth estimates for pink ling, *Genypterus blacodes* (Schneider), and gemfish, *Rexea solandri* (Cuvier), from eastern Bass Strait, Australia. *Australian Journal of Marine and Freshwater Research* **40**: 215–226.

8. Woodward, I. (1987) An analysis of catch statistics from the south-western sector of the Australian south-east demersal trawl fishery. *Tasmanian Department of Sea Fisheries, Technical Report* **23**. 90 pp.

9. Hall, D.N. and MacDonald, C.M. (1986) Commercial fishery situation report: net and line fisheries of Port Phillip Bay Victoria, 1914–1984. *Victorian Department of Conservation, Forests and Lands, Fisheries Division, Marine Fisheries Report* **10**. 121 pp.

10. Edgar, G.J., Last, P.R. and Wells, M.W. (1982) *Coastal fishes of Tasmania and Bass Strait.* Hobart: Tasmanian Underwater Photographic Society. 176 pp.

Contributors

Information on this species was originally provided by Richard Tilzey and supplemented by (in alphabetical order) Barry Bruce, Dianne Furlani, Ken Graham, Neil Klaer, Peter Last, Jeremy Lyle and Allan Williams. Drawing of adult by Rosalind Poole and of larva by Dianne Furlani. *(Details of contributors and their organisations are given in the Acknowledgements section at the back of this book.)*
Compilers Patricia Kailola, Christina Grieve (maps) and Phillip Stewart (statistics)

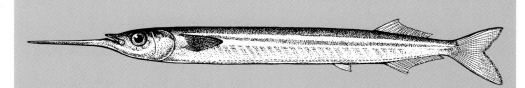

Garfish

Hyporhamphus species

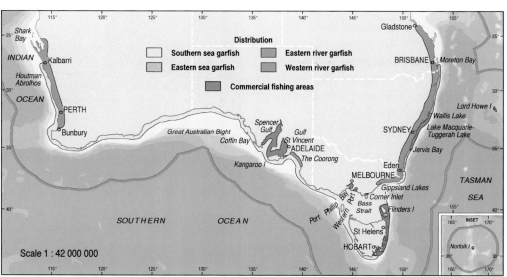

Garfish

This presentation is on 2 species, **southern sea garfish** and **eastern sea garfish**.

Southern sea garfish,
Hyporhamphus melanochir
(Valenciennes)

Other common names include
**South Australian garfish,
halfbeak** and **dusky garfish.**
FAO: no known name
Australian species code: 234001

Eastern sea garfish,
Hyporhamphus australis
(Steindachner)

Another common name is **sea garfish**.
FAO: no known name
Australian species code: 234014

Family HEMIRAMPHIDAE

Diagnostic features Southern sea garfish (pictured) are pale greenish blue on the back and upper sides, and have a broad, blue-edged silver band along the middle of the sides. Their fins are clear. They have 30–33 rakers along the first gill arch. Eastern sea garfish are similarly coloured but have 3 narrow brown lines along the back above the silvery band. They have 34–37 rakers along the first gill arch.

Distribution

Southern sea garfish and eastern sea garfish are endemic to Australian waters. Southern sea garfish are distributed from Eden in New South Wales, through Bass Strait and around Tasmania to Kalbarri in Western Australia.[1] Eastern sea garfish are distributed from Moreton Bay in Queensland to Eden. They are also present around Lord Howe and Norfolk Islands.[1]

Sea garfish live in sheltered bays, clear coastal waters and sometimes in estuaries (in south-western Australia).[2] They generally inhabit waters to about 20 m deep. In the South Australian gulfs, however, southern sea garfish may move into deeper water during winter, apparently to avoid the colder water temperatures of the shallows.[3] Garfish are schooling fish, generally near the surface at night and close to the sea floor over seagrass beds (eg *Zostera* and *Heterozostera* species) during the day.

Life history

Southern sea garfish spawn in the summer (October to March),[4,5,6] with a peak in spawning activity from October to November.[5] Studies in South Australian waters indicate that southern sea garfish probably spawn twice each year. An adult female can produce up to 10 000 eggs, averaging 1.5 mm in diameter.[4,5] The eggs have adhesive filaments for attachment to seagrasses.[7] There is no information on larval sea garfish. In south-western Australia, postlarvae or fish younger than 1-year-old live in estuaries from March to July and then in shallow, inshore marine waters for up to 2 years.[2] No studies have been reported on the spawning of eastern sea garfish.

Male and female southern sea garfish grow at a similar rate in South Australian

waters.[5,6] Their average total length (from the tip of the upper jaw to the tip of the tail fin) at 1.5 years is 22 cm, and at 3.5 years it is 28–30 cm.[5] The recorded maximum size for southern sea garfish is 52 cm total length[7] and 0.6 kg, and their estimated maximum age is 10 years.[6] Some southern sea garfish are mature at 2 years of age, but all fish are mature by 3 years of age.[5,6] The size at first maturity for southern sea garfish in south-western Australia is 25 cm fork length.[4] Eastern sea garfish are known to attain 40 cm total

length.[7] The age and size of eastern sea garfish at maturity is unknown.

Garfish are generally herbivorous. Seagrasses are a dominant food for sea garfish, and algal filaments are also important.[8,9] Together, they comprise about 75 % of the diet, the remainder consisting of diatoms, insect larvae, polychaete worms and small crustaceans.[8,10] Southern sea garfish have a different diet at night and day: they eat more algae during the day, other material

Geographic distribution and commercial fishing areas for garfish.

at night.[10] Eastern sea garfish consume a high proportion of crustaceans.[9] Tommy ruff (*Arripis georgianus*) and western Australian salmon (*A. truttaceus*) are known to feed on southern sea garfish.[8] Predators of eastern sea garfish include mulloway (*Argyrosomus hololepidotus*) and tailor (*Pomatomus saltatrix*). Garfish also fall victim to coastal water birds.

Stock structure

Some morphometric information on southern sea garfish has shown evidence for eastern (New South Wales, Victoria and Tasmania) and western (South Australia and Western Australia) populations.[7] No studies have been undertaken on eastern sea garfish.

Commercial fishery

The largest fishery for southern sea garfish is in Gulf St Vincent and Spencer Gulf (300–400 t a year from the gulfs), and around Kangaroo Island off South Australia.[11] Other significant fisheries exist along the Victorian coast (mainly Port Phillip Bay, also Western Port and Corner Inlet) and Flinders Island and eastern Tasmania. There is a small fishery for southern sea garfish in the estuaries of south-western Australia.

The garfish catch in Victorian waters consists of a mixture of southern sea garfish and river garfish, *Hyporhamphus regularis*. Southern sea garfish comprise most of the garfish catch from the more marine bays and inlets (eg Port Phillip Bay, where the average annual catch is around 82 t),[12] and river garfish are dominant in brackish inlets and estuaries (eg the Gippsland Lakes).

The fishery for eastern sea garfish is concentrated in large coastal bays and estuaries along the New South Wales coast such as Wallis, Macquarie, Tuggerah and Illawarra lakes and Jervis Bay. Small catches are also made by netting inshore in southern Queensland, mainly in Moreton Bay. Fishing is mostly done during the day using haul nets, power hauling nets, ring nets[6] and small mesh garfish seines[12] in water to about 5 m deep. About 10 % of the commercial catch in South Australia is, however, taken at night with dab nets, using lights to search for fish on the surface. Eastern sea garfish are mostly caught with specialised ring nets, sometimes with purse seines.

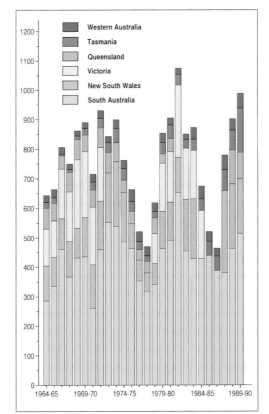

Total annual catch in t of all garfish for the period 1964–65 to 1989–90. Figures are unavailable for: New South Wales from 1984–85 to 1986–87; Victoria from 1972–73 to 1977–78 and 1985–86 to 1989–90; Queensland from 1981–82 to 1987–88. Catches for States that average less than 5 % of the total for all States are not shown. (Source: Fisheries Resources Atlas Statistical Database)

In South Australia, southern sea garfish are caught between November and June in Spencer Gulf and between March and July in Gulf St Vincent. There are large monthly fluctuations in catch rates.[11] For example, in upper Spencer Gulf during the April–June period of peak abundance, the average catch per unit effort ranges from 70 kg to 120 kg per person-day.[11]

Most southern sea garfish catches in Port Phillip Bay are taken in late summer.

Garfish are marketed fresh chilled, either whole or as butterfly fillets. Unlike the situation in most States, there is a high demand in South Australia for garfish in the fresh fish market, restaurant and 'take-away' food outlets. This demand is sometimes met by imports from other States. Garfish are also used as bait by recreational anglers; and small quantities are sold for 'sashimi' (raw fish) through the Sydney Fish Market. In 1991–92, prices for eastern sea garfish at the Sydney Fish Market averaged A$ 2.46 per kg. In South Australia there is a price differential depending on size: small garfish fetching up to A$ 2.50 per kg (1991 prices) and large garfish fetching A$ 5.00–7.50 per kg.

Management controls Minimum size limits apply in some States, and there are limited entry and non-transferable licences in the South Australian Marine Scale Fishery.

Recreational fishery

Sea garfish are a popular target fish for recreational anglers, especially during summer and early autumn.[13] They are caught with handlines from shore, boats and jetties, with bait nets in Western Australia and Queensland and dab nets in South Australia.

Boxing a catch of southern sea garfish, South Australia. (Source: South Australian Department of Fisheries)

In marine waters adjacent to Coffin Bay, the recreational catch is approximately one-third of the commercial catch.[14] In South Australia, southern sea garfish comprised 18–26 % of the fish caught by recreational anglers.[14] Southern sea garfish are the second most commonly angled fish after flathead (Platycephalidae) in Port Phillip Bay, especially over the summer months.[13]

Management controls Minimum size limits and licences apply in some States.

Resource status

In most States, the status of sea garfish resources is unknown. In South Australia there is recent evidence that excessive effort in the winter fishery for southern sea garfish in Gulf St Vincent has adversely affected the summer fishery.

The effect of seagrass bed degradation throughout the species' ranges could affect the resource status, as it appears to have affected garfish numbers in parts of Port Phillip Bay.[12]

Notes

River garfish, also known as needle garfish, are an important component of the garfish fishery in eastern and western Australia. River garfish can be distinguished from sea garfish by their wider and more rounded upper jaw (the upper jaw is pointed and longer in sea garfish). They are endemic to Australia. The east coast and west coast populations of river garfish are recognised at the level of subspecies:[7] *H. regularis ardelio* is the eastern form, present between Gladstone and the Gippsland Lakes; and *H. regularis regularis* is the western form, present in south-eastern South Australia and between Bunbury and Shark Bay.[1]

River garfish inhabit brackish and fresh waters. Maximum recorded standard lengths are 28 cm for eastern river garfish and 19.5 cm for western river garfish.[7] In eastern Australia, river garfish may comprise a significant incidental catch of sea garfish when fishing is conducted near estuaries or in brackish water — for example in the Gippsland Lakes and the Hawkesbury River estuary north of Sydney. New South Wales catches of river garfish since 1965 range from 19 t in 1978–79 to 136 t in 1973–74. In 1989–90,

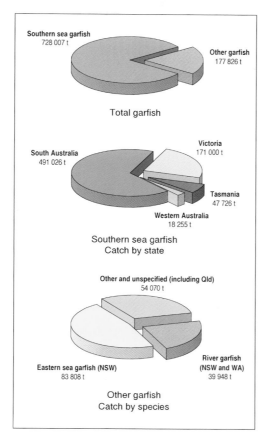

Composition of the total garfish catch for 1980–81. (top) Proportion of southern sea garfish in the total catch; (middle) proportion of southern sea garfish catch by State; (bottom) proportion of eastern sea garfish, river garfish, and other garfish species, including aggregated Queensland figures for all species. (Source: Fisheries Resources Atlas Statistical Database)

the catch totalled 53 t. They are also a significant catch in the Coorong in South Australia. There is a small fishery for western river garfish in the estuaries of south-western Australia.

References

1. Paxton, J.E., Hoese, D.F., Allen, G.R. and Hanley, J.E. (1989) *Zoological catalogue of Australia. Volume 7, Pisces. Petromyzontidae to Carangidae*. Canberra: Australian Government Publishing Service. 664 pp.

2. Lenanton, R.C.J. (1982) Alternative non-nursery habitats for some commercially and recreationally important fish species of south western Australia. *Australian Journal of Marine and Freshwater Research* 33: 881–900.

3. Jones, G.K., Hall, D.A., Hill, K.L. and Staniford, A.J. (1990) *The South Australian marine scale fishery: stock assessment, economics and management*. South Australian Department of Fisheries, Green paper. 186 pp.

4. Thompson, J.M. (1957) The size at maturity and spawning times of some Western Australian estuarine fishes. *Western Australian Department of Fisheries, Fisheries Bulletin* 8. 8 pp.

5. Ling, J. (1958) The sea garfish, *Reporhamphus melanochir* (Cuvier and Valenciennes) (Hemirhamphidae) in South Australia: breeding, age determination and growth rate. *Australian Journal of Marine and Freshwater Research* 9: 60–110.

6. Jones, G.K. (1990) Growth and mortality in a lightly fished population of garfish (*Hyporhamphus melanochir*), in Baird Bay, South Australia. *Transactions of the Royal Society of South Australia* 114 (1): 37–45.

7. Collette, B.B. (1974) The garfishes (Hemiramphidae) of Australia and New Zealand. *Records of the Australian Museum* 29(2): 1–105.

8. Thomson, J.M. (1957) The food of Western Australian estuarine fish. *Western Australian Department of Fisheries, Fisheries Bulletin* 7. 13 pp.

9. Thomson, J.M. (1959) Some aspects of the ecology of Lake Macquarie, NSW, with regard to an alleged depletion of fish. IX. The fishes and their food. *Australian Journal of Marine and Freshwater Research* 10: 365–374.

10. Klumpp, D.W. and Nichols, P.D. (1983) Nutrition of the southern sea garfish, *Hyporhamphus melanochir*: gut passage and daily consumption of two food types and assimilation of seagrass components. *Marine Ecology in Progress Series* 12: 207–216.

11. Jones, G.K. and Kangas, M. (1987) A review of the catch and effort in the commercial marine scale fishery in South Australian waters, 1976–1986. *South Australian Department of Fisheries, Fisheries Research Paper* 18. 113 pp.

12. Hall, D.N. and MacDonald, C.M. (1986) Commercial fishery situation report: net and line fisheries of Port Phillip Bay Victoria, 1914–1984. *Victorian Department of Conservation, Forests and Lands, Fisheries Division, Marine Fisheries Report* 10. 121 pp.

13. MacDonald, C.M. and Hall, D.N. (1987) A survey of recreational fishing in Port Phillip Bay, Victoria. *Victorian Department of Conservation, Forests and Lands, Fisheries Division, Marine Fisheries Report* 11. 40 pp.

14. Jones, G.K. (1983) Species composition and catch rates by recreational and commercial fishermen in southern Eyre Peninsula waters. *SAFIC* 7 (4): 9–18.

Contributors

Information on southern sea garfish was originally provided by Keith Jones. Additional contributions were made by (in alphabetical order) Rod Lenanton, Murray MacDonald, Kevin Rowling and Howel Williams. Drawing by Roger Swainston. *(Details of contributors and their organisations are given in the Acknowledgements section at the back of this book.)*

Compilers Kay Abel, Patricia Kailola and Christina Grieve (maps)

Orange roughy

Hoplostethus atlanticus

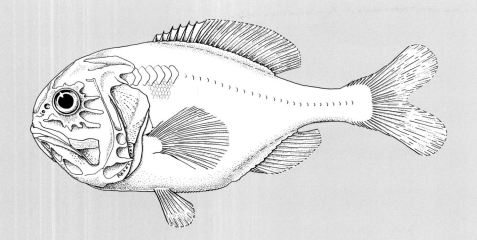

Hoplostethus atlanticus Collett

Orange roughy

Other common names include
deep-sea perch and **red roughy**.
FAO: **orange roughy**
Australian species code: 255009

Family TRACHICHTHYIDAE

Diagnostic features Orange roughy
have a bright reddish orange head and
body and their mouth and gill cavities
are black. Their head is covered with
bony ridges and deep mucus cavities.
The dorsal fin has 6 spines (the last one
being the longest) and 15–18 rays.
Orange roughy have large scales in the
lateral line which are 4–6 times the
height of the adjacent, rough-edged
body scales, and they have 19–25
weakly developed scutes along the belly
midline before the anus.

Distribution

Orange roughy principally inhabit deep,
cold (4 –7˚C) waters over steep
continental middle and lower slopes and
oceanic ridges. Orange roughy have been
reliably recorded from as deep as 1809 m
in the north Atlantic Ocean.[1] Their global
distribution extends from the north
Atlantic Ocean north-west of the British
Isles southwards to off north-west Africa,
the western Mediterranean Sea, the south
Atlantic Ocean off Namibia and through
the ridges of the southern Indian Ocean
from Africa to Australia, the Southern
Ocean and the south-west Pacific Ocean
including New Zealand.

In Australian waters, orange roughy
inhabit waters from 700 m to at least
1400 m, on the continental shelf slope
between Port Stephens in New South
Wales and Cape Naturaliste in Western
Australia. They are also found on the
South Tasman Rise, Cascade Plateau and
Lord Howe Rise.

Orange roughy appear to be dispersed
throughout these waters over both flat
bottoms and steep, rough ground such as
pinnacles and canyons. Adult fish form
dense spawning aggregations for several
weeks in winter and sporadically form

non-spawning aggregations, particularly
in summer and autumn. Aggregations of
orange roughy usually occur from 5 m to
10 m above the sea bed, with some
aggregations extending up to 100 m from
the sea floor.[2] Aggregations are usually
associated with submerged hills or
pinnacles.

Life history

Although several large orange roughy
spawning aggregations occur in New

Zealand waters, only 1, on a single hill
east of St Helens in Tasmania, has been
confirmed in Australian waters. There are
records however, of other spawning sites
in the Great Australian Bight[3] and south
of Tasmania, and small numbers of
spawning fish have been caught off
central New South Wales.[4] (No spawning
sites are known from the northern
hemisphere.) At the St Helens 'Hill',
spawning takes place from early July to
early August and the aggregation
disperses 3–4 weeks after spawning.[5,6]
However, spawning orange roughy from
the New South Wales sites have been
caught in May and June[4] and spawning
fish from the Great Australian Bight site
have been caught in late August.[3]

Orange roughy are synchronous
spawners, shedding eggs and sperm into
the water at the same time. Not all of the
adult population spawn each year.[7]
Individual males appear to spawn over a
1–2 week period and females spawn for
up to 1 week.[5] Orange roughy produce
between 10 000 and 90 000 large eggs,
2.0–2.5 mm in diameter.[7] The eggs are
positively buoyant when fertilised, and

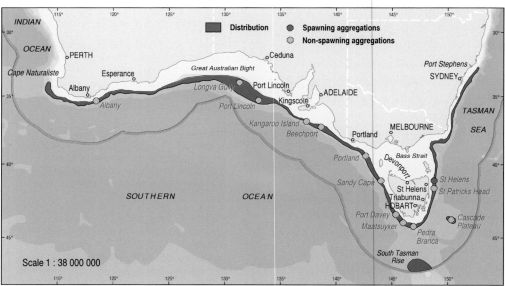

Geographic distribution and commercial fishing areas for orange roughy in Australian waters.

Large catch of orange roughy off St Helens, July 1989. (Source: Jeremy Lyle, Division of Sea Fisheries, Tasmanian Department of Primary Industry and Fisheries)

probably hatch 10–20 days after fertilisation. Little is known of the larvae and juveniles, which do not appear to aggregate. There are very few juveniles present with adults in spawning or non-spawning aggregations.

Orange roughy are believed to grow slowly and natural mortality is probably low. However, a validated ageing technique has yet to be developed for this species. Radiometric ageing techniques suggest orange roughy may live to at least 149 years.[8] Several other methods, including studies of juvenile length frequencies, studies of growth rings on sectioned ear bones (otoliths), and population modelling, also indicate that orange roughy are long lived. Although estimates of maximum age vary, it probably exceeds 100 years.

The largest specimens recorded, up to 56 cm standard length with weights of 5 kg or more, were from the Cascade Plateau.[9] Orange roughy in New Zealand waters attain only 45 cm standard length and up to 3.5 kg in weight.[10] Maturity is thought to occur between 20 and 32 years[7] when the fish are 28–32 cm long and weigh between 500 and 800 g.

Orange roughy feed opportunistically on bentho-pelagic and meso-pelagic fish such as viperfish (Chauliodontidae), lanternfish (Myctophidae) and whiptails (Macrouridae); on crustaceans such as carid prawns (particularly *Acanthephyra* species), amphipods (eg Lysianassidae) and mysids (eg *Gnathophausia* species); and on squid, particularly jewel squid (Histioteuthidae).[11] Juvenile orange roughy feed mainly on crustaceans, while mature fish eat predominantly fish and squid.[12,13] Orange roughy appear to have moderately high rates of food consumption.[12] Studies of gut contents suggest that juveniles may feed higher in the water column than do adults.[13] Gut content analyses suggest that oilfish (*Ruvettus pretiosus*) and large basketwork eels (*Diastabranchus* species) prey on orange roughy.

Stock structure

The stock structure of orange roughy in Australian waters remains uncertain.[14] Genetic studies suggest that there is a single population, but biological studies imply the existence of separate stocks. It is possible that separate stocks occur around Tasmania and in the Cascade Plateau, the Great Australian Bight and central New South Wales waters.[3,7,12] The presence of separate stocks in these regions is suggested by the size structure of populations, different spawning times, otolith microchemistry and different parasite loadings.[14]

Commercial fishery

Orange roughy were first recorded in Australian waters in trawl surveys off New South Wales conducted in 1972. The first promising catches were taken off Tasmania in 1981 by the research vessel *Challenger*, but it was not until 1986 that a large (non-spawning) aggregation was dicovered off western Tasmania. From 1986 until the discovery of the spawning aggregation off St Helens in 1989, the fishery was largely based on non-spawning aggregations and small catches from the dispersed population.

Orange roughy are caught in the South East Fishery and, to a much lesser extent, in the Great Australian Bight Trawl Fishery, mainly in depths of 800–1200 m. The bulk of the catch is taken off eastern and southern Tasmania. The few attempts to catch orange roughy north of the South East Fishery area have proved largely unsuccessful, although small catches have been made off Port Stephens.[4]

Commercial fisheries are based primarily on spawning and non-spawning aggregations of adult fish over 30 cm in length. Most fish in catches from the Cascade Plateau are 35–50 cm long (average 42 cm) with an average weight of 1–2 kg, whereas those from around Tasmania and the Great Australian Bight are 30–46 cm (average 36 cm). The aggregations tend to be highly localised. The 'Hill' east of St Helens supports a major fishery and minor aggregations,

Part of an orange roughy catch off Maatsuyker Island, July 1989. (Source: Jeremy Lyle, Division of Sea Fisheries, Tasmanian Department of Primary Industry and Fisheries)

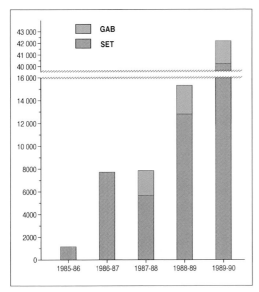

Total annual catch in t of orange roughy from the South East Fishery and the Great Australian Bight Trawl Fishery for the period 1985–86 to 1989–90. South East Fishery catch records for 1985–86 are incomplete. (Source: Australian Fishing Zone Information System)

also of spawning fish, have been fished in the Great Australian Bight and off southern Tasmania. Non-spawning aggregations have so far been found on the Cascade Plateau; at Port Davey, Maatsuyker and Pedra Branca (southern Tasmania); off Sandy Cape (western Tasmania); off Beachport, Kangaroo Island and Port Lincoln (South Australia); and off Albany (Western Australia).

Such aggregations provide very high catches. Trawl 'shots' of 30–40 t are not uncommon from a few minutes' trawling on an aggregation. Orange roughy usually comprise more than 90 % of such catches. The aggregations can be extremely dense: the 1990 management

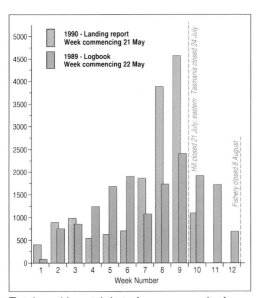

Total weekly catch in t of orange roughy from the St Helens Hill plus some east coast of Tasmania catches for the 1989 and 1990 fishing seasons. (Source: Australian Fishing Zone Information System)

quota of 12 000 t on the St Helens Hill was caught within only 3 weeks. Target fishing on aggregations involves large numbers of trawlers fishing a small area and requires considerable co-operation among fishers to achieve efficient and safe fishing practices.

Orange roughy caught in small quantities from the dispersed population include subadult fish and display a much wider range of sizes than do fish from the aggregations. Catches from dispersed populations show a bimodal distribution of sizes with peaks above and below the size at maturity. This phenomenon has not been fully explained.

Oreos (Oreosomatidae) are the main bycatch of the orange roughy fishery. Though usually in relatively small numbers, large catches (more than 10 t per haul) may occur. Dogfish (Squalidae) and whiptails are also commonly caught.

The orange roughy catch is sold as frozen, deep-skinned, boned fillets. Most is exported. Deep-skinning removes the skin and a 1–2 mm layer, consisting principally of fat beneath the skin, to leave the fillets virtually fat-free. The fat, 96 % wax esters, is similar to jojoba oil and refined orange roughy oil has been used both as a lubricant and in the cosmetic, pharmaceutical, leather, and textile industries.

The price for orange roughy fluctuates with supply and international exchange rates. The 1992 price to fishers averaged about A$ 2.50 per kg for whole fish. Domestic consumers paid from A$ 12.00 to A$ 18.00 per kg for white fillets.

Management controls The South East Fishery and the Great Australian Bight Trawl Fishery are managed by the Commonwealth of Australia. In September 1989, a total allowable catch of 15 000 t of orange roughy was introduced to protect the St Helens spawning aggregation, and 'Eastern' and 'Southern' management zones were created in the South East Fishery. Catches in the 2 management zones were regulated by total allowable catch limits in 1990 and 1991. From the beginning of 1992 this fishery was managed by individual transferable quotas, with total allowable catch limits applied to 3 management zones. The Great Australian Bight Trawl Fishery has restrictions on the number of vessels licensed to fish the region.

Recreational fishery

There is no recreational fishery for orange roughy.

Resource status

The Australian orange roughy fishery has developed relatively recently and the status of the resource is still uncertain.[15] Biomass assessment has proven particularly difficult because of this species' deep water habitat, wide distribution and alternating dispersed/ aggregating behaviour. Available evidence suggests that the long-term sustainable yield is low as orange roughy have a low fecundity, slow growth and a long life. The history of the New Zealand fishery, which has been operating since 1979, supports this view. An acoustic estimate of the St Helens spawning aggregation calculated the virgin (ie unfished) biomass as 110 000 t. No biomass estimates are available elsewhere in this fishery. The most recent maximum sustainable yield estimates for the South East Fishery are in the order of thousands of t rather than tens of thousands.

References

1. Merrett, N.R. and Wheeler, A. (1983) The correct identification of two trachichthyid fishes (Pisces, Berycomorphi) from the shore fauna west of Britain, with notes on the abundance and commercial importance of *Hoplostethus atlanticus*. *Journal of Natural History* **17**: 569–573.

2. Do, M.A. and Coombs, R.F. (1989) Acoustic measurements of the population of orange roughy (*Hoplostethus atlanticus*) on the north Chatham Rise, New Zealand, in winter 1986. *New Zealand Journal of Marine and Freshwater Research* **23**: 225–237.

3. Newton, G.M., Turner, D. and Riley, S.P. (1990) Spawning roughy in the GAB — a new find. *Australian Fisheries* **49**(10): 24–26.

4. Graham, K.J. (1990) *Kapala cruise report no. 107*. Sydney: NSW Agriculture and Fisheries. 22 pp.

5. Pankhurst, N.W. (1988) Spawning dynamics of orange roughy, *Hoplostethus atlanticus*, in mid-slope waters of New Zealand. *Environmental Biology of Fishes* **21**(2): 101–116.

6. Lyle, J.M., Kitchener, J.A. and Riley, S.P. (1990) St Helens roughy site — 1990 season. *Australian Fisheries* **48**(12): 20–24.

7. Bell, J.D., Lyle, J.M., Bulman, C.M., Graham, K.J., Newton, G.M. and Smith, D.C. (1992) Spatial variation in reproduction, and occurrence of non-reproductive adults, in orange roughy, *Hoplostethus atlanticus*

Orange roughy caught off St Helens and unloaded at Bicheno, east coast of Tasmania, prior to trucking to a Hobart processor. (Source: Lindsay Chapman, Bureau of Resource Sciences)

Collett (Trachichthyidae), from south-eastern Australia. *Journal of Fish Biology* **40**: 107–122.

8. Fenton, G.E., Short, S.A. and Ritz, D.A. (1991) Age determination of orange roughy, *Hoplostethus atlanticus* (Pisces: Trachichthyidae) using $^{210}Pb/^{226}Ra$ disequilibria. *Marine Biology* **109**: 197–202.

9. Lyle, J.M., Baron, M. and Cropp, R. (1991) Developmental trawling suggests potential for Remote Zone. *Australian Fisheries* **50** (2): 10–12.

10. Robertson, D.A. (1991) *The New Zealand orange roughy fishery — an overview.* Pp 38–48, in *Issues and opportunities — Proceedings of the Australian and New Zealand Southern Trawl Fisheries conference, Melbourne, 6–9 May 1990.* Ed by K. Abel, M. Williams and P. Smith. *Proceedings of the Bureau of Rural Resources* **10.**

11. Newton, G.M. and Burnell, S. (1989) 'Roughy rush' in the Great Australian Bight. *Australian Fisheries* **48**(7): 10–13.

12. Bulman, C.M. and Koslow, J.A. (1992) Diet and food consumption of a deep-sea fish, orange roughy *Hoplostethus atlanticus* (Pisces: Trachichthyidae), from southeastern Australian waters. *Marine Ecology in Progress Series* **82**(2): 115–129.

13. Rosecchi, E., Tracey, D.M. and Webber, W.R. (1988) Diet of orange roughy *Hoplostethus atlanticus* (Pisces: Trachichthyidae) on the Challenger Plateau, New Zealand. *Marine Biology* **99**: 293–306.

14. Lyle, J.M. (in press, 1992) Orange roughy *Hoplostethus atlanticus.* In, *The South East Fishery: a scientific review with particular reference to quota management.* Ed by R.D.J. Tilzey. *Bureau of Resource Sciences Bulletin.*

15. Bureau of Rural Resources (1992) South East trawl orange roughy. *Fishery Status Report*, February 1992. Canberra. 4 pp.

Contributors

The information presented here was originally provided by Jeremy Lyle and Gina Newton. Additional contributions were made by (in alphabetical order) Cathy Bulman, Tony Smith and Richard Tilzey. Drawing by Rosalind Poole. (*Details of contributors and their organisations are given in the Acknowledgements section at the back of this book.*)
Compilers Kay Abel, Patricia Kailola, Christina Grieve (maps) and Phillip Stewart (statistics)

R e d f i s h

C e n t r o b e r y x   a f f i n i s

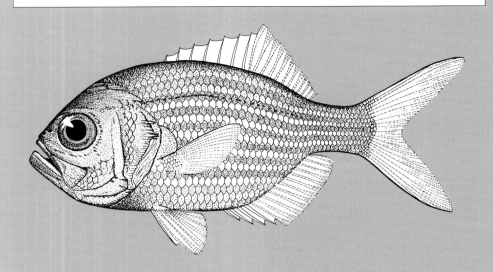

Centroberyx affinis (Günther)

Redfish

Other common names include **nannygai**, **red snapper** and **golden snapper**.
FAO: no known name
Australian species code: 258003

Family BERYCIDAE

Diagnostic features Redfish have moderately short compressed bodies, a spiny head, large eyes and rough scales. They have 7 spines and 11–12 rays in the dorsal fin. The upper parts of their head and body are red and the lower surface is silvery. The scales have red spots forming thin lines along their body and the eyes are red. The tail is red and other fins are pinkish.

Distribution

Redfish live in south-eastern waters of Australia from Moreton Bay in Queensland to western Bass Strait, including north-eastern Tasmanian waters, although the species is most abundant off the New South Wales coast. Redfish have been reported from trawl catches off western Victoria and South Australia but these specimens may have been confused with similar species such as Bight redfish (*Centroberyx gerrardi*). The distribution also extends to New Zealand where redfish are most common in northern waters.[1]

Juvenile redfish inhabit estuaries and shallow coastal waters while adults are found over reefs and mud substrates in continental shelf and slope waters to a depth of 450 m.[2] Trawl catches are highest in depths of 100 m to 300 m[3] and fish show some diurnal movement, forming schools near the sea bed at dawn and dusk.

Life history

Spawning takes place in late summer and autumn and is thought to occur throughout the species' distribution.[4] There is no information on the numbers of eggs released, spawning behaviour or larval biology although larvae have been collected in waters shallower than 100 m off central New South Wales.[5]

Redfish are relatively slow growing, maturing at approximately 4 years of age and lengths of 20–25 cm. They reach a maximum size of 38 cm fork length for females at age 16 years and 33 cm for males at 11 years.[6] These ages have been estimated by examination of otoliths, although the results of recent tagging studies suggest that redfish may grow more slowly than indicated by otolith structure.[4] Redfish in New Zealand waters have been reported to reach a total length of 50 cm.[1]

Tagging studies have shown considerable movement by individual fish although no seasonal migration has been reported. Redfish do move through the water column, schooling near the sea bed during the day and moving to upper layers to feed at night. This diurnal movement may not occur consistently however, as redfish are often caught near the sea floor by trawlers at night.[4]

Redfish eat small fish, crustaceans and molluscs.[7] There is no information on predators of redfish.

Stock structure

Tagging studies[8] indicate a single stock off New South Wales but the genetic relationship with fish from other areas is unknown.

Geographic distribution and commercial fishing areas for redfish in Australian waters.

Distribution
Commercial fishing area
Assumed limit

Scale 1 : 30 500 000

Tagged redfish prior to release. (Source: NSW Fisheries)

Redfish catch waiting to be unloaded, south coast of New South Wales, mid 1970s. (Source: Australian Fisheries Management Authority)

Commercial fishery

Prior to World War II most redfish caught by trawlers operating off New South Wales were discarded due to their low market price. Following the War, landings of redfish by steam trawlers increased and peaked at 2500 t in 1949, mainly as a result of declining tiger flathead (*Neoplatycephalus richardsoni*) catches.[9] Redfish catches declined as steam trawlers left the fishery and the catch during the late 1950s and the 1960s was taken primarily by Danish seiners. The entry of diesel powered trawlers into the fishery in the late 1960s again initiated an increase in catches, which peaked at about 2400 t in 1980.[4]

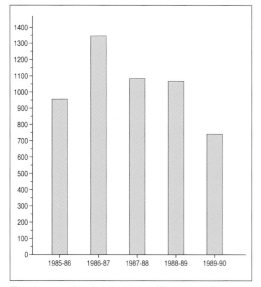
Total annual catch in t of redfish from the South East Fishery for the period 1985–86 to 1989–90. Catch records for 1985–86 are incomplete. (Source: Australian Fishing Zone Information System)

The main fishery for redfish is part of the South East Fishery, with most of the catch taken by demersal otter trawlers between Sydney and Eden.[4] Redfish are also caught by trawl vessels operating as far north as Crowdy Head, but in smaller quantities than off southern New South Wales. Modest catches are taken in eastern Bass Strait and small quantities of redfish are also taken as a bycatch of the trap fishery for snapper (*Pagrus auratus*) in New South Wales.

Redfish are commonly caught with tiger flathead and jackass morwong (*Nemadactylus macropterus*) in depths of less than 200 m. About half of the redfish catch is taken by target fishing, with the remainder caught as bycatch. Historically, redfish were caught in summer on the continental shelf, but in recent years 30 % of the catch has been caught in waters between 200 m and 450 m, mainly as bycatch in the winter gemfish (*Rexea solandri*) fishery.

The mean size of redfish in trawl catches has declined from 25 cm fork length in 1975[8] to less than 20 cm fork length, and fish as small as 17 cm fork length are common.[4] Redfish are an important component of the domestic fresh fish market and are sold mostly whole and chilled. Most of the redfish catch is sold at the Sydney Fish Market. In 1991–92 the average wholesale price there was A$ 0.90 per kg.

Management controls South of Barranjoey Head, the redfish fishery is managed by the Commonwealth of Australia under the South East Fishery

Management Plan with associated limited entry provisions, boat replacement policy and gear restrictions. A total allowable catch limit and individual transferable quotas were introduced for South East Fishery catches of redfish in January 1992. Fishers who trawl for redfish north of Barranjoey Head in New South Wales are subject to management by the New South Wales Government.

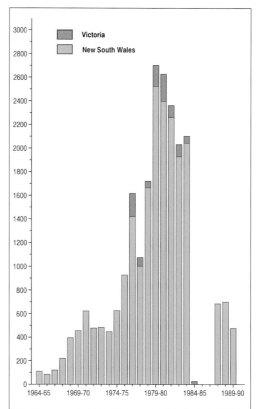
Total annual catch in t of redfish for the period 1964–65 to 1989–90. Figures are unavailable for: New South Wales from 1984–85 to 1986–87; and Victoria from 1970–71 to 1975–76 and 1985–86 to 1989–90. Catches for States that average less than 5 % of the total for all States are not shown. (Source: Fisheries Resources Atlas Statistical Database)

Recreational fishery

Redfish are an incidental catch of anglers fishing reefs for snapper and morwong, and open ground for flathead (Platycephalidae). They are normally caught on handlines or rod-and-line and are often used as live bait for yellowfin tuna (*Thunnus albacares*). The largest redfish caught by an angler under Australian Anglers Association rules was 2.0 kg, caught in 1984 off Sydney.

Management controls There are no management controls on anglers fishing for redfish.

Resource status

Redfish catches have decreased steadily since 1980. Trends in catch rates and size composition of commercial catches indicate a significant reduction in the population off New South Wales, mainly due to commercial fishing.[4] Pending the results of further research, the total allowable catch for the South East Fishery in 1992 was set at a level below the mean of historic catches. This catch limit was intended to encourage recovery of the redfish stock to a more productive state.

Notes

Bight redfish are closely related to redfish. They are distributed from Bass Strait to south-western Western Australia and inhabit the same depths as redfish.[2] Bight redfish grow to a larger size (66 cm total length) and can be identified by their red fins with white margins, silvery longitudinal lines along their body and 6 spines in their dorsal fin. Sampling of commercial catches indicate a single spawning period in March and April.[10] Bight redfish are most abundant in the Great Australian Bight where catches are taken by demersal trawlers licensed to operate in the Great Australian Bight Trawl Fishery. The total catch of Bight redfish from the trawl fishery was 57 t in 1988, increasing to 239 t in 1990. The bulk of the catch is taken at night.

References

1. Paul, L. (1986) *New Zealand fishes. An identification guide.* Auckland: Reed Methuen. 184 pp.

2. May, J.L. and Maxwell, J.G.H. (1986) *A field guide to trawl fish from temperate waters of Australia.* Hobart: CSIRO Division of Fisheries Research. 492 pp.

3. Tilzey, R.D.J., Zann-Schuster, M., Klaer, N.L. and Williams, M.J. (1990) The south east trawl fishery: biological synopses and catch distributions for seven major commercial fish species. *Bureau of Rural Resources Bulletin* **6**. 80 pp.

4. Rowling, K.R. (in press, 1992) Redfish. In *The South East Fishery: a scientific review with particular reference to quota management.* Ed by R.D.J. Tilzey. *Bureau of Resource Sciences Bulletin.*

5. Graham, K.J, Gibbs, P.J. and Gorman, T.B. (1987) *Kapala cruise report No. 102.* Fisheries Research Institute, NSW Department of Agriculture and Fisheries. 25 pp.

6. Diplock, J.H. (1984) A synopsis of available data on redfish *Centroberyx affinis* from NSW waters. *Demersal and Pelagic Fish Research Group workshop on trawl fish resources, Sydney, 27–29 March 1984. Working Paper.*

7. Rowling, K.R. (1990) Estimation of fishing mortality, stock unity and growth of redfish *Centroberyx affinis* by tagging. *Fisheries Research Institute, NSW Fisheries. FIRTA Project 85/71, Final report of the redfish tagging study.*

8. *Commercial fisheries of New South Wales* (1982) N.S.W. State Fisheries. 60 pp.

9. Fairbridge, W.S. (1952) The New South Wales tiger flathead, *Neoplatycephalus macrodon* (Ogilby) II. The age composition of the commercial catch, overfishing of the stocks and suggested conservation. *Australian Journal of Marine and Freshwater Research* **3**: 1–31.

10. Burnell, S. and Newton, G. (1989) Commercial stocks in the GAB. *Australian Fisheries* **48**(4): 20–24.

Contributors

Most of the information on this species was provided by Kevin Rowling. Additional information on Bight redfish was provided by Gina Newton and Danny Turner. Richard Tilzey provided further comment as well as (in alphabetical order) Barry Hutchins, Peter Last and Rosalind Poole. Drawing by Roger Swainston. (*Details of contributors and their organisations are given in the Acknowledgements section at the back of this book.*)
Compilers Phillip Stewart and Christina Grieve (maps)

Dories

Zenopsis nebulosus and *Zeus faber*

Dories

This presentation is on 2 species, **mirror dory** and **John dory**.

Mirror dory, *Zenopsis nebulosus* (Temminck and Schlegel)

Another common name is **silver dory**.
FAO: no known name
Australian species code: 264003

John dory, *Zeus faber* Linnaeus

Another common name is **kuparu**.
FAO: **John dory**
Australian species code: 264004

Family ZEIDAE

Diagnostic features Mirror dory (pictured) have a silvery body with a large faint greyish blotch on the side and no scales except along the lateral line. John dory are olive-green and have a large black spot with a white or yellow margin on each side. Their bodies are covered with minute scales. Both species have numerous bony scutes arranged adjacent to the dorsal and ventral profiles. Mirror dory have 3 scutes in front of the ventral fin and John dory have 7 or 8. Mirror dory have 8 or 9 spines in the dorsal fin and John dory have 10 spines with long filamentous membranes between them.

Distribution

Mirror dory are distributed throughout the continental shelf and upper slope waters off southern Australia from Broken Bay in New South Wales to the North West Shelf off Western Australia. Mirror dory are also recorded from New Zealand and Japan. John dory are present in continental shelf waters from Moreton Bay in Queensland to Cape Cuvier in Western Australia. They also inhabit the western Indian Ocean, eastern Atlantic Ocean, Mediterranean Sea, and the waters of New Zealand and Japan.

Mirror dory are recorded from waters as deep as 800 m[1] but are mostly caught in depths between 50 m and 600 m.[2] John dory inhabit depths from 5 m to 360 m[1,3] although they are uncommon in waters deeper than 200 m. Both species live close to the sea bed.

Life history

Mirror dory spawn during winter in New South Wales waters, apparently over a prolonged period from May to September.[2] The eggs are large, approximately 2 mm in diameter.[2] It is not known whether individuals undergo a single spawning or a series of spawnings over the winter months. Nothing is known about larval development or early life history for mirror dory, and no studies on ageing and growth rates have been undertaken for this species. Mirror dory grow to a maximum size of 70 cm total length and a weight of at least 3 kg.[1] Samples from trawl catches indicate that mirror dory reach maturity at about 35 cm total length.

John dory are known to spawn off the coast of New South Wales in late summer and autumn at depths of 50 to 100 m.[4] No studies of their reproductive development or early life history have been undertaken in Australia. John dory reach a maximum

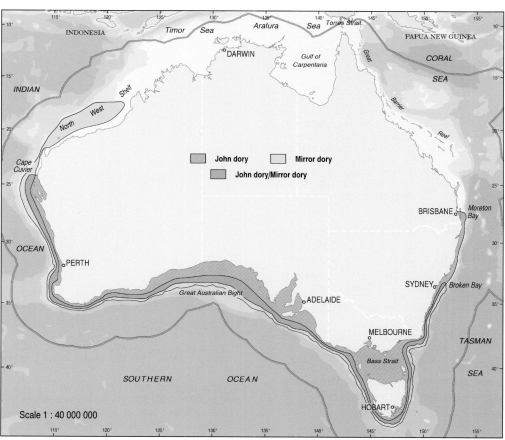

Geographic distribution of mirror dory and John dory in Australian waters.

size of 65 cm total length and a weight of 3 kg.[4] The otoliths of both mirror dory and John dory are small and the structure is difficult to interpret for ageing purposes. In New Zealand, John dory are reported to mature at an age of 3 to 4 years and live to a maximum of 9 years.[5]

No information is available on migration and movement of either dory species in Australia. Mirror dory are carnivorous, feeding on fish, crustaceans and molluscs.[6] John dory have a similar diet and are active predators.[5,6]

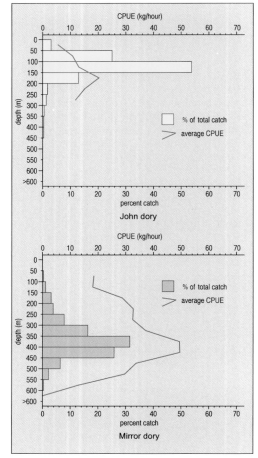

Percentage catch and average catch per unit effort (CPUE) of John dory and mirror dory from the South East Fishery by 50 m depth zone. CPUE values are not shown for John dory below 300 m depth due to possible misrecording of other dory species. (Source: Australian Fishing Zone Information System)

Stock structure

Nothing is known of stock structure for mirror dory and John dory in Australian waters.

Commercial fishery

Mirror dory are caught only by vessels using demersal otter trawls. The main Australian fishery is located off New South Wales and eastern Victoria, although some catch is taken throughout other areas of the South East Fishery.

Catches of mirror dory in the South East Fishery have ranged between 370 t and 460 t between 1986–87 and 1989–90. Small amounts are also caught in the Great Australian Bight Trawl Fishery, the Western Deepwater Trawl Fishery and the North West Slope Trawl Fishery. Up until 1992 the mirror dory catch was mainly taken as a bycatch of the winter fishery for gemfish (*Rexea solandri*). The catch consisted of large mature fish, between 40 and 50 cm total length.[2] Mirror dory are also taken throughout the year as a bycatch of trawling for various continental slope species.

John dory are taken primarily as a bycatch of the South East Fishery, although from shallower grounds than the mirror dory fishery. John dory are trawled from depths between 50 m and 200 m off New South Wales and eastern Victoria. The main species trawled on these grounds are tiger flathead (*Neoplatycephalus richardsoni*), jackass morwong (*Nemadactylus macropterus*) and redfish (*Centroberyx affinis*).[4] Catches of John dory from the South East Fishery showed little variation between 1985–86 and 1989–90, ranging from 180 t to 207 t. John dory are also commonly caught by Danish seine vessels in Victorian waters

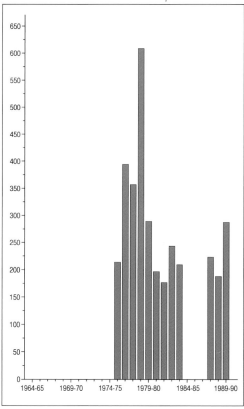

Total annual catch in t of mirror dory for the period 1975–76 to 1989–90 in New South Wales. Figures are unavailable from 1964–65 to 1974–75 and 1984–85 to 1986–87. (Source: Fisheries Resources Atlas Statistical Database)

John dory are an excellent table fish and command high prices on the domestic fresh fish market. (Source: Australian Fisheries Management Authority)

and occasionally by haul seines in bays and estuaries.

Both dory species are sold on the domestic fresh fish market as whole fish. John dory command higher prices than mirror dory, with an average wholesale price of A$ 5.69 per kg at the Sydney Fish Market during 1991–92. Mirror dory

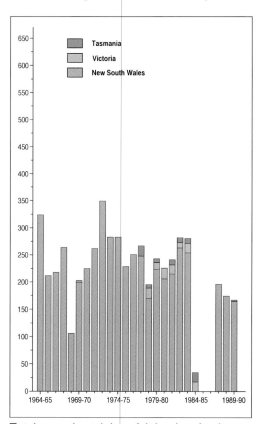

Total annual catch in t of John dory for the period 1964–65 to 1989–90. Figures are unavailable for: New South Wales from 1984–85 to 1986–87; Victoria from 1972–73 to 1977–78 and 1985–86 to 1989–90. Catches for States that average less than 5 % of the total for all States are not shown. (Source: Fisheries Resources Atlas Statistical Database)

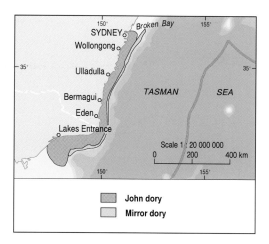

Commercial fishing areas for mirror dory and John dory in Australian waters.

averaged A$ 2.05 per kg for the same period.

Management controls Fishers trawling or Danish seining for dories in the South East Fishery are subject to management by the Commonwealth of Australia. Total allowable catch limits were introduced for each species in January 1992 with allocation of catch to fishers in the form of individual transferable quotas. The Commonwealth of Australia also manages the Great Australian Bight Trawl Fishery, the Western Deepwater Trawl Fishery and the North West Slope Trawl Fishery. Trawl vessels catching John dory north of latitude 33°35' S in New South Wales are managed by the State government. Fishers catching John dory within the coastal waters of a particular State, ie within 3 nautical miles of the coast, are subject to fisheries regulations of that State.

Recreational fishery

Mirror dory are rarely caught by anglers because of the depths they inhabit. In estuaries and bays, John dory are often caught by anglers using live fish baits, and on inshore reefs, anglers may catch John dory using whole fish or flesh baits.[7] The Australian Anglers Association record for John dory is 2.95 kg and was recorded from New South Wales in 1974.

Management controls There are no management controls which apply specifically to dories.

Resource status

Catches of mirror dory in south-eastern Australian waters have been relatively stable over recent years although there is some evidence of irregular recruitment.[2] Lack of biological information has precluded any estimates of biomass or sustainable yield.[2] The catch history for John dory has shown little variation and current catch levels seem to be sustainable.[4]

Notes

Two other species from the dory family are caught as bycatch in the South East Fishery, although these are landed in smaller quantities than mirror dory and John dory. They are king dory (*Cyttus traversi*) and silver dory (*C. australis*). King dory are caught in continental slope waters to 800 m depth and silver dory inhabit waters down to 350 m. Both

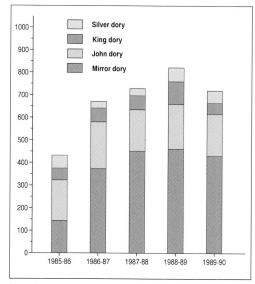

Total annual catch in t of mirror dory, John dory, king dory and silver dory from the South East Fishery for the period 1985–86 to 1989–90. The catch records for 1985–86 are incomplete. (Source: Australian Fishing Zone Information System)

species are distributed throughout southern Australian waters.[1]

References

1. Williams, A. (1990) *Deepwater fish guide: commercial trawl fish from the Western and North West Slope Deepwater Trawl Fisheries.* Hobart: CSIRO Division of Fisheries. 46 pp.

2. Rowling, K.R. (in press,1992) Mirror dory. In *The South East Fishery: a scientific review with particular reference to quota management.* Ed by R.D.J. Tilzey. *Bureau of Resource Sciences Bulletin.*

3. May, J.L. and Maxwell, J.G.H. (1986) *A field guide to trawl fish from temperate waters of Australia.* Hobart: CSIRO Division of Fisheries Research. 492 pp.

4. Rowling, K.R. (in press, 1992) John dory. In *The South East Fishery: a scientific review with particular reference to quota management.* Ed by R.D.J. Tilzey. *Bureau of Resource Sciences Bulletin.*

5. Paul, L. (1986) *New Zealand fishes. An identification guide.* Auckland: Reed Methuen. 184 pp.

6. *Commercial fisheries of New South Wales* (1982) N.S.W. State Fisheries. 60 pp.

7. Starling, S. (1988) *The fisherman's handbook. How to find, identify and catch the top Australian angling fish.* Sydney: Angus and Robertson Publishers. 263 pp.

Contributors

Most of the information on these species was originally provided by Kevin Rowling and supplemented by (in alphabetical order) Gina Newton, John Paxton and Richard Tilzey. Drawing by Rosalind Poole. (*Details of contributors and their organisations are given in the Acknowledgements section at the back of this book.*)
Compiler Phillip Stewart

A large catch of mirror dory trawled by the New South Wales Fisheries research vessel *Kapala*. (Source: Ken Graham, NSW Fisheries)

237

Oreos

Oreosomatidae

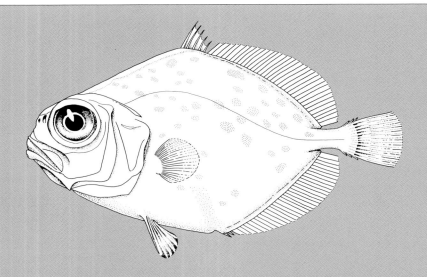

Oreos

This presentation is on 4 species, **smooth oreo**, **black oreo**, **warty oreo** and **spiky oreo**.

Smooth oreo, *Pseudocyttus maculatus* Gilchrist

Other common names include **smooth oreo dory**, **smooth dory**, **spotted dory** and **spotted oreo**.
FAO: no known name
Australian species code: 266003

Black oreo, *Allocyttus niger* James, Inada and Nakamura

Other common names include **black dory**, **black oreo dory** and **spiky dory**.
FAO: no known name
Australian species code: 266005

Warty oreo, *Allocyttus verrucosus* (Gilchrist)

Another common name is **warty dory**.
FAO: no known name
Australian species code: 266004

Spiky oreo, *Neocyttus rhomboidalis* Gilchrist

Other common names include **spiky dory** and **spiky oreo dory**.
FAO: no known name
Australian species code: 266001

Family OREOSOMATIDAE

Diagnostic features Oreos have a deep, laterally compressed body and a moderate to large head which is thicker than the body. Their eyes are large to very large, and their bodies vary in colour from bluish grey to greyish brown or greyish black. In smooth oreos (pictured), the first dorsal spine is longer than the other dorsal spines; the dorsal profile is curved and there are no wart-like scales on the belly. Black oreos have black fins and their first dorsal spine is shorter than the second. Warty oreos have 2 rows of wart-like scales on the belly. Their first dorsal spine is shorter than the second and the dorsal and anal spines are weak. The dorsal profile from the eyes to the dorsal fin is almost straight. Spiky oreos have strong dorsal and anal fin spines, and the first dorsal fin spine is shorter than the second. The dorsal profile from the eyes to dorsal fin is distinctly concave.

Warty oreos and spiky oreos are distributed widely through the southern hemisphere.[1] Warty oreos have an extensive distribution in Australia from Cape Hawke in New South Wales[2] through the continental slope waters of all southern states to the Exmouth Plateau off Western Australia. Spiky oreos are present on the continental slope from Broken Bay[1] north of Sydney to about 26° S latitude in Western Australia.[3]

Adult oreos live close to the sea bed in deep water. All 4 species have been recorded from depths well in excess of 1000 m. The recorded depth ranges for each species are: smooth oreo, 400 m to 1200 m;[1] black oreo, 560 m to 1180 m;[1] warty oreo, 338 m to 1600 m;[1,3] spiky oreo, 200 m[1] to 1240 m. Adult oreos form large shoals over rough ground near pinnacles and canyons. Immature fish tend to be dispersed over smooth grounds.

Life history

There is some variation in spawning time between the 4 oreo species. Smooth oreos and black oreos spawn in November and December in both Australian[4] and New Zealand waters.[5] Several spawning sites for them have been located off southern Tasmania.[4] In Tasmanian waters warty oreos spawn in May and June and spiky oreos show greatest spawning activity in September and October.[4] Spawning in oreos is synchronous and may be stimulated by annual events such as an increase in day length.[5] Oreos produce relatively few eggs[6], estimated[7] at up to 84 000 in smooth oreos and up to 62 000 in black oreos.

Oreo eggs float near the sea surface and the larvae also inhabit surface waters. Juvenile oreos are pelagic and inhabit oceanic waters.

Distribution

Smooth oreos are widespread throughout the southern hemisphere[1] but are most common in Australian and New Zealand waters. In Australia they are known to inhabit the continental slope from Broken Bay in New South Wales[2] to southern Western Australia;[3] and are also present on the Cascade Plateau and South Tasman Rise.

Black oreos inhabit New Zealand and Australian waters south of latitude 43° S.[1] Australian catches of black oreos have been confirmed only from southern Tasmania and the South Tasman Rise but it is likely that this species is also present on the Cascade Plateau.

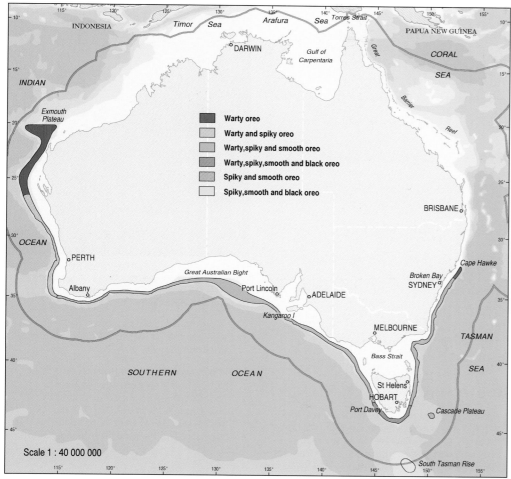

Geographic distribution for smooth oreos, black oreos, warty oreos and spiky oreos in Australian waters.

Information on growth rates and longevity for oreos is very limited due to the difficulty of ageing these species. However, preliminary results from studies on warty oreos at the University of Tasmania using radiometric ageing techniques and at the Victorian Marine Science Laboratories using sectioned otoliths, indicate that this species is long lived:[4] all 4 oreo species might live to ages of 100 years or more.

Smooth oreos are mature at a size of 32 cm total length for males and 41 cm for females.[4] Male black oreos from Tasmanian waters mature at about 33 cm total length and most females by 36 cm.[4] The majority of warty oreos are mature at a total length of 24 cm for males and 28 cm in females.[7] Male spiky oreos mature at about 29 cm total length and females at 34 cm.[7]

Smooth oreos have been recorded to a size of 61 cm total length and a weight of about 5 kg, but there are reports of larger fish in commercial catches. Black oreos in Tasmanian trawl catches range up to 47 cm total length and 1.5 kg. The maximum size for warty oreos is 42 cm total length and 2 kg.[3] Spiky oreos also grow to a total length of 42 cm and 2 kg.[7]

Feeding studies of oreos in New Zealand waters have revealed that smooth oreos feed mainly on salps (Thaliacea) at all ages.[8] Some planktonic crustaceans and fish are also consumed by larger smooth oreos. Salps dominate the diet of black oreos but fish between 30 cm and 40 cm total length consume more crustaceans than salps.[8] Warty oreos feed on crustaceans such as shrimps, amphipods and copepods as well as fish and squid.[7] Salps, fish, crustaceans and squid are probably common prey items for spiky oreos.[7] Many of the planktonic species consumed by oreos undergo daily migrations within the water column. However, trawl catch rates for oreos show no evidence of vertical migration during day or night.[8]

Stock structure

There is no information concerning stock structure of oreos in Australian waters.

Commercial fishery

The main fishing area for oreos is within the South East Fishery, on the continental slope south of Tasmania. There have also been significant catches taken from the Cascade Plateau by foreign vessels under developmental fishing arrangements.[9] Oreos are also landed from eastern Tasmanian waters as bycatch of target trawling on orange roughy (*Hoplostethus atlanticus*) aggregations.

Oreos are caught exclusively by vessels using demersal otter trawl gear. Oreo aggregations tend to be located over rough ground and require the use of 'target trawling' techniques similar to those used for orange roughy. They have been caught as a bycatch of orange roughy fishing for a number of years and, in the early stages of the orange roughy fishery, were normally discarded. Development of markets for oreos has led fishers to retain the oreo bycatch. Some fishers are now targeting aggregations of oreos off southern Tasmania,[7] especially during the closed season for orange roughy. Experienced skippers can often distinguish between orange roughy and oreos by their different acoustic target strengths on the echo sounder.

Smooth oreos are the most common species in oreo landings in Tasmania. However, the percentage of black oreos is increasing. Only small numbers of warty oreos and spiky oreos are landed. Smooth oreos are generally larger fish than the other species and give a more valuable return. Most of the smooth oreo catch has been taken in late spring and summer in the last few years, a seasonal trend probably more related to fishing patterns in the orange roughy fishery than to changes in abundance or catchability of oreos.

Landings of oreos in the South East Fishery were about 60 t per annum between 1985–86 and 1987–88. The catch

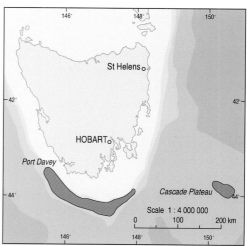

Commercial fishing area for oreos in Australian waters.

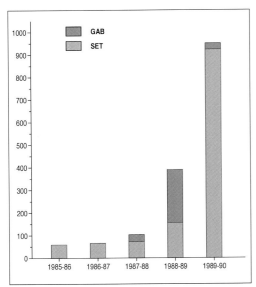

Total annual catch in t of all oreo species from the South East Fishery (SET) and Great Australian Bight Trawl Fishery (GAB) for the period 1985–86 to 1989–90. (Source: Australian Fishing Zone Information System.)

retained increased considerably in 1989–90 to just over 900 t.

Some oreos are caught by vessels fishing orange roughy aggregations in the Great Australian Bight Trawl Fishery. Approximately 200 t of oreos were landed from this fishery in 1988–89 but the 1989–90 catch was less than 30 t. Most of the oreo catch in the Bight is reported to be spiky oreos but they are normally discarded in favour of orange roughy.[10] Further west, exploitation of deepwater trawl grounds off Albany during 1991 has resulted in some significant catches of smooth oreos. However, the amount of oreo catch retained still appears to be determined by catch levels of orange roughy.

Oreos are usually processed into fillets and frozen for both domestic and export markets. Approximately 50 % of the oreo catch is now exported, mainly to Europe and the United States of America. The oreo 'frames' are processed into fertilizer or fishmeal and there is some interest in fish oil production from oreo waste. Fishers receive A$ 0.80 to A$ 1.20 per kg from processors. Wholesale prices on the Melbourne Wholesale Fish Market normally ranged between A$ 1.00 and A$ 1.70 per kg during 1991–92.

Management controls The oreo fishery off Tasmania is managed by the Commonwealth of Australia within the south-western sector of the South East Fishery. Oreos are not subject to a total allowable catch and individual transferable quotas. Fishing for oreos and other trawl species on the Cascade

Plateau and South Tasman Rise is subject to developmental management arrangements for the remote zone of the South East Fishery. Fishers trawling in the Great Australian Bight Trawl Fishery are also subject to Commonwealth management.

Recreational fishery

There is no recreational fishery for oreos.

Resource status

Australian oreo stocks are probably not fully fished at present. However, the low reproductive rate of oreos, their likely slow growth rate and their tendency to form dense aggregations may mean that there is limited scope for expansion of this fishery.

References

1. James, G.D., Inada, T. and Nakamura, I. (1988) Revision of the oreosomatid fishes (Family Oreosomatidae) from the southern oceans, with a description of a new species. *New Zealand Journal of Zoology* **15**: 291–326.

2. Paxton, J.E., Hoese, D.F., Allen, G.R. and Hanley, J.E. (1989) *Zoological catalogue of Australia. Volume 7, Pisces. Petromyzontidae to Carangidae.* Canberra: Australian Government Publishing Service. 664 pp.

3. Williams, A. (1990) *Deepwater fish guide: commercial trawl fish from the Western and North West Slope Deepwater Trawl Fisheries.* Hobart: CSIRO Division of Fisheries. 46 pp.

4. Lyle, J., Riley, S. and Kitchener, J. (1992) Oreos — an underutilised resource. *Australian Fisheries* **51**(4): 12–15.

5. Pankhurst, N.W., McMillan, P.J. and Tracey, D.M. (1987) Seasonal reproductive cycles in

A large catch of oreos in the cod-end of a trawl net. (Source: Sean Riley, Division of Sea Fisheries, Tasmanian Department of Primary Industry and Fisheries)

The net coming aboard a trawler off southern Tasmania. (Source: Sean Riley, Division of Sea Fisheries, Tasmanian Department of Primary Industry and Fisheries)

three commercially exploited fishes from the slope waters off New Zealand. *Journal of Fish Biology* **30**: 193–211.

6. Conroy, A.M. and Pankhurst, N.W. (1989) Size-fecundity relationships in the smooth oreo, *Pseudocyttus maculatus*, and the black oreo, *Allocyttus niger* (Pisces: Oreosomatidae) (Note). *New Zealand Journal of Marine and Freshwater Research* **23**: 525–527.

7. Lyle, J.M., Kitchener, J.A. and Riley, S.P. (1991) An assessment of the orange roughy resource off the coast of Tasmania. *Tasmanian Department of Primary Industry, Sea Fisheries Division. FIRDC Project 87/65, Final Report.* 129 pp.

8. Clark, M.R., King, K.J. and McMillan, P.J. (1989) The food and feeding relationships of black oreo, *Allocyttus niger*, smooth oreo, *Pseudocyttus maculatus*, and eight other fish species from the continental slope of the south-west Chatham Rise, New Zealand. *Journal of Fish Biology* **35**: 465–484.

9. Lyle, J., Baron, M. and Cropp, R. (1991) Developmental trawling suggests potential for remote zone. *Australian Fisheries* **50**(2): 10–12.

10. Newton, G. and Klaer, N. (1991) Deep-sea demersal fisheries resources of the Great Australian Bight: a multivessel trawl survey. *Bureau of Rural Resources Bulletin* **10**. 71 pp.

Contributors

Most of the information on this species was provided by Jeremy Lyle. Additional information was supplied by (in alphabetical order) Gwen Fenton, Gina Newton, Dave Smith, Bryce Stewart and Alan Williams. Drawing by Rosalind Poole. (*Details of contributors and their organisations are given in the Acknowledgements section at the back of this book.*)
Compiler Phillip Stewart.

Distribution

Ocean perch inhabit southern Australian waters from Coffs Harbour in northern New South Wales[1] to latitude 26° S in Western Australia,[2] including Bass Strait and Tasmania. They are also widespread in New Zealand waters.[3]

Adult ocean perch are present in depths from 50 m to 750 m. Two forms of ocean perch are recognised in waters off New South Wales (see 'Stock Structure'). They are referred to as 'inshore' and 'offshore' forms based on their preferred depth ranges. The inshore form is dominant in depths less than 300 m and the offshore form is most common in deeper waters.[1]

Life history

Reproduction in ocean perch is distinctive in that fertilisation is internal. Larvae stay within the female fish until they are approximately 1 mm long before they are released into the water. The reproductive season for ocean perch in New South Wales waters probably extends from June to November.[1] Studies in this region have shown that the inshore and offshore forms of ocean perch begin mating at different times and there is a difference in the length of their larval development prior to release.[1] Studies in New Zealand have shown that female ocean perch of 30 cm fork length produce between 150 000 and 200 000 eggs during the breeding season and may brood 40 000 to 50 000 larvae at any one time.[4]

Little is known of ocean perch larval development or early life history. Larvae with developed eyes and internal organs are found in females of the inshore form. Larvae have not been observed at this level of development in the offshore form. Juveniles of both forms are caught near the edge of the continental shelf by fishers targeting royal red prawns

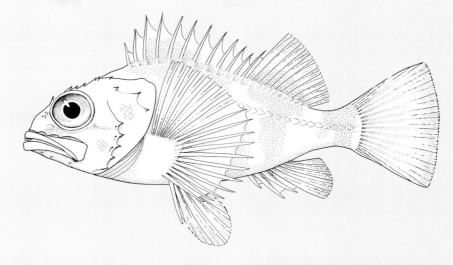

Ocean perch

Helicolenus species

Helicolenus species

Ocean perch

Other common names include **red gurnard perch**, **coral cod**, **coral perch**, **red perch**, **red rock perch** and **sea perch**.
FAO: no known name
Australian species code: 287001

Family SCORPAENIDAE

Diagnostic features Ocean perch are pink with reddish-brown or orange bands on the body that may be faint in some individuals. They have a few series of small spines on the top of the head and operculum, although the bony ridge below the eye is spineless.

(*Haliporoides sibogae*), but their full distribution is unknown.

Ocean perch have a slow growth rate and may be long-lived. The maximum age recorded from examination of otolith rings is 42 years.[5] Ocean perch reach a size of at least 44 cm fork length and 1.4 kg.[5]

The morphology of ocean perch indicates that they feed by resting on the sea bed and ambushing their prey. Squid, royal red prawns and cardinal fish (*Apogonops* species) have been identified in the stomachs of ocean perch in New South Wales waters.

Stock structure

The taxonomy and stock structure of ocean perch in Australia is not well defined. Distinct inshore and offshore forms are present in New South Wales waters. These forms may represent separate stocks or even valid species.[1] The stock structure of ocean perch for the remainder of its Australian distribution is

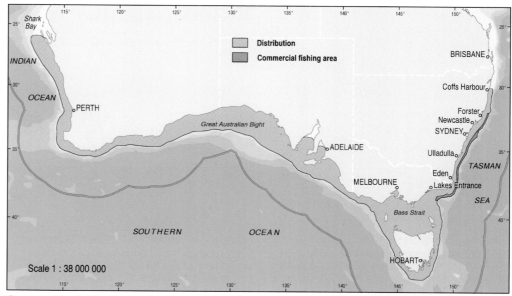

Geographic distribution and commercial fishing area for ocean perch in Australian waters.

unknown. Although ocean perch is normally identified by the scientific name *Helicolenus percoides* (Richardson), the generic term only is used in this presentation due to the uncertain taxonomy of this group.

A closely related species, *Helicolenus barathri*, is known from New Zealand and its distribution may also include southern Australian waters.[1,3]

Commercial fishery

Ocean perch was only a minor commercial species prior to the mid 1970s when the development of trawl fisheries commenced in deep waters off New South Wales and eastern Victoria. The present fishing area for ocean perch is mainly within the eastern sector of the South East Fishery, from Sydney to Lakes Entrance. Ocean perch are also taken as far north as Coffs Harbour although catches are greatest south of Forster. Most of the catch is taken in depths from 350 m to 550 m and there is little change in catch rates between seasons.

Demersal otter trawling is the main method used to catch ocean perch,

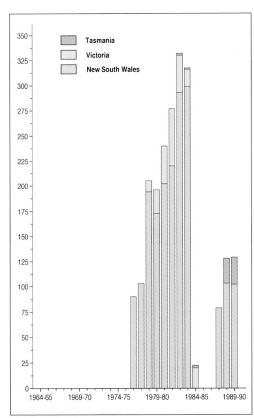

Total annual catch in t of ocean perch for the period 1964–65 to 1989–90. Figures are unavailable for: New South Wales from 1964–65 to 1975–76 and 1984–85 to 1986–87; and Victoria from 1964–65 to 1977–78 and 1985–86 to 1989–90. Catches for States that average less than 5 % of the total for all States are not shown. (Source: Fisheries Resources Atlas Statistical Database)

although only 20 % of the catch is caught by target fishing operations.[1] The remainder is taken as bycatch of target fishing for other demersal fish, and ocean perch are particularly common in catches of royal red prawns.[1] Ocean perch are an incidental catch of Danish seining and droplining, and small quantities are also caught in rock lobster (*Jasus* species) pots in southern Australia. Although ocean perch inhabit South Australian and Western Australian waters, the catch taken in these areas is minimal.

Ocean perch are sold whole and chilled on the domestic fresh fish markets, mainly in Sydney. They are normally sold whole and chilled. The average price obtained on the Sydney Fish Market in 1991–92 was A$ 2.47 per kg.

Management controls The ocean perch fishery is managed by the Commonwealth of Australia through the South East Fishery Management Plan. Limited entry provisions, boat replacement policy and gear restrictions apply. Ocean perch catches within the South East Fishery have been limited by a total allowable catch and transferable quotas since January 1992. Trawl fishers operating north of the South East Fishery are managed by the New South Wales Government.

Recreational fishery

Ocean perch are not targeted by recreational fishers, although they are occasionally caught by anglers fishing from boats in coastal waters.

Management controls There are no specific management controls on recreational fishing for ocean perch.

Resource status

The resource status of ocean perch for Australian waters is unclear. There is

Four examples of the inshore form of ocean perch and 1 example of the offshore form (bottom) from waters off New South Wales. (Source: Tim Park, Fisheries Research Institute, NSW Fisheries)

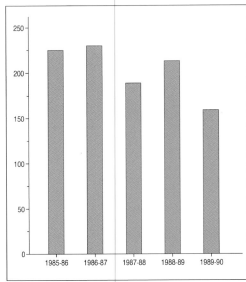

Total annual catch in t of ocean perch from the South East Fishery for the period 1985–86 to 1989–90. The catch records for 1985–86 are incomplete. (Source: Australian Fishing Zone Information System)

some evidence that abundance has decreased off the east coast since the early 1980s.[1]

References

1. Park, T. (in press,1992) Ocean perch. In *The South East Fishery: a scientific review with particular reference to quota management.* Ed by R.D.J. Tilzey. *Bureau of Resource Sciences Bulletin.*

2. Williams, A. (1990) *Deepwater fish guide: commercial trawl fish from the Western and North West Slope Deepwater Trawl Fisheries.* Hobart: CSIRO Division of Fisheries. 46 pp.

3. Paulin, C.D. (1989) Redescription of *Helicolenus percoides* (Richardson) and *H. barathri* (Hector) from New Zealand (Pisces, Scorpaenidae). *Journal of the Royal Society of New Zealand* **19**(3): 319–325.

4. Mines, A. (1975) *Aspects of reproductive biology of some demersal fish species in Wellington Harbour, New Zealand.* Unpublished MSc thesis, Victoria University of Wellington.

5. Withell, A.F. and Wankowski, J.W. (1988) Estimates of age and growth of ocean perch, *Helicolenus percoides* Richardson, in south-eastern Australian waters. *Australian Journal of Marine and Freshwater Research* **39**: 441–457.

Contributors

Most of the information on this species was originally provided by Tim Park and supplemented by (in alphabetical order) Keith Jones and Richard Tilzey. Drawing by Rosalind Poole. (*Details of contributors and their organisations are given in the Acknowledgements section at the back of this book.*)

Compiler Phillip Stewart

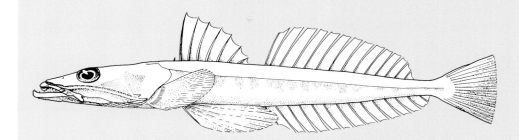

Deepwater flathead

Neoplatycephalus conatus

Neoplatycephalus conatus
(Waite and McCulloch)

Deepwater flathead

Another common name is **trawl flathead**.
FAO: no known name
Australian species code: 296002

Family PLATYCEPHALIDAE

Diagnostic features In deepwater flathead, the lower of the 2 preopercular spines is longer than the upper spine, and the gill rakers are short and thick. Deepwater flathead possess a swim bladder. Their body is greenish purple to grey on the back and whitish below. Their paler sides are often blotched grey and there is a dark blotch on the operculum. The pectoral, ventral and caudal fins are grey.

Distribution

Deepwater flathead are endemic to Australia, inhabiting southern waters from Marrawah in north-western Tasmania to latitude 27° S[1] off Western Australia. They live on the continental shelf and slope from a depth of 70 m[2] to at least 490 m. Deepwater flathead are demersal fish that are distributed over a range of sea bed types.[3]

Life history

In the Great Australian Bight, the spawning period of deepwater flathead lasts from October to February.[3] Spawning activity in the western-central Bight peaks in late summer.[3] There is no information on spawning of deepwater flathead outside the Great Australian Bight.

Little is known of the early life history of this species. Unvalidated ageing of deepwater flathead has produced a maximum age estimate of between 15 and 20 years. Analysis of age and length suggests that females are faster growing and longer lived than males. Female deepwater flathead as large as 94 cm total length and 4 kg have been caught in the Great Australian Bight, while the largest males caught were 62 cm and 1.5–2 kg. Male deepwater flathead reach maturity at about 40 cm total length and 4–5 years of age. Females mature at about 45 cm total length and 5–6 years of age. Catches often consist of up to either 80 % male or female fish, which suggests that this species may aggregate by sex.[3]

Analysis of deepwater flathead diet in the Great Australian Bight has revealed proportions of 60 % fish, 20 % crustaceans and 10 % squid in stomach contents. The remaining 10 % consists of polychaete worms, gastropod molluscs and echinoderms. Deepwater flathead from Victorian waters feed mainly on fish, including worm eels (*Muraenichthys* species), silversides (*Argentina australiae*) and cucumber fish (*Chlorophthalmus nigripinnis*).[4] There is no information on predators of deepwater flathead.

Stock structure

No studies have been carried out on stock structure for deepwater flathead. The average size of deepwater flathead from trawl catches is significantly greater from grounds near Kangaroo Island than for the western-central Great Australian Bight,[3] but it is not known if this size variation indicates the presence of discrete stocks.

Commercial fishery

Deepwater flathead have been trawled sporadically in the Great Australian Bight since the turn of the century. However, only since the Great Australian Bight Trawl Fishery was set up as a developmental fishery in 1988[5] has a commercial fishery for them become established. The most productive grounds for deepwater flathead are on the Ceduna Plateau in the central Bight and the Eyre Plateau further to the west. Catches are less frequent on continental shelf grounds south of Kangaroo Island, mainly as a result of lower fishing effort in that

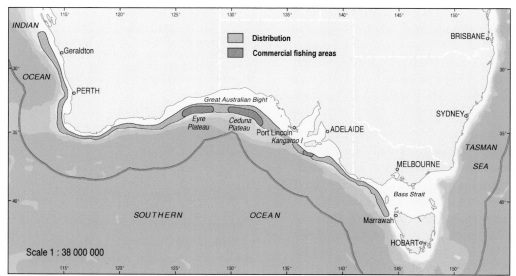

Geographic distribution and commercial fishing areas for deepwater flathead.

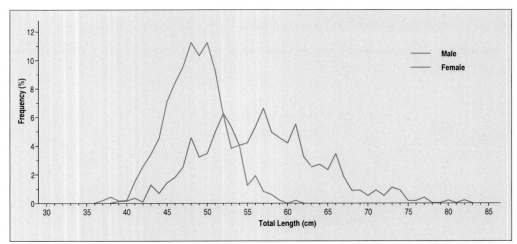

Size composition of deepwater flathead trawl catches from the Great Australian Bight showing differences in size between sexes. The graph is derived from a sample of 463 male fish and 541 females. (Source: Gina Newton, Bureau of Resource Sciences)

region. Small quantities of deepwater flathead are caught in the South East Fishery off western Tasmania and western Victoria, and in southern areas of the Western Deepwater Trawl Fishery.[1]

Deepwater flathead is the dominant species in the continental shelf component of the Great Australian Bight Trawl Fishery, accounting for 40–50 % of landings. Most of the deepwater flathead catch is taken at depths of 100–200 m, and the majority of the fish are between 45 cm and 60 cm total length; very few individuals shorter than 35 cm are caught. The catch includes a variety of other market species such as Bight redfish (*Centroberyx gerrardi*), jackass morwong (*Nemadactylus macropterus*), angel shark (*Squatina tergocellata*), boarfish (Pentacerotidae) and leatherjackets (Monacanthidae).

This fishery is worked by stern trawlers of 23–37 m overall length using demersal otter trawl nets. Deepwater flathead may be trawled at any time of the day and night.[3] The annual catch of deepwater flathead from the Great Australian Bight rose sharply in 1988–89 from previous levels. By 1990–91 it had reached 430 t. However, the average annual trawl catch rates for deepwater flathead have dropped from 127 kg per hour trawled in 1989 to 80–85 kg per hour in 1990 and 1991.[5]

Marketing of the deepwater flathead catch has changed greatly since 1988 when 75 % of landings were exported, mainly as frozen fillets. All of the catch is now sold on the domestic market as fresh, chilled or frozen fillets. The wholesale price for skinless, boneless fillets was about A$ 8.00 per kg in 1992. Fish heads are sold either for use as rock lobster (*Jasus* species) bait or to processors producing fish meal.

Management controls The deepwater flathead fishery is managed by the Commonwealth of Australia as part of the Great Australian Bight Trawl Fishery, the South East Fishery and the Western Deepwater Trawl Fishery. In the South East Fishery deepwater flathead catches are included in a total allowable catch limit applying to all flathead species.

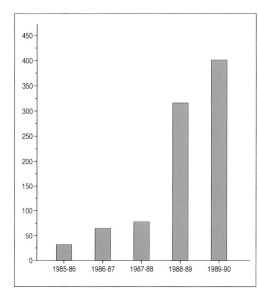

Total annual catch in t of deepwater flathead from the Great Australian Bight Trawl Fishery for the period 1985–86 to 1989–90. (Source: Australian Fishing Zone Information System)

Recreational fishery

There is no recreational fishery for deepwater flathead.

Resource status

Estimates of sustainable yield for deepwater flathead indicate that the resource is currently under-exploited in the Great Australian Bight. However,

Bight redfish is an unavoidable bycatch of target fishing for deepwater flathead and the annual catch of Bight redfish is currently within the range of sustainable yield estimates. In other words, although an increase in the catch of deepwater flathead would not endanger that stock, it would be difficult to take more of them without imposing a risk of over-fishing Bight redfish.

There is no information on the resource status of deepwater flathead stocks outside the Great Australian Bight.

References

1. Williams, A. (1990) *Deepwater fish guide: commercial trawl fish from the Western and North West Slope Deepwater Trawl Fisheries.* Hobart: CSIRO Division of Fisheries. 46 pp.

2. Last, P.R., Scott, E.O.G. and Talbot, F.H. (1983) *Fishes of Tasmania.* Hobart: Tasmanian Fisheries Development Authority. 563 pp.

3. Burnell, S. and Newton, G. (1989) Commercial stocks in the GAB. *Australian Fisheries* **48**(4): 20–24.

4. Coleman, N. and Mobley, M. (1984) Diets of commercially exploited fish from Bass Strait and adjacent Victorian waters, south-eastern Australia. *Australian Journal of Marine and Freshwater Research* **35**: 549–560.

5. Newton, G. and Klaer, N. (1991) *Great Australian Bight Developmental Trawl Fishery — progress report to GABIA.* Bureau of Rural Resources, unpublished report. 8 pp.

Contributors

The information on this species was originally provided by Gina Newton and Danny Turner. Additional comments were provided by (in alphabetical order) Alastair Graham, Dave Smith, Elizabeth Turner and Joe and Marcia Valente. Drawing by Rosalind Poole. (*Details of contributors and their organisations are given in the Acknowledgements section at the back of this book.*)

Compilers Alex McNee and Phillip Stewart

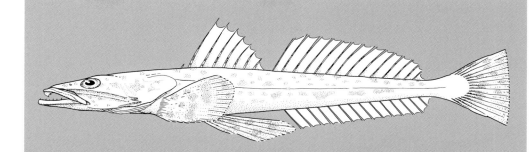

Tiger flathead

Neoplatycephalus richardsoni

Neoplatycephalus richardsoni
(Castelnau)

Tiger flathead

Other common names include **king flathead**, **trawl flathead** and **deep-sea flathead**.
FAO: no known name
Australian species code: 296001

Family PLATYCEPHALIDAE

Diagnostic features Tiger flathead are light brown on the head, back and upper sides. They have light brown to orange-brown spots on the upper body and sometimes grey blotches on the sides. Their undersurface is white. The ventral and pectoral fins and the upper half of the tail have lines of orange-brown spots. Tiger flathead have overlapping scales on their head and body, and 2 spines on the side of their head, in front of the operculum. The lower spine is longer but not more than twice the length of the upper spine. The gill rakers are elongate, their length much greater than their width. Tiger flathead have swim bladders.

Distribution

Tiger flathead are endemic to Australian waters and are distributed from Coffs Harbour in northern New South Wales[1] to Portland in Victoria, including Bass Strait and Tasmania. They inhabit depths of 10–400 m but are most common in waters less than 200 m deep.[2]

Tiger flathead are not active fish and will normally rest on the the sea bed during the day in areas of mud and sand substrate. They may migrate into the water column at night following prey species.[3]

Life history

Spawning grounds have not been defined for tiger flathead. Fish in spawning condition have been caught in northern and southern regions of the species' distribution. They spawn between October and May in New South Wales waters, and spawning tends to occur earlier in the north than in the south.[4] Tiger flathead in eastern Bass Strait spawn from December to February.[5] There is evidence that mature fish migrate to shallower waters prior to the spawning period and also tend to concentrate in 'shoals' on the inshore grounds.[4] Estimates of the maximum number of eggs produced by tiger flathead range from 1.5 million[5] to 2.5 million.[3] The eggs and larvae are thought to be pelagic but there is currently little known of the early life history of this species.[6]

Tiger flathead reach maturity at 4–5 years and a total length of about 30 cm for males and 36 cm for females.[4] Female fish live to an age of 12 years[6] and reach a total length of approximately 65 cm. Estimates of maximum age for males vary from 8 to 10 years.[6] However, male tiger

flathead grow more slowly than females and male fish larger than 50 cm total length are uncommon. Juvenile tiger flathead inhabit shallow waters of the continental shelf and move into the outer shelf zone as they reach maturity. The different sizes at maturity for each sex produce varying sex ratios in the commercial catch — most fish below 37 cm caudal fork length are male while females dominate the catch of larger fish.[7]

Adult tiger flathead feed mainly on small fish such as silversides (*Argentina australiae*) and three-spined cardinalfish (*Apogonops anomalus*).[8] Juveniles feed mainly on crustaceans including krill (*Nyctiphanes australis*). Tiger flathead leave the sea bed at night to feed on fish and crustaceans which migrate upwards in the water column.[3] Predators of tiger flathead include John dory (*Zeus faber*) and larger tiger flathead.[8]

Stock structure

Very little research has been undertaken on tiger flathead stock structure. Morphometric studies[4] and tagging programs[2] indicate the existence of a single stock, despite regional differences in growth rates and spawning periods.

Commercial fishery

The tiger flathead fishery has existed since the commencement of trawling by New South Wales Government steam trawlers in 1915. The fishery was limited to waters between Crowdy Head and Gabo Island up until 1930, when trawling began in eastern Bass Strait.[4] About 6000 t of tiger flathead were caught in 1929, an amount more than double the total Australian catch in recent years.[6] Tiger

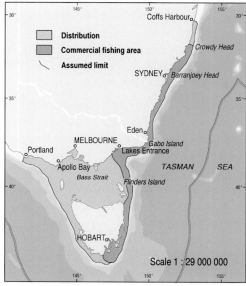

Geographic distribution and commercial fishing area for tiger flathead.

A tagged tiger flathead prior to release off New South Wales. (Source: Kevin Rowling, Fisheries Research Institute, NSW Fisheries)

flathead accounted for 80–90 % of the New South Wales trawl catch up until 1930 but the stock declined during the decade leading to World War II. Despite the entry of a number of Danish seine vessels into the fishery in 1937, catches did not rise to more than 3500 t in that year.[4] There was little fishing done during the War due to requisition of trawlers and Danish seiners as mine sweepers. Afterwards fishing effort increased but catches gradually fell to about 1000 t by 1948–49 and remained at levels near 1000 t until the introduction of diesel powered trawlers in the 1970s.[6] Catch levels have since increased and have ranged between 2000 t and 3000 t since 1985.

The commercial fishing area for tiger flathead extends along the south-eastern coast from Crowdy Head to the southern tip of Tasmania. Most of the catch is taken from eastern Bass Strait by demersal otter trawlers and Danish seine vessels. Very few tiger flathead are caught by any other method. Most tiger flathead landed are between 33 cm and 45 cm total length.[4]

The Danish seine fleet is based at Lakes Entrance in Victoria and restricts its fishing effort mainly to the eastern Bass Strait grounds.[9] Some Danish seine vessels take small amounts of tiger flathead from central Victorian waters as far west as Apollo Bay. A few Danish seiners also operate in south-eastern coastal waters of Tasmania. Most of the tiger flathead catch from Danish seine vessels is a result of target fishing.

Catches of tiger flathead are taken mainly from depths up to 150 m, the 100–150 m depth zone yielding the highest catch rate.[2] Most fish are caught from October to March in eastern Bass Strait.[9] The most common bycatch species are eastern school whiting (*Sillago flindersi*) and jackass morwong (*Nemadactylus macropterus*).[9]

Otter trawlers catch tiger flathead throughout the commercial fishing area but highest catch rates are recorded between Eden and Flinders Island, including the eastern Bass Strait grounds. Tiger flathead are caught by trawl fishers all year and over a wider depth range than by Danish seine boats. Maximum catch rates are obtained by trawlers in depths between 150 m and 200 m.[2,6] Trawl fishers target tiger flathead, especially in eastern Bass Strait, but a significant proportion of the catch is taken as bycatch when targeting species such as jackass morwong and redfish (*Centroberyx affinis*). Jackass morwong, redfish and John dory are also the main bycatch species when trawling for tiger flathead.[6]

Tiger flathead are reported in trawl catches from western Victorian waters although it is probably not the dominant flathead species in that area.[2] Trawl catches of flathead taken west of Bass Strait are most likely to consist of gold-spot flathead (*Neoplatycephalus aurimaculatus*) and deepwater flathead (*N. conatus*). Trawl and Danish seine catches reported as tiger flathead from waters east of Bass Strait also include unknown proportions of other flathead species, such as sand flathead

(*Platycephalus bassensis*) and yank flathead (*P. speculator*).[2]

Tiger flathead are sold on the domestic market usually as whole fresh fish. The majority of the catch is sold on the Sydney Fish Market but about 600 t is also sold by the Melbourne Wholesale Fish Market each year. The average price for tiger flathead at the Sydney market was A$ 1.72 per kg in 1991–92.

Management controls The tiger flathead fishery south of latitude 33°35' S is managed by the Commonwealth of Australia under the provisions of the South East Fishery Management Plan. Tiger flathead catches within the South East Fishery have been limited by a total allowable catch and individual transferable quotas applying to all flathead species since January 1992. The tiger flathead fishery north of 33°35' S is managed by the New South Wales Government.

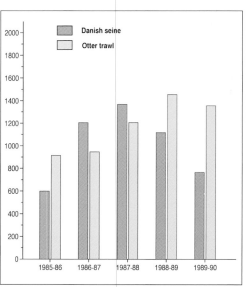

Total annual catch in t of tiger flathead from the South East Fishery by fishing method for the period 1985–86 to 1989–90. The catch records for 1985–86 are incomplete. (Source: Australian Fishing Zone Information System)

Recreational fishery

Tiger flathead are caught by anglers using handlines on inshore grounds in New South Wales and Victoria. Adult tiger flathead are commonly caught by recreational fishers in Tasmanian bays during spring (September-November).[10] The largest tiger flathead recorded by the Australian Anglers Association was 3 kg caught off the central New South Wales coast.

Management controls Minimum legal size restrictions apply to tiger flathead in New South Wales, Victoria and Tasmania.

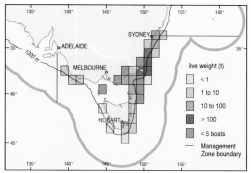

Total trawl catch in t of tiger flathead by 1-degree block from the South East Fishery for 1989–90. The catch for blocks fished by fewer than 5 boats is not shown. (Source: Australian Fishing Zone Information System)

Resource status

Separate estimates of sustainable yield for the New South Wales[7] and eastern Bass Strait[11] regions of the tiger flathead fishery gave a total of 2500 t as the maximum sustainable yield for the whole fishery. Catch levels in recent years have been close to this estimate, indicating that the resource is fully exploited.[6]

References

1. Paxton, J.R., Hoese, D.F., Allen, G.R. and Hanley, J.E. (1989) *Zoological catalogue of*

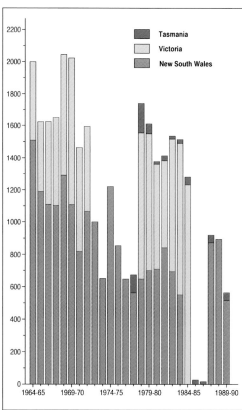

Total annual catch in t of tiger flathead for the period 1964–65 to 1989–90. Figures are unavailable for: New South Wales from 1984–85 to 1986–87; and Victoria from 1972–73 to 1977–78 and 1985–86 to 1989–90. Catches for States that average less than 5 % of the total for all States are not shown. (Source: Fisheries Resources Atlas Statistical Database)

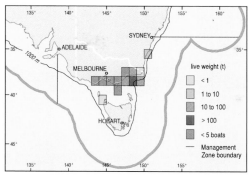

Total Danish seine catch in t of tiger flathead by 1-degree block from the South East Fishery for 1989–90. The catch for blocks fished by fewer than 5 boats is not shown. (Source: Australian Fishing Zone Information System)

Australia. Volume 7, Pisces. Petro-myzontidae to Carangidae. Canberra: Australian Government Publishing Service. 664 pp.

2. Tilzey, R.D.J., Zann-Schuster, M., Klaer, N.L. and Williams, M.J. (1990) The South East Trawl Fishery: biological synopses and catch distributions for seven major commercial fish species. *Bureau of Rural Resources Bulletin* **6**. 80 pp.

3. Colefax, A.N. (1938) A preliminary investigation of the natural history of the tiger flathead (*Neoplatycephalus macrodon*) on the south-eastern Australian coast. II. Feeding habits; breeding habits. *Proceedings of the Linnaean Society of New South Wales* **63**: 155–164.

4. Fairbridge, W.S. (1951) The New South Wales tiger flathead, *Neoplatycephalus macrodon* (Ogilby). I. Biology and age determination. *Australian Journal of Marine and Freshwater Research* **2**: 117–178.

5. Hobday, D.K. and Wankowski, J.W.J. (1987) Tiger flathead *Platycephalus richardsoni* Castelnau: reproduction and fecundity in eastern Bass Strait, Australia. *Victorian Department of Conservation, Forests and Lands, Fisheries Division, Internal Report* **154**. 15 pp.

6. Rowling, K.R. (in press, 1992) Tiger flathead. In, *The South East Fishery: a scientific review with particular reference to quota management.* Ed by R.D.J. Tilzey. *Bureau of Resource Sciences Bulletin.*

7. Montgomery, S.S. (1985) *Aspects of the biology of the tiger flathead* Platycephalus richardsoni *and the associated fishery.* Unpublished MSc thesis, University of New South Wales. 181 pp.

8. Coleman, N. and Mobley, M. (1984) Diets of commercially exploited fish from Bass Strait and adjacent Victorian waters, south-eastern Australia. *Australian Journal of Marine and Freshwater Research* **35**: 549–560.

9. Wankowski, J.W.J. (1983) The Lakes Entrance Danish seine fishery for tiger flathead, school whiting and jackass morwong, 1947–1978. *Victorian Department of Conservation, Forests and Lands, Fisheries and Wildlife Division, Technical Report* **30**. 21 pp.

10. Last, P.R., Scott, E.O.G. and Talbot, F.H. (1983) *Fishes of Tasmania.* Hobart: Tasmanian Fisheries Development Authority. 563 pp.

11. Wankowski, J.W.J. (1986) Surplus yield estimates for the eastern Bass Strait demersal trawl fishery: 3. Tiger flathead. *Victorian Department of Conservation, Forests and Lands, Fisheries Division, Technical Report* **53**. 22 pp.

Contributors

Most of the information on this species was provided by Kevin Rowling. Additional information was supplied by Clive Keenan. Drawing by Rosalind Poole. (*Details of contributors and their organisations are given in the Acknowledgements section at the back of this book.*)

Compiler Phillip Stewart

Flathead

Platycephalus species

Flathead

This presentation is on 2 species, **dusky flathead** and **sand flathead**.

Dusky flathead,
Platycephalus fuscus Cuvier

Other common names include **mud flathead, estuary flathead, dusky, river flathead** and **black flathead**.
FAO: no known name
Australian species code: 296004

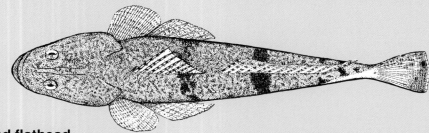

Sand flathead,
Platycephalus bassensis Cuvier

Other common names include **slimy flathead, southern sand flathead, sandy** and **bay flathead**.
FAO: no known name
Australian species code: 296003

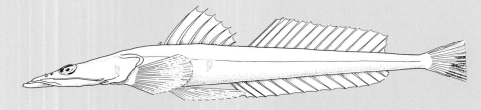

Family PLATYCEPHALIDAE

Diagnostic features Dusky flathead are distinguished by having a conspicuous black spot on the trailing edge of the upper lobe of their dusky caudal fins. Their preopercular spines are subequal, and their gill raker count is 10–12.

Sand flathead have a large (sometimes 2) dark spot on the lower lobe of their caudal fin. Their upper preopercular spine is approximately half the length of the lower spine and their gill raker count is 18–20.[1]

Life history

Both species of flathead spawn in bays and estuaries and in shallow, nearshore coastal waters,[7,8] sometimes over seagrass beds.[3] Spawning appears to take place in response to increasing day length and water temperature.[3,4]

Dusky flathead spawn during the warmer months of September to March in northern tropical waters,[8] November to February in Moreton Bay[2] and January to

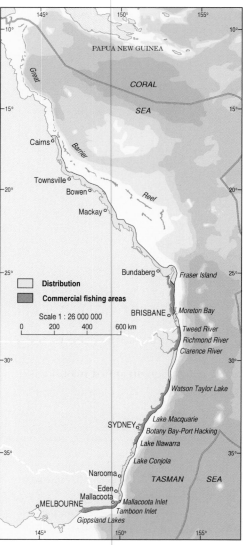

Geographic distribution and commercial fishing areas for dusky flathead.

Distribution

Both flathead species are endemic to Australia. Dusky flathead are present along the east coast between approximately Cairns in Queensland[1] and the Gippsland Lakes in eastern Victoria. Sand flathead are present from Red Rock in northern New South Wales, along the southern Australian coastline as far as Lancelin in Western Australia. They are most common in Victoria and Tasmania.

Dusky flathead generally inhabit shallow bays and inlets and can be found in estuaries as far as tidal limits;[2] they often invade freshwater. Dusky flathead occur over mud, silt, gravel, sand and seagrass (mainly *Zostera* species)[3] beds from intertidal areas to depths of 10 m in Queensland and to 30 m in southern New South Wales. Sand flathead inhabit coastal waters from shallow bays and inlets to depths of about 100 m, over sand, shell grit and mud substrates. In Port Phillip Bay they are most abundant at 15–25 m,[4,5] and in eastern Bass Strait they are found mostly in 35–64 m depths.[6]

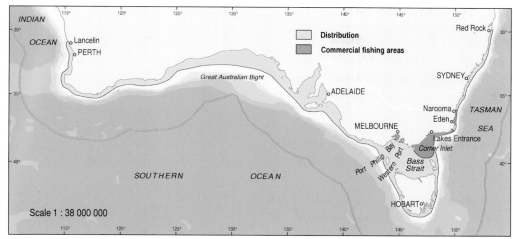
Geographic distribution and commercial fishing areas for sand flathead.

Sand flathead in Port Phillip Bay change their diet seasonally: crustaceans are the main food between October and March and fish are the main food over winter.[4] There is no information on predators of flathead.

Stock structure

There is no information on the stock structure of either dusky flathead or sand flathead.

Commercial fishery

Dusky flathead are one of the most valuable commercial estuarine fish in New South Wales.[7] They are usually caught in sheltered coastal embayments, estuaries, coastal lakes and river mouths. In Queensland, most fishing is in the south-east of the State and takes place from late autumn to early spring. In New South Wales most of the catch comes from north coast estuaries from the Tweed to the Clarence rivers, and from the central coast between Watson Taylor

March in New South Wales[3,7] and Victoria.[9] There is no information on the frequency of their spawning or fecundity. There is conflicting information[2,3,8] on whether dusky flathead are protandrous sex reversers or not (ie whether each fish first functions as a male and then changes to a female). Dusky flathead mature as males probably in their second year and sex reversal (if it occurs) probably takes place at 4 or 5 years of age.[2]

Sand flathead undertake a single, brief spawning between August and October in Port Phillip Bay.[4] There is no information about their reproduction from other areas.

Eggs and larvae of dusky flathead are dispersed along the coast by tidal and current movements.[7] Small juveniles less than 12 cm total length first appear in coastal bays 1–2 months after spawning (eg April in Botany Bay[3]). They mainly inhabit shallow mangrove and mud flats and seagrass beds.[2,3]

Dusky flathead attain a maximum size of approximately 15 kg and 1.2 m total length.[7,9] One-year-old dusky flathead in Queensland waters are about 18 cm total length.[2] By 3 years of age they average 40 cm, and by 8 years of age average 90 cm total length. Dusky flathead mature at a larger size in warmer waters than they do in cooler waters. For example, the average total length at first maturity is 46 cm (males) and 56 cm (females) in Queensland,[8] 32 cm (males) and 38 cm (females) in Botany Bay,[3] and about 26 cm[7,9] (both sexes) in southern New South Wales and Victoria.

Sand flathead are reported to reach a maximum total length of 46 cm[10] and weight of slightly more than 3 kg. In Victoria, they attain 10–12 cm total length after 1 year, 22–30 cm after 4 years and up to 43 cm after 9 years.[4,5] Maximum age is

estimated at 7 years for males and 9 years for females.[4] In Port Phillip Bay, all sand flathead are mature by 22 cm total length.[4]

Flathead are usually solitary but may form loose aggregations.[4,8] They sometimes move long distances. For example, a dusky flathead tagged at Fraser Island, Queensland, was recaptured 230 km south after 97 days' liberty.[11] Tagging studies in the Clarence and Richmond rivers in New South Wales indicate a northward movement, with a number of fish recaptured around Moreton Bay in southern Queensland.

Both species are active foragers and ambush predators, ie they lie partly concealed in mud or sand, lunging out to catch passing prey. They are also occasional scavengers. Prey items vary with locality and include small fish such as whiting (Sillaginidae), mullet (Mugilidae), hardyheads (Atherinidae) and gobies (Gobiidae), and crabs (Portunidae), prawns (eg *Penaeus plebejus*[3]) and other small crustaceans, octopus and squid (Cephalopoda) and polychaete worms. For dusky flathead in Botany Bay, the importance of crustaceans in the diet increases and of fish decreases as the flathead grow,[3] although the converse has been reported for the same species in Moreton Bay.[2]

Angler fishing for flathead, Moreton Island. (Source: Darren Cameron, Southern Fisheries Centre, Queensland Department of Primary Industries)

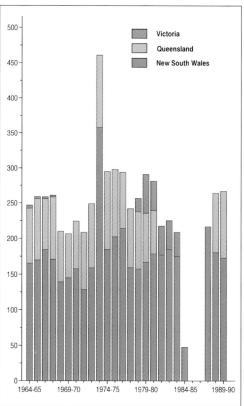
Total annual catch in t of dusky flathead for the period 1964–65 to 1989–90. Figures are unavailable for: New South Wales from 1984–85 to 1986–87; Victoria from 1972–73 to 1977–78 and 1985–86 to 1989–90; and Queensland from 1981–82 to 1987–88. Yank flathead catches are included in New South Wales and Victorian figures, and some northern sand flathead are included in Queensland figures. (Source: Fisheries Resources Atlas Statistical Database)

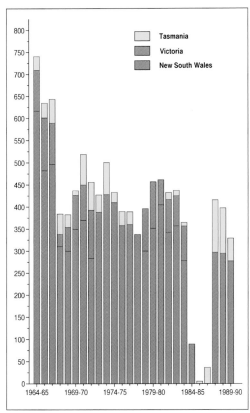

Total annual catch in t of sand flathead for the period 1964–65 to 1989–90. Figures are unavailable for: New South Wales from 1984–85 to 1986–87; Victoria from 1972–73 to 1977–78 and 1985–86 to 1989–90; and Tasmania for 1978–79 and 1979–80. Northern sand flathead catches may be included in the New South Wales figures. (Source: Fisheries Resources Atlas Statistical Database)

Lake and Lake Illawarra. Dusky flathead are caught mainly by gillnets in New South Wales and tunnel nets in Queensland, although in eastern Victoria small catches are also taken in inlets using haul seines or handlines, or in open coastal waters by demersal otter trawlers working inshore for prawns.[9]

Sand flathead are caught commercially by demersal otter trawling and Danish seining in open coastal waters, and by gillnets, haul seines, handlines and anchored longlines in bays and inlets. Commercial catches of sand flathead are taken mainly off southern New South Wales between Narooma and Eden, in eastern Bass Strait[6] and in several Victorian bays and inlets such as Port Phillip Bay[5] (where most catches are made from April to June and from October to November). Sand flathead are a secondary commercial species in Tasmania where tiger flathead (*Neoplatycephalus richardsoni*) are by far the main commercial flathead species. Although widespread in South Australia, sand flathead are not targeted but are caught incidentally on the continental shelf.

The New South Wales sand flathead catch includes an unknown proportion of northern sand flathead, *Platycephalus arenarius*, eastern blue-spotted flathead, *P. caeruleopunctatus* and yank flathead, *P. speculator*. In Port Phillip Bay (Victoria), sand flathead comprise 50–80 % of the total commercial flathead catch. The remainder consists mostly of rock flathead (*P. laevigatus*) and yank flathead.[5]

Flathead are sold whole, or gilled and gutted, or as fillets. For dusky flathead, the average price per kg at the Sydney Fish Market in 1991–92 was A$ 2.50, and the 1992 prices at the Brisbane wholesale market ranged from A$ 2.50 to A$ 4.00 per kg. For whole sand flathead, the average price at the Melbourne Wholesale Fish Market in 1991–92 ranged from A$ 0.84 to A$ 2.25 per kg.

Management controls Sand flathead catches off southern New South Wales and in eastern Bass Strait are controlled by the Commonwealth of Australia under regulations applying to the South East Fishery. Catches of dusky flathead and sand flathead in Queensland and Victorian bays and inlets are controlled under regulations applying to the State-administered multi-species, multi-method

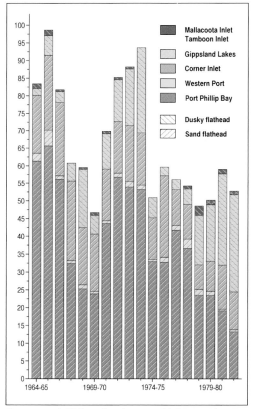

Commercial Victorian bay and inlet catches of sand flathead and dusky flathead for the period 1964–65 to 1981–82.(Source: Fisheries Division, Victorian Department of Conservation and Environment; Winstanley;[9] and Hall and MacDonald.[5])

commercial fisheries, and these include closed areas and gear restrictions. Access to nearshore areas is prohibited in Tasmania, and in New South Wales gillnets are not permitted in estuaries during the summer. Area and seasonal closures and other gear restrictions apply in New South Wales. Legal minimum lengths apply in Queensland, New South Wales, Victoria and Tasmania.

Angler with a large dusky flathead, Moreton Island. (Source: Darren Cameron, Southern Fisheries Centre, Queensland Department of Primary Industries)

Recreational fishery

Dusky flathead are very important in recreational fishing. They are commonly sought by anglers in and near Moreton Bay, Queensland, mainly from late spring to early autumn. In New South Wales and eastern Victoria, they are popular in estuaries and coastal lakes such as Lake Macquarie, Botany Bay, Sydney estuary[12] and Port Hacking, Lake Conjola, Mallacoota Inlet and Gippsland Lakes. In Gippsland Lakes, dusky flathead are the second most popular angling target species after black bream (*Acanthopagrus butcheri*)[13] and about 21 t a year are taken there by recreational anglers.

Anglers fishing from shoreline or boat generally use baited handlines or rods fitted with lures to catch dusky flathead. Seine nets are used in some States. Specialist anglers target large flathead with live fish (eg mullet) as bait. Lure fishing for dusky flathead is best in summer months and provides good sport.

In southern New South Wales and Port Phillip Bay, sand flathead is the main flathead species caught by anglers. Flathead are caught with handlines from drifting boats, jetties and shorelines and also with seine nets and gillnets. In Port Phillip Bay the recreational sand flathead catch is estimated to be more than 400 t a year, and is about 10 times that taken by commercial fishers.[14] In Tasmania, sand flathead are sought by anglers mostly during summer and are the most important recreational fish species in the State. A 1983 survey in Tasmania estimated that 20 % of the Tasmanian population fished specifically for sand flathead that year. The popularity of sand flathead has not diminished since then. In South Australia and Western Australia, sand flathead are caught incidentally.

According to Australian Underwater Federation spearfishing records, the largest dusky flathead taken weighed 10.4 kg (New South Wales) and the largest sand flathead weighed 3.1 kg (South Australia).

Management controls Gear restrictions and legal minimum lengths apply in all States.

Resource status

The resource status of both species is unclear. Queensland, New South Wales and Tasmanian catches appear stable, but evidence of long-term trends is lacking. Commercial catches of dusky flathead have declined in Tamboon Inlet[9] but not in other Victorian inlets. Commercial sand flathead catches in Port Phillip Bay have fallen from more than 160 t in the 1950s to less than 30 t a year in the 1980s.[5] The reasons for these lower catches may include changes in commercial fishing gear and/or target preferences in Port Phillip Bay, and market competition from trawl-caught flathead from other areas.[5] It is possible that populations of dusky flathead may be adversely affected by sedimentation, seagrass decline and other habitat changes in east coast inlets and estuaries.

Notes

Dusky flathead and sand flathead are often confused in catches with yank flathead, eastern blue-spotted flathead and northern sand flathead in New South Wales, Victoria and Tasmania.

References

1. Keenan, C.P. (1988) *Systematics and evolution of Australian species of flatheads (Pisces, Platycephalidae).* Unpublished PhD thesis, University of Queensland. 415 pp.

2. Dredge, M.C.L. (1976) *Aspects of the ecology of three estuarine dwelling fish in south east Queensland.* Unpublished MSc thesis, University of Queensland. 122 pp.

3. State Pollution Control Commission (1982) *The ecology of fish in Botany Bay — biology of commercially and recreationally valuable species. Environmental control study of Botany Bay.* Sydney. 287 pp.

4. Brown, I.W. (1977) *Ecology of three sympatric flatheads (Platycephalidae) in Port Phillip Bay, Victoria.* Unpublished PhD thesis, Monash University, Victoria. 324 pp.

5. Hall, D.N. and MacDonald, C.M. (1986) Commercial fishery situation report: net and line fisheries of Port Phillip Bay, Victoria, 1914–1984. *Victorian Department of Conservation, Forests and Lands, Fisheries Division, Marine Fisheries Report* **10**. 121 pp.

6. Wankowski, J.W.J. and Moulton, P.L. (1986) Distribution, abundance and biomass estimates of commercially important demersal fish species in eastern Bass Strait, Australia. *Victorian Department of Conservation, Forests and Lands, Fisheries and Wildlife Service, Technical Report* **62**. 57 pp.

7. *Commercial fisheries of New South Wales.* (1982) N.S.W. State Fisheries. 60 pp.

8. Russell, D.J. (1988) An assessment of the east Queensland inshore gill net fishery. *Queensland Department of Primary Industries, Information Series* **QI88024**. 57 pp.

9. Winstanley, R.H. (1985) Commercial fishery situation report: Tamboon Inlet. *Victorian Department of Conservation, Forests and Lands, Fisheries and Wildlife Service, Marine Fisheries Report* **7**. 28 pp.

10. Hutchins, B. and Swainston, R. (1986) *Sea fishes of southern Australia. Complete field guide for anglers and divers.* Perth: Swainston Publishing. 180 pp.

11. Australian National Sportfishing Association (1991) *Sportfish tagging program. Tag and release building on conservation and knowledge. 1990/91 report.* Ed by E. Sawynok. Rockhampton. 69 pp.

12. Henry, G.W. (1984) Commercial and recreational fishing in Sydney estuary. *Department of Agriculture, New South Wales, Fisheries Bulletin* **1**. 47 pp.

13. Hall, D.N. and MacDonald, C.M. (1985) A survey of recreational fishing in the Gippsland Lakes, Victoria. *Victorian Department of Conservation, Forests and Lands, Fisheries and Wildlife Service, Marine Fisheries Report* **3**. 25 pp.

14. MacDonald, C.M. and Hall, D.N. (1987). A survey of recreational fishing in Port Phillip Bay. *Victorian Department of Conservation, Forests and Lands, Fisheries Division, Marine Fisheries Report* **11**. 40 pp.

Contributors

Information on these species was provided by (in alphabetical order) Ian Brown, Darren Cameron, Mark Cliff, Les Gray, Gary Henry, Clive Keenan, Rod Lenanton, Murray MacDonald, Julian Pepperell, Alex Schaap, Ron West and Ross Winstanley. Dusky flathead drawing by Roger Swainston, and sand flathead drawing by Rosalind Poole. (*Details of contributors and their organisations are given in the Acknowledgements section at the back of this book.*)
Compilers Patricia Kailola and Christina Grieve (maps)

Catch of dusky flathead caught by a recreational angler, Lake Conjola, New South Wales. (Source: Gary Henry, Environment Protection Authority, New South Wales)

Barramundi

Lates calcarifer

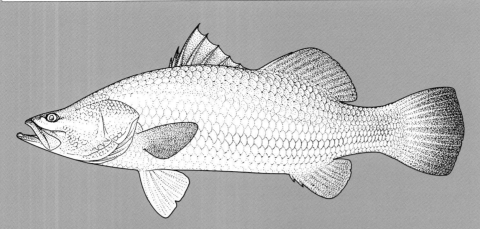

Lates calcarifer (Bloch)

Barramundi

Other common names include **sea bass** and **giant perch**.
FAO: **barramundi**
Australian species code: 310006

Family CENTROPOMIDAE

Diagnostic features Barramundi have a large mouth which reaches well behind the eye, and a protruding lower jaw. Their body scales are large. The spined and rayed parts of their dorsal fin are separated, and their caudal fin is rounded. Adult barramundi are dark greenish grey to golden brown above and silvery below. Juveniles have 3 prominent white stripes along their head.[1] Barramundi are noted for their brilliant pinkish orange eyes which 'glow' at night.

Distribution

In Australia, barramundi are distributed in tropical coastal and fresh waters from the Ashburton River in Western Australia to the Noosa River in Queensland. Globally, they are widely distributed in the Indo-West Pacific region from the Arabian Gulf to China, Taiwan, Papua New Guinea and northern Australia.[2]

Barramundi move between fresh and salt water during various stages of their life cycle. Mature barramundi live in estuaries and associated coastal areas or in the lower reaches of rivers. Larvae and young juveniles live in brackish temporary swamps associated with estuaries, and older juveniles inhabit the upper reaches of rivers. When in fresh water, barramundi can be found near submerged logs and overhanging banks.[1]

Life history

Maturing male barramundi migrate downstream from freshwater habitats at the start of the wet (monsoon) season to spawn with resident females in estuaries[3] and on tidal flats outside the mouths of rivers. In Australia the exact timing of spawning by barramundi varies through-out their range. In Western Australian rivers spawning occurs between

September and February after monsoonal rainfall. In the Northern Territory and the Gulf of Carpentaria it occurs between December and March, usually before substantial rainfalls. Populations on the

east coast of Queensland spawn between October and March with peaks in November and early December in the north[4] and late December to early January in the south.[5] Spawning occurs at water temperatures of between 27°C and 33°C,[6] and timing is closely related to lunar (or tidal) cycles.[7] Barramundi spawn on the full moon and new moon, primarily at the beginning of an incoming tide which carries the eggs into the estuary.[6]

Barramundi are broadcast spawners that aggregate to spawn. Spawning aggregations occur in or around the mouths of rivers.[3] While adults and juveniles are capable of living in fresh water, brackish waters are required for embryonic development.[8] Female barramundi are capable of producing

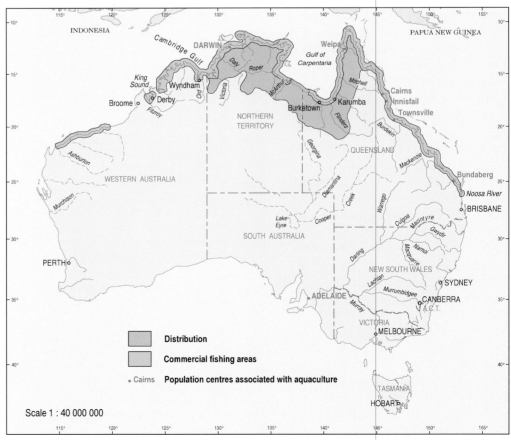

Geographic distribution, commercial fishing areas and population centres associated with aquaculture of barramundi in Australian waters.

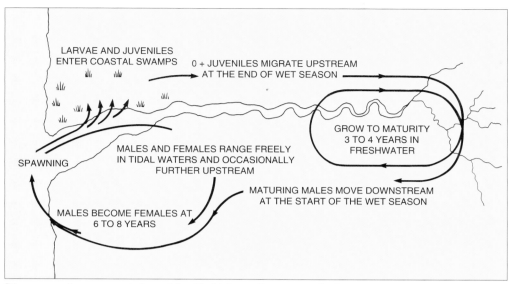

Diagrammatic representation of the life history of barramundi. (Diagram courtesy of the Fisheries Division, Northern Territory Department of Primary Industry and Fisheries)

large numbers of eggs, with estimates as high as 2.3 million eggs per kg of body weight.[9]

The fertilised eggs are pelagic and average 0.7 mm in diameter.[6] They are distributed by tidal movements[4] and hatch within a day at temperatures of 28°C. The newly hatched larvae are about 1.5 mm long.[6] Under hatchery conditions larvae grow to juveniles in 26 days.[7] The postlarvae (and possibly larvae) move from spawning areas to brackish water seasonal habitats.[4] Larval barramundi occupy these habitats as well as main channels of streams. Juveniles live in freshwater lagoons, swamps and creeks.[4] As these temporary habitats dry up, the juveniles move into the main stream and many migrate upstream to permanent freshwater habitats.

Barramundi are protandrous hermaphrodites, ie they undergo sex inversion during their life cycle. Females are generally absent in the smaller length classes, but dominate larger length classes. Most barramundi mature first as males and function as males for one or more spawning seasons before undergoing sex inversion. A few females will develop directly from immature fish.[3] Similarly, some males may never undergo sex inversion.[3] The time taken to first maturity varies. Males in Northern Territory waters reach maturity from 1 to 5 years of age, at 29-60 cm total length.[3] In Queensland, males have been found to mature at 3–5 years of age at about 55 cm total length.[10] Sex inversion occurs in Northern Territory fish aged between 4 and 8 years and 84–93 cm total length. Fish from the Gulf of Carpentaria undergo sex inversion when they are between 3 and 7 years of age and 68–90 cm total length.[10] Barramundi can grow to 180 cm total length and weigh up to 60 kg.[1]

Larval and juvenile barramundi feed on plankton. The adult diet is dominated by crustaceans and fish.[3] Prawns such as banana prawns (*Penaeus* species) and grooved tiger prawns (*Penaeus semisulcatus*) are commonly eaten by adult barramundi. Juvenile barramundi are often cannibalised by larger juveniles and adults.

Stock structure

Four major barramundi stocks have been identified in Western Australia[11] and recent work suggests the existence of at least 16 genetically isolated populations of barramundi in northern Australian waters east of the Ord River.[12] In the Northern Territory, genetically discrete stocks were found to exist in different groups of river systems.[13]

The linear coastal distribution of barramundi, combined with moderate levels of larval migration, can explain the differences observed between barramundi stocks.[14] Barramundi populations from geographically close rivers (within a 50 km radius) are probably part of a common stock.

Commercial fishery

Barramundi are fished in coastal waters and the tidal reaches of many of the accessible rivers of northern Australia. In Western Australia most fishing effort is centred in Cambridge Gulf, King Sound and along the Kimberley coast, although small quantities of barramundi are taken from tidal waters as far south as the Ashburton River.[11] In the Northern Territory, most fishing effort is centred on the rivers between the Victoria and McArthur rivers. In Queensland, most barramundi are caught in the rivers of the Gulf of Carpentaria, although barramundi are also caught in the east coast gillnet fishery.[15]

Gillnets are the primary method used to catch barramundi in all States. Gillnet fishers set nets in the tidal reaches of rivers and estuaries, and on coastal mud flats.[11,15] Small dinghies are used to check and clear the nets and return the catch to shore camps or larger boats where they are filleted, packed and frozen. Fixed tidal traps are used to catch barramundi in the Northern Territory.

In the Northern Territory small numbers of barramundi are taken live for sale in the aquarium trade.

Historically, Western Australian fishers supplied only local markets, often tethering their fish live in rivers until they could transport them to town. An increase in demand and higher prices in southern capital city markets has seen a marketing shift from whole fish to fillets, which are easier to process, pack and transport.[11] In Queensland, barramundi are sold either

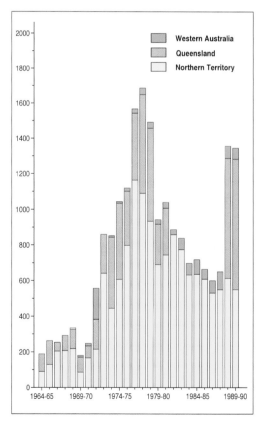

Total annual wild catch in t of barramundi for the period 1964–65 to 1989–90. Figures are unavailable for Queensland from 1981–82 to 1987–88. (Source: Fisheries Resources Atlas Statistical Database)[11]

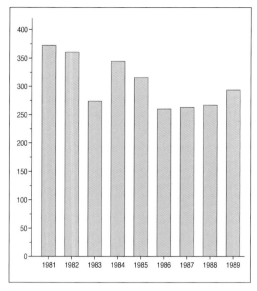

Total annual catch in t (fillet weight) of barramundi for the period 1981 to 1989 from the Queensland Gulf of Carpentaria Gillnet Fishery. (Source: Ross Quinn, Fisheries Branch, Queensland Department of Primary Industries)

whole or as fillets. Prices for barramundi vary around the country. In 1992 wholesale prices for barramundi fillets were A$ 12.00 per kg in Queensland and A$ 13.00 per kg in the Northern Territory. Wholesale prices for gilled and gutted fish in 1992 were A$ 7.50–8.50 per kg in Western Australia and A$ 8.00 per kg in the Northern Territory.

Management controls Commercial fisheries for barramundi have come under increasing regulation in recent years. Fishing effort is being reduced to sustain breeding stock levels. Freshwater reaches of rivers in Queensland, the Northern Territory and Western Australia are closed to commercial barramundi fishing, with fishing activity restricted to the lower estuarine areas and tidal flats around river mouths. Specific area closures are also enforced in Queensland and the Northern Territory. Closed seasons apply in the 3 States to protect spawning populations.[16] The fisheries in the Northern Territory, the Gulf of Carpentaria and the Queensland east coast are limited entry fisheries,[15] and the Western Australian fishery is limited entry for waters north of Broome.[16] Gear restrictions apply in all 3 States and minimum sizes apply in the Northern Territory and Queensland.[15,16] Provisions are also made in the Northern Territory's *Fisheries Act* for traditional Aboriginal fisheries for barramundi.

Aquaculture

Research into the culture of barramundi in Australia began in 1984 with studies carried out by the Queensland Department of Primary Industries. This work was aimed at adapting culture techniques developed in Thailand to Australian conditions.[17] Barramundi are now being farmed in Queensland, the Northern Territory and South Australia.

Eggs for culture operations initially came from wild broodstock, and after hatching, the larvae were reared in a flow-through tank system until they reached fingerling size (30–40 mm total length).[17] Most operations now retain captive broodstock, and use extensive systems of fertilised brackish or salt water earthen ponds for larval rearing. This method has the advantages of requiring less labour and hence is less expensive than tank system hatcheries and larval rearing facilities for the production of an equivalent number of larvae. Furthermore, in extensive systems, growth rates are 2 to 3 times faster and the number of observed deformities is lower than in tank systems.

Barramundi fingerlings are used either for stocking freshwater reservoirs for recreational fishing, or in 'grow-out' operations. In grow-out operations, fingerlings are usually stocked in floating cages in ponds where they are held until they reach a marketable size of about 400 g — usually in as little as 6 months. Growth rates vary, and regular grading of the fish reduces cannibalism on smaller fish.[17]

Farmed barramundi are sold as 'plate-sized' fish. These are scaled, gilled and gutted, packed on ice and sold as whole, fresh fish at the Brisbane, Sydney and Melbourne fish markets. In 1991-92 cultured barramundi were wholesaling for A$ 11.00 to A$ 12.00 per kg at these markets. Production of farmed barramundi (fingerlings and plate-sized) in 1990-91 was 120 t.[17]

Recreational fishery

Barramundi are caught by recreational fishers throughout their range, although fishing pressure is greatest on accessible rivers near population centres. Anglers fish for barramundi in freshwater billabongs and creeks, the upper tidal reaches of rivers, and throughout the estuarine and coastal habitats of barramundi. Most anglers use light rods

A recreational catch of barramundi from a Northern Territory river. (Source: Dave Pollard, Fisheries Research Institute, NSW Fisheries)

Recreational fishing for barramundi is a major industry in the Northern Territory.
(Source: Fisheries Division, Northern Territory Department of Primary Industry and Fisheries)

and lines or handlines rigged with flies, lures or occasionally live bait. They fish either from the bank or from small dinghies.

Recreational fishing effort for barramundi has increased in recent years, particularly with improved access to the more remote fishing areas in north Queensland and the Northern Territory. Barramundi is a recognised game fish under International Game Fishing Association rules, and is sought by anglers for both its eating and sporting qualities.[2] According to records of the Australian Anglers Association the largest barramundi landed by a recreational angler weighed 22.2 kg and was caught in the Northern Territory.

In the Northern Territory and Queensland, recreational barramundi fishing is a major industry. Many fishing charter operators in the Northern Territory specifically target barramundi,[2] catering for the increasing numbers of fishing tourists.

Management controls Minimum sizes and bag limits are applied in Queensland and the Northern Territory. Closed areas and closed seasons are also enforced to protect breeding stocks. A bag limit also applies in Western Australia.

Resource status

The exploitation rate of barramundi is low, largely because of the management policies effected in each State. The resource appears to be stable.

References

1. Larson, H.K. and Martin, K.C. (1989) *Freshwater fishes of the Northern Territory.* Darwin: Northern Territory Museum of Arts and Sciences. Handbook Series Number 1. 102 pp.

2. Grey, D.L. (1987) An overview of *Lates calcarifer* in Australia and Asia. Pp 15–21, in *Management of wild and cultured sea bass/barramundi* (Lates calcarifer). Ed by J.W. Copland and D.L. Grey. *ACIAR Proceedings* **20**. Canberra: Australian Centre for International Agricultural Research.

3. Davis, T.L.O. (1987) Biology of wildstock *Lates calcarifer* in northern Australia. Pp 22–29, in *Management of wild and cultured sea bass/barramundi* (Lates calcarifer). Ed by J.W. Copland and D.L. Grey. *ACIAR Proceedings* **20**. Canberra: Australian Centre for International Agricultural Research.

4. Russell, D.J. and Garrett, R.N. (1985) Early life history of barramundi, *Lates calcarifer* (Bloch), in north-eastern Queensland. *Australian Journal of Marine and Freshwater Research* **36**: 191–201.

5. Russell, D.J. (1988) An assessment of the Queensland inshore gill net fishery. *Queensland Department of Primary Industries, Information Series* **QI88024**. 57 pp.

6. MacKinnon, M.R., Garrett, R.N., and Russell, D.J. (1986) Report of pilot hatchery operations 1984–85. *Queensland Department of Primary Industries, Monograph Series*. Unpublished report.

7. MacKinnon, M.R. (1987) Rearing and growth of larval and juvenile barramundi (*Lates calcarifer*) in Queensland. Pp 148–153, in *Management of wild and cultured sea bass/barramundi* (Lates calcarifer). Ed by J.W. Copland and D.L. Grey. *ACIAR Proceedings* **20**. Canberra: Australian Centre for International Agricultural Research.

8. Shaklee, J.B. and Salini, J.P. (1985) Genetic variation and population subdivision in Australian barramundi, *Lates calcarifer* (Bloch). *Australian Journal of Marine and Freshwater Research* **36**: 302–318.

9. Davis, T.L.O. (1984) Estimation of fecundity in barramundi *Lates calcarifer* (Bloch), using an automatic particle counter. *Australian Journal of Marine and Freshwater Research* **35**: 111–118.

10. Davis, T.L.O. (1982) Maturity and sexuality in barramundi, *Lates calcarifer* (Bloch), in the Northern Territory and south-eastern Gulf of Carpentaria. *Australian Journal of Marine and Freshwater Research* **33**: 529–545.

11. Morrissy, N. (1985) The commercial fishery for barramundi (*Lates calcarifer*) in Western Australia. *Western Australian Department of Fisheries and Wildlife Report* **68**. 32 pp.

12. Shaklee, J.B., Phelps, S.R. and Salini, J. (1990) Analysis of fish stock structure and mixed stock fisheries by the electrophoretic characterisation of allelic isozymes. Pp 181–184, in *Electrophoretic and isoelectric focussing techniques in fisheries management*. Ed by D.H. Whitmore. Boca Raton: CRC Press.

13. Salini, J. and Shaklee, J.B. (1988) Genetic structure of barramundi (*Lates calcarifer*) stocks from northern Australia. *Australian Journal of Marine and Freshwater Research* **39**: 317-329.

14. Keenan, C.P. (in press, 1992). Rapid evolution of population structure in Australian barramundi, *Lates calcarifer* (Bloch): an example of isolation by distance in one dimension. *Evolution.*

15. Quinn, R.H. (1987) Analysis of fisheries logbook information from the Gulf of Carpentaria, Australia. Pp 92–95, in *Management of wild and cultured sea bass/barramundi* (Lates calcarifer). Ed by J.W. Copland and D.L. Grey. *ACIAR Proceedings* **20**. Canberra: Australian Centre for International Agricultural Research.

16. Brown, R.S. (1988) Control of barramundi gillnet fishing in the Kimberley. *Fisheries Department of Western Australia, Fisheries Management Paper* **15**. 49 pp.

17. Trendall, J. and Fielder, S. (1991) Barramundi — an industry perspective. *Austasia Aquaculture* **5**(8): 3–6.

Contributors

Information on this species was originally provided by (in alphabetical order) Roland Griffin, Noel Morrissy, Mike Rimmer and John Russell. Additional information was provided by Ray Clarke, Mark Elmer, Clive Keenan and Rosemary Lea. Drawing by Gavin Ryan. (*Details of contributors and their organisations are given in the Acknowledge-ments section at the back of this book.*)
Compiler Alex McNee

C o r a l   t r o u t

Plectropomus species

Coral trout

This presentation is on 3 species, **common coral trout**, **bluespot trout** and **bar-cheeked trout**.

Common coral trout,
Plectropomus leopardus
  Lacepède

Another common name is **leopard trout**.
FAO: **bluedotted coral-trout**
Australian species code: 311078

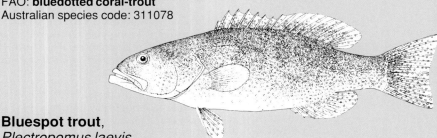

Bluespot trout,
Plectropomus laevis
  Lacepède

Other common names include **footballer trout, tiger trout** and **oceanic trout**.
FAO: **black-saddled coral-trout**
Australian species code: 311079

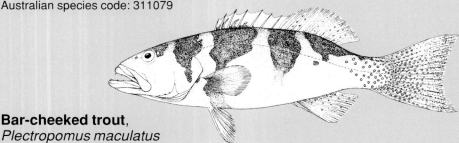

Bar-cheeked trout,
Plectropomus maculatus
  Bloch

Other common names include **coastal trout, red emperor** and **island trout**.
FAO: **spotted coral-trout**
Australian species code: 311012

Family SERRANIDAE

Diagnostic features Coral trout have 8 spines and 11 soft rays in the dorsal fin. They have a large mouth with a few large canine teeth including 1–4 along each side of the lower jaw. Their lower jaw is prominent and there are 3 large spines on the lower edge of the preoperculum. The caudal fin is blunt or slightly excavated. Body colouration and colour pattern distinguish these 3 species. Common coral trout are olive to orange-red with numerous very small, round blue spots on the head and body (more than 10 spots on the cheek). There are 2 colour forms of bluespot trout: either brown with numerous small dark blue spots or yellow with broad, saddle-like brown or black bars on the body. Bar-cheeked trout (not pictured — see photo on next page) are greenish grey, brown or orange-red with blue spots on the head and body (3–7 spots on the cheek); spots are of moderate size anteriorly, small posteriorly, and some spots on the head and anterior body are horizontally elongate.[1]

Distribution

Coral trout inhabit the tropical waters of the Indian and Pacific oceans.[1] Common coral trout range from southern Japan to Fiji, bluespot trout are present in most of the Indo-Pacific region from Africa to Tahiti, and bar-cheeked trout are distributed from Thailand to the Solomon Islands.[1]

In Western Australia, common coral trout are present from Dongara to the Monte Bello Islands and Dampier Archipelago. In Queensland, they are distributed from the Sir Charles Hardy Islands to Brisbane. Bluespot trout inhabit only Queensland waters, from Torres Strait to Gladstone. Bar-cheeked trout have the most extensive distribution in Australian waters, from the Houtman Abrolhos in Western Australia to Gladstone.[1]

Coral trout generally inhabit shallow water to 100 m, often in association with coral reefs — from inshore to the steep outer reef margins. On the Great Barrier Reef, bar-cheeked trout inhabit inshore reefs, common coral trout inhabit mid-shelf reefs and bluespot trout inhabit outer shelf reefs. Bar-cheeked trout and common coral trout replace each other in relative abundance on the Great Barrier Reef — from the north where bar-cheeked trout are more common, to the south where common coral trout are more abundant. Maximum densities of common coral trout are achieved in the Swain Reefs and Capricorn–Bunker Reefs.[2]

Life history

Coral trout are protogynous hermaphrodites, ie the same individuals function first as females and later as males. They are spring–summer spawners, the spawning period varying slightly with latitude along the east Queensland coast. For example, peak reproductive activity for common coral trout takes place between September and November in both the Lizard Island and Cairns areas[3,4,5] and over November–December in the southern reef areas such as the Capricorn Islands group.[6,7] Some coral trout migrate over short distances to spawn, forming aggregations. Common

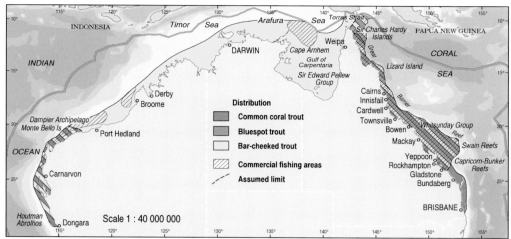

Geographic distribution and commercial fishing areas for 3 species of coral trout in Australian waters.

coral trout probably form several spawning aggregations on a reef, whereas bluespot trout form larger aggregations — maybe only 1 or 2 per reef. A 1990-91 study at Scott Reef off Cairns recorded that spawning coral trout aggregated in highest numbers in October and November, coinciding with the new moon and a water temperature of 25–26°C.[4] Coral trout spawn in pairs during a brief period around sunset, performing a characteristic 'rush' towards the water surface.[4]

Coral trout eggs float just below the surface. The pelagic larvae are present in Great Barrier Reef waters between October and January, and are found in habitats similar to those of the adults.[8] The larval stage of common coral trout lasts 3–4 weeks, the larvae appearing in northern Great Barrier Reef waters about 1 month after the peak spawning period there.[4] At Arlington and Green Island reefs off Cairns, common coral trout larvae settle at 16–17 mm standard length, and 2-month-old juveniles measure 45–85 mm standard length. Juvenile coral trout have a demersal existence in shallow water in reef habitats, especially around coral rubble.[4]

Young coral trout grow rapidly until about 3 years of age.[3] The maximum recorded sizes of the 3 species range from 76 cm total length for bar-cheeked trout,[5,9] 109 cm fork length for bluespot trout, to at least 80 cm fork length and 3.5–4 kg for common coral trout (an individual at One Tree Island was recently estimated at 120 cm standard length). Bar-cheeked trout of 60 cm fork length weigh approximately 3.3 kg, and fish of about 74 cm fork length weigh approximately 6.5 kg.[9] Age estimates are 11 years (at 58 cm fork length) for common coral trout, 18 years (at 109 cm

fork length) and 12 years[5] (at 68 cm fork length) for bar-cheeked trout. In north Queensland waters, common coral trout mature at 2 years of age as females and at 3–4 years as males[8] and bar-cheeked trout mature at 2 years of age as females, and between 3 and 7 years as males.[5] Sex change takes place between spawnings.[5] On the Great Barrier Reef, the size at maturity for common coral trout varies: for example, females mature at from 21–25 cm to 55-60 cm fork length.[3,6]

Common coral trout are home-ranging, moderately sedentary fish that associate with specific areas of reef slope for several months. They regularly range approximately 2 km along the reef slope and up to 7.5 km on occasions.[7] Longer range movements between reefs have been reported.[10] Coral trout also migrate short distances within particular reef systems to spawn.[4] Larger coral trout inhabit deeper waters (eg more than 20 m) outside of the spawning period.[3] They may also move into shallow water to feed.

Juvenile coral trout feed on small fish and invertebrates such as crustaceans and squid.[11] Adult common coral trout are

mainly fish eaters, their diet changing with season and region.[11,12] Many types of reef fish of a wide size range are consumed.[11] Larger common coral trout on the reef slope also eat small pelagic fish such as herrings (Clupeidae) and anchovies (Engraulididae), mainly in summer.[11] These coral trout feed during the day and exhibit different hunting strategies depending on the time of day. At dusk they appear to utilise an 'ambush' strategy whereas at dawn they 'prowl'. Groups of larger fish have been observed to hunt and chase small pelagic fish.[7]

Stock structure

No studies have been conducted on the stock structure of coral trout. Differences in maximum lengths of common coral trout populations between the Capricorn–Bunker Reefs and other Great Barrier Reef areas may indicate the existence of 2 stocks[2] although there is no known barrier to exchange between these areas.

Commercial fishery

Common coral trout and bluespot trout are fished on the Great Barrier Reef by handline, and common coral trout is handlined at the Houtman Abrolhos. Bar-cheeked trout are fished in western and northern Australian waters by demersal otter trawling, trapping, droplining and handlining (north of Carnarvon in Western Australia).

Coral trout are the major Queensland commercial finfish, worth about A$ 8.2 million in 1989–90. They are one of the target species groups of the Queensland East Coast Reef Line Fishery and comprise 31–34 % of the catch from that Fishery.[13,14] The fishing fleet operates

Specimen of a bar-cheeked trout, 46.5 cm standard length, from the North West Shelf. (Source: Peter Last, CSIRO Marine Laboratories, Hobart)

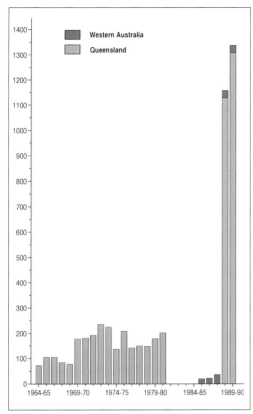

Total annual catch in t of coral trout for the period 1964–65 to 1989–90. Figures are unavailable for: Queensland from 1981–82 to 1987–88; and Western Australia from 1964–65 to 1982–83. Catches for States that are less than 20 t in a particular year are not shown. (Source: Fisheries Resources Atlas Statistical Database)

predominantly from ports between Cardwell and Mackay[14] and is very mobile. It concentrates in regions such as the Swain Reefs, the Whitsunday Island Group and the far northern Great Barrier Reef on a rotational basis. The Reef Line Fishery is daytime based and conducted by individuals operating small dories or dinghies ('tender vessels') working to a mother ship. Generally, coral trout are caught in commercial quantities from Torres Strait to just south of Rockhampton.[13] Catches peak in the waters off Mackay and only small catches are made south of Gladstone. Although coral trout are caught throughout the year, catches and fishing effort are higher from August to October.[14]

In north Queensland, coral trout are caught by shallow and deep water handlining off the reef crests. They may also be caught using rod-and-reel and by trolling ('wogging'). Vessel size and local weather conditions, such as currents and wind, influence gear modifications and fishing locations — either in open water or in the lee of reefs. Fishing vessels operating on the outer reefs have large freezer capacity and may stay out for up to 3 weeks.[13] Cut baits from oily fish such

as tunas and mackerel (Scombridae), frozen pilchards (*Sardinops neopilchardus*) from Western Australia and shark (*Carcharhinus* species), and also squid are commonly used.[3] Fishers often target spawning aggregations of common coral trout and bluespot trout, and also seek 'plate-sized' trout about 35 cm fork length.

In contrast to Queensland, coral trout are a minor part of Western Australian and Northern Territory fisheries. There, bar-cheeked trout are caught at depths of between 50 m and 100 m. Fish traps used in Western Australia are generally circular and they are usually baited with pilchards. The traps are left to fish from 20 minutes to 12 hours, the shorter times usually being the most productive. Coral trout caught in traps range from 41cm to 76 cm fork length.[9]

Between 1979 and 1991, first Taiwanese, and later Thai and Chinese, fleets operated a demersal trawl fishery in northern Australia from the North West Shelf to the Arafura Sea. They used pair trawlers and some stern trawlers. Taiwanese pair trawlers fished at 50–75 m on the North West Shelf,[15] each trawl lasting from 2 to more than 3 hours. Australian stern trawlers entered the Arafura Sea fishery after 1987 and the North West Shelf fishery in 1989. Coral trout comprised 38 % of the reported 'cod' catches in the demersal trawl fishery (based on an assessment of the Arafura Sea catches) and they are more abundant

in catches on the North West Shelf to 21° S and 120° E. Fishing was carried out all year although fishing effort was concentrated on the North West Shelf from October to March.[15]

Coral trout are an excellent table fish. Bar-cheeked trout caught in the trap-and-line fishery in north-western Western Australia used to be marketed with *Lutjanus sebae* as 'red emperor' but they are now marketed as 'coral trout'. Fresh, whole coral trout fetch A$ 7.00 to A$ 9.00 per kg on the Perth wholesale market. The Northern Territory 1992 wholesale prices for gilled and gutted fish averaged A$ 5.30 per kg. Coral trout are marketed mostly as fillets in Queensland, and in 1992 the wholesale price at the Brisbane fish market was A$ 12.00-14.00 per kg for frozen fillets and A$ 9.00 per kg for fresh whole fish.

Management controls The North West Shelf trap fishery is limited entry, and the trawl fishery is a developmental fishery over 3 years. In the Northern Territory, there is no access to marine parks and restrictions such as total allowable catch and limited entry apply generally to the demersal trawl fishery. In Queensland, the Reef Line Fishery is a licensed, limited entry fishery. Minimum legal size and gear restrictions also apply. Fishing is prohibited on some reefs within the Great Barrier Reef Marine Park.

Commercial spearfishing (except for ornate rock lobster, *Panulirus ornatus*) is prohibited in all States.

Common coral trout, Great Barrier Reef. (Source: Great Barrier Reef Marine Park Authority)

Recreational fishery

In north Queensland waters, considerable quantities of coral trout are taken by handline and rod-and-reel. The fish are caught mainly during the day in depths to about 25 m.[3] Coral trout are also caught by spearfishing to about 20 m depth. Small vessels are used on inshore reefs. Fishing in deeper water to 40 m is occasionally conducted from charter vessels.[13] Similar fishing activities are carried out in the other States. The quantity of coral trout taken in the recreational fishery in Queensland is estimated to be the same as, or more than, the quantity taken in the commercial fishery.

The largest recorded coral trout caught by a recreational fisher was 23.6 kg, from Queensland (Australian Underwater Federation records).

Management controls In Queensland, a bag limit is proposed and a minimum legal size, identical to that in the commercial fishery, applies. Fishing is prohibited on some reefs in the Great Barrier Reef Marine Park. In Western Australia, bag limits and legal minimum size restrictions apply. Spearfishing for coral trout using SCUBA gear is prohibited in the Northern Territory and Queensland.

Resource status

In Queensland there appears to be 'localised' over-fishing of common coral trout and bluespot trout on reefs near centres of population, and the average size of coral trout is smaller on reefs that are fished compared with the size of coral trout on closed reefs in the Capricorn Reefs area.[16] Over the whole Great Barrier Reef however, coral trout densities appear to have remained stable over a considerable time period. Despite both recreational and commercial fisheries targeting the same species using the same gear and methods, it appears that the resource has not been over-fished. However, fishing effort on coral trout is increasing from both fisheries.

There is no information on the resource status of bar-cheeked trout in Western Australian and Northern Territory fisheries.

Notes

Large coral trout may carry ciguatoxin and be the cause of ciguatera poisoning in some areas.

Squaretail coral trout (*Plectropomus areolatus*) are a minor component of the Queensland fishery. They inhabit the North West Shelf and north Queensland waters.

References

1. Randall, J.E. and Hoese, D.F. (1986) Revision of the groupers of the Indo-Pacific genus *Plectropomus* (Perciformes: Serranidae). *Indo-Pacific Fishes* **13**. 31 pp.

2. Ayling, A.M. and Ayling, A.L. (1986) *A biological survey of selected reefs in the Capricorn section of the Great Barrier Reef Marine Park*. Report to the Great Barrier Reef Marine Park Authority. 61 pp.

3. McPherson, G., Squire, L. and O'Brien, J. (1988) Demersal reef fish project 1984–85: age and growth of four important reef fish species. A report to the Great Barrier Reef Marine Park Authority. *Queensland Department of Primary Industries, Fisheries Research Branch, Technical Report* **FRB 88/6**. 38 pp.

4. Brown, I.W., McPherson, G., Samoilys, M.A., Doherty, P.J. and Russ, G. (1991) Growth, reproductive strategies and recruitment of the dominant demersal food-fish species on the Great Barrier Reef. *Progress report on FIRDC Project 90/18*. Queensland Department of Primary Industries, Australian Institute of Marine Science, James Cook University of North Queensland.

5. Fereira, B. and Russ, G. (in press, 1992) Age, growth and mortality of the inshore coral trout *Plectropomus maculatus*. *Australian Journal of Marine and Freshwater Research*.

6. Goeden, G.B. (1978) A monograph of the coral trout. *Queensland Fisheries Service, Research Bulletin* **1**. 42 pp.

7. Samoilys, M. (1987) *Aspects of the behaviour, movements and population density of* Plectropomus leopardus *(Lacepède, 1802) (Pisces: Serranidae) at Heron Island, southern Great Barrier Reef, Australia*. Unpublished MSc thesis, University of Queensland . 230 pp.

8. Williams, D.McB. and Russ, G.R. (in press, 1992) *Review of data on fishes of commercial and recreational fishing interest on the Great Barrier Reef. Volume 1*. Townsville: Great Barrier Reef Marine Park Authority.

9. Moran, M., Jenke, J., Burton, C. and Clarke, D. (1988) The Western Australian trap and line fishery on the North-west Shelf. *Western Australian Marine Research Laboratories. FIRTA Project 86/28, Final Report.* 79 pp.

10. Craik, W. and Mercer, G.W. (1981) *Tagging demersal fishes in the Capricornia section of the Great Barrier Reef Marine Park*. Abstract, Australian Society for Fish Biology annual conference, Brisbane, 31 July–3 August, 1991.

11. Kingsford, M. (in press, 1992) Diet of *Plectropomus leopardus* (Serranidae) and patterns of abundance at One Tree Island, Great Barrier Reef, Australia. *Coral Reefs*.

12. St John, J. (1991) *Regional differences in the diet of* Plectropomus leopardus. Abstract, Australian Coral Reef Society annual scientific meeting, Townsville, 10–11 August, 1991.

13. Gwynne, L. (1990) *A review of the reef line fishery and proposed management measures. A discussion paper*. Brisbane: Queensland Fish Management Authority. 16 pp.

14. Trainor, N. (1991) Commercial line fishing. *The Queensland Fisherman* **9**(3): 17–18, 23–24.

15. Ramm, D.C., Lloyd, J.A. and Coleman, A.P.M. (1991) *Demersal trawling in the northern sector of the Australian Fishing Zone: catch and effort 1980–90*. Northern Territory Department of Primary Industry and Fisheries, unpublished draft fisheries report.

16. Ayling, A.M. and Ayling, A.L. (1988) *Are coral trout counts useful to marine park managers?* Discussion paper prepared by 'Sea Research' for the Great Barrier Reef Marine Park Authority. 7 pp.

Contributors

Most of the information on these species was originally provided by Melita Samoilys and Peter Doherty. Additional comments were provided by (in alphabetical order) Wendy Craik, Beatrice Fereira, Tony Fowler, Laurie Gwynne, Steve Hillman, Mike Kingsford, Geoff McPherson, Mike Moran, Dave Ramm and Neil Trainor. Drawings courtesy of FAO, Rome. (*Details of contributors and their organisations are given in the Acknowledgements section at the back of this book.*)
Compiler Patricia Kailola

R o c k   c o d

Epinephelus species

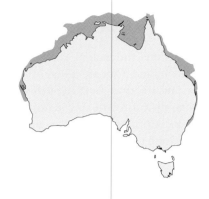

Rock cod

This presentation is on 3 species, **yellow-spotted rock cod**, **Rankin's rock cod** and **estuary rock cod**.

Yellow-spotted rock cod,
Epinephelus areolatus
(Forsskål)

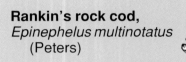

Other common names include **areolate rock cod** and **green-spotted rock-cod.**
FAO: **areolated grouper**
Australian species code: 311009

Rankin's rock cod,
Epinephelus multinotatus
(Peters)

Another common name is **Rankin's cod**.
FAO: **white-blotched grouper**
Australian species code: 311010

Estuary rock cod,
Epinephelus coioides
(Hamilton)

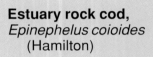

Another common name is **estuary cod**.
FAO: no known name
Australian species code: 311067

Family SERRANIDAE

Diagnostic features Rock cod have a large mouth with an exposed maxilla and 3 flat opercular spines. Rankin's rock cod are dark purplish grey with scattered whitish blotches and sometimes small dark spots. They have a deep body (about one-third of the standard length) and a truncate caudal fin.[1] Yellow-spotted rock cod are pale with many close-set brown to greenish yellow spots on head, body and fins and a distinct white margin to the caudal fin. The caudal fin is truncate. Estuary rock cod have a rounded caudal fin and large lateral line tubules. Their head, body and fins are covered with brownish orange spots, either rounded or oblong, and they have 5 blotchy dark bars across the body. They usually have 20 rays in the pectoral fin.[1]

Distribution

Rock cod (serranids) inhabit tropical and subtropical waters. Yellow-spotted and estuary rock cods are distributed from East Africa and the Red Sea or Persian Gulf to the Western Pacific and from southern Japan to Australia.[1,2] Rankin's rock cod is present in the Indian Ocean from East Africa and the Persian Gulf, including island groups, to southern Indonesia and Australia.[1]

In Australian waters, yellow-spotted rock cod are present around northern Australia from Exmouth Gulf to just south of Sydney. Rankin's rock cod are distributed from about Geraldton to about the Wessel Islands in the Northern Territory, and estuary rock cod are distributed from the Houtman Abrolhos to Newcastle.

Yellow-spotted rock cod inhabit a depth range of 6–200 m,[3] in turbid to clear water, over small coral heads or rocky outcrops, silty sand and seagrass areas (in shallower water). Rankin's rock cod inhabit clear to turbid water 2 m to at least 90 m deep, and adults are found in shallow as well as deep water.[1] Estuary rock cod occur on coral reefs and rocky sea beds in turbid areas to depths of 100 m,[2] and are often found in brackish water[3] over mud and rubble.

Life history

Rock cod are probably protogynous hermaphrodites, ie they function first as females and secondly as males. They probably spawn during restricted periods and form aggregations when doing so.[4] The eggs and early larvae of rock cod are probably pelagic. On the North West Shelf, rock cod larvae are present all year but are most abundant from late winter to late summer.[5] Around Lizard Island in Queensland, rock cod larvae are most abundant in spring and summer.[5]

Rock cod larvae inhabit relatively shallow continental shelf waters.[5] Juvenile estuary rock cod are common in shallow waters of estuaries over sand, mud and gravel and among mangroves, yet small (less than 20 cm total length) yellow-spotted rock cod are not uncommon at water depths to 80 m.

Little is known about growth rates in rock cod. Yellow-spotted rock cod attain 47 cm fork length and 1.4 kg.[6] They mature at 19 cm standard length, when about 2 years old[4] and are estimated to live for at least 15 years.[4] Rankin's rock cod attain 100 cm total length[1] and more than 9 kg.[7] A 76 cm fork length individual weighed 8.4 kg.[6] Estuary rock cod reach at least 100 cm total length and 15 kg.[2]

Movement patterns have not been investigated for these 3 species. Most rock cod make frequent use of shelters, suggesting an 'ambush' method of feeding. Rock cod are carnivores and major predators of fishes and benthic invertebrates, primarily prawns and crabs.[1,8] Yellow-spotted rock cod and Rankin's rock cod feed in water to more than 100 m depth.[8]

Stock structure

There is no information on the stock structure of rock cod in Australian waters.

Commercial fishery

In Australian waters, rock cod are caught by demersal otter trawling, traps, droplines and handlines. In general however, they are not targeted in these fisheries, instead forming a major bycatch of emperor (Lethrinidae) and sea perch (Lutjanidae) fisheries. The highest recorded catches of rock cod in domestic fisheries up to 1989–90, were 39 t (Queensland, 1975–76), 14 t (Northern Territory, 1986–87) and 287 t (Western Australia, 1989–90).

Estuary rock cod, yellow-spotted rock cod, 3-lined rock cod (*E. heniochus*) and six-banded rock cod (*E. sexfasciatus*) are the major serranid species in the Northern Fish Trawl Fishery[9] which includes the North West Shelf, Timor Sea and Arafura Sea. This fishery was mainly worked by Taiwanese pair trawlers and some Thai stern trawlers and Chinese pair trawlers from about 1971 to 1991. Up until 1990, yellow-spotted rock cod and estuary rock cod comprised 62 % of the reported 'cod' catches by foreign vessels in northern Australia (bar-cheeked trout, *Plectropomus maculatus*, was the other main species).[9]

Currently, the highest catches of rock cod are made by Australian stern trawlers on the North West Shelf. Larger rock cod are less abundant in the Gulf of Carpentaria and the Arafura Sea. Six-banded rock cod however, forms an important bycatch of the Northern Prawn Fishery, especially around Arnhem Land.

On the North West Shelf, demersal trap and line fishing occurs mainly in the Exmouth to Point Samson (114°–117° E) and Broome areas. Rankin's rock cod is the dominant rock cod in the fishery, comprising about 65 % of the serranid catch. The fish caught range from 31 cm to 82 cm fork length.[6] Other large rock cod harvested are estuary rock cod, greasy rock cod (*E. tauvina*) and

Processing a catch of Rankin's rock cod and red emperor (*Lutjanus sebae*) from an 'O' trap, North West Shelf. (Source: Allan Williams, CSIRO Marine Laboratories, North Beach)

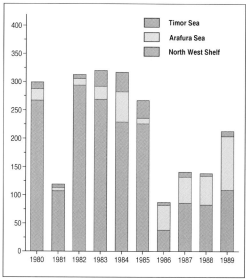

Total annual catch in t of rock cod (serranids) from northern Australian Fishing Zone foreign demersal trawling, for all fleets, between calendar years 1980 and 1989. (Source: Ramm et al[9])

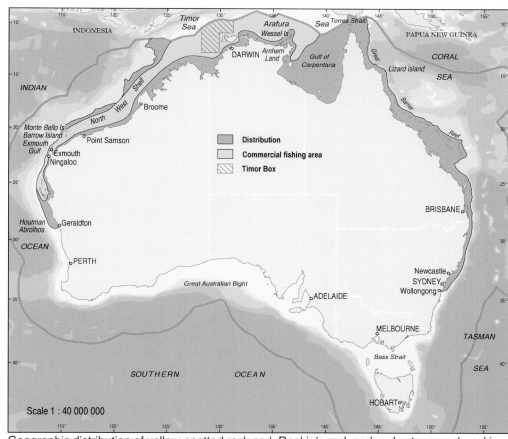

Geographic distribution of yellow-spotted rock cod, Rankin's rock cod and estuary rock cod in Australian waters, and commercial fishing areas.

camouflage rock cod, *E. polyphekadion*. Peak catches of all rock cod in this fishery are achieved between July and November. Yellow-spotted rock cod, trout cod (*E. maculatus*), and longfin rock cod (*E. quoyanus*) comprise a group of smaller species frequently caught in the traps.[6]

In the Northern Territory, demersal trap, handline and dropline fishing is carried out mainly in the 'Timor Box' (a region between 127.5° E and 131° E). In

1991, serranids comprised 22 % of the total catch from the Timor Box. Fish trapping is confined to areas with hard sea floor which are not worked by demersal trawlers. The traps are set mainly between 50 m and 100 m, sometimes deeper. They usually are circular 'O' traps with a single entrance, and are baited with pilchards (*Sardinops neopilchardus*). Traps are left to fish from 30 minutes to 12 hours. Droplines fish at 100–120 m and are normally baited with

Pair trawlers, North West Shelf. (Source: Wade Whitelaw, CSIRO Marine Laboratories, Hobart)

pilchards or squid. The main serranid caught in the Northern Territory trap and dropline fishery is yellow-spotted rock cod. Some yellow-lipped rock cod (*E. amblycephalus*), comet rock cod (*E. morrhua*), Rankin's rock cod and estuary rock cod are also caught.

In Queensland, rock cod are a component of the East Coast Reef Line Fishery. They are caught usually with handlines in shallower water and with droplines in deeper water. The main species caught are estuary rock cod, wire-netting cod (*E. merra*) and Maori cod (*E. undulatostriatus*). There is no information on the quantity of each species caught in Queensland.

Rock cod also form a small part of the bycatch from demersal otter trawling in Queensland. Throughout northern Australia they are an incidental catch in bottom set longlines and gillnets.

Smaller rock cod are marketed whole or gilled and gutted, either frozen or fresh chilled. Larger rock cod are sold whole but more often as fillets or cutlets. The catch from the North West Shelf trap and line fishery is sold in Western Australia and that from the Northern Territory trap and dropline fishery in Darwin, Brisbane and Sydney. Queensland rock cod are sold locally. Large fish command high prices. In 1991 and 1992, rock cod fetched A$ 2.50–4.00 per kg at the Perth wholesale market, about A$ 4.00 per kg in Brisbane and about A$ 4.30 per kg in Darwin.

Management controls The Commonwealth-managed Northern Fish Trawl Fishery is restricted to Australian vessels. From the beginning of 1992, trapping on the North West Shelf became a limited entry fishery, and trawling is by

licence endorsement only. In 1989, trawling for finfish was banned from the Timor Box.[9] There are no restrictions on trapping and droplining in the Northern Territory. Commercial fishers working in the Queensland East Coast Reef Line Fishery require vessel endorsements and there are restrictions on the number of tender boats per vessel.

Recreational fishery

Recreational fishers target large and small rock cod (eg Chinaman rock cod, *E. rivulatus*, and black-tipped rock cod, *E. fasciatus*) especially in inshore areas. They use lures, live bait or cut fish, jigs and deep-running troll lures. Rock cod can be hooked on single and double-handed casting tackle and jigs, or (for larger fish) heavy handlines.

According to records of the Australian Underwater Federation the largest rock cod (possibly *E. lanceolatus*) caught weighed 233 kg and was from southern Queensland.

Management controls In Queensland, a bag limit and minimum and maximum legal sizes apply. Large individuals of some rock cod species are protected.

Resource status

There is no information on the current status of rock cod stocks in Australian waters.

Notes

Identification of all brown saddled and spotted serranids has been confused until

recently. *Epinephelus coioides* is the correct name for the fish previously called *E. suillus* and often depicted as Malabar rock cod (*E. malabaricus*).[3]

References

1. Randall, J.E. and Heemstra, P.C. (1991) Revision of Indo-Pacific groupers (Perciformes: Serranidae: Epinephelinae) with descriptions of five new species. *Indo-Pacific Fishes* **20**. 332 pp.

2. Smith, M.M. and Heemstra, P.C. (1986) *Smith's sea fishes*. Johannesburg: Macmillan South Africa (Publishers) (Pty) Ltd. 1047 pp.

3. Randall, J.E., Allen, G.R. and Steene, R.C. (1990) *The complete divers' and fishermens' guide to fishes of the Great Barrier Reef and Coral Sea*. Bathurst: Crawford House Press. 507 pp.

4. Shapiro, D.Y. (1987) Reproduction in groupers. Pp 295–327, in *Tropical snappers and groupers. Biology and fisheries management*. Ed by J.J. Polovina and S. Ralston. Boulder and London: Westview Press.

5. Leis, J.M. (1987) Review of the early life history of tropical groupers (Serranidae) and snappers (Lutjanidae). Pp 189–237, in *Tropical snappers and groupers. Biology and fisheries management*. Ed by J.J. Polovina and S. Ralston. Boulder and London: Westview Press.

6. Moran, M., Jenke, J., Burton, C. and Clarke, D. (1988) The Western Australian trap and line fishery of the North-west Shelf. *Western Australian Marine Research Laboratories. FIRTA Project 86/28, Final Report*. 79 pp.

7. Allen, G.R. and Swainston, R. (1988) *The marine fishes of north-western Australia. A field guide for anglers and divers*. Perth: Western Australian Museum. 201 pp.

8. Parrish, J.D. (1987) The trophic biology of snappers and groupers. Pp 405–463, in *Tropical snappers and groupers. Biology and fisheries management*. Ed by J.J. Polovina and S. Ralston. Boulder and London: Westview Press.

9. Ramm, D.C., Lloyd, J.A. and Coleman, A.P.M. (1991) *Demersal trawling in the northern sector of the Australian Fishing Zone: catch and effort 1980–90*. Northern Territory Department of Primary Industry and Fisheries, unpublished draft fisheries report.

Contributors

Comments on this presentation were provided by (in alphabetical order) Anne Coleman, Mike Moran, Richard Mounsey, Dave Ramm, Keith Sainsbury and Neil Trainor. Drawings courtesy FAO, Rome. (*Details of contributors and their organisations are given in the Acknowledgements section at the back of this book.*)

Compiler Patricia Kailola

Golden perch

Macquaria ambigua

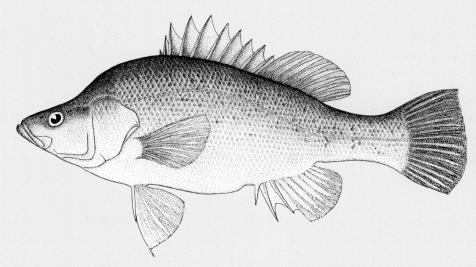

Macquaria ambigua
(Richardson)

Golden perch

Other common names include **callop**, **yellowbelly**, **perch**, **white perch**, **Murray perch**, **Murray bream**, **freshwater bream** and **tarki**.
FAO: no known name
Australian species code: 311075

Family PERCICHTHYIDAE

Diagnostic features Golden perch have a deep head and a tapered snout. Larger specimens have big eyes and mouth with a protruding lower jaw.[1] The dorsal profile behind the head is arched. The caudal fin is rounded, and the first ray of the ventral fin extends as a filament. Golden perch vary in colour depending on habitat, from dark olive green to bronze, yellow and pale cream.[2]

Distribution

Golden perch are endemic to Australia. They are distributed throughout the Murray–Darling river system, except for those streams at altitudes higher than about 600 m. The northern limit of the species' natural distribution is the headwaters of the Georgina River.[1] Golden perch also inhabit rivers in the eastern Lake Eyre and Bulloo drainages, the Dawson–Fitzroy river system in south-eastern Queensland and in many of the floodplain lakes of western Victoria and New South Wales. They have been stocked in farm dams and reservoirs outside their natural range.[2]

Golden perch live throughout the river systems, from the clear, fast flowing upper reaches to the turbid, slow flowing lower reaches and associated billabongs and backwaters. They favour deep pools with plenty of cover from fallen timber, rocky ledges or undercut banks.[2]

Life history

Golden perch spawn from early spring to late autumn. They most commonly spawn at night. A rise in water temperature above 23°C and inundation of the floodplain are required generally for successful spawning to occur.[3] Under favourable conditions female golden perch are capable of spawning more than once a season.[2] However, without suitable environmental cues they may fail to breed in a season, with the eggs being resorbed.[2] Females can produce up to 500 000 eggs, and the number produced is directly related to fish size.

Following fertilisation, the non-adhesive eggs swell to 4 mm in diameter, become transparent and semi–buoyant, and float downstream with the current. The eggs hatch within 32 hours at 23°C.

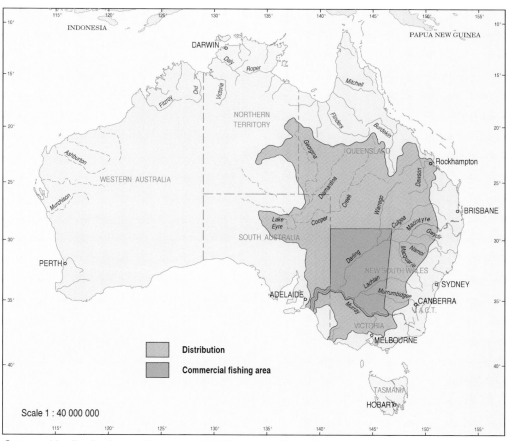

Scale 1 : 40 000 000

Distribution

Commercial fishing area

Geographic distribution and commercial fishing area for golden perch.

Larvae are 3.5–4.0 mm long and semi-buoyant on hatching.[2] They are strongly attracted to light and the presence of redgum (*Eucalyptus camaldulensis*) timber in the water[4] and so naturally prefer the shallower waters over the floodplain. However, if water quality is not suitable, the larvae may actively avoid floodplain habitats.[5] Juvenile fish disperse throughout the floodplain to find food and cover.[3]

Growth rates in golden perch vary and are primarily dependent on water temperature and the availability of food.[6] Approximate sizes are 16 cm in the first year, 29 cm at 2 years and 50 cm at 5 years. After the second year females grow faster than males.[2] The largest fish recorded weighed 24 kg and was estimated to be over 20 years old. However, it is exceptional to catch fish weighing over 6 kg. Male golden perch mature at 2 or 3 years of age and females at 4 or 5 years.[2]

Young golden perch feed on the abundant zooplankton on recently inundated floodplains. As they grow they feed on larger zooplankton and aquatic insects, and also on yabbies (*Cherax destructor*) and smaller forage fish. The diet of adult fish is dominated by yabbies and a variety of fish species.[2] Cormorants (*Phalacrocorax* species), redfin perch (*Perca fluviatilis*) and Murray cod (*Maccullochella peelii*) prey on smaller golden perch.

Golden perch is Australia's most migratory freshwater fish species. They have been recorded to travel up to 2000 km.[7] Migrations occur with floods and rises in river levels. Spawning probably needs to take place at least 500 km from the river mouth to ensure the pelagic juveniles are not carried into salt waters,[7] so migrations may well be part of ensuring the success of spawning.

Stock structure

Recent work[8] suggests that there are 3 distinct stocks of golden perch. The population in the Dawson–Fitzroy river system is a subspecies of that in the Murray–Darling basin. The population in the Cooper Creek–Barcoo River and Lake Eyre drainages may represent an undescribed species.

Commercial fishery

Golden perch have been part of the catch from the inland fishery since its inception in the mid to late 1800s.[9] In the early 1900s they constituted about 25 % of the

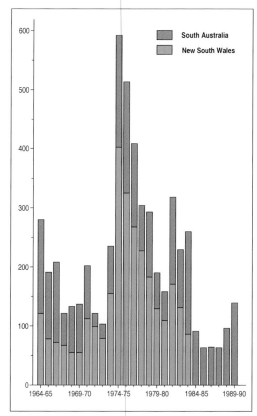

Total annual catch in t of golden perch for the period 1964–65 to 1989–90. Figures are unavailable for New South Wales from 1984–85 to 1989–90. Catches for States that average less than 5 % of the total for all States are not shown. (Source: Fisheries Resources Atlas Statistical Database)

catch, of which the rest was Murray cod.[9] With the decline in Murray cod numbers, golden perch has become the dominant native species in inland catches.

The inland fishery is centred on the lower reaches of the Murrumbidgee, Lachlan and Murray rivers and associated floodplain lakes in New South Wales and South Australia. Fishers also work in Lake Albert and Lake Alexandrina in South Australia and lakes and backwaters associated with the Darling River in New South Wales.[10,11] The fishery is opportunistic, ie it operates in response to seasonal flooding.

Drum nets and gillnets are used to catch golden perch. Drum nets are the favoured method in rivers. They are checked twice daily when fish are running, less frequently at other times.[12] Gillnets are used in the lake fishery and in slow flowing backwaters.

The fishery targets adult fish. The catch is strictly for domestic markets and is sold locally,[10] or as wet, gutted fish through the Sydney, Melbourne and Adelaide fish markets. The average price for this product at the Melbourne Wholesale Fish Market in 1991–92 was A$ 7.00 per kg.

Fisheries research staff carrying out river netting surveys. (Source: Glen Smith, Southern Fisheries Centre, Queensland Department of Primary Industries)

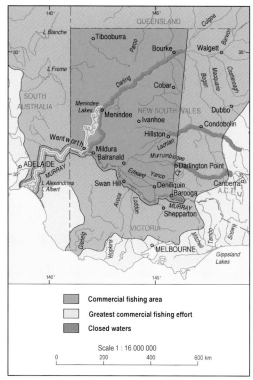

Commercial fishing area for golden perch showing areas of greatest fishing effort and waters closed to commercial fishing.

Management controls There are total closures during the breeding season to protect stocks. All States involved in the fishery have ceased issuing new commercial licences and the number of licensed fishers is being reduced either by natural attrition or return of licences.[11] State regulations set out minimum lengths for the types of gear that may be used and in South Australia and New South Wales some areas are closed to commercial fishing. For example, the main channel of the Darling River is closed to commercial fishing,[10] as are the Lachlan River upstream from Hillston and the Murrumbidgee River upstream from Darlington Point.

Recreational fishery

Golden perch are taken by anglers throughout their natural range. Most effort centres on impoundments throughout south-eastern Australia that have been artificially stocked. Fishing effort is heaviest in the spring and summer months. In rivers, effort increases during flooding when fish begin to migrate. Large numbers of fish may accumulate below weirs and barriers when migrating and so become easy targets for anglers.

Golden perch are caught using handlines, rod-and-line or set lines. Artificial lures have been used but live baits such as worms, yabbies (*Cherax*

species), 'bardi grubs' (burrowing moth and beetle larvae — Lepidoptera) and small fish are more successful. A creel survey of catch in a New South Wales reservoir in 1981–82 estimated a recreational catch of 50 t, equal to 13 % of the commercial catch for that year.[2] This suggests that the recreational catch is significant. The largest golden perch in the records of the Australian Anglers Association is a 7 kg fish taken in New South Wales in 1975.

Management controls State regulations set out gear restrictions and area closures. Minimum lengths apply in all States.[10,11] Separate bag limits for rivers and impoundments will be introduced in New South Wales in 1993.

Resource status

Catches of golden perch fluctuate widely, and abundance is thought to be related to flooding.[11] Construction of dams and weirs throughout the Murray–Darling river system has altered both flow and thermal regimes. Changes induced by such barriers in the Murray River flooding regime may also affect catch sizes. Furthermore, because golden perch move extensively, high barriers without facilities for fish passage limit the amount of river available to them.

While catches remain good, the range and abundance of golden perch has declined since European settlement.[13] Illegal use of drum nets and gillnets in remote western rivers is a major management problem.

References

1. Merrick, J.R. and Schmida, G.E. (1984) *Australian freshwater fishes: biology and management.* North Ryde: John R. Merrick. 409 pp.

2. Battaglene, S. and Prokop, F. (1987) Golden perch. *Department of Agriculture, New South Wales.* Agfact **A3.2.2**. 7 pp.

3. Lloyd, L.N., Puckridge, J.T. and Walker, K.F. (1989) The significance of fish populations in the Murray–Darling system and their requirements for survival. *Proceedings of the third Fenner conference on the environment, Canberra, September 1989.* Adelaide: Department of Enviroment and Planning.

4. Gehrke, P.C. (1990) Clinotactic responses of larval silver perch (*Bidyanus bidyanus*) and golden perch (*Macquaria ambigua*) to simulated environmental gradients. *Australian Journal of Marine and Freshwater Research* **41**: 523–528.

5. Gehrke, P.C. (1991) Avoidance of inundated floodplain habitat by larvae of golden perch (*Macquaria ambigua* Richardson): influence of water quality or food distribution? *Australian Journal of Marine and Freshwater Research* **42**: 707–719.

6. Barlow, C.G. and Bock, K. (1981) *Fish for farm dams.* New South Wales State Fisheries. Unpublished final report. 19 pp.

7. Reynolds, L.F. (1983) Migration patterns of five fish species in the Murray–Darling River system. *Australian Journal of Marine and Freshwater Research* **34**: 857–871.

8. Musyl, M.K. and Keenan, C.P. (in press, 1992) Population genetics of Australian freshwater golden perch, *Macquaria ambigua* (Richardson 1845)(Teleostei, Percichthyidae) throughout their distribution. *Australian Journal of Marine and Freshwater Research.*

9. Rowland, S.J. (1989) Aspects of the history and fishery of the Murray cod, *Maccullochella peeli* [sic] (Mitchell) (Percichthyidae). *Proceedings of the Linnaean Society of New South Wales* **111**: 201–213.

10. O'Connor, P.F. (1989) Fisheries management in inland New South Wales. Pp 19–23, in *Proceedings of the workshop on native fish management.* Ed by B. Lawrence. Canberra: Murray–Darling Basin Commission.

11. Rohan, G. (1987) *River fishery (South Australia) — review of management arrangements.* South Australian Department of Fisheries, Green paper. 31 pp.

12. Atkins, B. (1990) The Murray whalers. *SAFISH* **15**(1): 18–19.

13. Cadwallader, P.L. (1978) Some causes of the decline in range and abundance of native fish in the Murray–Darling river system. *Proceedings of the Royal Society of Victoria* **90**(1): 211–224.

Contributors

The information on this species was originally provided by Peter Gehrke, and supplemented by (in alphabetical order) Clive Keenan, Lance Lloyd, Richard Tilzey and John Timmins. Drawing by Jack Hannan, courtesy of Fisheries Research Institute, NSW Fisheries. (*Details of contributors and their organisations are given in the Acknowledgements section at the back of this book.*)
Compiler Alex McNee

Murray cod

Maccullochella peelii

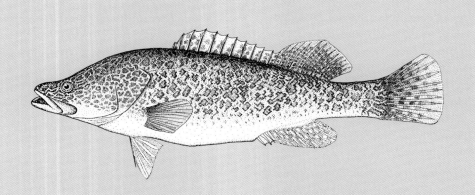

Murray cod
Maccullochella peelii (Mitchell)

Murray cod

Other common names include **cod**,
codfish, **goodoo** and **ponde**.
FAO: no known name
Australian species code: 311076

Family PERCICHTHYIDAE

Diagnostic features Murray cod have
a broad, depressed head with a rounded
snout and a concave forehead profile.
Their jaws are usually equal in length
but sometimes the lower jaw protrudes.
The mouth is large, extending beyond
the eye. There are 65–81 scales in the
lateral line. The caudal fin is rounded.
Body colour is variable with the back
and upper sides usually olive-green to
yellow-green and the upper flanks
mottled brown to pale green. The belly is
white.[1]

Distribution

The Murray cod is one of the world's
largest freshwater fish. Endemic to
Australia, the species was originally
distributed throughout the
Murray–Darling river system in
south-eastern Australia, except for the
upper reaches of the southern tributaries.
The cods' abundance has been drastically
reduced across their natural range and
they are now considered rare in many
Victorian tributaries.[2]

Murray cod have been widely
translocated to waters within their natural
range and introduced to waters outside it
throughout this and last century. Most
recently, Murray cod have been
introduced to the Cooper Creek system in
central Australia.[3] Very few of the earlier
stocked populations have survived,[4] but
more recently stocked populations are
still present in many farm dams and water
supply reservoirs.

Murray cod live in a wide range of
habitats, from clear, rocky streams to slow
flowing, turbid rivers and billabongs.[2]
They are generally found in waters to 5 m
deep, in sheltered areas with cover from
rocks, timber or overhanging banks.

Life history

Murray cod spawn from spring to early
summer. Rising water levels are not
required to initiate spawning as originally
thought[2] — it can take place in as little as
30 cm of water. A rise in water
temperature to 16–21°C may stimulate
spawning.[1] Murray cod often prefer to
spawn in protected sites.[2] Their eggs are
demersal and large, 3–3.5 mm in
diameter, and adhere to logs, rocks, and
similar hard substrates. A 2.5–3 kg female
Murray cod may produce about 10 000
eggs, a 5 kg female 14 000–30 000 eggs
and a 23 kg female 90 000 eggs.[2]

Hatching occurs 5–7 days after
fertilisation at a water temperature of
20–22°C. The larvae are 5–8 mm long on
hatching. Within 8–10 days they are
feeding on zooplankton and when they
reach 15–20 mm long they are able to
feed on aquatic insects.

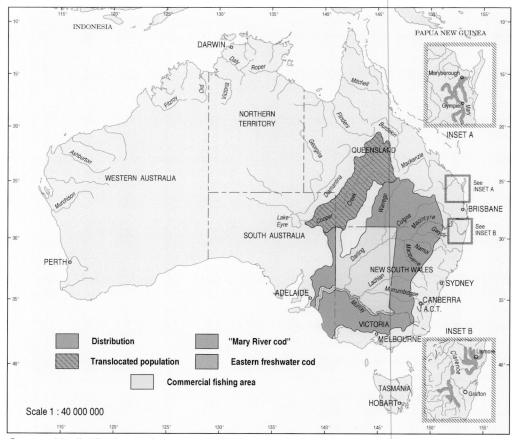

Geographic distribution and commercial fishing area for Murray cod. Distributions of the Mary
River cod (inset A) and the eastern freshwater cod (inset B) are also shown.

Early growth is rapid, most individuals attaining a length of 23 cm or 0.2 kg in weight after 1 year, 50 cm and 2 kg after 3 years and 64 cm and 5 kg after 5 years. The maximum recorded total length is 1.8 m (a fish weighing 83 kg), and the maximum recorded weight is 113.5 kg.[4] Murray cod are said to be long-lived. They attain maturity at 4–5 years of age, when weighing between 2.5 and 5 kg.

Adult fish are carnivorous, having a diet of invertebrates, fish, amphibians and occasionally reptiles, birds and aquatic mammals.[2] Cormorants (*Phalacrocorax* species) and large fish such as golden perch (*Macquaria ambigua*) or redfin (*Perca fluviatilis*) prey on juvenile Murray cod, while man is probably the only predator of large cod.

Murray cod are territorial, their 'territory' associated with a specific hole, snag (large woody debris) or area of a river or lake.[2] Tagging studies have shown that most adult cod move less than 10 km, although there are records of fish moving more than 200 km.[5] This movement is probably associated with breeding, although juveniles may undertake dispersal migrations.

Stock structure

The genetic status of the Murray cod stock in the Murray–Darling river system is unclear. Perceived differences are probably clinal given the length of riverine habitat and the species' limited movement. The relationships between Murray cod, the eastern freshwater cod (*Maccullochella ikei*) and the Mary River cod (*Maccullochella* species) remain unclear. Furthermore, the cod population of Cataract Dam (near Sydney) is a fertile hybrid of Murray cod and the trout cod (*Maccullochella macquariensis*).[6]

Commercial fishery

The Aborigines were the first to fish for Murray cod, using traps, spears, nets and poisons. Early European explorers were quick to realise its value. The first commercial inland fishery began on the Murray–Darling river system in the mid to late 1800s. Murray cod dominated the early catches, with records[4] showing that it comprised 75 % of the river fish available at the Melbourne Wholesale Fish Market in 1900. Total inland catch declined from a peak in 1918, yet in

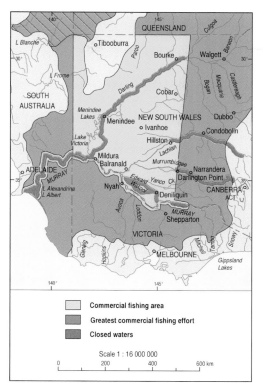

Commercial fishing area for Murray cod showing areas of greatest fishing effort and waters closed to commercial fishing.

(below) Collecting broodfish from a Murray River backwater for use at the Inland Fisheries Research Station, Narrandera. (Source: Stuart Rowland, NSW Fisheries)

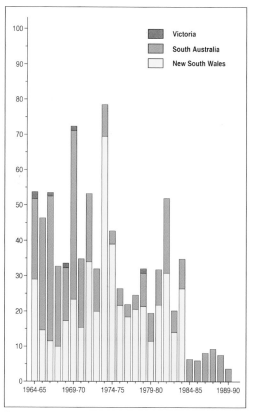

Total annual catch in t of Murray cod for the period 1964–65 to 1989–90. Figures are unavailable for New South Wales from 1984–85 to 1989–90 and Victoria from 1972–73 to 1982–83 and 1985–86 to 1989–90. (Source: Fisheries Resources Atlas Statistical Database)

1940–51 Murray cod still comprised 42–65 % of the total inland catch in New South Wales. It is now less than 10 % of this catch.[2] In South Australia Murray cod made up only 0.4 % of the State's inland catch by 1988–89.

The current commercial fishery for Murray cod is concentrated on the lower reaches of the Murray and Murrumbidgee rivers, from Deniliquin to the South Australian border, the Edward and Wakool rivers and Lake Victoria. Gillnets and drum nets are the main nets used. Drum nets are set close to the banks in

flowing water with their opening facing downstream. Gillnets are set in still waters and generally left overnight.[7]

All Murray cod caught are for domestic consumption. They are sold as wet, gutted fish in local markets and through the fish markets in Melbourne, Adelaide and Sydney. In 1991–92, prices at the Melbourne Wholesale Fish market varied between A$ 10.00 and A$ 23.00 per kg. The high variability in price reflects variations in demand and availability. The proportion sold locally is unknown but probably relatively high.

Management controls In all States a closed season is enforced and no new licences are issued. Natural attrition has seen the number of commercial licences in New South Wales fall from 214 in 1981–82[8] to 51 in 1990–91. South Australia has placed a moratorium on the taking of Murray cod by both commercial and recreational fishers.

Minimum mesh sizes for nets and minimum lengths for fish apply in most States and area closures apply.[8]

Although there has been concern about Murray cod stocks since 1880, there has been comparatively little management of the resource. Recent management steps have been confined to gradually reducing the number of commercial fishers.[8] In South Australia stock enhancement research is under way, with a view to lifting the moratorium when stocks recover.

Recreational fishery

Murray cod is a highly valued recreational species because of its size, its value for sport and its edibility. Recreational fishing for Murray cod is concentrated around the major towns on the lower Murray, Murrumbidgee and Lachlan rivers and the Darling River (downstream from Menindee) and impoundments on or near these river sections.[8] Murray cod are also

Recreational fisher landing a large Murray cod. (Source: Rod Harrison, *The Australian Angler's Fishing World*)

keenly sought in the Barwon, Macintyre and other northern rivers.

Anglers targeting Murray cod have most success using set lines with live bait such as small fish, yabbies (*Cherax* species) and 'bardi grubs' (burrowing moth and beetle larvae — Lepidoptera). Murray cod are also taken using rod-and-line with artificial lures.[2] The recreational catch of Murray cod probably now surpasses the commercial catch. Although individuals exceeding 50 kg are rarely taken, small numbers of fish between 20 kg and 40 kg are regularly caught by experienced anglers. According to records of the Australian Anglers Association the largest fish taken weighed 50.4 kg, and was caught in South Australia in 1967.

Management controls There are individual State regulations on gear, legal size and bag limits for recreational fishers, and area closures apply. In recent years most management effort has centred on habitat management plus hatchery production and stocking. The major regulatory problem is the illegal use of drum nets and gillnets in remote areas.

Resource status

Heavy commercial fishing pressure in the period up to the 1930s saw the decline of Murray cod in the inland catch. In the mid-1930s catches declined to levels unprofitable for large-scale operators. Catches of Murray cod increased again between 1940 and 1951, but declined in following years, stabilising around the current low levels in the 1960s.[4]

While much of the decline in Murray cod numbers up until the 1930s can been attributed to over-fishing, environmental changes such as those caused by removal of snags or by the construction of dams, levee banks, and high level weirs throughout the Murray–Darling river system have undoubtedly had a major effect since the 1950s. These constructions have altered the natural flow and temperature regimes of the river and reduced the incidence of seasonal flooding. Flooding promotes the production of zooplankton on which Murray cod larvae feed, and its suppression has probably reduced larval recruitment and hence Murray cod numbers. Poor juvenile recruitment is probably the main reason for the

continued decline in the Murray cod populations within the river system.[4]

Another possible factor contributing to the decline of Murray cod in the Murray–Darling river system is the introduced fish, redfin. The diets of these 2 fish species overlap extensively and it is also possible that juvenile redfin prey on cod larvae. Redfin also spawn earlier in water temperatures of around 12°C. As a result there is competition for resources, particularly during drought periods.[4]

References

1. Merrick, J.R. and Schmida, G.E. (1984) *Australian freshwater fishes: biology and management.* North Ryde: John R. Merrick. 409 pp.

2. Rowland, S.J. (1988) Murray cod. *NSW Agriculture & Fisheries. Agfact* **F3.2.4.** 10 pp.

3. Pierce, B. (1990) Murray cod invade South Australia's Cooper Creek. *SAFISH* **7**: 11–12.

4. Rowland, S.J. (1989) Aspects of the history and fishery of the Murray cod, *Maccullochella peeli* [sic] (Mitchell) (Percichthyidae). *Proceedings of the Linnaean Society of New South Wales.* **111**: 201–213.

5. Reynolds, L.F. (1983) Migration patterns of five fish species in the Murray-Darling River system. *Australian Journal of Marine and Freshwater Research* **34**: 857–871.

6. Harris, J.H. and Dixon, P.I. (1982) *Occurrence of the endangered fish species, trout cod* (Maccullochella macquariensis), *in a protected habitat in New South Wales.* Abstract, Australian Society for Fish Biology annual conference, Hobart, 30 July–2 August 1982.

7. Roughley, T.C. (1966) *Fish and fisheries of Australia.* Sydney: Angus and Robertson. 328 pp.

8. O'Connor, P.F. (1989) Fisheries management in inland New South Wales. Pp 19–23, in *Proceedings of the workshop on native fish management.* Ed by B. Lawrence. Canberra: Murray–Darling Basin Commission.

Contributors

The information on this species was originally provided by Richard Tilzey and supplemented by (in alphabetical order) John Harris, Hamar Midgley, Bryan Pierce and Stuart Rowland. Drawing by Jack Hannan, courtesy of Fisheries Research Institute, NSW Fisheries.(*Details of contributors and their organisations are given in the Acknowledgements section at the back of this book.*)
Compiler Alex McNee

Westralian jewfish

Glaucosoma hebraicum

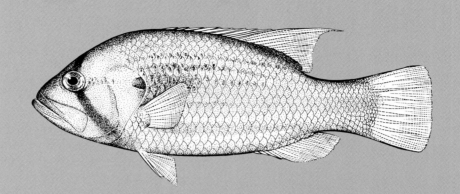

Glaucosoma hebraicum
Richardson

Westralian jewfish

Other common names include **jewie**, **dhufish** and **West Australian jewfish**.
FAO: no known name
Australian species code: 320004

Family GLAUCOSOMATIDAE

Diagnostic features Westralian jewfish are robust, deep bodied fish with a large, fully scaled head. They have large eyes and mouth, with small, canine-like teeth in the jaws. The rayed section of their dorsal fin is higher than the spined section and is tapered to a point. Their body is lilac-bronze above and silvery-grey on the sides and below, and there are 6 broad dark longitudinal bands on the side that fade with age. The roof of the mouth and tongue are pale.[1] Westralian jewfish have a black line through the eye that is often indistinct in larger fish.[2]

Distribution

Westralian jewfish are endemic to Australian waters, and are present only in Western Australia. They inhabit waters from the Recherche Archipelago off Esperance, to Beagle Island, although they are rare north of Shark Bay.

Westralian jewfish live in shallow inshore waters and depths to over 200 m.[3] They are present over hard, flat sea beds (eg limestone shelf) and in reefs, wrecks and underwater caverns and gutters. Adult fish move into shallower waters in the cooler months between April and June.[3,4]

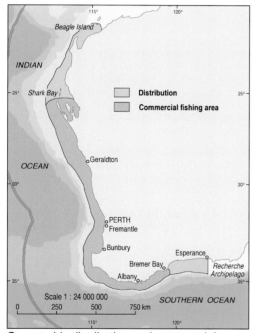

Geographic distribution and commercial fishing areas for Westralian jewfish.

Life history

Mature Westralian jewfish migrate to shallower waters during the spawning season. They aggregate around inshore reefs in about 20 m of water, although actual spawning appears to take place on isolated outcrops of reef or flat, weed-covered sandy substrates away from a main reef. Spawning occurs annually over a protracted period from December to March, with a peak in January and February when water temperatures are high and plankton is abundant.[3]

Female Westralian jewfish can produce between 300 000 and 3 million eggs (large fish). They are broadcast spawners, releasing floating eggs into the water column; these are pelagic and can be carried large distances on ocean surface currents. Larvae of Westralian jewfish feed on plankton. Juveniles tend to remain in shallower water than adults and are rarely found in waters more than 100 m deep.[3]

Westralian jewfish can grow to a total length of at least 1.22 m,[2] and weigh up to 26 kg. On average, fish in the commercial catch weigh around 7–8 kg.[3] Westralian jewfish grow to about 30 cm in total length after 1 year and 40–45 cm after 2 years. The growth rate slows after 2 years and 3-year-old and 5-year-old fish are, on average, 52 cm and 65 cm long respectively.[3] Males and females mature after 3 or 4 years, at 54–58 cm long.[3]

Westralian jewfish feed primarily on small fish, but will also eat rock lobsters (Palinuridae), crabs (Portunidae), squid (Loliginidae), octopus (*Octopus* species) and cuttlefish (*Sepia* species).[3]

Stock structure

There is no information on the stock structure of Westralian jewfish.

Commercial fishery

Westralian jewfish are taken commercially off the West Australian coast from Bremer Bay to Shark Bay, with the majority of the catch coming from the waters of the mid-west coast, off Geraldton. The main methods of capture are bottom set gillnets, droplines, bottom set longlines and handlines. The greatest part of the catch is taken by handline, with peak catches generally occurring between December and February, coinciding with the spawning season. Westralian jewfish are taken in gillnets and on longlines as bycatch of the Southwest Shark Fishery.

Westralian jewfish are sold whole, or gilled and gutted. In 1992, the wholesale price per kg in Western Australia was A$ 8.00 to A$ 11.00. The catch for the 1988–89 financial year was 216 t, with an estimated value of A$ 1.8 million.[5]

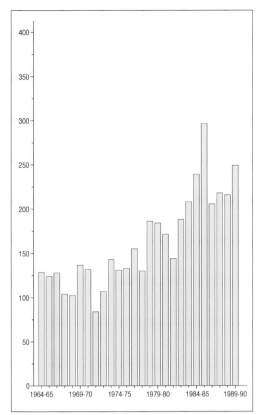

Total annual catch in t of Westralian jewfish for the period 1964–65 to 1989–90. (Source: Fisheries Resources Atlas Statistical Database)

(below) The Western Australian handline fishery targets several species including Westralian jewfish and snapper. (Source: Jerry Jenke, Western Australian Marine Research Laboratories, Fisheries Department of Western Australia)

Management controls There are no gear restrictions, quotas or closures specific to fishers targeting Westralian jewfish. A legal minimum total length applies.[6]

Recreational fishery

Westralian jewfish are taken by recreational fishers throughout their range and heaviest fishing effort centres on offshore reefs along the southern and south-western coasts.[3] The recreational Westralian jewfish catch is estimated to be greater than the commercial catch. They are fished throughout the year and their habit of migrating inshore in the cooler months makes larger fish more accessible.[3,4]

Experienced anglers suggest that the most productive time to fish for Westralian jewfish is late afternoon, through the night, and early in the morning. The main method used is boat-based handlining, either with the boat drifting, or by anchoring and berleying.[3]

Westralian jewfish rank with snapper (*Pagrus auratus*) as the fifth most popular fish targeted by anglers, and they are the most prized demersal species.[3] The largest Westralian jewfish caught by a recreational fisher was 25.9 kg (records of the Australian Anglers Association).

Management controls Minimum size limits and daily bag limits apply. In addition, Westralian jewfish are included in a mixed daily bag limit with other prize recreational species such as samson fish (*Seriola hippos*) and Spanish mackerel (*Scomberomorus* species).[3]

Resource status

The status of the resource is unknown. There is some evidence of increased fishing pressure in certain areas, where there has been a decrease in the average size of Westralian jewfish taken by anglers.[3]

Notes

Northern pearl-perch (*Glaucosoma burgeri*) and threadfin pearl-perch (*G. magnificum*) are caught on the North West Shelf of Western Australia. Northern pearl-perch can be distinguished from Westralian jewfish mainly by their black palate and tongue, and threadfin pearl-perch can be distiguished by their tasselated fins and by having 3 (not 1) dark bands across their head.[1]

References

1. Sainsbury, K.J., Kailola, P.J. and Leyland, G.G. (1985) *Continental shelf fishes of north-western Australia. An illustrated guide.* Canberra: Clouston and Hall and Peter Pownall Fisheries Information Service. 375 pp.

2. Hutchins, B. and Swainston, R. (1986) *Sea fishes of southern Australia. Complete field guide for anglers and divers.* Perth: Swainston Publishing. 180 pp.

3. Westralian jewfish (in press, 1992) *Fisheries Department of Western Australia, Fishing WA.*

4. Cusack, R. and Roennfeldt, M. (1987) *Fishing the wild west.* Perth: St George Books. 208 pp.

5. Australian Bureau of Statistics (1990) *Fisheries, Western Australia 1988–1989.* Catalogue No. **7601.5**. 19 pp.

6. *Government Gazette, W.A.* 20 May 1988. (1988) Perth: Government Printers.

Contributors

Additional information on this species was provided by Rod Lenanton. Drawing by Roger Swainston. (*Details of contributors and their organisations are given in the Acknowledgements section at the back of this book.*)
Compiler Alex McNee

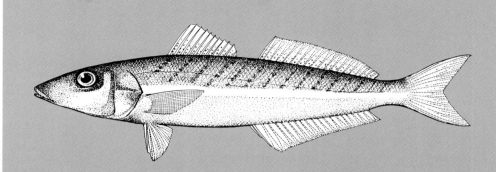

Distribution

School whiting are endemic to southern regions of the Australian continental shelf. Eastern school whiting are distributed from Moreton Bay in Queensland,[1] through New South Wales and Victoria to Anxious Bay in South Australia.[2] They are also present on the east coast of Tasmania. The distribution of western school whiting overlaps partly with the eastern species, ranging from Kangaroo Island in South Australia[2] to Geraldton in Western Australia.[1]

School whiting live close to the sea bed over sandy substrates. Eastern school whiting normally inhabit depths from the surf zone to about 80 m,[3] although small catches have been taken from deeper water.[1] Western school whiting are recorded from depths up to 42 m, but they probably also inhabit deeper waters.[1]

Life history

The spawning period of eastern school whiting varies throughout its range. Off northern New South Wales spawning activity peaks in winter.[4] In southern New South Wales and eastern Bass Strait spawning occurs from spring to late summer.[4,5] It is likely that eastern school whiting spawn more than once during these periods, and that some eggs are resorbed by females at the end of the spawning season.[5] Each female releases between 30 000 and 110 000 eggs in total during the season.[5]

No studies of reproduction have been conducted for western school whiting. The distribution of eastern school whiting larvae is patchy and influenced by ocean currents.[2] Juveniles of both school whiting species inhabit inshore waters. Western school whiting juveniles associate with accumulated seaweed in

School whiting

This presentation is on 2 species, **eastern school whiting** and **western school whiting**.

Eastern school whiting,
Sillago flindersi McKay

Other common names include **red spot whiting**, **silver whiting**, **trawl whiting** and **transparent whiting**.
FAO: no known name
Australian species code: 330014

Western school whiting,
Sillago bassensis Cuvier

Other common names include **silver whiting** and **transparent whiting**.
FAO: no known name
Australian species code: 330002

Family SILLAGINIDAE

Diagnostic features Both species of school whiting have a silver stripe along the side of their body but no dark blotch on the pectoral fin base. Eastern school whiting (pictured) have oblique red to orange bands on the upper sides of their body and a series of blotches just above the lateral line. Western school whiting have fine bands on their upper sides and no series of blotches. Eastern school whiting have a pink or white abdomen and a pale cream pectoral fin, while western school whiting have a pale silvery white abdomen and a dull yellow pectoral fin.

the surf zone during spring and summer in Western Australia. The seaweed provides shelter and suitable habitat for prey species.[6]

Male and female eastern school whiting have similar growth patterns. Maturity is reached at an age of 2 years and a size of 14–16 cm fork length.[5,7] A maximum age of 7 years has been recorded for females and 6 years for males.[8] Eastern school whiting grow to at least 32 cm total length.[1] There is some variation in growth rates between eastern school whiting from different areas. Fish from northern New South Wales grow more quickly than those from southern waters[4] but may not live as long as fish from Bass Strait. There is no information

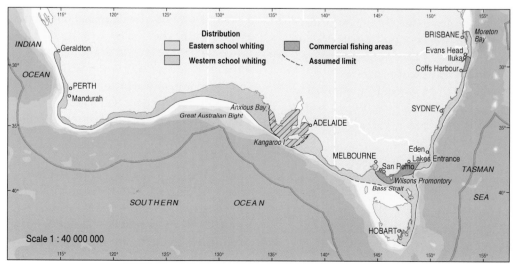

Geographic distribution of eastern school whiting and western school whiting, and commercial fishing areas for eastern school whiting.

on growth rates for western school whiting, but they are recorded to a maximum total length of 33 cm.[1]

The 2 school whiting species have similar diets. Crustaceans, particularly amphipods and prawns, are the main prey of adults.[7] Polychaete worms are also eaten. Juveniles consume mostly amphipods and polychaete worms.

Research into the genetics of eastern school whiting suggests that school whiting do not normally migrate.[2] There is no information on movements by western school whiting.

Stock structure

Genetic studies of eastern school whiting have identified 4 separate stocks.[2] Fish from northern New South Wales are distinct from southern New South Wales fish, and these appear to be part of a separate stock which extends through eastern and central Bass Strait. The other stocks are present in Tasmania and from western Victoria to Anxious Bay.[2]

Four samples of western school whiting analysed using electrophoresis showed significant genetic variation and may be from separate stocks.[2] Three of the samples were from South Australia and the other from Mandurah in Western Australia. Other stocks of western school whiting may also exist.

Commercial fishery

Eastern school whiting is much more important as a commercial species than is western school whiting. There are 2 main fisheries for eastern school whiting, the largest being located within the South East Fishery. Approximately 90 % of the South East Fishery catch is taken by Danish seine vessels fishing in eastern Bass Strait.[9] Most of the vessels operate from the port of Lakes Entrance in eastern Victoria. A few Danish seine vessels operate from the port of San Remo and fish grounds close to the port as well as grounds immediately east of Wilsons Promontory.[3]

Danish seine vessels have operated from Lakes Entrance since 1946, when the eastern Bass Strait grounds began to develop.[9] Up until 1970 the annual catch of school whiting from eastern Bass Strait varied between 30 t and 270 t, but with the development of an export market in Japan, target fishing for school whiting

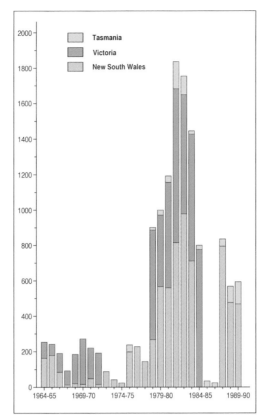

Total annual catch in t of eastern school whiting for the period 1964–65 to 1989–90. Figures are unavailable for: New South Wales from 1984–85 to 1986–87; and Victoria from 1972–73 to 1977–78 and 1985–86 to 1989–90. Catches for States that average less than 5 % of the total for all States are not shown. (Source: Fisheries Resources Atlas Statistical Database)

increased. Catches from the South East Fishery varied between 400 t and 800 t per annum from 1970 to 1985, mainly as a function of the number of Danish seine vessels operating in any year.[10] Catches have since increased to nearly 1400 t per annum. Catch rates of school whiting in Bass Strait are highest in autumn and winter[10] although some catch is taken all year. Almost 90 % of the catch comes from waters less than 50 m deep, regardless of season.[10]

Only small quantities of school whiting are caught by demersal otter trawl vessels within the South East Fishery. The trawl catches are widely distributed through southern New South Wales and eastern Victorian waters and normally form a bycatch of tiger flathead (*Neoplatycephalus richardsoni*) and jackass morwong (*Nemadactylus macropterus*).

The second major fishery for eastern school whiting is located off the northern New South Wales coast. Trawl vessels fishing from the port of Iluka catch school whiting as a bycatch of fishing for eastern king prawns (*Penaeus plebejus*). Some school whiting is also caught by vessels

from Coffs Harbour and Evans Head. The fishery commenced in the mid 1970s. It developed rapidly and catches reached about 700 t by the early 1980s,[10] stabilising at about 500 t by the mid 1980s.[4] Fishers target school whiting when prawn catches are low or when export demand is high.[11] The highest catch rates are recorded in late autumn and winter in this fishery.[12] Prior to 1986, fishers used modified prawn trawls to increase the catch rate of school whiting, but regulations were introduced to discourage this practice in Commonwealth waters from May 1986.[4] In northern New South Wales, stout whiting (*Sillago robusta*) form a significant bycatch of trawling for eastern school whiting, constituting about 10 % of the total whiting catch (see 'Notes').[12]

Minor school whiting fisheries exist in other areas. In recent years an inshore trawl fishery for eastern school whiting has started in eastern Tasmanian waters. The Tasmanian catch exceeded 100 t in 1989–90. School whiting are also caught with beach seines inshore in Victoria and Tasmania. Western school whiting are caught as a bycatch of trawlers fishing for prawns and scallops (*Pecten* species) off south-western Western Australia. They are rarely targeted by commercial fishers in Western Australia because of the high proportion of fish there that are smaller than the minimum legal size. The total Western Australian catch (mainly western school whiting) was about 18 t in 1988–89.

Only small amounts of school whiting are sold on the domestic market. All of

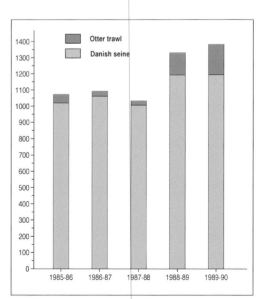

Total annual catch in t of eastern school whiting from the South East Fishery for the period 1985–86 to 1989–90. Catch records for 1985–86 are incomplete. (Source: Australian Fishing Zone Information System)

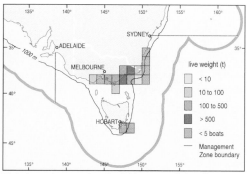

Total eastern school whiting catch in t by 1-degree block from the South East Fishery for the period 1986 to 1989. The catch for blocks fished by fewer than 5 boats is not shown. (Source: Australian Fishing Zone Information System)

the eastern school whiting landed at Iluka and Lakes Entrance are exported. Cartons of whole fish are frozen and sent either directly to Japan for processing or to Thailand for processing into 'butterfly' fillets and subsequent re-export to Japan.[11] In 1988–89, 745 t of frozen whole whiting was sent to Japan, 322 t to Thailand, and nearly 300 t shared between Taiwan, Singapore and China. The average wholesale price for eastern school whiting sold through the Sydney Fish Market in 1991–92 was A$ 1.40 per kg.

Management controls Fishers operating in the South East Fishery are regulated by the Commonwealth of Australia. Management regulations include licence limitations, gear restrictions and boat replacement provisions. A total allowable catch limit was introduced for school whiting in the South East Fishery in 1992 and fishers were allocated shares of the total allowable catch by means of individual transferable quotas. The northern New South Wales fishery is managed by the New South Wales Government.

Fishers trawling or Danish seining within State waters of Victoria, Tasmania and Western Australia are subject to management regulations of each State. A minimum legal size limit applies to western school whiting in Western Australian waters.

Recreational fishery

Eastern school whiting are caught occasionally by anglers in New South Wales, Victorian and Tasmanian waters.[10] Western school whiting are commonly caught by anglers in Western Australia along with other whiting species such as western trumpeter whiting (*Sillago*

maculata burrus) and yellowfin whiting (*S. schomburgkii*).

Management controls A daily bag limit applies in Western Australia.

Resource status

Estimates of biomass for eastern school whiting in the South East Fishery are variable and sensitive to estimates of catchability for the species. The more conservative estimates indicate that current catch levels are sustainable. Information on the northern New South Wales stock is insufficient for reliable assessment of the resource.

No information is available on resource status for western school whiting.

Notes

In recent years a trawl fishery for stout whiting has developed off southern Queensland in 20-100 m depths. About 300 t of this species was landed in 1989 and more than 1000 t in 1990. As with eastern school whiting, the product is frozen whole and exported for reprocessing in Thailand and subsequent re-export to Japan. All trawlers operating in this fishery use modified prawn trawls.

References

1. McKay, R.J. (1985) A revision of the fishes of the family Sillaginidae. *Memoirs of the Queensland Museum* **22**: 1–73.

2. Dixon, P.I, Crozier, R.H., Black, M. and Church, A. (1987) Stock identification and discrimination of commercially important whitings in Australian waters using genetic criteria. *Centre for Marine Science, University of New South Wales. FIRTA Project 83/16, Final Report.* 69 pp.

3. Winstanley, R.H. (1983) Fishery situation report: school whiting. *Victorian Department of Conservation, Forests and Lands, Fisheries and Wildlife Division, Commercial Fisheries Report* **9**. 22 pp.

4. Smith, D.C., Huber, D. and McGuren, M.E. (1987) Assessment of the New South Wales fishery for red spot whiting. Progress report number 2. *New South Wales Department of Agriculture, Fisheries Research Institute, Internal Report* **29**. 23 pp.

5. Hobday, D.K. and Wankowski, J.W.J. (1987) School whiting *Sillago bassensis flindersi*: reproduction and fecundity in eastern Bass Strait, Australia. *Victorian Department of Conservation, Forests and Lands, Fisheries Division, Internal Report* **153**. 24 pp.

6. Lenanton, R.C.J., Robertson, A.I. and Hansen, J.A. (1982) Nearshore

accumulations of detached macrophytes as nursery areas for fish. *Marine Ecology in Progress Series* **9**: 51–57.

7. Burchmore, J.J., Pollard, D.A., Middleton, M.J., Bell, J.D. and Pease, B.C. (1988) Biology of four species of whiting (Pisces: Sillaginidae) in Botany Bay, New South Wales. *Australian Journal of Marine and Freshwater Research* **39**: 709–727.

8. Hobday, D.K. and Wankowski, J.W.J. (1986) Age determination and growth of school whiting. *Victorian Department of Conservation, Forests and Lands, Fisheries Division, Internal Report* **130**. 29 pp.

9. Wankowski, J.W.J. (1983) The Lakes Entrance Danish seine fishery for tiger flathead, school whiting and jackass morwong, 1947–1978. *Victorian Department of Conservation, Forests and Lands, Fisheries and Wildlife Division, Technical Report* **30**. 31 pp.

10. Smith, D.C. (in press, 1992) Eastern school whiting. In *The South East Fishery: a scientific review with particular reference to quota management.* Ed by R.D.J. Tilzey. *Bureau of Resource Sciences Bulletin.*

11. 'By-catch' pays the bills for Clarence prawners (1984) *Australian Fisheries* **43**(7): 14–16.

12. Smith, D.C., Huber, D. and McGuren, M.E. (1987) Co-occurrence of red spot and stout whiting off northern New South Wales — preliminary results. *New South Wales Department of Agriculture, Fisheries Research Institute, Internal Report* **24**. 23 pp.

Contributors

Most of the information on eastern school whiting was provided by Dave Smith. Rod Lenanton contributed information on western school whiting and Adam Butcher provided notes on the stout whiting fishery in Queensland. Richard Tilzey provided comments. Drawing by Roger Swainston. (*Details of contributors and their organisations are given in the Acknowledgements section at the back of this book.*)
Compiler Phillip Stewart

Part of a trawl catch of eastern school whiting. (Source: Dave Smith, Marine Science Laboratories, Victorian Department of Conservation and Environment)

W h i t i n g

Sillago species

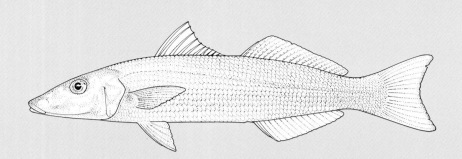

Whiting

This presentation is on 2 species, **sand whiting** and **trumpeter whiting**.

Sand whiting, *Sillago ciliata* Cuvier

Other common names include **summer whiting**, **silver whiting** and **blue-nose**.
FAO: no known name
Australian species code: 330010

Trumpeter whiting, *Sillago maculata maculata* Quoy and Gaimard

Other common names include **winter whiting**, **spotted whiting** and **diver whiting**.
FAO: no known name
Australian species code: 330004

Family SILLAGINIDAE

Diagnostic features Sand whiting (pictured) are silvery white, with plain yellowish sides (blotched dark in fish less than about 9 cm long) and with a distinctive dark blotch at the base of the pectoral fin. The dorsal fin has greenish hues and the remaining fins are yellowish.[1] There are 60–69 small scales in the lateral line.[2] Both adult and juvenile trumpeter whiting have a pattern of dark blotches on a silvery body, and they have a dark blotch at the base of the pectoral fin. There are 71–75 small scales in their lateral line.[2]

Distribution

Sand whiting are distributed from Cape York southwards to eastern Victoria and to Ulverstone, northern Tasmania,[3] although there are unsubstantiated reports of their presence on the east coast of Tasmania.[2] The species' distribution includes Lord Howe Island waters, and beyond Australia to New Caledonia and south-eastern Papua New Guinea.[2] Trumpeter whiting are endemic to Australia. They occur from Lizard Island in Queensland to Narooma in southern New South Wales.[2,3]

Sand whiting inhabit inshore waters including coastal beaches and sandbars, bays, coastal lakes, estuaries, and rivers as far as tidal limits. The whiting move in large schools across sand banks near river mouths, and in the surf zone.[1,2] Sand whiting favour shallow water over a sand or muddy sand substrate to about 6 m, where they are generally common all year or move into deeper water (to 46 m)

during winter.[2,4,5] Trumpeter whiting are the most abundant whiting in Moreton Bay, and they occupy depths from 1 m to 30 m.[5] In contrast to sand whiting, trumpeter whiting favour silty, muddy bays and inshore waters, and are especially common in turbid areas near river mouths and mangrove creeks.[2,4,6] Both species bury themselves in soft sand and mud when alarmed.

Life history

Sand whiting aggregate during the spawning period, and spawning takes place at the mouth of estuaries, in large embayments, in the sea[2,4,7,8,9] or on shallow banks close to breaking surf. It occurs at peak high tide, at night and 1–2 days prior to full moon.[10] The spawning period extends from September to February[10] in the north and from early summer to April in central New South Wales.[4,9] The onset of spawning may be related to water temperature and day

length.[4,9] Adults disperse after spawning, perhaps to deeper offshore waters. Sand whiting probably spawn twice each season.[4,8] Evidence for this comes from the presence of 2 prominent size groups of yolked ova (eggs) in sand whiting at Bribie Island early in the season and only 1 size group late in the season,[8] and from the high range in recorded fecundity (31 000 to 380 000 eggs). Fecundity increases with size.

Trumpeter whiting spawn throughout the year[2,10,11] with peaks in spawning activity in winter in Queensland[11] and from December to February in Botany

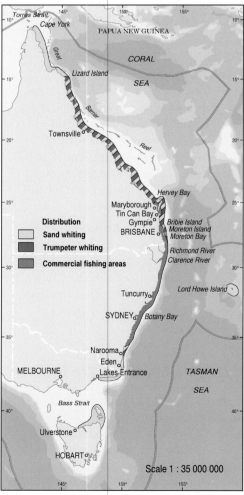

Geographic distribution and commercial fishing areas for sand whiting and trumpeter whiting in Australian waters.

Bay[9] — ie they spawn several times each year.[12] Trumpeter whiting exhibit a wide range in fecundity at given sizes: 141 000– 362 000 eggs.[11] They spawn in very shallow water on sandy beaches of sheltered bays and estuaries.

Whiting larvae (of various species) are present in river mouths and mangrove areas most of the year.[13] Their planktonic phase is restricted to early or mid summer. In sand whiting it lasts until the fish reach about 15.5 mm in length.[13] Juveniles and adolescents are abundant in shallow waters of rivers and creeks, over seagrass beds and in mangroves,[9] although they tend to move into deeper water as they grow older. Whereas adult sand whiting share the juvenile habitat, adult trumpeter whiting prefer deeper water.[5]

The growth rates of sand whiting from Queensland and New South Wales are comparable[4] although the growth rate itself is highly variable.[10] Summer measurements of sand whiting in southern Queensland gave average fork lengths of 11–19 cm for 1-year-old fish and up to 32–35 cm for 6-year-old fish.[10] The maximum recorded size for sand whiting is 50 cm total length,[4] and maximum age estimates vary from 9 years[2] to 22 years.[4] Male sand whiting are mature at about 2 years of age[2] and females at 3 years.[10] Size at first maturity ranges from 19 cm to 26 cm fork length.[2,4,8,9] In sand whiting populations at Bribie Island and Botany Bay, there are more males than females at sizes less than 24 cm fork length, but the proportions are reversed above that size.[8,9]

Trumpeter whiting grow to about 30 cm total length[1,9] and reach maturity at about 19 cm fork length[9] (21–22 cm total length). There is a change in sex ratio over size, with more females than males present in adult populations.[9,11] There are no maximum age estimates for trumpeter whiting.

Whiting forage for burrowing or benthic animals by using their conical snout to plough through sand or mud. Sand whiting eat invertebrates including crustaceans such as yabbies (*Callianassa* species), prawns and soldier crabs (Mictyridae), polychaete worms[10] and bivalve molluscs such as pipies (*Plebiodonax* species). In a Botany Bay study, polychaete worms (61 %) and crustaceans (37 %) were the dominant food items.[9] Food selection changes with fish size; smaller fish eat fewer polychaetes, and larger fish (31–40 cm fork length) eat large amounts of bivalve molluscs and yabbies.[9] Trumpeter whiting eat mainly polychaete worms, crustaceans (amphipods, shrimps, crabs), bivalve molluscs,[6,9] and a variety of other benthic animals and small fish.[6] As with sand whiting, trumpeter whiting change their dietary pattern as they grow larger.[9]

No studies of predation on sand or trumpeter whiting have been undertaken.

Stock structure

There are 2 schools of thought on the nature of the sand whiting stocks. One considers that separate stocks are associated with different river systems along the mainland coast and at Bribie and Moreton islands in southern Queensland.[14] The other, based on tagging studies, believes that sand whiting belong to a unit stock. A recent study[1] did not resolve the issue.

Trumpeter whiting are distinguished from western trumpeter whiting (*Sillago maculata burrus*) chiefly on swimbladder morphology,[2] although the subspecific status has not been confirmed by genetic studies.[1]

Commercial fishery

Whiting have been the basis of an established inshore fishery along the eastern seaboard since early last century. In 1947, three-quarters of the Queensland catch of whiting came from Maryborough, Gympie and Wynnum (Brisbane) co-operatives.[4] Moreton Bay and Tin Can Bay are now the major fishing areas in Queensland and an estimated 240 t each year was taken in southern Queensland in 1977 and 1978.[15] The 1989–90 value of the combined sand whiting/golden-lined whiting (*S. analis*) fishery in Queensland was A$ 2.2 million. The whiting fishery is also important in New South Wales.

Sand whiting are taken mostly in summer, mainly using beach seine nets off sandy beaches and in estuaries. Tunnel nets, bottom set gillnets and handlines are also used. Fish 23–42 cm fork length are targeted.[4,5] Catches around Bribie Island are highest from August to November and the fishery is usually associated with aggregations during the spawning period. In New South Wales estuaries and river mouths,

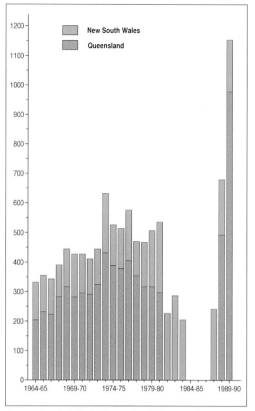

Annual catch in t of sand whiting and trumpeter whiting combined, for the period 1964–65 to 1989–90. Figures are unavailable for: Queensland from 1981–82 to 1987–88; and New South Wales from 1984–85 to 1986–87. Catches for States that average less than 5 % of the total for all States are not shown. (Source: Fisheries Resources Atlas Statistical Database)

particularly in the north of the State, are more popular for whiting fishing. Generally, the catch rates fluctuate with the ability of beach seine crews, weather conditions and seasonal whiting abundance. Some sand whiting are caught incidentally by prawn trawlers in Moreton Bay, and there is a moderately high incidental catch of other fish species in beach seine hauls.

Large numbers of trumpeter whiting are caught by haul seine in shallow water and by demersal otter trawl in slightly deeper water.[2] Trumpeter whiting are also caught with hook and line. They are the only commercial fish species taken regularly in large numbers by trawlers in Moreton Bay,[12] and the Queensland fishery for them is restricted to this area. Trumpeter whiting is regarded as a useful bycatch of prawn trawlers, especially when prawn catches are low over winter.

Whiting are marketed locally as chilled or fresh whole fish or fillets. All whiting species command high prices on local markets and sand, golden-lined and trumpeter whiting are often boxed together. Large quantities of trumpeter whiting are marketed during winter (hence, 'winter whiting'). The average 1991–92 price per kg at the Sydney Fish Market was A$ 6.68 for sand whiting and A$ 2.36 for trumpeter whiting.

Golden-lined whiting are caught with sand whiting in southern Queensland. They often form schools with sand whiting,[2] although they typically live in muddier areas than sand whiting. Golden-lined whiting are far more abundant in mangrove areas in Moreton Bay than are other whiting species.[16] Individuals up to 35 cm fork length are caught in the fishery and are marketed as 'summer whiting'. However, golden-lined whiting comprise only 10 % of the marketed Queensland whiting catch.[5]

Management controls Minimum legal sizes are imposed in Queensland and New South Wales. There are also gear restrictions in New South Wales.

Aquaculture

Research is being undertaken in Queensland into the commercial culture of sand whiting.

Recreational fishery

Whiting are caught by rod-and-line and handlines from shore and boat, using live baits of worms, soldier crabs and yabbies, or squid bait (only for trumpeter whiting).[5,14] They are popular angling species for their fighting ability and table value.

Sand, trumpeter and golden-lined whiting are some of the most popular recreational angling species in southern Queensland,[15] especially around Bribie Island and Moreton Island. Large catches are made on banks close to breaking surf and on spring high tides.

In New South Wales, whiting do not constitute a large proportion of anglers' catches despite their relative abundance in estuaries. Larger catches are generally made during the warmer summer months, and over sandbars at the entrance to estuaries. Sand whiting is a commonly caught recreational fish in Sydney Harbour. The largest sand whiting caught by a recreational fisher was 1.4 kg, from New South Wales (records of the Australian Underwater Federation). Trumpeter whiting are popular with anglers fishing in muddy bays.

Management controls Minimum legal sizes apply. Nevertheless, a large number of retained sand whiting are less than the legal minimum size, for example, 50 % in the 1980–81 season at Bribie Island.[7] A large amount of retained sand and trumpeter whiting in the Richmond River and Clarence River (New South Wales) are undersized.

An angler's catch of sand whiting taken in New South Wales. (Source: Gary Henry, Environment Protection Authority, New South Wales)

Resource status

There is no recent information on the resource status of sand whiting and trumpeter whiting. The number of fish caught in the 1980–81 season was more than in the previous 20 years, but the average fish size was less.[14]

References

1. Dixon, P.I., Crozier, R.H., Black, M. and Church, A. (1987) Stock identification and discrimination of commercially important whitings in Australian waters using genetic criteria. *Centre for Marine Science, University of New South Wales. FIRTA Project 83/16, Final Report.* 69 pp.

2. McKay, R.J. (1985) A revision of the fishes of the family Sillaginidae. *Memoirs of the Queensland Museum* 22(1): 1–73.

3. Paxton, J.R., Hoese, D.F., Allen, G.R. and Hanley, J.E. (1989) *Zoological catalogue of Australia. Volume 7, Pisces. Petromyzontidae to Carangidae.* Canberra: Australian Government Publishing Service. 664 pp.

4. Cleland, K.W. (1947) Studies on the economic biology of the sand whiting (*Sillago ciliata* C. & V.). *Proceedings of the Linnean Society of New South Wales* 72: 215–228.

5. Weng, H.T. (1986) Spatial and temporal distribution of whiting (Sillaginidae) in Moreton Bay, Queensland. *Journal of Fish Biology* 29(6): 755–764.

6. Maclean, J.L. (1971) The food and feedings of winter whiting (*Sillago maculata* Q. & G.) in Moreton Bay. *Proceedings of the Linnean Society of New South Wales* 96(2): 87–92.

7. Morton, R.M. (1982) *Reproductive biology and tagging studies of summer whiting* Sillago ciliata *(C.V.), at Bribie Island, Queensland.* Unpublished MSc thesis, University of Queensland.

8. Morton, R.M. (1985) The reproductive biology of summer whiting, *Sillago ciliata* C. & V., in northern Moreton Bay, Queensland. *The Australian Zoologist* 21(6): 491–502.

9. Burchmore, J.J., Pollard, D.A., Middleton, M.J., Bell, J.D. and Pease, B.C. (1988) Biology of four species of whiting (Pisces: Sillaginidae) in Botany Bay, New South Wales. *Australian Journal of Marine and Freshwater Research* 39: 709–727.

10. Dredge, M. (1976) *Aspects of the ecology of three estuarine dwelling fish in south east Queensland.* Unpublished MSc thesis, University of Queensland. 122 pp.

11. Maclean, J. (1969) *A study of the biology of winter whiting,* Sillago maculata *(Quoy and Gaimard), in Moreton Bay.* Unpublished MSc thesis, University of Queensland.

12. Maclean, J.L. (1973) An analysis of the catch of trawlers in Moreton Bay (Qld.) during the 1966–67 prawning season. *Proceedings of the Linnean Society of New South Wales* 98(1): 35–42.

13. Munro, I.S.R. (1945) Postlarval stages of Australian fishes — no.1. *Memoirs of the Queensland Museum* 12(3): 136–153.

14. Pollock, B. and Williams, M.J. (1983) An assessment of the angling fishery of summer whiting, *Sillago ciliata* and *S. analis*, in Moreton Bay, Queensland from 1959–1980. *Proceedings of the Royal Society, Queensland* 96: 19–23.

15. Pollock, B. (1980) Surprises in Queensland angling study. *Australian Fisheries* 39(4): 17–19.

16. Morton, R.M. (1990) Community structure, density and standing crop of fishes in a subtropical Australian mangrove area. *Marine Biology* 105: 385–394.

Contributors

Comments on this presentation were provided by (in alphabetical order) Alan Blackshaw, Mike Capra, Glen Cuthbert, Mike Dredge, Gary Henry, Rick Morton, Neil Trainor and Ron West. Drawing by Gavin Ryan. (*Details of contributors and their organisations are provided in the Acknowledgements section at the back of this book.*)
Compilers Patricia Kailola and Christina Grieve (maps)

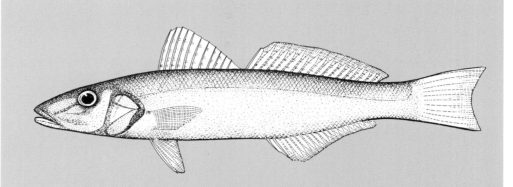

Yellowfin whiting

Sillago schomburgkii

Distribution

Yellowfin whiting inhabit Gulf St Vincent and Spencer Gulf waters in South Australia, and waters from Albany to Dampier in Western Australia.[1] It is not known whether they also occur in the intervening waters.

Yellowfin whiting generally frequent inshore sandbanks and sandbars and the mouths of estuaries in shallow water[2] from 1 m to about 10 m depth. These whiting are principally marine residents[3,4] and can tolerate upper Spencer Gulf waters with salinity as high as 40–50 parts per thousand. They may also penetrate to the limit of brackish water in tidal creeks, where salinity is as low as 1 part per thousand.[2,4] Juvenile yellowfin whiting inhabit warmer water, mangrove-lined creeks and inshore protected environments[4] over mud bottoms and seagrass beds. In Western Australia, adults prefer more open, firm sandy banks and beach areas all year, whereas in South Australia adults share the juvenile habitat during winter, moving onto the sandbanks and into deeper water during summer.

Life history

Yellowfin whiting congregate in sandy hollows and move in schools over sand flats with the tide. They are timid fish, and bury themselves in the muddy or sandy substrate when alarmed.

In Western Australia, yellowfin whiting spawn between September and January in Shark Bay[5] and slightly later along the coast to the south. In South Australia, the spawning period extends from December to February.[6] Spawning is preceded by a post-winter movement to inshore sheltered bays and sandy beaches.[6] Ripe fish in Shark Bay probably

Sillago schomburgkii Peters

Yellowfin whiting

Other common names include **silver whiting**, **western sand whiting** and **fine-scale whiting**.
FAO: no known name
Australian species code: 330012

Family SILLAGINIDAE

Diagnostic features Yellowfin whiting can be distinguished from other whiting by their plain body colouring and bright yellow or orange ventral and anal fins. The base of their pectoral fin is plain and there is no silvery stripe along their sides. They have small body scales (66–76 in the lateral line).

break off from the main yellowfin whiting schools and form smaller spawning schools.[5] In South Australia, large schools of mature whiting appear in the estuaries and inshore waters of southern Spencer Gulf and Gulf St Vincent, where spawning takes place.[6] After spawning, the fish disperse to offshore waters — such as northern Spencer Gulf.[6] In Shark Bay, yellowfin whiting spawn once each season.[3] The fecundity ranges from 170 000 to 217 000 eggs for each female

between 22.5 and 32.5 cm fork length. The average ripe egg diameter is 0.6 mm.[3]

Juveniles first appear in southern Western Australian estuaries in March.[4]

Yellowfin whiting grow moderately rapidly, and average 3 cm in length at 4 months of age.[6] Growth of older fish has been estimated at from 18 cm to 29 cm and from 60 g to 190 g in 1 year.[6] By 2 years of age, yellowfin whiting have an average total length of 24 cm.[1] Based on scale growth rings, Shark Bay yellowfin

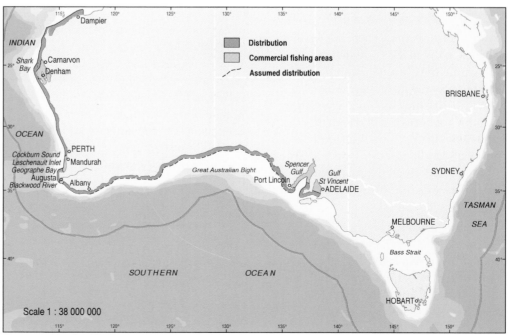

Geographic distribution and commercial fishing areas for yellowfin whiting.

whiting are approximately 8 cm total length at 1 year of age, 15 cm long at 2 years of age and 22–23 cm long at 3 years of age.[5] There is no difference in growth rate between males and females in Gulf St Vincent[6] but in Shark Bay, mature females grow more rapidly than do mature males. The maximum recorded size is 42 cm total length.[7] Ageing studies suggest that yellowfin whiting can live to at least 12 years of age in South Australia[1] and 11 years in Western Australia (Shark Bay).[5] The average fork length at first maturity is 22.5 cm for females and 20 cm for males.[3,8]

Adult yellowfin whiting eat polychaete worms and bivalve molluscs, small prawns and amphipod crustaceans and seagrass.[9] There is no information on whiting predators.

Stock structure

Western Australian and South Australian populations of yellowfin whiting do not differ morphologically.[2] The concentration of yellowfin whiting in the gulfs in South Australia and their sparse distribution along the west coast hints, however, at the existence of some level of population differentiation, and behavioural information on the 2 fished populations supports this. Electrophoretic work performed so far has been inconclusive.[10]

Commercial fishery

The major Australian fisheries for yellowfin whiting are Spencer Gulf and Gulf St Vincent in South Australia and Shark Bay in Western Australia — all large marine embayments.[4] There are smaller fisheries in the Blackwood River estuary, Geographe Bay, Leschenault Inlet and Cockburn Sound in Western Australia. In the late 1970s, the combined catch from northern Spencer Gulf and Gulf St Vincent made up 63–65 % of South Australia's landings for the species.[6] The highest recorded catch from the Shark Bay fishery was in 1961, when 204 t were landed.

In South Australia, yellowfin whiting are fished mostly with beach seines but also with bottom set gillnets along the edges of creeks. Ring netting using a drain-off shot method or power hauling are other techniques used. Nets are worked from the shore or from

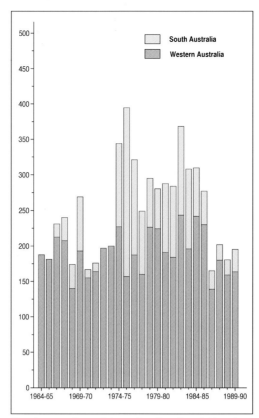

Total annual catch in t of yellowfin whiting for the period 1964–65 to 1989–90. Figures are unavailable for South Australia from 1964–65 to 1965–66 and 1972–73 to 1973–74.
(Source: Fisheries Resources Atlas Statistical Database)

shallow-hulled boats. In Shark Bay, the whiting are caught with long gillnets on sandbanks.[5]

Fishing for yellowfin whiting in South Australia usually takes place during the early morning when the fish are moving from shallow flats to deeper channels; but in Shark Bay, whiting are caught on the incoming high tide when the fish are moving from deeper to shallow water.[5] Large schools can be seined, yielding very high catch rates — up to 272 kg per person-day in northern Spencer Gulf.[2,11] For Shark Bay, peak catch rates were achieved in 1961 and 1985, with low catch rates in 1965 and 1971.[8] The yellowfin whiting fishery is conducted all year, although the highest catches are generally taken in winter (April to July) in the South Australian gulfs[11] or autumn to spring (March to September) in Shark Bay.[5] In contrast, gillnetters in northern Spencer Gulf make their highest catches of yellowfin whiting during the summer months, particularly from March to May, at the time the fish are moving to the southern Gulf to spawn.[11] The majority of yellowfin whiting taken in the Shark Bay fishery are in the 3–5 year age group.[5]

In Western Australia from Shark Bay

northwards, golden-lined whiting (*Sillago analis*) are harvested with yellowfin whiting and form a minor proportion of the catch. Tailor (*Pomatomus saltatrix*), mullet (Mugilidae), bream (Sparidae) and some snapper (*Pagrus auratus*) are other bycatch species. Inside Shark Bay, western trumpeter whiting (*Sillago maculata burrus*) and banded whiting (*S. vittata*) associate in shallow onshore waters with yellowfin whiting[2] and form an incidental catch.

Yellowfin whiting can be easily scaled[5] and are marketed as whole fish or fillets. The entire South Australian catch is consumed locally, and much of the Shark Bay catch is also sold in South Australia and the eastern States. The South Australian price was moderately high in 1989, with an average wholesale price of A$ 7.00 per kg, but by mid 1992 the price had dropped to an average of A$ 3.82 per kg. The average 1992 prices in Perth ranged from A$ 3.00 to A$ 4.50 per kg.

Management controls South Australian regulations are under review, but present restrictions include limited licence access and netting closures. Minimum legal sizes also apply in the South Australian and Western Australian fisheries.

Recreational fishery

Throughout their range, yellowfin whiting are a popular target fish for boat and shore anglers using handlines. Sometimes a shore set net is used in South Australia. In the river inlet and lake sections of the Blackwood River estuary, south-western Australia, yellowfin whiting and tommy ruff (*Arripis georgianus*) were the major species caught by recreational anglers in a 1-year survey from May 1974,[12] and yellowfin whiting were also important in the angling catch from the river. In the inlet and lake section the whiting alone, totalling 120 700 fish, formed approximately 55 % of the catch. Yellowfin whiting are most abundant in the estuary during early summer months.

Yellowfin whiting are commonly caught by shore anglers in metropolitan Adelaide waters,[13] where they are subject to considerable recreational fishing pressure.[6]

Management controls A minimum legal size applies in South Australia and Western Australia, and there is also a bag limit in Western Australia.

Seine netting — the major method used in commercial fisheries for yellowfin whiting. (Source: Gary Henry, Environment Protection Authority, New South Wales)

Resource status

There is evidence that yellowfin whiting stocks were overfished during the early to mid 1960s.[5] Current levels of catch per unit effort for this species in Shark Bay are well within the historical range for the fishery. However, there is no clear reason for both the low effort in the fishery and presence of fewer fish, despite the increased fishing capacity of the fleet over recent years.[8] The status of yellowfin whiting stocks in Shark Bay is uncertain.

There has been sufficient decline in the catches of yellowfin whiting in South Australia to warrant concern. In northern Spencer Gulf, there are large fluctuations in catches of yellowfin whiting over cycles lasting several years. When there are abundant fish during these cycles, individual catch rates can be very high (eg 200 kg per boat-day). Catches in Gulf St Vincent have decreased substantially since 1976–77 and were so low from 1983 to 1986 that they represented only a bycatch from other targeted species. The reason(s) for the decline is unknown.[11]

Notes

Golden-lined whiting (or coarse-scale whiting) form an incidental catch with yellowfin whiting from Shark Bay northwards. They receive the same market price as yellowfin whiting.[5] Golden-lined whiting comprise only a small proportion of the catch from Western Australia — between 2 % and 35 % (average 8 %) over the past 15 years.

Golden-lined whiting can be distinguished by their larger body scales (54–61 in the lateral line), presence of a golden-silver or golden-yellow stripe along the middle of their sides and fine black spots on their pectoral fin base. They reach about 45 cm total length.[2] Golden-lined whiting form schools with yellowfin whiting, the schools separating when the whiting become adults.[5] Juvenile golden-lined whiting share the estuarine habitat of yellowfin whiting, but mature adults prefer muddy, tidal streams.[5]

References

1. Jones, G.K., Hall, D.A., Hill, K.L. and Staniford, A.J.(1990) *The South Australian marine scalefish fishery: stock assessment, economics, management.* South Australian Department of Fisheries, Green paper. 186 pp.

2. McKay, R.J. (1985) A revision of the fishes of the family Sillaginidae. *Memoirs of the Queensland Museum* **22**: 1–73.

3. Thomson, J.M. (1957) The size at maturity and spawning times of some Western Australian estuarine fishes. *Western Australian Fisheries Department Fisheries Bulletin* **8**. 8 pp.

4. Lenanton, R.C.J. (1982) Alternative non-estuarine nursery habitats for some commercially and recreationally important fish species of south-western Australia. *Australian Journal of Marine and Freshwater Research* **33**: 881–900.

5. Lenanton, R.C.J. (1969) Whiting fishery — Shark Bay. *Western Australian Department of Fisheries and Wildlife, Fishing Industry News Service* **2**(1): 4–11.

6. Jones, G.K. (1981) Yellowfin whiting (*Sillago schomburgkii*) studies in South Australian waters. *SAFIC* **5**(4): 20–23.

7. Hutchins, B. and Swainston, R. (1986) *Sea fishes of southern Australia. Complete field guide for anglers and divers.* Perth: Swainston Publishing. 180 pp.

8. Sudmeyer, J.E., Hancock, D.A. and Lenanton, R.C.J. (in press, 1992) Synopsis of the biology of Western Australian whitings (Fam. Sillaginidae). *Western Australian Fisheries Department, Fisheries Research Report.*

9. Thomson, J.M. (1957) The food of Western Australian estuarine fish. *Western Australian Fisheries Department Fisheries Bulletin* **7**. 13 pp.

10. Dixon, P.I., Crozier, R.H., Black, M. and Church, A. (1987) Stock identification and discrimination of commercially important whitings in Australian waters using genetic criteria. *Centre for Marine Science, University of New South Wales. FIRTA Project 83/16, Final Report.* 69 pp.

11. Jones, G.K. and Kangas, M. (1987) A review of the catch and effort in the commercial marine scale fishery in South Australian waters, 1976–1986. *South Australian Department of Fisheries, Fisheries Research Paper* **18**. 113 pp.

12. Caputi, N. (1976) Creel census of amateur line fishermen in the Blackwood River estuary, Western Australia, during 1974–75. *Australian Journal of Marine and Freshwater Research* **27**: 583–593.

13. Jones, G.K. (1981) The recreational fishery in metropolitan coastal waters. *SAFIC* **5**(6): 9–11.

Contributors

The information on this species was originally provided by Keith Jones and Rod Lenanton. Drawing by Roger Swainston. *(Details of contributors and their organisations are included in the Acknowledgements section at the back of this book.)*
Compilers Patricia Kailola and Christina Grieve (maps)

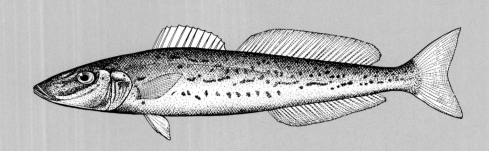

King George whiting

Sillaginodes punctata

Sillaginodes punctata (Cuvier)

King George whiting

Other common names include **spotted whiting** and **South Australian whiting**.
FAO: no known name
Australian species code: 330001

Family SILLAGINIDAE

Diagnostic features King George whiting have very small body scales (129–147 in the lateral line) and their dorsal fin has 12–13 spines and 25–27 rays. Generally they have a silvery body which is dusky yellow above and has irregular oblique rows of small bronze or brown spots on the back and upper sides.

Distribution

King George whiting are endemic to Australia. They live in temperate waters from Port Jackson (Sydney) in New South Wales, along southern coasts as far south as northern Tasmania, and westwards to Jurien Bay in Western Australia.[1]

King George whiting inhabit shallow inner continental shelf waters, including bays and inlets. For their first few years they live mainly where seagrasses (*Zostera* species, *Posidonia* species) grow, in sandy, muddy and broken bottom areas such as tidal estuaries, bays and creeks. Small juveniles favour water depths from 2 m to 20 m. Adults inhabit more exposed waters along coastal beaches and reef areas,[2,3] sometimes to depths as great as 200 m.

Life history

King George whiting spawn in offshore waters from late summer to winter: May to July in Victoria; late February to early June in South Australia. Spawning peaks in mid April in South Australia. King George whiting are serial batch spawners, yet the number of spawnings in a season is unknown. Fecundity increases as the female fish grow — from an average of 100 000 eggs at 34 cm total length to 800 000 eggs at 45 cm.

King George whiting eggs are buoyant and the larvae are planktonic. The larvae move inshore to sheltered areas and settle

out of the plankton when 60–80 days old and 15–18 mm long.[4] Juveniles remain in protected waters for 2–3 years. Older King George whiting (more than 25 cm total length) move to deeper water, particularly during winter.[2,3]

A maximum age of 15 years, and a maximum size of 72 cm total length and 4.8 kg have been recorded. Growth rates vary from region to region, depending on the water temperature. King George whiting grow very little in winter, but grow rapidly in the summer months of December to March. They can reach 28 cm in 2–3 years.[2]

Maturity is attained at 3 or 4 years of age when males are between 27 cm and 32 cm total length and females between 32 cm and 36 cm total length. The sex ratio at that time is even, but among older fish (greater than 50 cm total length), females are 4 times more numerous as males.[2]

Juvenile King George whiting feed on benthic amphipods and other crustaceans. As they grow larger, the fish's diet expands to include polychaete worms, molluscs and peanut worms (Sipuncula).[2,3]

Adult King George whiting are preyed upon mostly by sharks, whilst juveniles are eaten by other fish such as flathead (Platycephalidae), Australian salmon (*Arripis* species) and barracouta (*Thyrsites atun*).

Stock structure

In South Australia there appears to be only 1 spawning stock in the main commercial fishery. However, the distribution of host-specific parasitic trematode flatworms (*Microcotyle* species) suggests that at least 2 populations exist across the species' range[5] — 1 in the east, the other in the west. Enzyme analysis on a limited sample of King George whiting from Victoria and South Australia also gave indications of sub-structuring within the King George whiting population.[6]

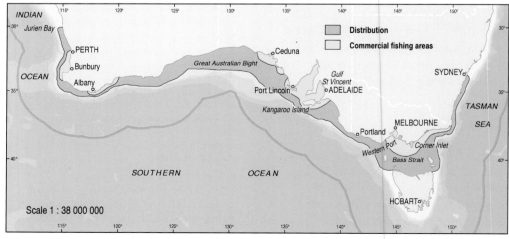

Geographic distribution and commercial fishing areas for King George whiting.

Commercial fishery

The fishery for King George whiting began at about the time of white settlement in South Australia and probably at about the same time in Victoria and Western Australia. The main commercial fishery is now located in South Australia, from Gulf St Vincent to Ceduna. Smaller fisheries are located in central Victoria and south-western Western Australia around Albany and Bunbury. The fisheries operate in spring and early summer (September to November) and to a lesser extent in autumn (April to June).

Fish are caught either with seine net, power hauling and gillnets from small vessels in shallow (3–10 m) water, or by handline in deeper water. Most fishing effort is directed at 2-year-old to 7-year-old fish. Fish caught in nets average 32 cm in total length and those handlined average 34 cm. King George whiting are targeted and there is little bycatch taken in these fishing operations. However, some King George whiting are caught as bycatch of the southern sea garfish (*Hyporhamphus melanochir*) fishery.[2]

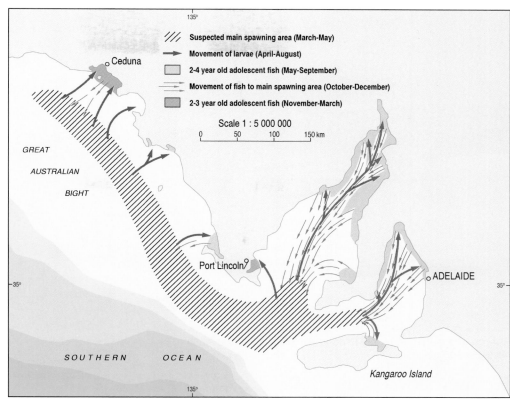

Representation of the distribution and movement of early age classes of King George whiting in South Australian waters. (Source: adapted from Jones et al[2])

King George whiting are sold either fresh or frozen, usually as fillets and sometimes whole. Most are consumed locally but excess fish are occasionally sent to Melbourne from South Australia. The 1988–89 wholesale price in South Australia ranged from A$ 7.00 to A$ 10.00 per kg, giving a total catch value of A$ 5 million. In mid 1992, the price averaged A$ 6.20 per kg. The 1991–92 price to fishers at the Melbourne Wholesale Fish Market ranged from A$ 5.50 to A$ 9.50 per kg. In Perth, the 1992 prices ranged from A$ 2.50 per kg for whole, small fish to A$ 8.00 per kg for large fish.

Management controls Regulations in effect in South Australia control entry to the fishery by licence, fishing area, seasonal closures and gear limitations. However, a number of these regulations are being reviewed. All States that have King George whiting fisheries impose limits on the size of fish retained from catches.

Recreational fishery

King George whiting are popular recreational fish throughout their range. Fishers use rod-and-line or handlines, mainly from boats but also from the shore and jetties. Nets may be used but are prohibited in some areas. Shore anglers target immature fish.

Significant quantities of King George whiting are caught by recreational fishers. For example, in South Australia, the recreational fishery accounted for nearly 38 % of the total annual catch (61 % in the Gulf St Vincent region) between 1979 and 1982.[2] The Australian Anglers Association records the largest King George whiting caught as 2.3 kg (from South Australia).

Management controls A minimum legal size is imposed in Victoria, South Australia and Western Australia. There is also a bag limit in Western Australia.

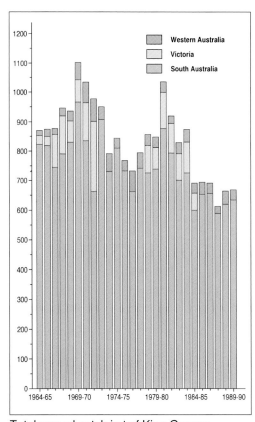

Total annual catch in t of King George whiting for the period 1964–65 to 1989–90. Figures are unavailable for Victoria from 1972–73 to 1977–78 and 1985–86 to 1989–90. (Source: Fisheries Resources Atlas Statistical Database)

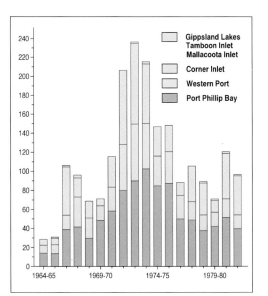

Commercial catch in t of King George whiting from Victorian bays and inlets for the period 1964–65 to 1981–82. (Source: Fisheries Division, Victorian Department of Conservation and Environment)

Beach seines are commonly used to catch King George whiting. (Source: Australian Fisheries Management Authority)

Resource status

King George whiting are probably fully exploited throughout most of their shallower coastal range. In South Australia there may be heavier fishing pressure than necessary for maximising catch per unit effort, yield per recruit and recreational fishing quality. This view is supported by the apparent reduction in size at first maturity of King George whiting in the South Australian fishery since the mid 1960s.[2]

Notes

Commercial catches in Western Port, Victoria, declined dramatically after a 70 % dieback of seagrass in the early 1970s.

Investigations into the potential for aquaculturing King George whiting are being conducted in South Australia.

References

1. Paxton, J.R., Hoese, D.F., Allen, G.R. and Hanley, J.E. (1989) *Zoological catalogue of Australia. Volume 7, Pisces. Petromyzontidae to Carangidae.* Canberra: Australian Government Publishing Service. 664 pp.

2. Jones, G.K., Hall, D.A., Hill, K.L. and Staniford, A.J. (1990) *The South Australian marine scalefish fishery: stock assessment, economics, management.* South Australian Department of Fisheries, Green paper. 186 pp.

3. Robertson, A.I. (1977) Ecology of juvenile King George whiting *Sillaginodes punctatus* (Cuvier and Valenciennes) (Pisces: Perciformes) in Western Port, Victoria. *Australian Journal of Marine and Freshwater Research* **28**: 35–43.

4. Bruce, B.D. (1989) Studying larval fish ecology. *SAFISH* **13**(4): 4–9.

5. Sandars, D.F. (1945) Five new microcotylids from fish from Western Australian waters. *Journal and Proceedings of the Royal Society of Western Australia* **29**: 107–135.

6. Dixon, P.I., Crozier, R.H., Black, M. and Church, A. (1987) Stock identification and discrimination of commercially important whitings in Australian waters using genetic criteria. *Centre for Marine Science, University of New South Wales. FIRTA Project 83/16, Final Report.* 69 pp.

Contributors

The information on this species was originally provided by Keith Jones. Additional contributions were made by (in alphabetical order) Albert Caton, Rod Lenanton and Murray MacDonald. Drawing by Roger Swainston. *(Details of contributors and their organisations are given in the Acknowledgements section at the back of this book.)*
Compilers Kay Abel, Patricia Kailola and Phillip Stewart (statistics)

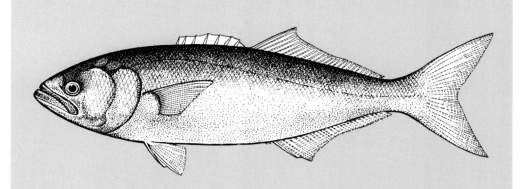

Tailor

Pomatomus saltatrix

Distribution

Tailor inhabit coastal waters of all Australian States except the Northern Territory, being distributed from the northern tip of Fraser Island in Queensland to Onslow in Western Australia. Catches of tailor are much less common in Tasmanian and western Victorian waters than off the east and west coasts, and they are rare in South Australia and the Great Australian Bight. Tailor are also distributed through temperate coastal waters of the south-eastern United States of America, the western and eastern coasts of southern Africa, the Mediterranean Sea and the Black Sea.

Tailor are present on the continental shelf to a depth of approximately 50 m and are occasionally found offshore near the sea surface. They are schooling fish, most common along surf beaches and rocky headlands in clean, high energy waters, although adults can also be found in estuaries and into brackish water.[1]

Life history

The only confirmed spawning ground in Australia is located inshore off the north-east coast of Fraser Island, in waters moderately exposed to wind and wave action.[2] Large schools of fish are found in the vicinity of the spawning ground during late winter and spring, their abundance reaching a peak in September and October. The location of spawning ground(s) off Western Australia are unknown but spawning probably takes place there in early spring, as it does near Fraser Island.[3] Overseas studies have shown that tailor are serial spawners, ie they release eggs and milt on a number of occasions during the spawning season.[4] Large females may produce more than

Pomatomus saltatrix (Linnaeus)

Tailor

Other common names include **skipjack**, **choppers**, **bluefish** and **elf**.
FAO: **bluefish**
Australian species code: 334002

Family POMATOMIDAE

Diagnostic features Tailor are greenish blue or blue on the back, and the sides and belly are silvery. Their fins are pale green, tinged with yellow and the base of the pectoral fins are bluish. Both jaws have numerous strong sharp teeth, and the lower jaw protrudes. There are 2 dorsal fins, the first with 7 or 8 short spines and the second with soft rays and a higher profile than the first dorsal. The rayed anal fin is almost as long as the second dorsal fin. Tailor have forked tails with broad lobes.

1 million eggs. The eggs are pelagic and 0.9–1.2 mm in diameter.[5]

No surveys of larval distribution have been carried out in Australian waters. Juvenile tailor first appear in estuarine waters when they are 35–45 mm total length. Juveniles form schools and move to oceanic waters during their second year. Tailor grow to a size of approximately 15 cm by the end of their first year and exceed 60 cm total length by the age of 5 years. They are reported

to reach a maximum size of 120 cm total length and 14 kg.[6] Male fish tend to reach maturity at a slightly smaller size than females but most individuals are mature at a total length of 30 cm and an age of 2 years.[7]

Tailor populations in South Africa and North America display definite seasonal migratory patterns, moving from higher latitudes to sub-tropical waters in winter.[4,5] Tagging studies conducted in Queensland and New South Wales have

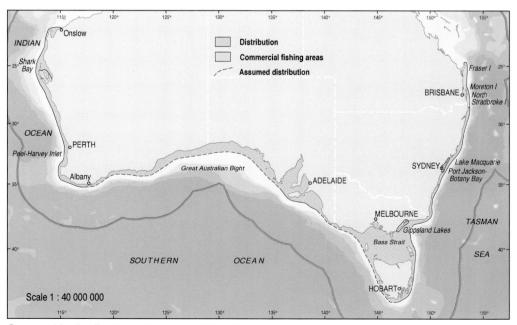

Geographic distribution and commercial fishing areas for tailor in Australian waters.

confirmed that a similar migratory pattern occurs in eastern Australian waters, at least north of Sydney. In New South Wales, schools of similarly sized fish show a definite movement northwards from late winter to early spring, with some tagged fish being recaptured as far north as Fraser Island. Recaptures of tailor tagged at Fraser Island show a pronounced movement south following the spring spawning, although the extent of this movement is not clear.[8] A drift of fish southwards through northern New South Wales waters is also evident in autumn. The extent of migration of tailor in southern New South Wales, Victoria and Western Australia is unknown.

Juvenile tailor feed upon small crustaceans, cephalopods and fish while adult tailor prey mainly on smaller schooling fish, particularly pilchards (*Sardinops neopilchardus*), sea garfish (*Hyporhamphus* species) and sea mullet (*Mugil cephalus*). Tailor are cannibalistic and can be caught readily by anglers using tailor flesh as bait although the extent of their predation upon other tailor is probably limited by the species' tendency to school by size.[7]

Stock structure

Electrophoretic studies on tailor have shown that the genetic variation between fish sampled from the eastern and western coasts of Australia is significant and the 2 groups should be considered as separate genetic stocks.[9] Tagging studies in Queensland and New South Wales waters indicate that tailor from Sydney north are part of a single stock, but more research is needed to confirm the stock status of fish from southern New South Wales and Victoria.

Commercial fishery

The major fishing grounds for tailor are on the east coast. In most years more than half the total Australian catch is taken in Queensland waters, particularly from North Stradbroke, Moreton and Fraser islands. Most of the Queensland catch is landed on the beaches of those islands using beach seines, although a small quantity is caught from estuaries using gillnets. The highest catches are taken from June to September, coinciding with the northern migration of tailor to the waters of Fraser Island.

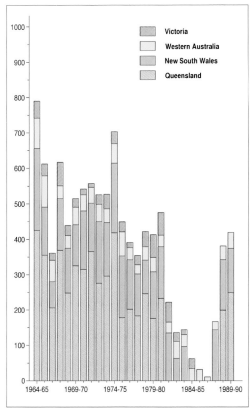

Total annual catch in t of tailor for the period 1964–65 to 1989–90. Figures are unavailable for: New South Wales from 1984–85 to 1986–87; Victoria from 1985–86 to 1989–90; and Queensland from 1981–82 to 1987–88. Catches for States that average less than 5 % of the total for all States are not shown. (Source: Fisheries Resources Atlas Statistical Database)

In New South Wales, tailor is not a major target species. A considerable quantity is taken incidentally in gillnets from Lake Macquarie and Sydney (Port Jackson and Botany Bay) and some catches are also taken with beach seines from northern New South Wales waters in late winter.[6]

In Victoria, tailor are a small component of catches in the eastern bay and inlet fisheries, with the bulk of landings coming from the Gippsland Lakes. Gillnets and beach seines are the main methods used in these fisheries.

Tailor is a minor commercial species in Western Australia. Most of the catch are adult fish taken in the Shark Bay area using beach seines, and the remaining catch consists mainly of 'choppers' (fish less than 35 cm total length) caught from the Peel–Harvey estuary using gillnets.

The tailor catch is sold on domestic markets, mostly as fresh and chilled product although some of the catch is smoked. If marketing delays cause deterioration in quality the catch is sold to pet food canners. The average price obtained for tailor at the Sydney Fish Market in 1991–92 was A$ 1.70 per kg,

and in Brisbane the average wholesale price was about A$ 2.00 per kg.

Management controls All fisheries for tailor are subject to State management regulations. In Queensland the number of fishers licensed to net tailor is limited, and commercial beach fishing from Fraser Island is restricted to a few licence holders during the period 1 September to 31 March. All forms of fishing are prohibited from the known spawning ground off north-eastern Fraser Island during the month of September. The net fisheries in the other States are subject to limited entry and restriction of mesh and net size.

Recreational fishery

Tailor is one of the most popular angling species in Queensland, New South Wales and Western Australia. Estimates of the recreational tailor catch in Queensland indicate that anglers take more fish than commercial operators, especially from Fraser Island beaches.[10] Recaptures of tailor tagged in New South Wales ocean waters were higher for recreational fishers than for the commercial sector, although estuarine recaptures were taken mainly by net fishers. A survey of anglers in Western Australia produced an estimate that 86 000 people fished for tailor in 1987.[3] The largest tailor recorded by the Australian Anglers Association weighed 12.1 kg and was caught near Shark Bay in Western Australia.

Anglers mainly fish for tailor using rod-and-line from beaches or rock platforms, using whole baits of pilchard or sea garfish. The baits are presented on 3 or 4 hooks joined or 'ganged' together and weighted with a lead sinker for beach fishing and usually unweighted for rock fishing. The use of metal lures or 'spinners' is also popular with anglers fishing from rocks and beaches. Tailor are most likely to be caught by anglers at dawn and dusk when fish tend to feed more actively and move closer inshore. However, some schools of fish remain within the range of anglers during the day, provided bait is used to maintain their feeding behaviour.[11]

Management controls To protect spawning fish, waters are closed to fishing during September in the vicinity of Waddy Point and Indian Head at Fraser Island. Minimum legal size limits are in effect in Queensland, Victoria and

Anglers fishing for tailor from the beach at Fraser Island, Queensland. (Source: Ian Halliday, Fisheries Branch, Queensland Department of Primary Industries)

Western Australia and a daily bag limit applies in Western Australia.

Resource status

Reports of reduced catch rates for recreational fishers have caused some concern about the status of Australian tailor stocks, particularly in Western Australia.[3] However, commercial catch levels have remained relatively stable over the past 20 years. More research is needed to determine whether current catch levels (both commercial and recreational) are sustainable.

References

1. Grant, E.M. (1982) *Guide to fishes.* Brisbane: Department of Harbours and Marine. 896 pp.

2. Halliday, I. (1990) Tailor tagging project: summary of 1988 and 1989 results. *Queensland Department of Primary Industries, Information Series* **QI90027**. 8 pp.

3. Tailor (1990) *Fisheries Department of Western Australia, Fishing WA* **4**. 4 pp.

4. van der Elst, R. (1976) Game fish of the east coast of southern Africa. I. The biology of the elf, *Pomatomus saltatrix* (Linnaeus), in the coastal waters of Natal. *South African Association for Marine Biological Research, Oceanographic Research Institute, Investigational Report* **44**. 59 pp.

5. Wilk, S.J. (1977) Biological and fisheries data on bluefish, *Pomatomus saltatrix* (Linnaeus). *United States Department of Commerce, National Marine Fisheries Service, Technical Series Report* **11**. 56 pp.

6. *Commercial fisheries of New South Wales* (1982) N.S.W. State Fisheries. 60 pp.

7. Bade, T.M. (1977) *The biology of tailor* (Pomatomus saltatrix *Linn.*) *from the east coast of Australia.* Unpublished MSc thesis, University of Queensland. 116 pp.

8. Morton, R. (1989) 1987 tagging shows tailor under 'moderate' pressure. *Queensland Fisherman* **5**(1): 23–26.

9. Nurthen, R.K., Cameron, R.C. and Briscoe, D.A. (in press, 1992) Population genetics of tailor, *Pomatomus saltatrix* (Linnaeus) (Pisces: Pomatomidae), in Australia. *Australian Journal of Marine and Freshwater Research.*

10. Pollock, B.R. (1979) Anglers probably take bulk of Queensland tailor catch. *Australian Fisheries* **38**(9): 31–32.

11. Chapman, G. (1982) The technique of tailor fishing. Pp 52–55, in *Fish and fisheries.* Sydney: New South Wales State Fisheries.

Contributors

Most of the information on this species was provided by Ian Halliday and supplemented by (in alphabetical order) Rod Lenanton, Murray MacDonald, Rod Nurthen and Julian Pepperell. Drawing by Roger Swainston. (*Details of contributors and their organisations are given in the Acknowledgements section at the back of this book.*)
Compiler Phillip Stewart

Silver trevally

Pseudocaranx dentex

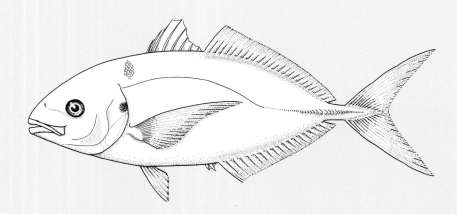

Pseudocaranx dentex (Bloch and Schneider)

Silver trevally

Other common names include **silver bream**, **skippy**, **white trevally**, **skipjack trevally** and **ranger**.
FAO: **white trevally**
Australian species code: 337062

Family CARANGIDAE

Diagnostic features Silver trevally have moderately elongate and compressed bodies. There is a low ridge bearing 20–26 bony scutes along the posterior part of the lateral line. Silver trevally have 2 dorsal fins, a deeply forked caudal fin and 2 small, detached spines just forward of the anal fin. These fish are bluish silver on the back, sometimes with a yellowish hue. Their sides are yellowish silver, and they have a small black blotch on the operculum.[1]

Distribution

Silver trevally are distributed from approximately Rockhampton on the central Queensland coast through the waters of all southern Australian States to North West Cape in Western Australia. They also inhabit the waters of Lord Howe Island, Norfolk Island, New Zealand and the sub-tropical to temperate waters of the Atlantic and Indian oceans.[2]

Juvenile silver trevally usually inhabit estuaries, bays and shallow continental shelf waters, while adults form schools near the sea bed on the continental shelf. Some older fish school near the surface in deeper shelf waters.[1] Adult trevally also live on inshore reefs and over open grounds of sand or gravel, or in large bays and inlets such as Botany Bay.

Life history

Silver trevally spawn in summer.[2] Individuals have been found in spawning condition in both estuaries and shelf waters.[3] Silver trevally seem to be serial spawners , releasing batches of eggs over a number of weeks.[4] Their planktonic eggs are about 0.8 mm in diameter.[5] There is no information on growth for silver trevally in Australian waters, but silver trevally in New Zealand waters

grow rapidly until the age of 5 years when they are about 37 cm total length.[2] Both sexes grow at the same rate. Some New Zealand fish have been aged to 46 years.[2] The maximum total length reported for silver trevally is 70 cm in New Zealand[6] and 76 cm in Australian waters.[1] Silver trevally from New South Wales waters mature from a size of 28 cm total length.[7]

There is no evidence of any seasonal migration of silver trevally in Australian waters. However, New Zealand studies indicate that adult fish may move between demersal and pelagic habitats on a seasonal basis.[2]

Silver trevally are carnivores and feed on polychaete worms, molluscs, and crustaceans such as amphipods on the sea bed.[3] Pelagic schools of silver trevally are also known to feed on planktonic crustaceans such as krill (Euphausiidae).[3,4]

Stock structure

There is no information on silver trevally stock structure in Australian waters.

Commercial fishery

The main fishery for silver trevally is located in New South Wales waters. Trevally are targeted by fishers using beach seines in bays, or from ocean beaches along the coast from Port Macquarie to the Victorian border. They are also caught in the New South Wales trap fishery which targets higher valued species such as snapper (*Pagrus auratus*) and ocean jackets (*Nelusetta ayraudi*).

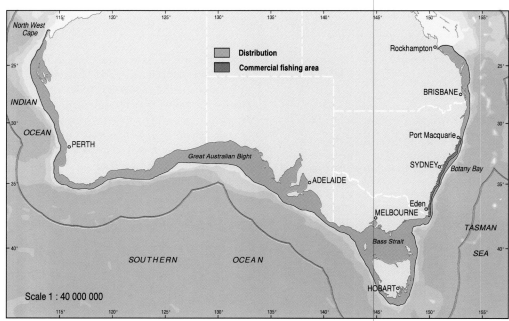

Geographic distribution and commercial fishing area for silver trevally in Australian waters.

Small quantities of silver trevally are caught in estuaries using coastal set gillnets. Catches are also made by demersal otter trawlers targeting other species in the South East Fishery off south-eastern Australia. Trawl catch rates are consistently low in the Fishery, eg total trawl catches ranged between 200 t and 400 t from 1985–86 to 1989–90. Most of the silver trevally trawl catch is taken from waters less than 100 m deep.[8] Silver trevally are also a bycatch of the Southern Shark Fishery, although the level of catch is uncertain due to misreporting of warehous (*Seriolella* species) as silver trevally. Small quantities of silver trevally are also trolled in Tasmanian coastal waters.

The New South Wales catch of silver trevally has increased over the last 10 years. Prior to the 1980s the low price obtained for silver trevally deterred fishers from targeting the species. Higher prices now encourage fishers to target silver trevally when the availability of other more valuable species is low.

Silver trevally are sold mainly as whole fish on the domestic fresh fish market.

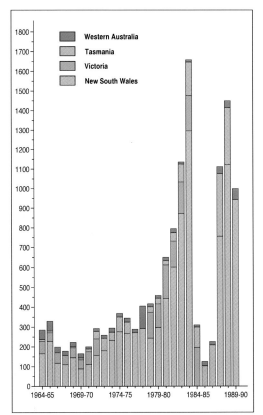

Total annual catch in t of silver trevally for the period 1964–65 to 1989–90. Figures are unavailable for: New South Wales from 1984–85 to 1986–87; Victoria from 1972–73 to 1977–78 and 1985–86 to 1989–90; and Tasmania for 1989–90. Catches for States that average less than 5 % of the total for all States are not shown. The figures for Tasmania include an unknown proportion of warehou (*Seriolella* species) catch. (Source: Fisheries Resources Atlas Statistical Database)

Some of the catch is air freighted to Japan as fresh, chilled product. The Sydney Fish Market is the main market for silver trevally, with 568 t sold in 1991–92. The Melbourne Wholesale Fish Market also handles significant quantities. The average wholesale price at the Sydney market in 1991–92 was A$ 1.22 per kg.

Management controls The inshore fisheries for silver trevally in New South Wales and Victoria are managed by State fisheries authorities. Fishers operating in the South East Fishery are licensed and regulated by the Commonwealth of Australia. The trawl fishery for silver trevally north of 33°35' S is managed by the New South Wales Government.

Recreational fishery

Silver trevally is a significant recreational species throughout the area it inhabits. The most common methods used to catch it are handlines and rod-and-line and most fish are caught by using baits of cut fish flesh, whole pilchards (*Sardinops neopilchardus*) or anchovies (*Engraulis australis*), squid, prawns (Penaeidae), crabs or cunjevoi (*Pyura stolonifera*).[9] The largest recorded silver trevally caught by a recreational angler weighed 10 kg and was taken off Lord Howe Island (Australian Anglers Association records).

Management controls Minimum size limits apply in Victoria and Western Australia. There is a bag limit in Western Australia and a similar limit will be introduced for New South Wales in 1993.

Resource status

There is insufficient information to assess the resource status of silver trevally.[8]

References

1. Last, P.R., Scott, E.O.G. and Talbot, F.H. (1983) *Fishes of Tasmania*. Hobart: Tasmanian Fisheries Development Authority. 563 pp.

2. James, G.D. (1984) Trevally, *Caranx georgianus* Cuvier: age determination, population biology, and the fishery. *New Zealand Ministry of Agriculture and Fisheries, Fisheries Research Bulletin* **25**. 51 pp.

3. Winstanley, R.H. (1985) Commercial fishery situation report: Tamboon Inlet. *Victorian Department of Conservation, Forests and Lands, Fisheries and Wildlife Service, Marine Fisheries Report* **7**. 28 pp.

Catch of silver trevally taken by demersal otter trawling. (Source: Australian Fisheries Management Authority)

4. James, G.D. (1978) Trevally and koheru — biology and fisheries. Pp 50–54, in *Proceedings of the pelagic fisheries conference, July 1977. New Zealand Ministry of Agriculture and Fisheries, Fisheries Research Division, Occasional Publication* **15**.

5. James, G.D. (1976) Eggs and larvae of the trevally, *Caranx georgianus* (Teleostei: Carangidae). *New Zealand Journal of Marine and Freshwater Research* **10**(2): 301–310.

6. Paul, L. (1986) *New Zealand fishes. An identification guide.* Auckland: Reed Methuen. 184 pp.

7. State Pollution Control Commission (1981) *The ecology of fish in Botany Bay — biology of commercially and recreationally valuable species. Environmental control study of Botany Bay.* Sydney. 287 pp.

8. Tilzey, R.D.J. (in press, 1992) Silver trevally. In *The South East Fishery: a scientific review with particular reference to quota management.* Ed by R.D.J. Tilzey. *Bureau of Resource Sciences Bulletin.*

9. Starling, S. (1988) *The fisherman's handbook. How to find, identify and catch the top Australian angling fish.* Sydney: Angus and Robertson. 263 pp.

Contributors

Information on this species was originally provided by (in alphabetical order) Gary Henry, Richard Tilzey and John Virgona. Drawing by Rosalind Poole. (*Details of contributors and their organisations are given in the Acknowledgements section at the back of this book.*)
Compilers Phillip Stewart and Christina Grieve (maps)

Kingfish and samson fish

Seriola species

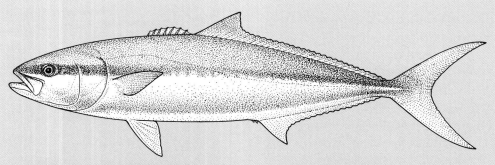

Kingfish and samson fish

This presentation is on 2 species, **yellowtail kingfish** and **samson fish**.

Yellowtail kingfish, *Seriola lalandi* Valenciennes

Other common names include **kingie**, **kingfish**, **yellowtail**, **amberjack** and **southern yellowtail**.
FAO: **yellowtail amberjack**
Australian species code: 337006

Samson fish, *Seriola hippos* Günther

Another common name is **sea kingfish**.
FAO: no known name
Australian species code: 337007

Family CARANGIDAE

Diagnostic features Yellowtail kingfish (pictured) and samson fish have elongate, moderately compressed bodies. Yellowtail kingfish have a slender head[1] longer than their body depth,[2] and they have 31–34 dorsal fin rays.[2,3] They are generally blue, bluish-green or purplish green above[3] and silvery-white below. Yellowtail kingfish can be distinguished by their yellow caudal fins.[1,3] Samson fish have a blunt head, shorter in length than the body depth,[2] and they have 23–25 rays in their dorsal fin.[2,3] Samson fish are variable in colour[3] yet are generally bronze or brown on the back and silvery below. Both species may have a golden stripe on the midsides.[3]

and from Marion Bay in South Australia to Shark Bay in Western Australia.[4]

Both species live in inshore and continental shelf waters where they are associated with reefs, jetties and pylons. Adult yellowtail kingfish are solitary or occur in small groups and can be found near rocky shores, reefs and islands. Schools of juveniles are generally found in offshore waters, often near or beyond the continental shelf.[1] Yellowtail kingfish and samson fish prefer water temperatures between 18°C and 24°C, although they are occasionally found in cooler water.[5]

Life history

Little is known about the life history of yellowtail kingfish in Australian waters. It has been suggested[1] that populations off New South Wales have a protracted spawning period, which varies between locations. Spawning occurs in July off Coffs Harbour, in October off Greenwell Point and in February off Narooma. Yellowtail kingfish appear to be pelagic spawners that move offshore to spawn.[1]

Yellowtail kingfish eggs are pelagic and about 1.4 mm in diameter. They hatch within 2 to 3 days, and the larval kingfish average 4 mm in length.[6] Yellowtail kingfish grow to at least 1.9 m total length,[7] and can weigh up to 70 kg.[8] The largest fish commonly taken are about 1 m long, weighing 10 to 15 kg.[1] They are thought to spawn first at 2 years of age when about 50 cm fork length.

Juvenile yellowtail kingfish less than 30 cm fork length often occur near floating objects offshore. Tagging studies[9,10] have shown that yellowtail kingfish up to 60 cm fork length remain in a limited area, at least for 12 months,[9] with most recaptured within 50 km of their release point. Tagging data have also

Distribution

Yellowtail kingfish are distributed globally in the cool temperate waters of the Pacific and Indian oceans off South Africa, Japan, southern Australia and the United States of America. However, samson fish are endemic to Australian waters.[4]

In Australian waters, yellowtail kingfish are distributed from North Reef in Queensland, around the southern coast to Trigg Island in Western Australia.[4] They also occur off the east coast of Tasmania[1] and around Lord Howe and Norfolk islands. Samson fish have a discontinuous distribution, from Moreton Bay to Montague Island off the east coast,

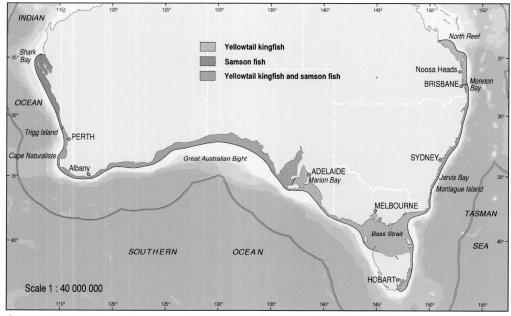

Geographic distribution for yellowtail kingfish and samson fish in Australian waters.

Underwater view of schooling yellowtail kingfish. (Source: Fisheries Research Institute, NSW Fisheries)

shown that larger fish travel further, with fish tagged off New South Wales being recaptured off Victoria, Lord Howe Island and New Zealand.[10]

Yellowtail kingfish are opportunistic daytime feeders consuming small fish, squid (Ommastrephidae) and crustaceans. Feeding schools will sometimes rise to the surface.[9]

There is little information on the life history of samson fish. They have been reported to grow to over 50 kg, but individuals over 30 kg are rare.[5]

Stock structure

A genetic study[1] of yellowtail kingfish stock structure in southern Australian waters revealed significant differences between samples from Greenwell Point in New South Wales. These differences may indicate the existence of distinct subpopulations in New South Wales waters. Tagging data however, point to the presence of a single stock in south-eastern Australia.[10] Genetic analyses failed to separate yellowtail kingfish samples from Australian, New Zealand or Californian waters.[1]

Commercial fishery

The major commercial fishery for yellowtail kingfish is in New South Wales, with fishing effort centred around Solitary Island (near Coffs Harbour), Crowdy Head, and around reefs and islands off Sydney, Greenwell Point and Bermagui. In Queensland, yellowtail kingfish are taken as an incidental catch in the snapper (*Pagrus auratus*) handline fishery. In Western Australia, yellowtail kingfish and samson fish are caught between Israelite Bay and Shark Bay,

although most of the catch is taken between Perth and Geraldton.

The main fishery techniques used in New South Wales are surface and subsurface traps. These account for 80 % of the catch. In northern areas, traps are often used as fish aggregating devices (FADs). Other techniques include trolling, bottom set longlines, poling and bottom set traps. Leadlines trolled with live bait are also commonly used at Greenwell Point and Coffs Harbour.

The New South Wales fishery operates all year, but there are large catches of small fish (comprising over 50 % of the total annual catch) made between December and February. Poling is carried out at Greenwell Point during October and November, when aggregations of medium size (2–4 kg) fish are targeted. Warehou (*Seriolella* species) are a bycatch in the trap fishery. Bonito (*Sarda* species) are sometimes taken by trolling, while a variety of tunas (Scombridae) are caught when poling.

Off south-western Western Australia, yellowtail kingfish and samson fish are

caught with handlines, droplines, longlines and bottom set gillnets. Samson fish form most of the catch and are taken on handlines and droplines. Gillnet and longline catches are usually considered a bycatch of the Southwest Shark Fishery.

Yellowtail kingfish are marketed as whole, gilled and gutted fish. Their average wholesale price at the Sydney Fish Market in 1991–92 was A$ 4.33 per kg. They are sold on domestic markets in cutlet or fillet form, with better quality fish sold for sashimi (raw fish) and fetching high prices. In the same period, yellowtail kingfish and samson fish sold for A$ 0.80–1.50 per kg on Perth wholesale fish markets.

Management controls In New South Wales there are restrictions on the number of traps for fishers targeting *Seriola* species and a minimum legal size applies. In Western Australia there are no gear restrictions, quotas or closed seasons that apply specifically to those fishers targeting samson fish or yellowtail kingfish. There is a minimum length set for samson fish but no limit applies to kingfish.[11]

Recreational fishery

Yellowtail kingfish and samson fish are important species for recreational anglers,[5,10] with most effort concentrated in the summer months. They are usually taken from boats by anglers using handlines and rod-and-line, although they are occasionally taken from the shore. Anglers often fish near traps and other fish aggregating devices.

The Australian Anglers Association records the largest yellowtail kingfish

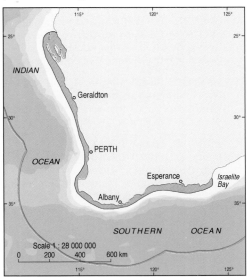
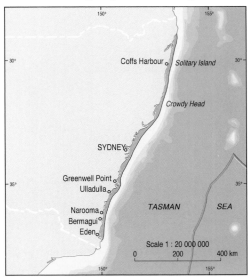

Commercial fishing areas for yellowtail kingfish and samson fish in Australian waters.

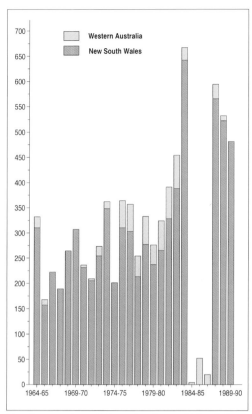

Total annual catch in t of yellowtail kingfish for the period 1964–65 to 1989–90 in Australia. Figures are unavailable for New South Wales from 1984–85 to 1986–87. Catches for States that average less than 5 % of the total for all States are not shown. (Source: Fisheries Resources Atlas Statistical Database.)

landed as 47.3 kg (from New South Wales) and the largest samson fish as 53.1 kg (from Western Australia).

Management controls Minimum legal sizes apply for yellowtail kingfish caught by recreational fishers in New South Wales and South Australia, and for samson fish caught in Western Australia. Bag limits apply for yellowtail kingfish in New South Wales and Western Australia and for samson fish in Western Australia.

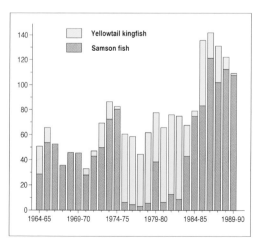

Total annual catch of yellowtail kingfish and samson fish in Western Australia for the period 1964–65 to 1989–90. (Source: Fisheries Resources Atlas Statistical Database.)

Resource status

The status of yellowtail kingfish and samson fish resources are unknown. New South Wales commercial catches of yellowtail kingfish have declined in recent years.

Notes

Amberjack (*Seriola dumerili*) are very similar to yellowtail kingfish and samson fish. They can be distinguished by their colour (brown back and purplish-brown caudal fin), torpedo-shaped body and dorsal ray count of 29–35. Amberjack are distributed throughout the Pacific Ocean and into the western Atlantic Ocean off Florida, the Caribbean and the Bahamas. They have a discontinuous distribution in Australia, from Noosa Heads to Jervis Bay on the east coast and Albany to Cape Naturaliste in the south-west of Western Australia.[4]

Amberjack live in warm continental shelf waters, and occur further offshore than adult yellowtail kingfish and samson fish. Little is known of the life history of amberjack in Australia. They are reported to grow to 60 kg,[5] but in Australian waters individuals weighing between 2 kg and 15 kg are commonly landed.[5]

Anglers target amberjack along with yellowtail kingfish and samson fish. The largest individual caught by an angler was 39.5 kg, from Western Australia (record of the Australian Anglers Association).

References

1. Smith, A.K. (1987) *Genetic variation and dispersal of the yellowtail kingfish*, Seriola lalandi, *from New South Wales waters.* Unpublished Honours thesis, University of New South Wales.

2. Scott, T.D., Glover, C.J.M. and Southcott, R.V. (1974) *The marine and freshwater fishes of South Australia.* Adelaide: South Australian Government. 392 pp.

3. Hutchins, B. and Swainston, R. (1986) *Sea fishes of southern Australia. Complete field guide for anglers and divers.* Perth: Swainston Publishing. 180 pp.

4. Paxton, J.R., Hoese, D.F., Allen, G.R., Hanley, J.E. (1989) *Zoological catalogue of Australia. Volume 7, Pisces. Petromyzontidae to Carangidae.* Canberra: Australian Government Publishing Service. 664 pp.

5. Starling, S. (1988) *The fisherman's handbook. How to find, identify and catch the top Australian angling fish.* Sydney: Angus and Robertson. 263 pp.

A sizeable specimen of an amberjack caught in southern Queensland. (Source: Lindsay Chapman, Bureau of Resource Sciences)

6. Akazaki, M. and Yoden, Y. (1990) The growth and metamorphosis of larvae and juvenile of Hiramasa, *Seriola lalandi. Bulletin of the Faculty of Agriculture, Miyazaki University* **37**(1): 41–47.

7. Smith, M.M. and Heemstra, P.C. (eds) (1986) *Smith's sea fishes.* Johannesburg: Macmillan South Africa (Publishers) (Pty) Limited. 1047 pp.

8. Roughley, T.C. (1968) *Fish and fisheries of Australia.* Sydney: Angus and Robertson. 328 pp.

9. *Commercial fisheries of New South Wales* (1982) N.S.W. State Fisheries. 60 pp.

10. Smith, A., Pepperell, J., Diplock, J. and Dixon, P. (1991) Study suggests NSW kingfish one stock. *Australian Fisheries* **50**(3): 34–36.

11. *Government Gazette WA.* 20 May 1988. Perth: Government Printer.

Contributors

Information on these species was originally provided by Adam Smith, and supplemented by (in alphabetical order) Mark Cliff, John Diplock and Doug Ferrell. Drawing by Gavin Ryan. (*Details of contributors and their organisations are given in the Acknowledgements section at the back of this book.*)
Compilers Alex McNee and Christina Grieve (maps)

Australia. Catches of juvenile Australian salmon are made throughout the year in South Australia, Victoria and Tasmania. Some fish are also taken in South Australian sea garfish and mullet (Mugilidae) catches.

Aircraft and land-based spotters are, or have been, used to locate schools of Australian salmon. Beach seine fishers rely on cliff-top spotters to locate schools of fish. In South Australia, spotter aircraft direct purse seine fishers in the placement of their nets. Australian salmon are sold as whole, fresh fish, or canned for human consumption or pet food, or used for rock lobster (*Jasus* species) bait. The highest demand for Australian salmon is for use as rock lobster bait; eg between 1983 and 1986 about 85 % of the South Australian catch was used for this purpose. Prices for Australian salmon vary Australia wide depending on the end use. Fish for local fresh fish markets fetched the highest prices. In 1992 Western Australian fishers received A$ 0.20–0.50 per kg for whole fish.

Management controls In Western Australia, commercial fishers are limited to fishing certain beaches. In South Australia, the South Australian Marine Scale Fishery licence quota limits Australian salmon fishers to fishing in

waters shallower than 5 m. Annual quotas also apply.

Recreational fishery

Australian salmon are taken by recreational anglers throughout their ranges. They are especially popular with beach and rock anglers[7] and smaller fish are sometimes netted. In Victoria, Australian salmon are targeted by shoreline fishers and by boat-based trolling. The most common method is the use of a pilchard bait on linked hooks although metal casting lures are also used. According to the Australian Anglers Association, the largest recorded Australian salmon is a 9.4 kg fish caught in South Australia in 1973.

The size of the recreational catch in South Australia has been estimated to be hundreds of t annually. Angler catch rates vary greatly depending on locality.[7] There are no data on recreational catch for other States.

Management controls Western Australia imposes minimum lengths and a bag limit on Australian salmon caught by anglers. South Australia and Victoria regulate catch using minimum lengths. Several South Australian beaches are closed to commercial netting to avoid conflict with recreational anglers. There are no restrictions in New South Wales or Tasmania.

Resource status

The Australian salmon fisheries in New South Wales and Western Australia are believed to be fully exploited, while the South Australian fishery is under-fished.

Western Australian salmon populations are vulnerable to the effects of over-exploitation[8] as they are characterised by high natural mortality, strong schooling habits, and the fish are often caught before their first spawning. The South Australian catch has declined since the 1970s, mostly through a reduction in the number of large purse seine operators. A 1984–86 estimate put the fishable population in South Australia at 3600 to 6000 t.[7] There is no information on the present status of eastern Australian salmon populations.

References

1. Hutchins, B. and Swainston, R. (1986) *Sea fishes of southern Australia. Complete field guide for anglers and divers.* Perth: Swainston Publishing. 180 pp.

2. Malcolm, W.B. (1966) Synopsis for F.A.O. species and stocks thesaurus of data on *Arripis trutta* (Bloch and Schneider). In *Commonwealth–States fisheries conference, Southern Pelagic Project Committee technical session, Cronulla 1966.* Vol. **3**. Cronulla: CSIRO.

3. Stanley, C.A. (1978) Area of distribution, movements, age composition and mortality rates of the Australian salmon population in Tasmania, Victoria and New South Wales. *Australian Journal of Marine and Freshwater Research* **29**: 417–433.

4. Stanley, C.A. (1980) Australian salmon. *Fisheries Situation Report* No. **5**. Cronulla: CSIRO. 11 pp.

5. Robertson, A.I. (1982) The population dynamics and feeding ecology of juvenile Australian salmon (*Arripis trutta*) in Western Port, Victoria. *Australian Journal of Marine and Freshwater Research* **33**: 369–375.

6. Stanley, C.A. and Malcolm, W.B. (1977) Reproductive cycles in the eastern subspecies of the Australian salmon, *Arripis trutta marginata* (Cuvier and Valenciennes). *Australian Journal of Marine and Freshwater Research* **28**: 287–301.

7. Cappo, M.C. (1987) The fate and fisheries biology of sub-adult Australian salmon in South Australian waters. *FIRTA Report* **84/75**. 162 pp.

8. Cappo, M.C. (1987) The biology and exploitation of Australian salmon in South Australia. *SAFISH* **12**(1): 4–14.

9. Nicholls, A.G. (1973) Growth in the Australian 'salmon' *Arripis trutta* (Bloch and Schneider). *Australian Journal of Marine and Freshwater Research* **24**: 159–176.

10. MacDonald, C.M. (1983) Population, taxonomic and evolutionary studies on marine fishes of the genus *Arripis* (Perciformes: Arripidae). *Bulletin of Marine Science* **33**(3): 780 (abstract).

Contributors

The information on this species was originally provided by Keith Jones and supplemented by (in alphabetical order) Mike Cappo, Murray MacDonald and Clive Stanley. Drawing by Roger Swainston. (*Details of contributors and their organisations are given in the Acknowledgements section at the back of this book.*)

Compilers Alex McNee, Kay Abel, Patricia Kailola and Christina Grieve (maps)

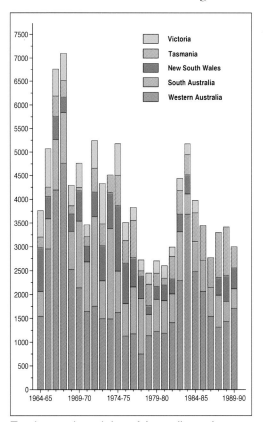

Total annual catch in t of Australian salmon for the period 1964–65 to 1989–90. Figures are unavailable for: New South Wales from 1984–85 to 1986–87; and Victoria for 1973–74 and 1985–86 to 1989–90. (Source: Fisheries Resources Atlas Statistical Database)

S e a   p e r c h

Lutjanus species

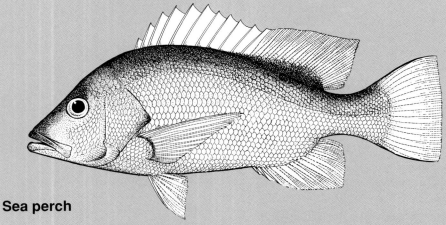

Sea perch

This presentation is on 3 species of sea perch, **saddle-tail snapper, red emperor** and **red snapper**.

Saddle-tail snapper, *Lutjanus malabaricus* (Schneider, in Bloch and Schneider)

Other common names include **large-mouthed nannygai, big-mouth nannygai, saddletail snapper, red jew, scarlet sea-perch, redfish, red snapper, silver, nannygai, red bream** and **red emperor**.
FAO: **Malabar blood snapper**
Australian species code: 346007

Red emperor, *Lutjanus sebae* (Cuvier)

Other common names include **government bream, king snapper, queenfish, redfish** and **red kelp**.
FAO: **emperor red snapper**
Australian species code: 346004

Red snapper, *Lutjanus erythropterus* Bloch

Other common names include **small-mouthed nannygai, high brow sea perch, red bream, scarlet snapper, black, redfish** and **red jew**.
FAO: **crimson snapper**
Australian species code: 346005

Family LUTJANIDAE

Diagnostic features These 3 species vary from pink to red. Red emperor can be distinguished from the other 2 species by having more (15–16) rays in the dorsal fin and a pronounced pre-opercular notch. Red emperor are deep pink with 3 bright red oblique lines crossing their body (less distinct with age) and the fins are usually edged white. Saddle-tail snapper (pictured) and red snapper have 12–14 rays in the dorsal fin and the pre-opercular notch is weak. Saddle-tail snapper have a smaller eye (4.2–6.7 in head length) and longer snout (2.4–3.1 in head length) than red snapper (eye 3.4–4.1, snout 3–3.4, both in head length), the predorsal profile is straight to slightly concave (evenly convex in red snapper) and the soft dorsal and anal fins tend to be pointed (rounded in red snapper). The body and fins of saddle-tail snapper are deep orange red to brownish red. Red snapper have bright pink to scarlet body and fins, often with narrow yellow lines along the scale rows. Juveniles of both species have a broad dark band from the snout through the eye to the origin of the dorsal fin and a prominent black band ('saddle') across the caudal peduncle.

Distribution

Sea perch (lutjanids) are demersal fish inhabiting tropical and subtropical waters.

Saddle-tail snapper and red emperors are present in Australian waters from Shark Bay in Western Australia to Sydney in New South Wales, and red snapper inhabit Australian waters between Shark Bay and Brisbane. Globally, these species are widespread in the Indo-West Pacific.[1]

Saddle-tail snapper are found from 10–12 m to at least 100 m depth.[1,2] They are present on coastal and offshore reefs and general mid-continental shelf waters. They tend to be associated with sponge and gorgonian-dominated habitats on the North West Shelf,[3] and hard mud areas of the Arafura Sea. Juveniles tend to inhabit shallow inshore waters and larger fish live in deeper waters.[2,4] Saddle-tail snapper often school with red snapper.[1]

Red emperors live in a variety of habitats including coral reef lagoons, reefs, sand flats and gravel patches.[1,2] They are found from shallow (5 m) water to at least 180 m. Small juveniles frequently form commensal associations with sea urchins.[1] Juveniles less than 20 cm long are common in nearshore, turbid waters,[2] in mangrove areas[1] or among both coastal and deeper water offshore reefs.[2] Red emperors move to deeper water as they grow larger,[4] with large fish often moving into shallower water during the winter months.[2,4] Red emperors form schools of similar-sized individuals or are solitary.

Red snapper inhabit waters from less than 5 m to at least 100 m deep.[1] They are present over shoals, rubble, corals, large epibenthos, hard or sandy mud substrates and offshore reefs. Juvenile red snapper from about 2.5 cm length inhabit shallow waters over muddy substrates.

Life history

Sea perch are batch or serial spawners.[5] Spawning is sometimes timed to coincide with spring tides and it usually takes place at night[5,6] near open water.[5] On the Great Barrier Reef however, 'redfish' (a common term for red sea perch) spawn throughout the full lunar cycle, over both spring and neap tides.[6]

Spawning seasonality in lutjanids is either over an extended summer period or year round with peaks in activity.[5] On the northern Great Barrier Reef, spawning activity extends over October to February in saddle-tail snapper, October to April in red emperors and September to April in red snapper. Peaks in activity occur from October through December for saddle-tail snapper and red emperors and slightly longer for red snapper.[7] In Northern Territory waters, spawning is more or less continuous over the year.

Sea perch are highly fecund, broadcast spawners.[5] Fecundity increases with size increase in the females.[6] Large females (eg 100 cm long) can produce up to at least 5–7 million eggs per season.[5] The eggs and larvae are pelagic.[5]

On the North West Shelf, sea perch larvae are found in shallow (40-75 m) open continental shelf waters,[7] and in the east, the open waters of the Great Barrier Reef lagoon are the more likely nursery areas for larval sea perch.[7] Sea perch larvae move into the surface waters at night and away from them during the day.

Ageing and growth studies on lutjanids in Australia are largely unvalidated. On the northern Great Barrier Reef, it has been estimated that saddle-tail snapper average 5–20 cm fork length at 1 year of age and 41 cm (females) and 44 cm (males) at 3 years of age.[8] In the Arafura Sea, 3-year-old saddle-tail snapper average 26 cm standard length and are about 55 cm at 10 years of age.[9] Saddle-tail snapper attain at least 100 cm total length[1] and live for at least 12 years.[1]

Similarly, red emperors on the Great Barrier Reef are estimated to be 20–21 cm fork length at 1 year of age and 40 cm at 3 years of age.[8] Red emperors attain a maximum total length of at least 100 cm,[1] possibly 116 cm fork length[8] and live to at least 10 years of age.[1] An individual from deep water on the Great Barrier Reef weighed 32.7 kg, gutted.[8]

Estimates on sizes of 1-year-old red snapper are 17 cm (males) and 20 cm (females) fork lengths, increasing to 40 cm (males) and 43 cm (females) at 3 years of age.[8] Maximum size estimates for red snapper vary, from at least 64 cm fork length (Great Barrier Reef)[8] and 73 cm and 81.6 cm fork length with age estimates of at least 8 years.[10]

On the Great Barrier Reef and North West Shelf, there appears to be variation in growth rates by 'redfish' before and after age at maturity, some of it sex-related.[8,10] Maturity in sea perch occurs at about 40–50 % of maximum length.[5,6]

In common with other sea perch, saddle-tail snapper, red emperors and red snapper are predaceous fish, consuming a broad range of prey dominated by fish, and with small amounts of crustaceans, cephalopods and other benthic invertebrates. They forage mostly at night.

Stock structure

No studies have been conducted. However, it is believed that there is

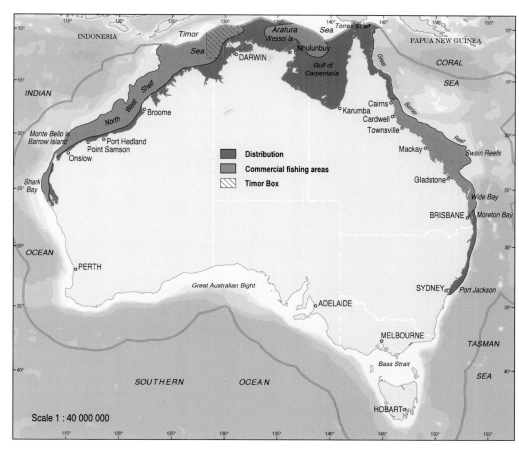

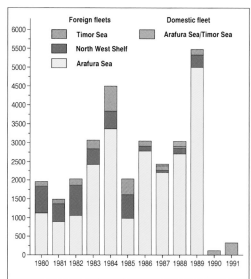

(above) Geographical distribution and commercial fishing areas for saddle-tail snapper, red emperor and red snapper in Australian waters.

(left) Retained catches in t of 'red snapper' for all foreign trawl fleets operating on the North West Shelf, Timor Sea and Arafura Sea between 1980 and 1989 and the domestic trawl fleet between 1987 and 1991. (Source: Australian Fishing Zone Information System and Ramm et al[12])

probably a unit stock for each of the 3 species in northern Australian waters.

Commercial fishery

In Western Australia and the Northern Territory, saddle-tail snapper, red emperors and red snapper are caught by demersal and semi-pelagic otter trawls, traps, droplines, and deepwater handlines (Western Australia). In Queensland, they are also longlined. The fisheries operate all year. Saddle-tail snapper and red snapper are more commonly caught by trawling in northern waters, while red emperors are as common in trap and line fisheries as in trawl fisheries.

Saddle-tail snapper are harvested by demersal otter trawling for fish on the North West Shelf, Timor Sea and Arafura Sea. They are the principal target species of domestic trawlers in the Arafura Sea and Timor Sea,[11] and historically (1930s[12] to 1991) for Taiwanese and Thai pair trawl and stern trawl fleets fishing in northern Australia.

Sea perch (mainly 'redfish') were a dominant group of fishes in Thai and Taiwanese trawler catches in the Arafura Sea and Timor Sea, comprising up to 30 % of the total catch; and between 1985 and 1987 on the North West Shelf, sea perch were the third most important fish group taken by demersal foreign trawling. The highest catches of 'redfish' per unit of effort by the foreign fleets in the period 1980-90 were achieved in the Arafura Sea and retained catches of 'redfish' per unit of effort by Taiwanese (and some Thai) trawlers of 100–150 kg/hour were common in the Timor Sea and higher in the Arafura Sea. The 'redfish' catch was dominated by saddle-tail snapper (70 % by weight) and red snapper (24 % by weight). Catches in the Timor Sea had a large component of red snapper (up to 670 t per year), and this species was also a major component of the Arafura catch (up to 3370 t per year),[12] where saddle-tail snapper is the dominant species taken.

Currently, the domestic Northern Fish Trawl Fishery operates in depths of 50–70 m offshore from prawn grounds in the Arafura Sea only, with vessels based at Gove and Karumba. Saddle-tail snapper are targeted and red snapper are an incidental catch. Juvenile saddle-tail snapper and red snapper are also a bycatch of the Northern Prawn Fishery.

Red emperors and saddle-tail snapper are caught in the Great Barrier Reef Reef Line Fishery as well as in east Queensland coastal waters. The Fishery operates all year between Torres Strait to south of the Swain Reefs and into Moreton Bay, with most of the catch being taken between Cardwell and Mackay.[2] There are seasonal peaks in catch and effort — especially during the period August-October.[2]

'Redfish' on the Great Barrier Reef are targeted primarily at night. Handlines, large, deck-mounted, hand-operated reels and bottom set longlines are used, and baits include squid, oily fish and lower quality reef fish.[13] Boats either fish while drifting or anchored, usually in about 100 m depth. Dinghies ('tender vessels')

(below) Large catch of 'redfish' by a Thai stern trawler, Arafura Sea. (Source: Kevin McLoughlin, Bureau of Resource Sciences)

work to a mother ship with freezers and the teams stay out for up to 3 weeks. Smaller vessels also work inshore waters.

In 1980–81, red emperors were the main 'redfish' recorded in catches, comprising 17 % of the total commercial catch around Cairns, 4 % around Townsville and 5 % around Mackay.[2] In recent years the proportion of saddle-tail snapper and red snapper in the Queensland catch has increased.

In the Northern Territory, red emperors are targeted in the trap fishery operating in the 'Timor Box' (refer p. 305). The traps are of various designs with a single entrance. Usually they are set during the day in water depths of about 100 m, on a coral rubble or reef bottom near the edge of the continental shelf. Boats operate 10–15 traps with soak time from 1–3 hours. The traps are baited with oily fish such as pilchards (*Sardinops neopilchardus*) placed inside bait boxes or bags. Tropical snappers (*Pristipomoides* species) and red emperors comprise nearly 50 % each of the catch from the trap fishery, in which rock cod and other species of sea perch comprise the small bycatch. The 3 'redfish' species are also caught as a bycatch of the Northern Territory dropline fishery for tropical snapper.

Red emperors are targeted in the Western Australian Trap and Line Fishery, which began on the North West Shelf in 1984.[3] Handlining had been carried out from boats working inshore and the islands before that year.[14] The main area for trapping is now north of Broome and some fishing is also carried out off Port Hedland. Fish traps used in Western Australia are mostly circular ('O' traps) and are baited usually with pilchards. They are left to fish from 45 minutes to a few hours, or even overnight. Depths fished are from 20 m to 100 m.

Red emperors are the dominant sea perch taken in the trap fishery.[14] Saddle-tail snapper, then red snapper comprise the next most dominant category.[14]

Sea perch are marketed either gilled and gutted, whole or as fillets, as fresh chilled or frozen product. Northern Territory and Queensland sea perch are marketed locally (eg in Darwin, and on the Reef island tourist resorts) and in Brisbane, Sydney and Melbourne. In Brisbane, late 1992 wholesale prices for gilled and gutted fish averaged A$ 3.50 per kg for saddle-tail snapper and red

snapper and A$ 5.00 per kg for red emperors.

Management controls The Northern Fish Trawl Fishery is managed by the Commonwealth of Australia. Six vessels are endorsed to fish in the Arafura Zone and 4 endorsements are available for the Timor Zone.

Various entry and gear restrictions apply in the Western Australian trawl, trap and line fisheries. In the Northern Territory, there are no restrictions. The Queensland Government manages the Reef Line Fishery in conjunction with zoning plans established by the Great Barrier Reef Marine Park Authority. Restrictions apply on commercial licences and some use of gear.[2] A legal minimum size applies for red emperors in Queensland.

Recreational fishery

Red emperors are caught by recreational fishers using handlines and sometimes rod-and-line. The most common baits are cut fish flesh, pilchards and squid. In Western Australia, the recreational fishery extends from the Houtman Abrolhos to Broome. In the Northern Territory, saddle-tail snapper are commonly caught inshore and on artificial reefs and red emperors are caught offshore. Recreational fishing on the Great Barrier Reef is carried out by small vessels (from 3 m long) working inshore reefs and larger charter vessels working the more remote outer reefs. Recreational landings of 'redfish' on the Great Barrier Reef are about the same as the commercial catch from the Reef. Red emperors are caught relatively more commonly in the Cairns region (17 % of the total recreational catch) than in areas further south such as Townsville and Mackay.[2]

The record size for sea perch in Australian waters is 17.6 kg, from Western Australia (Australian Anglers Association records).

Management controls Red emperors are the only species regulated. Bag limits apply in Western Australia, and a minimum legal size applies in Queensland and Western Australia.

Resource status

Lutjanids comprised 20–30 % of the fish biomass in the mid-shelf area of the North

West Shelf (115°30' and 118°30' E) during the 1960s and early 1970s.[3] By 1983 however, they comprised less than 10 % of the biomass following a period of intensive fishing by Taiwanese trawlers.[3]

Saddle-tail snapper stocks in the Northern Fish Trawl Fishery were assessed in 1991[11] and 1992. Stock biomass was estimated from research surveys and a yield-per-recruit analysis was used to derive sustainable yield estimates. The 1992 estimate of sustainable yield for the Arafura region was 3000–8000 t for saddle-tail snapper and 4000–10 000 t for 'redfish' (including Timor snapper, *L. timorensis*). The large ranges of the yield estimates are due to various uncertainties in the assessment including lack of information on growth and mortality and uncertainty in the biomass estimates.

Queensland fishers consider that the 'redfish' and emperor resources in the Reef Line Fishery are in decline.[13] Generally, the decline is concentrated very close to the coast, away from major commercial fishing activity on the Great Barrier Reef coral reefs — except possibly for Cairns.[2] The catch rates and the size of reef fish caught by the offshore charter boat fleet on the Reef since 1963 have remained fairly stable.[2]

Notes

There are several other species of sea perch caught in commercial fishing operations targeting 'redfish'. Timor snapper is caught in the Northern Fish Trawl Fishery and trap and dropline fisheries. With its red body and fins, it closely resembles saddle-tail snapper from which it is distinguished by its black pectoral fin axil. Striped sea perch *(L. vitta)* are a bycatch of demersal otter trawling in the Arafura Sea and the trap fisheries. They also formed a significant catch of the earlier Taiwanese and Thai fishing operations in northern Australia. Retained catch per unit of effort ranged from 10 kg to 20 kg per hour on the North West Shelf and the Timor Sea.[11] Moses sea perch *(L. russelli)* are also caught in demersal trawling operations and in trap fisheries. Stripey *(L. carponotatus)* are common on the Great Barrier Reef and mangrove jack *(L. argentimaculatus)* and fingermark sea perch *(L. johnii)* are common in inshore waters, mangrove areas and around headlands. All 3 species

Samples of saddle-tail snapper and red emperor from demersal trawling on the North West Shelf. (Source: Dave Evans, CSIRO Marine Laboratories, Perth)

are popular with recreational fishers and are caught with handlines, trolling gear and also fish traps.

References

1. Allen, G.R. (1985) FAO species catalogue, volume 6. Snappers of the world. An annotated and illustrated catalogue of the lutjanid species known to date. *FAO Fisheries Synopsis No. 125*, **6**. 208 pp.

2. Williams, D.McB. and Russ, G.R. (in press, 1992) *Review of data on fishes of commercial and recreational fishing interest on the Great Barrier Reef. Volume 1.* Townsville: Great Barrier Reef Marine Park Authority.

3. Sainsbury, K.J. (1987) Assessment and management of the demersal fishery on the continental shelf of northwestern Australia. Pp 465–503, in *Tropical snappers and groupers. Biology and fisheries management.* Ed by J.J. Ralston. Boulder and London: Westview Press.

4. McPherson, G., Squire, L. and O'Brien, J. (1988). Demersal reef fish project 1984-85: age and growth of four important reef fish species. A report to the Great Barrier Reef Marine Park Authority. *Queensland Department of Primary Industries, Fisheries Research Branch Technical Report* **FRB 88/6**. 33 pp.

5. Grimes, C.B. (1987) Reproductive biology of the Lutjanidae: a review. Pp 239–294, in *Tropical snappers and groupers. Biology and fisheries management.* Ed by J.J. Polovina and S. Ralston. Boulder and London: Westview Press.

6. McPherson, G., Squire, L. and O'Brien, J. (1992) Reproduction of three dominant *Lutjanus* species of the Great Barrier Reef inter-reef fishery. *Asian Fisheries Science* **5**: 15-24.

7. Leis, J.M. (1987) Review of the early life history of tropical groupers (Serranidae) and snappers (Lutjanidae). Pp 189–237, in *Tropical snappers and groupers. Biology and fisheries management.* Ed by J.J. Polovina and S. Ralston. Boulder and London: Westview Press.

8. McPherson, G. and Squire, L. (1992) Age and growth of three dominant *Lutjanus* species of the Great Barrier Reef inter-reef fishery. *Asian Fisheries Science* **5**: 25–36.

9. Edwards, R.R.C. (1985) Growth rates of Lutjanidae (snappers) in tropical Australian waters. *Journal of Fish Biology* **26**: 1–4.

10. Chen, C.Y., S.Y. Yeh and H.C. Liu (1984) Age and growth of *Lutjanus malabaricus* in the northwestern shelf off Australia. *Acta Oceanographica Taiwanica* **15**: 154–164.

11. *Northern fish trawl* (1992) Fishery status report, February 1992. Canberra: Bureau of Rural Resources. 4 pp.

12. Ramm, D.C., Lloyd, J.A. and Coleman, A.P.M. (1991) *Demersal trawling in the northern sector of the Australian Fishing Zone: catch and effort 1980–1990.* Northern Territory Department of Primary Industry and Fisheries, unpublished draft fisheries report.

13. Gwynne, L. (1990) *A review of the Reef Line Fishery and proposed management measures. A discussion paper.* Brisbane: Queensland Fish Management Authority. 16 pp.

14. Moran, M., Jenke, J., Burton, C. and Clarke, D. (1988) The Western Australian trap and line fishery of the North West Shelf. *Western Australian Marine Research Laboratories. FIRTA Project 86/28, Final Report.* 79 pp.

Contributors

Information on these species was provided by (in alphabetical order) Mike Cappo, Anne Coleman, Laurie Gwynne, Phil Hall, Aubrey Harris, Jim Higgs, Jerry Jenke, Kevin McLoughlin, Geoff McPherson, Dave Milton, Mike Moran, Dave Ramm, Dave Williams and Tim Wood. Drawing by Roger Swainston. (*Details of contributors and their organisations are given in the Acknowledgements section at the back of this book.*)
Compiler Patricia Kailola

Thai trawler, Arafura Sea. (Source: Kevin McLoughlin, Bureau of Resource Sciences)

Tropical snappers

Pristipomoides species

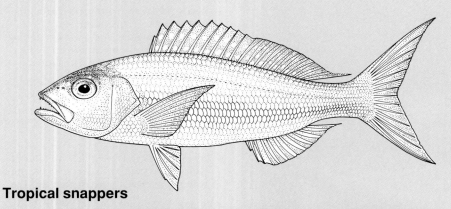

Tropical snappers

This presentation is on 2 species, **gold band snapper** and **sharptoothed snapper**.

Gold band snapper,
Pristipomoides multidens
(Day)

Another common name is **golden snapper**.
FAO: **goldbanded jobfish**
Australian species code: 346002

Sharptoothed snapper,
Pristipomoides typus Bleeker

There are no other common names.
FAO: **sharptooth jobfish**
Australian species code: 346019

Family LUTJANIDAE

Diagnostic features Tropical snappers are characterised by having the last ray of their dorsal and anal fins much longer than the preceding rays, and by the absence of scales on the bases of their dorsal and anal fins. Pectoral fins are much longer than the snout length. Jaw teeth usually include enlarged canines at the front. These 2 species have 47–52 scales in the lateral line.[1] Gold band snapper (pictured) have 2–3 orange-yellow stripes on their snout and under the eyes and there are thick yellow transverse stripes or markings on the interorbital (ie between the eyes). Sharptoothed snapper have no stripes on their snout, but there are thin yellow longitudinal stripes or scribblings on the interorbital.

Distribution

Tropical snappers are deepwater fish inhabiting tropical and sub-tropical waters. Gold band snapper are distributed from the Red Sea to southern Japan and Samoa, while sharptoothed snapper are distributed from Sumatra to the Ryukyu Islands and eastern New Guinea. In Australian waters, gold band snapper are present between Cape Pasley in Western Australia and Moruya in southern New South Wales, and sharptoothed snapper are distributed from about 19°19' S, 117°13' E on the North West Shelf to Tweed Heads in New South Wales.

Pristipomoides are deep-water snapper. Throughout their range, gold band snapper are recorded from 40–200 m and sharptoothed snapper from 40–100 m depth.[1] In the Timor Sea they are most likely to congregate at depths of 90–145 m;[2] in the northern Gulf of Carpentaria and Arafura Sea gold band snapper occur in depths of 48–59 m; and on the North West Shelf the depth range is 60–182 m. Tropical snappers are schooling fish and live in areas of hard, rocky and uneven sea floor and steep slopes off islands.[3]

Life history

There is little information on the reproductive activity of gold band snapper and sharptoothed snapper in Australia. It is likely that gold band snapper are multiple spawners, ie spawning several times during a season. On the North West Shelf, ripe gold band snapper are present from October to February. In Papua New Guinea,[4] the western Pacific and South China Sea,[5] some reproductively active fish were present all year. The fecundity (number of eggs) of gold band snapper 60–69 cm fork length has been estimated as 296 000–646 000.[4] Tropical snapper

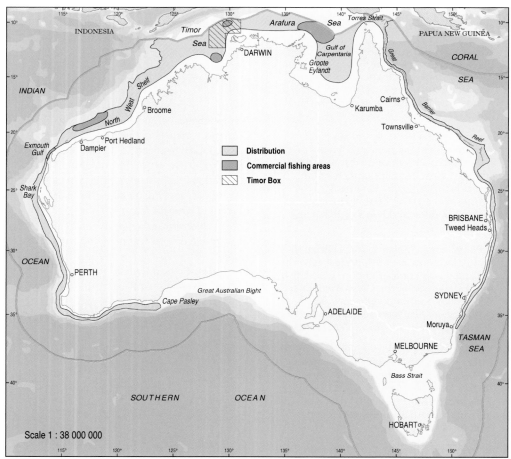

Geographic distribution and commercial fishing areas for gold band snapper and sharptoothed snapper in Australian waters.

larvae, and probably eggs, are pelagic.[6] Tropical snapper larvae have been collected only from the outer continental shelf and slope.[6]

There are several estimates of maximum age and length for gold band snapper. In the western Pacific Ocean, total length is estimated at about 90 cm.[1] In northern Australia, a 1985 study[7] estimated maxima of 14 years' age, 55 cm standard length and 3.7 kg. The maximum size recorded more recently from the North West Shelf is 65 cm fork length. New Guinea gold band snapper were estimated to reach 74 cm fork length.[4] Gold band snapper in Australian waters grow rapidly in the first 3 years and attain an average of 55 cm fork length by 10 years of age. The smallest mature gold band snapper recorded on the North West Shelf was 35 cm fork length, and 50 % of individuals are mature at approximately 50 cm fork length.

Sharptoothed snapper in Australian waters have been estimated to live for 11 years and to reach 47 cm standard length and 2.2 kg.[7] Larger individuals are caught in Papua New Guinea. Sharptoothed snapper in the western Pacific and South China Sea are mature from about 28 cm standard length.[5]

Tropical snapper are generalised, opportunistic carnivores. They feed both on the sea floor and in the water column.[3] Gold band snapper and sharptoothed snapper feed on fish, crustaceans (including prawns and crabs) and squid as well as pelagic items such as gastropod molluscs.[3] In 19 stomach samples of Papua New Guinea gold band snapper caught from 120 m to 290 m depth, the contents were fish (74 % — Priacanthidae, Bregmacerotidae, Triglidae), crustaceans (31 % — caridean shrimps, mainly *Heterocarpus ensifer*), and cephalopods (21 % — mainly squid).[4] Fish collected in May–June in Northern Territory waters had eaten large quantities of pelagic salps (Thaliacea).

Stock structure

There is no information on the stock structure of tropical snappers in Australian waters.

Commercial fishery

Gold band snapper and sharptoothed snapper are caught by demersal otter trawling and some semi-pelagic otter trawling on the North West Shelf, Timor Sea and Arafura Sea and by droplines and wire-meshed traps in the 'Timor Box', an area covering approximately 68 000 square km northwest of Darwin where finfish trawling is prohibited. The dropline and trap boats work at the northern edge of the Timor Box, although they are extending their range.

Gold band snapper and sharptoothed snapper made up part of the catch of foreign trawlers (Taiwanese, Thai, Chinese) operating in Australian waters since the 1930s.[8] They are generally taken in water from around 100 m to the edge of the continental shelf. The greatest catches are made during early winter (April–June). Trawled catches up to 490 t per year have been taken from the Timor Sea,[8] comprising by weight 91 % gold band snapper and 9 % sharptoothed snapper. In comparison, the ratio in a 1990 trawl survey off Northern Territory was 83 % and 17 % respectively. The highest catch rates by foreign trawl fleets were achieved in the Timor Sea (50–110 kg per hour) and the largest catches were taken between January and June.[8]

Trapping on a regular basis commenced in the Timor Box in 1988, after an 18-month trial period over 1982–83. One vessel trapped for tropical snapper in 1988 and was joined by 5 more vessels in 1989.

Seven trap designs have been used, the most successful being single entrance round traps and arrow traps and Western Australian 'D' or square traps. The traps are baited with oily fish, mostly pilchards (*Sardinops neopilchardus*). The traps are set in water 100–140 m deep and soak times vary from 0.5 to 10 hours — generally shorter during the day and longer overnight. After hauling, the traps are rebaited and set if catching is going well. During 1989, higher catch rates were achieved at neap tides. Gold band

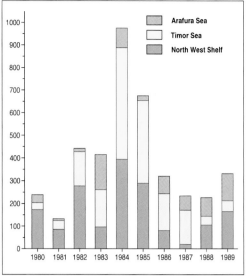

Retained catches in t of *Pristipomoides* species for all trawl fleets operating on the North West Shelf, Timor Sea and Arafura Sea, 1980–1989. Figures are unavailable for: the Taiwanese fleet from 1988 to 1989; the Thai fleet from November 1985 to 1989; the Chinese fleet in 1989. (Source: Australian Fishing Zone Information System and Ramm et al[8])

snapper (28–66 cm fork length) and sharptoothed snapper (30–60 cm fork length) dominate the catch (58 %) from deep-water trapping. However, this percentage is now decreasing as operators are targeting red emperor (*Lutjanus sebae*). A third species of tropical snapper, *Pristipomoides filamentosus* or rosy jobfish, is caught incidentally in the Northern Territory Trap and Dropline Fishery.

Droplining in the Timor Sea and the Arafura Sea by Japanese vessels from 1975 to 1981 caught large quantities of tropical snappers — 54 % of the catch over surveys conducted in October to December, 1980.[9] The vessels fished in depths of 70–140 m. Droplining by Australian vessels commenced in the Timor Sea in 1987 and by 1991, 3 boats were operating full-time. Highest catch rates are made in the early evening, and 80 % of the total dropline catch is made up of these 2 snappers. The hooks are

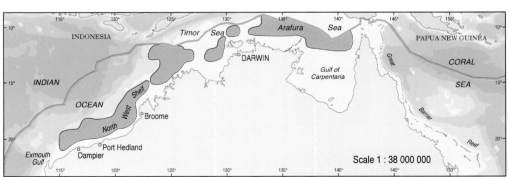

Historical extent of the demersal trawl fishery for *Pristipomoides* species in Australian waters since 1980. (Source: Australian Fishing Zone Information System logbook data)

Catch of red snapper (*Lutjanus* species) and gold band snapper on a retrieved dropline, Northern Territory. (Source: Julie Lloyd, Fisheries Branch, Northern Territory Department of Primary Industry and Fisheries)

baited with squid, pilchards or cuttlefish (*Sepia* species).

Handlining for gold band snapper is being carried out on a small scale off north-eastern Queensland, operating mainly out of Cairns. Fishing is conducted in depths from 80 m to 150 m on the continental shelf slope.

Tropical snapper are sold fresh, chilled or frozen, either as whole fish, gilled and gutted fish, or fillets. The Darwin market for these fish is small, so most tropical snapper are air-freighted to the bigger markets of Brisbane and Sydney. The 1992–93 price for chilled, fresh gold band snapper in Brisbane and Sydney wholesale fish markets ranged from A$ 6.00 to A$ 10.00 per kg. Trawled tropical snapper receive lower prices than droplined snapper.

Management controls There are no restrictions for vessels licensed to operate traps and droplines. Finfish trawlers are confined to defined fish management zones. Foreign trawling is no longer permitted. The Northern Fish Trawl Fishery is managed by the Commonwealth of Australia, and the Western Australian Government manages demersal fish trawling on the North West Shelf.

Recreational fishery

There is no recreational fishery for gold band snapper and sharptoothed snapper in the Northern Territory and Western Australia. However, off eastern Queensland these 2 species, rosy jobfish and other tropical snappers such as *P. argyrogrammicus* and *P. sieboldii* are caught incidentally as part of the general reef fish fishery for 'redfish' from boats fishing the outer reef and slopes in waters deeper than 50 m.

Management controls There are no specific management controls on recreational fishing for tropical snappers.

Resource status

The size of the resource in the Northern Territory is being investigated. As well as fishing by domestic fishing fleets, the entire northern Australian stock is also being fished by foreign trawlers operating just outside Australian waters in the Timor Sea. It is not known whether the trawl and dropline-trap fisheries are harvesting the same stocks.

References

1. Allen, G.R. (1985) FAO species catalogue, volume 6. Snappers of the world. An annotated and illustrated catalogue of the lutjanid species known to date. *FAO Fisheries Synopsis No. 125*, **6**. 208 pp.

2. Mounsey, R. (1990) Northern Territory offshore dropline fishing methods. *Northern Territory Department of Primary Industry and Fisheries,Fishnote* **4**. 3 pp.

3. Parrish, J.D. (1987) Trophic biology of snappers and groupers. Pp 405–463, in *Tropical snappers and groupers. Biology and fisheries management*. Ed by J.J. Polovina and S. Ralston. Boulder and London: Westview Press.

4. Richards, A.H. (1987) Aspects of the biology of some deep water bottomfish in Papua New Guinea with special reference to *Pristipomoides multidens* (Day). *Papua New Guinea Department of Fisheries and Marine Resources, Report* **87–01**. 17 pp.

5. Grimes, C.B. (1987) Reproductive biology of the Lutjanidae: a review. Pp 239–294, in *Tropical snappers and groupers. Biology and fisheries management*. Ed by J.J. Polovina and S. Ralston. Boulder and London: Westview Press.

6. Leis, J.M. (1987) Review of the early life history of tropical groupers (Serranidae) and snappers (Lutjanidae). Pp 189–237, in *Tropical snappers and groupers. Biology and fisheries management*. Ed by J.J. Polovina and S. Ralston. Boulder and London: Westview Press.

7. Edwards, R.R.C. (1985) Growth rates of Lutjanidae (snappers) in tropical Australian waters. *Journal of Fish Biology* **26**: 1–4.

8. Ramm, D.C., Lloyd, J.A. and Coleman, A.P.M. (1991) *Demersal trawling in the northern sector of the Australian Fishing Zone: catch and effort 1980–90*. Northern Territory Department of Primary Industry and Fisheries, unpublished draft fisheries report.

9. Stehouwer, P.J. (1981) Report on a dropline fishing operation. Observations of the 'Takuryo Maru No.11' during feasibility fishing operations in the Australian Fishing Zone. *Department of Primary Production Fishery Report* **6**. 28 pp.

10. Lloyd, J. (1990) *Off-shore droplining for Lutjanidae in the Timor Sea*. Abstract, Australian Society for Fish Biology conference, 25–26 August, Lorne, Victoria

Contributors

Information on these species was originally provided by Julie Lloyd. Additional comments were made by (in alphabetical order) Anne Coleman, Aubrey Harris, Geoff McPherson, Richard Mounsey, John Paxton and Dave Ramm. Drawing by Gavin Ryan. (*Details of contributors and their organisations are given in the Acknowledgements section at the back of this book.*)
Compiler Patricia Kailola

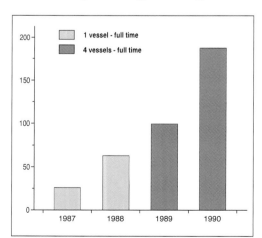

Landed catch in t of *Pristipomoides* species from the dropline fishery operating in the Timor Box, 1987 to 1990. The catch for 1990 is incomplete. (Source: Lloyd[10])

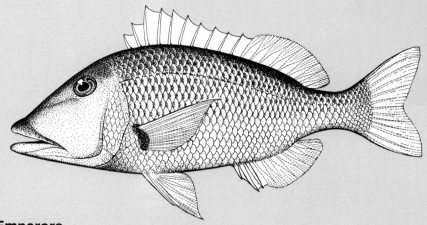

Emperors

Lethrinus species

Distribution

These 4 emperors are distributed in tropical and sub-tropical Indo-Pacific waters from East Africa through South-east Asia, Japan, Australia and New Caledonia. In Australia, red-throat emperors are distributed between the Houtman Abrolhos and Sydney Harbour; also Norfolk Island. They are reportedly absent from the Gulf of Carpentaria and Queensland waters north of Cooktown.[1] Spangled emperors are distributed between Rottnest Island (near Perth) and northern New South Wales. Blue-spotted emperors are found between the Houtman Abrolhos and Wollongong, New South Wales, and red-spot emperors between North West Cape and Hervey Bay.

Red-throat emperors are most abundant from the Houtman Abrolhos to North West Cape and on the Great Barrier Reef from near Townsville to the Capricorn-Bunker Reefs group. Blue-spotted emperors and red-spot emperors are more common in northern and north-western Australia. Spangled emperors appear to be more common in outer coastal waters to the west and east of Australia than they are in the north.

Emperors inhabit continental shelf waters including coral reef and lagoon areas over substrates of hard coral, gravel, sand or rubble. They are found in clear to turbid water in depths from less than 2 m to 76 m (or to 90 m for red-spot emperors).[1] On the North West Shelf, emperors are associated with sponge and gorgonian-dominated habitats.[2,3] Emperors are generally reef or site asociated, but tagging studies in Western Australia showed that individuals may move up to 60 nautical miles.

Life History

Red-throat, red-spot and blue-spotted emperors are protogynous

Emperors

This presentation is on 4 species, **red-throat emperor**, **spangled emperor**, **blue-spotted emperor** and **red-spot emperor**.

Red-throat emperor, *Lethrinus miniatus* (Bloch and Schneider)

Other common names include **north-west snapper, sweetlip, sweetlip emperor, lipper, trout, tricky snapper** and **trumpeter.**
FAO: **trumpet emperor**
Australian species code: 351009

Spangled emperor, *Lethrinus nebulosus* (Forsskål)

Other common names include **yellow sweetlip, sand snapper, tricky snapper, norwest snapper** and **north-west snapper.**
FAO: **spangled emperor**
Australian species code: 351008

Blue-spotted emperor, *Lethrinus choerorhynchus* Bloch and Schneider

Another common name is **lesser spangled emperor**
FAO: no known name
Australian species code: 351001

Red-spot emperor, *Lethrinus lentjan* (Lacepède)

Other common names include **pink-eared emperor, purple-eared emperor** and **purple-headed emperor.**
FAO: **redspot emperor**
Australian species code: 351007

Family LETHRINIDAE

Diagnostic features Red-throat emperors (pictured) are reddish orange around their eyes, with a red patch at the base of the pectoral fin, and a bright red dorsal fin. Spangled emperors and blue-spotted emperors have pearly-blue centres to the scales on their upper body and flanks, and 3 blue bands radiating from the eye over their cheeks and snout. They are very similar fish, only the presence of yellow stripes along the flanks, a brownish band from the eye to mouth and the spots on the head being elongate, distinguishing blue-spotted emperors from spangled emperors. Red-spot emperors have a red margin on their gill cover, a red spot at the base of the pectoral fin and an often mauve or purple head.

hermaphrodites, ie they function first as females and then as males.[4] The reproductive nature of spangled emperors is uncertain, although they also may be protogynous hermaphrodites.[1] A study on the Great Barrier Reef[5] found no clear evidence of sex change in spangled emperors within the size range 17–54 cm.

There is very little data on the actual spawning and fecundity in any species of emperor.[1] Spawning times of red-throat emperors change with latitude off east Queensland — from almost all year off Cairns and Townsville to June-July in north-central waters and October-November in southern waters. Spangled emperors spawn between May and October[5] (peaking in June-July[1,6]). In the Gulf of Carpentaria, blue-spotted and red-spot emperors spawn in November and December.[7]

Emperor eggs are pelagic, and they range from 0.6 mm to 0.9 mm in diameter.[6] Juvenile red-throat emperors

307

Close-up of a red-throat emperor, Great Barrier Reef. (Source: Russell Reichelt, Bureau of Resource Sciences)

2–3 cm long have been collected from shallow, shoreline seagrass beds near Townsville in November. Juvenile emperors (all species) appear to live in shallow, inshore waters such as seagrass and mangrove areas, the fish moving into deeper water as they age.[1,7]

One-year-old red-throat emperors are about 25 cm fork length. At 2 years of age they average 30 cm fork length, 38 cm by 4 years and 41 cm by 6 years. There is no information on growth rates for the other species. Red-throat emperors are mature at 31–35 cm standard length, spangled emperors at 28 cm[6] and red-spot emperors at about 16 cm.[7] Recorded maximum total lengths are 86 cm for spangled emperors and 90 cm for red-throat emperors, and 49 cm fork length for red-spot emperors.[1] Spangled emperors attain at least 4.4 kg in weight.[5] In Australian waters, red-throat emperors

have been estimated to live for up to 18 years,[1] spangled emperors to 25 years, and red-spot emperors for more than 10 years.[7]

Emperors are classed as carnivorous bottom feeders. They are also selective in their diet. Red-throat emperors consume mainly crabs, followed by sea urchins and sand dollars (Echinoidea), fish and benthic organisms.[8] Spangled emperors eat mostly bivalve molluscs, then gastropod molluscs and sand dollars; and red-spot emperors consume mainly small fish.[6]

Stock structure

The taxonomic position of blue-spotted, spangled and blue-lined (*L. fraenatus*) emperors has been confused, with reviews[9,10] suggesting they are mis-identifications for the 1 species. However, surveys and continuing studies consistently reveal morphological and ecological differences between them, and recent electrophoretic study in Western Australia has confirmed that the 3 taxa are reproductively isolated species.

No studies have been conducted on the stock structure of red-throat emperors and red-spot emperors in Australian waters. Western Australian populations of blue-spotted emperors and spangled emperors have been shown to be single

stocks, yet the relationship of these populations and blue-spotted and spangled emperors from other States is unknown.

Commercial fishery

Emperors are caught by handlines, rod-and-line, traps and demersal otter trawling — mainly stern trawling but also semi-pelagic trawling in the Northern Territory.

Emperors are trawled off north-western and northern Australia. From 1970[3,11] until 1991, Taiwanese and later Thai and Chinese fleets operated pair trawlers and stern trawlers on the North West Shelf and northern Australia. Emperors and butterfly bream (Nemipteridae) dominated catches on the North West Shelf for the 10 years from 1980,[12] peaking at a retained catch of 2200 t of emperor in 1982. Emperors were far less abundant in retained catches in the Timor and Arafura seas for the same period. The trawlers worked in depths between 30 m and 120 m, and concentrated on waters between 115° and 120° E.[3]

In the northern demersal fishery to 1991, red-spot emperors comprised 64 % of the emperor catch followed by blue-spotted emperors (29 %).[12] Catch rates were highest during October-December on the North West Shelf, in July in the Timor Sea and during April-June in the Arafura Sea.[12]

Domestic fishing interest in trawling in northern Australia commenced in 1985 and increased after 1988.[11] It is focused on grounds on the North West Shelf, the Arafura Sea and in the northern region of the Gulf of Carpentaria,[11] and has a large seasonal component caused by prawn trawlers converted to fish trawling during the closed seasons of the Northern Prawn Fishery.[11,12] Red-spot, blue-lined and blue-spotted emperors are the main emperors caught. Spangled emperors are taken by domestic trawlers near Barrow Island and Glomar Shoal, Western Australia.

Trap fishing began on the North West Shelf in 1984.[3,13] Fishing is carried out on hard-bottom areas to the west or inshore from main areas worked in the past by Taiwanese pair trawlers. It first concentrated on the Monte Bello-Barrow Island area mainly near the coastal towns of Onslow, Port Hedland and Point

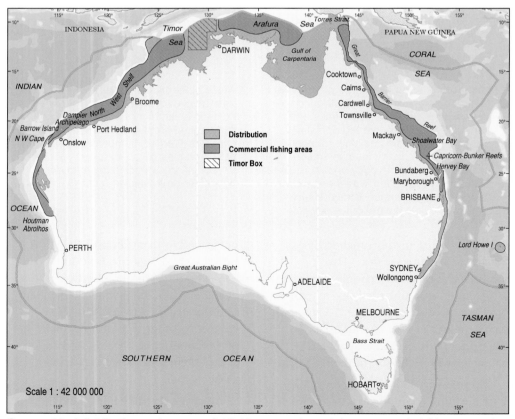

Geographical distribution and commercial fishing areas for red-throat, spangled, blue-spotted and red-spot emperors in Australian waters.

Samson.[13,14] The main area for trapping is now north of Broome.

Fish traps used in Western Australia are mostly circular ('O' traps) and are baited usually with pilchards (*Sardinops neopilchardus*). They are left to fish from 45 minutes to a few hours, or overnight, but the shorter times (1–4 hours)[14] are usually the most productive. The traps are set in water depths of 20–100 m. Peak catches are made in May[14] and July.[13] Catch rates can vary between sets.

Red-throat and spangled emperors are targeted by handline fishers on the west coast. A small quantity of emperors are also taken by dropline.

Spangled emperors are the most abundant emperor caught in the North West Shelf Trap and Line Fishery, followed next in abundance for red-throat emperors.[13] Yellow-tailed emperors (*L. atkinsoni*) and blue-spotted emperors are also taken in small quantities.

In the shallow water (10–50 m) fishery in the Northern Territory, spangled emperors comprise up to 50 % of the catch. Blue-lined emperors and yellow-striped emperors (*L. ornatus*) are also common. In the deepwater trap fishery, emperors comprise only a small — less than 1 — percent of the catch.

Smaller emperors, between 15 cm and 23 cm total length, comprise a very small component of the bycatch from the Northern Prawn Fishery.[15] The main species are red-spot emperors and threadfin emperors, (*L. nematacanthus*).

Red-throat emperors are the third largest component of the Queensland East Coast Reef Line Fishery and comprise 14 % of the catch or more than 500 t annually.[16] On the Great Barrier Reef this species comprises more than 90 % of the emperor catch. Catches of red-throat emperors are highest between August and October. They peak in the waters off Mackay, and are largely confined to waters between Cardwell and Shoalwater Bay, with small catches as far south as Maryborough.

Spangled and red-throat emperors are the only emperors of significance on the Great Barrier Reef although red-spot emperors are caught in fish traps on the outer slopes of mid-shelf reefs.[1] Red-throat emperors are caught with rod-and-line or handlines, baited usually with pilchards. Commercial vessels operate with 2–4 tender boats which

anchor over coral 'bombies' to fish. Bottom fishing in Great Barrier Reef shallow lagoons at night catches mainly spangled emperors, and red-throat emperors are caught both in the daytime and at night. There is also a handline fishery for red-throat emperors in Norfolk Island waters. Best catches are taken in summer months between November and February.[8]

Most fish from the North West Shelf fishery are sent to Perth as whole, chilled fish. Some are gutted and brined before freezing. In Queensland, 1992 prices for whole, chilled fish at the Brisbane wholesale fish market averaged A$ 6.40 per kg.

Management controls The number of vessels and tender boats in the Queensland East Coast Reef Line Fishery is regulated by the State Government. There are also restrictions on gear, and legal minimum sizes apply.

In Western Australia, most waters shallower than 50 m are closed to trap and trawl fishing. The Pilbara trap fishery is a limited entry fishery, and the Pilbara trawl and Kimberley trap and trawl fisheries are coming under developmental fishery management.

The Northern Fish Trawl Fishery (now operated only by domestic vessels) is managed by the Commonwealth of Australia. Separate total allowable catch limits apply for the Arafura Sea and Timor Sea areas. The North West Shelf fishery is regulated by the Western Australian Government.

Taiwanese stern trawler, North West Shelf. (Source: Glen Smith, Southern Fisheries Centre, Queensland Department of Primary Industries)

Recreational fishery

Red-throat emperors are 1 of the major target species by anglers on the Great Barrier Reef and the Queensland east coast. To a lesser extent anglers also target spangled emperors, both in Western Australia and Queensland. Emperors are caught with either fresh

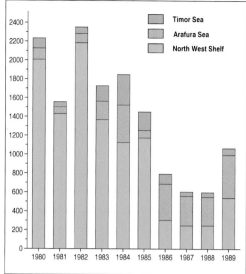
Retained catches in t of emperors for all trawl fleets operating on the North West Shelf, Timor Sea and Arafura Sea, 1980–1989. Figures are unavailable for: the Taiwanese fleet from 1988 to 1989; the Thai fleet from November 1985 to 1989; and the Chinese fleet in 1989. (Source: Australian Fishing Zone Information System and Ramm et al[12])

baits or whole or cut fish, crabs, prawns and squid, and tackle ranges from handlines to casting rigs. The largest emperor recorded by the Australian Anglers Association was 9.6 kg, from Queensland.

Spangled emperors are the largest component of recreational angling in the Ningaloo Marine Park, Western Australia. The recreational fishery in that State extends from the Houtman Abrolhos to Dampier Archipelago.

Management controls In Queensland, a minimum legal size for red emperor applies. Fishing is prohibited on some reefs in the Great Barrier Reef Marine Park. There are no regulations specific to emperors in Western Australia and the Northern Territory.

Resource status

Emperors comprised 47 % of demersal fish in retained catches taken by Russian survey vessels on the North West Shelf between 1962 and 1973. Emperors and sea perch (Lutjanidae) comprised 40–60 % by weight in 1962 but the amount dropped to about 10 % in 1983[3] (the emperor component of the total catch fell from 27.9 % in 1967 to 5.4 % in 1983[2]). This reduction in yield can partly be attributed to the removal of large epibenthos from the sea floor by the action of trawlers and to over-fishing these groups in the mixed species trawl fishery.[3,11] The size composition also changed, with emperors (probably blue-spotted emperors) larger than 0.6 kg disappearing from the catch after 8 months of fishing.[2] By 1986, the catch per unit of effort for emperors had declined by 65 % from a peak in 1973. Whereas the abundance of emperors has continued to decline in trawled areas, the catch rate has increased since 1986 due to concentration of fishing effort on emperors by Taiwanese fleets.[11]

There have been no studies on the resource status of emperors on the Great Barrier Reef and inshore areas of northern Australia. Although there have been reports of declining numbers of red-throat emperors on the Great Barrier Reef,[1] information from fishing clubs along the coast from Cairns to Bundaberg do not suggest a decline. Similarly, there is no information on the resource status of emperors in Western Australian fisheries.

Diver inspecting a fish trap, North West Shelf. (Source: Wade Whitelaw, CSIRO Marine Laboratories, Hobart)

References

1. Williams, D. McB. and Russ, G.R. (in press, 1992) *Review of data on fishes of commercial and recreational fishing interest on the Great Barrier Reef. Volume 1*. Townsville: Great Barrier Reef Marine Park Authority.

2. Sainsbury, K.J. (1987) Assessment and management of the demersal fishery on the continental shelf of northwestern Australia. Pp 465–503, in *Tropical snappers and groupers. Biology and fisheries management*. Ed by J.J. Polovina and S. Ralston. Boulder and London: Westview Press.

3. Sainsbury, K.J. (1991) Application of an experimental approach to management of a tropical multispecies fishery with highly uncertain dynamics. *ICES Marine Science Symposium* **193**: 301–320.

4. Young, P.C. and Martin, R.B. (1982) Evidence for protogynous hermaphroditism in some lethrinid fishes. *Journal of Fish Biology* **21**: 475–491.

5. McPherson, G., Squire, L. and O'Brien, J. (1988) Demersal reef fish project 1984–85: age and growth of four important reef fish species. A report to the Great Barrier Reef Marine Park Authority. *Queensland Department of Primary Industries,Fisheries Research Branch Technical Report* **FRB 88/6**. 33 pp.

6. Walker, M.H. (1975). *Aspects of the biology of emperor fishes, family Lethrinidae, in North Queensland Barrier Reef waters*. Unpublished PhD thesis, James Cook University of North Queensland.

7. Harris, A.N., Blaber, S.J.M., Brewer, D.T. and Milton, D.A. (in press, 1992) Aspects of the biology and factors affecting the distribution of commercial fishes in the Gulf of Carpentaria. *Australian Journal of Marine and Freshwater Research*.

8. Grant, C. (1981). High catch rates in Norfolk Island dropline fishery. *Australian Fisheries* **40**(3): 10–13.

9. Carpenter, K.E. and Allen, G.R. (1989) FAO species catalogue, volume 9. Emperor fishes and large-eye breams of the world (family Lethrinidae). An annotated and illustrated catalogue of lethrinid species known to date. *FAO Fisheries Synopsis No. 125*, **9**. 118 pp.

10. Randall, J.E., Allen, G.R. and Steene, R.C. (1990) *The complete divers' and fishermen's guide to fishes of the Great Barrier Reef and Coral Sea*. Bathurst: Crawford House Press. 507 pp.

11. Jernakoff, P. (1990) Part 1: a review. Pp 3–38, in *CSIRO's northern demersal finfish stock assessments: 1980 to 1989*, by P. Jernakoff and K.J. Sainsbury. *Bureau of Rural Resources Information Paper* **IP/6/90.**

12. Ramm, D.C., Lloyd, J.A. and Coleman, A.P.M. (1991) *Demersal trawling in the northern sector of the Australian Fishing Zone: catch and effort 1980-1990*. Unpublished draft fisheries report. Darwin: Northern Territory Department of Primary Industry and Fisheries.

13. Moran, M., Jenke, J., Burton, C. and Clarke, D. (1988) The Western Australian trap and line fishery of the North West Shelf. *Western Australian Marine Research Laboratories. FIRTA Project 86/28, Final Report.* 79 pp.

14. Whitelaw, A.W., Sainsbury, K.J., Dews, G.J. and Campbell, R.A. (1991) Catching characteristics of four fish-trap types on the North West Shelf of Australia. *Australian Journal of Marine and Freshwater Research* **42**: 369–382.

15. Pender, P.J. and Willing, R.S. (1990) Northern Prawn Fishery bycatch with market potential. *Northern Territory Department of Primary Industry and Fisheries, Fishery Report* **20**. 52 pp.

16. Trainor, N. (1991) Commercial line fishing. *The Queensland Fisherman* March 1991: 17–18, 23–24.

Contributors

The information in this presentation was compiled from contributions made by (in alphabetical order) Anne Coleman, Campbell Davies, Aubrey Harris, Mike Johnson, Richard Martin, Mike Moran, Keith Sainsbury, Wade Whitelaw and Glen Wilson. Drawing by Roger Swainston. (*Details of contributors and their organisations are given in the Acknowledgements section at the back of this book.*)

Compiler Patricia Kailola

Bream

Acanthopagrus species

Bream

This presentation is on 2 species, **yellowfin bream** and **black bream**.

Yellowfin bream,
Acanthopagrus australis
(Günther)

Other common names include **silver bream**, **sea bream**, **black bream** and **eastern black bream**.
FAO: no known name
Australian species code: 353004

Black bream,
Acanthopagrus butcheri
(Munro)

Other common names include **bream**, **southern bream**, **golden bream**, **silver bream**, **southern black bream**, **Gippsland bream** and **southern yellowfin bream**.
FAO: no known name
Australian species code: 353003

Family SPARIDAE

Diagnostic features Yellowfin bream have a silvery to olive-green body, varying from light coloured individuals in coastal waters to darker coloured fish in estuaries. Their pectoral, ventral and anal fins are yellowish. The upper body of black bream can vary from silvery to golden brown, bronze, green or black depending on habitat. Their chin and belly are usually white and their fins are dusky to greenish black. There are 43–46 scales in the lateral line of yellowfin bream and 52–58 scales in black bream. The dorsal and ventral profiles of adult black bream are similarly convex but the dorsal profile is more convex than the ventral profile in yellowfin bream.

Distribution

Yellowfin bream inhabit coastal and estuarine waters of eastern Australia from Townsville in Queensland to the Gippsland Lakes in Victoria.[1] Black bream inhabit estuarine waters from Myall Lake in central New South Wales to the Murchison River in Western Australia,[2] including Tasmania, the islands of Bass Strait and Kangaroo Island. They are absent from the Great Australian Bight region due to the lack of estuarine habitat there. Both species are endemic to Australia.

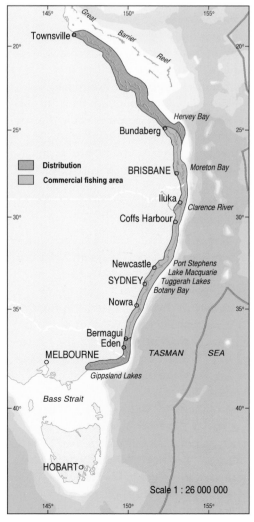

Geographic distribution and commercial fishing areas for yellowfin bream.

Yellowfin bream are most abundant in estuaries but also inhabit inshore reefs and waters adjacent to ocean beaches and rocky headlands. They live in rivers upstream to the limit of brackish waters but rarely enter fresh waters. Yellowfin bream are demersal fish and associate with a variety of substrates from sand and mud to rocky sections of river bed. Black bream are usually restricted to estuarine habitats and only leave them during periods of flooding. They can withstand a wide range of salinities and sometimes move into freshwater reaches of rivers.[2] Black bream are also demersal and tend to inhabit areas where rocky river beds, snags or structures such as jetties provide cover,[2] although they are caught in deeper open waters over sand or mud substrates in the Gippsland Lakes.[3]

Life history

Yellowfin bream spawn mainly during winter[4,5,6] but there can be considerable variation in spawning season between estuaries and between years. Spawning may commence as early as late autumn in southern and central New South Wales.[6] It takes place in the vicinity of river entrances — either over river bars or in the surf zone.[4,7] Adult yellowfin bream migrate from their feeding grounds to the spawning site. All mature male fish

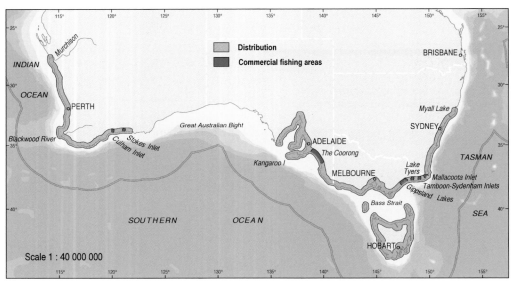

Geographic distribution and commercial fishing areas for black bream.

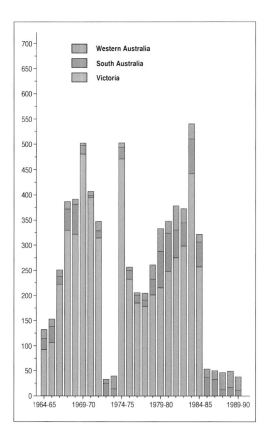

Total annual catch in t of black bream for the period 1964–65 to 1989–90. Figures are unavailable for Victoria from 1972–73 to 1973–74 and 1985–86 to 1989–90. Catches for States that average less than 5 % of the total for all States are not shown. (Source: Fisheries Resources Atlas Statistical Database)

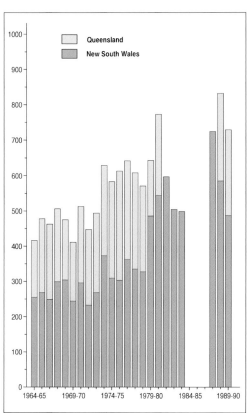

Total annual catch in t of yellowfin bream for the period 1964–65 to 1989–90. Figures are unavailable for: New South Wales from 1984–85 to 1986–87; and Queensland from 1981–82 to 1987–88. The Queensland catch figures include a small proportion of tarwhine (*Rhabdosargus sarba*) and pikey bream (*Acanthopagrus berda*). (Source: Fisheries Resources Atlas Statistical Database)

undertake the spawning migration but the proportion of mature females migrating to spawn increases as they age.[8] There are no estimates of fecundity for yellowfin bream but they probably produce similar numbers of eggs to black bream. Yellowfin bream eggs are planktonic and hatch after about 2.5 days into planktonic larvae. After 1 month the postlarvae enter estuaries on the flood tide[9] and settle out

of the plankton when they are about 13 mm total length.[9] Postlarvae and juveniles of yellowfin bream mainly inhabit seagrass beds in shallow estuarine areas.[4]

Black bream show considerable variation in spawning time between different estuaries.[2] In eastern Victoria the spawning season may begin as early as August but spawning occurs progressively later in more westerly

estuaries.[10] In the Gippsland Lakes black bream usually spawn from October to early December.[3] Black bream in South Australia usually spawn from November to January.[11] In Western Australia, spawning may start as early as mid-July and extend to November. Spawning occurs in the upper estuary near the interface between fresh and brackish waters. The optimum salinity range for spawning is reported to be 11–18 parts per thousand.[10] Female black bream release between 300 000 and 3 million eggs during the spawning season.[10,12] The eggs are small and pelagic, hatching approximately 2 days after fertilisation.[10] Black bream larvae and small juveniles are most abundant over seagrass beds in shallow estuarine waters.[2,13]

Growth in yellowfin bream is rapid prior to maturity. In Tuggerah Lakes, New South Wales, juveniles reach 13 cm fork length at an age of 1 year, 18 cm at 2 years and 23 cm at 3 years.[14] A more rapid growth rate is indicated in Moreton Bay (Queensland) where water temperatures are higher.[5] In Botany Bay, New South Wales, male fish reach maturity from 3 years of age and females from 4 years of age and a size of approximately 24 cm fork length.[6] A proportion of the population change sex from male to female after their first spawning season. Other fish remain functional males throughout their life and another small proportion develop directly into females at the age of 4 years.[4,8] The oldest and largest yellowfin bream are females that may reach at least 12 years of age and 39 cm fork length. Males have been aged at 10 years and a size of 30 cm fork length.[14]

The growth rate of black bream varies depending on locality. In South Australian estuaries black bream are about 10 cm fork length at an age of 1 year, 17 cm at 2 years and 23 cm fork length at 3 years.[15] In South Australia and Western Australia maturity is reached between 2 and 3 years of age.[2,12] Black bream grow more slowly in Victorian estuaries, reaching fork lengths of 6 cm, 11.5 cm and 16 cm after each of the first 3 years and maturity after 5 years.[3,10] Male black bream tend to reach maturity slightly earlier than females.[15] It is not known whether there is any sex inversion in black bream. Female black bream appear to grow to a larger size than males, their age estimates from scale growth rings ranging up to 17 years.[3] Black bream are reported to reach

Hauling a haul seine net, Tuggerah Lakes. (Source: Gary Henry, Environment Protection Authority, New South Wales)

a maximum size of 60 cm total length and 4 kg.[10]

Yellowfin bream consume a wide variety of prey species including small crabs, prawns (Penaeidae), molluscs such as oysters (Ostreidae) and pipis (*Plebidonax* species), and small fish. Black bream are also opportunistic feeders, consuming a range of plant and animal species. Their diet includes bivalve and gastropod molluscs, prawns and crabs, polychaete worms and small fish.[2]

Stock structure

The stock structure of yellowfin bream and black bream is uncertain. It has been proposed that both species consist of separate stocks for each estuary.[7] This theory is more plausible for black bream, where little movement of fish between estuaries occurs. However, recent tagging of yellowfin bream in northern New South Wales by NSW Fisheries has confirmed that some fish migrate considerable distances. These results indicate that a single stock of yellowfin bream exists.

Commercial fishery

The yellowfin bream fishery extends from Bundaberg in Queensland to Bermagui on the south coast of New South Wales. Most of the catch is taken from estuarine waters. The most important estuaries in New South Wales are Clarence River, Port Stephens, Lake Macquarie, Tuggerah Lakes and Botany Bay. In Queensland almost half of the yellowfin bream catch is taken from Moreton Bay.[16] Yellowfin bream are caught throughout the year but catches are greatest during autumn and winter.

Tunnel nets are the main gear used to catch yellowfin bream in Queensland, and some catch is taken with gillnets. In New South Wales gillnets and haul seines are the most common gear used.[10] Traps are employed in the lower regions of some estuaries and beach seines are sometimes used from ocean beaches. Fishing in estuaries is normally carried out at night.[10] Small quantities of yellowfin bream sometimes form a bycatch of inshore trawling and trapping.

Most of the commercial catch of black bream is taken from Victorian waters. Within Victoria, the Gippsland Lakes fishery is by far the most important, accounting for more than 80 % of the State catch. Black bream have been fished commercially there since the 1880s, and were the major species in the commercial catch prior to about 1920, when catches declined to less than 50 t per year from the previous level of about 250 t per year. Yellow-eye mullet (*Aldrichetta forsteri*) dominated the Gippsland Lakes fishery for the next 4 decades until black bream landings recovered in the mid 1960s. Catches since then have ranged between 200 t and 400 t per year. Other Victorian estuaries which produce significant commercial catches are Mallacoota Inlet, Tamboon Inlet and Lake Tyers in eastern Victoria.

In South Australia, most of the commercial catch of black bream is taken from the Coorong.[11] The size of the Coorong catch has varied between 10 t and 70 t annually over the last 25 years. The commercial catch of black bream in Western Australia is not large, ranging between 15 t and 30 t in most years. Small amounts are landed from most of the southern and south-western estuaries but Culham Inlet and Stokes Inlet account for most of the commercial catch.

The main commercial fishing methods used for black bream in Victoria and South Australia are gillnets and haul seines. In Western Australia almost all the commercial catch is taken with gillnets.

Both yellowfin bream and black bream are sold exclusively on domestic fresh fish markets. They are normally sold as whole chilled product. In 1991–92 the average wholesale price for yellowfin bream at the Sydney Fish Market was A$ 5.55 per kg. Monthly average prices for black bream at the Melbourne Wholesale Fish Market ranged between A$ 4.65 and A$ 6.16 per kg in 1991–92.

Management controls The commercial fisheries for yellowfin bream and black bream are managed by the respective State governments. Most States impose limited entry licensing for estuarine fisheries, and gear regulations, closed areas and closed seasons apply in many estuaries. Minimum legal size limits apply to bream species in all States.

Recreational fishery

Yellowfin bream are one of the most popular angling species in estuaries and from ocean beaches and headlands in southern Queensland and New South Wales. The recreational catch of yellowfin bream by southern Queensland anglers exceeds the commercial catch for that State.[17] Surveys in northern New South Wales rivers by NSW Fisheries have also shown higher catches by recreational fishers.

Black bream are one of the top angling species in Victoria, Tasmania, South Australia and Western Australia. They are the main target species in estuaries such as the Gippsland Lakes and Mallacoota Inlet,[18,19] and the Blackwood River in Western Australia.[20] The recreational catch of black bream in the Gippsland Lakes and Mallacoota Inlet is approximately equal to the commercial catch from those areas.[18,19]

Both yellowfin bream and black bream are caught mainly with baited rod-and-line or handline. Live yabbies (*Callianassa australiensis*), beachworms (Onuphidae), crabs and fresh baits of prawns, pipis, fish flesh or whole small fish are used to catch yellowfin bream. The most popular baits for black bream are prawns, bloodworms and sandworms (Nereidae), crabs, 'mullet gut' and sandy sprat or 'whitebait' (*Hyperlophus vittatus*).[18,19]

The Australian Anglers Association record for yellowfin bream is 4.5 kg for a fish caught in New South Wales in 1984. The largest black bream recorded by the Association is 3.5 kg from South Australia in 1969.

Management controls Minimum legal size limits apply to yellowfin bream and black bream in all States where they are caught. Daily bag limits apply to yellowfin bream and black bream in New South Wales and to black bream in Western Australia. A bag limit also applies in Sydenham Inlet in eastern Victoria. Regulations on numbers of lines and hooks used vary between States.

Resource status

The New South Wales and Queensland yellowfin bream stocks are probably fully exploited, yet population levels appear to be stable. The black bream population in the Gippsland Lakes also is probably fully exploited but nothing is known about the status of other black bream populations. Environmental and habitat changes in southern Australian estuaries as well as increased fishing effort by recreational anglers are likely to have an important influence on future population levels of both bream species.

References

1. Rowland, S.J. (1984). Hybridisation between estuarine fishes yellowfin bream, *Acanthopagrus australis* (Günther) and black bream, *A. butcheri* (Munro) (Pisces: Sparidae). *Australian Journal of Marine and Freshwater Research* **35**: 427-440.

2. Black bream (1991) *Fisheries Department of Western Australia, Fishing WA* **12**. 4 pp.

3. Hobday, D. and Moran, M. (1983) Age, growth and fluctuating year-class strength of black bream in the Gippsland Lakes, Victoria. *Victorian Ministry for Conservation, Marine Science Laboratories Internal Report* **20**. 19 pp.

4. Dredge, M.C.L. (1976) *Aspects of the ecology of three estuarine dwelling fish in south east Queensland*. Unpublished MSc thesis, University of Queensland. 122 pp.

5. Pollock, B.R. (1982) Spawning period and growth of yellowfin bream, *Acanthopagrus australis* (Günther), in Moreton Bay, Australia. *Journal of Fish Biology* **21**: 349-355.

6. State Pollution Control Commission (1981) *The ecology of fish in Botany Bay — biology of commercially and recreationally valuable species. Environmental control study of Botany Bay*. Sydney. 287 pp.

7. Munro, I.S.R. (1944) *The economic biology of the Australian black bream (*Roughleyia australis *(Günther))*. Unpublished MSc thesis, University of Queensland. 151 pp.

8. Pollock, B.R. (1984) Relations between migration, reproduction and nutrition in yellowfin bream *Acanthopagrus australis*. *Marine Ecology in Progress Series* **19**: 17-23.

9. Pollock, B.R., Weng, H. and Morton, R.M. (1983) The seasonal occurrence of postlarval stages of yellowfin bream, *Acanthopagrus australis* (Günther), and some factors affecting their movement into an estuary. *Journal of Fish Biology* **22**: 409-415.

10. Cadwallader, P.L. and Backhouse, G.N. (1983) *A guide to the freshwater fish of Victoria*. Melbourne: Victorian Government Printing Office. 249 pp.

11. Hall, D.N. (1984) The Coorong: biology of the major fish species and fluctuations in catch rates 1976-1983. *SAFIC* **8**(1): 3-17.

12. Harbison, I.P. (1973) *The black bream in the Onkaparinga estuary. A study of the age structure, spawning cycle and feeding relationships of* Acanthopagrus butcheri *(Munro) in the Onkaparinga estuary, South Australia, during the months May-December 1973*. Unpublished research paper, Salisbury College of Advanced Education. 105 pp.

13. Ramm, D.C. (1986) *An ecological study of the ichthyoplankton and juvenile fish in the Gippsland Lakes, Victoria*. Unpublished PhD thesis, University of Melbourne. 161 pp.

14. Henry, G.W. (1983) *Biology and fisheries of yellowfin bream* Acanthopagrus australis *(Teleostei: Sparidae) in Tuggerah Lakes, New South Wales*. Unpublished MSc thesis, University of New South Wales. 139 pp.

15. Weng, H.T. (1971) *The black bream,* Acanthopagrus butcheri *(Munro); its life history and its fishery in South Australia*. Unpublished MSc thesis, University of Adelaide. 90 pp

16. Queensland Fish Management Authority (1991) *Directions for change. Proceedings of the ocean beach net fishery seminar, Brisbane, 19-20 September, 1991*. Ed by A. Magee. Brisbane. 33 pp.

17. Pollock, B.R. (1980). Surprises in Queensland angling study. *Australian Fisheries* **39**(4): 17-19.

18. Hall, D.N. and MacDonald, C.M. (1985) A survey of recreational fishing in the Gippsland Lakes, Victoria. *Victorian Department of Conservation, Forests and Lands, Fisheries and Wildlife Service, Marine Fisheries Report* **3**. 25 pp.

19. Hall, D.N., MacDonald, C.M. and Kearney, J.D. (1985) A survey of recreational fishing in Mallacoota Inlet, Victoria. *Victorian Department of Conservation, Forests and Lands, Fisheries and Wildlife Service, Marine Fisheries Report* **5**. 21 pp.

20. Caputi, N. (1976). Creel census of amateur line fishermen in the Blackwood River estuary, Western Australia, during 1974-75. *Australian Journal of Marine and Freshwater Research* **27**: 583-593.

Contributors

Information on yellowfin bream was provided by Gary Henry and Ron West. Information on black bream was provided by (in alphabetical order) Mark Cliff, Keith Jones, Rod Lenanton, Murray MacDonald, Gina Newton and Dave Ramm. Drawing of yellowfin bream by Gavin Ryan, and of black bream by Roger Swainston. (*Details of contributors and their organisations are given in the Acknowledgements section at the back of this book.*)
Compilers Phillip Stewart and Christina Grieve (maps)

Recreational fisher with yellowfin bream catch. (Gary Henry, Environment Protection Authority, New South Wales)

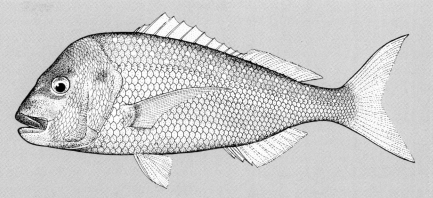

Snapper

Pagrus auratus

Pagrus auratus (Forster, in Bloch and Schneider)

Snapper

Other common names include **cockney bream** (small juveniles), **red bream**, **squire**, **old man snapper** and **pink snapper**.
FAO: **golden snapper**
Australian species code: 353001

Family SPARIDAE

Diagnostic features Snapper have a moderately compressed body and in adults, the dorsal profile is strongly arched anteriorly. Large individuals often have a prominent hump on the top of their head and a bulge on their snout. Snapper have low molar-like teeth at the sides of their mouth. They have 9–10 scale rows above the lateral line and 8–10 soft rays in the dorsal fin. Individuals vary in colour from red to golden pink to light grey on their back and sides, which have numerous small blue spots. The fins are reddish or pink.[1,2]

Distribution

Snapper have a continuous distribution around the southern coastline of mainland Australia. They inhabit waters from Hinchinbrook Island in Queensland to Barrow Island in Western Australia. They are occasionally found off the north coast of Tasmania, but no further south.[3] Abundance does not appear to be uniform throughout the species' range.[3] Snapper are also widely distributed in the Indo–Pacific region, from Japan and the Philippines to India and Indonesia and off New Zealand.[1]

Snapper are confined to warm temperate and subtropical waters.[3] Juveniles mainly inhabit inlets, bays and other shallow, sheltered marine waters, often over mud and seagrass. Adults often live near reefs, but are also found over mud and sand substrates. Adult snapper inhabit depths from less than 1 m to 200 m.[3]

Life history

Snapper are serial spawners, ie they spawn repeatedly during the breeding season.[4] Mature adults form large schools in preferred spawning areas.[3] Spawning generally occurs in waters less than 50 m deep[3] although on occasions schooling does take place at the surface. Generally, snapper do not spawn until the surface water temperature is around 18°C, yet snapper in Shark Bay spawn at water temperatures of about 21°C. Snapper populations in southern Australia spawn between late October and early March,[5] and the exact timing varies between different areas. Snapper in the north (eg Moreton Bay, Shark Bay) have a winter spawning period extending from late May or early June to August.

Little is known of the early life history of snapper in Australian waters, but it is thought that the fertilised eggs are buoyant and drift with the prevailing currents for a few days before hatching.

Juvenile snapper leave the midwater zone to inhabit reefs or rocky outcrops when they are 12 months of age and about 6 cm long. In New South Wales, Victoria and South Australia, the older juveniles and young adults progressively move to coastal and offshore waters and some individuals also migrate substantial distances along the coastline. Tagging studies in Victoria showed that snapper move considerable distances, eg from Port Phillip Bay to Kingston (South Australia) and from Mallacoota to southern Queensland.[6] In South Australia,

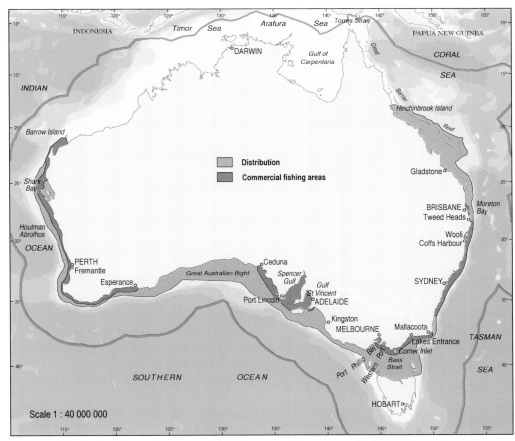

Geographic distribution and commercial fishing areas for snapper in Australian waters.

snapper move from the northern waters of the gulfs to Investigator Strait and offshore islands at the mouth of Spencer Gulf. In Western Australia, snapper from the inner areas of Shark Bay do not leave their 'home' area. However, snapper in the oceanic stock around the mouth of Shark Bay may move further away, some up to 200 nautical miles south — almost to the Houtman Abrolhos.

Snapper are long-lived and slow-growing fish which exhibit variable growth rates across their distribution. Differences in snapper growth rates are probably related to habitat type.[7] They reportedly live up to 35 years; 22-year-old fish are common in the South Australian fishery. Fish of up to 1.3 m in total length and weighing up to 16 kg have been recorded.[2] Age at first maturity also varies throughout their distribution. Snapper from New South Wales are, on average, 3 years old and 30 cm fork length at first maturity. Snapper in Port Phillip Bay first breed when they are about 4 years old and 27 cm total length,[3] while those from South Australian waters are about 28 cm total length at first maturity. In New Zealand, some juvenile snapper change sex from female to male but all such changes are completed by the onset of maturity.[8] There have been no investigations of sex reversals in Australian snapper populations.

Snapper in Victorian waters feed on crustaceans, bivalve molluscs and small fish.[9] Juveniles and small adults in South Australia feed on western king prawns (*Penaeus latisulcatus*), while larger fish feed on thick shelled animals such as blue swimmer crabs (*Portunus pelagicus*) and mussels (Mytilidae).[10] Whaler sharks (eg *Carcharhinus obscurus*) are known to accompany spawning aggregations of snapper, but their significance as a predator is unknown.

Stock structure

Tagging and genetic studies[3,7] have indicated the presence of several stocks or breeding populations of snapper in Australian waters. There is considerable overlap in the distributions of these populations.

Commercial fishery

Snapper are fished commercially throughout their range. In Queensland,

large numbers of juveniles are sometimes caught by demersal otter trawlers near reefs in Moreton Bay.[11] In New South Wales, the main fishery is on the north coast around Coffs Harbour and Wooli.[12] In Victoria, the main fishery is in Port Phillip Bay (80–90 % of the State's total catch), although small commercial catches are also taken from other bays and inlets and from open coastal waters.[13] In South Australia, commercial fishing effort is concentrated in Spencer Gulf and Gulf St Vincent. In Western Australia, snapper are fished from Esperance to Barrow Island but the major fishery targets stocks near Shark Bay. The Western Australian fishery is distinctly seasonal. In the north, 75 % of the catch is taken in winter (June and July), while in southern areas, summer is the peak fishing season.

In New South Wales, 70 % of the snapper catch is harvested by trap fishers and the rest by fishers using bottom set longlines and handlines. In Victoria over 80 % of the catch is taken on longlines, while in South Australia, snapper are caught using (in order of catch quantities) handlines, bottom set longlines, hauling nets, power hauling and large mesh gillnets. Most of the Western Australian catch is taken on handlines, although traps and droplines are also used. Large quantities of juveniles are often caught in prawn trawl nets in estuaries, although this is an incidental catch.

The design of snapper traps differs between States. Traps used in the New South Wales fishery tend to catch large numbers of smaller fish of 25–30 cm fork length. Fish taken on longlines and handlines vary in size. Line-caught fish are preferred for the fresh fish markets, particularly for export, as they are generally in better condition. Since 1988 considerable quantities of snapper caught in the Shark Bay fishery have been exported to Japan as whole chilled fish.

Most of the Australian snapper catch is sold on the domestic market, particularly in Sydney where large quantities are freighted from interstate and some imported from New Zealand. Snapper are usually sold as fresh whole or gilled and gutted fish. In 1991–92, snapper prices at the Sydney Fish Market averaged A\$ 7.76 per kg. Wholesale prices per kg in other State capitals in 1991–92 were: Melbourne, A\$ 5.00–7.50, Adelaide A\$ 7.00–11.00; and Perth, A\$ 3.50–5.80.

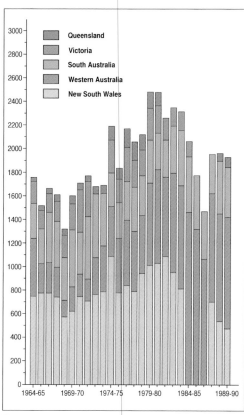

Total annual catch in t of snapper for the period 1964–65 to 1989–90. Figures are unavailable for: New South Wales from 1984–85 to 1986–87; Victoria from 1972–73 to 1973–74 and 1985–86 to 1989–90; and Queensland from 1981–82 to 1987–88. Catches for States that average less than 5 % of the total for all States are not shown. (Source: Fisheries Resources Atlas Statistical Database)

Management controls Snapper fisheries in Victoria, South Australia and at Shark Bay in Western Australia are limited entry fisheries and there are minimum sizes on the fish that can be retained. The New South Wales snapper fishery is managed by the State Government, and a minimum size applies. In Victoria snapper fishing is managed as part of the limited entry bay and inlet fishery, while the South Australian snapper fishery is managed as part of the Marine Scale Fishery. In Western Australia individual transferable quotas are applied to licence holders who fish the peak season

Commercial snapper fisher returning to port, Coffs Harbour. (Source: Gary Henry, Environment Protection Authority, New South Wales)

between May and August. South Australian net fishers are restricted by quota. The number of hooks on longlines are restricted in Victoria and South Australia. In Port Phillip Bay, snapper may not be caught with gillnets.

Recreational fishery

Snapper are an important recreational species, highly prized for both sport and eating.[3,14] In New South Wales anglers fish both in estuaries and offshore, while in Victoria most recreational fishing effort takes place in Port Phillip and Western Port bays. In South Australia most effort is concentrated on the inshore waters of Spencer Gulf and Gulf St Vincent, particularly around artificial reefs in their central and northern areas. In Western Australia the major areas fished are the inshore waters of Shark Bay and coastal waters in the south of the State.

Most of the recreational snapper catch is taken by handline or rod-and-line using pilchards (*Sardinops neopilchardus*) for bait. Snapper are caught by both shore and boat-based anglers. The largest snapper recorded by the Australian Anglers Association was a 16.2 kg fish caught in Western Australia in 1988.

The sizes of recreational catches of snapper are probably considerable. The angler catch of snapper for Coffs Harbour is probably equivalent to 25 % of the commercial catch in that area.[12] In Victoria the recreational catch of snapper in Port Phillip Bay in 1982–83 was conservatively estimated at 112 t or 44 % of the total catch from the Bay,[14] and in 1983, Western Australian anglers caught an estimated 10 % of the State's snapper catch from the Shark Bay region.

Management controls Minimum legal sizes for snapper are set in all States where snapper are fished. Bag limits also apply in New South Wales, South Australia and Western Australia.

Resource status

Commercial catch rates of snapper in New South Wales and Victoria have fallen in recent years while fishing effort has increased. It is not known whether this decline is due to natural population fluctuations, excessive fishing pressure or environmental degradation. The decline in the number of large fish in northern Spencer Gulf is due to excessive fishing effort.[15] In Western Australia, there has been a reduction in the average size of fish caught in the trap and line fisheries.

Notes

There has been preliminary work in New South Wales and South Australia on the possibility of culturing snapper.

References

1. Paulin, C.D. (1990) *Pagrus auratus*, a new combination for the species known as "snapper" in Australasian waters (Pisces: Sparidae). *New Zealand Journal of Marine and Freshwater Research* **24**: 259–265.

2. Hutchins, B. and Swainston, R. (1986) *Sea fishes of southern Australia. Complete field guide for anglers and divers.* Perth: Swainston Publishing. 180 pp.

3. MacDonald, C.M. (1982) Life history characteristics of snapper *Chrysophrys auratus* (Bloch and Schneider, 1801) in Australian waters. *Victorian Department of Conservation, Forests and Lands, Fisheries and Wildlife Division, Fisheries and Wildlife Paper* **29**. 16 pp.

4. Crossland, J. (1977) Seasonal reproductive cycle of snapper *Chrysophrys auratus* (Forster) in the Hauraki Gulf, New Zealand. *New Zealand Journal of Marine and Freshwater Research* **11**: 37–60.

5. Lenanton, R.C.J. (1974) The abundance and size composition of trawled juvenile snapper, *Chrysophrys unicolor* (Quoy and Gaimard) from Cockburn Sound, Western Australia. *Australian Journal of Marine and Freshwater Research* **25**: 281–285.

6. Sanders, M.J. (1974) Tagging indicates at least two stocks of snapper *Chrysophrys auratus* in south-east Australian waters. *New Zealand Journal of Marine and Freshwater Research* **8**: 371–374.

7. Francis, R.I.C.C. and Winstanley, R.H. (1989) Difference in growth rates between habitats of south-east Australian snapper (*Chrysophrys auratus*). *Australian Journal of Marine and Freshwater Research* **40**: 703–710.

8. Francis, M.P. and Pankhurst, N.W. (1988) Juvenile sex inversion in the New Zealand snapper *Chrysophrys auratus* (Bloch and Schneider, 1801) (Sparidae). *Australian Journal of Marine and Freshwater Research* **39**: 625–631.

9. Winstanley, R.H. (1983) The food of snapper *Chrysophrys auratus* in Port Phillip Bay, Victoria. *Victorian Department of Conservation, Forests and Lands, Fisheries and Wildlife Service, Commercial Fisheries Report* **10**. 14 pp.

10. Jones, K. (1981) Biological research on snapper (*Chrysophrys auratus* syn. *unicolor*) and an analysis of the fishery in northern Spencer Gulf. *SAFIC* **5**(6): 5–8.

11. Maclean, J.L. (1973) An analysis of the catch of trawlers in Moreton Bay (Qld) during the 1966–67 prawning season. *Proceedings of the Linnean Society of New South Wales* **98**(1): 35–42.

12. Henry, G. (1988) Snapper. *NSW Agriculture & Fisheries. Agfact* **F1.0.3**. 6 pp.

13. Hall, D.N. and MacDonald, C.M. (1986) Commercial fishery situation report: net and line fisheries of Port Phillip Bay Victoria, 1914–1984. *Victorian Department of Conservation, Forests and Lands, Fisheries Division, Marine Fisheries Report* **10**. 121 pp.

14. MacDonald, C.M. and Hall, D.N. (1987) A survey of recreational fishing in Port Phillip Bay, Victoria. *Victorian Department of Conservation, Forests and Lands, Fisheries Division, Marine Fisheries Report* **11**. 40 pp.

15. Jones, G.K. (1987) A review of the commercial fishery for snapper (*Chrysophrys auratus*) in South Australian waters (1983–1986). *South Australian Department of Fisheries. A discussion paper, no. 2.* 20 pp.

Contributors

The information on this species was originally provided by Keith Jones and supplemented by (in alphabetical order) Mike Cappo, Gary Henry, Murray MacDonald and Mike Moran. Drawing by Roger Swainston. (*Details of contributors and their organisations are given in the Acknowledgements section at the back of this book.*)
Compilers Alex McNee, Kay Abel and Christina Grieve (maps)

Anglers with a good snapper catch, Coffs Harbour. (Source: Gary Henry, Environment Protection Authority, New South Wales)

Mulloway

Argyrosomus hololepidotus

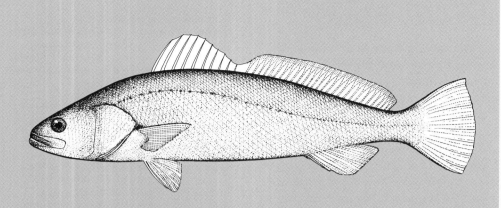

Argyrosomus hololepidotus
(Lacepède)

Mulloway

Other common names include **jewfish, silver jewfish, school jew, river kingfish** and **butterfish**. Small mulloway are often called **soapies**.
FAO: **mulloway, southern meagre**
Australian species code: 354001

Family SCIAENIDAE

Diagnostic features Mulloway are silvery blue or grey, and sometimes they have a large black blotch at the upper part of the pectoral fin base. The fins are grey or brown. The dorsal fin is long and notched after the spined section. Their mouth is terminal and there are 6 distinct pores on the chin. The caudal fin margin is generally rounded or sigmoid('}') shaped.

Distribution

Mulloway inhabit central and southern, mainland Australian waters from Bundaberg and the Burnett River in Queensland to North West Cape in Western Australia. Although these fish are common in western Victoria, they are much less abundant between Melbourne and southern New South Wales and have rarely been reported from Bass Strait. Mulloway are also found around southern Africa and Madagascar.[1]

These fish live in coastal environments, including the lower reaches of rivers, estuaries, rocky reefs, ocean beaches and embayments and the continental shelf out to 150 m.[2,3] Adults are generally found close to the estuary floor or around shallow coastal reefs or rocky shores. Mulloway are more prevalent in and around the mouths of larger rivers and embayments — eg the Coorong–Murray River mouth in South Australia — especially after periods of high summer rainfall ('freshes'). Juveniles, at least, have a wide salinity tolerance.[3]

Life history

In South Australia, spawning mulloway shoal in coastal marine waters adjacent to

the surf zone between late October and February.[4] In south-eastern Australia, the time of spawning is not known,[3] but is probably spring–summer. There is no information on the number of eggs produced. Larvae have not been identified, but it is believed that they develop at sea for several months before moving into the estuaries when about 10 cm long.[4] In many New South Wales rivers, mulloway less than 5 cm long have been found within the main river channel. Juveniles 1–2 years old are most abundant

in New South Wales estuaries from February to September[3] and young adult 'school jew' are common in lower rivers and embayments in September and October.

These fish are solitary or, particularly as juveniles, form loose schools. Movement between estuaries several hundred km apart has been recorded. For example, in New South Wales, tagging studies have shown that mulloway move hundreds of km both north and south from big rivers such as the Clarence and Richmond. In South Australian waters, the fish leave the Coorong during autumn and return to the adjacent coastal beaches in the following summer.[4]

Juvenile mulloway grow rapidly, especially from January to March.[3] Young mulloway in northern New South Wales can increase their length by an average of 2 cm each month.[5] Weight also increases rapidly.[3] In South Australian waters, fish 2–3 years old average 46 cm in total length and 1.5 kg in weight; for 5 to 6-year-old fish the corresponding sizes are 80 cm and 8 kg. Mulloway can live for

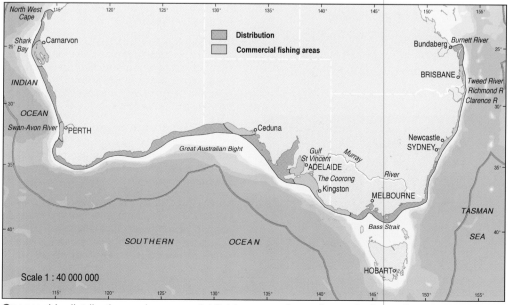

Geographic distribution and commercial fishing areas for mulloway in Australian waters.

30 years[4] or more and may grow to 2 m in length. The largest mulloway recorded in Australia weighed 43 kg, although fish up to 71 kg have been caught in South Africa.[1] Mulloway mature at about 6 years of age and when about 75 cm long.[4]

The feeding habits of these fish have been studied only in Coorong waters. There, mulloway feed throughout the water column. Adults eat a variety of fish including yellow-eye mullet (*Aldrichetta forsteri*), leatherjackets (Monacanthidae), garfish (*Hyporhamphus* species), blue mackerel (*Scomber australasicus*), bony bream (*Nematalosa erebi*), tommy ruff (*Arripis georgianus*), pilchards (*Sardinops neopilchardus*) and yellowtail (*Trachurus novaezelandiae*). They also consume sand crabs (*Ovalipes* species), prawns (Penaeidae), and worms.[4] In New South Wales, school jew are known to eat prawns and adult mulloway commonly feed on sea mullet (*Mugil cephalus*).

Adult mulloway also feed on juvenile mulloway.[4]

Stock structure

Preliminary stock identification studies, using electrophoresis on small samples from few localities, indicate the existence of 2 subpopulations of mulloway around Australia: one in Western Australia from about Carnarvon to Mandurah, south of Perth, the other from South Australia to New South Wales. There are also genetic differences between Western Australian, Great Australian Bight, the Coorong and New South Wales samples, suggesting the possibility of further population substructuring.[6] However, studies of mitochondrial DNA have so far hinted at a single interbreeding population of mulloway stretching from Sydney around the east coast to at least the south-west coast of South Australia.[7]

Commercial fishery

Mulloway are caught commercially throughout their range. They are generally caught near river mouths (eg, during floods) and in estuaries, although a reasonable number — mostly of spawning or spent adults — are caught off surf beaches. Some mulloway are taken as bycatch (in both coastal and more offshore waters) of the gillnet fisheries for mullet and sharks in Western Australia and South Australia, and of the

Small catch of mulloway on the Coorong, South Australia. (Source: South Australian Department of Fisheries)

demersal otter trawl fishery for prawns in New South Wales.

In South Australia the main fishery is in the Coorong, with lesser activity in south-east, Gulf St Vincent and west coast waters. In Victoria, the fishery is concentrated on the west coast, although there are incidental catches in most bays and estuaries. In New South Wales, mulloway are fished along the entire coast, although the largest catches are taken between Port Jackson (Sydney) and the Tweed River. Smaller, mostly offshore fisheries exist south of Sydney, in southern Queensland and in the Swan–Avon River estuary (near Perth) and Shark Bay in Western Australia.

Most mulloway are caught in bottom set gillnets and haul nets although larger fish are generally caught using swinger nets, beach seines and handlines or rod-and-reel with live or dead bait.

The year-round South Australian fishery is based on 3–6-year-old fish. Higher catches are generally taken from December to March in the Coorong with peaks in catch rates following peaks in the flow of the Murray River water through the 'barrages' (weirs or locks) 2 or 3 years earlier.[2,8] There is some evidence from the Coorong that freshwater inflow has an influence on the recruitment of juvenile fish. The Coorong fishery has declined over recent years,[8] and the fishing effort now switches between the marine Coorong area and the associated lakes Alexandrina and Albert, depending on the abundance of fish and the relative price of freshwater and marine fish. Approximately 20 % of

the mulloway catch is taken by shark fishers outside the Coorong.

The southern Queensland, New South Wales and Western Australian fisheries target adult fish, although significant quantities of juveniles (less than 38 cm long) are caught incidentally in estuaries by gillnetting and by trawlers.

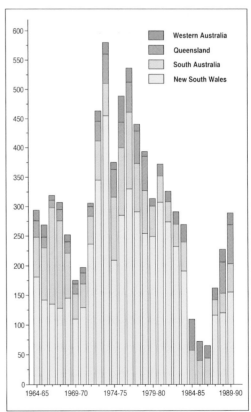

Total annual catch in t of mulloway for the period 1964–65 to 1989–90. Figures are unavailable for: New South Wales from 1984–85 to 1986–87; and Queensland from 1979–80 to 1987–88. Catches for States that average less than 5 % of the total for all States are not shown. The Queensland catch of 'mulloway' may include other jewfish species. (Source: Fisheries Resources Atlas Statistical Database)

Large mulloway caught off the beach on the Coorong, South Australia. (Source: South Australian Department of Fisheries)

In all southern mainland States, mulloway are sold on local markets as fresh, gutted fish. In 1991-92, the average wholesale price for 'jewfish' at the Sydney Fish Market was A$ 5.85, and the average monthly prices at the Melbourne Wholesale Fish Market ranged from A$ 4.07 to A$ 6.90 per kg.

Management controls Some States limit the number of licences issued. There are also local restrictions on the type and frequency of netting in, or access to, different estuaries or regions (such as the Coorong). Minimum legal fish sizes vary from State to State although there is no minimum size in Victoria. There is a total catch limit on mulloway from the South Australian shark fishery.

Recreational fishery

Mulloway are popular recreational fish along the entire Victorian coast, and are caught off beaches, around inshore reefs and river mouths. Catches near rivers escalate following 'freshes'. The fish are caught on handlines, rod-and-line, and with spears by snorkellers and occasionally with gillnets. Although large adults are sought by anglers, many of the fish caught are 'soapies' of less than 2.5 kg weight. The largest mulloway taken by a recreational angler was 43 kg from South Australia (Australian Anglers Association record).

Information from tag returns suggests that the recreational catch in South Australia may be up to one third of the commercial catch there; and mulloway is one of the most commonly caught species in Sydney Harbour, where 9 t were reported taken in 1980–81.[9] The recreational catch from offshore anglers in New South Wales waters is on average higher than the catch by commercial fishers, whereas the inshore recreational catch is comparable with, or less than, the commercial catch.

Management controls Bag and minimum legal size limits are imposed in New South Wales, South Australia and Western Australia. Restrictions on gear apply in some States.

Resource status

The status of the stocks is unknown in Queensland, Victoria and Western Australia. In New South Wales, where large numbers of small mulloway are taken by trawlers, decline in the commercial catch of mulloway in recent years is causing concern. The reduction in flow from the Murray River has affected the spawning potential of mulloway in South Australia, with some evidence of a decline in catches.[10]

References

1. Trewavas, E. (1977) The sciaenid fishes (croakers and drums) of the Indo-West Pacific. *Transactions of the Zoological Society, London* **33**(4): 253–541.

2. Lake, J.S. (1971) *Freshwater fishes and rivers of Australia*. Sydney: Thomas Nelson Australia Ltd. 61 pp.

3. Gray, C.A. and McDonall, V.C. (in press, 1992) Distribution of juvenile mulloway, *Argyrosomus hololepidotus* (Pisces: Sciaenidae), in the Hawkesbury River, south-eastern Australia. *Australian Journal of Marine and Freshwater Research* **44**(2).

4. Hall, D.A. (1986) An assessment of the mulloway (*Argyrosomus hololepidotus*) fishery in South Australia with particular reference to the Coorong Lagoon. *South Australian Department of Fisheries. A discussion paper.* 41 pp.

5. West, R.J. (1991) *Habitat use, growth and movement of estuarine fish in northern NSW.* Abstract, Australian Society for Fish Biology annual conference, Hobart, 20-25 August, 1991.

6. Dixon, P.I. (1988–90) Stock identification and discrimination of mulloway in Australian waters. *FIRTA Grant 86/16, Progress Reports.* Sydney: Centre for Marine Science, University of New South Wales.

7. Dixon, P.I. (1990) *Identification and discrimination of mulloway in Australian waters based on mitochondrial DNA sequence data.* Sydney: Centre for Marine Science, University of New South Wales. 38 pp.

8. Hall, D.A. (1984) The Coorong: biology of the major fish species and fluctuations in catch rates 1976–1984. *SAFIC* **8**(1): 3–17.

9. Henry, G.W. (1984) Commercial and recreational fishing in Sydney estuary. *Department of Agriculture, New South Wales, Fisheries Bulletin* **1**. 47 pp.

10. New restrictions for mulloway fishery (1988). *Australian Fisheries* **47**(8): 9–10.

Contributors

Information on this species was originally provided by Keith Jones and supplemented by (in alphabetical order) Glen Cuthbert, Pat Dixon, Dave Hall, Vince McDonall and Kevin Rowling. Drawing by Roger Swainston. (*Details of contributors and their organisations are given in the Acknowledgements section at the back of this book.*)
Compilers Patricia Kailola, Kay Abel and Christina Grieve (maps)

Luderick

Girella tricuspidata

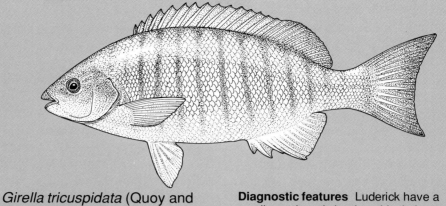

Girella tricuspidata (Quoy and Gaimard)

Luderick

Other common names include **blackfish**, **nigger**, **darkie** and **blackbream**.
FAO: no known name
Australian species code: 361007

Family GIRELLIDAE

Diagnostic features Luderick have a small mouth and slender, chisel-shaped teeth in each jaw. They have a single, unnotched dorsal fin with 13 or more spines and 14–16 rays. The caudal fin is concave. Their body is blackish, olive brown or grey and there are 8–12 dark, narrow vertical bands across the back and upper sides.

Distribution

Luderick live only in waters off eastern Australia and the north island of New Zealand. In Australia, they are present from Hervey Bay in Queensland southwards to Victoria, northern, eastern and western Tasmania as far as Macquarie Harbour, and South Australia as far west as the north coast of Kangaroo Island.

Luderick favour estuarine (including mangroves), rocky reef and inshore, coastal water habitats.[1,2] They flourish in seagrass areas. Commercial luderick catches are greatest where seagrass is most abundant.

Life history

Maturing luderick form large aggregations comprising equal numbers of male and female fish.[3,4] In about November in New South Wales, mature fish have been observed to undertake runs from inside the rivers and coastal lakes to the sea. Luderick have a protracted spawning period,[5] and spawn in the surf zone and estuary mouths.[4] Spawning times vary: July to August in southern Queensland,[1] August to December in central and northern New South Wales,[3,4] and October to February or March in the Gippsland Lakes in Victoria.[5] Although no studies have been undertaken on reproduction, these fish have large ovaries and are believed to be highly fecund. Estimates range from 300 000 to 400 000 ova.

Luderick larvae inhabit seagrass beds, moving out of them into mangrove-lined creeks and estuaries during their first year.

Luderick are moderately sedentary, schooling fish. They do however, move between and within estuaries and coastal lakes, with a more pronounced movement or migration occurring prior to

Geographic distribution and commercial fishing areas for luderick in Australian waters.

spawning.[1,3,4] The 'travelling season' takes place along the New South Wales coast in autumn and early winter, and large schools of luderick, mostly comprising fish 20–30 cm long, usually move in a northerly direction.

The maximum recorded sizes of luderick are 71 cm fork length and 4 kg. Growth rates are moderately slow. They vary between different regions and, as with many estuarine species, appear to be affected by water temperature. In Moreton Bay (Queensland), 3-year-olds have a mean length of 23 cm fork length and 11-year-olds have a mean length of 40 cm;[1] in Tuggerah Lakes (central New South Wales), 1-year-olds have a mean fork length of 17 cm,[3] 3-year-olds average 26 cm fork length and 5-year-olds average 31 cm fork length; in Gippsland Lakes, 1-year-olds have a mean fork length of 7 cm[5] and 3-year-old fish have a mean length of 22 cm.[5] Female luderick probably grow faster than males.[1] Infestations of isopod parasites can slow the growth rate.[6] At first maturity, male luderick are 22–25 cm fork length and female luderick are about 26 cm fork length.[3,4]

Luderick are herbivorous and feed primarily on seagrasses (eg *Zostera* species). Filamentous red algae (*Gracilaria* species), filamentous green algae (*Enteromorpha* species) and cabbage weed (*Ulva* species) also form part of their diet.[7] Detritus, molluscs, prawns (Penaeidae) and polychaete worms are occasionally consumed, more often during winter and spring.

The only information on predation on luderick is that dolphins (Delphinidae) feed on them in large numbers, both in estuaries and offshore.

Stock structure

There is no information on the stock structure of luderick.

Commercial fishery

Commercial fishing for luderick takes place all year in estuaries, along coastal shores and in coastal lakes, from southern Queensland to Port Phillip Bay and northern Tasmania. Luderick are mostly fished at night, but when the fish are 'travelling', day fishing is more common. The catch is seasonal; for example, in

southern Queensland the summer catch is about half the winter catch.

Along the central New South Wales coast, fish caught are between 22 cm and 36 cm fork length.[2,4] The highest catches, 2–3 times the rest of the year's catches, are made off the beaches during the autumn–early winter 'travelling season'.[1] For example, in April–May 1991, 66 t were caught on the beaches around Port Stephens in a 5-week period. Luderick taken from the Tuggerah Lakes to the Hastings River, including the Myall and Wallis lakes, comprise the bulk of the New South Wales commercial catch.

In Tuggerah Lakes, the luderick catch increased over the period 1946–1977,[3] the average annual catch over the period 1975 to 1978 being 62 t.[3] With the development of the Vales Point power station and associated increase in water temperature, the luderick catch in Lake Macquarie has increased over the last 10 years.[4]

In Moreton Bay, the commercial fishery targets 4-year-old to 6-year-old fish,[1] and about 50 t are taken each year. This represents about 90 % of the

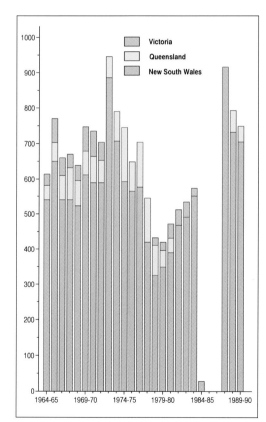

Total annual catch in t of luderick for the period 1964–65 to 1989–90. Figures are unavailable for: New South Wales from 1984–85 to 1986–87; Victoria from 1972–73 to 1977–78 and 1985–86 to 1989–90; and Queensland from 1981–82 to 1987–88. Catches for States that average less than 5 % of the total for all States are not shown. (Source: Fisheries Resources Atlas Statistical Database)

Queensland annual commercial catch of luderick, and much of that is taken south of Mud Island in the Bay.

In Queensland, most luderick are caught by tunnel nets staked and set out on intertidal areas.[1] The fish are trapped as the tide ebbs. The tunnel nets may be up to 1700 m long, and usually have a small mesh (5 cm stretched size). Gillnets up to 1450 m long are used in estuaries, and beach seine, haul and pound ('figure 6') nets are used for 'travelling' fish on ocean beaches in New South Wales from the Clarence River to Eden, in Victoria[3,2,4] and off northern Tasmania.

In the Tamboon Inlet, Victoria, luderick is a bycatch of the black bream (*Acanthopagrus butcheri*) fishery.[2] In Queensland and New South Wales, luderick schools move and shelter with mullet (family Mugilidae) and yellowfin bream (*Acanthopagrus australis*) schools, and form an incidental catch of those species.

Luderick should be bled immediately on capture, filleted and skinned, and washed in changes of seawater. The entire catch of luderick is sold on the domestic market in Australia. Salted luderick is also used as bait for the rock lobster (*Jasus* species) fishery in New South Wales. They do not fetch a high price. The Queensland market price in 1992 averaged about A$ 2.50 per kg. In New South Wales, market gluts created by big catches of 'travelling' luderick depress prices. In 1991–92, the average wholesale price paid for luderick at the Sydney Fish Market was A$ 0.78 per kg.

Management controls There are regulations controlling legal fish size, net size and mesh, area and time closures and fishing techniques employed in catching luderick in most fisheries. These regulations vary from State to State.

Recreational fishery

Luderick are keenly sought by amateur fishers. They rank among the most popular recreational fish in Moreton Bay, Lake Macquarie, Tuggerah Lakes, Sydney Harbour and associated waterways (Port Hacking, Botany Bay) and Port Phillip Bay. In 1 year alone (1978-79) in Tuggerah Lakes, 71 388 fish weighing 21.5 t were landed by amateur fishers.[3] The number of fish caught almost equalled the number taken in the commercial luderick fishery in the Lakes over the same period, although they represented only 85 % of the weight of the commercial fish yield (ie some fish were undersized). In Lake Macquarie, the amateur catch is only slightly less than the commercial catch.[4]

Fishing for luderick is considered by amateur fishers to be one of the more specialised techniques, requiring a generally high level of proficiency. Most fishing takes place in winter. Fish are caught with handlines and long rods with light lines, from boats, jetties and the shore (rock walls and rocky headlands). 'Green weed' (filamentous green algae), cabbage weed or prawns are used for bait. According to the Australian Anglers Association records, the largest luderick caught by an amateur weighed 3.88 kg (from New South Wales).

Management controls In Queensland and New South Wales, a minimum legal size is imposed.

Resource status

The resource status is largely unknown. Luderick abundance fluctuates widely, probably as a result of alterations to the habitat, vulnerability to seine nets and changing targeting preference by fishers.[2] In New South Wales, there have been recent reports that luderick numbers are increasing, probably because of increased algal abundance, itself the product of increased organic run-off into estuaries and coastal lakes.

Recreational fisher landing a luderick (above); and the prize (below). Port Hacking, Sydney, New South Wales. (Source: John Matthews, Fisheries Research Institute, NSW Fisheries)

References

1. Pollock, B.R. (1981) Age determination and growth of luderick, *Girella tricuspidata* (Quoy and Gaimard), taken from Moreton Bay, Australia. *Journal of Fish Biology* **19**: 475–485.

2. Winstanley, R.H. (1985) Commercial fishery situation report: Tamboon Inlet. *Victorian Department of Conservation, Forests and Lands, Fisheries and Wildlife Service, Marine Fisheries Report* **7**. 28 pp.

3. Henry, G.W. and Virgona, J.L. (1980) *The impact of the Munmorah power station on the recreational and commercial finfish fisheries of Tuggerah Lakes*. Sydney: New South Wales State Fisheries. 91 pp.

4. Virgona, J.L. (1983) *Lake Macquarie fish study*. Prepared for the Electricity Commission of NSW. Sydney: New South Wales State Fisheries. 131 pp.

5. Ramm, D.C. (1986) *An ecological study of the ichthyoplankton and juvenile fish in the Gippsland Lakes, Victoria*. Unpublished PhD thesis, University of Melbourne. 161 pp.

6. Lanzing, W.J.R. and O'Connor, P.F. (1975) Infestation of luderick (*Girella tricuspidata*) populations with parasitic isopods. *Australian Journal of Marine and Freshwater Research* **26**: 355–361.

7. Anderson, T.A. (1987) *Quantitative and qualitative aspects of the digestive system of the luderick*, Girella tricuspidata *(Pisces, Kyphosidae) (Quoy and Gaimard)* [sic]. Unpublished PhD thesis, University of Sydney. 119 pp.

Contributors

Most of the information on this species was provided by (in alphabetical order) Gary Henry, Murray MacDonald, Vince McDonall, Barry Pollock and John Virgona, and supplemented by Trevor Anderson, Glen Cuthbert and Alex Schaap. Drawing by Gavin Ryan. (*Details of contributors and their organisations are given in the Acknowledgements section at the back of this book.*)

Compilers Patricia Kailola and Christina Grieve (maps)

Morwong

Nemadactylus species

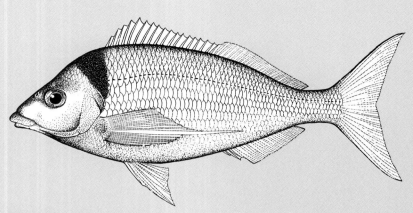

Morwong

This presentation is on 2 species, **jackass morwong** and **grey morwong**.

Jackass morwong,
Nemadactylus macropterus
(Bloch and Schneider)

Other common names include **sea bream**, **jackass fish**, **perch**, **silver perch**, **deepsea perch** and **mowie**.
FAO: no known name
Australian species code: 377003

Grey morwong, *Nemadactylus douglasii* (Hector)

Other common names include **rubberlip morwong**, **blue morwong**, **great perch** and **Douglas' morwong**.
FAO: no known name
Australian species code: 377002

Family CHEILODACTYLIDAE

Diagnostic features Morwongs are distinguished by having the lower 4–7 pectoral fin rays unbranched and somewhat thickened. At least 1 of these rays is elongated and produced beyond the remainder of the fin. Jackass morwong (pictured) have thinner lips than grey morwong, and 59–60 scales in the lateral line compared with 47–55 in grey morwong. Jackass morwong are greyish silver on the upper body and silvery white below. A broad grey to black band extends from in front of the dorsal fin to the posterior edge of the gill cover. Grey morwong are a pale silvery blue and sometimes have a brownish hue. They lack the dark band of jackass morwong.

Distribution

Jackass morwong are distributed throughout the southern areas of the Australian Fishing Zone from Moreton Bay in Queensland to Perth in Western Australia. They also inhabit the waters of New Zealand, southern South America, southern Africa and some islands in the Indian and Atlantic oceans.[1,2] Jackass morwong are demersal fish, living over open grounds at 40 m to 400 m depth. Juveniles tend to live near shallow reefs in Bass Strait and around Tasmania.[2,3]

Grey morwong inhabit continental shelf waters of south-eastern Australia from Moreton Bay to Wilsons Promontory in central Victoria, and as far south as Storm Bay in Tasmania. This species is also present in the waters of New Zealand's north island.[2] Grey morwong are demersal fish, commonly caught near reefs in depths of 10 m to 100 m.[2,4]

Life history

Jackass morwong spawn from late summer to autumn (February to May).[1,5] Female fish older than 10 years produce over 1 million eggs on average, compared with 100 000 eggs produced by 3-year-olds.[5] Jackass morwong may spawn more than once during the spawning season[5] and probably spawn throughout their adult Australian distribution.[1] They have an extended pelagic postlarval stage. Research in New Zealand has shown that metamorphosis to the juvenile stage occurs between 9 and 12 months after hatching.[6]

The only known nursery areas for juvenile jackass morwong are in Bass Strait and coastal waters of Tasmania. Juveniles are rarely caught on the trawling grounds of eastern Victoria and New South Wales and have not been reported from the Great Australian Bight.[7] Tagging studies have shown little movement by adults,[1] so it appears that older juveniles disperse from the nursery areas to the areas they will occupy as adults. Both sexes mature at 3 years of age at a size of approximately 25 cm fork length. Jackass morwong are relatively slow growing. Females grow more quickly than males and live to a greater age, and can attain 50 cm fork length and 16 years of age. Some males live to 11 years of age and reach a size of 45 cm fork length.[8] Jackass

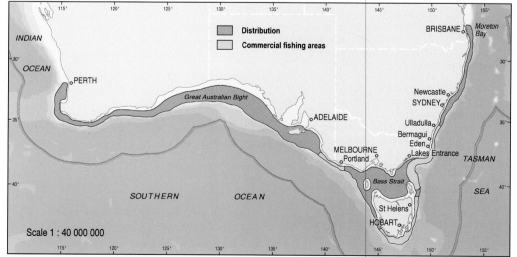

Geographic distribution and commercial fishing areas for jackass morwong in Australian waters

morwong from New Zealand waters are reported to live significantly longer than Australian fish, with some individuals aged to 50 years.[2]

There is no information on spawning and larval development in grey morwong. Juvenile grey morwong are abundant in eastern Bass Strait in July and are present in low numbers there in other months.[9] Juveniles are also caught by trawlers off north-eastern Tasmania.[3] Adult fish are most abundant in New South Wales waters. There are no estimates of growth rates or maximum age for grey morwong. They reach a greater size than jackass morwong, some fish growing to a total length of 74 cm and weights exceeding 4 kg.[3]

Jackass morwong feed mainly at night, on a diet of polychaete worms, crustaceans, molluscs and echinoderms.[10] Grey morwong probably consume a similar range of invertebrates.[2] There is no information on predators of morwong.

Stock structure

Studies of Australian and New Zealand jackass morwong using electrophoresis revealed genetic separation of the 2 populations but no population structuring was found for Australian fish.[11] However, recent research using microprobe analysis of otoliths indicates the presence of 3 Australian stocks, from New South Wales–Victoria, Tasmania, and the Great Australian Bight.[1] No research has been

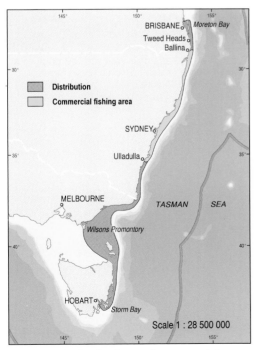

Geographic distribution and commercial fishing areas for grey morwong in Australian waters.

undertaken into the grey morwong stock structure in Australia.

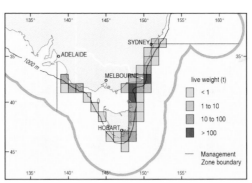

Total jackass morwong catch by 1-degree block from the South East Fishery for 1989–90. (Source: Australian Fishing Zone Information System)

Commercial fishery

Jackass morwong have been trawled since 1915 in south-eastern Australian waters although most of the catch was discarded prior to World War II in favour of tiger flathead (*Neoplatycephalus richardsoni*). The decline in tiger flathead catches following the War encouraged fishers to retain the lower priced morwong and redfish (*Centroberyx affinis*) components of the catch.[12] The jackass morwong catch taken by steam trawlers and Danish seine vessels off New South Wales was approximately 1800 t in 1946–47 and 1947–48. Catches then dropped to levels of about 1000 t per annum until the 1970s, when landings began to increase. Catches peaked in 1980–81 at an estimated 2300 t, including Victorian and Tasmanian catches.[1]

Southern New South Wales, eastern Bass Strait and eastern to south-western Tasmania are the main Australian fishing grounds for jackass morwong. Small amounts are also caught off western Victoria. The southern New South Wales port of Eden is the main landing point for jackass morwong from the fishery. Significant amounts are also landed at Lakes Entrance in eastern Victoria. Demersal otter trawls are the main type of fishing gear used, Danish seine vessels accounting for only 3 % of the jackass morwong catch in 1989–90. However, prior to the mid 1970s Danish seine fishers took the majority of jackass morwong catches. Minor catches of jackass morwong are also taken by traps, and small quantities of jackass morwong are caught in bottom set gillnets, by handline, and with bottom set longlines.[1] Jackass morwong are also trawled on the continental shelf in the Great Australian

Bight Trawl Fishery, with current annual catches of approximately 50 t. Approximately 80 % of the South East Fishery catch is taken in depths of 100 m to 200 m, although highest catch rates are made in slightly deeper water.[13] Jackass morwong catch varies with season, summer and autumn being the most productive period for some areas within the Fishery. However, off Eden, catches and catch rates are highest in spring and autumn.[1]

The grey morwong fishery is limited to New South Wales waters from Ballina to Ulladulla. Most of the catch is taken by trap fishers although a small percentage is caught on handlines and bottom set longlines. Grey morwong form a minor bycatch of trawlers fishing in shallower waters of the continental shelf. The highest recorded annual catch for grey morwong was about 960 t in 1980–81 but this figure probably includes an unknown amount of jackass morwong. The 1990–91 catch was approximately 190 t.

Both species of morwong are sold mainly on the domestic fresh fish market, either as whole fish or fillets. The average price obtained for jackass morwong at the Sydney Fish Market in 1991–92 was $A 1.97 per kg. Grey morwong prices averaged $A 3.08 per kg in 1991–92.

Management controls The jackass morwong fishery is managed by the Commonwealth of Australia as part of the South East Fishery with associated limited entry provisions, boat replacement policy and gear restrictions. Jackass morwong catches in the Fishery are limited by a

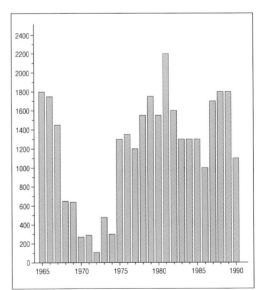

Total annual catch in t of jackass morwong from the South East Fishery for the period 1965 to 1990. (Source: South Eastern Fisheries Research Committee, Demersal and Pelagic Fish Research Group)

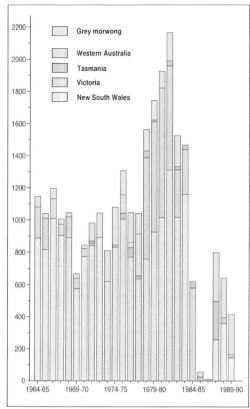

Total annual catch of jackass morwong and grey morwong in t for the period 1964–65 to 1989–90. Figures are unavailable for: New South Wales from 1984–85 to 1986–87; and Victoria from 1972–73 to 1977–78 and 1985–86 to 1989–90. Catches for States that average less than 5 % of the total for all States are not shown. (Source: Fisheries Resources Atlas Statistical Database)

total allowable catch and individual transferable quotas. Vessels operating in the Great Australian Bight Trawl Fishery are managed by limited entry. Operators using trap and line in the grey morwong fishery are managed by the New South Wales Government.

Minimum legal size limits apply to jackass morwong and grey morwong in New South Wales waters. A size limit also applies to jackass morwong caught in Tasmanian waters.

Recreational fishery

Both species of morwong are caught by anglers but grey morwong are more commonly taken. Anglers use handlines, deck winches or rod-and-line methods to catch morwong and favoured baits are fish flesh, prawns and pieces of squid.[14]

The Australian Anglers Association records list the largest morwong caught as 2.9 kg for jackass morwong and 5.9 kg for grey morwong, both from New South Wales.

Management controls Minimum legal size limits apply to recreational catches of jackass morwong and grey morwong in New South Wales. Jackass morwong are also subject to a size limit in Tasmania.

Resource status

Current total catches of jackass morwong are within estimates of sustainable yields. However, confirmation of stock structure is needed to allow more precise estimates of sustainable yields by region.[1] There are no biomass or sustainable yield estimates for grey morwong in Australian waters.

References

1. Smith, D.C. (in press, 1992) Jackass morwong. In *The South East Fishery: a scientific review with particular reference to quota management*. Ed by R.D.J. Tilzey. *Bureau of Resource Sciences Bulletin.*

2. Paul, L. (1986) *New Zealand fishes. An identification guide.* Auckland: Reed Methuen. 184 pp.

3. Last, P.R., Scott, E.O.G. and Talbot, F.H. (1983) *Fishes of Tasmania.* Hobart: Tasmanian Fisheries Development Authority. 563 pp.

4. May, J.L. and Maxwell, J.G.H. (1986) *A field guide to trawl fish from temperate waters of Australia.* Hobart: CSIRO Division of Fisheries Research. 492 pp.

5. Hobday, D.K. and Wankowski, J.W.J. (1987) Jackass morwong *Nemadactylus macropterus:* reproduction and fecundity in eastern Bass Strait, Australia. *Victorian Department of Conservation, Forests and Lands, Marine Science Laboratories, Internal Report* **155**. 17 pp.

6. Vooren, C.M. (1972) Post-larvae and juveniles of the tarakihi (Teleostei: Cheilodactylidae) in New Zealand. *New Zealand Journal of Marine and Freshwater Research* **6**: 601–618.

7. Smith, D.C. (1983) Annual total mortality and population structure of jackass morwong (*Nemadactylus macropterus* Bloch & Schneider) in eastern Australian waters. *Australian Journal of Marine and Freshwater Research* **34**: 253–260.

8. Smith, D.C. (1982) Age and growth of jackass morwong (*Nemadactylus macropterus* Bloch & Schneider) in eastern Australian waters. *Australian Journal of Marine and Freshwater Research* **33**: 245–253.

9. Wankowski, J.W.J. and Moulton, P.L. (1986) Distribution, abundance and biomass estimates of commercially important demersal fish species in eastern Bass Strait, Australia. *Victorian Department of Conservation, Forests and Lands, Marine Science Laboratories, Technical Report* **62**. 57 pp.

10. Godfriaux, B.L. (1974) Food of tarakihi in western Bay of Plenty and Tasman Bay, New Zealand. *New Zealand Journal of Marine and Freshwater Research* **8**: 111–153.

11. Richardson, B.J. (1982) Geographical distribution of electrophoretically detected protein variation in Australian commercial fishes. II. Jackass morwong, *Cheilodactylus macropterus* Bloch & Schneider. *Australian Journal of Marine and Freshwater Research* **33**: 927–931.

12. Fairbridge, W.S. (1952) The New South Wales tiger flathead, *Neoplatycephalus macrodon* (Ogilby) II. The age composition of the commercial catch, overfishing of the stocks, and suggested conservation. *Australian Journal of Marine and Freshwater Research* **3**: 1–31.

13. Tilzey, R.D.J., Zann-Schuster, M., Klaer, N.L. and Williams, M.J. (1990) The South East Trawl Fishery: biological synopses and catch distributions for seven major commercial fish species. *Bureau of Rural Resources Bulletin* **6**. 80 pp.

14. Starling, S. (1988) *The fisherman's handbook. How to find, identify and catch the top Australian angling fish.* Sydney: Angus & Robertson Publishers. 263 pp.

Contributors

Most of the information on these species was originally provided by Dave Smith. Additional information was provided by (in alphabetical order) Alastair Graham, Richard Tilzey and Elizabeth Turner. Drawing by Roger Swainston. (*Details of contributors and their organisations are given in the Acknowledgements section at the back of this book.*)
Compiler Phillip Stewart

A catch of jackass morwong on the deck of a Danish seine vessel. (Source: Dave Smith, Marine Science Laboratories, Victorian Department of Conservation and Environment)

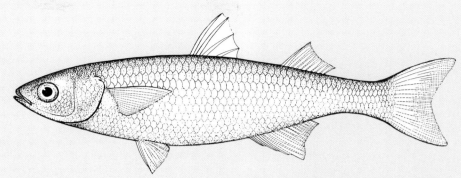

Yellow-eye mullet

Aldrichetta forsteri

Aldrichetta forsteri
(Valenciennes)

Yellow-eye mullet

Other common names include **pilch, Coorong mullet** and **Victor Harbor mullet**.
FAO: no known name
Australian species code: 381001

Family MUGILIDAE

Diagnostic features Yellow-eye mullet have a more pointed head and mouth than sea mullet, and their eyes lack adipose (fatty) eyelids. Their body scales are small (54–64 between gill opening and tail base) and thin, and are easily dislodged. Yellow-eye mullet have 2 widely separated dorsal fins, the first with 4 spines and the second with 1 spine and 9 soft rays. These fish are olive or bluish brown above and silvery on the sides, and their eyes are bright yellow or golden. Their fins have brown margins.[1]

Distribution

Yellow-eye mullet are schooling fish inhabiting bays, estuaries and open coastlines, from the Hunter River and Newcastle in New South Wales, along the temperate-water coasts of southern Australia, including Tasmania, to Shark Bay in Western Australia. They are possibly the most abundant and widespread fish in waters over sandy substrates near the Tasmanian coastline.[1] Yellow-eye mullet also inhabit shallow bays and estuaries around New Zealand.[2]

Yellow-eye mullet live in brackish and inshore coastal waters and beaches, over sand and mud sea beds to depths of 10–20 m. They have a wide tolerance of water temperatures, up to 28°C.[3] Juveniles in the Gippsland Lakes inhabit lower salinity water (about 20 parts per thousand) but generally from Victoria to south-western Australia, juveniles less than 1-year-old live in both estuarine and marine environments with salinity to 35 parts per thousand[4,5] and temperatures ranging from 14°C to 24°C.[6] As they grow older,[3] yellow-eye mullet gradually move into more open coastal waters, yet prior to spawning they undertake a more pronounced movement to the coast.[5]

Life history

Yellow-eye mullet form large aggregations prior to spawning.[5,6] They spawn in coastal waters[5] and protected marine embayments.[4,6,7] In the east, to as far as the gulfs in South Australia, spawning takes place between January and April;[8] and from western South Australia to Shark Bay, spawning takes place between March–May and October.[6,9] Yellow-eye mullet spawn only 1 set of moderately large (average 0.5 mm diameter)[8] eggs each season. The number of eggs produced increases as the

female grows larger, from about 125 000 at 24.5 cm total length to 630 000 at 39 cm total length.[9]

Recently hatched juvenile yellow-eye mullet probably enter the estuaries by active swimming.[6] Juveniles in Barker Inlet (near Adelaide, South Australia) enter estuaries and sheltered bays when they are 3–4 cm long, and remain there until they reach 25–30 cm total length.

Yellow-eye mullet reach a size of at least 40 cm total length[2,5] and about 950 g.[1] They grow rapidly during their first 2 years,[8] and after that, females grow more quickly than do males. Females also

achieve a larger size.[8] The relative size of yellow-eye mullet varies with locality: Gippsland Lakes fish attain average total lengths of 7.5 cm and 15.5 cm at 1 and 2 years of age respectively;[10] in the Coorong, lengths attained during the first 4 years are, on average, 14–15 cm, 20–22 cm, 24–26 cm and 30–32 cm respectively;[8] and in the Swan–Avon (Western Australia) estuary, the mean total lengths and weights of approximately 1-year-old fish are 16cm and 34 g, and of 2-year-old fish are 30 cm and 229 g respectively.[6] Western Australian yellow-eye mullet at all ages attain a larger size and grow more quickly

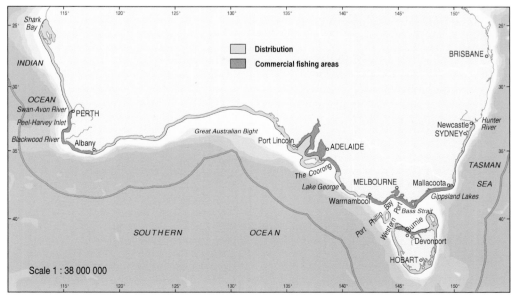

Geographic distribution and commercial fishing areas for yellow-eye mullet in Australian waters.

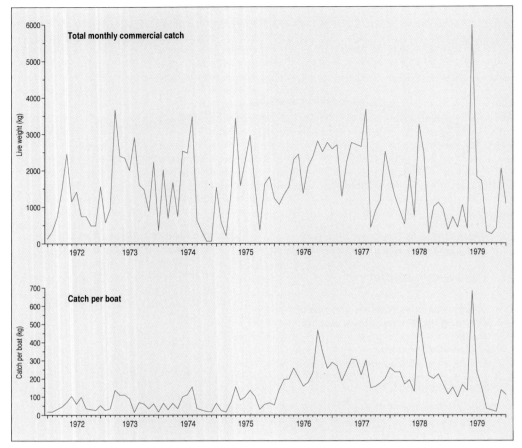

Total monthly commercial catch and catch per boat of yellow-eye mullet in the Swan–Avon river system for the period 1972 to 1979. (Source: Chubb et al[6])

than do yellow-eye mullet from Victoria, Tasmania and South Australia.[8,11] Water temperature and pattern of movement appear to affect the growth rate, as yellow-eye mullet in the Blackwood River do not attain the same length at a given age as do those in the Swan–Avon system to the north.[7] Yellow-eye mullet generally are mature at 2–3 years of age.[2,6,8] Eastern yellow-eye mullet populations reach maturity faster and at a smaller size than do western populations.

Yellow-eye mullet are omnivores, feeding on plankton (as juveniles), detritus, seagrass, microalgae and macroalgae (such as *Ulva* species), small animals (for example, amphipods, gastropod molluscs and polychaete worms) and epiphytes associated with rocks, seagrass and algae.[9] Mulloway (*Argyrosomus hololepidotus*) are predators of yellow-eye mullet.

Stock structure

There are 2 distinct populations of yellow-eye mullet: an eastern population which spawns in late summer and autumn, and a western population which spawns in winter. However, this difference may in part be due to the marked tendency for sandbars to form at

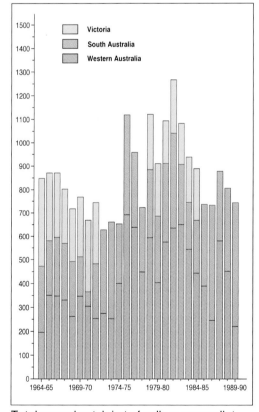

Total annual catch in t of yellow-eye mullet for the period 1964–65 to 1989–90. Figures are unavailable for Victoria from 1972–73 to 1977–78 and 1985–86 to 1989–90. Catches for States that average less than 5 % of the total for all States are not shown. (Source: Fisheries Resources Atlas Statistical Database)

the entrances to Western Australian estuaries during summer, effectively preventing the movement of ripe fish into coastal waters for spawning.[6] The only morphological difference between eastern and western yellow-eye mullet is the number of scales, fish from Western Australia and South Australia having 54–59 scale rows, those from eastern Australia having 59–64.[9] The genetics of the 2 populations has not been studied.

Commercial fishery

The main fishing areas for yellow-eye mullet are estuarine and inshore waters of Victoria (Mallacoota to Warrnambool), the north and north-west coasts of Tasmania, South Australia (Lake George, the Coorong and the 2 gulfs) and most of the river systems and protected marine embayments of south-western Australia.[6,9] The yellow-eye mullet fishery is locally important, for example around Burnie and Devonport in northern Tasmania, and the Gippsland Lakes and Port Phillip Bay in Victoria.[10]

The fishery for yellow-eye mullet continues throughout the year but with seasonal fluctuations in catch levels. Lower catches are reported over winter in Port Phillip Bay[10] and the South Australian gulfs, over late summer to autumn in the Coorong,[5] and over spring in the Swan–Avon estuary.[6] Yellow-eye mullet are caught using haul seines, coastal set gillnets and ring nets (New South Wales only).

Commercial catches from the Gippsland Lakes have decreased from about 220 t a year in the early 1960s, apparently in response to changes in fishing patterns and local market demand. In contrast, the Port Phillip Bay catch increased from 11–22 t a year prior to 1960 to an average of 56 t between 1973–74 and 1983–84.[10] In northern Tasmania, the catch per unit effort of yellow-eye mullet is as high as 100 kg per 50 m net haul. Most of it is caught inside the Tamar River and Mersey River estuaries and along the adjacent north coast. A fair proportion of the Tasmanian catch is not reported, being either sold direct to fish shops, or fished by shop proprietors themselves. From 1964–65 to 1989-90, the stated Tasmanian catch of yellow-eye mullet fluctuated between 3 t and 70 t a year. In Western Australia yellow-eye mullet traditionally have been sold as rock lobster (Palinuridae) bait. Now however, other bait sources are generally used. This tendency has led to a decrease in demand for yellow-eye mullet. The average catch per unit effort in the Peel–Harvey estuary in Western Australia between 1970 and 1979[12] was nearly 7 times higher than that in the Swan–Avon estuary. Yellow-eye mullet catches in the Peel–Harvey estuary were about 300–400 t in recent years.

Larger yellow-eye mullet are usually sold as fresh chilled fillets, occasionally as whole fish. Most of the catch is consumed locally, but the excess from the Coorong fishery (which historically provided approximately 75 % of the South Australian yellow-eye mullet catch[8]) is often sent to Victorian markets. Yellow-eye mullet are sold often in the 'fish-and-chips' trade in South Australia. In New Zealand, yellow-eye mullet are smoked as 'kippers' or soused as 'rollmops'.[2] The 1992 price at the Melbourne Wholesale Fish Market ranged from A$ 0.72 to A$ 1.04 per kg, the price in Tasmania fluctuated between A$ 0.70 and A$ 1.00 per kg, and the wholesale price in Western Australia was A$ 0.60 per kg.

Management controls There is limited entry to the fishery in South Australia and Western Australia. In Victoria, commercial fishing in bays and inlets is controlled by limited entry regulations. A legal minimum length applies in Tasmania, Victoria, South Australia and Western Australia. In Victoria there is a limit on net length; a legal minimum net mesh size applies in South Australia and Victoria; and in Western Australia there are fishing time and closed water restrictions.

Recreational fishery

Catching yellow-eye mullet is a popular, year-round fishing pastime in all States where it occurs, especially in Tasmania. The recreational catch is probably well in excess of the commercial catch. Yellow-eye mullet is one of the 3 most popular species for jetty and shore anglers in South Australia and comprises 44 % of the recreational catch in Port Lincoln waters.[13] Recreational fishers use gillnets, handlines and 'mullet' nets (gillnets with 6–7 cm mesh size). The fish respond well to small, baited hooks and to berleying. Adult yellow-eye mullet are targeted in inshore South Australian waters between

February and April, and during winter and early spring in the Gippsland Lakes, the northern part of Port Phillip Bay and in embayed and estuarine beaches in Western Australia when they are spawning near the beaches.

Management controls A legal minimum size applies in South Australia, Western Australia and Tasmania, and a legal minimum net mesh size is enforced in Tasmania. Gear restrictions apply in Victoria, although there are no minimum size and bag limits.

Resource status

The commercial fishery fluctuates in response to prices and market demand, notably in Western Australia and Victoria.[10] In Victoria, catches have remained generally stable over the past 25 years. Northern Tasmanian and Port Phillip Bay stocks are not fully utilised. In some Western Australian and South Australian estuaries there is evidence of increased catch rates due to increases in the growth and extent of macroalgae.[3,12]

References

1. Last, P.R., Scott, E.O.G. and Talbot, F.H. (1983) *Fishes of Tasmania*. Hobart: Tasmanian Fisheries Development Authority. 563 pp.

2. Paul, L.J. (1986) *New Zealand fishes. An identification guide.* Auckland: Reed Methuen. 184 pp.

3. Jones, G.K., Baker, J.L., Edyvane, K. and Wright, G.J. (in press, 1993) The nearshore fish community of the Port River – Barker Inlet estuary, South Australia. 1. The effect of thermal effluent on the distribution and growth of economically important fish species. *Marine Ecology in Progress Series.*

4. Lenanton, R.C.J. (1982) Alternative non-estuarine nursery habitats for some commercially and recreationally important fish species of south-western Australia. *Australian Journal of Marine and Freshwater Research* **33**: 881–900.

5. Hall, D. (1984) The Coorong: biology of the major fish species and fluctuations in catch rates 1976–1983. *SAFIC* **8**(1): 3–17.

6. Chubb, C.F., Potter, I.C., Grant, C.J., Lenanton, R.C.J., and Wallace, J. (1981) Age structure, growth rates and movements of sea mullet, *Mugil cephalus* L., and yellow-eye mullet, *Aldrichetta forsteri* (Valenciennes), in the Swan–Avon River System, Western Australia. *Australian Journal of Marine and Freshwater Research* **32**: 605–628.

7. Lenanton, R.C.J. (1977) Aspects of the ecology of fish and commercial crustaceans of the Blackwood River estuary, Western Australia. *Western Australian Fisheries Research Bulletin* **19**. 72 pp.

8. Harris, J.A. (1968) The yellow-eye mullet. Age structure, growth rate and spawning cycle of a population of yellow-eye mullet, *Aldrichetta forsteri* (Cuv. and Val.) from the Coorong lagoon, South Australia. *Transactions of the Royal Society of South Australia* **92**: 37–50.

9. Thomson, J.M. (1957) Biological studies of economic significance of the yellow-eye mullet, *Aldrichetta forsteri* (Cuvier & Valenciennes). *Australian Journal of Marine and Freshwater Research* **8**: 1–13.

10. Hall, D.N. and MacDonald, C.M. (1986) Commercial fishery situation report: net and line fisheries of Port Phillip Bay Victoria, 1914–1984. *Victorian Department of Conservation, Forests and Lands, Fisheries Division, Marine Fisheries Report* **10**. 121 pp.

11. Thomson, J.M. (1957) Interpretation of the scales of yellow-eye mullet *Aldrichetta forsteri* (Cuvier & Valenciennes) (Mugilidae). *Australian Journal of Marine and Freshwater Research* **8**: 14–28.

12. Lenanton, R.C.J., Potter, I.C., Loneragan, N.R. and Chrystal, P.J. (1984) Age structure and changes in abundance of three important species of teleost in a eutrophic estuary (Pisces: Teleostei). *Journal of Zoology, London* **203**: 311–327.

13. Jones, G.K. (1986) A review of the recreational and commercial marine scale fish resource in Pt Lincoln waters. *South Australian Department of Fisheries. A discussion paper.* 29 pp.

Sorting mullet caught in the Swan-Avon estuary, Perth, Western Australia. (Source: Australian Information Service)

Contributors

Information in this presentation was originally provided by Keith Jones and supplemented by (in alphabetical order) Rod Lenanton, Murray MacDonald and Alex Schaap. Drawing by Roger Swainston. *(Details of contributors and their organisations are given in the Acknowledgements section at the back of this book.)*

Compilers Patricia Kailola, Kay Abel and Christina Grieve (maps)

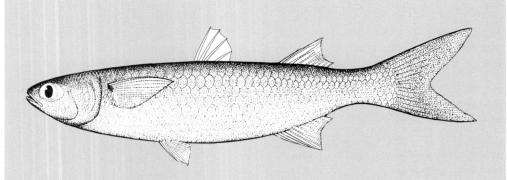

Sea mullet

Mugil cephalus

Mugil cephalus Linnaeus

Sea mullet

Other common names include **bully mullet**, **hardgut mullet**, **river mullet**, **mangrove mullet**, **grey mullet** and **striped mullet**.
FAO: flathead mullet
Australian species code: 381002

Family MUGILIDAE

Diagnostic features Sea mullet vary in colour depending on where they live. Those from oceanic waters are olive-green on the upper surface and silvery on the sides; while those from rivers are deep blue to brownish above and a dull silver on the sides. All sea mullet have a whitish or grey belly, pale yellow ventral fins, and a dark blue to violet blotch on the pectoral fin base. Their head is broad and flattened and a fatty eyelid almost covers the eye. There are 38–42 longitudinal rows of scales on the body, and 3 spines and 8 soft rays in the anal fin.

Distribution

Sea mullet inhabit coastal waters and estuaries in tropical and temperate waters of all seas of the world. They are distributed mainly between the latitudes of 42° N and 42° S.[1]

Sea mullet inhabit fresh, estuarine and coastal waters in all States of Australia.[2] In eastern Australia they commonly range from Townsville[2] in Queensland to Fowlers Bay in South Australia.[3] Sea mullet have a sporadic distribution in Tasmania and have only been recorded from northern and eastern waters as far south as the Derwent River.[2,4] They appear to be absent from the central and western Great Australian Bight but are common from Esperance[5] to Port Hedland in Western Australia. The distribution of sea mullet is reported by a number of sources to include Australian coastal waters north of latitude 20° S, but no detailed information on their abundance in this region is available.

Adult sea mullet typically inhabit freshwater reaches of coastal rivers except during the spawning season, when mature adult fish migrate through the estuaries to inshore waters.[6] In some areas such as Shark Bay and the Houtman Abrolhos in Western Australia, adults live in marine waters throughout the year.

This behaviour seems to occur only where estuarine and freshwater habitats are limited.[6] A small proportion (probably about 5 %)[6] of older juveniles may leave the estuaries and migrate along the beaches in early summer. The migration may be associated with flooding of rivers and is referred to as the 'hardgut' migration because the mullets' guts are empty.[6] Sea mullet normally feed close to the river bed in shallow water, but do move throughout the water column in river channels and individuals often jump high out of the water.

Sea mullet have a strong tendency to school as juveniles and during the spawning season as adults. Feeding schools of juveniles commonly disperse over sand and mud flats of estuaries during high tide and reform on the ebb tide.[6]

Life history

Sea mullet are known to spawn at sea each year but the exact location of

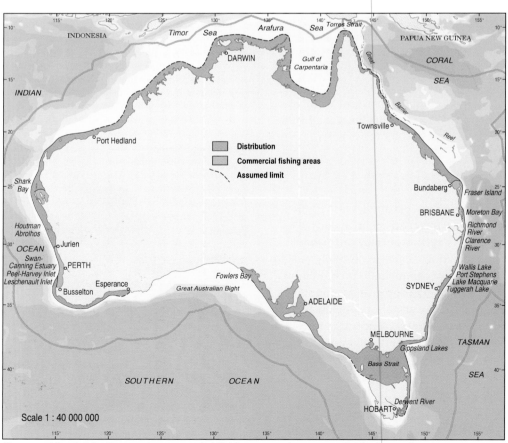

Geographic distribution and commercial fishing areas for sea mullet in Australian waters.

spawning grounds is not known.[6] However, from patterns of movement in Australian sea mullet stocks, it is assumed that spawning takes place adjacent to the surf zone of ocean beaches.[7,8] The mullet form large schools in the lower estuaries and tend to leave the estuary during periods of prevailing offshore winds.[6] They migrate in a northerly direction in inshore waters against the direction of prevailing ocean currents.[6] It appears that the fish enter more northerly rivers after spawning and do not undertake a return migration.[1] The timing of the spawning run varies with latitude and may start as early as February in southern New South Wales and as late as July in southern Queensland. The migration probably takes 1–2 months and individual fish may travel up to 740 km in that time.[9]

Sea mullet have a protracted spawning period from March to July[10] on the east coast and from March to September in the west. Some adult fish do not spawn each year, particularly if feeding is disrupted prior to the spawning run.[6] Depending on the size of fish, female sea mullet produce between 1.6 million and 4.8 million pelagic eggs, averaging 0.6 mm in diameter.[7] Knowledge of larval biology in sea mullet is limited to laboratory studies.

Postlarval sea mullet first enter estuaries when 2-3 cm long.[8] They tend to migrate in calm weather as a continuous stream of fish.[6] The fish form schools of a few hundred individuals after entering the estuary and move to shallow nursery areas, which may be located from the lower estuary to freshwater reaches of tidal creeks.[6]

Sea mullet from east and west coasts of Australia have similar growth rates, and there is no significant difference in growth patterns between sexes.[11] Juvenile fish reach an average size of 15 cm fork length at an age of 1 year, 24 cm at 2 years and 33 cm at 3 years.[10,11] Sea mullet reach maturity at the end of their third year, at sizes between 30 cm and 35 cm.[11] The maximum age recorded for sea mullet in Australian waters is 9 years, although ages up to 16 years have been reported from other countries.[1] In Australia, sea mullet are reported to reach a total length of 76 cm and a weight of 8 kg.[12]

In estuarine waters sea mullet feed on detritus, diatoms, algae and microscopic invertebrates which they filter from mud and sand through their mouth and gills.[1]

Beach seining is the most common method used to catch sea mullet. (Source: Australian Fisheries Management Authority)

A proportion of the sand is ingested to assist the grinding of food in the muscular stomach. Adult fish tend to feed mainly on algae while inhabiting fresh waters.[11] Migrating sea mullet do not feed during either the 'hardgut' migration or spawning migration. Juvenile sea mullet are eaten by a number of predator species including flathead (Platycephalidae), eels (*Anguilla* species) and tailor (*Pomatomus saltatrix*). Birds such as pelicans (*Pelecanus conspicillatus*) and cormorants (*Phalacrocorax* species) also feed on juveniles.[1] Adult sea mullet are preyed upon by dolphins (Delphinidae), and by larger fish species such as tailor, mulloway (*Argyrosomus hololepidotus*) and sharks.

Stock structure

There is no information on the stock structure of sea mullet in Australia. It is possible that there is no migration of fish between eastern and western populations because of the apparent discontinuous distribution in the Great Australian Bight. However, there are no significant morphological or physiological differences between eastern and western fish to support this hypothesis.[11]

Commercial fishery

There are 2 types of fishery for sea mullet in Australian waters. The first is an ocean beach fishery exploiting mainly mature fish on their spawning migration. The

second is located in estuaries, bays and inlets and is a 'mixed species' fishery.

The main areas for the ocean beach fishery on the east coast are from Bundaberg in Queensland to Port Stephens in central New South Wales. Some catches are also taken on the south coast of New South Wales. In Western

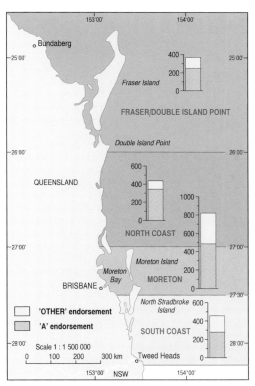

Average annual catch in t of sea mullet by subregions of the Queensland ocean beach fishery. Estuarine catch is represented by the 'OTHER' endorsement section of each bar and the catch from ocean beaches is represented by the 'A' endorsement section. (Source: Queensland Fish Management Authority and Queensland Department of Primary Industries[13])

Australia the ocean beach fishery is limited mainly to the southern regions between Jurien and Busselton and also to Shark Bay in the north. Beach seines are the dominant fishing method. On the east coast sea mullet are fished by teams of fishers using 4-wheel drive vehicles and small dories. Schools of migrating mullet are spotted from headlands or towers and the nets are then paid out around them using the dory. The net is then hauled to the beach by the team, and the fish are collected in the 'bunt' of the net. The season of the ocean beach fishery varies with the timing of the spawning migration. In central New South Wales, March and April are the peak season while April and May are the best months in the north of the State.[1] In Queensland most of the ocean beach catch is taken between May and July.[13] Some fishers follow the migration pattern, fishing in central New South Wales in March and travelling north as the season progresses. Some ocean beach catches may also be taken during the summer run of immature 'hardgut' fish.

The Shark Bay fishery differs from the other beach fisheries in use of fishing gear. There, fishers operate from mother vessels of 10–12 m length and use jet-powered boats of about 5 m length to shoot the nets in shallow waters. The Shark Bay fishery exploits mature, schooling fish. Tailor and yellowfin whiting (*Sillago schomburgkii*) are also caught in the Shark Bay fishery.

The estuarine fishery on the east coast operates mainly within the same regions as the ocean beach fishery. Moreton Bay is the most important estuarine fishery for sea mullet in Queensland. In New South Wales the Richmond and Clarence rivers, Wallis Lake, Port Stephens, Lake Macquarie and Tuggerah Lake are the most important areas. In Western Australia, the main estuarine fisheries are in the Swan–Canning Estuary and the Peel–Harvey and Leschenault inlets.

In New South Wales, the estuarine fishery accounts for the majority of the annual sea mullet catch, although during the spawning season landings are highest from ocean beaches.

Sea mullet are caught throughout the year in estuaries but the highest catches occur in late summer and autumn when movement of mature fish through the estuaries is greatest. The estuarine fisheries use several types of nets

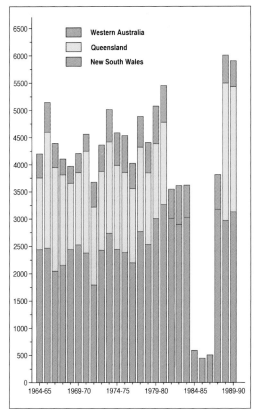

Total annual catch in t of sea mullet for the period 1964–65 to 1989–90. Figures are unavailable for: New South Wales from 1984–85 to 1986–87; and Queensland from 1981–82 to 1987–88. Catches for States that average less than 5 % of the total for all States are not shown. (Source: Fisheries Resources Atlas Statistical Database)

depending on the region. In Queensland, coastal set gillnets and tunnel nets are the most widely used gear[14] and, in New South Wales, haul seines, pound nets, coastal set gillnets and ring nets are used.[15] In Western Australia haul seines and gillnets are the main types of gear used.

Small amounts of sea mullet are taken by fishers from estuaries and ocean beaches in Victoria, Tasmania and South Australia, but these catches are normally a bycatch of effort targeted at other species.

The sea mullet caught in the ocean beach fishery in New South Wales and Queensland is generally intended for the export market of roe. Prices averaged about A$ 35.00 per kg for sea mullet roe on the Taiwanese and Japanese markets in 1991–92. Sea mullet are also common on the domestic fresh fish market and are the most common fish purchased in 'fish-and-chip' take-away outlets in Queensland and northern New South Wales. The fish are normally marketed whole and relatively low prices are paid at wholesale markets. In 1991–92, 843 t of sea mullet was sold at the Sydney Fish Market at an average price of A$ 1.01 per kg. Some of the estuarine catch from New

South Wales and Queensland is exported as whole frozen product, particularly to Middle East countries such as Saudi Arabia and the United Arab Emirates. Sea mullet sold to export processors yield higher prices than fish sold on domestic markets — in 1992 fishers received A$ 3.50 per kg for sorted roed females and A$ 1.50 per kg for unsorted fish. Fish which are damaged during handling are processed for local bait markets.

Management controls The sea mullet fisheries are managed by the respective State governments. The Queensland ocean beach fishery for sea mullet has a limited number of licence holders and a closed season during spring and summer. Restrictions also apply to net size and crew size.[13] Net fishers catching sea mullet in estuaries and from beaches north of Fraser Island are also regulated. In New South Wales there are regulations controlling the fishing gear used in the ocean beach and estuarine fisheries. The estuarine fisheries are also subject to closed areas and seasons in some areas. Limited-entry licence schemes, gear restrictions and area closures apply in Western Australian ocean beach and estuarine fisheries.

Minimum size limits apply to commercial catches of sea mullet in Queensland, New South Wales, Victoria, Tasmania and South Australia.

Recreational fishery

Sea mullet are not a common catch of anglers. In fresh water sea mullet will accept baits of dough or earthworm pieces presented on small hooks under a float.[2] The largest sea mullet caught on hook-and-line under Australian Anglers Association rules was a 4.9 kg fish, landed in New South Wales in 1974.

Sea mullet are a target species for recreational fishers in southern Western Australian estuaries using haul seines and gillnets and from ocean beaches using haul seines. Sea mullet may also be caught occasionally as a bycatch of fishers using coastal set gillnets and haul seines in South Australia, Victoria and Tasmania.

Management controls Minimum size limits apply to sea mullet in Queensland, New South Wales, Victoria, Tasmania and South Australia. A bag limit applies in Western Australia. Restrictions on type, number and size of nets, mesh size, closed seasons and closed waters apply to recreational net fishers in States where net methods are allowed.

Resource status

There is insufficient information to allow reliable assessment of the resource status for sea mullet in Australia. New South Wales annual catches have fluctuated to some extent over the 25 years to 1990, but there is no evidence of a decline in the sea mullet stock in that State.

References

1. Thomson, J.M. (1963) Synopsis of the biological data on the grey mullet *Mugil cephalus* Linnaeus 1758. CSIRO *Division of Fisheries and Oceanography, Fisheries Synopsis* **1**. 65 pp.

2. Thomson, J.M. (1980) Family Mugilidae. Grey mullets. Pp 162–166, in *Freshwater fishes of south-eastern Australia*. Ed by R.M. McDowall. Sydney: AH & AW Reed Pty Ltd.

3. Roughley, T.C. (1966) *Fish and fisheries of Australia.* Sydney: Angus and Robertson. 328 pp.

4. Last, P.R., Scott, E.O.G. and Talbot, F.H. (1983) *Fishes of Tasmania.* Hobart: Tasmanian Fisheries Development Authority. 563 pp.

5. Thomson, J.M. (1950) The effect of a period of increased legal minimum length of sea mullet in Western Australia. *Australian Journal of Marine and Freshwater Research* **1**: 199–220.

6. Thomson, J.M. (1955) The movements and migrations of mullet (*Mugil cephalus* L.). *Australian Journal of Marine and Freshwater Research* **6**: 328–347.

7. Grant, C.J. and Spain, A.V. (1975) Reproduction, growth and size allometry of *Mugil cephalus* Linnaeus (Pisces: Mugilidae) from north Queensland waters. *Australian Journal of Zoology* **23**: 181–201.

8. Chubb, C.F., Potter, I.C., Grant, C.J., Lenanton, R.C.J. and Wallace, J. (1981) Age structure, growth rates and movements of sea mullet, *Mugil cephalus* L., and yellow-eye mullet, *Aldrichetta forsteri* (Valenciennes), in the Swan–Avon River system, Western Australia. *Australian Journal of Marine and Freshwater Research* **32**: 605–628.

9. Kesteven, G.L. (1953) Further results of tagging sea mullet, *Mugil cephalus* Linnaeus, on the eastern Australian coast. *Australian Journal of Marine and Freshwater Research* **4**: 251–306.

10. Kesteven, G.L. (1942) Studies in the biology of Australian mullet. I. Account of the fishery and preliminary statement of the biology of *Mugil dobula* Günther. *Australian Council for Scientific and Industrial Research Bulletin* **157**. 147 pp.

11. Thomson, J.M. (1951) Growth and habits of the sea mullet, *Mugil dobula* Günther, in Western Australia. *Australian Journal of Marine and Freshwater Research* **2**: 193–225.

12. Grant, E.M. (1982) *Guide to fishes.* Brisbane: Department of Harbours and Marine. 896 pp.

13. Queensland Fish Management Authority (1991) *Directions for change. Proceedings of the ocean beach net fishery seminar, Brisbane, 19–20 September, 1991.* Ed by A. Magee. Brisbane. 33 pp.

14. Grant, E.M. (1967) *Synopsis of mullet and associated fisheries of southern Queensland.* Australian fisheries development conference, Canberra, 20–22 February, 1967. Background paper **20**. 9 pp.

15. *Commercial fisheries of New South Wales.* (1982) N.S.W. State Fisheries. 60 pp.

Contributors

Information on sea mullet fisheries was originally provided by (in alphabetical order) Mark Cliff, Terry Healy and Rod Lenanton. Additional comments were received from John Burke, Gary Hamer, Vince McDonall, Peter McNamara and Ron West. Drawing by Roger Swainston. (*Details of contributors and their organisations are given in the Acknowledgements section at the back of this book.*)

Compiler Phillip Stewart

A fisher retrieving sea mullet from a gillnet in a Queensland estuary. (Source: Glen Smith, Southern Fisheries Centre, Queensland Department of Primary Industries)

Threadfin salmon

Polydactylus and *Eleutheronema* species

Threadfin salmon

This presentation is on 2 species, **king threadfin** and **blue threadfin**.

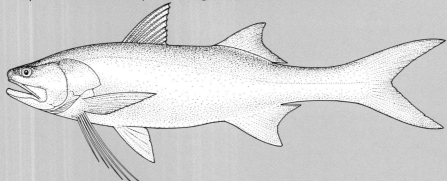

King threadfin, *Polydactylus sheridani* (Macleay)

Other common names include **Burnett salmon, king salmon, gold threadfin** and **Sheridan's threadfin**.
FAO: no known name
Australian species code: 383005

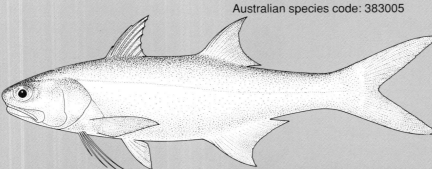

Blue threadfin, *Eleutheronema tetradactylum* (Shaw)

Other common names include **blue salmon, Cooktown salmon, Rockhampton salmon, giant threadfin, colonial salmon, blunt-nosed salmon, blind tassel-fish** and **bluenose salmon**.
FAO: **fourfinger threadfin**
Australian species code: 383004

Family POLYNEMIDAE

Diagnostic features These fish are characterised by having long, free filaments in the pectoral fin and a gelatine-like membrane over the eye ('adipose eyelid'). King threadfin have 5 pectoral fin filaments attached to the pectoral fin and are bluish grey above and silvery yellow below, with bright yellow or golden pectoral fins.[1] Blue threadfin have 3–4 pectoral fin filaments and are dusky bluish green on the upper sides, with yellowish fins. In mature fish, the edge of the pectoral fin is dark blue.[2]

Distribution

Threadfin salmon live in tropical inshore waters, estuaries and tidal reaches of rivers. In Australian waters, king threadfin are present from about Broome in Western Australia to the Noosa River in southern Queensland, and blue threadfin are present from the Ashburton River[3] in Western Australia to at least the Mary River and nearby Great Sandy Strait, or further south, in Queensland. King threadfin are known from the Bay of Bengal,[4] Australia and New Guinea, and blue threadfin are distributed from India through South-east Asia to Australia.

Threadfin salmon usually inhabit shallow, often turbid water over sandbanks and mud substrates to about 5 m, although blue threadfin are found occasionally in water as deep as 23 m off the central Queensland coast. Threadfin salmon usually form loose schools, although larger fish are more often observed in pairs or singly.

Life history

Threadfin salmon are protandrous hermaphrodites, ie mature fish function first as breeding males for several years and then change into functional females. King threadfin between 70 cm and 100 cm fork length may be transitional hermaphrodites (they possess mature male and immature female reproductive tissue, and function as males[2]). However, most king threadfin less than 80 cm fork length are males and most more than 95 cm fork length are females.[5] In the Gulf of Carpentaria and along the north-east Queensland coastline, transitional king threadfin are most often found in the months of June, July, August and September.

In northern waters, king threadfin spawn over the summer months from October to February–March, with a peak during December.[5]

Blue threadfin collected on surveys along the north-east Queensland coast in November–December had either recently spawned or were ready to. Around Townsville, spawning begins in late October.[2] The site of spawning is unknown. Although blue threadfin spawn only once each season,[2] the season is probably extended as ripe male and female fish are present in north Queensland as late as March and April. Ripe eggs are 0.4–0.9 mm diameter,[2,6] and in counts from 15 fish of 37.5–42 cm fork length and 0.9–1.2 kg in the Townsville region, the average number of eggs (ie fecundity) per female was 681 221.[2]

Threadfin salmon eggs are planktonic. There is little information on the larvae, although nursery areas are known to be inshore, shallow and of low salinity. Threadfin salmon from 3 cm fork length are present over inshore tidal flats and in

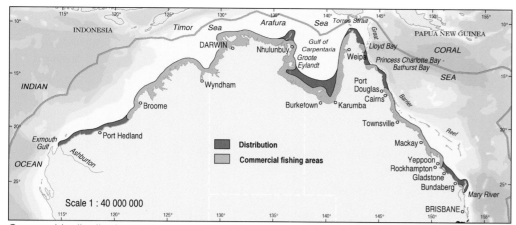

Geographic distribution and commercial fishing areas for blue threadfin (above) and king threadfin (below) in Australian waters.

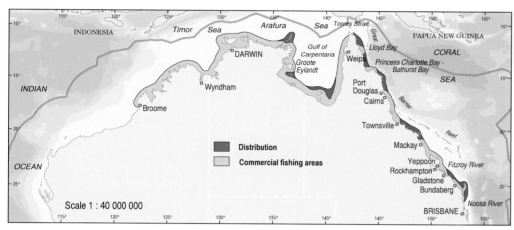

the lower estuaries and foreshores from October[7] to May — during and just after the wet season.[8]

King threadfin have been recorded at 140 cm fork length and 32 kg in the Gulf of Carpentaria, and more than 150 cm fork length in Princess Charlotte Bay. Validated ageing studies have shown that king threadfin can live for more than 20 years, with an estimated maximum attainable size of 170 cm fork length and more than 40 kg.

Blue threadfin in Australian waters are known to attain a maximum fork length of 82 cm, although they rarely exceed 60 cm. Elsewhere in their distribution their maximum recorded sizes are 2 m[9] and 145 kg.[1] Blue threadfin grow very rapidly in their first 6 months. At 1-year-old they average 30 cm fork length, and at 3 years old, 45 cm fork length.[2] Fish are males at 24–47 cm fork length, hermaphrodites at 25–46 cm, and females at 28–72 cm fork length. On the north-east Queensland coast, most blue threadfin are females by 45–50 cm fork length. Hermaphroditic blue threadfin develop from 1–2-year-old fish, and females first appear as 2–3-year-old individuals.[2] Male fish probably commence sex reversal immediately after spawning (ie about April–May) and this

condition may persist until after the next spawning period.[2] The progression from hermaphrodites to females is complete by the following season.

There is little information on the life cycle movements of threadfin salmon. Tagging programs[10] have shown that adult threadfin salmon move long distances along the coastline: at least

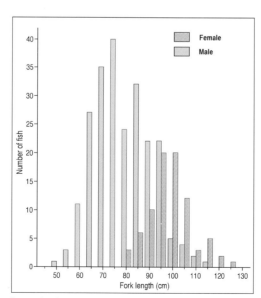

Length–frequency chart showing size of king threadfin at sex reversal, based on 1988 all-year measurements from the southern Gulf of Carpentaria. (Source: Rod Garrett, Northern Fisheries Centre, Queensland Department of Primary Industries)

550 km by king threadfin and 150 km by blue threadfin.

Threadfin salmon are carnivores, feeding at or just below the water surface. Blue threadfin feed on mainly ponyfish (*Leiognathus* species),[2] and also on a variety of other small fish including flathead (*Platycephalus* species), jewfish (Sciaenidae), scats (*Selenotoca* species), sardines (*Sardinella* species), grunters (*Pelates* species, *Pomadasys* species), whiting (*Sillago* species) and small sharks. Crustaceans such as penaeid and alphaeid prawns, crabs, mantis shrimp, stomatopods (*Oratosquilla* species), bay lobsters (*Thenus* species) and molluscs such as gastropods and bivalves, octopus (*Octopus* species), cuttlefish (*Sepia* species) and squid (*Loligo* species) are also consumed. King threadfin feed on crustaceans such as penaeid prawns, mantis shrimp and crabs (eg blue swimmer, *Portunus pelagicus*) and fish such as whiting, ponyfish and jewfish.

Predators of threadfin salmon are sharks, barramundi (*Lates calcarifer*) and other large fish (including larger threadfin salmon) and crocodiles (*Crocodylus porosus*).

Stock structure

There is no information on stock structure in Australian threadfin salmon populations.

Commercial fishery

Threadfin salmon are fished in the north of Western Australia, in the Northern Territory and in Queensland. In Western Australia they are fished all year from about 19° S northwards. In the Northern Territory, threadfin salmon comprise approximately 30 % of the total landings of the barramundi fishery. There, only licensed barramundi fishers may take king threadfin. Blue threadfin are taken in the mixed fish coastal gillnet fishery.

King threadfin and blue threadfin form part of a multi-species fishery (which includes barramundi) on the Queensland east coast from about Lloyd Bay southwards and in the Gulf of Carpentaria; although the landings vary between regions. For example, on the central Queensland coast blue threadfin dominate net fishery catches; in the southern Gulf of Carpentaria, king threadfin are more commonly harvested;

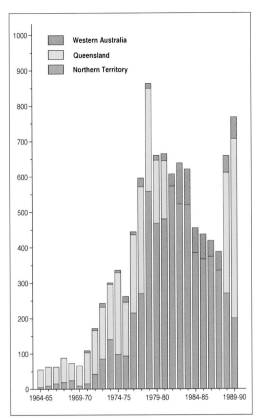

Total annual catch in t of combined blue threadfin and king threadfin for the period 1964–65 to 1989–90. Figures are unavailable for Queensland for the period 1981–82 to 1987–88. Catches for States that average less than 5 % of the total for all States are not shown. (Source: Fisheries Resources Atlas Statistical Database)

and the catch per unit effort for king threadfin is 5 times higher on the east coast south of about Mackay than it is between Mackay and Cairns.[11] From the Gulf of Carpentaria gillnet fishery between 1980 and 1987, king threadfin averaged 30 % by weight of total landings whereas blue threadfin averaged about 5 % of the total landings.

In terms of value to the inshore fishery in Queensland, king threadfin are second only to barramundi and form the main bycatch of the barramundi fishery. Especially in the Gulf of Carpentaria, king threadfin provide the basis for the foreshore fishery. Threadfin salmon are important during the late dry season cooler months (about June to September), while barramundi tend to dominate the river catches at other times. On the east Queensland coast, king threadfin and blue threadfin are caught throughout the year, both species exhibiting greater catch rates during winter months (May to July).[2,11] In general, however, barramundi fishers target king threadfin rather than blue threadfin because of their greater value. This targeting is facilitated by the mesh size permitted for gillnets. In other

words, large mesh nets set for barramundi also gill king threadfin, but blue threadfin — being smaller — often pass through the nets.

Threadfin salmon are caught mainly by coastal set gillnets, but also by fixed tidal traps, beach seines and ring nets, over sandbanks offshore or onshore, or in the mouths of rivers on tidal mud flats.

In the southern Gulf of Carpentaria, the fishery for king threadfin is largely based on male 3–6-year-old fish. Blue threadfin enter the commercial fishery from about 40 cm fork length when they are about 2 years of age.

Typically, threadfin salmon are marketed as fillets, either fresh and chilled on ice or frozen. They are shipped interstate or consumed locally. On the east Queensland coast south of Port Douglas and near Darwin in the Northern Territory, blue threadfin and king threadfin are often wholesaled as gilled and gutted whole fish, but in the Gulf of

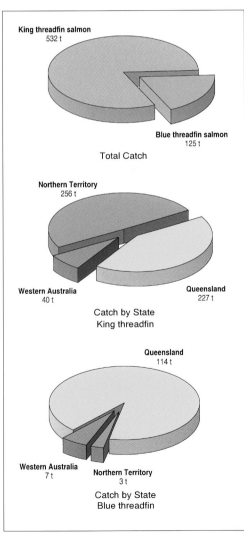

Relative composition of the total threadfin salmon catch for 1988–89 in kg live weight. (Source: Fisheries Resources Atlas Statistical Database)

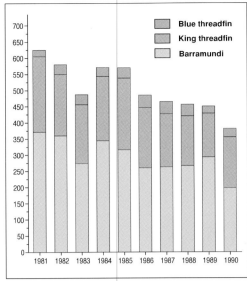

Catches in t fillet weight of threadfin salmon and barramundi from the Gulf of Carpentaria gillnet fishery for the calendar years 1981 to 1990. (Source: Queensland Fish Management Authority and Queensland Department of Primary Industries)

Carpentaria, the fishery is for fillets only. In the Northern Territory, threadfin salmon is used largely in the 'fish-and-chips' trade. King threadfin especially, fetch high prices and were frequently sold as 'barramundi B'. In 1992, wholesale prices for gilled and gutted threadfin salmon (both species) in Queensland averaged A$ 4.50 to A$ 5.50 per kg. Northern Territory prices for threadfin salmon fillets averaged A$ 6.50 to A$ 7.00 in 1992.

Management controls Management of the threadfin salmon fishery is effectively that of the barramundi fishery. Various restrictions on gear and access to areas apply in all States, and in Queensland and the Northern Territory commercial fishers require licences to fish for threadfin salmon. In the Northern Territory the fishery is closed from 1 October to 31 January. There is no closed season for threadfins in Queensland but restrictions on the use of gillnets during the barramundi closed season do affect the fishery.

Recreational fishing

Threadfin salmon are important sport fish. They are caught with rod-and-reel or handlines, from shore or boat. Live or very fresh baits of oily fish, prawns or crabs as well as lures are used. In Queensland, the fishery for blue threadfin is significant from about Port Douglas to Gladstone on the east coast, as well as in the Gulf of Carpentaria around the ports of Weipa and Karumba. The recreational fishing record for a threadfin salmon is 13.6 kg, from Queensland (Australian Anglers Association records).

Management controls Minimum gillnet mesh sizes apply in the Northern Territory and Queensland and minimum legal sizes of threadfin salmon apply in Queensland. The closed fishing season for barramundi around the end of the year also affects the threadfin salmon recreational fishery in the Northern Territory but not in Queensland.

Resource status

Fluctuations in catch rates of king threadfin generally mirror those for barramundi, but in central Queensland over recent years the catch rate of king threadfin compared with that of barramundi has dropped.[9] Better market acceptance of blue threadfin has produced a marked increase in the quantities of blue threadfin landed in Queensland. Threadfin salmon appear to be fully exploited on the east coast but catches are increasing in the Gulf of Carpentaria as better prices are being offered.

Notes

The threadfin salmons' trailing pectoral filaments are sensory and function in the location of food items in the typically turbid waters inhabited by these species.

References

1. Grant, E.M. (1978) *Guide to Fishes.* Brisbane: Queensland Department of Harbours and Marine. 768 pp.

2. Stanger, J.D. (1974) A study of the growth, feeding and reproduction of the threadfin, *Eleutheronema tetradactylum* (Shaw). Unpublished Honours thesis, James Cook University of North Queensland. 126 pp.

3. Whitley, G.P. (1948) A list of the fishes of Western Australia. *Western Australian Department of Fisheries Bulletin* **2**. 35 pp.

4. Kumari, S.G., Ratnamala, B. and Rao, B.V.S. (1985) A new record of the threadfin, *Polynemus sheridani* Macleay from India. *Matsya* **9** & **10**: 196–198.

5. Griffin, R.K. (in press, 1992) Evidence of protandry in threadfin, *Polynemus sheridani* (Macleay), in the Northern Territory, Australia. *Australian Journal of Marine and Freshwater Research*.

6. Kowtal, G.V. (1972) Observations on the breeding and larval development of Chilka 'Sahal' *Eleutheronema tetradactylum* (Shaw). *Indian Journal of Fisheries* **19**: 70–75.

(top) Fishing boat in a northern Australian estuary. (Source: Northern Territory Department of Primary Industry and Fisheries)

(bottom) Portrait of a king threadfin. (Source: Laurie Gwynne, Queensland Fish Management Authority)

7. Taylor, W.R. (1964) Fishes of Arnhem Land. *Records of the American–Australian Scientific Expedition to Arnhem Land* **4**: 45–307.

8. Russell, D.J. and Garrett, R.N. (1983) Use by juvenile barramundi, *Lates calcarifer* (Bloch), and other fishes of temporary supralittoral habitats in a tropical estuary in northern Australia. *Australian Journal of Marine and Freshwater Research* **34**: 805–811.

9. Menon, A.G.K. and Babun Rao, M. (1984) Polynemidae. Threadfins, tasselfishes. 18 pp. in *FAO species identification sheets for fishery purposes. Western Indian Ocean (Fishing Area 51)*. Vol. **3**. Ed by W. Fischer and G. Bianchi. Rome: FAO, United Nations.

10. Australian National Sportfishing Association (1991) *Sportfish tagging program. Tag and release building on conservation and knowledge. 1990/91 report.* Ed by E. Sawynok. Rockhampton. 69 pp.

11. Russell, D.J. (1988) An assessment of the Queensland inshore gill net fishery. *Queensland Department of Primary Industries, Information Series* **QI88024**. 57 pp.

Contributors

Most of the information on this species was originally provided by Rod Garrett, Roland Griffin and John Russell and supplemented by (in alphabetical order) Rik Buckworth, Mark Connell and Terry Healy. Drawings by Gavin Ryan. (*Details of contributors and their organisations are given in the Acknowledgements section at the back of this book.*)
Compilers Patricia Kailola and Phillip Stewart (statistics)

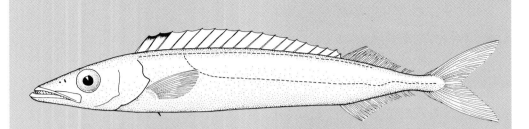

G e m f i s h

R e x e a   s o l a n d r i

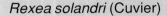

Rexea solandri (Cuvier)

Gemfish

Other common names include **hake, king couta, kingfish, silver kingfish** and **southern kingfish**.
FAO: **royal escolar**
Australian species code: 439002

Family GEMPYLIDAE

Diagnostic features Live gemfish are dark bronze to silvery; they turn bluish after death. Their second dorsal fin, anal fin and caudal fin are grey to black. There is a black blotch at the front of the first dorsal fin covering less than half of the fin membrane. Gemfish have 3 enlarged fang-like teeth at the front of their upper jaw. Their lateral line branches into 2 portions below or behind the fifth dorsal spine. Fish longer than 25 cm are entirely scaled. The pelvic fins consist of a distinct spine and 2 or 3 soft rays.

Distribution

Gemfish are distributed throughout southern Australian waters from Cape Moreton in southern Queensland[1] to the continental slope off the central Western Australian coast. They are also present in New Zealand waters.[2]

Gemfish inhabit deeper continental shelf and upper slope waters from 100 m to 700 m.[3] They are normally caught close to the sea bed but probably move into midwater at times.[3]

Life history

Mature gemfish undergo an annual spawning migration which begins with fish aggregating off north-eastern Bass Strait in autumn, followed by movement of the aggregated fish into waters off New South Wales.[2] The migrating schools usually reach the Sydney to Wollongong region by the end of June and typically peak in abundance during July. There can be some variability from year to year in the timing of the migration, but most fish reach the spawning grounds by early to mid-August. The only confirmed spawning area for gemfish in Australian waters is off the central to northern New South Wales coast,[3] although it is probable that some fish spawn in waters west of Bass Strait (see 'Stock Structure'). Gemfish larvae have been caught in surveys in central and northern New South Wales waters throughout the month of August, but the fast flowing water of the East Australian Current and associated eddies make precise location of spawning grounds difficult.[4]

Spawning takes place during August. The number of eggs produced by female gemfish varies according to the size of the fish. The majority of females release 1–2 million eggs.[3] The pelagic larva has been identified but there is little information on larval development or early life history.

Juvenile gemfish first appear in commercial catches at 1 or 2 years of age as a bycatch of the royal red prawn (*Haliporoides sibogae*) fishery in New South Wales. Gemfish exhibit moderate to fast growth rates throughout their lives, reaching 25–30 cm fork length after 1 year

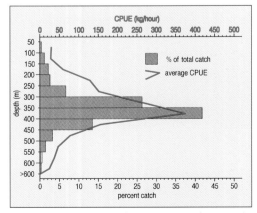

Percentage catch and average catch per unit effort (CPUE) of gemfish from the South East Fishery by 50 m depth zone. (Source: Australian Fishing Zone Information System)

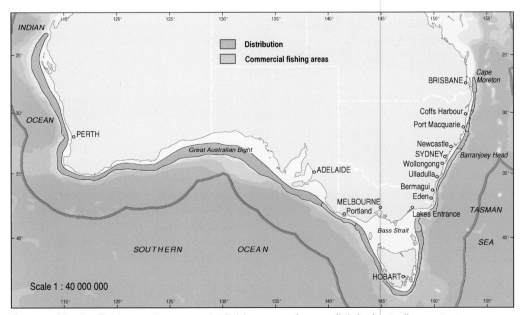

Geographic distribution and commercial fishing areas for gemfish in Australian waters.

and 65–75 cm after 5 years.[5,6] Female gemfish have a greater average size than males for a given age and also live longer. Maximum recorded sizes for gemfish are 116 cm fork length for females and 101 cm for males.[6] Estimates of age from examination of otolith rings have ranged up to 16 years for females and 11 years for males.[3] Estimates of age at maturity for fish sampled from New South Wales waters are 3–5 years for males and 4–6 years for females.[3] The ratio of female to male gemfish in the spawning stock varies from year to year.[7] For example, there was a higher percentage of females in the 1990 spawning run.[8]

Gemfish appear to disperse after spawning although reasonable catch rates can be taken in September and October from the 'back run', when some of the stock returns to southern waters.[6] No information is available on the movement of gemfish in the Great Australian Bight and off Western Australia. Gemfish are known to move throughout the water column at times but no studies have been carried out on the nature of these movements.

Gemfish are carnivorous, feeding mainly on fish such as whiptails (Macrouridae) and deepwater cardinalfish (*Apogonops anomalus*).[9] Gemfish also feed on royal red prawns and squid (Ommastrephidae).[1,9]

Stock structure

The stock structure of Australian gemfish is currently being studied and there is increasing evidence of 2 stocks — 1 in eastern Australian waters and another west of Bass Strait.[3] Juvenile gemfish less than 14 cm long have been caught in western Bass Strait and in the Great Australian Bight[2] and 'ripe' fish have been caught off Western Australia.[2]

Commercial fishery

Gemfish have a history of commercial exploitation beginning last century in Tasmanian waters. Up until 1880 gemfish was an important commercial species in southern Tasmania, where it was caught inshore at night on lines baited with jack mackerel (*Trachurus declivis*) or barracouta (*Thyrsites atun*). The cause of the disappearance of gemfish from the inshore fishery was never established.[10]

Juvenile gemfish have been an incidental catch of demersal otter trawlers

operating on the continental shelf since 1915.[6] It is only since the early 1970s that fishing effort has been targeted on migrating gemfish on the upper continental slope. The Australian gemfish catch rose from less than 100 t in the 1960s to a peak of more than 5000 t in 1978–79 but has since declined because

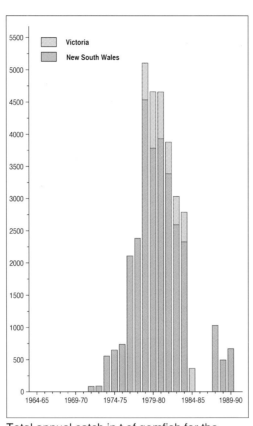

Total annual catch in t of gemfish for the period 1964–65 to 1989–90. Figures are unavailable for: New South Wales from 1964–65 to 1970–71 and 1984–85 to 1986–87; and Victoria from 1972–73 to 1977–78 and 1985–86 to 1989–90. Catches for States that average less than 5 % of the total for all States are not shown. (Source: Fisheries Resources Atlas Statistical Database)

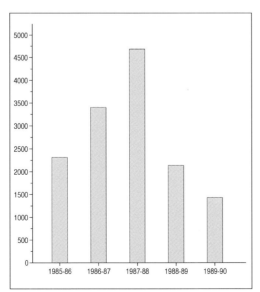

Total annual catch in t of gemfish from the South East Fishery for the period 1985–86 to 1989–90. Catch records for 1985–86 are incomplete. (Source: Australian Fishing Zone Information System)

of the lower availability of fish as well as government regulation of catches.

Gemfish are mainly caught from trawl vessels using demersal otter trawl gear and operating in the South East Fishery. The main trawl grounds are located from Newcastle to eastern Bass Strait in depths of 300 m to 400 m. Most of the catch is taken in June and July when migrating fish are targeted. In the South East Fishery, over 80 % of the annual gemfish catch is taken during winter. The fish caught from the spawning run are large, mature fish mostly between 60 cm and 90 cm fork length.[3]

During spring and autumn, some catches are taken from western Victoria and north-western Tasmania. Immature gemfish are also caught throughout the year as a bycatch of trawling operations targeted at other species such as redfish (*Centroberyx affinis*), jackass morwong (*Nemadactylus macropterus*) and royal red prawns. Small amounts of gemfish are caught in the Great Australian Bight Trawl Fishery.

A small dropline fishery exists for spawning gemfish off the coast of northern New South Wales. Catch rates of gemfish by dropline are low in this area except during August and early September. Some gemfish are also caught in bottom set gillnets (for sharks) in eastern Bass Strait.[3]

Most of the gemfish catch is sold on the domestic fresh fish market. The Sydney Fish Market is the main wholesale market for gemfish, although in recent years the bulk of the catch has been sent directly to processors. Significant quantities of frozen gemfish fillets were until recently exported to Japan, but catch reductions have limited development of a bigger export market. Gemfish are either headed and gutted on board the catching vessel if catches are small, or sold as whole fish when large catches are made. Prices for whole gemfish at the Sydney Fish Market averaged A$ 3.59 per kg in 1991–92. The lower catches taken in the 1990 and 1991 winter gemfish runs have significantly reduced the value of this fishery.

Management controls The main Australian gemfish fishery is managed by the Commonwealth of Australia as part of the South East Fishery. Management of the gemfish fishery is now based on the existence of separate 'eastern' and 'western' stocks. Gemfish catches taken

Hauling a catch of gemfish onboard; south-east of Eden, New South Wales. (Source: Ken Graham, NSW Fisheries)

east of Bass Strait have been subject to a total allowable catch limit since 1988. In 1990 an individual transferable quota system was introduced for the east coast fishery and in 1992 a total allowable catch limit and individual transferable quotas were introduced for the 'western' stock. Catches of gemfish by trawl and dropline north of Barranjoey Head in New South Wales are managed by the State Government. Fishers operating in the Great Australian Bight are also regulated by the Commonwealth of Australia.

Recreational fishery

As they live in deep water, gemfish are rarely caught by anglers. The Australian Anglers Association's record for gemfish is a 6.9 kg individual caught off New South Wales in 1979.

Management controls There are no specific management controls on recreational catches of gemfish.

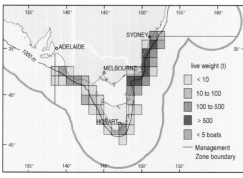

Total gemfish catch in t by 1-degree block from the South East Fishery for the period 1986–1989. The catch for blocks fished by fewer than 5 boats is not shown. (Source: Australian Fishing Zone Information System)

Resource status

A decline in catch rates and changes in mean size for gemfish caught in eastern Australian waters have been observed since the mid 1980s. These changes in the fishery may have been caused by excessive levels of fishing or unknown environmental factors. In any event the stock has been unable to produce sufficient numbers of juvenile fish to replace adults and the result has been a 'recruitment failure' from 1988 onwards. The total allowable catch of 3000 t introduced in 1988 has, of necessity, been greatly reduced in successive years. The present stock size in eastern Australian waters is well below that capable of producing maximum sustainable yields.[3,11]

References

1. Parin, N. and Paxton, J. (1990) Australia's east coast gemfish. *Australian Fisheries* **49**(5), supplement. 5 pp.

2. Tilzey, R.D.J., Zann-Schuster, M., Klaer, N.L. and Williams, M.J. (1990) The south east trawl fishery: biological synopses and catch distributions for seven major commercial fish species. *Bureau of Rural Resources Bulletin* **6**. 80 pp.

3. Rowling, K.R. (in press, 1992) Gemfish. In *The South East Fishery: a scientific review with particular reference to quota management.* Ed by R.D.J. Tilzey. *Bureau of Resource Science Bulletin.*

4. Gorman, T.B., Graham, K.J. and Miskiewicz, A. (1987) *Kapala cruise report no. 100.* Sydney: Division of Fisheries, New South Wales Department of Agriculture. 12 pp.

5. Withell, A.F. and Wankowski, J.W.J. (1989) Age and growth estimates for pink ling, *Genypterus blacodes* (Schneider), and gemfish, *Rexea solandri* (Cuvier), from eastern Bass Strait, Australia. *Australian Journal of Marine and Freshwater Research* **40**: 215–226.

6. Rowling, K.R. (1984) A synopsis of the available biological data on gemfish *Rexea solandri* from NSW waters. *Demersal and Pelagic Fish Research Group workshop on trawl fish resources, Sydney, 27-29 March, 1984. Working paper.* 33 pp.

7. Rowling, K.R. (1990) Changes in the stock composition and abundance of spawning gemfish *Rexea solandri* (Cuvier), Gempylidae, in south-eastern Australian waters. *Australian Journal of Marine and Freshwater Research* **41**: 145–163.

8. Rigney, H. (1990) Poor season indicates big problems for gemfish. *Australian Fisheries* **49**(9): 5–6.

9. Coleman, N. and Mobley, M. (1984) Diets of commercially exploited fish from Bass Strait and adjacent Victorian waters, south-eastern Australia. *Australian Journal of Marine and Freshwater Research* **35**: 549–560.

10. Roughley, T.C. (1966) *Fish and fisheries of Australia.* Sydney: Angus and Robertson. 328 pp.

11. Bureau of Rural Resources (1992) South East Trawl gemfish. *Fishery Status Report,* February 1992. 4 pp.

Contributors

Most of the original information on this species was provided by Kevin Rowling. Additional comments were given by John Paxton and Richard Tilzey. Drawing by Sharne Weidland. (*Details of contributors and their organisations are given in the Acknowledgements section at the back of this book.*)

Compilers Phillip Stewart and Christina Grieve (maps)

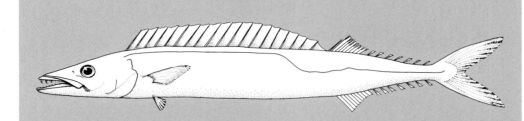

Barracouta

Thyrsites atun

Thyrsites atun (Euphrasen)

Barracouta

Other common names include **couta** and **snoek**.
FAO: **snoek**
Australian species code: 439001

Family GEMPYLIDAE

Diagnostic features Barracouta have an elongate, compressed body which is covered with minute, easily dislodged scales. The first dorsal fin is barely separated from the second dorsal fin and there are 5–7 finlets behind both the second dorsal fin and anal fins. A single lateral line runs along the back, turning sharply downwards below the rear of the first dorsal fin. Barracouta are steel blue to dark grey on their upper body and silvery below. Their first dorsal fin is black.

Distribution

Barracouta are distributed throughout coastal and continental shelf waters of the southern hemisphere between the latitudes 30° and 45°.[1] They inhabit southern waters of the Australian Fishing Zone from Moreton Bay in Queensland[2] to Shark Bay in Western Australia.[3]

Schools of barracouta are most common in surface waters of the continental shelf in water temperatures between 13°C and 18°C. They are occasionally caught from near the sea bed in depths to 550 m.

Life history

Spawning patterns of barracouta are complex, with different stocks spawning at different times of the year.[4] Off New South Wales and eastern Victoria spawning occurs mainly during winter and spring. In waters of Tasmania, Bass Strait and central Victoria the spawning period is spring to early autumn (October to March). In South Australia and Western Australia the spawning season is from late autumn to winter.[2]

Barracouta eggs are small, transparent and pelagic.[5] There are no estimates of egg numbers for mature female fish and little is known of larval ecology and development in barracouta. Juvenile barracouta inhabit sheltered waters of southern bays and estuaries.[6,7]

Barracouta grow quickly as juveniles, reaching 30 cm fork length by the end of their first year, and 45–50 cm by 2 years of age.[1] They may live for more than 10 years[2] and reach a total length of 140 cm.[8] There is no significant difference in growth rates between sexes. Faster growth is evident in fish from eastern Tasmania compared with the Bass Strait

stock.[1] Sexual maturity is reached between 2 and 4 years of age.[2]

The migration patterns in Australian barracouta are complex. Some stocks undertake annual migrations lasting 6–9 months that cover several hundred km.[4] The migrations appear to be related to water temperature or food availability, or a combination of both factors. Barracouta also move through the water column from depths of 200 m to the surface, where they are usually caught at dawn and at dusk.[4]

Barracouta feed on a variety of midwater species including euphausiid shrimps (*Nyctiphanes australis*), anchovy (*Engraulis australis*), pilchards

(*Sardinops neopilchardus*) and jack mackerel (*Trachurus declivis*).[2] Juvenile barracouta are important in the diet of adult barracouta. Juveniles are also a major food item for arrow squid (*Nototodarus gouldi*) in Bass Strait. School sharks (*Galeorhinus galeus*), gummy sharks (*Mustelus antarcticus*) and seals (Otariidae) also feed on barracouta.

Stock structure

There appear to be at least 5 stocks of barracouta in Australian waters, 3 of which are located in south-eastern waters and the remaining 2 in South Australia and Western Australia respectively.[1,4]

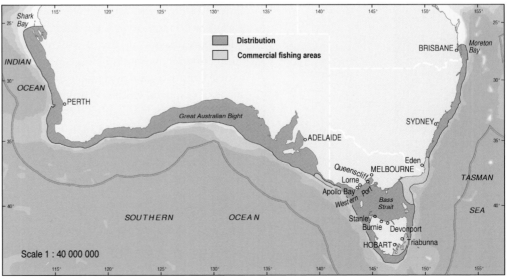

Geographic distribution and commercial fishing areas for barracouta in Australian waters.

These findings are based on studies of growth, spawning and migration factors and have not been validated by genetic studies.

Commercial fishery

The Australian barracouta fishery has operated since the mid 1800s, following the introduction of trolling methods at Queenscliff (Victoria) in the 1850s.[9] A barracouta fishery was also established in Tasmania in the second half of that century. Prior to the Second World War, barracouta was the second most important fish species in the Australian fishing industry, exceeded only by sea mullet (*Mugil cephalus*) in volume of landed catch. Production of barracouta increased during the war, peaking in 1945–46 at 9000 t. This peak was mainly the result of increased catches in Tasmania where effort was diverted from the southern rock lobster (*Jasus edwardsii*) fishery to produce bulk fish for canning.[10] Production of barracouta was low during the 1950s but increased from 1960, ranging from about 1900 t to 4100 t during the period 1960–61 to 1974–75.[2] Since 1975 fishing effort

Barracouta are a common bycatch of demersal otter trawling.
(Source: Ken Graham, N.S.W. Fisheries)

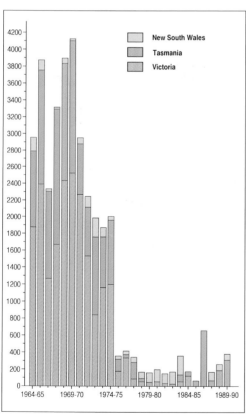

Total annual catch in t of barracouta for the period 1964–65 to 1989–90. Figures are unavailable for: New South Wales from 1984–85 to 1986–87; and Victoria from 1985–86 to 1989–90. Catches for States that average less than 5 % of the total for all States are not shown. (Source: Fisheries Resources Atlas Statistical Database)

targeted at barracouta has lessened, mainly as a result of competition from more popular trawled species in the domestic fresh fish market and low priced imported product for processing.

Historically, fishing for barracouta has been confined to southern New South Wales, Victoria and Tasmania. Most of the New South Wales catch was landed at Eden. In Victoria, the most productive waters were off Lorne, Apollo Bay, Queenscliff and Western Port[2] while Tasmanian barracouta vessels operated mainly from Hobart and Triabunna in the south-east and Devonport, Stanley and Burnie in the north. Trolling was the most widely used method in the fishery, with lines towed at the surface or weighted to attract deeper swimming fish. Lures used varied from wooden and plastic jigs to strips of coloured cloth and animal hide attached to hooks. Vessels used in the early fishery were open or half-decked sailing vessels up to 12 m in length. Diesel engines were introduced in the 1950s, but the vessel design remained basically the same.

Currently, catches of barracouta are taken as a bycatch of demersal otter trawling in New South Wales and Victoria as part of the South East Fishery, with the highest catches resulting from target

fishing for warehous (*Seriolella* species). Catches are also taken in south-eastern Tasmanian waters using trolling methods, although the level of catch has varied considerably since 1980 when it was less than 10 t, to 650 t in 1986–87.

Most of the catch is sold on the fresh fish market in headed and gutted form. Some of the catch is processed as smoked product or fish cakes, although processors rely mainly on imported barracouta for continuity of supply.[2] Barracouta heads are widely used as bait in rock lobster pots. Wholesale prices for barracouta at the Melbourne Wholesale Fish Market ranged between A$ 0.50 and A$ 1.00 per kg in 1991-92.

Management controls Trawl fishers in the South East Fishery are regulated by the Commonwealth of Australia through a management plan limiting licence numbers, gear specifications and vessel units. Barracouta catches are not currently subject to the total allowable catch limits and individual transferable quotas which were introduced for the major South East Fishery species in 1992. A specific total allowable catch limit may apply to barracouta in the future. Troll vessels operating in Tasmanian waters are managed under State Government regulations.

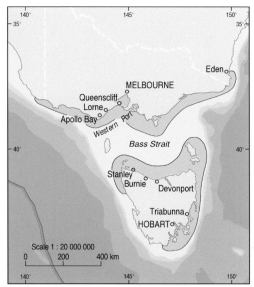

Historical fishing areas for barracouta in Australian waters.

Recreational fishery

Barracouta are targeted by anglers in all southern States except New South Wales. Surface feeding schools are fished by trolling or casting metallic lures or jigs.[7] The largest recorded barracouta was caught by a recreational angler in New South Wales and weighed 6.2 kg (Australian Anglers Association records).

Management controls There are no specific management controls on recreational fishing for barracouta.

Resource status

Current catches appear to be well below sustainable levels. This situation is due to market limitations rather than over-exploitation of stocks. Periodic fluctuations in apparent abundance of barracouta are well documented but the factors responsible are unknown.

Notes

Barracouta are susceptible to infestation by protozoan parasites, which cause the incidence of 'milky' fish. The flesh of infected individuals softens within 24 hours of capture to an unmarketable condition.[5] A small percentage of barracouta is also infected by nematode and cestode worms. Occurrence of these parasites has contributed to the low demand for barracouta on the fresh fish market although their presence is detected prior to sale and the affected fish discarded.

References

1. Grant, C.J., Cowper, T.R. and Reid, D.D. (1978) Age and growth of snoek, *Leionura atun* (Euphrasen), in south-eastern Australian waters. *Australian Journal of Marine and Freshwater Research* **29**: 435–444.

2. Winstanley, R.H. (1979) Snoek. *CSIRO Division of Fisheries and Oceanography, Fishery Situation Report* **4**. 16 pp.

3. Hutchins, B. and Swainston, R. (1986) *Sea fishes of southern Australia. Complete field guide for anglers and divers.* Perth: Swainston Publishing. 180 pp.

4. Blackburn, M. and Gartner, P.E. (1954) Populations of barracouta, *Thyrsites atun* (Euphrasen), in Australian waters. *Australian Journal of Marine and Freshwater Research* **5**: 411–468.

5. Cowper, T.R. (1960) A synopsis for FAO species and stocks thesaurus of data on *Leionura atun* (Euphrasen) 1791, barracouta. Document prepared for the *First meeting of the Standing Committee on Development of Pelagic Fisheries in South-east Australia, Melbourne, 30 November – 1 December, 1960.* Cronulla: CSIRO Division of Fisheries and Oceanography. 30 pp.

6. Paul, L. (1986) *New Zealand fishes. An identification guide.* Auckland: Reed Methuen. 184 pp.

7. Starling, S. (1988) *The fisherman's handbook. How to find, identify and catch the top Australian angling fish.* Sydney: Angus and Robertson Publishers. 263 pp.

8. May, J.L. and Maxwell, J.G.H. (1986) *A field guide to trawl fish from temperate waters of Australia.* Hobart: CSIRO Division of Fisheries Research. 492 pp.

9. Hall, D.N. and MacDonald, C.M. (1986) Commercial fishery situation report: net and line fisheries of Port Phillip Bay Victoria, 1914–1984. *Victorian Department of Conservation, Forests and Lands, Fisheries Division, Marine Fisheries Report* **10**. 121 pp.

10. Blackburn, M. (1950) The condition of the fishery for barracouta, *Thyrsites atun* (Euphrasen), in Australian waters. *Australian Journal of Marine and Freshwater Research* **1**: 110–128.

Contributors

Information on the trawl fishery for barracouta was originally provided by Richard Tilzey. Ross Winstanley and Howel Williams provided further comment. Drawing by Rosalind Poole. (*Details of contributors and their organisations are given in the Acknowledgements section at the back of this book.*)

Compilers Phillip Stewart and Christina Grieve (maps)

Antarctic fish

Channichthyidae *and* Nothotheniidae

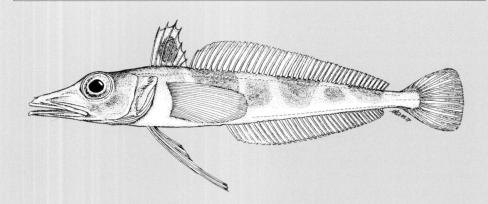

Antarctic fish species

This presentation is on 3 species, **spiny icefish**, **Antarctic silverfish** and **blunt scalyhead**.

Spiny icefish, *Chaenodraco wilsoni* Regan

There are no other common names.
FAO: **spiny ice fish**
Australian species code: 407790

Family CHANNICHTHYIDAE

Antarctic silverfish, *Pleuragramma antarcticum* Boulenger

There are no other common names.
FAO: **Antarctic silverfish**
Australian species code: 404790

Family NOTOTHENIIDAE

Blunt scalyhead, *Trematomus eulepidotus* Regan

There are no other common names.
FAO: no known name
Australian species code: 404791

Family NOTOTHENIIDAE

Diagnostic features Spiny icefish (pictured) have completely colourless blood. They are the only 'white-blooded' fish with 4 rays in the pelvic fin (others have 5). They have a large mouth with prominent teeth, 2 dorsal fins and no scales. Antarctic silverfish are herring-like Antarctic cod and have red blood. They are distinguished by having relatively large eyes and a long streamlined body with silvery deciduous scales. Blunt scalyheads are Antarctic cod with scales, 2 dorsal fins, red blood and no swim bladder. They can be distinguished from most other Antarctic cods by having scales on their snout, lower jaw and in the preorbital area.

Distribution

These 3 species — spiny icefish, Antarctic silverfish and blunt scalyhead — are distributed only within the waters of the Antarctic continental shelf and Antarctic offshore islands (South Orkney, South Shetland and Elephant islands).

Spiny icefish and blunt scalyheads inhabit depths of 100 m to 650 m.[1] Adults are described as benthopelagic, ie they live on the sea floor but rise frequently to feed. Both species are most common in shallower waters of the continental shelf, especially on banks less than 250 m deep in areas where local upwellings increase food supply.

Antarctic silverfish are described as the only truly pelagic fish species in Antarctic waters. They live throughout the water column from the surface to a depth of 700 m,[1] although they more commonly inhabit continental shelf waters in high latitudes where water temperatures do not exceed 2°C. Adult Antarctic silverfish generally inhabit deeper waters than do juveniles.

Life history

Spiny icefish spawn in winter.[1] Females produce a small number (100s per female) of large, yolky eggs that are probably demersal. The larvae spend their first summer in waters near the surface.[2]

Antarctic silverfish have been observed to spawn in winter or early spring in Prydz Bay[3] or winter in the Weddell Sea outside Australian Antarctic Territory waters.[4] Unlike other Antarctic species, Antarctic silverfish lay a large number (average of 7500 per female) of small eggs of about 1.5 mm diameter.[5] The eggs probably hatch in waters near the surface in November or December, where the larvae spend their first 2 or 3 years.[2]

Spawning activity has not been observed for blunt scalyheads but it is thought to occur in summer[6] on the continental shelf, with the pelagic eggs hatching in May to June[2] in near-surface waters. The eggs are about 4.5 mm in diameter and larvae average 18.6 mm standard length on hatching.[6] Larvae inhabit near-surface waters.

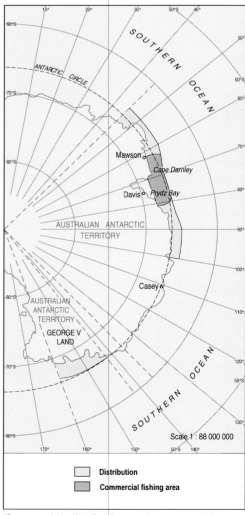

Geographic distribution and commercial fishing area for spiny icefish in Australian Antarctic Territory waters.

Juveniles of all 3 species are also found near the surface, often in association with Antarctic krill (*Euphausia superba*) swarms. Aggregations of spiny icefish, which are believed to be feeding aggregations, have been observed over shallow banks in summer. Juvenile blunt scalyheads are found in the surface layer of continental shelf waters until they are about 6–7 cm standard length when they adopt the adult benthic life.[6]

Spiny icefish grow to 43 cm total length,[7] and fish of 30 cm length are common.[1] Growth in Antarctic silverfish is slow. They live up to 15 years,[4] growing to a maximum total length of only 25 cm [1] and a weight of 200 g. Blunt scalyheads can grow to 34 cm total length.[7] There are no data on the size at maturity for spiny icefish or blunt scalyheads. Both sexes of Antarctic silverfish mature when 3–4 years old, and at about 13 cm in length.[3]

Spiny icefish appear to feed entirely on euphausiid shrimps. Juveniles feed on juvenile *Euphausia crystallorophias* and Antarctic krill whilst adults feed almost entirely on adult Antarctic krill, mostly in the top 100 m of the water column. Both juvenile and adult Antarctic silverfish feed on euphausiid shrimp larvae and copepod crustaceans.[8] Juvenile blunt scalyheads feed on small crustaceans, mainly copepods. In adults the diet shifts to one dominated by Antarctic krill, with bottom living crustaceans and polychaete worms comprising the remainder of the diet.

Adelie penguins (*Pygoscelis adeliae*) feed occasionally on juveniles of several icefish species (probably including spiny icefish) as well as Antarctic silverfish.[9] Juvenile fish associated with Antarctic krill swarms probably also contribute to the diet of baleen whales (Mysticeti). Adult spiny icefish and Antarctic silverfish are prey to Weddell seals (*Leptonychotes weddelli*). Antarctic silverfish are also a major forage species for emperor penguins (*Aptenodytes forsteri*), several species of petrels (Procellariidae), and crabeater seals (*Lobodon carcinophagus*).[9] Blunt scalyheads are a significant part of the diet of emperor penguins.

Stock structure

There is no information on the stock structure of Antarctic fish resources.

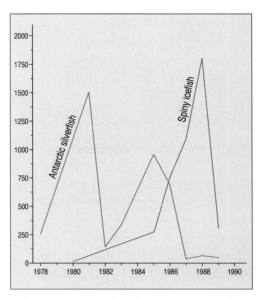

Total annual catch in t of spiny icefish and Antarctic silverfish for the period 1978 to 1989 in Australian Antarctic Territory waters. (Source: Williams and Nicol[10])

Commercial fishery

Within the Australian Antarctic Territory, spiny icefish are caught by demersal otter trawling on the continental shelf in Prydz Bay, while Antarctic silverfish are taken by mid-water trawling in the same area. Spiny icefish and blunt scalyheads are caught by demersal otter trawling on the shallow banks to the west, between Cape Darnley and Mawson. Antarctic silverfish are caught by mid-water trawling in shelf areas to the west of Prydz Bay and in the southern Pacific Ocean. Outside the Australian Antarctic Territory spiny icefish have been caught on the Gunnerus Bank (33° E), the Antarctic Peninsula and South Shetland Islands. Very small catches of Antarctic silverfish have been taken near the Antarctic Peninsula and South Orkney Islands.

All 3 species are taken in the Australian Antarctic Territory by trawlers from the Commonwealth of Independent States (CIS) of the former USSR.[10] Catches of spiny icefish have varied between 279 t and 1816 t annually since 1985. Small catches of Antarctic silverfish have also been made. In the Prydz Bay area, annual catches of Antarctic silverfish have varied between 30 t and 966 t, while in the southern Pacific Ocean, catches reached

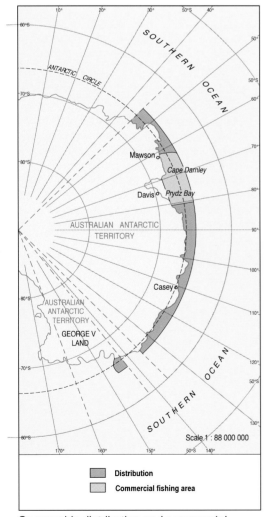

Geographic distribution and commercial fishing area for Antarctic silverfish in Australian Antarctic Territory waters.

Geographic distribution and commercial fishing area for blunt scalyheads in Australian Antarctic Territory waters.

1517 t in 1981. The first catches of blunt scalyheads were recorded in 1990 when trawlers from the CIS landed 148 t.[11]

In the Antarctic Peninsula area, outside the Australian Antarctic Territory, over 10 000 t of spiny icefish were caught in 1979, 4320 t in 1980 and virtually nothing since then. All catches were taken by vessels from the CIS.[8]

In the CIS spiny icefish and blunt scalyheads are marketed as frozen fillets or headed and gutted fish. Antarctic silverfish are small, the flesh has a high oil content[10] and is probably only suitable for industrial purposes such as oil production. There are currently no markets for these species in Australia.

Management controls All resources in Antarctic waters are under the control of the international Convention for the Conservation of Antarctic Marine Living Resources (CCAMLR) as well as national governments to the extent of their jurisdiction. There are no fishing restrictions in force in Australian Antarctic Territory waters, but all vessels wishing to fish in these waters require permits as resources are protected under the Commonwealth *Antarctic Marine Resources Act*. All fishing is prohibited in the Antarctic Peninsula region and the South Orkney Islands region.

Recreational fishery

There is no recreational fishing in Australian Antarctic Territory waters.

Resource status

In Australian Antarctic Territory waters, spiny icefish, Antarctic silverfish and blunt scalyheads are probably not fully exploited. However, the total resource in these waters is likely to be small.

References

1. Fischer, W. and Hureau, J.C. (eds) (1985) *FAO species identification sheets for fishery purposes. Southern Ocean (Fishing Areas 48, 58 and 88) (CCAMLR Convention Area)* Vol. **2**: 233–470. Rome: FAO.

2. Kellermann, A. (1990) Identification key and catalogue of larval Antarctic fishes. *Berichte fur Polarforschung* **67**: 1–136.

3. Shust, K.V., Parfenovich, S.S. and Gerasimchuk, V.V. (1984) Distribution of the Antarctic silverfish (*Pleuragramma antarcticum* Boulenger) in relation to oceanographical conditions within its area of habitat and in relation to biographical characteristics of the species. In *Problems of Geography, issue* **125**, *'Oceans and Life'*. Moscow: Mhysl.

4. Hubold, G. and Tomo, A.P. (1989) Age and growth of Antarctic silverfish *Pleuragramma antarcticum* Boulenger 1902 from southern Weddell Sea and Antarctic Peninsula. *Polar Biology* **9**: 205–212.

5. Gerasimchuk, V.V. (1987) On the fecundity of Antarctic sidestripe, *Pleuragramma antarcticum. Journal of Ichthyology* **28**: 98–100.

6. Ekau, W. (1989) Egg development of *Trematomus eulepidotus* Regan, 1914 (Nototheniidae: Pisces) from the Weddell Sea, Antarctica. *Cybium* **13**(3): 213–219, cited in O. Gon and P.C. Heemstra (eds) (1990). *Fishes of the Southern Ocean.*

7. Gon, O. and Heemstra, P.C. (eds) (1990) *Fishes of the Southern Ocean.* Johannesburg: Macmillan South Africa (Publishers) (Pty) Ltd. 462 pp.

8. Williams, R. (1985) Trophic relationships between pelagic fishes and euphausiids in Antarctic waters. Pp 452–459, in *Antarctic nutrient cycles and food webs*. Ed by W.R. Siegfried, P.R. Conde and R.M. Laws. Berlin: Springer.

9. Williams, R. (1988) Australian research on Antarctic bird and seal diets. *Scientific Commission for the Conservation of Antarctic Marine Living Resources, Selected scientific papers* **5**(2): 231–249.

10. Williams, R. and Nicol, S. (1991) Southern Ocean resources. Pp 207–215, in *Australian and New Zealand southern trawl fisheries conference: issues and opportunities. Bureau of Rural Resources Proceedings* **10**. Ed by K. Abel, M. Williams and P. Smith. Canberra: Bureau of Rural Resources and Australian Bureau of Agricultural and Resource Economics.

11. Commission for the Conservation of Antarctic Marine Living Resources (1990) *Statistical bulletin* **2** (1980–1989). Hobart, Australia. 109 pp.

Contributors

The information on this species was provided originally by Dick Williams. Drawing courtesy of FAO, Rome. (*Details of contributors and their organisations are given in the Acknowledgements section at the back of this book.*)

Compilers Alex McNee and Christina Grieve

Demersal trawl being hauled aboard the Australian Antarctic research vessel, *Aurora Australis*. (Source: Stephanie Davenport, CSIRO Marine Laboratories, Hobart)

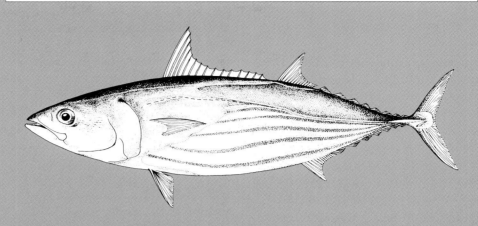

Skipjack tuna

Katsuwonus pelamis

***Katsuwonus pelamis* (Linnaeus)**

Skipjack tuna

Other common names include
skipjack, **striped tuna**, **stripey** and
oceanic bonito.
FAO: **skipjack tuna**
Australian species code: 441003

Family SCOMBRIDAE

Diagnostic features Skipjack tuna are
dark blue or purple on the back and
silvery on their lower sides and belly.
They have 3–5 prominent, dark
longitudinal bands on their lower sides.
These tuna have fine, slender teeth, a
strong median keel on the caudal fin
base between 2 smaller keels, and
barely separated first and second dorsal
fins. They have a total of 53–63 gill
rakers on the first gill arch.[1]

Distribution

Skipjack tuna are widespread in
Australia's oceanic waters. They inhabit
waters off the east coast from Lady Elliot
Island in Queensland to Storm Bay in
Tasmania, but are not present within the
Great Barrier Reef. The southern limit of
distribution on the east coast varies
seasonally,[2] such that in late winter and
spring the fish are not found south of the
New South Wales–Victorian border. In the
west, their distribution extends from
Kangaroo Island in the Great Australian
Bight to Cape Leeuwin in southern
Western Australia, and north to Broome.[2]

The global distribution of skipjack
tuna includes all tropical and subtropical
waters except for the eastern
Mediterranean Sea and the Black Sea.[1]
Skipjack tuna normally inhabit waters
with surface temperatures of 20°C to
30°C.[3] However, adults are sometimes
present in waters as cold as 15°C.[1,2]
Skipjack tuna also need a dissolved
oxygen level of 2.5 ml per l of sea water
to maintain a minimum swimming speed,
and require higher levels when active.[4]
This requirement generally restricts
skipjack tuna to water above the
thermocline and in some areas, such as
the eastern Pacific, may exclude them
from surface waters.[4]

The depth range of skipjack tuna can
be from surface waters to 260 m during
the day, but at night it is much shallower.[5]
Skipjack tuna are schooling fish having a
general tendency to school by size.[6] The
schools are often associated with albacore
(*Thunnus alalunga*) or yellowfin tuna
(*T. albacares*) and sometimes with
whales (Cetacea) or whale sharks
(*Rhiniodon typus*). Schools may also
occur close to floating objects such as
logs, and near seamounts and current
boundaries.

Life history

Skipjack tuna probably spawn in the
Coral Sea off north Queensland and in
waters off north-western Australia.[2] In
equatorial waters spawning occurs during
all months, but in subtropical waters the
season is restricted to summer and early
autumn. In the western Pacific Ocean
skipjack tuna larvae have been recorded
from latitudes between 35° N and 25° S,
and water temperatures of 23–30°C.[6,7] In
the Indian Ocean skipjack tuna larvae
have been recorded north of latitude
30° S.[7]

In tropical waters reproductively
active female skipjack tuna spawn almost
daily.[8] Ripe skipjack tuna eggs are about
1 mm in diameter and transparent and
buoyant. Estimates of the number of eggs

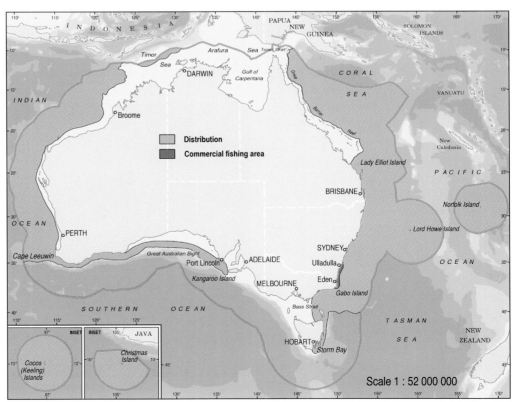

Geographic distribution and commercial fishing area for skipjack tuna in Australian waters.

released at each spawning range from about 100 000 eggs for the smallest mature females to 2 million for the largest fish.[6] Skipjack tuna eggs hatch after 1–1.5 days.

The warm East Australian Current distributes skipjack tuna larvae into subtropical waters off eastern Australia.[9] The larvae are generally limited to the upper 50 m of water and are most common in the sub-surface layers. Juvenile skipjack tuna less than 15 cm total length inhabit the same areas as larvae but generally move to cooler waters as they grow to maturity.[9]

There are no validated age estimates for skipjack tuna. Growth rates calculated from tag-recapture studies, length frequency data, and growth rings on otoliths and fin spines show large variation between regions and seasons.[10] Growth rates are reported to be faster in the western Pacific Ocean than in the eastern Pacific. Skipjack tuna probably live to about 4 years of age and in Australian waters they reach a maximum size of about 80 cm fork length.[2] Very large fish, greater than 100 cm fork length and 20 kg, are sometimes caught in central Pacific waters.[11] Skipjack tuna reach maturity at 40–45 cm fork length.[6] Estimates of age for a given size indicate that they are 1 or 2 years old at maturity.[6]

There is little information on migration patterns for skipjack tuna in Australian waters. Skipjack tuna tagged in the Coral Sea, off Norfolk Island and off New South Wales have been recovered in waters off the Solomon Islands, New Caledonia, French Polynesia and New Zealand.[12] The recapture in Australian waters of a few fish tagged in New Zealand and Papua New Guinea indicates that there could also be significant movement of skipjack tuna into the Australian Fishing Zone from the greater South Pacific.

Skipjack tuna are carnivorous and eat a wide variety of species. Juveniles have a high proportion of crustaceans in their diet and tend to consume more fish as they grow larger. Studies have shown that fish and squid are the most important food items in areas north of Sydney[12] and krill (*Nyctiphanes australis*) is most important in the south.[2] Adult skipjack tuna are also cannibalistic towards juveniles. The main predators of skipjack tuna are larger pelagic fish such as yellowfin tuna, bigeye tuna (*Thunnus obesus*), billfish (Istiophoridae) and whaler sharks (Carcharhinidae).[6]

Stock structure

The stock structure of skipjack tuna from the Pacific and Indian oceans has not been determined. Only 2 of the several hypotheses for Pacific Ocean skipjack tuna stock structure are widely supported. The first proposes at least 5 sub-populations within the Pacific, including 2 in the western Pacific;[4] and the alternative hypothesis proposes that whereas there are no distinct subpopulations, the probability of skipjack tuna schools interbreeding is proportional to the distance between each group.[12,13] There is no information on the stock structure of skipjack tuna in the Indian Ocean.

Commercial fishery

Skipjack tuna have been caught by Australian commercial fishers since the development of pole-and-line fisheries targeting southern bluefin tuna (*Thunnus maccoyii*) in the 1950s. However, only small amounts of skipjack tuna are targeted in this fishery in most years because of their lower value. Additionally, purse seine vessels operating in the southern bluefin tuna fishery have taken significant catches of skipjack tuna in some years, particularly in the Great Australian Bight. The total catch of skipjack tuna taken varied between 100 t and 1200 t per year between 1975–76 and 1989–90.

The main fishing area for skipjack tuna in Australia is in the south-east from Ulladulla to just south of Gabo Island. Two methods are used in the fishery: pole-and-line and purse seining. The

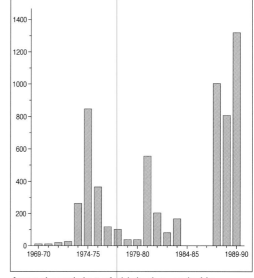

Annual catch in t of skipjack tuna in New South Wales for the period 1969–70 to 1989–90. Figures are unavailable for 1984–85 to 1986–87. (Source: Fisheries Resources Atlas Statistical Database)

fishery has developed from catches of about 150 t in 1985–86 to an estimated 6000 t in 1990–91 and 1991–92. Purse seine vessels generally land a greater proportion of the catch. Pole-and-line vessels often fish skipjack tuna schools in co-operation with purse seine vessels. Yellowfin tuna and albacore are taken as a bycatch of both fishing methods.

The fishing season normally extends from December to March. The skipjack tuna caught are usually between 2 kg and 3 kg, yet larger fish tend to be caught late in the season in southern waters.

The main port of landing for skipjack tuna is Eden, and the cannery there processes most of the Australian catch. Some skipjack tuna is processed at the Port Lincoln cannery in South Australia. Some of the skipjack tuna catch is sold for

Poling skipjack tuna off the southern New South Wales coast. (Source: Lindsay Chapman, Bureau of Resource Sciences)

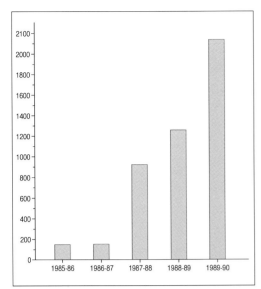

Annual landings in t of skipjack tuna at the Eden cannery for the period 1985–86 to 1989–90. (Source: H.J. Heinz Company Australia Ltd., Eden)

bait depending on demand from other fisheries and the prevailing price for canning fish. Only a small amount is sold on the domestic fresh fish market. Fishers supplying frozen skipjack tuna to the Eden cannery during the 1992–93 season, received A$ 590 per t for fish less then 2.3 kg and A$ 840 per t for larger fish.

Management controls The skipjack tuna fishery is managed as part of the East Coast Tuna Fishery. Tuna fisheries are managed by the Commonwealth of Australia in all States except New South Wales, which has jurisdiction to 3 nautical miles. Fishing by purse seining is subject to limited entry, net size restrictions, bycatch limits for yellowfin tuna and boat length restrictions for inshore waters.

Recreational fishery

Skipjack tuna are commonly caught by sport and recreational fishers in south-eastern Australian waters. Most fish are caught by trolling or casting small lures from a boat. Catches are also made using flies or baits of whole, small fish or flesh strips.[14] Skipjack tuna are often used as live or dead baits for larger tuna species and billfish. The flesh is also a popular bait amongst anglers for a variety of marine fish. The largest skipjack tuna caught under Game Fishing Association of Australia rules was 11.5 kg, landed in Queensland.

Management controls There are no management controls on recreational fishing for skipjack tuna.

Resource status

There are no estimates of sustainable yield or stock size for skipjack tuna in Australian waters. An estimated 780 000 t of skipjack tuna were caught in the western Pacific (which includes Australia) in 1990.[9] Exploitation rates calculated from tagging studies indicate that significantly higher catches can be sustained.[9,11,12]

References

1. Blackburn, M. and Serventy, D.L. (1981) Observations on distribution and life history of skipjack tuna, *Katsuwonus pelamis*, in Australian waters. *Fishery Bulletin (U.S.)* **79**: 85–94.

2. Collette, B.B. and Nauen, C.E. (1983) FAO species catalogue. Vol. 2. Scombrids of the world. An annotated and illustrated catalogue of tunas, mackerels, bonitos and related species known to date. *FAO Fisheries Synopsis No. 125*, **2**. 137 pp.

3. Forsbergh, E.D. (1980) Synopsis of biological data on the skipjack tuna, *Katsuwonus pelamis* (Linnaeus, 1758), in the Pacific Ocean. Pp 295–360, in *Synopsis of biological data on eight species of scombrids. Special Report* **2**. Ed by W.H. Bayliff. La Jolla, California: Inter-American Tropical Tuna Commission.

4. Sharp, G.D. (1978) Behavioural and physiological properties of tuna and their effects on vulnerability to fishing gear. Pp 397–450, in *The physiological ecology of tunas*. Ed by G.D. Sharp and A.E. Dizon. New York: Academic Press.

5. Dizon, A.E., Brill, R.W. and Yuen, H.S.H. (1978) Correlations between environment, physiology, and activity and the effects on thermoregulation in skipjack tuna. Pp 233–260, in *The physiological ecology of tunas*. Ed by G.D. Sharp and A.E. Dizon. New York: Academic Press.

6. Matsumoto, W.M., Skillman, R.A. and Dizon, A.E. (1984) Synopsis of biological data on the skipjack tuna, *Katsuwonus pelamis*. *U.S. Department of Commerce, NOAA Technical Report, NMFS Circular* **451**. 92 pp.

7. Nishikawa, Y., Honma, M., Ueyanagi, S. and Kikawa, S. (1985) Average distribution of larvae of oceanic species of scombrid fishes, 1965–1981. *Far Seas Fisheries Research Laboratory, Japan, S Series* **12**. 99 pp.

8. Hunter, J.R., Macewicz, B.J. and Sibert, J.R. (1986) The spawning frequency of skipjack tuna, *Katsuwonus pelamis*, from the South Pacific. *Fishery Bulletin (U.S.)* **84**: 895–903.

9. Wild, A. and Hampton, J. (1991) *A review of skipjack tuna biology and fisheries in the Pacific Ocean*. Background paper for the FAO expert consultation on interactions of Pacific tuna fisheries, Noumea, New Caledonia, 3–11 December 1991. 48 pp.

10. Sibert, J.R., Kearney, R.E. and Lawson, T.A. (1983) Variation in growth increments of tagged skipjack (*Katsuwonus pelamis*). *South Pacific Commission, Tuna and Billfish Assessment Programme Technical Report* **10**. 43 pp.

11. Kearney, R.E. (1991) Extremes in fish biology, population dynamics, and fisheries management: Pacific skipjack and southern bluefin tuna. *Reviews in Aquatic Sciences* **4**(2–3): 289–298.

12. South Pacific Commission (1984) An assessment of the skipjack and baitfish resources of eastern Australia. *South Pacific Commission, Skipjack Survey and Assessment Programme Final Country Report* **16**. 59 pp.

13. Richardson, B.J. (1983) Distribution of protein variation in skipjack tuna (*Katsuwonus pelamis*) from the central and south-western Pacific. *Australian Journal of Marine and Freshwater Research* **34**: 231–251.

14. Starling, S. (1988) *The fisherman's handbook. How to find, identify and catch the top Australian angling fish*. Sydney: Angus and Robertson. 263 pp.

Contributors

Information on this species has been provided by (in alphabetical order) John Hampton, Steve Jackson, Bob Kearney, Tony Lewis and Bob Miller. Drawing courtesy of FAO, Rome. (*Details of contributors and their organisations are given in the Acknowledgements section at the back of this book.*)
Compiler Phillip Stewart

Catch of skipjack tuna being loaded into the hold of a pole-and-line boat. (Source: Lindsay Chapman, Bureau of Resource Sciences)

Mackerel

Scomberomorus species

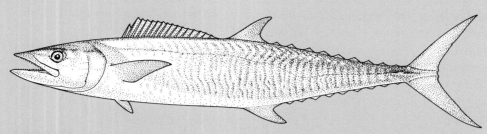

Mackerel

This presentation is on 4 species, **Spanish mackerel**, **spotted mackerel**, **school mackerel** and **grey mackerel**.

Spanish mackerel,
Scomberomorus commerson
(Lacepède)

Other common names include **narrow-barred Spanish mackerel, Spaniard, narrow-bar** and **macko**.
FAO: **narrow-barred Spanish mackerel**
Australian species code: 441007

Spotted mackerel,
Scomberomorus munroi
Collette and Russo

Another common name is **spotty**.
FAO: **Australian spotted mackerel**
Australian species code: 441015

School mackerel,
Scomberomorus queenslandicus Munro

Another common name is **doggie mackerel**.
FAO: **Queensland school mackerel**
Australian species code: 441014

Grey mackerel,
Scomberomorus semifasciatus (Macleay)

Other common names include **tiger mackerel** and **broad-barred Spanish mackerel**.
FAO: **broadbarred king mackerel**
Australian species code: 441018

Family SCOMBRIDAE

Diagnostic features Species of the genus *Scomberomorus* are distinguished from other mackerel and tunas by having strong teeth in their jaws and 2 small keels and a large median keel on the caudal peduncle. Spanish mackerel (pictured) have a deep dip in the lateral line below the end of the second dorsal fin. Their sides have narrow, slightly wavy dark bars, sometimes breaking into spots ventrally, and their first dorsal fin is uniformly bright blue. The other 3 species have an almost straight lateral line. Spotted mackerel have a faint band of small round spots along the midsides and their first dorsal fin is almost uniformly blackish blue. School mackerel have about 3 rows of bronze-grey blotches on their midsides and a large white area midway along the black first dorsal fin. Grey mackerel have broad dark bars along their upper sides and a white area on the centre of the blackish first dorsal fin.[1]

near the edge of the continental shelf to shallow coastal waters, often of low salinity and high turbidity.[2] Adults are commonly associated with coral reefs, rocky shoals and current lines[2] on outer reef areas and offshore. They are most frequently located on the up-current side of reefs or shoals.[3] Juvenile Spanish mackerel form loose schools. School mackerel often inhabit very turbid coastal waters shallower than 30 m. Grey mackerel are more common around coastal headlands and rocky reefs but are also caught offshore, and spotted mackerel are more common in offshore, open waters away from reefs and shoals.[2]

Life history

Most life history information on mackerel in Australia is based on Queensland studies. In Great Barrier Reef waters, Spanish mackerel spawn off the reef slopes and edges,[3] and there is evidence[3] that they form spawning aggregations in specific areas. The spawning period varies with locality. It extends from August to about March in Torres Strait, from October to early December between Lizard Island, Cairns and Townsville, and October to November between Gladstone and Bundaberg.[3]

There are no accurate fecundity assessments on Spanish mackerel. Each female spawns several times over the season, about 2 to 6 days apart,[4] depending on the locality.

The larvae, and probably the eggs, are pelagic. Small juveniles up to 10 cm fork length live in creeks, estuaries and along areas of sheltered mud flats in the early wet season (December–January) in north Queensland.[3] Juveniles of 15–40 cm fork length are caught by prawn trawlers working shallow water during February and March.[3] After May, Spanish mackerel

Distribution

Spanish mackerel are widespread in tropical and subtropical waters of the Indo-Pacific from Africa to Fiji, and they are also in the Mediterranean Sea.[1] In Australian waters, they are distributed from Geographe Bay in Western Australia to St Helens in Tasmania. The other species of *Scomberomorus* are endemic to the Australasian region. In Australian waters, spotted mackerel are present from Rottnest Island to Wollongong, school mackerel from Shark Bay to Sydney and grey mackerel from Shark Bay to northern New South Wales. The distribution of mackerel southwards in Australian waters is probably associated with the southern extension of warm currents in summer.

These 4 species of mackerel are pelagic, rarely occupying water deeper than 100 m. Spanish mackerel range from

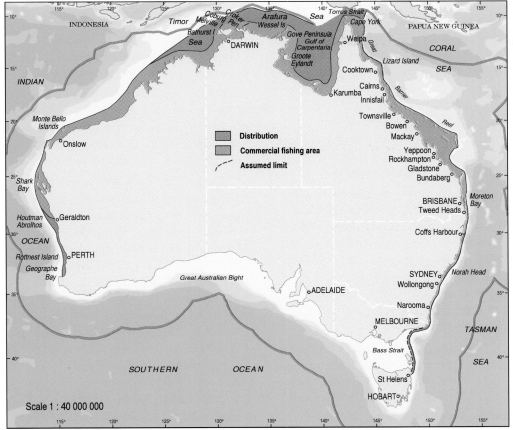

Geographic distribution and commercial fishing areas for 4 species of *Scomberomorus* in Australian waters.

of about 40 cm fork length are caught in reef waters in the commercial hook-and-line fishery.[3]

Little is known about spawning activities of other mackerel species except that they commence spawning earlier in the year than Spanish mackerel, and in inshore waters.[2]

Some Spanish mackerel undertake seasonal migrations whilst others remain in certain reef areas all year. The resident fish simply disperse from the reefs after spawning, while the migrating fish move up to 1000 nautical miles to the south.[5] On the Queensland east coast, migration from the Lizard Island–Townsville area takes place after the spawning season when a significant proportion of 2 and 3-year-old fish moves southwards. A return migration of 3 and 4-year-old fish commences during winter.[2] On the west coast, the mackerel follow the 22–24°C isotherm,[6] generally moving south in the late summer and north during the winter.

The maximum sizes recorded for Spanish mackerel are 240 cm fork length and 70 kg.[7] These larger fish are females, males rarely exceeding 17 kg in weight.[7] The maximum age estimate for females is 14 years (measuring 155 cm fork length and 35 kg)[3] and 10 years for males (124 cm and 19 kg).[7] The maximum recorded

fork lengths for other mackerel are: 104 cm for spotted, 100 cm for school and 120 cm for grey mackerel. The maximum recorded weights for these mackerel are, respectively, 10 kg, 12 kg and 8.4 kg.[1]

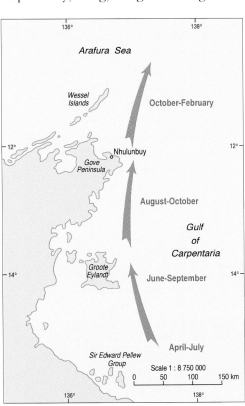

Presumed movement of Spanish mackerel in the western Gulf of Carpentaria, based on fishers' catch returns. (Source: Geoff McPherson, Northern Fisheries Centre, Queensland Department of Primary Industries)

Spanish mackerel attain an average size of 58–60 cm fork length and 2.2 kg after 1 year. Females grow faster than males after the first year.[3] Spanish mackerel in northern Australia grow more rapidly than those in eastern Queensland.[7] Maturity occurs generally at the end of their second year,[4] at about 65 cm fork length for males,[1] 80–82 cm fork length for northern females and 72–79 cm fork length for east coast females.[7]

Juvenile Spanish mackerel up to 50 cm fork length feed on small fish such as sardines (Clupeidae), trevally (Carangidae), ponyfish (Leiognathidae) and garfish (Hemiramphidae). Some of these fish as well as fusiliers (Caesionidae), squid and penaeid prawns are preyed upon by adult Spanish mackerel.[8] Spanish mackerel also feed readily on discarded fish from prawn trawlers.

Stock structure

There appear to be 2 genetically distinct stocks of Spanish mackerel.[9,10] Fish from the northern Great Barrier Reef to New South Wales form 1 stock, while fish from Torres Strait and the Gulf of Carpentaria are part of a northern stock distributed from the southern Gulf of Papua to Western Australia.[4,10,11] Evidence from tagging studies and historic fishing activity in the Gulf of Carpentaria and Torres Strait waters, although limited, suggests that Spanish mackerel move between the Gulf and Strait waters.[9]

Commercial fishery

In Western Australia, Spanish mackerel and spotted mackerel are fished north of approximately 28° S and grey mackerel and school mackerel are fished north of 24° S. Mackerel fishing is a major fishery on the North West Shelf. From the trap and line fishery there, Spanish mackerel comprised an average of 31 % of the catch of all fish during a recent 2-year study.[12] The fishery peaks in July and August, and weather conditions restrict fishing operations during the wet monsoon period (December–February).[5,12]

In the Northern Territory, Spanish mackerel have been targeted by local fishers since the late 1970s. The fishery extends along the whole coastline, with local concentrations south of Darwin, from Bathurst and Croker islands to the

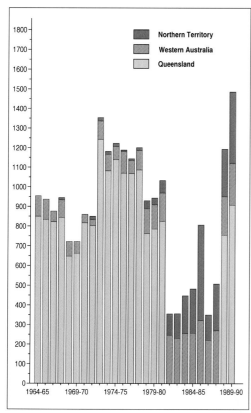

Total annual catch in t of all mackerel
(*Scomberomorus* species) for the period
1964–65 to 1989–90. Figures are
unavailable for Queensland from 1981–82 to
1987–88. New South Wales figures are not
shown as they average less than 5 % of the
total for all States. (Source: Fisheries Resources
Atlas Statistical Database)

Wessel Islands, and in the western Gulf of Carpentaria. Most fishing takes place during the second half of the year, peaking in September–November. Spanish mackerel are also targeted on their presumed migration path along the western Gulf of Carpentaria coastline. Since 1987, effort and catch have increased sharply in the Northern Territory Spanish mackerel fishery.

Taiwanese fleets fished for *Scomberomorus* species off northern Australia from 1974 to mid-1986[13] and in the Gulf of Carpentaria until the fleet's exclusion in 1978. The Taiwanese used drifting gillnets ranging in length from 8 km to more than 20 km.[13] Australian Government regulations in 1986 limited the gillnet lengths to 2.5 km or less, effectively making the Taiwanese gillnet fishery uneconomic in Australian waters.

The Queensland fishery for mackerel is the State's major offshore finfish fishery[8] and has been operating for at least 60 years.[11] In 1989–90, its value was estimated at A$ 3.4 million, of which more than 66 % was Spanish mackerel. The Queensland fishery extends from the southern Gulf of Carpentaria, through Torres Strait and along the east coast,

although most fishing takes place from north of Cooktown to Mackay. Mackerel fishers operate mostly from the ports of Cairns, Townsville, Yeppoon, Mackay and Bundaberg. Mackerel are fished to approximately 30° S (Coffs Harbour) in New South Wales. The east coast fishery targets mackerel during the spring spawning season and the northward migration[3] and later in summer–early autumn in southern Queensland.

The main fishing method for Spanish mackerel is trolling. Varying lengths of Bowden cable main line, wire trace and terminal rigs of ganged hooks are used.[2] Garfish are the preferred bait. Other fish baits and different combinations of rope and lures may be used. Another fishing technique for mackerel is drift-fishing using rod-and-reel.[2,3,8]

Catch rates vary depending on the time of day (early morning and evenings are preferred), moon phase, tides, water temperature, depth,[14] sea floor features,[6] trolling speed and the fishers' experience.[14] The size of the fishing operation varies, from a mothership up to 16 m long operating several dories through smaller vessels without dories, to dinghies operating from island locations.

All *Scomberomorus* are susceptible to drifting gillnets. There are localised gillnet fisheries for small mackerel through almost their entire distribution in Australia, from approximately Shark Bay to northern New South Wales. Sharks form an important part of the catch in these fishing operations,[6] and fishers target either shark or mackerel depending on availability and market demand. A small amount of mackerel is taken with offshore drifting gillnets by domestic fishers in north-eastern Queensland, where reasonable quantities of juvenile mackerel are also caught inshore.

Demersal otter trawlers targeting prawns in northern Australia may catch

A mothership with attendant dories fishing on the northern Great Barrier Reef. (Source: Campbell Davies, James Cook University of North Queensland)

substantial quantities of mackerel either as bycatch or by line fishing. Some boats engaged primarily in other fisheries in northern waters switch to trolling mackerel when the fish are biting.

Wahoo (*Acanthocybium solandri*) (in north-eastern Australia) and shark mackerel (*Grammatorcynus* species) (in north-western Australia) are important bycatches of the mackerel troll fishery.

Mackerel are marketed frozen, fresh or chilled as gilled-and-gutted whole fish or trunks, and are retailed as fillets or cutlets. In Western Australia, the mackerel are gutted or put in chilled brine for gutting later the same day.[12] In Queensland, some fish are filleted on the boats and stored on ice or frozen. Small local operations prepare smoked mackerel. Much of the Northern Territory product is trucked interstate, whereas Western Australian and Queensland product is sold both locally and interstate. Mackerel is in high market demand in Australia. It is a staple of the 'fish-and-chips' trade in Queensland. Queensland prices for headed and gutted Spanish mackerel ranged from A$ 3.50 per kg to A$ 8.50 per kg in 1992. In 1992 Northern Territory fishers received an average of A$ 6.74 per kg for Spanish mackerel fillets and A$ 4.00 per kg for trunks of school mackerel and grey mackerel. In Perth, wholesale prices for Spanish mackerel trunks ranged from A$ 3.50 to A$ 6.50 per kg in 1992.

Management controls In Western Australia, the fishery may only be accessed by licensed fishers. In the Northern Territory, it is managed through licences for particular fishing methods targeting different mackerel species, and by limited entry to defined management zones. Controls in Queensland differ by region. They include restrictions on the number of vessels, a catch quota (Torres Strait), a legal minimum retention size, prohibition of fishing in high-risk ciguatera areas (see Notes) and seasonal and area closures (eg in marine parks). Targeting Spanish mackerel with gillnets is prohibited east of Cape York.

Recreational fishery

In the Northern Territory and Queensland, most recreational fishing for Spanish mackerel takes place in waters within reach of pleasure boats from major coastal population centres. Spanish mackerel is the most widely sought-after pelagic fish for recreational fishers in Queensland waters and their annual catch from Great Barrier Reef waters is considerable.

Rod-and-reel gear is used almost exclusively with live bait, dead bait or lures.[8] Fishers troll from boats or drift rigged baits from the shore, sometimes using balloons to carry the baits well out into the currents. The Australian Anglers Association records the largest Spanish mackerel taken as 42.2 kg, caught in Western Australia in 1979.

Management controls In Queensland, mackerel may only be fished using line gear. Bag limits and legal minimum size restrictions are in effect in Queensland and Western Australia. In the Northern Territory only bag limits apply.

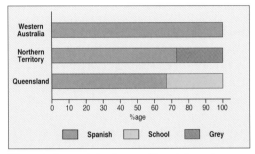

The relative catch of grey, Spanish and school mackerel in Australia for 1989–90. Figures are misleading, as only Spanish mackerel are recorded for Western Australia, Spanish mackerel and school mackerel for Queensland and grey mackerel and Spanish mackerel for Northern Territory. (Source: Fisheries Resources Atlas Statistical Database)

Resource status

No studies on the resource status of mackerel have been conducted.

The catch of Spanish mackerel from north-eastern Queensland has declined since the late 1970s,[11] while that from northern New South Wales has slightly increased.[11] Spanish mackerel stocks in the Northern Territory may be adversely affected by foreign fishers — mainly Taiwanese driftnetters operating under licence in Indonesian waters. These vessels catch substantial quantities of Spanish mackerel which are probably migrating into or out of Australian waters. Over-exploitation of the resource during the years of Taiwanese gillnet fishing in northern Australian waters was suggested[13] by declines in both catch per unit effort and body length of mackerel. The Taiwanese fleet operating in the Gulf

of Papua in the first half of the 1980s was also implicated in reduced mackerel catches in the Torres Strait troll fishery.[11]

Notes

Ciguatera poisoning is associated with mackerel. A lipid-soluble toxin, similar to ciguatoxin, has been found in individual mackerel caught between 24° S and 26° S off Queensland[1] and also in mackerel from the Gove Peninsula area, Northern Territory.

References

1. Collette, B.B. and Nauen, C.E. (1983) FAO species catalogue.Vol. 2. Scombrids of the world. An annotated and illustrated catalogue of tunas, mackerels, bonitos and related species known to date. *FAO Fisheries Synopsis No. 125*, **2**. 137 pp.

2. McPherson, G.R. (1985) Northern line fishery for mackerels still important. *Australian Fisheries* **44**(8): 12–14.

3. McPherson, G.R. (1981) Preliminary report: investigations of Spanish mackerel, *Scomberomorus commerson* in Queensland waters. Pp 51–58, in *Northern pelagic fish seminar. Darwin, Northern Territory, 20–21 January, 1981.* Ed by C.J. Grant and D.G. Walter. Canberra: Australian Government Publishing Service.

4. McPherson, G.R. (in press, 1992) Reproductive biology of narrow-barred Spanish mackerel (*Scomberomorus commerson* Lacepède, 1800) in Queensland waters. *Asian Fisheries Science.*

5. McPherson, G.R. (1989) North-eastern Australian mackerel (*Scomberomorus*) fishery. Pp 341–348, in *Proceedings of the workshop Australia–Mexico on marine sciences, Quintana Roo, Mexico, 6–17 July 1989.* Ed by E.A. Chavez. Mexico: Quintana Roo.

6. Donohue, K., Edsall, P., Robins, J. and Tregonning, R. (1982) Exploratory fishing for Spanish mackerel in waters off Western Australia during the period June 16 to October 16, 1981. *Report of the Department of Fisheries and Wildlife, Western Australia* **57**. 46 pp.

7. McPherson, G.R. (in press, 1992) Age and growth of the narrow-barred Spanish mackerel (*Scomberomorus commerson*

Lacepède, 1800) in north-eastern Queensland waters. *Australian Journal of Marine and Freshwater Research* **42**.

8. McPherson, G.R. (1987) Food of narrow-barred Spanish mackerel in north Queensland waters, and their relevance to the commercial troll fishery. *Queensland Journal of Agriculture and Animal Sciences* **44**(1): 69–73.

9. McPherson, G.R. (1988) Search for Spanish mackerel stocks. *Australian Fisheries* **47**(6): 34–35.

10. Shaklee, J.B., Phelps, S.R. and Salini, J. (1990) Analysis of fish stock structure and mixed-stock fisheries by the electrophoretic characterization of allelic isozymes. Pp 173–196, in *Electrophoretic and isoelectric focussing techniques in fisheries management.* Ed by D.H. Whitmore. Boca Raton: CRC Press.

11. McPherson, G.R. (1985) Development of the northern Queensland mackerel fishery. *Australian Fisheries* **44**(8): 15–17.

12. Moran, M., Jenke, J., Burton, C. and Clarke, D. (1988) The Western Australian trap and line fishery on the North-west Shelf. *Western Australian Marine Research Laboratories. FIRTA Project 86/28, Final Report.* 79 pp.

13. Stevens, J.D. and Davenport, S. (1991) Analysis of catch data from the Taiwanese gill-net fishery off northern Australia, 1979 to 1986. *CSIRO Marine Laboratories Report* **213**. 51 pp.

14. Rohan, G. and Church, A. (1979) A review of the Northern Territory mackerel and reef fisheries. *Northern Territory Department of Primary Production, Fisheries Division, Fishery Report* **3**. 48pp.

Contributors

Information on these species was originally provided by Geoff McPherson. Additional information was provided by (in alphabetical order) Andrew Bartleet, Rik Buckworth, Chris Calogeras, Kevin Donohue, Rosemary Lea, Mike Moran and Neil Trainor. Drawing by Gavin Ryan. (*Details of contributors and their organisations are given in the Acknowledgements section at the back of this book.*)
Compiler Patricia Kailola

A recreational catch of Spanish mackerel, school mackerel and rock cod (Serranidae) from the Great Barrier Reef. (Source: Great Barrier Reef Marine Park Authority)

Albacore

Thunnus alalunga

Thunnus alalunga (Bonnaterre)

Albacore

Other common names include
albacore tuna and **longfin tuna**.
FAO: **albacore**
Australian species code: 441005

Family SCOMBRIDAE

Diagnostic features Albacore can be
recognised by their very long pectoral
fins, usually one third or more of the fork
length, and extending past the insertion
of the anal fin. In fish smaller than 50 cm
fork length, however, the pectoral fins
are proportionally smaller than in other
tunas such as bigeye (*T. obesus*). Body
depth in albacore is greatest at or
slightly before the level of the second
dorsal fin; and the ventral surface of the
liver is striated. Albacore have a dark
yellow first dorsal fin, pale yellow second
dorsal and anal fins, and a white
posterior margin to their caudal fin.[1]

The migration pattern of albacore in
the south Pacific Ocean has recently been
described.[4] Juveniles move from the
tropics into temperate waters and then
eastwards along the subtropical
convergence zone. At maturity, albacore
return to the tropics but go back to
temperate waters after spawning.

Life history

In southern hemisphere oceanic waters
between 5° S and 25° S albacore spawn at
least twice[1] each summer (October to
March), with peak activity during
December and January.[2,5] The fish form
small spawning aggregations.[2] A mature
female will produce between 2 and 3
million eggs each season, released in at
least 2 batches. The larvae inhabit the
upper 60 m where the water is warmer
than 24°C.[6] In Australian waters, larvae
are present on the North West Shelf all
summer, but are present off north-eastern

Distribution

Albacore are pelagic fish distributed from
about 45° N to 50° S in all tropical,
subtropical and temperate oceans[1] and
the Mediterranean Sea. Their abundance
is greater in subtropical and temperate
regions. Their distribution expands
polewards in summer and contracts in
winter following changes in the
distribution of warm water.[2] In Australian
waters, albacore are present in the east,
south and west from east of Torres Strait
to the North West Shelf.[3]

Albacore are oceanic fish. Their
distribution is related to oxygen
concentration and water temperature.[1,2]
The minimum oxygen concentration
requirement for albacore is probably the
same as for yellowfin tuna (*T. albacares*),
which is about 2 ml per l.[1,2] Off southern
Australia and New Zealand, they are
usually present in sea surface
temperatures of 16–22°C in association
with oceanic temperature fronts —
although they have been recorded in
water ranging in temperature from 9.5°C
to 25.2°C.[1,2] Albacore feed at the surface
but otherwise live at the thermocline, the
sharp temperature boundary between the
warm surface waters and cooler deep

waters. The thermocline depth in the
Tasman Sea in summer tends to vary
between 50 m and 150 m. Albacore have
been found at least as deep as 500 m in
the Pacific Ocean.

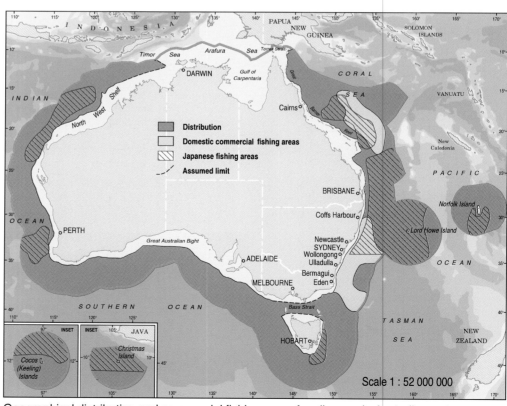

Geographical distribution and commercial fishing areas for albacore in Australian waters.

Australia mainly between October and December.[5]

Juvenile albacore of 40–80 cm fork length form loose schools in the upper 100 m of the water column. In Australia the juveniles are found off New South Wales from September to November, and during summer they follow the warmer waters of the East Australian Current southwards. Albacore may reach eastern Tasmanian waters by December, where they remain until about April. As autumn approaches and warm waters recede, the juveniles move northwards and are present again off New South Wales until May.[7] Adult albacore travel in independent, small groups,[2] and are common throughout much of the species' range.

Different methods of ageing have produced estimates of growth for Pacific albacore ranging from 38 cm to 57 cm fork length in their first year.[8] Until age 6 or 7, the annual growth rate is estimated at 8–15 cm, after which it slows. Males tend to grow more quickly than females. Adults reach a maximum size of about 127 cm fork length (more than 40 kg) at an age of 10 or more years.[1] Maturity is reached at about 85 cm fork length in females[8] and possibly as small as 50 cm fork length in males.[9]

Albacore are opportunistic carnivores, ie they forage when and where food becomes available. Albacore eat swarming planktonic crustaceans such as krill (*Nyctiphanes australis*), squid (Cephalopoda), and a variety of small fish including skipjack tuna (*Katsuwonus pelamis*), frigate mackerel (*Auxis* species), mackerel tuna (*Euthynnus* species), jack mackerel (*Trachurus declivis*), lanternfish (Myctophidae) and sauries (Scomberesocidae).[10] Albacore are preyed upon by larger tunas such as southern bluefin (*Thunnus maccoyii*), yellowfin and bigeye, billfish (Istiophoridae) and various sharks (Lamnidae, Carcharhinidae, Sphyrnidae).[2]

Stock structure

In the Pacific Ocean, albacore are considered to comprise separate northern and southern hemisphere stocks, each with distinct spawning areas. Currently, there is no firm evidence that these stocks mix across the equator.[3,11] Scientists presently regard south Pacific albacore as a functional, or discrete, unit stock.[8,11]

Albacore off the west coast and north-west coast of Australia are part of the Indian Ocean stock, while albacore off the east coast are part of the south Pacific Ocean stock. It is possible that albacore along the east coast move around southern Tasmania and mix with the albacore stock of the Indian Ocean[12] although the interchange is probably minimal.

Commercial fishery

Albacore are a premium canning species. They are esteemed for their white, dry flesh and are often referred to as 'chicken of the sea'.

In the south Pacific Ocean, albacore are caught mainly by longline vessels from Taiwan, Korea and Japan, and trolling vessels from the United States of America and New Zealand. The longline vessels operate from off the Australian mainland east to about 100° W. Combined catches by all fleets over the 10 years to 1988 has averaged 32 700 t per year.[8] While a major Japanese and Taiwanese driftnet fishery for albacore operated in the southern Tasman Sea between Australia and New Zealand during the mid and late 1980s, there is now no commercial fishery that targets albacore in the Australian Fishing Zone.

The largest catches of albacore in the Zone are usually taken as a bycatch by Japanese fishing vessels longlining for southern bluefin, yellowfin and bigeye tunas.[13] Japanese longlining mainly takes place off the east and south-east coast

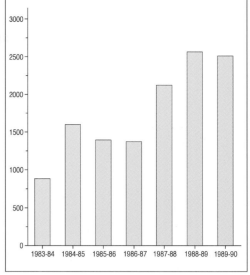

Total annual catch in t of albacore for the period 1983–84 to 1989–90 by foreign and domestic vessels. (Source: Australian Fishing Zone Information System)

with lesser activity off the west coast. Hooks are set between 50 m and 150 m below the sea surface, with up to about 3300 hooks per line. The lines are 80–100 km long.

The Japanese freeze their albacore catch whole and take it back to Japan for canning. From 1984 to 1988 an annual average of 1300 t of albacore was caught by Japanese longliners working in Australian waters.[14]

Domestic vessels using drifting longlines have successfully fished for various species of tuna off eastern Australia since the early 1950s, the fishing activity escalating after 1984.[14] The target species are the more valuable yellowfin tuna and bigeye tuna, with albacore as bycatch.[13] Logbooks record that the

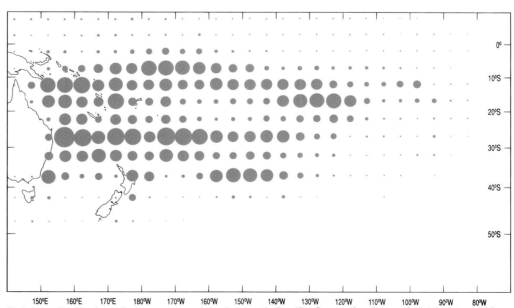

Relative distribution of albacore catch in the south Pacific Ocean for the period 1962 to 1990
Each circle is located at the centre of each 5-degree grid. (Source: South Pacific Commission)

Recreational fisher landing a trolled albacore. (Source: Lindsay Chapman, Bureau of Resource Sciences)

domestic tuna longline fleet catches about 100 t of albacore annually,[14] although the catch is probably higher. The Australian longlines are shorter than the Japanese longlines: up to 30 km long and set with 200–800 hooks. Albacore from domestic longliners are sold through the Sydney and Melbourne fish markets, to wholesale buyers in Melbourne, or to local canneries.

Albacore were previously a minor bycatch of pole-and-line and purse seining operations for southern bluefin tuna off New South Wales, South

Australia and Western Australia. In 1 year (1981–82) the catch was around 2000 t.[12] More recently, small quantities of albacore have been taken by pole-and-line vessels targeting skipjack tuna off the New South Wales south coast. The catch of albacore from pole-and-line is sold mainly to the cannery at Eden.

Small quantities of albacore are also caught off the east coast by domestic trolling, although these operations are more opportunistic. Domestic longliners, after setting their gear, may troll adjacent to the area. Vessels troll up to 15 lines with single lures spaced 5–50 m behind the boat. Trolling is also carried out off Tasmania's east coast to target southern bluefin tuna with albacore a significant bycatch in those waters. The trolled albacore catch — along with any bycatch from longlining — is sold locally either as fresh fish or as processed, smoked fillets.

The albacore catch in domestic fisheries off the southern and western coast is incidental and trivial.

The Australian cannery price in 1992 for whole albacore averaged A$ 1500 per t (A$ 1.50 per kg), which is about the same as the cannery price for yellowfin tuna. The world canning price for albacore in 1991–92 was about US$ 2250 per t. Fresh albacore prices at Sydney and Melbourne wholesale fish markets in 1991–92 fluctuated between A$ 1.50 and A$ 3.00 per kg.

Management controls There are no specific controls in place for albacore

caught in Australian waters apart from the Commonwealth licence and longline endorsements.

Recreational fishery

The recreational fishery for albacore is small but growing steadily as amateur fishers venture further off the coast in search of fish. Anglers use rod-and-reel to take albacore by trolling artificial lures and live or dead baits, or drifting using live bait or fish pieces with the assistance of a berley trail. Albacore are mainly caught off New South Wales from September to December and again in April and May, while off Tasmania they are caught from January to April. Mainly juveniles (40–90 cm fork length) are taken. The record size for an albacore caught by an angler in Australia is 23.2 kg (records of the Game Fishing Association of Australia). Angler clubs reported a catch of 642 albacore off eastern Australia in 1988–89.[15]

There has been a noticeable increase in the numbers of albacore tagged and released by game fishers on Australia's east coast. Figures provided by the NSW Fisheries Research Institute's database show that from 1986 to the end of 1990–91, 2450 albacore were tagged and released. Up to July 1992, a total of 21 tagged fish have been recovered from a total of 3646 releases since 1973.

Management controls There are no specific controls on the taking of albacore by anglers in Australian waters. New

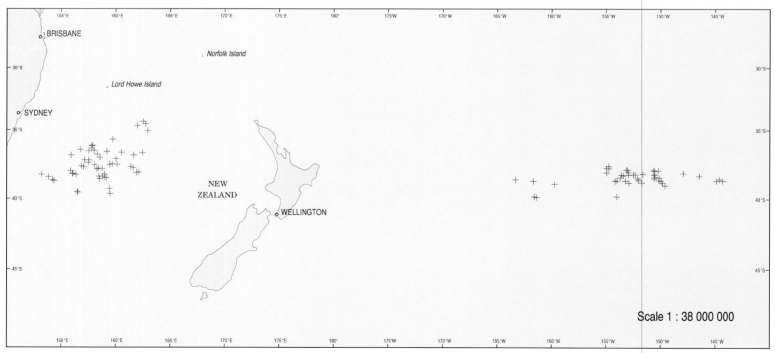

Positions of drifting gillnet vessel sightings made during the 1989–90 (October–April) albacore fishing season. (Source: South Pacific Commission)

South Wales has a general number and size limit on tunas.

Resource status

Albacore stocks are considered to be under-utilised in Australian waters and there is potential for development of a fishery.[12] A review of the status of the broader south Pacific Ocean stock[7] by the South Pacific Albacore Research working group, an informal group of albacore scientists from the South Pacific and distant water fishing nations, suggests that the withdrawal of the driftnet fleet from the Tasman Sea and broader south-west Pacific has considerably lessened earlier concern about the potential impact of that fleet on the south Pacific Ocean stock of albacore. Nevertheless, the south Pacific albacore troll fishery has the capacity to reduce yields in the south Pacific longline fishery.

References

1. Collette, B.B. and Nauen, C.E. (1983) FAO species catalogue.Vol. 2. Scombrids of the world. An annotated and illustrated catalogue of tunas, mackerels, bonitos and related species known to date. *FAO Fisheries Synopsis No. 125*, **2**. 137 pp.

2. Foreman, T.J. (1980) Synopsis of biological data on the albacore tuna *Thunnus alalunga* (Bonnaterre, 1788) in the Pacific Ocean. Pp 17–70, in *Synopsis of biological data on eight species of scombrids. Special Report* **2**. Ed by W.H. Bayliff. La Jolla, California: Inter-American Tropical Tuna Commission.

3. Caton, A.E. and Ward, P.J. (1991) Albacore tuna and its fisheries in the Australian fishing zone. *Bureau of Rural Resources Working Paper* **WP/3/91**. 43 pp.

4. Jones, J.B. (1991) Movements of albacore tuna (*Thunnus alalunga*) in the South Pacific: evidence from parasites. *Marine Biology* **111**: 1–9.

5. Nishikawa, Y., Honma, M., Ueyanagi, S. and Kikawa, S. (1985) Average distribution of larvae of oceanic species of scombrid fishes, 1965–1981. *Far Seas Fisheries Research Laboratory, Japan, S Series* **12**. 99 pp.

6. Ueyanagi, S. (1969) Observations on the distribution of tuna larvae in the Indo-Pacific Ocean with emphasis on the delineation of the spawning areas of albacore, *Thunnus alalunga. Bulletin of the Far Seas Fisheries Research Laboratory* **2**: 177–256.

7. Garvey, J.R. (1991) Albacore and the east coast tuna longline fishery. *Australian Fisheries* **50**(2): 22–26.

8. Murray, T. (1991) A review of information on the biology of albacore, *Thunnus alalunga*, and fisheries for this species in the south Pacific Ocean. *FAO expert consultation on interactions of Pacific tuna fisheries, Noumea, New Caledonia, 3–11 December 1991.* **TIC/91/BP 8**. 18 pp.

9. Ratty, F., Kelly, R. and Laurs, R.M. (1989) Testes morphology, histology and spermatogenesis in South Pacific albacore tuna. *Second South Pacific albacore research workshop, Suva, Fiji, 14-16 June 1989. Working Paper* **19**. South Pacific Commission.

10. Bailey, K. (1986) A preliminary analysis of the stomach contents of albacore, *Thunnus alalunga*, from the subtropical convergence zone east of New Zealand. *First South Pacific albacore research workshop, Auckland, New Zealand, 9–12 June 1986. Working Paper* **17**. South Pacific Commission.

11. Lewis, A.D. (1990) South Pacific albacore stock structure: a review of available information. *Third South Pacific albacore research workshop, Noumea, New Caledonia, 9–12 October 1990. Working Paper* **5**. South Pacific Commission.

12. Caton, A.E. (1991) The commercial potential of albacore in Australia. *Australian Fisheries* **50**(2): 14–16.

13. Caton, A.E. and Ward, P.J. (1991) Albacore in the AFZ. *Australian Fisheries* **50**(2): 17–21.

14. Caton, A.E. and Ward, P.J. (1989) Albacore tuna and its fisheries in the Australian fishing zone. *Second South Pacific albacore research workshop, Suva, Fiji, 14–16 June 1989. Working Paper* **4**. South Pacific Commission.

15. West, L. (1990) A review of existing and potential data systems for recreational fishing for tunas and billfishes — east coast of Australia. *Internal report for the Department of Primary Industries and Energy and the East Coast Tuna Management Advisory Committee.* Kewagama Research, Tewantin. 69 pp.

Contributors

The information on this species was originally provided by Lindsay Chapman and Albert Caton. It was supplemented by comments from (in alphabetical order) John Garvey, John Hampton, Marc Labelle, Talbot Murray and Peter Ward. Drawing courtesy of FAO, Rome. (*Details of contributors and their organisations are given in the Acknowledgements section at the back of this book.*)

Compilers Patricia Kailola, Phillip Stewart and Cesar Ramirez (statistics), and Christina Grieve (maps)

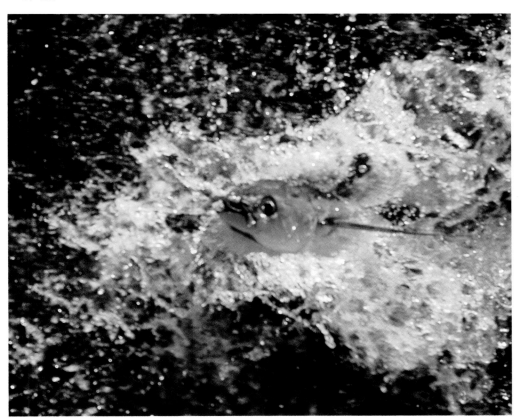

A trolled albacore about to be landed. (Source: Talbot Murray and Peter Sharples, Ministry of Agriculture and Fisheries, New Zealand)

Yellowfin tuna

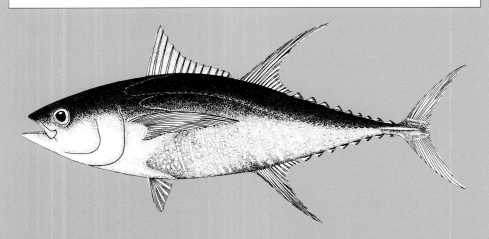

Thunnus albacares

Thunnus albacares (Bonnaterre)

Yellowfin tuna

Other common names include
yellowfin, **yellowfinned albacore**, **'fin**
and **Allison tuna**.
FAO: **yellowfin tuna**
Australian species code: 441002

Family SCOMBRIDAE

Diagnostic features The caudal fin of
yellowfin tuna is distinctly notched in an
'm' shape at the centre of its fork.
Behind the second dorsal fin and the
anal fin, the body profile of yellowfin
tuna is somewhat flat. The ventral
surface of the liver is smooth and the
right lobe is longer than the central lobe.
Yellowfin tuna adults are distinguished
by having a moderately long pectoral fin
that is one third to one quarter the body
fork length. In juveniles there are about
20 broken pale lines crossing the lower
sides. In large fish the second dorsal
and anal fins may be exceedingly
elongate and bright yellow. Yellowfin
tuna less than 75 cm fork length (10 kg
whole weight) may be difficult to
distinguish from small bigeye tuna
(*T. obesus*).

Yellowfin tuna smaller than 15 kg
often form surface schools of similar sized
fish. Schools may be mono-specific (ie,
consist of only 1 species) or include other
tunas, such as skipjack tuna (*Katsuwonus
pelamis*). Dolphins often associate with
surface feeding schools in the eastern
Pacific Ocean, but a similar association is
not found in the western Pacific. Adult
yellowfin tuna tend to be more solitary off
south-eastern Australia. Fish larger than
15 kg inhabit the deeper waters above the
thermocline and tend not to school in
Australian waters. A behavioural study in
Hawaiian waters using ultrasonic tags[3]
showed that during the day yellowfin
tuna inhabited waters just above the
thermocline (50–90 m), with occasional
short descents to depths as great as 250
m. At night the tuna tended to stay within
50 m of the surface.

Distribution

Yellowfin tuna inhabit all oceans and
tropical and subtropical seas except the
Mediterranean Sea, between about 40° N
and 40° S. They are present in Australian
waters from Torres Strait to eastern
Tasmania as far as 43° S, and from
south-western Australia at about 128° E to
Northern Territory waters at about 136° E.

Yellowfin tuna distribution is limited
by sea surface temperature less than 15°C,
salinity extremes and low dissolved
oxygen concentrations. For these reasons,
they are not usually caught below 250 m
in the tropics.[1,2] Yellowfin tuna are often
caught in frontal regions ie regions
between water masses characterised by
strong gradients in physical conditions,
such as temperature, where prey species
are concentrated by currents or
favourable nutrient levels.[3] Yellowfin
tuna are oceanic fish, but are occasionally
caught in the brackish waters of estuaries
or shallow bays.

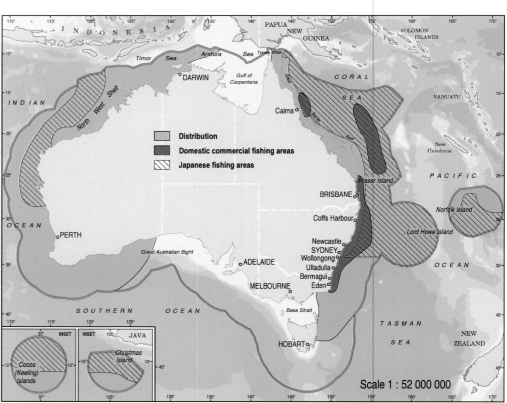

Geographic distribution and commercial fishing areas for yellowfin tuna in Australian waters.

Tagged yellowfin tuna about to be released.
(Source: Kevin McLoughlin, Bureau of Resource
Sciences)

Life history

Yellowfin tuna spawn throughout the tropical and equatorial waters of the major oceans. Spawning may continue throughout the year. However, it tends to be restricted to summer months in higher latitudes. In Australian waters, reproductively active yellowfin tuna have been reported from the north-western Coral Sea[4] and North West Shelf.[5] In the north-western Coral Sea, mature fish aggregate and spawn between October and January during periods of the full moon.[5] Off eastern Australia, yellowfin tuna probably do not spawn south of 25° S.[6] During spawning activity in the north-western Coral Sea, sea surface temperatures are 25–26°C.[4]

Yellowfin tuna are multiple spawners, ie they spawn every few days over the spawning period. The numbers of ripe ova in ovaries sampled from 7 mature female yellowfin tuna (15–60 kg) were between 200 000 and 1 500 000.[4] Eggs and sperm are released into the water for fertilisation. The eggs are epipelagic, ie they float at the water surface.

Large concentrations of larvae and eggs are reported from the western Pacific, including the Coral Sea, and from the Indian Ocean adjacent to Australia's North West Shelf.[7] Yellowfin tuna larvae are pelagic.

Recreational anglers report that juveniles less than 1-year-old are present off southern Queensland and northern New South Wales during the summer. In Australian waters yellowfin tuna grow rapidly. Females average 55 cm (5 kg) by the end of their first year and 155 cm (55 kg) by their fifth year. Although the world record for the largest yellowfin tuna caught on sport fishing gear is 209 cm (176 kg),[8] those caught off eastern Australia rarely exceed 190 cm (100 kg). Yellowfin tuna rarely live for more than

8 years. Large fish are usually males, with few reports of female yellowfin tuna larger than 170 cm (70 kg). In the north-western Coral Sea female yellowfin tuna were reported to reach maturity by about 2 years of age (101 cm fork length or 17 kg).[4]

Tagged yellowfin tuna have been reported to move 1000 km or more over a 12-month period, but no directed migration has been demonstrated. Recoveries from a tagging study of yellowfin tuna on the Australian east coast between 27° S and 38° S suggested that most yellowfin tuna form local groups that moved no more than a few hundred miles over several years. This northward and southward movement of yellowfin tuna along the south-eastern Australian coast is probably associated with the seasonal movement of the warm East Australian Current.[9]

Adult yellowfin tuna are opportunistic carnivores, ie they feed on what animals are available. Their diet includes squid and other cephalopods, other scombrids such as skipjack tuna, frigate mackerel (*Auxis* species), mackerels (*Scomber* species), mackerel tuna (*Euthynnus* species), bonito (*Sarda* species) and smaller yellowfin tuna, as well as trevallies (Carangidae), pilchards (*Sardinops neopilchardus*) and pelagic crabs (Portunidae). They also feed on deepwater lanternfish, *Diaphus* species.[4]

Yellowfin tuna are preyed upon by larger tunas, billfish (Istiophoridae) and, possibly, sharks.[8] In deeper waters, cookie cutter sharks (*Isistius brasiliensis*) may bite flesh from the bodies of yellowfin and other tunas and billfishes.[10]

Stock structure

Yellowfin tuna are presumed to form separate stocks in each of the major oceans. Limited mixing may occur between the Pacific and Indian oceans through Indonesia, and there is probably some mixing between the major fisheries regions in the eastern Pacific and western Pacific oceans.[11] Yellowfin tuna appear to form local groups off south-eastern Australia, and there is limited evidence of mixing with yellowfin tuna of other western Pacific areas.[6] Stock structure of Western Australian yellowfin tuna has not been investigated.

Commercial fishery

Yellowfin tuna support substantial commercial fisheries in the warm waters of the eastern and western Pacific oceans and western Indian Ocean.[9] Yellowfin tuna are commonly caught off south-eastern Australia where sea surface temperatures are between 18°C and 22°C.

Fishing with drifting longlines accounts for most of the commercial catch of yellowfin tuna in Australian waters.

As part of their global fishing operations, the Japanese fish for yellowfin tuna with longlines off eastern Australia, but further offshore and over more northerly waters than the Australian longline fishery. Japanese vessels are usually 200–300 t (40–45 m) in size. On average, each Japanese longliner spends 1 or 2 months in the Australian Fishing Zone during its 6–18 month fishing campaign. Some also fish off north-western Australia and in the vicinity of the Cocos-Keeling and Christmas islands.

The Japanese commenced longlining off eastern and western Australia during the early 1950s. However, since the declaration of the Australian Fishing Zone in 1979, Australian Government restrictions on access have modified Japanese fishing patterns in Australian waters. Now, fishing patterns in the Australian Fishing Zone are variable: some vessels fish off the east coast between 25° S and 34° S in July to October; others operate in more northerly waters between October and January. Most Japanese vessels leave the Australian Fishing Zone by January, having fished as

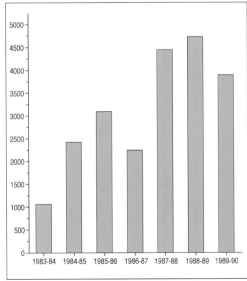

Total annual catch in t of yellowfin tuna for the period 1983–84 to 1989–90 by foreign and domestic vessels. (Source: Australian Fishing Zone Information System)

far as north Queensland waters. A few remain there until February or March. In some years, during full moons in October–December, yellowfin tuna and bigeye tuna are caught by pole-and-line and handline in warm (>25°C) waters off north Queensland.[4,12]

Yellowfin tuna caught by the Japanese are frozen and sold as 'sashimi' (raw fish) in Japan. They target adult yellowfin (30 kg average dressed weight), bigeye tuna, broadbill swordfish (*Xiphias gladius*) and striped marlin (*Tetrapturus audax*). Albacore (*Thunnus alalunga*), black marlin (*Makaira indica*) and blue marlin (*M. mazara*) are also taken. Off north-western Australia, Japanese longliners fish for yellowfin tuna, bigeye tuna and striped marlin during summer.

Australian fishers catch yellowfin tuna mainly off south-eastern Australia, where they have fished with longlines for tunas since the 1950s. The Australian longline fleet grew rapidly with the successful air-freighting of yellowfin tuna to Japan in 1984. Vessels range from 25 t to 150 t (10–28 m) in size. The fishery targets adult yellowfin tuna (25 kg average dressed weight) and bigeye tuna.

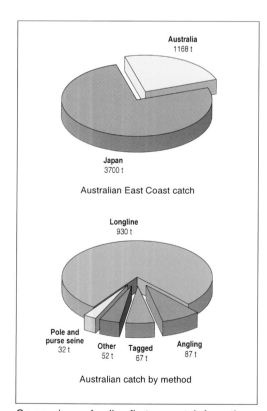

Australia
1168 t

Japan
3700 t

Australian East Coast catch

Longline
930 t

Pole and purse seine
32 t

Other
52 t

Tagged
67 t

Angling
87 t

Australian catch by method

Comparison of yellowfin tuna catch from the eastern Australian Fishing Zone (north of 40° S and east of 140° E) for 1988–89 reported by: Japanese and Australian fishers (upper chart); Australian fishers by fishing method (lower chart). (Sources: Australian Fishing Zone Information System; David Bateman, Eden; 'Form 49' data provided by Bruce Pease, Fisheries Research Institute, NSW Fisheries; and estimates from data presented in West[14])

(above) Yellowfin tuna caught by longline off eastern Australia. (Source: Albert Caton, Bureau of Resource Sciences)

(below) Processing yellowfin tuna caught by longline off eastern Australia. (Source: Peter Ward, Bureau of Resource Sciences)

Broadbill swordfish and albacore are the main bycatch of the Australian longline fishery. The domestic longline season commences off southern Queensland and northern New South Wales in August and spreads southwards following the warm East Australian Current along the coast. Sporadic catches are reported from north-eastern Tasmania in February and March. Catches are reported from the far south coast of New South Wales as late as May or June. A few vessels occasionally longline for yellowfin tuna off north Queensland during October–January. In Western Australia, there is almost no fishing by Australians for yellowfin tuna.

The longlines consist of a main line and a series of branch lines with baited hooks. Longlines set by Australians are generally shorter than those used by the Japanese operating further offshore. Australians set 250–600 hooks each day whereas the Japanese set 2500–3250 hooks on a line of about 100 km length. Both Japanese and Australians target yellowfin tuna, setting the lines to fish at 50–150 m depth. Deeper sets to 250 m — which target bigeye tuna — are occasionally made.

During the late 1980s, most yellowfin tuna caught by Australian longline fishers were sold fresh at sashimi markets in Japan. However, in recent years the Australian sashimi market has accounted for an increasing proportion of the catch and by 1990 almost half of the Australian yellowfin catch was sold at domestic markets.

The price for yellowfin tuna on sashimi markets is variable. Average monthly prices for sashimi-grade yellowfin tuna at the Sydney Fish Market ranged from A$ 4.00 per kg to A$ 10.50 per kg in 1991–92. In 1991–92, average monthly prices for frozen longline-caught yellowfin tuna ranged from A$ 3.50 per kg to A$ 6.30 per kg at the fish market in Yaizu, Japan. Fish sold on the fresh-chilled sashimi market in Japan receive higher prices. Yellowfin tuna from waters south of 25° S are of particularly high quality and fetch much better prices than those caught in warmer waters.

Yellowfin tuna are also caught by other fishing methods in Australia. These tuna are a bycatch of Australian vessels using pole-and-line and purse seine to target skipjack tuna. Most of the yellowfin tuna caught by these methods are taken off southern New South Wales, and canned in Australia. Other fishing methods for this species include trolling, handlining and droplining.

The annual Australian yellowfin tuna catch of around 3000 t is dwarfed when compared with the catch taken in the tropical western Pacific. The South Pacific Commission[13] estimated that over 300 000 t of yellowfin tuna were caught in that region in 1990. Over 200 000 t of this were landed by purse seine, with longlining and poling accounting for most of the remainder.

Management controls There are no catch restrictions for yellowfin tuna. The Japanese fleet is not allowed to fish by methods other than handline and longline. New entry by Australian vessels to the longline and purse seine fisheries off eastern Australia is restricted. In 1990, about 220 Australian vessels were registered to operate in the East Coast Tuna Fishery. Of these, fewer than 45 operated full-time.

Fishing operations of the Japanese in the Australian Fishing Zone are controlled by the Commonwealth Government. The Japanese pay access fees and are excluded from certain areas. For example, since 1990 they have not been permitted to fish with longlines within 50 nautical miles of the east coast. From November 1991 to October 1992 the Japanese were limited to 9.5 million hooks and a maximum of 50 vessels off the east coast.

Recreational fishery

Yellowfin tuna are prized by gamefishers in Australia and are the prime target of gamefishing on the south coast of New South Wales — 1 of the few locations where they can be caught from the shore. More commonly, though, these tuna are caught by trolling lures or baits. Baits include small skipjack tuna, pilchards and mackerel (Scombridae). Yellowfin tuna are also caught from drifting boats by anglers using dead or live bait such as nannygai or redfish (*Centroberyx* species) along with berley.

Anglers fish in the same areas as Australian longliners, but generally closer to shore. They take a wide size range of yellowfin tuna, but often tag and release those smaller than 20 kg. The Game Fishing Association of Australia's record for yellowfin tuna is 102 kg. Angler clubs in eastern Australia reported landing almost 2887 yellowfin tuna in 1988–89, with a further 2233 tagged and released.[14]

Management controls There is no limit on total catch. A bag limit was introduced in New South Wales in 1990. Angler associations and management agencies strongly promote tagging and release of tunas and billfishes.

Resource status

Longline catch rates of yellowfin tuna in the western Pacific declined by about 50 % between 1952 and 1982, then were fairly stable during the remainder of the 1980s. Preliminary assessment of yellowfin tuna in the western Pacific based on a long time-series of longline data suggested a maximum sustainable yield for the longline fishery of 68 000–112 000 t in the area west of 180° E.[11] However, since the mid 1980s, large-scale purse seining, targeting yellowfin tuna of a smaller average size, has grown to be the major fishing method in the region. Yellowfin tuna catches in the western Pacific exceeded 300 000 t by 1990.[13] Recent analyses of tag-recapture results suggest that the purse seine catch of yellowfin tuna could be increased to 500 000 t without causing a significant decline in their abundance.

For many years, catches from the Australian Fishing Zone have varied around current levels, so are probably sustainable with the present fishing pattern and levels of effort. Links between yellowfin tuna in the eastern Australian Fishing Zone and those of the wider western Pacific Ocean are uncertain. As a result, the impact of the steadily expanding western Pacific yellowfin catches is also uncertain.

References

1. Sharp, G.D. (1978) I. Behavioral and physiological properties of tunas and their effects on vulnerability to fishing gear. Pp 397–450, in *The physiological ecology of tunas*. Ed by G.D. Sharp and A.E. Dizon. New York: Academic Press.

2. Brill, R.W. and Holland, K.N. (1990) Horizontal and vertical movements of yellowfin tuna associated with fish aggregation devices. *Fishery Bulletin (U.S.)* **83**(3): 493–507.

3. Power, J.H. and May, L.N. (1991) Satellite observed sea-surface temperatures and yellowfin tuna catch and effort in the Gulf of Mexico. *Fishery Bulletin (U.S.)* **89**(3): 429–439.

4. McPherson, G.R. (1988) Reproductive biology of yellowfin tuna in the eastern Australian Fishing Zone, with special reference to the north-western Coral Sea. *Australian Journal of Marine and Freshwater Research* **42**: 465–477.

5. Shung, S.H. (1973) The sexual activity of yellowfin tuna caught by the longline fishery in the Indian Ocean based on the examination of ovaries. *Bulletin of the Far Seas Research Laboratory* **9**: 123–142. (cited in Stequert and Marsac (1989) *FAO Fisheries Technical Paper* **282**).

6. A biological study of east coast tunas and billfishes, with particular emphasis on yellowfin tuna (*Thunnus albacares*).

Review of results and recommendations for research. (1989) *Bureau of Rural Resources, Working Paper* **11/89**. 35 pp.

7. Nishikawa, Y., Honma, M., Ueyanagi, S. and Kikawa, S. (1985) Average distribution of larvae of oceanic species of scombrid fishes, 1965–1981. *Far Seas Fisheries Research Laboratory, Japan, S Series* **12**. 99 pp.

8. Cole, J.S. (1980) Synopsis of biological data on the yellowfin tuna, *Thunnus albacares* (Bonnaterre, 1788), in the Pacific Ocean. Pp 71–150, in *Synopsis of biological data on eight species of scombrids. Special Report* **2**. Ed by W.H. Bayliff. La Jolla, California: Inter-American Tropical Tuna Commission.

9. Pepperell, J.G. and Diplock, J.H. (1989) Seasonal migration of yellowfin tuna (*Thunnus albacares*) off south eastern Australia. Evidence for a possible localised stock. *New South Wales Department of Agriculture and Fisheries, Fisheries Research Institute Internal Report* (unpublished).

10. Jones, E.C. (1971) *Isistius brasiliensis*, a squaloid shark, the probable cause of crater wounds on fishes and cetaceans. *Fishery Bulletin (U.S.)* **69**(4): 791–798.

11. Suzuki, Z. (1991) Status of world yellowfin tuna fisheries and stocks. *Tuna Newsletter* May: 5–8.

12. Hisada, K. (1973) Investigation of tuna hand-line fishing ground and some biological observations on yellowfin and bigeye tunas in the northwestern Coral Sea. *Bulletin of the Far Seas Fisheries Research Laboratory* **8**: 35–69. [transl. by Green (1988) *CSIRO Marine Laboratories Report* **194**]

13. South Pacific Commission (1991) Status of tuna fisheries in the SPC area during 1990, with annual catches since 1952. *Fourth Standing Committee on Tuna and Billfish, Port Vila, Vanuatu, 17–19 June, 1991. Working Paper* **3**. 75 pp.

14. West, L. (1990) A review of existing and potential data systems for recreational fishing for tunas and billfishes — east coast of Australia. *Internal Report for the Department of Primary Industries and Energy and the East Coast Tuna Management Advisory Committee.* Kewagama Research, Tewantin. 69 pp.

Contributors

Most of the information on this species was provided by Peter Ward. Additional contributions were made by (in alphabetical order) Albert Caton, Geoff McPherson, Julian Pepperell and Thim Skousen. Drawing courtesy FAO, Rome. (*Details of contributors and their organisations are given in the Acknowledgements section at the back of this book.*)

Compilers Patricia Kailola, Christina Grieve (maps), Cesar Ramirez and Phillip Stewart (statistics)

Southern bluefin tuna

Thunnus maccoyii

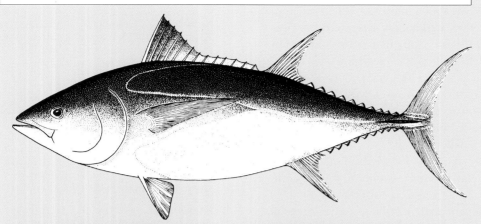

Thunnus maccoyii (Castelnau)

Southern bluefin tuna

Another common name is **SBT**.
FAO: **southern bluefin tuna**
Australian species code: 441004

Family SCOMBRIDAE

Diagnostic features Southern bluefin tuna are distinguished by their yellow median caudal keels and moderately short pectoral fins which are 4–5 times shorter than the body fork length. The upper body is blackish blue and the lower sides and belly are silvery white with alternating rows of clear dots and lines. The anal fin and finlets are yellow, edged with black. Northern bluefin tuna (*T. thynnus*) are similar to southern bluefin tuna, but are distinguished by their dark caudal keels and shorter pectoral fins (5–6 times shorter than the body fork length).

Distribution

Southern bluefin tuna have a probable circumglobal distribution between 30° S and 50° S. They are highly migratory pelagic fish. In Australian waters, southern bluefin tuna range from northern New South Wales around the south of the continent to north-western Australia.[1] At certain times of the year, they form large surface schools off southern and (until recently) south-eastern Australia.

Life history

Southern bluefin tuna in spawning condition are found only in the Indian Ocean. The single spawning ground has been identified as between 7° S and 20° S in the north-eastern Indian Ocean south of Java.[2] The tuna spawn from September to March. The highest larval catches are made from January to February.[3] In the area to the south of the spawning grounds, large southern bluefin tuna with ripening or spent gonads accumulate from September to March. It is not known whether all mature fish spawn each year, every few years, or even only once in their lifetime.[4] After spawning, southern bluefin tuna migrate southwards.

The migration pattern of these tuna is revealed by the capture of progressively larger fish along the migration route. Juveniles 6–8 cm long have been collected on the North West Shelf of Australia and larger juveniles (20–60 cm fork length) have been caught on the continental shelf further south (22–34° S).[3] Off the south-west of Australia, 1–3-year-old (35–75 cm) southern bluefin tuna are common in surface catches; and further eastwards 2–6-year-olds (50–120 cm) and sometimes fish up to 9 years old (145 cm) are taken in surface catches.

Young fish are generally closely associated with coastal and continental shelf waters, although some immature fish, from 3 years of age, move away from the shelf to feed in the waters of the West Wind Drift (40–45°S) of the Southern Ocean.[2] They are caught by longline as far away as South Africa. By maturity, most southern bluefin tuna lead an oceanic, pelagic existence.

Southern bluefin tuna are known to attain 200 kg and 200 cm fork length.[2]

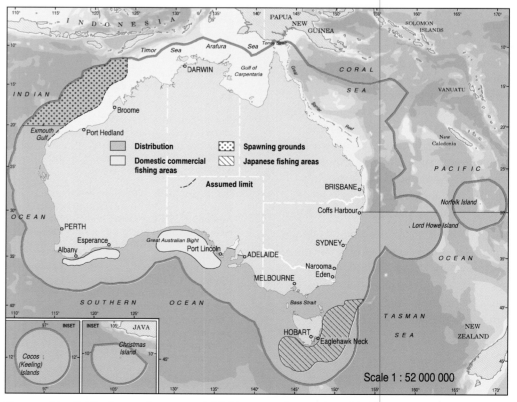

Geographic distribution and commercial fishing area for southern bluefin tuna in Australian waters.

They live for at least 20 years. Fish 2 years old are estimated to range from 46 cm to 56 cm fork length, 8-year-olds from 125 cm to 137 cm and 14-year-olds from 157 cm to 175 cm.[3] Fish appear to grow faster during summer and early autumn, probably in response to warmer sea surface temperatures. Maturity can occur at about 120 cm fork length, but it is more common at 130 cm (about 8 years old). An estimate of the number of eggs, 0.5–1 mm in diameter, produced in a spawning period by a 158 cm fork length female was 14–15 million.[5]

Juvenile and adult southern bluefin tuna are opportunistic feeders, chiefly of cephalopods, crustaceans, fish and salps (Thaliacea). Smaller southern bluefin tuna feed mainly on crustaceans and adults feed mainly on fish. Sharks, other tunas and fish, seabirds and killer whales (*Orcinus orca*) are possible predators at different stages of the southern bluefin tuna's life cycle.

Stock structure

Southern bluefin tuna have a single spawning area and are morphologically uniform; studies have shown that tagged fish disperse rapidly over long distances. These phenomena indicate that southern bluefin tuna form a single stock in the southern hemisphere.[4]

Commercial fishery

Australian and Japanese fleets fish for southern bluefin tuna in the Australian Fishing Zone, and elsewhere these tuna are or have been fished by Japanese, Taiwanese, New Zealand, Indonesian and Korean fleets.[6] In Australian waters, southern bluefin tuna are caught with drifting longlines, pole-and-line, purse seines, by trolling and sometimes with rod-and-reel.

Southern bluefin tuna were occasionally caught by trolling before the 1940s. Experimental canning was undertaken in 1936 at a small cannery in southern New South Wales and in 1939 at the cannery at Port Lincoln, South Australia. However, the fishery did not become commercial until the early to mid 1950s off New South Wales and mid 1950s off South Australia when pole-and-line techniques were introduced.[4] Catches in these States steadily expanded during the 1960s, and were supplemented during

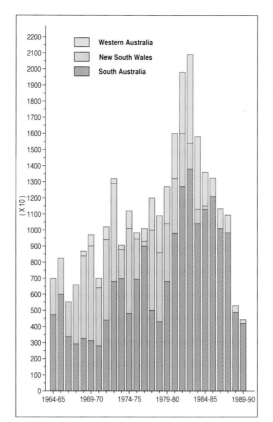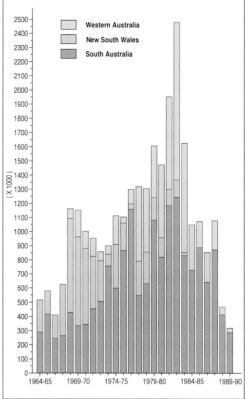

State catches of southern bluefin tuna from 1964–65 to 1989–90 by 'quota year' (1 October to 30 September) in t live weight (left) and number of fish (right). (Source: CSIRO, Australian Fisheries Management Authority and Bureau of Resource Sciences)

the 1970s by a rapidly growing Western Australian pole-and-line fishery. Aerial spotting extended the efficiency of locating fish and the range of the New South Wales and South Australian activities during the 1960s.

Purse seining was successfully introduced in these areas in the mid 1970s (earlier attempts in 1953 and 1966 were largely unsuccessful). An effective joint operation was developed, using a pole vessel to hold fish at the surface with live bait while a purse seine was set around both the fish and pole boat. Catches expanded quickly, with the greater proportion of the South Australian and New South Wales catches taken by this combined pole and purse seine technique. However, after a production peak of 21 500 t in 1982, the Australian surface fishery catches were rapidly reduced by the imposition, and progressive reduction, of catch quotas. In 1991, the southern bluefin tuna catch by domestic vessels was less than 3000 t with the surface fishery located almost entirely off South Australia. The Western Australian fishery, after peaking at just over 6000 t in 1982–83, declined because of the transfer of quota to South Australia. The New South Wales surface fishery, on the other hand, collapsed in the early 1980s, when the occurrence of surface

schools first declined and then virtually ceased.[3]

During the late 1980s the developing New South Wales small vessel longline fishery began to take southern bluefin tuna. Commercial trolling for southern bluefin tuna and albacore (*Thunnus alalunga*) has recently started off the Tasmanian east coast. Quantities taken are small but the return to fishers is good because the southern bluefin tuna are air-freighted fresh chilled to the Japanese 'sashimi' (raw fish) market.

Japanese fishing for southern bluefin tuna with drifting longlines first commenced on the spawning grounds, spread south to the region of the West Wind Drift, then eastwards and westwards. By the late 1960s their fishing grounds extended from eastern New Zealand in the east to the South Atlantic in the west.[2] Production peaked at 78 000 t in 1961 but had declined to around 20 000–30 000 t by the end of the 1970s despite continually increasing longline effort. During the 1980s, the catch declined to 11 500 t, then to 6065 t as quotas were implemented.

The main areas of the Australian Fishing Zone fished for southern bluefin tuna by Japanese longliners were the waters adjacent to southern New South Wales, southern Tasmania and the Great

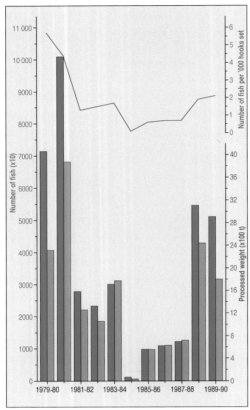

Japanese longline catch of southern bluefin tuna from 1979–80 to 1989–90 by 'AFZ year' (1 November to 31 October) in the Australian Fishing Zone in t processed weight, number of fish and number of fish per thousand hooks set. Processed weight is 85 % of live weight. Catch rates may be misleading here, as a substantial amount of the fishing effort is directed towards species other than southern bluefin tuna. (Source: Australian Fisheries Management Authority and Bureau of Resource Sciences)

Australian Bight; but incidental catches were taken from most areas of the Zone where southern bluefin tuna are present. Access restraints have recently confined Japanese southern bluefin tuna longlining in the Australian Fishing Zone to the Tasmanian region. However, joint venture arrangements between the Australian and Japanese industries have resulted in a portion of the Australian quota now being longlined. The joint venture fishers have access to some of the area closed to licensed Japanese longliners.

Southern bluefin tuna become available to the Western Australian surface fishery when approximately 40 cm fork length (when about 1 kg and 1–2 years old) and to the South Australian fishery when about 2 years old. In general, they are fished by the Japanese longliners from approximately 90 cm (when about 15 kg and 4 years old),[3] but longline operations in the Great Australian Bight take small quantities of younger fish as well.

Initially, most of the surface catch was canned. Towards the end of the 1980s

about 30 % of the Australian catch was still landed whole for canning. Now, virtually all southern bluefin tuna are gilled and gutted then air-freighted fresh, or shipped frozen, for the Japanese 'sashimi' market. Southern bluefin tuna taken by Japanese longliners are killed, gilled and gutted and frozen (to minus 60°C) during voyages lasting up to 15 months. The 1989 price for fish for canning was approximately A$ 1.20 per kg. The sashimi price varies considerably depending on quality. In 1992, Australian exports of frozen southern bluefin tuna to Japan received average prices of A$ 11.00 to A$ 15.00 per kg (1100 –1400 yen per kg).

Management controls Shortly after the purse seining technique was introduced to the southern bluefin tuna fishery, catches rapidly expanded. Purse seining for southern bluefin tuna was banned off Western Australia in the mid 1970s, and a limit placed on the number of purse seiners permitted to operate off south-eastern Australia. Subsequently, a 'freeze' was placed on the entry of further

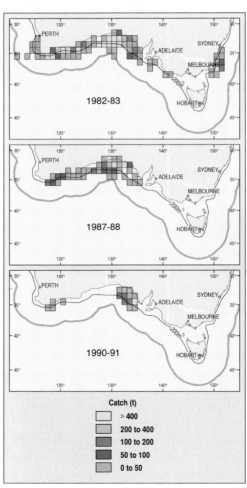

Annual distributions of southern bluefin tuna catch (t live weight) reported by Australian fishing vessels, for 'quota years' (1 October to 30 September) a) 1982–83, b) 1987–88, c) 1990–91. (Source: Australia Fishing Zone Information System)

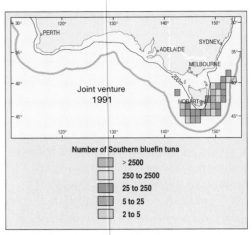

Distribution of southern bluefin tuna catch reported by Australia–Japan joint venture longliners in the Australian Fishing Zone for 1991. (Source: Australian Fishing Zone Information System)

pole-and-line vessels. These controls were replaced in the 1983–84 season by interim catch quotas for the south-eastern and western components of the fishery, after which individual transferable quotas were introduced and are still in use. An additional objective of management was that fishers target away from small fish. Consequently, commercial capture of southern bluefin tuna along the west coast north of 34° S is prohibited.

Since the establishment of the Australian Fishing Zone in 1979 access arrangements for Japanese longline vessels have been negotiated annually. During the early 1980s, access areas were progressively reduced and in 1985 southern bluefin tuna fishing by Japanese longliners was prohibited in the Zone pending establishment of a global southern bluefin tuna quota for that fleet.

Frozen southern bluefin tuna on sale at the Tsukiji market in Japan. (Source: Albert Caton, Bureau of Resource Sciences)

The Tasmanian region was the only area of the Zone subsequently reopened to licensed Japanese longliners.[3]

Australia, Japan and New Zealand have co-operated to establish a global quota on the catch of southern bluefin tuna. Quotas for 1991–92 were fixed at the same levels as 1990–91, ie 5265 t for Australia, 6065 t for Japan and 420 t for New Zealand. However, the expansion of catches by countries outside this trilateral arrangement is a serious obstacle to achieving effective global restraint. Catches of southern bluefin tuna by vessels from Taiwan (perhaps as much as 1000 t) and to a lesser extent Indonesia and Korea, are now quite significant compared with catch allowed by the quota arrangement.

Recreational fishery

Southern bluefin tuna of 7–20 kg were common in recreational catches off southern New South Wales until surface schools virtually disappeared there in the early 1980s. The Eaglehawk Neck area off eastern Tasmania was similarly affected, but troll catches resumed after the mid 1980s. Recreational troll catches off western Victoria and south-eastern South Australia failed for much of the 1980s, but showed a small recovery at the end of the decade. In Western Australia between Perth and Albany, 1–7 kg southern bluefin tuna are taken in small quantities by anglers. The Game Fishing Association

of Australia record for southern bluefin tuna is 126 kg.

Management controls A bag limit for all tunas was introduced in New South Wales in 1990. In recognition of the fragile condition of the resource, many anglers have ceased targeting southern bluefin tuna (eg the New South Wales Gamefishing Association). Furthermore, tagging and release of southern bluefin tuna and other tunas is encouraged by recreational angling associations.

Resource status

Trilateral scientific meetings between Australia, Japan and New Zealand have been held each year since 1982. The major conclusion of all assessments has been that the parent stock has continuously declined since the 1950s, the decline becoming more rapid in the early 1980s. Scientists have progressively become more pessimistic about the capacity of the stock to maintain adequate recruitment of young fish into the fishery.

The 11th trilateral scientific meeting, in October 1992 in Japan, again concluded that the parent stock is at historically low levels, so the risk of recruitment collapse and the potential for parental stock collapse is at least as high as it has ever been. The meeting could not predict with certainty whether stocks would recover or decline in future under current catch levels.[6]

On a positive note, however, indications are that abundance of the

juvenile stock has increased since 1986, mainly as a result of the drastic reduction of surface fishing in recent years.

Different interpretations of the 1992 assessment lead to different predictions of appropriate catch levels: that there is a very high probability that the stock will increase not only under current catch levels but also under slightly higher catch levels; or, that there is a significant possibility that the stock is already in the process of recruitment collapse.

While southern bluefin tuna currently support a valuable fishery, the value could be far greater if spawning populations could be rebuilt and the recruitment of young fish to the fishery enhanced.

References

1. Robins, J.P. (1963) Synopsis of biological data on bluefin tuna, *Thunnus thynnus maccoyii* (Castelnau) 1872. *FAO Fisheries Report* **6**(2): 562–587.

2. Shingu, C. (1978) Ecology and stock of southern bluefin tuna. *Japan Association of Fishery Resources Protection. Fisheries study* **31**. 81 pp. (In Japanese. English translation in *CSIRO Division of Fisheries and Oceanography report* **131**. 1981.)

3. Caton, A.E. (1991) Review of aspects of southern bluefin tuna biology, population and fisheries. Pp 181–357, in *World meeting on stock assessment of bluefin tunas: strengths and weaknesses. Special report* **7**. Ed by R.B. Deriso and W.H. Bayliff. La Jolla, California: Inter-American Tropical Tuna Commission.

4. Caton, A., McLoughlin, K. and Williams, M.J. (1990) Southern bluefin tuna: scientific background to the debate. *Bureau of Rural Resources Bulletin* **3**. 41 pp.

5. Kikawa, S. (1964) Estimated number of eggs spawned out of the ovaries of an indomaguro (*Thunnus thynnus maccoyii?*). *Report of the Nankai Regional Fisheries Research Laboratory* **20**: 27–34. (In Japanese with an English summary.)

6. *Report to management of the eleventh meeting of Australian, Japanese and New Zealand scientists on southern bluefin tuna* (1992) Unpublished report of the meeting. Shimizu-shi, Japan, 5–10 October 1992.

Contributors

The information in this presentation was originally provided by Albert Caton. Additional comments were made by (in alphabetical order) Kevin McLoughlin, Tom Polacheck and Peter Ward. Drawing courtesy FAO, Rome. (*Details of contributors and their organisations are given in the Acknowledgements section at the back of this book.*)
Compilers Patricia Kailola and Christina Grieve (map)

South Australian tuna polefishing in its hey-day when large loads were taken for canning. Now, boats take small loads with careful handling of individual fish for the fresh-chilled 'sashimi' market. (Source: Kevin McLoughlin, Bureau of Resource Sciences)

365

B i g e y e   t u n a

Thunnus obesus

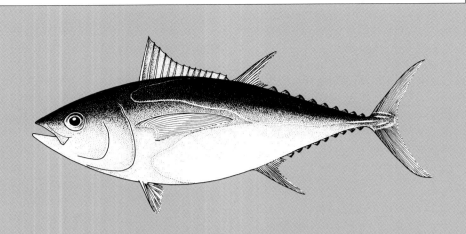

Thunnus obesus (Lowe)

Bigeye tuna

Another common name is **bigeye**.
FAO: **bigeye tuna**
Australian species code: 441011

Family SCOMBRIDAE

Diagnostic features Bigeye tuna have a shallow notch at the centre of the caudal fin fork and, in adults, the eye is relatively large compared with that of other tunas. Their entire dorsal and ventral body profiles are evenly curved. The liver has noticeable striations and its central lobe is the longest. The pectoral fin in adult bigeye tuna is one-quarter to one-third the body fork length, whereas the pectoral fin in juvenile bigeye tuna is longer and always extends beyond a line drawn between the anterior edges of the second dorsal and anal fins. Bigeye tuna less than 75 cm fork length (10 kg whole weight) have longer pectoral fins than yellowfin tuna (*T. albacares*) of comparable sizes. Juvenile bigeye tuna often have 7–10 white unbroken stripes crossing the lower sides vertically, substantially fewer than in juvenile yellowfin tuna.

Distribution

Bigeye tuna inhabit the tropical and subtropical waters of the Pacific, Indian and Atlantic oceans between about 45° N and 40° S.[1] They are oceanic fish, present throughout Australian waters where sea surface temperatures exceed 17°C — from east of Torres Strait to 43° S and from approximately 140° E in the Great Australian Bight to the North West Shelf.

Temperature and dissolved oxygen limit the vertical and geographic distributions of bigeye tuna. They are more tolerant of lower temperatures and lower dissolved oxygen concentration than are other tunas and tend to occupy deeper waters.[2] For example, during the day adult bigeye tuna inhabit the thermocline zone at about 150–250 m in tropical waters where temperatures descend to almost 10°C, provided dissolved oxygen concentration is more than 1 mg per l.[3,4] The tuna make occasional short ascents to 100 m or shallower.

Young bigeye tuna have not been reported outside tropical waters.[2] Here, bigeye tuna smaller than 20 kg may form surface-dwelling schools of similar sized fish with other species such as yellowfin tuna and skipjack tuna (*Katsuwonus pelamis*). Schools of only bigeye tuna are less common.[1] In tropical waters, young bigeye tuna are often caught 50–100 m below floating objects such as logs and fish aggregating devices.[2]

Adults tend to be solitary. Behavioural studies in Hawaiian waters using ultrasonic tags[5] found that the distribution of adult bigeye tuna was closely correlated with the 15°C isotherm during the day. Like yellowfin tuna, bigeye tuna move into the warmer surface waters (within 50 m of the surface) at night.

Life history

Bigeye tuna spawn throughout tropical waters of the eastern Indian Ocean and

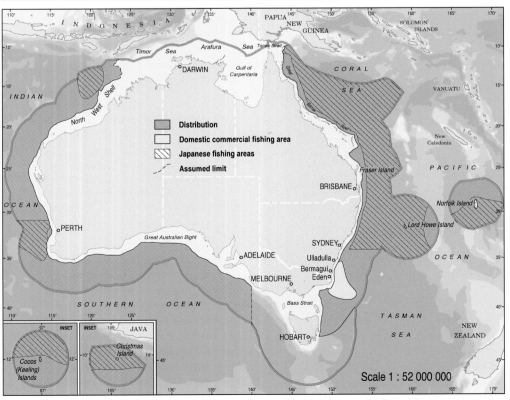

Geographic distribution and commercial fishing areas for bigeye tuna in Australian waters.

the eastern and western Pacific oceans. In Australian waters, reproductively active bigeye tuna have been reported from south of Indonesia,[6] north of Australia[2] and from the north-western Coral Sea.[7]

Spawning tends to be restricted to summer months: April–September in the northern hemisphere and January–March in the southern hemisphere.[2,8] In the north-western Coral Sea, bigeye tuna and yellowfin tuna aggregate and spawn over periods of the full moon during October– January. Aggregations are associated with frontal regions where sea surface temperatures are 25–26°C.[8,9] Like yellowfin tuna, bigeye tuna are multiple spawners that may spawn every 1 or 2 days over several months.[10]

The eggs are epipelagic, ie they float at the water surface. Little is known of the life history of bigeye tuna larvae except that they are pelagic. From October to March, particularly high concentrations of larvae and eggs are reported from south of Indonesia, including north-western areas of the Australian Fishing Zone. Larvae are also reported from the north-western Coral Sea.[11]

Although bigeye tuna have been reported to grow to over 200 cm fork length (210 kg), individuals larger than 180 cm (150 kg) are rare in Australian waters. Several studies have estimated that

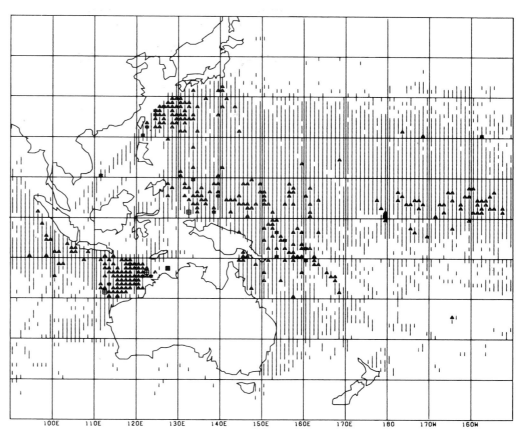

Distribution of bigeye larvae in waters adjacent to Australia (adapted from Nishikawa et al[11]). Vertical lines indicate sites of larvae net tows where no larvae were reported; other symbols indicate sites where up to 3 larvae were reported per cubic km of water strained.

Tagging bigeye tuna in the Coral Sea.
(Source: Thor Carter, CSIRO Marine Laboratories, Hobart)

bigeye tuna may live for 8 to 11 years.[2] Male bigeye tuna are more common than females in longline catches, with few reports of female bigeye tuna larger than 150 cm (90 kg) in Australian waters.

In the north-western Coral Sea female bigeye tuna were reported to reach maturity at 100–125 cm,[7] when 3 or more years old. There are, however, reports from other regions of mature bigeye tuna of 67 cm and 92 cm long.[2]

Adult bigeye tuna are opportunistic carnivores and, like yellowfin tuna, have a diverse diet. Bigeye tuna are known to feed on squid and other cephalopods, pomfrets (*Brama brama*), other scombroid fish such as skipjack tuna, yellowfin tuna, frigate mackerel (*Auxis* species), mackerels (*Scomber* species), mackerel tuna (*Euthynnus* species) and bonito (*Sarda* species). They also feed on trevallies (Carangidae), pilchards (*Sardinops neopilchardus*), flying fish (Exocoetidae), deepwater lanternfish (*Diaphus* species), pelagic crabs (Portunidae) and other crustaceans.[1]

Bigeye tuna are preyed upon by larger tunas, billfish (Istiophoridae) and toothed whales (Odontoceti).[1] It is known that in deeper waters, cookie cutter sharks (*Isistius brasiliensis*) may take bites of flesh from bigeye tuna.[12]

Stock structure

Few biological studies of bigeye tuna have been conducted and there is uncertainty regarding stock structure. Limited tag-recapture results indicate that bigeye tuna are capable of long-range movements of several thousand nautical miles, but separate Pacific Ocean and Indian Ocean stocks are assumed for the purpose of stock assessment. Bigeye tuna taken in Australian waters are members of larger, possibly trans-oceanic stocks.

Commercial fishery

Bigeye tuna are an important target species of Japanese, Korean and, more recently, Taiwanese fleets using longlines in the tropical waters of the Pacific, Indian and Atlantic oceans. Bigeye tuna also form a significant bycatch of purse seining for yellowfin tuna in the Western Indian Ocean and for yellowfin tuna and skipjack tuna in the western Pacific.

Longlining using drifting lines accounts for almost all of the catch of bigeye tuna in Australian waters. During October–December in some years, bigeye tuna are also caught from Japanese vessels with pole-and-line and handline off north Queensland.[7,9]

The Australian longline fishery for tunas off south-eastern Australia has been in operation since the 1950s. With the successful air-freighting of yellowfin tuna and bigeye tuna to Japan in 1984, a longline fishery for these tunas grew rapidly, stabilising during the late 1980s. Domestic longliners, mostly 10–20 m long, commence fishing off southern Queensland and northern New South Wales in about August. Many vessels follow the movement of the warm East Australian Current southwards along the coast, fishing off southern New South Wales until May and sometimes as late as June. During the 1980s there were several attempts to establish small-scale longline operations for bigeye tuna off south-western Australia. These operations were unsuccessful and now few Australians fish for bigeye tuna off Western Australia.

The Japanese commenced longlining off eastern and western Australia during the early 1950s. Before the declaration of the Australian 200-mile fishing zone in 1979, Japanese longline vessels would commence fishing off southern New South Wales during July and gradually move north over August–September to areas such as off Fraser Island and Lord Howe Island. Since 1979 however, access restrictions to the Zone have modified Japanese fishing patterns in Australian waters. Off eastern Australia, the Japanese vessels, usually 40–45 m long, fish further offshore and usually over more northerly waters than do the Australian vessels. Some Japanese vessels fish off the east coast between 25° S and 34° S from July to October while others operate in more northerly waters between October and January. Most vessels leave the Australian Fishing Zone by January although a few remain until February or March. On average, each longliner spends up to 2 months in the Zone during its 6–18 month global fishing campaign.

Longlines used by Australian fishers are 10–30 km long and are set each day with 250–800 baited hooks. Japanese vessels daily set a line 80–100 km long bearing 2500–3250 hooks . Both Japanese and Australian fishers target yellowfin tuna, setting the lines to fish between 50 m and 150 m depth. In tropical waters outside the Australian Fishing Zone, the Japanese use mostly deeper sets to 250–300 m to target bigeye tuna,[4] but such deep sets are not used by either fleet within the Zone unless other catches in

Branchlines are retrieved by the crew of a Japanese longline vessel fishing for bigeye tuna and yellowfin tuna in the Australian Fishing Zone. (Source: Peter Ward, Bureau of Resource Sciences)

the area suggest the presence of bigeye tuna.

In north-eastern Australian waters the Japanese target adult yellowfin tuna, bigeye tuna, broadbill swordfish (*Xiphias gladius*) and striped marlin (*Tetrapturus audax*). Albacore (*Thunnus alalunga*), black marlin (*Makaira indica*) and blue marlin (*M. mazara*) are also taken. Off south-western Australia, the Japanese specifically target bigeye tuna during October–April as an adjunct to fishing for southern bluefin tuna (*Thunnus maccoyii*). Whereas bigeye tuna comprise only 5–10 % of the catch off the east coast, they account for over 70 % of the catch in the south-west. Off north-western Australia and around the Cocos–Keeling and Christmas islands during the summer, a small bycatch of bigeye tuna is taken by the Japanese targeting yellowfin tuna and striped marlin.

Bigeye tuna is a highly valued item on the 'sashimi' (raw fish) market in Japan, second only to southern bluefin tuna and northern bluefin tuna (*Thunnus thynnus*). Most bigeye tuna caught in Australian waters are sold fresh (Australian vessels) or frozen (Japanese vessels) to such markets. In Japan, bigeye tuna fetched an average of about A$ 18.00 per kg on the fresh-chilled sashimi market in 1992 and A$ 12.00 per kg on the frozen sashimi market. Bigeye tuna from cooler waters south of 30° S are often large and particularly high in quality.

Management controls There are no catch restrictions for bigeye tuna. Only the Australian fleet is allowed to fish by methods other than handline and longline and entry to the longline and purse seine fisheries off eastern Australia is restricted.

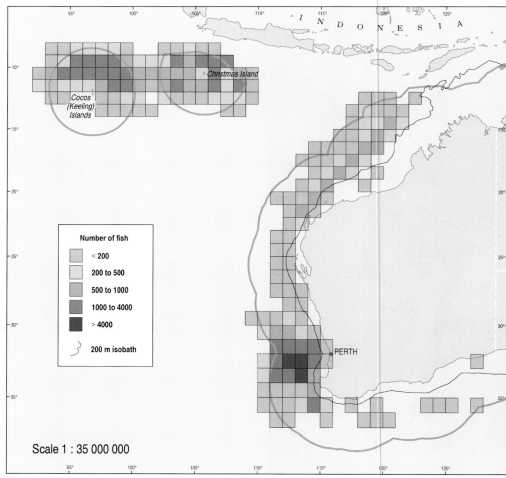

Total Japanese catch of bigeye tuna in number of fish by 1-degree block from the Australian Fishing Zone west of 130° E, for the period 1979 to 1989. (Source: Australian Fishing Zone Information System)

Fishing operations of the Japanese fleet in the Australian Fishing Zone are controlled by access restrictions imposed by the Commonwealth of Australia. Japanese fishers pay access fees and are not permitted to fish in certain areas, eg within 50 nautical miles off the east coast. In 1991, restrictions on the number of fishing days were introduced off the east coast because of concern over expansion in Japanese longline fishing effort.

Recreational fishery

Bigeye tuna are rarely taken by recreational anglers. According to records of the Game Fishing Association of Australia, the record bigeye tuna caught weighed 120 kg and was taken off Bermagui in New South Wales.

Management controls A bag limit for all tunas was introduced in New South Wales in 1990. Angler associations and management agencies strongly promote tagging and release of all billfishes and tunas.

Resource status

Longline catch rates of bigeye tuna declined from the late 1950s to the late 1960s, then stabilised in the 1970s as the Japanese commenced targeting bigeye tuna.[4,13] Preliminary assessments[13] suggest a fairly constant stock size in the Pacific Ocean over this time.

The South Pacific Commission estimated that over 32 000 t of bigeye tuna were caught by longline in the

western Pacific in 1990.[14] No bigeye tuna are reported to have been caught by purse seining, yet it may go undetected. Port sampling suggests that bigeye tuna may comprise a significant portion — perhaps as much as 10–15 % — of the 177 000 t of yellowfin tuna reported by purse seiners. The ability of the resource to support these catches is not known. Uncertainty over links between bigeye tuna of the eastern Australian Fishing Zone and the wider western Pacific hamper assessment of the condition of local groups off eastern Australia.

References

1. Calkins, T.P. (1980) Synopsis of biological data on the bigeye tuna, *Thunnus obesus* (Lowe, 1839), in the Pacific Ocean. Pp 215–259, in *Synopsis of biological data on eight species of scombrids. Special Report 2*. Ed by W.H. Bayliff. La Jolla, California: Inter-American Tropical Tuna Commission.

2. Stequert, B. and Marsac, F. (1989) Tropical tuna — surface fisheries in the Indian Ocean. *FAO Fisheries Technical Paper 282*. 238 pp.

3. Sharp, G.D. (1978) I. Behavioral and physiological properties of tunas and their effects on vulnerability to fishing gear. Pp 397–450, in *The physiological ecology of tunas*. Ed by G.D. Sharp and A.E. Dizon. New York: Academic Press.

4. Sakagawa, G.T., Coan, A.L. and Bartoo, N.W. (1987) Patterns in longline fishery data and catches of bigeye tuna, *Thunnus obesus. Marine Fisheries Review 49*(4): 57–66.

5. Brill, R.W. and Holland, K.N. (1990) Horizontal and vertical movements of yellowfin tuna associated with fish aggregation devices. *Fishery Bulletin (U.S.) 83*(3): 493–507.

6. Ueyanagi, S. (1969) Observation on the distribution of tuna larvae in the Indo-Pacific with emphasis on the spawning areas of albacore, *Thunnus alalunga. Bulletin of the Far Seas Fisheries Research Laboratory 2*: 177–256. (cited in Stequert and Marsac, 1989)

7. McPherson, G.R. (1988) Reproductive biology of yellowfin and bigeye tuna in the eastern Australian fishing zone, with special reference to the north western Coral Sea. *Queensland Department of Primary Industries, Northern Fisheries Research Centre, Fisheries Research Branch Technical Report FRB 88/10*. 66 pp.

8. Collette, B.B. and Nauen, C.E. (1983) FAO species catalogue. Vol. 2. Scombrids of the world. An annotated and illustrated catalogue of tunas, mackerels, bonitos and related species known to date. *FAO Fisheries Synopsis No. 125, 2*. 137 pp.

9. Hisada, K. (1973) Investigation of tuna hand-line fishing ground and some biological observations on yellowfin and bigeye tunas in the northwestern Coral Sea.

Bulletin of the Far Seas Fisheries Research Laboratory 8: 35–69. [translated by Green (1988) *CSIRO Marine Laboratories Report 194*]

10. Nikaido, H., Miyabe, N. and Ueyanagi, S. (in press, 1992) Spawning time and frequency of bigeye tuna, *Thunnus obesus. Bulletin of the National Research Institute of Far Seas Fisheries*. (cited in Miyabe (1991) *FAO expert consultation on interactions of Pacific tuna fisheries, Noumea, New Caledonia, 3–11 December 1991*. **TIC/91/BP 9**)

11. Nishikawa, Y., Honma, M., Ueyanagi, S. and Kikawa, S. (1985) Average distribution of larvae of oceanic species of scombrid fishes, 1965–1981. *Far Seas Fisheries Research Laboratory, Japan, S Series 12*. 99 pp.

12. Jones, E.C. (1971) *Isistius brasiliensis*, a squaloid shark, the probable cause of crater wounds on fishes and cetaceans. *Fishery Bulletin (U.S.) 69*(4): 791–798.

13. Miyabe, N. (1989) Preliminary stock assessment of Pacific bigeye tuna. Pp 122–130, in *Report of the Third Southeast Asian tuna conference, Indo-Pacific Tuna Development and Management Programme*. Ed by FAO, Rome.

14. South Pacific Commission (1991) Status of tuna fisheries in the SPC area during 1990, with annual catches since 1952. *Fourth Standing Committee on Tuna and Billfish, Port Vila, Vanuatu, 17–19 June, 1991. Working Paper 3*. 75 pp.

Contributors

Most of the information on this species was provided by Peter Ward. Additional contributions were made by (in alphabetical order) Albert Caton and John Hampton. Drawing courtesy of FAO, Rome. (*Details of contributors and their organisations are given in the Acknowledgements section at the back of this book.*)

Compilers Patricia Kailola, Christina Grieve (maps), Cesar Ramirez and Phillip Stewart (statistics)

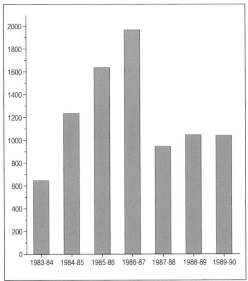

Total annual catch in t of bigeye tuna for the period 1983–84 to 1989–90 by foreign and domestic vessels. (Source: Australian Fishing Zone Information System)

Black marlin

Makaira indica

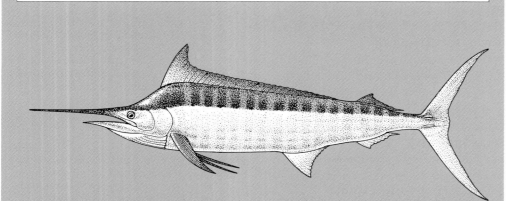

Makaira indica (Cuvier)

Black marlin

Other common names include **Pacific black marlin** and **silver marlin**.
FAO: black marlin
Australian species code: 444006

Family ISTIOPHORIDAE

Diagnostic features Black marlin can be distinguished from other marlin because their body depth is greater than the height of the front lobe of the first dorsal fin, and their second dorsal fin begins slightly forward of the second anal fin. Adults are more easily identified, as they have a well-elevated nape and their pectoral fins are rigid and cannot be pressed back against the sides of their body. There are usually no blotches or dark stripes along the body.[1]

Distribution

Black marlin are present in tropical and subtropical waters of the Indian and Pacific oceans, between approximately 25–40° N and 30–45° S[1] and in surface water temperatures of 20–30°C.[2] Australian records note that black marlin extend throughout northern waters and can be found as far south as Tasmania and Albany in Western Australia. Black marlin are recorded from the western Gulf of Carpentaria to the south of Groote Eylandt, but their presence has not been confirmed in the eastern Gulf of Carpentaria. They are also reported in Torres Strait.[3]

Black marlin are pelagic fish which inhabit almost any depth of water. They are more closely associated with land masses than are blue marlin (*Makaira mazara*) and striped marlin (*Tetrapturus audax*). Catch rates of black marlin in the eastern Australian Fishing Zone are higher close to the continental slope and in the East Australian Current than further offshore. Young juvenile black marlin (10–25 kg) are seasonally common in continental shelf waters, whereas adults are usually restricted to oceanic waters or those in close proximity to the continental slope.

Black marlin are highly mobile. Seasonal changes in distributions of catch

rates, reflecting concentrations of fish, do take place but individuals do not follow clear migration routes.[4] Such seasonal concentrations are known to occur in the north-west Coral Sea, off the North West Shelf of Australia, in the Banda Sea and the east China Sea. There have been suggestions that the distributions and

migrations of black marlin are sex-dependent.[5] Knowledge of seasonal changes in distribution and migration patterns of this highly mobile species is largely based on catch data collected by the Japanese longline fleet. Tagging has also assisted greatly in interpretation of movement patterns.[4,6]

From the Coral Sea aggregation in September–December, presumed 1–2-year-old fish and 1 or 2 older groups move south parallel to the eastern Australian coastline from north Queensland to central New South Wales, apparently in association with the southward movement of the East Australian Current.[4] By April, however, the fish have probably dispersed eastwards (catch rates in eastern Australia between April and August are generally very low). Fish can move large distances

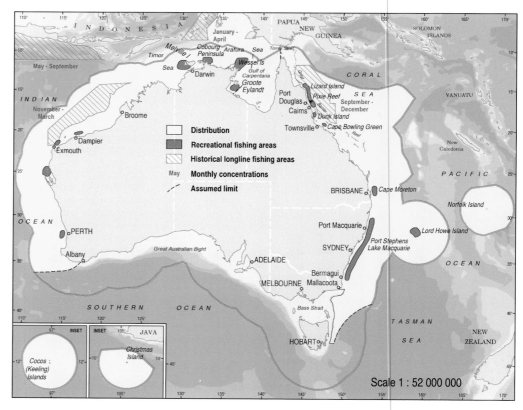

Geographic distribution, commercial and recreational fishing areas for black marlin in Australian and adjacent waters.

(up to 7200 km in 359 days) and recaptures from tagging studies over several years strongly suggest annual homing of at least part of the (western Coral Sea) population.[4] It appears that fish also migrate from north-western Australia to Indian Ocean waters south of Indonesia in late March–April, and fish migrate back to north-western Australia during October.[3] High catch rates occur in the Banda Sea north of Australia between January and April.

Life history

In Australian waters, black marlin spawn between October and December in the north-west Coral Sea. This conclusion is based on seasonal aggregations of sexually mature fish and the presence of black marlin larvae. Spawning may also take place off the north-western Australian continental shelf and in the Timor Sea sometime between October and March. In the northern hemisphere, spawning may occur in the South China Sea in May and June and around Taiwan from August to October.[1] In 13 female black marlin weighing 322–477 kg caught in the north-west Coral Sea between mid October and November 1979, egg counts suggested that the number of viable eggs per female ranged from 67 million to 226 million. It is not known whether all eggs are released simultaneously or serially in batches over the spawning season.

Black marlin larvae have been found only in the north-west Coral Sea off Queensland and off north-western Australia, south of 10° S (where they were misidentified as sailfish larvae, *Istiophorus platypterus*).[7,8] Off Lizard Island in north Queensland, concentrations of black marlin larvae have been found in close proximity (within half a mile) to the outer slopes of coral reefs on the edge of the continental shelf.[8]

The maximum recorded total length for black marlin is 448 cm[1] and the maximum weight is 709 kg. Males are smaller than females. Although the maximum weight of males is unknown, data from the Coral Sea longline fishery suggest they rarely, if ever, exceed 200 kg. The size of fish at maturity is uncertain, although males appear to mature at much smaller sizes than females.[9] The sex ratio of juveniles of 10–60 kg approximates 1:1 but in the longline fishery, 9 males are caught for every female.[6]

Methods for ageing black marlin other than by size-frequency have yet to be determined. Eastern Australian black marlin show the following presumed age-weight relationship: 1-year-old fish average 15–20 kg, 2-year-olds average 30 kg, 3-year-olds average 50–55 kg and 4-year-olds average 70 kg.[4]

Juvenile (less than 40 kg) black marlin consume tropical pilchards and herrings (Clupeidae) whereas tuna-like fishes (Scombridae) and scad and trevally (Carangidae) dominate the adult diet. Sharks, larger billfish (Istiophoridae), tunas, trevallies and dolphin fish (*Coryphaena* species) probably prey on juvenile black marlin.[1]

Stock structure

The stock structure of black marlin is unclear, although there may be several stocks: the eastern Pacific, the south-west Pacific, the north-west Pacific–East China Sea and the north-east Indian Ocean stocks.[3] The extent of movement between these stocks is not known. There is slight evidence of a relationship between the eastern Pacific population and the south-west Pacific stock.[4,6]

Commercial fishery

There is no domestic fishery for black marlin off eastern Australia, based on a voluntary agreement by the East Coast Longline Tunamens' Association. Elsewhere, domestic fleets catch black marlin incidentally in longline tuna fisheries.

Japanese vessels began making significant catches of black marlin in both the north-west Coral Sea and off north-western Australia in 1953. Since the commencement of operation of the 200-mile Australian Fishing Zone in 1979, access of this fleet to Australian waters is subject to bilateral agreements. In the Australian Fishing Zone, Japanese fleets fish for tunas such as yellowfin tuna (*Thunnus albacares*) and bigeye tuna (*T. obesus*) and billfish such as striped marlin and broadbill swordfish (*Xiphias gladius*). Black marlin and blue marlin usually form an incidental catch of the Japanese drifting longline fishery. A few longliners used to target spawning and pre-spawning aggregations of black marlin in the Coral Sea during the summer.

The Japanese longline boats range up to 350 t and 45 m in size and each boat generally spends about 60 days in the Australian Fishing Zone during its fishing campaign. The longlines are 70–110 km long and may carry more than 3000 hooks. One set of a single main line is made in any 24 hour period, and traditionally the lines are set to fish at between 50 m and 150 m depth. Deeper sets to 250 m — which target bigeye tuna — may occasionally be made.

The maximum catch rate for black marlin off north-western Australia occurs between November and April,[3] mostly between 12° S and 24° S, peaking offshore between Exmouth and Broome. The north-west Coral Sea longline grounds, which were historically bounded by 142–150° E and 10–20° S, accounted for the major part of the south-west Pacific black marlin catch. Catch and catch rates there peaked between October and December between 14° S and 19° S in the Queensland and Townsville troughs. The present fishing grounds are much more restricted due to area closures.

Black marlin in the Coral Sea longline fishery typically range from 50–120 kg (processed weight) with an average size of 85–90 kg. In this fishery, fish less than 100 kg are usually male and all fish more than 190 kg are female. This size difference suggests that immature females may not be present in the Coral Sea longline fishery — only about 10 % of the total north-west Coral Sea longline catch is comprised of females. The whereabouts of immature females larger than 60 kg is unknown.

The vast majority of black marlin caught by Japanese longliners is sold as processed, frozen sashimi in Japan. The average price per kg at the Yaizu fish market was 532 yen (A$ 5.08) in 1988, 525 yen (A$ 4.82) in 1989[10] and 448 yen (A$3.87) in 1990. In 1991–92, monthly

Small black marlin hooked off Bermagui, New South Wales. (Source: Julian Pepperell, Pepperell Research & Consulting Pty Ltd, Sydney)

average prices at Yaizu market ranged from 230–440 yen (A$ 2.20 –4.80) per kg.

Domestically, black marlin is banned from sale in New South Wales because mercury and selenium levels usually exceed government health limits in that State. Although the levels are highly variable between individuals, they are correlated with size.[11]

Management controls The number of Japanese longliners is limited under access agreements which are reviewed each year. An area between 12° S and 19° S in the Coral Sea has been closed to pelagic longline fishing by the Japanese fleet since 1980 to reduce perceived competition between the fishery and the established recreational fishery for black marlin at the outer edge of the Great Barrier Reef. A further area closure to the south of that area was legislated in 1990. In addition, all black marlin and blue marlin taken alive at the time of longline retrieval are voluntarily released by the Japanese. The domestic fleet size is also restricted and all live marlin have to be released.

Recreational fishery

The black marlin recreational fishery off eastern Australia is large in terms of value and interest. The game fishery off Cairns to Lizard Island occurs at the same time as the longline fishery (September– December) on the outside of the coral reefs but within several km, often hundreds of m, of the reef crests. The Cairns–Lizard Island charter boat fishery targets females of greater than 450 kg ('thousand pounders') associated with the spawning/pre-spawning aggregation previously targeted by the commercial fleet. The size of fish caught generally ranges from 10 kg to 500 kg.[4] Of the total catch (including tagged fish), 47 % are larger than 200 kg. The largest black marlin recorded by the Gamefishing Association of Australia, caught off Cairns, was 654 kg. Most captures of black marlin in eastern Australia are made off Queens-land, where a high proportion are tagged and released (the fate of about 90 % of black marlin caught by charter boats and in tournaments). Tagging of black marlin in New South Wales is steadily growing in popularity. Under the New South Wales Fisheries Research Institute's gamefish tagging program, 16 412 black marlin were tagged from the end of 1973 to mid-1992 and there have been 108 recaptures.

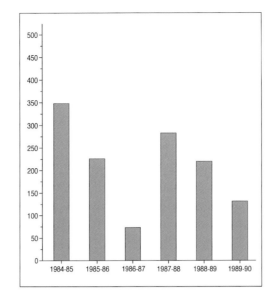

Total annual catch in t of black marlin for the period 1984–85 to 1989–90 by foreign and domestic longliners. (Source: Australian Fishing Zone Information System)

Light-tackle fisheries for 10–40 kg fish take place from July to October at Pixie Reef, Dunk Island and Cape Bowling Green. Fishing for 20–50 kg fish off Cape Moreton peaks in January–February. The range of sizes of fish caught in north-central New South Wales is 25–120 kg, with the peak season occurring from January to March. Some larger fish are caught off Bermagui further south, mostly around March.[4] Angler clubs located in eastern Australia reported landing approximately 600 marlin (mostly black, also blue and striped) in 1988–89.

There is a small fishery in Northern Territory waters concentrated around Melville Island, Cobourg Peninsula, the Wessel Islands and south of Groote Eylandt. Landed fish range in size from 50 kg to 200 kg.

Management controls There are none. A number of gamefishing clubs have introduced voluntary or mandatory size limits. The practice of voluntary release of most fish caught may act as a significant control on the fishery, although no analysis of its effectiveness has been performed. The results of billfish tagging suggest good survival of released fish. There is no routine catch data collection from the recreational fishery.

Resource status

The Pacific-wide catch of black marlin by the Japanese fleet has remained moderately stable since the mid 1960s although fishing effort (measured as thousands of hooks set) has increased.[12] Exclusion of the fleet from inshore areas of the Australian Fishing Zone has contributed to the reduced catch per unit effort as it denies access to the coastal habitats of black marlin. This in turn results in a change in the species targeted: the longline boats now fish primarily in cooler and deeper waters than those normally frequented by black marlin.

The black marlin catch of the Taiwanese distant water fleet has been increasing over the same period, and to some extent has offset the declining Japanese catches — although the Taiwanese do not fish in Australian waters and their Coral Sea catch is small compared with that of the Japanese.

The recreational fisheries of Cairns–Lizard Island and north-western Australia fish the same stock as the Japanese longline fishery. The extent of their combined pressure on the stock is unknown.

Because of uncertainty in total (global) catch figures and stock structure,[13] together with an apparently sustained total catch level over a wide range of fishing effort, stock production models have not been successfully applied to black marlin in either the Pacific or Indian oceans.[12] There have been apparent declines in the catch per unit effort for both oceans, but the extent to which these declines have been due to reductions in stock size or to changes in targeting and area closures are presently unclear.

References

1. Nakamura, I. (1985) FAO species catalogue. Vol. 5. Billfishes of the world. An annotated and illustrated catalogue of marlins, sailfishes, spearfishes and swordfishes known to date. *FAO Fisheries Synopsis No. 125*, **5**. 65 pp.

2. Goadby, P. (1987) *Big fish and blue water. Gamefishing in the Pacific.* Sydney: Angus and Robertson. 5th, revised edition. 334 pp.

3. Howard, J.K. and Ueyanagi, S. (1965) Distribution and relative abundance of billfishes (Istiophoridae) of the Indian Ocean. *Studies in Tropical Oceanography* **2**: 1–134.

4. Pepperell, J.G. (1990) Movements and variations in early year class strength of black marlin, *Makaira indica* off eastern Australia. Fisheries Research Institute, Cronulla, NSW. Pp 51–66, in *Planning the future of billfishes. Research and management in the 90's and beyond.* Ed by R.H. Stroud. *Proceedings of the second international billfish symposium, Kailua–Kona, Hawaii, 1–5 August, 1988.* Part 2. Contributed papers.

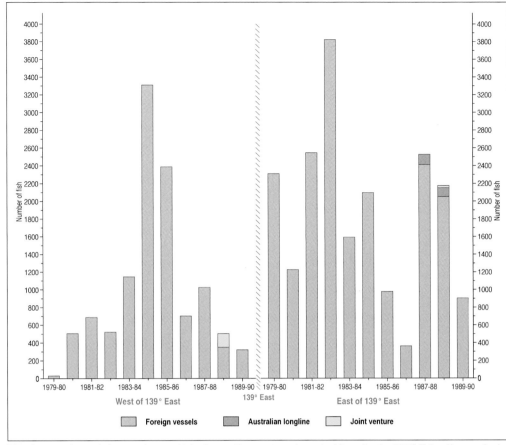

Total annual catch in numbers of black marlin west and east of longitude 139° E for the period 1979–80 to 1989–90 by vessel type. Catch is not stated for Australian longline vessels in years where fewer than 5 vessels landed black marlin. (Source: Australian Fishing Zone Information System)

5. Koto, J., Furukawa, I. and Kodama, K. (1960) Studies on tuna long-line fishery in the East China Sea IV. Ecological studies on the so-called white marlin *Marlina marlina*. *Bulletin of the Japanese Society of Scientific Fisheries* **26**: 887–893. [In Japanese]

6. Squire, J.L. and Nielsen, D.V. (1983) Results of a tagging program to determine migration rates and patterns for black marlin, *Makaira indica*, in the Southwest Pacific Ocean. *NOAA Technical Report NMFS, SSRF* **772**: 1–19.

7. Ueyanagi, S. (1974) On an additional diagnostic character for the identification of billfish larvae with some notes on the variation in pigmentation. *NOAA Technical Report NMFS, SSRF* **675**: 73–78.

8. Leis, J.M., Goldman, B. and Ueyanagi, S. (1987) Distribution and abundance of billfish larvae (Pisces: Istiophoridae) in the Great Barrier Reef lagoon and Coral Sea near Lizard Island, Australia. *Fishery Bulletin (U.S.)* **85**(4): 757–765.

9. Ueyanagi, S. (1960) On the larvae and the spawning areas of the shirokajiki, *Marlina marlina* (Jordan and Hill). *Report of the Nankai Regional Fisheries Research Laboratory* **12**: 85–96.

10. Bergin, T.J. (1990) *Marlin — cause for reviewing Japanese longline operations in the Australian Fishing Zone.* Paper prepared for the Australian Recreational and Sport Fishing Confederation Inc. 32 pp.

11. Mackay, N.J., Kazacos, M.N., Williams, R.J. and Leedow, M.I. (1975) Selenium and heavy metals in black marlin. *Marine Pollution Bulletin* **6**: 57–61.

12. Suzuki, Z. (1989) Catch and fishing effort relationships for striped marlin, blue marlin and black marlin in the Pacific Ocean, 1952 to 1985. Pp 165–177, in *Planning the future of billfishes. Research and management in the 90's and beyond.* Ed by R.H. Stroud. *Proceedings of the second international billfish symposium, Kailua–Kona, Hawaii, 1–5 August, 1988.* Part 1. Fishery and stock synopses, data needs and management.

13. Wetherall, J.A. and Yang, R.T. (1980) Black marlin, *Makaira indica.* Pp 56–63, in *Summary report of the billfish stock assessment workshop, Pacific Resources.* Ed by R.S. Shomura, Honolulu Laboratory SWFC, 5–14 December, 1977. *NOAA Technical Memorandum, NMFS* **5**. 63 pp.

Contributors

Most of the information on this species was provided by Dave Williams with contributions from Julian Pepperell. Additional comments were provided by (in alphabetical order) Alex Julius, Neil Patrick and Peter Speare. Drawing by Gavin Ryan. (*Details of contributors and their organisations are given in the Acknowledgements section at the back of this book.*)

Compilers Patricia Kailola, Dave Williams and Christina Grieve (maps)

Blue marlin

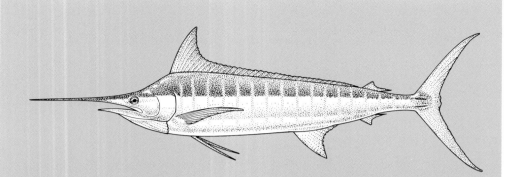

Makaira mazara

Makaira mazara (Jordan and Snyder)

Blue marlin

There are no other common names.
FAO: **Indo-Pacific blue marlin**
Australian species code: 444003

Family ISTIOPHORIDAE

Diagnostic features Blue marlin, like black marlin have a body depth greater than the height of the front lobe of their first dorsal fin. Their second dorsal fin begins slightly behind the beginning of the second anal fin. In blue marlin, the pectoral fin can be folded back against the side of the body. Pale blue round dots and narrow bars form about 15 rows of bands along the body.[1]

Distribution

Blue marlin have the most tropical distribution of all the marlins, although their range extends throughout the tropical and subtropical waters of the Indian and Pacific oceans between approximately 35–45° N and 25–45° S.[1] They are distributed throughout eastern and western Australian waters and, depending on the extent of warm currents, as far south as north-eastern Tasmania and Rottnest Island. Blue marlin rarely, if ever, occur in continental shelf waters and have not been recorded from northern Australia.

Blue marlin are pelagic, oceanic fish rarely found in waters shallower than 100 m, or close to land. Their abundance increases with their distance offshore from the continental slope. Although they can be found in waters with surface temperatures as low as 21°C,[2] blue marlin generally inhabit waters of 24°C or more.[1] Acoustic tagging studies[3] suggest that blue marlin primarily inhabit the surface mixed layer, which is the relatively uniform layer of water between the surface and the top of the thermocline where water temperatures start to drop suddenly. Recent studies have also suggested that fish spend more time close to the surface at night than during the day.

In the Pacific Ocean, blue marlin concentrate year-round in tropical waters, but a part of the population undertakes large seasonal movements away from equatorial waters to about 30° S.[4] These movements, mostly undertaken by males of 35–75 kg,[4] occur as waves in the northern and southern hemisphere summers. Fish moving into eastern Australian waters in the summertime are probably part of 1 of these migrations.

Blue marlin also live year-round in the Eastern Indian Ocean between north-western Australia, Java and the Lesser Sunda Islands, with maximum concentration during the Northwest Monsoon (November to April), and between the equator and 13° S during the Southeast Monsoon (April to October).

Life history

The reproductive activity of blue marlin in Australian waters has not been studied, although the presence of larvae in the Coral Sea[5] indicates that some spawning does occur off eastern Australia. Spawning probably takes place year-round in equatorial waters to 10° latitude (although 1 study has suggested this needs verification) and during summer periods in both hemispheres to 30° latitude, in both the Indian and Pacific oceans. In the southern hemisphere, concentrations of spawning fish probably occur around French Polynesia.[4]

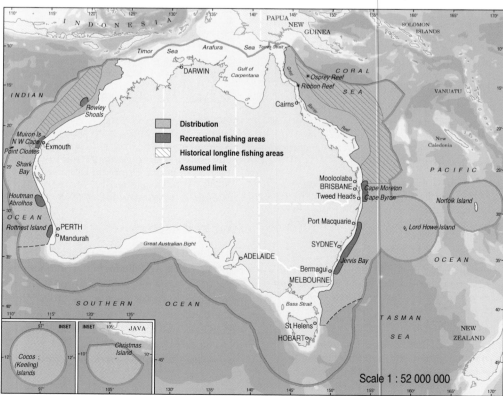

Geographic distribution, commercial and recreational fishing areas for blue marlin in Australian waters.

Limited sampling has collected blue marlin larvae in the Coral Sea between October and December[6] and from late January to mid-February around the Ribbon and Osprey reefs off Queensland.[5] Large numbers of blue marlin larvae have also been collected off north-western Australia[6] between October and March.

Blue marlin are serial spawners,[7] with each female spawning several times in a season. Estimates of the number of eggs (based on 4 ripe females) range from 31.5 million for a 127 kg fish to 98.9 million for a 420 kg fish.[7] Blue marlin eggs are transparent and 1.0–1.5 mm in diameter when ripe.

Female blue marlin reach sizes of more than 906 kg[1] and males grow to approximately 170 kg. The maximum total length of blue marlin is more than 450 cm.[1] Unvalidated age estimates of blue marlin have been made on fish caught off Hawaii, the maximum being 21 years for males and 28 years for females.[8,9] The size at a given age (based on these estimates) appears to be very variable,[8] a 175 kg female being between 5 and 17 years of age, and a 75 kg male between 3 and 17 years.[8] Males grow rapidly for the first 3–4 years and become mature at about 80 kg. Females grow at a highly variable rate, mature when about 4 years old, and keep growing (in contrast to most males).[8,9] Comparable age and growth estimates have come from fish caught in Mauritius in the Indian Ocean.[10]

Blue marlin are known to feed on squid and fishes, particularly scombroids (tuna-like fish). Large pelagic sharks and killer whales (*Orcinus orca*) have been observed attacking billfish hooked on longlines, but such attacks are very unlikely under natural conditions.[1]

Stock structure

A single stock in each of the Pacific and Indian oceans is assumed, based on the homogeneous distribution of larvae and adults.[4,11]

The identity of the blue marlin in the Indian and Pacific oceans remains an issue of contention. Some authors[1] consider it is distinct from the Atlantic Ocean blue marlin, whilst others[7,9] consider the 2 are 1 species. These nominal species can be distinguished only by differences in the lateral line pattern,[1] although very recent mitochondrial DNA work on blue marlin

suggests isolation between the Pacific and Atlantic populations.

Commercial fishery

Unlike black marlin (*Makaira indica*) and striped marlin (*Tetrapturus audax*), blue marlin are not targeted by any commercial fishery. However, they are caught as a bycatch or incidental catch of longliners targeting other billfish, bigeye tuna (*Thunnus obesus*) and yellowfin tuna (*T. albacares*), and purse seiners targeting yellowfin tuna and skipjack tuna (*Katsuwonus pelamis*) throughout the Indian and Pacific oceans. In the Western Pacific purse seine fishery individual blue marlin are frequently caught when sets are made around floating logs.[12]

Japanese drifting longline fisheries began in both the western Coral Sea (off north-eastern Australia) and off north-western Australia in 1953. Since the declaration of the 200-mile Australian Fishing Zone in 1979, access of this fleet to Australian waters has been subject to bilateral agreements. The Japanese boats range from 200 t to 350 t and are 35–45 m long. They spend about 60 days in the Zone during their long fishing campaign in the south-west Pacific.

Highest catch rates of blue marlin by Japanese vessels in both the Coral Sea and off the north-west of Australia occur between January and March and further offshore than for black marlin. In both the Pacific and Indian oceans the size of blue marlin tends to increase from east to west.[4,13] The usual size of blue marlin in the Japanese fishery on the east coast during the 1980s was 40–100 kg processed weight, with most between 50 kg and 70 kg. Pre-1965 data from the longline fishery off north-western Australia indicate modal sizes between 50–90 kg north of 20° S and 105–160 kg south of 20° S.[13]

The longline catch of blue marlin is exported to Japan, where it is not a high value fish. The average annual price of processed, frozen fish per kg at the Yaizu fish market was 227 yen (A\$ 2.08) in 1988, 275 yen (A\$ 2.52) in 1989 and 316 yen (A\$ 2.73) in 1990. Although black marlin and blue marlin fetched similar prices for fresh fish in 1970 — to 500 yen per kg — blue marlin was worth less than half the price of black marlin by 1986.[14] In 1992, average monthly prices for blue marlin at Yaizu market were 236–375 yen (A\$ 2.55–3.75) per kg.

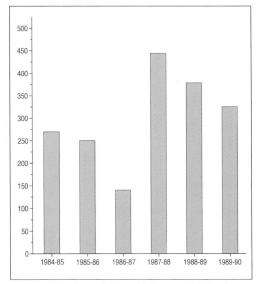

Total annual catch in t of blue marlin for the period 1984–85 to 1989–90 by foreign and domestic longliners. (Source: Australian Fishing Zone Information System)

Management controls The numbers of Japanese longliners fishing the Australian Fishing Zone is limited by access agreements. In 1987, the Japanese agreed to a voluntary release in Australian waters of all blue marlin and black marlin alive at the time of longline retrieval and this agreement is still in effect. Domestic sale of blue marlin and black marlin is banned in some States.

Recreational fishery

Blue marlin are caught less frequently by recreational anglers in Australian waters than are black marlin.

A blue marlin caught from a Japanese longline vessel is killed using the 'iki-jime' method. (Source: Peter Ward, Bureau of Resource Sciences)

The fishery is centred over continental slope waters 150–300 m deep. In recent years, exceptional catch rates of blue marlin have been made from grounds off south-eastern Queensland from Mooloolaba and Tweed Heads beyond the 200 m line. Blue marlin are caught in these depths generally, all the way from Cape Moreton to Bermagui — wherever serious attempts have been made. Other grounds fished by recreational anglers are (eastern Australia) off Cape Byron and from Port Macquarie to Jervis Bay; (Western Australia) Rottnest Trench west of Perth, the Houtman Abrolhos, Point Cloates, north of North West Cape to Muiron Islands, and off Rowley Shoals.

The recreational fishery for blue marlin has grown dramatically in the last 4–5 years. They were rare in the catch 10 years ago, and now are quite common. This is partly a result of boats fishing further offshore and using Hawaiian-type straight running lures.

The fishery targets fish to 350 kg,[15] but some individuals as small as 50 kg were caught off New South Wales in 1989. The Game Fishing Association of Australia's blue marlin record is 364 kg for a fish landed off Cape Moreton, Queensland in 1989. Recreational fishers in eastern Australia landed approximately 600 marlin (3 species, most of them black marlin) in 1988–89, 80 % of them caught by gamefishing club members. In the same period, almost 1300 marlin were tagged and released by recreational anglers in Queensland and New South Wales. In the 19 years to mid 1992, 586 blue marlin have been tagged under the New South Wales Fisheries Research Institute's gamefish tagging program.

Management controls There are none, although a number of gamefishing clubs have introduced voluntary size limits. A feasibility study to gather catch data from gamefishing clubs is current, and there is no routine catch data collection from the fishery.

Resource status

The Japanese longline catch of blue marlin dominates in the Pacific Ocean. Total catch peaked in the early 1960s, exhibited a decreasing trend in the mid 1970s and was followed by a moderate recovery in the early 1980s.[11] The longline catch rate has shown a comparable trend. A surplus production

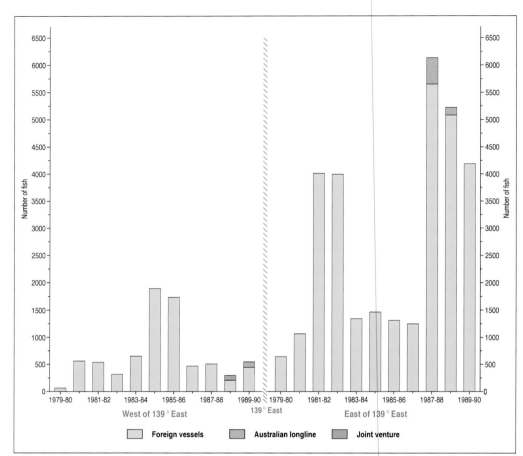

Total annual catch in numbers of blue marlin west and east of longitude 139° E for the period 1979–80 to 1989–90 by vessel type. Catch is not stated for Australian longline vessels in years where fewer than 5 vessels landed blue marlin. (Source: Australian Fishing Zone Information System)

model based on the equatorial Western Pacific led to the conclusion[16] that the Pacific blue marlin stock is overfished (ie more effort is expended than needed to take the maximum sustainable yield) but that some recovery of the stock from 1975 to 1980 is indicated. Despite this recent assessment, overfishing remains a possibility.

Lack of appropriate data prevents an accurate assessment of the Indian Ocean blue marlin stock.

References

1. Nakamura, I. (1985) FAO species catalogue. Vol. 5. Billfishes of the world. An annotated and illustrated catalogue of marlins, sailfishes, spearfishes and swordfishes known to date. *FAO Fisheries Synopsis No. 125*, **5**. 65 pp.

2. Goadby, P. (1987) *Big fish and blue water. Gamefishing in the Pacific.* Sydney: Angus and Robertson. 5th, revised edition. 334 pp.

3. Holland, K., Brill, R. and Chang, R.K.C. (1990) Horizontal and vertical movements of Pacific blue marlin captured and released using sportfishing gear. *Fishery Bulletin (U.S.)* **88**: 397–402.

4. Howard, J.K. and Ueyanagi, S. (1965) Distribution and relative abundance of billfishes (Istiophoridae) of the Pacific Ocean. *Studies in Tropical Oceanography* **2**: 1–134.

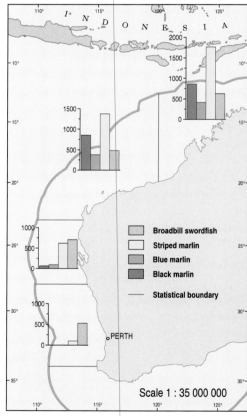

Average catch rates of billfish species for 1979 to 1988 from the Japanese longline fishery off north-western Australia. Data are in number of fish per million hooks within statistical regions of the Australian Fishing Zone. (Source: Australian Fishing Zone Information System and Bureau of Resource Sciences)

5. Leis, J.M., Goldman, B. and Ueyanagi, S. (1987) Distribution and abundance of billfish larvae (Pisces: Istiophoridae) in the Great Barrier Reef lagoon and Coral Sea near Lizard Island, Australia. *Fishery Bulletin (U.S.)* **85**(4): 757–765.

6. Nishikawa, Y., Honma, M., Ueyanagi, S. and Kikawa, S. (1985) Average distribution of larvae of oceanic species of scombrid fishes, 1965–1981. *Far Seas Fisheries Research Laboratory, Japan, S Series* **12**. 99 pp.

7. Hopper, C.N. (1990) Patterns of Pacific blue marlin reproduction in Hawaiian waters. Pp 29–40, in *Planning the future of billfishes. Research and management in the 90's and beyond.* Ed by R.H. Stroud. *Proceedings of the second international billfish symposium, Kailua–Kona, Hawaii, 1–5 August, 1988.* Part 2. Contributed papers.

8. Wilson, C.A. III (1984) *Age and growth aspects of the life history of billfishes.* Unpublished PhD thesis, University of South Carolina. 180 pp.

9. Hill, K.T., Cailliet, G.M. and Radtke, R.L. (1989) A comparative analysis of growth zones in four calcified structures of Pacific blue marlin, *Makaira nigricans. Fishery Bulletin (U.S.)* **87**: 829–843.

10. Cyr, E.C., Dean, J.M., Jehangeer, I. and Nallee, M. (1990) Age, growth and reproduction of blue marlin and black marlin from the Indian Ocean. Pp 309–316, in *Planning the future of billfishes. Research and management in the 90's and beyond.* Ed by R.H. Stroud. *Proceedings of the second international billfish symposium, Kailua–Kona, Hawaii, 1–5 August, 1988.* Part 2. Contributed papers.

11. Suzuki, Z. (1989) Catch and fishing effort relationships for striped marlin, blue marlin and black marlin in the Pacific Ocean, 1952 to 1985. Pp 165–177, in *Planning the future of billfishes. Research and management in the 90's and beyond.* Ed by R.H. Stroud. *Proceedings of the second international billfish symposium, Kailua–Kona, Hawaii, 1–5 August, 1988.* Part 1. Fishery and stock synopses, data needs and management.

12. Gillett, R.D. (1986) Observations on two Japanese purse seining operations in the equatorial Pacific. *South Pacific Commission, Tuna and Billfish Assessment Program, Technical Report* **16**. 35 pp.

13. Howard, J.K. and Stark, W.A., III (1975) Distribution and relative abundance of billfishes (Istiophoridae) of the Indian Ocean. *Studies in Tropical Oceanography* **13**: 1–31.

14. Ueyanagi, S., Shomura, R.S., Watanabe, Y. and Squire, J.L. (1989) Trends in fisheries for billfishes in the Pacific. Pp 147–158, in *Planning the future of billfishes. Research and management in the 90's and beyond.* Ed by R.H. Stroud. *Proceedings of the second international billfish symposium, Kailua–Kona, Hawaii, 1–5 August, 1988.* Part 1. Fishery and stock synopses, data needs and management.

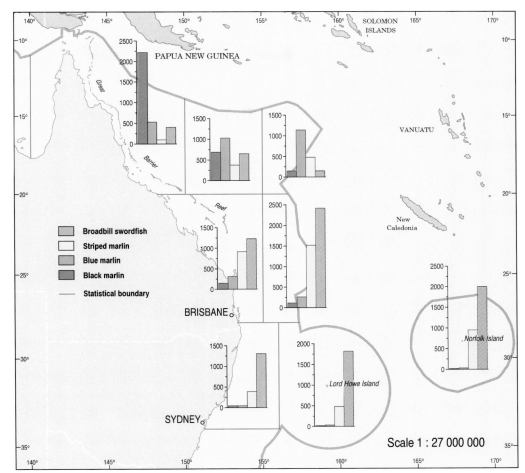

Average catch rates of billfish species for 1979 to 1988 from the Japanese longline fishery off north-eastern Australia. Data are in number of fish per million hooks within statistical regions of the Australian Fishing Zone. (Source: Australian Fishing Zone Information System and Bureau of Resource Sciences)

15. Starling, S. (1988) *The fisherman's handbook. How to find, identify and catch the top Australian angling fish.* North Ryde: Angus and Robertson Publishers. 263 pp.

16. Skillman, R.A. (1989) Status of Pacific billfish stocks. Pp 179–195, in *Planning the future of billfishes. Research and management in the 90's and beyond.* Ed by R.H. Stroud. *Proceedings of the second international billfish symposium, Kailua–Kona, Hawaii, 1–5 August, 1988.* Part 1. Fishery and stock synopses, data needs and management.

Contributors

Most of the information on this species was originally provided by Dave Williams, with contributions from Julian Pepperell. Additional comments and assistance were provided by (in alphabetical order) Albert Caton, Kerrie Deguara, Neil Patrick, Cesar Ramirez and Peter Ward. Drawing by Gavin Ryan. (*Details of contributors and their organisations are given in the Acknowledgements section at the back of this book.*)

Compilers Patricia Kailola, Christina Grieve (maps) and Phillip Stewart (maps and statistics)

Striped marlin

Tetrapturus audax

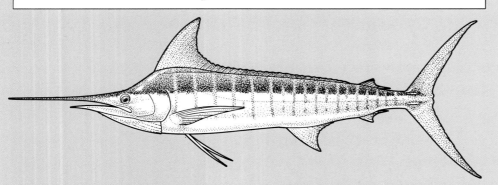

Tetrapturus audax (Philippi)

Striped marlin

Other common names include **stripey**, **beakie** and **beak**.
FAO: **striped marlin**
Australian species code: 444002

Family ISTIOPHORIDAE

Diagnostic features Striped marlin are distinguished from other marlin by their body depth being less than, or equal to, the height of the front lobe of the first dorsal fin, and by the anus being near the origin of the first anal fin.[1] The lower jaw is longer, and the body more compressed than in similar-sized blue marlin and black marlin. The pectoral fin in striped marlin can be folded back against the side of the body. Striped marlin are dark blue or black above, with 12–16 blue vertical bars on their lower sides.

Distribution

Striped marlin inhabit tropical to temperate waters of the Pacific and Indian oceans between approximately 45° N and 30–45° S.[1] Their distribution in the Pacific Ocean is unique among billfishes and tunas in that it forms a horseshoe-shaped pattern from the north-west Pacific through the eastern Pacific to the south-west Pacific.[2] In the Indian Ocean, fish are more densely distributed in equatorial regions with higher concentrations off eastern Africa, in the western Arabian Sea, the Bay of Bengal and off north-western Australia.[3]

Within the Australian Fishing Zone, striped marlin are present in the east from off Torres Strait to Tasmania, and in the west from the North West Shelf to about 125° E off southern Australia.

Striped marlin generally inhabit cooler water than either black or blue marlin.[1] Their abundance increases with distance from the continental shelf. Like blue marlin, striped marlin are a true oceanic species and are usually seen close to shore only where deep drop-offs occur.

Life history

Striped marlin spawn between 10° S and 30° S in the south-west Pacific in November and December and between 10° S and 20° S in the north-eastern Indian

Ocean from about October to December.[4] Major concentrations of pre-spawning and spawning striped marlin occur in the southern Coral Sea off eastern Australia from late September.[4] Each female fish probably only spawns once each season.

There is little information on the distribution of striped marlin eggs and larvae. Juveniles are relatively rare in the south-west Pacific Ocean.[2] Fish of

4–10 kg (80–100 cm fork length) are regularly caught on longlines in the region but concentrations of fish this size are mostly restricted to the north-central Pacific Ocean.[2]

Unlike black marlin and blue marlin, there is little difference in growth rate and maximum size between the sexes.[5] Growth model calculations of striped marlin in the Hawaiian longline fishery up to the onset of spawning suggest that average-sized 2-year-old fish are about 180 cm fork length or 23 kg, 3-year-old fish are 215 cm or 43 kg and 4-year-old fish are approximately 227 cm or 52 kg (male) and 235 cm or 59 kg (female).[5] From a dorsal spine and otolith study of striped marlin in New Zealand,[6] estimates of weight at a given age included 92.8 kg for 3-year-olds, 108.6 kg for 5-year-olds and 125.6 kg for 7-year-olds. The much larger size of striped marlin at a given age

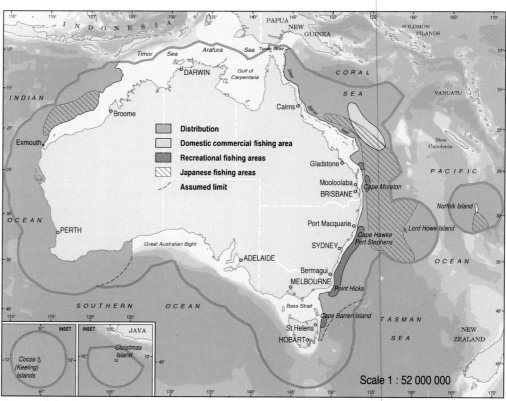

Geographic distribution, commercial and recreational fishing areas for striped marlin in Australian and adjacent waters.

in New Zealand waters suggests they are faster growing than striped marlin studied in other areas.

Striped marlin grow to at least 350 cm total length and 200 kg.[1] The size at first maturity for Coral Sea fish is about 29 kg,[4] about 2–3-year-old fish. The sex ratio of adults varies, females usually predominating in longline catches except on the spawning grounds where males are more prevalent.

Striped marlin are carnivorous, non-selective feeders whose diet includes more epipelagic organisms (ie those living in the surface layers) than the diets of other billfish and larger tunas. Their diet changes with season and locality and includes flutemouths (*Fistularia* species), squid, lancetfish (*Alepisaurus* species), anchovy (Engraulididae), trevally (Carangidae) and small tuna-like fishes (Scombridae). Large pelagic sharks and toothed whales (Odontoceti) may be predators of adult striped marlin.[1]

Stock structure

The stock structure of striped marlin in the Pacific Ocean is uncertain. Analyses of catch-effort data with morphometrics[7] and time[8] provided some evidence for separate northern and southern hemisphere stocks. However, evidence from catch-effort and tagging data and studies of spawning areas, body proportions and changes in body length related to geography[2] suggests that there is general movement of striped marlin between several widely separated areas of the Pacific. Some fish may range further than others, yet the overall diffusive movements (not migration) could permit management of different core areas of high catch rates as if they represented separate stocks.[2] The stock structure of striped marlin in the Indian Ocean is unknown.

Commercial fishery

Striped marlin are targeted by Japanese fleets of drifting longline vessels in the eastern Pacific, and off Japan and New Zealand. They are also targeted in tropical waters of the Australian Fishing Zone by these fleets, as are yellowfin tuna (*Thunnus albacares*), bigeye tuna (*T. obesus*) and broadbill swordfish (*Xiphias gladius*).

Striped marlin caught in the Japanese longline fishery off eastern Australia range from 70–170 kg processed weight. Those in the west coast fishery range from 10 kg to 140 kg, with modes at 21–27 kg and 50–60 kg. Maximum catch rates occur from September to November: on the east coast offshore between Gladstone and the Queensland-New South Wales border; and in the west, offshore between Exmouth and Broome. Highest catch rates of striped marlin occur further offshore than those of black marlin. Off Western Australia (and other areas of the species' distribution) the best fishing grounds for striped marlin are centred at the boundary of currents and where the sea surface temperature is 20–22°C.[9]

The Australian (domestic) catch of striped marlin by longline fleets is very much less than the catch by the Japanese longline fleet.

The Japanese longline boats range in size up to 350 t and 45 m in length and each boat generally spends about 30–60 days in the Australian Fishing Zone during its fishing campaign in the south-west Pacific. The longlines comprise a main line 70–110 km long with a series of branch lines bearing a

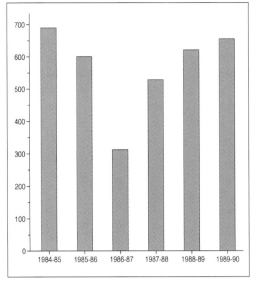

Total annual catch in t of striped marlin for the period 1984–85 to 1989–90 by foreign and domestic longliners. (Source: Australian Fishing Zone Information System)

total of about 3000 hooks. One set of a single main line is made in any 24 hour period, and traditionally the lines are set to fish at between 50 m and 150 m depth.

The primary market for striped marlin is the Japanese raw fish ('sashimi' and 'sushi') market. Striped marlin are the most valuable of all marlins. The prices paid for fresh striped marlin easily exceed those paid for any other species of billfish

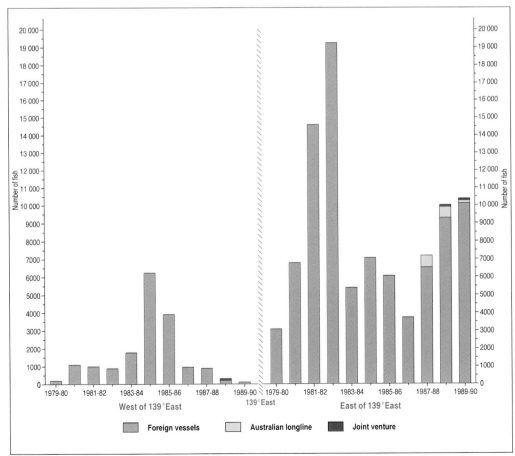

Total annual catch in numbers of striped marlin west and east of longitude 139° E for the period 1979–80 to 1989–90 by vessel type. Catch is not stated for Australian longline vessels in years where fewer than 5 vessels landed striped marlin. (Source: Australian Fishing Zone Information System)

and are similar to those paid for bigeye tuna. The 1991–92 average monthly price for frozen striped marlin at the Yaizu market in Japan ranged from A$ 6.00 to A$ 12.00 per kg. Compared with a lower summer price, fresh chilled striped marlin caught in Australian waters in winter fetches approximately A$ 15.00–A$ 30.00 per kg in Japanese markets.

Management controls The number of Japanese longliners permitted to fish in the 200 mile Australian Fishing Zone is limited under annually reviewed bilateral access agreements. In addition, Japanese longliners are excluded from all waters within 50 nautical miles of the east coast north of Sydney and from all waters off southern New South Wales.

Striped marlin may not be sold in Western Australia, and in New South Wales striped marlin may only be sold for export to Japan.

Recreational fishery

Striped marlin are mainly caught by trolling or by handlining from anchored or drifting boats. Lures are live or dead bait of oily fish such as mackerel and small tunas (Scombridae), kingfish (*Seriola* species) or mullet (Mugilidae). Striped marlin are fished over continental shelf and slope waters. Generally the recreational fisheries for striped marlin are located off Queensland from about Mooloolaba to Cape Moreton, from about off Cape Hawke in New South Wales to Point Hicks in eastern Victoria and off Tasmania from Cape Barren Island to St Helens. The Western Australian fishery for striped marlin is centred off Exmouth. Most striped marlin are caught off the active New South Wales gamefishing

centres of Port Stephens, Sydney and Bermagui. The largest striped marlin angled in Australia was 172 kg, from off Bermagui in 1988 (Game Fishing Association of Australia record).

Up until mid 1992, 812 striped marlin had been tagged under the New South Wales Fisheries Research Institute's gamefish tagging program, 410 of them off New South Wales. Six striped marlin had been recaptured.

Management controls There are none. A number of gamefishing clubs have introduced voluntary size limits, and the clubs encourage the voluntary release of marlin caught alive.

Resource status

The results of production models based on Pacific-wide catches from 1952 to 1980 and in 1985 suggest that striped marlin stocks are not over-fished. They are either close to an optimal level of fishing[7] or are below it.[8] The status of the resources off eastern or western Australia is unknown.

References

1. Nakamura, I. (1985) FAO species catalogue. Vol. 5. Billfishes of the world. An annotated and illustrated catalogue of marlins, sailfishes, spearfishes and swordfishes known to date. *FAO Fisheries Synopsis No. 125*, **5**. 65 pp.

2. Squire, J.L., Jr and Suzuki, Z. (1990) Migration trends of striped marlin (*Tetrapturus audax*) in the Pacific Ocean. Pp 67–80, in *Planning the future of billfishes. Research and management in the 90's and beyond*. Ed by R.H. Stroud. *Proceedings of the second international billfish symposium, Kailua-Kona, Hawaii, 1–5 August, 1988.* Part 2. Contributed papers.

3. Pillai, P.P. and Ueyanagi, S. (1977) Distribution and biology of the striped marlin, *Tetrapterus* [sic] *audax* (Philippi) taken by the longline fishery in the Indian Ocean. *Bulletin of the Far Seas Fishery Research Laboratory* **16**: 9–32.

4. Hanamoto, E. (1977) Fishery oceanography in striped marlin — II. Spawning activity of the fish in the Southern Coral Sea. *Bulletin of the Japanese Society for Scientific Fisheries* **43**: 1279–1286.

5. Skillman, R.A. and Yong, M.Y.Y. (1976) Von Bertalanffy growth curves for striped marlin, *Tetrapturus audax*, and blue marlin, *Makaira nigricans*, in the central North Pacific Ocean. *Fishery Bulletin (U.S.)* **74**: 553–566.

6. Davie, P.S. and Hall, I. (1990) Potential of dorsal and anal spines and otoliths for assessing the age structure of the recreational catch of striped marlin. Pp 287–294, in *Planning the future of billfishes. Research and management in the 90's and beyond*. Ed by R.H. Stroud. *Proceedings of the second international billfish symposium, Kailua-Kona, Hawaii, 1–5 August, 1988.* Part 2. Contributed papers.

7. Suzuki, Z. (1989) Catch and fishing effort relationships for striped marlin, blue marlin and black marlin in the Pacific Ocean, 1952 to 1985. Pp 165–177, in *Planning the future of billfishes. Research and management in the 90's and beyond*. Ed by R.H. Stroud. *Proceedings of the second international billfish symposium, Kailua-Kona, Hawaii, 1–5 August, 1988.* Part 1. Fishery and stock synopses, data needs and management.

8. Skillman, R.A. (1989) Status of Pacific billfish stocks. Pp 179–195, in *Planning the future of billfishes. Research and management in the 90's and beyond*. Ed by R.H. Stroud. *Proceedings of the second international billfish symposium, Kailua-Kona, Hawaii, 1–5 August, 1988.* Part 1. Fishery and stock synopses, data needs and management.

9. Squire, J.L., Jr (1985) Relationship of sea surface temperature isotherm patterns off northwestern Mexico to the catch of striped marlin, *Tetrapterus* [sic] *audax*, off southern California. *Marine Fisheries Review* **47**: 43–47.

Contributors

Most of the information on this species was provided by Dave Williams. Contributions came from (in alphabetical order) Albert Caton, Julian Pepperell and Peter Ward. Additional comments were provided by Bill Causebrook, Lindsay Chapman, Kerrie Deguara, Steve Jackson and Neil Patrick. Drawing by Gavin Ryan. (*Details of contributors and their organisations are given in the Acknowledgements section at the back of this book.*)

Compilers Patricia Kailola and Christina Grieve, Cesar Ramirez and Phillip Stewart (maps and statistics)

Processing a longline-caught striped marlin on deck. (Source: Peter Ward, Bureau of Resource Sciences)

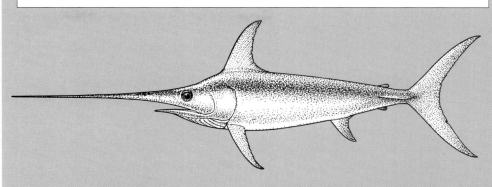

Broadbill swordfish

Xiphias gladius

Xiphias gladius Linnaeus

Broadbill swordfish

Other common names include
broadbill and **swordfish**.
FAO: **swordfish**
Australian species code: 442001

Family XIPHIIDAE

Diagnostic features Broadbill swordfish are blackish-brown on the upper body, fading to light brown on the belly. Their fins are brown or blackish-brown. Their upper jaw extends into a long bill which has a flattened oval cross section. Adults have no teeth or scales and they have a large keel on each side of the body in front of the tail. The dorsal fins are broadly separated and there are no pelvic fins.

Distribution

Broadbill swordfish are oceanic fish distributed through tropical and temperate waters of the Pacific, Indian and Atlantic oceans between 45° N and 45° S.[1] They inhabit all Australian waters beyond the edge of the continental shelf.

Japanese longline vessels have reported high catch rates of broadbill swordfish in the south-western Pacific between latitudes 15° S and 40° S, from the edge of the Australian continental shelf to northern New Zealand.[1,2] In the Indian Ocean, catch rates by Japanese longliners are high in a region south of the south-western corner of Western Australia.[1]

Broadbill swordfish tolerate a broad range of water temperatures, from 5–27°C, but normally inhabit waters with surface temperatures greater than 13°C.[3] Juveniles are common only in tropical and sub-tropical waters and migrate to higher latitudes as they mature.[4] In south-eastern Australian waters, sharp temperature and salinity gradients across oceanic fronts provide favourable conditions for concentrations of broadbill swordfish.

Little is known of large scale movements by adult broadbill swordfish. Mature fish make only limited local movements.[1] Tracking of fish using acoustic tags has shown that broadbill swordfish typically move to surface waters at night and inhabit deeper waters during the day, reaching depths up to 600 m.[5] These vertical movements may be rapid and involve changes in water temperature as great as 19°C. Some tagged fish spend daylight hours near the sea bed close to the continental shelf break or submerged banks and move offshore at night. In the eastern Pacific broadbill swordfish are commonly seen basking at the sea surface for short

periods during the day, a behaviour that may allow the fish to recover from stress associated with low temperature and dissolved oxygen levels in deep water.[5] Broadbill swordfish are normally solitary, but pairs of fish are regularly observed at the surface off the Californian coast.[5]

Life history

The distribution of larval broadbill swordfish in the Pacific Ocean indicates that spawning occurs mainly in waters with a temperature of 24°C or more. Spawning appears to occur in all seasons in equatorial waters, but is restricted to spring and summer at higher latitudes.[6] In Australian waters larvae are common in spring in the Coral Sea.[7] Broadbill swordfish with mature ovaries have also been caught in this area in October.[4] In western waters the greatest numbers of larvae have been collected between north-western Australia and Java, where

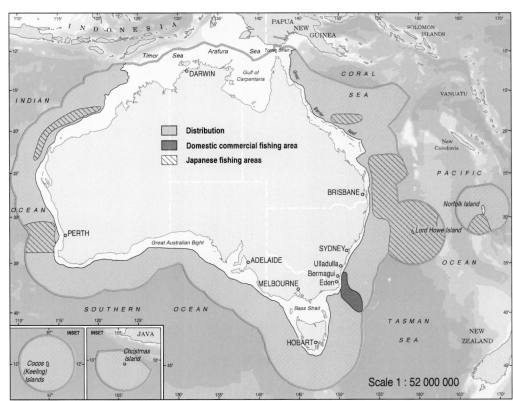

Geographic distribution and commercial fishing areas for broadbill swordfish in Australian waters.

they are common during spring and summer.[7] This area is also a spawning ground for other large pelagic fish including blue marlin (*Makaira mazara*) and southern bluefin tuna (*Thunnus maccoyii*).[7]

Fertilisation in broadbill swordfish is external and pairing of solitary males and females is thought to occur when spawning.[1] Broadbill swordfish are reported to spawn in the upper layers of the water column, from the surface to a depth of 75 m.[3] Estimates of egg numbers vary considerably, from 1 million to 16 million in a 68 kg female[1] and 29 million in a 272 kg female.[8] Eggs are pelagic and 1.6–1.8 mm in diameter.[1] Larvae are most common within a few m of the surface during the day but may move to depths of 30 m at night.[6] Swordfish larvae longer than 10 mm feed almost exclusively on larvae of other fish species.

There has been little research on ageing and growth rates of broadbill swordfish from the Pacific and Indian oceans. Available estimates for the Pacific Ocean indicate that 1-year-old fish are 50–60 cm in eye fork length.[4] Females grow more rapidly than males from the age of 2 years and reach a much larger size. There are no maximum age estimates of broadbill swordfish from the Pacific and Indian oceans. The only estimate of age at maturity for the Indo-Pacific is 5 to 6 years corresponding to an eye fork length of 150–170 cm.[4] Few male broadbill swordfish are reported at sizes above this range in the Atlantic Ocean so it is likely that male fish in the Pacific mature at a smaller size.[8] Broadbill swordfish are reported to reach a total length of 445 cm and a weight of 540 kg.[3]

Juvenile broadbill swordfish feed on squid, fish and pelagic crustaceans.[1] Adults living in deep oceanic waters feed mainly on pelagic fish and squid but swordfish living in shallower continental shelf waters are opportunistic feeders, preying on pelagic and demersal fish.

Adult broadbill swordfish have few predators except for large sharks and perhaps killer whales (*Orcinus orca*) or sperm whales (*Physeter macrocephalus*).[1] Juveniles are preyed upon by larger tunas (Scombridae), marlin (Istiophoridae), sailfish (*Istiophorus platypterus*), shortbill spearfish (*Tetrapturus angustirostris*) and sharks (Lamnidae).[4]

Stock structure

There is little information on stock structure of broadbill swordfish in the Pacific Ocean although 2 hypotheses are currently proposed. The first identifies a single stock which is distributed throughout the Pacific but has local areas of high abundance. The second proposes 3 stocks based on the regional centres of high abundance in the north-western, south-western and eastern Pacific.[2] There is no information on stock structure in Indian Ocean broadbill swordfish.

Commercial fishery

Broadbill swordfish do not represent a commercial fishery for Australian fishers. They are a significant bycatch of pelagic longlining in the East Coast Tuna Fishery but are not normally targeted because of difficulties in marketing the species. The main target species of the longline fishery are yellowfin tuna (*Thunnus albacares*) and bigeye tuna (*T. obesus*).

About 90 t of broadbill swordfish were caught by domestic tuna longline vessels in 1989–90. Most of the catch was taken from the Tasman Sea in waters off southern New South Wales and eastern Victoria. Fishing trials have shown that broadbill swordfish can be targeted at night by using squid baits set at shallow depths. The attachment of 'lightsticks' to the baits is reported to significantly increase the catch rate of broadbill swordfish.

Most of the broadbill swordfish caught off the east coast weigh less than 100 kg.

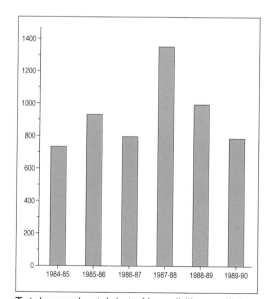
Total annual catch in t of broadbill swordfish for the period 1984–85 to 1989–90 by foreign and domestic longliners. (Source: Australian Fishing Zone Information System)

A broadbill swordfish caught from a Japanese longline vessel. (Source: Peter Speare, Australian Institute of Marine Science)

They are headed and gutted on board the fishing vessel and sold as fresh chilled product on the domestic fresh fish market. Broadbill swordfish are popular amongst Sydney consumers but health regulations have caused a reduction in supply in recent years. Broadbill swordfish sold in New South Wales must be individually tested for mercury content. The larger fish are likely to exceed the limit, which is lower than the amount specified for other States. Much of the broadbill swordfish landed is therefore sold through Brisbane and Melbourne markets. In 1988–89, 15.6 t of broadbill swordfish were sold through the Sydney Fish Market at an average wholesale price of A\$ 10.48 per kg but only 1.1 t were sold in 1989–90 at an average price of A\$ 13.88 per kg. In 1990–91 and 1991–92, less than 1 t of broadbill swordfish were sold through the Sydney Fish Market. The average price of broadbill swordfish on Japanese markets in 1991–92 was about 700 yen (A\$ 7.00–8.00) per kg.

The Japanese longline fleet catches large numbers of broadbill swordfish throughout the Pacific and Indian oceans. Japanese longline vessels have operated near the eastern and western coasts of Australia since the 1950s. These vessels are normally between 35 m and 45 m in length and set approximately 3000 hooks per day on mainlines which are 70–110 km long. Within the Australian Fishing Zone the most productive areas are in the east, off southern Queensland and surrounding Lord Howe Island. Significant catches are also taken south of Norfolk Island, in the Coral Sea off north Queensland and off north-western Australia. Catches from north-eastern and north-western waters are mainly bycatch of vessels fishing for yellowfin tuna. Significant catches of broadbill swordfish

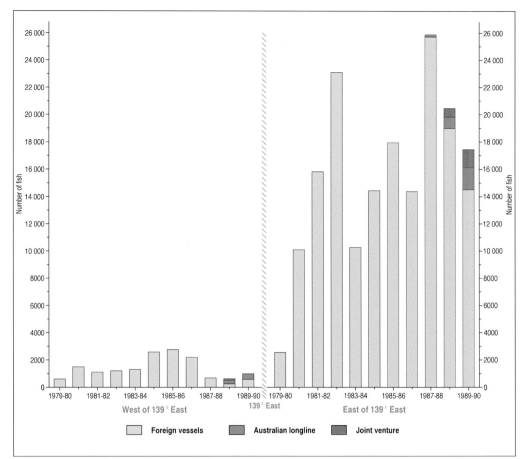

Total annual catch in numbers of broadbill swordfish west and east of longitude 139° E for the period 1979–80 to 1989–90 by vessel type. Catch is not stated for Australian longline vessels in years where fewer than 5 vessels landed broadbill swordfish. (Source: Australian Fishing Zone Information System)

are also recorded by Japanese longliners targeting bigeye tuna off south-western Australia from October to April each year. The annual Japanese catch of broadbill swordfish from the Australian Fishing Zone normally ranges between 700 t and 1000 t.

Management controls Fishers catching broadbill swordfish in the Australian Fishing Zone are subject to management by the Commonwealth of Australia. The East Coast Tuna Management Plan limits the number of longline vessels licensed to operate in eastern Australian waters and restricts fishing areas for some vessels.

The fishing activities of Japanese vessels within the Australian Fishing Zone are regulated by the Commonwealth of Australia. The Japanese pay access fees and are not permitted to fish in certain areas, for example within 50 nautical miles of the east coast north of Sydney. Restrictions on total annual fishing effort and numbers of vessels also apply.

Recreational fishery

Broadbill swordfish are popular sport and gamefish in the eastern Pacific Ocean,

particularly off California, Ecuador, Peru and northern Chile.[1] In these areas basking broadbill swordfish are targeted using trolled whole fish or flesh baits.

For many years, rare catches of small broadbill swordfish have been reported by anglers in Australian waters. However, it was not until June 1989 that a broadbill swordfish was landed that qualified for record status under international game fishing regulations. A number of fish weighing in excess of 50 kg have since been caught from southern New South Wales waters. The Game Fishing Association of Australia's record for a broadbill swordfish is 106 kg for a fish caught off Eden in May 1991. The larger fish landed by anglers in Australia have all been caught on baits drifted at night near the edge of the continental shelf.

Management controls There are no management controls on recreational and sport fishing for broadbill swordfish.

Resource status

Stock assessments based on Japanese longline catch rates indicate that Pacific stocks of broadbill swordfish are not

over-exploited.[2] However, the data used for these assessments are incomplete for the period since 1980.

References

1. Palko, B.J., Beardsley, G.L. and Richards, W.J. (1981) Synopsis of the biology of the swordfish, *Xiphias gladius Linnaeus. U.S. Department of Commerce, NOAA Technical Report, NMFS Circular* **441**. 21 pp.

2. Bartoo, N.W. and Coan, A.L. (1989) An assessment of the Pacific swordfish resource. Pp 137–151, in *Planning the future of billfishes. Research and management in the 90's and beyond.* Ed by R.H. Stroud. *Proceedings of the second international billfish symposium, Kailua-Kona, Hawaii, 1–5 August, 1988.* Part 1. Fishery and stock synopses, data needs and management.

3. Nakamura, I. (1985) FAO species catalogue. Vol. 5. Billfishes of the world. An annotated and illustrated catalogue of marlins, sailfishes, spearfishes and swordfishes known to date. *FAO Fisheries Synopsis No. 125*, **5**. 65 pp.

4. Yabe, H., Ueyanagi, S., Kikawa, S. and Watanabe, H. (1959) Study on the life history of the swordfish, *Xiphias gladius* Linnaeus. *Report of the Nankai Regional Fisheries Research Laboratory* **10**: 107–150.

5. Carey, F.G. and Robison, B.H. (1981) Daily patterns in the activities of swordfish, *Xiphias gladius*, observed by acoustic telemetry. *Fishery Bulletin (U.S.)* **79**(2): 277–292.

6. Nishikawa, Y. and Ueyanagi, S. (1974) The distribution of the larvae of swordfish, *Xiphias gladius*, in the Indian and Pacific Oceans. Pp 261–264, in *Proceedings of the international billfish symposium, Kailua-Kona, Hawaii, 9–12 August, 1972.* Part 2. Review and contributed papers. *US Department of Commerce, NOAA Technical Report, NMFS SSRF* **675**

7. Nishikawa, Y., Honma, M., Ueyanagi, S. and Kikawa, S. (1985) Average distribution of larvae of oceanic species of scombrid fishes, 1965-1981. *Far Seas Fisheries Research Laboratory, Japan, S Series* **12**. 99 pp.

8. Wilson, C.A. (1984) *Age and growth aspects of the life history of billfishes.* Unpublished PhD thesis, University of South Carolina. 180 pp.

Contributors

Most of the information on this species was provided by Dave Williams and supplemented by (in alphabetical order) Bob Miller and Kevin Williams. Drawing by Gavin Ryan. (*Details of contributors and their organisations are given in the Acknowledgements section at the back of this book.*)
Compilers Phillip Stewart and Dave Williams

Blue eye

Hyperoglyphe antarctica

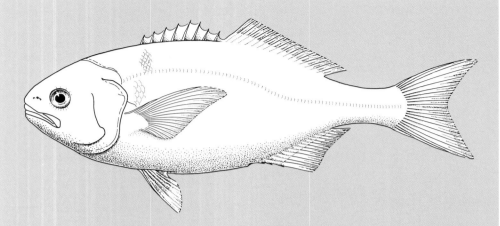

Hyperoglyphe antarctica
(Carmichael)

Blue eye

Other common names include **deep sea trevalla, trevalla, big eye, sea trevally, deep sea trevalla** and **deepsea trevally**.
FAO: **bluenose warehou**
Australian species code: 445001

Family CENTROLOPHIDAE

Diagnostic features Blue eye are dark bluish grey above and metallic blue below, sometimes nearly black. Larger fish often have a bronze sheen along their sides. The eye is large and either dark blue or orangey. Their dorsal fin has 8 strong spines anteriorly and 19–21 elevated rays posteriorly. The pectoral fin is pointed.

Distribution

Blue eye inhabit the outer continental slope and shelf waters of southern South America, South Africa, New Zealand and Australia. In Australia they are present along the southern continental margin from off Moreton Island, Queensland to 30° S in Western Australia. Blue eye also occur on the seamounts off the eastern Australian coast and south of Tasmania, around Lord Howe Island and probably also Norfolk Island.

Adult blue eye are present at depths between 200 m and 900 m.[1,2] Juveniles inhabit surface waters, sometimes in association with floating debris. Generally, blue eye remain close to the sea bed during the day and move up in the water column at night, following concentrations of food. The fish are found over rough ground and at the edges of canyons and steep drop-offs. Blue eye appear to prefer cold water as part of their general behaviour.

Life history

Spawning in blue eye appears to be correlated with water temperature and nutrient upwellings.[3] Blue eye spawn as early as February–March in Tasmanian

waters,[1] from April to June off mainland Australia,[2] and later than June off northern New South Wales. It appears that mature fish move up the continental slope into shallow depths (320–400 m) and aggregate in specific grounds for spawning.

There is no information on the number of eggs blue eye produce nor on the egg and larval stages of their life history. Fish move to the deeper demersal habitat at about 2 years of age when 47–50 cm long.[4] Juveniles appear to grow rapidly.[1,4] Growth studies suggest that fish of 55–70 cm fork length and approximately 5.5 kg from the South

Australian continental slope are 6 to 8 years old, while fish 90 cm long are approximately 13 years old.[3] Large fish of 30–50 kg have been caught off eastern Australian seamounts and the continental slope off central New South Wales. Blue eye are known to attain a total length of 140 cm.[5] More than half of the larger fish caught are females[3,6] and most fish more than 70 cm fork length are females. The maximum age estimate for blue eye is 15 years.[4] Both sexes are mature at between 5 and 7 years of age[1,6] at about 61 cm fork length and 4.5 kg.[1,5]

Adult blue eye feed primarily on the pelagic tunicate *Pyrosoma atlantica*, which is found near the sea bed during the day but dispersed throughout the water column at night.[3,7] They also eat squid, molluscs and crustaceans[2,7] and fish ranging from small lanternfish (Myctophidae) to large fish such as gemfish (*Rexea solandri*). Blue eye are also cannibalistic. Juveniles consume small planktonic and sedentary organisms.[8] Although there is no direct information on blue eye predators, there are records of deepwater dogsharks (Squalidae), gemfish and killer whales (*Orcinus orca*)[9] having scavenged on hooked blue eye in the dropline fishery.

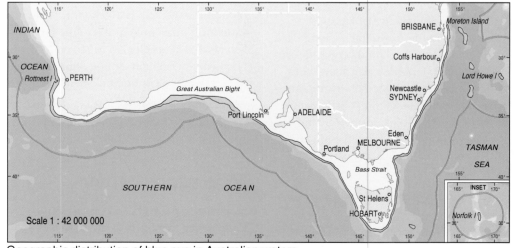

Geographic distribution of blue eye in Australian waters.

Stock structure

Preliminary allozyme analyses indicate that blue eye off south-eastern Australia belong to a common stock. A second and possibly undescribed species, similar in general appearance to blue eye, is now known from New South Wales seamounts.

Commercial fishery

Blue eye were first taken on bottom set longlines (for sharks) off the continental shelf off Tasmania in the early 1950s, and later off western Victoria.[8] A dropline and trotline fishery for them developed on the continental slope in these areas and in south-eastern New South Wales from the late 1960s–early 1970s. The dropline and trotline fishery targets adult fish. The fishery spread to the continental slope off South Australia in the early 1980s[3] and is now the main method for catching blue eye. Fishing on the seamounts off southern Queensland and New South Wales is carried out mostly during summer months.

In 1974 significant catches of blue eye were made off Tasmania by deepwater gillnetting and some gillnetting was conducted off eastern Victoria in the early 1980s. Since the early 1970s, blue eye have been caught by demersal otter trawling off south-eastern Australia and more recently some have been trawled in

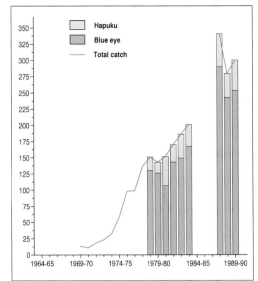

Blue eye and hapuku catch in t for New South Wales from 1969–70 to 1989–90. Figures are not available for 1984–85 to 1986–87 and catch of both species is combined for 1969–70 to 1977–78. (Source: Fisheries Resources Atlas Statistical Database)

the Great Australian Bight. Blue eye at first were a bycatch of trawling for target species such as blue grenadier (*Macruronus novaezelandiae*). However, catches have gradually increased with most blue eye taken during the day in depths of 300–600 m.

Demersal trawlers are now taking the occasional large catch of blue eye near grounds for orange roughy (*Hoplostethus atlanticus*) (ie in deeper water over rough ground) and can target aggregations of breeding and feeding adult fish.

However, this practice is being discouraged in the South East Fishery by management authorities. Blue eye have also been caught by mid-water trawling at night, either as a target species or as an incidental catch of blue grenadier. Blue eye are sometimes caught incidentally in shark netting and longline fisheries.[2]

Generally, hapuku (*Polyprion oxygeneios* — see 'Notes'), sea bass (*Polyprion moeone*) and dogsharks are significant bycatch species in the blue eye fishery. Pink ling (*Genypterus blacodes*), gemfish and ocean perch (*Helicolenus* species) are also locally significant bycatches.

Blue eye are sold as both whole, and headed and gutted fish at State wholesale markets. They are sold on retail markets as cutlets and fillets. There is some interstate trade and fillets have been marketed in Japan and the United States of America. Smoked roe is sold locally in Tasmania. Small quantities are also sold for 'sashimi' (raw fish). The price in the Sydney Fish Market averaged A$ 5.17 per kg in 1991-92.

Management controls Licence limitations apply in South Australia and

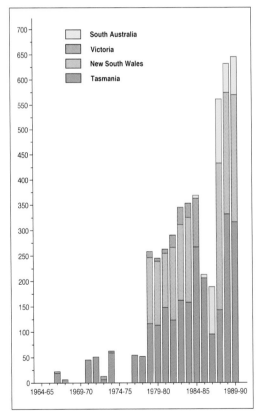

Total annual catch in t of blue eye for the period 1964–65 to 1989–90. Figures are unavailable for: New South Wales from 1964–65 to 1977–78 and 1984–85 to 1986–87; Victoria from 1974–75 to 1977–78 and 1985–86 to 1989–90; and Tasmania for 1964–65. Catches for States that average less than 5 % of the total for all States are not shown. (Source: Fisheries Resources Atlas Statistical Database)

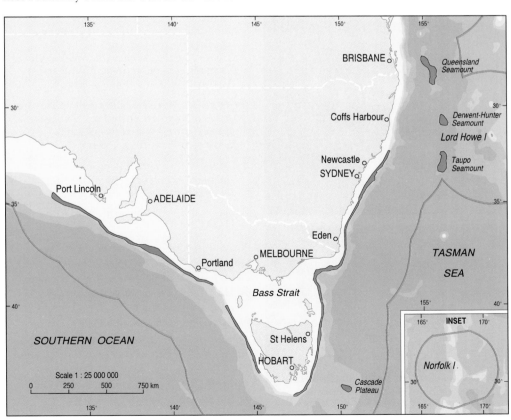

Commercial fishing areas for blue eye in Australian waters.

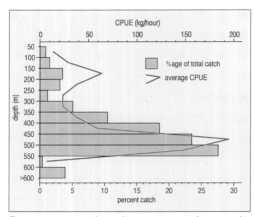

Percentage catch and average catch per unit effort (CPUE) of blue eye from the South East Fishery by 50 m depth zone. (Source: Australian Fishing Zone Information System)

Tasmania. Catches from the South East Fishery have been managed by the imposition of a 500 kg 'trip limit' in 1991, then by an individual transferable quota system since 1992. A ban on gillnetting below 200 m is in effect off Tasmania.

Recreational fishery

Blue eye are very rarely caught by recreational fishers.

Resource status

There are insufficient data to determine the status of the stock as a whole, but available information suggests that blue eye may be vulnerable to intense local fishing and are probably fully exploited in certain areas. Fish size was decreasing prior to the expansion of the fishery to the south and west coasts of Tasmania and the Cascade Plateau, although the catch per unit effort data indicated stability.[1] Blue eye are heavily exploited, with increased fishing effort realising increased catches over recent years. An assessment is being made of the impact of the developing trawl fishery in traditional droplining grounds, especially with regard to the vulnerability of blue eye to the different gears and their impact on yields from both fisheries.

Notes

Hapuku and sea bass are often caught with blue eye and may constitute up to 10 % of the catch. These demersal fish inhabit waters from shallow inshore to a depth of about 450 m, over soft sea beds and reefs. Hapuku and sea bass are distributed in Australia on the continental shelf from Sydney to Rottnest Island.[10]

Hapuku may reach 180 cm in total length and weigh up to 50 kg.[3] Females reach a slightly larger size than males.[11]

Droplining for blue eye on the Derwent Hunter seamount off New South Wales. (Source: Gary Henry, Environment Protection Authority, New South Wales)

References

1. Webb, B.F. (1979) Preliminary data on the fishery for deep-sea trevalla (*Hyperoglyphe antarctica*). *Tasmanian Fisheries Research* **22**: 18–29.

2. Jones, G.K. (1988) The biological status of the deepsea trevalla (*Hyperoglyphe antarctica*) offshore line fishery in South Australian waters. *South Australian Department of Fisheries. A Discussion Paper*. 15 pp.

3. Jones, G.K. (1985) An exploratory dropline survey for deepsea trevalla (*Hyperoglyphe antarctica*) in continental slope waters off South Australia. *South Australian Department of Fisheries, Research Paper* **15**. 20 pp.

4. Horn, P.L. (1988) Age and growth of bluenose, *Hyperoglyphe antarctica* (Pisces: Stromateoidei) from the lower east coast, North Island, New Zealand. *New Zealand Journal of Marine and Freshwater Research* **22**(3): 369–378.

5. *Commercial fisheries of New South Wales* (1982) N.S.W. State Fisheries. 60 pp.

6. Horn, P.L. and Massey, B.R. (1989) Biology and abundance of alfonsino and bluenose off the lower east coast, North Island, New Zealand. *New Zealand Fisheries Technical Report* **15**.

7. Winstanley, R.H. (1978) Food of the trevalla *Hyperoglyphe porosa* (Richardson) off southeastern Australia. *New Zealand Journal of Marine and Freshwater Research* **12**(1): 77–79.

8. Winstanley, R.H. (1979) Exploratory droplining for deepsea trevalla *Hyperoglyphe porosa* off Victoria. *Department of Fisheries and Wildlife Paper* **23**. 17 pp.

9. Tasmanian Fisheries Development Authority (1981) *Assessment of the impact of interference of Orcynus orca (killer whales) on the Tasmanian dropline fishery*. Unpublished report to the Australian National Parks and Wildlife Service.

10. Hutchins, B. and Swainston, R. (1986) *Sea fishes of southern Australia. Complete field guide for anglers and divers*. Perth: Swainston Publishing. 180 pp.

11. Roberts, C.D. (1989) Reproductive mode in the percomorph fish genus *Polyprion* Oken. *Journal of Fish Biology* **34**: 1–9.

Contributors

The information in this presentation was originally provided by (in alphabetical order) Keith Jones, Kate Paulovics, Kevin Rowling, Richard Tilzey, Howel Williams and Ross Winstanley. Drawing by Rosalind Poole. (*Details of contributors and their organisations are given in the Acknowledgements section at the back of this book.*)
Compilers Kay Abel, Patricia Kailola and Phillip Stewart (statistics)

Warehous

This presentation is on 2 species, **blue warehou** and **spotted warehou**.

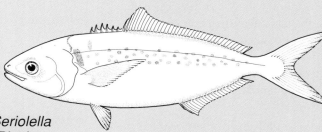

Blue warehou, *Seriolella brama* (Günther)

Other common names include **Tasmanian trevally, snotty trevally, sea bream, snotty nose trevalla, warehou, snotty, snotgall, snotgall trevalla, trevally, black trevally** and **haddock**.
FAO: no known name
Australian species code: 445005

Spotted warehou, *Seriolella punctata* (Forster, in Bloch and Schneider)

Other common names include **silver warehou, spotted trevally, spotted trevalla, snotty nose trevalla, trevally** and **mackerel trevalla**.
FAO: no known name
Australian species code: 445006

Family CENTROLOPHIDAE

Diagnostic features Blue warehou have a moderately deep body (body depth 2.3–3.2 in standard length) and a low keel in front of their tail. They have 25–29 rays in the second dorsal fin and their pectoral fin is long, extending at least to the anal fin origin. Spotted warehou have a slender body (body depth 2.9–4 in standard length) and lack a tail keel. There are 34–39 rays in the second dorsal fin and their pectoral fin is short, not reaching the anal fin.[1] Blue warehou are bluish green above and silvery white below with bluish grey blotches along their sides. Spotted warehou are bluish grey above and silvery below and have many spots along the sides that may be faint in older fish. Both species have a dark blotch above the pectoral fin but it is more distinct and bar-shaped in spotted warehou.

Distribution

The distribution limits of blue warehou and spotted warehou are uncertain but both species have been recorded from waters of central New South Wales to South Australia.[1] Blue warehou have been caught as far west as 131° E in the Great Australian Bight and spotted warehou have been recorded from Spencer Gulf. Both species are also present in New Zealand waters.[1]

Adult warehous inhabit continental shelf and slope waters from a depth of 50 m to 400 m for blue warehou[2] and up to 600 m for spotted warehou.[3] They are schooling species, usually aggregating close to the sea bed[1] although there is some evidence that they move into the middle water column at night.[4]

Life history

Knowledge of warehou reproduction in Australian waters is limited. In western Bass Strait warehous are close to spawning condition in late winter and early spring.[2,3] In New Zealand, spring spawning periods have been documented for both species.[5,6] Female fish produce a large number of eggs — up to 1.6 million for spotted warehou.[3] The eggs of both species are pelagic, about 1.5 mm in diameter for blue warehou and 1.1 mm diameter for spotted warehou.[5] Small juvenile warehous are also pelagic. They inhabit offshore areas and are often associated with jellyfish (Scyphozoa).[1] Older juvenile warehou move inshore and large numbers of them are often found in bays and inlets.

Juveniles of both warehou species grow rapidly, reaching a fork length of 23–27 cm at 1 year of age. Blue warehou are reported to reach a maximum size of 76 cm total length compared with spotted warehou which achieve a maximum of 66 cm.[1] Warehou mature by 3 or 4 years of age or a size of 40 cm fork length.[2,3] In Australian waters, blue warehou have been recorded to live for up to 10 years and spotted warehou to 11 years of age.[2,3]

Seasonal trends in the presence of both species in trawl catches indicate that some form of schooling behaviour may be associated with spawning activity. In New Zealand, spotted warehou are thought to undertake a southerly migration following spawning on the Chatham Rise in spring.[6]

The migration of warehous in Australian waters has not been studied.

Adult warehous mainly eat planktonic tunicates (*Iasis zonaria* and *Pyrosoma atlantica*).[2,3] Blue warehou are also known to feed on small crustaceans. There is no information on predators of warehous.

Stock structure

The stock structure of warehous in Australian waters is unknown.

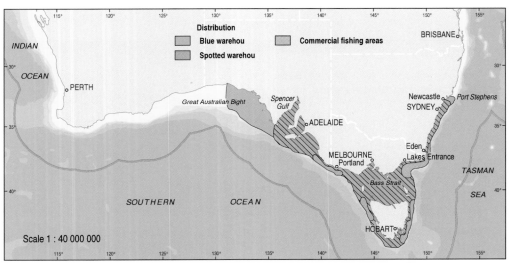

Geographic distribution and commercial fishing areas for warehous in Australian waters.

Commercial fishery

The warehou fishery has developed only since the late 1970s. Increases in the number of trawlers fishing southern New South Wales and eastern Victoria and greater market acceptance of warehous saw annual landings reach about 1800 t by 1986.[3]

Prior to 1987, most of the warehou catch was taken by trawlers using demersal otter trawl nets. Since then landings have increased greatly due to the targeting of blue warehou by fishers using bottom set gillnets in the Southern Shark Fishery. Most of the blue warehou catch from this fishery comes from grounds off eastern Victoria and is landed at Lakes Entrance.[7] Both species of warehou also form a bycatch of gillnet fishing for school sharks (*Galeorhinus galeus*) and gummy sharks (*Mustelus antarcticus*) in the Southern Shark Fishery. The amount of warehou landed by gillnet fishers operating in Victorian waters has increased from 80 t in 1984 to over 1700 t in 1990.

Both warehou species are also caught in Tasmanian waters by coastal set gillnets. Tasmanian fishers target schooling warehou by setting the gillnets on reefs in depths up to 20 m. There is also potential for the use of mid-water trawl nets to target schooling warehou.[4]

The main trawling grounds for warehous are off southern New South Wales, eastern and western Victoria, and north-western Tasmania where significant catches of spotted warehou are taken.[2,3] Spotted warehou catches are greatest from depths between 150 m and 250 m and significant catches are also recorded between 400 m and 550 m.[3] Most of the blue warehou trawl catch is taken from depths of 50 m to 250 m in the trawl fishery and from 60 m to 75 m in the gillnet fishery, although the highest catch rates from gillnets have been recorded in 150–175 m.[7] Trawl catches of warehou show a distinct seasonal trend with late winter and early spring producing the largest catches of both species.[7] Gillnet catches of blue warehou exhibit less seasonal variation but catches do tend to be higher in late summer and autumn.[7]

Most of the warehou catch is sold on the domestic fresh fish market, mainly through the Melbourne Wholesale Fish Market. The 2 species are often marketed together but when they are marketed separately, blue warehou tend to gain higher prices. Warehou prices at the Melbourne market in 1991–92 averaged between A$ 0.80 and A$ 2.50 per kg.

Management controls The trawl fishery for warehous is managed by the Commonwealth of Australia as a component of the South East Fishery. A total allowable catch covering both species was introduced for the South East Fishery in January 1992 along with allocation of individual transferable quotas to fishers. Separate catch limits for each species have been introduced for the 1993 season. Fishing activity targeting blue warehou in the shark gillnet fishery is also subject to management by the Commonwealth under the provisions of the Southern Shark Fishery Management Plan. The Tasmanian Government manages the gillnet fishery for warehous in coastal waters of that State.

Recreational fishery

Anglers catch juveniles of both warehou species in large bays and estuaries, with blue warehou more common in recreational catches than are spotted warehou. Warehous are normally caught by anglers during the colder months of the year, on baits of prawn (Penaeidae), rock lobster (*Jasus* species) or fish flesh.[8] Recreational fishers in Tasmania use coastal set gillnets to catch warehou.

Management controls There are no specific controls on angling for warehous in any State. In Tasmania there are restrictions on mesh size, net length and closed areas for fishers using gillnets.

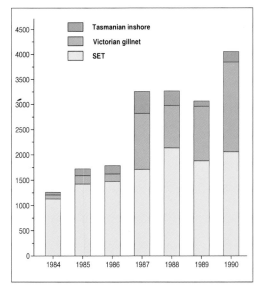

(left) Total annual catch in t of both warehou species (combined) for the period 1984 to 1990. Catch is presented separately for the South East Fishery (SET), the Victorian gillnet fishery and the Tasmanian inshore trawl and gillnet fisheries. (Source: Australian Fishing Zone Information System, Lakes Entrance Fishermens' Cooperative, Southern Shark Monitoring Database, and the Tasmanian Department of Primary Industry and Fisheries)

(right) A large catch of blue warehou taken by bottom set gillnetting. (Source: Dave Smith, Marine Science Laboratories, Victorian Department of Conservation and Environment)

Fishers removing blue warehou as a bottom set gillnet is hauled. (Source: Dave Smith, Marine Science Laboratories, Victorian Department of Conservation and Environment)

Resource status

There is insufficient information to determine the status for each species in Australian waters. No reliable biomass estimates are available for blue warehou and estimates of biomass for spotted warehou in some areas of the South East Fishery have varied considerably: hence, further research is needed to better estimate biomass by allowing for seasonal changes in local abundance.[3] The lack of sound biomass estimates means that it is not possible to determine whether current catch levels are sustainable for either species.

References

1. Last, P.R., Scott, E.O.G. and Talbot, F.H. (1983) *Fishes of Tasmania*. Hobart: Tasmanian Fisheries Development Authority. 563 pp.

2. Smith, D.C. (in press, 1992) Blue warehou. In *The South East Fishery: a scientific review with particular reference to quota management*. Ed by R.D.J. Tilzey. *Bureau of Resource Sciences Bulletin*.

3. Smith, D.C. (in press, 1992) Spotted warehou. In *The South East Fishery: a scientific review with particular reference to quota management*. Ed by R.D.J. Tilzey. *Bureau of Resource Sciences Bulletin*.

4. Boyes, J. (1983) Pelagic trawling off Tasmania takes warehou. *Australian Fisheries* **42**(8): 4–6.

5. Grimes, P.J. and Robertson, D.A. (1981) Egg and larval development of the silver warehou, *Seriolella punctata* (Pisces: Centrolophidae). *New Zealand Journal of Marine and Freshwater Research* **15**: 261–266.

6. Paul, L. (1986) *New Zealand fishes. An identification guide*. Auckland: Reed Methuen. 184 pp.

7. Smith, D.C. (1989) Summary of data available on the warehous, *Seriolella brama* and *S. punctata*. *Victorian Department of Conservation, Forests and Lands, Fisheries Division, Internal Report* **183**. 9 pp.

8. Starling, S. (1988) *The fisherman's handbook. How to find, identify and catch the top Australian angling fish*. North Ryde: Angus and Robertson Publishers. 263 pp.

Contributors

Most of the information on these species was provided by Dave Smith. Additional information was provided by (in alphabetical order) Barry Bruce, Terry Sim, Alex Schaap and Richard Tilzey. Drawings by Rosalind Poole. (*Details of contributors and their organisations are given in the Acknowledgements section at the back of this book.*)
Compiler Phillip Stewart

Ocean jacket

Nelusetta ayraudi

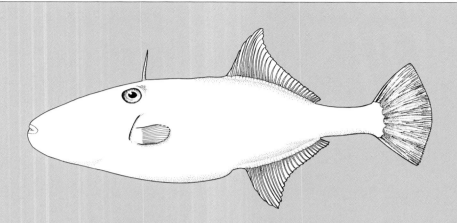

Nelusetta ayraudi (Quoy and Gaimard)

Ocean jacket

Other common names include **Chinaman leatherjacket**, **yellow jacket** and **chunks**.
FAO: no known name
Australian species code: 465006

Family MONACANTHIDAE

Diagnostic features Ocean jackets have a long snout and their head length is much greater than their body depth. The anterior rays of their dorsal and anal fins are much longer than the remaining rays, and there are 31–32 rays in the dorsal fin. Adult females and juveniles are yellowish brown, with orangey or yellowish fins, and the juveniles have 1–4 longitudinal dark brown stripes along their body. Adult males are greenish grey, sometimes with 2 or 3 dark blotches on their sides, and they have bright yellow fins.

Distribution

Ocean jackets inhabit waters of southern Australia from Cape Moreton in Queensland to North West Cape in Western Australia, but excluding Tasmania. The species is considered to be endemic to Australia, although a single specimen has been reported from New Zealand.[1]

Ocean jackets are found from very shallow water (2 m) to water as deep as 200 m. There is a tendency for their average size to increase with water depth.[2] Juvenile ocean jackets have been caught in seagrass, over bare sand and on rocky reefs. Adults however, tend to be absent from seagrass areas. In northern New South Wales, ocean jackets are occasionally present in reef areas, but in South Australian waters, they are common over sand and 'coral' (bryozoans — Ectoprocta) sea beds.

Life history

Ocean jackets spawn off South Australia between late April and early May[3] in waters 85–200 m deep several hundred km offshore. Spawning probably occurs more than once during this brief period.[3] Seasonal migration (in South Australia)

appears to be associated with spawning: movement is predominantly to the west prior to spawning, and to the east just after spawning. Tagging studies conducted in this region have recorded movements by individual ocean jackets of up to 350 nautical miles along the continental shelf over a 12 month period.

Each season, female ocean jackets averaging 40 cm total length produce about 700 000 spherical eggs[3] measuring approximately 0.6 mm in diameter when ripe. Fecundity increases with length

however, and some large females can produce up to 2 million eggs.[3]

In South Australian waters, the generally south-westerly direction of winter surface currents in the eastern Great Australian Bight possibly facilitates the inshore movement of ocean jacket larvae from the offshore spawning areas. Juvenile ocean jackets averaging 12 cm total length first appear in the gulfs and sheltered bays and inshore coastal waters in November, ie at approximately 6 months of age.[3] In May and June, when they are about 1-year-old, young ocean jackets begin to move out of inshore areas to more open waters up to about 60 m depth. This general offshore migration continues with age, such that older fish inhabit the deepest waters at the edge of the continental shelf.

Growth is rapid[3] and juveniles attain 22 cm total length by about 1 year of age. The maximum recorded length of ocean jackets is 79 cm fork length, and the maximum recorded weight is 3.5 kg.[4] Ocean jackets have been aged up to 9 years by counting the rings on their vertebrae.[3] However, because it is

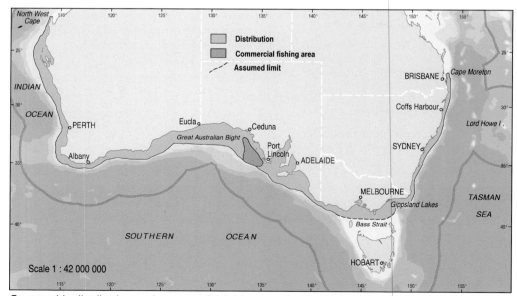

Geographic distribution and commercial fishing area for ocean jacket.

increasingly difficult to distinguish growth rings in older fish, some individuals may exceed that age.

A small proportion of females mature at 2–2.5 years of age and full maturity is reached at 3–4 years of age in fish longer than approximately 37 cm total length.[3] From approximately 23 cm total length, sexual dichromatism (ie sexes differently coloured) is apparent.[2] Male and female fish occur in equal numbers up to 4 years of age but the ratio decreases until by 6 years of age, males comprise less than 20 % of the catch.[3] This phenomenon is probably because of a higher mortality rate among males than females.

Adult ocean jackets are carnivorous, feeding mainly on salps (Thaliacea), gastropod molluscs, crustaceans and fish.[2] Fishers have reported that squid are also commonly eaten. Ocean jackets form loose, small schools when feeding.[5] Predation on ocean jackets has not been recorded.

Stock structure

Tagging studies[3] have demonstrated that ocean jackets from the eastern Great Australian Bight and the south-east of South Australia are a common stock. Relationships with populations from other areas are unknown.

Commercial fishery

Ocean jackets were intensively fished in northern New South Wales during the 1940s and 1950s but, after a dramatic decline in their numbers there, the fishery was replaced by a snapper (*Pagrus auratus*) fishery. Ocean jackets were also fished in the Albany region of Western Australia during the 1970s.

The South Australian fishery commenced in 1984 largely as a supplement to southern rock lobster (*Jasus edwardsii*) fishing and shark fishing, and has developed rapidly. Commercial catches of ocean jackets are now taken mainly in South Australia and to a much lesser extent along the entire New South Wales coast, to the edge of the continental shelf. The South Australian fishery operates all year, although catches are lower in winter.

The principal fishery uses traps. The traps used in South Australia have a single, 80 mm wide opening[5] and are set at depths from 60 m to 150 m. The traps

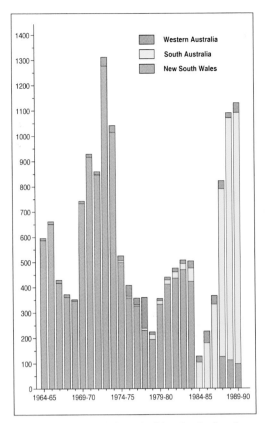

Total annual catch in t of all leatherjacket for the period 1964–65 to 1989–90. Figures are unavailable for: New South Wales from 1984–85 to 1986–87; and South Australia from 1964–65 to 1973–74. Catches for States that average less than 5 % of the total for all States are not shown. (Source: Fisheries Resources Atlas Statistical Database)

are baited with rock lobster heads and set at dawn, and are retrieved about 2 hours later. After removal from the trap, the fish are immediately headed, gutted and chilled. The traps are rebaited and set in the same general area, to be pulled up again in a further 2–3 hours' time. The process continues over the day. Because the fishing grounds in South Australia are at least 7–8 hours' steaming time offshore, fishers usually stay at sea for 3–5 days at a time.

Ocean jackets are not fully recruited to the commercial trap fishery until they are about 4 years of age[3] and the average total length of fish taken is 40 cm — although fish over 57 cm are common.

Demersal otter trawling takes only a small proportion of the South Australian ocean jacket catch. In the Great Australian Bight Trawl Fishery, trawling for these fish is generally conducted between 150 m and 180 m depth. Most ocean jacket catches in the Bight are made around 126° E.

In New South Wales, ocean jacket are caught as a bycatch of demersal trawling and Danish seining.[2] In addition, snapper trap fishers occasionally target ocean

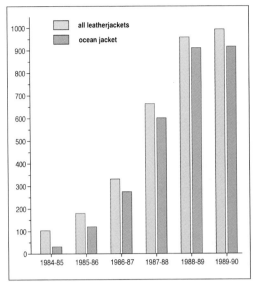

Total annual catch in t of ocean jacket compared with total annual catch of all leatherjacket species (including ocean jackets) for South Australia, for the period 1984–85 to 1989–90. (Source: Fisheries Resources Atlas Statistical Database and Grove-Jones and Burnell[3])

jackets by changing from a fish to a meat bait.

Most ocean jackets caught in South Australian waters are sold in New South Wales as fresh trunks and some are sold in Victoria. In comparison, demand in South Australia and Western Australia is poor. The 1991–92 Sydney Fish Market price averaged A$ 2.28 per kg, the large offerings of ocean jackets from South Australia keeping prices low.

Management controls In South Australia, regulations control the number of vessels licensed to take ocean jackets by trap, the depth of set, and the number and size of traps that may be used. The size of the trap opening is also regulated to prevent capture of adult southern rock lobsters.

Recreational fishery

There is no established recreational fishery for ocean jacket, although juveniles may be caught in bays as incidental catch to the King George whiting (*Sillaginodes punctata*) and snapper fisheries. Generally, children fish for these small leatherjackets.

Resource status

Ocean jackets are fast growing and have a short life span. A recent assessment[3] of the South Australian ocean jacket resource indicated that it would probably sustain high fishing pressure. However,

Retrieving ocean jacket traps, South Australia. (Source: Rod Grove-Jones, South Australian Department of Fisheries)

the extent of the resource is not known, and this uncertainty suggests that catches should not be increased at this stage.

The New South Wales stocks of ocean jacket were fished down from the early days of the fishery, although some quantities remain. For example, ocean jackets are among the top 10 (of approximately 100) species landed at the Coffs Harbour Fishermens' Cooperative, and comprise 3–5 % of the total catch.

The species has not been exploited recently in Western Australia, although it is plentiful there between Albany and Eucla (at least). High transport costs to eastern markets have so far impeded the development of a fishery in that State.

Notes

Other leatherjacket species are caught in shallower, temperate waters and inshore areas around Australia, mostly by trawl. For example, the annual catch from East Gippsland in Victoria is 2–11 t. These fish supply local markets.

Ocean jackets are commonly parasitised by the leatherjacket louse *Ourozeuktes owenii* (Isopoda).[6] This condition does not affect the flesh quality.

References

1. Ayling, T. and Cox, G.J. (1982) *Collins' guide to the sea fishes of New Zealand.* Auckland: Collins. 343 pp.

2. Lindholm, R. (1984) Observation on the ocean jacket *Nelusetta ayraudi* (Quoy and Gaimard) in the Great Australian Bight.

Australian Journal of Marine and Freshwater Research **35**: 597–599.

3. Grove-Jones, R.P. and Burnell, A.F. (1991) Fisheries biology of the ocean jacket (Monacanthidae: *Nelusetta ayraudi*) in the eastern waters of the Great Australian Bight. *South Australian Department of Fisheries. FIRDC Project DFS01Z, Final Report.* 107 pp.

4. Hutchins, B. and Swainston, R. (1986) *Sea fishes of southern Australia. Complete field guide for anglers and divers.* Perth: Swainston Publishing. 180 pp.

5. Grove-Jones, R.P. and Burnell, A.F. (1990) Ocean jacket traps assessed. *SAFISH* **15**(1): 10–11.

6. Hale, H.M. (1929) *The crustaceans of South Australia.* Part 2. Pp 201–380. Adelaide: South Australian Museum.

Contributors

Most of the information on the South Australian fishery was provided by Rod Grove-Jones. Substantial additional contributions were made by (in alphabetical order) Andrew Burnell, Gary Henry, Barry Hutchins, Keith Jones and Gina Newton. Peter Petrusevics provided information on sea surface currents. Drawing by Rosalind Poole. *(Details of contributors and their organisations are given in the Acknowledgements section at the back of this book.)*
Compilers Patricia Kailola and Christina Grieve (maps)

compiled by Patricia Kailola
and Alex McNee

The annual catch for species discussed in this chapter varies from less than 100 t to more than 1000 t. However, they are of secondary importance to those comprising Chapter 5. The species here are of primarily commercial rather than recreational significance. Some of the species mentioned are taken regularly as bycatch. Others have only recently been recognised as a potential fishery or aquaculture resource and their production is low.

In this chapter, species are presented alphabetically in the order of plant, invertebrate and vertebrate. Details of contributors are given in the Acknowledgements section at the back of this book, and, if available, at least 1 reference source is cited for each presentation.

Kelp is harvested from the beaches of King Island in Bass Strait. The kelp that is cast onto the beach during storms is harvested and hung from racks to dry before it is transferred to a processing plant where it is shredded and pelletised. The end product is exported for further processing into alginates. Alginates are used in the food and pharmaceutical industries (for example as sauce thickeners in meat pies) and some varieties are eaten by humans. More recently some of the kelp has been used as food in abalone mariculture operations. Kelp harvesting also occurs off the east coast of Tasmania. Vessels mounted with aquatic 'mowers' are used to trim beds of giant kelp about 1 m below the surface. The cut seaweed is transferred up a conveyor into the hull of the vessel as it moves through the kelp bed. The kelp is unloaded from the cutting vessel and transferred to an onshore factory for processing. Estimated production from both these operations is 21 000–25 000 wet t per annum, which is equal to about 3000–3200 dry t per annum. Some 273 000 wet t of kelp have been harvested since 1976.

There are 4 major species of kelp found in Australia. Two brown kelp species are distributed from southern Queensland to southern Western Australia and the Houtman Abrolhos, including Tasmania. Bull kelp and giant kelp largely replace these brown kelps south of Bermagui and extend to Kangaroo Island in South Australia and into Western Australia.

Japanese kelp, an exotic species probably introduced to Australian waters in ships' ballast water, is spreading along the Tasmanian coast. In Japan, this kelp is a major seaweed variety, where its dried blades are known as 'wakame'. Japanese kelp is the third largest mariculture plant crop in Japan. Quantities existing in Tasmania appear to be commercially harvestable.

Taxonomy — Family DURVILLAEACEAE, *Durvillaea potatorum*, bull kelp; Family LESSONIACEAE, *Macrocystis pyrifera*, giant kelp; Family SEIROCOCCACEAE, *Phyllospora comosa*, brown kelp; Family ALARIACEAE, *Ecklonia radiata*, brown kelp; *Undaria pinnatifida*, Japanese kelp

Contributors — Marc Wilson and Shirley Slack-Smith

Bait worms (including **blood worms** and **beach worms**) are favoured as bait by recreational fishers and are collected commercially from Moreton Bay in Queensland to Victoria. Bait worms are caught by digging on mudflats and in shallow water, often using yabby (bait) pumps, and (for beach worms) by hand at the surfline using pieces of meat as bait.

In Victoria and New South Wales the possibility of aquaculturing bait worms has been investigated.

There are numerous species of bait worms distributed throughout Australia. They are common and widespread but mostly in low numbers throughout Queensland, New South Wales and Western Australia. Little life history information is available. Most species probably have distinct males and females, and breeding occurs over a restricted time period: gametes are discharged into the water column where fertilization occurs. The pelagic larvae settle after 2–3 weeks. Blood worms grow to 25 cm long. They inhabit fine mud and muddy sand in salinities of 11–33 parts per thousand and in eelgrass (*Zostera* species) beds. Other bait worms attain larger sizes; for example beach worms reach at least 2.5 m.

The size and value of the bait worm resource is largely unknown. Domestic use is as live, salted or frozen product.

Taxonomy — Family EUNICIDAE, *Marphysa* species, blood worms; Family GLYCERIDAE, *Glycera* species; Family ONUPHIDAE, *Onuphis* species, *Australonuphis* species, beach worms; Family NEREIDIDAE, *Australonereis* species.

Contributors — Pat Hutchings, Cassie Rose and Robin Wilson

Further reading

Hutchings, P.A. and Murray, A. (1984) Taxonomy of polychaetes from the Hawkesbury River and the southern estuaries of New South Wales. *Records of the Australian Museum* **36**, Supplement 3. 118 pp.

Paxton, H. (1979) Taxonomy and aspects of the life history of Australian beachworms (Polychaeta: Onuphidae). *Australian Journal of Marine and Freshwater Research* **30**: 265–294.

Forbes, A.J. (1984) The bait worm fishery in Moreton Bay, Queensland. *Queensland Department of Primary Industries, Project report* **Q084009**. 18 pp.

Bêche-de-mer (also called **sea cucumbers**, **sea slugs** and **trepang**) are collected by hand picking from reefs at low tide, spearing from dinghies with weighted spikes, or by diving. They also form part of the incidental catch from trawlers off the coast of north-western Australia.

Collected bêche-de-mer is cleaned, boiled, sun or machine dried and then smoked. The processing is labour intensive but the product stores well. Prices received are very dependent on the species and quality. Processed bêche-de-mer is used for food and medicinal purposes, particularly amongst Chinese communities; and the main markets are in Singapore, Hong Kong, Malaysia and Thailand. Research into processing and storage methods for export is being carried out.

Bêche-de-mer fisheries were historically important in Torres Strait and the northern part of the Great Barrier Reef. Commercial fishing for bêche-de-mer probably began during the 1700s with Macassan vessels controlled by the Dutch East India Company regularly calling in northern Australia. Reefs such as Rowley Shoals off Western Australia have been fished also by Timorese in the past. The bêche-de-mer fishery expanded through to the early 1900s (annual catches from Queensland waters between 1895 and 1948 ranged from 51 t to 5420 t), but as demand and prices dropped the fishery declined. Between 1986 and 1992 catches in Queensland peaked at 218 t, with up to 29 collecting operations. The 1992 Northern Territory catch was 100 t. The bêche-de-mer fishery is largely developmental, pending clearance of export restrictions.

Black and white teatfish are found on reefs off the north-west coast of Australia through to Torres Strait. Sand fish are found inshore along the Kimberley and Pilbara coasts, through Torres Strait and along the east coast as far south as Moreton Bay. Prickly redfish are found from offshore reefs off western Australia (eg Rowley Shoals, Kimberley and Pilbara coasts) and across northern Australia. Deepwater redfish are found in Torres Strait.

Little is known of the life history of bêche-de-mer species. At about 60 cm, prickly redfish attain the largest size.

Taxonomy — Family HOLOTHURIIDAE, *Holothuria (Microthele) nobilis*, black teatfish; *H. (Microthele) fuscogilva*, white teatfish; *H. (Metriatyla) scabra*, sand fish; *H. (Halodeima) atra*, lolly fish; *Actinopyga echinites*, deepwater redfish; *A. mauritiana*, surf redfish; Family STICHOPODIDAE, *Thelenota ananas*, prickly redfish

Contributors — Loisette Marsh, Geoff Williams, Tim Wood and Malcolm Dunning

Further reading

Cannon, L.R.G. and Silver, H. (1986) *Sea cucumbers of northern Australia*. Brisbane: Queensland Museum. 60 pp.

Shelley, C.C. (1986) The potential for re-introduction of a bêche-de-mer fishery in Torres Strait. Pp 140–150, in *Torres Strait fisheries seminar, 11–14 February, 1985, Port Moresby*. Ed by A.K. Haines, G.C. Williams and D. Coates. Canberra: Australian Fisheries Service, Department of Primary Industry.

Bêche-de-mer of the tropical Pacific (1979). South Pacific Commission, Handbook No. **18**. Noumea, New Caledonia. 29 pp.

Carid prawns are caught by demersal trawling in the North West Slope Trawl Fishery. White carids are often discarded as meat recovery and market value on them is low (and peeling costs prohibitive), but red carids are important commercially. Prawns are sorted, graded and frozen whole on board and most of the catch is exported, primarily to Japan. These species are caught mainly during the day as they migrate upwards in the water column at night to feed. The red carid prawn catch in the North West Slope Trawl Fishery was 135 t in 1987–88 and 115 t in 1988–89. Catches have declined in recent years.

White carids inhabit western and north-western Australian waters in depths of 247–850 m and red carids inhabit north-western and eastern Australian waters in depths of 290–655 m. White carids also occur in eastern Atlantic, Indian and south-western Pacific oceans and red carids are widely distributed in the tropical Indo-West Pacific. There is little information on spawning and early life history of carid prawns. Red carids grow to 39 mm carapace length (females) and white carids reach 41 mm carapace length (females).

Source: Dave Evans

Taxonomy — Family PANDALIDAE, *Heterocarpus woodmasoni*, red carid prawn; *H. sibogae*, white carid prawn

Contributors — Vicki Wadley and John Garvey

Further reading

Wadley, V. and Evans, D. (1991) *Crustaceans from the deepwater trawl fisheries of Western Australia*. Marmion: CSIRO Division of Fisheries. 44 pp.

Phillips, B. and Jernakoff, P. (1991) The north west slope trawl fishery. What future does it have? *Australian Fisheries* **50**(7): 18–20.

Clams are harvested by Aborigines and Torres Strait Islanders who have fishing rights to take them for their own consumption. Six species of clam are harvested in Australia: giant, smooth giant, fluted, great, boring and strawberry. Apart from traditional harvest, clams are totally protected in Australian waters. Australia has the only major stocks of clams that are not threatened by overfishing.

Clams are collected by reef walking at low tide and by diving. Most parts of the clam are usable although the adductor muscle is a prize delicacy. In South-east Asia, the mantle is also eaten. Clam shells are used for craft items. Whole boring clams were selling in Japan for A$ 100.00 per kg wet weight in 1992, and frozen mantle and adductor muscle meat of giant, fluted and strawberry clams were selling for A$ 50.00 per kg. Recent work in Australia has been directed at developing successful mariculture techniques for production of juveniles to re-seed natural beds as well as production of adults to supplement or replace natural harvest. Most effort has been put into

producing the faster growing giant clams and smooth giant clams.

Clams inhabit coral reef waters north of the Tropic of Capricorn in Australia, in water to about 20 m depth. They spawn from early to late summer and there may be a number of spawnings over a season. All are protandrous hermaphrodites, maturing first as males when 2–3 years old, then maturing as females from 5 years of age (in smaller species). Growth varies widely between species. Giant clams are the largest and fastest growing species, reaching 110 cm in length and 200 kg. Most adult giant clams are less than 20 years old.

Poaching of clams by Taiwanese fishers — mostly from outer reefs — was a problem in northern Australia in the 1970s and early 1980s.

Taxonomy — Family TRIDACNIDAE, *Tridacna gigas*, giant clam; *T. derasa*, smooth giant clam; *T. squamosa*, fluted clam or scaly clam; *T. maxima*, great clam or rugose giant clam; *T. crocea*, boring clam or crocus clam; *Hippopus hippopus*, horse's hoof, bear paw or strawberry clam

Contributors — John Lucas, Julie Macaranas and Bill Anderson

Further reading

Copland, J.W. and Lucas, J.S. (1988) Giant clams in Asia and the Pacific. *Australian Centre for International Agricultural Research, Monograph series* **9**. 274 pp.

Cuttlefish are taken as bycatch by Australian fishers, especially in prawn fisheries. Larger species are usually kept for sale while smaller species are only marketed if sufficient quantities are caught. Cuttlefish are sold for human consumption and bait. Most landings are made in New South Wales, where 183 t were recorded in 1989–90.

Australian giant cuttlefish are mainly caught by recreational fishers using lures or baited hooks from jetties, piers or the shore. Pharaoh's cuttlefish are taken incidentally by Australian fishers using trawls, jigs, lures and baited hooks. They were a widely exploited bycatch of foreign (mainly Taiwanese) demersal otter trawlers fishing in north-western Australian waters between 1978 and 1991. The highest catches were made on the North West Shelf, peaking at more than 8400 t in 1982.

Australian giant cuttlefish occur only in coastal waters and bays to about 35 m depth in subtropical and temperate Australia. Pharaoh's cuttlefish inhabit shallow waters (to 110 m) across northern Australia and along the west coast as far south as Rottnest Island. Little is known on the biology of these 2 species in Australian waters. Australian giant cuttlefish spawn in October-December, grow to over 40 cm mantle length and reach more than 5 kg. Timing of spawning in Pharaoh's cuttlefish varies with localities in southern Asia. They migrate shorewards and aggregate when spawning. Pharaoh's cuttlefish grow to 43 cm mantle length and weigh up to 4 kg. Cuttlefish feed primarily on demersal fish and crustaceans.

Taxonomy — Family SEPIIDAE, *Sepia apama*, Australian giant cuttlefish; *S. esculenta*, golden cuttlefish; *S. pharaonis*, Pharaoh's cuttlefish

Contributors — Wolfgang Zeidler and Malcolm Dunning; drawing by Leslie Newman

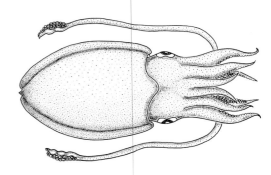

Doughboy scallops were historically part of the Tasmanian commercial catch and are now targeted by recreational divers in the D'Entrecasteaux Channel in Tasmania, along with Queen scallops. About 1200 divers participate in the dive fishery and daily bag limits apply.

The D'Entrecasteaux Channel commercial fishery was closed in 1970 when stocks were assessed as not commercially viable. It re-opened in 1982 but was closed again in 1985. Small quantities of doughboy scallops are landed in South Australia, but the main population appears to be in Bass Strait where very large catch rates have been recorded.

Doughboy scallops are distributed from New South Wales, around Tasmania and the Bass Strait islands to about Shark Bay in Western Australia, in depths of 2–120 m. They are dioecious (ie, unisexual) and attain up to 110 mm shell height. The low market value for this species is probably because of their low meat yield and because they require extra processing as they are sold 'roe-off'.

Taxonomy — Family PECTINIDAE, *Chlamys (Mimachlamys) asperrimus*

Contributors — Will Zacharin and Richard McLoughlin

Further reading

Zacharin, W. (in press, 1993) Reproduction and recruitment in the doughboy scallop (*Chlamys asperrimus*) in the D'Entrecasteaux Channel, Tasmania. In, *Proceedings of the second Australasian scallop workshop, 22–26 March, 1993, Triabunna, Tasmania*. Brisbane: Queensland Museum

---

Jellyfish are harvested in South-east Asia for human consumption. They are sold salted and dried. There is a small domestic market for them in Australia.

Two jellyfish species (brown jellyfish and brown jelly blubbers) are caught commercially in Australia. In the early 1980s research in Australia developed methods for processing brown jelly blubbers. Since then efforts were made to establish fisheries for them in the Clarence River and Lake Illawarra in 1990 and for brown jellyfish on the Swan River in 1989–90 (now ceased).

Brown jelly blubbers are distributed along the east coast of Australia from far north

Queensland to Port Phillip Bay in Victoria. Brown jellyfish are distributed from Queensland to New South Wales and eastern Victoria, and they are also present in south-western Australia. Both species also occur in the Philippines. Stocks of brown jelly blubbers are very large, and stocks of brown jellyfish on the west coast are also considerable. The stocks are technically easily harvested and have rapid seasonal replacement. However, processing is long and labour intensive, with a low recovery rate. Variations in colour from blue to brown to white may affect the demand and price.

Both jellyfish species live in estuaries and inshore coastal waters. Jellyfish spawn from mid summer to autumn, when about 20–25 cm long. The larvae metamorphose into a polyp which survives the winter. Most adult jellyfish die at the end of the summer.

Taxonomy — Family MASTIGIIDAE, *Phyllorhiza punctata*, brown jellyfish; Family CATOSTYLIDAE, *Catostylus mosaicus*, brown jelly blubber

Contributors — Ken Pulley and Loisette Marsh

Further reading

Davis, P. (1982) Acceptable salted jellyfish produced. *Australian Fisheries* **41**(3): 34.
Coleman, A., Micin, S., Mulvay, P. and Rippingale, R. (1990) The brown jellyfish (*Phyllorhiza punctata*) in the Swan-Canning Estuary. *Swan River Trust, Waterways Information no. 2*. 4 pp.
Wells, R.W. and Wellington, R. (1992) The potential exploitation of the brown jelly blubber, *Catostylus mosaicus*, in eastern Australian waters. *Sydney Basin Naturalist* **1**: 57–61.

King crabs (also called **giant crabs, giant southern Australian crab** and **Tasmanian king crab**) used to be an incidental catch in southern Australian rock lobster and trawl fisheries but in recent years they have been targeted increasingly. King crabs are commonly fished off Albany and Esperance in Western Australia, where they are caught in lobster pots, usually in over 100 m water depth. King crabs have also been caught off south-eastern South Australia and out of Portland in Victoria. King crabs are caught occasionally in Tasmanian lobster catches, but as yet there is no target fishery there.

Most product is exported, although it is appearing on local markets in southern capital cities — including a live market for the restaurant trade. Prices in early 1993 ranged from A$ 4.50 to A$ 10.00 per kg. The 1991–92 catch in Western Australia was 47 t.

King crabs are distributed from central New South Wales to the south-western tip of Western Australia, usually at depths between 100 m and 180 m, although they have been recorded in shallower waters. Little is known on the life history of this large crab, but they are probably long-lived and slow growing. Maximum recorded sizes are 40.6 cm carapace width and 13.6 kg.

Taxonomy — Family XANTHIDAE, *Pseudocarcinus gigas*

Contributors — Diana Jones, Gary Morgan, Elizabeth Turner, Robin Wilson and Jim Sutton

Further reading

Healy, A. and Yaldwyn, J. (1970) *Australian crustaceans in colour*. Sydney: A.H. and A.W. Reed. 112 pp.

Pipis (also called **Goolwa cockle** and **ugari**) were historically gathered commercially for bait and food in southern New South Wales. Pipis are currently harvested commercially in South Australia and New South Wales. In 1989–90, 560 t were landed. Pipis are used in soups and chowders and can be stored live, frozen or pickled.

Pipis are distributed on surf beaches from southern Queensland to Eyre Peninsula in South Australia. They are found along high energy coastlines but not outside the surf zone. In South Australia, pipis spawn mainly over September and October. They mature at about 13 months of age when more than 36 mm in shell length and reach a maximum length of more than 60 mm at 3–3.5 years of age. Pipis live for 4–5 years and growth varies with season and age.

Pipi abundance is subject to enormous natural fluctuations in size, and they are affected by phenomena such as reduced water salinities.

Taxonomy — Family DONACIDAE, *Plebidonax deltoides*

Contributors — Mike King and Will Zacharin; drawing by Leslie Newman

Further reading

King, M. (1985) The life history of the Goolwa cockle, *Donax (Plebidonax) deltoides* (Bivalvia: Donacidae), on an ocean beach, South Australia. *South Australian Department of Fisheries, Internal report* **85**.
A review of the Goolwa cockle (1985). *SAFISH* **9**(5): 14.

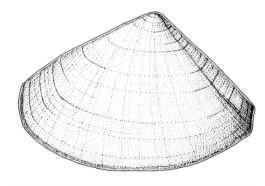

Roe's abalone are fished commercially from the Western Australian border westwards to South Passage, Western Australia. The fishery is small (about 120 t a year) and most of the abalone meat is canned and exported to Japan and South-east Asia. Roe's abalone are collected by hand by divers. There is also a popular recreational fishery for this abalone, largely because they inhabit nearshore waters.

Roe's abalone are distributed from Corner Inlet, Victoria to Shark Bay, Western Australia. They prefer rough water coasts or rocky reef platforms and are found in depths from 10 cm to 4 m. Roe's abalone can spawn year round, although winter spawning occurs in Western Australia. The larvae are free swimming and move inshore with currents and settle on coralline algae. Most abalone move to deeper

waters as they mature in their second year. These abalone reach 12.5 cm in length and probably live for up to 10 years. Roe's abalone is the smallest commercial abalone species in Australia.

Taxonomy — Family HALIOTIDAE, *Haliotis roei*

Contributor — Lindsay Joll; drawing by Leslie Newman

Further reading

Keesing, J.K. and Wells, F.E. (1989) Growth of the abalone *Haliotis roei* Gray. *Australian Journal of Marine and Freshwater Research* **40**: 199–204.
Wells, F.E. and Keesing, J.K. (1990) Population characteristics of the abalone *Haliotis roei* on intertidal platforms in the Perth metropolitan area. *Journal of the Malacological Society of Australia* **11**: 65–71.

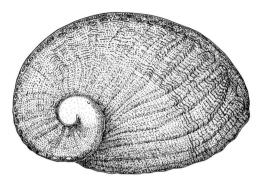

Sand crabs are fished commercially from Coffin Bay and Gulf St Vincent-Investigator Strait in South Australia. The main fishing methods used are traps and hoop nets. Catches have been increasing from around 25 t in the mid 1980s to 142 t in 1989–90. In Western Australia and South Australia, sand crabs are dredged or trawled occasionally and may be marketed if the catches are large.

Sand crabs are distributed mainly across southern Australia from Wide Bay in Queensland to Rottnest Island in Western Australia, including Tasmanian waters. They are common on surf beaches and in sandy bays and inlets and also occur offshore to a depth of 100 m. There is no information on spawning times or maturity. Sand crabs attain 15 cm carapace width at least.

Taxonomy — Family PORTUNIDAE, *Ovalipes australiensis*

Contributors — Diana Jones, Wolfgang Zeidler and Will Zacharin

Further reading

Stephenson, W. and Rees, M. (1968) A revision of the genus *Ovalipes* Rathburn, 1898 (Crustacea, Decapoda, Portunidae). *Records of the Australian Museum* **27**(11): 213–261.
Healy, A. and Yaldwyn, J. (1970) *Australian crustaceans in colour*. Sydney: A.H. and A.W. Reed. 112 pp.
Jones, G.K., Hall, D.A., Hill, K.L. and Staniford, A.J. (1990) The South Australian marine scale fishery. Stock assessment, economics and management. *South Australian Department of Fisheries, Green paper*. 186 pp.

Scampi have been fished commercially since 1985. They are caught in demersal trawls similar to those used for prawns in the Northern Prawn Fishery. Velvet scampi and australiensis scampi dominate the scampi catch. The annual catch (mainly of velvet scampi) in the North West Slope Trawl Fishery has varied between 92 t (1987–88) and 166 t (1988–89). It is now about 50 t. Scampi are graded, packed and frozen whole on board. The product is sold on domestic and export markets.

Australiensis scampi are known only from north-western Australian waters in depths of 420 m to 500 m. Velvet scampi and Boschi's scampi are distributed from north-western Australia to Eucla in Western Australia and also inhabit waters near the Philippines. Scampi are demersal species which probably inhabit burrows and each species has a particular preference for sediment type. Females attain a slightly larger maximum size than males, to 76 mm (carapace length) for australiensis scampi, 57 mm for Boschi's scampi and 68 mm for velvet scampi.

Taxonomy — Family NEPHROPIDAE, *Metanephrops velutinus*, velvet scampi; *M. australiensis*, australiensis scampi; *M. boschmai*, Boschi's scampi

Contributors — Phil Stewart, Vicki Wadley and John Garvey

Further reading

Carter, D. (1990) Finding the right market for north west shelf products. *Australian Fisheries* **49**(6): 31–32.

Wadley, V. and Evans, D. (1991) *Crustaceans from the deepwater trawl fisheries of Western Australia*. Marmion: CSIRO Division of Fisheries. 44 pp.

Phillips, B. and Jernakoff, P. (1991) The north west slope trawl fishery. What future does it have? *Australian Fisheries* **50**(7): 18–20.

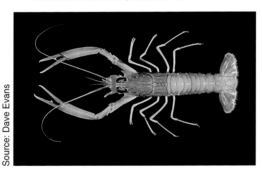

Source: Dave Evans

Shovel-nosed lobsters (including **smooth bugs, Balmain bugs** and **Wollongong bugs**)

are mostly taken as a bycatch of demersal trawling operations, although some targeting occurs in lightly fished areas. Most of the bugs marketed in New South Wales are smooth bugs, Balmain bugs and, to a lesser extent, Wollongong bugs. Smooth bugs are caught mainly at night by the New South Wales north coast prawn fleet. Balmain bugs are caught by inshore fish trawlers in New South Wales, and by Danish seiners in Victorian waters. In Victoria, most Balmain bugs are caught from March to July off East Gippsland. Wollongong bugs are caught incidentally in South Australia.

Five species of shovel-nosed lobsters are present in Australia. Balmain bugs are distributed from New South Wales to Western Australia, including Tasmania; Wollongong bugs from New South Wales to South Australia; Bruce's bugs from Queensland and New South Wales; nine-toothed bugs and hairy bugs only in Western Australia; and smooth bugs only in New South Wales. The deeper-dwelling species are rarely caught by commercial fishers.

Balmain bugs mainly inhabit water less than 80 m deep, yet have been reported to 150 m. Smooth bugs are present in depths from 50 m to 150 m. Bugs live on sand, mud or gravel substrates and are probably inactive during the day. Berried individuals of Balmain bugs have been caught in May, September and October.

Balmain bugs are known to reach 8.8 cm carapace length and 377 g weight, and smooth bugs to attain 8.0 cm carapace length and 300 g. The maximum carapace length of other shovel-nosed lobsters in Australia ranges from 5.0 cm to 7.2 cm.

The size of the resources is unknown. There has been an observed decline in the size of harvested individuals since the early 1970s. Catches are low in heavily fished prawn grounds and higher in lightly fished areas.

Taxonomy — Family SCYLLARIDAE, *Ibacus peronii*, slipper lobster, sand lobster, butterfly lobster, squagga, flapjack, shovel-nosed lobster and Balmain bug; *I. alticrenatus*, prawn killer, deepwater bug, sandy bug and Wollongong bug; *I. brucei*, Bruce's bug; *I. novemdentatus*, nine-toothed bug; *I. ciliatus pubescens*, hairy bug; and *Ibacus* species, smooth bug

Contributors — Dianne Brown and Ken Graham

Trochus

Trochus meat is of secondary importance to the shell which is used primarily for button manufacture, production of cosmetics, ceramics, luminescent paints and ornaments. Button production is mostly carried out in Japan and European countries (eg Spain, Germany, Italy).

Trochus are collected from remote reefs in Western Australia and Queensland using small dinghies which operate from mother ships. Harvesting is done by walking on the reef top at low tide (dry picking) or using mask and snorkel, or sometimes hookah in subtidal areas. Flesh is usually extracted after cooking the shell for 5–10 minutes, and may be eaten immediately, or dried or frozen for later use.

Trochus are naturally distributed between Sri Lanka, the Ryukyu Islands, New Caledonia and northern Australia and the Wallis Islands. Since the 1920s trochus have been translocated extensively — eg to the Cook Islands and French Polynesia, where important fisheries for this species now exist. Trochus inhabit coral reef habitats. They live in the intertidal and shallow subtidal areas of coral reefs, primarily just behind the reef crest in exposed reef aspects.

Trochus spawn throughout the year in warmer areas (northern Great Barrier Reef and equatorially) but only in summer at higher latitudes (southern Great Barrier Reef, New Caledonia). Spawning is linked to the lunar cycle and appears to be synchronised primarily with spring tides. Onset of maturity generally occurs at 5–6 cm basal shell diameter (age about 2 years). The maximum size attained is about 15–16 cm basal diameter and they live for 15–20 years.

Trochus resources are probably fully exploited in Australia. Poaching by Indonesian fishers is a major problem facing Australian managers.

Taxonomy — Family TROCHIDAE, *Tectus niloticus*

Contributors — Warwick Nash, Bill Anderson and Noel Moore

Further reading

Nash, W.J. (1985) Aspects of the biology of *Trochus niloticus* (Gastropoda: Trochidae) and its fishery in the Great Barrier Reef region. *Unpublished report to the Queensland Department of Primary Industries and to the Great Barrier Reef Marine Park Authority.* 210 pp.

Hyland, S. (1993) A background paper for the management of the trochus fishery in Queensland. *Queensland Department of Primary Industries, Fisheries Division.* Brisbane. 48 pp.

Turban shells

Turban shells (also called **periwinkles** or **wavy turbos**) form 1 of Tasmania's oldest fisheries as they appear to have been well represented in the diets of Tasmanian Aborigines. They are currently harvested in waters 2–20 m deep in small amounts by commercial divers collecting over subtidal reefs and platforms off the north-east and south-east coasts. Turban shells are harvested also from the intertidal zone. Catches have been stable, at around 15 t between 1988 and 1990, with reported catch rates of 20–50 kg per hour. Early attempts to export whole turban shells and meat to Asia were not profitable. Currently turban shells are being exported live to mainland markets — primarily Melbourne — or sold to local processors and restaurants. Prices are between A$ 2.00–4.00 per kg. Some processors purge animals for 2–3 days to improve texture by removing sand from the gut.

Turban shells are distributed from New South Wales south to Tasmania and west to Hopetoun in Western Australia.

The turban shell fishery is developmental, while potential markets and products are being evaluated.

Taxonomy — Family TURBINIDAE, *Turbo undulatus* [Note: the name 'periwinkle' is used for a number of gastropod mollusc species, including members of the family Littorinidae]

Contributors — Will Zacharin, Shirley Slack-Smith and Russell Reichelt

---

Venus shells

Venus shells (also called **clams** or **cockles**) are gathered for food and bait along southern coasts to Western Australia, where they are locally important (Oyster Harbour). Venus shells are collected by digging with large forks in the sandy shores of bays and estuaries, and by wading. They are sold live in the shell to local restaurants or distributors. Two species are harvested commercially. Tasmanian production is small with 15.5 t and 14 t landed in 1990 and 1991 respectively, and Western Australian production is about 10 t per year. Venus shells were selling in Tasmania for A$ 3.50 per kg in 1991.

Venus shells are bivalve molluscs, and are distributed from New South Wales to southern Western Australia, including Tasmania. They inhabit tidal flats to 5 m depth. They reach a maximum diameter of about 8 cm.

Taxonomy — Family VENERIDAE, *Katelysia scalarina* and *K. rhytiphora*

Contributors — Mike King, Will Zacharin, Lindsay Joll and Shirley Slack-Smith

---

Angel sharks are occasionally taken by demersal otter trawlers or net fishers in southern Australian waters. Their flap-like pectoral fins are often cut off and served as steaks. Landings of angel sharks in the 5 years since 1985–86 averaged 63 t a year.

Angel sharks live on or near the sea bed, and are distributed from off New South Wales to southern Western Australia, from close inshore to 256 m depth (Australian angel shark) or 128–366 m depth (ornate angel shark). Angel sharks grow to at least 1.5 m.

Taxonomy — Family SQUATINIDAE, *Squatina australis*, Australian angel shark; *S. tergocellata*, ornate angel shark

---

Blue mackerel (also called **slimy** or **slimy mackerel**) are caught commercially by small purse seines for use as both live and dead bait in domestic tuna fisheries. They are also caught with ring nets and in otter trawls in New South Wales. The main fisheries for them are in New South Wales and Tasmania: New South Wales catches ranged from 40 t to 670 t over the 25 years to 1989–90, and Tasmanian catches ranged from 0 to 1183 t in the same period. In Tasmania, blue mackerel are taken mainly as bycatch of the jack mackerel fishery.

Blue mackerel are distributed across southern Australia from southern Queensland to Western Australia, including Tasmania. They are also found through the western Pacific Ocean, Hawaii and the eastern Pacific. Juveniles and small adult fish usually inhabit inshore waters while larger adult fish form schools in 40–200 m of water over the continental shelf. Little is known of their biology. They spawn in summer; and grow to 50 cm fork length and weigh up to 2 kg.

Blue mackerel produce a good smoked product. There is potential for domestic markets for fresh chilled and processed product, for export as smoked product and for bait in tuna longline fisheries.

Taxonomy — Family SCOMBRIDAE, *Scomber australasicus*

Contributors — Grant Pullen and Albert Caton

Further reading

Stevens, J.D., Hausfeld, H.F. and Davenport, S.R. (1984) Observations on the biology, distribution and abundance of *Trachurus declivis*, *Sardinops neopilchardus* and *Scomber australasicus* in the Great Australian Bight. *CSIRO Marine Laboratories Report* **164**. 27 pp.

Blue sharks (also called **blue whalers**) are a bycatch of Japanese longline vessels fishing for tuna within the Australian Fishing

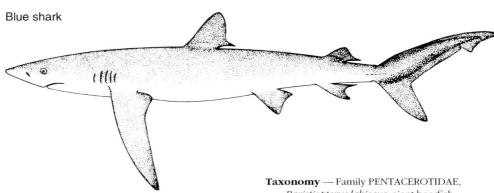

Blue shark

Zone. Highest catch rates are recorded in the southern part of the Zone. The blue shark catch off Tasmania is estimated to be about 275 t a year. The fins are the most prized parts of the sharks. Blue sharks are a common catch of gamefish anglers off south-eastern Australia: in southern New South Wales blue sharks accounted for about 20 % of the catch between 1961 and 1990.

Blue sharks are distributed circumglobally in temperate and tropical waters. They are pelagic fish, ranging from the surface to at least 150 m depth. They are mainly oceanic but occasionally move into inshore continental shelf waters, especially at night. Off New South Wales, mating occurs in October. The gestation period lasts 9–12 months. Pups are born during October and November off New South Wales, and probably between December and March off Western Australia.

Taxonomy — Family CARCHARHINIDAE, *Prionace glauca*

Contributors — John Stevens and Kevin McLoughlin; drawing courtesy FAO, Rome

Further reading

Stevens, J.D. (1989) Blue sharks — a wasted resource? *Fishing Today* **2**(5): 23–24.

Pepperell, J.G. (1992) Trends in the distribution, species composition and size of sharks caught by gamefish anglers off south-eastern Australia, 1961–90. Pp 213–225, in *Sharks: biology and fisheries*. Ed by J.G. Pepperell. *Australian Journal of Marine and Freshwater Research* **43**.

Stevens, J.D. (1992) Blue and mako shark by-catch in the Japanese longline fishery off south-eastern Australia. Pp 227–236, in *Sharks: biology and fisheries*. Ed by J.G. Pepperell. *Australian Journal of Marine and Freshwater Research* **43**.

Boarfish (also called **armourheads**, **duckfish** and **diamond fish**) are caught in demersal otter trawling and gillnet fisheries in southern Australia. The 1991 retained catch (Great Australian Bight and Western Deep-Water Trawl Fishery) was about 115 t.

Boarfish are distributed in temperate waters from north-central New South Wales to southern Western Australia. They are demersal, inhabiting the continental shelf to about 260 m (giant boarfish, yellow-spotted boarfish) and slope to 500 m. Their maximum size ranges from 33 cm (black-spotted boarfish) to 1 m (giant boarfish).

Boarfish are high quality table fish. Difficulties with marketing and processing have hindered development of this resource.

Taxonomy — Family PENTACEROTIDAE, *Paristiopterus labiosus*, giant boarfish; *P. gallipavo*, yellow-spotted boarfish; *Zanclistius elevatus*, black-spotted boarfish, long-finned boarfish; *Pentaceros decacanthus*, big-spined boarfish

Contributor — John Garvey

Further reading

Williams, A. (1990) *Commercial trawl fish from the Western and North West Slope Deepwater Trawl fisheries*. Marmion: CSIRO Division of Fisheries. 46 pp.

Butterfish (also called **driftfish** and **eyebrowfish**) were exploited by Taiwanese pair trawlers in the Arafura Sea up until 1988–89. Highest catch rates were recorded during December-February — up to 120 kg per hour. Retained catches by the Taiwanese fleet from the Arafura Sea peaked at 3373 t in 1983. Butterfish are seasonally abundant (November to April) off Cape Wessel in the Arafura Sea, and it appears that the Taiwanese fishing masters were well aware of the seasonalities of the resource in the region as they concentrated fishing effort during those seasons. Black spot butterfish comprised about 79 % of the catch and Indian eyebrowfish comprised the remainder.

There is no Australian market for butterfish, yet in South-east Asia it is held in very high esteem.

In Australia, butterfish are most abundant in offshore, continental shelf waters, 70–120 m depth. Greatest catches were taken in areas where the habitat was damaged by trawling or over flattened substrates. At the present biomass, the annual sustainable yield in the Arafura Sea is estimated to be about 3400 t a year.

Indian eyebrowfish reach about 25 cm fork length. They form shoals, and appear to be pelagic at night and demersal during the day.

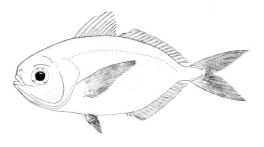

Taxonomy — Family CENTROLOPHIDAE, *Psenopsis anomala*, black-spot butterfish; Family ARIOMMATIDAE, *Ariomma indica*?, Indian eyebrowfish

Contributor — drawing courtesy FAO, Rome

Further reading

Ramm, D.C. and Xiao, Y. (in press, 1993) Demersal fisheries of northern Australia. *Proceedings of the Third Asian Fisheries Forum.*

Butterfly bream

Butterfly bream (also called **threadfin bream**) are the dominant species group in terms of catch biomass in the Arafura Sea. There is a small fishery north of Dampier in Western Australia, in which they are caught in small mesh nets and by otter trawling. However, butterfly bream are primarily caught by foreign fishing fleets working off northern and north-western Australia. They are exported to Asian markets as whole fish and very little is sold in Australia. Small quantities appear in local Darwin and Perth markets.

Source: Anne Coleman

Butterfly bream are tropical fish distributed in northern Australian coastal and offshore waters in depths of 20–200 m. They are demersal in habit, occurring over mud or sand substrates to about 100 m. Males are larger than females, and these fish may be sequential hermaphrodites. The largest species in Australian waters attains about 27 cm standard length.

Butterfly bream are dominant on the North West Shelf, Taiwanese pair trawlers catching up to 3950 t per year during the foreign trawling period 1973–91. On the North West Shelf, butterfly bream accounted for up to 21 % of the total catch by weight; and in the Arafura Sea they comprised 7–10 % of the total catch. In the period 1974 to 1986, an average of 3222 t of butterfly bream was retained from northern Australian waters.

At present biomass estimates, butterfly bream would sustain a 10 000 t a year fishery in the Arafura Sea and North West Shelf. Properly prepared, they are a good quality fish but they are soft-bodied and easily damaged in transport.

Taxonomy — Family NEMIPTERIDAE, *Nemipterus furcosus*, rosy threadfin bream; *N. peronii*, notched threadfin bream; *N. hexodon*, ornate threadfin bream

Contributors — Mike Moran, Barry Russell and Wade Whitelaw

Further reading

Sainsbury, K.J. and Whitelaw, W. (1984) Biology of Peron's threadfin bream, *Nemipterus peronii* (Valenciennes) from the North West Shelf of Australia. *Australian Journal of Marine and Freshwater Research* **35**: 167–185.

Russell, B.C. (1990) FAO species catalogue. Vol. 12. Nemipterid fishes of the world (threadfin breams, whiptail breams, monocle breams, dwarf monocle breams, and coral breams). Family Nemipteridae *FAO Fisheries Synopsis No. 125*, **12**. 149 pp.

Dogfish

Dogfish (also called **spurdogs**) are taken as part of southern mixed species fisheries. They are an important component of the continental slope fishery outside of the gemfish, mirror dory and blue grenadier season. Dogfish liver may be processed into squalene which is used by the vitamin and cosmetics industries. The oil from livers of deepwater dogfish commonly comprises 50–70 % squalene. Dogfish are a potential source of other products including fishmeal and corneas.

Several species of dogfish are caught commercially off southern Australia. They generally are caught by otter trawlers although some are caught with droplines and longlines (in deeper water) and gillnets (inshore waters). Occasionally they form a large part of the bycatch in the orange roughy fishery.

Most dogfish species inhabit depths between 50 m and 900 m. Dogfish can reach 1.5 m in total length. They are ovoviviparous and bear 1–9 young (up to 20 in white-spotted dogfish) each litter.

There is a significant Australian resource of dogfish which could become increasingly important with marketing promotion, although some problems with heavy metal residues may occur in deepwater species. Reported catches in 1988–89 totalled 257 t.

Taxonomy — Family SQUALIDAE, including *Centrophorus harrissoni*, dumb dogfish; *C. scalpratus*, endeavour dogfish; *C. uyato*, southern dogfish; *Squalus acanthias*, white-spotted dogfish; *S. megalops*, spiked dogfish; *S. mitsukurii*, green-eyed dogfish; *Centroscymnus* species, velvet dogfish; *Etmopterus* species, lantern sharks; and *Dalatias* species, seal sharks

Contributors — Ken Graham, Peter Last, Stephanie Davenport and Kevin McLoughlin

Further Reading

Davenport, S. and Deprez, P. (1989) Market opportunities for shark liver oil. *Australian Fisheries* **48**(11): 8–10.

Dolphinfish

Dolphinfish (also called **mahi-mahi**) are caught by trolling, using either bait or lures. Mariculture of dolphinfish was being investigated in Western Australia as there is potential for increased domestic consumption of this species, as well as export markets.

Dolphinfish provide excellent eating and are highly regarded as sport fish.

Dolphinfish are tropical fish widely distributed in the Indo-west Pacific Ocean, and in Australian waters they are present from the Recherche Archipelago in Western Australia to Montague Island in New South Wales. They are schooling, generally pelagic fish found in deeper, offshore waters, often associating with fish attraction devices (FADs). They grow to about 2 m in length.

Taxonomy — Family CORYPHAENIDAE, *Coryphaena hippurus*

Further reading

Nel, S. (1990) Mahimahi mariculture. *Infofish International*, March 1990: 32–34.

Elephant fish

Elephant fish are taken as a bycatch of the Southern Shark Fishery and the South East Fishery. They are caught with large meshed monofilament gillnets, demersal trawls, Danish seines and occasionally with hooks, mostly in Bass Strait but also on the continental shelf around southern Australia. The catch is sold and processed at the Melbourne Fish Market and marketed as 'white fillets' or 'flake' in the fish-and-chips trade. The livers are also sold for liver oil and processed as squalene.

Elephant fish are particularly abundant in shallow bays and large estuaries but are also commonly found at 100 m on the continental shelf in temperate, southern Australian waters. They have been recorded at a depth of 1000 m in western Bass Strait. Adults aggregate on the continental shelf in February to spawn. The eggs are deposited in shallow water from the surf line to 50 m in sand or mud, frequently near river mouths and estuaries. Juveniles remain in shallow coastal waters at first but gradually move into deeper water up to 100 m before they mature. Males do not grow much bigger than 79 cm (2.5 kg) while females just reach maturity at 70 cm and grow to at least 102 cm and 7.2 kg and possibly to 110 cm (9 kg).

The 1991 catch of elephant fish from the Southern Shark Fishery was 51 t. The trawl and Danish seine bycatch of elephant fish is not known as it is either discarded or not recorded by species. An estimated total landed

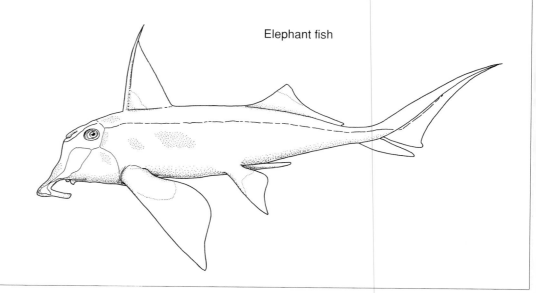

Elephant fish

catch of approximately 100 t had a wholesale value of A$ 160 000 in 1992. Very little is known about the biomass, growth and dynamics of elephant fish populations, although their declining catch rate from gillnets suggests that the stocks may be fully to over exploited.

Taxonomy — Family CALLORHINCHIDAE, *Callorhinchus milii*

Contributors — Patrick Coutin and Terry Walker; drawing by Rosalind Poole

Further reading

Walker, T.I., Moulton, P.L. Dow, N.G. and Saddlier, S.R. (1989) Reproduction studies of four species of shark and one species of elephant fish commercially fished in southern Australian waters. 88 pp, in *Southern shark assessment project, Final FIRTA Report, Part B. Department of Conservation, Forests and Lands, Fisheries Division, Internal Report* **175b**.

Flat-tail mullet (also called **jumping mullet** or **tiger mullet**)

Flat-tail mullet (also called **jumping mullet** or **tiger mullet**) are mainly taken as a bycatch by fishers targeting yellow-eye mullet or bream. They are caught in seine nets and gillnets. Catches in New South Wales over the 25 years to 1989–90 peaked at about 360 t in 1967–68 and 1976–77 and are now around 100 t a year.

Flat-tail mullet are distributed in estuarine waters around most of the Australian mainland, and they are most abundant in New South Wales and Queensland. They inhabit tidal creeks and estuaries; and schools travel considerable distances along shorelines. Flat-tail mullet spawn between December and June when freshwater run-off occurs or when water temperatures are raised. These fish grow to about 45 cm total length.

There is potential for export of flat-tail mullet roe but it is of lower quality than sea mullet roe.

Taxonomy — Family MUGILIDAE, *Liza argentea*

Contributors — Keith Jones and Vince McDonall

Further reading

State Pollution Control Commission (1981) *The ecology of fish in Botany Bay — biology of commercially and recreationally valuable species. Environmental control study of Botany Bay.* Sydney. 287 pp.

Fork-tailed catfish

Fork-tailed catfish are taken by commercial fishers mainly in river systems; either by gillnets, handline or trapping. They are also an incidental catch of demersal otter trawlers in northern Australia.

Fork-tailed catfish inhabit tropical fresh and marine waters. In Australia, 4 of the 18 species are harvested commercially. Giant salmon catfish are marine and are trawled to 150 m depth. Lake Argyle silver cobbler is the basis of a small gillnet fishery in Lake Argyle, Ord River system, Western Australia. Silver cobbler are sold in Perth and Darwin markets, attracting prices up to A$ 14.00 per kg for fillets in recent years. Properly processed fish are good eating.

Fork-tailed catfish attain 1.3 m fork length. Silver cobbler have been recorded to 28 kg. These catfish have a low fecundity and large (to 1.5 cm diameter) eggs. The eggs and larvae

are incubated by the male parent for up to 6 weeks. The low fecundity and habit of inshore and/or spawning aggregations makes fork-tailed catfish susceptible to over-exploitation. There is good potential for aquaculture of the freshwater and estuarine species.

Taxonomy — Family ARIIDAE, *Arius thalassinus*, giant salmon catfish; *A. midgleyi*, Lake Argyle silver cobbler; *A. leptaspis*, golden cobbler; *Arius* species, yellow-mouth catfish

Contributors — Patricia Kailola and Barry Russell

Further reading

Kailola, P.J. and Pierce, B.E. (1989) Potential for culturing Australian fork-tailed catfishes. Pp 38–46, in *Advances in aquaculture. Proceedings of the Australian Society for Fish Biology workshop, 15 August 1986, Darwin.* Ed by R.R. Pyne. *Northern Territory Department of Primary Industry and Fisheries, Technical Report* **3**.

Goatfish (called red mullet in southern Australia)

Goatfish (called **red mullet** in southern Australia) are caught in demersal otter trawl fisheries in northern Australia and they formed a fair proportion of the catch of Taiwanese trawlers (up to 900 t, 1981–82) in northern Australia. In southern Australia, goatfish are caught as bycatch in inshore seine net fisheries. There is a limited high value market for domestic consumption of larger fish. The smaller red mullet are popular with South Australian consumers, where about 5 t are landed each year.

Goatfish are demersal fish and use their barbels to search for food. They reach maximum sizes of 35–50 cm fork length.

Taxonomy — Family MULLIDAE, mainly *Parupeneus* species; *Upeneichthys* species, red mullet, barbounia

Contributor — Wade Whitelaw

Greenback flounder

Greenback flounder are caught commercially mainly in coastal waters of eastern Victoria and the Coorong in South Australia. They are harvested with bottom set gillnets, seine nets and by spearing, and incidental catches in Tasmanian and Victorian waters are made in otter trawls and Danish seines. The harvest has declined to about 50 t a year in both Victorian and South Australian fisheries, and about 40 t in Tasmania. In Port Phillip Bay, 65 % of the catch is taken during summer, and Coorong catches either remain stable throughout the year or are highest in February-April.

Greenback flounder are a common temperate species distributed in estuaries, marine embayments and inshore coastal waters of New South Wales, Victoria, Tasmania, South Australia and eastern Western Australia. They are found over silty sand substrates and have a wide temperature and salinity tolerance, with juveniles occasionally penetrating upstream into freshwater and adults distributed to depths of 100 m. Flounder feed with the rising tide at night on shallow mud banks. Their offshore spawning coincides with a protracted period of cold water temperatures between June and October and larval abundance is greatest

between June and August. Fish are 19–30 cm long at maturity. Greenback flounder reach a maximum size of about 40 cm (0.6 kg) at 3–4 years of age.

Very little is known about the biomass, growth and dynamics of greenback flounder populations. Aquaculture of the species is being investigated. An export market for live fish has been opened up recently with large fish (at least 500 g) commanding a higher price.

Taxonomy — Family PLEURONECTIDAE, *Rhombosolea tapirina*

Contributors — Patrick Coutin, Dave Hall, Piers Hart, Keith Jones and Murray MacDonald

Further reading

Crawford, C.M. (1986) Development of eggs and larvae of the flounders *Rhombosolea tapirina* and *Ammotretis rostratus* (Pisces: Pleuronectidae) *Journal of Fish Biology* **29**: 325–334.

Jenkins, G.P. (1987) Comparative diets, prey selection, and predatory impact of co-occurring larvae of two flounder species. *Journal of Experimental Marine Biology and Ecology* **110**: 147–170.

Hall, D.A. (1984) The Coorong: biology of the major fish species and fluctuations in catch rates 1976-1984. *SAFIC* **8**(1): 3–17.

Lizardfish

Lizardfish are a bycatch in the Northern Prawn Fishery, with an estimated 3650 t caught each year. Prior to 1989, up to 1200 t a year were retained by Thai and Taiwanese demersal fish trawlers from the North West Shelf, Timor and Arafura seas. Retained catch rates up to 60 kg per hour were achieved on the North West Shelf and Timor Sea. The catch consisted mainly of short-finned lizardfish and checkered lizardfish, from depths of 11 m to 120 m. Most lizardfish are trashed, although there is a market in Taiwan for checkered lizardfish (a very low grade but prolific species) which is dried and stored onboard.

Lizardfish are distributed across northern Australia, and their populations have increased in size as a result of seabed modification by heavy trawling.

There are potential uses for lizardfish as pet food, feed for marine park and zoo animals, and bait for the commercial rock lobster industry.

Taxonomy — Family SYNODONTIDAE, *Saurida undosquamis*, checkered lizardfish; *S. micropectoralis*, short-finned lizardfish

Contributors — Graham Baulch, Wade Whitelaw and Bill Anderson

Further reading

Pender, P.J., Willing, R.S. and Ramm, D.C. (1992) Bycatch from the NPF mixed species fishery. *Northern Territory Department of Primary Industry and Fisheries, Fisheries Report* **26**. 70 pp.

Source: Glen Smith

Thresher, R.E., Sainsbury, K.J., Gunn, J.S. and Whitelaw A.W. (1986) Life history strategies and recent changes in population structure in the lizardfish genus, *Saurida*, on the Australian Northwest shelf. *Copeia (1986)* **4**: 876–885.

Ramm, D.C. and Xiao, Y. (in press, 1993) Demersal fisheries of northern Australia. *Proceedings of the Third Asian Fisheries Forum.*

Longtail tuna (also called **northern bluefin**)

were caught by Taiwanese gillnetters in northern Australia between 1978 and 1986. Catches were between 750 t and 6000 t a year, peaking in 1977. The fishery was stopped in mid 1986 because of unacceptably high levels of dolphin bycatch.

Longtail tuna are also taken by trolling and as an incidental handline catch by prawn trawlers in Shark Bay, the Gulf of Carpentaria and Moreton Bay. Small amounts are taken by beach seining in northern New South Wales. Catches range from 10 t to 130 t a year. Longtail tuna are popular with recreational fishers on the east coast.

Longtail tuna are distributed across northern Australia from Cockburn Sound, Western Australia to Twofold Bay, New South Wales. They also occur throughout the Indo-west Pacific Ocean. Longtail tuna are a neritic species that appear to make a north-south migration following southern intrusions of warm water. Spawning occurs in summer and they first spawn at 60–70 cm fork length. The maximum size is unknown, however fish 136 cm long, weighing 30 kg have been recorded from southern Queensland.

Longtail tuna are usually eaten fresh or smoked and are used for canning. The size of the Taiwanese catches indicates that the stock may be considerable, although it is under-exploited.

Taxonomy — Family SCOMBRIDAE, *Thunnus tonggol*

Contributor — Marc Wilson

Further reading

Lyle, J.M. and Read, A.D. (1985) Tuna in northern Australian waters: a preliminary appraisal. *Northern Territory Department of Ports and Fisheries, Fisheries Report* **14**. 41 pp.

Wilson, M.A. (1981) Some aspects of the biology and production of longtail tuna in Oceania. Pp 24–34, in *Northern pelagic fish seminar, Darwin, Northern Territory, 20–21 January, 1981.* Ed by C.J. Grant and D.G. Walter. Canberra: Australian Government Publishing Service.

Marine aquarium fish

are collected commercially mainly from the Great Barrier Reef and Western Australian reefs. The collectors are licensed. The most common method used is for divers with SCUBA or hookah breathing systems to trap fish using hand-nets in conjunction with barrier nets.

Australian marine aquarium species are currently exploited at low levels, mostly for the domestic market. Only small numbers of Australian species are exported. Most marine aquarium fish sold in Australia are imported, 80 % of them from the Philippines.

Taxonomy — numerous families, but predominantly CHAETODONTIDAE, coralfish; LABRIDAE, wrasse; and POMACANTHIDAE, angelfish or boarfish.

Further reading

Kailola, P.J. (1985) *The marine aquarium fish industry in Australia, with an appraisal of the criteria associated with the import of fishes, a taxonomic review of the list of fishes currently imported, associated amendments and recommendations for the future trade in marine aquarium fish in this country.* Report for the Australian National Parks and Wildlife Service, Canberra.

Whitehead, M., Gilmore, J., Eager, E., McGinnity, P., Craik, W. and Macleod, P. (1986) Aquarium fishes and their collection in the Great Barrier Reef region. *Great Barrier Reef Marine Park Authority Technical Memorandum* **GBRMPA-TM-13**. 39 pp.

Perth herring

were previously caught in Western Australia to provide bait for the western rock lobster fishery. Gillnets and seine nets were the primary fishing methods. Landings were 50–150 t per year and 35 % of the State's total catch was taken in the Swan estuary. Perth herring are no longer fished commercially.

Perth herring are endemic to Western Australia, distributed from Bunbury to Broome. They inhabit inshore marine and estuarine environments and are particularly abundant in the Swan and Peel-Harvey river estuaries. Between November and February, Perth herring migrate from inshore marine waters to spawn in the upper reaches of estuaries. Perth herring live for up to 8 years, reaching a maximum size of 36 cm standard length.

Taxonomy — Family CLUPEIDAE, *Nematalosa vlaminghi*

Contributor — Franco Neira

Further reading

Chubb, C.F. and Potter, I.C. (1986) Age, growth and condition of the Perth herring, *Nematalosa vlaminghi* (Munro) (Dorosomatinae) in the Swan Estuary, south-western Australia. *Australian Journal of Marine and Freshwater Research* **37**: 105–112.

Chubb, C.F., Hall, N.G., Lenanton, R.C.J. and Potter, I.C. (1984) The fishery for Perth herring, *Nematalosa vlaminghi* (Munro). *Department of Fisheries and Wildlife, Western Australia, Report* **66**. 17 pp.

Purple stargazers (also called **scaled stargazers** or **monkfish**)

are taken in commercial quantities in the Great Australian Bight and off Tasmania. They are a bycatch of deepwater trawling operations, and are marketed either as whole fish or fillets. They have been taken in large quantities (42 kg per hour mean catch rate; nearly 140 kg per hour maximum) in the Great Australian Bight. The 1988–89 landing was 36 t.

Purple stargazers inhabit southern Australian waters in the 400–900 m depth range. They attain 70 cm total length and can weigh at least 8 kg.

Taxonomy — Family URANOSCOPIDAE, *Pleuroscopus pseudodorsalis*

Queen snapper (also called **blue morwong**)

are taken as a bycatch in shark gillnet fisheries and demersal trawl fisheries. They are a major bycatch component of the Southwest Shark Fishery in Western Australia, with about 50 t landed each year.

Queen snapper are distributed from western Victoria to southern Western Australia. They are demersal fish, found from inshore reefs to offshore at depths of 40 m to 240 m. They can grow to 90 cm length.

Taxonomy — Family CHEILODACTYLIDAE, *Nemadactylus valenciennesi*

Redbait

are taken as bycatch in jack mackerel purse seine fisheries or are targeted when they occur in independent schools. They are caught off the east coast of Tasmania, where catches peaked at 1090 t in 1986–87 and 1280 t in 1987–88. Redbait are a potentially good bait in longline fisheries, though presently they are turned mainly into fishmeal. There is potential for development of the redbait fishery.

Redbait are distributed off southern Australia from New South Wales to South Australia, including Tasmanian waters. They also occur in southern African and New Zealand waters. They form surface or midwater schools over the continental shelf. Spawning takes place between October and January in Tasmanian waters. Redbait mature at about 21 cm fork length and grow to about 36 cm in length.

Taxonomy — Family EMMELICHTHYIDAE, *Emmelichthys nitidus*

Contributors — Grant Pullen and Howel Williams

Further reading

Williams, H., Pullen, G., Kucerans, G. and Waterworth, C. (1987) The jack mackerel purse seine fishery in Tasmania, 1986–87. *Tasmanian Department of Sea Fisheries, Technical Report* **19**. 32 pp.

Source: Neil Klaer

Redfin perch

are the basis of a small commercial fishery in western Victoria and South Australia. In South Australia most of the redfin catch comes from the lakes fishery (lakes Alexandrina and Albert). A popular angling species, redfin perch are also good to eat.

Redfin perch were first introduced from Europe into Tasmania in 1862. They were introduced into Victoria in 1868, and this introduction is thought to be the source of all redfin in mainland Australia. Redfin perch are widespread in cooler waters across south-eastern Australia, including southern New South Wales, Victoria, South Australia and Tasmania. They inhabit still and slowly flowing waters, especially amongst aquatic vegetation.

Redfin perch spawn in spring, with eggs dispersed amongst aquatic weeds or submerged logs. They are mature in their first year. Their maximum size is 60 cm total length and 10.4 kg.

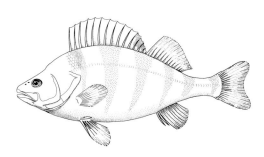

Taxonomy — Family PERCIDAE, *Perca fluviatilis*

Contributor — drawing by Rosalind Poole

Further reading

McDowall, R.M. (1980) Family Percidae. Freshwater perches. Pp 158–159, in *Freshwater fishes of south-eastern Australia*, ed by R.M. McDowall. Sydney: A.H. & A.W. Reed Pty Ltd.

Red gurnards and **latchets** are bycatch species from demersal trawling off central and southern New South Wales, Victoria and Tasmania although latchet are occasionally targeted. They are also caught with Danish seines, longlines and gillnets. Catches of up to 160 t of red gurnard and more than 120 t of latchet have been taken in New South Wales and Victoria but catches have declined since 1985. New South Wales catches for 1989–90 were 51 t of red gurnard catch and 54 t of latchet. Between 50 t and 100 t of red gurnard and latchet are taken in the South East Fishery, mainly in summer.

Red gurnards are distributed from Moreton Bay in Queensland to Shark Bay in Western Australia, including Tasmania. They are also found in New Zealand, South Africa, Japan and China. They mostly inhabit shallow coastal waters over sandy substrates, but have been reported from shelf waters to 180 m depth. Spawning appears to take place in summer and larvae are found off eastern Tasmania in late January. Juveniles inhabit inshore nursery areas. Both males and females are mature at 20–24 cm fork length, when they are 2–3 years old. Red gurnards live for over 10 years, growing to 60 cm length and about 3 kg.

Latchet are distributed from about Port Stephens, New South Wales to Perth in Western Australia, including Tasmania. They also occur off northern New Zealand. Latchet inhabit mid to outer continental shelf waters at depths of 20–220 m. Spawning occurs in July-August in New South Wales waters, latchet first spawning when about 45 cm length. Juveniles enter bays and estuaries in

autumn. Latchet can attain 62 cm fork length and 2.6 kg.

Red gurnard and latchet are sold whole chilled on domestic markets. Their resources are limited, yet there is potential for export as fresh or chilled product.

Taxonomy — Family TRIGLIDAE, *Chelidonichthys kumu*, red gurnard; *Pterygotrigla polyommata*, latchet

Contributors — Ken Graham, Wes Ford and Martin Gomon

Further reading

Lyle, J.M. and Ford, W.B. (in press, 1992) Trawl research surveys (1979–87) with summaries of biological information for fourteen species of finfish. *Tasmanian Department of Primary Industry and Fisheries, Technical Report*.

Elder, R.D. (1976) Studies on age and growth, reproduction, and population dynamics of red gurnard, *Chelidonichthys kumu* (Lesson and Garnot) in the Hauraki Gulf, New Zealand. *New Zealand Fisheries Research Bulletin* **12**: 1–70.

Sandy sprat (also called **white pilchard, glassy** or **whitebait**) are normally caught by beach seine methods in estuaries, bays, inlets and from ocean beaches, although purse seines are occasionally used. The main fishery for them is in Western Australia, centred on the Fremantle to Bunbury area. In the Bunbury fishery most of the catch is taken from November to March when the prevailing weather conditions are most favourable. This captures 100–180 t per year. The value is A$ 1.50 per kg for sprat to be used as bait, and up to A$ 3.50 for their sale to restaurants. From 1975–76 to 1989–90 the Western Australian catch ranged from 61 t to 240 t. The 1991 catch was 178 t. Fish are sold fresh or frozen. After the sandy sprat season, fishers tend to target Australian salmon.

Small fisheries for sandy sprat exist in New South Wales and Victoria: up to 30 t a year through the Sydney Fish Market, and up to 118 t a year through the Melbourne Wholesale Fish Market. In Victoria most of the sandy sprat is caught in Port Phillip Bay in purse seines.

Spandy sprat are distributed from southern Queensland to Kalbarri, Western Australia. They form large schools in estuary mouths and coastal bays. Juveniles are found in estuaries and bays while adults are found in inshore and offshore regions. Very little is known of their life history. Sandy sprat have a protracted spawning season, peaking in late winter to early spring. Spawning occurs outside of the estuaries. The maximum size is 13 cm total length and the maximum age is probably 2 years.

Taxonomy — Family CLUPEIDAE, *Hyperlophus vittatus*

Contributor — Rick Fletcher

Further reading

Parry, G.D., Campbell, S.J. and Hobday, D.K. (1990) Marine resources off east Gippsland, southeastern Australia. *Department of Conservation and Environment, Fisheries Division, Technical Report* **72**. 166 pp.

Saw sharks are caught as a bycatch of the Southern Shark Fishery and the South East Fishery. Saw sharks are caught with large meshed monofilament gillnets, demersal trawls and Danish seines mostly in Bass Strait, but also in the Great Australian Bight. The annual catch of saw sharks from the Southern Shark Fishery was 180 t in 1991, while the trawl and Danish seine bycatch of saw sharks was about 50 t. The catch is sold and processed in Melbourne and marketed as 'flake' to retailers in the 'fish-and-chips' trade. Saw shark flesh is of high quality and the 1992 Melbourne market price was A$ 3.50 per kg.

Two species are caught — southern saw shark and common saw shark. Saw sharks are common temperate and subtropical species inhabiting continental shelf and upper slope waters off southern Queensland (southern saw shark), New South Wales, Victoria, Tasmania, South Australia and Western Australia. They are found at all depths from the shore to about 300 m but are most abundant between 40 m and 150 m. Gestation and embryo development take place between October and January. The average number of young produced is 9–10 per female. Female saw sharks mature at 90–115 cm total length and males at 80–100 cm. Saw sharks grow to at least 1.5 m long.

Very little is known about the growth and dynamics of saw shark populations. The declining saw shark catch from gillnets suggests that the stocks may by fully to over-exploited.

Taxonomy — Family PRISTIOPHORIDAE, *Pristiophorus nudipinnis*, southern saw shark; *Pristiophorus cirratus*, common saw shark

Contributors — Patrick Coutin, Ken Graham, Peter Last, Terry Walker

Further reading

Coleman, N. and Mobley, M. (1984) Diets of commercially exploited fish from Bass Strait and adjacent Victorian waters, South-eastern Australia. *Australian Journal of Marine and Freshwater Research* **35**: 549–560.

Walker, T.I., Moulton, P.L., Dow, N.G. and Saddlier, S.R. (1989) Reproduction studies of four species of shark and one species of elephant fish commercially fished in southern Australian waters. 88 pp, in *Southern shark assessment project, Final FIRTA Report, part B. Department of Conservation, Forests and Lands, Fisheries Division, Internal Report* **175b**.

Scaly mackerel form part of the catch of the Fremantle purse seine fishery. The catch varies from 100 t to 1000 t per year. Only 100 t was taken in 1991. There is also a developing purse seine fishery off Geraldton where 100 t was caught in 1991. Scaly mackerel are used for rock lobster bait.

Scaly mackerel are distributed off the Western Australian coast from Fremantle to Broome. They are also abundant in Indonesia. Little is known on the life history of scaly mackerel. They probably spawn in summer; and maximum size is about 24 cm fork length.

The status of the scaly mackerel stock in Western Australia is being investigated. The catch in the Geraldton area will probably increase to 1000 t.

Taxonomy — Family CLUPEIDAE, *Sardinella lemuru*

Contributor — Rick Fletcher

Silver biddies (also called **roach**) are marketed in Sydney and Perth. The largest quantities are from New South Wales waters — 100–176 t a year over the 10 years to 1990.

Silver biddies are caught with beach seines in inshore waters. They are small, silvery fish reaching about 23 cm total length. They are distributed in temperate waters between central New South Wales and southern Western Australia. Other species inhabit tropical waters.

Taxonomy — Family GERREIDAE, *Gerres subfasciatus*

Skates are a low value bycatch group taken in trawl fisheries throughout their distribution. Their flaps are eaten.

Skates are most abundant on the continental shelf and upper slope of temperate Australia, and on the continental slope in the tropics. There are over 40 species of edible skates. Skates reach a range of sizes, from 36 cm to 2 m total length. Spawning is probably continuous.

Skates are a highly under-utilised resource and there is good potential for a developing fishery.

Taxonomy — Family RAJIIDAE, *Raja* species

Contributor — Peter Last

Snook (also called **short-finned seapike**) are taken as bycatch in the inshore fisheries targeting King George whiting, garfish and calamary in the north of Gulf St Vincent and Spencer Gulf, South Australia. They are caught with seine nets and also set gillnets, mainly between April and August. There is also a troll fishery for snook off the west coast of South Australia and in the southern waters of both gulfs. The South Australian snook fishery landed 100 t in 1991–92. Small catches of snook are also taken in Victoria, Tasmania and Western Australia. Snook are a high quality table fish.

Snook are distributed in temperate waters from southern Queensland to southern Western Australia. The exact distribution is uncertain. Snook are also found off South Africa and New Zealand. They are highly migratory pelagic fish that occur in shoals of 50 or more individuals.

Spawning probably takes place from October to January. The largest fish landed in Australia was 109 cm long, weighing 5.6 kg. Growth studies on South Australian fish have estimated the maximum age at about 20 years.

Snook appear to be under-utilised. The potential of this fishery is unknown.

Taxonomy — Family SPHYRAENIDAE, *Sphyraena novaehollandiae*

Contributor — Malcolm Bertoni

Further reading

Blaber, S.J.M. (1982) The ecology of *Sphyraena barracuda* (Osteichthyes: Perciformes) in the Kosi system with notes on the Sphyraenidae of other Natal estuaries. *South African Journal of Zoology* **17**: 171–176.

Bertoni, M. (1992) Snook fishery review (*Sphyraena novaehollandiae*): present fishery review and future research requirements. *SAFISH* **16**(4): 4–7.

Southern frostfish are taken in small amounts (10–36 t a year) as bycatch in the South East Fishery and Great Australian Bight Trawl Fishery. Significant catches are also taken by trawling off New South Wales and eastern Bass Strait in winter as a bycatch of gemfish fishing. Most frostfish are discarded at sea because of poor market acceptability; however between 50 t and 100 t are marketed through the Sydney Fish Market each year (average price less than A$ 1.00 a kg).

Southern frostfish are distributed in temperate waters from New South Wales to Western Australia, at depths of 300–600 m on the continental slope. They are also distributed through the north-west Atlantic, Mediterranean, southern Indian and Pacific oceans. Southern frostfish off New South Wales spawn in winter at depths of 300–500 m. Frostfish attain a maximum length in excess of 2 m, and weight of 3–4 kg. Nothing is known of age at maturity or maximum ages.

There is no biological data available to assess the status of southern frostfish. The species is considered to be under-utilised, but exploitation level and yield estimate have not been derived. There is significant potential for a hook and line fishery for them since exports of trawl fish meet resistance due to poor condition. There is already significant domestic and export potential for a handline fishery for hairtail (*Trichiurus lepturus*), a related tropical inshore species.

Taxonomy — Family TRICHIURIDAE, *Lepidopus caudatus*

Contributor — Kevin Rowling

Sweetlips are caught in the northern trawl, dropline and trap fisheries. They are sensitive to trawling, but there is a possibility for the development of a trap fishery. Sweetlips are a limited volume, low value species with limited foreign and domestic markets.

Sweetlips inhabit tropical Australian and Indo-Pacific waters in the depth range 10–120 m. They attain a maximum length of 60 cm.

Source: Kevin McLoughlin

Taxonomy — Family HAEMULIDAE, *Diagramma pictum*, *Plectorhinchus* species

Contributors — Wade Whitelaw and Bill Anderson

Tarwhine commonly form schools in coastal waters of eastern and western Australia. They are distributed from Queensland to the Gippsland Lakes in Victoria and from Albany to Coral Bay in Western Australia. They are occasionally taken as bycatch with yellowfin bream and black bream. About 35 t are recorded each year, mainly from New South Wales waters. Tarwhine grow to about 80 cm long.

Taxonomy — Family SPARIDAE, *Rhabdosargus sarba*

Teraglin are highly rated table fish with fine eating qualities. They are sought after by recreational fishers, and are also taken by commercial handline fishers and occasionally by trap fishers in northern New South Wales. Annual catches have historically been moderate (at least 120 t) but in recent years catches have declined (35 t in 1989–90).

Teraglin are distributed off the east coast of Australia in coastal waters from Brisbane to Montague Island. Juvenile fish are found in inshore waters, including deeper estuaries, while the largest schools of adult fish are found at depths of 20–80 m over gravel or broken reef substrates. They stay close to the sea bed during the day and rise to mid-water or the surface to feed during the night. Teraglin can be found in southern waters during summer, moving north during winter.

Teraglin can grow to around 1 m in length and weigh nearly 20 kg.

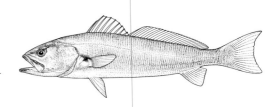

Taxonomy — Family SCIAENIDAE, *Atractoscion aequidens*

Contributors — Vince McDonall and Kevin Rowling; drawing by Gavin Ryan

Tropical trevallies are caught year-round by commercial fishers in Western Australia, the Northern Territory and Queensland, mainly as bycatch in demersal trawl and gillnet fisheries. They are generally discarded, although it is estimated that at least 2000 t are caught each year. A number of species are caught.

Adult trevallies are found throughout northern Australian waters, from Exmouth Gulf to Brisbane. Juveniles are occasionally found as far south as Perth and Sydney. Tropical trevallies spawn in spring and summer.

Taxonomy — Family CARANGIDAE, mainly *Carangoides* species, *Caranx* species and *Scomberoides* species

Contributor — John Gunn

Trumpeter are mainly caught in Tasmania, South Australia and Victoria. Stripey trumpeter are caught on droplines while bastard trumpeter are caught with gillnets. The 1991 Tasmanian combined catch was 718 t.

Stripey trumpeter are distributed from Sydney to Kangaroo Island in South Australia, as well as Tasmania. They are found also in New Zealand and South American waters. Stripey trumpeter from the west coast of Tasmania spawn from late winter to early spring. Stripey trumpeter grow to at least 1.2 m total length and 25 kg.

Bastard trumpeter are distributed from Montague Island, New South Wales, to Albany, Western Australia, as well as Tasmania. They also inhabit New Zealand inshore waters.

Bastard trumpeter spawn in late winter. They grow to 65 cm total length and 4.3 kg, and live for approximately 30 years.

Trumpeter are a potential resource, although stocks of both species are susceptible to overfishing. There is also significant pressure on the resource from recreational fishing. Stripey trumpeter are 1 of the best table fish caught in southern Australia. They have potential for aquaculture and trials are being carried out in Tasmania.

Taxonomy — Family LATRIDAE, *Latris lineata*, stripey trumpeter or Tasmanian trumpeter; *Latridopsis forsteri*, bastard trumpeter

Contributors — Dianne Furlani and Peter Last

Whiptails are a bycatch of deepwater trawling in southern Australian waters. More than 2000 t were reported in 1988–89. Most of the catch is discarded, although whiptails are used successfully as bait in tuna longline fisheries.

Taxonomy — Family MACROURIDAE, several species

Whitebait commercial fishing in Tasmania began in the early 1930s with significant catches obtained in the early 1940s (515 t in 1947). Catches declined however, such that the fishery was closed in 1974. Trial fishing in recent years has indicated a modest stock recovery. If stocks recover sufficiently, they could support controlled recreational and commercial fishing. Illegal fishing for whitebait remains a major problem, with fishers receiving A$ 15.00–20.00 per kg.

Whitebait are caught with scoop nets and 'fyke' nets (known locally as 'D' nets). They are eaten whole.

Whitebait inhabit coastal waters and rivers of Tasmania. Adult fish are caught in large runs as they move into estuaries to spawn.

Females lay a few hundred eggs and die soon after spawning. Whitebait attain 77 mm total length.

Juveniles of small native trout also comprise part of the whitebait run.

Source:Mick Olsen

Taxonomy — Family APLOCHITONIDAE, *Lovettia sealei*; Family GALAXIIDAE, *Galaxias* species, native trout

Contributors — Wayne Fulton and Richard Tilzey

Further reading

Fulton, W. and Pavuk, N. (1988) The Tasmanian whitebait fishery. Summary of present knowledge and outline of future management plans. *Inland Fisheries Commission Occasional Report* **88–01**. 27 pp.

McDowall, R.M. (1980) Family Aplochitonidae, Tasmanian Whitebait. Pp 70–71, in *Freshwater fishes of South-eastern Australia*, ed by R.M. McDowall. Sydney: A.H. & A.W. Reed Pty Ltd.

Yank flathead (also called **southern blue-spotted flathead**) are generally caught as bycatch of other commercial fishing operations. For example, in Western Australia they are caught in the gillnet fishery for cobbler, and are occasionally taken by scallop trawlers operating off the south-west coast. Yank flathead are taken also in trawls in the Great Australian Bight and off south-eastern Australia. Yank flathead are an important recreational species in Victoria, Tasmania and Western Australia.

Yank flathead are distributed along the southern coast of Australia from Lakes Entrance, Victoria to Albany, Western Australia, including Tasmania. They inhabit nearshore to continental shelf and slope waters (70–360 m depth). They are found in marine and estuarine environments over sandy and weedy substrates. In Western Australia yank flathead spawn several times over a protracted period from December to March in both the sea and estuaries. Males mature at 1 year of age (19–31 cm total length) and females mature at 2 years of age (25–40 cm total length). Yank flathead are estimated to live for at least 12 years; and the largest individual recorded was 76 cm long.

Taxonomy — Family PLATYCEPHALIDAE, *Platycephalus speculator*

Contributors — Glen Hyndes and Peter Last

Further reading

Hyndes, G.A., Neira, F.J. and Potter, I.C. (1992) Reproductive biology and early life history of the marine teleost *Platycephalus speculator* Klunzinger (Platycephalidae) in a temperate Australian estuary. *Journal of Fish Biology* **40**: 859–874.

Hyndes, G.A., Comeragan, N.R. and Potter, I.C. (1992) Influence of sectioning otoliths on marginal increment trends and age at growth for the flathead *Platycephalus speculator*. *Fishery Bulletin (U.S.)* **90**: 276–284.

Yellowtail (also called **scad, bung** or **yakka**) are a traditional bait for recreational and commercial fishers (eg as live and dead bait for tuna). Fish put straight onto ice slurry are used for human consumption, fetching about A$ 3.00 per kg in the Sydney Fish Market. Yellowtail are caught with handlines and seine nets, and are often associated with schools of pilchards. Yellowtail are mainly caught in New South Wales (139 t in 1989–90), with small catches from Western Australia (46 t).

Yellowtail are distributed around southern Australia from southern Queensland to Exmouth Gulf in Western Australia, although they are most abundant in New South Wales waters. They are pelagic fish that form large schools in marine inshore areas such as estuaries and bays. Adult fish are generally found over offshore rocky reefs, while juveniles are generally found in shallow, soft substrate areas. Spawning is thought to occur in the open ocean. Yellowtail first mature at 20 cm (females) and 22 cm (males) fork length. They grow to 33 cm total length.

There is potential for an export market for yellowtail for both human consumption and bait in tuna longline fisheries.

Taxonomy — Family CARANGIDAE, *Trachurus novaezelandiae*

Contributors — Johann Bell; drawing by Rosalind Poole

Further reading

Commercial fisheries of New South Wales (1982) N.S.W. State Fisheries. 60 pp.

State Pollution Control Commission (1981) *The ecology of fish in Botany Bay — biology of commercially and recreationally valuable species. Environmental control study of Botany Bay*. Sydney. 287 pp.

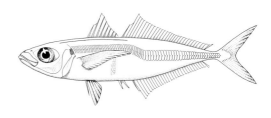

Summary table

compiled by Ebenezer Adjei,
Christina Grieve and Phillip Stewart

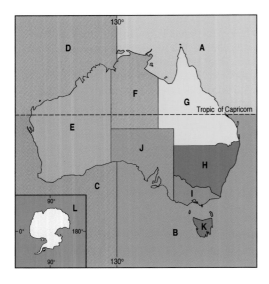

This 4-page table summarises the primary information on each species or species group discussed in Chapter 5. Readers are advised to check details on each of the species in Chapter 5, as there is insufficient space in this table to explain all of the variation displayed.

The following codes apply to some attributes in the table and indicate where there is variation.

L – variation between localities is known

S – variation between species is known

X – variation between sexes is known

unknown – information on this subject was not available while the book was being compiled.

Sizes

CL – carapace length

EFL – eye fork length

FL – fork length

ML – mantle length

SHL – shell length

SHT – shell height

SL – standard length

TD – test diameter

TL – total length

Common name (Number of species)	Age at maturity (years)	Size at maturity (cm)	Spawning period	Maximum age (years)	Maximum size (cm)	Maximum weight (kg)	Habitat
Greenlip abalone	3	unknown	Spring–Autumn	unknown	22 SHL	unknown	Reefs
Blacklip abalone	3–10 (L)	7.5–12.0 SHL (L)	Spring–Autumn (L)	unknown	21 SHL	unknown	Reefs
Blue mussel	2	4.5 SHL	Winter–Summer (L)	25	unknown	unknown	Estuarine,Neritic
Pearl oyster	1	11.0–13.5 SHL (X)	Spring–Autumn (L)	unknown	unknown	unknown	Neritic,Reefs
Pacific oyster	1	unknown	Spring–Autumn	unknown	30 SHL	unknown	Estuarine,Intertidal
Sydney rock oyster	1	unknown	Spring–Autumn (L)	10	unknown	unknown	Estuarine, Intertidal
Southern scallop	1	4–5 SHT (L)	Winter–Spring (L)	10	14.5 SHT	unknown	Neritic
Saucer scallops (3)	1	9 SHT	Variable (L)	4	14 SHT	unknown	Neritic
Inshore squid & calamary (4)	1	16 ML (S)	All year	1.5	38 ML (S)	2.1	Neritic,Oceanic
Arrow squid	unknown	22–30 ML (X)	All year	1.0	40 ML (X)	1.6 (X)	Neritic,Oceanic
Octopus (4)	unknown	5 ML (S)	Summer	1.5	35–120 TL (S)	0.3–9.0 (S)	Neritic,Oceanic,Reefs
Antarctic krill	2	3 TL	Spring–Autumn	11	6 TL	0.001	Oceanic
Royal red prawn	unknown	2.1–2.5 CL (X)	Summer–Winter	unknown	16–20 TL (X)	unknown	Oceanic
Greasyback prawn	1	1.6–2.0 CL (X)	All year	unknown	8–11 TL (X)	unknown	Estuarine,Neritic
Endeavour prawns (2)	unknown	1.8– 2.6 CL (LX)	All year	unknown	3.3–4.7 CL (SX)	unknown	Neritic
School prawn	unknown	1.8–3.0 CL (LX)	unknown	1.5	13–16 TL (X)	unknown	Estuarine,Neritic
Tiger prawns (2)	0.5	2.6–3.0 CL (S)	All year	2	3.9–5.5 CL (SX)	unknown	Neritic,Reefs
Banana prawns (2)	0.5	2.6–3.4 CL	Spring, Autumn	1.5	19–24 TL (X)	0.07 (X)	Estuarine,Neritic
Western king prawn	1–2	2.3–2.7 CL (X)	Variable (L)	4	5.1–7.6 CL (LX)	unknown	Neritic
Red spot king prawn	unknown	2.4–3.3 CL (L)	Autumn–Spring	unknown	15–18 TL (X)	unknown	Neritic,Reefs
Eastern king prawn	1.0–1.5	4 CL	Summer–Winter	3	19–30 TL (X)	unknown	Neritic
Giant tiger prawn	unknown	unknown	Spring,Autumn	unknown	33.6 TL (X)	0.15	Neritic
Yabby	0.2	3–5 CL (X)	Spring–Autumn	unknown	unknown	unknown	Freshwater
Redclaw	1	unknown	All year	5	9CL	0.6	Freshwater
Marron	1–3 (X)	2.5–3.0 CL (X)	Spring	10	38 TL	2.2	Freshwater
Southern rock lobster	3.5–4.5	6.5–11.5 CL	Autumn–Winter	20	23 CL (LX)	unknown	Neritic,Reefs
Eastern rock lobster	unknown	16 CL	Spring–Summer	10	26 CL	8	Neritic,Reefs
Western rock lobster	5	6.5–9.5 CL	Winter–Summer	20	20 CL	4.5	Neritic,Reefs
Ornate rock lobster	2.5	8.5 CL	Spring–Autumn	5	14CL	5	Neritic,Reefs
Bay lobsters (2)	1–2	5.2–5.8 CL (S)	Winter–Summer	7	9–10 CL (S)	0.42–0.56 (S)	Neritic
Spanner crab	2	6.4CL	Spring–Summer	9	12–15 CL (X)	0.4–0.9 (X)	Neritic
Blue swimmer crab	1	8–15 CL (L)	Variable (L)	3	21.8 CL (L)	1	Neritic
Mud crab	1.5–2.0	unknown	unknown	3	24 CL	3.25	Estuarine, Intertidal,Neritic
Purple sea urchin	3	4–5 TD	Summer–Autumn	8	14 TD	unknown	Intertidal,Neritic,Reefs
Whiskery shark	unknown	120 TL	Summer–Autumn	unknown	160 TL	unknown	Neritic
School shark	12	140 TL	Summer	50	175 TL	37.2	Neritic,Oceanic
Gummy shark	unknown	85–130 TL (X)	Spring–Summer	16	145–175 TL (X)	24.8	Neritic,Oceanic
Dusky & bronze whalers (2)	13–19 (X)	280 TL	Summer	30–35 (SX)	295–370 TL (S)	227–323 (S)	Neritic,Oceanic
Tropical sharks (2)	2–4	90–115 TL (S)	Summer	8–12 (S)	160–200 TL (S)	28–52 (S)	Neritic

Australian Distribution

Codes A – L indicate the adult distribution of each species or group of species. The map on the opposite page displays the limits of each area. Within these codes, A – D extend to the limits of the Australian Fishing Zone and E – K include all waters within the coastline (eg estuaries, rivers, lakes).

Resource Status

F – fully exploited

H – heavily exploited

O – over-exploited

U – under-exploited

Type of Fishery

A – aquaculture

B – bycatch

C – commercial

R – recreational

Manager of the Commercial Fishery

CA – Commonwealth of Australia

CCAMLR – Commission for the Conservation of Antarctic Marine Living Resources

NSW – New South Wales Government

NT – Northern Territory Government

PNG – Papua New Guinea Government

Qld – Queensland Government

SA – South Australian Government

Tas – Tasmanian Government

Vic – Victorian Government

WA – Western Australian Government

Common name (Number of species)	Depth range (m)	Australian distribution	Distribution outside Australia	Resource status	Type of fishery	Fishing method and / or gear used	Manager of the commercial fishery
Greenlip abalone	10–40	BC	None	F	A,C,R,	diving	Vic,Tas,SA,WA
Blacklip abalone	0–40	BC	None	F	A,C,R	diving	NSW,Vic,Tas,SA
Blue mussel	0–10	BC	New Zealand	unknown	A,C,R	diving,long line culture	NSW,Vic,Tas,SA,WA
Pearl oyster	0–85	AD	Indo-Pacific	F	A,C	diving	CA,WA,NT,Qld
Pacific oyster	unknown	ABGHIK	Indo-Pacific,France	unknown	A	tray & raft culture	NSW,Vic,Tas,SA
Sydney rock oyster	0–3	ABGHI	None	unknown	A,R	stick & tray culture	Qld,NSW
Southern scallop	< 120	BC	None	O	A,C,R	diving,dredging	CA,Vic,Tas
Saucer scallops (3)	10–75	ABCD	New Caledonia	uncertain	C	nets	CA,WA,NT,Qld
Inshore squid & calamary (4)	< 300 (S)	ABCD	Indo-Pacific	U	B,C,R	jigging,nets	CA,Qld,Vic,Tas,SA,WA
Arrow squid	0–825	BC	New Zealand	unknown	C	jigging,nets	CA,Vic
Octopus (4)	0–550	BC	None	unknown	B,C	traps	WA
Antarctic krill	< 500	L	other Antarctic waters	uncertain	C	nets	CA,CCAMLR
Royal red prawn	230–825	ABCD	Indo-West Pacific	uncertain	C	nets	CA,NSW
Greasyback prawn	0–22	BGH	None	unknown	C	nets	Qld,NSW
Endeavour prawns (2)	0–95	ABCD	Indo-West Pacific	F	C	nets	CA,Qld,WA
School prawn	1–55	AB	None	H	C,R	nets	Qld,NSW,Vic
Tiger prawns (2)	0–200	ABCD	Indo-West Pacific	F	C	nets	CA,Qld,WA
Banana prawns (2)	0–90	ADEFG	Indo-West Pacific	F	C,R	nets	CA,Qld,WA
Western king prawn	0–90	ABCD	Indo-Pacific	F	C,R	nets	CA,Qld,SA,WA
Red spot king prawn	18–60	ACD	Indonesia,Malaysia,South China Sea	unknown	C	nets	Qld
Eastern king prawn	1–220	AB	None	H	C,R	nets	Qld,NSW,Vic
Giant tiger prawn	< 110	ABCD	Indo-West Pacific	unknown	A,B,C	nets,pond culture	Qld,NSW
Yabby	0–5	EFGHIJ	None	unknown	A,C,R	traps,nets, pond culture	NSW,Vic,SA,WA
Redclaw	0–5	FG	Papua New Guinea	unknown	A,R	lines,pond culture	NT,Qld
Marron	unknown	E	North America,Southern Africa,Asia (Introduced)	uncertain	A,R	nets,pond culture	WA
Southern rock lobster	1–200	BC	New Zealand	F	C,R	traps	NSW,Vic,Tas,SA,WA
Eastern rock lobster	0–220	B	New Zealand	H	C,R	diving,traps	NSW
Western rock lobster	1–200	CD	None	F	C,R	traps	WA
Ornate rock lobster	1–200	ABCD	Indo-West Pacific	U	C,R	diving,nets	PNG,CA,WA,NT,Qld
Bay lobsters (2)	10–60	ABCD	Indo-West Pacific	H	B,C	nets,traps	CA,Qld,NSW,WA
Spanner crab	0–100	ABC	Indo-Pacific	uncertain	C,R	traps	Qld,NSW
Blue swimmer crab	0–50	ABCD	Indo-West Pacific, Mediterranean Sea	F	C,R	nets,traps	SA,WA,NT,Qld,NSW
Mud crab	unknown	ABDEFGH	Indo-West Pacific	H	C,R	nets,traps	WA,NT,Qld,NSW
Purple sea urchin	0–35	BC	None	U	C,R	diving	Vic,Tas,SA
Whiskery shark	< 220	BC	None	O	C	lines,nets	WA
School shark	0–550	BC	Pacific, Atlantic & Southern oceans	O	C,R	lines,nets	CA,Vic,Tas,SA
Gummy shark	0–350	BC	None	O	C,R	lines,nets	CA,Vic,Tas,SA,WA
Dusky & bronze whalers (2)	0–400	ABCD	Indian, Pacific & Atlantic oceans	unknown	C,R	lines,nets	SA,WA
Tropical sharks (2)	< 150 (S)	ABD	Indo-Pacific	unknown	C,R	lines,nets	CA,WA,NT,Qld

Common name (Number of species)	Age at maturity (years)	Size at maturity (cm)	Spawning period	Maximum age (years)	Maximum size (cm)	Maximum weight (kg)	Habitat
Bony bream	2	13–20 TL *(X)*	Spring–Autumn *(L)*	10	48 TL	unknown	Freshwater
Pilchard	1–3 *(L)*	7–13 TL *(L)*	Variable *(L)*	6	21 SL	unknown	Neritic
Australian anchovy	1	6 TL	Spring–Autumn *(L)*	6	15.7 TL	unknown	Neritic
Freshwater eels (2)	8–10	unknown	Variable *(L)*	32–41 *(S)*	158 TL *(SX)*	unknown	Freshwater,Estuarine
Trout & salmon (3)	2–3	unknown	Autumn–Spring *(S)*	5–9 *(S)*	90 FL	8–14 *(S)*	Freshwater,Estuarine
Carp & goldfish (2)	1–5 *(SX)*	20–25 TL *(S)*	Spring–Summer	20 *(S)*	85 TL *(S)*	15 *(S)*	Freshwater
Cobbler	2–3	38.5–40.5 TL *(X)*	Spring–Summer	13	76 TL	2.5	Estuarine,Neritic
Blue grenadier	4	73 TL	Winter–Spring	25	110 SL	unknown	Oceanic
Pink ling	unknown	unknown	Winter–Spring	unknown	160 TL	20	Oceanic
Garfish (2)	2	25 FL	Spring–Autumn	10	40–52 TL *(S)*	0.6	Estuarine,Neritic
Orange roughy	20–32	28–32 SL	Autumn–Winter	> 100	56 SL	5	Oceanic
Redfish	4	20–25 FL	Summer–Autumn	11–16 *(X)*	38 FL *(X)*	unknown	Neritic,Oceanic
Dories (2)	3	35 TL	Summer–Winter *(S)*	9	65–70 TL	3	Neritic,Oceanic
Oreos (4)	unknown	24 –41 TL *(S)*	Winter–Spring *(S)*	100	42–61TL *(S)*	1.5–5.0 *(S)*	Oceanic
Ocean perch	unknown	unknown	Winter–Spring	42	44 FL	1.4	Neritic,Oceanic
Deepwater flathead	4–6	40–45 TL *(X)*	Spring–Summer	15–20 *(X)*	62–94 TL *(X)*	2–4 *(X)*	Neritic,Oceanic
Tiger flathead	4–5	30–36 TL *(X)*	Spring–Autumn *(L)*	10–12	50–65 TL *(X)*	unknown	Neritic,Oceanic
Flathead (2)	2–4	22–56 TL *(LSX)*	Variable *(LS)*	9	46–120 TL *(S)*	3–15 *(S)*	Estuarine,Neritic
Barramundi	1–5 *(LX)*	29–60 TL *(LX)*	Spring–Summer *(L)*	unknown	180 TL	60	Freshwater,Estuarine
Coral trout (3)	2 *(X)*	21–60 FL *(LX)*	Spring–Summer	11–18 *(S)*	76 TL–109 FL *(S)*	3.3–6.5 *(S)*	Neritic,Reefs
Rock cod (3)	2	19 SL	All year	15 *(S)*	100 TL *(S)*	1.4–15 *(S)*	Estuarine,Neritic,Reefs
Golden perch	2–5 *(X)*	29–50 TL *(X)*	Spring–Autumn	20	unknown	24	Freshwater
Murray cod	4–5	unknown	Spring–Summer	unknown	180 TL	113.5	Freshwater
Westralian jewfish	3–4	54–58 TL	Summer	unknown	122 TL	26	Neritic,Reefs
School whiting (2)	2	14–16 FL	Variable *(L)*	7	32–33 TL	unknown	Neritic
Whiting (2)	2–3	19–26 FL	Variable *(L)*	22	30–50 TL *(S)*	unknown	Estuarine,Neritic
Yellowfin whiting	2–3	20–22.5 FL *(X)*	Spring–Summer	12	42 TL	unknown	Neritic
King George whiting	3–4	27–36 TL *(X)*	Summer–Winter	15	72 TL	4.8	Estuarine,Neritic,Reefs
Tailor	2	30 TL	Spring	unknown	120 TL	14	Estuarine,Neritic
Silver trevally	unknown	28 TL	Summer	unknown	76 TL	unknown	Neritic
Kingfish & samson fish (2)	2	50 FL	Winter–Summer *(L)*	unknown	190 TL	70	Neritic,Reefs
Jack mackerel	3–4	27 FL	Summer	16	47 FL	unknown	Neritic,Oceanic
Tommy ruff	2–4	unknown	Autumn–Winter	7	41 FL	0.8	Estuarine,Neritic,Reefs
Australian salmon (2)	3–6 *(LS)*	39–54 FL *(S)*	Summer–Winter	9	80 FL	7.0–10.5 *(S)*	Neritic
Sea perch (3)	unknown	unknown	Spring–Autumn	8–12 *(S)*	100 TL	unknown	Neritic,Reefs
Tropical snappers (2)	unknown	28–50 FL *(S)*	Spring–Summer *(L)*	11–14 *(S)*	65 FL *(S)*	2.2–3.7 *(S)*	Neritic
Emperors (4)	2–3	16–35 SL *(S)*	Variable *(LS)*	10–25 *(S)*	49–90 TL *(S)*	4.4–9.6 *(S)*	Neritic,Reefs
Bream (2)	2–5 *(LSX)*	24 FL	Winter–Summer*(LS)*	12–17 *(S)*	60 TL	4	Estuarine,Neritic,Reefs
Snapper	3–4	27 TL–30 FL *(L)*	Winter–Summer *(L)*	35	130 TL	16	Neritic,Reefs
Mulloway	6	75 TL	Spring–Summer	30	200 TL	43	Estuarine,Neritic,Reefs
Luderick	3	22–26 FL	Winter–Summer *(L)*	unknown	71 FL	4	Estuarine,Neritic,Reefs
Morwong (2)	3	25 FL	Summer–Autumn	16	50 FL–70 TL *(S)*	2.9–5.9 *(S)*	Neritic,Oceanic
Yellow-eye mullet	2–3	unknown	Variable *(L)*	unknown	40 TL	0.95	Estuarine,Neritic
Sea mullet	3	30–35 FL	Autumn–Winter *(L)*	9	76 TL	8	Freshwater,Estuarine,Neritic
Threadfin salmon (2)	unknown *(X)*	unknown *(X)*	Spring–Autumn	20	150–200 FL *(LS)*	40–145 *(LS)*	Estuarine,Neritic
Gemfish	3–6 *(X)*	unknown	Winter	11–16 *(X)*	101–116 FL *(X)*	unknown	Neritic,Oceanic
Barracouta	2–4	unknown	Variable *(L)*	10	140 TL	6.2	Neritic,Oceanic
Antarctic fish(3)	3–4	13 TL	Winter–Summer *(S)*	15	25–43 TL *(S)*	unknown	Neritic,Oceanic
Skipjack tuna	1–2	40–45 FL	All year	4	100 FL *(L)*	20 *(L)*	Neritic,Oceanic
Mackerel (4)	2	65–82 FL *(LX)*	Variable *(LS)*	10–14 *(X)*	100–240 FL *(S)*	8.4–70.0 *(S)*	Neritic
Albacore	unknown	50–85 FL *(X)*	Summer	10	127 FL	40	Oceanic
Yellowfin tuna	2	101 FL	All year *(L)*	8	170–190 TL *(X)*	70–100 *(X)*	Neritic,Oceanic
Southern bluefin tuna	8	120 FL	Spring–Summer	20	200 FL	200	Oceanic
Bigeye tuna	3	100 FL	Summer	11	200 FL	210	Oceanic
Black marlin	unknown *(X)*	unknown *(X)*	Spring–Summer	unknown	448 TL	709	Neritic,Oceanic
Blue marlin	3–4	unknown	Summer	21–28 *(X)*	450 TL *(X)*	170–906 *(X)*	Oceanic
Striped marlin	2–3	unknown	Spring–Summer	unknown	350 TL	200	Oceanic
Broadbill swordfish	5–6	150–170 EFL	Spring–Summer	unknown	445 TL *(X)*	540 *(X)*	Oceanic
Blue eye	5–7	61 FL	Summer–Winter	15	140 TL	50	Oceanic
Warehous (2)	3–4	40 FL	Winter–Spring	10–11	66–76 TL *(S)*	unknown	Neritic,Oceanic
Ocean jacket	3–4	37 TL	Autumn	9	79 FL	3.5	Neritic

Common name (Number of species)	Depth range (m)	Australian distribution	Distribution outside Australia	Resource status	Type of fishery	Fishing method and / or gear used	Manager of the commercial fishery
Bony bream	0–3	EFGHIJ	None	uncertain	C	nets	SA
Pilchard	0–200	BC	cosmopolitan	uncertain	C	nets	NSW,Vic,WA
Australian anchovy	0–20	BC	New Zealand	unknown	C	nets	NSW,Vic,WA
Freshwater eels (2)	0–300	ABGHIJK	West Pacific Islands,New Zealand	unknown	A,C,R	lines,nets,traps	Qld,NSW,Vic,Tas
Trout & salmon (3)	unknown	EGHIJK	Europe,Iceland,Western Asia,North Americas	unknown	A,R	cage/pond culture,lines	NSW,Vic,Tas,SA,WA
Carp & goldfish (2)	unknown	EGHIJ	Introduced to most countries	uncertain	C,R	electrofishing,lines,nets	NSW,Vic,SA
Cobbler	0–30	BC	None	unknown	C,R	lines,nets,traps	WA
Blue grenadier	200–1000	BC	New Zealand	uncertain	C	nets	CA
Pink ling	20–800	BC	New Zealand,South America	uncertain	B,C	lines,nets	CA
Garfish (2)	0–20	BC	None	unknown	C,R	lines,nets	NSW,Vic,Tas,SA
Orange roughy	700–1400	BC	Atlantic,Indo-Pacific,Southern Ocean	uncertain	C	nets	CA
Redfish	< 450	B	New Zealand	O	B,C,R	lines,nets,traps	CA,NSW
Dories (2)	5–800 (S)	BCD	Indian & Atlantic oceans,New Zealand,Japan	unknown	B,C,R	lines,nets	CA,NSW,Vic
Oreos (4)	200–1600 (S)	BCD	throughout southern hemisphere	unknown	C	nets	CA
Ocean perch	50–750	BC	New Zealand	uncertain	B,C,R	lines,nets	CA,NSW
Deepwater flathead	70–490	BC	None	U	C	nets	CA
Tiger flathead	10–400	B	None	F	C,R	lines,nets	CA,NSW,Vic,Tas
Flathead (2)	0–100	ABCEGHIJK	None	uncertain	C,R	lines,nets	CA,Qld,NSW,Vic,Tas
Barramundi	unknown	ADEFG	Indo-West Pacific	U	A,C,R	lines,nets,pond culture	WA,NT,Qld
Coral trout (3)	0–100	ABCD	Indo-Pacific	H	C,R	lines,nets,traps	CA,WA,NT,Qld
Rock cod (3)	2–200 (S)	ABCD	Indo-West Pacific	unknown	C,R	lines,nets,traps	CA,WA,NT,Qld
Golden perch	unknown	FGHIJ	None	unknown	C,R	lines,nets	NSW,Vic,SA
Murray cod	0–5	GHIJ	None	O	C,R	lines,nets	NSW,Vic,SA
Westralian jewfish	20–200	CD	None	unknown	C,R	lines,nets	WA
School whiting (2)	0–80	BC	None	uncertain	C,R	lines,nets	CA,NSW,Vic,Tas
Whiting (2)	0–46	ABGHIK	New Caledonia,Papua New Guinea	unknown	C,R	lines,nets	NSW,Qld
Yellowfin whiting	1–10	BCD	unknown	uncertain	C,R	lines,nets	SA,WA
King George whiting	0–200	BC	None	F	C,R	lines,nets	Vic,SA,WA
Tailor	0–50	BCEGHIK	cosmopolitan	uncertain	C,R	lines,nets	Qld,NSW,Vic,WA
Silver trevally	unknown	BC	Indo-West Pacific,Atlantic Ocean	unknown	B,C,R	lines,nets,traps	CA,NSW,Vic
Kingfish & samson fish (2)	unknown	BC	Indo-Pacific	unknown	C,R	lines,nets,traps	NSW,WA
Jack mackerel	< 460	BC	New Zealand	unknown	C,R	lines,nets	CA,NSW,Vic,Tas,SA
Tommy ruff	unknown	BCEIJ	None	U	C,R	lines,nets	SA,WA
Australian salmon (2)	0–80	BC	New Zealand,Kermadec Islands	F	C,R	lines,nets	NSW,Vic,Tas,SA,WA
Sea perch (3)	5–180	ABD	Indo-West Pacific	U	C,R	lines,nets,traps	CA,WA,NT,Qld
Tropical snappers (2)	40–200	ABCD	Indo-West Pacific	unknown	C	lines,nets,traps	CA,WA,NT
Emperors (4)	2–90	ABCD	Indo-Pacific	unknown	C,R	lines,nets,traps	CA,WA,NT,Qld
Bream (2)	unknown	ABEGHIJ	None	F	C,R	lines,nets,traps	Qld,NSW,Vic,SA,WA
Snapper	1–200	ABCD	Indo-Pacific	F	C,R	lines,nets,traps	NSW,Vic,SA,WA
Mulloway	0–150	BCEGHIJ	southern Africa,Madagascar	uncertain	C,R	lines,nets	Qld,NSW,Vic,SA,WA
Luderick	unknown	BGHIJK	New Zealand	unknown	C,R	lines,nets	Qld,NSW,Vic,Tas
Morwong (2)	10–400	BC	New Zealand,Indian & Atlantic oceans	uncertain	C,R	lines,nets,traps	CA,NSW
Yellow-eye mullet	0–20	BC	New Zealand	F (L)	C,R	lines,nets	Vic,Tas,SA,WA
Sea mullet	unknown	ABCDEGHIJK	cosmopolitan	unknown	C,R	nets	Qld,NSW,WA
Threadfin salmon (2)	0–23	ADEFG	India,South-east Asia	uncertain	C,R	nets,traps	WA,NT,Qld
Gemfish	100–700	BC	New Zealand	O	C	lines,nets	CA,NSW
Barracouta	< 550	BC	circumglobal between latitudes 30° S & 45° S	U	B,R	lines,nets	CA,Tas
Antarctic fish (3)	100–700 (S)	L	other Antarctic waters	unknown	C	nets	CA,CCAMLR
Skipjack tuna	0–260	ABCD	tropical & sub-tropical waters	unknown	C,R	lines,nets	CA,NSW
Mackerel (4)	0–100	ABCD	Indo-Pacific,Mediterranean Sea	unknown	C,R	lines,nets	WA,NT,Qld,NSW
Albacore	50–500	ABCD	cosmopolitan	U	B,C,R	lines	CA
Yellowfin tuna	0–250	ABCD	cosmopolitan(except Mediterranean Sea)	uncertain	B,C,R	lines,nets	CA,NSW
Southern bluefin tuna	unknown	BCD	circumglobal between latitudes 30° S & 50° S	O	C,R	lines	CA
Bigeye tuna	150–250	ABCD	circumglobal between latitudes 45° N & 40° S	unknown	B,C	lines	CA
Black marlin	unknown	ABCD	Indo-Pacific	uncertain	B,R	lines	CA
Blue marlin	unknown	ABCD	Indo-Pacific	O	B,R	lines,nets	CA
Striped marlin	unknown	ABCD	Indo-Pacific	uncertain	C,R	lines	CA
Broadbill swordfish	< 600	ABCD	circumglobal between latitudes 45° N & 45° S	uncertain	B,C,R	lines	CA
Blue eye	200–900	BC	New Zealand,South America,South Africa	H	C	lines,nets	CA,Qld,NSW,Tas,SA
Warehous (2)	50–600 (S)	B	New Zealand	unknown	C,R	lines,nets	CA,Tas
Ocean jacket	2–200	BC	None	uncertain	B,C	nets,traps	SA

407

Acknowledgements

While the 'main players' are acknowledged at the front and throughout, this book is also the product of many other people's time and expertise. The assistance received from the people and institutions listed here varies immensely in content and magnitude. Their combined talents and generosity accorded us in compiling *Australian Fisheries Resources* surely reflect their dedication to and interest in Australian fish and fisheries as well as their recognition that the most accurate reference book on Australian fisheries could only be achieved through their combined support. Although the listing is alphabetical, we trust that each individual accepts our thanks for their particular contributions
— the editors

Institutions

Australian Antarctic Division
Australian Bureau of Agricultural and Resource Economics
Australian Bureau of Statistics
Australian Fisheries Management Authority
Australian Information Service, Dept of Foreign Affairs and Trade
Australian Institute of Marine Science
Australian Quarantine and Inspection Service

Commonwealth Scientific and Industrial Research Organisation, Division of Fisheries
Commonwealth Scientific and Industrial Research Organisation, Division of Oceanography
Demersal and Pelagic Fish Research Group, South Eastern Fisheries Research Committee
Dept of Foreign Affairs and Trade
Division of Sea Fisheries, Tasmanian Dept of Primary Industry and Fisheries

Fisheries Dept of WA
Fisheries Research and Development Corporation
Fisheries Research Institute, NSW Fisheries
Fisheries Policy Branch, Dept of Primary Industries and Energy
Food and Agriculture Organisation of the United Nations, Rome
Great Barrier Reef Marine Park Authority
Lakes Entrance Fishermen's Cooperative
Marine Science Laboratories, Victorian Dept of Conservation and Environment
Melbourne City Council
Murray-Darling Basin Commission
New Zealand Ministry of Agriculture and Fisheries
Northern Fisheries Centre, Queensland Dept of Primary Industries
NSW Fish Marketing Authority
NSW Fisheries
NT Dept of Primary Industry and Fisheries
Queensland Commercial Fishermen's Organisation
Queensland Dept of Primary Industries

Queensland Fish Management Authority
SA Dept of Fisheries
South Pacific Commission
Southern Fisheries Centre, Queensland Dept of Primary Industries
Southern Shark Assessment Group, South Eastern Fisheries Research Committee
Tasmanian Salmonid Growers Association
Victorian Dept of Conservation and Environment
WA Marine Research Laboratories, Fisheries Dept of WA

The following abbreviations are used: 'ACT' for Australian Capital Territory; 'Dept' for Department; 'MSL' for Marine Science Laboratories; 'NSW' for New South Wales; 'NT' for Northern Territory; 'NT DPI & F' for NT Dept of Primary Industry and Fisheries; 'QDPI' for Queensland Dept of Primary Industries; 'Qld' for Queensland (not always); 'SA' for South Australia; 'Tas' for Tasmania (not always); 'Tas DPI & F' for Tas Dept of Primary Industry and Fisheries; 'Vic' for Victoria; 'WA' for Western Australia; 'WAMRL' for WA Marine Research Laboratories.

Individuals

Ebenezer Adjei – Bureau of Resource Sciences, Canberra
Phil Alderslade – Fish Section, Museum and Art Gallery of the NT, Darwin
Geoff Allan – Brackish Water Fish Culture Research Station, Salamander Bay, NSW
Gerry Allen – Fish Section, WA Museum, Perth
Bill Anderson – Australian Fisheries Management Authority, Canberra
Malcolm Anderson – Fisheries Dept of WA, Perth
Trevor Anderson – Deakin University, Geelong, Vic
Neil Andrew – Fisheries Research Institute, NSW Fisheries, Sydney
James Andrews – WAMRL, Fisheries Dept of WA, Waterman, WA
Tom Angelakis – Angelakis Brothers Pty Ltd, Adelaide
Pat Appleton – Qld Fish Management Authority, Brisbane
Leon Arundell – Bureau of Resource Sciences, Canberra
Fred Austin – Fisheries Division, Vic Dept of Conservation and Environment, Melbourne
Pascale Baelde – Division of Sea Fisheries, Tas DPI & F, Taroona, Tas
Diane Balanger – formerly of MSL, Vic Dept of Conservation and Environment, Queenscliff, Vic

Chris Barlow – Fisheries Branch, QDPI, Brisbane
Anna Barry – Fisheries Division, NT DPI & F, Darwin
Andrew Bartleet – NSW Fisheries, Sydney
David Bateman – H.J. Heinz Company Australia Ltd, Eden, NSW
Tony Battaglene – Australian Bureau of Agricultural and Resource Economics, Canberra
Graham Baulch – Fisheries Division, NT DPI & F, Darwin
Johann Bell – Forum Fisheries Agency, Honiara, Solomon Islands
Susan Bennett – SA Dept of Fisheries, Adelaide
Penny Berents – Crustaceans Section, Australian Museum, Sydney
Tom Bergin – Noosa, Qld
Tim Berra – Ohio State University, Mansfield, United States of America
Gregg Berry - Bureau of Resource Sciences, Canberra
Malcolm Bertoni – SA Dept of Fisheries, Adelaide
John Beumer – Fisheries Division, QDPI, Brisbane
Jo-Anne Bicanic – International Food Institute of Qld, Hamilton, Qld
Ron Billyard – Inland Fisheries Research Station, Narrandera, NSW
Mick Bishop – Australian Fisheries Management Authority, Canberra

Alan Blackshaw – Dept of Physiology and Pharmacology, University of Qld, Brisbane
Jeff Blaney – North Stradbroke Island, Qld
Stuart Blight – WAMRL, Fisheries Dept of WA, Waterman, WA
Walter Boles – Ornithology Section, Australian Museum, Sydney
Bernard Bowen – formerly of Fisheries Dept of WA, Perth
Rusty Branford – Dept of Primary Industries and Energy, Canberra
Darren Brasher – Dept of Zoology, University of Tas, Hobart
Heather Brayford – Fisheries Dept of WA, Perth
Allan Bremner – International Food Institute of Qld, Hamilton, Qld
Clare Bremner – Crustaceans Section, Qld Museum, Brisbane
Dave Brewer – CSIRO Marine Laboratories, Cleveland, Qld
Debbie Brown – Australian Bureau of Agricultural and Resource Economics, Canberra
Diane Brown – Crustaceans Section, Australian Museum, Sydney
Ian Brown – Southern Fisheries Centre, QDPI, Deception Bay, Qld
Michael Brown - Publishing Services, QDPI, Brisbane
Rhys Brown – Fisheries Dept of WA, Perth

Paul Browne – Australian Quarantine and Inspection Service, Dept of Primary Industries and Energy, Canberra
Barry Bruce – formerly of SA Dept of Fisheries, Adelaide
Don Buckmaster – Fisheries Division, Vic Dept of Conservation and Environment, Melbourne
Rik Buckworth – Fisheries Division, NT DPI & F, Darwin
Cathy Bulman – CSIRO Marine Laboratories, Hobart
Jenny Burchmore – NSW Fisheries, Sydney
John Burke – Southern Fisheries Centre, QDPI, Deception Bay, Qld
Andrew Burnell – formerly of SA Dept of Fisheries, Adelaide
Steven Burnell – formerly of SA Dept of Fisheries, Adelaide
Adam Butcher – Southern Fisheries Centre, QDPI, Deception Bay, Qld
Alan Butler – Zoology Dept, University of Adelaide, Adelaide
Kevin Cahart – WAMRL, Fisheries Dept of WA, Waterman, WA
Chris Calogeras – Fisheries Division, NT DPI & F, Darwin
Darren Cameron – Southern Fisheries Centre, QDPI, Deception Bay, Qld
Merle Cammiss – formerly of SA Dept of Fisheries, Adelaide
David Campbell – Australian Bureau of Agricultural and Resource Economics, Canberra

Judith Campbell – Bureau of Resource Sciences, Canberra

Robert Campbell – CSIRO Marine Laboratories, Hobart

Tim Cansfield-Smith – Great Barrier Reef Marine Park Authority, Townsville, Qld

Mike Cappo – Australian Institute of Marine Science, Townsville, Qld

Mike Capra – Dept of Public Health and Nutrition, Qld University of Technology, Brisbane

Nick Caputi – WAMRL, Fisheries Dept of WA, Waterman, WA

Neil Carrick – SA Dept of Fisheries, Adelaide

Thor Carter – CSIRO Marine Laboratories, Hobart

Ian Cartwright – Australian Maritime College, Beauty Point, Tas

Albert Caton – Bureau of Resource Sciences, Canberra

Bill Causebrook – Fisheries Policy Branch, Dept of Primary Industries and Energy, Canberra

Peter Channells – formerly of Dept of Primary Industries and Energy, Thursday Island, Qld

Lindsay Chapman – formerly of Bureau of Resource Sciences, Canberra

Jean Chesson – Bureau of Resource Sciences, Canberra

Chris Chubb – WAMRL, Fisheries Dept of WA, Waterman, WA

Ray Clarke – Fisheries Dept of WA, Perth

Steve Clarke – SA Dept of Fisheries, Adelaide

Mark Cliff – WAMRL, Fisheries Dept of WA, Waterman, WA

Anne Coleman – Fisheries Division, NT DPI & F, Darwin

Noel Coleman – MSL, Vic Dept of Conservation and Environment, Queenscliff, Vic

Phil Coleman – Malacology Section, Australian Museum, Sydney

Rob Coles – Northern Fisheries Centre, QDPI, Cairns, Qld

Kathy Colgan – Bureau of Resource Sciences, Canberra

Mark Connell – formerly of Northern Fisheries Centre, QDPI, Cairns, Qld

Rod Connolly – Zoology Dept, University of Adelaide, Adelaide

Andrew Constable – Division of Environmental Sciences, Griffith University, Brisbane

John Coombs – Port Karama, NT

Lisa Cooper – Division of Sea Fisheries, Tas DPI & F, Taroona, Tas

Rob Cordover – formerly of Fisheries Division, Vic Dept of Conservation and Environment, Melbourne

Tony Courtney – Southern Fisheries Centre, QDPI, Deception Bay, Qld

Patrick Coutin – MSL, Vic Dept of Conservation and Environment, Queenscliff, Vic

Jim Craig – Fisheries Research Institute, NSW Fisheries, Sydney

Wendy Craik – Great Barrier Reef Marine Park Authority, Townsville, Qld

George Cresswell – CSIRO Division of Oceanography, Hobart

Andrew Cribb – Fisheries Dept of WA, Perth

Millin Curtis – Fisheries Research Station, QDPI, Walkamin, Qld

Glen Cuthbert – NSW Agriculture, Grafton, NSW

Bill Dall – formerly of CSIRO Marine Laboratories, Cleveland, Qld

Trevor Dann – Australian Bureau of Agricultural and Resource Economics, Canberra

Stephanie Davenport – CSIRO Marine Laboratories, Hobart

Brian Davies – SA Dept of Fisheries, Adelaide

Campbell Davies – Zoology Dept, James Cook University of North Qld, Townsville, Qld

Jeffrey Davies – formerly of Fisheries Division, Vic Dept of Conservation and Environment, Melbourne

Peter Davies – Crustaceans Section, Qld Museum, Brisbane

Suzie Davies – Great Barrier Reef Marine Park Authority, Townsville, Qld

Rob Day – Dept of Zoology, University of Melbourne, Melbourne

Kerrie Deguara – Fisheries Research Institute, NSW Fisheries, Sydney

Henry Dekker – Neetos Pty Ltd, Canberra

Kurt Derbyshire – Northern Fisheries Centre, QDPI, Cairns, Qld

David Die – Southern Fisheries Centre, QDPI, Deception Bay, Qld

John Diplock – NSW Fisheries, Sydney

Pat Dixon – Centre for Marine Science, University of NSW, Sydney

Ruth Dodd – Australian Surveying and Land Information Group, Canberra

Peter Doherty – Australian Institute of Marine Science, Townsville, Qld

Kevin Donohue – WAMRL, Fisheries Dept of WA, Waterman, WA

Joe Doyle – Hydrographic Office, Royal Australian Navy, Sydney

Peter Doyle Snr – Watsons Bay, NSW

Mike Dredge – Southern Fisheries Centre, QDPI, Deception Bay, Qld

Ignatius Duivenvoorden – Vic Dept of Conservation and Environment, Melbourne

Malcolm Dunning – Fisheries Division, QDPI, Brisbane

Echo Radar Pty Ltd, Port Adelaide, SA

Bob Edwards – CSIRO Division of Oceanography, Hobart

Karen Edyvane – SA Dept of Fisheries, Adelaide

Mark Elmer – Qld Fish Management Authority, Brisbane

Jenny Ensbey – Australian Information Service, Dept of Foreign Affairs and Trade, Canberra

Dave Evans – CSIRO Marine Laboratories, North Beach, WA

Rick Fallu – Fisheries Division, Vic Dept of Conservation and Environment, Melbourne

Gwen Fenton – Zoology Dept, University of Tas, Hobart

Beatrice Fereira – Dept of Marine Biology, James Cook University of North Qld, Townsville, Qld

Doug Ferrell – Fisheries Research Institute, NSW Fisheries, Sydney

Greg Finlay – Fisheries Dept of WA, Shark Bay, WA

Rick Fletcher – WAMRL, Fisheries Dept of WA, Waterman, WA

Wes Ford – Division of Sea Fisheries, Tas DPI & F, Taroona, Tas

Tony Fowler – formerly of Australian Institute of Marine Science, Townsville, Qld

Ian Freeman – Australian Fisheries Management Authority, Canberra

Stewart Frusher – Division of Sea Fisheries, Tas DPI & F, Taroona, Tas

Wayne Fulton – Tas Inland Fisheries Commission, Hobart

Teresa Fumo – Division of Sea Fisheries, Tas DPI & F, Hobart

Dianne Furlani – CSIRO Marine Laboratories, Hobart

Rod Garrett – Northern Fisheries Centre, QDPI, Cairns, Qld

John Garvey – Bureau of Resource Sciences, Canberra

Anne Gason – MSL, Vic Dept of Conservation and Environment, Queenscliff, Vic

Gerry Geen – Forum Fisheries Agency, Noumea, New Caledonia

Peter Gehrke – Inland Fisheries Research Station, Narrandera, NSW

Jack Gibson – MSL, Vic Dept of Conservation and Environment, Queenscliff, Vic

Linda Gibson – Mammals Section, Australian Museum, Sydney

Neville Gill – Fisheries Division, NT DPI & F, Darwin

Noel Gillespie – Bribie Island Aquaculture Research Centre, QDPI, Bribie Island, Qld

John Glaister – Fisheries Branch, QDPI, Brisbane

Fred Glasbrenner – Australian Abalone Exporters, Laverton North, Vic

Martin Gomon – Fish Section, Museum of Vic, Melbourne

Alastair Graham – CSIRO Marine Laboratories, Hobart

Ken Graham – Fisheries Research Institute, NSW Fisheries, Sydney

Anne Grant – CSIRO, Melbourne

Charlie Gray – Fisheries Research Institute, NSW Fisheries, Sydney

Les Gray – SA Dept of Fisheries, Adelaide

Joe Greco – Eden, NSW

Darryl Grey – Fisheries Division, NT DPI & F, Darwin

Neil Gribble – Northern Fisheries Centre, QDPI, Cairns, Qld

Roland Griffin – Fisheries Division, NT DPI & F, Darwin

Rod Grove-Jones – formerly of SA Dept of Fisheries, Adelaide

John Gunn – CSIRO Marine Laboratories, Hobart

Laurie Gwynne – Qld Fish Management Authority, Brisbane

Dave Hall – Fisheries Dept of WA, Perth

Doug Hall – formerly of Vic Dept of Conservation and Environment, Melbourne

Phil Hall – Fisheries Division, NT DPI & F, Darwin

Ian Halliday – Fisheries Branch, QDPI, Brisbane

Ian Hamdorf – Bureau of Resource Sciences, Canberra

Gary Hamer – formerly of NSW Fisheries, Sydney

John Hampton – South Pacific Commission, Noumea, New Caledonia

Jack Hannan – Fisheries Research Institute, NSW Fisheries, Sydney

Karina Hansen – Kaleen, ACT

Des Harrington – Fisheries Division, Vic Dept of Conservation and Environment, Melbourne

Aubrey Harris – CSIRO Marine Laboratories, Cleveland, Qld

John Harris – Fisheries Research Institute, NSW Fisheries, Sydney

Peter Harris – Ocean Sciences Institute, University of Sydney, Sydney

Rod Harrison – *Australian Angler's Fishing World* magazine, Sydney

Piers Hart – University of Tas, Launceston, Tas

Mary Harwood – Fisheries Policy Branch, Dept of Primary Industries and Energy, Canberra

Charles Hausman – Mareeba, Qld

Terry Healy – Qld Fish Management Authority, Brisbane

H.J. Heinz Company Australia Ltd, Eden, NSW

Gary Henry – Environment Protection Authority, Bankstown, NSW

Neil Hickman – MSL, Vic Dept of Conservation and Environment, Queenscliff, Vic

Jim Higgs – James Cook University of North Qld, Townsville, Qld

Burke Hill – CSIRO Marine Laboratories, Cleveland, Qld

Steve Hillman – Great Barrier Reef Marine Park Authority, Townsville, Qld

Patrick Hone – SA Dept of Fisheries, Adelaide

Dorothea Huber – formerly of Division of Sea Fisheries, Tas DPI & F, Hobart

Pat Hutchings – Worms Section, Australian Museum, Sydney

Barry Hutchins – Fish Section, WA Museum, Perth

Stuart Hyland – Southern Fisheries Centre, QDPI, Deception Bay, Qld

Glen Hyndes – School of Biological and Environmental Sciences, Murdoch University, Murdoch, WA

Steve Jackson – Australian Fisheries Management Authority, Canberra

John Jefferson – SA Dept of Fisheries, Adelaide

Jerry Jenke – WAMRL, Fisheries Dept of WA, Waterman, WA

Peter Jernakoff – CSIRO Marine Laboratories, North Beach, WA

John Johnson – SA Dept of Fisheries, Adelaide

Mike Johnson – Zoology Dept, University of Western Australia, Perth

Lindsay Joll – WAMRL, Fisheries Dept of WA, Waterman, WA

Clive Jones – Fisheries Branch, QDPI, Brisbane

Diana Jones – Aquatic Invertebrate Zoology Section, WA Museum, Perth

Keith Jones – SA Dept of Fisheries, Adelaide

Madeleine Jones – Bureau of Resource Sciences, Canberra

Alex Julius – Conservation Commission of the NT, Darwin

Christine Julius – Fisheries Division, NT DPI & F, Darwin

Theo Kailis – Kailis Bros Pty Ltd, Canning Vale, WA

Mervi Kangas – SA Dept of Fisheries, Adelaide

Allan Kaufmann – Eels Pty Ltd, Skipton, Vic

Barry Kaufmann – Australian Fisheries Management Authority, Canberra

Bob Kearney – Fisheries Research Institute, NSW Fisheries, Sydney

Clive Keenan – Southern Fisheries Centre, QDPI, Deception Bay, Qld

Bob Kennedy – Division of Sea Fisheries, Tas DPI & F, Taroona, Tas

Terry Kennedy – NSW Fish Marketing Authority, Sydney

Steve Kennelly – Fisheries Research Institute, NSW Fisheries, Sydney

Matt Kenway – Australian Institute of Marine Science, Townsville, Qld

Steve Kerr – Bureau of Resource Sciences, Canberra

Mike King – Australian Maritime College, Beauty Point, Tas

Mike Kingsford – School of Biological Sciences, University of Sydney, Sydney

John Kitchener – Division of Sea Fisheries, Tas DPI & F, Taroona, Tas

Neil Klaer – Bureau of Resource Sciences, Canberra

Ian Knuckey – Fisheries Division, NT DPI & F, Darwin

John Koehn – Arthur Rylah Institute, Vic Dept of Conservation and Environment, Melbourne

Felicia Kow – Australian Maritime College, Beauty Point, Tas

Marc Labelle – South Pacific Commission, Noumea, New Caledonia

Jeremy Langdon – deceased, Animal Health Laboratories, WA Dept of Agriculture, Perth

Helen Larson – Fish Section, Museum and Art Gallery of the NT, Darwin

Peter Last – CSIRO Marine Laboratories, Hobart

Laurie Laurenson – WAMRL, Fisheries Dept of WA, Waterman, WA

Brian Lawrence – Murray-Darling Basin Commission, Canberra

Rosemary Lea – Fisheries Division, NT DPI & F, Darwin

Mervyn Lee – Trident Seafoods Pty Ltd, Hobart

Mark Lees – Seafresh Products, Mackay, Qld

Rod Lenanton – WAMRL, Fisheries Dept of WA, Waterman, WA

Robert Lester – Dept of Parasitology, University of Qld, Brisbane

Rob Lewis – SA Dept of Fisheries, Adelaide

Tony Lewis – South Pacific Commission, Noumea, New Caledonia

Guy Leyland – WA Fishing Industry Council, Osborne Park, WA

Julie Lloyd – Fisheries Division, NT DPI & F, Darwin

Lance Lloyd – State Water Laboratory, Armadale, Vic

Ian Lock – Malacology Section, Australian Museum, Sydney

Peter Long – Fisheries Division, QDPI, Rockhampton, Qld

Rocco Losordo – Springvale North, Vic

C.C. Lu – Invertebrate Zoology Section, Museum of Vic, Melbourne

John Lucas – James Cook University of North Qld, Townsville, Qld

Jeremy Lyle – Division of Sea Fisheries, Tas DPI & F, Taroona, Tas

Julie Macaranas – Centre for Biological Population Management, Qld University of Technology, Brisbane

Murray MacDonald – MSL, Vic Dept of Conservation and Environment, Queenscliff, Vic

Michael Mackie – Marine Biology Dept, James Cook University of North Qld, Townsville, Qld

Mathew M. Maliel – Bureau of Resource Sciences, Canberra

Bruce Mapstone – Great Barrier Reef Marine Park Authority, Townsville, Qld

Loisette Marsh – Aquatic Invertebrate Zoology Section, WA Museum, Perth

Jenny Martin – Bureau of Resource Sciences, Canberra

Richard Martin – CSIRO Marine Laboratories, Hobart

John Matthews – Fisheries Research Institute, NSW Fisheries, Sydney

Vince McDonall – NSW Commercial Fishing Advisory Council, Sydney

Mark McGrouther – Fish Section, Australian Museum, Sydney

Kevin McLoughlin – Bureau of Resource Sciences, Canberra

Richard McLoughlin – CSIRO Marine Laboratories, Hobart

Peter McNamara – A. Raptis & Sons, Colmslie, Qld

Geoff McPherson – Northern Fisheries Centre, QDPI, Cairns, Qld

Frank Meany – Australian Fisheries Management Authority, Canberra

Grahame Mehrtens – Qld Commercial Fishermen's Organisation, Brisbane

Anna Menegazzo – MSL, Vic Dept of Conservation and Environment, Queenscliff, Vic

Jason Middleton – School of Mathematics, University of New South Wales, Sydney

Hamar Midgley – Bli Bli via Nambour, Qld

Alf Mikolajczyk – formerly of Fisheries Division, NT DPI & F, Darwin

Ed Miles – Institute for Marine Studies, University of Washington, Seattle, United States of America

Bob Miller – formerly of Fisheries Research Institute, NSW Fisheries, Sydney

Peter Millington – Fisheries Dept of WA, Perth

Dave Milton – CSIRO Marine Laboratories, Cleveland, Qld

Dave Molloy – MSL, Vic Dept of Conservation and Environment, Queenscliff, Vic

Steven Montgomery – Fisheries Research Institute, NSW Fisheries, Sydney

Noel Moore – Fisheries Branch, QDPI, Brisbane

Mike Moran – WAMRL, Fisheries Dept of WA, Waterman, WA

Gary Morgan – formerly of Crustaceans Section, WA Museum, Perth

Sandy Morison – MSL, Vic Dept of Conservation and Environment, Queenscliff, Vic

Noel Morrissy – WAMRL, Fisheries Dept of WA, Waterman, WA

Rick Morton – WBM Oceanics Pty Ltd, Brisbane

Richard Mounsey – Fisheries Division, NT DPI & F, Darwin

Talbot Murray – Ministry of Agriculture and Fisheries, Wellington, New Zealand

Warwick Nash – Division of Sea Fisheries, Tas DPI & F, Taroona, Tas

Franco Neira – School of Biological and Environmental Sciences, Murdoch University, Murdoch, WA

John Nell – Brackish Water Fish Culture Research Station, Salamander Bay, NSW

Leslie Newman – Crustaceans Section, Qld Museum, Brisbane

Gina Newton – Bureau of Resource Sciences, Canberra

Steve Nicol – Australian Antarctic Division, Hobart

Chris Nowak – Camperdown, NSW

Gabrielle Nowara – WAMRL, Fisheries Dept of WA, Waterman, WA

Rod Nurthen – School of Biological Sciences, Macquarie University, Sydney

Mick Olsen – Newton, SA

Colin Olsson – Albany Creek, Qld

Justine O'Regan – CSIRO Marine Laboratories, Hobart

Dos O'Sullivan – University of Tas, Launceston, Tas

Jenny Ovenden – Zoology Dept, University of Tas, Hobart

Tim Park – Fisheries Research Institute, NSW Fisheries, Sydney

Neil Patrick – Halco Tackle Company, Fremantle, WA

Kate Paulovics – Division of Sea Fisheries, Tas DPI & F, Taroona, Tas

John Paxton – Fish Section, Australian Museum, Sydney

Alan Pearce – CSIRO Marine Laboratories, North Beach, WA

Bruce Pease – Fisheries Research Institute, NSW Fisheries, Sydney

Peter Pender – Fisheries Division, NT DPI & F, Darwin

Jim Penn – WAMRL, Fisheries Dept of WA, Waterman, WA

Julian Pepperell – Pepperell Research and Consulting P/L, Caringbah, NSW

Peter Petrusevics – SA Dept of Fisheries, Adelaide

Bruce Phillips – Australian Fisheries Management Authority, Canberra

Bryan Pierce – SA Dept of Fisheries, Adelaide

Roland Pitcher – CSIRO Marine Laboratories, Cleveland, Qld

Rhyllis Plant – Invertebrate Zoology Section, Museum of Vic, Melbourne

Tom Polacheck – CSIRO Marine Laboratories, Hobart

Dave Pollard – Fisheries Research Institute, NSW Fisheries, Sydney

Barry Pollock – Fisheries Branch, QDPI, Brisbane

Phil Pond – Qld Fish Management Authority, Brisbane

Winston Ponder – Malacology Section, Australian Museum, Sydney

Rosalind Poole – Fish Section, Museum of Vic, Melbourne

Ian Potter – School of Biological and Environmental Sciences, Murdoch University, Murdoch, WA

Jim Prescott – SA Dept of Fisheries, Mt Gambier, SA

Jim Puckridge – Zoology Dept, University of Adelaide, Adelaide

Grant Pullen – Division of Sea Fisheries, Tas DPI & F, Taroona, Tas

Ken Pulley – Shorncliffe, Qld

Rex Pyne – Fisheries Division, NT DPI & F, Darwin

Qld Commercial Fishermen's Organisation, Line Fishery Committee, Brisbane

Ross Quinn – Southern Fisheries Centre, QDPI, Deception Bay, Qld

Tarmo Raadik – Arthur Rylah Institute, Vic Dept of Conservation and Environment, Melbourne

Cesar Ramirez – formerly of Bureau of Resource Sciences, Canberra

Dave Ramm – Fisheries Division, NT DPI & F, Darwin

Sally Reader – Fish Section, Australian Museum, Sydney

Andy Richards – Forum Fisheries Agency, Honiara, Solomon Islands

Sean Riley – Division of Sea Fisheries, Tas DPI & F, Taroona, Tas

Mike Rimmer – Northern Fisheries Centre, QDPI, Cairns, Qld

Jane Robertson – Kailis Bros Pty Ltd, Canning Vale, WA

John Robertson – Great Barrier Reef Marine Park Authority, Townsville, Qld

Dave Rochford – formerly of CSIRO Division of Oceanography, Hobart

David Rodgers – formerly of Fisheries Research Institute, NSW Fisheries, Sydney

Cassie Rose – Worms Section, Australian Museum, Sydney

Peter Rothlisberg – CSIRO Marine Laboratories, Cleveland, Qld

Stuart Rowland – NSW Fisheries, Grafton, NSW

Kevin Rowling – Fisheries Research Institute, NSW Fisheries, Sydney

Nick V Ruello – Ruello and Associates, Henley, NSW

Trevor Rule – SA Gamefishing Club, Adelaide

Barry Russell – Fish Section, Museum and Art Gallery of the NT, Darwin

John Russell – Northern Fisheries Centre, QDPI, Cairns, Qld

Gavin Ryan – Magnetic Island, Townsville, Qld

Margot Sachse – Australian Fisheries Management Authority, Darwin

Steve Saddlier – Arthur Rylah Institute, Vic Dept of Conservation and Environment, Melbourne

Keith Sainsbury – CSIRO Marine Laboratories, Hobart

Melita Samoilys – Northern Fisheries Centre, QDPI, Cairns, Qld

Andrew Sanger – Tas Inland Fisheries Commission, Hobart

Bill Sawynok – Australian National Sportfishing Association, Rockhampton, Qld

Alex Schaap – Division of Sea Fisheries, Tas DPI & F, Taroona, Tas

Rick Scoones – Broome Pearls Pty Ltd, Broome, WA

Zena Seliga - Fisheries Library, QDPI, Brisbane

James Sgherza – WAMRL, Fisheries Dept of WA, Waterman, WA

Peter Sharples – Ministry of Agriculture and Fisheries, Wellington, New Zealand

Scoresby Shepherd – SA Dept of Fisheries, Adelaide

John Short – Crustaceans Section, Qld Museum, Brisbane

Terry Sim – Fish Section, SA Museum, Adelaide

Colin Simpfendorfer – Dept of Marine Biology, James Cook University of North Qld, Townsville, Qld

Tim Skewes – CSIRO Marine Laboratories, Cleveland, Qld

Thim Skousen – Australian Fisheries Management Authority, Canberra

Dick Slack-Smith – Fisheries Division, NT DPI & F, Darwin

Shirley Slack-Smith – Aquatic Invertebrate Zoology Section, WA Museum, Perth

Hazel Small – Bureau of Resource Sciences, Canberra

Martin Smallridge – Zoology Dept, University of Adelaide, Adelaide

Adam Smith – The Ecology Lab, Balgowlah, NSW

Dave Smith – MSL, Vic Dept of Conservation and Environment, Queenscliff, Vic

Glen Smith – Southern Fisheries Centre, QDPI, Deception Bay, Qld

Ian Smith – Brackish Water Fish Culture Research Station, Salamander Bay, NSW

Kevin Smith – Fish Section, WA Museum, Perth

Perry Smith – Australian Bureau of Agricultural and Resource Economics, Canberra

Tony Smith – CSIRO Marine Laboratories, Hobart

Ian Somers – CSIRO Marine Laboratories, Cleveland, Qld

Peter Speare – Australian Institute of Marine Science, Townsville, Qld

Lucy Spence – Bureau of Resource Sciences, Canberra

Viv Spencer – Tas Inland Fisheries Commission, Hobart

Roger Springthorpe – Marine Invertebrates Section, Australian Museum, Sydney

Laurie Squires – Northern Fisheries Centre, QDPI, Cairns, Qld

Clive Stanley – CSIRO Marine Laboratories, Hobart

Simon Stanley – Division of Sea Fisheries, Tas DPI & F, Hobart

Derek Staples – Bureau of Resource Sciences, Canberra

John Stevens – CSIRO Marine Laboratories, Hobart

Mark Stevens – Yanco Agricultural Institute, NSW Agriculture, Yanco, NSW

Bryce Stewart – MSL, Vic Dept of Conservation and Environment, Queenscliff, Vic

Tim Stranks – Invertebrate Zoology Section, Museum of Vic, Melbourne

Wayne Sumpton – Fisheries Branch, QDPI, Brisbane

Jim Sutton – Fisheries Dept of WA, Esperance, WA

Roger Swainston – Fremantle, WA

Augy Syahailatua – formerly of Centre for Marine Science, University of NSW, Sydney

Graham Sykes – Fisheries Branch, QDPI, Brisbane

Paul Tauriki – Forum Fisheries Agency, Honiara, Solomon Islands

Brian Taylor – CSIRO Marine Laboratories, Cleveland, Qld

Laurie Thomas – Kailis Bros Pty Ltd, Canning Vale, WA

Marshall Thomson – Kailis Bros Pty Ltd, Canning Vale, WA

Tina Thorne – Animal Health Laboratories, WA Dept of Agriculture, Perth

John Thorogood – Wellington Point, Qld

Ron Thresher – CSIRO Marine Laboratories, Hobart

Stephen Thrower – International Food Institute of Qld, Hamilton, Qld

Richard Tilzey – Bureau of Resource Sciences, Canberra

John Timmins – NSW Fisheries, Sydney

John Tompkin – MSL, Vic Dept of Conservation and Environment, Queenscliff, Vic

Neil Trainor – Fisheries Branch, QDPI, Brisbane

Lindsay Trott – Australian Institute of Marine Science, Townsville, Qld

Angelo Tsolos – SA Dept of Fisheries, Adelaide

Don Tuma – Fisheries Division, QDPI, Brisbane

Clive Turnbull – Northern Fisheries Centre, QDPI, Cairns, Qld

Danny Turner – formerly of Bureau of Resource Sciences, c/- SA Dept of Fisheries, Adelaide

Elizabeth Turner – Tas Museum and Art Gallery, Hobart

Marcia and Joe Valente – Valente Seafoods, Port Lincoln, SA

Peter Vanderdrift – Eels Pty Ltd, Skipton, Vic

John Virgona – Fisheries Research Institute, NSW Fisheries, Sydney

Vicky Wadley – CSIRO Marine Laboratories, North Beach, WA

Terry Walker – MSL, Vic Dept of Conservation and Environment, Queenscliff, Vic

John Wallace – formerly of Australian Maritime College, Beauty Point, Tas

Bruce Wallner – CSIRO Marine Laboratories, North Beach, WA

Marie Wapnah – WAMRL, Fisheries Dept of WA, Waterman, WA

Peter Ward – Bureau of Resource Sciences, Canberra

Reg Watson – Northern Fisheries Centre, QDPI, Cairns, Qld

W. Richard Webber – National Museum of New Zealand, Wellington, New Zealand

Sharne Weidland – Mosman, NSW

Sally Wells – Bureau of Resource Sciences, Canberra

Grant West – CSIRO Marine Laboratories, Hobart

Ron West – Fisheries Research Institute, NSW Fisheries, Sydney

Wade Whitelaw – CSIRO Marine Laboratories, Hobart

Alan Williams – CSIRO Marine Laboratories, North Beach, WA

Dave McB. Williams – Australian Institute of Marine Science, Townsville, Qld

Dick Williams – Australian Antarctic Division, Hobart

Geoff Williams – Bureau of Resource Sciences, Canberra

Howel Williams – Division of Sea Fisheries, Tas DPI & F, Taroona, Tas

Kevin Williams – WW Fisheries Consultants, Sydney

Lew Williams – Fisheries Branch, QDPI, Brisbane

Russell Willing – Fisheries Division, NT DPI & F, Darwin

Steve Willmore – Fisheries Division, NT DPI & F, Darwin

Bob Wilson – Vic Dept of Agriculture, Langata, Vic

Glen Wilson – Zoology Dept, James Cook University of North Qld, Townsville, Qld

John Wilson – Division of Sea Fisheries, Tas DPI & F, Taroona, Tas

Marc Wilson – Australian Maritime College, Beauty Point, Tas

Robin Wilson – Crustaceans Section, Museum of Vic, Melbourne

Ross Winstanley – MSL, Vic Dept of Conservation and Environment, Queenscliff, Vic

Eve Witney – formerly of Fisheries Branch, QDPI, Brisbane

Des Wolfe – Division of Sea Fisheries, Tas DPI & F, Hobart

Peter Wolfe – formerly of NSW Fisheries, Sydney

Tim Wood – Fisheries Division, NT DPI & F, Darwin

Simon Woodley – Great Barrier Reef Marine Park Authority, Townsville, Qld

Linda Worland – Centre for Marine Science, University of NSW, Sydney

Dave Wright – CSIRO Marine Laboratories, North Beach, WA

Ken Yasuda – Oceania Trading Pty Ltd, Sorell, Tas

Gordon Yearsley – CSIRO Marine Laboratories, Hobart

Peter Young – CSIRO Marine Laboratories, Hobart

Peter J. Young – formerly of Vic Dept of Conservation and Environment, Melbourne

Will Zacharin – Division of Sea Fisheries, Tas DPI & F, Taroona, Tas

Wolfgang Zeidler – Marine Invertebrates Section, SA Museum, Adelaide

Alex Ziolkowski – Abalone Fishermen's Cooperative Ltd, Mallacoota, Vic

G l o s s a r y

compiled by Albert Caton and Steve Kerr, with contributions from Madeleine Jones, Kevin McLoughlin, Russell Reichelt, Patricia Kailola, Derek Staples and Richard Tilzey

Acoustic tag – underwater sound transmitter attached to **fish**

Adductor muscle – muscle which holds together the 2 shells of **bivalve molluscs**

Adipose eyelid – fleshy gelatinous eyelid present in some **fish** species

Adipose fin – fin remnant, in the form of a dorsal fleshy lobe, present in some **fish** species

Adrostral ridge – ridge running down the length of the large spine (**rostrum**) on the front of a prawn

Age validation – in many **species**, growth rings can be seen on bony parts (such as **otoliths**, scales, vertebrae or fin spines) or on the shell; validation involves confirming that these rings coincide with the period (eg year, day) assumed

Aggregation – may refer to '**schooling**', which involves behavioural grouping of animals; but 'aggregation' is also used to reflect concentration (of fish) for unknown or direct causes such as the concentration of food organisms, or **spawning**

Air bladder – see: **swim bladder**

Amphipods – type of small, flattened crustaceans (eg freshwater shrimps, sand fleas)

Annelid – worm whose body consists of a series of rings or segments; eg earthworms, leeches, beach worms

Antennae – second pair of feelers in crustaceans

Antennular flagellae – long whip-like extensions of the antennules (see: **antennules**)

Antennules – in crustaceans, the first pair of feelers, usually sensory in function

Aquaculture – commonly termed '**fish farming**' but broadly the commercial growing of marine (**mariculture**) or freshwater animals and plants in water

Artesian bores – wells tapping underground water reserves (sandwiched between 2 impervious layers of rock) and producing water supply at the surface via little or no pumping

Artisanal fisheries – fisheries involving skilled but non-industrialized operators; typically subsistence fisheries although the catch may be sold

Australian Fishing Zone – Australia has proclaimed a 200 nautical mile wide zone around its coast within which it controls domestic and foreign access to **fish** resources

Bag limit – restriction in the number of **fish** that an angler may retain

Barbels – fleshy 'feelers' protruding from the lower jaw of some **fish species**, commonly used for locating food

Batch fecundity – number of viable eggs usually released by a **serial spawner** in a pulse of **spawning**

Beach price – 'raw' price for a product at the landing point, not taking account of any transportation or handling costs

Benthic; bentho; benthos – associated with the bottom of a water body such as a sea or lake

Berley – animal or plant matter spread in water to attract **fish** to its source

Berried – female crabs, lobsters, etc which have eggs attached to the appendages of the underside of the abdomen ('tail section') are described as berried or 'in berry'

Billabong – section of river bed fully isolated from the main stream except at flood times when it refills

Billfish – marlins and swordfish; ie **fish** where the snout is extended into a bill or 'spear'

Bimodal distribution – see: **length distribution**

Biomass [standing stock] – weight of a **stock** or of a component of a **stock** eg 'spawning biomass' is the combined weight of mature animals [Standing stock is an alternative term for biomass]

Bivalves – 2-shelled shellfish such as oysters and scallops (bivalve molluscs)

Bloom – see: **phytoplankton**

Brackish – saline water where the salinity is not as high as in the sea

Broadcast spawners – fish which release their **gametes** into the water, where fertilizaton may occur

Bryozoans – small aquatic animals, usually grouped together in a 'mat-like' or 'coral-like' colony

Burley – see: **berley**

Butterfly fillets – fillets from each side of a **fish** left joined together (usually at the gut region) after removal from the backbone

Bycatch – **species** taken incidentally in a **fishery** where other **species** are the target; bycatch **species** may be of lesser value than the target **species**, and are often discarded ('**trash**' species). In many cases, bycatch **species** are of commercial value and are retained for sale

Byssus – silky or coarse threads by which some **bivalve** molluscs attach themselves to a **substrate**

Carapace – in crustaceans, the 'shield' covering the upper surface of part of the body of various **species** (eg the broad shield forming the upper body cover of crabs, and of the front portion of prawns and rock lobsters)

Catch per unit (of) effort; CPUE – catch taken for a given amount of **fishing effort** expressed as a ratio

Catchability – in a general sense the extent to which a **stock** is susceptible to fishing; quantitatively, the proportion of the **stock** removed by 1 unit of **fishing effort**

Caudal [caudal peduncle; caudal keels] – pertaining to the tail (caudal fin) ['caudal peduncle' is the narrow 'stalk' from which the tail fans out; 'caudal keels' are elongate projections at the sides of the tail-base in fish such as tunas]

Cephalopods – literally 'head-foot'; animals like squid and octopus where the tentacles ('feet') converge at the head

Cephalothorax – head and chest (thoracic) region of a crustacean; the region of the body usually covered by the **carapace** when one is present

Cestode worms – parasitic flatworms, usually known as tapeworms

Cetaceans – whales, dolphins, porpoises; Order Cetacea

Chaetognaths – 'arrow worms'; small arrow-shaped aquatic animals

Chemoreception – capacity to detect and differentiate certain chemicals in the surrounding environment

Ciguatera poisoning – some tropical **fish** may accumulate toxin (poison) from the algae they eat, and **fish** preying on them may accumulate the toxin. Consumption of contaminated fish by humans may cause nerve and muscle reactions which can result in death

Cirri – hair-like structures in animals and plants

Clinal – gradual but continuous change of form of a **species** across its range, usually linked with differences in environment

Clupeoids – literally **fish** of the herring family Clupeidae (eg herrings, sardines) but used in a wider sense to include related families (eg anchovies, Engraulididae)

Cohort – those individuals of a **stock** born in the same **spawning** season. For annual **spawners**, a year's **recruitment** of new individuals to a **stock** is a single cohort or '**year-class**'

Conspecific – individuals that are members of the same **species**

Continental shelf – sea bed from the shore to the edge of the **continental slope**

Continental slope – region of the outer edge of a continent between the generally shallow **continental shelf** and the deep ocean floor, usually demarcated by the 200 m **isobath**

Copepod – aquatic crustacean; usually microscopic and **plankton**ic

Coralline algae – algae with a coral-like, calcareous outer covering

Correlation – mutual relation between 2 or more things; interdependence of variables

Cosmopolitan species – **species** with a distribution belonging to many, or all, parts of the world

Creel survey – estimation of anglers' catches, usually by a sampling program involving interviews and inspection of individual catches

Decapods – literally '10 feet'; types of crustaceans with 10 feet. Prawns and lobsters are decapod crustaceans: while they have paired limbs on all body segments, they have 5 pairs of main walking and grasping legs. Squid are decapod molluscs as they have 10 tentacles

Deciduous scales – loosely-affixed scales, easily shed when **fish** are handled or rubbed

Demersal – found on or near the bottom of the sea or lake; cf **pelagic**

Dendritic organ – branching or 'tree-like' organ possessed by cobbler; function unknown

Detritus [detritus feeders] – decomposing organic debris or remains [animals that feed on detritus]

Development (of fisheries) – transition through exploratory and experimental fishing, and establishment of commercial activities and markets, with the ultimate goal of sustained long term exploitation within bounds which the **stock** can support

Diatoms – microscopic single-celled algae which have 2 ornate interfitting outer 'shells' containing silica

Dichromatic – members of the 1 species having different colouration

Disjunct distribution – discontinuous or separated distribution

DNA – deoxyribonucleic acid; long chain molecules found in the nucleus of individual cells which form the genetic coding responsible for **species**' and individuals' characteristics

Ebb tide – out-flowing tide from high tide to low tide; *cf* **flood tide**

Ecosystem – community of plants, animals and other living organisms, together with the non-living components of their environment, found in a particular habitat and interacting with each other

Electrophoresis – technique for separating charged molecules — particularly proteins such as enzymes — based on their different mobilities in an electric field. It is used to differentiate between morphologically similar **taxa** (see: **isozymes**)

Endemic – so-called 'native species', which are confined to a given region; eg a **species** endemic to Australia is not found beyond Australia

Epibenthos – animals and plants that live at the surface of the sea bed or lake floor; *cf* **benthic**

Epipelagic – associated with the surface layer of a water body (eg sea or lake); *cf* **pelagic**

Epiphytes – plants attached to other plants for support, but not parasitic upon them

Euphausiid – small shrimp-like crustaceans; eg krill

Eutrophication – rapid increase in the nutrient status of a water body, both natural and occurring as a by-product of human activity. Excessive production leads to anaerobic conditions below the surface waters.

Eviscerated – having the gut removed

Exploited – fished; harvested and put to use

Eye fork length – measurement of the length of a **fish** (eg billfish) from the eye to the 'V' of the **caudal** fin; *cf* **fork length**

Fecundity – number of eggs an animal produces each reproductive cycle; the potential reproductive capacity of an organism or **population**

Fertile (viable) hybrid – individual formed by the sexual union of individuals from 2 genetically distinct varieties (or species) that is capable of reproducing

Fish [fishes; finfish; scalefish] – literally, a vertebrate (animal with a backbone) that has gills and lives in water, but generally (and here) used more broadly to include any harvestable animal living in water ['fishes' refers to more than 1 type of fish; 'finfish' refers to sharks, some rays and bony fishes, and 'scalefish' refers to fish bearing scales]

Fishery [fisher] – term to describe the collective enterprise of taking **fish**, usually used in conjunction with reference to the **species**, gear or area involved [a person participating in a fishery (in preference to the previously used term 'fisherman')]

Fishing effort – amount of fishing taking place, usually described in terms of gear type and frequency or period for which it is in use; for example 'hook-sets', 'trawl hours'

Fishmeal – protein-rich animal feed product based on fish

Flagellum – whip-like projection or 'appendage' (see also **antennular flagellae**)

Flood tide – in-flowing tide, from low tide to high tide; *cf* **ebb tide**

Food web – food cycle; network of food chains in a community

Forage species – prey or food **species** of an animal

Foraminifers – minute single-celled organisms having calcareous shells

Fork length (sometimes called 'caudal fork length') – length from the tip of the snout of a **fish** to the most anterior point of the 'fork' or 'V' of the tail; *cf* **eye fork length**, **standard length**, **total length**

Free on board; f.o.b. – price without freight costs

Front (temperature front; frontal region) – region where a sharp gradient in temperature occurs, often indicating the demarcation between 2 current systems or water masses; usually associated with high biological activity

Gametes – reproductive cells; eggs or sperm

Gastropods [gastropod molluscs] – literally 'stomach-foot'; a large group of molluscs [single-shelled molluscs such as abalone, turban shells and snails]

Gene pool – genes in an interbreeding population at a particular time

Gill arches – bony arches in the throat of **fish** to which the filaments and rakers of the gills are attached

Gill rakers – projections from the inner surfaces of **fishes**' gill arches which strain water for food particles

Gonads – reproductive organs of animals and plants which produce eggs and sperm

Gorgonians – sea whips and sea fans

Green prawns – uncooked prawns

Grow-out operations – pond or enclosure rearing of hatchery-bred animals

Growth model – mathematical 'description' or representation of the rate at which an animal or plant grows at different sizes or ages

Habitat – particular 'living space' or environment in which an animal or plant lives

'Height' of shells – perpendicular distance from the '**hinge**' end of a **bivalve** mollusc shell to the outermost edge

'Hinge' of shells – junction of the 2 shells of **bivalve** molluscs. The shells pivot at the hinge, which often has teeth or ridges that prevent sideways slipping (see: **adductor muscle**)

Hookah – underwater breathing device involving an above-water pump and an air supply tube to a diver's mouthpiece or helmet; *cf* **SCUBA**

Host-specific – parasites which are associated with only 1 type of host

Hypersaline embayments – bays where the water is extremely salty — much saltier than normal sea water

Ikijime; ike-jime – method of quickly killing **fish** such that quality is retained; used for **sashimi**. First the skull is pierced or cored and the brain destroyed, then the spinal cord is destroyed by inserting a thin rod along its length

Incidental catch – see: **bycatch**

Individual transferable quota – see: **quota**

Input controls – management controls on type or amount of fishing as a means of limiting catches, eg by gear restrictions, closed seasons (*cf* **output controls**); see: **limited entry fishery**

Insertion of fins – point along the body of a fish at which the front or rear edge of a fin emerges

Inshore waters – waters of the shallower part of the **continental shelf**; *cf* **nearshore waters**

Inter-orbital – bones on the roof of the skull between the eyes; space between the eyes across the top of the head

Ischial spine – spine on the base of the legs of prawns

Isobath – contour line linking regions of the same depth

Isopod – type of small, flat crustaceans (eg garden slaters, true sea lice)

Isotherm – contour line linking regions of the same temperature

Isozymes [isozyme analysis] – variants of the same enzyme which can be separated on special conducting media using **electrophoresis** [analysis of isozymes]

Landing(s) – weight of the catch landed at the wharf

Larvaceans – tiny transparent animals belonging to the Subphylum Urochordata (**tunicates**) and found in marine plankton; Class Larvacea

Larval settlement – settlement phase of some sedentary or **benthic** animals which commence life as free-swimming larvae

Lateral line – row of sensory organs along the body in most **fish**, usually appearing as pored scales or scales differently-shaped to the other body scales

Lee – sheltered side; side out of the wind or protected from the current

Length distribution [modal size; bimodal distribution] – 'length distribution' of a catch is the number of individuals in each length group ['modal size' is the length group in which most individuals occur; 'bimodal distribution' indicates that there are 2 length groups within which individuals are most abundant, with other less abundant length groups around them]. Some distributions may show several modes, reflecting different **fish** ages

Limited entry fishery – **fishery** where the number of operators is restricted to control the amount of **fishing effort**; frequently involves controls on the number and size of vessels, and conditions relating to the transfer of fishing rights or the replacement of vessels; *cf* **open access fishery**

Lipid – large group of organic compounds including fats, oils, waxes and sterols

Longevity – life span

Macro-algae – large algae; eg kelp

Macrophytes – large plants

Mantle – shellfish such as oysters and snails have a 'mantle' or tissue which secretes and lines the shell. In squid it is represented by the 'tube'

Mariculture – fish farming or **aquaculture** of marine animals

Marine – pertaining to the sea, from the open oceans to high water mark and into estuaries

Medusa – bell-shaped, free-swimming form of a group of animals including jellyfish, sea anemones and corals; *cf* **polyp**

Megalopa – larval stage of a crab

Mesopelagic – **pelagic** zone of intermediate depth, 200–1000 m

Metamorphosis – rapid change of body shape; eg the change from a larval form to an adult form

Microencapsulated diets – special feeds developed for the rearing of larvae or some forms of animal where their normal food items are microscopic and of a particular size

Microprobe analysis – examination of the chemical composition of material at a microscopic level with an X-ray probe

Minimum size – legislated size below which individuals of some **fish** species are not to be retained after being caught

Mitochondrial DNA – DNA of the mitochondria (the energy-producing structures within a cell); carrier of genetic information useful in examining genetic identity of an individual

Model (population) – hypothesis of how a population functions; often uses mathematical descriptions of growth, **mortality** and **recruitment**

Modes; modal size – see: **length distribution**

Moon closures – because prawn movements are linked to moon cycles, some **fishery** closures are timed to coincide with moon phases and hence with prawn activity patterns

Morphometric; morpho- – to do with the measurement of the shape of an individual; body proportions

Mortality rate [natural mortality] – rate of deaths (usually on an annual basis in terms of proportion of the **stock** dying) from various causes ['natural mortality' rate includes only deaths generated by factors such as ageing, predation and disease; ie it does not include mortality from fishing]

Mother-ships – in some **fisheries**, catching vessels are serviced on the fishing grounds by a 'mother-ship' to which they land their catches and which may process those catches before storing them for transport or trans-shipping

Moult cycle – Crustaceans grow in a series of 'moults' whereby the body covering is periodically shed and a new covering develops

Mysids; mysid shrimps – group of small, shrimp-like crustaceans characterised by possessing a ventral brood pouch

Nauplius – early egg-shaped larval stage of prawns and other crustaceans. It is unsegmented and bears 3 pairs of appendages

Neap tides – tides occurring at first and third moon quarters, where the range between high tide and low tide is smallest; *cf* **spring tides**

Nearshore waters – shallow **inshore** waters (*qv*)

Nematodes – unsegmented round worms, some of which are parasitic

Neritic – to do with that part of the sea over the **continental shelf**; *cf* **oceanic**

'Nuclei' for pearl culture – pearls are composed of a smooth glossy covering which has been layed down by the pearl oyster over a solid irritant. Pearl culture involves the insertion of such an irritant body or 'nucleus' into the oyster which then covers it with 'nacre', the lustrous 'mother-of-pearl' material

Nutrient upwelling – divergence of water currents or the movement of surface water away from land can lead to a 'welling-up' of deeper water which commonly is richer in nutrients than is surface water

Oceanic – to do with the open ocean waters beyond the edge of the **continental shelf**; *cf* **neritic**

Offshore Constitutional Settlement (OCS) – arrangement commenced in 1982 whereby the States and Commonwealth sought to introduce legislation on a **fishery** by **fishery** basis passing responsibility for control to 1 or the other administration. Arrangements are not finalized, and there are still **fisheries** where joint control or the *status quo* remains

Offshore waters – tend to be the more oceanic waters, though they still may relate to outer **continental shelf** waters; *cf* **onshore waters**

Onshore waters – waters abutting the coastline; *cf* **nearshore waters**

Oocyte – cell which develops into an **ovum**

Open access fishery – **fishery** where there is no limit on the number of operators (see: **limited entry fishery**)

Operculum – bony covering over the gill slits of **fish**; or, in **gastropod molluscs**, the calcareous plate over the shell opening that protects the body when the animal withdraws into its shell

Opportunistic (feeding) – taking of food as it becomes available

Ostracods – group of small crustaceans with a **bivalve**d **carapace** which can be closed to completely cover the body

Otoliths – calcareous deposits or bones found in chambers at the base of the skull in **fish** (and inner ear of other vertebrates). These bones frequently show rings or layers which can be used to determine age

Output controls – management measures directly limiting fish catch or **landings** (eg by **quota**); *cf* **input controls**

Overfishing – fishing beyond a desirable, **sustainable**, or 'safe' **population** or **stock** level

Ovum; ova – unfertilized egg cell

Palaeohistory – fossil history

Parameter – characteristic feature or measure of some aspect of a **stock**, usually expressed as a numerical value; eg 'natural mortality rate'

Parts per thousand – way of expressing chemical concentrations in solutions; 1 part per thousand is roughly equivalent to 1 gram per litre

Pathogen – disease-causing (micro)organism

Pectoral – to do with the shoulder; in **fish**, the pectoral fins are those at the sides behind the **operculum**

Pelagic – associated with the surface or middle depths of a body of water; *cf* **demersal**, **epipelagic** and **mesopelagic**

Photoperiod – light phase of a light-dark cycle. Many animals and plants are sensitive to the seasonal variation in the relative length of day and night, and their biochemical activities respond to it

Phyllosoma – leaf-like, early larval stage of lobsters. It is followed by the **puerulus** stage which settles

Phytoplankton – plant **plankton**; a rapid build-up in abundance of phytoplankton — usually in response to nutrient build-up — can result in a '**bloom**'

Plankton – aquatic, free-drifting, suspended organisms; usually small animals (**zooplankton**) and plants (**phytoplankton**)

Pleopods – paddle-like swimming limbs on the abdomen of prawns

Polychaetes – segmented marine worms with bristles along the body; beach worms (see: **annelid**)

Polyp – cylindrical stalk-like body attached at 1 end and the mouth at the other end surrounded by tentacles. Phylum Coelenterata; eg jellyfish, coral

Population – group of individuals of the same species, forming a breeding unit and sharing a **habitat**

Population structuring – composition of a **population** in terms of size, **stock** (genetic or regional), age class, sex, etc

Postlarvae – animals that have changed from the **larval** form to juvenile or adult form; usually refers only to the stage immediately following the larva

Post-rostral ridge – ridge running along the carapace of a prawn behind the large frontal spine (**rostrum**)

Pre-opercular bone – a cheek bone on the side of the 'face' of **fish** in front of the **operculum**

Pre-orbital – in the 'face' of **fish**, the bone in front of the eye

Protandrous – **fish** which mature first as males and later become females

Protogynous – **fish** which mature first as females and later become males

Protozoans – group of single-celled animals

Puerulus – see: **phyllosoma**

Quota – amount of catch allocated; could refer to a **fishery** as a whole (a 'total allowable catch') or to that amount allocated to an individual or company (an 'individual quota') of the total allowable catch from a **stock**; also transferable shares in the total quota for a **stock** (an 'individual transferable quota')

Radiometric ageing techniques – X-ray examination of the biochemical composition across bony structures of **fish** to identify periodic (eg daily, annual) patterns and permit determination of age

Recruitment – usually refers to the addition of new individuals to the fished component of a **stock**. It may also refer to new additions to sub-components; eg 'recruitment to the fishery' refers to fish entering the actual **fishery**, and this is determined by the size and age at which they are first caught

Resorption of ova; resorbed – not all **ripe ova** are released during a **spawning** season. Those remaining may be broken down and the breakdown products absorbed by the adult's body

Riparian – pertaining to the river bank

'Ripe' fish – female **fish** with enlarged, fully mature eggs ready to be fertilized. Female **fish** with eggs in that condition are referred to as 'running ripe'

'Roe-off' – when abalone or scallops are shelled ('**shucked**'), the 'gut' (including the roe) is removed from the meat (the white muscle block which joins the shells). Usually these shellfish are marketed with the red or orange roe (**gonad**) still attached; however in some markets or for some species, meat without the roe is preferred (eg doughboy scallops)

Rostrum – central, forward-projecting and occasionally long spine between the eyes of crustaceans

Run – seasonal migration undertaken by fish, usually as part of their life history, eg spawning run of gemfish; upstream migration of whitebait. Fishers may refer to increased catches as a 'run' of fish, a usage often independent of their migratory behaviour

Salp – small, transparent, barrel-shaped free-swimming **plankton**ic animal belonging to the Subphylum Urochordata (**tunicates**); Class Thaliacea

Sashimi – Japanese term for sliced **fish** — especially tuna — served raw as a delicacy

Scalefish – see: **fish**

Schooling – behavioural grouping together of **fish**, which then usually move together as a group; *cf* **aggregation**; **shoal**

SCUBA – 'self-contained underwater breathing apparatus'; aqualung equipment, providing air without the need of an airtube to the surface; *cf* '**hookah**'

Scutes – projecting, modified (strongly-ridged and rough) scales in some **fish**, usually associated with the **lateral line**, or at the side in the tail region, or along the ventral profile

Sequential hermaphrodite – having male and female reproductive organs which mature at different times; see: **protandry** and **protogyny**

Serial (or batch) spawning – **spawning** in bursts or pulses more than once in a spawning season in response to an environmental cue; *cf* **synchronous spawning**

Sessile – attached to the **substrate**

Sexual dichotomy – differences between males and females of a species

'Shamateurs' – so-called amateur fishers who illegally sell their catch

Shelf break – region where the **continental shelf** and **continental slope** meet, ie where the more gently-shelving region of the sea bed adjacent to a land-mass rather abruptly slopes more steeply down towards the ocean depths; commonly around 200 m

Shellfish – aquatic animals with shells, eg crustaceans (prawns, lobsters) and molluscs (eg oysters, scallops, clams)

Shoals (of fish) – **schools** of fish, but usually inferring **schools** at the surface or in shallow water

Shucked – see: 'roe-off

Sipunculids – group of unsegmented, bottom dwelling marine worms; sometimes called 'peanut worms'; usually sedentary, some living in empty snail shells or other refuges

Size-at-age – length or weight at a particular age

Size frequency – see: **length distribution**

Spat ['settling' of spat; spatfalls] – fertilized shellfish larvae, eg of oysters or mussels. [Spat commence life as free-swimming individuals in the plankton, then 'settle' onto suitable **substrates** (a 'spatfall')]

Spatial and temporal closures – area and seasonal closures of a fishery

Spawning [spawning stock] – release or deposition of **spermatozoa** or **ova**, of which some will fertilize or be fertilized to produce offspring ['spawning stock' is the part of a **stock** which is mature and breeding]

Speciation – formation of new species

Species – group of animals or plants having common characteristics and able to breed together to produce fertile (capable of reproducing) offspring, so that they maintain their 'separateness' from other groups. For example, yellowfin tuna and bigeye tuna are 2 distinct tuna species; whereas general terms like 'tuna' and 'trout' each represent groups of species

'Spent' fish – male or female **fish** after **spawning**, where the gonads have released their sperm or eggs; in many species the condition of the **fish** is poor and they may die or take some time to regain commercial quality (eg **salmon, trout**)

Spermatheca – organ which receives and stores sperm from the male pending fertilization of the eggs; eg on female prawns and lobsters

Spermatophore – 'package' of sperm produced by some animal species with internal fertilisation

Spring tides – tides occurring at new and full moons, where the range between high and low tides is greatest; *cf* **neap tides**

Standard length – length from the tip of the snout of a **fish** to the most distal edge of the last bone in the backbone, from which

the tail rays radiate; *cf* **fork length; total length**

Standing stock – see: **biomass**

Stock – group of individuals of a **species** which can be regarded as an entity for management or assessment purposes. Some **species** form a single stock (eg southern bluefin tuna) and other species are composed of several stocks (eg albacore tuna in the Pacific Ocean, where there are separate northern Pacific and southern Pacific stocks). The impact of fishing on a **species** cannot be determined without knowledge of this stock structure

Stomatopods – group of crustaceans including mantis shrimps (*Squilla* species)

Subspecies – somewhat distinct morphological and reproductively isolated sub-group of a **species**. Inter-breeding between different subspecies is possible, but it is not as common as breeding among the individuals of a subspecies

Substrate – sea bed or lake bed, or other solid surface to which animals or plants attach, or on which they move

Sub-tropical convergence zone – ocean region where warmer water of tropical origin interfaces with water originating in colder regions; in the southern hemisphere in the general vicinity of latitude 40°S

Surplus production model – mathematical representation of the way a **stock** of **fish** responds to fishing or other removals of individuals, with the central assumption that at large **stock** size, reproductive rates and rate of **stock** growth is slowed by self-regulating mechanisms, and that **stock** growth rates are faster after removals as the **stock** attempts to rebuild. In theory, fishing can be moderated to take advantage of the more productive **stock** growth rates, provided that it does not exceed the **stock** recovery capacity

Sustainable yield; maximum sustainable yield; MSY – maximum catch that can be removed over an indefinite period without causing the **stock** to be depleted, assuming that removals and natural mortality are balanced by stable recruitment and growth. [In reality this is never the case: environmental variability causes **stock**s to change regardless of fishing, and fishing at the assumed level of MSY can lead to over-exploitation.]

Swim bladder; air bladder – in some **fish species** there is a gas (or oil-filled) chamber in the body cavity above the gut and near the backbone, used to assist in the regulation of buoyancy at different depths

Swimmerets – paired limbs on the body segments beneath the tail of lobsters, prawns, and similar crustaceans. They are egg-holding in lobsters, and serve breathing and movement functions in other crustaceans

Symbiosis – living together of members of 2 different **species** with (usually) beneficial consequences for 1 or both of the parties

Synchronous spawning – spawning of all individuals in unison, usually in response to an environmental trigger; *cf* **serial spawning**

Tagging – marking, or attaching a tag to an individual or group of individuals, so that it or they can be identified on recapture; used for the study of movement, migration and **stock** delineation, for the examination of growth, for the estimation of numbers in a **stock**, and for the recovery of biological specimens

Taxonomic [taxon; taxa] – to do with the naming and categorization of the

relationships of animals or plants and animal or plant groups; eg **fish** are grouped into **taxa** including **species**, genera (groups of similar **species**), families (groups of similar genera), etc ['taxon' (taxa) is a named unit or level within the group]

Telson – extension of the body, in the centre of the 'tail fan' of prawns, yabbies, rock lobsters, etc

Temperate waters – waters in the region of higher (cooler; more poleward) latitudes than tropical latitudes; literally those between the Tropic of Cancer and the Arctic Circle in the northern hemisphere, and the Tropic of Capricorn and the Antarctic Circle in the southern hemisphere

Thermocline – region below the surface layer of the sea or lake, where temperature declines abruptly with increasing depth; *cf* **front**

Total allowable catch – see: **quota**

Total length – length of a **fish** measured from the tip of its snout to the most distal tip of its **caudal** (tail) **fin**; *cf* **standard length**

Translocation – movement of native or introduced (exotic) **species** to waters or **habitat**s outside their natural or previous distribution

Trash fish – **fish** of no commercial value that have been caught but are discarded ('trashed')

Trematode – type of flat parasitic worm (eg liver fluke)

Tube feet – starfish and sea urchins (echinoderms) have fluid-filled, extendable, suction-capable tube 'limbs' by which they can either hold themselves to the **substrate** or drag themselves along

Tubercle – projection on the surface of the skin or a scale

Tunicate – sea squirt (eg **larvaceans, salps,** cunjevoi)

200-mile zone – see: **Australian Fishing Zone**

Univalve – mollusc with a single shell

Uropods – appendages on the side of the **telson** which make up the tail fan in crustaceans

Vegetated substrate – plant or vegetable matter forming a base for attachment

Vertebral counts – number of bones in the backbone is a feature — like the number of rays in fins — used to classify **fish species**

Vertical migration – movement up and down in the **water column** often with a daily cycle

Volumetric unit quotas – **quotas** based on the volume of animals taken, eg in the Tasmanian scallop fishery

Water column – vertical section of the sea or lake

Year-class – individuals **spawned** in the same year (or **spawning** season, when that spans the end of 1 year and the beginning of the next)

Yield-per-recruit – analysis of how growth and natural **mortality** interact to determine the best size of animals to harvest; ie is it most beneficial economically for **fish** to be caught when they are young and plentiful, or when they are older and larger but reduced in number by natural causes?

Zoea; zoeae – early larval stage of lobsters and crabs (and prawns)

Zooplankton – animal portion of the **plankton**

> – more than

< – less than

Page numbers and common names in **bold** type indicate species that have a detailed presentation in Chapters 5 and 6 of the text. Their other common names are not bolded. Species are not indexed in their role as prey or predator of other species. Family names are in CAPITALS. Fishing **gear** is indexed only to Chapter 3 ('Fishing Gear').